The **Rough Guide**

East Coast
Australia

written and researched by
Emma Gregg

with additional contributions by
**Margo Daly, Anne Dehne, David Leffman,
Helen Marsden and Chris Scott**

ROUGH
GUIDES

Contents

East coast ecotourism
colour section following
p.184

Take the plunge!
colour section following
p.376

◀◀ Heron Island ◀ Looking across Port Phillip Bay to Melbourne

Introduction to

East Coast Australia

Fascinatingly diverse, Australia's East Coast hogs a high proportion of the country's finest features – from Sydney's iconic Opera House and Melbourne's sophisticated restaurant scene, to natural wonders such as the Daintree Rainforest, the Whitsunday Islands and the Great Barrier Reef.

Best of all, perhaps, are the staggeringly beautiful **beaches** that dot the coast all the way from southeast Victoria to Far North Queensland and the islands beyond. Here, you'll find dozens of different ways to enjoy the Pacific breezes: **swimming** and **surfing** are the classic East Coast pastimes, but with sailing, snorkelling, kayaking, kitesurfing, scuba diving and skydiving on offer, too, there's really no excuse for just snoozing in the shade.

Those with an appreciation for **nature** will want to explore the coast's dramatic backdrop of hills, gullies and escarpments, crisscrossed by ancient Aboriginal people walking tracks. While all too many coastal Aborigines now live in disadvantaged urban communities, those who

4
■

work as national park guides willingly share something of their traditions with visitors, explaining their time-honoured relationship with the land and its native flora and fauna.

The first European to take an active interest in the coast and its potential was **Captain Cook**, who set about charting its salient features in 1770; within twenty years, the British had capitalized on his discoveries by founding a penal colony on the coast's most spectacular bay, and naming it **Sydney**. The harsh conditions of the Australian interior forced the young colony to grow along the seaboard, seeking

◀ Uluru (Ayers Rock; 2800km from Sydney)

▶ Lord Howe Island (700km from Sydney) & Norfolk Island (1600km from Sydney)

5 ■

out fresh water and safe harbours; even now, the vast majority of Australians live within a couple of hours' drive of the Pacific.

Still barely two centuries old, Sydney and the other **East Coast cities** are dynamic and ambitious. Urban Australians embrace the New World values of material self-improvement through hard work and hard play

Fact file

• Australia's East Coast connects **four states** – Queensland, New South Wales, Australian Capital Territory and Victoria.

• The state capitals of **Brisbane**, **Sydney**, **Canberra** and **Melbourne** all lie within easy reach of the open ocean. Together, they house over half of Australia's twenty million **citizens**; another five million live elsewhere on the East Coast.

• The **coastal highway** from Melbourne to Cooktown, where tarmac gives way to unsealed roads, is approximately 4060km long.

• The **Great Barrier Reef**, which shelters the northern East Coast, is the largest organic complex on the planet.

with an easy-going, outdoorsy vitality that visitors, especially Europeans, often find refreshingly hedonistic. Away from the cities, the pace is gentler and opportunities abound to enjoy the towering forests, tumbling waterfalls, pristine islands and spotless sands of the coastal wilderness.

Where to go

B y far the most popular long-distance route on the coast is the northbound run from **Sydney to Cairns**. Sydney, one of the world's most exciting cities, is a great launchpad for an action-packed trip taking in **Byron Bay**, the **Gold Coast**, **Brisbane**, the **Sunshine Coast**, **Fraser Island**, the **Whitsundays** and the **Great Barrier Reef**.

While there's nothing wrong with hopping from one blockbuster attraction to another, there are magical experiences to be had by plotting your own itinerary, and keeping it flexible. By following your nose around Victoria's **Mornington Peninsula** and **Yarra Valley**, you'll discover boutique wineries that the tour groups overlook; and by exploring the coastal back roads of southern New South Wales, you'll come across long, empty beaches of dazzling sand – particularly near **Jervis Bay** and **Batemans Bay** – where you can pad barefoot along kangaroo tracks. By heading inland from the busy beach Meccas of northern New South Wales and southeast Queensland, you'll discover appealing country villages, such as **Bellingen**, peopled by arty, alternative types, and the stunning

▲ Flying over the Great Barrier Reef

The open road

With the Pacific to the east, the Great Dividing Range to the west and interesting detours at regular intervals, a journey along the **East Coast highway** is the ultimate road trip. Allow at least two months to travel the entire region by public transport, motorbike, campervan or car, or five weeks to cover the classic **Sydney-to-Cairns** section, and you can feast on its highlights. If you'd rather zoom in on a smaller area for an adventure lasting two or three weeks, you're spoilt for choice: for details of some of the coast's most picturesque self-drive routes, see Basics, p.41.

bushwalking country of **Dorrigo**, **Springbrook** and **Lamington national parks**. Camp out here, or in any of the coast's many other beautiful conservation areas, and you'll almost certainly be rewarded with sightings of native birds, frogs, butterflies, reptiles and marsupials. Offshore, particularly in Queensland, there are dozens of islands to explore, all the way up to **Thursday Island** at the very tip of the continent.

When to go

Australia's East Coast spans over 28 degrees of latitude and encompasses several **climate** zones. The region south of Sydney has the same sequence of four seasons as northern Europe and the US, but six months out of sync; by contrast, the tropical north switches gradually between its two seasons – dry and wet – with no discernible spring or summer. The subtropical region from northern New South Wales to southeast Queensland has a climate that lies between these two extremes.

As a rule of thumb, the **best time to visit the south** is during the warmest, sunniest months of October to March, while **the far north** is best visited during the relatively cool dry season,

◄ Lifeguards, Queensland

The great outdoors

With a climate that lends itself to active pursuits, the East Coast is a great place to charge your inner dynamo through **watersports** or **bushwalking**: just about every coastal city has inviting waterways and wilderness within easy reach. For maximum thrills, there are masses of extreme adventures on offer, from **abseiling** and **canyoning** in the Blue Mountains to **V8 Supercar racing** on the Gold Coast. Suggestions are given throughout the book; for an overview, start on p.62.

from April to November. The **subtropical region** enjoys good sunshine and manageable temperatures all year round. The **inland highlands** are noticeably cooler than the seaboard. All the **coastal cities** experience summer heatwaves; the offshore islands tend to be fresher.

Times you may prefer to **avoid** are the Christmas and Easter holidays, when crowds and prices peak; May to August in the far south, when winter brings short, chilly days; and December to March in the far north, when extreme humidity and tropical downpours can make conditions uncomfortable. Between November and May, you need to guard against dangerous jellyfish before swimming in the coastal waters of northern Queensland (see p.47).

Average temperatures and rainfall

	Jan	Feb	Mar	Apr	May	Jun	Jul	Aug	Sep	Oct	Nov	Dec
Cairns												
Av temp °C	31	31	30	29	28	25	25	27	27	28	30	31
Av rainfall mm	400	400	450	180	100	50	30	25	35	35	90	160
Brisbane												
Av temp °C	27	27	26	25	23	21	23	22	24	25	26	27
Av rainfall mm	160	160	150	80	70	60	55	50	50	75	100	140
Sydney												
Av temp °C	25	25	24	23	20	17	16	17	19	22	23	24
Av rainfall mm	100	105	125	130	125	130	110	75	60	75	70	75
Melbourne												
Av temp °C	26	26	24	21	16	15	14	15	17	19	21	20
Av rainfall mm	45	50	55	60	55	50	50	50	55	65	55	55

28

things not to miss

It's not possible to see everything that Australia's East Coast has to offer in one trip – and we don't suggest you try. What follows, in no particular order, is a selective taste of the region's highlights, including beautiful beaches, outstanding national parks, fascinating wildlife encounters and unforgettable urban experiences. They're arranged in five colour-coded categories, which you can browse through to find the very best things to see and experience. All highlights have a page reference to take you straight into the guide, where you can find out more.

01 Sydney Opera House Pages **233–235** • Take in an opera, concert or play and revel in the glittering harbour views as you sip your interval gin and tonic.

02 **Wilsons Promontory National Park** Page **165** • Victoria's most popular coastal wilderness offers superb bushwalks and inspirational scenery.

03 **The Melbourne Cup** Page **91** • For Australians everywhere, Melbourne's famous horse race is a great excuse for a get-together – complete with Ascot-style hats.

04 **Turtle hatching season, Bundaberg coast** Page **497** • Witness the tiny, vulnerable hatchlings making a scramble for the sea between January and early April.

05 **Bondi Beach** Page **269** • Sand, surf and laid-back style – all within Sydney's city limits.

06 **Watching a match at the MCG** Page **109** • Joining the crowd at the Melbourne Cricket Ground for the cricket – or, even better, Aussie Rules football – is a must for sports fans.

07 **Café society, Melbourne** Page **122** • Sit back and enjoy the perfect flat white or soy latte at one of the many mellow hangouts in the East Coast's coolest capital.

08 **The Daintree and Cape Tribulation** Page **605** • Lush rainforest tumbles down to pristine beaches in this glorious tropical wilderness.

09 **Whale migration, Hervey Bay** Page **485** • Catch sight of frolicking humpbacks as they take a break from their long annual migration between the Antarctic and the Whitsundays.

10 **Sailing in the Whitsundays** Page **522** • Waltz around the archipelago's crystal-clear waters by yacht, mooring overnight in beautiful, sheltered coves.

11 **Platypus-watching, Broken River** Page **513** • Watch quietly to spot these charmingly industrious creatures in their natural environment.

12 **Surfing on the Gold Coast** Page **407** • For many Australians, surfing is life – join them if you dare.

13 Sydney Harbour ferries Page **218**
• The classic way to cross from Circular Quay to the North Shore or Manly, with million-dollar views en route.

14 Walking in the Blue Mountains Page **318** • Australia's answer to the Grand Canyon is laced with rugged forest tracks, perfect for hiking.

16 Australia Zoo Page **464** • Forget the standoffish zoos that don't let you near the animals – this upbeat place is all about good-humoured, hands-on encounters.

15 Fraser Island Page **487** • Bowl along the beach in a 4WD, trek across the giant dunes or take a relaxing dip in the freshwater lakes.

17 **South Bank, Brisbane** Page **449** • World-class art, leafy gardens and a pleasant urban beach add up to the perfect day out in the River City.

18 **Hugging a koala**
Page **453** • Cuddle a sleepy, furry bundle in one of Queensland's, many well-kept wildlife parks.

19 **Feeding wild dolphins, Tangalooma** Page **437** • Just a short boat trip from Brisbane, this is the closest you'll ever get to a wild cetacean.

20 **Highland waterfalls, Atherton Tablelands** Page **571** • Get right back to nature by bathing under a cool cascade.

21 New Year's Eve fireworks, Sydney Page **213** • The Harbour City sees out the year in style with a pyrotechnical tour de force – nowhere else in the world comes close.

23 Nocturnal wildlife-watching Page **63** • Explore the bush with a spotlight to track down fascinating tree-dwelling creatures.

22 Whitehaven Beach Page **525** • One of the contenders for the beach with the whitest sand in the world, this is a little piece of paradise.

24 Little penguin colony, Phillip Island Page **163** • Watch the little chaps walk the walk as they make their way up the beach to their burrows.

25 **Climbing Sydney Harbour Bridge** Page 235 • Scale the giant coathanger for a 360-degree panorama of the East Coast's most thrilling city.

27 **Lord Howe Island** Page 387 • Though just a speck on the map, this Pacific island harbours rare birds galore, amid dramatic, untamed scenery.

26 **Diving the Great Barrier Reef** Page 500 • With a lifetime's worth of dive sites to explore, the Reef is truly one of the world's natural wonders.

28 **Sydney Mardi Gras** Page 296 • Strut your stuff among the sequinned-and-feathered beautiful people at this annual festival of all things outrageous.

East Coast wildlife

Since Australia broke away from the ancestral supercontinent Gondwana about ninety million years ago, its plants and animals have developed in splendid isolation from the rest of the world. Its few mammalian species, most of which are marsupials, are particularly distinctive, and less elusive than you might think. The lush rainforest and dense bush found along many stretches of the East Coast are also home to a great diversity of birds, reptiles and amphibians, while offshore reefs and rock formations harbour a dazzling variety of marine life.

This brief guide provides a quick reference to help you identify some of the most common species. Straightforward photos show markings and other physical features, while the notes for each fish, animal or bird give you pointers about the kind of habitat in which you are likely to see it, and distinguishing characteristics that you may observe when sighting it in the wild. For further details and background, see p.640.

Racoon butterflyfish

Chaetodon lunula

☞ swims in pairs around areas of living coral

🖋 false "eye" is to fool predators as to which way it will escape

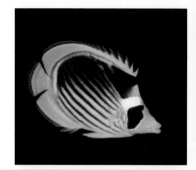

Feather-fin bullfish

Heniochus acuminatus

☞ swims in pairs close to coral reefs

🖋 often mistaken for bannerfish or moorish idol

Anenomefish or Clownfish

Amphiprion melanopus

☞ hides in anenomes on coral reefs

🖋 male changes gender if the dominant female dies

Parrotfish

Chlorurus microrhinus

☞ nibbles at coral on shallow reefs

🖋 ingests coral, excreting it as sand; sleeps in a mucus cocoon

Humpheaded maori wrasse
Cheilinus undulatus

☞ swims around shallow coral reefs

✐ commonly grows to well over 100kg

Bluespot stingray
Amphotistius kuhlii

☞ hovers on sandy seabed in warm waters

✐ tail carries two stinging spines

Whitetip reef shark
Triaenodon obesus

☞ hunts around reefs in warm tropical waters

✐ timid and passive; eats fish

Green turtle
Chelonia mydas

☞ feeds on seagrass beds and coral reefs

✐ named "green" since its innards are greenish

☞ WHERE FOUND   ✐ NOTES

Dugong

Dugong dugon

☞ feeds on seagrass beds, rising to
breathe every one to three minutes

✎ rare, slow-moving, herbivorous
marine mammal

Humpback whale

Megaptera novaeangliae

☞ breaches in open ocean, from the
Whitsundays south

✎ migrates up the East Coast in winter
to breed

Estuarine crocodile

Crocodylus porosus

☞ inhabits fresh and saltwater coastal
areas in northern Australia

✎ basks on banks by day, hunts by night;
dangerous to humans

Agile wallaby

Macropus agilis

☞ mobs inhabit grasslands of central and
northern Queensland coast

✎ widespread; males are much larger
than females

Red-necked pademelon

Thylogale thetis

☞ solitary; grazes on rainforest margins

✐ shy marsupial; eats leaves and grasses round the clock

Eastern grey kangaroo

Macropus giganteus

☞ mobs feed on grass in scrubland and forest in eastern Australia

✐ active from late afternoon to early morning; widespread

Brushtail possum

Trichosurus vulpecula

☞ lives in tree hollows and roof spaces; agile climber

✐ nocturnal; common; well-adapted to life in towns

Koala

Phascolarctus cinerus

☞ solitary; sleeps in eucalyptus trees for twenty hours per day

✐ highly specialized diet of eucalyptus leaves; habitat is dwindling

☞ WHERE FOUND ✐ NOTES

Common wombat

Vombatus ursinus

☞ solitary and nocturnal ground-dweller, from northeastern NSW south

✎ stocky marsupial; digs burrows to sleep and nest in

Sugar glider

Petaurus breviceps

☞ shy and nocturnal arboreal possum

✎ membrane between fore and hind paws; can glide up to 50m

Black flying fox

Pteropus alecto

☞ roosts in trees by day, hanging upside down, wrapped in its wings

✎ entire colony departs for feeding grounds at dusk

Platypus

Ornithorhynchus anatinus

☞ swims in mountain creeks; active around dawn and dusk

✎ shy; egg-laying aquatic mammal; suckles young after they hatch

Rainbow lorikeet

Trichoglossus haematodus

☞ flocks and pairs are common in woodlands and backyards

✐ gregarious and noisy; eats nectar, pollen and some insects

Laughing kookaburra

Dacelo novaeguineae

☞ perches on branches in woodlands; distinctive cackling call

✐ member of the kingfisher family, but eats insects and worms

Southern cassowary

Casuarius casuarius

☞ strides through gullies and rainforests of the Far North Queensland coast

✐ chicks are striped and are cared for by male parent

Superb lyrebird

Menura novaehollandiae

☞ lives on forest floor in NSW and VIC coastal regions

✐ expert mimic: call imitates natural and mechanical sounds

☞ WHERE FOUND ✐ NOTES

Basics

Basics

Getting there

You can fly pretty much any day of the week to the main East Coast cities of Melbourne, Sydney, Brisbane and Cairns from Europe, North America and Southeast Asia, and regional connections are excellent. Airfares always depend on the season, with the highest fares being the two weeks either side of Christmas. Fares drop during the "shoulder" seasons – mid-January to March and mid-August to November – and you'll get the best prices during the low season, April to June. Because of the distance from most popular departure points, flying at weekends does not alter the price.

While plenty of tour operators offer East Coast packages including flights, accommodation and transport or tours, it's straightforward enough – and sometimes cheaper – to create your own independent itinerary by booking everything separately. If Australia is only one stop on a longer journey, you might want to consider buying a Round-the-World (RTW) ticket (see p.28). Students and under-26s may be able to cut costs by using a **specialist travel agent** who can fix up discount fares plus travel insurance, bus or rail passes, tours and the like.

From the UK and Ireland

Flying to Sydney and the other East Coast cities takes a minimum of 21 hours, including stopovers. If you break the trip in Southeast Asia or North America, getting to Australia need not be the tedious, seat-bound slog you may have imagined.

Sydney and Melbourne are served by the greatest number of airlines, and carriers such as Qantas charge around the same price to fly to Sydney or Melbourne, with Brisbane and Cairns costing extra (4–12 percent and 15–30 percent, respectively). **Open-jaw fares** (flying into one city and out from another) fall into the same range as ordinary returns.

London's Heathrow airport is the main departure point, although you can also fly from Manchester to Sydney with Emirates (via Dubai) or Singapore Airlines (via Singapore). For flights from other UK regional airports via Heathrow, Qantas is generally the best option.

The cheapest standard **fare to Sydney or Melbourne** is around £550 return, available from April to June, though special offers can go as low as £450. Standard fares with Qantas, British Airways or Singapore Airlines start from around £800, with special offers from £600. Mid-January to March and mid-August to November, you should expect to pay around £700–950, depending on the airline. Prices are higher during the European summer holidays (late June to mid-Aug), and peak in the two weeks before Christmas, when you'd be lucky to find anything for under £1000 return unless you book at least six months in advance.

An excellent alternative to a long direct flight is to make **one or more extended stopovers**; this can cost little more than an ordinary return, unless the routing is particularly unusual. A popular option is to build an overland trip through Southeast Asia into your itinerary: though a bit more demanding than Australia, it's a fascinating region that's unlikely to make a big dent in your budget. Since many Asian airlines stop in Bangkok, Kuala Lumpur, Singapore, Jakarta or Denpasar on the way to Australia, breaking your journey in these cities may be free. If you'd like to include a lengthy overland journey such as the classic Bangkok to Bali route, you could buy a multi-city or Round-the-World ticket (see p.28) with an overland component. If you're considering combining your East Coast trip with a visit to New Zealand or the Southwest Pacific, you may be able to save money with a **Boomerang Pass**, available to anyone flying from Europe to Australia with Qantas or BA – it allows you

Fly less – stay longer! Travel and Climate Change

Climate change is perhaps the single biggest issue facing our planet. It is caused by a build-up in the atmosphere of carbon dioxide and other greenhouse gases, which are emitted by many sources – including planes. Already, **flights** account for three to four percent of human-induced global warming: that figure may sound small, but it is rising year on year and threatens to counteract the progress made by reducing greenhouse emissions in other areas.

Rough Guides regard travel as a **global benefit**, and feel strongly that the advantages to developing economies are important, as are the opportunities for greater contact and awareness among peoples. But we also believe in travelling responsibly, which includes giving thought to how often we fly and what we can do to redress any harm that our trips may create.

We can travel less or simply reduce the amount we travel by air (taking fewer trips and staying longer, or taking the train if there is one); we can avoid night flights (which are more damaging); and we can make the trips we do take "climate neutral" via a carbon offset scheme. **Offset schemes** run by climatecare.org, carbonneutral .com and others allow you to "neutralize" the greenhouse gases that you are responsible for releasing. Their websites have simple calculators that let you work out the impact of any flight – as does our own. Once that's done, you can pay to fund projects that will reduce future emissions by an equivalent amount. Please take the time to visit our website and make your trip climate neutral, or get a copy of the *Rough Guide to Climate Change* for more detail on the subject.

www.roughguides.com/climatechange

to book flights between destinations in New Zealand and the Southwest Pacific at a discount rate (from £65 per leg).

Most of the routings **from Ireland** involve a stopover and change of airlines in London, but it's also possible to fly direct from Dublin to Los Angeles with Aer Lingus and pick up a Qantas flight to Sydney from there. Fares typically range from €1150 to €2000 according to season. Airlines offering flights ticketed through from Dublin, Shannon or Cork to Sydney include Singapore Airlines (via London and Singapore), Malaysia Airlines (via London and Kuala Lumpur), BA and Qantas (both via London).

RTW tickets

Round-the-World (RTW) tickets incorporating Australia provide a chance to see the world on your way to – and from – Down Under; RTW flights come pre-packaged in a tantalizing variety of permutations, with stopovers chiefly in Asia, the Pacific and North America, but you can pretty much devise your fantasy itinerary and get it priced. A good agent should be able to piece together sector fares from various airlines: providing you keep your itinerary down to

three continents, you can bag a simple London–Bangkok–Sydney–LA–London deal for little more than a standard return to Sydney. For six or more stops, or complicated routings, prices start at around £1100.

From the US and Canada

The main departure point for East Coast Australia is Los Angeles, which is fourteen and a half hours from Sydney by **non-stop flight**. Qantas, American Airlines and United all fly direct; other airlines making the run include Air New Zealand (via Auckland) and Air Canada (via Vancouver). Qantas also have direct flights from LA to Brisbane or Melbourne (non-stop), from New York to Sydney (via LA) and from San Francisco to Sydney (non-stop or via LA). Flying from either the west or east coast on a national Asian airline will most likely involve a stop in their capital city (Tokyo, Hong Kong, Kuala Lumpur, Singapore), a longer and costlier routing. If a Pacific Rim or South Pacific stopover appeals, you can build this into your itinerary, even if you're flying with Qantas or an American airline: there will either be a flat surcharge on your ticket, or you will be offered a higher-priced ticket allowing you to make as many stops as you like, within certain parameters, over a fixed period of time.

The starting prices for standard scheduled **fares to Sydney** in low/high seasons are approximately as follows: from Chicago or New York (US$1550/2000); Los Angeles or San Francisco (US$1150/1700); Montréal or Toronto (CDN$1500/2500); Vancouver (CDN$1400/2000). You can expect to pay eight percent more for a flight to Melbourne and Brisbane, or thirteen percent for Cairns. The price of an **open-jaw ticket** (flying into one city and returning from another) should be approximately the average of the return fares to the two cities. If you plan on flying between several East Coast cities or elsewhere in Australia, you can save money with the **Qantas AirPass**, which includes an international flight from LA or San Francisco plus three domestic flights in Australia (from US$1249).

RTW or Circle Pacific tickets

If you don't mind planning your itinerary in advance, you can extend your travels with a **Round-the-World (RTW)** ticket, or a **Circle Pacific** ticket, which limits your trip to a series of destinations in Australia, New Zealand, Asia and South America. A sample RTW itinerary would be: Los Angeles–Sydney–Singapore–Bangkok–Delhi–London–Los Angeles (US$4220), while a sample Circle Pacific route would be: NY–Santiago (Chile)–Sydney–Perth–Hong Kong–NY (US$4100).

From New Zealand and South Africa

Routes from **New Zealand** are busy and competition is fierce, resulting in an ever-changing range of deals and special offers; your best bet is to check the latest with a specialist travel agent (see p.30) or the relevant airlines' websites. It's a relatively short hop across the Tasman Sea: **flying time** from Auckland to Sydney is around three and a half hours.

All the **fares** quoted below include tax and are for travel during low or shoulder seasons; flying at peak times (primarily Dec to mid-Jan) can add substantially to the prices.

Ultimately, what you pay for your flight will depend on how much flexibility you want; many of the cheapest deals are hedged with restrictions – typically, a maximum stay of thirty days and a fourteen-day advance-purchase requirement. Pacific Blue flies from Auckland, Christchurch and Wellington to Gold Coast (Coolangatta), Brisbane, Sydney and Melbourne, with connections to many other East Coast cities, from around NZ$400 return. The cheapest regular return fare from Auckland to Sydney is usually with Aerolineas Argentinas (also to Melbourne) for around NZ$380–500, but flights tend to be heavily booked.

Flying **from South Africa**, the journey time is around twelve hours from Johannesburg to Sydney. The main carriers are Qantas and South African Airways, which both offer ten flights a week from around ZAR7800 in low season and ZAR11,800 in high season.

Airlines, agents and tour operators

Travel websites and the airlines' own websites offer the best deals and cut out the cost of agents and middlemen. If your time is short and you're reasonably sure of what you want to do, it may not be a bad idea to pre-book some of your accommodation and tours. See below for a list of operators and Australian holiday specialists. Local tour operators are listed in the Guide, by region.

Online booking

Ⓦ www.expedia.co.uk (UK), Ⓦ www.expedia .com (US), Ⓦ www.expedia.ca (Canada)
Ⓦ www.lastminute.com (UK)
Ⓦ www.opodo.co.uk (UK)
Ⓦ www.orbitz.com (US)
Ⓦ www.travelocity.co.uk (UK), Ⓦ www .travelocity.com (US), Ⓦ www.travelocity.ca (Canada)
Ⓦ www.zuji.com.au (Australia), Ⓦ www.zuji .co.nz (New Zealand)
Ⓦ www.travelshop.com.au (Australia)

Airlines

Aerolineas Argentinas UK ☏ 0800/096 9747, US ☏ 1-800/333-0276, Canada ☏ 1-800/688-0008; Ⓦ www.aerolineasargentinas.com.

Air China UK ☎020/7744 0800, US ☎212/371-9898, Canada ☎416/581-8833, Australia ☎02 9232 7277; ⓦwww.fly-airchina.com.

Air New Zealand Australia ☎13 24 76, NZ ☎0800/737 000; ⓦwww.airnz.co.nz.

Air Pacific UK ☎0870/572 6827, US ☎1-800/227-4446, Australia ☎1800 230 150, NZ ☎0800/800 178; ⓦwww.airpacific.com.

All Nippon Airways (ANA) UK ☎0870/837 8866, Republic of Ireland ☎1850/200 058, US & Canada ☎1-800/235-9262; ⓦwww.anaskyweb.com.

American Airlines UK ☎0845/7789 789, Republic of Ireland ☎01/602 0550, US ☎1-800/433-7300, Australia ☎1300 650 747, NZ ☎0800 887 997; ⓦwww.aa.com.

British Airways UK ☎0870/850 9850, Republic of Ireland ☎1890/626 747, US & Canada ☎1-800/AIRWAYS, Australia ☎1300 767 177, NZ ☎09/966 9777; ⓦwww.ba.com.

Cathay Pacific UK ☎020/8834 8888, US ☎1-800/233-2742, Australia ☎13 17 47, NZ ☎09/379 0861; ⓦwww.cathaypacific.com.

China Airlines UK ☎020/7436 9001, US ☎1-917/368-2003, Australia ☎02/9231 5588, NZ ☎09/308 3364; ⓦwww.china-airlines.com.

Emirates UK ☎0870/243 2222, US ☎1-800/777-3999, Australia ☎02 9290 9700, NZ ☎09/968 2200; ⓦwww.emirates.com.

Garuda Indonesia UK ☎020/7467 8600, US ☎1-212/279-0756, Australia ☎02 9334 9944 or 1300 365 330, NZ ☎09/366 1862; ⓦwww.garuda-indonesia.com.

JAL (Japan Air Lines) UK ☎0845/774 7700, Republic of Ireland ☎01/408 3757, US & Canada ☎1-800/525-3663, Australia ☎02 9272 1111, NZ ☎09/379 9906; ⓦwww.jal.com or www.japanair.com

Jetstar US ☎1-866/397-8170, Australia ☎13 15 38, NZ ☎0800/800 995; ⓦwww.jetstar.com.

KLM (Royal Dutch Airlines) UK ☎0870/507 4074, Republic of Ireland ☎1850/747 400, US ☎1-800/225-2525, Australia ☎1300 303 747, NZ ☎09/921 6040, SA ☎11/961 6767; ⓦwww.klm.com.

Korean Air UK ☎0800/413 000, Republic of Ireland ☎01/799 7990, US & Canada ☎1-800/438-5000, Australia ☎02 9262 6000, NZ ☎09/914 2000; ⓦwww.koreanair.com.

Malaysia Airlines UK ☎0870/607 9090, Republic of Ireland ☎01/676 2131, US ☎1-212/697-8994, Australia ☎13 26 27, NZ ☎0800/777 747; ⓦwww.malaysia-airlines.com.

Olympic Airways UK ☎0870/606 0460, US ☎1-800/223-1226, Canada ☎1-416/964-2720, Australia ☎02/9251 2044; ⓦwww.olympic-airways.com.

Pacific Blue NZ ☎0800/670 000, outside NZ ☎07/3295 2284, ⓦwww.flypacificblue.com.

Qantas Airways UK ☎0845/774 7767, Republic of Ireland ☎01/407 3278, US & Canada ☎1-800/227-4500, Australia ☎13 13 13, NZ ☎09/357 8900 or 0800 808 767, SA ☎11/441 8550; ⓦwww.qantas.com.

Royal Brunei UK ☎020/7584 6660, Australia ☎1300 721 271, NZ ☎09/977 2209; ⓦwww.bruneiair.com.

Singapore Airlines UK ☎0844/800 2380, Republic of Ireland ☎01/671 0722, US ☎1-800/742-3333, Canada ☎1-800/663-3046, Australia ☎13 10 11, NZ ☎0800/808 909, SA ☎11/880 8560 or 8566; ⓦwww.singaporeair.com.

South African Airways UK ☎0870/747 1111, US & Canada ☎1-800/722-9675, Australia ☎1800 221 699, NZ ☎09/977 2237, SA ☎11/978 1111; ⓦwww.flysaa.com.

Thai Airways UK ☎0870/606 0911, US ☎1-212/949-8424, Canada ☎1-416/971-5181, Australia ☎1300 651 960, NZ ☎09/377 3886; ⓦwww.thaiair.com.

Tiger Airways Australia ☎03 9335 3033, Singapore ☎+65 6580 7630; ⓦwww.tigerairways.com.au.

United Airlines UK ☎0845/844 4777, US ☎1-800/UNITED-1, Australia ☎13 17 77; ⓦwww.united.com.

Virgin Atlantic UK ☎0870/380 2007, US ☎1-800/821-5438, Australia ☎1300 727 340, SA ☎11/340 3400; ⓦwww.virgin-atlantic.com.

Virgin Blue Australia ☎13 67 89, outside Australia ☎07/3295 2296, ⓦwww.virginblue.com.au.

Agents and tour operators

Abercrombie and Kent US ☎1-800/554-7016, ⓦwww.abercrombiekent.com. Offers eight- to twenty-one-day high-end tours, often with a special-interest component, and customized itineraries. Extensions available to Papua New Guinea, New Zealand and Fiji.

Air Brokers International US ☎1-800/883-3273, ⓦwww.airbrokers.com. US consolidator and specialist in RTW and Circle Pacific tickets.

Airtreks.com US & Canada ☎415/977-7100 or 1-877/AIRTREKS, ⓦwww.airtreks.com. RTW and Circle Pacific tickets for North Americans. The website features an interactive database that lets you build and price your own round-the-world itinerary.

Asia Transpacific Journeys US ☎1-800/642-2742, ⓦwww.asiatranspacific.com. Long-established outfit with a wide range of customized itineraries and group tours including nature, adventure and Aboriginal rock art.

ATS Tours US ☏ 1-888/781 5170, ⓦ www
.atstours.com. Huge Australian and New Zealand
specialist; dive deals, fly-drives, city stopovers, rail/
bus passes, motel vouchers and other add-ons.
Australia Travel Centre Republic of Ireland
☏ 01/804 7188, ⓦ www.australia.ie. Flights and
holiday packages.
Austravel UK ☏ 0870/166 2020, Republic of
Ireland ☏ 01/642 7009; ⓦ www.austravel.com.
Specialists for flights and tours to Australia with a
huge range of packages, including self-drive trips, rail
journeys, escorted tours and sailing holidays.
Contiki UK ☏ 020/8290 6422; ⓦ www.contiki
.com. Big-group, bus and 4WD tours at budget prices
for fun-loving 18- to 35-year-olds, with plenty of
optional extras (climbing, diving, etc).
ebookers UK ☏ 0800/082 3000, Republic of
Ireland ☏ 01/488 3507; ⓦ www.ebookers.com. Low
fares on an extensive selection of scheduled flights
and package deals.
Explore UK ☏ 0845/013 1537, Republic of Ireland
☏ 01/677 9479; ⓦ www.explore.co.uk. Bus and
4WD adventure tours; their eighteen-day East Coast
Experience costs from £2674 including return flight
from London.
Flight Centre UK ☏ 0870/499 0040, US
☏ 1-866/967-5351, Canada ☏ 1-877/967-5302,
Australia ☏ 13 31 33, NZ ☏ 0800/243 544, SA
☏ 0860/400 727; ⓦ www.flightcentre.com.
Competitive discounts on airfares, and a wide range of
package holidays and adventure tours.
Holiday Shoppe NZ ☏ 0800/808 480, ⓦ www
.holidayshoppe.co.nz. One of New Zealand's
largest travel agencies. Good for budget airfares and
accommodation packages.
Lee's Travel UK ☏ 0870/027 3338, ⓦ www
.leestravel.com. Good deals from the UK, especially
on Southeast Asian airlines.
North South Travel UK ☏ 01245/608 291,
ⓦ www.northsouthtravel.co.uk. Friendly,
competitive travel agency, offering discounted fares
worldwide. Profits are used to support projects in
the developing world, especially the promotion of
sustainable tourism.
Qantas Holidays UK ☏ 020/8222 9125, ⓦ www
.qantasholidays.co.uk. Australia specialists with a
vast array of flight-plus-accommodation packages
and bespoke holidays.
Quest Travel UK ☏ 0845/263 6963, ⓦ www
.questtravel.com. UK agent dealing in long-haul
flights and holidays.
STA Travel UK ☏ 0870/1630 026, Australia
☏ 1300 733 035, US ☏ 1-800/781-4040,
Canada ☏ 1-888/427-5639, NZ ☏ 0508/782 872,
SA ☏ 0861/781 781; ⓦ www.statravel
.com. Worldwide specialists in independent travel;

also student IDs, travel insurance, car rental, rail
passes and more. Good discounts for students and
under-26s.
Student Universe US & Canada ☏ 1-800/272-
9676, ⓦ www.studentuniverse.com. Competitive
student-travel specialists for North Americans; no card
or membership required.
Swain Australia Tours US ☏ 1-800/227-9246,
ⓦ www.swainaustralia.com. Excellent range of
customized tours, including trips specifically designed
for families.
Trailfinders UK ☏ 0845/058 5858, Republic of
Ireland ☏ 01/677 7888, Australia ☏ 1300 780 212;
ⓦ www.trailfinders.com. One of the best-informed
and most efficient agents for independent travellers.
Travelbag UK ☏ 0800/082 5000, ⓦ www
.travelbag.co.uk. Specialists in RTW tickets, many
with Australian components, with good deals aimed
at the backpacker market. Also car and campervan
rental, farmstays and bus and 4WD tours.
Travel Cuts Canada ☏ 1-866/246-9762, US
☏ 1-800/592-2887; ⓦ www.travelcuts.com.
Canadian student-travel organization with offices in
many North American cities.
Usit Republic of Ireland ☏ 01/602 1904, ⓦ www
.usit.ie. Student and youth specialists for flights,
accommodation and transport.

Special-interest holiday companies

Auswalk Australia ☎ 03 5356 4971, ⓦ www
.auswalk.com.au. Walking holidays run by
enthusiasts.

Birdquest UK ☎ 01254/826 317, ⓦ www
.birdquest.co.uk. Extended birdwatching tours, led by
ornithological experts.

Hands Up Holidays UK ☎ 0800/783 3554,
ⓦ www.handsupholidays.com. Adventurous, offbeat
trips through Queensland, taking in wilderness areas,
rock-art sites and conservation projects.

I-to-I UK ☎ 0800/011 1156, ⓦ www.i-to-i.com.
Voluntourism specialist, currently offering the chance
to help create cassowary corridors in the Mission
Beach rainforest or assist at a wallaby conservation
project near Rockhampton.

Naturetrek UK ☎ 01962/733 051, ⓦ www
.naturetrek.co.uk. Wildlife holiday specialist, offering
two-week trips to Queensland focusing on birds and
nocturnal animals.

Oxley Travel Australia ☎ 1800 671 536, ⓦ www
.oxleytravel.com.au. Lord Howe Island and Norfolk
Island travel specialists.

Pure Vacations UK ☎ 0845/299 0045, ⓦ www
.purevacations.com. Surfing holidays on the
Sunshine Coast, with tuition at all levels.

Real Gap Experience UK ☎ 01892/516 164,
ⓦ www.realgap.co.uk. Working holidays, volunteer
opportunities and overland trips for young gap
year travellers.

Responsible Travel UK ☎ 01273/600 030,
ⓦ www.responsibletravel.com. Innovative agency
offering a wide selection of accommodation options
and trips, including hiking, wildlife-watching and
overland camping safaris, from providers that
have been assessed for their responsible-tourism
credentials.

Sunsail Australia ☎ 07 4948 9509 or 1800 803
988, ⓦ www.sunsail.com.au. Whitsundays-based
sailing holiday company, offering luxury yacht cruises
and RYA courses. Their MileCatchers Voyages, hosted
by professional instructors, allow sailing enthusiasts
to clock up knots in the Coral Sea between Cape York
and Fraser Island.

Talpacific Australia ☎ 07 3218 9900, UK ☎ 020/
8288 8400; ⓦ www.talpacific.com.au. Trips to Lord
Howe Island and Norfolk Island.

Walks Worldwide UK ☎ 01524/242 000, ⓦ www
.walksworldwide.com. Escorted and self-guided
hiking itineraries.

World Expeditions UK ☎ 0800/074 4135, US
☎ 1-888/464-8735, Canada ☎ 1-800/567-2216,
Australia ☎ 1300 720 000, NZ ☎ 09/368 4161;
ⓦ www.worldexpeditions.co.uk. Australian-owned
adventure company; small-group active wilderness
holidays, including a seven-day Hinchinbrook Island
and Coral Sea trip.

Entry requirements

All visitors to Australia, except New Zealanders, require a visa to enter the
country. You can apply online, a fast and efficient process – it's unlikely that you'll
need to visit an Australian high commission, embassy or consulate in person.

The best option for nationals of the UK, the
Republic of Ireland, the US, Canada,
Malaysia, Singapore, Japan and most
European countries who intend to make one
or more short trips to Australia is to get an
ETA (Electronic Travel Authority), a virtual
visa valid for multiple entry over one year
(max three months per visit). ETAs can only
be obtained outside Australia, and do not
entitle you to accept paid employment during
your visit. It's easy to apply online (ⓦ www
.eta.immi.gov.au) or through travel agents

and airlines. There's no visa fee, only a A$20
service charge, payable by credit or debit
card, and successful applicants typically
receive their visa the same day (max three
days). You don't need to have booked your
flights at the time you apply, and you don't
need to send off your passport: instead, the
ETA system records your details in the
Australian immigration database and emails
you a confirmation code. You're unlikely to
be asked for this at flight check-in or
passport control, but it's worth keeping for

reference: you can use it to double-check the details of your visa online at any time.

If you want to stay longer than three months, or your nationality is not included in the ETA scheme, you should apply for a **Tourist Visa (676)** instead, available for A$75 and typically valid for three, six or twelve months, for either single or multiple visits (depending on the purpose of your visit and your personal circumstances). It doesn't entitle you to accept paid work in Australia, but it does allow you to work as an unpaid volunteer as an incidental part of your trip. You can apply online (Ⓦwww.immi.gov.au; normal turnaround 48 hours or less, maximum three weeks) or in person at an Australian visa office (see below).

If, having entered Australia with an ETA or a Tourist Visa, you decide you'd like to stay longer than your allotted time, your only option is to apply for a new Tourist Visa at least two weeks before your old visa expires. However, you'll be subject to a A$215 fee and extra administrative tasks, such as supplying proof of your medical and financial status and a police statement confirming you have no criminal convictions, so it's wiser to obtain a Tourist Visa valid for the full period of your stay before you travel.

Citizens of the UK, the Republic of Ireland, Belgium, Canada, Cyprus, Denmark, Estonia, Finland, France, Germany, Hong Kong, Italy, Japan, Korea, Malta, the Netherlands, Norway, Sweden and Taiwan aged 18–30 are entitled to apply for a twelve-month **Working Holiday Visa (417)**. The stress is on casual employment: you're not permitted to work for the same employer for more than six months. Again, you can apply online (Ⓦwww.immi.gov.au; most visas are issued within 48 hours) or in person at an Australian visa office; the fee is A$190. You can begin your trip at any time within twelve months of the issue date of your visa, which expires a year after you first enter Australia, even if you don't spent the entire year there. If during that time you have spent at least 88 days (or three months full time) doing seasonal work for a primary producer (such as a farm, fishery, plantation or mine) in regional Australia, you can apply for a second Working Holiday Visa for another A$190.

In a separate but similar scheme, tertiary-educated US citizens aged 18–30 can apply for a twelve-month **Work and Holiday Visa (462)** for A$180.

Australia has strict **quarantine laws** that apply to bringing fruit, vegetables, fresh and packaged food, seed and some animal products into the country; there are also strict laws prohibiting drugs, steroids, firearms, protected wildlife and associated products. You are allowed to carry A$900 worth of goods into Australia, including gifts and souvenirs, while those over 18 can take advantage of a duty-free allowance on entry of 2.25 litres of alcohol and 250 cigarettes or 250g of tobacco. Families travelling together (married couples and children under 18) can pool their allowances.

Australian embassies and consulates abroad

The following accept visa applications.

Canada Australian High Commission, Suite 710, 50 O'Connor St, Ottawa, ON K1P 6L2 ☎1888/990 888 or 613/236-0841, Ⓦwww.canada.embassy.gov.au.
France Australian Embassy, 4 rue Jean Rey, 75724 Paris ☎+33 1 40 59 33 06, Ⓦwww.france.embassy.gov.au.
Germany Australian Embassy, Wallstrasse 76–79, 10179 Berlin ☎+49 30 700 129 129, Ⓦwww.germany.embassy.gov.au.
India Australian High Commission, 1/50G Shantipath, Chanakyapuri, New Delhi 110021 ☎+91 11 4122 1000, Ⓦwww.india.embassy.gov.au.
Indonesia Australian Consulate, Australian Consulate-General, Jalan Hayam Wuruk No 88B, Tanjung Bungkak, Denpasar, Bali 80234 ☎+62 361/241 118, Ⓦwww.bali.indonesia.embassy.gov.au. Australian Embassy, Jalan HR Rasuna Said Kav C15–16, Jakarta Selatan 12940 ☎+62 21/2550 5700, Ⓦwww.indonesia.embassy.gov.au.
Republic of Ireland The Australian Embassy in Dublin has no visa office; Irish citizens should apply to the London office or online.
Italy Australian Embassy, Via Antonio Bosio 5, Rome 00161 ☎+39 06 852 721, Ⓦwww.italy.embassy.gov.au.
Malaysia Australian High Commission, 6 Jalan Yap Kwan Seng, Kuala Lumpur ☎+60 2146 5642, Ⓦwww.malaysia.embassy.gov.au.
The Netherlands The Australian Embassy in The Hague has no visa office; Dutch citizens should apply to the Berlin office or online.
New Zealand Australian Consulate-General, Level 7, Price WaterHouse Coopers Tower, 188

Quay St, Auckland ☎09/921 8800, ⓦwww
.newzealand.embassy.gov.au.

Singapore Australian High Commission, 25 Napier
Rd, Singapore ☎+65 6836 4100, ⓦwww
.singapore.embassy.gov.au.

South Africa Australian High Commission,
292 Orient St, Arcadia, Pretoria ☎12/423 6000,
ⓦwww.australia.co.za.

Thailand Australian Embassy, 37 South Sathorn

Rd, Bangkok ☎+66 2/344 3476, ⓦwww.thailand
.embassy.gov.au.

UK Australian High Commission, Australia House,
Strand, London WC2B 4LA ☎020/7379 4334
(recorded information), ☎0906/550 8900 (premium
rate), ⓦwww.uk.embassy.gov.au.

USA Australian Embassy, 1601 Massachusetts Ave
NW, Washington, DC 20036-2273 ☎1888/990-8888
or 202/797-3000, ⓦwww.usa.embassy.gov.au.

Getting around

The East Coast is Australia's main transport corridor. The coastal highway from Melbourne to Cooktown varies in condition along its 4060-kilometre length but is generally good, and long-distance bus services to the major towns are frequent and affordable. Many areas are also connected by train. With 28 regional airports dotted along the coast, flying is a speedy and efficient alternative: low-cost airlines are keeping fares competitive. Frequencies and journey times of long-distance bus, train and plane services can be found under "Travel details" at the end of each chapter, with local buses and trains covered in the main text. Guided tours can be an excellent way to see some of the more interesting wilderness areas, but to get right off the beaten track and explore at your own pace, self-drive is the best option, either by buying or renting a vehicle.

However you're travelling, plan your routes carefully: first-time visitors from smaller, more densely populated countries often underestimate Australia's vast distances. While you can cover ground fairly rapidly on the highways and freeways, any lengthy excursion into the hinterland is likely to take you onto narrow, steep and winding minor roads, while in remote areas, including some national parks, the roads may be graded gravel instead of tarmac. Consider the season, too; in the summer, you'll be glad of a vehicle with air-conditioning. If you'll be visiting Far North Queensland at the height of the rains, self-drive may not be the most comfortable option.

By plane

Between them, Qantas, Jetstar, Tiger Airways and Virgin Blue cover most of the **East Coast airports**, with regional specialists and private charters (such as those

serving the island resorts) filling in the gaps. **Melbourne**, **Sydney**, **Brisbane** and **Cairns** are the hubs. One-way fares vary from month to month; examples include: Sydney to Cairns with Qantas from A$142; Sydney to the Fraser Coast with Virgin Blue from A$85; Melbourne to Cairns with Jetstar from A$172; and Melbourne to the Gold Coast with Tiger Airways from A$60. It's worth checking online for the latest deals, which are often very good, especially when you consider the time and money you'd otherwise spend on a long bus or train journey.

By train

It's possible to visit much of the region by **train**: interstate railways connect all the major cities from Melbourne to Cairns, though some main lines run many kilometres inland, skirting the smaller coastal towns. The principal **long-distance services** are

Transport information

Domestic airlines

Aeropelican ☎02 4928 9600, ⓦwww.aeropelican.com.au. Newcastle to Sydney.

Brindabella Airlines ☎1300 668 824, ⓦwww.brindabellaairlines.com.au. From Canberra and Brisbane to Coffs Habour, Newcastle and Port Macquarie.

Jetstar ☎13 15 38, ⓦwww.jetstar.com.au. Many East Coast destinations.

Norfolk Air ☎+6723 24272 or 1800 612 960, ⓦwww.norfolkair.com. Brisbane, Sydney and Melbourne to Norfolk Island.

Qantas ☎13 13 13, ⓦwww.qantas.com.au. Australia's most comprehensive regional service.

Regional Express ☎02 6393 5550 or 13 17 13, ⓦwww.rex.com.au. From Sydney to Brisbane and the New South Wales coast, plus Melbourne to Merimbula.

Skytrans ☎1300 7598 7267, ⓦwww.skytrans.com.au. From Cairns to Townsville, Cooktown and Cape York.

Tiger Airways ☎03 9335 3033, ⓦwww.tigerairways.com.au. From Melbourne to Canberra, Newcastle and the Queensland coast.

Virgin Blue ☎07 3295 2296 or 13 67 89, ⓦwww.virginblue.com.au. Many East Coast destinations.

Bus, train, tram and ferry companies

CityRail ☎02 8202 2000 or 13 15 00, ⓦwww.cityrail.info. Rail network for Greater Sydney, including the Blue Mountains, the North Coast New South Wales to Newcastle and South Coast New South Wales to Bomaderry (Nowra).

CountryLink ☎02 8202 2000 or 13 23 32, ⓦwww.countrylink.info. State provider for regional New South Wales. Long-distance train services from Sydney to Canberra, Melbourne and Brisbane, supplemented by bus services to regions lying off the main lines including the far north and far south New South Wales coastal towns.

Firefly Express Coaches ☎03 8318 0318 or 1300 730 740, ⓦwww.fireflyexpress .com.au. Melbourne to Sydney bus service.

Greyhound Australia ☎1300 473 946, ⓦwww.greyhound.com.au. National long-distance bus service: covers the inland route from Melbourne to Sydney, and the coast from Sydney to Cairns, but not the southeastern coast.

Premier Motor Service ☎02 4423 5233 or 13 34 10, ⓦwww.premierms.com.au. Long-distance bus service covering the entire East Coast from Melbourne to Cairns, including the southeastern coast.

Queensland Rail ☎07 3606 5555, ⓦwww.qr.com.au. State provider for Queensland. Runs long-distance trains from Brisbane to Cairns, Citytrain services within Southeast Queensland, and the Kuranda Scenic Railway.

TransLink ☎13 12 30, ⓦwww.translink.com.au. Integrated transport network (buses, trains and ferries) for Brisbane and southeast Queensland.

V/Line ☎03 9697 2076 or 13 61 96, ⓦwww.vline.com.au. State provider (buses and trains) for regional Victoria.

Timetables, fares and journey planning

Metlink ☎13 16 38, ⓦwww.metlinkmelbourne.com.au. Melbourne and Victoria.

TransLink ☎13 12 30, ⓦwww.translink.com.au. Brisbane and southeast Queensland.

Transport Infoline ☎13 15 00, ⓦwww.131500.com.au. Sydney and New South Wales.

Traveltrain ☎1800 872 467, ⓦwww.traveltrain.com.au. Regional Queensland, including Sunlander and Tilt Train reservations.

the CountryLink XPT from Melbourne to Sydney and Brisbane (twice daily), the Queensland Rail Sunlander from Brisbane to Cairns (twice weekly) and the Tilt Train (three times weekly from Brisbane to Cairns; twice daily except Sat from Brisbane to Bundaberg or Rockhampton). Australian trains are comfortable enough but, unlike their European equivalents, they're not particularly fast: despite the higher price, some are no speedier than buses. Each state also operates commuter services and branch lines that radiate out from the state capitals.

While long-distance nonstop train travel is considerably more expensive than flying, suburban line fares are very reasonable, and passes that allow you to break a longer journey into multiple segments can also be a good deal. CountryLink and Queensland Rail offer a range of **rail passes**, of which the most useful are the East Coast Discovery Pass, valid for six months' unlimited travel in one direction on the XPT, Sunlander and Tilt Train, between specified stops (A\$130–500), and the Backtracker Rail Pass, valid for unlimited travel between Melbourne and Brisbane in either direction for between two weeks and six months (A\$232–420).

By bus

Bus travel is reasonably comfortable, with air-conditioning, drinking water and meal breaks, but it can be tiresome. Even though the bus network reaches much further than the railways, routes stick firmly to the main highways, and while almost all East Coast towns and cities have at least one service a day, in smaller places this may be in the middle of the night.

If you're planning to cover a lot of ground, be realistic about your powers of endurance and aim for a stopover at least every twelve hours or so. In theory, it's possible to travel all the way from Melbourne to Cairns in one marathon sixty-hour trip with just an hour or two changing buses in Sydney and Brisbane, but if all you want to do is get from A to B without stopping, flying is far faster and kinder to your constitution – and often far cheaper.

Of the main players, **Premier Motor Service** is better value than **Greyhound**. Both offer decent fares for relatively short trips such as Melbourne to Sydney, or Townsville to Cairns, including online specials, but both are expensive for

Travelling between states

When travelling across state borders by car or bus, bear in mind that you may be subject to a customs search by officers on the lookout for **fruit and fresh produce**, which often cannot be carried from one state, to minimize the spread of pests and viruses. You'll see large bins at the side of the road as you approach a state border line for this purpose: dump any perishables here before crossing, otherwise you risk receiving a large fine if caught with them.

non-stop trips over long distances – from Melbourne, for example, a single to Cairns costs A$450 with Greyhound or A$361 with Premier, less than the train but far more than the standard airfare. **Passes** that offer unlimited stops over an extended period are a much better deal; both companies offer a wide choice of these, typically valid for one, two, three, six or twelve months, allowing travel between specified points (in one direction) or over a specified total distance (in any direction). A six-month Melbourne-to-Cairns pass costs A$350 from Premier or A$445 from Greyhound; other options include Premier's two-month Sydney-to-Cairns pass (A$250) and Greyhound's ninety-day Central Coaster (Sydney to Brisbane; A$193). **Discounts** of around ten percent are available to card-carrying students, pensioners and backpackers (see "Costs", p.73).

By guided tour

The following companies offer extended **tours**, with a wide choice of East Coast itineraries. It's also possible to build short local tours of anything between a few hours and a few days into your trip: details are given in the Guide.

AAT Kings UK ☎020/8225 4220, US & Canada ☎714/456-0505, Australia ☎03 9915 1500 or 1300 556 100, NZ ☎09/300 1520 or 0800/500 146, ⓦwww.aatkings.com. Long-established Australian bus-tour operator offering escorted and independent trips, the best of which are 4WD Wilderness Safari tours and camping adventures.

Adventure Tours Australia ☎08 8132 8230 or 1300 654 604, ⓦwww.adventuretours.com.au. A variety of overland trips for backpackers, lasting four to fourteen days and starting from Sydney, Byron Bay, the Gold Coast, Brisbane or Cairns.

Australian Pacific Touring UK ☎020/8879 7444, US & Canada ☎1-800/290 8687, Australia ☎03 9277 8555 or 1300 656 985, NZ ☎0800-278/687, ⓦwww.aptouring.com.au. Comprehensive range of all-inclusive bus tours.

Oz Experience Australia ☎02 9213 1766 or 1300 300 028, ⓦwww.ozexperience.com. Hop-on-hop-off bus tours geared towards up-for-it young travellers, with optional extras such as surfing, zorbing and white-water rafting along the way. Start at Melbourne, Sydney, Byron Bay, Brisbane or Cairns and travel up or down the coast, taking as long as you like up to a maximum of six months per pass (A$250–770 plus food, accommodation and activities).

By car

To explore the East Coast at your own pace, you'll need **your own vehicle**. This is the easiest way to get to the national parks, isolated beaches and country villages that make the region such a special place. If your trip is a long one – three months or more – then **buying a vehicle** may well be the cheapest plan. On shorter trips, you should consider **renting** – if not for the whole time then at least for short periods, thereby allowing you to explore an area in depth.

Most foreign **licences** are valid for a year for those visiting Australia as a tourist or working holidaymaker. An International Driving Permit (available from national motoring organizations) may be useful if you come from a non-English-speaking country. **Fuel** prices went through a rapid rise in 2008, peaking at just under A$1.50 per litre for unleaded, with diesel about five percent more: prices are typically ten to fifteen percent higher at remote stations. The **rules of the road** are similar to those in the UK and US. Most importantly, drive on the left (as in the UK), remember that seatbelts are compulsory for all, and that the speed limit in all built-up areas is 50kph or less unless indicated otherwise. Elsewhere, the limit varies, so you need to watch for signs. On open highways, the standard maximum is 100kph, though some newer stretches have a 110kph maximum.

East Coast driving distances (km)

	Airlie Beach	Batemans Bay	Brisbane	Byron Bay	Cairns	Coffs Harbour	Cooktown	Hervey Bay	Lakes Entrance
Airlie Beach		2317	1096	1266	620	1498	942	878	2760
Batemans Bay	2317		1217	1063	2902	819	3224	1515	443
Brisbane	1096	1217		167	1681	398	2003	294	1660
Byron Bay	1266	1063	167		1851	243	2173	464	1506
Cairns	620	2902	1681	1851		2083	323	1463	3345
Coffs Harbour	1498	819	398	243	2083		2423	696	1262
Cooktown	942	3224	2003	2173	323	2423		1785	3692
Hervey Bay	878	1515	294	464	1463	696	1785		1958
Lakes Entrance	2760	443	1660	1506	3345	1262	3692	1958	
Melbourne	3153	836	2053	1962	3738	1655	4060	2351	398
Mission Beach	507	2789	1568	1738	141	1988	463	1350	3236
Narooma	2386	69	1286	1132	2971	888	3293	1584	374
Newcastle	1891	446	791	636	2476	393	2798	1089	889
Noosa	996	1348	127	297	1581	528	1903	196	1791
Rockhampton	482	1836	615	785	1066	1017	1388	397	2292
Surfers Paradise	1178	1140	79	89	1763	320	2085	376	1583
Sydney	2030	278	931	776	2615	532	2937	1228	721
Townsville	273	2555	1334	1504	349	1802	671	1116	2998

· With such long distances between towns in many areas, it's particularly important to monitor your fuel consumption, carry a mobile phone and drinking water, and avoid driving when tired – get out of the car every two hours. The Australian authorities are extremely tough on drivers who drink alcohol or take drugs; random breath-tests are common even in rural areas, especially over weekends and public holidays. Beware of fifty-metre-long **roadtrains**: these colossal trucks can't stop quickly or pull off the road safely, so if there's the slightest doubt, get out of their way; only overtake a roadtrain if you can see well ahead and are certain that your vehicle can manage it. Wild **animals** can be a hazard, too, particularly at dawn, dusk and night-time. If you find an animal in your path, slow down if you're certain it's safe to do so, resisting the urge to swerve. Remember that cattle, kangaroos and wallabies generally move in groups, so if one appears, others may soon follow. In the unlucky event of a collision, your first priority should be to attend to your own safety and that of other road users; if you're also concerned about an animal's condition, call one of the wildlife rescue organizations listed on p.80, or contact the nearest vet or national park office.

Around the cities, watch out for local quirks such as Melbourne's "hook turn" system (see p.95), Sydney's obscure motorway toll systems (see p.215), and inept signposting – all too often, the first sign for a junction is positioned at the junction itself, too late for you to change lane. One rule that might catch you out is that **roadside parking** must be in the same direction as the traffic; in other words, don't cross oncoming traffic to park on the right.

Elsewhere on the East Coast, you can explore extensively, even in the hinterland, without leaving the tarmac. The main **A1/M1 East Coast highway**, variously known as the Princes Highway (in southeast Australia), the Pacific Highway (between Sydney and Brisbane) and the Bruce Highway (from Brisbane to Cairns), is single-carriageway for most of its length, with overtaking lanes at intervals. Often shaded by trees, it's generally in good condition bar a few rough patches in North Coast New South Wales where, unusually for the East Coast, many minor roads are also in terrible shape.

In remote areas, including some national parks, you may come across steep, winding climbs, which can be tiring to negotiate, and graded gravel roads: here, it's wise to keep

Melbourne	Mission Beach	Narooma	Newcastle	Noosa	Rockhampton	Surfers Paradise	Sydney	Townsville
3153	507	2386	1891	996	482	1178	2030	273
836	2789	69	446	1348	1836	1140	278	2555
2053	1568	1286	791	127	615	79	931	1334
1962	1738	1132	636	297	785	89	776	1504
3738	141	2971	2476	1581	1066	1763	2615	349
1655	1988	888	393	528	1017	320	532	1802
4060	463	3293	2798	1903	1388	2085	2937	671
2351	1350	1584	1089	196	397	376	1228	1116
398	3236	374	889	1791	2292	1583	721	2998
	3625	767	1282	2184	2672	1975	1114	3391
3625		2858	2363	1468	953	1650	2502	236
767	2858		515	1417	1905	1209	347	2624
1282	2363	515		922	1410	714	159	2129
2184	1468	1417	922		515	209	1061	1234
2672	953	1905	1410	515		697	1549	719
1975	1650	1209	714	209	697		853	1416
1114	2502	347	159	1061	1549	853		2292
3391	236	2624	2129	1234	719	1416	2292	

your speed down to 80kph, stick to the best section and never assume that the road is free from potholes and rocks. Long corrugated stretches can literally shake the vehicle apart – check radiators, fuel tanks and battery connections afterwards. Windscreens can shatter when hit by flying stones from passing traffic, so slow down and pull over to the left.

Some so-called **"4WD only" tracks** are easily navigable in ordinary cars as long as you take it easy – high ground clearance is often the crucial factor – but it would be madness to tackle the roughest or sandiest tracks, such as those on Fraser Island and in Queensland's extreme north, in a 2WD vehicle. For advice specific to Fraser, see p.490; for Cape York, see p.618.

After severe **storms**, roads may be closed due to landslides, floods or fallen debris, particularly in the hinterland mountains (such as Lamington and Springbrook national parks), the low-lying valleys and plains (such as the New South Wales Northern Rivers region between Grafton and Tweed Heads) and the tropical north. The highway from Cairns to Townsville is notorious for floods during the summer cyclone season. Seek reliable advice (from local police or a roadhouse) before starting out, making it clear what sort of vehicle you're driving and remembering that their idea of "good" and "bad" conditions may be radically different from yours.

Car, 4WD and campervan rental

To **rent** a car you need a full, clean driver's licence and be at least 21 years old, rising to 25 for 4WDs and motorcycles (see p.44). Rental agencies are detailed under "Listings" in the guide: check on any distance limits, other restrictions, extras and liabilities before signing. The multinational operators Hertz, Budget, Avis and Thrifty, which have offices in all the major cities, charge from A$70–80 a day for a small car with unlimited kilometres and reduced-excess insurance. Local firms are almost always better value: A$45 a day is typical, while some companies offer budget vehicles, which may be older than average, for even less. One-way rental (whereby you pick up in one town and drop off in another) might appear handy, but usually incurs an extra fee of at least A$200.

Four-wheel drive rental starts at around A$120 a day. Combined with steep fuel costs this is a pricey option for everyday

Four-wheel driving: some tips

If you're planning to tackle some of Queensland's off-road tracks, the following basic tips should help; see also the advice on creek crossings in the box on p.618.

- Be aware of your limitations, and those of your vehicle.
- Know how to operate everything – including free-wheeling hubs (where present) and how to change a wheel – before you need it.
- If safe to do so, cross deep water and very muddy sections on foot first.
- Don't persevere if you're stuck – avoid wheel spin (which will only dig you further in), and reverse out. Momentum is key on slippery surfaces such as mud, sand and snow – as long as you're moving forward, however slowly, resist the temptation to change gear, and so lose traction.
- Reducing tyre pressures down to 1 bar (15lb psi) dramatically increases traction in mud and sand, but causes tyre overheating, so keep speeds down. Carry a compressor or re-inflate as soon as possible.
- If stuck, clear all the wheels with your hands or a shovel, create a shallow ramp (again, for all wheels), engage four-wheel drive, lower tyre pressures if necessary, and drive or reverse out in low-range second.
- Keep to tracks – avoid unnecessary damage to the environment.
- Driving on beaches can be great fun, but is treacherous – observe other vehicles' tracks and be aware of tidal patterns.
- Consider a rented satellite phone for remote travel (see "Phones" on p.77).

driving, so it's wise to only book one for those parts of your trip where you really need it. Some agents don't allow their vehicles to be driven on unsealed roads, however, let alone off-road, so check the fine print.

Touring by **campervan** is a classic East Coast experience: a well-equipped vehicle can be the key ingredient in a trip of a lifetime. Rates start at A$50 a day for a two-berth campervan in low season (up to A$175 high season) with unlimited kilometres – amazing value when you consider the independence, comfort and the saving on accommodation costs. Again, one-way rental is possible, for an extra fee; check whether you're allowed to drive on unsealed roads. Be aware that the sleeping capacity stated is usually a maximum, which you wouldn't want to endure for too long. Furthermore, in the tropics, the interior will never really be cool enough overnight unless you leave the doors open – which brings the bugs in. Consider sleeping outside under a mozzie dome or inner tent.

Britz, Apollo and Kea, to name a few, rent **4WD campervans**, notably Toyota Troop Carriers, tough all-terrain vehicles that will only be stopped off-road by your experience or the height of the roof, as long as you understand the operation of the free-wheeling hubs on the front axle in engaging 4WD. Their main drawback is their high fuel consumption, around 7kpl. Chunky six-berthers use even more fuel. Lighter 4WD utes (utility vehicles) fitted with a cabin and a pop-up roof can't take the same hammering but are more economical. With any 4WD camper it's vital to appreciate the altered driving dynamics of an already high vehicle fitted with a heavy body. In the hands of an inexperienced driver they can easily topple over. Prices for 4WD campers start around A$150 a day in the low season, up to A$250 in the high season.

Car-rental agencies

Avis UK ☏ 0870/606 0100, Republic of Ireland ☏ 021/428 1111, US ☏ 1-800/230-4898, Canada ☏ 1-800/272-5871, Australia ☏ 02/9353 9000 or 13 63 33, NZ ☏ 09/526 2847 or 0800/655 111; ⓦ www.avis.com.

Budget UK ☏ 0870/156 5656, US ☏ 1-800/527-0700, Canada ☏ 1-800/268-8900, Australia ☏ 1300 362 848, NZ ☏ 0800/283 438; ⓦ www.budget.com.

Europcar UK ☏ 0870/607 5000, Republic of Ireland ☏ 01/614 2800, US & Canada ☏ 1-877/940-6900, Australia ☏ 393/306 160; ⓦ www.europcar.com.

East Coast scenic drives

With your own wheels, you're free to explore some of the coast's most picturesque routes: the following will knock you out.

Ballina to Byron Bay NSW. Unspoilt headlands, hang-gliding and huge ocean-scapes. See p.372.

Bloomfield Track QLD. Creek crossings and rainforest wildlife, from reptiles and amphibians to cassowaries. 4WD only. See p.613.

Cairns to Port Douglas QLD. The winding Captain Cook Highway passes perfect little beaches as it hugs the tropical shore. See p.596.

Eungella National Park QLD. A steep climb leading through ancient rainforests, with superb views. See p.511.

Far North Coast hinterland NSW. Rolling green landscapes, very evocative of the "old" South Wales. See p.384.

Gold Coast Hinterland QLD. Rainforest-cloaked highlands, home to thousands of birds. See p.423.

Grand Pacific Drive NSW. Towering cliffs, rolling surf and the Sea Cliff Bridge. See p.197.

Great Ocean Road VIC. Pristine coastal forests and striking offshore rock formations. See p.157.

Lakes Way NSW. Peaceful lakes, quiet beaches and beautiful forested slopes. See p.352.

South Coast tourist drives NSW. Detours off the Princes Highway skirt tranquil coastal lagoons and paperbark swamps. See p.186 & p.189.

Hertz UK ☎020/7026 0077, Republic of Ireland ☎01/870 5777, US & Canada ☎1-800/654-3131, Australia ☎13 30 39, NZ ☎0800/654 321; ⊛www.hertz.com.

Holiday Autos UK ☎0870/400 4461, Republic of Ireland ☎01/872 9366, Australia ☎1300 554 432; ⊛www.holidayautos.co.uk.

National UK ☎0870/400 4581, US ☎1-800/CAR-RENT, Australia ☎0870 600 6666, NZ ☎03/366 5574; ⊛www.nationalcar.com.

Thrifty UK ☎01494/751 540, Republic of Ireland ☎01/844 1950, US & Canada ☎1-800/847-4389, Australia ☎1300 367 227, NZ ☎09/256 1405; ⊛www.thrifty.com.

Campervan- and motorhome-rental agencies

Apollo Motorhome Holidays ☎07 3265 9200 or 1800 777 779, ⊛www.apollocamper.com.au.
Backpacker Campervans ☎03 8379 8893 or 1800 670 232, ⊛www.backpackercampervans.com.

Britz ☎03 8379 8890 or 1800 331 454, ⊛www.britz.com.
Kea Campers ☎02 8707 5540 or 1800 252 555, ⊛www.keacampers.com.
Maui ☎03 8379 8891 or 1300 363 800, ⊛www.maui-rentals.com.

Wicked Campers ☎07 3634 9000 or 1800 24 68 69, ⊛www.wickedcampers.com.au.

Buying a car

Buying a used vehicle needn't be an expensive business, and a well-kept car should resell at about two-thirds of the purchase price at the end of your trip. If you're lucky, or a skilful negotiator, you might even make a profit.

Buying and registering a car

If you don't know your axle from your elbow but are not too gullible, **car yards** and **dealerships** can provide some advice – in Sydney, some cater specifically for travellers (see p.307) – but don't forget you're dealing with used-car salesmen whose worldwide reputation precedes them; a buy-back guarantee, for example, is often just a guarantee to pay you a fraction of the car's potential value (typically thirty to fifty percent of the price you originally paid). Assuming you have a little time and some mechanical knowledge, you'll save money by **buying privately**: newspaper classifieds and online ads offer plenty of options. Backpackers' noticeboards in Melbourne, Sydney, Brisbane and Cairns are good places to look for something cheap, with Sydney being the busiest marketplace. One of the advantages of buying from a fellow traveller is that you may get all sorts of stuff thrown in, such as camping gear, eskies and spares. The disadvantage is that the car may have been maintained on a backpacker's budget.

A **thorough inspection** is essential. Rust is one thing to watch for, especially in the tropics where humidity and salt air will turn scratches to holes within weeks – look out for poorly patched bodywork. Take the car for a spin and check the engine, gearbox, clutch and brakes for operation, unusual noises, vibration and leaks; repairs on some of these parts can be costly. Don't expect perfection, though: worn brake-pads and tyres, grating wheel-bearings and defective batteries can be fixed inexpensively, and if repairs are needed, it gives you a good excuse to haggle over the price. All tyres should be the same type and size. If you lack faith in your own abilities, the various state automobile associations can recommend mechanics who will conduct rigorous pre-purchase inspections for about A$100, which isn't much to pay if it saves you from buying a wreck. To make sure the vehicle has never been written off and has no outstanding payments owing on it, you can check its registration, engine number and VIN/chassis number against a database managed by the Register of Encumbered Vehicles or REVS (Ⓦ www.revs.nsw.gov.au).

Car-buying **procedure** differs slightly from state to state but a common requirement is that the seller must provide a receipt and a roadworthiness or safety certificate, recently issued (at the seller's expense) by a state-accredited garage, stating that the car is basically mechanically sound. You take the receipt, certificate, your driver's licence, passport and proof of local address to the local transport registry office, where you will be charged a transfer fee plus duty (calculated as a percentage of the purchase price) to have the vehicle registration transferred to your name. If you're buying from a dealer, they will sort out all this paperwork for you and add the fees to the bill.

To keep a car on the road, you're required to pay an annual **vehicle registration fee** ("rego", pronounced "redge-o"), which amounts to a state tax plus compulsory third-party insurance (CTP) against personal injury claims. Each state runs a separate system; rates vary but, for a standard car, A$550–570 is typical, payable by phone, online or in person at transport registry offices. When buying a car, you usually acquire the unexpired portion of the rego; this can be a bargaining point between buyers and sellers. It's fine to drive a vehicle outside its home state as long as your permanent address remains unchanged (while travelling, you can have mail forwarded on request), but if you move to another state permanently, you are required to re-register your car in the new state within fourteen days, by paying for a mechanical inspection, duty, a registration fee and number plate fee.

Third-party property or comprehensive **insurance** are optional but well worth considering, as is motoring club membership; check first whether your home club has a reciprocal arrangement with one of the Australian outfits.

Best second-hand buys

Big-engined, mid-1980s **Holden Kingswood** or **Ford Falcon** station wagons are popular travellers' cars: cheap, roomy, reliable, mechanically simple and durable, with spares available in just about any city supermarket, roadhouse or wrecker's yard. Chances are, if a vehicle has survived this long, there's nothing seriously wrong with it and you should be able to nurse it through a bit further. Real bargains (from A$2000) can be secured from travellers desperate to get rid of their vehicle before flying out. Ideally, though, you should plan to pay at least A$4000 in total for a sound, well-equipped vehicle. Manual transmission models are more economical than old automatics, with the four-speed versions superior to the awkward, three-speed, steering-column-mounted models. Smaller and less robust, but much more economical to run, are old Japanese station wagons or vans such as **Mazda L300s** (also in 4WD version), suitable for one or two people.

Four-wheel drives are expensive and, with poor fuel economy and higher running costs, worth it only if you have some actual off-tarmac driving planned; to do that, you can't buy an old wreck. **Toyota FJ** or **HJ LandCruisers** are legendary, especially the long-wheelbase (LWB) models: tough, reliable and with plenty of new and used spares all over the country. If nothing goes wrong, a diesel (HJ) is preferable to a petrol (FJ) engine, being sturdier and more economical – although all Toyota engines, particularly the six-cylinder FJs, seem to keep on running, even if totally clapped out. The trouble with diesels is that problems, when they occur, tend to be serious and repairs expensive. Generally, you're looking at A$8000 for a twenty-year-old model.

If you're going to be sticking to the tarmac and have a little more money to spend, there's a lot to be said for buying a **Hyundai** or **Toyota** runabout – these are common, reliable, economical to run, and easy to get serviced or repaired.

Equipping your car

Even if you expect to stick mostly to the main highways, you'd be wise to carry some **spares**: there are plenty of very isolated spots, even between Sydney and Melbourne. For ordinary cars, the cheapest place to buy spares is at a supermarket – head for the racks of any branch of K-Mart or Coles. A **towrope** is a good start; passing motorists are far cheaper than tow trucks. If your vehicle is past its prime, you should have a set of spark plugs, points, fuses, fuel filters (for diesels), fan belt and radiator hoses – you need to check and maybe replace all these anyway. A selection of **spares** such as hose clamps, radiator sealant, water-dispersing spray, jump leads, tyre pump/compressor, and a board to support the jack on soft ground will also come in handy. Establish the engine oil consumption early on; if the level drops too much, the engine will cook itself. Get hold of a **Gregory's workshop manual** for your vehicle; even if you're not confident following it, someone might help who knows how to. A ten-litre or bigger **fuel container** is also useful in case you run out.

Before you set off, check **battery** terminals for corrosion, and the battery for charge – buy a new one if necessary. Carry a spare tyre. In fact, one of the best things you can do is start a long road trip with five new tyres, oil, filters, and radiator coolant, as well as points (if present) and plugs on a petrol engine. **Off-road** drivers in remote regions should add to the list a puncture repair kit, bead breaker and tubes – and know how to use them. Keeping tyres at the correct pressure and having a wheel balance/ alignment will reduce wear.

Cars and driving: information and resources

Valuation and sales
Car Point Ⓦ www.carpoint.com.au
Car Sales Ⓦ www.carsales.com.au
Red Book Ⓦ www.redbookasiapacific.com.au
Trading Post Ⓦ www.autotrader.com.au

Motoring associations
Australian Automobile Association (AAA) ☎ 02 6347 7311, Ⓦ www.aaa.asn.au
National Roads and Motorists' Association (NRMA, covers NSW and ACT) ☎ 13 11 22, Ⓦ www.mynrma.com.au
Royal Automobile Club of Queensland (RACQ) ☎ 13 19 05, Ⓦ www.racq.com.au
Royal Automobile Club of Victoria (RACV) ☎ 03 9790 2211, Ⓦ www.racv.com.au

Vehicle registration
Queensland Transport ☎ 13 23 90, Ⓦ www.transport.qld.gov.au
Roads and Traffic Authority, NSW ☎ 13 22 13, Ⓦ www.rta.nsw.gov.au
VicRoads ☎ 13 11 71, Ⓦ www.vicroads.gov.au

Selling your car

When the time comes **to sell**, you will need to fix up a roadworthiness/safety inspection (unless you're selling to a trade dealer; see below) and assemble the other paperwork: proof of purchase, registration certificate and log book with service history. Your options include advertising to travellers or the general public in print or online, or leaving the car with a dealer to sell on consignment (by agreeing a reserve price, commission and expenses in advance). If the odometer (clock) is past 200,000km, local buyers won't be interested, so your best avenue is to advertise to travellers. It's the buyer's responsibility to make sure the rego is transferred to them – from this point, they will be liable for fees and traffic fines – but it's worth requesting confirmation of transfer from the transport registry when you notify them of the sale.

If your car is registered **interstate** (outside the state in which you're selling it), you can't transfer the rego to a local buyer. One option is to sell the car unregistered: once the sale is agreed, you cancel the rego by removing the windscreen sticker and number plates and notifying the transport authority, who will refund you the unexpired portion by cheque (this can be sent to an overseas address on request). It's then up to the dealer or buyer to re-register the car in its new home state. Some buyers are put off by the hassle of re-registering a car, though; you may get a quicker sale and a better overall price if you re-register the car yourself.

If you need to sell your car fast, you could try tracking down a **trade buyer**. The advantages of selling to a trade buyer are that they will be happy to take a vehicle registered in another state, will not require you to present a roadworthiness/safety certificate, and will offer you cash or a cheque on the spot; however, they will expect a heavily discounted price – typically thirty percent less than the sum you might expect from a private sale.

By motorcycle

Motorcycles, especially large-capacity trail bikes, are ideal for the Australian climate, although long distances place a premium on their comfort and fuel range. Japanese trail bikes, such as Yamaha's XT600, sell for around A$4000 and allow 100kph on-road cruising, are manageable on dirt roads and have readily available spares. A bike like the Honda XL650V Transalp is heavier but has a much smoother engine and fairing, which add up to better long-range comfort and reasonable gravel manners.

If it's likely that you'll return to your starting point, look out for dealers offering buy-back options that guarantee a resale at the end of your trip; bikes can be more difficult to sell privately than cars. Whether you're planning to ride off or on the tarmac, plenty of water-carrying capacity is essential. **Night-riding** carries risks from collisions with wildlife from which a rider always comes off badly; all you can do is make sure your lights and brakes are up to it and keep your speed down to under 100kph.

Motorcycle **rental** is widely available in the main cities; for extended touring, you can't beat something like a BMW GS1150: comfortable, economical and a pleasure to ride loaded, two-up, day in, day out (although tyre choice will be critical for unsealed roads and it weighs a ton). Among other outlets, 1150s are available from Ⓦwww.carconnection.com.au from around A$105 a day, or at a flat rate of A$6050 for three months (plus various deposits and bonds). *The Adventure Motorcycling Handbook* (Trailblazer) is a definitive manual for preparation and riding off the beaten track.

Health

Australia has high standards of hygiene, and there are few exceptional health hazards – at least in terms of disease. No vaccination certificates are required unless you've come from a yellow-fever zone within the past week. Standards in Australia's hospitals are also very high, and medical costs are reasonable in comparison to Europe and the US. Sun protection is crucial, but wildlife dangers tend to be overstated: snake, spider, crocodile and shark attacks, though widely publicized, are extremely rare.

The national healthcare scheme, **Medicare** (☏ 13 20 11, ⓦ www.medicareaustralia.com .au), offers a reciprocal arrangement – free essential healthcare and subsidized medicines – for citizens of the UK, the Republic of Ireland, New Zealand, Italy, Malta, Finland, the Netherlands, Norway and Sweden. Of these nationalities, all are entitled to treatment in public hospitals and casualty departments; citizens of New Zealand and the Republic of Ireland are also entitled to free treatment by GPs, while the others are required to pay GPs up front and then either provide bank details or fill out a claim form and post or take it to a Medicare office (of which there are many branches) to get two-thirds of the fee reimbursed.

To enrol in the scheme, you should obtain a **Medicare Card** from a Medicare office by showing your passport and National Health ID from home: anyone eligible who's staying in Australia for a while, particularly those on working holidays, is advised to do this. Without a card, you will need to pay for all treatment up front and reclaim later.

Ambulance journeys aren't covered – you'll need to claim on your travel insurance. Nor is dental treatment included – in one of the larger cities, try the dental hospital, where dental students may treat you cheaply or for free.

The sun

Australia's biggest health problem is also one of its chief attractions: **sunshine**. A sunny day in London, Toronto or even Miami is not the same as a cloudless day on the East Coast, where the intensity of the sun's damaging ultraviolet rays is far greater.

Whether this is because of Australia's proximity to the ozone hole is a matter of debate, but there's absolutely no doubt that the southern sun burns extremely fiercely, and you need to take extra care.

Australians of European origin, especially those of Anglo-Saxon or Celtic descent, could not be less suited to Australia's outdoor lifestyle, which is why two out of three Australians are likely to develop **skin cancer** in their lifetime, the world's worst record. About five percent of these will develop potentially fatal melanomas, and about a thousand die each year. Looking at the ravaged complexions of some older Australians (who had prolonged exposure to the sun in the days before there was an awareness of the great dangers of skin cancer) should be enough to make you want to cover yourself with lashings of the highest factor **sun block** (SPF 35+), widely used and sold just about everywhere. Sunscreen should not be used on babies less than six months old: instead, keep them out of direct sunlight. What looks like war paint on the noses of surfers and small children is actually zinc cream, good for a total blockout.

These days, Australians are fully aware of the sun's dangers, and you're constantly reminded to **"Slip, Slop, Slap"**, the government-approved catchphrase reminding you to slip on a T-shirt, slop on some sun block and slap on a hat – sound advice. Pay attention to any moles on your body: if you notice any changes, either during or after your trip, see a doctor; cancerous melanomas are generally easily removed if caught early. To prevent headaches and – in the long term – cataracts, it's a good idea to wear sunglasses with 100% UV protection.

The sun can also cause **heat exhaustion** and **sunstroke**, so in addition to keeping well covered up, stay in the shade if you can. Drink plenty of liquids: on hot days when walking, experts advise drinking a litre of water an hour – which is a lot to carry. Alcohol and sun don't mix well; when you're feeling particularly hot and thirsty, remember that a cold beer, however refreshing, does a poor job of hydrating you.

Tropical complaints

Cuts and bites should be dressed with extra care in the hot and humid north, to prevent infection. Take care to dry your ears after swimming or showering to avoid **swimmers ear** or **tropical ear**, a very painful fungal infection of the ear canal. Treatment is with ear drops: if you think you might be susceptible, use them anyway after getting wet. When hiking, watch out for stinging trees, found on the fringes of tropical rainforests: their large heart-shaped leaves are covered in nettle-like hairs, which cause an agonizing sting if touched.

Dangerous wildlife

Australia has more than its fair share of **deadly animals**, some large and aggressive, others small and poisonous – but with common sense, your chances of an encounter are much reduced.

Insects, leeches and spiders

Although **mosquitoes** are found across the whole of the country, malaria is not endemic; however, in the tropical north, there are regular outbreaks of similarly transmitted Ross River fever and dengue fever, chronically debilitating viruses that are potentially fatal to children and the elderly. Pharmacies and supermarkets sell insect repellent: the most effective are those that contain DEET (diethyl toluamide), such as Bi-Lo Roll-on, Aerogard, Black & Gold and Autan. Bushman, though pricey, is the most water resistant; Kids Rid has a reduced DEET content. Natural alternatives such as tea tree oil, citronella and eucalyptus are unreliable unless reapplied every thirty minutes or so,

and are not recommended in areas where disease-carrying mozzies are found.

Ticks, **mites** and **leeches** are the bane of bushwalkers, though spraying repellent over shoes and leggings will help keep these pests away in the first instance. **Ticks** are poisonous – spring is the time when they produce the most toxins during feeding – and can cause local discomfort, allergic reactions and, in extreme cases, paralysis and death. They attach themselves to long grass and bushes and latch on to passing animals and humans. Check yourself over after a hike: look for local stinging and swelling (usually just inside hairlines) and you'll find either a tiny black dot, or a pea-sized animal attached, depending on which species has bitten you. Use fine-pointed tweezers and grasp it as close to the skin as possible, and gently pull the tick out, trying to avoid squeezing the animal's body, which will inject more venom. Seek medical attention if you are not successful. A lot of bushwalkers advocate dabbing kerosene, alcohol or insect repellent on the ticks before pulling them out, but the official medical advice is don't – it will cause the tick to inject more toxins into the host's body. **Mites** cause an infuriating rash known as "scrub itch", which characteristically appears wherever your clothes are tightest, such as around the hips and ankles. Unfortunately, there's not much you can do except take antihistamines and wait a day or two for the itching to stop. **Leeches** are gruesome but harmless, though bites may bleed heavily for some time: a firm flick of the fingernail, insect repellent, fire or salt gets them off the skin.

Two **spiders** whose bites can be fatal if untreated are the **funnel web**, a black, stocky burrow-dwelling creature found south of Gladstone, and the small **redback**, a relative of the notorious black widow of the Americas, which lives in dark, dry locations all over Australia (including outdoor toilets, shrubberies and piles of rocks or logs). Treat funnel-web bites as for snakebites, and apply ice to redback wounds to relieve pain; if bitten by either, get to a hospital – antivenins are available. Other spiders (including the large, hairy and alarming-looking huntsman), centipedes and scorpions can deliver painful bites but generally only cause serious problems if you have allergies.

Crocodiles, snakes, stingrays, jellyfish and sharks

Estuarine or **saltwater crocodiles** (which can grow up to 6m in length and have no natural predators apart from each other) are not to be trifled with. The way to minimize danger is to keep your distance. They're found in the coastal belt north of Rockhampton in Queensland, ranging up to 100km inland: if you're thinking of hiking, bush-camping or swimming in this area, seek local advice first. When camping near a creek, always make sure your tent is at least 2m above, or 50m away from, the high-water mark, and don't collect water at the same spot every day or prepare food close to the water's edge. Never leave any rubbish around.

Australia is home to three quarters of the world's deadliest **snakes**, including, on the coast, death adders, taipans, copperheads, common browns, king browns and tiger snakes. However, snakes almost always do their best to avoid people, and you'll probably never see one. Wear boots and long trousers when hiking through under-growth, take care when collecting firewood and, in the event of a confrontation, back off. As long as you never try to threaten, kill or catch a snake, you're not likely to be bitten, but they're unpredictable when provoked. Killing native Australian animals is illegal: national park rangers and wildlife-rescue organizations (see p.80) can offer advice on how to deal with snakes that have found their way into areas of human habitation.

If **bitten** by a snake, use a crepe bandage to bind the entire limb firmly and splint it, as if for a sprain; this slows the distribution of venom into the lymphatic system. Don't clean the bite area (venom around the bite can identify the species, making treatment easier), and don't slash the bite or apply a tourniquet. Treat all bites as if they were serious and always seek immediate medical attention, but remember: not all snakes are poisonous, not all poisonous snakes inject a lethal dose of venom every time they bite, and death from snakebite is rare.

Sea snakes sometimes find divers intriguing, wrapping themselves around limbs or staring into masks; they're able to bite but are seldom aggressive. **Stingrays** generally only sting if badly provoked, perhaps by being stepped on; injuries should be doused with hot water, and medical help sought.

More serious is the threat from various types of **jellyfish** (also known as stingers), which occur in coastal tropical waters through the summer months. Two to avoid are the tiny irukandji and the saucer-sized box jellyfish; both are virtually invisible in water and extremely dangerous. **Irukandji** have initially painless stings, but their venom causes elevated heart rate, increased blood pressure, excruciating pain and extreme anxiety or dread. **Box jellyfish** stings leave permanent red weals; if more than half a limb has been stung, the venom can cause rapid unconsciousness by paralyzing the heart muscles. Treat stinger victims by dousing the sting area with liberal amounts of vinegar, supplied in small stands on affected beaches. Never rub with sand or towels, or attempt to remove tentacles from the skin – both could trigger the release of more venom; apply mouth-to-mouth resuscitation if needed, and get the victim to hospital for treatment. Avoidance is best: always wear a protective Lycra suit when swimming in the sea in Queensland during the stinger season (Nov–May). The stinger nets found in some tourist areas block box jellyfish but don't offer full protection against irukandji, which are tiny enough to pass through the mesh. For other underwater hazards specific to the tropics, see p.501.

A common type of jellyfish called the **bluebottle**, which may show up anywhere on the East Coast, delivers a nasty sting, which can cause severe pain for up to an hour. If affected, wash the wound with seawater and carefully remove the tentacles; the best way to soothe the pain is with hot water. Lifeguards will close beaches if ocean currents are bringing bluebottles into the area.

Bull sharks, **tiger sharks** and **great whites**, much feared by surfers, inhabit the temperate coastal waters around southeast Queensland, New South Wales and Victoria, but attacks are very rare: when a teenager died after being bitten on the leg while bodyboarding at a deserted beach near Ballina in 2008, it was the first fatal attack in New South Wales in fifteen years. The safest plan is to stick to the patrolled beaches, many of which are protected by nets.

For more background on Australian fauna, see "Wildlife" on p.640.

Bushfires

Although you're unlikely to find yourself in the path of a raging **bushfire**, it helps to know how to survive one. If you're in a car, don't attempt to drive through smoke but park at the side of the road in the clearest spot, put on your headlights, wind up the windows and close the air vents. Although it seems to go against common sense – and your natural instincts – it's safer to stay inside the car. Lie on the floor and cover all exposed skin with a blanket or any natural-fibre covering at hand. The car won't explode or catch fire, and a fast-moving wildfire will pass quickly overhead. If you smell or see smoke and fire while walking, find a cleared rocky outcrop or an open space: if you're trapped in the path of the fire and the terrain and time permits, dig a shallow trench – in any event, lie face down and cover all exposed skin.

Medical resources for travellers

UK and Republic of Ireland

Hospital for Tropical Diseases Travel Clinic ☏0845/155 5000 or 020/7387 4411, ⊚www.thehtd.org.
Liverpool School of Tropical Medicine ☏0151/708 9393, ⊚www.liv.ac.uk/lstm.
MASTA (Medical Advisory Service for Travellers Abroad) ☏0113/238 7575, ⊚www.masta.org.
Tropical Medical Bureau Republic of Ireland ☏1850/487 674, ⊚www.tmb.ie.

US and Canada

Canadian Society for International Health ⊚www.csih.org.
CDC ☏1-877/394-8747, ⊚wwwn.cdc.gov/travel.
International Society for Travel Medicine ☏1-770/736-7060, ⊚www.istm.org.

Australia, New Zealand and South Africa

The Travel Doctor ☏1300 658 844, ⊚www.tmvc.com.au.

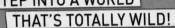

Accommodation

Tourism is booming on the East Coast, with new or revamped accommodation options opening on a regular basis. Finding somewhere to bed down is rarely a problem, even in the smallest of places, but it's a good idea to book ahead for Christmas, January, the Easter holidays, long weekends, and popular events such as festivals and sporting fixtures; at these times, you can expect above-average prices in the busy tourist areas.

The sheer variety of places on offer means that holidaying on the East Coast is a realistic prospect for travellers on all budgets: if you're exploring extensively, you could mix it up by spending part of your time in a lively urban pad, part getting back to basics in an ecolodge, and part spoiling yourself silly in a luxury resort. If funds are tight, there's no need to miss out: this is a region in which an exorbitantly priced luxury retreat may share an island with a bushcamping site where you can pitch a tent for next to nothing. **Single travellers** are at a disadvantage, however: hostels take bookings on a per-person basis, but elsewhere you'll nearly always have to fork out the full rate for a double room.

Watch out for the term "**hotel**", which in Australia is traditionally used to denote a pub or bar. Pubs were once legally required to provide somewhere for customers to sleep off a skinful, and many still do provide accommodation, but while some are great value, the facilities are often by no means luxurious. Many places that would call themselves hotels elsewhere prefer to use another name – hence so many "**motels**" and "**resorts**". Many small places opt for describing themselves as "boutique hotels", but to avoid misunderstanding, when reviewing hotels in this book we reserve the term "**boutique**" for places that are not only small but also chic and luxurious.

Other accommodation options on the East Coast include **country B&Bs**, often in characterful houses; **farmstays** where you can join in with farm life; **hostels**, which are usually aimed at young backpackers; **tourist parks**, which offer a choice of camping, caravanning or self-catering cabins; and **national park campsites**, often in fabulously beautiful areas. Visitor

---

Accommodation price codes

The accommodation listed in this book has been categorized according to eight **price codes**, reflecting the price of the cheapest standard double or twin room in high season (ignoring premium rates, which are only charged on a handful of dates per year, such as Dec 24–26, the Easter weekend or New Year's Eve).

Where **hostels** offer the option of booking one single bed or single bunk in a shared room or dormitory, we give the price in dollars per person per night in high season, followed by the price code for a private room for two, if available.

For **campsites**, we give the price in Australian dollars per tent or van in high season, while for self-catering units and cabins, we give a price code. In some cases, there's an additional charge if more than two people share.

In the lower categories, most rooms will be without private shower or bath, though there may be a washbasin in the room, and the option of paying more for an en suite. From code ❸ upwards, you'll most likely have private facilities.

❶ Under A$50	❹ A$101–150	❼ A$301–400
❷ A$51–75	❺ A$151–225	❽ Over A$400
❸ A$76–100	❻ A$226–300	

Information Centres are often a mine of information on the options in their locality; some run online booking systems, while others will ring around to find you a place that fits your requirements.

Useful websites

Bed and Breakfast and Farmstay Australia ⓦ www.australianbedandbreakfast.com.au. City and country accommodation, listed by state.
Stayz ⓦ www.stayz.com.au Self-catering-accommodation booking site.
Wotif ⓦ www.wotif.com Discounted rates for late availability (within four weeks).

Hotels, guesthouses and motels

Cheap, basic **hotels** with shared bathrooms, plain furnishings and no TV are increasingly rare on the East Coast, but some of the older pubs still offer accommodation of this sort. In country areas, they are often the social centre of town, so don't expect peace and quiet, especially at weekends. But with double rooms at around A$50–70 and singles from A$40 (often with breakfast included), they can be better value – and more private – than hostel accommodation.

In cities, the cheapest **places** can be rather sleazy, but by spending just a little more (from around A$75, or A$100 in the state capitals) you can stay at simple but pleasant family-run **guesthouses**. Mid-range hotels (A$125–225), aimed at tourists and business travellers who don't need five-star fuss but don't want to rough it either, are often excellent value, particularly if you manage to pick up a discount (just ask). Top-end city hotels charge upwards of A$225 per night, or from A$300 in Sydney, where the plushest rooms go for A$700 plus – pricey for Australia, but still reasonable by international standards. For something truly individual, there's a growing array of **boutique hotels** in the state capitals, and a thin scattering elsewhere; these often provide more luxury for your money.

Motels are typically a comfortable, bland choice, often found en masse at the edge of provincial towns and cities to catch weary drivers, and priced on average upwards of A$70 for an en-suite double room with TV;

often, the rooms have basic cooking facilities. Many have larger units for families. There are numerous nationwide **chains** with reliable standards, among them familiar names such as Best Western and Travelodge, as well as Australian ones including Budget, Golden Chain and Flag.

Resorts

The northern New South Wales and Queensland coasts have plenty of **resort complexes** aimed specifically at holiday-makers. At the bottom end, these are very similar in price, appearance and facilities to motels, while top-flight places can be exclusive hideaways costing hundreds of dollars a night. Almost all have restaurants, bars and outdoor swimming pools; some also offer spas, sports facilities and a busy programme of activities. On islands and other remote locations, it's often possible to opt for an all-inclusive rate covering transfers, drinks, meals, sports and anything else on offer. These places tend to be picturesque – the Great Barrier Reef islands swarm with them – and are often brilliant value if you can wangle a stand-by or off-season rate.

Self-catering accommodation

Self-catering units, **apartments**, **villas** and **cottages** are found all over the region and can be a very good deal, particularly for families and larger groups; there are excellent options for couples, too, with far more space than a similarly priced hotel room. The places themselves range from purpose-built city apartments to cottages on country estates and even lighthouses, and many have truly beautiful locations: some are within easy walking distance of restaurants and bars, while others are gloriously isolated, perfect if you have your own transport and would like to feel totally immersed in the environment. Cooking, bathroom and laundry facilities vary from the basic to the luxurious, according to price, but there'll always be a TV and fridge. In top-end places, the price covers everything, including linen, towels, daily cleaning and a stash of breakfast goodies; in cheaper accommodation, these are optional extras.

Top ten eco-friendly accommodation

Along with the region's many national park campsites, the following lodges, resorts and retreats deserve special mention.

1. *The Sanctuary*, Mission Beach (see p.562)
2. *Heron Island Resort* and its sister resorts on Wilson and Lizard islands (see p.503 & p.620)
3. *Head Lighthouse Keeper's Quarters*, Montague Island (see p.188)
4. *Paperbark Camp*, Jervis Bay (see p.195)
5. *Kingfisher Bay Resort*, Fraser Island (see p.491)
6. *Rose Gums Wilderness Retreat*, Atherton Tablelands (see p.570)
7. *Broken River Mountain Resort*, Eungella National Park (see p.513)
8. *Binna Burra Mountain Lodge*, Lamington National Park (see p.428)
9. *Mount Quincan Crater Retreat*, Atherton Tablelands (see p.570)
10. *Worrowing*, Jervis Bay (see p.196)

Eco-retreats, farmstays and country B&Bs

Dotted around the East Coast's most beautiful wilderness areas, including its coastal rainforests and rugged highlands, are a small but growing number of lovely places to stay designed and run on ecologically sound principles. Many are specifically styled as **eco-retreats**, offering guided tours of the surrounds in the company of botanical, ornithological or zoological experts. For some of our favourites, see the box above.

Other options in rural and wilderness areas, particularly in Victoria and New South Wales, include farmstays on working farms, and country B&Bs. Some **farmstays** provide very upmarket comforts, while at others you make do with the basic facilities in vacant shearers' quarters; their attraction is that they are always in out-of-the-way locations, and you'll often get a chance to participate in the working of the farm, or take advantage of guided tours around the property on horseback or by 4WD. **Bed and breakfasts** can be anything from a bedroom in someone's home to your own colonial cottage.

Hostels

Australia has a huge number of **backpacker hostels**, aimed primarily, but by no means exclusively, at young international travellers. You'll find at least one in practically every tourist town on the East Coast, with big concentrations in Melbourne, Sydney, Byron Bay, Surfers Paradise, Brisbane, Airlie Beach and Cairns; the next busiest spots are Magnetic Island, Port Douglas and Cape Tribulation. Key to their appeal, apart from their low prices, are their popular communal areas – kitchens, barbecue areas, Internet rooms and lounges – and social events, conducive to meeting other travellers and getting on the grapevine. There's often a choice of private or shared rooms: the latter may be single-gender or mixed dormitories, usually with enough bunks for between four and twelve people, and are booked on a per-person basis (if you're travelling in a small group and don't want to share with strangers, you could opt for booking all the beds in a dorm). Only a few places have single beds rather than bunks, but an increasing number have at least some en-suite doubles and dorms.

As you'd expect, the atmosphere of a hostel is partly determined by its size and whether it's in a city, in the country or by the beach, but standards vary across the board: while some are simply grubby, rapid-turnover dives, the best places are fantastic value, great fun and stylish to boot. **YHA hostels** are pretty dependable and have the broadest spread on the East Coast.

Standard rates are A\$22–42 for a dorm bunk, with A\$25–29 the norm; doubles start from just under A\$50. Sheets, and sometimes towels, are provided; sleeping bags are usually banned, to curb the spread of bed bugs.

Hostel associations and networks

You don't need to join an association to stay in a hostel, but if you do join, you'll receive discounted accommodation and many other benefits (see "Costs", p.49).

Hostelling International (HI) and Youth Hostel Association (YHA) England & Wales ⓦ www.yha .org.uk; Scotland ⓦ www.syha.org.uk; Northern Ireland ⓦ www.hini.org.uk; Republic of Ireland ⓦ www.irelandyha.org; US ⓦ www.hiusa.org; Canada ⓦ www.hihostels.ca; Australia ⓦ www .yha.com.au; New Zealand ⓦ www.yha.co.nz; other countries ⓦ www.hihostels.com. In Australia, YHA hostels are found in interesting, offbeat areas as well as the big cities, and tend to be run by genuine enthusiasts, many of them brilliant at organizing tours and social activities for guests. Despite the name, YHAs cater for all ages and tend to be more inclusive of older travellers than other hostels. As an international member, you get a discount of at least ten percent. You can pay the annual fee online, or at a hostel or YHA travel centre in your home country: Australia A$32, or A$37 including ISC or IYTC (see p.74); UK £15.95, or £9.95 for under-26s; Republic of Ireland €20; US US$28; Canada CAN$35; New Zealand NZ$40.

Nomads ⓦ www.nomadsworld.com. There are Nomads hostels in Australia, New Zealand and Fiji, including snazzy options in Melbourne, Sydney, Cairns and Cape Tribulation. A Nomads Adventure Card (A$34/year) gets you A$1 off nightly rates.

VIP Backpackers ⓦ www.vipbackpackers.com. Worldwide hostel network: one-year membership A$43, two years A$57.

Camping and caravan parks

Perhaps because Australian hostels are so widespread and inexpensive, **camping** is an option little used by foreign travellers. But don't let this put you off: national parks and nature reserves offer a host of camping grounds, which, depending on the location, may have an amenities block with flushing toilets, hot and cold showers and drinking water, plus a barbecue and picnic tables. Others, however, provide nothing at all, so come prepared, especially in national parks, where **bushcamping** is often the only option for staying overnight. Vital equipment includes ground mats and a range of pegs – some wide (for sand), others narrow (for soil). A hatchet for splitting firewood is light

to carry and doubles as a hammer. Fuel stoves are recommended (propane or butane ones tend to be handier and safer than other options), but if you're going to be camping in one of the few areas where fires, and the collection of firewood, are permitted, it's worth taking a light hatchet; this can double as a hammer. You'll usually need to purify your drinking water, by boiling or other means.

The cost of camping in national parks is universally low, and sometimes free, though you'll usually need a permit from the local national parks office (see p.54). Payment may be in advance (by phone or online), or on arrival, either direct to a park ranger doing the rounds, or by self-registration (fill in a form, put it into an envelope together with the required money, and drop it off in a box on the camp ground). You'll be issued with a payment reference to display on your tent. A few sites are so popular that that in order to nab a spot during the summer holidays you'll have to enter a ballot held around six months beforehand; details are given in the Guide.

Camping rough on beaches and in towns is not allowed, and doing the same just outside a town is not ideal, both from a security and an environmental point of view, even if you take the usual precautions of setting up away from the roadside and avoiding dry riverbeds. If you have to do it, animals are unlikely to pose a threat, except to your food – keep it in your tent or a secure container, or be prepared to be woken by their nocturnal shenanigans.

All over the East Coast, commercial or council-run camping and **caravan parks** (sometimes called holiday or tourist parks) are usually well equipped: in addition to an amenities block and a coin-operated laundry, very often you'll get a camp kitchen, coin-operated barbecues, a kiosk and a swimming pool, maybe even a children's playground and a tennis court. If you are travelling without a tent, renting an on-site van or cabin (with cooking facilities but shared amenities) is a cheap, if somewhat basic, accommodation option. Some upmarket caravan parks have large, well-equipped en-suite cabins, which are usually cheaper than a motel room or apartment of similar size, and good for families or groups.

Expect to pay A$20–30 per tent for an unpowered holiday park site; vans and cabins can cost anything from A$55 to over A$300 per night, depending on location, size and standard.

National park campsite bookings

New South Wales National Parks and Wildlife Service ☎ 1300 361 967, ⊛ www .nationalparks.nsw.gov.au. Bookings are handled locally, during business hours: call or check the website for details of the NPWS office nearest the site you'd like to visit. Campgrounds A$5–14 per adult or A$3–7 per child, depending on amenities, plus, in some parks, a daily entrance

fee of A$7–11 per vehicle; bushcamping, where permitted, is free.
Parks Victoria ☎ 13 19 63, ⊛ www.parkweb .vic.gov.au. You can book selected sites including Buchan Caves online at ⊛ www.parkstay.vic.gov .au; for others, contact the nearest Park Visitor Centre. Campgrounds A$13–22.50 for a tent site for one or two people, bushcamping A$6.90 per person per night.
Queensland Parks and Wildlife Service ☎ 13 13 04, ⊛ www.qld.gov.au/camping. Central, 24hr booking system for all sites, with the facility to book specific slots or buy general-purpose credits in advance and fine-tune your itinerary later. Campgrounds and bushcamping (where permitted) A$4.50 per person per night.

Food and drink

Australia's East Coast is riding a wave of interest in gourmet food. The state capitals' outstandingly cosmopolitan restaurants and cafés between them offer almost every cuisine imaginable, from cheap and delicious Asian dishes and fresh local seafood to elaborate degustation menus featuring many a mini masterpiece. Melbourne, in particular, has an exceptionally high ratio of eating places to people, and its restaurants survive because people eat out so much – three times a week is not unusual. The effect is rubbing off on provincial towns and well-to-do country villages, too, where outposts of excellence keep appearing among the more mundane restaurants and pubs serving old favourites such as pies, grills, pizza and pasta. All East Coast restaurants and bars are non-smoking, though some have an outside area where you can smoke but not eat.

Two things have helped shape Australia's culinary inventiveness: **immigration** and an extraordinary range of superb, **locally produced ingredients**. Various ethnic cuisines are briefly discussed below, but in addition to introducing their own cuisine, immigrants have had at least as profound an effect on mainstream Australian food. Contemporary Australian (or **Mod Oz**) cuisine is an exciting blend of tastes and influences from around the world – particularly Asia but also the Mediterranean – and many not specifically "ethnic" restaurants will have a menu that includes properly prepared curry, dolmades and fettuccine alongside steak and prawns. This healthy, eclectic – and above all,

fresh – cuisine has a lot in common with Californian cooking styles, and goes under the banner of "East meets West" or fusion cuisine.

Australian food

In Australia, **meat** is plentiful, cheap and excellent. Steak forms the mainstay of the pub-counter meal and of the ubiquitous **barbie**, as Australian an institution as you could hope to find: free or coin-operated barbecues can be found in car parks, campsites and beauty spots across the region. As an alternative to beef, lamb and pork, local game may be served, especially in more upma rket restaurants: occasionally emu, but more commonly kangaroo, which is rich, tender and virtually fat-free, or crocodile, which has a mild, meaty flavour and is at its best when simply grilled. Local fish and **seafood**, both in restaurants and in humble fish 'n' chip shops, is nothing short of tremendous: you can expect to feast on prawns, oysters, mud crabs, Moreton Bay bugs (a sweet-tasting crustacean), yabbies (crayfish), lobsters, calamari and a wide variety of fish (barramundi has a reputation as one of the finest, but is easily beaten by sweetlips or coral trout).

Fruit is good, too, from Tasmanian apples and pears to tropical bananas, pawpaw (papaya), mangoes, avocados, citrus fruits, custard apples, lychees, pineapples, passion fruit, star fruit and coconuts – few of them native, but delicious nonetheless. **Vegetables** are also fresh, cheap and good, and include everything from European cauliflowers and potatoes to Chinese pak choi and Indian bitter gourds. Note that aubergine is known as eggplant, courgettes as zucchini, and red or green peppers as capsicums.

Vegetarians might assume that they'll face a narrow choice of food in "meatocentric" Australia, and in the country areas that's probably true. But elsewhere, most restaurants will have one vegetarian option at least, and in the cities, veggie cafés have cultivated a wholesome, trendy image that suits Australians' active, health-conscious nature.

Finally, a word on **eskies** – these insulated food containers vary from handy "six-pack" sizes to cavernous sixty-litre trunks capable of refrigerating a weekend's worth of food or beer. No barbie or camping trip is complete without them.

Ethnic food

Since World War II, wave after wave of **immigrants** have brought a huge variety of ethnic cuisines to Australia: first North European, then Mediterranean and most recently Asian.

Chinese

Chinese restaurants were on the scene early in Australia – a result of post-gold rush Chinese enterprise; Sydney and Melbourne have Chinese connections dating back to the 1850s. Most of the Chinese restaurants you'll find in the smaller East Coast towns are rather old-fashioned and heavily reliant on MSG, but Melbourne, Sydney and Brisbane each have a Chinatown area where you can sample regional Chinese dishes as well as the usual Cantonese fare. *Yum cha* restaurants specialize in **dim sum**, lots of little titbits, such as steamed buns and dumplings, served from trolleys; also worth trying is **steamboat**, an Asian version of fondue, where you and your companions cook fresh morsels in a wok of simmering stock.

Only in Australia

Anzac biscuit Chewy oatmeal cookies with a distinctive caramel flavour, named after the hard biscuits sent in care packages to the Australian and New Zealand Army Corps (ANZAC) soldiers in World War I.

Chiko roll Imagine a wrapper of stodgy dough covered in breadcrumbs, filled with a neutered mess of chicken, cabbage, thickeners and flavourings, and then deep-fried. You could only get away with it in Australia.

Damper Sounding positively wholesome in this company, "damper" is the swagman's staple – soda bread baked in a pot buried in the ashes of a fire. It's not hard to make after a few attempts – the secret is in the heat of the coals and a splash of beer.

Lamington A chocolate-coated sponge cube rolled in shredded coconut.

Pavlova A "pav" is a dessert concoction of soft, very sweet meringue with layers of cream and fruit, named after the eminent Russian ballerina.

Vegemite Regarded by the English as an inferior form of Marmite and by almost every other nationality with total disgust, Vegemite is an Australian institution – a strong, dark yeast spread for bread and toast.

Bushtucker

The first European colonists decided that the country was not "owned" by the **Aborigines** because they didn't systematically farm the land. As many frustrated pastoralists later came to realize, this was a direct response to Australia's erratic seasons, which don't lend themselves to European farming methods with any degree of long-term security. Instead, Aborigines followed a nomadic lifestyle within extensive tribal boundaries, following seasonal game and plants, and promoting both by annually burning off grassland.

Along the coast, indigenous people speared turtles and dugong from outrigger canoes, caught **fish** in stone traps, piled emptied oyster shells into giant middens, and even cooperated with dolphins to herd fish into shallows. They also caught possums, snakes (highly prized), goannas, emus and kangaroos. These animals were thrown straight onto a fire and cooked in their own juices, and sometimes their skin, bones and fat used as clothing, tools and ointment, respectively. More meagre pickings were provided by honey and green ants, water-holding frogs, moths and various **grubs** – the witchetty (or *witjuti*) being the best known. Thirty-centimetre-long ooli worms were drawn out of rotten mangrove trunks, and tiny native bees were tagged with strands of spider web and then followed to their hives for honey; another sweet treat was **mulga resin**, picked off the tree trunk.

Plants, usually gathered by women, were used extensively and formed the bulk of the diet. The cabbage palm, sea almond, mangrove seeds, pandanus and dozens of fruits, including tropical coconuts, plums and figs, all grew along the coast. Inland were samphire bush, wild tomatoes and "citrus", grasstree hearts, cycad nuts (very toxic until washed, but high in starch), native millet, wattle seeds, waterlily tubers, nardoo seeds (a water fern), fungi, macadamia nuts, quandongs and bunya pine nuts – the last had great social importance in southern Queensland, where they were eaten at huge feasts. In Queensland's far north, meat and vegetables are wrapped in banana leaves (*kup maori*) and roasted in an underground oven; one of the Torres Strait Islanders' few surviving traditional styles of cooking.

It's tempting to taste some bushfoods, and a good few city restaurants are now experimenting with them as ingredients; otherwise, you'll need expert guidance, as many plants are poisonous. Safari guides will often point out key species.

Other Asian cuisines

Immigrants from Southeast Asia have been energizing Australian cuisine since the 1970s. **Vietnamese** restaurants not only offer some of the cheapest meals anywhere, they also come with the freshest of ingredients: accompanying most meals is a plate of red chillies, lemon wedges and beansprouts.

There are numerous **Malaysian** and **Indonesian** restaurants and market stalls, where hearty noodle soups and satays with hot peanut sauce are served up. Hawker-style stalls in city food-courts often serve *laksa*, a huge bowl of hot and spicy coconut-milk-based soup full of noodles, tofu and chicken or prawns.

The biggest success, however, are the **Thai** restaurants, and it's hard to believe that they've been around for less than twenty years. Dishes can be fiery, yet subtly flavoured, with ingredients such as basil, lemongrass, garlic, chilli and coriander.

Because so much fresh seafood is available in Australia, **Japanese** food is less expensive than it is in many other countries. There may not be a large Japanese population, but there is a huge number of Japanese visitors, and plenty of places catering for them (you'll find lots on the Gold Coast and in Cairns, for example).

Mongolian barbecues are an unusual, fast and inexpensive complement to an already diverse Asian food culture. Thinly sliced meat or seafood is added to a selection of sliced vegetables, and stir-fried in a soy-type sauce before your eyes on a giant wok – a Mongol warrior's shield is said to have been the original cooking utensil.

Italian – and coffee

The Italian influence on Australian cooking has been enormous. Second in number only to the English as an ethnic group, the Italians brought with them their love of food, which was a perfect complement to the Australian climate and way of life, and from the 1950s pizzerias, espresso and *gelati* bars, and the then-exotic taste of garlic, conquered palates countrywide. One particularly Australian metamorphosis is **focaccia**, now a staple of every city café and even beginning to make an appearance in country towns.

Australia can also thank the Italians for elevating **coffee** to a pastime rather than just a hot drink. Melburnians and Sydneysiders are particularly proud of their sophisticated café culture, but nowadays every suburban café on the coast has an espresso machine; it's only on the breakfast buffets of resort hotels that you're likely to find dreary jugs of percolated coffee. You can order a cappuccino or a latte, but other varieties have uniquely Australian names: a "flat white" is an espresso with steamed milk (less milk than a latte and less froth than a cappuccino), a "short black" is an espresso, transformed by a splash of milk into a macchiato, and a "long black" is an espresso diluted with hot water.

Other European and Middle Eastern cuisines

In Melbourne, Australia's food capital, one of the strongest culinary influences comes from the **Greek** population. *Taverna*-style restaurants and *souvlaki* bars, with spiced lamb rotating on a spit, abound. **Turkish** and **Lebanese** takeaways, found in all the East Coast cities, offer spicy filled rolls, while some Turkish places also make *börek*, small, simple variants on a pizza. Turkish bread is as popular as focaccia in cafés and sandwich shops. Lebanese restaurants are especially good for vegetarians, with falafel rolls (pitta bread stuffed with chickpea patties, hummus and *tabbouleh*) making an inexpensive, filling meal.

Central European influences are most obvious in baking, particularly in Melbourne, which has a large **Jewish** community descended from immigrants from pre-war Poland; as well as cake shops, there are also a few **Polish** restaurants serving hearty, peasant-style dishes.

Eating out

Restaurants are astonishingly good value compared with the UK and North America, particularly as many restaurants allow you to "BYO" (bring your own – usually understood to mean wine only) and you're rarely far from a bottle shop. Corkage starts at around A$1, rising to A$10 per bottle at smarter places, which typically also have their own wine list. You should have no problem finding an excellent two-course meal in a simple restaurant for A$25 or less; a main course at a moderate restaurant is around A$17–24 and it's not hard to find places where you can spend a whole evening eating amazingly well without spending more than A$100.

There are also lots of excellent **cafés** and coffee shops, many of which serve big breakfasts and other great meals as well as good coffee, tea and cold drinks. In the cities and resorts, they will be open from early in the morning until late at night; in the country, they stick more or less to shop hours. Ordering and paying at the counter before taking a seat is the usual system.

The **hotel** (pub) or surf club counter meal is another mainstay, consisting of simple, substantial bar food such as grills with chips and salad for around A$10–15, and daily specials for less; serving times are typically noon to 2pm and from 6pm to 8pm, daily except Sunday evenings. Slightly more upmarket is the **bistro** or motel restaurant where you sit down to be served much the same food. These places often have a help-yourself salad bar; the most expensive thing on the menu is likely to be a huge steak for around A$30.

In cities and bigger resorts, you'll find fantastic fast-food in **food courts**, often in the basements of office buildings or the top floors of shopping malls, where dozens of counters compete to offer Thai, Chinese, Japanese or Italian food, as well as burgers, steaks and sandwiches. On the road, you may be reduced to what's available at the **roadhouse**, usually the lowest common denominator of reheated meat-pies and microwave ready-meals.

East Coast food fads

Australian restaurant habits can be rather faddy, with much use and abuse of borrowed names. The French word for a wine tasting – **dégustation** – has become the preferred term for a fashionable meal of gourmet titbits, with or without matching wines; while "high tea", all the rage in smart hotel dining rooms, thankfully bears no resemblance to its English boarding-school namesake but instead evokes afternoon tea at *The Ritz* with a feast of dainty sandwiches, cakes, and tea poured from a china pot. Tea with scones, jam, and cream squirted out of a can is known, with a generous dollop of poetic licence, as a "**Devonshire tea**", much touted by country teashops.

Other terms are more faithfully used, however, such as the Cantonese **yum cha** for the ritual of eating dim sum with Chinese tea sometime between late morning and mid-afternoon. **Brunch**, hugely popular at weekends, is likely to feature eggs benedict or a giant pile of pancakes, syrup and bacon with fresh juice and coffee, as in North America. Finally, in this region where fresh fish is so abundant, **sashimi** is as delicious and authentic as you'd expect.

Drink

Australians have a reputation for enjoying a drink, and **hotels** (also called pubs, inns, taverns or bars) are where it mostly takes place. Traditionally, public bars are male enclaves, the place where mates meet after work on their way home, with the emphasis more on the beer and banter than the surroundings. While changing attitudes have converted many city hotels into comfortable, relaxed bars, a lot of provincial pubs are still pretty spartan and daunting for strangers of either sex, but you'll find barriers will come down if you're prepared to join in the conversation.

Friday and Saturday are the serious party nights, when there's likely to be a band. **Standard opening hours** are usually 10am to 11pm or midnight (10pm on Sun), but places with an extended licence stay open often much later, sometimes with a 3am lockout (after which those inside can stay in, but nobody else can enter).

In Australia, shops selling wine, beer and spirits by the bottle or case (**bottle shops**) are often sections attached to pubs or supermarkets – **drive-in** versions allow you to load bulk purchases directly into the boot of your car. If you plan to visit **Aboriginal communities**, bear in mind that some of them are "dry". Respect their regulations and don't take any alcohol with you.

In towns, **tap water** is safe to drink; mineral water is also widely available. In remote areas, purify tap water before drinking.

Beer

As anyone you ask will tell you, the proper way to drink **beer** in a hot country such as Australia is ice cold (the English can expect to be constantly berated for their warm-beer preferences) and fast, from a small container so it doesn't heat up before you can down the contents. Tubular foam or polystyrene coolers are often supplied for **tinnies** (cans) or **stubbies** (short-necked bottles) to make sure they stay icy. Glasses are always on the small side, and are given confusingly different names state by state. The standard 285ml serving is known as a **pot** in Victoria and Queensland, and a **middy** in New South Wales; all three states call a larger glass a schooner but the size varies (425ml in New South Wales and Queensland, 485ml in Victoria). A **carton** or **slab** is a box of 24 to 30 tinnies or stubbies, bought in bulk from a bottle shop and always cheaper when not chilled.

Australian beers are **lager-** or **pilsner-style**, and even the big mass-produced varieties are pretty good – at least once you've worked up a thirst. They're considerably stronger than their US equivalents, and marginally stronger than the average British lager at just under five percent alcohol. Each state has its own **label** and there are fierce local loyalties, even though most are sold nationwide: East Coast favourites include Fourex (XXXX; see p.452) and Powers in Queensland, VB in Victoria, and Tooheys in New South Wales. Almost all of these companies produce more than one beer – usually a light, low-alcohol version and a premium "gold" or bitter brew. There are also a number of smaller "boutique" breweries and specialist beermakers. Fosters is treated as a joke in Australia, something that's fit only for export. Larger bottle shops might have imported beers, but outside cities (where Irish pubs serve surprisingly authentic-tasting Guinness), it's rare that you'll find anything foreign on tap.

Wine and spirits

Australian **wines** have long been appreciated at home, and it's not hard to see why; even an inexpensive bottle (around A$12) will be better than just drinkable, while pricier varieties compare favourably with fine French wines – though some critics complain that Australian reds have become a bit too "woody" in recent years. If you're new to Australian wines, you'll always find Yalumba, Lindemans and Wolf Blass will give satisfaction, but the secret is to be adventurous: you're extremely unlikely to be disappointed. Even the "chateau cardboard" four-litre bladders or wine casks that prevail at parties and barbecues are perfectly palatable.

Whatever the colour, a mid-range bottle of wine will set you back about A$16.

The biggest wine-producing **regions** are the Hunter Valley in New South Wales, noted for its Sémillons, and the Barossa Valley in South Australia, which produces superb Shiraz. Restaurant wine lists and bottle shops also often feature Cabernet Sauvignon from Margaret River in Western Australia, or Coonawarra in South Australia, while Victoria's Yarra Valley and Mornington Peninsula are known for their Pinot Noirs and Chardonnay. For more information, check out Ⓦwww.australianwines.com.au or get hold of one of the annual guides to Australian wines and wineries, such as James Halliday's *Australian Wine Companion*.

The Australian wine industry also makes **port** and **brandy** as a sideline, though these are not up to international standards. Two excellent dark **rums** from Queensland's sugar belt are well worth tasting, however: the sweet, deliciously smoky Bundaberg (see p.495) and the more conventionally flavoured Beenleigh. They're of average strength, normally 33 percent alcohol, but beware of "overproof" variations, which will have you flat on your back if you try to drink them like ordinary spirits.

The media

Local papers are always a good source of listings, if not news. You should be able to track down some international papers, or their overseas editions – British, American, Asian and European – in the state capitals. Australian television isn't particularly exciting unless you're into sport, of which there's plenty; commercial stations put on frequent advertising breaks throughout films.

Newspapers and magazines

The Murdoch-owned *Australian* (Ⓦwww .theaustralian.news.com.au) is the country's only national daily (that is, Mon–Sat) **newspaper**; aimed mainly at the business community, it has good overseas coverage, but local news is often built around statistics.

Each state (or more properly, each state capital) has its own daily paper, the best of which are two Fairfax-owned papers, the *Sydney Morning Herald* (Ⓦwww.smh.com.au) and Melbourne's venerable *The Age* (Ⓦwww .theage.com.au) – both are available across the southeast (the two papers share similar content in their weekend-edition magazines).

If you're interested in wildlife, pick up a copy of the quarterly *Australian Geographic* magazine (related only in name to the US mag) for some superb photography and in-depth coverage of Australia's remoter corners, or the quarterly *Australian Wildlife* magazine, published by the Wildlife Preservation Society. There are some first-rate glossy Australian-focused adventure-travel magazines, too, such as the quarterly *Wild*. The bimonthly *Australian Traveller* is good for mainstream and luxury travel, as is the excellent *Australian Gourmet Traveller*, which also celebrates fine food. You'll find Australian versions of all the fashion mags, from *Vogue* to *Marie Claire*, plus enduring publications such as the *Australian Women's Weekly*. As elsewhere, there's also a slew of gossipy magazines giving the lowdown on the antics of international and Australian celebs.

Television

Australia's first **television** station opened in 1956, and the country didn't get colour television until 1974 – both much later than other Westernized countries. Australian TV is governed by content rulings, which means that there are a good amount of Australian dramas, series and soap operas, many of which go on to make it big overseas, from *Neighbours* and *Home and Away* to *The Secret Life of Us*. However, there's a predominance of American programmes, and lots of repeats.

There are three predictable commercial stations: Channel Seven; Channel Nine, which aims for an older market with more conservative programming; and Channel Ten, which tries to grab the younger market with some good comedy programmes. In addition, there is also the more serious ABC – a national, advertisement-free station still with a British bias, showing all the best British sitcoms and mini-series – and the livelier SBS, a government-sponsored, multicultural station, which has the best coverage of world news, as well as interesting current-affairs programmes and plenty of foreign-language films. In more remote areas, you won't be able to access all five channels, and often only ABC and one commercial offering are receivable. There are over 35 pay-TV stations, though the pay-TV culture is not as firmly established yet as in other countries.

Radio

The best **radio** is on the various ABC stations, both local and national. ABC Radio National – broadcast all over Australia – offers a popular mix of arty intellectual topics. Another ABC station, 2JJJ ("Triple J"), a former Sydney-based alternative-rock station, is aimed at the nation's youth, and is available across the country in watered-down form.

Festivals and major sporting events

Each of the East Coast capitals tries to elevate its sophistication quotient with a regular showcase of art and culture. Excellent though these events often are, it's the big sporting fixtures and public holidays that really unite the region – and the nation – in celebration: barbies are fired up and bars fill to capacity as families and groups of mates get together for a party fuelled by plenty of beer, wine and seafood.

Besides the major festivals, there's a host of smaller, local events, many of which are detailed throughout the Guide. Also, all cities and towns have their own agricultural "shows", which are high points of the local calendar. National holidays such as

Christmas, New Year, Australia Day (Jan 26), Easter and ANZAC day (April 25) are always marked by celebrations all over the region.

January

Sydney Festival NSW. Over three weeks of world-class arts events. See p.212.

Tamworth Country Music Festival NSW. Third week. Ten days of music inspired by Slim Dusty and his ilk, culminating in the Australian Country Music Awards. ⓦ www.tamworthcountrymusic.com.au.

Big Day Out Various locations. Late Jan. Australia and New Zealand's largest outdoor music festival, with over 250,000 people gathering at six different locations including, on the East Coast, Melbourne, Sydney and the Gold Coast, to see bands such as Silverchair, Rage Against the Machine and Björk. ⓦ www.bigdayout.com.

February

Sydney Gay and Lesbian Mardi Gras NSW. Early Feb to early March. Sydney's proud LGBT festival. See p.296.

March

Australian Grand Prix Melbourne, VIC. First or second weekend. Formula One racing in Albert Park. See p.90.

Moomba Waterfest Melbourne, VIC. Second weekend. A long weekend of water-based fun. See p.90.

April

Melbourne International Comedy Festival VIC. Starts first week. Features comics from around the world. See p.90.

June

Sydney International Film Festival NSW. Mid-June. Celebration of Australian and world cinema. See p.301.

Laura Dance and Cultural Festival Cape York, QLD. Third weekend; biennial, held in odd-numbered years. Three-day, alcohol-free celebration of authentic Aboriginal culture.

July

Brisbane Festival Brisbane, QLD. Mid-July; biennial, held in even years. Huge festival of arts and culture. See p.462.

Melbourne International Film Festival VIC. End July to mid-Aug. The country's most prestigious film festival. See p.91.

August

Riverfestival Brisbane, QLD. Late Aug. Hugely enjoyable waterfront events. See p.451.

September

AFL Grand Final Melbourne, VIC. Last Sat. Massive, testosterone-charged sporting event. See p.91.

October

Manly Jazz Festival Sydney, NSW. First weekend. Long-established, free festival. See p.231.

Melbourne International Arts Festival VIC. Mid-Oct. Two-week celebration of the arts. See p.91.

November

Melbourne Cup Flemington Racecourse, VIC. First Tues. Australia's Ascot. See p.91.

December

Christmas Day Sydney, NSW. 25 Dec. Backpackers flock to Bondi Beach to celebrate in the sun. See p.270.

Sydney–Hobart Yacht Race Sydney, NSW. 26 Dec. The classic regatta starts with a flourish. See p.213.

New Year's Eve Sydney, NSW. 31 Dec. Stupendous fireworks display from Sydney Harbour Bridge. See p.213.

Outdoor activities and special interests

Though the cities are fun, what really makes the East Coast special is the great outdoors: the vast and remote wilderness of the bush, and the thousands of kilometres of unspoilt coastline. There's tremendous potential here to indulge in a huge range of outdoor pursuits, including hiking, fishing, surfing and diving – especially in the multitude of national parks that cover the region. Further information on all of these is available from local tourist offices, which publicize what's available in their area, and from the national parks offices in each state, which have detailed maps of parks with walking trails, climbs, swimming holes and other activities. In addition, virtually any activity can be done as part of an organized excursion, often with all the gear supplied. If you want to go it alone, you'll find plenty of places ready to rent or sell you the necessary equipment.

As with any wilderness area, the Australian interior does not suffer fools, and the coast conceals **dangers**, too: sunstroke and dehydration are risks everywhere, with riptides, currents and unexpectedly large waves to be wary of on exposed coasts. In the more remote regions, isolation and lack of surface water compromise energetic outdoor activities such as bushwalking or mountain biking: if you're less than fully confident, you should stick to the cooler climes and more populated locations of the south. Before indulging in adventure activities, check your insurance cover (see "Travel essentials" on p.74). For the latest weather forecasts and warnings, go to Ⓦwww.bom.gov.au. Once your careful preparations are complete, you're likely to have an outstanding experience.

Bushwalking

Bushwalking on the East Coast doesn't mean just a stroll in the bush: it also refers to self-sufficient hikes, from a day to a week or longer. It's an increasingly popular activity, and you'll find trails marked in almost every national park, as well as local bushwalking clubs whose trips you may be able to join.

The Great Dividing Range, which runs roughly parallel to the East Coast, is the fourth-longest mountain range in the world. Much of it is covered with lush forests that provide spectacular bushwalking country. Near Sydney, the popular **Blue Mountains** region, a system of escarpments and canyons also renowned for rock-climbing, caving and canyoning, is a genuine "land that time forgot" – near here, bushwalkers discovered the dinosaur-contemporary Wollemi pine, a tree previously believed to have been extinct for more than two million years. In Far North Queensland, the **Daintree rainforest** is a region of unmatched biodiversity, made accessible by easy-going boardwalks and more challenging tracks. Other national parks that offer superb bushwalking include Wilson's Promontory, Lamington, Fraser Island, Eungella and Hinchinbrook Island. Queensland has an ambitious network of **Great Walks** for long-distance enthusiasts (see p.424).

It's essential to be **properly equipped** for the conditions you'll encounter – and to know what those conditions are likely to be. Carry a map (often on hand at the ranger station in popular national parks), know how the trail is marked, and stay on the route. If your trip is a long one, let someone know where you're going, and confirm to them that you've arrived back safely – park rangers are useful contacts for this, and some will insist on it for overnight walks, which may require registration. Depending on the gradient, a walking speed of 3kph to 4kph is average on park tracks. The essentials, even for a short walk, are adequate clothing including a wide-brimmed hat, enough food and, above all, plenty of water. Other useful items include a torch, matches or lighter, penknife, sun block, insect

Bush essentials

Four things above all:

Fire The driest continent on earth is always at risk from bushfires. At least three times since 1997 Sydney has been ringed with burning bushland, and during the terrible bushfire season of 2002/2003 a large part of the Alpine region in Australia's southeast was ablaze for almost two months. Only a few human lives were lost, however, mainly owing to the skills, resilience and determination of the fire fighters and local residents. Even in wet years, there's a constant red alert during summer months; periodic total fire bans – announced in the local media when in effect – prohibit any fire in the open, including wood, gas or electric barbecues, with heavy fines for offenders. In areas where fires are permitted, always use an established fireplace if available, or dig a shallow pit and ring it with stones. Keep fires small and make absolutely sure embers are smothered before going to sleep or moving on. Never discard burning cigarette butts.

Check on the local fire danger before you go bushwalking – some walking trails are closed in the riskiest periods (summer, Dec–Feb, in the south; the end of the dry season, Sept–Oct, in the north). If driving, carry blankets and a filled water container, listen out for radio announcements and watch for roadside fire-danger indicators. See also "Health", p.48.

Water Carry plenty with you and do not contaminate local water resources. Soaps, detergents and sunscreen can render water undrinkable and harm livestock and wild animals. Avoid washing in standing water, especially tanks and small lakes or reservoirs.

Waste Take only photographs, leave only footprints. That means carrying all your rubbish out with you – never burn or bury it – and making sure you urinate (and bury your excrement) at least 50m from a campsite or water source.

Hypothermia In southeast Australia, where the weather is notoriously changeable, prepare as you would for a walk in Scotland or Vermont.

---

repellent, toilet paper, first-aid kit, and a whistle or mirror to attract attention if you get lost. A lot of this gear can be rented, or bought cheaply at disposal stores, which can often also put you in touch with local clubs or specialists.

Two of Australia's best-regarded bushwalkers are John Chapman and Tyrone T. Thomas, who both publish a range of **walking guides**. Try to get hold of the latest edition of Chapman's rigorously updated *Bushwalking in Australia*, which details the country's best bushwalks.

Wildlife watching

Daytime **bushwalks** may bring excellent encounters with native birds, insects, reptiles and marsupials, but since many of the region's species are **nocturnal**, wildlife enthusiasts shouldn't miss the opportunity to camp or lodge in wilderness areas overnight in order to head out on after-dark walks,

preferably in the company of a guide. Ecolodges and national park rangers organize regular **guided nature walks**, by day or by night, in the most popular wilderness areas. Discreet use of a powerful torch may pick out a surprising variety of creatures: pademelons and bandicoots bounding through the bush, sugar gliders peering down from flowering trees, frogs chirruping beside billabongs, and geckos gobbling insects.

Snorkellers and **scuba divers** with a specific zoological interest – be it tropical or temperate species, sharks, turtles, seals, dolphins or weedy sea dragons – will find sites to suit. If all you want to do is find Nemo, however, very few Great Barrier Reef sites will disappoint. For a good chance of spotting marine mammals such as dolphins, seals and dugongs without getting wet, you can head out on a **wildlife-watching cruise**: you'll find these on offer in Hervey Bay, Moreton Bay, Port Stephens and several spots along South Coast New South Wales. Cruises run all year round but are busiest during the annual whale-watching season: humpback whales migrate north up the East Coast in mid-winter, and south again in spring (see p.485). There are excellent vantages all the way from southeast Australia to the Whitsundays, with particularly good whale-watching trips running from Hervey Bay and Jervis Bay.

For an overview of some of the more common species found on the East Coast, see the Wildlife section on p.18 and Contexts, p.640, and for a rundown of the best places to see them, see the *East Coast ecotourism* **colour section**.

Watersports

The oceans and seas around Australia are a national playground, not just for lying around or playing volleyball on the beach. Always take local advice on the waves, which must be treated with respect. See also the *Take the plunge!* **colour section**.

Surfing

In Australia, you'll find **surfing** fanatics wherever there's surf; on the East Coast, this means all the way from Melbourne to Agnes Water, just south of the Great Barrier Reef's sheltering influence: **key spots** include southeast Queensland, Byron Bay, and the Sydney area from Newcastle to Wollongong. Mark Warren's *Atlas of Australian Surfing* is a useful reference, with details of many good spots.

If you've never tried surfing before, boogie-boarding – catching the waves on a small, light board that you lie on – is a good way to practice your timing. To progress to something big enough to stand on, it's worth investing in a few **lessons** – you'll find scores of surf schools in the most popular surfing areas, some of them run by former champions.

Confident surfers can set out on their own – every surfing town has shops where you can rent gear, and hostels sometimes lend out boards for free – but don't expect the local surfie community to be too friendly at first: they're often cliquey and fiercely territorial about their patches. Before you set out, it's worth checking the conditions: daily reports are posted online at ⓦwww.swellnet .com.au and ⓦwww.coastalwatch.com, while in New South Wales the Beachwatch Bulletin

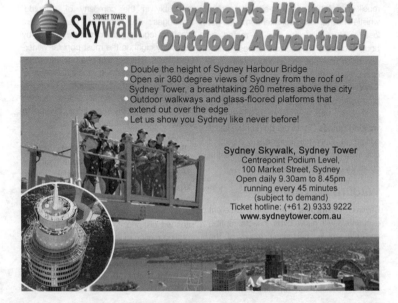

(☎1800 036 677, ⊕www.environment.nsw .gov.au/beach) monitors marine pollution.

Throughout the year, the coast plays host to a number of high-profile **competitions** such as the Quiksilver Roxy Pro Surf Championships at Kirra Beach, Gold Coast, in February; Newcastle's Surfest in late March; and the legendary Rip Curl Pro Surf and Music Festival, held each Easter at Bell's Beach, southwest of Melbourne – all good opportunities to watch some wave-riding action. One peculiarly Australian institution is the **surf carnival**, when teams of volunteer lifesavers demonstrate their skills; it makes for a great day out on the beach.

Windsurfing, boating and rafting

Windsurfing, kitesurfing and sailing are also extremely popular, and you'll be able to rent equipment and get instruction in almost any resort, though some of the best **sailing** in the country can be found around Queensland's Whitsunday Islands. Other options include powerboating, wakeboarding, waterskiing, white-water rafting, sea-kayaking and canoeing.

Diving and snorkelling

The Great Barrier Reef (see p.500) is rightly famous for its **scuba diving** opportunities (Cairns is by far the busiest starting point for trips), but there are also many other excellent sites within reach of the coast. Queensland has two particularly good wreck dives: the *Yongala* (see p.531) and the *Brisbane* (see p.468). Dive facilities in Australia are of a high standard, with good rental gear, and scuba courses are not that expensive, though for those who simply want to try it once most operators offer closely supervised "try dives". **Snorkelling**, the low-tech alternative, still allows you to get dramatically close to the aquatic life around a reef.

Swimming

All the East Coast cities and resorts have at least one stretch of beach that is patrolled by life savers, making **swimming** reasonably safe: at the first sight of danger, you'll hear an announcement or an emergency siren. Red flags mean you shouldn't enter the water.

Fishing

Fishing is an Australian obsession, conducted on rivers and lakes, off piers or small boats ("tinnies"), or out at sea where – if your bank balance is up to the challenge – marlin and other game fish are caught. All the equipment – even boats – can be rented in most good fishing areas. Barramundi, renowned for its fighting qualities, is the thing to go for up north. Bear in mind that recreational fishing licenses may be required depending on the state or territory.

Adventure pursuits

The East Coast's buzzing backpacker hubs – particularly Sydney, Byron Bay, Surfers

---

Beach safety

- Protect yourself against the sun.
- Only swim "between the flags" – red and yellow flags indicate that the beach is patrolled by lifeguards or lifesavers and it's safe to enter the water. Boogie-boards are allowed between the flags; fibreglass surfboards are not.
- On beaches affected by stingers (see p.47), don't swim without a protective Lycra suit.
- Never swim or surf alone.
- If you hear a siren, clear the water: it could signal dangerous waves, a shark sighting, or a swarm of bluebottles (stinging jellyfish).
- If you get into difficulty, raise your arm to attract help.
- A rip tide is a strong oceanward current, typically found between sand bars. If caught in one, don't attempt to swim against it – you will tire quickly. If you're not a strong swimmer, let the rip carry you (and your surfboard, if you have one). As soon as you can, try to swim or paddle at right angles to the rip, parallel to the shore, towards the breaking waves, which will carry you back to the beach.

Paradise, Brisbane, Airlie Beach and Cairns – offer no end of opportunities to test your nerve and boost your adrenaline in **adventurous activities** such as skydiving, jetboating and ziplining. The Blue Mountains are famous for rock-climbing, abseiling and canyoning.

Horseback riding is offered in many rural areas, and there are also a few spots where you can gallop, romantically, along the beach. **Cycling** is tremendously popular, too; just about all hostels rent out bikes, and we've listed other outlets throughout the Guide.

Australia's wilderness is an ideal venue for extended **off-road driving** and **motorbiking**, although permission may be needed to cross Aboriginal-owned lands, and the fragile desert ecology should be respected at all times. Northern Queensland's Cape York is the most adventurous destination, 4WD-accessible in the dry season only.

Jumping aboard a helicopter, light aircraft or seaplane for a **scenic flight** is a thrilling

way to get a new perspective on the landscape, admiring the rich textures of the rainforest canopy or spotting turtles as they swim over coral reefs. In Melbourne, Canberra, the Hunter Valley and Brisbane, you can enjoy the gentle adventure of **hot-air ballooning** at dawn.

Cultural, wine and food tours

A growing number of Aboriginal guides – some of them national park rangers, others independent operators – offer **cultural tours**, which include a brief introduction to Aboriginal bush lore, ritual and botanical knowledge, possibly built around a visit to a rock art site or another heritage area.

The wine-making regions of the Yarra Valley, the Mornington Peninsula, the Hunter Valley and southeast Queensland are all good places to indulge your gourmet inclinations with guided visits to **wineries** and other producers including cheesemakers, olive growers and chocolate specialists.

National parks, beaches, islands and marine reserves

Australia has a highly active conservation movement, and national parks account for almost four percent of the country's gigantic landmass – impressive when compared to the total area used for farming, which is a little over six percent. The populated East Coast has a surprisingly high concentration of parks, including six World Heritage regions and four biosphere reserves (see Contexts, p.639). Many are compelling places to visit: as well as being areas of natural or cultural significance, they're well set up for activities such as bushwalking, wildlife-watching and camping.

Almost all of Australia's **national parks** are public land, owned by the federal government and protected by the Department of the Environment, Water, Heritage and the Arts (🔵www.environment.gov.au); the task of running them and conserving their flora, fauna, landforms and heritage sites lies with dedicated management authorities in each state, each of which operates separately. However, Booderee National Park near

Jervis Bay is co-managed by the government and the local Aboriginal community, one of very few Australian parks to be run in this way (other notable examples being Uluru-Kata Tjuta and Kakadu in the Northern Territory).

Parks are typically unfenced; all parks in Queensland – and many others – can be entered for **free**. In Victoria, New South Wales and ACT, parks for which there's a vehicle-entry charge either have manned gates (which may be locked at night) or ticket machines. If you'll be "going bush" for more than ten days, you can save money with an annual pass for your vehicle, available from the relevant state authority (each pass covers that state only; see p.68).

The national park authorities employ teams of **rangers** whose responsibilities include informing the general public on conservation matters and on practicalities such as camping, hiking, bushfire prevention and wildlife rescue. Some also offer guided bushwalks (free, or for a small fee) with a botanical, zoological or heritage theme. The **New South Wales Discovery Programme** (details available from New South Wales NPWS, at regional offices or online) is excellent – this is a series of ranger-led walks, talks and tours, each one focusing on one species, topic or activity, be it visiting the shearwater nesting burrows on Muttonbird Island, watching wildlife in the Dorrigo rainforest, or learning about bushtucker or wild flowers. Many events (some free, others A$5–25, child A$2–15) are one-offs, timed to fit in with the seasons. Participants need to get themselves to the starting point. In southeast Queensland, the **QPWS Go Bush Programme** (☎1300 723 684) is run along similar lines.

Outstanding national parks on the East Coast mainland include, in Victoria: Mornington Peninsula, Wilson's Promontory and Croajingolong; in New South Wales: Murramarang, Royal, Blue Mountains, Ku-Ring-Gai Chase, Myall Lakes, Barrington Tops and Dorrigo; and in Queensland: Lamington, Springbrook, Eungella, Daintree and Cape Tribulation. All the most popular parks have simple, rustic **campgrounds** (see p.53); some also have desirable and eco-friendly self-catering accommodation, in safari tents, cabins or even lighthouse keepers' cottages.

Beaches are also public land (there are no private beaches on the East Coast) and while not all are national parks, state law governs what you can and can't do – campers need to stick to designated campsites, for example, and four-wheel-drivers should only use established tracks, to minimize sand and dune erosion. Australia – which has a great deal of space, but limited fresh-water supplies – has so far largely

escaped the high-density coastal develop-ment found in many other countries, and the Pacific seaboard is refreshingly uncluttered. Most of the coastal towns, with a few glaring exceptions, are predominantly low-rise, and the beaches themselves tend to be backed by grassy dunelands or headlands rather than shops, hotels and apartments.

Numerous **islands** dot the coastal waters, particularly in Queensland. Many are havens for rare flora, seabirds and turtles, or are protected for their unique landscapes. Montague, Lord Howe, Moreton Bay, Fraser, Lady Elliott, Hinchinbrook, the Whitsundays, Heron, Wilson and Lizard are particularly worth visiting. While some are within boat-trip distance, others are served by scheduled or charter plane; accommodation options range from the simplest of bushcamps to the swankiest of resorts. The Australian Pacific itself is also carefully managed, zoned so that different groups such as ecologists, scuba-diving operations and commercial fishermen each have areas they can access without interference.

The **marine reserves** at Wilsons Promon-tory, Jervis Bay, the Solitary Islands (near Coffs Harbour), Port Stephens and the Great Lakes are home to a fascinating array of wildlife, while the Great Barrier Reef Marine Park, the largest ocean reserve in the world, protects a region of remarkable biodiversity. All can be visited by boat, for wildlife-watching, scuba diving or snorkelling.

National parks authorities

Australian Capital Territory

ACT Parks, Conservation and Lands ☎13 22 81, ⓦ www.tams.act.gov.au. Free entry to parks.

New South Wales

New South Wales National Parks and Wildlife Service (NPWS) ☎1300 361 967, ⓦ www .nationalparks.nsw.gov.au. Vehicle entry fees (A$7–11/day) apply at the most popular parks; see the Guide for details. Annual pass for all parks in New South Wales apart from Booderee and Kosciuszko A$65 per vehicle; access to all except Booderee A$190 (☎02 9585 6068, ⓦ www.environment .nsw.gov.au).

Queensland

Queensland Parks and Wildlife Service (QPWS) ☎1300 130 372, ⓦ www.epa.qld.gov .au. Visitors to the Great Barrier Reef Marine Park are required to pay an Environmental Management Charge (A$5 per person per day, collected by boat operators on behalf of the Great Barrier Reef Marine Park Authority). All other national parks in Queensland are free.

Victoria

Parks Victoria ☎13 19 63, ⓦ www.parkweb .vic.gov.au. Vehicle entry fees (A$4.30–10/day, discounted multi-day passes available) apply at Wilsons Promontory, Mornington Peninsula and some other parks; see the Guide for details. Annual pass for all parks in Victoria: A$70.50 per vehicle.

Travelling with children

Australians have an easy-going attitude to children, and in most places they are made welcome. With plenty of beautiful beaches, parks and playgrounds, travel-ling with children in Australia can be great fun.

Getting around

Most forms of **transport** within Australia offer child concessions. Throughout the country, metropolitan buses and trains give discounts of around fifty percent for children, and many allow children under 4 or 5 to travel free. Most interstate buses offer around twenty percent off for children under the age of 14. Long-distance train travel is more expensive, but has the advantage of sleepers and a bit more freedom of movement. Domestic airlines offer discounts of around fifty percent of the full adult fare for children between 2 and 11. However, it's worth checking for adult discount deals, which are likely to be even cheaper. Infants usually travel free of charge.

Otherwise, there's always the option of **self-drive**. Car rental is reasonably priced, and motorhomes and campervans are also available for rental. They're an excellent way of seeing Australia and make it possible to camp in some spectacular national parks, as well as the many family-friendly caravan parks. It's important to remember, however, that Australia is a huge place and that driving between cities almost always involves long distances; you'll need to take more activities for the car – music, books, magnetic games, cards – than usual. Stop regularly for breaks: most towns in Australia have public playgrounds.

Accommodation

Many **motels** and **resorts** give discounts for children and some offer a baby-sitting service – it's worth checking when you book. The family-oriented places, of which there are many, often have kids' clubs, organized children's activities and baby-sitting services, a boon for those moments when you'd like a quiet whinge-free bushwalk or cocktails by the pool. Many **hostels** provide affordable family rooms – some en suite. Hostels tend to be well located and all have communal kitchens, lounge areas and TV rooms, plus plenty of books and games. **Self-contained apartments** can also be excellent value, particularly if you're happy to cook your own meals. The most economical way to travel is to **camp** or stay in **caravan parks**, found in every coastal town (though in the state capitals, they're some distance from the centre). As well as tent spaces, most have on-site vans or self-contained cabins at very reasonable rates for families.

Eating out

Many Australian **restaurants** are welcoming to children, often providing highchairs, toys, blackboards, drawing materials and a reasonable children's menu. There are also plenty of standard **fast-food outlets**, which often have enclosed play areas. Children are allowed in the dining section of **pubs** for counter meals; many provincial towns also have **RSL clubs** (Returned and Services League) or surf clubs serving very reasonably priced, family-friendly meals.

Kids' gear

Car- and van-rental companies provide **child safety seats**. Taxis will also provide child seats if you request them when making a booking, although there may be a longer wait. Airlines will allow you to carry a pram or travel cot for free, and it's possible to rent baby equipment from some shops – check the local *Yellow Pages* for listings. When planning a day that involves a lot of walking, check to see if you can rent a pushchair, as this can make the difference between a pleasant and an awful day out.

Activities

Most tours and visitor attractions sell child **tickets** at approximately half the price of an adult ticket; many also offer discounted family tickets for two adults plus two or three children. Museums often have special children's areas. During **school holidays** (see p.77 for dates), museums, attractions and national parks run entertaining and educational activities including storytelling, performances and ranger-led walks.

Sun care

The Australian **sun** is ferocious, making it essential to combine outdoor activities with sensible skin care. A broad-spectrum, water-resistant sunscreen (minimum SPF of 30) is essential; see "Health" for more on sunscreens. There's a "no hat, no play" policy in school playgrounds, and most kids wear legionnaire-style caps, or broad-brimmed sun hats, which are cheap and easy to find in surf shops and department stores. All sunglasses in Australia are UV-rated, and most kids also wear UV-resistant Lycra swim tops or wetsuit-style all-in-ones to the beach. The Cancer Council Australia has shops in most Australian cities selling a high-quality and colourful range of all these items; for locations, consult Ⓦwww .cancer.org.au.

Helpful publications

In Sydney, look for *Sydney's Child* (🖰www
.sydneyschild.com.au), a free monthly
magazine listing kids' activities in and around
the city and advertising a range of services
including baby-sitting. Spin-offs published in
Melbourne, Brisbane and Canberra have the
same format; all can be picked up at libraries
and museums, and you can read some of
the content online. Visitor Information Centres
can also help with suggestions for planning a
child-friendly itinerary.

Working in Australia

Most visitors' visas clearly state that no employment of any kind is to be undertaken during a visit to Australia. However, if you're in possession of a Working
Holiday Visa (see "Entry requirements" on p.32) and are prepared to try anything,
there are plenty of possibilities for finding a short-term job. There are also
organized work programmes – both paid and voluntary.

Since Working Holiday Visa (WHV) regulations disallow working holidaymakers from
remaining with the same employer for more
than six months, and professionals often
need Australian accreditation before they
can take on work, in practice the only jobs
open to travellers are unskilled, temporary
ones such as farm or factory work, hospitality, catering, clerical and construction.
Even then, there may be a few hoops to
jump through: in order to work in a bar, for
example, you will need to take one-day
courses in Responsible Service of Alcohol
and Conduct of Gambling; to work on a
building site, you have to complete a one-
day Occupational Health and Safety course.

The National Harvest Hotline (☎1800 062
332, 🖰www.jobsearch.gov.au/harvesttrail)
has information about **harvesting** or **farm-
labouring jobs** and will put you in touch with
potential employers. One advantage of such
work is that it may qualify you to extend your
stay by taking out a second WHV (see p.33).
Just remember that crop picking is hard graft
for low wages (usually paid on a commission
basis) and farms or plantations are often some
distance away from the nearest town. There
may be a minibus (sometimes free) to shuttle
workers between a hostel in town and the
farm; in other cases, you may be given some
basic accommodation or tent space on site.

Websites such as 🖰www.jobmap.com.au
and 🖰www.travellersxpress.com carry ads for
casual jobseekers, and all towns and cities
have local employment agencies. A good
place to enquire is **Travellers' Contact Point**
(☎1800 647 640, 🖰www.travellers.com.au),
which has branches in Melbourne, Sydney,
Brisbane, Airlie Beach and Cairns. Services
include a job noticeboard, skills testing, CV
updating and help with the required
paperwork; they also run a specialist recruit-
ment agency, Travellers at Work (☎02 9221
4810 or 1300 797 810, 🖰www.taw.com.au).
The travel centre **Backpackers World**
(☎1800 676 763, 🖰www.backpackersworld
.com.au) also runs a jobs agency, with
branches all up the East Coast. All of these
places can help with all aspects of working,
from organizing tax file numbers to actually
getting you jobs; some charge a membership
fee of around A$40 for this service.

If you have a **marketable skill** (computer
training, accountancy, nursing, cooking and
the like), it's worth trying 🖰www.mycareer
.com.au, Australia's largest **online jobsearch engine**, or the relevant temping
agencies in the cities. Newspaper job ads
are worth checking out, especially in smaller
local papers. Quite a few hostels have a
permanently staffed employment desk, but
you can pick up good local leads at any

hostel: from fellow travellers, staff and notice-boards. Hostels also occasionally hire casual workers, particularly for cleaning duties.

Australia is becoming increasingly tough on people working illegally, either on tourist visas or on expired working visas. If you're caught, you will have any visa cancelled and will be asked to leave the country immediately; you may be taken into detention if immediate arrangements cannot be made. It is extremely unlikely that you will be granted another visa under normal circumstances. Employers can be fined up to A$10,000 for employing illegal workers, and are liable for prosecution; there are also heavy fines for paying or accepting cash-in-hand without declaring it to the taxation office.

Study and work programmes

AFS Intercultural Programs UK ☎0113/242 6136, US ☎1-800/AFS-INFO, Canada ☎1-800/361-7248 or 514/288-3282, Australia ☎1300 131 736, NZ ☎0800/600 300, SA ☎11/447 2673, international enquiries ☎1-212/807-8686, ⓦwww .afs.org. Intercultural exchange organization with programmes in over fifty countries.
American Institute for Foreign Study ☎1-866/906-2437, ⓦwww.aifs.com. Offers the opportunity to study at university in Cairns or Sydney.
ATCV (Australian Trust for Conservation Volunteers) Australia ☎1800 032 501, ⓦwww .atcv.com.au. Volunteer work (unpaid) on conservation projects across Australia. The projects are usually four to six weeks long; volunteers pay around A$33 a day for food and accommodation.
BTCV (British Trust for Conservation Volunteers) ☎01302/572 244, ⓦwww.btcv .org.uk. One of the largest environmental charities in

Britain, with a programme of national and international working holidays (as a paying volunteer).
BUNAC UK ☎020/7251 3472, US ☎1-800/GO-BUNAC; ⓦwww.bunac.org. Organizes working holidays in a range of destinations for students.
Council on International Educational Exchange (CIEE) UK ☎020/8939 9057, US ☎1-800/40-STUDY or 1-207/533-7600; ⓦwww .ciee.org. Leading NGO offering study programmes and volunteer projects around the world.
Earthwatch Institute UK ☎01865/318 838, US ☎1-800/776-0188 or 978/461-0081, Australia ☎03 9682 6828; ⓦwww.earthwatch.org. Scientific expedition projects spanning over fifty countries, with environmental and archeological ventures worldwide.
Visitoz UK ☎01865/861 516, Australia ☎07 4168 6106; ⓦwww.visitoz.org. Provides work on farms and stations and rural hospitality. Previous knowledge is not required. Participants must attend a four-day preparation and orientation course, and during this period a job is chosen from a few suitable ones offered. Driving licences are necessary for most of the jobs.
WWOOF (Willing Workers on Organic Farms) Australia ☎03 5155 0218, ⓦwww.wwoof.com .au. Wwoofing is a great way to experience a side of Australia that you'd never see if you just worked in an office and then beachbummed your way up the East Coast. As you are not paid cash, a work visa is not required: you put in about half a day's work at your host's place in exchange for full board and lodging, and the rest of the time is yours to go exploring. You are expected to stay at least two nights; everything else is negotiable. The *Australian WWOOF Book* lists over one thousand organic farms and one hundred non-farm hosts (such as organic nurseries and greengrocers, or alternative schools). By ordering the book you become a member (A$55 single, A$65 for two people travelling together); the membership includes basic work-insurance for one year.

Tax and paperwork

Income tax (levied at the non-resident rate of 29 percent for earnings under A$30,000 per annum) and **superannuation**, a compulsory retirement fund (nine percent) are deducted at source. To become part of the system you have to obtain a **tax file number** (TFN) from the Australian Taxation Office (☎13 28 61, ⓦwww .ato.gov.au); if you have a Working Holiday Visa, you can apply online by quoting your personal details and passport number. You'll also need to open an Australian bank account (see p.76) and get a Medicare card (see p.45). If you don't have a TFN, you'll be subject to higher deductions, though your employer may be able to give you a couple of weeks' grace. At the end of your trip, you can claim back some of the money that's been deducted; employment agencies will explain the tax-return procedure.

Gay and lesbian travellers

Australia is now well and truly planted on the Queer map, as year after year the beautiful people flock Down Under, lured by the conducive climate and laid-back lifestyle. Sydney, home of Mardi Gras, is Australia's gay-friendly capital. Despite its reputation as a macho culture, the country revels in a large and active scene: you'll find an air of confidence and a sense of community that is often missing in other parts of the world.

It wasn't until the 1980s that Victoria and New South Wales (generally thought of as liberal states) decriminalized homosexual practices; Queensland only took the plunge in 1991. The **age of consent** varies from state to state, and in some cases is discriminatory: in ACT and Victoria, it's 16 years for all; in New South Wales, it's 16 for lesbians, and 18 for gay men; while in Queensland, it's 16 for all with the exception of anal sex, which is outlawed until 18. The foreign partner in a **de facto** gay relationship can apply to reside permanently in Australia, a much better situation than in many countries, but the current battle the gay and lesbian lobby groups are waging is to make same-sex relationships completely equal in the eyes of the law to heterosexual ones in terms of marriage, parenting, next-of-kin rights, superannuation and age of consent.

On the East Coast, an abundance of gay venues, services, businesses, travel clubs, country retreats and the like bear witness to the power of the **pink dollar**. The climate attracts those who enjoy sun and sport, so to get into the scene it's a good idea to pack your swimming, snorkelling and clubbing gear.

Australian dykes are refreshingly open and self-possessed – a relief after the more closed and cliquey scene in Europe. The flip side of their fearlessness is the predominance of S&M on the scene: you'll see a good deal of tattoos and pierced flesh around.

Dyke and gay scenes are nothing if not mercurial, and Australia is no exception. We've done our best to list bars, clubs and meeting places, but be warned that venues open, change their names, shut for refurbishment, get relaunched and finally go out of business with frightening rapidity.

Where and how to go

Sydney is the jewel in Australia's luscious navel. Firmly established as one of the world's great gay cities – only San Francisco can really rival it – it attracts lesbian and gay visitors from around the world, particularly during Mardi Gras (see p.296). Melbourne closely follows, but for a change of pace, take a trip to Brisbane and the Gold Coast.

Away from the cities, things get more discreet, but a lot of **country areas** do have very friendly local scenes – tricky to pinpoint, but easy to stumble across. Australians on the city scene are a friendly bunch, but in a small country town they get really friendly, so if there's anything going on you'll probably get invited along.

Gay and lesbian contacts

Personal contacts

Pinkboard ⓦ www.pinkboard.com.au. Popular, long-running Australian website featuring personal ads and classifieds sections with everything from houseshares and party tickets for sale to employment and a help-and-advice section. It's free to run your own personal or classified.

Media and resources

Each major capital has excellent free gay **newspapers**, such as the *Sydney Star Observer* (ⓦ www.ssonet.com.au), *SX News* (ⓦ www.sxnews.e-p.net.au) and the *Melbourne Community Voice* (ⓦ www.mcv .e-pnet.au), which give the local lowdown.

ALSO Foundation ⓦ www.also.org.au. Based in Victoria, they have a good website with an excellent nationwide business and community directory.
DNA ⓦ www.dnamagazine.com.au. National glossy – an upmarket lifestyle magazine for gay men.
Gay and Lesbian Counselling and Community Services of Australia ⓦ www.glccs.org.au. Nationwide support network.
Joy FM ⓦ www.joy.org.au. Melbourne-based gay and lesbian radio station broadcasting nationally on 94.9FM.
LOTL (Lesbians on the Loose) ⓦ www.lotl .com. A monthly publication available at lesbian and gay venues.
The Pink Directory ⓦ www.thepinkdirectory.com .au. Online directory of gay and lesbian business and community information.

Tourist services and travel agents

GALTA (Gay and Lesbian Tourism Australia) ⓦ www.galta.com.au. An online resource and nonprofit organization set up to promote the gay and lesbian tourism industry. Website has links to accommodation, travel agents and tour operators, and gay and lesbian printed and online guides.
Gay Travel ⓦ www.gaytravel.com. Online travel agent, concentrating mostly on accommodation.
International Gay and Lesbian Travel Association ⓦ www.iglta.org. Trade group with lists of gay-owned or gay-friendly travel agents, accommodation and other travel businesses.
Q Beds ⓦ www.qbeds.com. An online accommodation directory and booking service for gay- and lesbian-owned, -operated or -friendly businesses.

Travel essentials

Costs

If you've travelled down from Southeast Asia, you'll find Australia expensive on a day-to-day basis, but fresh from Europe or the US you'll find prices comparable or cheaper; note, though, that in Sydney the cost of living has crept up over the years, and any prolonged length of time spent in the city will quickly drain any savings you might have unless you have a contingency plan in place, such as finding work.

If you're prepared to camp, you might get by on a **daily budget** of A$50 (£24/US$47/€30), but you should count on around A$75 (£36/US$71/€45) a day for food, board and transport if you stay in hostels, travel on buses and eat and drink fairly frugally. Stay in motels and B&Bs (assuming you're sharing costs) and eat out regularly, and you'll need to budget A$120 (£58/US$113/€73) or more: extras such as scuba-diving courses, clubbing, car rental, petrol and tours will all add to your costs. **Tipping** is not customary in Australia, however (see p.79).

A **Goods and Services Tax** (GST) of ten percent applies to most goods and services. Under the Tourist Refund Scheme (TRS),

visitors can claim GST refunds for goods purchased in Australia as they clear customs (goods need to be taken within hand luggage), providing individual receipts exceed A$300, and the claim is made within thirty days of purchase.

Most Australian transport services, museums and attractions offer **concessions** to under 16s, over 60s, and students producing appropriate ID; museums and attractions also usually offer reduced-price admission to family groups of two adults and two children. Other travellers can benefit from a wide range of discounts (including ten to fifteen percent off the price of Greyhound bus passes, tours, attractions and certain hostels) just by getting hold of a youth or backpacker discount card; these can be used worldwide.

Useful discount cards

Euro<26 ⓦ www.euro26.org. Youth card available to young Europeans aged under 26, both students or non-students, for a small fee (£10 in the UK).
Hostelling International (HI) and Youth Hostels Association (YHA) The annual or life membership card of this worldwide hostelling association (see p.53) gets you masses of discounts.

ISIC, IYTC and ITIC ⓦwww.istc.org. Issued by the International Student Travel Confederation, the ISIC (International Student Identity Card) is globally recognized. The IYTC (International Youth Travel Card; for non-students under 26) and the ITIC (International Teacher Identity Card; for teaching professionals) provide similar benefits. A one-year card costs £9 in the UK and $22 in the US from ⓦwww.isiccard.com or student travel agents.

Nomads Adventure Card From Nomads, a network of hostels in Australia, New Zealand and Fiji; see p.53.

VIP Backpackers Annual discount card offered by a worldwide hostelling network (p.53).

Crime and personal safety

Australia can pride itself on being a safe country: violent **crime** is relatively rare. This is not to say there's no petty crime, or that you can leave normal caution behind, though you're more likely to fall victim to a fellow traveller or an opportunist. Theft is not unusual in hostels, and many therefore provide lockable boxes. But if you leave valuables lying around, or on view in cars, you can expect them to be stolen.

One place where violence is commonplace is at the ritual **pub "blue"** (fight), usually among known protagonists on a Friday or Saturday night in smaller, untouristed towns. Strangers are seldom involved without at least some provocation. Be aware also of drug- and drink-related crime, especially around known hotspots such as Kings Cross in Sydney. Exercise caution and be street-wise, and you should be fine.

Ecotourism

Australia's **EcoCertification programme** was set up to encourage and recognize good practice in tour companies, tourist attractions, accommodation and service providers and guides. There are three levels of **certification**: Nature Tourism (for ecologically sustainable operations with a primary focus on experiencing natural areas), Ecotourism (for those that also foster environmental and cultural understanding, appreciation and conservation)

The number to call for emergencies – police, ambulance or fire brigade – is ⓣ000

---

and Advanced Ecotourism (for those whose practices far exceed minimum standards). To qualify, the operation must undergo a thorough assessment of its economic, environmental and social sustainability, and its contribution to conservation and community work. Qualifying operations can display the EcoCertified logo. For further details, contact Ecotourism Australia (ⓣ07 3229 5550, ⓦwww.ecotourism.org.au). For more, see the *East Coast Ecotourism* colour section.

Electricity

Australia's **electrical current** is 240/250v, 50Hz AC. British appliances will work with an adaptor for the Australian three-pin plug. American and Canadian 110v appliances will also need a transformer.

Insurance

Even if you're entitled to free emergency healthcare from Medicare (see "Health"), some form of **travel insurance** is essential to help plug the gaps and cover you in the event of losing your baggage, missing a plane and the like. A typical travel-insurance policy usually provides cover for the loss of baggage, tickets and – up to a certain limit – cash and cheques, as well as cancellation or curtailment of your journey. If you're thinking of doing any "high-risk" activities such as scuba diving, skiing or even just hiking, you may need to pay an extra premium; check carefully before you take out any policy what exactly you are covered for in case of an accident. If you do take medical coverage, ascertain whether benefits will be paid as treatment proceeds or only after return home, and whether there is a 24-hour medical-emergency number. When securing baggage cover, make sure that the per-article limit – typically under £500/US$1000 – will cover your most valuable possession. If you need to **make a claim**, you should keep receipts for medicines and medical treatment, and in the event you have anything stolen, you must obtain an official written statement from the police.

Internet

Internet access is becoming increasingly widespread across Australia, though, compared to the UK or the US, free access is surprisingly rare: public libraries are the exception, with many branches offering a few terminals that anyone can book for short periods, plus free Wi-Fi. In towns and cities, Internet cafés are everywhere, typically charging A$3–8 an hour for terminals or Wi-Fi. Many places to stay – especially hostels – also provide terminals and, increasingly, Wi-Fi for their guests; in the more enlightened places, Wi-Fi is cheap or free but some hotels charge extortionate rates (up to A$20/hr). Some shopping centres and fast-food joints have Telstra-operated hotspots, which also overcharge (A$12/hr plus a connection fee of 25¢ per session). Even worse, a few places still opt for the user-reviled coin-op booths. **Mobile broadband** for your laptop or phone currently requires a long-term contract, but affordable pay-as-you-go systems may appear during the lifetime of this book.

Laundry

Known as **laundromats** or **laundrettes**, these are rare outside urban centres. Hostels always have a laundry with at least one coin-operated washing machine and a dryer, as do most caravan parks, holiday units and a lot of motels. Five-star hotels, of course, will do it for you.

Mail

Every town of any size will have a **post office**, or at least an Australia Post agency in a general store or stationer's; you can also buy standard 50¢ stamps at newsagents. Post offices are officially open Monday to Friday 9am to 5pm; big city GPOs sometimes open late or on Saturday morning as well. Out in the country, it's rare to see post boxes.

The domestic **mail service** can be slow over long distances, making guaranteed Express Post worth the expense for important packages. On the other hand, international mail is extremely efficient, taking three to four working days to New Zealand, four to five to the UK and four to seven to the US, Canada and South Africa. Sending a standard letter or postcard within Australia costs 50¢ or A$4.30 for Express; to Europe, the US, Canada, South Africa and New Zealand postcards cost A$1.30 and regular airmail letters start at A$2. Large **parcels** are reasonably cheap to send by international surface mail, but this may take up to three months; standard airmail is generally delivered within ten working days, with optional insurance; express delivery (3–7 days) costs considerably more. For full details, consult ⓦwww.austpost.com.au. As an alternative, all the major international **couriers** are represented in Australia, and there are a number of commercial shippers offering budget overseas delivery.

Maps

A **map** of Australia, or maps of the state or states you intend to visit, can be useful for basic route planning. For Australia, options include *The Rough Guide Map* (1:4,500,000), printed on rip- and waterproof paper; alternatively, *GeoCenter* (including NZ) and *Nelles*, both 1:4,000,000, have good topographical detail. For individual states and regions, Hema maps (ⓦwww .hemamaps.com.au), widely available in Australia and overseas, are clear and useful.

Rough Guides travel insurance

Rough Guides has teamed up with Columbus Direct to offer you **travel insurance** that can be tailored to suit your needs. Products include a low-cost **backpacker** option for long stays; a **short-break** option for city getaways; a typical **holiday-package** option; and others. There are also annual **multi-trip** policies for those who travel regularly. Different sports and activities (trekking, skiing, etc) can be usually covered if required.

See our website (ⓦwww.roughguides.com) for eligibility and purchasing options. Alternatively, UK residents should call ☏0870/033 9988; Australians should call ☏1300 669 999 and New Zealanders should call ☏0800/559 911. All other nationalities should call ☏+44 870/890 2843.

If you're planning a **self-drive trip**, however, you'll need far more detail. Surprisingly, perhaps, the best (and in some cases, the only) large-scale regional maps are very inexpensive or even free: the RACQ (@www.racq.com.au) produces extremely useful maps of Queensland, and the excellent Cartoscope (@www.maps.com.au) series covers most sections of the New South Wales and Victoria coast. Some of these are available free from tourist offices; all can be ordered online for a small charge. Tourist offices also often have good-quality town plans, but to explore beyond the main tourist areas in Melbourne, Sydney or Brisbane you'll need a city directory; the main publisher is UBD (@www.ubd.com.au).

Money

Australia's **currency** is the Australian dollar, or "buck", written as $, AUD or A$ – which is how it's written in this Guide – and divided into 100 cents. The colourful plastic notes with forgery-proof clear windows come in A$5, A$10, A$20, A$50 and A$100 denominations, along with 5¢, 10¢, 20¢, 50¢, A$1 and A$2 coins; bills are rounded up or down to the closest multiple of 5¢, which can be confusing at first.

At the time of writing, the Australian dollar had an **exchange rate** of A$2.07 to £1; A$1.06 to US$1; A$1.05 to CDN$1; A$0.81 to NZ$1; and A$0.14 to ZAR1. To check the latest exchange rate, log onto @www.xe.com.

The major **banks**, with branches countrywide, are ANZ (@www.anz.com.au), Commonwealth (@www.commbank.com.au), National (@www.nab.com.au), St George (@www.stgeorge.com.au) and Westpac (@www.westpac.com.au); Bendigo (@www.bendigobank.com.au) is considered more ethical than most. Standard opening hours are Monday to Friday 9am to 5pm, but a few branches close at 4pm on Thursdays and some open on Saturday mornings. **ATMs** are widespread in all East Coast city and town centres, petrol stations and country stores.

If you're planning to **work in Australia**, it makes life a great deal easier if you **open a bank account**. To save time, you can get this in motion before you leave home by researching the options and applying online. You can then activate the account when you arrive in Australia by taking the required ID into your nominated branch. The Commonwealth Bank and Westpac are the most widespread options, and their cards give you access not only to ATM machines but also **EFTPOS** facilities (Electronic Funds Transfer at Point of Sale), where you can use your card to pay directly for goods and to withdraw cash as well, similar to cashback in the UK. Bear in mind that **bank fees** and charges are high in Australia. Many accounts have a monthly fee (typically A$5), which may only cover a few free withdrawal transactions per month; some charge extra whenever you use a competitor's ATM. It's well worth shopping around before you open an account. If you will not be working during your stay, it's likely to be easier, and no more expensive, to use your home account, assuming you have an internationally recognized bank card.

Opening hours and holidays

Shops and **services** in provincial towns are generally open Monday to Friday 9am to 5pm and until lunchtime on Saturday. In cities and larger towns, many shops stay open late on Thursday or Friday evening – usually until 9pm – and all day on Saturday and Sunday. Many city supermarkets are open practically or literally round the clock.

City **petrol stations** and country **roadhouses** provide all the essential services for the traveller; those on the major highways are generally open 24 hours a day. **Tourist offices** are often open every day although, since they tend to be run by volunteers, hours sometimes vary. **Most tourist attractions** such as museums, galleries and attended historic monuments are open daily. See "Mail" and "Money" for post office and bank opening hours.

Practically without exception, shops and attractions are **closed** on Good Friday and Christmas Day. Specific opening hours are given throughout the Guide.

National holidays, Australia Day (which originally marked the arrival of the First Fleet in Sydney Cove in 1788 but is now a more inclusive national celebration) and ANZAC

Day (commemorating the 1915 Gallipoli landing) bring a show of patriotic fervour. If any **public holiday** falls on a Saturday or Sunday, the following Monday is usually a holiday. Each district may also have a local holiday – for example, Melbourne Cup Day in early November is a holiday in Melbourne, as is the Royal Queensland Show Day (mid-Aug) in Brisbane.

During **school holidays**, all the popular tourist areas are full to overflowing: the busiest times are January, when Australians go on summer holiday after spending Christmas at home, and the Easter long weekend. All East Coast schools have four terms; dates vary from state to state, so you can sometimes avoid the crush by state hopping.

East Coast public holidays

New Year's Day January 1
Australia Day January 26
Labour Day (VIC only) Second Monday in March
Good Friday Date varies (March/April)
Easter Monday Date varies (March/April)
ANZAC Day April 25
Labour Day (QLD only) First Monday in May
Queen's Birthday Second Monday in June
Labour Day (NSW and ACT only) First Monday in October
Christmas Day December 25
Boxing Day December 26

East Coast school holidays

Spring Two weeks between late September and mid-October.
Summer Six weeks between mid-December and the end of January, including Christmas, New Year and Australia Day.

Autumn One week in early or mid-April, often including the Easter long weekend.
Winter Two weeks between late June and mid-July.

Phones

Public telephones are becoming rarer, as mobiles become more and more widespread. They take coins or phone cards, which are sold through newsagents and other stores, and do not accept incoming calls.

Local calls are **untimed**, allowing you to talk for as long as you like; from a public phone this is likely to cost 40¢. Many businesses and services operate free-call numbers, prefixed ☏1800, while others have numbers beginning ☏13 or 1300 that are charged at the local-call rate – both can only be dialled from within Australia. Numbers starting ☏1900 are premium-rate private information services.

Discount phonecards are a cheap way to call cross-country or abroad. Various brands are available from newsagents, phone shops, Internet cafés, hostels or online; most give you the option of topping up your credit by signing up for an online account. Rates start from as low as 4¢ a minute from a landline, though are considerably higher from a mobile. Some systems charge a small connection fee per call.

High-street outlets sell **pre-paid mobile phones**; alternatively, you could buy a SIM card to use in any unlocked mobile (dual or tri-band, 2G or 3G, CDMA or GSM; most phones can be unlocked with a download-able code, which, in many cases, is free). Telstra, the main provider, has the widest out-of-town coverage; the alternatives

---

Making international calls

Calling Australia from home
Dial your country's international access code + 61 + city code, omitting the initial zero.

In the UK, the Republic of Ireland, New Zealand and South Africa, the **international access code** is ☏00; in the US and Canada, it's ☏011.

Calling home from Australia
Dial the Australian **international access code** (☏0011) + country code + city or area code, omitting the initial zero if calling the UK, the Republic of Ireland or New Zealand.

Country codes include: UK +44, Republic of Ireland +353, US and Canada +1, New Zealand +64, South Africa +27.

(Optus, Virgin, Vodafone and 3 Mobile) sometimes have better deals.

If you'll need phone reception in remote areas, the best, though priciest, solution is a **satellite phone**. Little bigger than a conventional mobile, they can be rented from ⓦ www.rentasatphone.com.au for A$21 per day, discounted for rentals of fifteen days or more, and can run both GSM as well as the special satellite SIM cards. Outgoing calls cost A$1 per thirty seconds.

Police and the law

Things to avoid, most of all, are misuse of **alcohol** and **drugs**. A lot of marijuana is grown, and its use is widespread, but you'd be foolish to carry it when you travel, particularly if you intend to drive, and crazy to carry any other illicit narcotic. Each state has its own penalties, and though a small amount of grass may mean no more than confiscation and an on-the-spot fine, they're generally pretty tough – especially in Queensland. Driving under the influence of alcohol or drugs is taken extremely seriously, so don't risk it – random breath tests are common around all cities and larger towns. There are extensive **controls** on where and when you can drink – restrictions may be imposed in public areas such as beaches, while taking alcohol onto Aboriginal lands can be a serious offence. **Smoking** is banned in bars, restaurants, clubs and many other public places. **Nude** or **topless sunbathing** is quite acceptable in many places, but absolutely not in others – follow the locals' lead.

Seasons

In the southern hemisphere, **summer** lasts from November to February, **winter** from June to September. In **southeast Australia**, the intervening seasons (spring and autumn) mark a transition in the weather.

In the **tropical north**, the important seasonal distinction is between the Wet (effectively summer) and the Dry (winter). The **dry season** normally begins in April, when rains stop and humidity decreases somewhat. It may take a couple of months for vehicular access to be restored to the most far-flung tracks, but the bush is at its greenest and the waterfalls at their most impressive. From April to October, skies are generally cloud free; June and July brings the coolest nights (around 10°C). The end of the year brings the **"build up"** when temperatures and humidity rise and the unprepared may go "troppo". Storms begin to break in late December, and the rains usually commence at the turn of the year, lasting a couple of months. The **cyclone season** lasts from October to April, with peaks in late December and late February.

Shopping

Australians love to shop, and you'll find plenty of **outlets** to tempt you to part with your cash, from designer boutiques to large department stores. Australians also do vintage very well, and there are some excellent **thrift shops** to be found, especially around Chapel Street in Melbourne and Paddington in Sydney.

Worth a browse are the **weekly markets** that take place in most cities and resort towns, selling everything from second-hand clothes and New Age remedies to fresh seafood and mouthwatering delicacies; popular ones include Queen Victoria Market in Melbourne (see p.107) and, in Sydney, the markets in Glebe and Paddington (p.253 & p.258).

For **souvenirs**, there's no shortage of shops selling Australiana, mass-produced tat such as stuffed koalas, painted boomerangs and the like. If you're looking for something more authentic, most tourist towns have at least one gallery shop selling gemstone jewellery, contemporary art and handcrafted didgeridoos: there are a number of good ones around The Rocks in Sydney, while Melbourne has a fine selection of independent art and craft galleries including some specializing in Aboriginal work. Australian opals and cultured pearls are a popular purchase, though the quality and price varies so be sure to shop around before you buy. Note that if you purchase goods worth more than A$300 in one single transaction, you can **claim the tax back** under the Tourist Refund Scheme (see p.73).

Time

The East Coast is on **Eastern Standard Time** (EST), which is eight hours ahead of South Africa Standard Time, ten hours ahead of Greenwich Mean Time (London), fifteen hours ahead of Eastern Standard Time (New York), eighteen hours ahead of Pacific Standard Time (Los Angeles) and two hours behind New Zealand Standard Time.

However, Victoria, New South Wales and ACT observe **daylight saving time** (DST) from the last Sunday in October to the last Sunday in March, so in practice Melbourne, Sydney and Canberra are eleven hours ahead of London during the Australian summer, and nine hours ahead for the rest of the year.

In Queensland, the clocks don't change, so if you cross the Queensland border between November and March, you have to put your watch forward by an hour. The time difference between London and Brisbane or Cairns is ten hours from November to March and nine hours from April to October.

Tipping

Tipping is not customary in Australia, and cab drivers and bar staff don't generally expect anything. In fact, cab drivers often round the fare down rather than bother with change. In cafés and restaurants, you might leave the change, or ten percent if the service is exceptional.

Tourist information

Australian tourism abroad is represented by **Tourism Australia**, whose website (see below) has links to everything you need to start planning your trip.

More detailed information is available by the sackful once you're in the country. Each state

Clothing and shoe sizes

Women's clothes

American	6	8	10	12	14	16	18	
Australian	8	10	12	14	16	18	20	
British	8	10	12	14	16	18	20	
Continental	36	38	40	42	44	46	48	

Women's shoes

American	5	6	7	8	9	10	11	
Australian	5	6	7	8	9	10	11	
British	3	4	5	6	7	8	9	
Continental	35.5	36.6	38	39	40.5	42.5	44	

Men's suits

American	44	46	48	50	52	54	56	58
Australian	34	36	38	40	42	44	46	48
British	34	36	38	40	42	44	46	48
Continental	44	46	48	50	52	54	56	58

Men's shirts

American	14	15	15.5	16	16.5	17	17.5	18
Australian	36	38	39	41	42	43	44	45
British	14	15	15.5	16	16.5	17	17.5	18
Continental	36	38	39	41	42	43	44	45

Men's shoes

American	7	7.5	8	8.5	9.5	10	10.5	11	11.5
Australian	6.5	7	7.5	8	9	9.5	10	10.5	11
British	6.5	7	7.5	8	9	9.5	10	10.5	11
Continental	39	40	41	42	43	44	44	45	46

or territory has its own **tourist authority**, and a level below this are a host of regional and community-run **Visitor Information Centres** – every East Coast town has one, or at the very least an information board located at a rest spot at the side of the road. **Visitor Information Centres** offer a wealth of leaflets, maps and advice on their local area and, sometimes, a selection of material relating to other areas, plus cheap Internet access.

Hostels are excellent places to pick up information, with noticeboards where you'll often find details of trips, restaurants and bars recommended by the staff, offers of cheap excursions or ride shares, and comments and advice from people who've already passed that way.

Finally, most tourist hotspots will have a **travellers' centre**, such as Backpackers World Travel (Ⓦ www.backpackersworld .com.au) and Travellers Contact Point (Ⓦ www.travellers.com.au). Once you've signed up with them, they can help you find work and pre-book travel and accommodation as you move around; you also get discounted phone and Internet rates, cheap drinks at selected pubs, use of noticeboards, and help with work.

Useful websites

Tourism Australia Ⓦ www.australia.com
Tourism New South Wales Ⓦ www.visitnsw.com
Tourism Queensland Ⓦ www.queensland holidays.com.au
Tourism Victoria Ⓦ www.visitvictoria.com

Government travel advice

Australian Department of Foreign Affairs
Ⓦ www.dfat.gov.au, Ⓦ www.smartraveller.gov.au
British Foreign & Commonwealth Office
Ⓦ www.fco.gov.uk
Canadian Department of Foreign Affairs
Ⓦ www.dfait-maeci.gc.ca
Irish Department of Foreign Affairs Ⓦ www .foreignaffairs.gov.ie
New Zealand Ministry of Foreign Affairs
Ⓦ www.mft.govt.nz
South African Department of Foreign Affairs
Ⓦ www.dfa.gov.za
US State Department Ⓦ www.travel.state.gov

Wildlife rescue

The following regional organizations care for injured, orphaned and distressed **wild animals and birds**, and respond to emergencies wherever possible. They also

offer advice on how best to deal with **snakes** and other wildlife matters.

New South Wales and ACT

Fawna ☎0500 861405, ⓦwww.fawna.org.au. New South Wales Mid-North Coast.
Koala Hospital ☎02 6584 1522, ⓦwww.koalahospital.org.au. Port Macquarie.
Native Animal Network Association ☎0418 427 214, ⓦwww.nana.asn.au. South Coast New South Wales.
Native Animal Trust Fund ☎0500 502 294, ⓦwww.users.bigpond.com.natf. Hunter region.
Sydney Wildlife ☎02 9413 4300, ⓦwww.sydneywildlife.org.au. Greater Sydney.
Wildcare ☎02 6299 1966 ⓦwww.wildcare.com.au. Canberra region.
Wildlife Information and Rescue Service (WIRES) ☎1300 094 737, ⓦww.wires.org.au. Branches in the Blue Mountains, New South Wales Mid-South Coast, Northern Beaches and Northern Rivers.

Queensland

Australian Wildlife Hospital ☎1300 369 652, ⓦwww.wildlifewarriors.org.au. Sunshine Coast.
FNQ Wildlife Rescue ☎07 4053 4467, ⓦwww.fnqwildliferescue.org.au. Tropical north Queensland.
Queensland Parks and Wildlife Service ☎1300 130 372, ⓦwww.epa.qld.gov.au. Will put you in touch with a wildlife expert in your area.
Wildcare Australia ☎07 5527 2444, ⓦwww.wildcare.org.au. Southeast Queensland.

Victoria

Wildlife Victoria ☎1300 094 535, ⓦwww.wildlifevictoria.org.au. State-wide service for Victoria.

Travellers with disabilities

The vast distances between Australia's cities and popular tourist resorts present visitors with mobility difficulties with a unique challenge but, overall, travel in Australia for people with disabilities is rather easier than it would be in, say, the UK and Europe.

The federal government provides **information** and various nationwide **services** through the National Information Communication Awareness Network (NICAN) and the Australian Council for the Rehabilitation of the Disabled (ACROD) – see below for contact details.

Much of Australia's tourist **accommodation** is well set-up for people with disabilities, because buildings tend to be built outwards rather than upwards; all new buildings in Australia must comply with a legal minimum accessibility standard. Public **transport** options are steadily increasing.

Disability needn't interfere with your **sightseeing** either: the attitude of the management at Australia's major tourist attractions is excellent, and they will provide assistance where they can. For example, you can snorkel unhindered on the Great Barrier Reef, go on a cruise around Sydney Harbour, and see the penguins at Phillip Island. Many national parks have wheelchair-accessible walks.

For a good overview of accessible travel in Australia, *Easy Access Australia* (A\$27.45; ⓦwww.easyaccessaustralia.com.au) is a comprehensive **guide** written by wheelchair-user Bruce Cameron for anyone with a mobility difficulty, and has information on all the states, with maps, and a separate section with floor plans of hotel rooms.

Useful contacts

Accessibility ⓦwww.accessibility.com.au. Online lists of accommodation and transport in Australia for people with disabilities, as well as Access Maps of major Australian cities.
National Disability Services ☎02 6283 3200, ⓦwww.nds.org.au. Regional offices provide lists of state-based help organizations, accommodation, travel agencies and tour operators.
NICAN (National Information Communication Awareness Network) ☎02 6241 1220 or 1800 806 769, ⓦwww.nican.com.au. A national, non-profit, free information service on recreation, sport, tourism, the arts and much more, for people with disabilities. Has a database of over 4500 organizations – such as wheelchair-accessible tourist accommodation venues, sports and recreation organizations, and rental companies who have accessible buses and vans.
ParaQuad Victoria ☎03 9415 1200, ⓦwww.paraquad.asn.au. Serves the interests of the spinally injured.
People with Disability Australia ☎02 9319 6622, ⓦwww.pwd.org.au. Disability support group.

Women and sexual harassment

The stereotyped image of the Aussie male is of a boozy bloke interested in sport, his car and his mates, with his wife or girlfriend a poor fourth. The Australian ethos of "mateship" traditionally excluded **women** – the hard, tough life of the early days of white settlement, when women were scarce, fostered a **male culture** that's to some extent still current. In the main cities, attitudes are generally enlightened, but in the more remote areas the older outlooks are more tenacious and sexual harassment can be commonplace – if rarely threatening.

In public life, Australia has one of the best records for **sexual equality** in the world – it was the second country to give women the vote (after New Zealand in 1893) – but anomalies abound; women are still fighting over workplace issues such as the right to paid maternity leave.

Country pubs are still very much male bastions. That doesn't mean women should avoid them altogether, however – many are frequented by decent salt-of-the-earth Aussie blokes, some of the nicest people you could wish to meet.

As always, common sense prevails: avoid travelling to remote areas on your own, and don't walk home alone late at night.

Guide

Guide

Melbourne

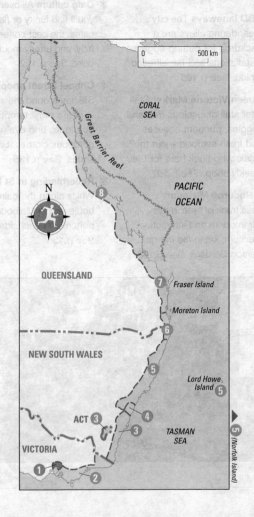

CHAPTER 1 # Highlights

✱ **Chinatown** The narrow, nineteenth-century streets once housed Chinese gold rushers but now brim with bars and bustling *yum cha* joints. See p.105

✱ **CBD laneways** The city's meandering alleys are a backdrop for cutting-edge art installations and fab alfresco dining. See p.105

✱ **Queen Victoria Market** Stall after stall of luscious fruit and veggies, pungent cheeses and fresh seafood – join the locals who flock here for their weekly shop. See p.107

✱ **Melbourne Museum** Lose track of time in this ultramodern and interactive museum, set in the tranquil Carlton Gardens. See p.108

✱ **Aussie Rules match at the MCG** Join the cheering Melbourne crowds for an action-packed footy game at the "G". See p.109

✱ **Café culture** All over town, you'll find funky or flashy cafés, the best coffee outside Italy, and utterly mouthwatering cake. See p.122

✱ **Chapel Street shopping** Sashay around the style capital's most tempting boutiques and eye up gorgeous clothes, bags and shoes. See p.135

✱ **Rollerblading in St Kilda** Whizz along the palm-lined boulevard in Melbourne's bohemian beachside suburb. See p.136

▲ St Kilda Esplanade

Melbourne

MELBOURNE is Australia's second-largest city, with a population of 3.8 million, around half a million less than Sydney. In the minds of Melburnians, competition between the two cities – in every sphere from cricket to business – is intense to the point of childishness. In truth, Sydneysiders, whose show-stoppingly glamorous metropolis stole a march on Melbourne as the nation's financial centre way back in the 1980s, are far too self-confident to participate; nonetheless Melburnians never tire of pointing out that, unlike their rivals, they inhabit "one of the world's most liveable cities". While Melbourne's Port Phillip Bay and Yarra River can't hope to match the glitter of Sydney Harbour, the city centre's charms grow on all who stay for more than a couple of days, while time spent exploring the characterful inner suburbs usually creates a wistful desire to up sticks and open your own artfully distressed pub there.

In many ways, Melbourne is the most European of all Australian cities: magnificent landscaped gardens and parks provide green spaces near the centre, while beneath the colourful skyscrapers of the Central Business District (CBD), an understorey of solid, Victorian-era facades ranged along tree-lined boulevards present the city on a more human scale. The **European influence** is perhaps most obvious in winter, as trams rattle past warm cafés and bookshops, and promenaders dress stylishly against the chill. Melbourne's influences are truly multicultural: large-scale immigration since World War II has shaken up the city's formerly self-absorbed, parochial WASP mindset for good. Whole villages have come here from Southeast Asia and all over Europe, especially from Greece, furnishing the well-worn statistic that Melbourne is the third-largest Greek city behind Athens and Thessaloniki. Not surprisingly, the immigrant blend has transformed the city into a **foodie Mecca**, where tucking into a different cuisine each night is entirely possible, and oft achieved by food-obsessed locals. Where there's food there's usually **drink**, and Melbourne is rightly proud of its café and bar culture. The city's laneways are stuffed with cool hangouts, from funky basements to slick rooftop terraces, with something to suit everyone – usually with a dollop of quirky Melbourne style.

Melbourne's strong claim to being the nation's **cultural capital** is well founded: the city's artistic life – laced with a healthy dash of counterculture – flourishes. Throughout the year, arts, film, comedy and music festivals abound, with more than enough heavyweight classical music, theatre, design hubs and wacky small galleries to occupy culture-buffs in between time. **Sport**, too, especially Australian Rules Football, is almost a religion here, while the Melbourne Cup horserace in November is a metropolitan public holiday, celebrated with gusto.

The phrase "four seasons in one day" could have been written about Melbourne's notoriously unpredictable **climate**. But while winter is generally cool and damp, the rest of the year tends to be sunny and pleasant, bar occasional barbaric hot spells in high summer (Dec–Feb) when temperatures can climb into the forties.

Some history

Five Aboriginal groups, together known as the **Kulin Nation**, lived in the Port Phillip and Yarra River region prior to the arrival of the Europeans. They shared a common language, an ordered society and a sophisticated belief system, but were little prepared for invasion. Colonists landed at Sorrento in 1803 and surveyed the bay; deterred by the apparent shortage of fresh water, they promptly departed to settle on Van Dieman's Land (Tasmania) across the Bass Strait instead. In due course, Tasmanians began crossing to the mainland in search of pasture, and in 1834, they established Melbourne, in defiance of a British government edict forbidding settlement in the territory, then part of New South Wales. Such was Britain's demand for wool that more and more squatters moved to the region to graze their flocks, with Melbourne evolving into the hub of a prosperous pastoral community. The Aboriginal tribes resisted this invasion, but were beaten back by warfare and disease.

City tours

It's definitely worth taking one of these tours to get to know a few of Melbourne's secrets. Two of the best are free.

Chocoholic Tours ☎03 9686 4655, ⊕www.chocoholictours.com.au. Tours are mainly on Friday or Saturday and take in sweet locations throughout the city. Naturally, lots of tastings are included, from chocolate ice cream to indulgent cakes in the city's finest bakeries. 1hr 30min–2hr; A$30.

Melbourne City Tourist Shuttle ☎03 9658 9658, ⊕www.thatsmelbourne.com.au. Free hop-on-hop-off bus with on-board commentary. Whisks you around eleven stops in the city centre, including the Arts Precinct, Federation Square, Melbourne Museum, Lygon Street and Queen Victoria Market; one complete circuit takes an hour. Daily 9.30am–4.30pm, every 15–20min.

Melbourne Food Tours ☎0408 555 679, ⊕www.melbournefoodtours.com. Local chef and food writer Allan Campion runs these excellent expeditions, which take in South Melbourne Market, Prahran Market, Fitzroy and the CBD amongst others, either on foot or by bus. From A$115 for a three-hour walking tour.

Melbourne Greeter Service ☎03 9658 9658, ⊕www.thatsmelbourne.com .au/greeter. The City of Melbourne's free tourist-orientation service matches up visitors with local volunteers for half a day (starting at 10am), for a walking or tram tour that gives an unparalleled insider's view of the city. Book at least three days in advance.

Melbourne on the Move Tram Bus ☎1300 558 686, ⊕www.melbourneonthemove .com.au. Decorated like a tram, this hop-on-hop-off tour bus starts from City Square on Swanston Street and does a circuit of twenty stops in the CBD and adjacent suburbs, taking in the Arts Centre, the Royal Botanic Gardens, the sports grounds and gardens of East Melbourne, the CBD and Carlton. Daily 10am–3pm; every 30min; 24hr ticket A$32, child A$16; 48hr ticket A$50/A$25; available by phone, online or on board.

Real Melbourne Bike Tours ☎0417 339 203, ⊕www.rentabike.net.au/biketours. Get a handle on the city by joining a guided cycling tour from Federation Square. The price includes coffee and cake in Little Italy, lunch, bike hire and equipment. Daily 10am–2pm; $89, child A$69.

Tullamarine Freeway (M2) to ▲ Melbourne Airport   ▲ Hume Highway (M31) to Canberra & Sydney

MELBOURNE

Museum of Modern Art at Heide & Montsalvat ▶

Eastern Freeway (M3) to Lilydale & Yarra Valley ▶

CityLink/Monash Freeway (M1) to Warragul, Sale, Bairnsdale & Lakes Entrance ▶

Dandenang Ranges ▶

Princes Highway to Gibbsland via M420 ▶

Westgate Freeway (M1) to Aralan Airport & Great Ocean Road ◀

CityLink

BULLA RD
LINCOLN RD
MOUNT ALEXANDER ROAD
PASCOE VALE ROAD
WATERFIELD ST
WaVerley RD
BUCKLEY ST
MOORE ST
ASCOT VALE RD
RACECOURSE ROAD
MARIBYRNONG ROAD
BALLARAT ROAD
DYNON ROAD
WHITEHALL STREET
DOCKLANDS HIGHWAY
FLEMINGTON ROAD

MOONEE PONDS
Moonee Valley Racecourse
BRUNSWICK
COBURG ROAD
MORELAND ROAD
THORNBURY
NORMANBY AVE
NORTHCOTE
NICHOLSON ST
ST GEORGES RD
HIGH STREET
MERRI PDE
WESTGARTH STREET
HEIDELBERG ROAD
Yarra Bend Park
Eastern Freeway
STUDLEY PARK ROAD
JOHNSTON STREET
ALEXANDRA PARADE
QUEENS PDE
HODDLE STREET
SIDNEY ROAD
LYGON STREET
NICHOLSON STREET
BRUNSWICK ROAD

Flemington Racecourse
Royal Park
Melbourne Zoo
University of Melbourne
ROYAL PARADE
RACECOURSE ROAD
CARLTON
FITZROY
COLLINGWOOD
VICTORIA STREET
VICTORIA STREET
Fitzroy Gardens
BRIDGE ROAD

CBD
Telstra Dome
Southern Cross Station & Bus Station
Flinders Street Station
Docklands
Yarra River
FLINDERS ST
MCG
Yarra Park
RICHMOND
SWAN STREET

Westgate Bridge
WESTGATE FREEWAY
GRAHAM STREET
PORT MELBOURNE
SOUTH MELBOURNE
Kings Domain
Royal Botanic Gardens
KINGS WAY
ST KILDA ROAD
CityLink
SOUTH YARRA
SOUTH EAST FREEWAY
TOORAK ROAD
GRANGE RD

Station Pier
BAY STREET
BEACONSFIELD PARADE
ALBERT PARK
Albert Park Lake
MIDDLE PARK
Albert Park
ALBERT ROAD
QUEENS ROAD
PUNT ROAD
TOORAK
COMMERCIAL ROAD
PRAHRAN
WINDSOR
HIGH STREET
WILLIAMS STREET
WILLIAMS ROAD

Melbourne Sports & Aquatic Centre
Jewish Museum
St Kilda Pier
FITZROYS STREET
BARKLY STREET
CHAPEL ST
HOTHAM ROAD

Commonwealth Reserve
NELSON PLACE
WILLIAMSTOWN
Point Gellibrand
Shelly Beach
ST KILDA
St Kilda Botanical Gardens
Ripponlea House
GLEN EIRA ROAD
NEPEAN HIGHWAY
Elwood Beach
ORMOND ESP

N

Port Phillip Bay

0   2 km

NORTH ROAD
ST KILDA STREET
NEW STREET

Nepean Highway to the Mornington Peninsula & Phillip Island ▼

By 1851, the **white population** in the area was large and confident enough to demand separation from New South Wales, achieved, by a stroke of luck, just nine days before **gold** was discovered in the new colony. Over the next thirty years, more gold was mined in Victoria than in the celebrated California Gold Rush of the 1840s and 50s, transforming the state into Australia's economic

Dates for your diary: festivals and events

Melbourne is Australia's premier events city. From January to December, and from sports to the arts, there's usually something on the go. *EG*, published with *The Age* on Fridays, carries events listings and features, as does the paper's Saturday magazine.

January

Australian Open ⓦ www.australianopen.com. Unlike the Grand Prix (see below), Melburnians get behind their famous tennis tournament in droves. You can get ground passes and wander around the outside courts, or buy a ticket for the Rod Laver Arena for a guaranteed sighting of a big star. Two weeks from mid-January.

Midsumma ⓦ www.midsumma.org.au. Midsumma is Melbourne's biggest lesbian and gay arts and cultural festival, an eclectic celebration of queer culture that incorporates spoken word, cabaret, comedy, film and sports amongst others. Three weeks from mid-January to early February.

February

St Kilda Festival ⓦ www.stkildafestival.com.au. With its full programme of music, indigenous arts and sporting events, the St Kilda Festival just feels like normal St Kilda times ten, with plastic cups. It's a fun way to spend a sunny weekend, though. Eight days in early February.

St Jerome's Laneway Festival ⓦ www.lanewayfestival.com.au. One-day event that brings live music and a street-party atmosphere to the city's vibrant laneways.

Melbourne Food and Wine Festival ⓦ www.melbournefoodandwine.com.au. In late February and early March, the city celebrates its foodie reputation with picnics, coffee education, wine-tasting, A$30 lunches, and a smorgasbord of talks, tours and cooking classes.

Brunswick Music Festival ⓦ www.brunswickmusicfestival.com.au. Ethnic, indigenous, acoustic and traditional music is showcased in the funky northern suburb of Brunswick over two weeks in late February and early March.

March

Moomba Waterfest ⓦ www.melbourne.vic.gov.au. City of Melbourne-run festival with a community focus; firework displays and dragon-boat races are amongst the watery events taking place along the banks of the Yarra over a weekend in early March.

Australian Grand Prix ⓦ www.grandprix.com.au. Petrolheads dig the cars (not to mention the pit bunnies), but the rest of Melbourne is heartily fed up of the Grand Prix, which creates a huge amount of noise and restricts public access to Albert Park over the race weekend in mid-March, and in the run-up.

April

Melbourne International Comedy Festival ⓦ www.comedyfestival.com.au. This three-week festival of Aussie and overseas acts is based at Melbourne Town Hall; other venues worth a look include the Festival Lounge over the road, which kicks off around midnight and has a riotous feel. From late March or early April.

Melbourne Jazz Festival ⓦ www.melbournejazz.com. People who favour horn-rimmed specs and black polo necks rejoice for eleven days in late April and early May, as various venues around the city centre and inner suburbs host mellow events.

powerhouse. Melbourne quickly mushroomed into a filthy, seething fortune seekers' town, only gradually pulling itself together to become a prosperous and elegant city whose inhabitants modelled their houses, parks, gardens and manners on middle–class England. Following Federation in 1901, it became the political capital, a title it retained until Canberra became fully operational in 1927.

May
Next Wave Festival www.nextwave.org.au. This biennial event, held over two weeks from mid-May, celebrates Victoria's young artists, writers and musicians; little-known public spaces around the CBD and suburbs are common venues.

July
Melbourne International Film Festival (MIFF) www.melbournefilmfestival .com.au. The forty-year-old film festival brings new flicks by the hundreds to Melbourne each year; the programme often has themed sections, and shorts feature heavily. The Festival Lounge, where you can dissect the day's screenings, is always popular. Two weeks in late July and early August.

August
Melbourne Writers' Festival www.mwf.com.au. Writers flock to the city in late August, for an orgy of talks, book launches and debauched drinking.

September
Melbourne Underground Film Festival (MUFF) www.muff.com.au. The much younger cousin to MIFF (see above) screens much more left-field films, and continues to grow in popularity. Dates vary.

Melbourne Fringe Festival www.melbournefringe.com.au. Cutting-edge riot of fringe arts, which starts in late September and aims to bring the most innovative and trend-setting work by independent artists to a broad Melbourne audience.

AFL Grand Final Day www.afl.com.au. The last day of the Australian Football League season (last Sat in Sept) is generally marked by communal barbecues, beer and betting.

October
Melbourne International Arts Festival www.melbournefestival.com.au. This admirable festival cherry-picks the very best of visual and performing arts from Australia and overseas for the delight of the Melbourne public, as well as putting on plenty of free events at Federation Square and around the city. Two and a half weeks in mid-October.

November
Melbourne Cup and the **Spring Racing Carnival** www.springracingcarnival.com.au. You know it's racing season when girls dressed in frocks and fascinators leave Flinders Street Station in the morning looking relatively demure, and return looking rather worse for wear. Who knows what goes on in the intervening period? Some horse racing, apparently. Worth getting tickets for, if only to dress up to the nines, see what all the fuss is about, and lose a fortune at the bookies. Starts in October, peaks in November.

December
Boxing Day Test www.mcg.org.au. See the Aussie cricketers take on some hapless chaps at the MCG on the 26th. Much revelry generally ensues, particularly if it's an Ashes match against the Poms.

The 1930s were marked by rapid industrial development on the city's fringes and the growth of suburban settlement; this continued post-war when Melbourne's population was boosted by a flood of immigrant workers. In 1956, the **Olympic Games** finally put Melbourne – and the MCG – on the world map. Multinational companies made the city their Australian base, and it remained the country's capital of business and finance until the focus shifted to Sydney in the early 1980s. When recession hit in the early 1990s, Melbourne rode out the worst of it under the leadership of controversial Victorian premier Jeff Kennett, who initiated high-profile developments such as the CityLink tollway, the Melbourne Museum and Federation Square, and championed Aboriginal causes. His successor Steve Bracks had a less dynamic style, but picked up Kennett's leads by fostering racial and religious tolerance, and encouraging docklands redevelopment and the expansion of the city's motorway network. After a successful eight years in office, Bracks resigned in July 2007, and his treasurer John Brumby took over a city with a high rate of economic and population growth, holding fast to its title of Australia's capital of sport, culture and diversity.

Arrival and information

Melbourne's international and domestic airports offer an efficient entry point into the city. Long-distance buses and trains will deliver you right into the centre with minimal fuss, while driving into town is straightforward as long as you familiarize yourself with the motorway toll system and a few rules of the road designed to keep the trams on track.

By air

Most international and domestic flights into Melbourne land at **Melbourne Airport** (MEL; ⓦ www.melbourneairport.com.au) on the Tullamarine Freeway, Tullamarine, 25km northwest of the city centre. Airlines flying to Melbourne from other East Coast cities include Jetstar, Qantas, Norfolk Air, Regional Express, Tiger Airways and Virgin Blue (see p.35). Airport **shuttle buses** provide public transport to the city. The Skybus Super Shuttle (every 10–15min 5.30am–9.30pm, every 30min 9.30pm–12.30am & 4.30–5.30am, hourly 12.30–4.30am; 20min; A\$16 one way, A\$26 return; ⓣ 03 9335 2811, ⓦ www.skybus.com.au) runs to the Southern Cross Bus Terminal on Spencer Street, where passengers can transfer to a complimentary minibus service (Mon–Fri 6am–9.30pm, Sat & Sun 7.30am–5.30pm) serving hotels in the CBD and some inner suburbs, or jump aboard a taxi, tram or bus. The Frankston and Peninsula Airport Bus (40–65min; ⓣ 03 9783 1199, ⓦ www.fapas.com.au) serves the southern and bayside suburbs including St Kilda (A\$18 one way, A\$30 return). A **taxi** from Melbourne Airport costs around A\$40 to the city centre, A\$50 to St Kilda.

Jetstar flies from a limited number of Australian and Asian cities to **Avalon Airport** (AVV; ⓦ www.avalonairport.com.au), located 55km southwest of Melbourne, just off the Princes Freeway to Geelong. Transport is provided by Sunbus (45min; A\$20 one way, A\$36 return; ⓣ 03 9689 6888, ⓦ www.sunbusaustralia.com.au), who meet all arriving flights and drop passengers at Southern Cross; they also run to other central and suburban destinations if pre-booked.

By train, bus or ferry

Melbourne has five railway stations, of which the main arrival point for inter-state and country trains (see p.35) is **Southern Cross Station** on Spencer Street, on the west side of the city. The adjacent **Southern Cross Bus Terminal** is the terminus for Greyhound, V/Line and Firefly long-distance buses (see p.35). From here, various trams run to the CBD and the inner suburbs: the 86 or 96 will take you down Bourke Street, the 109 down Collins and the 75 along Flinders. Some hostels pick up from Southern Cross Station, as well as from the **Tasmanian ferry terminal** located about 4km southwest of the city centre at Station Pier in Port Melbourne. Tram 109 runs from the ferry terminal along Collins Street in the CBD.

By car

Three **freeways** converge on central Melbourne: the Tullamarine Freeway from the airport, the West Gate/Princes Freeway from Geelong and the Great Ocean Road, and the Monash Freeway from southeast Victoria. All three are connected by a city-centre toll road, the **CityLink**. It's not possible to pay CityLink tolls in cash: you must either have an e-tag fitted to your windscreen, or buy a virtual pass for your car before or within three days of your first use of the toll roads, by phone or online (A$11.55; ☏ 13 26 29, ⓦ www.citylink.com.au). A pass allows you unlimited journeys on the CityLink from noon on Friday to midnight on Sunday or for 24 hours on other days. With an e-tag, tolls for the CityLink and any other electronic toll roads in Australia are charged to your account on a pay-as-you-go basis; you can order one online from CityLink by paying a deposit, but it will take two weeks to be delivered by post.

Other routes into the city include the Hume Highway from Canberra and Sydney, the Nepean Highway from the Mornington Peninsula and the Princes Highway from Gippsland.

Information

The **Melbourne Visitor Centre** on Federation Square, directly opposite Flinders Street Station (daily 9am–6pm; ☏ 03 9658 9658, ⓦ www .visitmelbourne.com.au), has a tour-and accommodation-booking service (same hours; ☏ 03 9650 3663), plus brochures and maps galore about Melbourne and the rest of the state. The pocket-sized *Melbourne Walks* series is useful: each one describes a themed, self-guided walk (1hr 30min–2hr 30min) around the city and has a good reference map. There's also a **Visitor Information Booth** in the middle of Bourke Street Mall (Mon–Sat 9am–5pm, Sun 10am–5pm). **City Ambassadors** – volunteers in red uniforms – roam the CBD between Elizabeth, Russell, La Trobe and Flinders streets (Mon–Fri 10am–4pm, Sat 11am–2pm) to assist with all kinds of tourist enquiries.

Other useful resources include the **Information Victoria Bookshop** at 505 Little Collins St (Mon–Fri 8.30am–5pm; ☏ 03 9603 9900 or 1300 366 356,

---

See Melbourne & Beyond Smartvisit Card

Providing free entry to over sixty attractions in Melbourne and Victoria, the **See Melbourne & Beyond** card is well worth the expense if you intend doing some serious sightseeing. It's available from visitor information centres, or by phone or online (1 day A$69, child A$49; 2 days A$105/65; 3 days A$135/79; 7 days A$205/135; ☏ 1300 66 17 11, ⓦ www.seemelbournecard.com).

@ www.bookshop.vic.gov.au), for maps, other publications and a noticeboard of city events, and **Tourism Victoria** (information service: daily 8am–6pm; @ 13 28 42, @ www.visitvictoria.com), for state-wide visitor information; see also p.66 for details of environment and conservation organizations.

City transport

Melbourne has an efficient if slightly confusing public transport system of trams, trains and buses under one umbrella called **Metlink** (telephone enquiries 6am–10pm on @ 13 16 38; online information @ www.metlinkmelbourne.com.au), with an equally confusing ticketing system that the Victorian government is currently overhauling by introducing a smart-card system called Myki (@ www .myki.com.au). In the meantime, the options are as follows.

A **Two-hour Metcard** (Zone 1 A$3.50; Zones 1 & 2 A$5.50) is valid for two hours after the next full hour it was bought or validated (or until 3am if bought after 6pm). A **Daily Metcard** (Zone 1 A$6.50; Zones 1 & 2 A$10.10) is more useful if you're making a few trips in Zone 1, or taking a trip to the outer suburbs. For longer stays, a **Weekly Metcard** (Zone 1 A$28; Zones 1 & 2 A$47.40) is an even better bargain. The **Sunday Saver Metcard** (just A$2.90) entitles the bearer to travel in Zones 1 and 2 throughout Sunday. The **City Saver Metcard** (A$2.60) is valid for a single trip on one vehicle in the City Saver area (the CBD and adjacent areas). Metcards comprised of ten two-hour or five daily tickets are also available.

With the exception of the City Saver, all Metcards can be used on the tram, train or bus – or a combination of these – until they expire. Almost everything of interest lies within Zone 1, including St Kilda and Williamstown. You'll need to **validate** your Metcard in one of the green validation machines every time you board a new vehicle.

For tram and train travel, City Saver, Two-hour and Daily Metcards can only be bought from **vending machines** on board (not from the driver); these only accept coins but give change. Some minor train stations only have these machines available. The reverse applies on buses: there are no vending machines, so buy your ticket from the driver (exact change preferred). You can can buy all Metcards and get travel advice from major stations, the Melbourne Visitor

---

Melbourne's vintage trams

Some of Melbourne's trams are vintage wooden vehicles dating back to the 1930s (though none is quite as ancient as the system, which dates from 1885).

The elegant, burgundy-coloured **City Circle trams** (free) run clockwise and anti-clockwise in a loop along Flinders, Spring, Nicholson, La Trobe and Spencer streets (every 12min; Thurs–Sat 10am–9pm, Sun–Wed 10am–6pm).

The **Colonial Tramcar Restaurant** (@ 03 9696 4000, @ www.tramrestaurant .com.au) is a 1927 tram that has been converted into a restaurant complete with white linen napkins and the best china, which trundles around Melbourne as you enjoy some good food. The service starts at Normanby Road near the Crown Casino; the restaurant offers a three-course early sitting (daily 5.45–7.15pm; A$70) and a five-course dinner (daily 8.35–11.30pm; A$115 Mon–Thurs & Sun, A$130 Fri & Sat), plus a four-course lunch (daily 1–3pm; A$75). All drinks are included. You'll need to reserve at least three weeks ahead, or up to four months in advance for Friday and Saturday evenings.

Centre at Federation Square, the MetShop at the Melbourne Town Hall on the corner of Swanston and Little Collins streets, and at most newsagents, a few milk bars and pharmacies – look for the flag with the **Metcard logo**.

Trams, trains and buses

Melbourne's **trams** give the city a distinctive character and provide a pleasant, environmentally friendly way of getting around: the **City Circle** (see box, p.94) is particularly convenient – and free. Trams run down the centre of the road (the "Central Melbourne" map on p.96, shows the main routes in the centre); the stops (green) are either at the side of the road or at a central island. Trams only stop when someone is getting on or off – it can be worth flagging them down to make sure the driver has seen you. Remember to keep an eye out for trams when crossing the road.

   Trains are the fastest way to reach the outer suburbs. An underground loop system feeding into seventeen suburban lines connects the CBD's five stations: **Southern Cross**, which also serves as the station for interstate and country trains; **Flagstaff**, on the corner of La Trobe and William streets; **Melbourne Central**, on the corner of Swanston and La Trobe streets; **Parliament**, on Spring Street; and **Flinders Street**, the main suburban station. Bikes can be carried free, but are banned during peak periods (Mon–Fri 7–9.30am & 4–6pm).

   Train and tram services operate Monday to Saturday from 5am until midnight, and Sunday from 8am until 11pm. Regular **buses** often run on the same routes as trams, as well as filling gaps where no train or tram lines run. In general, they are the least useful mode of public transport for visitors, with the exception of the **NightRider buses** (Sat & Sun; hourly 12.30–4.30am; A$6), which head from Swanston Street (City Square) to the outer suburbs of Frankston, Dandenong, Belgrave, Lilydale, Eltham, Epping, Craigieburn, St Albans, Werribee and Melton (A$8.20), more or less in the same direction as the suburban train routes. Each bus has an **onboard mobile phone**, on which the driver can book a taxi to meet you at a bus stop (free call), or you can call a friend (A$1) to meet you. The buses also operate during big events such as New Year's Eve and the Melbourne Grand Prix.

Accommodation

Most accommodation is concentrated in the CBD and adjoining suburbs of **North Melbourne**, **Carlton**, **Fitzroy**, **East Melbourne** and **Richmond**;

Driving and cycling in Melbourne

Driving in Melbourne requires some care, mainly because of the trams. You can overtake a tram only on the left and must stop and wait behind it while passengers get on and off, as they step directly into the road (though there's no need to stop if there's a central pedestrian island). A peculiar rule has developed to accommodate trams at major intersections in the city centre, which can take some getting used to: when turning right, you pull over to the left-hand lane and wait for the lights to change to amber before turning – a "**hook turn**". Signs overhead indicate when this rule applies.

Cyclists should also watch out for tram lines – tyres can easily get wedged in them. This apart, Melbourne is generally well set up for cycling, and you'll be in good company as it's a popular way of getting around. Helmets are compulsory. For cycle hire and touring possibilities, see p.136.

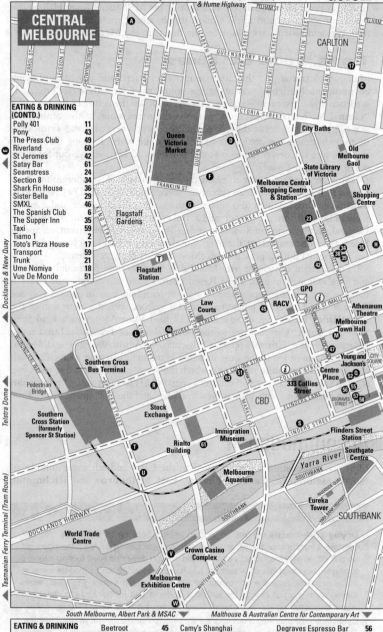

CENTRAL MELBOURNE

Melbourne Airport & Bendigo ▲ ▲ *Melbourne Zoo, Brunswick, & Hume Highway*

❶, ❷ & ❸

CARLTON

EATING & DRINKING (CONTD.)

Polly 401	11
Pony	43
The Press Club	49
Riverland	60
St Jeromes	42
Satay Bar	61
Seamstress	24
Section 8	34
Shark Fin House	36
Sister Bella	29
SMXL	46
The Spanish Club	6
The Supper Inn	35
Taxi	59
Tiamo 1	2
Toto's Pizza House	17
Transport	59
Trunk	21
Ume Nomiya	18
Vue De Monde	51

Queen Victoria Market

Flagstaff Gardens

City Baths

Old Melbourne Gaol

State Library of Victoria

Melbourne Central Shopping Centre & Station

QV Shopping Centre

Flagstaff Station

Law Courts

GPO

RACV

Athenæum Theatre

Melbourne Town Hall

Young and Jackson's

Southern Cross Bus Terminal

Pedestrian Bridge

Centre Place

333 Collins Street

CBD

Southern Cross Station (formerly Spencer St Station)

Stock Exchange

Rialto Building

Immigration Museum

Melbourne Aquarium

Flinders Street Station

Southgate Centre

Yarra River

SOUTHBANK

Eureka Tower

SOUTHBANK

World Trade Centre

Crown Casino Complex

Melbourne Exhibition Centre

Docklands & New Quay ◄

Telstra Dome ◄

Tasmanian Ferry Terminal (Tram Route) ◄

DOCKLANDS HIGHWAY

South Melbourne, Albert Park & MSAC ▼   *Malthouse & Australian Centre for Contemporary Art* ▼

EATING & DRINKING

100 Mile Cafe	23	Beetroot	45	Camy's Shanghai		Degraves Espresso Bar	56
Abla's	4	Bennetts Lane	22	Dumpling and Noodle		Ding Dong Lounge	31
Babka	7	Big Harvest	5	Restaurant	39	Double Happiness	27
Bar Lourinhã	44	Bimbo Deluxe	12	Cherry	48	The European	26
Bar Open	10	Blue Chillies	15	City Wine Shop	28	Ezard at the Adelphi	50
		Brunetti	1	Cookie	38	Flora's	52

96

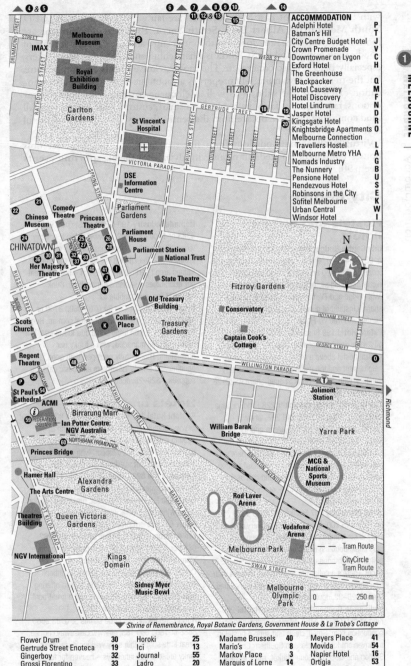

with the exception of East Melbourne, all are fairly lively. South of the CBD, **South Melbourne**, **Albert Park**, **South Yarra**, **Prahran** and **Windsor** are more upmarket and handy for both the city centre and the beach, with lots of good eating options; while **St Kilda** is a happening enclave where backpackers, especially Brits, tend to congregate. The most exclusive **hotels** are in the centre, but the trend for revamping old properties as boutique-style luxury accommodation extends to the suburbs as well. Melbourne has plenty of **backpacker** options, ranging from fairly basic places to smart, custom-built hostels with all mod cons. Though some distace from the centre, the city's **campsites** are useful if you have transport.

Virtually all accommodation, from five-star hotels to the scruffiest doss houses, tends to be booked out months in advance for the big **sporting events** (see p.90).

City centre

Hostels and budget hotels

City Centre Budget Hotel 22–30 Little Collins St ☎03 9654 5401, ⓦwww.citycentrebudgethotel .com.au. One step up from a standard hostel, with nicely designed singles, doubles, twins and triples (with fridge and TV; bathrooms and kitchen are shared) instead of dorms, plus a great rooftop garden and free Wi-Fi. ❸

Exford Hotel 199 Russell St ☎03 9663 2697, ⓦwww.exfordhotel.com.au. Secure, clean and central hostel above a refurbished pub. Friendly, helpful staff and the usual amenities, plus a tiny sundeck with a BBQ. Bunk in quad-share A$22–26, double/twin ❷

The Greenhouse Backpacker 228 Flinders Lane ☎03 9639 6400 or 1800 249 207, ⓦwww .friendlygroup.com.au. Large, clean and friendly place in a superb sixth-floor location amidst the characterful alleys of Melbourne's CBD. There's a big, well-equipped kitchen and a pleasant rooftop garden; staff offer good freebies and can assist with finding work. Bunk in four- or six-share A$27–30, double/twin ❸

Hotel Discovery 167 Franklin St ☎03 9329 7525 or 1800 645 200, ⓦwww.hoteldiscovery.com.au. Around six hundred beds (in dorms sleeping 4–16, plus basic doubles) in a converted former school building brightened up with colour-coordinated decor. There's a cellar bar and a small cinema with free screenings; a very basic breakfast is included. Bunk A$25–32, double/twin ❸

Melbourne Connection Travellers Hostel 205 King St ☎03 9642 4464, ⓦwww.melbourne connection.com. Small, clean and simple hostel in a convenient location close to Southern Cross Station and Queen Victoria Market; rates include breakfast. Bunk in four- or eight-share A$23–28, double/twin ❸

Nomads Industry 196 A'Beckett St ☎03 9328 4383 or 1800 44 77 62, ⓦwww.nomadsindustry .com. "Flashpacker" hostel that favours style over practicality – the kitchen is small, and the snazzy fittings aren't particularly well kept – but the great bar guarantees a sociable atmosphere. Bunk A$29–31, en-suite double ❹

Urban Central 334 City Rd ☎03 9693 3700 or 1800 631 288, ⓦwww.urbancentral.com.au. Huge, flashy hostel – a bit impersonal due to the size, but clean and well managed, with a funky bar downstairs. Thoughtfully equipped with good bedding and towels, hairdryers and basic catering supplies. A$29–25, double ❸

Hotels and motels

Adelphi Hotel 187 Flinders Lane ☎03 9650 7555, ⓦwww.adelphi.com.au. Stylish hotel with a striking exterior and sparse, ultramodern interior design throughout – it's topped with a glass-bottomed pool that overlooks the street. ❽

Batman's Hill 623 Collins St ☎03 9614 6344, ⓦwww.batmanshill.com. Behind the elegant Edwardian facade lies a modest, functional interior and a wide range of facilities. Good value, and handy for Southern Cross Station. ❺

Crown Promenade 8 Whiteman St ☎03 9262 6688 or 1800 776 612, ⓦwww.crownpromenade .com.au. Very close to the Melbourne Exhibition Centre and within easy reach of the Southbank entertainment precinct, this large, stylish offering has spacious rooms, good views and a great pool. Discounts make it affordable. ❽

Hotel Causeway 275 Little Collins St ☎03 9660 8888 or 1800 660 188, ⓦwww.causeway.com.au. Great little spot within easy walking distance of funky arcades and laneways – heaven for foodies and browsers. Fuss-free contemporary styling, and a roof terrace. Generous off-peak discounts. ❻

Hotel Lindrum 26 Flinders St ☏ 03 9668 1111, ⓦ www.hotellindrum.com.au. Named after Australia's most famous billiard-player, Walter Lindrum (the billiard room has one of his original tables), this luxurious hotel has a boutique feel about it. Rooms are designed with rich wood furnishings: the ones facing the front are by far the best. ❽

Jasper Hotel 489 Elizabeth St ☏ 03 8327 2777 or 1800 46 83 59, ⓦ www.jasperhotel.com.au. In what was once prime backpacker territory, this former YMCA is now a mid-range hotel with boutique-style decor, thanks to a radical refit. Guests have free access to the nearby Melbourne City Baths health club and pool. ❺

Kingsgate Hotel 131 King St ☏ 03 9629 4171 or 1300 734 171, ⓦ www.kingsgatehotel.com.au. Huge, renovated budget hotel with a choice of en-suite rooms or no-frills, economy rooms with shared bathroom; all are good value. Facilities include a pleasant TV lounge and a bar and café. ❸–❹

Pensione Hotel 16 Spencer St ☏ 03 9621 3333 or 1800 816 168, ⓦ www.pensione.com.au. Groovy, affordable little boutique hotel with a choice of rooms: simple, for a snip, or smarter and decorated with style-mag flourishes, for a slightly higher rate. ❸–❹

Rendezvous Hotel 328 Flinders St ☏ 03 9250 1888, ⓦ www.rendezvoushotels.com.au. Superbly central, this grand building has been revamped to great acclaim. Stylish without feeling overindulgent, it's aimed at both business travellers and tourists. Rates are very reasonable. ❺

Robinsons in the City 405 Spencer St, West Melbourne ☏ 03 9329 2552, ⓦ www.robinsonsinthecity.com.au. Boutique B&B with just six opulently spacious double rooms in a former bakery built in the 1850s. Immaculate service, perfect for those looking for a personal touch. ❺

Sofitel Melbourne 25 Collins St ☏ 03 9653 0000 or 1300 656 565, ⓦ www.sofitelmelbourne.com.au. An I.M. Pei-designed hotel, set on the top floors of a fifty-storey building, with marvellous views across Melbourne and surrounds, gloriously comfortable rooms and a good spread of cafés and restaurants, including the airy *Café La*. ❻

Windsor Hotel 103 Spring St ☏ 03 9633 6000, ⓦ www.thewindsor.com.au. A Melbourne landmark. This luxurious Victorian-era hotel has lavishly decorated suites and surprisingly affordable standard doubles with a pleasantly old-fashioned ambience. Room ❺, suite ❼

North Melbourne, Carlton and Fitzroy

Downtowner on Lygon 66 Lygon St, Carlton ☏ 03 9663 5555 or 1800 800 130, ⓦ www.downtowner.com.au. Great-value hotel in the heart of Carlton, with smart contemporary decor, and rooms with all mod cons, some with spa baths. ❹

Melbourne Metro YHA 78 Howard St, North Melbourne ☏ 03 9329 8599, ⓦ www.yha.com.au. This huge modern hostel – really more like a smart budget hotel – has a host of amenities including a rooftop garden with BBQ, bicycle hire and a licensed cafe. Bunk in four- or eight-share A$26–33.50, twin/double ❸

The Nunnery 116 Nicholson St, Fitzroy ☏ 03 9419 8637 or 1800 032 635, ⓦ www.nunnery.com.au. In three old buildings close to Brunswick Street's cafés and pubs, this has a quiet, characterful guesthouse section with shared bathrooms and kitchen, and a hostel wing with rather crammed dorms. Bunk A$26–30, double ❸–❹

East Melbourne

Knightsbridge Apartments 101 George St ☏ 03 9419 1333, ⓦ www.knightsbridgeapartments.com.au. Bright, serviced self-catering studios and two-bedroom apartments with a contemporary finish, 1km from the centre. Compact but good value. ❹

Richmond

Freeman Lodge 153 Hoddle St ☏ 03 8430 2978, ⓦ www.freemanlodge.com.au. With more character than the average hostel, this well-equipped guesthouse has a funky sharehouse feel. Just around the corner from West Richmond station, within walking distance of busy Bridge Rd. Bunk in quad-share A$25, room ❷

Richmond Hill Hotel 353 Church St ☏ 03 9428 6501 or 1800 801 618, ⓦ www.richmondhillhotel.com.au. Set in a stately Victorian mansion in a pretty garden, with spacious, cosy dining and sitting rooms. The guesthouse section offers apartments or B&B rooms, some en suite; the budget section has small, clean dorms and singles with shared facilities. Bunk A$30, room ❸, apartment ❻

🏃 **Villa Donati** 377 Church St ☎ 03 9428 8104, ⓦ www.villadonati.com. With a

stunning facade and an interior furnished like an elegant Italian villa, this chic B&B is the perfect place to savour suburban Melbourne's *dolce vita.* ❺

Albert Park, Middle Park, South Yarra, Prahran and Windsor

Hostels and budget hotels

The Beach Accommodation 97 Beaconsfield Parade, Albert Park ☎ 03 9690 4642, ⓦ www .thebeachaccommodation.com.au. Budget rooms above a pub, in a hard-to-beat location overlooking the beach, opposite a tram stop. Pleasant, though noisy and fairly basic. Price includes breakfast. Bunk A$21, twin/double ❷

Chapel Street Backpackers 22 Chapel St, Windsor (opposite Windsor station, Sandringham line) ☎ 03 9533 6855, ⓦ www.csbackpackers.com.au. Friendly hostel at the southern, quieter end of Chapel St, with very clean, comfy rooms, some en suite, and a small outdoor courtyard with a BBQ. Basic breakfast included. Bunk A$28, twin/double ❸

College Lawn Hotel 36 Greville St, Prahran ☎ 03 9810 0074, ⓦ www.collegelawnhotel.com .au. Simple, good-value backpacker accommodation above a great pub (with excellent nosh) on funky Greville St. Try your luck in the popular quiz on Wed evenings. Bunk A$21, double ❷

St Kilda

Hostels and budget motels

🏃 **Base** 17 Carlisle St ☎ 03 8598 6222, ⓦ www.basebackpackers.com. A swish, custom-built hostel with an unforgettable glossy red facade, minimalist decor and unusual features, such as the sunken fish-tank spanning the breezy lounge. All dorms and rooms are en suite, have a/c and are scrupulously clean. The bar lends a party vibe. Bunk A$28–34, en-suite double ❸

Cooee on St Kilda 333 St Kilda Rd ☎ 03 9537 3777, ⓦ www.cooeeonstkilda.com. Quality hostel with good, clean facilities, a host of activities, and bonuses such as free "Sausage Sizzle" nights and gated parking. Travellers congregate to swap stories in the huge kitchen and courtyard. Bunk A$24–32, en-suite double/twin ❹

Hotels and B&Bs

Annie's B&B 93 Park St, St Kilda West ☎ 03 9534 8705, ⓦ www.anniesbedandbreakfast.com.au.

Gunn Island 102 Canterbury Rd, Middle Park ☎ 03 9690 1882, ⓦ www.gunnisland.com.au. Inexpensive dorms and simple, pleasant rooms with shared facilities above a refurbished pub-cum-brewery. Great location close to the beach and the city, right in the midst of Armstrong Street's brunch bars and delis. Bunk A$21, double ❷

Hotels

🏃 **The Hatton Hotel** 65 Park St, South Yarra ☎ 03 9868 4800, ⓦ www.hatton.com.au. Charming and distinctive, this place is highly comfortable – with a grand aspect, individually styled rooms and pleasing luxury touches – but as relaxed as a B&B. Excellent value. ❺

Hotel Charsfield 478 St Kilda Rd, South Yarra ☎ 03 9866 5511, ⓦ www.charsfield.com. Posh Victorian mansion with a reading room, snooker room and a terrace that ooze old-money elegance; many of the bedrooms, which vary in splendour, have ornate ceilings and fireplaces. ❻

Small, family-run B&B in a renovated Edwardian house with en-suite rooms. Guests can use the courtyard garden and BBQ, and are served a great breakfast: treats include muffins, home-made bread and frittata, or fish cakes made from sweet potato and salmon. ❺

Cosmopolitan Hotel 8 Carlisle St ☎ 03 9534 0781 or 1800 333 073, ⓦ www.cosmopolitanhotel .com.au. Slick, contemporary outfit with a range of room types, all generously fitted out for the price. The least expensive ones are tiny but others have spacious balconies; all have comfy beds stacked with pillows. ❹–❻

Hotel Tolarno 42 Fitzroy St ☎ 03 9537 0200, ⓦ www.hoteltolarno.com.au. Pleasant, small and incredibly funky boutique hotel in a restored building located right in the thick of things. There's no escaping the street noise, but the arty vibe – with original paintings and retro-chic furniture – is fab. ❺

🏃 **The Prince** 2 Acland St ☎ 03 9536 1111, ⓦ www.theprince.com.au. This boutique

Gay and lesbian accommodation

The following options are run by gay owner/managers. If you're staying a while and want to find a house share, contact Gay Share (℡03 9691 2290, ⓦwww.gayshare.com.au).

169 Drummond Street 169 Drummond St, Carlton ℡03 9663 3081, ⓦwww .169drummond.com.au. B&B in a refurbished Victorian terraced house with cosy and homely rooms. ❺

Cotterville 204 Williams Rd, Toorak ℡03 9826 9105, ⓦwww.cotterville.com. Classy B&B owned by a style-conscious couple, with cheery, refreshingly colourful decor, a beautifully maintained garden, and elegant touches aplenty. ❻

Opium Den 176 Hoddle St, Collingwood ℡03 9417 2696, ⓦwww.opiumden.com.au. Good-value, pub-style rooms with a touch of exotic opulence at an intimate cabaret bar (see p.133). Bathrooms are shared. Price includes breakfast. ❸

hotel is one of the most elegant places in Melbourne to lay your head. The rooms have minimalist decor and Bose stereos; downstairs, there's a day-spa, the extremely swish *Circa* restaurant (see p.127), *Mink* vodka bar (see p.130), and a legendary club/band room (see p.131). ❻

Urban St Kilda 35–37 Fitzroy St ℡03 8530 8888, ⓦwww.urbanstkilda.com.au. Cutting-edge design features elevate this hip boutique hotel above the norm; nice touches include good entertainment systems and stashes of Aveda goodies in the bathrooms. ❺

Camping and caravan parks

There are no campsites close to the centre; the nearest are the two Big 4 holiday parks on the outskirts.

Big 4 Melbourne Ashley Gardens 129 Ashley St, Braybrook (9km west of the CBD) ℡1800 061 444 or 03 9318 6866, ⓦwww.big4ashleygardens .com.au. Well-equipped park for tents, vans and caravans, with spacious cabins and a great outdoor solar-heated swimming pool. Camping A$38–50, cabin ❸, villa ❹

Crystal Brook Holiday Centre 182 Heidelberg-Warrandyte Rd, East Doncaster (21km northeast of the CBD) ℡03 9844 3637,

ⓦwww.crystalbrook.net.au. Modern campsite and holiday park with tennis courts and a pool. Camping A$31–36, cabin or van ❷, villa ❹

Melbourne Big 4 Holiday Park 265 Elizabeth St, Coburg (9km north of the CBD) ℡03 9354 3533 or 1800 802 678, ⓦwww.melbournebig4holidaypark .com.au. Shady park with good facilities including a kids' playground and a pool. Camping A$32–55, cabin 2, unit ❹

The City

Melbourne is a place of few sights but plenty of lifestyle, and you'll get to know the city just as well by relaxing over a coffee or strolling in the park as by traipsing around museums or attractions. At the heart of the city lies the **Central Business District (CBD)**, bounded by La Trobe, Spring, Flinders and Spencer streets, dotted with fine public buildings, lots of shops and intriguing laneways. Sights include the ghoulish **Old Melbourne Gaol**, just north of La Trobe Street, and the **Immigration Museum** in the Old Customs House. The CBD is surrounded by gardens on all sides (save the downtown west): few cities have so much green space so close to the centre. To the north of the CBD, a wander through the lively **Queen Victoria Market** will repay foodies, collectors of Australiana and people-watchers alike, while the **Melbourne Museum** in tranquil Carlton Gardens draws on the latest technology to give an insight into Australia's flora, fauna and culture. The east of the CBD is home to **Parliament House** and other government buildings as well as the landscaped **Fitzroy Gardens**; from here it's a short walk to the venerable **Melbourne Cricket Ground (MCG)**, a must for sports fans.

Bordering the south side of the CBD, the muddy **Yarra River** lies at the centre of the massive high-rise developments that have transformed the face of the city. The shift towards the Yarra River kicked off in the mid-1990s with the waterfront development of **Southgate**, **Crown Casino** and the **Melbourne Exhibition Centre**. **Federation Square**, on the north bank of the Yarra River opposite Flinders Street Station, is considered the centre of the city; its adjacent park, Birrarung Marr, links the square with the sports arenas further east. South of Federation Square, the **Victorian Arts Centre** forms a cultural strip on one side of St Kilda Road, while on the other, Government House and the impressive Shrine of Remembrance front the soothing **Royal Botanic Gardens**.

Federation Square and around

The huge, orange-and-brown **Flinders Street Station**, the city's main suburban railway station, lies sandwiched between the southern edge of the CBD and the Yarra. Melburnians traditionally meet "under the clocks" at the station's entrance, whose row of clocks show the next departure on each line.

This famous old city landmark is faced by the very modern **Federation Square** (or Fed Square), which occupies an entire block between Flinders Street and the Yarra River. Variously loved or loathed, it nevertheless provides Melbourne with the central focus it previously lacked. It's a popular after-work drinking spot and crowds gather at the frequent events staged here, including short art films, live music and sporting events shown on the big screen. Rising up from St Kilda Road in a gentle incline, the square narrows into a horseshoe shape where it is hemmed in by the Ian Potter Centre, one of Melbourne's most interesting art museums (see p.103); the Melbourne Visitor Centre (see p.93); numerous cafés and restaurants; and the Alfred Deakin Building. The latter houses the **Australian Centre for the Moving Image** (ACMI; daily 10am–6pm; free; ℡03 8663 2200, ⓦwww .acmi.net.au), devoted to exploring the moving image in all its forms: film,

▲ Federation Square

television, games, art and new media. Worth checking out is the Screen Gallery, an underground exhibition space spanning the entire length of Federation Square featuring changing exhibitions of screen-based art; and Memory Grid on the ground floor, which displays film work by independent filmmakers, students and participants in ACMI workshops. Two state-of-the-art cinemas screen themed programmes and host film festivals and events. Group tours can be arranged by appointment, giving a lot of background information on architectural and technological aspects of ACMI and Federation Square.

Ian Potter Centre: NGV Australia

Walk from Flinders Street through the **Atrium** – a unique passageway of glass, steel and zinc – or from the main square through the similarly narrow **Crossbar** to reach the home of the National Gallery of Victoria's collection of Australian art, the **Ian Potter Centre: NGV Australia** (Tues–Sun 10am–5pm, Thurs until 9pm; free, except for special exhibitions; Ⓦ www.ngv.vic.gov.au), named in honour of Sir Ian Potter (1902–94), a local financier, philanthropist and patron of the arts. Occupying three floors, the centre showcases one of the best collections of Australian art in the country, with some seventy thousand works, of which about 1800 are usually on display (exhibits are rotated regularly). Traditional and contemporary indigenous art is displayed in four galleries on the ground floor, historic and modern Australian collections are housed on the second floor, and the galleries on the third floor are reserved for special temporary exhibitions. The artworks are complemented by interactive videos, which feature an overview of artists' works, with biographies and interviews.

The building itself is as much a work of art as its exhibits, constructed from two overlapping wings forming a slightly crooked "X" and offering constantly shifting views, with glimpses of the Yarra River and nearby parklands through the glass walls in the southern part of the building. The best way to get a handle on the collection, as well as the building, is to participate in a **free guided tour** (Mon–Fri 11am, noon & 2pm, Sat & Sun 11am & 2pm), which depart from the foyer on the ground floor.

Galleries 1–4 on the ground floor give an excellent overview of the art produced in Australia's **indigenous communities**, showcasing works in both traditional and contemporary styles. Traditional art is represented by carved and painted figures from Maningrida, masks from Torres Straits Islands, Pukumani poles from the Tiwi Islands north of Darwin, the Wandjina paintings from the north of Western Australia and bark paintings from Yirrkala and other places in Arnhem Land. One of the highlights is undoubtedly *Big Yam Dreaming* (1995), an enormous canvas by Emily Kam Kngwarray (*c.*1910–96) showing tangled, spidery webs of white against a black background, representing the pencil yam that grows along the creek banks at the artist's birthplace northeast of Alice Springs. In her brief career – she didn't take up painting until she was in her mid-70s – Emily produced a staggering three thousand-plus works, transcending the Western Desert-style dot paintings and developing a uniquely personal abstract and vibrantly coloured style, sometimes reminiscent of late Monet or Jackson Pollock.

On the second floor, galleries 5–11 contain paintings, sculptures, drawings, photographs and decorative arts from the mid-nineteenth century to the 1980s displayed in chronological order. One leitmotif is the harsh beauty of the Australian landscape, and European peoples' place in it. The early **colonial paintings** – with works by artists such as John Glover, Henry Burn, Frederick McCubbin and Tom Roberts – are particularly interesting, showing European artists struggling to come to terms with an alien land, as well as offering pictorial records of the growth of new cities and the lives of immigrants and pioneers.

Highlights of the twentieth-century collection include paintings by Albert Tucker, Russell Drysdale, John Perceval and, especially, **Sidney Nolan** (1917– 92). Dissatisfied with his Eurocentric art training at Prahran Technical College, Nolan strived to express the Australian experience in a fresh style, exploring new ways of seeing and painting the nation's landscapes, as in his *Wimmera* painting of the 1940s. Nolan also showed a unique interest in the histories of convicts, explorers and bushrangers, resulting in pictures such as his well-known *Ned Kelly* series (1946–48). Another highlight is the gallery dedicated to the overwhelming *Pilbara* collection of Fred Williams, painted in 1979 in the Pilbara region of Western Australia.

The CBD

Seen from the river, Melbourne's **Central Business District** presents a spectacular modern skyline; on close inspection, however, what you notice are the florid nineteenth-century facades, grandiose survivors of the great days of the gold rushes and after. The former Royal Mint on William Street near Flagstaff Gardens is one of the finest examples, but the main concentrations are south on **Collins Street** and along **Spring Street** to the east. At the centre of the CBD, trams jolt through the busy main shopping strip of **Bourke Street Mall**. A stone's throw from these central thoroughfares, narrow lanes, squares and arcades with quaint, hole-in-the-wall cafés, small restaurants, shops and boutiques add a cosy and intimate feel to the city.

Collins Street and around

Collins Street is *the* smart Melbourne address, becoming increasingly exclusive as you climb the hill to its eastern, rather hopefully named "Paris End". At the western end, the Stock Exchange squares up to the massive **Rialto Building** opposite: it was usurped as Melbourne's tallest structure by the Eureka Tower (see p.111) in 2006, but the reflective surface of its twin towers still lends the skyline a bit of oomph, and a trip to the **Melbourne Observation Deck** on the 55th floor provides a great view, particularly at dusk (daily 10am–10pm; A$14.50; Ⓦwww.melbournedeck.com.au). Nearby, at no. 333, the former **Commercial Bank of Australia** has a particularly sumptuous interior, with a domed banking chamber and awesome barrel-vaulted vestibule, which you can admire during business hours.

Further up Collins Street, shops become the focus of attention. Running north to Little Collins Street, the 1890s **Block Arcade** at nos. 282–284 is one of Melbourne's grandest shopping strips, its name taken from the tradition of "doing the block" – promenading around the city's fashionable shopping lanes. Restored in 1988, the L-shaped arcade sports a mosaic-tiled floor, ornate columns and mouldings, and a glass-domed roof. Almost opposite on the other side of Collins Street, **Centre Place** is an arcade of seamier nature, full of arty graffiti, funky shops of every calling and the best lunch joints in the city. Continue over Flinders Lane to **Degraves Street** for more of the same. **Flinders Lane** itself is worth a look, stuffed from Elizabeth Street to Spring Street with tiny, avant-garde galleries, cafés, bars and snazzy shops. The Anna Schwartz Gallery at no.185 (Tues–Fri noon–6pm, Sat 1–5pm; free; Ⓦwww .annaschwartzgallery.com) and Craft Victoria at no. 31 (Tues–Sat 10am–5pm; free; Ⓦwww.craftvic.asn.au) are among the best offerings.

Back on Collins, at the corner with Swanston Street, the Neoclassical **Melbourne Town Hall** squats on City Square. On the south side of the square is an unmissable landmark: the splendid **St Paul's Cathedral**, built in the 1880s to a Gothic Revival design by English architect William Butterfield (who never

Art in the city

Melbourne has a buzzing artistic community: there are over thirty **commercial gallery spaces** in the CBD, while further pockets of contemporary creative cool dot the inner suburbs of Fitzroy, Collingwood and Richmond (for listings, see ⓦwww .art-almanac.com.au). Head into the city centre's laneways and you may encounter thought-provoking sculptural works, video projections or light shows: the City of Melbourne nurtures and harnesses local talent by commissioning exciting **public installations** on a regular basis. In 2007, a particularly enlightened City initiative invited graffiti writers to give up on mindless tagging and channel their energies into **street art** instead. The owners of a large wall-space in **Union Lane**, off Bourke Street, gave full permission for a mentored group of young offenders to let rip; the resulting mural is a vivid addition to the streetscape.

actually visited Australia). Across from the cathedral, at 21–47 Swanston St, is the Art Deco **Nicholas Building** (see p.135), filled with niche boutiques, the Victorian Writers' Centre and various studios. Almost next door to the south, the restored *Young and Jackson's Hotel* is now protected by the National Trust, not for any intrinsic beauty but as a showcase for a work of art that has become a Melbourne icon: **Chloe**, a full-length nude, which now reclines upstairs in *Chloe's Bar and Bistro*. Exhibited by the French painter Jules Lefebvre at the Paris Salon of 1875, it was sent to an international exhibition in Melbourne in 1881 and has been here ever since.

Returning to Collins Street, the pompous **Athenaeum Theatre** next to the Town Hall is an important ingredient in the rising streetscape leading up past **Scots Church**, whose Gothic Revival design merits a peek, though it's famous mainly as the place where Dame Nellie Melba first sang in the choir. Further up, beyond expensive boutiques and souvenir shops, Collins Place and the towering **Hotel Sofitel** next door dominate the upper part of Collins Street: *Café La* on the 35th floor is worth a visit for the stunning panoramas from its windowside tables. Opposite, overshadowed by the *Sofitel* tower, stands one of the last bastions of Australian male chauvinism (in theory at least): the very staid, men-only **Melbourne Club**.

The Immigration Museum

Off the western end of Collins Street, at the corner of Flinders and William streets, the **Immigration Museum** (daily 10am–5pm; A\$6; ☎13 11 02, ⓦwww .immigration.museum.vic.gov.au) is dedicated to one of the central themes of Australian history. Housed in the beautifully restored Old Customs House, the museum builds a vivid picture of immigration history and personal stories using the spoken word, music, moving images, light effects and interactive screens, evoking the experiences of being a migrant on a square-rigger in the 1840s, a passenger on a steamship at the beginning of the twentieth century, or a postwar refugee from Europe. In the **Tribute Garden**, the outdoor centrepiece of the museum, a film of water flows over polished granite on which are engraved the names of migrants to Victoria, symbolizing the passage over the seas to reach these faraway shores. The names of all the Koorie people living in Victoria prior to white settlement are listed separately at the entrance to the garden.

Bourke Street Mall and Chinatown

Melbourne's main high-street shopping strip, **Bourke Street Mall**, extends west from Swanston Street to Elizabeth Street. After a fire gutted most of its interior in 2003, the Melbourne **General Post Office (GPO)**, an imposing

Victorian-era building at the mall's western end, was restored and reopened in late 2004 as a light and airy shopping complex for high-end designer clothes stores and upmarket eateries. Running off Bourke Street Mall, the lovely **Royal Arcade** is Melbourne's oldest (1839), paved with black-and-white marble and lit by huge fanlight windows. A clock on which two two-metre giants, Gog and Magog, strike the hours adds a hint of the grotesque. As you climb the hill east of here, Bourke Street keeps up the interest: the cafés and bars whose tables line the pavement at night include *Pellegrini's*, Melbourne's first espresso bar and still buzzing – with reams of laneway bars and late-opening book and record stores adding further colour.

Running parallel to the north of Bourke Street is Little Bourke Street, with the majestic **Law Courts** by William Street at the western end, and Chinatown in the east between Exhibition and Swanston streets. Australia's oldest continuous Chinese settlement, Melbourne's **Chinatown** began with a few boarding houses in the 1850s (when the gold rushes attracted Chinese people in droves) and grew as the gold began to run out and Chinese fortune-seekers headed back to the city. Today, the area still has a low-rise, narrow-laned, nineteenth-century feel, and is packed with restaurants, bars and stores. The **Chinese Museum**, in an old warehouse on Cohen Place (daily 10am–5pm; A$7.50; ☎03 9662 2888, ⓦwww.chinesemuseum.com.au), covers the Chinese role in the development of Melbourne, and is home to the Millennium dragon, the longest Chinese dragon in the world. The museum organizes the **Chinatown Heritage Walk**, a guided tour of the building and Chinatown (hours vary; 2hr A$18 or 3hr A$34 including Chinese banquet lunch; booking required).

QV, the State Library of Victoria and Melbourne Central

North of the Chinese Museum rises the latest bulk development in the CBD, the **QV precinct**, which takes up much of the block between Russell, Lonsdale, Swanston and La Trobe streets. The precinct is named after the Queen Victoria Women's Hospital, which occupied this site from 1896 until the late 1980s; it houses a shopping complex with a gym, supermarket, restaurants and bars, crisscrossed by open-air lanes.

Next to QV on Swanston Street is the **State Library of Victoria** (Mon–Thurs 10am–9pm & Fri–Sun 10am–6pm; ⓦwww.slv.vic.gov.au), which has free Wi-Fi. The building, dating from 1856, is a splendid example of Victorian architecture, and houses the state's largest research and reference library accessible to the public. The interior has been painstakingly refurbished and is well worth a visit, in particular the Cowen Gallery, which has a permanent display of paintings illustrating the changing look of Melbourne; the La Trobe Reading Room with its imposing domed roof; and the Dome Gallery dedicated to the history of Victoria. Also worth a mention is the **Chess Collection**: with almost 12,000 chess-related items, it's one of the three largest public collections in the world – you can play here, too. If you've been crunching the books for too long, pop into the fabulous attached *Mr Tulk* for a spot of brain food.

Opposite the State Library is the **Melbourne Central** shopping centre, which mirrors the QV concept of alleys and passageways lined with cafés, sushi bars and boutiques. On its top levels are several restaurants, a gym and a cinema complex.

Old Melbourne Gaol

A block north of the State Library, the **Old Melbourne Gaol** on Russell Street (daily 9.30am–5pm; A$18, child A$9.50; ☎03 8663 7228, ⓦwww .oldmelbournegaol.com.au) is one of the most fascinating sights in the CBD.

It's certainly the most popular, largely because outlaw and Australian folk hero **Ned Kelly** was hanged here in 1880 – the site of his execution, the beam from which he was hanged and his death mask are all on display, as is assorted armour worn by his gang of accomplices. The Hangman's Night Tour (2–4 nights a week: April–Oct 7.30pm, Nov–March 8.30pm; A\$30, child A\$22.50; advance bookings required with Ticketek, ☎13 28 49) uses the spooky atmosphere of the prison to full effect.

The bluestone prison was built in stages from 1841 to 1864 – the gold rushes of the 1850s caused such a surge in lawlessness that it kept having to be expanded. A mix of condemned men, remand and short-sentence prisoners, women and "lunatics" (often, in fact, drunks) were housed here; long-term prisoners languished in hulks moored at Williamstown, or at the Pentridge Stockade. Much has been demolished since the jail was closed in 1923, but the entrance and boundary walls at least survive, and it's worth walking round the building to take a look at the formidable arched brick portal on Franklin Street.

The gruesome collection of **death masks** on show in the tiny cells bears witness to the nineteenth-century obsession with phrenology, a wobbly branch of science which studied how people's characters were related to the size and shape of their skulls. Accompanying the masks are compelling case histories of the murderers and their victims. Most fascinating are the women: Martha Needle, who poisoned her husband and daughters (among others) with arsenic; and young Martha Knorr, the notorious "baby farmer", who advertised herself as a "kind motherly person, willing to adopt a child". After receiving a few dollars per child, she killed and buried them in her backyard. The jail serves up other macabre memorabilia, including a scaffold still in working order, various nooses, and a triangle where malcontents were strapped to receive lashes of the cat-o'-nine-tails. Perhaps the ultimate rite of passage for visitors is the "Art of Hanging", an interpretive display that's part educational tool and part setting for a medieval snuff-movie.

Queen Victoria Market

Opened in the 1870s, the **Queen Victoria Market** (Tues & Thurs 6am–2pm, Fri 6am–5pm, Sat 6am–3pm, Sun 9am–4pm; market office ☎03 9320 5822, Ⓦwww.qvm.com.au) is a much-loved Melbourne institution. The general merchandise market, housed in a collection of huge, open-sided sheds, is a boisterous, down-to-earth affair where you can buy anything from socks and sunglasses to boomerangs and sheepskin. The quaint high-roofed decorative halls, fronted along Victoria Street by restored shops, have a more hallowed feel, and contain reams of produce stalls. Here, stallholders and shoppers seem just as diverse as the goods on offer: Vietnamese, Italian and Greek greengrocers pile their colourful produce high and vie for your attention; Chinese and true-blue Aussie butchers and fishmongers raucously flog their last rump steak or kilo of prawns; and deliciously smelly cheeses from around the world effortlessly draw customers to the old-fashioned deli hall. Saturday morning, the best time to visit, marks a weekly social ritual as Melbourne's foodies turn out for their weekly grocery shop with trolleys in tow. The market office handles bookings for the guided **Foodies Dream Tour** (Tues, Thurs, Fri & Sat 10am–noon; A\$30 including food sampling and coffee), taking in all the culinary delights of the market, and classes at the resident **Cooking School** (from A\$80 for a 2hr 30min session). The action-packed **Night Market** (weekly on Wed from late Nov to late Feb, 5.30–10pm) has music, bars and over thirty stalls offering curries, Dutch pancakes and paella, amongst other delights.

Royal Exhibition Building and Melbourne Museum

Just beyond the CBD's northeast corner are the tranquil **Carlton Gardens**, home to one of Melbourne's most significant historic landmarks – the **Royal Exhibition Building**. It was built by David Mitchell (father of Dame Nellie Melba) for the International Exhibition of 1880 and visited by 1.5 million people. In later years this is where Australia's first parliament sat in 1901, and the Victorian State Parliament from 1901–27. It was also used as a sporting venue for the 1956 Melbourne Olympics. The magnificent Neoclassical edifice, with its soaring dome and huge entrance portal, is the only substantially intact example in the world of a Great Hall from a major exhibition; its scale and grandeur reflect the values and aspirations attached to industrialization, so much so that in 2004 Carlton Gardens and the Royal Exhibition Building were inscribed on the UNESCO World Heritage List. Tours of the building (daily 2pm; 1hr; A$5) depart from the Melbourne Museum next door.

Melbourne Museum (daily 10am–5pm; A$6, free for children; Ⓦwww .melbourne.museum.vic.gov.au) is an ultramodern, state-of-the-art museum, which makes a dramatic contrast to its nineteenth-century neighbour with its geometric forms, vibrant colours, immense blade-like roof and greenhouse accommodating a lush fern gully flanked by a canopy of tall forest trees. The museum, which includes a permanent collection exploring life in Victoria, and a hall for major touring exhibitions, has been designed with the multimedia generation in mind – glass-covered display cabinets are few and far between.

Highlights of the museum include the **Science and Life Gallery**, which covers the plants and animals inhabiting the southern lands and seas; **Bunjilaka**, the Museum's Aboriginal Centre, showcasing an extraordinary collection of Koori Aboriginal culture from Victoria and further afield (curving for 30m at the entrance is *Wurreka*, a wall of zinc panels etched with Aboriginal artefacts, shells, plants and fish); and the **Australia Gallery**, focusing on the history of Melbourne and Victoria, and featuring the legendary racehorse Phar Lap (reputedly Australia's most popular museum exhibit) and a kitchen set from the TV show *Neighbours*. Also of interest are the **Evolution Gallery**, which looks at the earth's history and holds an assortment of dinosaur casts, and the **Children's Museum**, where the exhibition gallery, "Big Box", is built in the shape of a giant, tiled cube painted in brightly coloured squares. One of the most striking exhibits is the **Forest Gallery**, a living, breathing indoor rainforest containing over 8000 plants from more than 120 species, including 25-metre-tall gums, as well as birds, insects, snakes, lizards and fish. **Tours** are available (daily, ask for start times; 45–60min; free). Also part of the museum, the **IMAX Melbourne Museum** boasts a huge screen and shows films with reels so big it takes a forklift truck to shift them. It shows some standard-format films but majors in 3D: mostly adventure documentaries or anything involving a Tyrannosaurus Rex (up to 7 different screenings daily; A$17.50–20 or A$20.50–23 including museum admission, child A$12.50–15; Ⓣ03 9663 5454, Ⓦwww .imaxmelbourne.com.au).

Parliament House and around

The area east of Spring Street has many fine public buildings, centred around **Parliament House**. Erected in stages between 1856 and 1930, the parliament buildings (daily guided tours on non-sitting days 10am, 11am, noon, 2pm, 3pm & 3.45pm; free; Ⓣ03 9651 8568, Ⓦwww.parliament.vic.gov.au) have a theatrical presence, with a facade of giant Doric columns rising from a high flight of steps, and landscaped gardens either side. Nearby, the 1857 **Old Treasury Building** and adjacent State Government Office, facing the lush Treasury Gardens, are equally imposing. The **City Museum** in the Old Treasury features a multimedia exhibition, *Built on Gold*, displayed in the old gold-vaults deep in the basement (Mon–Fri 9am–5pm, Sat & Sun 10am–4pm; A\$8.50, child A\$5; ⓣ03 9651 2233, ⓦwww.citymuseummelbourne.org), which illustrates the impact of the Victorian gold rushes on the fledgling colony. Three other permanent exhibitions on various aspects of Melbourne's history share the ground floor with temporary shows.

East of Parliament House, the beautiful **Fitzroy Gardens** offer great views of the city skyscrapers, and are a favourite getaway from the CBD for locals and tourists alike. Originally laid out in the shape of the Union Jack flag, the paths here still just about conform to the original pattern, and the attractive flower displays at the **Conservatory** (daily 9am–5pm; free), statuary, and tropical and native plants on show offer more interest than the traditional-style Carlton Gardens. The gardens' much-touted main attraction is really only for kitsch fans: **Captain Cook's Cottage** (daily 9am–5pm; A\$4.50, child A\$2.20; ⓣ03 9419 4677) was rebuilt in Melbourne in 1934 after being shipped over from England. Captain James Cook, the English navigator who first "discovered" Australia's East Coast, is supposed to have lived in the cottage in his formative years and visited his father there on his return from Australia.

The MCG and around

South of Fitzroy Gardens lies **Yarra Park**, containing the hallowed **Melbourne Cricket Ground (MCG)** – also easily reached by tram 75 from Flinders Street or train to Jolimont station. Hosting state and international cricket matches and some of the top Aussie Rules football games, the "G" is one of sports-mad Melbourne's best-loved icons, especially when its six immense 85-metre towers pour light into the surrounding area during night matches. Home to the Melbourne Cricket Club since 1853, the complex was totally reconstructed for the 1956 Olympic Games – only the historic members' stand survived – before redevelopments for the Commonwealth Games in 2006 pushed the ground's capacity to approximately 100,000. Bronze statues of cricketing, AFL and athletic greats surround the ground, with Dennis Lillee the latest to be unveiled in 2007. **Tours** of the ground (daily except event days 10am–3pm; every 30min; 1hr 15min; A\$15, child A\$8; tour plus NSM entrance A\$22/A\$12; ⓣ03 9657 8879, ⓦwww.mcg.org.au) depart from Gate 3 in the Olympic Stand and offer the chance to visit the players' changing rooms and coaches' boxes, plus a walk on the hallowed turf if you're lucky.

In 2008, the **National Sports Museum** opened in the MCG's Olympic Stand (daily 10am–5pm, call or check website for event-day restrictions; A\$15, child A\$8; entry plus MCG Tour A\$22/A\$12; ⓣ03 9657 8879, ⓦwww.nsm .org.au), incorporating many old sporting attractions such as the Australian Cricket Hall of Fame, AFL World and the Australian Gallery of Sport and Olympic Museum. Items such as Ian Thorpe's swimsuit, Don Bradman's "Baggy Green" cap and more prosaic headgear belonging to Shane Warne also feature, along with displays on the myriad other sports at which Aussies excel. In the Australia's Game section, Aussie Rules aficionados have the chance to step into the imaginary shoes of a footy player and follow his journey through the build-up of Grand Final week, culminating in the finale on Saturday.

From the MCG, pedestrian bridges over Brunton Avenue lead to **Melbourne Park**; here, Rod Laver Arena and Vodafone Arena play host to the Australian

Open tennis championship in January (see p.90), with cycling, basketball and music concerts throughout the rest of the year. Over Swan Street, **Melbourne Olympic Park** is where the Melbourne Storm rugby league team play their matches – the area will soon be redeveloped to include a new stadium for "the Storm" and their soccer counterparts, Melbourne Victory.

Birrarung Marr

Melbourne's newest park, **Birrarung Marr**, lies alongside the Yarra River and forms a striking link between the Melbourne Park sports precinct and Federation Square. "Birrarung" means "River of Mists", while "Marr" refers to the side the river. The 525-metre-long, musical William Barak **footbridge** intersects the park from the MCG in the northeast to the Yarra River in the southwest, giving spectacular views of the city skyline, the sports arenas and the river, particularly at sunset. A popular events space, the park contains a play area, children's arts centre and gallery, the colourful two-headed "Angel" sculpture and the **Federation Bells**; a collection of 39 variously sized, computer-controlled bells, created to commemorate the Centenary of Federation in 2001, they ring out across Birrarung Marr three times a day (8–9am, 12.30–1.30pm & 5–6pm).

The Yarra River and around

Despite its brownish tinge, a walk along the **Yarra River** offers some of the finest views in town; the riverside promenades are especially ambient at dusk or at night. The much-mocked **river** has always been – and still is – an important part of the Melbourne scene. Traditionally home to the city docks, tidal movements of up to 2m meant frequent flooding, a problem only partly solved by artificially straightening the river and building up its banks – this also had the incidental benefit of reserving tracts of low-lying land as recreational space, which are now pleasingly crisscrossed by paths and cycle tracks and backed by pretty boathouses. Five **bridges** cross the river from the CBD: Spencer Street Bridge at the end of Spencer Street; Kings Bridge on King Street; Queens Bridge, not quite at the end of Queen Street; the

▲ Riverboat cruising the Yarra

River and bay cruises

Cruise boats ply the Yarra River on a daily basis: the main departure points are **Princes Walk** (Northbank Promenade) on the southern side of Federation Square, and the **Southgate precinct**, Southbank. Tickets can be bought from the wharfside booths, or on board. All cruises run, weather permitting, in the cooler months (May–Sept), the last scheduled departures of the day may be cancelled. It's also possible to visit a **penguin colony** in Port Phillip Bay, or to cruise the western suburbs' **Maribyrnong River**, for a side of Melbourne tourists don't usually get to see – contrary to the prejudices of eastern suburbanites, it's not all factory yards and oil-storage containers.

City River Cruises Princes Walk Berth 4 and Southbank Berth C ☎03 9650 2214, ⓦwww.cityrivercruises.com.au. Head downstream to the Port of Melbourne and Docklands, or upstream to Herring Island (Como), passing many famous landmarks on the way – or combine both trips (4–5 daily; 1hr; A$19.80, child A$11; 2hr A$38.80/A$20).

Maribyrnong Cruises Saltriver Place, Footscray (15min walk from Footscray station on the Sydenham/Werribee line, or 5min walk from bus stop 17 on route 216 or 219 from Queen St) ☎03 9689 6431, ⓦwww.blackbirdcruises.com.au. The Maribyrnong River Cruise shows the tranquil and pretty side of the supposedly drab western suburbs (Tues, Thurs, Sat & Sun 1–3pm; A$16, child A$5), while the Port of Melbourne Cruise takes in the industrial areas and dockland developments of the lower Maribyrnong and Yarra rivers (Tues, Thurs, Sat & Sun 4–5pm; 1hr; A$8, child A$5).

Melbourne River Cruises Lower Promenade Berth 5, Southgate ☎03 8610 2600, ⓦwww.melbcruises.com.au. The River Gardens Cruise heads upriver past South Yarra and Richmond to Herring Island; the Port and Docklands Cruise runs downriver past Crown Casino and Melbourne Exhibition Centre to the Westgate Bridge (5–6 daily; 1hr 15min each; A$22 for one cruise, child A$11, or A$29/A$16 for both cruises).

Penguin Waters Cruises Lower Promenade Berth 1, Southgate ☎03 9386 8488, ⓦwww.penguinwaters.com.au. Sunset cruise along the Yarra to a little penguin colony in Port Phillip Bay, 4km from the mouth of the Yarra. They're the same species as the Phillip Island penguins (see p.163); this is the only cruise vessel permitted to visit them (daily; 2hr; A$55, child A$30, includes dinner and wine).

Williamstown Ferries Lower Promenade Berth 1, Southgate ☎03 9682 9555, ⓦwww.williamstownferries.com.au. These boats cruise the lower Yarra, heading southwest to Williamstown, via the Scienceworks museum (see p.121) in Spotswood (8 daily; 1hr; A$15 one way, child A$7.50; A$25/A$12.50 return).

sculpture-heavy Sandridge Bridge; and finally Princes Bridge, which carries Swanston Street across. There's also a pedestrian bridge from the bank below Flinders Street station to the Southgate Centre. The best way to see the Yarra is on a cruise – see the box above.

On the south side of Princes Bridge you can **rent bikes** to explore the riverbanks (see p.136); on fine weekends, especially, the Yarra comes to life, with people messing about in boats, cycling and strolling. **Southgate**, immediately west of Princes Bridge, is an upmarket shopping complex with lots of smart cafés and restaurants, and a huge food court.

Southbank and Melbourne Aquarium

Southbank continues west of Southgate; behind all the riverfront eateries lies Melbourne's tallest building, the soaring **Eureka Tower** on Riverside Quay, whose distinctive golden tip gleams as it catches the sun. From the tower's 88th-floor SkyDeck (daily 10am–10pm; A$16.50, child A$9; ⓦwww.eurekalookout .com.au) the CBD's skyscrapers stand out like Lego buildings from the mostly flat city. For an additional A$12 (chilld A$8) you can take on The Edge, a glass-walled, glass-floored cube that suspends you 300m above the ground.

At the western end of Southbank lies the **Crown Casino**, Australia's largest gambling and entertainment venue, stretching across 600m of riverfront between Queens Bridge and Spencer Street Bridge. Next door, the **Melbourne Exhibition Centre** is a whimsical example of the city's dynamic new architec-tural style: facing the river is an immense 450-metre-long glass wall, while the street entrance has an awning resembling a ski jump propped up by wafer-thin pylons. At the time of writing, the interesting **Maritime Museum** was closed for extensive renovations (due to reopen in late 2008). The museum's most popular exhibit, the *Polly Woodside*, remains outside on the river for viewing. A small, barque-rigged sailing ship, it was built in Belfast in 1885 for the South American coal trade and retired only in 1968, when it was the last deep-water sailing vessel in Australia still afloat.

On the other side of the river, near the corner of Flinders and King streets, is the **Melbourne Aquarium** (daily: Jan 9.30am–9pm; Feb–Dec 9.30am–6pm; A$26.50, child A$16; ⓦwww.melbourneaquarium.com.au). The curved, four-storey aquarium harbours thousands of creatures from the Southern Ocean. Part of it is taken up by the Oceanarium tank, which rests 7m below the Yarra, holding over two million litres of water and containing 3200 animals from 150 species. There's also a stingray-filled tank with a wave machine, and a glass-walled room that's like a fish bowl turned inside out: you stand in the middle to watch the sharks swim around you. You can even **dive** with the sharks and stingrays (3 times daily; certified divers with equipment A$150; certified divers plus equipment hire A$242; non-divers $A349).

Docklands and Telstra Dome

Downstream from the aquarium lies the old **Docklands**, now transformed into a new waterfront city district. Melburnians have been slow to take to the area's snazzy apartments and slightly sterile cafés and bars, although plenty of big companies have moved in. The pleasant promenades merit an hour's stroll, particularly for the urban art scattered around, including the "cow up a tree" and the Webb Bridge, whose design alludes to Koorie fishing traps. Squat in the middle of it all sits another of Melbourne's giant sporting venues, **Telstra Dome**, a 54,000-seater stadium for AFL, soccer and rugby-union matches, as well as concerts by big-name artists. A wide pedestrian footbridge crosses the railway tracks at Southern Cross Station, connecting Telstra Dome and the Docklands district with Spencer Street and the CBD.

The Arts Centre, NGV and around

Just south of the Yarra over Princes Bridge is **The Arts Centre** on St Kilda Road (ⓦwww.theartscentre.com.au), comprising the Hamer Hall, the Theatres Building and the Sidney Myer Music Bowl, an open-air venue across St Kilda Road in Kings Domain (see p.113). At the top of the Theatres Building is a 162-metre-tall **spire** whose curved lower sections are meant to evoke the flowing folds of a ballerina's skirt; the spire turns an iridescent blue at night. A **guided tour** of Hamer Hall and the Theatres Building provides an insight into the history of the centre and gives an overview of the architecture and design (Mon–Sat 11am; A$11), while the **backstage tour** ventures behind the curtains, taking in the dressing rooms and costumes (Sun 12.15pm; A$11);

tickets for both can be bought from the foyer in the Theatres Building. The many other studios and spaces in the centre host visual-arts collections, avant-garde drama productions and concerts – check the website for listings.

The bluestone building next to the Theatres Building is home to the **National Gallery of Victoria (NGV)**, Australia's oldest public art museum. After extensive refurbishments, it reopened in late 2003 and now houses a collection of international works under the name **NGV International** (daily except Tues 10am–5pm; free, fee for temporary exhibitions; Ⓦwww.ngv.vic.gov.au), having moved its Australian collection to the Ian Potter Centre (see p.103). Overall exhibition space was increased, while features such as the **Waterwall** at the entrance – a water curtain flowing down a twenty-metre-wide glass wall – and the **Great Hall** on the ground floor, with its beautiful stained-glass ceiling, were retained, as were the landscaped **Grimwade Gardens**. The ground floor contains three large rooms for temporary exhibitions plus galleries dedicated to Oceanic Art, Pre-Columbian, Egyptian and Near Eastern, as well as Greek and Roman Antiquities. Level 1 has rooms displaying paintings, decorative arts and sculpture from the fourteenth to the seventeenth century, whilst level 2 focuses on the seventeenth to the mid-twentieth centuries: the Flemish and Dutch masters, including the Rembrandt Cabinet, are some of the highlights here. The contemporary era is represented using installations and photos on level 3. A couple of cafés are complemented by the pleasant *Garden Restaurant* (daily 11.30am–3pm), overlooking the Grimwade Gardens. Along with **tours** of the collection (Mon & Wed–Fri 11am, noon & 2pm, Sat & Sun 11am & 2pm; free) the NGV has a regular programme of talks, lectures, and other activities – check the gallery's website for details.

Further south, at 111 Sturt St, the **Australian Centre for Contemporary Art** (ACCA; Tues–Fri 10am–5pm, Sat & Sun 11am–6pm; free; Ⓦwww.accaonline.org.au) has consistently challenging exhibitions of contemporary international and Australian art.

On Sunday (10am–6pm), a touristy but highly browsable **arts and crafts market** lines the pavement outside The Arts Centre, extending onto the footpath under the Princes Bridge.

Kings Domain

Across St Kilda Road from the National Gallery of Victoria, the grassy open parkland of **Kings Domain** encompasses the **Sidney Myer Music Bowl**, an outdoor music arena that is part of The Arts Centre. South of the bowl on Government House Drive, behind imposing iron gates with stone pillars and a British coat of arms, you can glimpse the flag flying over **Government House**, the ivory mansion of the governor of Victoria, set in extensive grounds. The National Trust runs **guided tours** of the house (Mon & Wed by appointment; A\$15; ☏03 9656 9841, Ⓦwww.nattrust.com.au), the highlight being the opulent state ballroom, which occupies the entire south wing.

Further south on Dallas Brooks Drive is Victoria's very first Government House, **La Trobe's Cottage** (Sun 1–4pm; gold-coin donation; or included in Government House tour). Relocated from its original site at Jolimont, it serves as a memorial to Lieutenant-Governor Charles Joseph La Trobe, who lived in this tiny house from 1840 to 1854. The cottage, featuring interesting displays on La Trobe and the early days of the colony, presents a compelling contrast to the current governor's residence.

The Shrine of Remembrance, in formal grounds in the southwestern corner of Kings Domain, was completed in 1934. It's a rather Orwellian monument, apparently half-Roman temple, half-Aztec pyramid, given further chill when a mechanical-sounding voice booms out and calls you in to see the symbolic light inside. The shrine is designed so that at 11am on Remembrance Day (11 Nov) a ray of sunlight strikes the memorial stone inside – an effect that's simulated every half-hour.

Royal Botanic Gardens

East of Kings Domain, the **Royal Botanic Gardens** (daily 7.30am–dusk; free) contain 12,000 different plant species and over 50,000 individual plants, as well as native wildlife such as cockatoos and kookaburras, in an extensive landscaped setting. Melbourne's much-maligned climate is perfect for horticulture: cool enough for temperate trees and flowers to flourish, warm enough for palms and other subtropical species, and wet enough for anything else. The bright and airy **visitor centre** at the Italianate Observatory on Birdwood Avenue (Mon–Fri 9am–5pm, Sat & Sun 9.30am–5pm; ☎03 9252 2429, ⊛www.rbg.vic.gov.au) is the best place to start your wanderings.

Highlights include the **herb garden**, comprising part of the medicinal garden established in 1880; the **fern gully**, a lovely walk through shady ferns; the large ornamental **lake** full of ducks, black swans and eels; and various **hothouses** where exotic cacti and fascinating plants such as the Venus Flytrap thrive. A topical feature, given Australia's battle against drought, is the **Water Conservation Garden**, where lush florals are out and plants that can tolerate dry conditions are in. The *Observatory Gate Café,* next to the visitor centre (daily 7am–5pm), and *The Terrace* by the lake (daily: May–Sept 9.45am–4pm; Oct–April 9am–5pm) will keep you fed and watered.

The visitor centre takes bookings for a multitude of seasonal **guided walks** and **workshops**, including stargazing experiences and Aboriginal Heritage walks (prices vary, some free). Every second Saturday of the month, the **Gardens Market** (9am–2pm; ⊛www.marketsinthegarden.com.au) is held, where one hundred stallholders sell plants, art and gourmet food.

On summer evenings, plays are often performed in the gardens, and cinema buffs can swap popcorn for picnic baskets from mid-December to mid-March when art-house, cult and classic films are projected onto a big outdoor screen at the **Moonlight Cinema** (A$16 or A$14 online; ⊛www.moonlight.com.au). Enter at D Gate on Birdwood Avenue; films start at sunset – don't forget to take an extra layer of clothing, a rug and, most importantly, insect repellent. Skirting the Botanic Gardens is **The Tan**, a 3.8-kilometre running track with some killer hills; it's always swarming with casual joggers and footy teams putting in the hard yards.

Melbourne suburbs

Far more than in the city centre, it's in Melbourne's **inner suburbs** that you'll really get a feel for what life here is really all about. Many have quite distinct characters, whether as ethnic enclaves or self-styled artists' communities. What's more, all can easily be reached by a pleasurable tram ride from the centre.

Browsing through markets and shops, cruising across Hobsons Bay, sampling the world's foods and, of course, sipping espresso are the primary attractions of the suburbs. Café society finds its home to the north among the alternative galleries and secondhand shops of **Fitzroy**, while Italian espresso bars that once fuelled the Beat Generation still thrive on Lygon Street in nearby **Carlton**, though boutiques now far outnumber bookshops. Grungier **Richmond**, to the east, was originally a working-class area, and the reams of workers' cottages that remain make it a popular residential suburb. South of the river is the place to shop until you drop, whether at wealthy **South Yarra** and **Toorak**, self-consciously cool **Prahran** or up-and-coming Windsor. To the south, **St Kilda** has the advantage of a beachside location to go with its trendy but raucous nightlife. To firm up your itinerary with something more concrete, make for the well-designed **Melbourne Zoo** in Parkville, or **Scienceworks**, a hugely enjoyable interactive museum in Spotswood. Also of interest is the **Heide Museum of Modern Art** in Bulleen and, a bit further along in the same direction, **Eltham**, with its artists' colony of **Montsalvat**.

Carlton and Parkville

Carlton lies just north of the city (tram 1 or 8 from Swanston Street) but, with its university presence and its long-established Italian restaurant scene, it could be a million miles away. **Lygon Street** is the centre of the action, and it was here, in the 1950s, that espresso bars were really introduced to Melbourne; exotic spots such as *Caffe Sport*, *La Gina*, *University Caffe* and *Toto's* (which claims to have introduced pizza to Australia) had an unconventional allure in staid Anglo-Melbourne, and the local intelligentsia soon made the street their second home. Victorian terraced houses provided cheap living, and Carlton became the first of the city's "alternative" suburbs. These days, the area is no longer bohemian – its residents are older and wealthier, and Lygon Street has gone definitively upmarket. The strip's smart fashion shops, delis, and bookshops still draw the crowds though, especially for a bowl of pasta or *gelati* on a summer's evening.

Whilst Lygon Street itself is the obvious place to explore, the elegant architecture also spreads eastwards to Drummond, Rathdowne and Nicholson streets. Running along the western side of the university, Royal Parade gives onto **Royal Park**, with its memorial to nineteenth-century explorers Robert O'Hara Burke and William John Wills, from where it's a short walk through the park to the zoo.

Melbourne Zoo

When it opened in 1862, **Melbourne Zoo** (daily 9am–5pm; A\$23, child A\$11.50; tram 55 from William Street or train from Flinders Street Station to Royal Park on the Upfield line; Ⓦwww.zoo.org.au) was the first in Australia. On hot days, the leafy trails around the zoo offer a great escape from the sun, and the animals are housed in more natural and spacious enclosures than you tend to see elsewhere. The Australian area contains a central lake with waterbirds, open enclosures for koalas and a bushland setting where you can walk among emus, kangaroos and wallabies. The monkey enclosures and Thai-inspired elephant sanctuary are amongst the most popular here, and the dark **Platypus House** is also worth a look, since the mammals are notoriously difficult to see in the wild – even here, there's no guarantee you'll get lucky. The entrancing **Butterfly House**, a steamy tropical hothouse with hundreds of colourful butterflies flitting about, is also highly enjoyable. You can **camp overnight** at the zoo on its Roar 'n' Snore programme (\$180, child A\$130; Ⓣ03 9285 9355, bookings required). On Saturdays and Sundays from mid-January to mid-March, the zoo stays open until 9.30pm for the **Zoo Twilights** concert series, with jazz, swing and rock bands playing on the central lawn (A\$34, child A\$27).

Fitzroy

In the 1970s, **Fitzroy** took over from Carlton as the home of the city's artistic community. The district's focus is **Brunswick Street** (tram 112 from Collins

Street), especially between Gertrude Street and Alexander Parade. In the shadow of Housing Commission tower blocks, welfare agencies rub shoulders with funky shops of every description, quirky bars, bustling restaurants, and thriving bookstores that open as late as the bars and are usually just as busy. Most are full of urban hipsters, artists, writers and musicians, inevitably dressed in the Fitzroy uniform of grey and black layers. Amongst the stream of attractive coloured shopfronts, the **Fitzroy Nursery** at 390 Brunswick St has an eye-catching wrought-iron gate with fairy-tale motif, and a garden-envy-inducing Artists Garden upstairs, which exhibits sculptures and other outdoor bits and bobs. Many of the rough old hotels have been done up to match the prevailing mood: *Café Provincial* is a good example, with its distressed paint-job, although some great pubs (see p.129) have remained untouched down the pretty sidestreets, which are jammed with desirable warehouse-style apartments.

Close to Brunswick Street, secondary Fitzroy precincts are being forged with their own distinct characters: on **Johnston Street**, lively Spanish bars are the mainstay, while a block to the south, **Gertrude Street** is *the* new trendy address, with vintage clothes and retro homewares mixed in with cool bars, cafés and restaurants.

The much-loved Brunswick Street Parade traditionally kicked off the Melbourne Fringe Festival, until celebrations got too big to handle. Fitzroy's fringe culture leanings are still reflected though, with plenty of band rooms, wacky "street installations" including mosaic chairs, and sculptures such as *Mr Poetry*. Fitzroy also boasts the unique **Rose Street Artists Market** at 60 Rose St (Sat 11am–5pm), where fashion designers, painters, photographers, ceramicists, sculptors and other artists sell their work. The **Fitzroy Pool** (see "Listings", p.139), in the north of the suburb on the corner of Young and Cecil streets, is a fifty-metre outdoor pool where in summer people occasionally swim between posing sessions.

Collingwood, Abbotsford and Richmond

In a city that's constantly looking for the next big thing, whisperings that Brunswick Street is "over" have been heard for some time, with many of its cool cats decamping a block east to **Smith Street** (tram 86 from Bourke St) in **Collingwood**. Smith Street is catching up with Brunswick Street fast, but you'll still find quite a few charity shops, ethnic butchers and cheap supermarkets that the edgy bookshops and record stores, warehouse lofts, quirky little cafés and revamped pubs haven't managed to push out of business. The **Lost and Found Market** at no. 127A (Mon–Fri from noon, Sat & Sun from 11am) is a treasure trove of books, furniture and clothes, mostly of a retro bent. The top end of Smith Street past Johnston Street is bargain-shopping territory, especially for heavily reduced sportswear and outdoor equipment.

To the east, **Collingwood Children's Farm** – not strictly in Collingwood but in St Heliers Street, Abbotsford – is nestled on a bend of the Yarra River (daily 10am–5pm; ⓦ www.farm.org.au). The farm's raison d'être is to teach city-dwelling folk about the joys of country living, and in that it succeeds admirably; only 5km out the city, it feels more like five hundred, and you can milk a cow, feed the chooks and visit the *Farm Café* to boot. The Farmers Market here, held every second Saturday of the month, is well worth the trip. On the same site is the wonderful **Abbotsford Convent** (ⓦ www.abbotsfordconvent.com.au), an emerging centre for artists, filmmakers and designers; check the website to see what classes and workshops are scheduled, or just wander around the restored building and gardens. Catch the Epping line train from Flinders Street Station and get off at Victoria Park, from where it's a five-minute walk along Johnston Street.

Richmond, directly south, can be divided up into the three huge strips that run through it: Swan Street, home to a diverse pub-music scene; Bridge Road, with a wealth of discount designer stores; and Victoria Street, the city's most accessible Vietnamese enclave.

The southeastern suburbs

Southeast of the river, the suburbs of South Yarra, Prahran and Toorak are home to the city's biggest **shopping** area, both grungy and upmarket. **Chapel Street** is the main drag: in **South Yarra**, it extends for a golden mile of trendy shopping, cooler-than-thou nightclubs and chic cafés full of skinny blondes with swishy hair; heading south beyond Commercial Road through **Prahran** and **Windsor**, the glossy streetscape takes on a refreshingly chequered, ruddier appearance. Crossing Chapel Street at right angles in South Yarra, Toorak Road boasts equally ritzy designer boutiques and, if that's possible, becomes even more exclusive east of Grange Road, as it enters **Toorak**, a suburb synonymous with wealth. Tram 8 heads via the northern end of Chapel Street to Toorak, while the 72 and 6 drop you in downtown Prahran, and the 64 and 5 in Windsor – all run via St Kilda Road from Swanston Street in the city. South Yarra, Prahran and Windsor can all be reached by train – take the Sandringham line from Flinders Street Station.

South Yarra, Toorak and Armadale

Standing out like a sore thumb amidst Chapel Street's wall-to-wall chic is the **Jam Factory** shopping complex, named after its former incarnation, and now full of middle-of-the-road shops and a cinema. To escape the endless air-kissing head to **Como Historic House and Gardens**, overlooking the river from Lechlade Avenue in South Yarra (daily 10am–5pm; house on garden A$12, garden only A$5; access to the house on one-hour guided tour only). This elegant white mansion, a mixture of Regency and Italianate architectural styles, is a good example of the townhouses built by wealthy nineteenth-century landowners. To reach the house, walk east along Toorak Road from Chapel Street, and then north on Williams Road; from the city centre, take tram 8 from Swanston Street.

Toorak has never been short of a bean: when Melbourne was founded, the wealthy built their stately homes here on the high bank of the Yarra, leaving the flood-prone lower ground for the poor; in addition, many European Jews who made good after arriving penniless celebrated their new wealth by moving to Toorak in the 1950s and 60s. There's little to see or do in the suburb save wander around and try to hide your jealousy: the hilly, tree-lined streets are full of huge mansions in extensive private gardens, while Toorak Village is stuffed with wickedly expensive designer boutiques. A suburb to the south, **Armadale** is well known for its antique shops – take tram 6 from Swanston Street or St Kilda Road.

Prahran and Windsor

Beyond Commercial Road in **Prahran** proper, Chapel Street still focuses on fashion, but in a more street-smart vein, becoming progressively more downmarket as it heads south. Landmarks include **Prahran Market** (Tues & Sat dawn–5pm, Thurs & Fri dawn–6pm, Sun 10am–3pm), round the corner on Commercial Road, an excellent though expensive food market selling fruit, veggies, meat, fish and deli produce. **Chapel Street Bazaar**, on the western side of Chapel Street, has good secondhand clothes, Art Deco jewellery, furniture and bric-a-brac. Just opposite, tucked away in Little Chapel Street, **Chapel off Chapel** (☎03 8290 7000 for bookings and information) provides a venue for an eclectic mix of theatre performances, music and art exhibitions. Heading a further 100m south along Chapel Street brings you to **Greville Street**, in the heart of Prahran, which has taken over from Chapel Street as the corridor of cutting-edge cool, with retro and designer boutiques, music outlets, bookshops, and groovy bars and restaurants. Things really hot up over the weekend, and every Sunday the small **Greville Street Market** sells arts, crafts and secondhand clothes and jewellery on the corner of Gratton Street in Gratton Gardens (noon–5pm).

As Chapel Street crosses High Street the suburb changes to **Windsor** and becomes more interestingly ethnic. Discount furniture and household-appliance shops sit cheek by jowl with inexpensive Asian noodle bars, organic-produce shops and up-and-coming café-bars. Busy Dandenong Road marks the boundary of Windsor and **St Kilda East**. Just across Dandenong Road on Chapel Street lies the **Astor Theatre** (ⓦwww.astor-theatre.com), a beautifully decorated cinema in an Art Nouveau building.

South Melbourne, Albert Park and Port Melbourne

If it's the bay you're heading for, then **St Kilda** is the obvious destination, but further west, South Melbourne, Albert Park and Port Melbourne provide compelling alternatives. **South Melbourne**'s focus is the **South Melbourne Market** on the corner of Coventry and Cecil streets (Wed, Sat & Sun 8am–4pm, Fri 8am–6pm), an old-fashioned, value-for-money place where you can browse stalls selling everything from fruit and vegetables to clothes and continental delicacies. At the other end of Coventry Street, **Clarendon Street** is South Melbourne's main shopping precinct, and a fine example of a nineteenth-century streetscape, with original Victorian awnings overhanging numerous cafés, clothing shops and restaurants. Tram 112 runs from Collins Street down Clarendon Street, while the 96 from Bourke Street stops closer to the market.

Exclusive **Albert Park** maintains a cosy, village-like atmosphere. The many lovely old terraced houses here line quiet, stylish streets that run into central Dundas Place, which is filled with mouthwatering delis and bakeries. The number 1 tram from Swanston Street runs through Dundas Place and down restaurant-lined Victoria Avenue to Albert Park's popular **beach**, where workers congregate to cool off during the summer heat. East of Dundas Place is the **Melbourne Sports and Aquatic Centre** or MSAC (see p.139), the venue for swimming events at the 2006 Commonwealth Games. Adjacent to MSAC, in the shadow of the St Kilda Road office buildings, lies Albert Park itself, home of the Australian Grand Prix in March and popular with joggers due to the five-kilometre running track that edges the large, pretty lake.

West of Albert Park is **Port Melbourne**; the main strip here, Bay Street, has similarly enticing pubs and boutiques, and leads down to the port from where the majestic *Spirit of Tasmania* sets off on her nightly journey across the pond.

St Kilda

The former seaside resort of **St Kilda** has an air of shabby gentility, which enhances its current schizophrenic reputation as a sophisticated yet seedy suburb, largely residential but blessed with a busy café scene and raging nightlife.

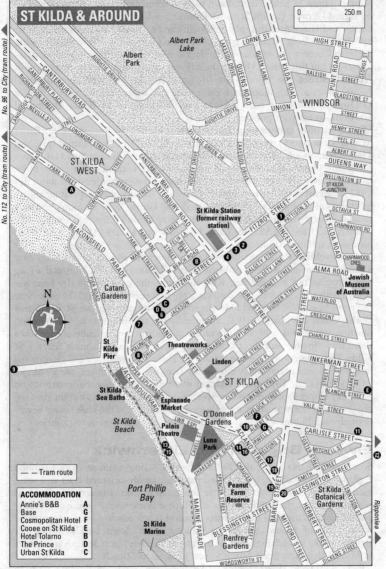

ST KILDA & AROUND

No. 16 to City (tram route)

No. 96 to City (tram route)

No. 112 to City (tram route)

0   250 m

Albert
Park

Albert Park
Lake

LORNE ST

HIGH STREET

QUEEN LANE

QUEENS ROAD

LAKESIDE DRIVE

ST KILDA ROAD

RALEIGH STREET

PUNT ROAD

GEORGE ST

GLADSTONE ST

UNION STREET

WINDSOR

STREET

HENRY STREET

PEEL ST

ALBERT ST

QUEENS WAY

WELLINGTON ST

ST KILDA
JUNCTION

OCTAVIA ST

CHARNWOOD RD

ST KILDA ROAD

CHARNWOOD
CRES

ALMA ROAD

Jewish
Museum
of Australia

WATERLOO

BARKLY STREET

CRESCENT

CHARLES STREET

INKERMAN STREET

STREET

MARKET STREET

LYELL ST

BLANCHE STREET

VALE STREET

GREEVES STREET

CARLISLE STREET

FOSTER STREET

MITCHELL ST

SMITH STREET

BLESSINGTON STREET

St Kilda
Botanical
Gardens

JENNINGS STREET

Ripponlea

St Kilda Station
(former railway
station)

FITZROY STREET

PATTISON ST

PRINCES STREET

DALGETY LANE

DALGETY STREET

BURNETT STREET

GURNER STREET

GREY STREET

ACLAND STREET

ST LEONARDS AV

NEPTUNE STREET

ROBE STREET

ALFRED PL

JACKSON STREET

EILDON ROAD

CANTERBURY ROAD

AUGHTIE DRIVE

AUGHTIE DRIVE

VILLAGE GREEN DR

HOTHAM DRIVE

LAKESIDE DRIVE

RICHARDSON STREET

CANTERBURY PLACE

NEVILLE ST

LANGRIDGE ST

FRASER STREET

YORK STREET

PARK STREET

ST KILDA
WEST

COMO PLACE

DEAKIN STREET

BEACONSFIELD PARADE

CANTERBURY WAY

CANTERBURY ROAD

LOCH STREET

PARK STREET

MARY STREET

W BEACH ROAD

FELIX LA

PARK LANE

ST KILDA ROAD

PIER ROAD

Catani
Gardens

St Kilda
Pier

POLINGTON ST

VICTORIA ST

UPPER ESPLANADE

JACKA BOULEVARD

St Kilda
Sea Baths

St Kilda
Beach

LWR ESPLANADE

CAVELL ST

Esplanade
Market

Palais
Theatre

Luna
Park

SHAKESPEARE GROVE

SPENCER STREET

MARINE PARADE

Peanut
Farm
Reserve

Renfrey
Gardens

CHAUCER STREET

St Kilda
Marina

Port Phillip
Bay

WORDSWORTH ST

BLESSINGTON STREET

MITFORD STREET

HERBERT STREET

DICKENS STREET

Theatreworks

Linden

ST KILDA

GLYDE STREET

FAWKNER STREET

HAVELOCK STREET

O'Donnell
Gardens

ALBERS ST

BURWELL ST

BELFORD ST

ACLAND STREET

BARKLY STREET

N

— — — Tram route

ACCOMMODATION

Annie's B&B	A
Base	G
Cosmopolitan Hotel	F
Cooee on St Kilda	E
Hotel Tolarno	B
The Prince	D
Urban St Kilda	C

EATING AND DRINKING

Baker D Chirico	2
Bala's	14
Bar Santo	7
Big Mouth	18
Chinta Blues	6
Cicciolina	17
Circa,The Prince	D

Donovan's	15
Elephant and Wheelbarrow	1
The Espy Kitchen	8
Galleon Café	10
George Lane Bar	4
Jackie O	20
La Roche Café	19

Las Chicas	12
Le Bon Continental Cake Shop	16
Melbourne Wine Room	3
Mink Bar	D
Pelican	5
St Kilda Pier Café	9
Stokehouse	13
Wall Two 80	11

Running from St Kilda Road down to the Esplanade, **Fitzroy Street** (reached on tram 112 from Collins St) is Melbourne's red-light district – usually pretty tame – and epitomizes this split personality, since it's lined with dozens of smart cafés and bars from which to gawp at the strip's goings-on. On weekend nights, these and others throughout St Kilda are filled to overflowing with a style-conscious but fun crowd. During the day, the same group line the main strip of **Acland Street** (on tram route 96 from Bourke St), with its wonderful European-style cake-shops and cafés; you can sit under the palm trees of **O'Donnell Gardens** next door to Luna Park, or in **St Kilda Botanical Gardens**, to eat your goodies.

St Kilda's most famous icon, **Luna Park**, is located on the Esplanade (Easter to Sept Sat & Sun 11am–6pm; Oct to Easter Fri 7–11pm, Sat 11am–11pm, Sun 11am–6pm; on school and public holidays also Mon–Thurs & Sun 11am–6pm Fri & Sat 11am–11pm; ⓦwww.lunapark.com.au), entered through the huge, laughing clown's face of "Mr Moon". There's nothing very high-tech about this 1912 amusement park: the Scenic Railway, the world's oldest operating roller-coaster, runs along wooden trestles, and the Ghost Train wouldn't spook a toddler – but then that's half the fun. Wandering around is free, but you pay A\$7 (child A\$5.50, toddler A\$3) for individual rides, or A\$35.95 (A\$25.95/A\$12.95) for a day's unlimited rides.

The **beachfront** is a popular weekend promenade all year round, with bars, separate cycling and walking paths running to Elwood and Brighton, and a long pier thrusting out into the bay. **Kite-surfing** is the craze of the day here (see p.136), with the colourful sails creating a pretty scene just beyond the pier. Near the pier's base is the botched redevelopment of a historic site, the **St Kilda Sea Baths**, which dates back to 1931, a heroically bad mix of shopping complex and function centre with a Moorish twist. Local residents are currently engaged in a fierce battle to save waterfront land next to Luna Park from a similar fate; the **St Kilda Triangle** complex – comprising the Palais Theatre, shops and recreational facilities – would undoubtedly change the face of St Kilda if it gets the go-ahead.

On Sundays, the **Esplanade Market** of art and crafts lines the waterfront on St Kilda's Upper Esplanade (10am–5pm); it's something of an institution, drawing big crowds in warm weather, even though all too many of the stalls favour bewilderingly awful homewares and accessories over genuine artiness or craftiness.

Elwood, Brighton and Elsternwick

South of St Kilda along the bay is **Elwood**, whose seafront road, Ormond Esplanade, runs past lovely kite-filled parkland, family-oriented cafés and some nice strips of sand. Slightly further south, **Brighton** attracts crowds to its pleasant beaches, the northernmost of which is home to the iconic and much-photographed Brighton **beach huts**. Elwood is best reached by taking tram 96 to the end of Acland Street and walking south down Barkly Street. For Brighton, take a Sandringham line train from Flinders Street Station and get off at Middle Brighton (for Church Street) or Brighton Beach.

East of Elwood, **Elsternwick** (take the same Sandringham line train to Ripponlea) is a largely Orthodox Jewish area. The original 1918 fittings and facade of Brinsmead's Pharmacy at 73 Glen Eira Rd are protected by the National Trust, as is **Rippon Lea Estate** at 192 Hotham St (daily 10am–5pm, closed Mon during winter; A\$12, child A\$6.50; ⓣ03 9523 6095, ⓦwww .ripponleaestate.com.au), which shows how Melbourne's wealthy elite lived a century ago. The 33-room mansion has magnificent gardens, complete with ornamental lake and fernery, and a way-over-the-top interior. The grounds are popular for picnics at weekends, when the tearoom is also open (11am–4pm).

Ten to fifteen minutes' walk away in East St Kilda, at 26 Alma Rd opposite the St Kilda Synagogue, is the **Jewish Museum of Australia** (Tues–Thurs 10am–4pm, Sun 11am–5pm; A$10, child A$5; ℡03 9534 0083, Ⓦwww .jewishmuseum.com.au; tram 3 or 67 to stop 32 from Swanston Street in the city or from St Kilda Road). The museum's permanent exhibitions focus on Australian and world Jewish history, and there are also displays and special exhibitions on Jewish beliefs and rituals, with a focus on festivals and customs.

Spotswood and Williamstown

Docks and industry dominate the area west of the city centre, reached by suburban train, Williamstown Ferries (see box, p.111), or by heading out on the Westgate Freeway across the huge Westgate Bridge. A good reason for visiting **Spotswood**, the first suburb across the Yarra, is the **Scienceworks and Melbourne Planetarium** at 2 Booker St (daily 10am–4.30pm; Scienceworks A$6, free for children; A$11 for combined Scienceworks and Planetarium ticket, child A$3.50; additional charges for some exhibitions; Ⓦwww.museumvictoria .com.au/scienceworks). Inside a space-age building, set in appropriately desolate wasteland, the displays and exhibitions are ingenious, fun and highly interactive. Part of the museum consists of the original Spotswood Pumping Station, an elegant early industrial complex with working steam pumps. The Planetarium features state-of-the-art digital technology, taking visitors on a virtual journey through the galaxy (Mon–Fri 2pm, Sat & Sun on the hour 11am–3pm; the 11am and noon shows are aimed at younger children).

On a promontory at the mouth of the Yarra, the peaceful streets of **Williamstown** are a mix of rich and poor, of industry, yachting marinas and working port. The street along the waterfront, Nelson Place, is nowadays lined with restaurants, cafés and *gelati* shops; the monthly **Williamstown Craft Market** is held here (third Sun, 10am–4pm; Ⓦwww.williams towncraftmarket.com.au).

Bulleen and Eltham

The northeastern suburbs of **Bulleen** and **Eltham** are home to two attractions of interest to art enthusiasts: the Heide Museum of Modern Art and Montsalvat. You could make a day of it by visiting them en route to the Yarra Valley wineries or the Healesville Sanctuary (see p.148).

The **Heide Museum of Modern Art** (Tues–Fri 10am–5pm, Sat & Sun noon–5pm; exhibition space A$12, free for children; gardens and sculpture park free; ℡03 9850 1500, Ⓦwww.heide.com.au), on Templestowe Road in Bulleen, was the home of Melbourne art patrons **John Reed** (1901–81) and **Sunday Reed** (1905–81), who in the mid-1930s purchased what was then a derelict dairy farm on the banks of the meandering Yarra River. During the following decades the Reeds fostered and nurtured the talents of young unknown artists and played a central role in the emergence of Australian art movements such as the Angry Penguins, the Antipodeans and the Annandale Realists; the painters Sidney Nolan, John Perceval, Albert Tucker and Arthur Boyd were all members of the artistic circle at Heide at one time or another. The **Heide I Gallery** is set in the farmhouse where the Reeds lived from 1934 until 1967. The gallery exhibits pieces from the museum's extensive collection of paintings and other works purchased by the Reeds over four decades, including works by famous Australian artists of the mid- to late twentieth century, including Nolan, Perceval and Boyd. Exhibits change every six months. In mid-2006, at a cost of A$3 million, two new galleries, an education centre, an outdoor sculpture area and restoration of Heide II (the latter house of John and Sunday built in the mid-1960s) were completed; at the time of writing, a further programme of works is underway. The most prominent addition to date is the Albert & Barbara Tucker Gallery (Heide III), which features over two hundred artworks from Albert's personal collection. There is also an excellent **café** (Tues–Fri 11am–4pm, Sat & Sun 11am–5pm), which serves gourmet produce and local wine. The museum is located 14km from the city centre; take the suburban train to Heidelberg station (Eltham line) then bus 291 to Templestowe Road (frequent services).

Eltham, a bushy suburb further northeast, about 24km from the city, is known as a centre for **arts and crafts**. Its reputation was established in 1935 when the charismatic painter and architect Justus Jorgensen moved to what was then a separate town and founded **Montsalvat**, a European-style artists' colony. Built with the help of his students and followers, the colony's eclectic design was inspired by medieval European buildings with wonderful quirky results; Jorgensen died before it was completed and it has deliberately been left unfinished. He did, however, live long enough to see his community thrive, and to oversee the completion of the mud-brick Great Hall, whose influence is evident in other mud-brick buildings around Eltham. Today Montsalvat, a two-kilometre walk from Eltham station, contains a gallery and is still home to a colony of painters and craftspeople (gallery open daily 9am–5pm; A$10, child A$6; ☎03 9439 7712, ⓦwww.montsalvat.com.au).

Eating

Melbourne is a foodie haven and Australia's premier city for **eating out**. Sydney may have the big-name chefs, but Melbourne has the best food from across the globe and the hippest restaurants – almost all of them exceptionally good value. While the CBD is the powerhouse of the restaurant scene, there's a thriving café society in most suburbs, where everyone has a favourite place for eggs benedict or an evening pizza. Lygon Street, in inner-city **Carlton**, is just one of many places across the city with a concentration of Italian restaurants; nearby, Brunswick Street in **Fitzroy** and Smith Street in neighbouring **Collingwood** both harbour a huge variety of international cuisines and trendy cafés by the dozen. **St Kilda** also has great restaurants, bakeries and delis, while in **Richmond**, Vietnamese restaurants and supermarkets dominate Victoria Street.

In March each year, the city celebrates all this culinary diversity with the **Melbourne Food and Wine Festival** (see box, p.90). If you're going to be around for a while, *The Age Cheap Eats* and its more upmarket companion, *The Age Good Food Guide*, are worthwhile investments.

City centre

In a relatively small CBD, you wonder how quite so many cafés and restaurants stay in business; the answer, of course, lies in the average Melburnian's never-ending quest for good food, be it the perfect toasted Turkish, the hippest new fusion concoction or the most sumptuous degustation menu. At lunchtime, cheap, hole-in-the-wall Japanese joints, cafés and shopping-centre food courts, such as those at **QV** and **Melbourne Central**, keep hungry workers in sushi, noodles and paninis. For provisions, the posh food hall at **David Jones** and the **Queen Victoria Market** come up trumps.

Cafés

Beetroot 123 Hardware Lane ⊕ 03 9600 0695. Top-notch brekkie and lunch fare is doled out with crisp efficiency, while the hot chocolate is an event: hot milk is added to a tall glass filled with chocolate beans, and topped with candy floss. Mon–Fri 7am–3.30pm.

Degraves Espresso Bar 23 Degraves St ⊕ 03 9654 1245. Old, faithful café, one of the solid-gold spots that line both sides of Degraves St and Centro Place: atmospheric, graffiti-daubed alleyways off Flinders Lane. Mon–Fri 7am–late, Sat 8am–6.30pm, Sun 8am–5.30pm.

Hopetoun Tea Rooms Block Arcade, 282 Collins St ⊕ 03 9650 2777. Tea and scones have been served in these elegant green-and-black surrounds for more than one hundred years. One for your nan. Mon–Thurs 9am–5pm, Fri 9am–6pm, Sat 10am–3.30pm.

Journal 253 Flinders Lane ⊕ 03 9650 4399. Bookish types decamp from the City Library next door to share the wooden communal tables, flick through art journals, and lunch on big baguettes and antipasto. Mon–Fri 7am–late, Sat 8am–6pm.

Little Cupcakes 7 Degraves St ⊕ 03 9077 0413. Cute-as-a-button shop specializing in adorable cupcakes. Mon–Fri 9am–6.30pm, Sat 10am–5.30pm.

Ortigia 442 Little Collins St ⊕ 03 9670 0774. Deep in the city's financial district, hungry workers gather in this airy shop to wolf down upper-class pizza slices loaded with antipasti and fancy cheeses. Mon–Fri 7.30am–5pm.

Pellegrini's Espresso Bar 66 Bourke St ⊕ 03 9662 1885. Melbourne's first espresso bar, and still an institution, with a classic 1950s interior and great cheap pasta. As Italian as they come. Mon–Sat 8am–11.30pm, Sun noon–8pm.

Satay Bar Corner of Flinders & Custom House lanes ⊕ 03 9629 1466. The addictive chicken, lamb, prawn and veggie skewers here are covered in a delectable peanut sauce and accompanied by crunchy achar salad, rice and crackers. Mon–Fri 8am–5pm.

SMXL 542 Little Bourke St ⊕ 03 9642 8611. A deserving winner of the city's best sandwich award, this cheery place majors in tasty wrap melts, innovative salads and healthy baguettes. Mon–Fri 7am–5pm.

Restaurants

100 Mile Cafe Level 3, Melbourne Central ⊕ 03 9654 0808. All produce at this eco-friendly place is sourced within one hundred miles. Luckily, it seems that quite a lot can be grown, caught or shot around these parts, hence the wide-ranging and tasty upmarket menu. Mon–Fri lunch & dinner, Sat dinner only.

The European 161 Spring St ⊕ 03 9654 0811. More than a few locals swear the best coffee in town is served in this old-style bistro complete with panelling, mirrors and black-and-white chequered floor. The Spanish-Italian hybrid menu is pretty good, too. Daily 7.30am until late.

Ezard at the Adelphi 187 Flinders Lane ⊕ 03 9639 6811. This sleek, dimly lit place is one of Melbourne's coolest eateries, with an exquisite range of East-meets-West dishes. With class, though, comes damage to the wallet – mains cost A$40–50. Mon–Fri noon–2.30pm & 6pm–late, Sat 6pm–late.

Flora's 238A Flinders Lane ⊕ 03 9663 1212. Noisy, robust and inexpensive Indian canteen, where students queue up for a metal tray loaded with tasty curries, rice and breads. Mon–Thurs & Sun 10am–10pm, Fri & Sat 10am–11pm.

Grossi Florentino 80 Bourke St ⊕ 03 9662 1811. A Melbourne institution. Downstairs, inexpensive minestrone and home-style pastas are doled out in the atmospheric *Cellar Bar* (Mon–Sat 7.30pm–1am); upstairs, choose between simple meat and fish grills in *The Grill* or stunning Italian food in *The Restaurant* (Mon–Sat noon–3pm & 6–11pm).

Hako Shop 7, 250 Flinders St (enter from Degraves St) ⊕ 03 9650 0207. Tiny hole-in-the-wall Japanese, whose pale pine tables are always full of people noshing on lunchtime bento boxes, noodle soups or heartier evening dishes. Mon–Fri lunch & dinner, Sat dinner only.

Horoki 19 Liverpool St ⊕ 03 9663 2227. The industrious staff in this contemporary, red-hued newcomer are as good to watch as the food is to eat. Grab a seat at the counter and watch the sashimi show in the open kitchen. Excellent tuna carpaccio. Moderate. Mon–Fri noon–3pm & 6–11pm, Sat 6–11pm.

Movida 1 Hosier Lane ⊕ 03 9663 3038. Down an unlikely laneway, this place can't seem to put a foot wrong: tables are so hard to come by that the bar brims with people "making do" with drinks and nibbles. Great service and a mix of hearty and delicate tapas explain the clamour. Moderate–expensive. Daily noon–late.

The Press Club 72 Flinders St ⊕ 03 9677 9677. Food critics and restaurant-goers alike are in thrall to the modern Greek food served here. The fresh, gentleman's-club decor is as far from the taverna as you can get, but for all its innovation, the food stays true to its roots. Mon–Sat lunch & dinner, Sun dinner only.

Taxi *Transport Hotel*, Federation Square ⊕ 03 9654 8808. *Taxi*'s prestigious, tourist-friendly location and up-to-the-minute vibe would guarantee a buzz even if the food were average – but it's actually rather good. The theme is modern Japanese. Prices are high. Daily lunch & dinner.

Trunk 275 Exhibition St ☎ 03 9663 7994. This former synagogue, now a cavernous, industrial Italian bistro, is the new darling of Melbourne's food-and-drink media mafia: the great pizzas, flavoursome mains and well-chosen wines are the reason why. Mon–Fri lunch & dinner, Sat dinner.

Chinatown

Dim sum is available at lunchtime almost everywhere on **Little Bourke Street**; on Sundays, the city's Chinese families flock here for their weekly dumpling ritual, meaning tables are at a premium.

Camy's Shanghai Dumpling and Noodle Restaurant Tattersalls Lane ☎ 03 9663 8555. Formica tables and plastic mugs are the scene here, along with unbelievably cheap steaming noodles and basic, filling dumplings. It's always packed out, despite the amusingly vague service. Daily 11am–10pm.

Flower Drum 17 Market Lane ☎ 03 9662 3655. This is where the city's powerbrokers come to eat, lured by the outstanding Cantonese cuisine, extensive wine list, and top-notch service. These all come at a price: at least A$90 per person for three courses. Mon–Sat noon–3pm & 6–10pm, Sun 6–10pm.

Gingerboy 27–29 Crossley St ☎ 03 9662 4220. Glossy black communal tables and starry lighting are

Vue De Monde 430 Little Collins St ☎ 03 9691 3888. Chef Shannon Bennett, a star of the Melbourne food scene, conjures dish after surprising dish – some at your table – for the evening degustation menu (A$150); in comparison the two- or three-course lunch appears a steal (A$55/A$70). One for serious foodies. Tues–Sat noon–2pm & 6.30–10pm, Sat 6.30–10pm.

teamed with spicy, hawker-style Southeast Asian food to share. Sister to the *Ezard*, and less expensive. Mon–Fri noon–2.30pm & 6pm–late, Sat 6pm–late.

Shark Fin House 131 Little Bourke St ☎ 03 9663 1555. Three storeys of converted warehouse devoted to dim sum. Steamed dumplings of every description, Chinese greens and sweet pork buns are trolleyed around at breakneck speed. Daily 11.30am–3pm (Sat & Sun from 11am) & 5.30–11pm. Also at 50 Little Bourke St (daily until 1.30am).

The Supper Inn 15 Celestial Ave ☎ 03 9663 4759. Insanely popular, old-school Chinese, which has the mother country down pat. The food is dirt-cheap and consistently excellent. Daily 5.30pm–2.30am.

Carlton and North Melbourne

Wall-to-wall Italian pizza and pasta restaurants – mediocre but inexpensive and fun – spill out onto **Lygon Street**'s footpaths between Grattan and Elgin streets; all but the most resolute-looking passers-by will be accosted by their touts. Meanwhile, cheap Asian noodle bars, popular with the Asian students at Melbourne University and RMIT, are cropping up every month around Carlton, breaking the Italian monopoly.

Cafés

Big Harvest 151 Elgin St ☎ 03 9348 0066. Super-small shop with one communal table that only fits about six people; the quality pasta bakes and salads – which are of the hearty, vegetarian variety – compensate for the lack of elbow room. Mon–Fri 7.30am–5pm.

Brunetti 194–204 Faraday St ☎ 03 9347 2801. A mouthwatering selection of chocolates, pastries, biscuits and cakes are arrayed in the display cases here, and there's great coffee, too. Mon–Thurs & Sun 6am–11pm, Fri & Sat 6am–midnight.

Restaurants

🏃 **Abla's** 109 Elgin St ☎ 03 9347 0006. Take a trip to Mamma Abla's and partake of the

best Lebanese food in the city. The moreish hummous and famous *kibbeh* (a spiced meat and nut combo) are both stand-outs in the great-value banquet (A$50 or A$55 with fish). Mon–Sat 6–11pm, plus Thurs & Fri noon–3pm.

Tiamo 1 303 Lygon St ☎ 03 9347 5759. One-time beatnik hangout and still popular with students, with layers of browning 1950s posters and a good-value blackboard menu of spaghetti dishes. Mon–Sat 7.30am–11pm, Sun 8.30am–10pm.

Toto's Pizza House 101 Lygon St ☎ 03 9347 1888. Melbourne's first pizzeria, dating from the 1950s; cheap, cheerful and noisy – none of those fancy pizzas here thank-you-very-much. Mon–Thurs & Sun noon–11pm, Fri & Sat noon–midnight.

Fitzroy and Collingwood

Adjacent **Fitzroy** and **Collingwood** brim with achingly hip places serving food from every country imaginable.

Brunswick Street and around

Babka 358 Brunswick St ☏ 03 9416 0091. This Russian-influenced café always has a queue out of the door, and not just because it's tiny. The cakes are divine, as are the breakfast-time *blintzes* (pancakes) or lunchtime *borscht* (tangy beetroot soup). Tues–Sun 7am–7pm.

Bimbo Deluxe 376 Brunswick St ☏ 03 9419 8600. Almost worth going for the name alone, this place offers big pizzas, early-hours nosh-ups, cool music and a casual vibe. Daily noon–2.30am.

Blue Chillies 182 Brunswick St ☏ 03 9417 0071. Dark, smooth and jazzy Malaysian restaurant at the southern end of Brunswick St, serving food that's a step up from the usual noodles and curries. Daily lunch & dinner.

Ici 359 Napier St ☏ 03 9417 2274. A much-loved, pretty local on a peaceful, very-Fitzroy sidestreet. Join the throngs dithering over the menu: spiced poached fruit, or something eggy? Daily breakfast & lunch.

Mario's 303 Brunswick St ☏ 03 9417 3343. This European-style café has dauntingly smart staff and decor, but is neither expensive nor dressy. An interesting mixture of poseurs, celebrities and scruffs fill the cramped tables and window seats. Daily 7am–11pm.

Gertrude Street

Birdman Eating 238 Gertrude St ☏ 03 9416 4747. Intriguing café, modishly done out with designer furniture. Delightfully retro breakfasts such as salty kippers, boiled eggs and soldiers, or sausage with bubble and squeak contrast nicely with the decor. Sun & Mon 8am–6pm, Tues–Sat 8am–10.30pm.

Ladro 224 Gertrude St ☏ 03 9415 7575. Thousands have been won over by *Ladro*'s sensational yet simple Italian-style pizzas, excellent wines, delightful service and irresistible Melbourne vibe. Never less than absolutely rammed. Wed–Sun 6pm–late.

Ume Nomiya 197 Gertrude St ☏ 03 9415 6101. In Japan, a "nomiya" is a place serving drinks and snacks, and so it is in this dark, funky place, where sake and Asian tapas such as *edamame* and *gyoza* are the mainstays. Tues–Sun 6–10pm, bar until 1am.

Smith Street and Johnston St

Café Rosamund 191 Smith St (rear) ☏ 03 9419 2270. Titchy, cosy hideaway that squeezes every ounce of mileage from its miniature kitchen, churning out great brunchables, toasties and soups. Daily breakfast & lunch.

The Commoner 122 Johnston St ☏ 03 9415 6876. Draws on a wide range of influences, with beignets and Arab pancakes for breakfast, Galician octopus salad for lunch, and lamb potato cake with smoky eggplant salad for dinner. Enjoy it all in the shabby-chic interior or stylish courtyard. Wed–Fri noon–late, Sat & Sun 9am–11pm.

Old Kingdom 197 Smith St ☏ 03 9417 2438. Word is well and truly out on this place. It looks nondescript, and the service can be laughingly abrupt, but it serves the best cheap Peking duck in town: for the banquet, order a day in advance. Tues–Fri lunch & dinner, Sat & Sun dinner only.

Richmond

Swan Street and Bridge Road have their fair share of restaurants, but it's down-at-heel **Victoria Street** that's the place to go in Richmond, lined as it is with Vietnamese supermarkets and dozens of cheap, authentic restaurants.

Fenix 680–682 Victoria St ☏ 03 9427 8500. Great views over the Yarra, especially in summer on the deck. As for the food, you can dive into steak, fish and steamed pudding, all of it decently priced and well presented. Tues–Sat lunch & dinner, Sun lunch.

Minh Minh 94 Victoria St ☏ 03 9427 7891. Good, cheap Indochinese food (Vietnamese, Laotian and Thai dishes) served in often-riotous surroundings that are a little bit more stylish than most on this street. Tues 4–10pm, Wed–Sun 11.30am–10pm.

Pacific Seafood BBQ House 240 Victoria St ☏ 03 9427 8225. The duck here is a particular favourite, and the fish is tank-fresh. Great no-frills ambience and reasonable prices. Mon–Thurs & Sun 10.30am–10.30pm, Fri & Sat 10am–11.30pm.

Richmond Hill Café and Larder 48–50 Bridge Rd ☎03 9421 2808. Founded by Melbourne foodie Stephanie Alexander, this rustic café still bears her hallmarks: a charcuterie-and-cheese lunch can be followed up by a visit to the adjacent produce store. Daily breakfast & lunch.

Vlado's 61 Bridge Rd ☎03 9428 5833. This fifty-year-old steakhouse, where you pick the cut of meat you want from passing waiters, isn't easy on the waistline or the wallet, but the results are always delicious. Lunch Mon–Fri, dinner Mon–Sat.

South Yarra, Prahran and Windsor

The **Chapel Street** area is full of chic little eateries catering for footsore designer shoppers.

Borsch, Vodka & Tears 173 Chapel St, Windsor ☎03 9530 2694. This velvet-draped Polish bar-restaurant offers over one hundred different vodkas, soaked up with dumplings, schnitzels and strudels. Mon–Fri 8.30am–late, Sat & Sun 9.30am–late.

Botanical Hotel 169 Domain Rd, South Yarra ☎03 9820 7800. Premier gastro-pub run by a British chef, serving excellent breakfasts; lunches and dinners have flair, and there's a long wine list. Nearly always full. Mon–Fri 7am–11pm, Sat & Sun 8am–11pm.

Caffe e Cucina 581 Chapel St, South Yarra ☎03 9827 4139. Trades heavily on its reputation as one of Melbourne's coolest Italian eateries, but still attracts a smart clientele. Pricey. Mon–Fri 7am–11.30pm, Sat 8am–11.30pm, Sun 9am–11.30pm.

France-Soir 11 Toorak Rd, South Yarra ☎03 9866 6589. Charmingly traditional French bistro that checks all the boxes: mirrored walls; cosy tables; Franglais-speaking waiters; long wine list; great onion soup; perfect steak-frites and unctuous crème brûlée. Daily noon–3pm & 6pm–midnight.

Globe Café 218 Chapel St, Windsor ☎03 9510 8693. Serves breakfast all day, plus globally inspired dishes for lunch and dinner. Great hand-made cakes and bread. Moderate. Mon–Fri 8am–late, Sat & Sun 9am–late.

Ice Café Bar 30 Cato St, Prahran (off Commercial Rd, opposite Prahran Market) ☎03 9510 8788. This switches from lively breakfast joint to hip lunch spot and smooth cocktail bar as the day progresses. Popular gay meeting place. Cheap-moderate. Daily 8am–late.

Orange 126 Chapel St, Windsor ☎03 9529 1644. Epitomizes the grunge-chic of the Windsor end of Chapel St: a great place to chill out over a light meal or a cocktail or two. Great garden at the back. Mon & Tues 7am–6pm, Wed–Fri & Sun until 2am, Sat until 3am.

Oriental Tea House 455 Chapel St, South Yarra ☎03 9826 0168. Great for those who find dim sum on trolleys a bit stressful: here, you order your Shanghai-style tea and dumplings from a menu instead. Mon–Wed & Sun 10am–10pm, Thurs–Sat 10am–11pm.

South Melbourne, Albert Park and Middle Park

There are cafés and delicatessens aplenty around here. The evening options are low-key but consistently high quality, in keeping with the wealthy local residents' tastes. In South Melbourne, lovely pavement cafés and great takeaway stalls surround the market.

Albert Park Deli 129 Dundas Place, Albert Park ☎03 9699 9594. One of many swish café-delis around Dundas Place. Lots of "Yummy Mummies" popping in to get some fresh pumpkin-and-porcini ravioli for later. Daily 5am–8pm.

Albert Park Hotel Corner of Montague St & Dundas Place, Albert Park ☎03 9690 5459. Very rah-rah renovated pub, full of bright young things and the odd celeb, with a serious restaurant putting out some sublime gastro-pub food. Daily lunch & dinner.

Jocks 83 Victoria Ave, Albert Park ☎03 9686 3838. Only serves ice cream, but this is ice cream

extraordinaire, seen on all the smartest restaurant menus. Try them all. Mon–Fri noon–9.30pm, Sat & Sun noon–10.30pm.

Mart 130 107A Canterbury Rd (Middle Park Light Rail Stop) ☎03 9690 8831. Hop off tram 96 to sit in the too-cute interior or on the sunny terrace, and tuck into divine bircher muesli with poached fruit, amazing corn fritters or home-made baked beans on toast. Daily 7am–5pm.

Misuzu's 7 Victoria Ave, Albert Park ☎03 9699 9022. Smart-yet-casual Japanese eatery, serving great sashimi and delicious mains to young crowds who spill out onto pavement tables lit by swinging red lanterns. Daily noon–3pm & 5.30–10pm.

Santiagos 14 Armstrong St, Middle Park ☎03 9696 8884. Cosy, very red Spanish eatery in pretty Middle Park. The tapas is excellent, or you can come for paella night (Wed & Sat) or to hear Spanish guitar (Sun). Mon–Wed & Sun 5–11pm, Thurs–Sat 5pm–1am.

St Ali 12–18 Yarra Place, South Melbourne ☎03 9686 2990. Award-winning coffee, which says a lot in this bean-obsessed city. Tucked away in a laneway warehouse, you can get a toasted Turkish or syrupy French toast to go with your flat white. Mon–Sat 7.30am–5pm, Sun 8am–4pm.

St Kilda

St Kilda's café and restaurant scene revolves around **Acland Street** and **Fitzroy Street**. While the former is good for late breakfasts and cholesterol-troubling bakeries, the latter has the edge in the evening.

Baker D Chirico 149 Fitzroy St ☎03 9534 3777. You'll find the exquisite breads made here in many a city breadbasket; St Kilda residents buy them at source, perhaps stopping for a coffee and croissant or a moreish savoury pastry while they're here. Tues–Sun 7am–5pm.

Bala's 1D Shakespeare Grove, just off Acland St near Luna Park ☎03 9534 6116. Excellent, cheap Asian takeaway food, including *lassis* and lots of stir-fried dishes with ultra-fresh ingredients. There are a few tables for eating in. Mon–Sat noon–10.30pm, Sun 10am–9.30pm.

Bar Santo 7 Fitzroy St ☎03 9534 1236. Peaceful Italian where a lot of idling goes on. The menu includes hearty, southern Italian pastas and sublime ricotta cake. Tues–Fri 11am–late, Sat & Sun 8am–late.

Chinta Blues 6 Acland St ☎03 9534 9233. The huge open windows at this Malaysian hawker-style restaurant mean that punters can check out the Acland St goings-on as they slurp their soup noodles and listen to blues. Consistently good. Daily lunch & dinner.

Cicciolina 130 Acland St ☎03 9525 333. The no-bookings policy at this seductive modern-Italian restaurant has the locals cramming into the back bar to nibble on antipasti, in the hope that a table will come up. Fabulously fresh ingredients. Daily lunch & dinner.

Circa, The Prince 2 Acland St ☎03 9536 1122. Going to *Circa* for dinner is a real event: with a magnificently theatrical fit-out, superb contemporary European food and a bewilderingly long wine list, it's something to save up for at least once. Daily 6.30–10.30pm, plus breakfast & lunch Mon–Fri & Sun.

Donovan's 40 Jacka Blvd ☎03 9534 8221. With a bright and breezy seaside feel, this restaurant offers sophisticated Mediterranean-influenced cuisine. It's so popular your only hope of a window table at weekends is to beg. Daily lunch & dinner.

The Espy Kitchen *Esplanade Hotel*, 11 Upper Esplanade ☎03 9534 0211. The huge, white *Espy* is a real Melbourne icon. Some new-fangled foods have been brought in, but most punters still come for the parmas, pizzas and hangover-reducing breakfasts. Daily lunch & dinner, plus Sat & Sun breakfast.

Galleon Café 9 Carlisle St ☎03 9534 8934. This distressed-retro hangout is a long-standing St Kilda favourite: the coffee is excellent, the atmosphere breezy, and the healthy, hearty breakfasts and lunches top notch. Daily 9am–5pm.

La Roche Café 185 Acland St ☎03 9534 1472. Popular and unpretentious eatery that has a rustic and jovial feel. The tables that spill onto the street are taken early in the day, so get in fast. Daily lunch & dinner.

Las Chicas 203 Carlisle St, Balaclava ☎03 9531 3699. Just east of St Kilda, this funky industrial place is somewhere to see and be seen. The breakfasts and lunches are legendary, and often have an Asian or Spanish twist. Daily 7am–5pm.

Le Bon Continental Cake Shop 93 Acland St ☎03 9534 2515. Perennial pastry shop and café – it's been tempting passers-by with European-style tarts and cakes, plus classic Aussie vanilla slices, for decades. Daily 8am–late.

Pelican 16 Fitzroy St ☎03 9525 5847. At the weekend, you could spend the whole afternoon and evening here, grazing on Middle Eastern share plates, before moving on to a cocktail or two. Mon–Fri noon–4pm, Sat & Sun noon–1am.

St Kilda Pier Café St Kilda Pier ☎03 9525 5545. Recently reborn, this little charmer is idyllically situated right at the end of the pier. The walk works up a bit of an appetite, which can be satiated with pancakes, sandwiches and cakes whilst enjoying the bay views and breezes. Mon–Fri 8.30am–5.30pm, Sat & Sun 8am–6pm.

Stokehouse 30 Jacka Blvd ☎03 9525 5555. The very affordable downstairs section serves upmarket pub food plus pizza and pasta. Upstairs, superb views of the bay and excellent Italian-inspired food combine to make a very pleasant dining experience. Daily lunch & dinner.

Wall Two 80 280 Carlisle St (rear), Balaclava ⓣ 03 9525 5555. Cool, relaxed and bohemian hole-in-the-wall café – a coffee lifeline on the eastern fringe of St Kilda. Daily 6.30am–6pm.

Entertainment, nightlife and culture

Melbourne has a rich arts and music scene, and there's always plenty to do in the evening. The line between restaurants, cafés, bars, clubs, music pubs and other performance venues is increasingly blurred as many places serve several purposes. To find out **what's on**, check *EG*, published with *The Age* on Fridays; pick up the great free magazines *Beat* and *Inpress* at record shops, cinemas and cafés; or refer to the online listings (see below). Annual **festivals** further enliven the scene – see p.90 for the low-down.

Credit-card **bookings** for most major events can be made through Ticketek (ⓣ 13 28 49, ⓦ www.ticketek.com.au) or Ticketmaster (ⓣ 13 61 00, ⓦ www.ticketmaster.com.au). For cut-price theatre, concert, opera, dance, comedy and festival tickets on the day of the performance, drop in to Half-Tix, Melbourne Town Hall (Mon 10am–2pm, Tues–Thurs 11am–6pm, Fri 11am–6.30pm, Sat 10am–4pm; cash only; ⓣ 03 9654 9420, ⓦ www .halftixmelbourne.com); you'll also find last-minute discounts online at Lucky Last (ⓦ www.luckylast.com.au).

Pubs and bars

Melbourne is the most exciting place to drink in Australia: cheap laneway rents have spawned hundreds of new über-stylish **bars**, designed to within an inch of their lives. This doesn't necessarily mean flashy; the interior of your favourite drinking spot is just as likely to be filled with op-shop finds. Bar-hopping is almost a certified sport, and an adrenalin sport at that, as people dash between basement hideaways and rooftop terraces in search of the new cool. As a rule of thumb, save the **pub** trips for the suburbs, where you'll find the most easygoing hangouts. Throughout Melbourne, drinking holes stay open very late, and many offer **live music**: the best of these are listed on p.130. For more options, see ⓦ www.melbournepubs.com.au.

What's on in Melbourne: useful websites

General listings
The Age ⓦ www.theage.com.au
City of Melbourne ⓦ www.thatsmelbourne.com.au
Melbourne Citysearch ⓦ www.melbourne.citysearch.com.au
Only Melbourne ⓦ www.onlymelbourne.com.au
Tourism Victoria ⓦ www.visitmelbourne.com

Gigs and clubs
Beat ⓦ www.beat.com.au
Clubs Guide ⓦ www.clubsguide.com.au/whatson
Live Guide ⓦ www.liveguide.com.au/melbourne
Your Gigs ⓦ www.yourgigs.com.au/melbourne

City centre

Bar Lourinhã 37 Little Collins St. Cosy up around small tables and choose from the excellent European wines chalked on the blackboard behind the bar. Extremely stylish in a low-key way, with superb tapas. Closed Sun.

City Wine Shop 159 Spring St. It's in the city, and it most definitely does wine (and how). The foodie tidbits in this simple, very European bar and bottle shop aren't to be missed either. Mon–Fri 7am–late, Sat & Sun 9am–late.

Cookie 252 Swanston St. Top-quality option: cute wallpaper and French bistro tables fill an industrial-sized space that draws hundreds of post-work drinkers. They also do great Thai food. The upstairs cocktail bar, *The Toff in Town*, has seductive private booths.

Double Happiness 21 Liverpool St. Chinese communist-influenced decor, inspiring cocktails and Asian nibbles. Up on the first floor is *New Gold Mountain* – similar, but as if communism had lost its appeal and interior designers with better taste in cocktails had taken over. Sours are the house speciality.

Madame Brussels Level 3, 59 Bourke St. Fake grass and stripy garden furniture – and that's just the inside. Outside, the fantastic garden patio looks through to the city spires. Pimms in jugs, and cute waiters, often wearing pink, complete the scene. Definitely one for the girls.

Melbourne Supper Club 161 Spring St. Made for winter, when you can cast off your hat and scarf, curl up on a leather sofa and get stuck into a great bottle of red from the amazing wine list. Jazzy music adds to the ambience.

Meyers Place 20 Meyers Place. One of the very first laneway bars, this place still exudes quintessential Melbourne style. The tiny space is matched by a tiny drinks list, but it works, hence the crowds spilling out onto the street.

Riverland 1 Federation Wharf (under Princes Bridge). Grab an outside table and watch boats float down the river, with the Arts Centre soaring in the background. A perfect summer venue, especially now they have a BBQ.

Seamstress 113 Lonsdale St. Ex-brothel and ex-sweatshop, in its latest incarnation this Chinatown spot hits the jackpot. In the third-floor bar, bartenders dole out excellent wine and cocktails under brightly coloured silk cheongsams; downstairs, you can tuck into succulent Asian tapas.

Section 8 27 Tattersalls Lane. Whole evenings have been lost in *Section 8*, which started life as a temporary trailer bar but now seems set to stay. Crates and cushions serve as seats, while thrown-together art installations, occasional bingo sessions, dizzying caipirinhas and bewildering bands (guitarist in a diving helmet anyone?) provide the entertainment.

Sister Bella 22 Drewery Place. This hangout looks like the inside of a particularly stylish op-shop. The limited drinks list is a bit of a minus, but it attracts all the cool kids anyway.

St Jeromes 7 Caledonian Lane. The quintessential laneway bar: a dark entrance in a spectacularly grungy alleyway leads to a surprisingly spacious outdoor courtyard. Longneck beers are dirt cheap and the wine comes in tumblers, so expect to see fewer suits and more artists and students. Home to the excellent St Jeromes Laneway Festival (see p.90).

Transport Federation Square. This madly popular watering hole takes the zinc jigsaw theme of its surroundings as its own decorative leitmotif. Big windows make it a great place for people-watching.

Carlton, Fitzroy and Collingwood

Gertrude Street Enoteca 229 Gertrude St, Fitzroy. A perfect, classy neighbourhood local and working bottle shop: you can open a wine from the hundreds lining the walls for only a small mark up, and there are cheeses, terrines and antipasti to snack on.

Lambsgo Bar 135 Greeves St, Fitzroy. This unassuming bluestone cottage is a beer-lover's dream, with over a hundred local and imported varieties. Dark and cosy, with quirky amusement machines, Connect 4 and killer tunes, it's a cult favourite of locals in the know.

Markov Place 350 Drummond St, Carlton. Enter via a tiny alley off Elgin St and prepare to be surprised by a huge converted warehouse with exposed beams, funky lightshades, retro advertising posters and moderately priced bistro food.

Marquis of Lorne 411 George St, Fitzroy. Yet another great local with modern twists and a summery roof terrace that looks out across the Fitzroy skyline. Epic pub food, with posher options in the second-floor restaurant, completes the picture.

Napier Hotel 210 Napier St, Fitzroy. Sweetly old-fashioned Fitzroy pub that's always busy. Try to finish their Bogan Burger (includes chicken schnitzel, steak, egg, potato cake, beetroot, huge wedges and salad) then sit in the relaxed beer garden and think thin thoughts.

Panama Dining Rooms 231 Smith St, Collingwood. This warehouse conversion is very Smith St, featuring retro wallpaper, low-slung lamps and horizon-skimming views from the huge arched windows. A central pool table, table tennis and good bistro food mean you might want to live here.

Polly 401 Brunswick St, Fitzroy. A decadent old favourite on happening Brunswick St. Low ceilings, lots of red velvet, chandeliers and a huge cocktail list make for an intimate, not to mention sophisticated, evening.

The Spanish Club 59 Johnston St, Fitzroy. Second home to the city's wannabe-Hispanic (ie salsa dancing) communities, this is a bit dated but lots of fun, with basic drinks, A$2 happy hour (daily 5–6pm), and mixture of Latin and rock music.

Richmond, Windsor and South Melbourne

Butterfly Club 204 Bank St, South Melbourne. The word "kooky" could have been invented just for this bar, which specializes in cabaret, dolls-house-style furnishing and lots of lace. A real one-off, with great drinks and people-watching opportunities.

Der Raum 438 Church St, Richmond. This small, groovy bar favours rat-pack swing tunes, German beers and creative cocktails – the Martinis, in particular, are worth crossing town for.

Lucky Coq 179 Chapel St, Windsor. From the *Bimbo Deluxe* crew, this bohemian-feel pub hosts late-night DJ sessions, making it a prime destination for party people. There's cheap gourmet pizza, too, with specials from A$4. Daily noon–3am.

Platform 3 472 Church St, Richmond. Named because it perches over East Richmond Station, this classy, minimalist lounge bar doesn't look much from outside, but huge windows with wide

city views and an extensive drinks list make it a popular venue.

St Kilda

Big Mouth 168 Acland St. Two floors full of great vibes – the ground floor is chilled in the day, and great for people-watching, while the more opulent upstairs is good for flirting come Fri and Sat night.

Elephant and Wheelbarrow 169 Fitzroy St. Corny English theme-pub that is enormously popular with backpackers looking for love and good times. Bands play Thurs–Sun; other events include *Neighbours* nights on Mon. Harold is a regular, we're led to believe.

George Lane Bar 129 Fitzroy St. Unusually for St Kilda, this is a small, intimate bar. Enter from Grey St, enjoy the lack of backpackers and settle into the ornate furniture.

Jackie O 204 Barkly St. Comfy, atmospheric surroundings complemented by relaxed service, good cocktails and value-for-money food. Daily 7.30am–1am.

Melbourne Wine Room *The George Hotel*, 125 Fitzroy St. An airy, classy St Kilda institution, where you can sit at an outside table and look cool, or work the room quaffing fine wine.

Mink Bar *The Prince*, 2B Acland St. This subterranean bar has shelves stacked high with an astonishing array of Russian, Polish, Swedish, Finnish, Lithuanian and – gulp – Japanese vodka. A great place for convivial consumption and mellowing.

Live music: rock, blues and jazz

Melbourne's **band** culture is the best on the East Coast – only Brisbane comes close. As in Sydney, gentrification of the inner suburbs has dealt a blow to the scene, with newcomers complaining about the noise from **music pubs** that have been in business for decades, prompting closures. Nonetheless, a great many venues still thrive, particularly in grungy Richmond, Fitzroy and St Kilda. The places listed below usually have at least two bars, so you can escape the band room for a chat if you want to. Local band nights are often free, but there may be a **cover charge** of A$5–25 for touring acts playing pubs, rising to A$100–120 for the big venues (see box, p.131). Local radio stations Triple R (102.7FM, Ⓦwww.rrr.org.au) and PBS (106.7FM, Ⓦwww.pbsfm.org.au) air alternative music and are a good source of gig information.

City centre and the northern suburbs

Bar Open 317 Brunswick St, Fitzroy ☎03 9415 9601, Ⓦwww.baropen.com.au. The beauty of this totally unpretentious place is that you never know what you're going to get: comedy, acoustic folk, funk and visual performances all feature. With

comfy couches dotted over the two floors, it's a perfect place to see what Fitzroy music is all about.

Bennetts Lane 25 Bennetts Lane, City ☎03 9663 2856, Ⓦwww.bennettslane.com. One of Melbourne's most interesting jazz venues, now expanded to include a larger back room to complement the original cramped, 1950s-style cellar.

Multi-purpose performance venues

Bookings for many major events are handled by Ticketek or Ticketmaster (see p.128).

The Arts Centre 100 St Kilda Rd, Southbank ☎03 9281 8000, ⓦwww.theartscentre.com.au

Billboard 170 Russell St, City ☎03 9693 4000, ⓦwww.billboardnightclub.com

BMW Edge Federation Square, City ⓦwww.federationsquare.com.au

Festival Hall 300 Dudley St, West Melbourne ☎03 9329 9699, ⓦwww.festivalhall.com.au

Forum Theatre 154 Flinders St, Corner of Russell St, City ☎03 9299 9700, ⓦwww.marrinertheatres.com.au

Palais Theatre Lower Esplanade, St Kilda ☎03 9525 3240, ⓦwww.palaistheatre.net.au

Rod Laver Arena Batman Ave, Melbourne Olympic Park ☎03 9286 1600, ⓦwww.mopt.com.au

Telstra Dome 740 Bourke St, Docklands ☎03 8625 7700, ⓦwww.telstradome.com.au

Vodafone Arena Swan St, Melbourne Olympic Park ☎03 9286 1600, ⓦwww.mopt.com.au

---

Cherry AC/DC Lane, City ☎03 9639 8122. This grungy basement bar has serious rock pedigree – the band themselves joined the campaign for the renaming of the laneway where it stands. Great tunes at all times, especially late at night, when big dance moves take the floor.

Ding Dong Lounge 18 Market Lane, City ☎03 9662 1020, ⓦwww.dingdonglounge.com.au. Small and busy Chinatown bar hosting indie rock bands and DJs. Strictly no electronica.

Empress Hotel 714 Nicholson St, North Fitzroy ☎03 9489 8605, ⓦwww.theempresshotel.com.au. Lots of bands play here, the bar meals are big, if somewhat unsophisticated, and there's a great beer garden.

Gem Bar and Dining Room 289 Wellington St, Collingwood ☎03 9419 5170. Free nightly blues, folk and jazz in a pub with a comfy restaurant area; Brazilian fish stew and halloumi burgers feature on the eclectic menu.

The Night Cat 141 Johnston St, Fitzroy ☎03 9417 0090, ⓦwww.thenightcat.com.au. The place to come for Latin, soul and funk – be prepared to dance with a fun, hip crowd. Thurs–Sun from 9pm.

Pony 68 Little Collins St, City ☎03 9662 1026, ⓦwww.pony.net.au. Gritty music bar deep in the heart of the CBD, open till 7am at weekends (5am Mon–Fri). People who don't have to get up next morning come here to immerse themselves in all things rock.

The Tote 71 Johnston St, Collingwood ☎03 9419 5320, ⓦwww.thetotehotel.com. A Melbourne institution with a good beer garden, and a dark and dingy band room for those who like their rock loud and raw. Many consider this Melbourne's best place to hear live music.

Richmond and the southern suburbs

Corner Hotel 57 Swan St, Richmond ☎03 9427 7300, ⓦwww.cornerhotel.com. Hosts big-name, alternative independent bands from both Australia and overseas. Also has a great beer garden on the roof with city, train and tram views. Closed Mon.

The Esplanade Hotel 11 Upper Esplanade, St Kilda ☎03 9534 0211, ⓦwww.espy.com.au. The "Espy" is the soul of St Kilda and of Melbourne's eclectic band scene (huge bouncers make it look rougher than it actually is), hosting an interesting nightly line-up on three stages.

The Greyhound 1 Brighton Rd, St Kilda ☎03 9543 4189, ⓦwww.thegreyhoundhotel.webs.com. Old-fashioned, relaxed local pub with cosy band room hosting live music most nights of the week.

Prince Band Room 29 Fitzroy St, St Kilda ☎03 9536 1168, ⓦwww.princebandroom.com.au. Another St Kilda icon, showcasing big-name inter-national acts, from DJs to indie bands and singer-songwriters.

Clubs

Some club nights have no cover charge, while others cost A$5–25; look out for flyers giving free or discounted entry at hostels, record shops and boutiques.

3rd Class Duckboard Place, City ☎03 9662 4555. Moving into the space previously occupied by much-loved club *HonkyTonks*, this had a hard act to follow – but its winning combination of imaginative DJs and esoteric, dressed-down artiness fits the bill. Thurs–Sat.

Altitude 163 Russell St, City ☎03 9663 8990, ⊛www.baraltitude.com.au. Trance, progressive house and electrofunk in a smooth lounge bar. Thurs & Fri 4pm–late, Sat 9pm–late.

Alumbra Shed 9, Central Pier, Docklands ☎03 8606 4466, ⊛www.alumbra.com.au. Sophisticated joint with a sleek, ethnic-inspired look. A cocktail-drinking crowd piles in at weekends to sway to Latin, house and disco. Wed–Sun.

Chasers 386 Chapel St, South Yarra ☎03 9827 7379, ⊛www.chasersnightclub.com.au. Long-running club that plays pounding house and R&B; plush, imperial-style cocktail lounges add glamour. Fri–Sun.

First Floor 393 Brunswick St, Fitzroy ☎03 3419 6380, ⊛www.firstfloor393.com.au. Turning retro music appreciation into an art form, this place goes for a madcap mix of new romantic, reggae, funk, Motown classics and swing. Fri–Sun.

Lounge 243 Swanston St, City ☎03 9663 2916, ⊛www.lounge.com.au. Not just a dance-music venue, but also a café, bar and gallery, this place has real cross-generational appeal – a rare and precious thing in clubland. Wed–Sat.

Queensbridge Hotel (QBH) 1 Queensbridge St, South Melbourne ☎03 9686 2944, ⊛www .queensbridge.com.au. Megaclub with a massive capacity and mind-spinning lighting effects. Big- (and biggish) name DJs play on Sat nights.

Revolver Upstairs 229 Chapel St, Prahran ☎03 9521 5985, ⊛www.revolverupstairs.com.au. Hosts a busy blend of club nights – from minimalist electronica to mega-disco – and live sets. Best known for its all-day sessions on Sun, with Thai food to keep the crowd fuelled up. Daily.

Seven 52 Albert Rd, South Melbourne ☎03 9690 7877, ⊛www.sevennightclub.com. Stylish venue that plays quality dance music and pulls in well-groomed party people. Thurs–Sat.

Viper Room 373 Chapel St, Prahran ☎03 9827 1771. Temple of trance and progressive house, attracting hordes of glossy young followers. Thurs–Sun.

Comedy

Melbourne is the comedy capital of Australia, with the highlight of the year being the **Melbourne International Comedy Festival** (see box, p.90).

Caz Reitop's Dirty Secrets 80 Smith St, Collingwood ☎03 9415 8876, ⊛www.crds.com.au. Decked out like a 1920s speakeasy, this cavern-like basement is perfect for intimate comedy and acoustic gigs. Tues–Sat.

Comedy Club Athenaeum Theatre, 188 Collins St, City ☎03 9650 6668, ⊛www.comedyclub.com.au.

Slick, cabaret-style set-up featuring mainstream comedians.

The Comics Lounge 26 Erroll St, North Melbourne ☎03 99348 9488, ⊛www.thecomicslounge .com.au. Stand-up comedy and cabaret shows in a classic down-to-earth supper-club format. Mon–Sat.

Theatre, classical music, opera and dance

Melbourne offers a rich array of dramatic and musical productions, from fringe to mainstream, with outdoor performances in summer.

Athenaeum Theatre 188 Collins St, City ☎03 9650 1500, ⊛www.melbourneathenaeum.org.au. One of numerous small Victorian theatre buildings in the CBD, hosting guest performances – mainly plays and concerts. Home of the Australian Shakespeare Company (⊛www.australianshakespeare company.com.au), who also perform alfresco in the Royal Botanic Gardens in the summer months.

Comedy Theatre 240 Exhibition St, City ☎03 9299 4950, ⊛www.marrinertheatres.com.au. Not a comedy venue, but a small theatre hosting events similar to the *Athenaeum*.

Hamer Hall The Arts Centre, 100 St Kilda Rd ☎03 9281 8000, ⊛www.theartscentre.com.au. Principal performance venue for the Melbourne Symphony Orchestra (⊛www.mso.com.au).

Gay and lesbian Melbourne

Melbourne's gay and lesbian scene may not be as in-your-face as Sydney's, but it's almost as big. Fitzroy, Collingwood, Carlton, St Kilda, South Yarra and Prahran are favourite **districts**, but younger individuals, in particular, resist ghettoization; as a symptom of this, the era of massive LGBT-only events is waning. One that keeps on running, however, is the fabulous **Midsumma Festival** in January (see p.90): free weekly **papers** Bnews (Ⓦwww.bnews.net.au) and MCV (Melbourne Community Voice; Ⓦwww.mcv.com.au) list other happenings. See also p.101 for gay-run places to stay.

Venues and club nights

DT's Hotel 164 Church St, Richmond ☎03 9428 5728, Ⓦwww.dtshotel.com.au. Relaxed broad-appeal pub: dance your socks off on club nights or get a little squiffy at a wine-appreciation session. Tues–Thurs 4pm–midnight, Fri & Sat 4pm–1am, Sun 2pm–1am.

The Glasshouse 51 Gipps St, Collingwood ☎03 9419 4748, Ⓦwww.glass-house .com.au. Supercool venue with regular women-only club nights, raunchy cabaret and burlesque shows. Wed & Thurs 11am–1am, Fri 11am–5am, Sat noon–5am, Sun noon–midnight.

Laird Hotel 149 Gipps St, Collingwood ☎03 9417 2832, Ⓦwww.lairdhotel.com. Men-only venue that hosts leather nights and underwear parties for macho types and their admirers. Daily.

Love Machine Corner of Little Chapel St & Malvern Rd, South Yarra ☎03 9533 8837, Ⓦwww.lovemachine.net.au. This glam-it-up club hosts a big LGBT dance party on Sunday nights, from 10pm.

The Market 143 Commercial Rd, South Yarra ☎03 9826 0933, Ⓦwww.markethotel .com.au. Full-on dance club with a mainstream feel and a weekly menu of top-notch DJs, drag acts and performance art. Fri 10pm–8am, Sat 10pm–11am.

Opium Den 176 Hoddle St, Collingwood ☎03 9417 2696, Ⓦwww.opiumden.com.au. Drag shows, lesbian DJs and cabaret acts all come out to play at this decadent little nightspot. Wed–Sun.

The Peel 113 Wellington St (Corner of Peel St), Collingwood ☎03 9419 4762, Ⓦwww .thepeel.com.au. Dance floor, music videos and shows, drawing a large and appreciative crowd, mainly men. Thurs–Sat 9pm–dawn.

Xchange Hotel 119 Commercial Rd, South Yarra ☎03 9867 5144, Ⓦwww.xchange .com.au. Lounge bar for gay men with drag shows (Wed–Sun), and a roof terrace for balmy nights. Mon–Thurs & Sun 4pm–1am, Fri & Sat 2pm–3am.

Organizations and resources

ALSO Foundation 1st Floor, 6 Claremont St, South Yarra ☎03 9827 4999, Ⓦwww .also.org.au. Campaigning organization that publishes the ALSO Directory, free online or from community outlets, listing everything from gay vets to lesbian psychologists.

Beat Books 157 Commercial Rd, Prahran ☎03 9827 8748. Gay bookshop with a large range of magazines, books, sex toys and leather goods.

Hares and Hyenas 63 Johnston St, Fitzroy ☎03 9495 6589. Gay and lesbian bookshop.

Gay and Lesbian Switchboard ☎1800 184 527 or 03 9827 8544 (Mon, Tues & Thurs 6–10pm, Wed 2–10pm, Fri–Sun 6–9pm). For counselling, referral and information.

Joy 94.9 FM ☎03 9699 2949, Ⓦwww.joy.org.au. Gay and lesbian radio station, with 24hr music ranging from classical to R&B and world music, plus news and updates about the arts and club scene.

Her Majesty's Theatre 219 Exhibition St, City ☎03 9663 3211 (bookings ☎1300 795 012), Ⓦwww.hmt.com.au. Full-scale musicals and ballet productions in a fabulously ornate old theatre.

La Mama 205 Faraday St, Carlton ☎03 9347 6142, Ⓦwww.lamama.com.au. Tiny studio theatre: a place for new playwrights and poets to cut their teeth.

Malthouse 113 Sturt St, Southbank ☎03 9685 5111, Ⓦwww.malthousetheatre.com.au. An eco-friendly complex of four venues that host opera, dance, concerts and readings. The resident theatre company produces contemporary plays, including edgy Australian work.

Playhouse Theatre The Arts Centre, 100 St Kilda Rd ☎03 9281 8000, Ⓦwww.theartscentre.com.au. Mainstream theatre productions, mainly from the Melbourne Theatre Company (Ⓦwww.mtc.com.au).

Princess Theatre 163 Spring St, City ☎03 9299 9800, Ⓦwww.marrinertheatres.com.au. Small but lavish old-fashioned theatre, which stages musicals and mainstream plays.

Regent Theatre 191 Collins St, City ☎03 9299 9500, Ⓦwww.marrinertheatres.com.au. Lovingly restored old theatre staging big-name musicals.

State Theatre The Arts Centre, 100 St Kilda Rd ☎03 9281 8000, Ⓦwww.theartscentre.com.au. Stages productions by Opera Australia (Ⓦwww.opera-australia.org.au) and the Australian Ballet Company (Ⓦwww.australianballet.com.au).

Theatreworks 14 Acland St, St Kilda ☎03 9534 4879, Ⓦwww.theatreworks.com.au. Ground-breaking new Australian plays.

Cinemas

The **cinemas** in Crown Casino and Melbourne Central show blockbuster movies, while the city's independents screen less obviously commercial US flicks and foreign-language films. Some venues offer a discount on Mondays or Tuesdays. In summer, you can watch classic, art-house and indie films under the stars at the Moonlight Cinema in the Royal Botanic Gardens (see p.114), the Rooftop Cinema (Ⓦwww.rooftopcinema.com.au) or at St Kilda Sea Baths (Ⓦwww.stkildaopenair.com.au); come winter, Melbourne's **film festivals**, MIFF and MUFF, bring all the buffs out to play (see box, p.90).

ACMI Federation Square City ☎03 8663 2583, Ⓦwww.acmi.net.au. Home from home for the city's film buffs, with regular themed seasons.

Astor Theatre Corner of Chapel St & Dandenong Rd, St Kilda ☎03 9510 1414, Ⓦwww.astor-theatre.com. Classic and cult double bills in a beautiful Art Deco cinema.

Cinema Nova Lygon Court Plaza, 380 Lygon St, Carlton ☎03 9347 5331, Ⓦwww.cinemanova.com.au. A rabbit warren of small, recently refurbished and comfortable cinemas showing mainly

art-house and local movies, but with the odd Hollywood release.

Como Gaslight Gardens, corner of Toorak Rd & Chapel St, South Yarra ☎03 9827 7533, Ⓦwww.palacefilms.com.au. Belongs to the Palace Cinemas chain, which shows latest releases of Hollywood movies as well as art-house films.

IMAX Melbourne Museum See p.108.

Kino Dendy 45 Collins St, City ☎03 9650 2100, Ⓦwww.dendy.com.au. In the Collins Place atrium, mainly showing art-house and indie flicks.

Shopping

Melbourne is most definitely the country's shopping capital: whether it's the weather, or just to maintain that famous Melbourne street style, locals blitz the shops with gusto. The city's big two **department stores**, David Jones and Myer, are amusingly competitive; "DJs" definitely has the edge at the moment. Both are in the Bourke Street Mall area, the city's high-street focus. Dig a little deeper around the laneways, arcades and suburbs and you'll uncover any number of fascinating little stores. Many streets or precincts have clusters of shops of a particular type, making it possible to go clothes hunting by district. **Opening hours** are generally daily from 9am to 5.30pm, with late-night shopping until 7pm on Thursday and 9pm on Friday.

▲ Shopping for groceries at Queen Victoria Market

Retail districts

Bridge Road, Richmond (between Punt Rd and Church St). This is Melbourne's inner-city bargain district: lots of factory outlets and clothes and shoe shops selling seconds, samples and end-of-season stock.

Brunswick Street, Fitzroy Interspersed with cafés, bars and cutting-edge hairdressers you'll find lots of small, groovy clothes boutiques, accessories shops, and design and housey bric-a-brac stores. Tea- and coffee-drinkers should get themselves down to T2 and Jasper respectively, whilst ladies might like to check out Kleins, a treasure trove for pampering prouducts.

Chapel Street: South Yarra, Prahran and Windsor Upmarket fashion outlets at the northern (South Yarra) end give way to progressively less expensive, younger and grungier stores towards Prahran and Windsor in the south.

City arcades and lanes In the city blocks bordered by Flinders, Swanston, Bourke & Elizabeth sts, lots of boutiques and small shops selling designer brands, unusual fashion and shoes are tucked away down the arcades and laneways.

Elizabeth Street, City A haven for computer nerds, electronics aficionados, and petrolheads (the motorbike variety) respectively as you move north from Collins St to Franklin St.

Gertrude Street, Fitzroy Up-and-coming street full of "directional" clothes shops, vintage stores and homewares, including the fantastic Industrial (furniture), Crumpler (makers of bags you'll see on a good proportion of Melbourne backs) and Aesop (local, delicious and entirely necessary pampering items).

GPO Building, City This grand, magnificently restored Victorian building is now home to high-fashion outlets.

Greville Street, Prahran More kooky clothes, funky shoes and vibeful record stores.

Hardware Lane & Little Bourke Street, City This is the place to head for if you want to kit yourself out for your skiing, hiking or rafting trip, or any other outdoor pursuits you care to name.

Lygon Street, Carlton Good shoe shops and fashion outlets ranging from the high street to the more upmarket, most of them at the northern end between Grattan & Elgin sts.

Nicholas Building 21–47 Swanston St, City. Art Deco building stuffed with niche boutiques, including the incredibly popular Retrostar, Alice Euphemia and Genki.

QV and Melbourne Central, City Large developments again offering high-street shops (but undercover) and some pricier clothes, too. QV is notable for its indoor laneways, and Melbourne Central for the striking glass cylindrical tower at its centre.

Smith Street, Collingwood Secondhand clothing stores plus discount sportwear and camping equipment at the northern end.

Books, magazines and music

Basement Discs 24 Block Place, off Little Collins St, City. Great range of jazz and world music.

Blue Moon Records 54 Johnston St, Fitzroy. Specializes in world music, particularly Latin and Spanish.

Book Affair 200–202 Elgin St, Carlton. Very good secondhand bookshop, particularly for novels.

Books for Cooks 233 Gertrude St, Fitzroy.

Charming bookshop that stocks Australia's largest range of cookbooks and related titles.

Borders There are branches of this American monolith at the Jam Factory in South Yarra, Lygon St in Carlton and in Melbourne Central in the CBD.

Brunswick Street Bookstore 305 Brunswick St, Fitzroy. Great independent bookseller with occasional launches and readings.

Tours and activities from Melbourne

Melbourne can be used as a base for days out in the **Yarra Valley**, the **Dandenongs**, the **Mornington Peninsula**, or longer trips to the **Great Ocean Road** (see box, p.157), **Phillip Island** or the gorgeous "Prom" (**Wilson's Promontory National Park**). Day-trips to the latter are possible, but rushed; see Chapter 2 for full details of all these destinations. Thanks partly to the damper climate, there are fewer activity companies in the Melbourne area than further up the coast, but there's still much to keep you busy, particularly in summer.

Cycling

You don't have to pedal too hard to get out of the city and into the bush: bike rides and events are listed on the **Bicycle Victoria website** (ⓦwww.bv.com.au), along with a rundown of good bike paths in and around the city, the best of which (and one of the most pleasant ways to spend a day in Melbourne) is the 69-kilometre **Bay Trail**. The most-used part of the trail runs from Brighton Beach through St Kilda, affording riders spectacular sea and city views, before continuing around the bay to Port Melbourne, from where, at weekends, the Westgate Punt will ferry you and your bike across the Yarra River to Williamstown (Sat, Sun & public holidays; A$3). The useful *Bike Paths: Safe Escapes* (A$24.95) is available at Bicycle Victoria (Level 10, 446 Collins St), bookshops and newsagents. **Rentabike** on the riverbank at Federation Square (daily 10am–5pm, weather permitting; ⓣ03 9654 2762 or 0417 339 203, ⓦwww.rentabike.net) has road bikes, mountain bikes and tandems (A$15/hr, A$35/day; helmets, locks, maps and backpacks provided). The owner also runs Real Melbourne Bike Tours (see p.88). In St Kilda, try the helpful **St Kilda Cycles**, 150 Barkly St (A$15/hr, A$25–35/day; ⓣ03 9534 3074, ⓦwww.stkildacycles.com.au), which runs river and beachfront bike tours (A$48).

Diving

There's good diving within easy reach of the city in Port Phillip Bay, particularly off the Mornington Peninsula. **DIVA** (the Dive Industry of Victoria Association; ⓣ1800 816 151, ⓦwww.underwatervictoria.com.au) lists members in the Greater Melbourne area who rent equipment, organize trips and offer courses.

Kite-surfing

Local specialists **Kiteboarding Australia** (ⓣ0409 133 561 or 0416 155 719, ⓦwww .kiteboardingaustralia.com.au) can sort you out with lessons and equipment.

Roller blading

Pick up some kit from one of the bike shops in St Kilda or from **Bayside Blades** in Highett, close to Highett station on the Frankston line (A$10/hr, A$25/24hr; ⓣ03 9555 7988, ⓦwww.baysideblades.com.au) and get ready to pose like the 90s never ended.

Chronicles 91 Fitzroy St, St Kilda. Small, well-stocked independent bookseller.
Discurio 113 Hardware Lane, City. Classical music, jazz, blues and folk.
Grub Street Bookshop 379 Brunswick St, Fitzroy. Secondhand and antiquarian books.
Mag Nation 88 Elizabeth St, City. Excellent magazine store, with everything from the mainstream to the extremely niche. Almost uniquely, they encourage you to try before you buy.

Map Land 372 Little Bourke St, City. Good stock of maps and travel books.
Missing Link 405 Bourke St, City. Melbourne's premier alternative music store and ticket-seller to gigs around town.
Northside Records 238 Gertrude St, Fitzroy. Appropriately, this deeply funky store specializes in funk.
Readings Books & Music 309 Lygon St, Carlton, also at 253 Bay St, Port Melbourne and Acland St, St Kilda. One of Melbourne's best independents.

Tours

Adventure Tours Australia ☏1300 654 604, ⓦwww.adventuretours.com.au. Safari-tour operator that runs from Melbourne to Sydney via southeast Victoria, the Snowy Mountains and Canberra (3 days including meals and bunk accommodation; A\$405; accommodation upgrade optional) and day-trips to see the Phillip Island Penguin Parade (A\$109).

Autopia Tours ☏03 9419 8878 or 1800 000 507, ⓦwww.autopiatours.com.au. Long-established outfit running popular day-trips by minibus along the Great Ocean Road (A\$105), to Phillip Island (A\$109) or the Yarra Valley (A\$98) and to Sydney via the Snowy Mountains and Canberra (3 days including meals and bunk accommodation; A\$395; accommodation upgrade optional).

Bunyip Bushwalking Tours ☏03 9531 0840, ⓦwww.bunyiptours.com. Nature-focused small-group tours, mainly to Wilson's Promontory (1–3 days; A\$110–225). For the longer trips you need to be reasonably fit and able to carry a pack with your own tent and supplies. The one-day tour can be combined with the Phillip Island Penguin Parade on the way back to Melbourne. They also offer a day on the Great Ocean Road (A\$95).

Echidna Walkabout ☏03 9646 8249, ⓦwww.echidnawalkabout.com.au. Long-running upmarket ecotour operator, with very small groups and enthusiastic, knowledgeable guides, focusing on native wildlife. Programme includes a Great Ocean Road trip (3 days; A\$990) and interesting East Gippsland bushwalking and wildlife-watching tours (4 days; A\$1450). Accommodation is in B&Bs or very comfortable camps.

Eco Platypus Tours ☏1800 819 091, ⓦwww.ecoplatypustours.com. Offers a very long day-trip along the Great Ocean Road, going as far as Loch Ard Gorge and staying at the Twelve Apostles for sunset, then returning via the faster inland route (A\$95, less for groups), plus Yarra Valley and Phillip Island trips.

Go West ☏1300 736 551, ⓦwww.gowest.com.au. This family-run tour company offers entertaining and informative day-trips, primarily aimed at the backpacker market, on a 21-seater minibus travelling the Great Ocean Road (A\$105) or visiting Phillip Island (A\$109).

Oz Experience ☏1300 300 028, ⓦwww.ozexperience.com.au. One-way hop-on-hop-off trips from Melbourne to Sydney and, if you choose, on up the coast to Brisbane or Cairns with a backpacker bus-company. Attracts a young, party crowd; hands-on activities such as surfing, hiking, mountain biking add to the fun.

Phillip Island Penguin Tours ☏03 9629 5888, ⓦwww.penguinislandtour.com.au. Concentrates on Phillip Island day-trips (A\$109) in good minibuses equipped with DVD players for an onboard penguin presentation.

Yoga

Yoga schools abound in Melbourne. Practice your Downward Dog at **Action Yoga**, 275 Smith St, Collingwood (☏03 9415 9798, ⓦwww.actionyoga.com).

Rhythm and Soul Records 128 Greville St, Prahran. Funk, electronic, trance and techno grooves.

Markets

The Arts Centre Arts and crafts, Sun; see p.112.
Camberwell Station St, Camberwell. Large flea market with lots of good retro clothes stalls, books, records, bric-a-brac, and plenty of food vans and cafés. Take the train to Camberwell, and get there early if you want to bag some good stuff. Sun 7am–3pm.
Collingwood/Abbotsford Monthly farmers market; see p.116.
Federation Square New and secondhand books are sold in The Atrium. Sun 11am–4pm.

Traveller's Bookstore 294 Smith St, Collingwood. Stocks a wide range of travel writing and travel guides.

Prahran General, Tues & Thurs–Sun; see p.117.
Queen Victoria Market General, Tues & Thurs–Sun, plus Wed nights in summer; see p.107.
Royal Botanic Gardens Monthly horticultural market; see p.114.
South Melbourne General, Wed & Fri–Sun; see p.118.
St Kilda Arts and crafts, Sun; see p.120.
Telstra Dome Concourse Arts and crafts. Sun 9am–4pm.

Listings

Airlines (domestic) Jetstar ☎03 8341 4901; Qantas ☎13 13 13; Virgin Blue ☎3 67 89.
Airlines (international) Alitalia ☎03 9920 3799; British Airways ☎03 8696 2633; Garuda Indonesia ☎1300 365 330; Japan Airlines ☎03 8662 8333; KLM ☎1300 303 747; Lauda Air ☎1800 642 438; Malaysia Airlines ☎13 26 27; Qantas ☎13 13 13; Singapore Airlines ☎13 10 11; Thai Airways ☎1300 651 960; United Airlines ☎13 17 77.
Banks and foreign exchange All major banks can be found on Collins St; ATMs are widespread. There are foreign-exchange desks at Melbourne Airport; city outlets include Travelex at 251 Collins St, 136 Exhibition St and 565 Bourke St.
Campervan hire Apollo Motorhomes ☎1800 777 779; Backpacker Campervan Rentals ☎03 8379 8768; Britz ☎1800 331 454; Kea Campers Australia ☎1800 252 555; Maui ☎1300 363 800; NQ Australia Rentals ☎1800 079 529; Wicked Campers ☎1800 246 869.
Car rental Apex ☎03 9330 3877; Ascot ☎13 24 94; Avis ☎13 63 33; Budget ☎13 27 27; Hertz ☎1300 132 607; Network ☎1800 736 825; Thrifty ☎1300 367 227. For budget rentals: Rent-A-Bomb (☎13 15 53); Travellers Auto Barn ☎1800 647 374.
Consulates Canada, Level 50, 101 Collins St ☎03 9653 9674; France, Level 7, 160 Queen St ☎03 9602 5024; Germany, 480 Punt Rd, South Yarra ☎03 9864 6888; UK, Level 17, 90 Collins St ☎03 9652 1600; USA, 553 St Kilda Rd ☎03 9526 5900.
Environment and conservation Conservation Volunteers, 162 Adderly St, West Melbourne ☎03 9326 8250 or 1800 032 501,

ⓦwww.atcv.com.au; Department of Sustainability and Environment (DSE) Information Centre, 8 Nicholson St, East Melbourne ☎03 9637 8325, ⓦwww.dse.vic.gov.au; National Trust, Tasma Terrace, 4 Parliament Place ☎03 9656 9800, ⓦwww.nattrust.com.au; Parks Victoria information service ☎13 19 63, ⓦwww.parkweb.vic.gov.au; the Melbourne Visitor Centre (see p.93), for general information on national parks and heritage sites.
Flat-hunting and sharing Check the Saturday edition of *The Age*; websites such as ⓦwww.flatmatefinders.com.au and ⓦwww.flatmates.com.au; or the notice boards of hostels, cafés and bookshops in Fitzroy, Carlton and St Kilda. Alternatively, try Traveller's Contact Point (see Travel agents, p.139).
Hospitals and medical centres Alfred Hospital, Commercial Rd, Prahran ☎03 9276 2000; Royal Children's Hospital, Flemington Rd, Parkville ☎03 9345 5522; Royal Melbourne Hospital, Grattan St, Parkville ☎03 9342 7000; St Vincent's Hospital, Victoria Parade, Fitzroy ☎03 9288 2211; Melbourne Sexual Health Centre, 580 Swanston St, Carlton ☎03 9347 0244 or 1800 032 017. For vaccinations, anti-malaria tablets and first-aid kits, contact the Travel Doctor (TMVC), 2nd Floor, 393 Little Bourke St ☎03 9602 5788, ⓦwww.tmvc.com.au.
Internet access Melbourne's public libraries (see opposite) offer free access (Wi-Fi plus terminals). There are plenty of cybercafés throughout Melbourne, with most charging between A$3–7 per hour. Many accommodation options also have Internet access; rates vary wildly.

Laundries Almost all of the hostels and hotels have their own laundry. Commercial self-serve coin laundries include Melbourne City Dry Cleaners, 244 Russell St, corner of Lonsdale St (Mon–Fri 7am–6.30pm, Sat 9am–8.30pm); World Wide Wash Corner at 381 Brunswick St, Fitzroy (daily 9.30am–10pm); The Soap Opera Laundry & Cafe, 128 Bridport St, Albert Park (Mon–Fri 7.30am–7.30pm, Sat 8am–6pm, Sun 10am–6pm); and Blessington St Launderette, 22 Blessington St, St Kilda (daily 7.30am–9pm).

Left luggage and luggage forwarding Most hostels and many hotels store luggage; hostels usually don't charge an extra fee for this service. Southern Cross Station has lockers (daily 6am–10pm; A$8 for medium locker; emptied nightly), as does Flinders St Station (8am–8pm; A$8 for medium locker). Traveller's Contact Point (see below) stores luggage and forwards it.

Libraries The Redmond Barry Reading Room at the State Library of Victoria, 328 Swanston St (Mon–Thurs 10am–9pm, Fri–Sun 10am–6pm), has current Australian and overseas magazines; the Newspaper Room has Australian and overseas papers. The State Library and city libraries (253 Flinders Lane, City; 122 George St, East Melbourne; 66 Errol St, North Melbourne) offer free Internet access.

Motorbikes The northern end of Elizabeth St in the city centre has a string of motorbike shops. Garner's Motorcycles, 179 Peel St, North Melbourne (T03 9326 8676, W www.garnersmotorcycles .com.au), does rentals and sells secondhand machines with buy-back deals.

Newspapers Melbourne's *The Age* is one of Australia's better papers; the pulpy *Herald Sun* is the city's only other daily and known mostly for its sport coverage. Foreign newspapers can be perused at the State Library (see above).

Pharmacies Late-opening pharmacies include My Chemist, 128–132 Elizabeth St (Mon–Fri 7.30am–9pm, Sat 9am–6pm, Sun 10am–6pm); My Chemist, 244 Smith St, Collingwood (Mon–Fri 8.30am–9pm, Sat 9am–6pm, Sun 10am–6pm); Leonard Long Pharmacy, corner of Williams Rd & High St (daily 8am–midnight).

Police Melbourne East City Police Station, 226 Flinders Lane T03 9650 7077; emergency T000.

Post office In the CBD: 250 Elizabeth St (Mon–Fri 8.30am–5.30pm, including poste restante) and 45 Collins St (Mon–Fri 9am–5pm). Traveller's Contact Point (see below) offers a mail-forwarding service.

RACV The RACV Shop at 438 Little Collins St sells good maps of Melbourne, Victoria and the rest of Australia (discounted for RACV members and members of affiliated overseas motoring associations; W www.racv.com.au). RACV also books

accommodation listed in its guides and package holidays; members get special rates.

Swimming pools Melbourne City Baths, 420 Swanston St, corner of Franklin St, has a thirty-metre heated indoor pool (Mon–Thurs 6am–10pm, Fri 6am–8.30pm, Sat & Sun 8am–6pm; swim A$4.90, child A$3.90; swim, sauna and spa A$10.25 or A$18 including gym; T03 9663 5888). In the state-of-the-art Melbourne Sports & Aquatic Centre, Aughtie Drive, off Albert Park Rd in Albert Park (via tram 112 from Collins St or 96 from Bourke St), there's a pool for every purpose and a giant waterslide (Mon–Fri 6am–10pm, fifty-metre pool Mon–Fri 5.30am–8pm, Sat & Sun 7am–8pm; swim A$6, child A$4.50; swim, spa, sauna and steam room A$9.70; T03 9926 1555, W www.msac.com.au). Fitzroy Pool, Alexandra Parade, Fitzroy (Mon–Thurs 6am–9pm, Fri 6am–8pm, Sat & Sun 8am–6pm; A$4.20, child A$2.40) is a fifty-metre heated outdoor job.

Taxis Taxi rank on Swanston St outside Flinders St Station, and plenty to flag down. Call Yellow Cabs T13 22 27; Embassy Taxis T13 17 55; or Silver Top T13 10 08.

Travel agents For flight bookings: Flight Centre (T13 18 66, W www.flightcentre.com.au), 150 Queen St (T03 9600 1919) and Shop 2, 250 Flinders St (T03 9663 6266), plus many branches throughout the city; STA Travel (T13 47 82, W www .statravel.com.au), 240 Flinders St, City, and 144 Acland St, St Kilda, plus other branches; Student Flights (T1800 046 462, W www.studentflights.com .au), Shop 4, 250 Flinders St or 357 Little Bourke St, plus other branches. General agents: Backpackers World, Shop 1, 250 Flinders St (Mon–Fri 9am–6pm, Sat 10am–4pm; T03 9654 8477); Traveller's Contact Point, Level 1, 361 Little Bourke St (Mon–Fri 9am–5.30pm Sat 9am–12.30pm; T03 9642 2911, W www.travellers.com.au); YHA Travel, 359B Lonsdale St (T03 9670 9611, W www.yha.com.au).

Travellers Aid Centre 2nd Floor, 169 Swanston St (Mon–Fri 9am–5pm; T03 9654 2600). As well as information, there's also a café serving budget meals, plus nappy-changing facilities, showers (for a fee), toilets, lounge rooms, lockers, wheelchairs for rent, and assistance for disabled and frail persons. There's another branch at Southern Cross Station (T03 9670 2873).

Travellers with disabilities Railway-station staff can offer assistance, and some trams and buses are wheelchair-accessible; check with Metlink (T13 16 38, W www.melbournemetlink.com.au). The Melbourne City Council produces a free mobility map of the CBD showing accessible routes and toilets, available from the front desk of the Melbourne Town Hall. For wheelchair-accessible taxis, call T1300 364 050. TADAS (Travellers Aid

Disability Access Service) at Level 2, 169 Swanston St, corner of Bourke St (Mon–Fri 9am–5pm, Sat & Sun 11am–4pm; ⊕03 9654 1938, ⓦwww .travellersair.org.au/tadas), provides personal care and various services, including wheelchair rental. **Work** Hostels that offer advice and contacts include *Coffee Palace*, 24 Grey St, St Kilda (⊕03 9534 2003, ⓦwww.coffeepalace backpackers.com.au); *Greenhouse Backpacker*, 228 Flinders Lane (jobsearch online at ⓦwww .friendlygroup.com.au); *Hotel Discovery*, 167 Franklin St (⊕1800 154 664, ⓦwww .downunderjobs.com). Alternatively, try Traveller's Contact Point (see Travel agents, p.139).

Moving on from Melbourne

Long-distance public **transport** services heading **up the East Coast** from Melbourne are operated by CountryLink (trains to Sydney); V/Line (trains and buses to regional Victoria, Canberra and the south coast of New South Wales; see p.145 & p.180 for details); Firefly (buses to Sydney via the inland route); Greyhound (buses to Canberra, Sydney and nationwide); and Premier Motor Service (buses to Sydney via the coastal route, and to the rest of the East Coast to Cairns), all of which operate from the city's transport hub, Southern Cross Station, which has staffed information and booking desks. Transport information is available online at ⓦwww.metlinkmelbourne.com.au and the operators' websites (see p.35). Long-distance V/Line trains from Southern Cross Station have an optional airport-style check-in service for luggage, bicycles and surfboards, which are then carried in the goods van; arrive at least thirty minutes early to take advantage.

For **Tasmania**, the alternative to flying is the *Spirit of Tasmania* **ferry** from Station Pier, Port Melbourne (on tram route 109 from Collins Street) to Devonport, which takes ten hours (daily at 9pm; additional departure at 9am mid-Dec to mid-Jan; from A\$123 one-way, plus A\$61 for a car or A\$50 for a motorbike; ⊕13 20 10, ⓦwww.spiritoftasmania.com.au).

If you're driving out of town via the **CityLink tollways**, you'll need an e-toll tag or pass (see p.93). Some car rental companies issue their vehicles with tags, and include the tolls in the final bill.

Travel details

Trains

Melbourne to: Bairnsdale (3 daily; 3hr 30min–3hr 35min); Belgrave (every 30min; 1hr 20min); Frankston (4–8 hourly; 1hr); Lilydale (2–5 hourly; 1hr 5min); Sale (3 daily; 2hr 35min–2hr 45min); Sydney (twice daily; 11hr).

Buses

Melbourne to: Bairnsdale (daily; 5hr 15min); Brisbane (daily; 23hr); Canberra (4–5 daily; 8hr–8hr 30min); Cann River (daily; 7hr 35min); Cowes (daily; 3hr 5min); Foster (daily; 2hr 40min); Genoa (daily; 7hr 35min); Lakes Entrance (daily; 5hr 45min); Orbost (daily; 6hr 30min); Sale (daily; 3hr 20min); Sydney via Narooma (daily; 17hr); Sydney via Canberra (4–5 daily; 12–14hr).

Flights

Melbourne to: Ayers Rock Resort (3 daily; 3hr 30min); Brisbane (many daily; 2hr 5min); Cairns (many daily; 3hr 20min direct); Canberra (many daily; 1hr 5min); Coffs Harbour (twice daily; 3hr 50min with one stopover); Gold Coast (many daily; 2hr); Hamilton Island (daily; 2hr 55min); Mackay (6 daily; 4hr 15min with one stopover); Newcastle (twice daily; 1hr 25min); Rockhampton (5–6 daily; 3hr 30min with one stopover); Sunshine Coast (twice daily; 2hr 10min); Sydney (many daily; 1hr 20min); Townsville (many daily; 5hr–6hr 30min with one stopover).

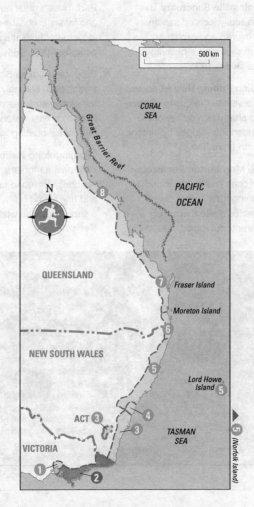

2

Southeast Victoria

CHAPTER 2 # Highlights

* **Yarra Valley** Enjoy bucolic landscapes and sample the wares of some great wineries, within easy reach of central Melbourne. See p.146

* **Healesville Sanctuary** This beautifully located sanctuary for injured and orphaned animals is also a bushland zoo. See p.149

* **Riding Puffing Billy** All aboard for a visit to the quaint villages and shady fern gullies of the Dandenong Ranges by vintage steam train. See p.151

* **The Mornington Peninsula** Beaches lined with colourful bathing huts and excellent wineries make this a truly characterful region. See p.151

* **Seal Rocks** Sail out to Seal Rocks, to see the largest known colony of Australian fur seals. See p.163

* **Wilsons Promontory National Park** There's great bushwalking and fantastic coastal scenery at Victoria's favourite national park. See pp.165–167

* **Gippsland Lakes** Black swans glide serenely across the glossy surfaces of these scenic coastal waterways, perfect for boating. See p.167

* **Croajingolong National Park** With pristine forests, wild beaches, secluded campsites and fine hiking trails, this is a superb coastal wilderness. See p.173

▲ Yarra Valley vineyard

Southeast Victoria

Victoria, Australia's second-smallest state, punches above its weight with an unrivalled variety of natural attractions. It's the country's most densely populated and industrialized state, but it also contains stunning tracts of wilderness, including three of Australia's fourteen **UNESCO Biosphere Reserves** – the Mornington Peninsula and Western Port, Wilsons Promontory Marine Park and Reserve, and Croajingolong National Park – all of which are found on the scenic Tasman coast, east of Melbourne.

You're never too far from civilization in southeast Victoria – by road, even the remotest areas near the New South Wales border are little more than seven hours from Melbourne, or eight hours from Sydney – but there are plenty of opportunities to get away from it all among easy-going wine regions, sleepy fishing villages, pristine national parks and beaches pounded by roaring surf. In the hinterland, the lowlands are spread with lakes and farming pastures, while the highlands offer glimpses of the state's wilder days when gold prospectors, bushrangers and horse breakers roamed the territory, immortalized by classic Australian balladeers such as Banjo Paterson.

Several of the region's highlights can be reached in a short trip from Melbourne, but this part of the state also lends itself to lengthy exploration, staying overnight in pretty country guesthouses or campsites. For those who enjoy quiet rural towns and secluded wilderness experiences, the 1054-kilometre coastal route between Melbourne and Sydney, covered by this chapter and the next, is one of Australia's most rewarding long-distance road trips.

Inland from Melbourne's eastern suburbs, the **Yarra Valley** and the **Dandenong Ranges** offer beautiful countryside, wine tasting and bushwalking, while to the south, the **Mornington Peninsula** on the east side of the huge **Port Phillip Bay** has some of Victoria's finest wineries, on gently rolling hills. On summer weekends, its smart resorts, popular beaches and surfing spots are packed with urban escapees. **Western Port Bay**, on the east side of the peninsula, encloses two fascinating islands – little-known **French Island**, much of whose wildlife is protected by a national park, and **Phillip Island**, whose nightly Penguin Parade, when masses of little penguins waddle ashore to roost, is among Australia's biggest tourist attractions. A regular ferry service operates from Phillip Island and French Island to the Mornington Peninsula and from there on to the Bellarine Peninsula on the western side of Port Phillip Bay, start of the **Great Ocean Road**, one of the most enjoyable drives in the state, a winding 280km of spectacular coastal scenery.

Gippsland, the green lowland region that stretches from Western Port Bay to the New South Wales border, between the Great Dividing Range and Bass Strait, has been the centre of Victoria's dairy industry since the 1880s. Jutting

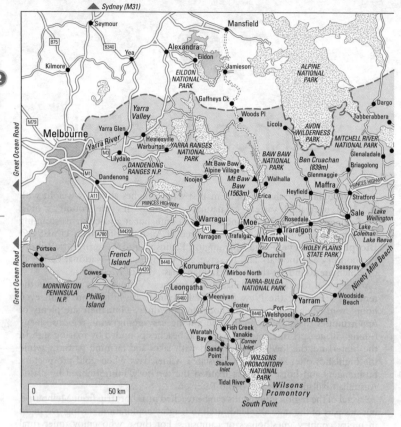

out into the strait to the south is the idyllic **Wilsons Promontory National Park** (the "Prom"), with superb scenery and fascinating bushwalks. Northeast of here are **Ninety Mile Beach** and the **Gippsland Lakes**, a region which, though beautifully untouched, is easy to access from the towns of Sale, Bairnsdale and Lakes Entrance. Further east, a diversion into the hinterland gives you a glimpse of the stunning Snowy River National Park, offering white-water rafting, horse-riding and lungfuls of fresh mountain air. East of Orbost, near Cann River and **Mallacoota**, Victoria's easternmost stretch is fringed by the **Croajingolong National Park**, a tremendous wilderness of rocky capes, high dunes and endless sandy beaches, extending all the way to the New South Wales border.

Regional practicalities

The parts of southeast Victoria within easy reach of Melbourne – the Yarra Valley, the Dandenongs and the Mornington Peninsula – have a good range of **accommodation** including luxury country and beach retreats aimed at Melburnians on weekend getaways. Elsewhere, you'll find a mixture of modest B&Bs, motels and campsites, plus a few backpacker hostels, but very few resort-style hotels – holidays in this region tend to be low-key.

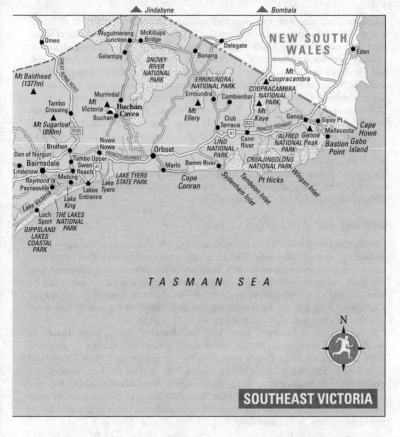

To make the most of the area's highlights, including offbeat wineries, secluded beaches and unspoilt campsites, **self-drive** is by far the best option. From Melbourne, access to the region is via the highways that radiate northeast, east and southeast out of the city: the Princes Highway (A1; which leads all the way to the south coast of New South Wales and is single-carriageway beyond the suburbs), Monash Freeway (M1; a faster alternative to the Melbourne end of the Princes Highway, for the Dandenongs), Eastern Freeway (M3; for the Yarra Valley), and the Nepean Highway and Frankston/Moorooduc Highway (A3 and A11; for the Mornington Peninsula). A scenic, though lengthy, alternative to the dull inland stretch of the Princes Highway between the end of the Monash Freeway and East Gippsland is to turn off onto the South Gippsland Highway, which loops down towards Phillip Island and Wilsons Promontory and rejoins the Princes Highway at Sale. From Sale, the Princes Highway continues east to the New South Wales border, typically skirting the East Gippsland coast by 10 to 25km as you drive first through farmland and later, east of Orbost, through tall, dense eucalyptus forests. At well-spaced intervals along this route, little-travelled side roads head south through the fields or trees towards the ocean.

Public transport in southeast Victoria, by bus and train, is monopolized by V/Line (see p.35) and subsidiary country bus lines. However, services are fairly infrequent, and places off the main highways can be reached only with difficulty, if at all. Suburban trains and buses from Melbourne will get you to the Yarra Valley, the Dandenongs and the Mornington Peninsula. The region's only **long-distance railway service**, the V/Line Gippsland Line from Melbourne's Southern Cross and Flinders Street stations, follows the Princes Highway to Dandenong, Yarragon and Sale, terminating at Bairnsdale. From Bairnsdale, a connecting bus runs to Lakes Entrance, Orbost, Cann River, Genoa and on to Eden, Merimbula, Bega, Narooma and Batemans Bay in New South Wales. There are also V/Line **buses** from Melbourne to Cowes (Phillip Island), and to Foster (for Wilsons Promontory). Subsidiary bus services run from Bairnsdale to Paynesville and from Genoa to Gipsy Point and Mallacoota. Premier Motor Service (see p.35), the main alternative to V/Line, runs a daily bus between Melbourne and Sydney along the coast, but it's not very convenient if you want to get off in East Gippsland, as it runs overnight. The closest **airports** to the region are in Melbourne, Canberra (ACT), Merimbula and Moruya (New South Wales).

Weather and seasons

One of the few drawbacks to the region, from the visitor's point of view, is the frequently cursed **climate**. Winter is generally mild, and the occasional heatwaves in summer are mercifully limited to a few days at most. However, hot, dry spells can spark bushfires that last for weeks; spring and autumn days can be immoderately hot; and cool, rainy "English" weather can descend in any season. The unpredictability can be frustrating, but as the local saying goes, if you don't like the weather, just wait ten minutes and it'll change.

As well as the Christmas, New Year and Easter holidays, **busy times** in southeast Victoria include March, when the Rip Curl Pro Surfing Championships are held on Bells Beach near Torquay on the Great Ocean Road, and Gippsland's many food and wine producers hold harvest markets, tastings and events. Wine festivals crop up in the Mornington Peninsula throughout the year but one of the biggest is the Winter Wine Weekend in June. The Australian Motorcycle Grand Prix in late September or early October brings hordes of motorsports fans to Phillip Island.

The Yarra Valley and the Dandenongs

Northeast of Melbourne, the **Yarra Valley** stretches out towards the foothills of the Great Dividing Range, with the towns of **Lilydale**, **Yarra Glen** and **Healesville** the targets for excursions into the wine country and the superb forest scenery beyond. Healesville also has an excellent **wildlife sanctuary**. Roughly east of Melbourne, and still within the suburban limits, the cool **Dandenong Ranges** are as pretty as anywhere in Australia, with quaint villages, fine old houses, beautiful flowering gardens, shady forests of eucalypts and tree ferns, and a century-old steam train, the **Puffing Billy**.

Getting there

To get to all these destinations and have a good look round, you really need **your own vehicle**. Travelling **by road**, the Yarra Valley region is 45 to 65km from central Melbourne via the Eastern Freeway and the Maroondah Highway, or, if you're approaching from the east, around 60km north of the Princes Highway via the C411. The Dandenong villages of Upper Ferntree Gully, Olinda and Belgrave (starting point of Puffing Billy) are 36 to 48km from central Melbourne via the Monash Freeway (the shortest route from the city, via the Burwood Highway, takes longer) or 17 to 26km north of the Princes Highway via Harkaway.

It's also possible, although less easy, to see the region by **public transport** from Melbourne. From the Melbourne City Loop stations, Connex train services run via Ringwood to Croydon and Lilydale or Upper Ferntree Gully and Belgrave. Direct buses or coaches to the Yarra Valley from Melbourne's Southern Cross Station include the V/Line Mansfield service, which stops at Lilydale and Yarra Glen; the V/Line Eildon service, which stops at Healesville and Marysville; and bus 684 to Lilydale, Healesville and Marysville; the journey takes 1hr 15min–2hr 35min. There are no direct buses from Melbourne to the Dandenongs. Within the region, bus 685 runs from Lilydale to Healesville, stopping at the Healesville Sanctuary (see p.149); bus 694 travels from Belgrave via the Mount Dandenong Tourist Road to Olinda township in the Dandenong Ranges; bus 688 runs from Olinda via the northern part of Mount Dandenong Tourist Road to Croydon railway station; and bus 695 runs from Belgrave to Emerald. For timetables and fare information for all routes, consult the Metlink information service (☎03 9619 2727 or 13 16 38, ⓦwww.metlinkmelbourne.com.au).

The Yarra Valley

An easy drive from Melbourne, the **Yarra Valley** is home to over thirty of Victoria's best small **wineries**. The combination of good wine and fine food is really taking off in the valley, and in recent years quite a few winery restaurants have made a name for themselves in culinary circles. Like the Hunter Valley in New South Wales, it's much loved as a weekend getaway destination; sophisticated urbanites come here not only for the wine but also to soak up the atmosphere at open-air concerts. There's also good bushwalking country nearby.

The wine country begins north of the Maroondah Highway near Lilydale. The densest concentrations are around Yarra Glen to the north and Healesville to the northeast; as you head towards Healesville on the Maroondah Highway, the Melba Highway to Yarra Glen branches off to the left. There's another cluster of vineyards east of Lilydale, along the Warburton Highway. The **Yarra Valley Visitor Information Centre** at The Old Courthouse, Harker St, Healesville (daily 9am–5pm; ☎03 5962 2600, ⓦwww.visityarravalley.com.au) has detailed brochures and maps.

Accommodation

Big4 Badger Creek Holiday Park 419 Don Rd, Healesville ☎03 5962 4328 or 1800 009 225, ⓦwww.badgercreekholidays.com.au. Budget, family-friendly option within easy reach of Healesville Sanctuary, with an adventure playground and pool. Camping A$30–47, cabin ④

Chateau Yering 42 Melba Hwy, Yering (1km south of Yarra Glen) ☎03 9237 3333, ⓦwww.chateauyering.com.au. Close to the Yering Station winery, this heritage-listed mansion with lovely gardens offers oodles of old-fashioned comfort. For the ultimate indulgence, wine and dine at its very posh restaurant, *Eleonore's* (lunch Sat & Sun, dinner daily), then sink into a four-poster bed in one of the period-style rooms. ⑧

Sanctuary House Resort Motel Badger Creek Rd, Healesville ☎02 5962 5148. Good-value option with a small pool and kids' playground; you can choose from a range of rooms, from simple doubles and twins to larger rooms with pine four-posters. ④–⑤

Susan's in the Valley 108 Badger Creek Rd, Healesville ☎03 5962 6233, ⓦwww.susansinthevalley.com.au. Luxury B&B in a strikingly contemporary house, with conservative but comfortable rooms and a small, attractive heated outdoor pool. ⑥

Yarra Glen Grand Hotel 19 Bell St, Yarra Glen ☎03 9730 1230, ⓦwww.yarraglengrand.com.au. Splendidly restored Victorian hotel with very comfy en-suite rooms and suites, some of them with

Yarra Valley wineries

Most of the valley's many wineries have a **cellar door** (tasting and sales room), which welcomes visitors any day of the week. Some also offer gourmet restaurants, bars and cafés, informative tours and wine-appreciation classes. A good alternative to driving is to join a **winery tour**: the Australian Wine Tour Company (☎03 9419 4444, ⓦwww.austwinetourco.com.au) picks up from several locations in Melbourne to spend a day visiting four premium wineries (daily; A$95 including transport, tastings, a good restaurant lunch and a food platter in the afternoon).

De Bortoli Pinnacle Lane, Dixon's Creek (10km north of Yarra Glen, off the Melba Highway) ☎03 5965 2271, ⓦwww.debortoli.com.au. With unbeatable views over gently rolling hills, this was one of the first places in the valley to offer gourmet food along with its wine; its restaurant, which serves Italian-inspired cuisine, is now run by a chef who has previously worked at two of London's top restaurants: *The River Café* and the *Connaught* (under Gordon Ramsay). Cellar door daily 10am–5pm. Lunch daily, dinner Sat.

Domaine Chandon Green Point, Maroondah Highway, near Coldstream ☎03 9738 9200, ⓦwww.domainechandon.com.au. Produces fine *méthode champenoise* sparkling wine, which you can sample (A$7–9 per glass) in a modern, bright and airy tastings room with brilliant views. Daily 10.30am–4.30pm; free thirty-minute tours hourly from 11am.

Rochford Maroondah Highway, corner of Hill Road, near Healesville ☎03 5962 2119, ⓦwww.rochfordwines.com. Winery known for its sparkling Pinot Chardonnay, with a restaurant that specializes in dishes made using locally produced ingredients. Hosts open-air concerts in summer. Cellar door daily 10am–5pm; restaurant Mon–Fri noon–3pm, Sat & Sun 9am–3pm.

Yarra Burn 60 Settlement Rd, Yarra Junction (off the Warburton Highway) ☎03 5967 1428, ⓦwww.yarraburn.com.au. Low-key, long-established winery, famous for its Chardonnays and Pinot Noirs made from hand-picked fruit. Cellar door daily 10am–5pm.

Yering Station 38 Melba Hwy, Yering (3km south of Yarra Glen) ☎03 9730 0100, ⓦwww.yering.com. This winery is located on the site of Victoria's first vineyard, dating back to 1838; the cellar door operates from the original brick building. There's a stylish, glass-walled restaurant offering views across the valley; a bar serving wines and plates of nibbles to share; and a shop selling regional produce. Hosted tastings and guided tours on request. Cellar door daily 10am–6pm; restaurant 10am–5pm, bar 10am–4pm.

antique furniture and balconies, plus a casual bistro (open daily) and smarter restaurant (lunch Sun, dinner Thurs–Sat). ⑤

Yering Gorge Cottages 215 Victoria Rd, Yering (8km north of Lilydale, 7km south of Yarra Glen) ☎03 9739 0110, ⓦwww.yeringcottages .com.au. This collection of twelve bright, ultra-modern cottages, scattered over a large estate beside the Yarra River, brings a breath of fresh air to the valley. Guests receive a hand-delivered breakfast hamper, complete with newspaper, each morning. ⑥

Yarra Glen

The small town of **YARRA GLEN**, 58km from Melbourne, is the focus of the Yarra Valley wine region and the heart of a long-established farming community. Hugging the banks of the Yarra River, it's surrounded by fields and vineyards, with the foothills of the Great Dividing Range as a backdrop. For a flavour of the region's agricultural heritage, you can visit the **Gulf Station** (daily 10am–4pm; A$10, children free; ☎03 9730 1286, ⓦwww.gulfstation.com.au), on the

Melba Highway just northeast of town. This well-preserved pioneer farm, dating back to the 1850s, features barns made from solid timber slabs – the most complete set of slab buildings in Victoria – plus a restored cottage garden and a stock of farm animals representative of the breeds introduced by the nineteenth-century settlers.

Besides wine, there's plenty of good local produce on offer throughout the year. Once a month, the Yering Station winery just south of town (see box opposite) hosts the lively **Yarra Valley Regional Farmers' Market** (third Sun 10am–2pm), with an array of fruit, vegetables and delicacies such as smoked trout, honey and jams. Nearby on McMeikans Road, the **Yarra Valley Dairy** (daily 10.30am–5pm; Ⓦwww.yvd.com.au) sells gourmet cheeses, as does the **Yarra Valley Cheese Room** at De Bortoli on the north side of town (see box opposite).

Healesville, Marysville and around

HEALESVILLE is a small, pleasant town whose main attraction, apart from its wineries, is the renowned **Healesville Sanctuary** (daily 9am–5pm; A$23, child A$11.50; Ⓣ03 5957 2800, Ⓦwww.zoo.org.au), a bushland zoo with more than two hundred species of Australian animals and a refuge for injured and orphaned animals, some of which are subsequently returned to the wild; those that stay join the sanctuary's programmes for education and the breeding of endangered species. It's a fascinating place in a beautiful setting, with a stream running through park-like grounds, dense with gum trees and cool ferns, and 3km of walking tracks. Many of the animals are in enclosures, but there are paddocks of emus, wallabies and kangaroos you can stroll through. The informative "meet the keeper" presentations are worth joining, especially the one featuring birds of prey (noon & 2.30pm, weather permitting).

As you continue north from Healesville on the Maroondah Highway over the Black Spur and Dom Dom Saddle towards Alexandra, the scenery becomes progressively more attractive. The **Maroondah Reservoir Lookout**, just off the highway 3km north of Healesville, is worth a brief stop, with picturesque views across the forest-fringed dam, and popular **picnic grounds** and **gardens** in the park on the southwest side of the reservoir. Soon after the reservoir, the highway meanders along bush-clad mountain slopes and enters luxuriant wet eucalypt forest with incredibly tall mountain ash, moss-covered myrtle beech, manna gum, gurgling creeks and waterfalls. The **Fernshaw Reserve and Picnic Ground** is a good place to stop and view the scenery. After the Dom Dom Saddle, 509m above sea level and 16km past Healesville, the highway descends towards Narbethong, where it enters drier country.

Three kilometres beyond Narbethong there's a worthwhile detour down a turn-off to scenic **MARYSVILLE**, 9km off the highway. The village nestles in the foothills of the Great Dividing Range, with **Lake Mountain** (1400m), a very popular area for cross-country skiing and tobogganing, 20km to the west. In summer, Marysville makes an excellent base for **bushwalking**, being surrounded by forests with many waterfalls. The best known, **Steavenson's Falls**, can be reached from the village by a walking trail or by road and is floodlit at night until 11pm. Marysville's visitor information centre is on Murchison Street (daily 9am–5pm; Ⓣ03 5963 4567, Ⓦwww.marysvilletourism.com).

Just out of Marysville, the unsealed **Lady Talbot Forest Drive** turns off Lake Mountain Road and then winds 46km through the forest, past picnic areas and walking tracks (suitable for conventional vehicles, though after heavy rainfall it's best to check in Marysville for road conditions). Return to Marysville via the Buxton Road, or turn right and head north to Buxton, where you rejoin the Maroondah Highway. Further north, the highway passes the drier **Cathedral Range State Park**: west of the road here the mighty sandstone cliffs of Cathedral Mountain rise almost vertically behind the paddocks, overlooking the Acheron Valley.

Warburton and the Upper Yarra Track

WARBURTON, east of Lilydale, is a pretty, old-fashioned town on the Upper Yarra River, and the starting point for the **Upper Yarra Track**, which follows old timber tram and vehicle tracks upstream for over 80km. The track can be covered as a series of short walks or as a continuous five- to seven-day trek, finishing in **Baw Baw National Park**, where it joins the Alpine Walking Track. For more information, contact Parks Victoria (☎13 19 63, ⓦwww.parkweb.vic.gov.au).

The Dandenongs

Like the Blue Mountains of New South Wales, the **Dandenong** hills are enveloped in a blue haze rising from the forests of gum trees that cover much of the area. These, interspersed with fern-lined gullies and impressive stands of mountain ash, blackwood and silver wattle, provide a habitat for superb lyrebirds, sulphur-crested cockatoos, crimson rosellas and numerous marsupial and reptile species. Rain ensures the area stays cool and lush, while adding to the scenery are fine old houses, their gardens glowing with colour in spring and early summer when the daffodils, tulips, azaleas and rhododendrons are in bloom. The **Dandenong Ranges and Knox Visitor Information Centre** at 1211 Burwood Hwy, Upper Ferntree Gully (daily 9am–5pm; ☎03 9758 7522, ⓦwww.dandenongrangestourism.com.au), offers a booking service for the region's many pretty country B&Bs and holiday cottages.

▲ Puffing Billy

Parts of the **Dandenong Ranges National Park** can be explored by car – a sealed forest road runs from Upper Ferntree Gully to Olinda – but this is also excellent bushwalking country, with hikes of various levels of difficulty through the Ferntree Gully and Sherbrooke Forest sections. Alternatively, a pleasant way to enjoy the forests and fern gullies is to take a ride on the **Puffing Billy** steam train (T 03 9754 6800, W www.puffingbilly.com.au), which runs for 13km from the Puffing Billy station in Belgrave to Lakeside on Lake Emerald (A$37 return, child A$19), stopping at Menzies Creek and Emerald: one train a day continues a further 9km from Lake Emerald to Gembrook (A$49 return from Belgrave, child A$25). The Puffing Billy station is a short, signposted walk from **Belgrave** station (served by Connex trains from Melbourne). The train has run more or less continuously since the early twentieth century, though its operation now depends on dedicated volunteers; on total-fire-ban days, diesel locomotives are used. Timetables vary seasonally, but there are generally several services daily until late afternoon. There's also a regular programme of special events including Thomas the Tank Engine days for the kids, and an annual Beat-the-Train fun run (early May).

Just outside Emerald, the man-made **Emerald Lakes** have paddle-boats to rent and a swimming pool, as well as walking trails around the perimeter or through the adjacent bushland and forest.

The Mornington Peninsula

The **Mornington Peninsula**, south of Melbourne, curves right around Port Phillip Bay, culminating in Point Nepean. The western shoreline, facing the bay, is beach-bum territory, though the well-heeled denizens of **Sorrento** and **Portsea** at the tip of the peninsula might well resent that tag. Two-thirds of the way down this shore and a little inland, the area around **Arthurs Seat** and **Red Hill** is particularly scenic: a bucolic landscape of rolling hills, orchards, paddocks and vineyards. On the largely straight, ocean-facing southwest coast, **Mornington Peninsula National Park** encompasses some fine seascapes, with several walking trails marked out. The eastern side of the peninsula, looking over the sheltered, shallow waters of **Western Port Bay** and out towards French Island and Phillip Island, has a much quieter, rural feel. Northeast of the pleasant township of **Flinders**, the coastline of rocky cliffs flattens out to sandy beaches, while north of **Stony Point** are mudflats and saltmarshes lined by white mangroves – not particularly visually appealing, but an internationally recognized and protected habitat for migratory waterbirds.

Getting there and information

For a sightseeing trip taking in Arthurs Seat and the Mornington Peninsula's many wineries and beaches, you'll need to join a tour from Melbourne (see p.136 & p.153) or take your own vehicle. **By road**, the region is a straightforward drive south from Melbourne via the Nepean or Moorooduc highways: from the city centre, it's 41km to Frankston on the northwest shore, 70km to Dromana on the fringe of the wine region, 92km to Sorrento and 95km to Portsea. Approaching from Gippsland, you reach the peninsula by turning southwest off the Princes Highway, or west off the South Gippsland Highway. **Public transport** will get you to the main beach resorts on Port Phillip Bay and to Western Point Bay: you can take a Connex train from Melbourne's City Loop stations to Frankston and change there for Stony Point, or pick up a

Mornington Peninsula community markets

Village markets selling regional produce and crafts attract many city dwellers as well as locals. There's usually at least one on every weekend; the following is just a sample.

Balnarring Racecourse Market Coolart Rd, Balnarring. Nov–April, third Sat of the month 8am–1pm.

Dromana Drive-in Sunday Market Dromana Drive-in Cinema, Nepean Hwy, Dromana. Year-round, every Sun 7am–1pm.

Mornington Farmers Market Mornington Primary School, Mornington. Year-round, second Sat of the month 8am–1pm.

Mornington Main Street Market Main St, Mornington. Year-round, every Wed 8am–1pm.

Mornington Racecourse Market Racecourse Rd, Mornington Year-round, second Sun of the month 9am–2pm.

Red Hill Community Market Red Hill Recreation Reserve, Arthurs Seat Road, 10km east of Dromana. Sept–May, first Sat of the month 8am–1pm. The largest and longest established of the "grow it, bake it or make it" markets.

Portsea Passenger Service bus 788 from Frankston to Dromana, Sorrento and Portsea. From Sorrento there's a community bus to Dromana via Blairgowrie, Rye and Rosebud (4 daily Mon–Fri), but no transport to Arthurs Seat. For timetables and fare information for all routes, consult the Metlink information service (☎03 9619 2727 or 13 16 38, ⑩www.metlinkmelbourne.com.au).

On the Port Phillip Bay shore, there are **visitor information centres** at Pier Promenade, Frankston (☎1300 322 842, ⑩www.visitfrankston.com); 320 Main St, Mornington (☎03 5975 1644, ⑩www.mcisc.org.au); and 359B Point Nepean Rd, Dromana (☎03 5987 3078 or 1800 804 009, ⑩www .visitmorningtonpeninsula.org). All are open daily (9am–5pm).

Port Phillip Bay shore: Frankston to Dromana

The peninsula's northwestern flank starts at suburban **FRANKSTON**, 40km from central Melbourne. From here on down, the western shore, flanked by the Nepean Highway, sports beach after beach, all crowded and traffic-snarled in summer. Twelve kilometres southwest of Frankston, the fishing port of **Mornington** preserves some fine old buildings along Mornington Esplanade. Five kilometres further on, near Mount Martha, **The Briars Park** (daily 9am–5pm; A\$4.90, child A\$3.75) comprises an 1840s homestead complete with a collection of furniture and memorabilia given to one of its former owners by Napoleon Bonaparte, and an enclosed wildlife reserve with woodlands and extensive wetlands (daily 9am–5pm, closed during total fire bans; free). The **visitors centre** near the homestead has an audiovisual display giving you an overview of how the affluent upper crust lived in early pioneering days, as well as a rundown on the present-day facilities of the park. Two walkways through the woodlands start near here; the adjacent **wetlands** are visited by more than fifty species of waterbirds, which can be observed at close distance from two bird-hides, accessible via a boardwalk from the visitor information centre.

At **DROMANA**, 29km southwest of Frankston, seaside development begins in earnest: colourful beach huts line the shore and tourists – particularly Italians

Activities on the Mornington Peninsula

Dolphin and seal encounters

Swimming with dolphins and seals is one of Port Phillip Bay's prime attractions. Operators include the environmentally conscious **Polperro Dolphin Swims** (T 03 5988 8437 or 0428 174 160, W www.polperro.com.au), which takes smaller groups, and **Moonraker** (T 03 5984 421, W www.moonrakercharters.com.au). Weather permitting, both run three- to four-hour trips twice daily during the season (Sept/Oct to April/May) for roughly the same prices: A$99–110 for swimmers, including wetsuit and snorkelling equipment; A$44–50 for sightseers.

Horse-riding

You can trot along the water's edge or follow bushland trails with **Ace-Hi Beach Rides**, Cape Schanck (T 03 5988 6262, W www.ace-hi.com.au) or **Gunnamatta Trail Rides**, Rye (T 03 5988 6755, W www.gunnamatta.com.au). From A$35–39 for an hour's ride, or A$77–99 for two hours.

Scuba diving, snorkelling and sea kayaking

Wildlife species snorkellers and divers may spot beneath the surface of Port Phillip Bay include sea dragons, sea horses and octopus; heading out to a site by boat you're also likely to see seals, dolphins and penguins. **Bayplay** in Blairgowrie (T 03 5984 0888, W www.bayplay.com.au) offers PADI training (all levels) and guided dives. They also run a guided kayaking trip along the Port Phillip Bay shoreline (daily; 3hr; A$75, child A$55).

Surfing

Whether you're a beginner or an improver, the tutors at **East Coast Surf School** at Point Leo (T 03 5989 2198, W www.eastcoastsurfschoool.net.au) or **Mornington Peninsula Surf School** in Frankston (T 03 9787 6494, W www.greenroomsurf.com.au) will show you the ropes. Two-hour group lessons cost A$44–50. For gear, **Peninsula Surf** (W www.peninsulasurf.com.au) has several shops dotted over the region.

Winery tours

Mornington Peninsula winery specialists include **Amour of the Grape** (T 0403 500 528, W www.amourofthegrape.com.au), **Vines By The Bay** (T 1300 667 603, W www.vinesbythebay.com.au) and **Wallace's Winery Tours** (T 03 9347 3039, W www.wmptours.com.au). All offer fixed itineraries or bespoke small-group tours, and will fix overnight stays on request; a full day including gourmet lunch typically costs around A$125, with pick-ups from Melbourne for around A$20 extra.

– pack out the resort's many holiday houses and restaurants in the summer season. From here, it's a quick hop into the wine region.

Arthurs Seat and the wine region

Inland from Dromana, the granite outcrop of **Arthurs Seat State Park** rises 305m, providing breathtaking views of Port Phillip Bay. The Arthurs Seat Chairlift, which used to whisk visitors up, ski-lift-style, is currently closed following a series of headline-making mechanical failures; while its future is decided, you can drive up the steep and winding Arthurs Seat Road from the Mornington Peninsula Freeway. At the summit, **Arthurs Seat Maze** (daily 10am–6pm; $15, child A$9; T 03 5981 8449, W www.arthursseatmaze.com.au) combines four landscaped mazes with theme gardens, a sculpture park and a children's animal farm, and offers lots of family-oriented activities and a good restaurant. *Arthurs Hotel* near the top of the Arthurs Seat Road (breakfast, lunch & dinner daily; ☎03 5981 4444) is a pleasant spot for a drink or a bite, with a large sunny terrace and live music on Friday and Saturday evenings and Sunday afternoons.

The Mornington Peninsula **wine region**, spread out around Arthur Seat, Red Hill and Red Hill South, is one of Victoria's best; its two hundred or so **vineyards** produce superb, if pricey, Pinot Noir and Shiraz wines, as well as decent whites. As in the Yarra Valley, good **winery restaurants** have proliferated here in recent years, some of them in truly spectacular settings. Among the best are *Stillwater* at Crittenden Wines, 25 Harrison's Rd, Dromana (cellar door daily 11am–4pm; lunch daily, dinner Thurs–Sat; ☎03 5981 9555, Ⓦwww.crittendenwines.com.au), which makes superb use of fresh organic or free-range ingredients, sourced locally; and *Max's* at the Red Hill Estate, 53 Shoreham Rd, Red Hill South (cellar door daily 11am–5pm; lunch daily, dinner Fri & Sat; ☎03 5931 0177, Ⓦwww.redhillestate.com.au), which has stunning views over the hills and Western Port Bay from its airy dining room and terrace, and a well-prepared Mod Oz menu. Another superb choice is the scenic and highly praised restaurant at *Montalto Vineyard and Olive Grove*, 33 Shoreham Rd, Red Hill South (cellar door daily 11am–5pm; lunch daily, dinner Fri & Sat; ☎03 5989 8412, Ⓦwww.montalto.com.au), offering gourmet dining in a clean-lined, contemporary setting. For more details, see the *Peninsula Wine Country Annual*, published by the Mornington Peninsula Vignerons Association, or *Wine Regions of Victoria*, available from visitor information centres. If you're in the mood for a beer instead, the Red Hill Brewery at 88 Shoreham Rd, Red Hill South (Thurs–Sun 11am–5pm; ☎03 5989 2959, Ⓦwww.redhillbrewery.com.au), has an excellent range of European-style varieties straight from the vat; its in-house bistro, the *Red Hill Brewery Eatery*, does delicious handmade nibbles and lunches.

Sorrento and around

West of Arthurs Seat, the peninsula arcs and narrows down to a strip that's less than 2km wide, with rugged ocean surf crashing onto its "back" beaches, and the calmer waters of the bay washing its "front" beaches. With some of the most expensive Victorian real estate outside the Melbourne CBD, **SORRENTO** is the traditional haunt of the city's rich during the "season" from Boxing Day to Easter. Well-heeled outsiders also make it their playground in January and on summer weekends, flocking here to swim, surf and dive at the bay and ocean beaches. Exploring beautiful rock formations and low-tide pools, and swimming with bottlenose dolphins add to the attraction. The smell of money is everywhere – in the wide, tree-lined residential streets, the clifftop mansions boasting million-dollar views, and the town-centre cafés, restaurants, galleries and antique shops, running along Ocean Road down to the beach.

Sullivan Bay, 3km southeast, was in 1803 the site of the first white attempt to settle in what is now Victoria; the settlers struggled here for four months before giving up and moving on to what is now Tasmania. One of the convicts in the expedition was the infamous William Buckley who, having escaped, was adopted by the local Aborigines and lived with them for 32 years. When the "wild white man" was seen again by settlers he could scarcely remember how to speak English; his survival against all odds has been immortalized in the phrase "Buckley's chance". You can walk along the cliffs and around the pioneer cemetery; there's a signposted turn-off from the main road.

From Sorrento, you can hop across the mouth of Port Phillip Bay by ferry, landing at Queenscliff on the Bellarine Peninsula: this is an interesting though little-used approach to the very scenic Great Ocean Road from Torquay to Warrnambool (see box, p.157).

Accommodation

Sorrento has a sophisticated mix of accommodation including elegant **B&Bs**, smart little **hotels** and holiday **apartments** with above-average rates for regional Victoria; the following is a very small selection.

Bayplay Adventure Lodge 46 Canterbury Jetty Rd, Blairgowrie (6km east of Sorrento) ☎ 03 5984 0888, ⓦ www.bayplay.com.au. Comfortable budget accommodation in a bushland setting near the beach, with a shared kitchen and swimming pool, plus a PADI dive centre (see box, p.153). The Frankston–Portsea bus stops just outside. Bunk A$35, double/twin ❸

Carmel of Sorrento 142 Ocean Beach Rd, Sorrento ☎ 03 5984 3512, ⓦ www.carmelof sorrento.com.au. Delightful period B&B with comfortably furnished rooms, smack in the middle of town; as well as guest rooms, it offers a couple of small but attractive apartments. ❻–❻

Hotel Sorrento 5 Hotham Rd, Sorrento ☎ 03 5984 8000, ⓦ www.hotelsorrento.com.au. In a secluded spot on a hill above the jetty, this charming 1870s building has been given a smart contemporary makeover, with modern furniture set against exposed limestone walls. The best suites and apartments have tremendous bay views. Room or suite ❺–❻, apartment ❼

Sorrento Beach Motel 780 Melbourne Rd, Sorrento ☎ 03 5984 1356, ⓦ www.sorrentobeach motel.com.au. Mid-range, well-managed motel with a pleasingly quirky design – the outside of each unit looks like an old bathing house. ❺

Sorrento YHA 3 Miranda St, Sorrento ☎ 03 5984 4323, ⓦ www.yha.com.au. Cosy and friendly hostel, with stacks of local information on offer. The rooms and dorms, though rather small, are well kept. Bunk A$25–40, double/twin ❸

Eating and drinking

As is to be expected in this posh part of the peninsula, most **eating places** tend to be on the pricey side, but some come with great water-views as a bonus. In winter, a lot of eateries have restricted opening times or are only open at weekends.

The Baths 3278 Point Nepean Rd, Sorrento ☎ 03 5984 1500. A stylish take on a beach house, this contemporary restaurant (daily 9am–late) has the best location in Sorrento, and highish prices. The *Fish and Chippery* around the side (daily noon–8pm) is a more affordable option.

Continental Hotel 21 Ocean Beach Rd, Sorrento ☎ 03 5984 2201. This venerable old-timer has a good café-restaurant with an Italian slant, and a wide range of local wines; at weekends, there's occasional live music and regular club nights. Daily from 8.30am for breakfast, lunch & dinner.

Hotel Sorrento 5 Hotham Rd ☎ 03 5984 8000. Run by a Kenyan chef with a vibrant contemporary style, this hotel restaurant serves hearty grills and seafood dishes, but the prime attraction is the view across the bay. Breakfast, lunch & dinner daily, afternoon spread Sat & Sun.

Shells Café 95 Ocean Beach Rd, Sorrento ☎ 03 5984 5133. This light-filled, breezy café serves good coffee and cakes plus the standard café fare, and is a prime spot for people-watching. Popular with surfers. Daily 8am–5pm.

Smokehouse Pizza Kitchen 182 Ocean Beach Rd ☎ 03 5984 1246. Since 1992, the *Smokehouse* has been dishing up some of the best pizzas this side of Melbourne. Takeaway available. Daily noon–late.

Spargo's 113 Ocean Beach Rd ☎ 03 5984 3177. Big, sometimes chaotic café with nice outdoor seating in which to get stuck into their excellent wine list and seafood specials. Open for breakfast, lunch & dinner daily.

Stringers Store 2 Ocean Beach Rd ☎ 03 5984 2010. Part gourmet supermarket, part great café that serves up the best continental breakfasts in town. Daily 8am–5pm.

Portsea and Point Nepean

PORTSEA, 4km west of Sorrento and 96km from Melbourne via the coast road, has an elegant, exclusive air: dotted with nineteenth-century mansions, mature gardens and tennis courts, it's another long-established retreat for wealthy Melburnians. Its Port Phillip Bay beaches – Shelley Beach, on the east side of town, and Portsea Front Beach, by the pier – feature wall-to-wall beautiful people. Overlooking Front Beach are the extensive lawns of *Portsea Hotel* on Point Nepean Road (℡03 5984 2213), a hugely popular drinking spot featuring salsa nights on Wednesdays and bands at weekends. The waters at this end of the peninsula attract playful dolphins, and are a Mecca for **divers**, with excellent dives off Port Phillip Heads; there are a couple of good dive shops running trips from the pier throughout the summer. On the southwest-facing shore, Portsea Ocean (or Back) Beach has challenging surfing, and a natural rock formation known as London Bridge (not to be confused with the other London Bridge near Port Campbell, further west); the cliffs near here are a favourite launch site for hang-gliders.

The tip, **Point Nepean**, with its fortifications, quarantine station and former army base, is part of a patchwork of parks sprinkled over the southern end of the peninsula, collectively known as Mornington Peninsula National Park. Because of its fragile sandy environment, visitors to Point Nepean are limited to six hundred at any one time (A\$7.70, child A\$3.70); if you'd like to visit at the weekend or during the school holidays, it's advisable to call the **visitor centre** at the entrance to the park to check whether you need to book (℡03 5984 4276). You can explore the park on foot, rent a bike at the visitor centre (A\$16/3hr) or board the Transporter – a few carriages pulled by a tractor (hourly; 9.30am–12.30pm plus 2pm & 3pm; A\$13, child A\$7.50 one way, A\$16/A\$9.50 return including park admission). It runs to the fortifications at Point Nepean, with four optional drop-offs for walks: the first, the **Walter Pisterman Heritage Walk** (1km), leads through coastal vegetation to the Port Phillip Bay shoreline; the second (1km) leads to the top of Cheviot Hill, where you can look across to Queenscliff, then continues to **Cheviot Beach** where on December 17, 1967, **Harold Holt**, Australia's then prime minister, went for a swim in the rough surf of Bass Strait and disappeared, presumed drowned: his body was never found. The third walk, the **Fort Pearce and Eagle's Nest Heritage Trail** (2km), crosses through defence fortifications. A fourth walk takes you around **Fort Nepean**, right at the tip of the peninsula. Built at the same time as Fort Queenscliff opposite to protect wealthy post-gold rush Melbourne from the imagined threat of Russian invasion, the fort comprises two subterranean levels, whose tunnels lead down to the Engine House at water level.

The south and east coasts

Mornington Peninsula National Park continues along the southwest-facing ocean coast (vehicle access A\$4.30 per day). An enjoyable two-day walk (27km) runs from London Bridge along the coast to **Cape Schanck**, the peninsula's southernmost point, with a lighthouse dating back to 1859. Here, walkways lead down to the sea along a narrow neck of land, providing magnificent coastal views. The two **lighthouse keepers' cottages** offer the most scenic accommodation on the peninsula (*Cape Schanck Light Station*, 420 Cape Schanck Rd; ℡0500 527 891, ⓦwww.austpacinns.com.au; ❹); each sleeps up to eight and has a cosy lounge and kitchen. The lighthouse, which incorporates a small maritime museum, is open daily for tours at half-hourly intervals (10am–5pm; A\$14, child A\$11).

The nearby **Bushrangers Bay Nature Walk** (6km; 2hr) heads from the cape to Main Creek, beginning as a leisurely walk along the clifftop, then

The Great Ocean Road

It's no coincidence that so many photos of Victoria's **Great Ocean Road** feature a shiny convertible bowling along in glorious sunshine: this is one of Australia's most picturesque drives, and a journey to be savoured. Winding its way around cliffs and through gullies between **Torquay** and **Warrnambool**, southwest of Melbourne, the road passes some spectacular sights including the legendary rollers of **Bells Beach** – nirvana for hard-core surfers – and the towering forests of **Otway National Park**. Travelling from east to west, you reach the most breathtaking section two thirds of the way along – the **Shipwreck Coast** west of Moonlight Head, with the **Twelve Apostles** and **London Bridge**, iconic rock formations, poised dramatically offshore. It's possible to cover the entire return route in a long day's excursion from Melbourne (for tour options, see p.136), but with appealing places to stay along the way, it's well worth spinning out the trip over a few days as a meandering add-on to your East Coast explorations.

The road was conceived in 1918 as a scenic drive to rival California's Pacific Coast Highway and the French Riviera, and a memorial to those who lost their lives in World War I. The arduous task of carving the 285-kilometre route out of this notoriously rugged and densely forested coastal wilderness commenced promptly the following year, but took thirteen years to complete. The road has drawn streams of tourists ever since, but the coast remains remarkably unspoilt.

By car or motorbike, there are two possible **approaches to Torquay**, the east end of the road. Following the Princes Freeway (M1) southwest out of Melbourne to Geelong and then continuing south along the Surf Coast Highway (B100) is a straightforward enough option: it's around 96km from central Melbourne to Torquay. For a more interesting journey, you could start from the Mornington Peninsula, hopping from Sorrento to Queenscliff by ferry, and heading west across the Bellarine Peninsula, bypassing both Melbourne and Geelong. The ferry, run by Searoad, operates all year round (hourly departures from both Sorrento Pier and Queenscliff Harbour 7am–6pm, extra services at 7pm from 26 Dec to early April; foot passenger A$9 one way, child A$7; vehicle plus two people A$58–64; motorbike plus rider A$27–31; ℡03 5258 3244, Ⓦwww.searoad.com.au). It's also possible, though challenging, to tackle the road by bicycle, or to hike along part of the coast: the 100-kilometre **Great Ocean Walk** along the central, southernmost section from Apollo Bay (served by a V/Line bus from Geelong) to Princetown via the Otway National Park follows the coast more closely than the road and is one of Australia's most magnificent trails. Parks Victoria manages seven hikers' campsites along this route (for details, see Ⓦwww.greatoceanwalk.com.au), and there are gorgeous ecolodges and B&Bs, plus more modest hostels and motels, throughout the region: for recommendations, consult the *Rough Guide to Australia* or contact the various **visitor information centres** along the way, the principal of which is at Stead Park on the Princes Highway, Geelong (daily 9am–5pm; ℡03 5275 5797 or 1800 620 888, Ⓦwww.greatoceanroad.org).

leading down to a wild beach facing Elephant Rock. More energetic activities in this part of the peninsula include **horse rides** along Gunnamatta Beach or through bushland and **surfing** at various spots near Point Leo (see box, p.153).

The pleasant village of **FLINDERS**, at the point east of Cape Schanck, has a good B&B, *Samburu*, on Eastern Grey Rise, off Meakins Road, 14km west of Flinders (℡03 5989 0093, Ⓦwww.samburu.com.au; ❹): the main farmhouse has a guest wing and a separate studio with great views. A decent budget option is the shady *Flinders Caravan Park* at 1/17 The Avenue (℡03 5989 0458, Ⓦwww.flinderscaravanpark.com.au; camping A$25–35, cabin ❷–❸).

Set in bushland near the northern end of Westernport Bay, 15km southeast of Frankston, the **Moonlit Sanctuary Conservation Park** at 55 Tyabb–Tooradin Rd, Pearcedale (daily 11am–5pm; day visit A\$9.50, child A\$6.50; ☎03 5978 7935, ⓦwww.moonlit-sanctuary.com), is home to lots of kangaroos, wallabies, emus and waterbirds. However, the park's emphasis is on rare nocturnal Australian animals, so it's well worth joining their **evening tour** (1hr 30min; A\$22, child A\$12; reservations required). Starting at dusk, this offers the chance to see eastern quolls, eastern bettongs, pademelons, gliders and tawny frogmouths in bushland enclosures.

French Island

FRENCH ISLAND, in Western Port on the eastern side of the Mornington Peninsula, is well off the beaten track. A former prison farm, about two-thirds of the island is a national park, with the remaining third used as farmland. The island is renowned for its rich **flora** and **fauna**, especially raptors, wading birds, long-nosed potoroos, a flourishing koala colony and many species of wild orchid. Virtually vehicle-free, it's a great place to cycle, an activity that is encouraged, with all walking tracks open to bikes. It's also one of Kylie Minogue's favourite retreats – she owns a house there.

Arrival and information

Inter Island Ferries (☎03 9585 5730, ⓦwww.interislandferries.com.au) carry foot passengers and bikes to **Tankerton jetty** on French Island from Stony Point, near Hastings, on the eastern side of the Mornington Peninsula (15min; Mon, Wed & Fri 8.30am & 4.15pm, Tues & Thurs 8.30am, noon & 4.15pm, Sat & Sun 8.30am, 10am, noon & 4.15pm; A\$20 return, child A\$10, plus A\$8 per bike). Stony Point jetty is 82km from central Melbourne by road, or a five-hundred-metre walk from Stony Point station, which you can reach in one and a half to two hours from Melbourne's Flinders Street Station, changing at Frankston. Inter Island Ferries also run one to three crossings per day between Cowes on Phillip Island (see p.159) and Tankerton (30min; same fares). The French Island Barge, which carries vehicles across from Corinella, is only available to residents, to avoid the spread of pest plants.

The island's **information centre** is 10km inland from the jetty on Bayview Road (☎03 5980 1241 or 1800 804 009), as is the **Parks Victoria office** (☎03 5980 1294). The French Island Tourist Association runs a telephone information service on ☎03 5985 5730.

Practicalities

Places to stay include *McLeod Ecofarm* on McLeod Road (☎03 5678 0155, ⓦwww.mcleodecofarm.com; bunk A\$39, double/twin ❻, including meals made from fresh farm produce and transfers from the ferry jetty 29km away), which incorporates the island's old prison buildings: cells have been converted into guest bunkrooms sleeping two, while the former officers' quarters are, as you'd expect, more comfortable; all rooms have shared facilities. Situated on the east side of the island, *t*he fully functional organic farm, where visitors can get involved in tending pigs and chickens, is surrounded by national park and has 8km of beach frontage. Also in the national park is the small and basic *Fairhaven Campground* on the west coast foreshore (bookings ☎03 5980 1294, 03 5986 9100 or 13 19 63); it has a pit toilet and tank water, but no showers. Camping is free, but must be booked in advance – two weeks ahead is advised during the summer school holidays and at Easter. Near the jetty on Tankerton Road, the small *Tortoise Head Lodge* (T03 5980 1234, Wwww.tortoisehead.net; ❸–❹) offers eco-friendly B&B accommodation in guest rooms with shared facilities, or four en-suite cabins with water views; moderately priced lunches and dinners are also available. *French Island B&B* is a cottage with two bedrooms, 2.5km from the jetty (T03 5980 1209, Wwww.frenchislandbandb.com.au; ❹); it's operated by the general store, who also provide well-priced lunches and dinners. The *Bayview Chicory Kiln Tea Room* on Bayview Road, 10km from the jetty (T03 5980 1241; camping A$10), has a private campsite with toilets and shower. In addition, scrumptious lunches and Devonshire teas are served here.

For a brief visit, the best way to see the island's natural attractions and the historic prison is to book a locally run bus tour. **French Island Tours** (4hr; Tues, Thurs & Sun 12.15pm; A$18, child A$10 including Devonshire tea; T03 5980 1241 or 0412 671 241, Wwww.frenchislandtours.com.au), operated by the owners of the *Bayview Chicory Kiln Tea Room*, offer an afternoon spent wildlife-watching, orchid-spotting, walking along the coast and visiting the Chicory Kiln and Ecofarm. **French Island Eco Tours** (4hr; Thurs & Sun, 12.15pm; A$40 including organic lunch; T1300 307 054 or 0429 177 532, Wwww .frenchislandecotours.com.au) have a similar offering, and can organize special-interest nature tours on request. Both operators meet the incoming ferry at Tankerton and drop guests at the jetty at the end of the tour. **Wildlife Coast Cruises** (6hr; Wed & Sun 9.30am; A$62, child A$42 including organic lunch; T03 5953 3501, Wwww.wildlifecoastcruises.com.au) run tours starting from Phillip Island.

Phillip Island

The hugely popular holiday destination of **PHILLIP ISLAND**, on the south side of Western Port, is famous above all for the nightly return to roost of hundreds of little penguins at Summerland Beach – the so-called **Penguin Parade** – but the island also boasts some dramatic coastline, plenty of challenging surfing, fine swimming beaches and a couple of well-organized wildlife parks. Motorsports fans will know it as the home of the annual **Australian Motorcycle Grand Prix**. Connected to the mainland by a bridge, the island is considerably more accessible than its northern neighbour, French Island. **Cowes**, on the sheltered bay side, is the main town and a lively, though somewhat tacky, place to stay. Other, smaller, communities worth a visit are **Rhyll**, to the east, close to an inlet where hundreds of wading birds gather to feed, and **Ventnor**, just west of Cowes.

Arrival and information

By **road**, Cowes is 143km southeast of central Melbourne via the Monash Freeway or Princes Highway, the South Gippsland Highway (M420) and the Bass Highway (A420). From Lakes Entrance, it's 405km via the Princes Highway and Strzelecki/Bass Highway (B460); from Foster, it's 104km via Buffalo, Tarwin and Inverloch. A direct **V/Line bus** to Cowes departs from Melbourne's Southern Cross station at 3.50pm daily, arriving around 7pm and returning at 8.50am (A$10, child A$5 one way). Alternatively, **Inter Island Ferries** (T03 9585 5730, Wwww.interislandferries.com.au) carry foot passengers and bikes to Cowes from Stony Point, near Hastings, on the eastern

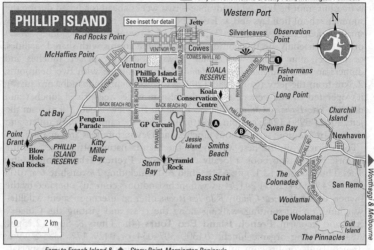

Ferry to French Island & Stony Point, Mornington Peninsula

PHILLIP ISLAND

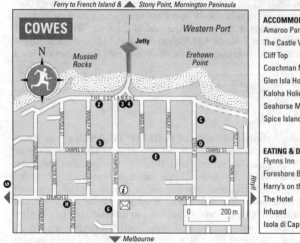

Ferry to French Island & Stony Point, Mornington Peninsula

COWES

ACCOMMODATION	
Amaroo Park	**H**
The Castle Villa by the Sea	**C**
Cliff Top	**A**
Coachman Motel	**E**
Glen Isla House	**G**
Kaloha Holiday Resort	**D**
Seahorse Motel	**F**
Spice Island	**B**

EATING & DRINKING	
Flynns Inn	**5**
Foreshore Bar and Restaurant	**1**
Harry's on the Esplanade	**2**
The Hotel	**4**
Infused	**6**
Isola di Capri	**3**

side of the Mornington Peninsula (30min; Mon & Wed 8.30am & 5pm; Tues, Thurs, Sat & Sun 8.30am, noon & 5pm; Fri 8.30am, 5pm & 7pm; A$20 return, child A$10, plus A$8 per bike). For routes to Stony Point from Melbourne and details of ferries between French Island and Cowes, see p.158. There's no public transport on Phillip Island itself, so without a car it can be tricky getting around and to the Penguin Parade, 15km from Cowes: joining a **tour** solves this (see p.136 for operators running day-trips from Melbourne), though since it's a long way to travel just for the day, you may prefer to stay at least one night, getting around by hire car or bicycle.

If you're **driving** here, the scenic lookout on the mainland just east of the island, about 3km before San Remo, is worth a stop, for fantastic views of Western Port Bay and the surrounding countryside; **SAN REMO** itself has a picturesque fishing fleet by its wharf and a co-operative selling fresh fish and crayfish.

Phillip Island has two **visitor information centres** (both daily 9am–5pm; ☎1300 366 422, ⊛www.visitphillipisland.com): at 895 Phillip Island Tourist Rd, Newhaven (just west of the bridge; ☎03 5956 7447) and at 91 Thompson Ave, Cowes (☎03 5951 3396); both can book accommodation and trips, including Three Park Passes for the Penguin Parade, Churchill Island Heritage Farm and Koala Conservation Centre (A$34, child A$17; also available online at ⊛www.penguins.org.au).

SOUTHEAST VICTORIA | Phillip Island

Accommodation

Other than *Cliff Top* and *Spice Island*, all of the following recommendations are in Cowes. Some rates increase steeply at Christmas and Easter.

Amaroo Park 97 Church St ☎03 5952 2548, ⊛www.amaroopark.com. Accommodation comprises a good YHA hostel and a caravan park; facilities include a convivial bar, heated swimming pool, cheap meals and bike rental. They also run tours of the island. Camping A$60, bunk A$30–40, room ❷, cabin ❹

The Castle Villa by the Sea 7–9 Steele St ☎03 5952 1228, ⊛www.thecastle.com.au. Delightful, imaginatively furnished boutique hotel with a choice of rooms, suites and mini-apartments in a pleasant and quiet location just around the corner from The Esplanade. Great restaurant as well. ❹–❻

Cliff Top 1 Marlin St, Smiths Beach ☎03 5952 1033, ⊛www.clifftop.com.au. Stunning views over the water make this the island's best accommodation option. The seven rooms are named after explorers and offer everything for the perfect romantic getaway. ❻

Coachman Motel 51 Chapel St ☎03 5952 1098, ⊛www.coachmanmotel.com.au. Comfortable and affordable – though rather dated – motel with self-contained units and suites. Facilities include a heated outdoor pool and spa. ❹

Glen Isla House 230–232 Church St ☎03 5952 1882, ⊛www.glenisla.com. Luxury B&B with a country-house feel; the rooms are classically decorated, some with sumptuous four-poster beds, and there's a spacious, beautifully landscaped garden. Breakfast is a first-class event. ❻

Kaloha Holiday Resort Steele St, corner of Chapel St ☎03 5952 2179, ⊛www.kaloha.com.au. Located in shady grounds close to The Esplanade, with easy access to its quiet swimming beach, this is a family-friendly resort with plain but decent rooms and self-contained units, and a solar-heated pool. ❹

Seahorse Motel 29–31 Chapel St ☎03 5952 2003, ⊛www.seahorsemotel.com.au. This above-average, centrally located motel has well-kept rooms and apartments, and helpful management. ❹

Spice Island 1A Hill St, Sunderland Bay ☎03 5956 7557, ⊛www.spiceisland.com.au. Luxury B&B offering a choice of three exceptionally cool and contemporary split-level studio apartments, set on rolling hills in a quiet part of the island. Furnished with flair, they're excellent value. ❻

Eating and drinking

All of the below, except the *Foreshore Bar and Restaurant*, are on or close to the lively strip facing the jetty in Cowes.

Flynns Inn 72 Chapel St ☎03 5952 1800. Homely Irish pub serving the usual fare such as beef and Guinness pie and Irish stew. Great place to go on cold nights. Tues–Sun 6pm–late.

Foreshore Bar and Restaurant 11 Beach Rd, Rhyll ☎03 5952 1300. Only a ten-minute drive away from Cowes, this stylish, contemporary bistro uses excellent locally sourced ingredients, from sausages to steaks. Light lunches such as chicken and artichoke salad are under A$20; heartier mains A$21–35. Lunch & dinner daily; closed Tues in winter.

Harry's on the Esplanade Shop 5, 17 The Esplanade ☎03 5952 6226. Steaks and grills served up in a nice setting: the balcony has tremendous views of the bay. Tues–Sun 11am–late, plus Sun breakfast.

The Hotel 11–13 The Esplanade ☎03 5952 2060. Relaxed restaurant with a mid-priced menu including pasta, seafood and grills; stays open late on Fri and Sat, when DJs spin a few tunes. Lunch & dinner daily.

Infused 115 Thompson Ave ☎03 5952 2655. One of the best places to eat in Cowes, this offers freshly shucked oysters, excellent seafood and juicy steaks in stylish but laidback surroundings. Above-average prices. Lunch & dinner daily.

161

Activities on Phillip Island

The island's coastal wilderness offers enjoyable walking, cycling, boating and birdwatching; for something to get the heart pounding, head for the Grand Prix racetrack or try surfing the wilder swells.

Cruises

From October to April, **Wildlife Coast Cruises** (☎03 5952 3501 or 1300 763 739, ⓦwww.wildlifecoastcruises.com.au) offer various trips from Cowes jetty, the best being the tour to Seal Rocks (2hr; A$58, child A$40) to see Australian fur seals close up. They also run trips to neighbouring French Island (see p.158).

Cycling and hiking

The island has plenty of trails to explore. You can hire mountain bikes (A$15/hr, A$35/day) and tandems (A$20/hr, A$60/day) from **Ride on Bikes** at 17 The Esplanade, Cowes (☎03 5952 2533, ⓦwww.rideonbikes.com.au).

Phillip Island Circuit HSV Hot Laps

Strap yourself in beside an experienced V8 Supercar racing driver for three lightning-fast laps round the **Grand Prix circuit** (30min including briefing; A$199; ☎03 5952 9400, ⓦwww.phillipislandcircuit.com.au). For a fun alternative, there's a miniature replica of the circuit beside the main track, which you can whizz round in a go-kart (from A$25 for 10min).

Surfing

The island is pounded with consistently good waves: hard-core types head for Cat Bay and Cape Woolamai, but Smiths Beach is safer for beginners. The island's surf shops include **Island Surfboards** (ⓦwww.islandsurfboards.com.au) with branches at 147 Thompson Ave, Cowes (☎03 5952 2578) and 65 Smiths Beach Rd, Smiths Beach (☎03 5952 3443), and **Islantis Surboards** at 10–12 Phillip Island Rd, Newhaven (☎03 5956 7553, ⓦwww.islantis.com.au); all sell and rent gear, and fix up lessons for around A$50 for two hours. For a recorded weather and surf forecast, call the Phillip Island Surf Report on ☎1902 243 082.

Isola di Capri 2 Thompson Ave ☎03 5952 2435. Long-established, friendly and moderately priced Italian restaurant, offering everything from coffee and *gelati* to pizzas, pasta or a classic seafood blow-out. Takeaway available. Lunch & dinner daily.

Phillip Island Grand Prix Circuit

Looping around a scenic section of the south coast, the **Phillip Island Grand Prix Circuit** (☎03 5952 9400, ⓦwww.phillipislandcircuit.com.au) hosts V8 Supercar endurance races (ⓦwww.v8supercar.com.au) in September and the Australian Motorcycle Grand Prix (ⓦwww.motogp.com.au) in September or October. The island is always jam-packed for these events. If there's no racing scheduled, you can get a taste of the action by booking a triple lap with a V8 racing driver (see box, above) or just dropping in at the History of Motorsport display at the visitor centre off Back Beach Road (daily 9am–7pm; A$13.50, child A$6.50), featuring snapshots and memorabilia of the crazy exploits and heroics of Australia's early racers.

Phillip Island Reserve and the Penguin Parade

The **Phillip Island Reserve** includes all the public land on the narrow **Summerland Peninsula** at the island's western extremity. The reason for the reserve is the **little penguin**, smallest of the penguins at only 33cm tall, which is found only in southern and southeastern Australian waters and whose largest colony – numbering over a thousand – breeds at Summerland Beach. Phillip Island Nature Parks, the organization that manages the reserve, hosts a penguin-watching event every day at sunset, the famous **Penguin Parade** (A\$20, child A\$10; ☎03 5956 8300, ⓦwww.penguins.org.au). The concept may sound horribly commercial – and with four thousand visitors a night at the busiest time of the year (the summer holidays and Easter, when bookings are essential), it can hardly fail to be. But don't be too hard on it: ecological disaster would ensue if the site wasn't managed properly, since visitors would still flock here, harming the birds and eroding the sand dunes; furthermore, entrance fees help fund research.

Spectators sit in concrete-stepped stadiums looking down onto a floodlit beach, with taped narrations in Japanese, Taiwanese and English. Photography and filming is prohibited, with or without flash. You can pay A\$15–50 extra for a more exclusive, close-up experience from an elevated viewing platform or a private section of beach, with a ranger on hand to answer questions, but even if you don't, the parade manages to transcend the setting, as the penguins come pouring onto the beach, waddling comically once they leave the water. They start arriving soon after dark; fifty minutes later the floodlights are switched off and it's all over, at which time (or before) you can move on to the extensive boardwalks over their burrows, with diffused lighting at regular intervals enabling you to watch them for hours after the parade finishes – they're active most of the night.

The excellent **Penguin Parade Visitor Centre** (daily from 10am; A\$4, child A\$2, free with a parade ticket) includes a simulated underwater scene of the hazards of a penguin's life, and there are also interactive displays, videos and even nesting boxes to which penguins have access from the outside, where you can watch the chicks (Nov–April).

If you want to avoid the worst of the crowds, the quietest **time to visit** the reserve is during the cold and windy winter (you'll need weatherproof clothing at any time of year), but you'll see more penguins if you visit during the laying and hatching season, or when the chicks are very young (Sept–Jan). Remember, too, that you can also see little penguins close to St Kilda Pier in Melbourne (see p.118) and at many other coastal locations in southern and southeastern Australia, notably Montague Island and Jervis Bay in New South Wales (see p.188 & p.194) – perhaps not in such large numbers, but with far fewer onlookers.

The Nobbies and Seal Rocks

At the tip of the Summerland Peninsula is **Point Grant**, where **The Nobbies**, two huge rock-stacks, are linked to the island at low tide by a wave-cut platform of basalt, affording views across to Cape Schanck on the Mornington Peninsula. From the point, a boardwalk leads across spongy greenery – vibrant in summer with purple and yellow flowers – along the rounded clifftops to a lookout over a blowhole. This is a wild spot, with views along the rugged southern coastline towards Cape Woolamai, a granite headland at the eastern end of the island. From September to April, you may see muttonbirds (shear-waters) here – they arrive in September to breed, and head for the same burrows each year after an incredible flight from the Bering Strait in the Arctic Circle. Further off Point Grant, **Seal Rocks** are two rocky islets with the largest known colony of Australian fur seals, estimated to number around 16,000. It's possible to see seals here all year round, though their numbers peak during the breeding season between late October and December. The **Nobbies Centre** near Point Grant (summer 10am–8pm; winter 11am–4pm; free; ☎03 5951 2800, ⓦwww.nobbies.org.au) has high-tech cameras trained on the colony, relaying footage to large screens; you can also watch the action through telescopes. The centre is a three-kilometre drive west of the Penguin Parade, from where there's a free shuttle at busy times. **Cruises** to Seal Rocks are available from Cowes (see box, p.162).

Phillip Island Wildlife Park and the Koala Conservation Centre

Two further parks complete Phillip Island's rich collection of wildlife attractions. **Phillip Island Wildlife Park**, on Thompson Avenue just over 1km south of Cowes (daily 10am–5pm; A$12; ☎03 5952 2038), provides a shady sanctuary for Australian animals – beautiful pure-bred dingoes, Tasmanian devils, fat and dozy wombats – as well as an aviary and a koala reserve. There are also freely ranging emus, Cape Barren geese, wallabies, eastern grey kangaroos and pademelons.

The **Koala Conservation Centre**, on Phillip Island Road between Newhaven and Cowes (daily 10am–5.30pm; A$10, child A$5), aims to keep the bushland habitat as natural as possible while still giving people a close-up view: there are elevated boardwalks through part of the park, and at 4pm the rangers provide fresh gum leaves – a very popular photo opportunity. You can learn about koalas in the excellent interpretive centre.

Rhyll Inlet and Rhyll

The **Conservation Hill Lookout**, just off the Cowes–Rhyll Road further north, provides a good view of the **Rhyll Inlet**, a significant roosting and feeding ground for migratory wading birds, which come from as far as Siberia. A boardwalk starting at the car park takes visitors into the middle of the inlet, a landscape of mangroves, saltmarshes and mudflats.

Unlike most other places on the island, the fishing village of **RHYLL** has managed to retain a sleepy charm. There are a couple of cafés and a tavern on the foreshore, with splendid views of the tranquil, shallow waters of Western Port Bay and the South Gippsland coast.

Churchill Island

Just north of Newhaven and connected to the mainland by a bridge, **Churchill Island** is mostly occupied by a working **Heritage Farm** (daily 10am–5pm; A$10; ☎03 5956 7214, ⓦwww.penguins.org.au); founded by pioneer Lieutenant James Grant in 1801, it was the first estate in Victoria to be cultivated. Now a low-key tourist attraction, it's stocked with suitably retro animals including Clydesdale horses and highland cattle. Visitors can nose around the restored homestead, which dates back to the late nineteenth century and is furnished with antiques; there are also pretty, English-style gardens to explore, surrounded by ancient moonah trees, home to abundant birdlife. A leisurely two-hour **walk** leads around the perimeter of the island, with views of the unspoilt coastline, while in the middle of the island there's a visitor centre with a café.

Wilsons Promontory

WILSONS PROMONTORY, or "the Prom", the southernmost part of the Australian mainland, was once joined by a land bridge to Tasmania. Its barbed hook juts out into Bass Strait, with a rocky coastline interspersed with sheltered sandy bays and coves; the coastal scenery is made even more stunning by the backdrop of granite ranges. It's understandably Victoria's most popular **national**

▲ Wilsons Promontory

park, and though the main campsite gets totally packed in summer, the park's big enough to allow you to escape the crowds, with plenty of walking tracks and opportunities for bushcamping in areas rich in native flora and fauna, including tea-trees and banksias, koalas, wallabies and rat kangaroos. The waters surrounding the Prom are a marine park and World Biosphere Reserve; you can swim and snorkel at several of the beaches, and the rockpools among the granite boulders are full of life.

Arrival and information

By **road**, the entrance to the Prom (day pass A$10 per car, multi-day pass A$15.80/A$30 for 2/5 consecutive days) is around 200km southeast of Melbourne, 116km east of Phillip Island and 250km southwest of Lakes Entrance; Tidal River, the principal destination, is 30km further south. Access to the region is via the South Gippsland Highway, turning south at Meeniyan or Foster to head towards the park. You can get to Foster on the **V/Line bus** service between Melbourne and Yarram via Dandenong; there's no public transport from Foster to Tidal River but Prom Country Taxis in Foster will take you there (around A$100 one way; ℡03 5682 2188); alternatively you could fix up a lift into the park with the owners of Foster's *YHA* (see p.167) for A$15–20 per person. Bunyip Bushwalking Tours run recommended **guided tours** of the Prom, starting from Melbourne (see box, p.136).

The **Prom Country Information Centre** is 105km northwest of Tidal River at Korumburra, on the South Gippsland Highway from Melbourne (daily 9am–5pm; ℡03 5655 2233 or 1800 630 704, ⊛www.visitpromcountry.com). The **Wilsons Promontory National Park Office** at Tidal River (daily 8.30am–4.30pm; ℡03 5680 9555 or 1800 350 552, ⊛www.parkweb.vic .gov.au) has plenty of visitor information, though not all of it is on display, so ask. The National Parks Association guide *Discovering the Prom* (A$14.95) is invaluable if you're attempting any of the longer **walks**; you can pick up or download information on short walks for free.

Accommodation

Most visitors to the park stay at **Tidal River** on Norman Bay, where there's a choice of camping (A$22.50), simple one-room huts (❷), motel-style self-catering units (❹) and comfortable, eco-friendly cabins (❺), all run by Victoria Parks (℡13 19 63, ⊛www.parkweb.vic.gov.au). The Prom is so popular that accommodation for the summer holidays (from the week before Christmas to late Jan) is allocated the previous winter by a ballot, for which you must apply online in June or July; the remainder of the summer (until April) is also extremely busy. Facilities at Tidal River include a general store, laundry, takeaway, petrol station and an outdoor cinema (summer holidays).

An alternative is to plan a hike of two or more days, staying at the **bush campsites** that are scattered throughout the park. To do so, you need to obtain an overnight hike permit (A$6.90 per person per night) by submitting your itinerary to the Tidal River park office, by phone or in person; there's a maximum stay of one night at some sites and two nights at others. Numbers are limited so it's best to book in advance. Hikers' campsites, most of which are only accessible on foot, have only the most basic facilities.

Committed hikers can book a night or two in the restored keepers' cottages at the **Wilsons Promontory Lightstation** (❻), which can also only be reached on foot – you should allow at least six hours for the walk of 19km from Telegraph Saddle car park, or 24km from Tidal River via Oberon Bay, carrying water and supplies. The granite lighthouse was completed in 1859; its four cottages are the Australian mainland's southernmost residences.

Another possibility is to base yourself outside the park boundary in **Prom Country**, which includes Foster, Waratah Bay, Walkerville, Sandy Point and Yanakie: the Prom Country Information Centre (see p.166) and Prom Accom (☎1800 458 382, ⓦwww.promaccom.com.au), an independent accommodation agency, have details of numerous B&Bs, motels and cottages in the area. Foster's several modest places to stay include the small, cosy *Prom Coast Backpackers YHA* at 40 Station Rd (☎03 5682 2171, ⓦwww.yha.com.au; bunk in quad-share A$25–30, double ❷), and the simple units at *Wilsons Promontory Motel*, 26 Station Rd (☎03 5682 2055; ❹). Further south you'll find some truly gorgeous country retreats with inspiring sea views: *Bear Gully Coastal Cottages*, 33 Maitland Court, Walkerville (☎03 5663 2364, ⓦwww.beargullycottages .com.au; ❺), are fresh, airy and contemporary, and perfect for an away-from-it-all stay; while *Limosa Rise*, 40 Dalgleish Rd, Yanakie (☎03 5687 1135, ⓦwww .limosarise.com.au; ❼), closer to the park, is a collection of three strikingly stylish glass-fronted villas.

Walks

Many short walks in the national park, including the wheelchair-accessible **Loo-Errn Track**, begin from Tidal River. One of the best is the **Squeaky Beach Track** (50min each way), which crosses Tidal River, heads uphill and through a tea-tree canopy, finally ending on a beach of pure quartz sand that is indeed squeaky underfoot. **The Lilly Pilly Gully Circuit** (3hr return) is very rewarding, as it affords an excellent overview of the Prom's diverse vegetation from low-growing shrubs to heathland to open eucalypt forest, as well as scenic views. The walk starts at the Lilly Pilly Gully car park near Tidal River, follows a small valley and returns to the car park along the slopes of Mount Bishop.

The tracks in the southern section of the park are well defined and not too difficult. The most popular walk is the two- to three-day (36km) circuit from Telegraph Saddle car park to **Sealers Cove**, **Refuge Cove**, **Waterloo Bay** and back to the start. The remote north of the park has limited fresh water and is only suitable for experienced, properly equipped bushwalkers.

The Gippsland Lakes region

The **Gippsland Lakes**, Australia's largest system of inland waterways, are fed by the waters of the Mitchell, Nicholson and Tambo rivers, and are separated from the sea by a long, straight, southeast-facing stretch of sand, Ninety Mile Beach. Placid and glittering, lakes Coleman, Wellington, Reeve, Victoria and King are home to a great many water birds including pelicans and black swans. **Sale** and **Bairnsdale**, inland, are feasible bases from which to explore the region, though to many travellers they're little more than punctuation marks on the Princes Highway. The focal point of the area is **Lakes Entrance**; though not the most inspiring of towns, it's one of Victoria's most popular holiday spots, with the foothills of the high country within easy reach to the north. Less known, but more attractive, are the nearby villages of **Metung** and **Paynesville**; a short hop by ferry from the latter is **Raymond Island**, one of the easiest places in Australia to spot wild koalas.

Sale

SALE, at the junction of the South Gippsland Highway and the Princes Highway, 213km east of Melbourne and 105km west of Lakes Entrance, is a good point from which to head off to explore the Gippsland Lakes Coastal Park and Ninety Mile Beach. From Seaspray, 35km south, a coastal road hugs the shore for 20km to Golden Beach, from where a scenic drive heads through the Gippsland Lakes Coastal Park to Loch Sport; here you're faced with the enviable dilemma of lakes on one side and ocean beaches with good surfing on the other. An unsealed road then continues on to Sperm Whale Head in The Lakes National Park. Sale's **visitor information centre**, as you come into town from the west on the Princes Highway (daily 9am–5pm; ☎1800 677 520, ⓦwww.tourismwellington.com.au), can provide you with all the details. They have Internet access (A$3 per 15min) and can also give information about the **Bataluk Cultural Trail**, which starts in Sale and links sites of cultural and spiritual significance to the Gunai/Kurnai people, the original inhabitants of the Gippsland coast.

If you'd like to get friendly with the locals, opt for a stay off the beaten track in **Maffra**, a small dairy-farming town, 20km north of the Princes Highway in the foothills of the Great Dividing Range. Its small, central hostel, *Cambrai Backpackers* at 117 Johnston St (☎03 5147 1600 or 1800 101 113, ⓦwww .maffra.net.au/hostel; bunk in eight-share A$25, double ❷), is in a lovely, refurbished building; the owners can pick you up from the bus stop, arrange walks in the high country, and put you in touch with work contacts.

Bairnsdale, Paynesville and Raymond Island

BAIRNSDALE is the next major town on the highway, 69km east of Sale and 36km west of Lakes Entrance; it serves as another departure point for the lakes to the south. The efficient staff at the **visitor information centre** on the Princes Highway, known locally as Main Street (daily 9am–5pm; ☎03 5152 3444 or 1800 637 060, ⓦwww.discovereastgippsland.com.au), will provide all the local information you'll need. Next door is **St Mary's**, Bairnsdale's Roman Catholic church, an imposing Italianate building with an interior painted with fine murals. Near the station at 37–53 Dalmahoy St, signposted off the Princes Highway, a small exhibition at the **Krowathunk-ooloong Keeping Place** explains the history of the Gunai/Kurnai people of Aboriginal East Gippsland (Mon–Fri 9am–noon & 1–5pm; A$3.50, child A$2.50; ☎03 5152 1891). Budget **accommodation** options in Bairnsdale include the *Grand Terminus Hotel* at 98 McLeod St (☎03 5152 4040, ⓦwww .grandterminus.com.au; ❸), with decent pub rooms, or the *Bairnsdale Holiday Park*, a pleasant, shady site just west of the town at 139 Princes Hwy (☎03 5152 4066 or 1800 062 885, ⓦwww.bairnsdaleholidaypark.com; camping A$27–50, cabin ❷, unit ❹).

A far prettier place to stay, though, is the lakefront village of **PAYNESVILLE**, 16km south of town. Here, the luxurious and arty *Lake Gallery B&B* at 2A Backwater Court (☎03 5156 0448, ⓦwww.lakegallerybedandbreakfast.com; ❺) has two designer-decorated guest suites at the water's edge, and its own jetty; the *Mariners Cove* at 2 Victoria St (☎03 5156 7444, ⓦwww.marinerscoveresort .com; room ❸, apartment ❻) offers comfortable waterside accommodation in a modish, dark-painted timber building.

A ten-minute ferry ride from Paynesville across the McMillan Strait takes you to **Raymond Island**, poised between Lake King and Lake Victoria, which is an idyllic place to visit or stay. The island's abundant wildlife includes a particularly large and successful breeding population of koalas – at one time, there was a concern that they might munch their way through Raymond's entire stock of eucalyptus. You're almost guaranteed to see some of the chubby fellows snoozing in the crooks of trees in the middle of the island, around a ten-minute walk from the wharf. The Raymond Island Ferry runs roughly every half-hour throughout the day (Mon–Thurs 7am–10.30pm, Fri & Sat 7am–midnight, Sun 8am–11pm; cars A$7 return, foot passengers free). Accommodation options on the island include *Montague's*, 1 Third Parade (☎03 5156 7880, ⓦwww.raymondisland.com; ④), a pretty B&B with an old-fashioned feel and a veranda with lake views.

Forty-five kilometres northwest of Bairnsdale is another site on the Bataluk Cultural Trail, the **Den of Nargun** in the **Mitchell River National Park**. According to a Gunai legend, the small cave here was inhabited by a large female creature, a *nargun*, who would abduct people who wandered off on their own. As the Den of Nargun was a special place for Gunai women and may have been used for initiation ceremonies, the story served the purpose of keeping unauthorized people away. The cave is located in a small, beautiful valley; follow the loop track from the park picnic area via a lookout to the Mitchell River (30min), then take the track along Woolshed Creek to the cave and climb up the steep path back to the starting point (40min).

Metung

The refined charms of **METUNG**, an upmarket boating and holidaying village in a pretty setting, are an appealing alternative to the commercial clatter of its larger neighbour, Lakes Entrance, 10km east along the shoreline. It's reached via a southbound turn-off from the Princes Highway between Bairnsdale and Lakes Entrance. There is a small **visitor information office** at 50 Metung Rd (9am–5pm daily; ☎03 5156 2969), which books accommodation and hires out boats.

A good **accommodation** option is *McMillans of Metung* at 155 Metung Rd (☎03 5156 2283, ⓦwww.mcmillansofmetung.com.au; ⑤–⑦), which has very comfortable, fully equipped cottages of different sizes in a garden setting, with a solar-heated pool, a tennis court and a private jetty. *The Moorings at Metung*, 28 Main Rd (☎03 5156 2750, ⓦwww.themoorings .com.au; ④–⑦), offers luxury rooms and apartments with sun decks overlooking Bancroft Bay, while the reasonably priced *Metung Hotel* on Kurnai Avenue (☎03 5156 2206, ⓦwww.metunghotel.com.au; bunk in six-share A$30; double ③) has simple rooms with shared facilities and a bistro with a fantastic waterside table area, dishing up steaks and other standards (lunch & dinner daily). Good **restaurants** in town include *Season* at the Kings Cove Club golf course on Kings Cove Blvd (lunch daily, dinner Wed–Sat; ☎03 5156 2927), serving modern cuisine in a smart, contemporary setting, and *The Metung Galley* at 59 Metung Rd (breakfast & lunch daily, dinner Tues–Sat; ☎03 5156 2330), with chic dishes such as coconut and lime fish cakes, or salt and pepper squid. *Nina's* at 53 Metung Rd (☎03 5156 2474) is a tiny café offering great pancakes, wraps and coffee.

Lakes Entrance

LAKES ENTRANCE is a large, popular tourist town strung out along the Princes Highway beside the Cunninghame Arm of Lake King. This long coastal waterway is separated from the Tasman Sea by a six-thousand-year-old sandy barrier, fringed by **Ninety Mile Beach**. When Europeans first surveyed the area in the 1840s, the only way through from the ocean to the Gippsland Lakes was via a seasonal, intermittent outlet, unsuitable for reliable trade; in 1889, the present stable Entrance was cut through the sandbar, and the town has since spread east from this point. A footbridge connects the town centre with the section of Ninety Mile Beach that was isolated by the creation of the gap.

Despite its impressive waterside location, Lakes Entrance itself is not particularly attractive; local families spend their holidays here, but for most other independent travellers it's either a base for boat trips or a stopover on the road between Melbourne and New South Wales. Most of its shops, restaurants and motels are spread out along the Princes Highway, which runs right through town along the shore of the Cunninghame Arm, and is called the Esplanade in the town centre. The **Griffiths Sea Shell Museum** at 125 Esplanade (daily 9am–5pm; A$5; ☎03 5155 1538), with its rather off-putting 1950s-style facade, has a huge collection of shells and marine life, as well as an aquarium containing an intriguing assortment of fish from the Gippsland Lakes. Lakes Entrance is also a big **fishing port**: the **Fishermans Cooperative Wharf** on Bullock Island has a viewing platform where you can watch the catch being unloaded, as well as a tantalizing fish shop.

Lakes Entrance Surf Beach, the section of Ninety Mile Beach nearest town, is patrolled in season by surf lifesavers; its surf is rarely better than average, but it does have attractive golden sand. A stand on the south shore of Cunninghame Arm, near the footbridge, hires canoes, paddleboats, aquabikes and catamarans. Of the many **lake cruises** on offer, one of the most popular is the trip from the Post Office Jetty at the western end of town, up North Arm to the Wyanga Park Winery (☎03 5155 1508, ⓦwww.wyanga.com.au), the most famous local winery, on the fringe of the Colquhoun Forest,. Tours use the winery's own boat, the *Corque* (daily lunch cruise A$45, Fri & Sat dinner cruise A$70; book at Lakes Entrance Visitor Centre, or through the winery). Peels Cruises (☎03 5155 1246, ⓦwww.peelscruises.com) run a Sunday lunchtime cruise to the *Metung Hotel* (see p.169; A$44), whilst Sea-Safari (☎03 5155 5027) run trips with an interesting ecological slant, getting involved in bird surveys and testing the water for salinity (Thurs–Sun 10am; from A$12 for 1hr, child A$8). Other waterside activities include three-hour lake **fishing** trips with Mulloway Fishing Charters (☎0427 943 154; A$40).

Lakes Entrance Tourist Information on the Esplanade (daily 9am–5pm; ☎03 5155 1966 or 1800 637 060, ⓦwww.discovereastgippsland.com.au) can

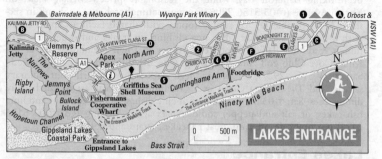

ACCOMMODATION				EATING & DRINKING		Lakes Entrance	
Deja Vu	D	Lakes Waterfront Motel	C	Ferryman's		Bowls Club	2
Goat and Goose B&B	A	Riviera Backpackers YHA	E	Seafood Café	5	L'Ocean Fish & Chips	3
Kalimna Woods	B	Waters Edge Holiday Park	F	Henry's Café	1	Tres Amigos	4

book accommodation and tickets for cruises. There's Internet access at the public library on Mechanics Street (free) and at the Bowls Club on the corner of Rowe Street and Bulmer Street.

Accommodation

Many of the town's **motels** and **tourist** parks are fairly forgettable, but there's no shortage of them.

Deja Vu 17 Clara St, Kalimna (5km north of central Lakes Entrance) ☎03 5155 4330, ⊛www .dejavu.com.au. A rather special B&B in a pleasant location, with spacious rooms, studios, cottages and apartments overlooking the waterway of North Arm. ⑤–⑥

Goat and Goose B&B 16 Gay St ☎03 5155 3079, ⊛www.goatandgoose.com. Recommended B&B in a timber house on a hill, with great ocean views from the balconies. Breakfast is huge and scrumptious, and, to top it all off, guests can request a tour of Lakes Entrance in the owner's Rolls Royce. ④

Kalimna Woods Kalimna Jetty Rd ☎03 5155 1957, ⊛www.kalimnawoods.com.au. Fully self-contained timber cottages, some with log fires, in a nice, peaceful bush setting. ④–⑤

Lakes Waterfront Motel 10 Princes Hwy ☎03 5155 2841, ⊛www.lakeswaterfrontmotel.com.

The motel rooms here are just average, but the self-contained two-bedroom lakeside cottages (sleeping up to three) are good value, and there's a pool. ③

Riviera Backpackers YHA 669 The Esplanade ☎03 5155 2444, ⊛www.yha.com.au. This friendly place, close to a beautiful stretch of the Cunninghame Arm, has a spacious site; its decent dorms and en-suite rooms are good value, and there's a large, spotless kitchen/common room, and a small pool. Bunk A$19–24, double or twin ①

Waters Edge Holiday Park 623 The Esplanade ☎03 5155 1914 or 1800 679 327, ⊛www .watersedgeholidaypark.com.au. Popular option with great amenities such as two pools, games room, playground and modern holiday units. Camping A$26–48, cabin ③

Eating

The **restaurants** in town tend to be cheap and basic. Most are found on or just off the Esplanade.

Ferryman's Seafood Café Middle Boat Harbour, The Esplanade ☎03 5155 3000. In a converted ferry, this offers surprisingly well-priced seafood in a lakeside setting you'd think would be more expensive. Lunch & dinner daily.

Henry's Café Wyanga Park Winery, Baades Rd (8km north of central Lakes Entrance) ☎03 5155 1508. Offers excellent cuisine sourced from local producers. Daily 10am–4pm, dinner Fri & Sat.

Lakes Entrance Bowls Club Corner of Rowe & Bulmer sts ☎03 5155 3578. Perhaps not trendy, but you can't go wrong with the generous portions

at very cheap prices: lunch dishes are A$7. Lunch & dinner daily.

L'Ocean Fish & Chips 19 Myer St ☎03 5155 2253. Fantastic fresh seafood place that, despite its modest exterior, has become an institution. Located just off The Esplanade, they cook with gluten-free and wheat-free batter. Daily 11am–8pm.

Tres Amigos 521 The Esplanade ☎03 5155 2215. A backpacker/surfer favourite since 1977, dishing out cheap Mexican fare. Takeaway available. Open daily for dinner.

Buchan and the Snowy River Loop

For a scenic detour off the Princes Highway between Lakes Entrance and the New South Wales border, it's worth turning north off the Princes Highway at Nowa Nowa or Orbost for a satisfying loop through the Snowy River National Park.

Turning off at Nowa Nowa and travelling clockwise, you start by heading for the small town of **BUCHAN**, in the foothills of the Australian Alps, which boasts over six hundred **caves**, the most famous of which – the Royal Cave and the Fairy Cave – can be seen on **guided tours** (daily: April–Sept 11am, 1pm & 3pm; Oct–March 10am, 11.15am, 1pm, 2.15pm & 3.30pm; A$13, child A$7). In the extensive Buchan Caves Reserve surrounding the caves there's an icy, spring-fed swimming pool, a playground, walking tracks and an attractive campsite (book through Parks Victoria, see p.54; camping A$22, cabin ❷), plus lots of wildlife.

On the north bank of the Buchan River in the town is *Buchan Lodge* on Saleyard Rd (☎03 5155 9421, ⓦwww.buchanlodge.com; bunk A$20), a smallish backpackers **hostel** with three bunkrooms, a country-style kitchen, a log fire in winter and a nice outdoor area. The owner will advise about activities in the area, including caving, trail riding and rafting. For more space, the *Buchan Valley Log Cabins*, 16 Gelantipy Rd (☎03 5155 9494, ⓦwww.buchanlogcabins.com.au; ❸), offers two-bedroom self-catering cabins in a garden setting. The *Caves Hotel* is good for pub grub (lunch Wed–Sun, dinner Tues–Sun; ☎03 5155 9203); alternatively, head to the *Café Caves* across the road for their kangaroo pie.

Snowy River National Park

The road continues north from Buchan through hilly country, following the Murrindal River and slowly winding its way up to the plateau of the Australian Alps. The sealed road ends at Wulgumerang Junction, about 55km north of Buchan; turning right here enables you to make a scenic, yet at certain times terrifying, arc through part of the **Snowy River National Park**, following the road towards Bonang (check road conditions in advance, as this is an unsealed road that can deteriorate badly in adverse weather conditions). **Little River Falls** are well worth a stop on this stretch: a short walk leads from the car park past snow gums to a lookout with breathtaking views of Little River Gorge and the falls. Equally stunning is the view from the second lookout from the top of the northeastern cliff-face of **Little River Gorge** (about 10min from the car park).

Further on, you descend to the valley of the Snowy River, which you cross at **McKillops Bridge**, set in the landscape that inspired Banjo Paterson's famous ballad, *The Man from Snowy River*. The river's sandy banks are a favourite swimming spot, and are also the place to set out on a **rafting** trip through deep gorges, caves, raging rapids and tranquil pools. *Karoonda Park* (☎03 5155 0220, ⓦwww.karoondapark.com; bunk A$24, double room ❷, cabin ❸), a small country **lodge** situated on a beef and sheep farm in Gelantipy, is the base for Snowy River Expeditions, specializing in adventurous white-water rafting and camping trips of one to four days (A$135–660), and, for an authentic taste of *Man from Snowy River* country, horse-riding (from A$30). They also offer good-value abseiling and zip-wiring (A$30), plus guided hikes (A$85), wild caving (A$85) or a full day of abseiling, caving and climbing (A$125), with a discount for overnight guests.

Bonang to Orbost

The road through the Snowy River National Park continues until it meets the Bonang–Orbost road. The general store at **Bonang**, a former goldrush town, sells takeaway food, groceries and fuel, and has some information about the area.

The winding, mostly unsealed, road down from the plateau to the highway leads past the **Errinundra National Park**, which protects magnificent wetland eucalypt forests containing giant, centuries-old specimens, as well as Victoria's largest surviving stand of **rainforest**. At **Errinundra Saddle**, in the heart of the park, there's a delightful picnic area and a self-guided boardwalk through the forest (about 40min). Take special care while driving, as all the roads in the area are heavily used by logging trucks.

The road from Bonang eventually leads to the old-fashioned town of **ORBOST**, on the Princes Highway where it crosses the Snowy River. The **Orbost Visitor Information Centre**, in an old slab hut at 39 Nicholson St (daily 9am–5pm; ☎03 5154 2424 or 1800 637 060, ⓦwww.discovere astgippsland.com.au), books accommodation and tours. There's a tranquil picnic spot opposite the pleasant *Snowy River Orbost Camp Park*, on the corner of Lochiel and Nicholson streets (☎03 5154 1097; camping A$25, cabin ❷), with huge gums lining one bank and cows roaming the paddocks on the other. The venerable *Orbost Club Hotel* at 63 Nicholson St (☎03 5154 1003; ❷) has rooms with shared bathrooms, and offers unusually good Chinese food. *A Lovely Little Lunch* at 125A Nicholson St (☎03 5154 1303) is appropriately named. From Orbost, a southbound side road follows the Snowy River down to the coast. Close to the mouth of the river is **Marlo**, a fishing hamlet with an undiscovered feel; it overlooks the coastal arm of Lake Corringle, home to a great many pelicans and other waterbirds, with rugged beaches nearby.

Croajingolong National Park

Extending for 100km along the Victorian coast between Sydenham Inlet (40km east of Marlo) and the New South Wales border, **Croajingolong National Park** encompasses little-visited beaches, estuaries and one of Australia's most impressive tracts of coastal forest. Remote and relatively undisturbed, it's one of only fourteen World Biosphere Reserves in the country, and an important area for botanical, zoological and environmental research. For visitors, it offers outstandingly varied bushwalking and camping, in a region rich in native wildlife: the rainforests and eucalyptus stands are home to possums, gliders, wallabies and lyrebirds; the rivers support an unusually diverse population of fish; and butterflies hover over the banksias, common heaths and boronias that dot the heathlands.

A number of southbound turn-offs from the Princes Highway take you into the park; the obvious starting points are the small towns of **Cann River**, 76km east of Orbost and 61km west of the New South Wales border, or **Mallacoota**, further east (see p.174). Parks Victoria (☎13 19 63, ⓦwww .parkweb.vic.gov.au) run two information centres, which provide information on the park's **hiking trails** and its back-to-basics **campsites** (A$11.50–19.50, payable on site): the Cann River centre is on the Princes Highway (Mon–Fri 9am–noon & 12.30–3.30pm; ☎03 5158 6351); the Mallacoota office is on Buckland Drive, near the wharf (daily 9.30am–3.30pm; ☎03 5158 0219, ⓦwww.parkweb.vic.gov.au).

Most of Croajingolong's campsites are on, or close to, thrillingly wild sections of coast, from where short walks are marked out. While most can be reached by 2WD-accessible unsealed roads, you'll need 4WD or a mountain bike to explore the park's more rugged tracks. Some sites are best approached by boat: the Parks Victoria rangers can provide full details. As an alternative to camping, you can stay overnight in a restored keeper's cottage (self-catering, sleeping up to eight) or a purpose-built one-bedroom bungalow at **Point Hicks Lighthouse** (℡03 5158 4268, ⊛www.pointhicks.com.au; ❸–❻), which overlooks the Tasman Sea at the end of an unsealed road leading south through the park from Cann River. A three-night **bushwalking safari** run by OzStyle Adventures (A$625; ℡02 6495 6997 or 1800 000 824, ⊛www.ozstyle.net.au) is a good option without roughing it too much: the tour leaves Cann River every Thursday afternoon and includes a tour of Point Hicks Lighthouse and gourmet catering.

For self-reliant walkers, there's an inspiring long-distance hike all the way from Sydenham Inlet to the Nadgee Nature Reserve over the border in NSW, the **Wilderness Coast Walk**. For this, you need to obtain a hiking permit from Parks Victoria or the NPWS office in Merimbula (see p.183).

Mallacoota and Gipsy Point

MALLACOOTA is a tranquil, unspoilt village in a gorgeous location close to the ocean on the lake system of the **Mallacoota Inlet**, within easy reach of the Croajingolong National Park. The village is approached by turning southeast off the Princes Highway at the hamlet of **Genoa**, 123km east of Orbost and 14km southwest of the New South Wales border. On the way, about 7km from Genoa and 15km before Mallacoota, a turn-off to the left leads to **Gipsy Point**, an idyllic spot near the confluence of the Genoa and Wallagaraugh rivers on the upper reaches of the Mallacoota Inlet. A **bus** service, the Mallacoota Explorer, runs to both Gipsy Point and Mallacoota from Genoa (twice daily on Mon, Thurs & Fri; also on Sun in summer holidays; ℡03 5158 0116), connecting with the V/Line Sapphire Coast Link service between Melbourne, Narooma and Batemans Bay.

Mallacoota, though seemingly remote, teems with holidaymakers in summer. The very helpful **visitor information centre** in a shed on the main wharf (daily, hours vary; ℡03 5158 0800) gives advice on accommodation and activities around town. The local **Parks Victoria office** (see p.173) has details of secluded camping spots, local bushwalks, and longer hikes through the Croajingolong National Park. You can also explore the beautiful waterways of the Mallacoota Inlet (Bottom Lake and Top Lake) by renting a boat or canoe from Mallacoota Hire Boats, 200m along the waterfront from the information centre (℡03 5158 0704).

Accommodation

Most of the **accommodation** in the area has a low-key feel; camping is a very popular option, but there are also a few good guesthouses.

Genoa and Gipsy Point

Coopracambra Cottages 1606 Wangarabell Rd, Wangarabell (18km north of Genoa) ℡03 5158 0802, ⊛www.mallacoota.com/coopracambra. These imaginatively designed, solar-powered timber self-catering cottages are very good value; they're remote but ideal for those wanting a bit of space. ❷

Gipsy Point Lakeside 261 Gipsy Point Rd, Gipsy Point ℡03 5158 8200 or 1800 688 200, ⊛www .gipsy.com.au. In a garden setting beside the upper Mallacoota Inlet, this resort offers luxury apartments with attractive views of the water, and a prettily landscaped, solar-heated pool. ❻

Gipsy Point Lodge MacDonald St, Gipsy Point ℡03 5158 8205 or 1800 063 556, ⊛www .gipsypoint.com. This appealing lakefront lodge, in an excellent area for bird-watching, offers a choice of rooms (with three delicious meals included in the rate) or self-catering cottages. All guests have free use of the lodge's rowing boats, canoes and tennis court. Room (full board) ❼, cottage ❹

Mallacoota

Adobe Flats 17 Karbeethong Ave ☎03 5158 0329, ⍵www.adobeholidayflats.com.au. Spacious self-contained, eco-friendly mud-brick apartments with bags of quirky, rustic character, close to the water, and with canoes to rent. ❷–❹

Karbeethong Lodge 16 Schnapper Point Drive ☎03 5158 0411, ⍵www.karbeethonglodge.com.au. A renovated, old-style guesthouse with a nice country feel. Attractive singles and doubles, most en suite, and use of the kitchen and living room, which has a wood-burning fireplace. ❺

Mallacoota Foreshore Caravan Park Allan Drive ☎03 5158 0300. In a great location, right on the lakeshore, this is easily the best place in town to pitch a tent. The office also offers good advice about where the fish are biting. Camping A$16.50–37.

Mallacoota Hotel 51 Maurice Ave ☎03 5158 0455, ⍵www.mallacootahotel.com.au. Very central, on the main shopping strip, this has good-value motel rooms and shared units for backpackers. Bunk A$22, motel room ❸

Wave Oasis 36 Vista Drive ☎03 5158 0995, ⍵www.thewaveoasis.com.au. One of the best options in town, with compact but comfortable modern apartments, and great views of the surrounding inlet. ❺

Eating

Choices for **food** in Mallacoota are very limited, although the standard is high. The *Croajingolong Café* on Allan Drive (daily except Mon 8.30am–4pm; ☎03 5158 0098) serves brunch, light meals and good coffee, while the *Mallcoota Bakery* next door is the pride of the town, selling award-winning pies. The *Tide Restaurant & Cocktail Bar* on Maurice Ave (daily from 6pm; ☎03 5158 0100) is the best place in town for dinner, sometimes having **live music**; otherwise, counter meals and cold beer are served at the *Mallacoota Hotel* (see above), where there's live music every night in January. A summer **cinema** operates at the Mallacoota Community Centre, Allen Drive.

Travel details

Trains

Bairnsdale to: Melbourne (3 daily; 3hr 30min–3hr 35min); Sale (3 daily; 50min).

Belgrave to: Melbourne (every 30min; 1hr 20min).

Frankston to: Melbourne (4–8 hourly; 1hr); Stony Point (8 daily; 40min).

Lilydale to: Melbourne (2–5 hourly; 1hr 5min).

Sale to: Bairnsdale (3 daily; 50min); Melbourne (3 daily; 2hr 35min–2hr 45min).

Stony Point to: Frankston (8 daily; 40min).

Buses

Bairnsdale to: Batemans Bay (1–2 daily; 6hr 45min–7hr 20min); Canberra (2–3 weekly; 6hr 20min); Cann River (2–3 daily; 2hr 20min–25min); Genoa (twice daily; 2hr 50min–3hr 25min); Lakes Entrance (2–3 daily; 30–35min); Melbourne (daily; 5hr 15min); Narooma (twice daily; 5hr 40min–6hr 20min); Orbost (2–3 daily; 1hr 15min–1hr 25min); Sale (daily; 1hr 30min); Sydney (daily; 12hr).

Cann River to: Bairnsdale (2–3 daily; 2hr 20min–25min); Batemans Bay (1–2 daily; 4hr 30min–4hr 35min); Canberra (2–3 weekly; 3hr 30min); Genoa (twice daily; 30–35min); Lakes Entrance (2–3 daily; 1hr 45min–1hr 50min); Melbourne (daily; 7hr 35min); Narooma (twice daily; 3hr 20min–3hr 30min); Orbost (2–3 daily; 1hr–1hr 5min); Sale (daily; 3hr 50min); Sydney (daily; 10hr 20min).

Cowes to: Melbourne (daily; 3hr 5min).

Foster (for Wilson's Promontory NP) to: Melbourne (daily; 2hr 40min).

Genoa to: Bairnsdale (twice daily; 2hr 20min); Batemans Bay (1–2 daily; 5hr 55min); Cann River (twice daily; 30–35min); Lakes Entrance (twice daily; 2hr 20min); Melbourne (daily; 7hr 35min); Narooma (twice daily; 2hr 50min–2hr 55min); Orbost (twice daily; 1hr 30min–1hr 35min); Sale (daily; 4hr 20min); Sydney (daily; 9hr 40min).

Lakes Entrance to: Bairnsdale (2–3 daily; 30–35min); Batemans Bay (1–2 daily; 6hr 15min); Canberra (2–3 weekly; 5hr 50min); Cann River (2–3 daily; 1hr 45min–1hr 50min); Genoa (twice daily; 2hr 20min); Melbourne (daily; 5hr 45min); Narooma (twice daily; 5hr 10min–5hr 15min); Orbost (2–3 daily; 45–50min); Sale (daily; 2hr); Sydney (daily; 12hr).

Orbost to: Bairnsdale (2–3 daily; 1hr 15min–1hr 25min); Batemans Bay (1–2 daily; 5hr 25min–5hr 30min); Canberra (2–3 weekly; 5hr); Cann River (2–3 daily; 1hr–1hr 5min); Genoa (twice daily; 1hr 30min–1hr 35min); Lakes Entrance (2–3 daily; 45–50min); Melbourne (daily; 6hr 30min); Narooma (twice daily; 4hr 25min); Sale (daily; 2hr 45min); Sydney (daily; 11hr 15min).

Sale to: Bairnsdale (daily; 1hr 30min); Batemans Bay (daily; 8hr 15min); Cann River (daily; 3hr 50min); Genoa (daily; 4hr 20min); Lakes Entrance (daily; 2hr); Melbourne (daily; 3hr 20min); Narooma (daily; 7hr 10min); Orbost (daily; 2hr 45min); Sydney (daily; 14hr).

3

South Coast
New South Wales

CHAPTER 3 # Highlights

✳ **Wallaga Lake** Just one of the Sapphire Coast's many wild and beautful coastal waterways, in a region rich in Aboriginal heritage. See p.186

✳ **Central Tilba** Insanely pretty heritage village from the gold rush era, chock full of tea rooms, gift shops and rampant floral displays. See p.187

✳ **Montague Island** Try a taste of the lighthouse keeper's life by staying here among the shearwaters, penguins and seals. See p.188

✳ **Murramarang National Park** Fragrant forests and pristine beaches, where you may find yourself sharing the sand with friendly kangaroos. See p.190

✳ **New Parliament House, Canberra** The stunning angular design of New Parliament House is contemporary Australian architecture at its best. See p.193

✳ **Jervis Bay** With sparkling water and dazzling sand, this is the perfect place for watching whales and dolphins, or just chilling out. See p.194

✳ **Grand Pacific Drive** Feel like the star of a car commercial as you zoom through stunning coastal scenery: cliffs to one side, the Pacific to the other. See p.197

▲ Crested tern, Montague Island

South Coast
New South Wales

A peaceful region of lakes, rivers, undulating dairylands and unassuming fishing villages, the South Coast of New South Wales is delightful in a timeless sort of way – an area for casting a rod, catching a wave, or sharing a beach with pelicans and kangaroos. With over thirty national parks, marine parks and reserves between the Victorian border and Sydney, there's more than enough wilderness to explore. The South Coast towns may be thin on cultural and architectural attractions, but they're refreshingly easy-going; unspoilt by hectic resorts or sprawling commercial developments, they have a back-to-basics appeal that's drawn many "sea changers" to jack in their stressful city lives and settle here instead.

As a holiday destination, the South Coast is low key and family oriented, with a few wildlife and amusement parks to keep the children happy, and plenty of country cafés and simple restaurants dishing up local produce such as oysters, mussels, fresh-off-the-boat fish and artisan-made cheese. Outdoor pursuits tend towards the traditional: the more exposed parts of the coast are perfect for **surfing**, while the numerous coastal lakes, bays and inlets are suited for **swimming**, windsurfing, sailing, canoeing, or heading out by boat to watch **dolphins** and, in season, **whales**. Away from the ocean, the forest-clad, mountainous hinterland offers great **bushwalking** through superb, rugged scenery.

The inland road from Melbourne to Sydney via the Snowy Mountains – the Hume Highway – takes most of the southeast Australian traffic, leaving the longer but more attractive coastal route, the **Princes Highway**, satisfyingly quiet. The 1054-kilometre journey along the entire southeast coast, covered by this and the preceding chapter, is so replete with unsung highlights that it's worth allowing at least four or five days to appreciate the beautiful New South Wales section, making detours as you go, or ten or more for the whole trip.

In the region closest to the state border, the **Sapphire Coast**, the calls of bellbirds and superb lyrebirds ring out from ancient melaleuca forests, swans glide across broad lagoons and, in fishing villages such as **Eden**, **Pambula** and **Merimbula**, pelicans, gulls and terns jostle for scraps. Offshore from Narooma on the **Eurobodalla Coast** is one of the state's most intriguing wilderness sanctuaries, **Montague Island**, while north of Batemans Bay, the stunning **Murramarang National Park** is home to beach-loving kangaroos. The jewel of the **Shoalhaven region**, further north, is **Jervis Bay**, an eco-paradise with spotless white beaches and superb opportunities for watching dolphins and whales. North of here you begin to feel the proximity of Sydney as the resorts get busier (and pricier) – in the **Illawarra region**, city-dwellers flock to **Kiama**, a favourite coastal playground with easy access to beautiful forest parks, while the bustling city of **Wollongong** is the South Coast's answer to Newcastle, north of Sydney. Of all the region's many inspiring **coastal drives**, one of the best lies along this stretch of coast, the Grand Pacific Drive from Nowra to the Royal National Park, one of Sydney's great green buffer zones.

Also included in this chapter is the **Australian Capital Territory (ACT)**, just over 280km southwest of Sydney, a tiny state that was carved out of New South Wales at the beginning of the twentieth century as an independent base for the new national capital, **Canberra**. Though saddled with a dull image, Canberra is actually a pleasant city, with fine museums and good access to the Snowy Mountains and Mount Kosciuszko, Australia's highest peak.

Regional practicalities

Most of the **accommodation** on the South Coast is aimed squarely at Australian families and retirees – there's no shortage of modest motels, country campsites and holiday houses, but very few glitzy hotels. South Coast hostels, which are equally scarce, attract nature-loving types rather than party animals. Just as rare, but well worth seeking out, are the region's thoughtfully designed ecolodges and luxury B&Bs, which, though comfortable, tend to be refreshingly free from urban-boutique style clichés.

Like southeast Victoria, the region has a great many offbeat places of interest, making **self-drive** the best way to explore. The **Princes Highway** (A1) is the main road through, running all the way along the South Coast from the Victoria border to Sydney, boosted between Wollongong and the Royal National Park by the Southern Freeway. Apart from its northernmost reaches, which chug through Sydney's southern suburbs, it's a quiet, single-carriageway highway; its scenic diversions take you along even quieter roads. From Canberrra, which lies 58km south of the Melbourne–Sydney Hume Highway, the main routes to the Princes Highway are via the Kings Highway to Batemans Bay, or via the Monaro Highway to Cooma followed by the Snowy Mountains Highways to Bega.

While the inland route between Melbourne, Canberra and Sydney is well travelled, **public transport** from these cities to the southern New South Wales coast is relatively limited, which partly explains why beach-loving travellers often overlook the entire region. Premier Motor Service (see p.35) runs the only **long-distance bus** service along the Princes Highway: they have an overnight run between Melbourne and Sydney and a daytime one between Sydney and Eden, both of which run daily in each direction. Both call at Sydney airport and all the South Coast towns, the overnight buses arriving on the coast in the early hours. Greyhound (see p.35) run buses from Melbourne to Sydney via the Hume Highway, stopping at Canberra; they don't have a coastal service.

An alternative route to the south of the region **from Melbourne** is to take the V/Line (see p.35) Gippsland Line train to Bairnsdale, which connects with the V/Line Sapphire Coast Link bus service to Eden, Merimbula, Bega, Narooma and Batemans Bay, arriving in the late afternoon. Three companies run buses to the coast **from Canberra**: CountryLink (see p.35) to Eden, Pambula, Merimbula and Bega; Transborder (T02 6241 0033, Wwww.transborderexpress.com.au) to Nelligen, Batemans Bay and Ulladulla; and Murrays Coaches (T32 22 51, Wwww.murrays.com.au) to Batemans Bay, Moruya and Narooma, or to Wollongong. The CountryLink railway line between Canberra and Sydney runs inland,

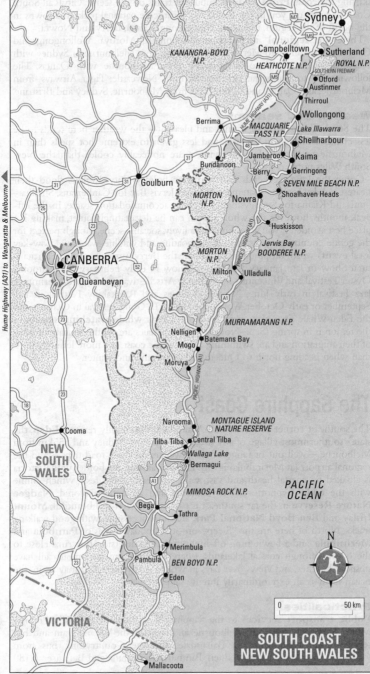

SOUTH COAST NEW SOUTH WALES

Sydney

KANANGRA-BOYD N.P.

Campbelltown
Sutherland
HEATHCOTE N.P.
ROYAL N.P.
Otford
Austinmer
Thirroul
Wollongong
Lake Illawarra
Shellharbour

Berrima
MACQUARIE PASS N.P.
Jamberoo
Kaima
Bundanoon
Berry
Gerringong

Goulburn
MORTON N.P.
Nowra
SEVEN MILE BEACH N.P.
Shoalhaven Heads

Huskisson

MORTON N.P.
Jervis Bay
BOODEREE N.P.

CANBERRA
Milton
Ulladulla
Queanbeyan

MURRAMARANG N.P.

Nelligen
Mogo
Batemans Bay
Moruya

Cooma

Narooma
MONTAGUE ISLAND NATURE RESERVE
Tilba Tilba
Central Tilba
Wallaga Lake
Bermagui

NEW SOUTH WALES

PACIFIC OCEAN

MIMOSA ROCK N.P.

Bega
Tathra

N

Merimbula
Pambula
BEN BOYD N.P.
Eden

0   50 km

VICTORIA

Mallacoota

SOUTH COAST
NEW SOUTH WALES

skirting the coast. **From Sydney**, suburban trains on the scenic CityRail South Coast line will get you to the Royal and Heathcote national parks and towns in the north of the region, including Wollongong, Kiama, Berry and Nowra.

There are **regional airports** in Merimbula, Moruya, Wollongong and Canberra. You can fly to Merimbula or Moruya from Melbourne or Sydney with Regional Express, and to Wollongong from Melbourne with Qantas. The following fly to Canberra: Brindabella, from Newcastle; Tiger Airways, from Melbourne; and Qantas and Virgin Blue, from Melbourne, Sydney and Brisbane.

Weather and seasons

The South Coast **climate** is mild and pleasant – the weather here tends to be less changeable than in Victoria, and less given to extreme hot spells than in Melbourne or Sydney, but the winters are noticeably cooler than the New South Wales north coast.

Come the long weekends and **summer** holidays, city-dwellers flood their nearest holiday towns – Batemans Bay and Jervis Bay for Canberrans, Shellharbour and Kiama for Sydneysiders – making accommodation scarce. In the off-peak months, however, the whole region can be devastatingly quiet, making it a place best avoided if you're looking for a lively, sociable scene, though perfect for the gentle country pursuits of walking, boating and wildlife-watching. Low-key local **events** worth dropping in for include the Berry Agricultural and Horticultural Show in late January, the Nowra Show in early February, the Narooma Oyster Festival and Vincentia's See Change Arts Festival in May, the Merimbula Jazz Festival in early June, Narooma's Blues and Rockabilly Festival in late September or early October, Wollongong's Viva La Gong Festival in October and the Eden Whale Festival in early November. Peak **whale-watching season** in the region is in spring (Sept–Nov), when the whales are on the southbound leg of their migration and are swimming closer to the coast, at a more leisurely pace, than when heading north to Queensland in autumn and winter.

The Sapphire Coast

The southeast corner of New South Wales feels thoroughly remote: **Eden**, the state's southernmost village of any size, is 478km from Sydney and 555km from Melbourne – well out of range of city-dwellers on short road trips – and the regional airport (at Merimbula) is tiny. The area around the border with Victoria is cloaked by coastal heath and vast, wild, temperate rainforests, which chime with the oddly hypnotic call of bellbirds, and are little explored. **Nadgee Nature Reserve** in the far southeast is particularly wild and beautiful; **Mount Imlay** and **Ben Boyd National Park** are more accessible, with good walking tracks. North of here are the "Sleepy-on-Sea" holiday towns of **Pambula** and **Merimbula**, and a bewitching off-highway scenic diversion that runs close to the ocean through coastal lakelands. Eden, Pambula and Merimbula all have unspoilt beaches, and views over bays in which, corny though it may seem, the ocean really is an extraordinarily intense sapphire blue.

Practicalities

Public transport services to the Sapphire Coast include the daily Premier Motor Service buses from Melbourne and Sydney; the V/Line train and bus service from Melbourne via Bairnsdale; and the CountryLink bus from Canberra, all of which stop at Eden, Pambula, Merimbula and Bega (see p.180

for a summary, and p.35 for contact details).You can also **fly** direct to Merimbula from Sydney or Melbourne. **Local bus** companies include Deane's Buslines (℡02 6495 6452, Ⓦwww.deanesbuslines.com.au), connecting Eden, Pambula and Merimbula and Bega, and Tathra Bus Service (Ⓦwww.tathrabus .com.au) serving Tathra, Merimbula and Bega.

Merimbula is the region's main tourist hub, with a **Visitor Information Centre** on Beach St (daily 9am–4.30pm; ℡02 6495 1129, Ⓦwww .sapphirecoast.com.au) and a **NSW National Parks and Wildlife office** on the corner of Merimbula Drive and Sapphire Coast Drive (Mon–Fri 8.30am– 4.30pm; daily in holiday periods; ℡02 6495 5000, Ⓦwww.nationalparks.nsw .gov.au). There are smaller Sapphire Coast visitor information centres on the Princes Hwy, Eden (daily 8.30am–5pm; ℡02 6496 1953 or 1800 150 457); on Lagoon St, Bega (daily 9am–5pm; ℡02 6491 7645); and Lamont St, Bermagui (daily 10am–4pm; ℡02 6493 3054).You'll also find a list of B&Bs and farmstays online at Ⓦwww.southcoastbnbs.com.au.

Nadgee Nature Reserve, Ben Boyd National Park and Mount Imlay

In this remote part of the state, the coast is edged with russet cliffs topped with melaleucas, a striking combination against the intensely blue ocean. **Nadgee Nature Reserve**, the eastern extension of southeast Victoria's mighty Croajin- golong National Park (see p.173), is one of the least visited of all Australia's coastal parks: to protect its forest, heathland and clifftop habitats, NSW National Parks and Wildlife Service limit the number of hikers exploring the park at any one time through a permit system (for details, contact the NPWS office in Merimbula; see above). Rugged hiking trails such as the long-distance Wilder- ness Coast Walk connect Nadgee with Croajingolong, and with the magnificent **Ben Boyd National Park**, which hugs the coast further north. With an NPWS permit, you can bushcamp in either park (A$5 per person per night); Ben Boyd also has vehicle-accessible campsites (A$10 per person per night) at Bittangabee Bay and Saltwater Creek, close to the coastal trail.

Inland, another hiking trail starting from the picnic grounds on Burrawang Road, a turning off the Princes Highway 30km north of the state border and 18km south of Eden, leads to the summit of **Mount Imlay** (3hr return). The steep, strenuous ascent rewards you with a panoramic view over the coast and across the dense forests of the hinterland onto the Monaro Plain: in clear condi- tions, you can see all the way south to Mallacoota and north to Narooma.

Eden

EDEN, just off the Princes Highway on pretty Twofold Bay, 48km northeast of the state border, is one of the nicest coastal villages south of Sydney. In 1818, the first **whaling station** on the Australian mainland was established here, and whaling remained a major industry until the 1920s; the descendants of the skippers now run whale-watching trips instead.

The village is touristy in a quiet sort of way – reminders of the old days, including the large wharf, can be reached by following the main drag, Imlay Street, downhill to Snug Cove.Trawlers still pull up at the wharf, which is home to a cluster of restaurants, and is earmarked for development; projects in the pipeline include a new **Sapphire Coast Marine Discovery Centre** (Ⓦwww .edenmarinediscovery.org.au), which, when it opens, will be a ground-breaking aquarium, whale-study centre and marine-ecology research facility.

Uphill from the wharf on Imlay Street is the aging but excellent **Killer Whale Museum** (Mon–Sat 9.15am–3.45pm, Sun 11.15am–3.45pm; A$7.50, child A$2; ☎02 6496 2094, ⓦwww.killerwhalemuseum.com.au). The star attraction is the huge skeleton of "Old Tom", an orca that used to herd baleen whales into the bay then lead whaling boats towards the pods, in order to get his chops around the discarded bits of carcass. There are also plenty of old whale bones, boats, some interesting Aboriginal history, and a (literally) incredible account of a man being swallowed by a sperm whale and coming out alive fifteen hours later.

Eden's two pretty **beaches**, Aslings and Cocora, are quiet and good for a snooze, swim or stroll. Cat Balou Cruises, based at Snug Cove (☎0427 962 027 or 0427 260 489, ⓦwww.catbalou.com.au), offer two-hour dolphin-spotting tours (A$30, child A$17) plus whale-watching **cruises** (Sept–Nov; 3hr 30min; A$65, child A$40; short cruise A$40). Freedom Charters (☎02 6496 1209, ⓦwww.freedom charters.com.au), the town's **fishing** specialists, also offer whale-watching in season (3hr 30min; A$70, child A$55), with a maximum of 12 passengers per trip. Ocean Wilderness (☎02 6496 9066, ⓦwww.oceanwilderness.com.au) run **kayaking** adventures in Twofold Bay (half day A$80, full day A$125).

Accommodation

The visitor information offices in Eden and Merimbula (see p.183) can advise on **accommodation** options.

Cocora Cottage 2 Cocora St ☎02 6496 1241, ⓦwww.cocoracottage.com. Pretty, heritage-listed B&B with fine rooms, a cute garden bedecked with flowers, and a stunning sun deck – with views over the bay – at the rear. ❹

Crown & Anchor Inn 239 Imlay St ☎02 6496 1017, ⓦwww.crownandanchoreden.com.au. This beautiful, historic house is the best B&B on the South Coast, with superlative ocean views from most of its exceedingly comfy rooms. The lovely owners offer complimentary champagne on arrival, and serve breakfast on the back deck, overlooking the water. ❺

Eden Tourist Park Aslings Beach Rd ☎02 6496 1139, ⓦwww.edentouristpark.com.au. Peaceful, leafy park, with Lake Curalo on one side and Aslings Beach on the other. Camping A$20–24, cabin ❷

Heritage House Motel & Units 178 Imlay St ☎02 6496 1657, ⓦwww.heritagehouseunits.com. Pleasant motel rooms and one- or two-bed units right in the centre of Eden; it's all a cut above the average, with free Wi-Fi, and some rooms boasting striking views over Twofold Bay. ❸–❹

Eating

There are a few **places to eat** in the middle of town, but you're better off heading down to the wharf.

Taste of Eden Snug Cove Wharf, Imlay St ☎02 6496 1304. The best choice for breakfast or lunch, this bright and breezy café, styled like a beach shack, has a cute, shaded front terrace. Dig into tasty free-range eggs in the morning, or drop by later for super-fresh seafood.

Wharfside Café Snug Cove Wharf, Imlay St ☎02 6496 1855. Though overpriced, this place produces

great brekkies, including apple and banana fritters with ricotta and honey, as well as good coffee, gourmet salads and seafood lunches.

The Wheelhouse Snug Cove Wharf, Imlay St ☎02 6496 3392. An excellent, airy seafood restaurant with an upstairs balcony looking out over the bay. Daily from 6pm.

Pambula and Merimbula

Around 19km north of Eden is the small town of **Pambula**, which lies a couple of kilometres inland. Its coastal hamlet, **Pambula Beach**, is a blissfully quiet little spot set on the wide, shallow inlet of Pambula River, at the northern fringe of the Ben Boyd National Park – a pleasant place to potter along the sand, with

East Coast ecotourism

When visitors fall in love with the East Coast's natural wonders, they tend to do so with a passion. This is a region packed with ecological drama and interest, from the biodiversity of the Great Barrier Reef to the intricate mysteries of the rainforests, dunes and paperbark swamps. The coast's native flora and fauna are survivors, highly evolved to withstand droughts, floods and pounding heat – and deserving of our protection. Among the species you may encounter a host of fascinating and endearing creatures found nowhere else on earth.

Parks and reserves

The primary purpose of the region's many **national parks** and **marine reserves** is to preserve important habitats and environmental features, but the park rangers in each state also devote considerable energy and resources into making wilderness areas visitor-friendly. In Queensland's Daintree National Park, you can wander through tracts of otherwise impenetrable rainforest on **boardwalks** built with minimal damage to the environment. In New South Wales, rangers lead regular Discovery events such as **hikes**, **botanical tours** or specialist **wildlife-watching trips**, possibly heading out after dark to look for echidnas, sugar-gliders and other shy, nocturnal species. Parks Victoria keeps an excellent database of companies running activities such as guided **bushwalking**, **mountain biking** and **bird-watching** in areas of superb natural beauty.

Eco-retreats

In the main, Australia's hoteliers seem slow to pick up on the interest in all things eco-friendly, but the places that genuinely deserve the term "**eco-retreat**" – not only for their location but also for their outlook and practices – are well worth seeking out. Among the best are *The Sanctuary*, Mission Beach (see p.562), a wonderfully stripped-down lodge set in coastal rainforest, with inspirational views; *Heron Island Resort* and its sister resorts on Wilson and Lizard islands (see p.503 & p.620), luxury hideaways run on sound ecological principles; and the *Head Lighthouse Keeper's Quarters* on Montague Island (see p.188), where guests can play an active role in ongoing nature conservation work. For further recommendations, see p.52.

Boardwalk in Daintree National Park ▲

The Sanctuary, Mission Beach ▼

Ecotourism Australia

Australia was one of the first countries in the world to develop a scheme to assess hotels, lodges, campsites, activity companies and guides for their adherence to ecologically sustainable practices. The exacting standards of non-profit accreditation agency **Ecotourism Australia** (Ⓦwww.ecotourism.org.au) are now a global benchmark. If you'd like to make your trip as eco-friendly as possible, then looking out for the **Advanced Ecotourism logo** when you're booking accommodation or tours is a good way to start.

Ecotourism in action

Ten ways to help minimize the environmental impact of your East Coast trip.

▶▶ Offset your road- and air-travel carbon emissions through a recognized scheme.

▶▶ If you have a vehicle, share journeys and plan your routes with fuel efficiency in mind.

▶▶ Avoid driving through country areas after dark, when wildlife is most active.

▶▶ Take an interest in the eco-policy of the accommodation and tour companies that you choose.

▶▶ In hotel rooms, limit your use of the air-con, and regulate the temperature responsibly.

▶▶ Conserve water by turning off taps promptly and taking short showers.

▶▶ When walking in national parks, always stick to the tracks to minimize erosion.

▶▶ Show respect for wildlife habitats by curbing noise, disturbance and use of bright lights.

▶▶ Offering food to wild animals or birds can cause malnutrition and aggression – don't be tempted.

▶▶ In all wilderness areas, try to "tread lightly", and leave everything exactly as you found it.

▲ Egret at the eco-certified Kingfisher Bay Resort, Fraser Island

▼ Water lily in a billabong

Humpback whale, Hervey Bay ▲

Looking for dugongs around Moreton Island ▼

Top wildlife hotspots

▶▶ **Great Barrier Reef**
Rich in tropical marine life including clownfish, manta rays and reef sharks.

▶▶ **Hervey Bay**
One of the best places to watch humpback whales on their winter migration.

▶▶ **Murramarang National Park**
Mobs of laid-back eastern grey kangaroos hang out on the beautiful beaches.

▶▶ **Atherton Tablelands**
Cool tropical forests harbour pademelons and rare Lumholtz's tree kangaroos.

▶▶ **Jervis Bay**
Resident pods of bottlenose dolphins play in the bay's crystal-clear waters.

▶▶ **Montague Island**
Gaggles of Australian fur seals loll and squabble on the rocks fringing the island.

▶▶ **Raymond Island**
In its eucalyptus groves, there's a wild koala snoozing in every third tree.

▶▶ **Lord Howe Island**
Remote haven for shearwaters and scores of other seabirds.

▶▶ **Mission Beach**
Here, the rainforest is home to the formidable southern cassowary.

▶▶ **Bundaberg Coast**
Important nesting ground for marine turtles.

▶▶ **Broken River, Eungella National Park**
An excellent spot to see platypuses at dawn or twilight.

▶▶ **Moreton Island**
Offshore, you may see a rare and unusual-looking mammal, the dugong.

▶▶ **Phillip Island**
Long-term residence of a large population of little penguins.

▶▶ **Fraser Island**
Home to a thriving and unusually pureblooded dingo population.

▶▶ **Daintree River**
The haunt of fearsome estuarine crocodiles.

the option of walking all the way along the coast to Merimbula, 7km further north. Pambula is best known for its **oysters** – to slurp a few down, you can take a table at oyster emporium *Wheelers* on Arthur Kaine Drive, the road to Merimbula (lunch daily, dinner Tues–Sat plus Mon & Sun in summer; ☎02 6495 6089), which also offers free tours of its oyster beds (Mon–Sat 11am).

The prettily located town of **MERIMBULA** is surrounded by lagoons, lakes, rivers and ocean, making it ideal for watery endeavours or an evening stroll along the various shores. By day, you can take a **boat trip** on Merimbula Lake (actually the wide mouth of the Merimbula River) and Pambula Lake with Merimbula Marina at the public jetty on Market Street (☎02 6495 1686, ⓦ www.merimbulamarina.com; or book through the tourist office – see p.182); options include dolphin tours (2hr; A\$25, child A\$20), whale-watching tours (2hr 30min; Feb–May & Sept–Nov; A\$69, child A\$39) and lunch or dinner cruises (2hr 30min; A\$25, child A\$14). Merimbula Lake is also a popular spot for **windsurfing** and **kitesurfing**, with an annual tournament held at the end of November, and an active local club (☎02 6495 6617). For **surfers**, there are good breaks at the river mouths at both Merimbula and Pambula; you can hire gear at Cycle 'n' Surf, 1B Marine Parade (☎02 6495 2171).

There are some good **dive** sites around town: the people to call are *Merimbula Diver's Lodge* (see below). You've a chance in a million of seeing a whale while you're under water, but it has happened. For a close-up glimpse of captive sharks and tropical fish, check out the **aquarium** at the end of Lake Street (daily 10am–5pm; A\$9.90, child A\$5.50; ☎02 6495 4446, ⓦ www.merimbulawharf .com.au), which has a café and a popular seafood restaurant (see p.186).

Accommodation

There are dozens of **motels** and **holiday apartments** in Merimbula; during the summer holidays, their rates increase and many only accept weekly bookings. The tourist office (see p.183) has listings.

Mandeni Resort Sapphire Coast Drive (7km north of Merimbula on TD11 to Tathra) ☎02 6495 9644 or 1800 358 354, ⓦ www.mandeni.com.au. Fully equipped timber cottages in a bushland setting; facilities include tennis courts, two swimming pools, walking trails and, intriguingly, a needlecraft centre. ❺

Merimbula Beach Cabins 47–65 Short Point Rd ☎02 6495 1216 or 1800 825 555, ⓦ www .beachcabins.com.au. Spacious studios and cabins with inspiring ocean views, in a pleasant location overlooking Short Beach and Back Lake. Small pool and BBQ area. ❹–❻

Merimbula Beach Holiday Park 2 Short Point Rd ☎02 6495 1269 or 1300 787 837, ⓦ www .merimbulabeachholidaypark.com.au. Scenically located in a breezy spot above the lovely Short

Point Beach, this is the nicest caravan park in town, with a great pool. Good for families. Camping A\$30, cabin or villa ❸–❼

Merimbula Divers Lodge 15 Park St ☎02 6495 3611, ⓦ www.merimbuladiverslodge.com.au. PADI dive centre offering accommodation in shared two-bedroom apartments, each sleeping up to eight people, with secure gear storage. Fully equipped kitchens; bring your own linen and towels. Bunk A\$28.

Wandarrah Lodge YHA 8 Marine Parade ☎02 6495 3503, ⓦ www.yha.com.au. Modern, purpose-built youth hostel close to both the beach and lake, with bright, clean accommodation, good communal areas and masses of local info. Bunk in four-share A\$26–29, private double/twin ❷

Eating

The following are all on or close to the waterfront in Merimbula.

Cantina 56 Market St ☎02 6495 1085. Funky place with a modern-Latin vibe, run by a music nut who plays good background tunes and often hosts live bands. Tasty plates of tapas to share. Daily noon–late.

Limetree Café 4 Alice St ☎02 6495 1977. Bright little joint serving good coffee and great lunchtime burgers, wraps and home-made cakes. Daily from 7.30am.

Sante Fe 23 Beach St ☎02 6495 4073. The chilli fanatics here do big wraps, nachos, tostados and Mexican-themed wood-fired pizzas. Open daily for lunch, dinner & takeaway.

Waterfront Café The Promenade, Beach St ☎02 6495 2211. Smart, popular place with a sunny lakeside terrace, packed at weekends. Delicious brunch options and imaginative salads. Daily from 8am for breakfast, lunch & dinner.

Wharf Restaurant Merimbula Aquarium, Lake St ☎02 6495 4446. Located on top of the aquarium but worth a trip in its own right, this casual spot has great sea views and seafood. Daily 11.30am–3pm, plus dinner Wed–Sun 6–8.30pm Dec–April.

Zanzibar Café Main St, corner of Market St ☎02 6495 3636. Town-centre restaurant with a modern feel, famous for its seafood soups and stews including a luscious Eden mussel chowder. Tues–Sat 6–9pm.

Sapphire Coast Drive, Tathra-Bermagui Road and Wallaga Lake

Head due north out of Merimbula (or, if you're travelling south, turn off the Princes Highway 19km south of Narooma, just beyond Tilba Tilba), and you'll find yourself on one of the South Coast's best scenic detours. While the Princes Highway heads inland to trundle innocuously through the cheesemaking town of **Bega** and its surrounding dairylands, **Sapphire Coast Drive** (Tourist Drive 11) and the **Tathra-Bermagui Road** (Tourist Drive 9) offer a serene alternative, leading you through gorgeous coastal lakelands where wooden bridges span shimmering lagoons, fringed by bush and beach. Along the way you pass several national parks, including **Bournda** and **Mimosa Rocks**, which both have lakeside and beachfront hiking trails, picnic spots and campsites (for details, contact Merimbula NPWS – see p.183), and the pleasant fishing villages of **Tathra** and **Bermagui**.

Some 5km north of Bermagui lies **Wallaga Lake**, one of the largest saltwater lakes on the Australian coast. The area around the lake is home to a thriving local **Yuin** community, who run the Umbarra Aboriginal Cultural Centre (Mon–Fri 9am–5pm, Sat & Sun 9am–4pm; free; ☎02 4473 7232, ⊛www.umbarra.com.au). The centre operates daily **tours** (A$20–60) to local sacred sites, including Gulaga (Mount Dromedary) and Mystery Bay, and offers hands-on activities such as face painting with ochres, building bark huts, and sampling bushtucker and traditional medicine (small fee per activity). They also run cruises on Wallaga Lake, a wild and lovely place where flocks of black swans and pelicans perch on the sand bars as the tide washes in and out. There's accommodation nearby at *Wallaga Lake Park* in a

Burnum Burnum: Aboriginal activist

Wallaga Lake is the birthplace of one of Australia's most important Aboriginal figureheads, the elder named **Burnum Burnum**, an ancestral name meaning "Great Warrior". He is best known for his flamboyant political stunts, which included planting the Aboriginal flag at Dover to claim England as Aboriginal territory in Australia's bicentennial year, in order to highlight the dispossession of his native country. He was born under a sacred tree by Wallaga Lake in January 1936. His mother died soon afterwards and he was taken by the Aborigines Protection Board and placed in a mission at Bomaderry, constituting one of the "stolen generation" of indigenous children removed from their families in this period. After graduating in law and playing professional rugby union for New South Wales, he became a prominent political activist in the 1970s. He was involved in various environmental and indigenous protests, including erecting the Aboriginal Tent Embassy outside the Federal Parliament in Canberra, and standing twice, unsuccessfully, for the senate. Burnum Burnum died in August 1997 and his ashes were scattered near the tree where he was born.

terrific location backing onto the lake, 400m from the wild Camel Rock Beach (℡02 6493 4655, Ⓦwww.bestonparks.com.au; camping A$25–45, cabin ❶–❺).

Eurobodalla Coast

Known to the coastal Aborigines as the Land of Many Waters, the Eurobodalla Coast, stretching from the country villages of **Tilba Tilba** and **Central Tilba** to the fragrant eucalyptus groves of **Murramarang National Park**, is so rich in creeks, inlets and lakes that fishermen, birdwatchers and kayaking fanatics find it hard to tear themselves away. The region's two main towns, **Narooma** and **Batemans Bay**, are understated little places situated between calm inland waters and wild ocean beaches.

Practicalities

The daily Premier Motor Service **buses** from Melbourne, Eden and Sydney stop at Tilba Tilba, Narooma and Batemans Bay, and the V/Line train and bus service from Melbourne via Bairnsdale stops at Narooma and Batemans Bay. From Canberra, Transborder and Murrays run to Batemans Bay; Murrays also serve Narooma (see p.180 for a summary, and p.35 for contact details). You can also **fly** into the region from Melbourne or Sydney, landing between Narooma and Batemans Bay at Moruya.

The region's main **Visitor Information Centre** is on the Princes Highway in Batemans Bay (corner of Beach Rd; daily 9am–5pm; ℡02 4472 6900 or 1800 802 528, Ⓦwww.eurobodalla.com.au). On the Princes Highway in Narooma, there's a smaller information centre (near Bluewater Drive; daily 9am–5pm; ℡02 4476 2881 or 1800 240 003), and an NPWS office (near Field Street; Mon–Fri 8.30am–4.40pm; ℡02 4476 2888).

Tilba Tilba and Central Tilba

Just off the highway, around 93km north of Merimbula and 15km south of Narooma, are the picturesque inland villages of **Tilba Tilba** and **Central Tilba**. **TILBA TILBA** is a sweet, sleepy little spot; if you're feeling energetic, follow the walking trail that starts from Pam's Store and leads through a forest to the summit of **Mount Dromedary**, or **Gulaga** (797m); the return walk is about 11km (allow 5–6hr). The larger of the Tilbas, **CENTRAL TILBA**, is by far the quaintest village on the South Coast, set beautifully against forested slopes; with many an old timber shop selling art, fudge, jewellery and gourmet foodstuffs, it invariably gets packed at weekends. The area is famous for its cheeses, and Central Tilba's hundred-year-old **ABC Cheese Factory**, on the main street (daily 9am–5pm), is open for visits and free tastings.

The next logical step is some wine-tasting: on the shores of Corunna Lake, 5km northeast of Central Tilba, is **Tilba Valley Wines** (reached via Tourist Drive 6, signposted off the Princes Highway; May–July & Sept Wed–Sun 11am–4pm; Oct–April daily 10am–5pm; ℡02 4473 7308, Ⓦwww .tilbavalleywines.com), an idyllic spot for a home-made lunch on the terrace, a game of croquet, chess or draughts, or to while away an afternoon listening to live jazz, soul and blues (first and third Sun of the month 12.30pm; free).

The villages have a few suitably cute and countrified **places to stay**. In Tilba Tilba, ⚑ *Green Gables B&B* at 269 Corkhill Drive (℡02 4473 7435, Ⓦwww .greengables.com.au; ❺) is a pretty, weatherboarded house with a dramatic mountain backdrop, home comforts, and gourmet cooking: as well as the full-on breakfast, other meals are available to order. Central Tilba's historic and popular pub, *Dromedary Hotel* on Bate St (℡02 4473 7223; ❷), offers guest accommodation in simple rooms. *The Two Story Bed and Breakfast*, also on Bate St (℡02 4473 7290 or 1800 355 850, ⓦwww.tilbatwostory.com; ❹), is a delightful, deeply homely place, with tasteful decor (if you can forgive the chintz) and very friendly owners. Out of town, 500m northwest along the Tilba–Punkalla Road is *The Bryn* (℡02 4473 7385, ⓦwww.thebrynattilba .com.au; ❹), a great B&B boasting bucolic views and a huge guest-lounge with a wood-burning stove. Back on Bate Street, the *Rose & Sparrow Café* (daily from 7.30am; ℡02 4473 7229) and *The Tilba Teapot* (daily from 9am; ℡02 4473 7811) both offer scrumptious cream teas and light **meals**.

Narooma and Montague Island

Surrounded on three sides by ocean, inlets and coastal lakes, **NAROOMA** is perfect for watery pursuits and is famous for its succulent **freshwater oysters**. The town is spread out over a headland with glorious views of Wagonga Inlet and the Forsters Bay marina to the west, and beautiful Pacific beaches to the east. The Princes Highway, known locally both as Wagonga Street and Campbell Street, runs through the centre. Southern right and humpback **whales** can be seen migrating south along the coast from September to November; there's also a decent chance of seeing **seals** from the lookout at the end of Bar Rocks Road, particularly in spring.

A compelling reason to visit Narooma is to take a trip out to **Montague Island**, an NPWS-managed nature reserve and ecotourism destination, 9km offshore. Narooma Charters (℡0407 909 111, ⓦwww.naroomacharters .com.au) carry groups to the island by boat, leaving them in the hands of an NPWS warden for a fascinating tour of the island's lighthouse, built in the 1870s from granite blocks that were hand-hewn in situ, and its ecological features. Depending on the season, visitors may see breeding colonies of little penguins (Oct–Jan), shearwaters (Dec–April) or malodorous gaggles of Australian fur seals (present all year round, but most numerous Oct–Dec). If you visit in summer, before the penguin chicks have fledged, you can watch the parent birds waddle ashore from the day's fishing and head up to their burrows for the evening feeding session. Half-day **trips** run daily (4hr; A$110, child A$88); if you'd like longer on the island, you can sign up for a Conservation Volunteers tour, staying for one or two nights in the *Head Lighthouse Keeper's* quarters, a lovingly restored five-bedroom Victorian house that sleeps up to twelve, and participating in conservation projects such as botanical management and penguin monitoring (1 night, full board A$370–475, 2 nights A$495–670; ℡03 5330 2600 or 1800 032 501, ⓦwww.conservationvolunteers.com.au). Alternatively, you could just book the entire house for a short, uniquely peaceful **stay** (A$1250–1500 per night, self-catering; min stay 2 nights, max 4 nights; ℡02 4476 2888, ⓦwww .montagueisland.com.au). Finally, another way to experience the island is to head out with Narooma Charters and instead of landing, go **snorkelling** among the seals (A$77, child A$55).

Back on the mainland, the *Wagonga Princess*, a charming little pine ferry very different from the usual glass-bottomed tourist hulks, takes passengers on scenic **cruises** through the mangroves of Wagonga Inlet (departs Taylor's Boatshed Wed, Fri & Sun 1pm; 3hr; A$33, child A$22; ℡02 4476 2665, ⓦwww .wagongainletcruises.com), whilst the Narooma Marina Centre on Riverside Drive (℡02 4476 2126) rents out **kayaks** and boats. **Diving** is available with several outfits, the best of which is Montague Island Diving on Riverside Drive (℡02 4476 1741, ⓦwww.montagueislanddiving.com.au); you'll need to rent gear with Ocean Hut, 123 Princes Hwy, if you don't have your own. If catching marine life is more your thing, try Island Charters (☏02 4476 1047, ⓦwww .islandchartersnarooma.com) for reef and game **fishing**.

Narooma gets into party mode in May, with the annual **Oyster Festival**, and in late September or early October, when the **Great Southern Blues and Rockabilly Festival** (ⓦwww.bluesfestival.tv) takes over the town.

Accommodation

Anchors Aweigh 5 Tilba St ☏02 4476 4000, ⓦwww.anchorsaweigh.com.au. Fresh, comfortable B&B in a modern house with traditional, homely character in a handy location right in the middle of town. ❺

Ecotel 44 Princes Hwy ☏02 4476 2217, ⓦwww .ecotel.com.au. Good-value with simple motel rooms on the north side of town; environmentally conscious features include solar and wind power, responsible water management and a saltwater pool. Guests can join yoga and meditation sessions. ❷

Narooma YHA 243 Princes Hwy ☏02 4476 4440, ⓦwww.yha.com.au. Friendly hostel in a former motel on the south side of town, with welcome extras such as a fridge, TV and kettle in each room, a free pick-up service and free use of bikes. Bunk in en-suite four- or five-share A$29, en-suite double ❷

Pub Hill Farm Wagonga Scenic Drive (10km west of Narooma on TD 4) ☏02 4476 3177, ⓦwww .pubhillfarm.com. Country-style B&B with four well-decorated en-suite rooms. It's extremely scenically situated, between Wagonga Inlet and Punkallah Creek, overlooking Mount Dromedary. ❹

Surfbeach Holiday Park Ballingalla St ☏02 4476 2275 or 1800 762 275, ⓦwww.naroomagolf.com.au. Adjoining the highly scenic golf club, the beach and a creek, this spacious site is the best holiday park in Narooma. Camping A$25–30, cabin ❷–❺

Eating

Casey's Café Wagonga St, corner of Canty St ☏02 4476 1241. A bright, cheery establishment, serving healthy, hearty food, with many veggie options, giant smoothies and the best coffee in town. Mon–Fri 8am–4.30pm, Sat & Sun 8am–2pm.

Lynch's Restaurant 138 Wagonga St, corner of Montague St ☏02 4476 3002. Posh pub serving counter meals at lunchtime, with an excellent Mod Oz restaurant specializing in local oysters (Mon–Sat from 6pm).

Pelicans 31 Riverside Drive ☏02 4476 2403. An upmarket, nautical-style option offering big break-fasts and excellent seafood, including Thai seafood lasagne and lemongrass swordfish. Tues–Thurs 8am–5pm, Fri & Sat 8am–late, Sun 8am–4pm.

Quarterdeck Marina 13 Riverside Drive ☏02 4476 2723. An eclectic and colourful restaurant on the shore of Wagonga Inlet, with a great deck, grilled or fresh oysters, imaginative fish dishes, °and live music sessions. Lunch & dinner daily.

Taylor's Boatshed Riverside Drive ☏02 4476 2127. Just how a fish 'n' chip restaurant should be – speedy service, super-fresh fare (the squid in sweet chilli sauce is rightly famous), and a waterfront deck on which to enjoy the sunset. Tues–Sun 10am–8pm; daily in school holidays.

Batemans Bay, Mogo and Murramarang National Park

At the mouth of the Clyde River and the end of the highway from Canberra, **BATEMANS BAY** is a favourite escape for the landlocked residents of the

The coast between Narooma and Batemans Bay

Scattered in pockets all the way up the central Eurobodalla Coast, the **Eurobodalla National Park**, which protects spotted gum forests, coastal wetlands and untouched white beaches, is an important wildlife reserve: to explore it, take your pick from the side roads that lead east off the Princes Highway between Narooma and Batemans Bay. There are a couple of memorable **tourist drives** in this region, too, notably Tourist Drive 5, north of Narooma, for great ocean views, and Tourist Drive 7, from Moruya to Batemans Bay, which runs right along the brink of the Moruya River and plunges into shimmering wetlands before meandering along the coast past laidback seaside settlements.

capital, just 152km away. It's not the most exciting place on the coast, but there's plenty to do in the vicinity. The town itself has a clutch of relaxed bars and eateries on Clyde and Orient streets. which run along the river foreshore, near the bridge.

The main road through town is Beach Road, which runs to the pleasant marina, then southeast to the beach suburbs of Batehaven, Denham's Beach and beyond – the further you go, the nicer the beaches get. It's also possible to head inland from town by taking a **cruise** on the Clyde River with Merinda Cruises (3hr; A\$27, child A\$14, lunch A\$10; tickets from The Boathouse on Clyde Street; ℡02 4472 4052), whose trips include a stop at the pretty village of **Nelligen**, just upstream. Alternatively, Straight Up Kayaks (℡0418 970 751, ⓌWwww .straightupkayaks.com.au) offer dusk paddles and full-day tours to Nelligen.

There are several small zoos and theme parks around Batemans Bay. You can meet wombats, koalas and wallabies at the **Birdland Animal Park**, just southeast of town at 55 Beach Rd in Batehaven (daily 9.30am–4pm; A\$16, child A\$8; ℡02 4472 5364, Ⓦwww.birdlandanimalpark.com.au), while in the heritage village of **MOGO**, 10km to the south, you can step back in time at the open-air **Old Mogo Town Goldrush Theme Park** (daily 10am–4pm; A\$15, child A\$8; Ⓦwww.oldmogotown.com.au), a reconstruction of a mid-nineteenth-century gold-rush town. Nearby **Mogo Zoo** (daily 9am–5pm; feeding at 10.30am & 1.30pm; A\$20, child A\$10; Ⓦwww.mogozoo.com.au) began life as a small sanctuary, and has grown to something more akin to the Serengeti, housing giraffes, monkeys and lions plus, famously, snow leopards.

North of Batemans Bay, between the highway and the ocean, are the serene eucalyptus groves of **Murramarang National Park** (A\$7 per car per day). There are rewarding hiking trails through the bush and along the coastal fringes, but the park is most famous for its unspoilt beaches where, at dawn and dusk, you may see kangaroos hopping along the shore, nibbling on the grassy banks or badgering campers for handouts (strongly discouraged by the National Park rangers). Two of the beaches, Pretty (℡02 4457 2019) and Depot (℡02 4478 6582), have NPWS-run **campsites** where you can rent a cabin (ⓒ) or pitch a tent in sublime surroundings for next to nothing (A\$10 per person per night, child A\$5). There's also a campsite at Pebbly Beach (A\$10 per person per night, child A\$5; ℡02 4478 6023).

Accommodation

There are plenty of **motels** in town, plus pleasant **B&Bs** in the nearby villages of Nelligen and Sunshine Bay; the visitor information centre (see p.187) has full details.

Batemans Bay Beach Resort 51 Beach Rd ℡02 4472 4541 or 1800 217 533, Ⓦwww .beachresort.com.au. Smart, spacious resort with some prime camping spots overlooking the water, and a choice of cabins, from budget to beachfront. Camping A\$41–56, cabin ❸–❼

Batemans Bay YHA Old Princes Hwy, corner of South St ℡02 4472 4972, Ⓦwww.yha.com.au. Small, quiet YHA in a decent, though somewhat cramped, holiday park, *Shady Willows*, on the south side of town, quite a walk from the river, shops and beaches. Bunk A\$22–27, private double/twin ❶

Murramarang Resort Mill Beach, Banyandah St, South Durras (17km northeast of Batemans Bay)

℡02 4478 6355, Ⓦwww.murramarangresort .com.au. Beautifully located beach resort run by an eco-sensitive company; it offers a wide choice of self-catering cabins and villas, the best of which have uninterrupted views of unspoilt coastline. ❸–❼

The Sun House 14 Kauzal Crescent, Surf Beach (8km southeast of Batemans Bay) ℡02 4471 1152. Modern B&B with just one elegantly designed and furnished guest apartment with use of the house's pretty gardens, swimming pool and tennis court. ❺

Eating

There are a number of decent **places to eat** in Batemans Bay, especially down Clyde and Orient streets and on the esplanade.

The Boatshed Clyde St ☏ 02 4472 4052. Classic fish 'n' chips from a family-run business that's a local institution, with a nice simple menu and a shaded river deck, lapped by gentle waves. Mon–Thurs & Sun 9am–7pm, Fri & Sat 9am–8pm.

Monet's 3/1 Orient St ☏ 02 4472 5717. Cute little café serving all-day breakfasts, pancakes, and yummy ciabattas loaded with bacon and pesto to a background of world music. Tues–Thurs 9am–4pm, Fri & Sat 9am–4pm & 6.30pm–late.

On the Pier Old Punt Rd ☏ 02 4472 6405. Over the bridge on the north bank of the Clyde, this is the nicest restaurant in town by a stretch. It's a bright, breezy place with a great Aussie wine list and imaginative seafood mains. As promised, you can actually eat on the pier. Daily noon–2.30pm & 6–8.30pm.

South Bank 11 Clyde St ☏ 02 4472 5622. With an unusually sleek feel for easy-going Batemans Bay, this serves of-the-moment dishes such as pork belly with Asian greens or ocean trout with beetroot jam (A\$21–27), and good-value lunchtime specials.

Starfish Deli 1 Clyde St ☏ 02 4472 4880. Popular place with river views and a modern menu, including a variety of wood-fired pizzas. Open daily for breakfast, lunch & dinner.

The Shoalhaven region

The well-watered Shoalhaven region is an odd combination of forgettable towns and memorably beautiful wilderness. While **Ulladulla**, **Nowra** and **Bomaderry** are themselves rather thin on attractions, they're close to inspiring scenery, including Kangaroo Valley and the Grand Pacific Drive. The jewel of the region is without doubt **Jervis Bay**, a beautiful natural arena in which dolphins and whales regularly make star appearances. **Berry**, in the north, is worth a stop for its true-blue heritage-village character.

Practicalities

You can travel to the north of the region by **train**: Bomaderry and Berry are on the CityRail South Coast line from Sydney's Central Station via Thirroul, Wollongong and Kiama (Bomaderry, near Nowra, is the southernmost stop). The daily Premier Motor Service (see p.35) **buses** from Melbourne, Eden and Sydney stop at Ulladulla, Nowra and Berry, and Transborder (see p.180) run to Ulladulla from Canberra and Batemans Bay. Local bus services are provided by Nowra Coaches (☏ 02 4423 5244, ⓦ www.nowracoaches.com.au).

The region's **visitor information centres** (ⓦ www.shoalhavenholidays .com.au) have an accommodation- and activities-booking service. The main centre is at Nowra, just south of the road bridge that carries the Princes Highway across the Shoalhaven River (daily 9am–5pm; ☏ 02 4421 0778 or 1300 662 808); there's also a branch in Ulladulla's Civic Centre on the Princes Highway (Mon–Fri 10am–6pm, Sat & Sun 9am–5pm; ☏ 02 4455 1269).

Ulladulla and around

ULLADULLA is a fairly uninspiring fishing port whose saving grace is its small, pretty harbour and its proximity to beautiful scenery: there are attractive river mouths, beaches and lakes along the coast in both directions. **Lake Tabourie** and **Lake Burrill** to the south and **Lake Conjola** to the north are all popular with fishermen, canoeists and campers, while Wheelbarrow Road, 8km south of town between Tabourie and Burrill, leads to the start of a marked walking trial (4hr return) to the top of the 720-metre **Pigeon House Mountain** in the Budawang Ranges, part of **Morton National Park**, where

Canberra, Australia's custom-built capital, has been the seat of government since 1927. Being such an overtly planned place populated by civil servants and politicians, it's in many ways a city in search of a soul: while there are all the galleries, museums and attractions that there should be, many seem to exist simply because it would be ridiculous to have omitted them from a national capital.

A few key sights are genuinely worth an overnight stay, however, namely the extraordinary, partly subterranean **Parliament House**, the **Australian War Memorial**, and the **National Botanic Gardens**. The city's other main draw – that of being surrounded by the unspoilt wilderness of the **Brindabella Ranges** and the **Namadgi National Park** – took a severe battering in 2003, when seventy percent of rural ACT was destroyed in a terrible **bushfire**. The forests were so badly burnt that they will take decades to recover, and are barely worth the effort to see at the present. However, the scenic **Kosciuszko National Park** and **Snowy Mountains** are within easy driving distance.

Canberra's **nightlife** – in term time at least – is alive and kicking. The two universities here (and the Duntroon Military Academy) mean there's a large and lively **student population** (good news for those who have student cards, as most attractions offer hefty discounts), and the city is also said to have more **restaurants** per capita than any other in Australia, which is saying something.

Some history

When the Australian colonies united in the **Commonwealth of Australia** in 1901, a capital city had to be chosen, with Melbourne and Sydney the two obvious and eager rivals. After much wrangling, and partly in order to avoid having to decide on one of the two, it was agreed to establish a brand-new capital instead. In 1909, Limestone Plains, south of Yass, was chosen out of several possible sites. An area of 2368 square kilometres was excised from the state of New South Wales and named the **Australian Capital Territory**, or **ACT**. The name for the future capital was supposedly taken from the language of local Aborigines: Canberra – the Meeting Place.

In 1912, **Walter Burley Griffin**, an American landscape architect from Chicago, won the international competition to create Canberra's urban design. His plan envisaged a garden city for about 25,000 people based in five main centres, each with separate functions, located on three axes: land, water and municipal. Roads were to be in concentric circles, with arcs linking the radiating design. The present-day population of over 300,000 completely outstrips his original estimates – though Canberra's decentralized design means that the city never feels crowded.

Practicalities

Canberra's **airport**, 7km east of the city, is connected to the centre by a twice-hourly bus service; **trains** arrive at the station on Wentworth Avenue, Kingston, southeast of the centre; and **long-distance buses** arrive at the Jolimont Centre on Northbourne Avenue, Civic.

With Canberra's sights so spread out, you'd have to be very enthusiastic to consider walking everywhere. City buses are run by Action (☏13 17 10, ⓦwww .action.act.gov.au); the hub is the **City Bus Interchange** at the eastern end of Alinga Street, Civic. A good option is to rent a **bike** and take advantage of the city's excellent network of cycle paths; some buses have special bike-racks on the front.

The **Canberra Visitor Information Centre** is inconveniently located 3km north of the centre at 330 Northbourne Avenue (Mon–Fri 9am–5pm, Sat & Sun 9am–4pm; ☏02 6205 0044, ⓦwww.visitcanberra.com.au); there's also an information desk at the airport (Mon–Fri 8.30am–5.30pm; ☏1300 554 114).

Recommended **places to stay** include the stylish and expensive *Hyatt* on Commonwealth Avenue, Yarralumla (☏02 6270 1234, ⓦwww.canberra.park.hyatt .com; ❼); *Olim's*, close to the War Memorial on the corner of Ainslie and Limestone Avenues, Braddon (☏02 6248 5511, ⓦwww.olimshotel.com; ❺), with a National

Trust-listed main building; and *Canberra City YHA* at 7 Akuna St, Civic (☎02 6257 3999, ⓦwww.yha.com.au; bunk A$25–33.50, twin/double ③), a cavernous, organized, centrally located hostel with comprehensive facilities.

Finding somewhere to eat around Civic and Kingston is never a problem; the restaurants feature a definite bias towards Southeast Asian food. There are also cafés at Parliament House, the National Gallery, Botanic Gardens and other sights.

Parliament House

Built into the side of Capital Hill, **Parliament House** (daily 9am–5pm; free; ⓦwww .aph.gov.au), is an extraordinary construction, though only the landmark, four-piece **flagpole** is visible from the outside. Designed by the American-based architect Romaldo Giurgola and opened in May 1988, it's certainly impressive in scale and concept, despite having numerous detractors – the former prime minister Malcolm Fraser, who commissioned the building, described it later as "an unmitigated disaster" and "my one very serious political mistake". Make sure you catch one of the free **guided tours**, which run every half hour between 9am and 4pm.

Outside the ground-floor entrance level is a **mosaic** by the Aboriginal artist Michael Tjakamarra Nelson – a piece that conveys the idea of a sacred meeting place. Inside, the impressive **foyer** is dominated by over forty columns clad in grey-green and rose-pink marble, representing a eucalypt forest. The floors are made of native woods, and the walls feature marquetry panels detailing native plants. Beyond the foyer, the **Great Hall** sports a twenty-metre-high **tapestry** based on a painting by Arthur Boyd showing the opposing forces of life and death meeting in blackened trees set against a powerful sky (look for the cockatoo). Other chambers are adorned with paintings by artists such as Albert Tucker, Sidney Nolan and Ian Fairweather, as well as portraits of political figures, photographs and ceramics. Important documents in the country's political history are also displayed.

When Parliament is in session – usually around seventy to eighty days a year – you can sit in the **public galleries** and watch the proceedings in the House of Representatives (the lower chamber of Parliament) or the Senate (the upper chamber of the legislature); Question Time in both chambers starts at 2pm, with the House of Representatives making for better viewing. To guarantee a seat at busy times (such as budget day), book in advance on ☎02 6277 5399.

The Australian War Memorial

Due east of Civic on Limestone Avenue, the **Australian War Memorial** (daily 10am–5pm; free) does a good job of commemorating Australia's war dead whilst avoiding any glorification of war itself – a notable achievement for a country that sees participation in world wars as a key part of its identity. The centrepiece is the Byzantine-style, domed **Hall of Memory**, approached past an eternal flame that rises from a rectangular pond. Look up at the ceiling to see mosaics depicting veterans of World War II, while the lovely blue stained-glass windows commemorate those who fought in World War I. In the centre is the tomb of the Unknown Australian Soldier, while over 100,000 names of the fallen are etched onto the walls outside. Wings either side house paintings by war artists, battle dioramas and military relics including huge naval guns and giant bombers, as well as countless films, and sound-and-light shows.

National Botanic Gardens

The **National Botanic Gardens** on Clunies Ross Street (daily 8.30am–5pm; free; free guided tours daily at 11am & 2pm) recreate a wide swathe of native habitats, including rainforest, in what was a sheep paddock in the 1970s. You can spend a couple of tranquil hours here walking through the undergrowth and spotting reptiles and birds, including rare **gang-gang cockatoos**. An outdoor **café** (same hours) is beautifully set amongst shaded fern-gardens and lawns.

③

there are also Aboriginal cave sites and numerous waterfalls. **Milton**, the village 6km north of Ulladulla on the Princes Highway, has a clutch of antique shops, craft galleries and cafés.

In Ulladulla itself, there's swimming at the free **seawater pool** by the wharf (Nov–March Mon & Wed–Sun 7–11am & 2–6pm), and **scuba diving** run by Ulladulla Dive & Adventure, 211 Princes Hwy (℡02 4455 3029, @www .ulladulladive.com.au). The local Budamurra Aboriginal community (℡02 4455 5883) has constructed an interesting wheelchair-accessible **cultural trail** called One Track For All at Ulladulla Head; turn off the highway at North Street and keep going. Guided tours (A$10) are also offered by the Budamurra people, and include tips on boomerang throwing, didgeridoo playing and fire making, as well as some bushtucker.

Accommodation

Bannister's Point Lodge 191 Mitchell Parade, Mollymook (5km north of Ulladulla) ℡02 4455 3044, @www.bannisterspointlodge.com.au. High-spec designer pad, with glamorous, modern rooms and a spectacular clifftop infinity pool adjoining a chic cocktail bar; an indulgent restaurant (see opposite) and day spa are also on site. ❼–❽

Ulladulla Guesthouse 39 Burrill St ℡02 4455 1796, @www.guesthouse.com.au. Pleasantly cluttered guesthouse with comfortable rooms, a palm-fringed swimming pool, art for sale, and a charming restaurant serving French cuisine at way-below-Parisian prices (dinner Mon & Thurs–Sat). ❺

Ulladulla Headland Tourist Park South St ℡02 4455 2457, @www.holidayhaven.com.au. Superb clifftop location, plus excellent amenities, including a swimming pool, tennis court, children's playground and smart cabins. Camping A$20–40, cabin ❷–❻

Eating

🏃 **Bannister's** Bannisters Point Lodge, 191 Mitchell Parade, Mollymook (5km north of Ulladulla) ℡02 4455 3044, @www .bannisterspointlodge.com.au. One of the best restaurants on the South Coast, with ocean views, award-winning food, and a particularly good wine cellar. Dinner Tues–Sun.

Edge Café Green St, corner of Boree St ℡02 4454 3565. The best lunch option in town, this spacious hideaway does gourmet pizza, pasta, salads and lots of veggie plates, plus great brunches. Mon–Thurs 8am–5pm, Fri 8am–10pm, Sat 9am–10pm.

Millard's Cottage 81 Princes Hwy ℡02 4455 3287. This striking pink building is one of Ulladulla's oldest; the menu offers very fine dining with some unusual seafood, and meat mains such as pork with strawberry-and-balsamic-vinegar sauce. Lunch Thurs–Sat, dinner Mon–Sat.

Jervis Bay

Around 107km north of Batemans Bay, 25km south of Nowra and 240km east by road from Canberra, the sheltered waters of **Jervis Bay** are a marine sanctuary; they're also, by a political quirk, technically part of the ACT, in order to provide the capital with access to the sea. The area attracts a lot of visitors due to its proximity both to Canberra and to Sydney, but it rarely feels crowded – the unspoilt coast is fringed with a variety of utterly lovely **beaches**, including the famously white Hyams Beach, so there's more than enough room for allcomers. Wildlife-watching opportunities are superb, making this one of the best places on the South Coast for ecotourists to explore.

Nowra Coaches (℡02 4423 5244, @www.nowracoaches.com.au) run **buses** to Jervis Bay from Nowra and Bomaderry, but the easiest way to get around is with your own transport. Of the several villages dotted around the bay and its vicinity, the main focus is **HUSKISSON**, a small settlement with a few shops and eateries; a cosy little cinema, Huskisson Pictures (℡02 4441 5076, @www.huskipics.com.au); and a couple of excellent operators who will get you waterborne, either to **dive** or **snorkel** in the pristine bay, or to observe marine wildlife such as dolphins, whales and little penguins by boat. The main scuba outfit, Deep 6 Diving at 64 Owen St (℡02 4441 5255,

@www.deep6divingjervisbay.com.au), offers courses, dive trips and snorkelling, with a chance to see schools of fish, anenomes, clams and, if you're very lucky, weedy sea dragons. Of the two companies that offer **wildlife-watching cruises**, Dolphin Watch Cruises at 50 Owen St (2hr 30min; A$24–30, child A$15; ☎02 4441 6311 or 1800 246 010, @www.dolphinwatch.com.au) have the edge for their wholehearted commitment to local ecological causes. You're almost certain to see dolphins in the bay throughout the year, while between September and November this becomes one of the best places in Australia to watch whales: the mighty mammals regularly duck into the bay with their calves to take a breather on their long journey south. Cruises also operate between late May and late July, when the whales are heading north.

The beautiful coast of **Booderee National Park** ("Bay of Plenty", or "Plenty of Fish"), at the southern end of the bay, is very popular: rugged cliffs face the pounding ocean along its eastern boundary, while the park's northern side, within the confines of the bay, is marked by tranquil beaches of dazzling white sand and clear water. Inland, heaths, wetlands and forests offer strolls and bushwalks; there's also great snorkelling from the park and around nearby Bowen Island, with a chance of spotting a range of marine life including dolphins, stingrays and – around the island – a penguin colony. The park (entry fee A$10 per vehicle per 48hr) is co-managed by the Australian government and the Wreck Bay Aboriginal Community, who also run the **visitor centre** at the entrance on Jervis Bay Rd (daily 10am–4pm; ☎02 4443 0977, @www .booderee.gov.au), where detailed walking maps are available. In summer, there's a cultural interpretation programme, Wreck Bay Walkabouts (free; bookings through the visitor centre), which covers diet and medicines, archeology and wildlife; alternatively, try the highly recommended Barry's Bushtucker Tours (☎02 4442 1168).

Booderee Botanic Gardens, on Cave Beach Road (daily 8am–6pm during DST; 9am–4pm rest of the year; free), focuses on regional coastal flora and has a number of pleasant walks with interpretive boards.

Accommodation

The Booderee Visitor Centre handles bookings for the three immensely popular, unpowered **campsites** (A$20) in the park – a ballot is held in August for spots over the Christmas holiday period. The *Cave Beach* site is the most sought-after, despite its cold showers, but *Bristol Point* and *Green Patch* also get plenty of guests; the latter is the only one of the three suitable for campervans.

Bay of Plenty Lodges Ellmoos Rd, Booderee National Park ☎02 4441 2018, @www .bayofplentylodges.com.au. In a unique location tucked away in the park, sandwiched between bush, beach and Sussex Inlet, these well-equipped cottages and cabins are great for nature-lovers. ⑤

Huskisson B&B 12 Tomerong St, Huskisson ☎02 4441 7551, @www.huskissonbnb.com.au. Lovely, beachy B&B in a 1913 weatherboard cottage with well-decorated shabby-chic rooms, nourishing breakfasts and a multitude of home comforts. ⑤

Huskisson Beach Tourist Park Beach St, Huskisson ☎02 4441 5142, @www.holidayhaven .com.au. Campsite in an unbeatable location, very close to the village and right on the beach, with

good amenities, including a pool. Camping A$50–56, cabin ⑤

Jervis Bay Backpackers 37 Owen St, Huskisson and 16 Elizabeth Drive, Vincentia ☎0402 299 309, @www.jervisbaybackpackers.com.au. This welcoming outfit with two bases offers budget accommodation with a homely feel. Bunk A$30, double/twin ②

Paperbark Camp Woollamia Rd, Woollamia (5km northwest of Huskisson) ☎02 4441 6066, @www.paperbarkcamp.com.au. Unusually lovely luxury resort, like a forward-thinking African safari camp transported to the Australian bush, with romantic en-suite safari tents on stilts, huge beds, private verandas, eco-conscious features and an amazing restaurant (see p.196). ⑦

Worrowing 81 The Wool Rd, Worrowing Heights (11km southwest of Huskission) ☎02 4443 8912, ⓦwww.jervisbay-getaways.com .au. These cute self-catering eco-cabins – lovingly

constructed from reclaimed materials – are so well spaced you'll feel it's just you, the wallabies, roos and forest birds in a huge tract of parkland. The owners also offer fabulous beach and lakefront houses. ❺

Eating and drinking

The Jervis Bay villages have a mixed bag of **eating places** – happily, the best ones are excellent.

The Gunyah *Paperbark Camp*, Woollamia Rd, Woollamia (5km northwest of Huskission) ☎02 4441 6066, ⓦwww.paperbarkcamp .com.au. This eco-friendly forest pavilion is a superbly atmospheric setting for intimate dinners with bushtucker touches, such as salmon baked in bark and yoghurt perfumed with lemon myrtle (mains A$28–34). Daily 6–9pm.

Huskisson Hotel 73 Owen St, Huskisson ☎02 4441 5001. The famous *Husky Pub*, currently let down by average bistro food and a shabby atmosphere, is overdue for a revamp, but you can't fault its location, right on the beachfront in the middle of town.

Husky Bakery 11 Currambene St, Huskisson ☎02 4441 5015. Chirpy bakery-café with

mouthwatering pies and other goodies, which you can enjoy at inside tables or on the veranda. Breakfast & lunch daily.

Jervis Blue Café 76 Cyrus St, Hyams Beach ☎02 4443 3874. Close to Hyams' whiter-than-white sands, this simple spot is just right for perfectionists, with consummate coffee and faultless light lunches. Breakfast (from 8am) & lunch daily.

Seagrass Brasserie 13 Currambene St, Huskisson ☎02 4441 6124. In a charming timber building with the cosiness of a country café, the cooking here is cutting edge, with delicious dishes such as braised pork belly with caramelized black vinegar and rice noodles, or seared trout with asparagus and macadamia salsa (mains A$29–33). Dinner daily, lunch Sat & Sun.

Nowra, Bomaderry and Kangaroo Valley

With so many beautiful places to explore nearby – and well-signposted **tourist drives** to follow – it's worth skipping the unremarkable towns of **Nowra**, a sizeable commercial centre on the Pacific Highway around 14km from the coast, and **Bomaderry**, which faces Nowra across the Shoalhaven River and marks the end of the South Coast railway line from Sydney. The main reasons to stop would be to drop in at Nowra's regional **visitor information centre** (see p.191) or to grab a bite or a **coffee** at *River Deli*, 84 Kinghorne St, Nowra (Mon–Sat 7am–2pm; ☎02 4423 1344).

Of the several worthwhile scenic routes that start from here, the **Grand Pacific Drive** (see box, p.197) is particularly inspirational; there are also some satisfying shorter options. Just north of Nowra Bridge over the Shoalhaven, **Tourist Drive 5/6** leaves the Princes Highway to run along the north bank of the river to Shoalhaven Heads, from where Tourist Drive 5 loops back inland to Berry (see p.197). On the opposite side of the Princes Highway, around 2.5km north of Nowra Bridge, **Tourist Drive 8** heads northwest to the pioneer dairy-farming village of **Kangaroo Valley**, which lies 20km inland on what was once a crucial overland route for the agricultural community. The kangaroos have, sadly, long since disappeared, but this pretty region is very popular with Sydneysiders on weekends away. **Hampden Bridge**, its most notable feature, is the oldest surviving suspension bridge in Australia, built over the Kangaroo River gorge between 1895 and 1898. From here, you can continue inland to the glorious **Fitzroy Falls** in the far northeast of Morton National Park, and on via Robertson to Budderoo National Park (see p.201), for a satisfying scenic loop, rejoining the Princes Highway at Kiama. A shorter route back to the coast from Kangaroo Valley is to pick up **Tourist Drive 7** (Kangaroo Valley Rd), which leads to Berry.

The Grand Pacific Drive

The 140-kilometre coastal route between Bomaderry, in the Shoalhaven region, and Royal National Park, just south of Sydney, is without doubt one of the East Coast's classic drives. Unlike Victoria's Great Ocean Road (see p.157), much of which is buried in bush, the **Grand Pacific Drive** rarely loses sight of the water. Consisting of a series of diversions from the Princes Highway, it's easy enough to break it into small sections if you so choose, switching onto the highway whenever you need to gather some speed. The most dramatic section of the route lies in the north, between Thirroul and Otford, where it runs between the Illawarra Escarpment and the ocean: here, the emblematic new **Sea Cliff Bridge** (see p.204), which lifts you high above the waves between Clifton and Coalcliff, is a genuine highlight. If you take the time to stop and follow the bridge on foot as it snakes around the cliffs, you can gulp in gigantic ocean views.

To cover the entire Grand Pacific Drive from south to north, you start just north of the Nowra Bridge, turning east off the Princes Highway onto **Tourist Drive 6**, which follows the Shoalhaven River to the coast then veers northward to scoot along the back of Seven Mile Beach National Park (see p.199) to Gerroa and Gerringong, rejoining the Princes Highway 7km south of Kiama. Having passed Kiama, you veer off the highway once more at Dunmore, taking **Tourist Drive 10** (Lawrence Hargrave Drive) along the oceanward side of Lake Illawarra to Wollongong. Tourist Drive 10 continues north along the scenic run from Wollongong, hugging the coast all the way to Otford; from here you can head inland via **Route 68**, which winds its way through Royal National Park (see p.204) to meet the Princes Highway once more.

Berry

Set amid rolling hills on the Princes Highway 16km north of Nowra and 62km south of Wollongong, **BERRY** is a pretty, historic village with many listed buildings. The highway, known as **Queen Street** as it runs through the centre, has two country pubs and a crush of upmarket homeware shops, little art galleries, cafés and restaurants. Always popular with visitors, Berry is particularly busy on Country Fair day, the first Sunday of the month. The *Berry Hotel* (see below) offers tours of the region's **wineries** (Sat 11am–1.30pm; A\$25): the Coolangatta Estate, 11km south of Berry on Bolong Road, Shoalhaven Heads (daily 10am–5pm; ☎02 4448 7131, ⓦwww.coolangattaestate.com.au) is the best, while The Silos Estate, 7km southwest of town at Jasper's Brush (Wed–Sun 10am–5pm; ☎02 4448 6082, ⓦwww.thesilos.com) also has a good reputation.

Accommodation

There are a great many rural **B&Bs** in the hills around the village; check out ⓦwww.shoalhavenholidays.com.au for listings.

The Berry Hotel 120 Queen St ☎02 4464 1011, ⓦwww.berryhotel.com.au. A really lovely old coach house offering shared-bathroom pub rooms with old-fashioned character. Midweek rates are lower but don't include the full breakfast that's served up at weekends. ❹

The Bunyip Inn 122 Queen St ☎02 4464 2064, ⓦwww.stayz.com/29878. Pleasant option in an imposing National Trust-classified former bank, with a leafy garden and swimming pool; some of the thirteen olde-worlde rooms have four-poster beds. ❹

Coolangatta Estate 1335 Bolong Rd, Shoalhaven Heads (11km southwest of Berry) ☎02 4448 7131, ⓦwww.coolangattaestate.com.au. Sympathetically converted outbuildings with a historic feel, from a cosy timber cottage with flowery fabrics and a pretty iron bedstead to a large split-level lodge. Midweek (bed & breakfast) ❻; weekend (half board) ❼

Silos Estate 640B Princes Hwy, Jasper's Brush (7km southwest of Berry) ☎02 4448 6082, ⓦwww.thesilos.com. This winery offers luxury accommodation in four different-sized suites with vineyard and escarpment views, and a complimentary bottle of bubbly. ❺–❼

Eating

Key to Berry's popularity with weekenders is its good selection of country-style **gourmet eateries**.

The Berry Hotel 120 Queen St. This much-loved place boasts the best food in town, served in either the pub itself, the large courtyard at the back, or a cosy dining room with open fire. Posh pub tucker at lunch, and affordable Mod Oz offerings in the evening, including a delicious cumin-spiced lamb rump with puy lentils, aubergine and yoghurt.

Berry Wood-Fired Sourdough Bakery 23 Prince Alfred St, Berry ☎02 4464 1617. Far more than just a purveyor of luscious bread and delectable cakes and croissants, this bakery-café also produces tasty lunch options including unforgettable seafood pizza and stuffed bream. Wed–Sun 8am–3pm.

Cuttlefish 98 Queen St ☎02 4464 3065. Stylish upstairs pizza bar serving modern Italian mains and wicked desserts. Lunch Fri–Sun, dinner Wed–Sun.

Emporium Food Co 127 Queen St ☎02 4464 1570. Opposite *The Berry Hotel*, this gourmet deli serves posh sandwiches, savoury pies, beautiful little cakes and excellent coffee – try and grab one of the little ornate tables at the front of the shop. Mon–Sat 9am–5pm, Sun 10am–4.30pm.

The Silos Winery *Silos Estate*, 640B Princes Hwy, Jasper's Brush (7km southwest of Berry) ☎02 4448 6082, ⓦwww .thesilos.com. The finest dining in the area, with an eclectic contemporary menu that draws on Asian, South American and European influences. Beautifully crafted desserts and idyllic views. Pricey. Feb–Nov lunch Thurs–Sun, dinner Thurs–Sat; Dec & Jan lunch daily, dinner Mon–Sat.

The Illawarra region

The section of the South Coast closest to Sydney has enough in the way of natural beauty to attract the most discerning of country-loving city-dwellers. Mercifully, however, its beach resorts aren't as crowded as you might expect – many Sydneysiders, put off by the thought of the grinding drive through the southern suburbs, head north instead – and, for the time being, much of Illawarra has managed to escape over-development. The beach hamlet of **Gerringong** and the small seaside town of **Kiama**, with its famously effervescent Blowhole, certainly have plenty of charm. North of Lake Illawarra, **Wollongong**, the region's largest city, is in many ways the counterpart to Newcastle on the north coast – a beach city with a heavy industrial past, now hoping to reinvent itself as supremely "liveable", and attract a few tourists in the process. To its advantage, it has the most scenic stretch of the **Grand Pacific Drive** on its doorstep: the coastal route to the **Royal National Park** via the Sea Cliff Bridge.

Practicalities

It's easy to travel through the region by **train**: Gerringong, Kiama, Wollongong, Thirroul, Wombarra and Scarborough are on the CityRail South Coast line (see p.35) from Bomaderry to Sydney's Central Station, as are Otford, Waterfall, Heathcote, Engadine and Loftus (for Royal and Heathcote national parks). Gerringong, Kiama, Wollongong, Heathcote and Engadine are all served by the daily Premier Motor Service (see p.35) **long-distance buses** from Melbourne, Eden and Sydney, while Murrays Coaches run to Wollongong from Canberra (see p.180). You can also **fly** to Wollongong from Melbourne. Local bus services are provided by Kiama Coachlines (Kiama, Jamberoo and Gerringong; Mon–Fri only; ☎02 4232 3466, ⓦwww .kiamacoachlines.com.au); Premier Illawarra (Kiama to Wollongong; ☎02 4271 1322, ⓦwww.premierillawarra.com.au); Dion's (Wollongong to Thirroul; ☎02 4228 9855, ⓦwww.dions.com.au) and Greens (Wollongong to Stanwell Park; ☎02 4267 3884; ⓦwww.greensnortherncoaches.com.au).

The region's main **visitor information centres** are on Blowhole Point Road, Kiama (daily 9am–5pm; ☎02 4232 3322, ⊛www.kiama.com.au) and at 93 Crown St, Wollongong, near Crown Street Mall (Mon–Fri 9am–5pm, Sat 9am–4pm, Sun 10am–4pm; ☎02 4227 5545 or 1800 240 737, ⊛www .tourismwollongong.com).

Gerroa and Gerringong

The adjacent villages of **Gerroa** and **Gerringong**, on the coast 15km northeast of Berry and 10km south of Kiama, are wonderfully scenic, set against green hills. They're connected by Tourist Drive 6 (see p.196), a scenic detour off the Princes Highway from just north of Nowra to just south of Kiama. Gerroa has glorious sweeping views of **Seven Mile Beach National Park**, a spotless beach backed by dunes and tea trees. Camping in the park is not permitted, but there's a family-friendly site nearby, *Seven Mile Beach Holiday Park* on Crooked River Road, Gerroa (☎02 4234 1340 or 1800 666 665, ⊛www.kiama.net/holiday/sevenmile; camping A$40–60, hut or safari tent ❹, cabin ❹–❻), located beside Crooked River and within walking distance of Gerringong and its cafés. As well as conventional options, it has safari tents complete with corny zebra-pattern bedspreads. The vanguard of boutique-hotel style in these parts is *Bellachara* at 1 Fern St, Gerringong (☎02 4234 1359, ⊛www.bellachara.com.au; room ❻, suite ❽), a sleek modern place with modish chandeliers and an attractive pool. Gerroa's *Seahaven Café* at 19 River-leigh Ave (☎02 4234 3796) does imaginative lunches and tasty cakes, while inland, the region's largest wine estate has a pleasant restaurant, the *Crooked River Winery Café*, 11 Willowdale Rd, Gerringong (Thurs–Sun 11am–3pm; ☎02 4234 0976), with views of hills and vines.

Kiama and around

Though not quite as charming as some of the region's quieter corners, the fishing centre and resort town of **KIAMA** is easily the most attractive of the South Coast destinations within two hours of Sydney. Its most famous natural feature is the **Blowhole** on Blowhole Point, a five-minute walk from the railway station. Stemming from a fault in the basalt-like rock, the Blowhole explodes like a geyser when a wave hits the cliffs below with sufficient force. It's impressive, but also potentially dangerous – freak waves can be thrown more than 60m into the air and have swept several over-curious bystanders into the raging sea – so stand behind the barrier. There's also a smaller blowhole to the south, on the point between Easts Beach and Kendalls Beach, which can shoot out plumes of water and compressed air up to 30m high. Other coastal wonders include **Cathedral Rocks**, a mysteriously monumental rock formation 3km to the north, best viewed from Cliff Drive, Kiama Downs, and there are further attractions just inland in the area around Jamberoo (see p.201).

Accommodation

There's an abundance of **B&Bs**, **motels** and **holiday houses** around town and in the leafy hinterland near Jamberoo (see p.201); the tourist office (see above) has a comprehensive list and can book places for free. As this is prime holiday territory for Sydneysiders, prices are above average for the South Coast.

Grand Hotel 49 Manning St ☎02 4232 1037, ⊛www.grandhotelkiama.com.au. Built in 1891 and listed by the National Trust, this traditional hostelry has old-fashioned share-bathroom pub rooms. ❸

Grand Mercure Kiama Blue Minnamurra St ☎02 4230 7500, ⊛www.grandmercure.com. Swish, modern rooms and apartments within easy walking distance of the station and Kiama Terrace, a row of

▲ Blowhole, Kiama

shops in weatherboarded houses dating back to the 1880s. ⑥

Kiama Backpackers Hostel 31 Bong Bong St ℡ 02 4233 1881. Budget option, handy for the station and Surf Beach. Bunk A$22, room ②

Kiama Harbour Cabins Blowhole Point ℡ 02 4232 2707 or 1800 823 824, ⓦ www.kiama.net /holiday/blowhole. Smart, modern self-catering cabins in a prime location within earshot of the Blowhole. ⑥

Surf Beach Holiday Park Bourroul St ℡ 02 4232 1791 or 1800 222 334, ⓦ www.kiama.net/holiday /surf. The closest campsite to the centre, and with a pool (rare in Kiama), this family-friendly place is up on the headland between Surf Beach and Kendalls Beach. The top-of-the-range cabin has amazing ocean views. Camping A$30–32, van or cabin ④–⑦

Eating and drinking

There are plenty of **places to eat** in Kiama, with a concentration on Manning and Terralong streets.

55 on Collins 55 Collins St ℡ 02 4232 2811. This appealing place does gourmet café food such as duck and cognac sausages by day, and dresses up a bit in the evening for its contemporary dinner menu (main courses A$26–32). Breakfast & lunch daily, dinner Mon, Tues & Thurs–Sat.

Grand Hotel 49 Manning St ℡ 02 4232 1037. Landmark pub with a reliable restaurant serving decent, filling meals such as pizzas, pasta and grills, using locally sourced meat.

Manning St Deli 14 Manning St ℡ 02 4232 4030. Hugely popular for coffee, cake and light meals, this classy deli-café also sells tempting cheese, chutneys and groceries. Breakfast & lunch daily.

Sugarbag 31 Shoalhaven St ℡ 02 4232 2890. Fresh, contemporary café, overlooking the ocean and hard to beat for classy fish 'n' chips. Breakfast & lunch daily.

Inland from Kiama

West of Kiama, Tourist Drive 4 leads steeply to **Mount Saddleback Lookout**, from where on a clear day you can get an incredible view of the entire coast, from Royal National Park in the north to Jervis Bay in the south.

Beyond the lookout, the road continues north to join Tourist Drive 9, which runs inland from Kiama to the old foresters' and dairy farmers' village of **Jamberoo** and beyond. The waterslides at **Jamberoo Action Park**, 4km north of Jamberoo (Sept–April daily 10am–5pm; A$35, child A$28; ℡ 02 4236 0114, Ⓦ www.jamberoo.net) are a big hit with young families. Around 6km west of Jamberoo and 15km west of Kiama via Minnamurra Falls Road is the most popular section of **Budderoo National Park**, the **Minnamurra Rainforest** (daily 9am–5pm, visitor centre and *Lyrebird Café* 9am–4pm; car entry A$11; ℡ 02 4236 0469). Thanks to its relative inaccessibility, this pocket of subtropical and temperate rainforest escaped the loggers' axes in the early years of the colony. To the sound of whipbirds and lyrebirds, you can explore via an elevated **boardwalk** (first 900m section wheelchair-accessible; to walk the entire 1.6km circuit set off before 4pm), which winds around cabbage tree palms, staghorn ferns and impressive Illawarra fig trees. Another walking track (2.6km; 2hr return; start before 3pm) takes you to viewing platforms overlooking the **Minnamurra Falls**. **Camping** is not permitted in the Minnamurra Rainforest, but you can bushcamp for free elsewhere in Budderoo, as long as you're more than 1km from the nearest road, lookout or picnic area.

Close to the Minnamurra Rainforest but just outside the Budderoo park boundary is the **Illawarra Fly Tree Top Walk** (daily 9am–5pm; A$19, child A$9; ℡ 02 4885 1010 or 1300 362 881, Ⓦ www.illawarrafly.com), reached by heading west from Jamberoo on the steep and winding Jamberoo Mountain Road section of Tourist Drive 9, and turning north onto Knights Hill Road after 15km. This new, high-level steel walkway, 500m long and 25m up, has impressive views of the surrounding greenery; a spiral staircase then takes you to the top of a 45-metre-high observation tower for panoramic vistas across the Illawarra Escarpment. The **Carrington Falls**, within Budderoo, are also worth a visit – you get a good view from the lookout points reached by turning off the Jamberoo Mountain Road 19km west of Jamberoo. From here, you can continue via Robertson to Fitzroy Falls (see p.196) and, for a scenic loop, head back to the coast via Kangaroo Valley and Berry. Alternatively, you can take Tourist Drive 8 (the Illawarra Highway) from Robertson to the **Macquarie Pass**, the gateway to the Southern Highlands. The **Macquarie Pass National Park**, 32km northwest of Kiama, is one of the southernmost stands of Australia's subtropical rainforest, with more waterfalls and excellent bushwalking; again, you can bushcamp here for free, 1km or more from the nearest road.

Wollongong

Although it's New South Wales' third-largest city, **WOLLONGONG**, 80km south of Sydney, has a staunchly provincial feel. The students of Wollongong University give it extra life in term time, and it has a big dose of surf culture, as the city is set right on the ocean, but it's essentially a working-class industrial centre. The huge steelworks at nearby Port Kembla looms unattractively over Wollongong City Beach, but the **Illawarra Escarpment** (see p.203) rises dramatically beyond the city and provides a lush backdrop.

There's not really much to see in the **city centre**, concentrated between Wollongong City railway station and the beach. A large chunk of the centre has been swallowed up by the giant **Crown Street Mall**, which includes Myer and David Jones department stores and a multitude of other shops. **Wollongong City Gallery** on Kembla St, near the mall (Tues–Fri 10am–5pm, Sat & Sun noon–4pm; free; T02 4228 7500, Wwww.wollongongcitygallery.com), shows changing exhibitions and has a permanent collection with an emphasis on contemporary Aboriginal and colonial Illawarra artists. If you continue east down Crown Street and cross Marine Drive, you'll hit **Wollongong City Beach**, a surf beach that stretches over 2km. Most locals choose the more salubrious **North Wollongong Beach**, where you can notch up some surf training with Taupu Surf School (from A\$59; T02 4268 0088). Between the two beaches, sheltering beside Flagstaff Point, is the city's highlight, **Wollongong Harbour**, with its fishing fleet in Belmore Basin, a fish market, a few seafood restaurants, and a picturesque nineteenth-century lighthouse on the breakwater; there's also gentle swimming from its beach.

At the end of October, the **Viva la Gong festival** spices up the city with a sculpture exhibition along the seafront and events every night including circus, dance, and music.

Away from the centre, science and religion provide the most interest. To the north, near the University of Wollongong at the southern end of **Fairy Meadow Beach** and next to Brandon Park, is the A\$6 million **Science Centre** on Squires Way (daily 10am–4pm; A\$10, child A\$7, or A\$13/A\$10 including the planetarium; T02 4286 5000, Wsciencecentre.uow.edu.au; train to Fairy Meadow station, then a 10–15min walk); attractions include over a hundred themed kid-friendly hands-on exhibits, while the **planetarium** is the state's best (daily shows noon & 3pm; 30min; laser concert Sat, Sun & school holidays 1pm).

Around 8km south of the centre, the vast **Nan Tien Temple** (Tues–Sun 9am–5pm; T02 4272 0600, Wwww.nantien.org.au), the largest Buddhist temple in Australia, is on Berkeley Road, Berkeley, reached via the Southern Freeway or by South Coast line train to Unanderra, from where it's twenty minutes on foot or ten minutes by bus (Route 34). Raised on a hill and surrounded by extensive, peaceful gardens, it's every bit as serene a spot as you'd expect, with sumptuously ornate Chinese-style shrines, a pagoda and a conference centre and museum (A\$1.10). The Fo Guang Shan Buddhists welcome visitors to the temple, where you can take part in chanting, origami, calligraphy or tai chi sessions for a small charge, join a guided tour (Sat & Sun 1–2.30pm; A\$4), have a vegetarian lunch in the dining room (Tues–Fri 11.30am–2pm, Sat & Sun 11.30am–2.30pm; A\$9), or traditional tea in the tea room (Tues–Sun 9am–5pm). There's also a surprisingly upmarket **guesthouse**, *Pilgrim Lodge*, which is open to all and is the base for weekend meditation and Buddhist activity retreats (T02 4272 0500; ➍).

Accommodation

Wollongong is more geared up for business travellers than tourists, but its **Visitor Information Centre** (see p.199) can advise on **accommodation** options. There's nowhere central to **camp**, but the city council runs three tourist parks on out-of-town beaches, with reasonably priced cabins and space for tents and vans – for details, see Ⓦtouristparks.wollongong.nsw.gov.au.

Boat Harbour Motel Wilson St ☏02 4228 9166, Ⓦwww.boatharbourmotel.com.au. Though somewhat dated in look and feel, this place has a good central location near the harbour, with comfortable and spacious rooms with balconies, some with sea views. ❹

Keiraview (Wollongong YHA) 75–79 Keira St ☏02 4229 1132, Ⓦwww.yha.com.au. Modern hostel with a central alfresco courtyard; the twin rooms have the luxury of en-suite facilities and shared balconies. Bunk in four-share A$26–29, private twin ❷

Medina Executive 19 Market St ☏02 4250 5000, Ⓦwww.medina.com.au. Shiny new top-end option bang in the centre, between the mall and the beach, with modern, executive-friendly studios, apartments with smart little kitchens, plus a swimming pool, sauna and gym. ❺–❼

Pleasant Heights 77 New Mount Pleasant Rd (6km from central Wollongong) ☏02 4283 3355, Ⓦwww.pleasantheights.com.au. Classy and exotic B&B on the northwest edge of town, with three themed luxury suites: Japanese, with oriental furnishings, a black marble bath and a private Zen garden; jaunty Mexican; and warm-white Italian. ❻

Eating and drinking

The Gong isn't renowned for its **restaurants**, which can be a bit hit or miss: the best of the bunch are on Keira Street. There are plenty of places for a quick coffee in and around Crown Street Mall.

Caveau 112 Keira St ☏02 4226 4855. Dazzles with complex, French-influenced dishes (two-course lunch A$45, two-course dinner A$57, three A$70) and, as the name suggests, superb wine. Lunch Thurs & Fri, dinner Tues–Sat 6pm–late.

Diggies 1 Cliff Rd, North Beach ☏02 4226 2688. Trendy modern beach café serving everything from big breakfasts for hungry surfers to super-cool tapas for the cocktail-sipping set. Daily 6.30am–5pm, plus dinner Fri & Sat in summer.

Five Islands Brewing Company Entertainment Centre, Crown St ☏02 4220 2854. Breezy modern bar with a large beachside terrace, an imaginative menu of plates to share, and a delicious and varied selection of additive-free ales, made on the premises.

Lorenzo's Diner 119 Keira St ☏02 4229 5633. Well-regarded eatery that serves top-notch contemporary Italian food in hearty portions (main courses A$29–34). Lunch Thurs & Fri, dinner Tues–Sat.

Monsoon 193 Keira St ☏02 4229 4588. Hip Vietnamese restaurant with an Australian slant. Lunch & dinner Tues–Sat.

North of Wollongong

The scenic route along the coast between Wollongong and Royal National Park is arguably the very best section of the **Grand Pacific Drive** (see box, p.197), treating you to panoramic views of bush-topped cliffs, beaches and rolling waves. The following account traces the northbound route along Tourist Drive 10 (Lawrence Hargrave Drive) from Wollongong; if you're starting your journey from Sydney's southern suburbs and travelling south, the most attractive approach is via the northern section of Route 68, which winds through Royal National Park (see p.204) and emerges above the cliffs at Otford.

The ruggedly primeval-looking cliffs of the **Illawarra Escarpment** dominate the coast all the way from Wollongong to the northern edge of Royal National Park. Between Bulli and Thirroul, just beyond the Wollongong's limits, a detour off the coast road climbs uphill via Bulli Pass to the **Bulli Lookout** and **Sublime Point Lookout**, each with fantastic views, a picnic area and access to walking tracks. Nearby is the site for an ambitious new regional visitor centre and museum of indigenous culture, the Southern Gateway Centre, which was still in the planning stages at the time of writing.

Back at sea level, there's impressive cliff scenery as you pass through **THIRROUL**, the spot where the English novelist D.H. Lawrence wrote *Kangaroo* during his short Australian interlude. The town and surrounding area are the backdrop to a substantial part of the novel, though he renamed the then-sleepy village Mullumbimby. Thirroul's other artistic connection is more sinister: it was here that avant-garde artist Brett Whiteley (see p.259) died of a drugs overdose in 1992. The town is now gradually being swallowed up in the suburban sprawl of Wollongong and is busy, with plenty of shops and cafés, including the excellent and appropriately literary *Oskar's Wild Bookstore & Coffee Bar* at 289 Lawrence Hargrave Drive. At the southern end of the beach, **Sandford Point**, as it's known (it's actually Bulli Point on maps) is a famous surf break. *Ryan's Hotel*, 138 Philip St (℡02 4267 1086, ⓦwww.ryanshotel .com.au; ❸), a modern bistro-pub with three dining rooms serving Australian, Italian and Thai food, has simple en-suite **rooms**, while *The Beaches Hotel*, 272 Lawrence Hargrave Drive (℡02 4267 2288, ⓦwww.beacheshotel.com.au; ❸), has budget rooms with shared bathrooms and a popular beer garden where you can barbecue your own steaks. Thirroul also has a good modern Italian restaurant, *Frati*, at 245 Lawrence Hargrave Drive (Tues–Sat lunch & dinner, Sun lunch; ℡02 4268 3404).

At **AUSTINMER**, you're at a break in the stunning cliffs and into some heavy surf territory. The down-to-earth town has a popular, very clean, patrolled beach that gets packed out on summer weekends. North of here, there's more impressive, craggy scenery to admire from clifftop pubs as you pass through **Wombarra**, **Scarborough** and **Clifton**. The historic *Scarborough Hotel* on the clifftop at Scarborough is well worth a stop for a drink; it also has a restaurant serving standard pub fare (breakfast & lunch daily, dinner Wed–Sat; ℡02 4267 5444).

Under the Illawarra Escarpment between Clifton and Coalcliff is the Grand Pacific Drive's engineering tour de force: the **Sea Cliff Bridge**, opened in late 2005 to replace a tricky stretch of road prone to landslides. The bridge solves this problem by lifting the road up and away from the cliffs, while following the curves of the coastline. You can park at either end to walk along the 1.2-kilometre bridge on foot, inhaling lungfuls of ocean air as you go.

North of Coalcliff is the village of **Stanwell Park**; from here the road climbs steeply up to the impressive Bald Hill clifftop lookout, with breathtaking views south towards the Sea Cliff Bridge. Bald Hill is a favourite launch point for **hang-gliders**: the Sydney Hang Gliding Centre (℡0400 258 258, ⓦwww .hanggliding.com.au) offers tandem flights with an instructor (A\$195 during the week, A\$220 weekends) and runs courses (A\$275 per day). Near here, a junction gives you the choice of heading inland to the Princes Highway for the fastest route to Sydney, or continuing along the cliffs to the **Otford** lookout and then into Royal National Park.

Royal National Park

Royal National Park is a huge nature reserve right on Sydney's doorstep, only 36km south of the city. Established in 1879, it was the second national park in the world (after Yellowstone in the USA), and offers a glimpse of what Gondwanaland's great forests might have been like. The railway between Wollongong and Sydney marks its western border, and from the **train** the

▲ Royal National Park

scenery is fantastic – streams, waterfalls, rock formations and rainforest flora fly past the window. If you want to explore more closely, get off at one of the stations along the way – Otford, Waterfall, Heathcote, Engadine or Loftus – all starting points for walking trails into the park.

You can also cross the park **by car** (A$11 per car per day; gates open 7am–8.30pm). Approaching via the Grand Pacific Highway from the south, you can enter via Wakehurst Drive (Route 68) from Otford; alternatively, if you're travelling up the Princes Highway or Southern Freeway from Wollongong, you can take McKell Avenue from Waterfall. From the north, Farnell Drive, the first left turn off the Princes Highway south of Loftus, takes you to the **NPWS Visitor Centre** at Audley Heights, 2km from Loftus railway station (daily 9am–4.30pm; ℡02 9542 0648, Ⓦ www.nationalparks.nsw.gov.au); the staff have a range of local information and can issue camping permits, which are also bookable over the phone (℡02 9542 0683). The easy one-kilometre **track** from here to the Bungoona Lookout boasts panoramic views and is wheelchair-accessible. A couple of kilometres south at **Audley**, a picturesque picnic ground on the Hacking River, there's a kiosk and a boatshed (℡02 9545 4967) where you can rent mountain bikes or canoes.

On the far side of the park, the terrain falls away abruptly to the ocean, creating a spectacular coastline of steep cliffs broken here and there by creeks cascading into the sea and little coves with fine sandy beaches; the remains of **Aboriginal rock carvings** are the only traces of the original Dharawal people. The beaches at **Wattamolla** and **Garie**, accessible by road and connected by a walking track, have kiosks and good waves for surfing.

It's possible to **stay in the park** overnight, if you're happy to rough it a bit. There's a small, basic, eco-friendly **hostel** with cold-water showers, *Garie Beach YHA*, in a secluded spot inside the park, 1km from Garie Beach (advance booking and key collection from Sydney or Cronulla required; ℡02 9261 1111, Ⓦ www.yha.com.au; bunk A$14). An alternative is the NPWS-run *Weemalah Cottage* on the Hacking River east of Audley (℡02 9542 0632; Ⓢ), which sleeps up to eight. Hikers can stay at the park's two bushcamps (A$5 per person per night, child A$3): North Era on the Coastal Track from Otford to Garie, and Uloola Falls on the Uloola Track inland between Waterfall and Audley. There's also a vehicle-accessible NPWS **campsite** at Bonnie Vale (A$14, child A$7) on the shore of Port Hacking in the north of the park. All NPWS-run camps are often fully booked, so it's best to apply in advance (see p.205).

Heathcote National Park

Heathcote National Park, across the Princes Highway from Royal National Park, is much smaller and quieter. This is a serious bushwalkers' park with no roads and a ban on trail bikes. You can access the park from Waterfall or Heathcote, which are both on the South Coast train line and are connected by a twelve-kilometre trail through the park. On the way, you pass through quite a variety of vegetation and alongside several swimmable pools, the carved sandstone of the **Kingfisher Pool** making it the most picturesque. Near here there's a small, basic bushcamp (no drinking water), and another at Mirang Pool. **Camping** permits (A$5 per person per night, child A$3) and maps are available from the Royal National Park NPWS Visitor Centre (see p.205).

Woronora Dam Road, which leads off the Princes Highway 4km south of Waterfall to run along the western border of the park, takes you to **Woronora Dam**, where there's a picnic area overlooking the reservoir.

Travel details

Trains

Berry to: Sydney (18 daily; 2hr 45min); Wollongong (18 daily; 1hr 5min).
Canberra to: Sydney (twice daily; 4hr 20min).
Kiama to: Sydney (18 daily; 2hr 25min); Wollongong (18 daily; 45min).
Nowra to: Sydney (18 daily; 2hr 55min); Wollongong (18 daily; 1hr 15min).
Wollongong to: Sydney (18 daily; 1hr 40min).

Buses

Batemans Bay to: Bairnsdale (twice daily; 7hr 20min); Sydney (twice daily; 5hr 50min).
Berry to: Sydney (twice daily; 3hr).
Canberra to: Batemans Bay (2–3 daily; 2hr 25min); Melbourne (3 daily; 8hr 30min); Sydney (16 daily; 3hr 30min).
Eden to: Bairnsdale (twice daily; 4hr 15min); Sydney (2 daily; 10hr).

Kiama to: Sydney (twice daily; 3hr 25min).
Merimbula to: Bairnsdale (twice daily; 4hr 45min); Sydney (2 daily; 9hr 35min).
Narooma to: Bairnsdale (twice daily; 6hr 20min); Sydney (2 daily; 7hr 25min).
Nowra to: Sydney (twice daily; 4hr 30min).
Wollongong to: Sydney (twice daily; 1hr 55min).

Flights

Canberra to: Brisbane (many daily; 1hr 55min); Melbourne (many daily; 1hr); Newcastle (many daily; 45min); Sydney (many daily; 35min).
Merimbula to: Melbourne (daily; 1hr 30min); Sydney (5 daily; 50min).
Moruya to: Melbourne (twice daily; 1hr 30min); Sydney (5 daily; 50min).
Wollongong to: Melbourne (1–2 daily; 1hr 50min).

Sydney

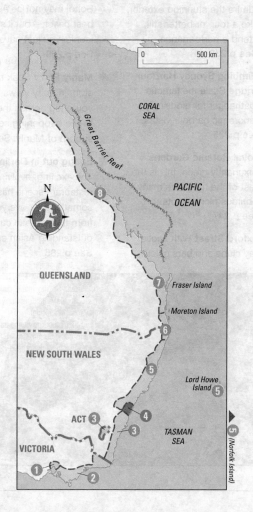

CHAPTER 4

Highlights

✳ Mardi Gras The biggest celebration of gay and lesbian culture in the world.
See p.212

✳ Sydney Opera House Admire the stunning exterior, take a tour, or better still, attend a performance.
See p.233

✳ Climbing Sydney Harbour Bridge Scale the famous coathanger for giddyingly panoramic harbour vistas.
See p.235

✳ Royal Botanic Gardens Luxuriantly green, this is the best of the harbour's many fabulous picnic spots.
See p.247

✳ Oxford Street With hectic gay clubs and bars galore, this is nightlife central; while on Saturdays, Paddington market is a must.
See p.257

✳ Bondi Beach Bold, brash Bondi may not be Australia's best beach – but it's so iconic, you just have to go.
See p.269

✳ Manly Ferry Soak up stunning city views as as you chug across the harbour to the happening seaside suburb of Manly. See p.275

✳ Eating out in Darlinghurst The exciting, evolving restaurant scene has something for everyone, from funky urban cafés to outstanding Asian eateries.
See p.285

▲ Sydney Harbour Bridge

Sydney

Flying into **SYDNEY** provides the first snapshot of Australia for most overseas visitors: toy-sized images of the Harbour Bridge and the Opera House, tilting in a glittering expanse of blue water. The Aussie city par excellence, Sydney stands head and shoulders above any other in Australia. Taken together with its surrounds, it's in many ways a microcosm of Australia as a whole – if only in its ability to defy your expectations and prejudices as often as it confirms them. A thrusting, high-rise business centre, a high-profile gay community and inner-city deprivation of unexpected harshness are as much part of the scene as the beaches, the bodies and the sparkling harbour. Its sophistication, cosmopolitan population and exuberant nightlife are a long way from the Outback, and yet Sydney has the highest Aboriginal population of any Australian city.

It's also as beautiful a city as any in the world, with a **setting** that perhaps only Rio de Janeiro can rival: the water is what makes it so special. No introduction to Sydney would be complete without paying tribute to one of the world's great **harbours**: Port Jackson is a sunken valley that twists inland to meet the fresh water of the Parramatta River; in the process it washes into a hundred coves and bays, winds around rocky points, flows past the small harbour islands, slips under bridges and laps at the foot of the Opera House. Sydney is seen at its gleaming best from the deck of a harbour ferry, especially at weekends when the harbour's jagged jaws fill with a flotilla of small vessels, racing yachts and cabin cruisers.

Getting away from the city centre and exploring is an essential part of Sydney's pleasures. Twenty minutes from the heart of the business district by bus, the high-rise office buildings and skyscrapers give way to colourful inner-city suburbs where you can get an eyeful of sky and watch the lemons ripening above the sidewalk. In the summer, people abandon their hot city offices for the remarkably unspoilt **beaches** strung along the Pacific coast to the north and south of town, or the largely intact corridors of bushland further inland, where many have built their dream homes. During every heat wave, however, bushfires threaten the city, bringing sophisticated Sydney abruptly down to earth.

It might seem surprising that Sydney is not Australia's capital. The creation of Canberra in 1927 – intended to stem the intense rivalry between Sydney and Melbourne – has not affected the view of many Sydneysiders that their city remains the true capital of Australia, and certainly in many ways it feels like it. This is partly down to a tangible sense of history: the old stone walls and well-worn steps in the backstreets around The Rocks serve as a reminder that it's well over two centuries since Europeans first settled here, while the area's Aboriginal heritage dates back over forty thousand years.

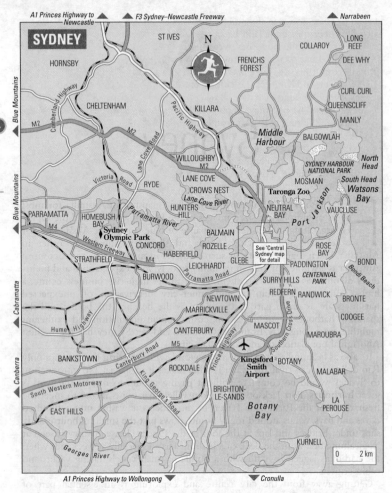

Some history

The early history of the city is very much the history of white Australia, right from its founding as a penal colony, amid brutality, deprivation and despair. In January 1788, the **First Fleet**, carrying over a thousand people, 736 of them convicts, arrived at **Botany Bay** expecting the "fine meadows" that Captain James Cook had described eight years earlier. In fact, what greeted them was mostly swamp, scrub and sand dunes: a desolate sight even for sea-weary eyes. An unsuccessful scouting expedition prompted Commander Arthurs Phillip to move the fleet a few kilometres north, to the well-wooded Port Jackson, where a stream of fresh water was found. Based around the less than satisfactory Tank Stream, the settlement was named **Sydney Cove** after Viscount Sydney, then Secretary of State in Great Britain. In the first three years of settlement, the new colony nearly starved to death several times; the land around Sydney Cove proved to be barren. When supply ships did arrive, they inevitably came with hundreds more convicts to further burden the colony. It was not until 1790, when land was successfully farmed further west at **Parramatta**, that the hunger began to abate. Measure this suffering with that of the original occupants, the **Eora Aborigines**: their land had been invaded, their people virtually wiped out by smallpox, and now they were stricken by hunger as the settlers shot at their game – and even, as they moved further inland, at the Eora themselves.

By the early 1800s, Sydney had become a stable colony and busy trading post. Army officers in charge of the colony, exploiting their access to free land and cheap labour, became rich farm-owners and virtually established a currency based on rum. The **military**, known as the New South Wales Corps (or more familiarly as "the rum corps"), became the supreme political force in the colony in 1809, even overthrowing the governor (mutiny-plagued Captain Bligh himself). This was the last straw for the government back home, and the rebellious officers were finally brought to heel when the reformist Governor **Lachlan Macquarie** arrived from England with forces of his own. He liberalized conditions, supported the prisoners' right to become citizens after they had served their time, and appointed several to public offices.

By the 1840s, the transportation of convicts to New South Wales had ended, the explorers Lawson and Blaxland had found a way through the Blue Mountains to the Western Plains, and **gold** had been struck in Bathurst. The population soared as free settlers arrived in ever-increasing numbers. In the Victorian era, Sydney's population became even more starkly divided into the **haves** and the **have-nots**: while the poor lived in slums where disease, crime, prostitution and alcoholism were rife, the genteel classes – self-consciously replicating life in the mother country – took tea on their verandas and erected grandiloquent monuments such as the Town Hall, the Strand Arcade and the Queen Victoria Building in homage to English architecture of the time. An outbreak of the plague in The Rocks at the beginning of the twentieth century made wholesale slum clearances inevitable, and with the demolitions came a change in attitudes. Strict new vice laws meant the end of the bad old days of backstreet knifings, drunk-filled taverns and makeshift brothels.

Over the next few decades, Sydney settled into comfortable **suburban living**. The metropolis sprawled westwards, creating a flat, unremarkable city with no real centre, an appropriate symbol for the era of shorts and knee socks and the stereotypical, barbecue-loving Bruce and Sheila – an international image that still plagues Australians. Sydney has come a long way since the parochialism of the 1950s, however: over the following decades, skyscrapers at the city's centre rocketed heavenward and constructions such as the **Opera House** began to reflect the city's dynamism. The clichés of cold tinnies of beer and meat pies with sauce were tossed out, giving way to a city confident in itself and its culinary attractions, too.

The **2000 Olympics** were a coming-of-age ceremony for Sydney. The impact on the city was all-embracing, with fifty years' worth of development compressed into four years under the pressure of intense international scrutiny. Transport infrastructure was greatly improved and a rash of luxury hotels and waterside apartments added to the skyline. The City of Sydney Council spent A\$200 million on enhancing and beautifying the city streets, public squares and parks; and licensing laws changed, too, creating a European-style bar culture. Sydney now has all the vigour of a world-class city, with the reputation of its restaurants in particular turning any lingering "cultural cringe" – that distinctively Aussie brand of self-deprecation – to confidence bordering on smugness. Today, Sydney's citizens don't look inwards – and they certainly don't look towards England. Thousands of immigrants from around the globe have given Sydney a truly cosmopolitan air and it's a city as thrilling and alive as any.

Sydney is famous for its kaleidoscopic programme of annual events – particularly packed during the summer months. For citywide websites that detail what's coming up, see the box on p.289.

January–April

Sydney Festival (Jan)

Lasting for most of the month, this exhaustive arts event ranges from concerts, plays and outdoor art installations to circus performances. Big international names take part and ticket prices can be high; about half the events are free, however. Venues include Circular Quay, The Domain, Darling Harbour, and Sydney Olympic Park. ☏02 8248 6500, ⊛www.sydneyfestival.org.au

Australia Day (26 Jan)

This is huge in Sydney – it starts with a dawn celebration of the region's Aboriginal heritage, then concentrates on waterborne racing: yachts speed to Botany Bay, ferries battle it out across the harbour, and tall ships parade up to the Harbour Bridge, with formation flying from the RAAF Roulettes overhead. Spectators decked out in patriotic kit gather anywhere with good harbour views, particularly the Royal Botanic Gardens, Opera House, Milson's Point and Cremorne Point. Other free events include Gabun in Victoria Park (an alcohol-free gig featuring Aboriginal and Torres Strait bands; ☏02 9564 5090, ⊛www.gadigal.org.au), museum open days, outdoor rock concerts, and fireworks over Darling Harbour. On or around the same date is **The Big Day Out** (see p.61) at the Sydney Showground (Sydney Olympic Park), featuring a storming line-up of bands and DJs. ⊛www.australiaday.com.au

Chinese New Year (late Jan to Feb)

Sydney's celebration of the Lunar New Year is the biggest outside China, with more than three weeks of events including dragon-boat races, and an exuberant parade of floats, dancers, lions and dragons along George Street and through Chinatown. ☏02 9265 9333

Mardi Gras (Feb–March)

This massive gay and lesbian festival engulfs the city – events include Fair Day, an afternoon picnic in Victoria Park (Camperdown); Sol y Luna, a ticket-only harbourside dance party at Mrs Macquarie's Point; and the glamorous after-dark Parade along Oxford Street from Hyde Park to Moore Park, followed by revelry and mayhem. See box, p.296. ☏02 9568 8600, ⊛www.mardigras.org.au

Sydney Royal Easter Show (late March/early April)

The country comes to the city for this two-week agricultural and garden show at the Sydney Showground, with a frantic array of amusement-park rides, fireworks, parades of prize animals, a rodeo, and wood-chopping displays. A$32, child A$21.50. ☏02 9704 1111, ⊛www.eastershow.com.au

Arrival

The dream way to **arrive** in Sydney is, of course, by ship – a privilege enjoyed by over 100,000 ocean-going travellers a year, their gleaming vessels cruising into the Overseas Passenger Terminal next to Circular Quay, or under the great coathanger of the Harbour Bridge to Darling Harbour. Flying in can be romantic, too, with great views on the approach, and there's a definite grandeur to Central Station, the main railway terminus in the heart of the city. Arriving by bus, you'll find the coach terminal functional and convenient, but if you're driving, you'll need to prepare yourself for poor signage and a motorway, bridge and tunnel toll system that seems deliberately designed to alienate outsiders.

May–September

Sydney Writers Festival (May)
A week-long series of free and ticketed events, including readings, walking tours, workshops and debates. ☎02 9252 7729, ⒲www.swf.org.au

Sydney Film Festival (June)
Three weeks of world cinema and documentary screenings (see box, p.301).

Biennale of Sydney (June–Sept in even-numbered years)
Contemporary art showcase, with provocative exhibitions at the Art Gallery of New South Wales, the Museum of Contemporary Art and various public spaces around town. ☎02 9368 1411, ⒲www.biennaleofsydney.com.au

City to Surf (Aug)
A fourteen-kilometre fun run from Park Street to Bondi.

October–December

Good Food Month (Oct)
A feast of gourmet happenings, including culinary workshops, a fundraising wine and food fair in Hyde Park, and special offers at some of the city's alluring eateries. ⒲www.gfm.smh.com.au

Manly International Jazz Festival (Oct)
Beachfront jazz over the New South Wales Labour Day weekend, with several free events in the spring sunshine, and a few ticket-only indoor concerts. ⒲www.manly .nsw.gov.au/manlyjazz

Surf carnivals (Oct–April)
Sydney's various Surf Lifesavers test their mettle at a summer-long programme of competitive events held by the Lifesaving Clubs up and down the coast. ☎02 9984 7188, ⒲www.surflifesaving.com.au

Sculpture By The Sea (Nov)
For two weeks, the two-kilometre coastal walk between Bondi and Tamarama is transformed by this magical exhibition. ☎02 8399 0233, ⒲www.sculptureby thesea.com

Sydney to Hobart Yacht Race (26 Dec)
Half of the city turns up at the harbour, on foot or by boat, to watch the colourful spectacle of two hundred or so yachts setting sail for a 630-nautical-mile slog. ⒲www.rolexsydneyhobart.com

New Year's Eve (31 Dec)
The old year gives way to the new with a spectacular, multi-million-dollar fireworks display from the Harbour Bridge and Darling Harbour. From early morning, Sydney-siders start jostling for the best vantage points in the harbour or on the shore: for suggestions, see ⒲www.cityofsydney.nsw.gov.au/nye.

By air

Sydney's **Kingsford Smith Airport (SYD)**, referred to as "Mascot" after the suburb where it's located, is 8km south of the city, near Botany Bay (international flight times ☎13 12 23, ⒲www.sydneyairport.com.au). Aeropelican, Jetstar, Norfolkair, Qantas, Regional Express and Virgin Blue (see p.35) run direct flights from most Australian cities; it's also a hub for international arrivals. Domestic and international terminals are linked by a free shuttle bus if you're travelling with Qantas (every 30min), or you can take the **T-Bus** (A$5). The fast **Airport Link** underground railway, though very pricey for inter-terminal transfers (A$13.40), is useful for getting you to Central and the other City

Airport buses

Sydney Buses

There are no regular public buses between the airport and the city centre, but routes 400 and 410, which run east–west between Bondi Junction and Burwood, stop at the international and domestic terminals (A$4).

Shuttle services

Shared shuttle buses are almost as convenient as taxis – they're slower, but much cheaper. Although it's best to book a place a day in advance, if you fly into Mascot without a booking and head for the bus park outside the Arrivals Hall there's a fair chance that you'll find a driver with a spare seat.

KST Sydney Transporter ⓣ02 9666 9988, ⓦwww.kst.com.au. Drops off at hotels or hostels in the area bounded by Kings Cross and Darling Harbour (every 30 min; 5am–7pm; A$12 one way, A$20 return). Book your return pick-up at least three hours in advance.

Sydney Super Shuttles ⓣ02 9311 3789 or 1300 765 635, ⓦwww.supershuttle .com.au. Quick call-out minibus service to and from the city and eastern beaches – Bondi, Coogee, Randwick, Clovelly and Bronte – and dropping off at all hostels, motels and hotels (A$15 one way). Book your return pick-up at least an hour in advance.

Airport Shuttle North ⓣ02 9997 7767 or 1300 505 100, ⓦwww.airportshuttlenorth .com. Covers the North Shore, including Manly and Collaroy (from A$33–38). Book at least a day in advance.

Circle stations – Town Hall, Wynyard, Circular Quay, St James and Museum – in ten to twenty minutes (daily every 10–15min; one way A$13.80, return A$20.80; ⓦwww.airportlink.com.au). One return Airport Link transfer is included in the excellent-value SydneyPass tourist pass (see box, p.218); with other transport passes, you can use the Airport Link service at a reduced rate – ask for a Gate Pass (one way A$10.80, return A$14.80). Tourist passes and a car-rental and accommodation booking service are available from the **Sydney Visitor Centre** (daily 5am until last arrival; ⓣ02 9667 6050), on the ground floor (Arrivals) of the international terminal. The cheapest way into the city centre is by shuttle bus (see box above), while a **taxi** costs A$32–36.

Bureau de change offices at both terminals are open daily from 5am until last arrival with rates comparable to major banks. There's an **accommodation freephone** line near the visitor centre; some places will pick you up for free or refund your bus fare.

By train and bus

All local and interstate **trains** arrive at **Central Station** on Eddy Avenue, just south of the city centre. There are no lockers at the station, but you can store your luggage at Wanderers' Travel, 810 George St, a three-minute walk around the block (daily 7am–8pm; A$4 per day). From outside Central Station, and neighbouring **Railway Square**, you can hop onto nearly every major bus route, and from within Central Station you can take a CityRail train to any city or suburban station (see p.216).

All **buses** to Sydney arrive and depart from Eddy Avenue and Pitt Street, bordering Central Station. The area is well set up, with decent cafés, a 24-hour police station and a huge YHA hostel as well as the **Sydney Coach Terminal** (Mon–Fri 6am–7.30pm, Sat & Sun 9am–6pm; ⓣ02 9281 9366), which has a luggage-storage room (A$5–15 per 24hr, depending on size) and can **book accommodation**, tours and all coach tickets and passes. Greyhound Australia has separate ticket offices/departure lounges also on Eddy Avenue.

By car

Driving into Sydney is a very different experience to driving into the smaller coastal cities – traffic jams can be vexing, poor signage can thwart your best attempts at navigation and a confusing array of different **toll systems** are in force on the Harbour Bridge (southbound), Sydney Harbour Tunnel (southbound), the Cross City Tunnel and the motorways. You can pay the Harbour Bridge toll in cash, but both tunnels and some stretches of motorway are cashless and require you to have a tag or pass whereby tolls are automatically charged to your credit card. If you drive through a cashless toll zone without a tag or pass, you have 48 hours to register and pay. Several operators issue **tags** to attach to your windscreen (for drivers) or armband (for motorcyclists); these work on all motorways. Best value are New South Wales Roads and Traffic Authority e-toll tags, which require a deposit and opening balance totalling at least A$80. You can order one online at ⓦ www.rta.nsw.gov.au, but it will take ten days to arrive in the post; the alternative is to pick one up in person from an RTA e-toll registry (listed online). If you don't want to open an e-toll tag account you can buy e-toll **passes**, which are virtual and temporary, and are issued immediately by paying a small registration fee over the phone or, for a discount, online. You'll also be charged an administration fee on top of each toll. Infuriatingly, the motorways are managed by several different companies, each requiring you to buy a separate pass: for details, see ⓦ www.sydneymotorways.com.

Information

There are three **Sydney Visitor Centres** offering comprehensive information, free accommodation-and tour-booking facilities, and selling sightseeing passes. One is at the international airport terminal (see p.214); the others are centrally located at The Rocks, on the corner of Argyle and Playfair streets, and at Darling Harbour, near the IMAX Theatre (both daily 9.30am–5.30pm; ⓣ 02 9240 8788 or 1800 067 676, ⓦ www.sydneyvisitorcentre.com). Free **maps** and brochures can be picked up at all three, including the very useful *Sydney: The Official Guide*. There are also **information kiosks** (daily 9am–5pm) at Circular Quay (on the corner of Pitt and Alfred streets), Martin Place (corner of Elizabeth Street) and George Street (near the Town Hall). Tourism New South Wales publishes detailed **online information** on Sydney, as well as the rest of the state (ⓦ www.visitnsw.com).

City transport

Sydney's **public transport network** is extremely good, though the system relies heavily on buses, and traffic jams can be a problem. The city's buses, ferries, railways, light rail and monorail are all run by separate companies, but the systems mesh well, and one fare, route and timetable information service, the Greater Sydney Transport Infoline, covers all (daily 6am–10pm; ⓣ 13 15 00, ⓦ www.131500.info). For details of daily DayTripper tickets, weekly TravelPasses and the great-value SydneyPass, which enables travel on all buses, ferries and trains, see p.218. Trains stop around midnight, as do most regular buses, though several services towards the eastern and northern beaches, such as the 380 to Bondi Beach, the 372 and 373 to Coogee and the 151 to Manly, run through the night. Otherwise, a pretty good network of **Nightride buses** shadows the train routes to the suburbs, departing from Town Hall station (outside the Energy Australia Building on George Street) and stopping at train stations – where licensed taxis wait at designated ranks.

Buses

Within the central area, **Sydney Buses** – blue and white, hailed from yellow-signed bus stops – are the most convenient, widespread mode of transport, and cover more of the city than the trains. With few exceptions buses radiate from the centre, with major interchanges at Railway Square near Central Station (especially southwest routes), at Circular Quay (range of routes), from York and Carrington streets outside Wynyard station (North Shore), and Bondi Junction station (eastern suburbs and beaches). Single-ride **tickets** can be bought on board from the driver and cost from A$1.80 for up to two distance-measured sections, with a maximum fare of A$5.80; A$3.00 (up to 5 sections) is the most typical fare. Certain routes are "prepay only" and only accept passes (see box, p.218 for options). Bus **information**, including route maps, timetables and passes, is available from handy booths at Carrington Street, Wynyard; at Circular Quay on the corner of Loftus and Alfred streets; and at the Queen Victoria Building on York Street; there's also detailed information online at ⓦ www.sydneybuses.info.

Trains

Trains, operated by **CityRail** see Sydney Rail map, will get you where you're going faster than buses, especially at rush hour and when heading out to the suburbs, but you need to transfer to a bus or ferry to get to most harbourside or beach destinations. There are seven train lines, mostly overground, each of which stops at Central and Town Hall stations. Trains run from around 5am to midnight, with **tickets** starting at A$2.60 for a single on the City Circle and for short hops; buying off-peak returns (after 9am and all weekend) means you can save up to thirty percent.

Automatic ticket-vending machines (which give change) and barriers (insert magnetic tickets; otherwise show ticket at the gate) have been introduced just about everywhere. On-the-spot fines for fare evasion start from A$200, and transit officers patrol frequently. All platforms are painted with designated "nightsafe" waiting areas and all but two or three train carriages are closed after

---

Smartvisit Card

All three Sydney Visitor Centres sell the **See Sydney & Beyond Smartvisit Card** (☎ 1300 661 711, ⓦ www.seesydneycard.com), which comes in two-, three- and seven-day versions (to be used over consecutive days) with or without a transport option (two-day A$129/$169, three-day A$159/$215, seven-day A$219/$285; cheaper children's passes are available) and includes admission to forty well-known attractions in Sydney and the Blue Mountains, as well as a range of discounts. If an action-packed, fast-paced itinerary is your thing, the card can be good value and it's certainly a convenient way to bypass the queues.

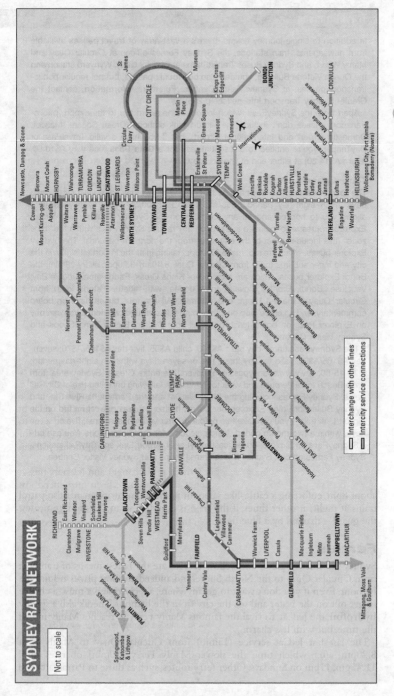

SYDNEY RAIL NETWORK

Not to scale

CITY CIRCLE

St James
Museum
Kings Cross
Edgecliff
BONDI JUNCTION
Martin Place
Green Square
Mascot
Domestic ✈
International ✈
Circular Quay

Newcastle, Dungog & Scone →

Cowan
Berowra
Mount Kuring-gai
Asquith
HORNSBY
Mount Colah
Waitara
Wahroonga
Warrawee
TURRAMURRA
Pymble
GORDON
Killara
LINDFIELD
Roseville
CHATSWOOD
Artarmon
ST LEONARDS
Wollstonecraft
Waverton
NORTH SYDNEY
Milsons Point

WYNYARD
TOWN HALL
CENTRAL
REDFERN

Normanhurst
Thornleigh
Pennant Hills
Beecroft
Cheltenham
EPPING
Eastwood
Denistone
West Ryde
Meadowbank
Rhodes
Concord West
North Strathfield

Proposed line

Erskineville
St Peters
SYDENHAM
TEMPE
Wolli Creek

Arncliffe
Banksia
Rockdale
Kogarah
Carlton
Allawah
HURSTVILLE
Penshurst
Mortdale
Oatley
Como
Jannali
SUTHERLAND

Gymea
Miranda
Caringbah
Woolooware
CRONULLA
Kirrawee

Loftus
Engadine
Heathcote
Waterfall
HELENSBURGH

Wollongong City, Port Kembla
Bomaderry (Nowra) →

Macdonaldtown
Newtown
Stanmore
Petersham
Lewisham
Summer Hill
Ashfield
Croydon
Burwood
STRATHFIELD
Homebush
Flemington

OLYMPIC PARK

Auburn
LIDCOMBE
Berala
Regents Park
BANKSTOWN

Turrella
Bardwell Park
Bexley North
Kingsgrove
Beverly Hills
Narwee
Riverwood
Padstow
Revesby
Panania
East Hills
Holsworthy

Dulwich Hill
Marrickville
Hurlstone Park
Canterbury
Campsie
Belmore
Lakemba
Wiley Park
Punchbowl

PARRAMATTA
BLACKTOWN
RICHMOND
East Richmond
Windsor
Mulgrave
Vineyard
Schofields
Quakers Hill
Marayong
Clarendon
RIVERSTONE

CARLINGFORD
Telopea
Dundas
Rydalmere
Camellia
Rosehill Racecourse
CLYDE

Toongabbie
Pendle Hill
Wentworthville
Westmead
Seven Hills
Harris Park

WESTMEAD

Clyde
GRANVILLE
Merrylands
Guildford
Yennora
Fairfield
Canley Vale

FAIRFIELD

Chester Hill
Sefton
Birrong
Yagoona

Leightonfield
Villawood
Carramar

Warwick Farm
LIVERPOOL
Casula

PENRITH
Emu Plains
Springwood,
Katoomba & Lithgow →

Mount Druitt
Doonside
Rooty Hill
St Marys
Kingswood
Werrington

Macquarie Fields
Ingleburn
Minto
Leumeah
CAMPBELLTOWN
GLENFIELD
MACARTHUR

Mittagong, Moss Vale
& Goulburn →

— Interchange with other lines
— Intercity service connections

SYDNEY

4

217

In addition to single-journey tickets, there's a vast array of **travel passes** available from newsagents, train stations, the Sydney Ferries offices at Circular Quay and Manly Wharf, and Sydney Buses TransitShops at Circular Quay, Wynyard station and the Queen Victoria Building; you can also buy tourist passes, but not regular public-transport passes, at Sydney Visitor Centres. For more **information**, contact the Greater Sydney Transport Infoline (see p.215).

Apart from the SydneyPass, which includes one return trip to the airport, public-transport passes don't include the Airport Link stations (Green Square, Mascot, Domestic Airport and International Airport), but if you have a valid TravelPass or DayTripper, you're entitled to a discount: ask for a **Gate Pass** (one way A$10.80, return A$14.80) at either end of your journey.

Tourist passes

The **Explorer Pass** (one-day pass A$39, child A$19; two-day pass, valid for any two days in an eight-day period A$68/A$34; ☎13 15 00, ⊛wwww.sydneypass.info) allows you to hop on and off any tour bus on the **Sydney Explorer** and **Bondi Explorer** routes; also included is travel on any regular Sydney Bus within the "blue zone" (this includes most of the city apart from the northern beaches). The Sydney Explorer buses, which are red, make 27 stops, taking in all the important sights in the city and inner suburbs (daily from Circular Quay 8.40am–5.20pm; every 20min); the Bondi Explorer buses, which are blue, cover Kings Cross, Paddington, Double Bay, Vaucluse, Bondi, Bronte, Clovelly and Coogee, with nineteen stops (daily from Circular Quay 8.45am–4.15pm; every 30min). All the tour buses have on-board commentary, and an entire loop on either route takes around two hours. You can buy an Explorer Pass on board (cash only), or from Sydney Buses TransitShops and Sydney Visitor Centres.

The **SydneyPass** (three-day pass A$110, child A$55; five-day A$145/A$70; seven-day A$165/A$80; valid for any three, five or seven days within an eight-day period; ☎13 15 00, ⊛wwww.sydneypass.info) covers the entire Greater Sydney area from Palm Beach to La Perouse and west to Parramatta, allowing unlimited use of CityRail trains, Sydney Ferries including the Manly JetCat and the Parramatta RiverCat, and Sydney Buses including Explorer tour buses. It also includes one return trip on the Airport Link train – you can take this before or after your chosen three, five or seven days, within a two-month period – and discounts for many attractions. You can buy a SydneyPass on Explorer buses (cash only) or at Airport Link and CityRail stations, Sydney Ferries offices, Sydney Buses TransitShops and Sydney Visitor Centres.

about 8pm, enforcing a cattle-like safety in numbers. Security guards also patrol trains at night; at other times, if the train is deserted, sit in the carriage nearest the guard – marked by a blue light.

Ferries

Sydney's distinctive green-and-yellow **ferries** are the fastest means of transport from Circular Quay to the North Shore, and, indeed, to most places around the harbour. Even if you don't want to go anywhere, a ferry ride is a must, a chance to get out on the water and see the city from the harbour. There's also a speedy **hydrofoil**, the JetCat, to rival the famous Manly Ferry; it reaches Manly in half the time, but with less charm.

The last fast JetCat service (15min) from Circular Quay to Manly is at 8.20pm, after which time the slower Manly Ferry (30min) operates until 11.45pm, 11pm on Sundays. Other ferry routes, such as those to Parramatta and

Combined bus, train and ferry passes

DayTripper tickets (valid for one day until 4am the next; A$16, child A$8) allow unlimited use of regular public buses, trains and ferries (not Explorer buses, the Manly JetCat, the Metro Monorail or the Metro Light Rail) within Greater Sydney.

TravelPasses are similar but with longer validity (a week, a quarter or a year, starting on any day) and different prices for different zones. The most useful options are the **Red TravelPass** (A$35/week), which covers the city, inner suburbs and harbour, and the **Green TravelPass** (A$43), which covers the same area plus the Manly Ferry and the RiverCat beyond Meadowbank. Passes covering a wider area cost A$50–57 a week.

Both Daytrippers and TravelPasses allow you to use the Airport Link at a discount (see p.218). Both can be bought from CityRail stations and Sydney Ferries offices (to start immediately), or from Sydney Buses TransitShops (to start on first use). DayTrippers can also be bought onboard buses (except prepay buses) and ferries.

If you don't intend to use the trains, you can opt for a pass that covers buses and ferries only. Options include the **Blue TravelPass** (same area as the Red; A$32 a week), the **Orange TravelPass** (same area as the Green; A$40) or the **Pittwater TravelPass** (unlimited travel on all buses and ferries; A$55).

Bus pass

A **TravelTen** ticket gives you ten single trips for the price of eight; the journeys can be taken at any time, and can be shared between two or more people. The tickets are colour-coded according to how many sections they cover: the Brown TravelTen (A$24), for example, is the choice for trips from Leichhardt to the city, while the Red TravelTen (A$32) is the one to buy if you're staying at Bondi.

Ferry pass

A **FerryTen** ticket is similar to a bus TravelTen, giving you ten single trips for the price of eight (Inner Harbour A$33.50, Manly Ferry A$48.10, JetCat A$67.80).

Train pass

Seven Day RailPass tickets allow unlimited travel between any two nominated stations and those in between, with savings of about twenty percent on the price of five return trips. For example, a pass between Bondi Junction and Town Hall would cost A$25.

Pyrmont Bay, operate only until early evening, while ferries to closer locations including Neutral Bay and Balmain continue to around 11.30pm. Except for the Manly Ferry, services on Sunday are greatly reduced and often finish earlier. Timetables for each route are available at Circular Quay and on the Sydney Ferries website ⓦwww.sydneyferries.info.

One-way **fares** are A$5.20 (A$6.40 for the Manly Ferry); return fares are doubled. The pricier JetCat to Manly and RiverCat to Parramatta are A$8.20 and A$7.70 respectively. Travelpasses and FerryTen tickets can offer substantial savings – see box above for details.

Monorail and light rail

The city's monorail and the light-rail system are run by **Metro Transport Sydney** (ⓣ02 9285 5600, ⓦwww.metromonorail.com.au; see the Central Sydney map for routes).

SYDNEY FERRIES

Not to scale

MANLY
(THE ESPLANADE)

MOSMAN BAY
(AVENUE ST)

Old Cremorne
(Green St)

South Mosman
(Musgrave St)

Cremorne Point
(Milsons Rd)

Taronga Zoo
(Bradleys Head Rd)

Kuraba Point
(Kuraba Rd)

Neutral Bay
(Hayes Street)

North Sydney
(High Street)

Kirribilli
(Holbrook Street)

Milsons Point
(Alfred St South)

McMahons Point
(Henry Lawson Ave)

WATSONS BAY
(MILITARY RD)

Rose Bay
(Lyne Park)

Double Bay
(Bay St)

Darling Point
(McKell Park)

Garden Island
(Navy Heritage Centre)

CIRCULAR QUAY FERRY TERMINAL

WHARF 2

WHARF 3

WHARF 4

WHARF 5

WHARF 6

DARLING HARBOUR
(KING ST WHARF 3)

PYRMONT BAY
(CASINO/MARITIME MUSEUM)

Darling Harbour
(Aquarium)

Balmain East
(Darling Street)

Balmain
(Thames Street)

Birchgrove
(Louisa Rd)

Cockatoo Island

Greenwich
(Mitchell St)

Woolwich
(Valentia St)

Drummoyne
(Wolseley St)

Huntleys Point
(Huntleys Point Rd)

Chiswick
(Bortfield Dr)

Abbotsford
(Great North Rd)

Bayview Park
(Burwood Rd)

Cabarita
(Cabarita Pt)

Kissing Point
(Kissing Point Park)

Meadowbank
(Bowden Rd)

Sydney Olympic Park
(Bennelong Rd)

Rydalmere
(John St)

PARRAMATTA
(CHARLES ST)

BIRKENHEAD POINT
(HENLEY MARINE DRIVE)

Balmain West
(Elliot Street)

N

Ferry Services

Manly JetCat

Sunday Only Services

The **Metro Monorail** is essentially a tourist shuttle designed to loop around Darling Harbour every three to five minutes, connecting it with the city centre. Thundering along tracks set above the older city streets, the "monster rail" – as many locals know it – doesn't exactly blend in with its surroundings. Still, the elevated view of the city, particularly from Pyrmont Bridge, makes it worth investing A\$4.80 (day-pass A\$9.50) and ten minutes to do the whole eight-stop circuit (Mon–Thurs 7am–10pm, Fri & Sat 7am–midnight, Sun 8am–10pm).

Metro Light Rail (MLR) runs from Central Station to the Pyrmont Peninsula and on to Lilyfield in the inner west. There are fourteen stops on the route, which links Central Station with Chinatown, Darling Harbour, the fish markets at Pyrmont, Star City Casino, Wentworth Park's greyhound racecourse, Glebe (with stops near Pyrmont Bridge Road, at Jubilee Park, and at Rozelle Bay by Bicentennial Park) and Lilyfield, not far from Darling Street, Rozelle. The air-conditioned light rail vehicles can carry 200 passengers, and are fully accessible to disabled commuters. The service operates 24 hours every ten to fifteen minutes to the casino (every 30min midnight–6am), with reduced hours for stops beyond to Lilyfield (Mon–Thurs & Sun 6am–11pm, Fri & Sat 6am–midnight). There are two zones: zone 1 covers Central to Convention Centre in Darling Harbour, and zone 2 spans Pyrmont Bay to Lilyfield. Tickets can be purchased at vending machines by the stops; singles cost A\$3.20/\$4.20 for zone 1/zone 2, returns A\$4.60/\$5.70, a day-pass costs A\$9 and a weekly one A\$20. A TramLink ticket, available from any CityRail station, combines a rail ticket to Central Station with an MLR ticket.

If you plan on using the monorail and light rail a lot, it might be worth purchasing a **METROcard** (A\$20), which gives six rides on either the monorail or light rail; the card can then be topped up for subsequent rides at A\$2.50 per ride. TravelPasses cannot be used on either system.

Taxis

Taxis are vacant if the rooftop light is on. They are notoriously difficult to find at 3pm, when the shifts change over. The four major city **cab ranks** are outside the *Four Seasons Hotel* at the start of George Street, The Rocks; on Park Street outside Woolworths, opposite the Town Hall; outside David Jones department store on Market Street, and on Pitt Street at the CountryLink entrance to Central Station. Drivers don't expect a tip but often need directions – try to have some idea of where you're going. Check the correct tariff rate is displayed: tariff 2 (10pm–6am) is twenty percent more than tariff 1 (6am–10pm). See "Listings", p.308, for phone numbers.

Accommodation

There are a tremendous number of places to stay in Sydney, and fierce competition helps keep prices down. Finding somewhere is usually only a problem just before Christmas and throughout January, in late February or early March during Mardi Gras, and at Easter: at these times, **book ahead**. All types of accommodation offer a (sometimes substantial) discount for **weekly bookings**, and may also cut prices considerably during the **low season** (from autumn to spring, school holidays excepted). Executive-oriented hotels offer reduced rates at weekends, but at the boutique hotels the opposite tends to apply.

Sydney's top-end **international hotels** are as stylish and comfortable as you'd expect; while some charge a fortune, you'll generally get far more luxury for your money here than in, say, London or New York, with some superb options in the A$300–400 range for a double room with breakfast. For something comfortable, stylish and intimate, head for one of the **boutique hotels** in the CBD, Potts Point or Darlinghurst, which charge a little less. Dotted around the more modest suburbs are characterful **guesthouses** charging A$100–200, while in many neighbourhoods – including The Rocks and the CBD – you'll find basic **pub** rooms for around A$100. Sydney has no shortage of **hostels**, but despite the rivalry between them standards are variable; the best, which have impressively modern facilities and an upbeat urban vibe, are good value at A$65–90 for a private double or A$23–40 for a room-share bunk. **Serviced holiday apartments** give you far more space than a hotel room, and can be very good value for a group.

For longer stays, the places to look for a **flat-share** include Saturday's *Sydney Morning Herald*; websites such as ⓦwww.flatmatefinders.com.au and ⓦwww.flatmates.com.au; or noticeboards in cafés and health-food stores in King Street (Newtown), Glebe Point Road (Glebe), or Hall Street (Bondi Beach). Competition for the best places is fierce. The average price for an unfurnished room in a shared house is around A$175 per week (paid two weeks in advance, with a bond/deposit of four weeks' rent). If you're prepared to share a room in a furnished house-share, you'll find something cheaper: Sydney Terraces (ⓣ1800 888 887, ⓦwww.sydneyterraces.com) rents beds in six-person townhouses (A$145/week), while Sleeping With The Enemy (ⓣ1300 309 468 or 02 9211 8878, ⓦwww.sleepingwiththeenemy.com) has some funky, well-equipped options (from A$120/week). Both are aimed at students and young travellers and require you to stay at least a month.

For **camping**, Sydney has a new mid-river site, Cockatoo Island, just a short ferry trip inland from Darling Harbour or Circular Quay; there are also a few options out in the suburbs.

Where to stay

The listings below are arranged by area. For short visits, you'll want to stay in the **city centre** or the immediate vicinity: **The Rocks** and the **CBD** have the greatest concentration of top-end hotels, while the area around Central Station and Chinatown, known as **Haymarket**, has some cheaper, more downmarket places and numerous backpackers' hostels, led by the huge YHA. West of here, leafy and peaceful **Glebe** is another slice of prime independent travellers' territory, featuring several backpackers' and small guesthouses. The cheap dives around **Kings Cross**, east of the centre, have fallen out of favour with backpackers – all but the most hard-up head to Haymarket or Glebe instead to avoid the sleaze of Darlinghurst Road, the hardcore red-light strip – but paradoxically the surrounding neighbourhoods harbour some upmarket gems. The adjacent suburbs of **Woolloomooloo**, **Potts Point** and **Elizabeth Bay**, though not as convenient as King's Cross, are quieter and smarter, while **Darlinghurst** is a good place for boutique hotels and gay-friendly guesthouses.

For longer stays, consider somewhere further out. On the **North Shore**, you'll get more for your money and more of a feel for Sydney as a city: **Kirribilli**, **Neutral Bay** or **Cremorne Point**, only a short ferry ride from Circular Quay, offer some serenity and affordable water views as well. Large, old private hotels out this way are increasingly being converted into hostels, particularly on Carabella Street in Kirribilli. Alternatively, you can soak up Sydney's beach culture at the seaside suburb of **Manly**, tucked away in the northeast corner of

Campsites in and around Sydney

Cockatoo Island Parramatta River (3km west of the city: 18min from Circular Quay or 10min from Darling Harbour by Sydney Ferry) ☏02 8898 9774, ⓦwww.cockatooisland.gov.au. The closest site to central Sydney, this mid-harbour island was once a prison, and later a commercial dock; old buildings still remain, lending a dramatic, though stark, post-industrial backdrop. Facilities are simple. You can hire a tent plus essential kit for A$30/day on top of the site fee. Tent site A$45.

Grand Pines Tourist Park 289 The Grand Parade, Sans Souci (18km southwest of the city: trian to Allaway then bus 478) ☏02 9529 7329. Within easy reach of the airport, this Botany Bay site has old-style but reasonably well-equipped cabins, and space for campervans (not tents). Van site A$39, cabin ④

Lakeside Caravan Park Lake Park Rd, Narrabeen (26km north of the city: bus 190 or L90 from Wynyard) ☏02 9913 7845 or 1800 008 845, ⓦwww.sydneylakeside.com.au. Great spot by Narrabeen Lakes with free gas BBQs, camp kitchen, nearby shop and a good range of shady areas for tents, caravans and vans, plus en-suite cabins and villas. Camping A$55–65, cabin ⑤, villa ⑥

Lane Cove River Tourist Park Plassey Rd, North Ryde (15km northwest of the city: train to Chatswood then bus 545) ☏02 9888 9133 or 1300 729 133, ⓦwww.lanecoverivertouristpark.com.au. Eco-friendly site in a wonderful bush location beside Lane Cove National Park, right on the river. Great facilities including a swimming pool. Camping A$34–36, cabin ④

Sheralee Tourist Caravan Park 88 Bryant St, Rockdale (16km southwest of the city: train to Rockdale) ☏02 9567 7161, ⓦwww.sydneycaravanpark.com.au. This simple, budget option has space for tents, vans or caravans, and a shared kitchen. Camping A$28–33.

---

the harbour, just thirty minutes from Circular Quay by ferry; or at the eastern suburbs of **Bondi** and **Coogee** closer to the city – all have lively but fairly shabby hostels, plus a few smarter options.

The Rocks

For the lisitings below, see map, p.237.

Lord Nelson Brewery Hotel Corner of Argyle & Kent sts ☏02 9251 4044, ⓦwww.lordnelson.com.au. This freshly presented B&B in a historic, colonial-style pub is excellent value, with small but very cosy rooms, some with shared bathrooms. Serves beer brewed on the premises, plus bar food daily and upmarket meals from its first-floor brasserie (lunch Thurs & Fri, dinner Tues–Sat). ④

Mercantile 25 George St ☏02 9247 3570. High-spirited Irish pub with a stash of cheap and decent rooms upstairs, which are often booked out. Some rooms have shared bathrooms; several have fireplaces and other original features. ④

Observatory 89 Kent St ☏02 9256 2222, ⓦwww.observatoryhotel.com.au. Astronomically priced, but worth it if money really is no object, this very beautiful hotel has impeccable service, an utterly luxurious spa, and a heavenly pool with a dark ceiling, which, charmingly, twinkles like the night sky. ⑧

Old Sydney Holiday Inn 55 George St ☏02 9252 0524, ⓦwww.sydneyhotels.holiday-inn.com. Four-and-a-half star in a great location right in the heart of The Rocks, with impressive architecture: eight levels of rooms around a central atrium create a remarkable feeling of space. The best rooms have harbour views; the rooftop swimming pool is a bonus. ⑦

Park Hyatt 7 Hickson Rd ☏02 9241 1234, ⓦwww.sydney.park.hyatt.com. With multi-million-dollar, pure-essence-of-Sydney views of the Opera House from its best rooms, the serene, top-end *Park Hyatt* is an obvious choice if a sense of place is all. The rooms are spacious but not showy. Rates are extreme. ⑧

Shangri-La 176 Cumberland St ☏02 9250 6000, ⓦwww.shangri-la.com. Hard to beat for glamour and comfort in the city centre, this luxurious towerblock with stunning harbour views offers Asian hospitality served up with cutting-edge style. ⑦

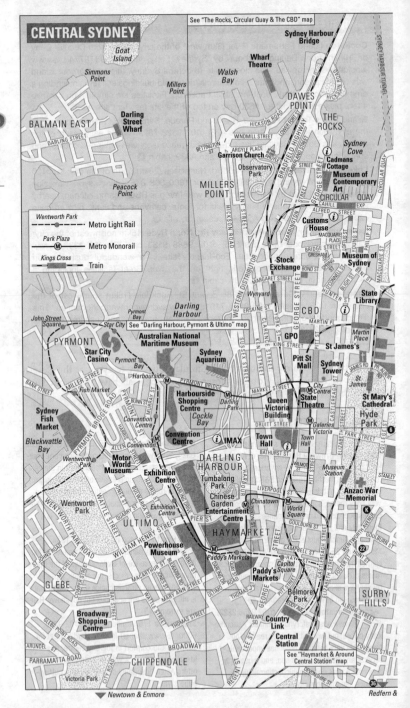

CENTRAL SYDNEY

See "The Rocks, Circular Quay & The CBD" map

Goat
Island

Simmons
Point

Millers
Point

Walsh
Bay

Sydney Harbour
Bridge

Wharf
Theatre

DAWES
POINT

HICKSON ROAD

SYDNEY HARBOUR TUNNEL

THE
ROCKS

Sydney
Cove

Darling
Street Wharf

BALMAIN EAST

DARLING STREET

HICKSON ROAD

WINDMILL STREET

BETTINGTON STREET

LOWER FORT ST

BRADFIELD HIGHWAY

CUMBERLAND STREET

ARGYLE STREET

GEORGE STREET

Cadmans
Cottage

Museum of
Contemporary
Art

Peacock
Point

ARGYLE PLACE

Garrison Church

Observatory
Park

MILLERS
POINT

KENT STREET

HARRINGTON STREET

CIRCULAR QUAY

CIRCULAR QUAY

Customs
House

CAHILL EXP

ALFRED STREET

Wentworth Park — — — Metro Light Rail

Park Plaza —Ⓜ— Metro Monorail

Kings Cross — Train

HICKSON ROAD

WESTERN DISTRIBUTOR

MARGARET STREET

ERSKINE ST

Stock
Exchange

BRIDGE STREET

GRESHAM

BOND ST

MACQUARIE
PLACE

YOUNG ST

PHILIP ST

Museum of
Sydney

BENT ST

HUNTER ST

MACQUARIE STREET

State
Library

John Street
Square

PYRMONT

Star City
Casino

Star City

Pyrmont
Bay

Pyrmont
Bay

Darling
Harbour

See "Darling Harbour, Pyrmont & Ultimo" map

Australian National
Maritime Museum

Sydney
Aquarium

CLARENCE STREET

KENT STREET

SUSSEX STREET

GEORGE STREET

Wynyard

KING STREET

MARTIN PL

Martin
Place

GPO

St James's

PITT STREET

Pitt St
Mall

Sydney
Tower

ST JAMES RD

PR ALBERT

St
James

BANK STREET

MILLER STREET

Fish Market

Harbourside

PYRMONT BRIDGE ROAD

BUNN ST

MURRAY ST

HARRIS ST

Harbourside
Shopping
Centre

PYRMONT BRIDGE

Ⓜ

Darling
Park

Cockle
Bay

MARKET STREET

Queen
Victoria
Building

DRUITT STREET

City
Centre

Ⓜ

State
Theatre

Galeries
Victoria

Ⓜ

St Mary's
Cathedral

Hyde
Park

ELIZABETH STREET

CASTLEREAGH STREET

PARK STREET

COLLEGE STREET

6

Sydney
Fish
Market

Blackwattle
Bay

Convention
Centre

Ⓜ

Convention

ALLEN

Convention
Centre

Ⓜ

IMAX
ⓘ

Town
Hall

Ⓜ

Town
Hall
ⓘ

BATHURST STREET

Museum
Station

Anzac War
Memorial

Wentworth
Park

Motor
World
Museum

HARRIS STREET

Exhibition
Centre

Exhibition
Centre

PIER ST

DARLING DRIVE

DARLING
HARBOUR

Tumbalong
Park

Chinese
Garden

Entertainment
Centre

LIVERPOOL

WILMOT
ST

PITT STREET

World
Square

GOULBURN STREET

ELIZABETH STREET

CASTLEREAGH STREET

STANLEY

K

WENTWORTH AVENUE

WENTWORTH PARK ROAD

WATTLE STREET

QUARRY ST

JONES ST

BOWMAN ST

WILLIAM HENRY STREET

ULTIMO

Ⓜ

Chinatown

Ⓜ

HAYMARKET

CAMPBELL ST

GOULBURN ST

22

GLEBE

ST JOHNS ROAD

MITCHELL ST

Powerhouse
Museum

MACARTHUR ST

JONES ST

BLACKBURN ST

MARY ANN STREET

HARRIS STREET

ULTIMO STREET

DARLING DRIVE

QUAY ST

Paddy's Markets

Paddy's
Markets

Capitol
Square

HAY

THOMAS STREET

GEORGE STREET

Belmore
Park

EDDY AVENUE

SURRY
HILLS

ALBION STREET

FOVEAUX STREET

Broadway
Shopping
Centre

GLEBE POINT ROAD

BAY STREET

WATTLE STREET

THOMAS STREET

RAILWAY
SQ

Country
Link

Central
Station

LEE ST

REGENT ST

See "Haymarket & Around
Central Station" map

ARUNDEL

CITY ROAD

PARRAMATTA ROAD

BROADWAY

CHIPPENDALE

Victoria Park

DEVONSHIRE STREET

36

▼ Newtown & Enmore

Redfern &

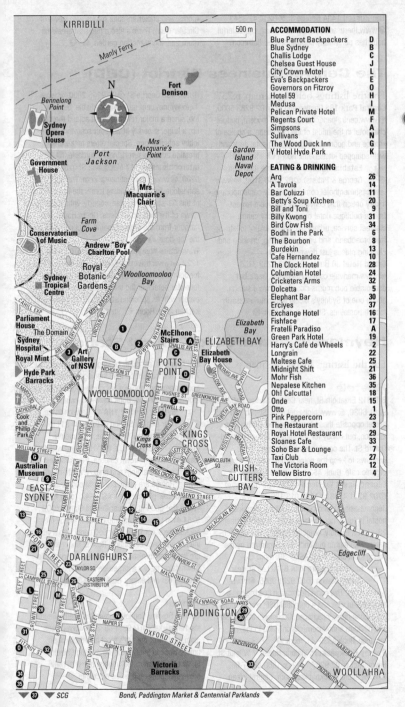

KIRRIBILLI

Manly Ferry

0   500 m

N

Bennelong
Point

Fort
Denison

Sydney
Opera
House

Government
House

Port
Jackson

Mrs
Macquarie's
Point

Garden
Island
Naval
Depot

Conservatorium
of Music

Farm
Cove

Andrew "Boy"
Charlton Pool

Mrs
Macquarie's
Chair

Sydney
Tropical
Centre

Royal Botanic
Gardens

Woolloomooloo
Bay

Parliament
House

The Domain

Sydney
Hospital

Royal Mint

Hyde Park
Barracks

Art
Gallery
of NSW

Elizabeth
Bay

McElhone
Stairs

ELIZABETH BAY

Elizabeth
Bay House

POTTS
POINT

Cook
and
Phillip
Park

WOOLLOOMOOLOO

KINGS
CROSS

Kings
Cross

Australian
Museum

EAST
SYDNEY

RUSH-
CUTTERS
BAY

Edgecliff

DARLINGHURST

Taylor Sq

PADDINGTON

Victoria
Barracks

WOOLLAHRA

SCG

Bondi, Paddington Market & Centennial Parklands

ACCOMMODATION

Blue Parrot Backpackers	D
Blue Sydney	B
Challis Lodge	C
Chelsea Guest House	J
City Crown Motel	L
Eva's Backpackers	E
Governors on Fitzroy	O
Hotel 59	H
Medusa	I
Pelican Private Hotel	M
Regents Court	F
Simpsons	A
Sullivans	N
The Wood Duck Inn	G
Y Hotel Hyde Park	K

EATING & DRINKING

Arq	26
A Tavola	14
Bar Coluzzi	11
Betty's Soup Kitchen	20
Bill and Toni	9
Billy Kwong	31
Bird Cow Fish	34
Bodhi in the Park	6
The Bourbon	8
Burdekin	13
Cafe Hernandez	10
The Clock Hotel	28
Columbian Hotel	24
Cricketers Arms	32
Dolcetta	5
Elephant Bar	30
Erciyes	37
Exchange Hotel	16
Fishface	17
Fratelli Paradiso	A
Green Park Hotel	19
Harry's Café de Wheels	2
Longrain	22
Maltese Cafe	25
Midnight Shift	21
Mohr Fish	36
Nepalese Kitchen	35
Oh! Calcutta!	18
Onde	15
Otto	1
Pink Peppercorn	23
The Restaurant	3
Royal Hotel Restaurant	29
Sloanes Cafe	33
Soho Bar & Lounge	7
Taxi Club	27
The Victoria Room	12
Yellow Bistro	4

225

The Russell 143A George St ☎02 9241 3543, ⓦwww.therussell.com.au. This small, characterful hotel has perennially popular shared-bathroom rooms, and pricier en-suite rooms with views of Circular Quay. There's also a pleasant breakfast room and sunny rooftop garden. ④–⑥

The Central Business District (CBD)

For the listings below, see map, p.237.

Central Park 185 Castlereagh St ☎02 9283 5000, ⓦwww.centralpark.com.au. Small, modern, budget-chic hotel in the midst of the city bustle; a choice of studios and good-sized rooms, with sofa, desk and well-equipped kitchenette. Room ⑤, studio ⑥

🏃 Establishment 5 Bridge Lane (between George & Pitt sts) ☎02 9240 3100, ⓦwww.establishmenthotel.com. Thoroughly contemporary, luxury option that delivers all that you'd expect from a boutique hotel bang in the city centre – discreet service, urban-chic decor, luxury toiletries, free broadband, and very cool eating, drinking and clubbing places just downstairs. ⑦

Grand Hotel 30 Hunter St ☎02 9232 3755, ⓦwww.merivale.com.au/thegrand. Basic but acceptable pub rooms close to Wynyard station, above one of Sydney's oldest (but not necessarily nicest) hostelries. Shared bathrooms. ③

Hilton 488 George St ☎02 9266 2000, ⓦwww.hiltonsydney.com.au. Always reliable, but now hip, too, since a major refurbishment spiced the place up; a huge, superbly lit abstract sculpture in the lobby sets the tone. Special offers make this prestige address surprisingly affordable. ⑥

Intercontinental 117 Macquarie St ☎02 9230 0200, ⓦwww.intercontinental.com. The old sandstone Treasury building forms the lower floors of this 31-storey, five-star property, with stunning views of the Botanic Gardens, Opera House and harbour from the priciest rooms. Pool and gym on the top floor. ⑦

Travelodge Wynyard 7–9 York St ☎02 9274 1222, ⓦwww.travelodge.com.au. Central position for both the CBD and The Rocks. This 22-storey four-star hotel has the usual motel-style rooms but excels with its spacious studios, which come with kitchen area. Room ⑤, studio ⑥

Haymarket and around Central Station

For the listings below, see map, p.243.

Hostels

BIG 212 Elizabeth St, near Central Station ☎02 9281 6030, ⓦwww.bighostel.com. Stylish 140-bed hostel opposite the railway line – an unattractive location, but handy for the station, Chinatown and Oxford St. The comfy rooms have extra-thick windows to keep the noise at bay, and there's an organic café. Bunk A$28–31, room ③

Legend Has It Westend 412 Pitt St, Haymarket ☎02 9211 4588 or 1800 013 186, ⓦwww.legendhasitwestend.com.au. Not the swankiest hostel in town, nor the quietest – one dorm sleeps 28 – but a friendly, outgoing atmosphere compensates, with nights out and tours organized by the young local staff. Bunk A$28–30, room ③

🏃 Railway Square YHA 8–10 Lee St, near Central Station ☎02 9281 9666, ⓦwww.yha.com.au. This converted station building has a swish urban vibe and a delightful USP: some rooms are replica railway carriages. Occasional train noises and platform announcements only add to the romance. Bunk A$30–41, room ③

Sydney Backpackers Victoria House, 7 Wilmot St, Haymarket ☎02 9267 7772 or 1800 88 77 66, ⓦwww.sydneybackpackers.com. Central, clean and spacious, although lacking a little atmosphere. There's a choice of dorms sleeping between four and sixteen, or spacious twins (no doubles); all rooms have air-con. Bunk A$28–33, twin ③

🏃 Sydney Central YHA 11 Rawson Place, near Central Station ☎02 9281 9111, ⓦwww.yha.com.au. This huge, dynamically managed hostel reinvents the YHA brand with fresh ideas (a cushion-strewn cinema, free salsa lessons, rooftop scuba training) and snazzy, contemporary styling. Rooms are plain, but it still outclasses many pricier places. Bunk A$30–42, room ③

Wake Up! 509 Pitt St, near Central Station ☎02 9264 4121, ⓦwww.wakeup.com.au. Trendy mega-backpackers' complex (over 500 beds) with a vibrant interior and bags of attitude. Rooms, some en suite, are light, well furnished and, above all, serviceable. Downstairs, there's a streetside café and a late-opening bar and eatery. Bunk A$28–36, room ③

Hotel

Capitol Square Capitol Square, Campbell & George sts, Haymarket ☎02 9211 8633, ⓦwww.rydges.com.au. One of the city's most affordable chain hotels, close to the Capitol Theatre and Chinatown. Small enough not to feel impersonal, with tidily presented rooms and online discounts. ③–⑥

Darling Harbour, Ultimo and Pyrmont

For the listings below, see map, p.249. **Glasgow Arms** 527 Harris St, Ultimo ☎ 02 9211 2354. These high-ceilinged pub rooms – nicely decorated down to the polished floorboards – are good value, all with en suite, air-con and TV; the pleasant bar downstairs serves good food. ❹

Inner west: Glebe and Newtown

For the listings below, see map, pp.224 –225.

Hostels

Billabong Gardens 5–22 Egan St, off King St, Newtown ☎ 02 9550 3236, ⊛ www.billabong gardens.com.au. In a sidestreet but close to the action, this long-running purpose-built hostel is arranged around an inner courtyard with a small pool; noisy, but with useful facilities including parking and free broadband. Bunk A$23–25, room ❷

Glebe Point YHA 262–264 Glebe Point Rd, Glebe ☎ 02 9692 8418, ⊛ www.yha.com.au. Run by friendly, knowledgeable managers, this relaxed hostel is a favourite with travellers on working holidays looking for something less frantic than the city-centre party hostels; the large rooftop terrace is a good spot to lounge with a book. Bunk A$25–33, room ❷

Glebe Village Backpackers 256 Glebe Point Rd, Glebe ☎ 02 9660 8133 or 1800 801 983, ⊛ www .glebevillage.com. Three large houses with a mellow, sociable atmosphere – the generally laid-back guests socialize in the leafy streetside fairy-lit garden. Staffed by young locals who know what's going on around town. Bunk A$26–28, room ❸

Rooftop Travellers Lodge 146 Glebe Point Rd, Glebe ☎ 02 9660 7711, ⊛ www.rooftoptravellerslodge.com. This good-value budget retreat for short and long stays is right in the heart of Glebe with fabulous city views from the rooftop. Each room has a fridge and a PC with free broadband. Bunk A$27, room ❹

Guesthouses and B&Bs

Ardmore House 24A Albemarle St, Newtown ☎ 02 9516 2251, ⊛ www.ardmorehouse.com.au. Very pretty house with Italianate balconies, period features, a homely feel and just two guest rooms. The charming, accommodating hosts produce memorable breakfasts and will arrange bespoke tours on request. ❹

Australian Sunrise Lodge 485 King St, Newtown ☎ 02 9550 4999, ⊛ www.australiansunriselodge .com. Small, modest hotel with a shared guest kitchen and a choice of basic and en-suite rooms at low prices; the best are upstairs, with cute, sunny balconies. ❸

Tricketts Bed and Breakfast 270 Glebe Point Rd, Glebe ☎ 02 9552 1141, ⊛ www .tricketts.com.au. Luxury B&B in an 1880s mansion, furnished with antiques and Persian rugs; the lounge was originally a small ballroom. Also a self-contained one-bedroom garden apartment with its own veranda. Generous and sociable breakfast. ❺

Woolloomooloo, Potts Point and Kings Cross

For the listings below, see map, pp.224 –225.

Hostels

Blue Parrot Backpackers 87 Macleay St, Potts Point ☎ 02 9356 4888, ⊛ www.blueparrot.com.au. Well located in the trendy (and quieter) part of Potts Point and with helpful staff, this converted mansion is sunny, airy, brightly painted and tastefully furnished. The huge courtyard garden has wooden furniture and big shady trees. Bunk A$27–31, room ❸

Eva's Backpackers 6–8 Orwell St, Potts Point ☎ 02 9358 2185, ⊛ www.evasbackpackers.com.au. Family-run hostel away from Darlinghurst Road's clamour; colourful, clean, safe and friendly. There's a peaceful rooftop garden with table umbrellas, BBQ area, and fantastic views over The Domain. The guest kitchen/dining room is sociable, though this isn't a "party" hostel. Dorms A$26, rooms ❺

The Wood Duck Inn 49 William St, East Sydney ☎ 02 9358 5856 or 1800 110 025, ⊛ www.woodduckinn.com.au. Fun, spacious dorm-only hostel with fine views over Hyde Park from the sunny rooftop. Run by two switched-on brothers who can fix up trips or help you kick-start a working holiday. Bunk A$22.

Hotels

Blue Sydney The Wharf, 6 Cowper Wharf Rd, Woolloomooloo ☎ 02 9331 9000,

Ⓦ www.tajhotels.com/sydney. This luxury, water's-edge warehouse conversion has bags of style and a smooth, contemporary design that confidently leaves old iron beams and braces exposed. There's a day spa, pool and gym, and fashionable restaurants nearby. Room ❻, suite ❽

Challis Lodge 21–23 Challis Ave, Potts Point ⓉⓉ 02 9358 5422, Ⓦ www.budgethotelssydney.com. A wonderful old mansion on a peaceful, tree-filled street, close to some of the area's trendiest eateries. It's functionally furnished, and the cheapest rooms are tiny, but the larger ones are good value. ❷–❹

🏃 **Hotel 59** 59 Bayswater Rd, Kings Cross ⓉⓉ 02 9360 5900, Ⓦ www.hotel59.com.au. Small, very popular hotel, reminiscent of a pleasant European guesthouse; benefits include a friendly owner, petite but tasteful rooms, a quiet, leafy location and a downstairs café where delicious cooked breakfasts are served. ❹

🏃 **Regents Court** 18 Springfield Ave, Potts Point ⓉⓉ 02 9358 1533, Ⓦ www.regentscourt.com.au. Raved about by international style mags for its decor and ambience, this arty place is a little piece of glam without an outrageous price tag. Each apartment-style room has a sleek kitchen area and classic designer furniture. Instead of a bar, there's a well-chosen wine list downstairs (at bottle-shop prices), and help-yourself coffee and biscotti. The crowning glory is a small but elegant rooftop garden. ❻

Simpsons 8 Challis Ave, Potts Point ⓉⓉ 02 9356 2199, Ⓦ www.simpsonspottspoint.com.au. Delightful little hotel with the feel of an upmarket B&B, *Simpsons* is crammed with homely character, from marble fireplaces to antique oddments – the perfect antidote if Sydney's modern, minimalist hotels aren't your style. ❺

Darlinghurst, Paddington, Woollahra and Surry Hills

For the listings below, see map, pp.224 –225.

Chelsea Guest House 49 Womerah Ave, Darlinghurst ⓉⓉ 02 9380 5994, Ⓦ wwww.chelseaguesthouse.com.au. Quiet, tastefully decorated terraced house with a lovely courtyard and pleasant rooms, tucked away in a leafy area, but within walking distance of shops and restaurants. ❹

City Crown Motel 289 Crown St, corner of Reservoir St, Surry Hills ⓉⓉ 02 9331 2433, Ⓦ www.citycrownmotel.com.au. Though plain inside and out, this motel has a fantastic location in the heart of the fashionable Surry Hills scene. The rooms aren't huge but they're well equipped for the price, and parking is available. ❹

Governors on Fitzroy 64 Fitzroy St, Surry Hills ⓉⓉ 02 9331 4652, Ⓦ www.governors.com.au. Long-established gay B&B in a restored Victorian terrace just a few blocks from Oxford St. The five guest rooms – big and well appointed – have basins and shared bathrooms. Guests – mostly men – can also meet and mingle in the spa pool. ❹

🏃 **Medusa** 267 Darlinghurst Rd, Darlinghurst ⓉⓉ 02 9331 1000, Ⓦ www.medusa.com.au. This boutique hotel is a modernist's dream, set in a grand heritage mansion decorated with dramatic, cutting-edge furniture and fittings. The seventeen luxurious rooms all have mini-kitchens; some also have access to a stunning interior courtyard. Glamorous and attentive staff. ❼

Pelican Private Hotel 411 Bourke St, Darlinghurst ⓉⓉ 02 9331 5344, Ⓦ www.pelicanprivatehotel.iwarp.com. Comfortable budget accommodation in one of Sydney's oldest gay guesthouses, a short walk from Oxford St. The tree-filled garden is an inner-city oasis and the communal kitchen makes it even more sociable. Bathrooms are shared. ❹

Sullivans 21 Oxford St, Paddington ⓉⓉ 02 9361 0211, Ⓦ www.sullivans.com.au. Medium-sized, conservatively furnished modern hotel in a trendy location, run by staff tuned into the local scene.

Gay-friendly accommodation

Sydney has a vibrant gay and lesbian scene; to be in the thick of it, you'll want to stay in Darlinghurst or Paddington, where the most welcoming places include the *Chelsea Guest House*, *Medusa*, *Pelican Private Hotel* and *Sullivans* (see above). Elsewhere, it's worth checking out *Ardmore House* in Newtown (see p.227) or, for the ultimate indulgence, the *Observatory* in The Rocks (see p.223). For Mardi Gras, anywhere in the centre is worth a try; you'll need to book way ahead.

Lots of useful free extras including parking, bicycles, Wi-Fi and a guided walking tour of Paddington; there's also a swimming pool and small gym. ❺
Y Hotel Hyde Park 5–11 Wentworth Ave, Darlinghurst ☎02 9264 2451 or 1800 994 994, ⓦwww.yhotel.com.au. Great location just off Oxford St for this former hostel; it's remodelled itself as a stylish budget hotel, catering for all ages, but retains some quad rooms (single beds, not bunks); it also has studios with mini-kitchens. Bed in quad-share A$35, room ❸, studio ❹

North Shore

Cremorne Point Manor 6 Cremorne Rd, Cremorne Point (near Cremorne Point wharf) ☎02 9953 7899, ⓦwww.cremornepointmanor.com.au. Huge, restored Federation-style villa with the atmosphere of a comfortable old English guesthouse, but with modern touches such as iPod docks and free Wi-Fi. As well as en-suite doubles there are a few good-value rooms with shared bathrooms. ❸–❺
Elite Private Hotel 133 Carabella St, Kirribilli (near Kirribilli wharf and Milsons Point station) ☎02 9929 6365, ⓦwww.elitehotel.com.au. Bright and in a pleasant residential area, but with simple rooms at bargain rates. Most have shared bathrooms; some have good harbour views. ❷
Glenferrie Lodge 12A Carabella St, Kirribilli (near Kirribilli wharf and Milsons Point station) ☎02 9955 1685, ⓦwww.glenferrielodge.com. Another made-over Kirribilli mansion: a clean, light and secure budget option with 24hr reception and a garden. Simple, tidy rooms with shared bathrooms. Bunk in quad-share A$40–45, double/twin ❹

Bondi Beach

Bondi Beachhouse YHA 63 Fletcher St, corner of Dellview St ☎02 9365 2088, ⓦwww.yha.com.au. Between Tamarama Beach and Bondi, in a splendid Art Deco building. The dorms, doubles and bathrooms are rather cramped, but the location keeps it perennially popular; there are great ocean views from the rooftop deck and some of the rooms. Lots of local info; free surf talks. Bunk A$25–30, basic double/twin ❷, en-suite room ❹
Bondi Serviced Apartments 212 Bondi Rd ☎02 8837 8000 or 1300 364 200, ⓦwww .bondi-serviced-apartments.com.au.
Underwhelming but good-value apartments halfway between Bondi Junction and Bondi Beach – all the basics are provided, and there's a rooftop pool. Some units have balconies with ocean views. ❹
Ravesi's Campbell Parade ☎02 9365 4422, ⓦwww.ravesis.com.au. Nobody comes to Bondi for peace and quiet, but some hope, at least, for a little style – this boutique hotel is one of the few places in town that delivers. Though pricey, the rooms are refreshingly hip, and are booked out whenever the bar downstairs hosts A-list parties. ❻

Coogee

Coogee Bay Hotel Coogee Bay Rd ☎02 9665 0000, ⓦwww.coogeebayhotel.com.au. This very busy pub has a choice of crisply decorated boutique-hotel-style rooms in a modern wing, and cheaper, older rooms in the main building – all are surprisingly stylish and many have fantastic ocean views. Parking included. ❺–❻

Holiday apartments

Medina Executive Apartments Head office, Level 1, 355 Crown St, Surry Hills ☎02 9360 1699 or 1300 300 232, ⓦwww.medina.com.au. Upmarket apartment-hotel chain with luxury units sleeping up to six, in salubrious locales all over Sydney, including Darling Harbour, Martin Place and Coogee. All include parking. Bookable by the day, except at peak times, for A$220–720.

The Park Agency 190 Arden St, Coogee ☎02 9315 7777, ⓦwww.parkagency .com.au. Spacious, well-set-up studios and apartments near Coogee Beach. All fully furnished, including washing machine and linen. From A$1350 per week, with substantial low-season discounts. Cheaper quarterly leases available.

Dive Hotel 234 Arden St ☎ 02 9665 5538, ⓦ www.divehotel.com.au. A wonderful small hotel opposite the beach; features include Art Deco tiling, high, decorative-plaster ceilings and a pleasant, bamboo-fringed courtyard. The rooms at the front have splendid ocean views; all have funky little bathrooms and a handy mini-kitchen. ⑥

Surfside Backpackers Coogee 186 Arden St ☎ 02 9315 7888, ⓦ www.surfsidebackpackers .com.au. On Coogee's main beachfront drag, Coogee's largest hostel tends to attract a drinking, party crowd – try elsewhere for quiet. Modern

facilities and great views from its high balconies, but a bit of a concrete-block feel, and not as clean as it should be. Bunk A$36, room ④

Wizard of Oz Backpackers 172 Coogee Bay Rd ☎ 02 9315 7876, ⓦ www .wizardofoz.com.au. Top-class hostel in a big and beautiful Californian-style house with a huge veranda, a pleasant backyard and polished wooden floors. Spacious, vibrantly painted dorms and some doubles, plus good-value apartments for longer stays. Bunk A$25–45, double/twin or apartment ④

Manly and the northern beaches

Avalon Beach Hostel 59 Avalon Parade, Avalon ☎ 02 9918 9709, ⓦ www.avalonbeach.com.au. At one of Sydney's best – and most beautiful – surf beaches, this rather tired-looking hostel has an airy beach-house feel with breezy balconies. Bathroom facilities are stretched at peak times. Boat trips on Pittwater can be organized; surfboard rental available. Bunk A$20–25, room ①

Manly Backpackers 24 Raglan St, Manly ☎ 02 9977 3411, ⓦ www.manlybackpackers .com.au. One block from the surf, this large, purpose-built, two-storey "hostel with lifestyle" tends to attract an all-out party crowd; depending on who's staying, it can get pretty grubby. The best dorm, at the front, has a balcony; some doubles are en suite. Dorms A$26, rooms ④

Manly Pacific Sydney 55 North Steyne, Manly ☎ 02 9977 7666, ⓦ www.accorhotels.com. On the beachfront, this multi-storey, three-star hotel is

rather bland in style, but has decent facilities including a spa, sauna, gym and a small, heated rooftop pool with spectacular ocean views. ⑤

Palm Beach Bed and Breakfast 122 Pacific Rd, Palm Beach ☎ 02 9974 1608, ⓦ www .palmbeachbandb.com.au. Incredibly friendly and slightly quirky B&B with a car collection scattered about the front lawn. All rooms have balconies and water views of either Pittwater or the Pacific, and the emphasis is on easy-going relaxation. Some rooms share a bathroom. ⑥

Periwinkle Guesthouse 18–19 East Esplanade, corner of Ashburner St, Manly ☎ 02 9977 4668, ⓦ www.periwinkle.citysearch.com.au. Pleasant B&B in a charming restored 1895 villa on Manly Cove. Close to the ferry, shops and the harbour, and perfect for swimming, sailing or just listening to the lorikeets chatter. Shared facilities include a kitchen, laundry and courtyard with BBQ. ④

Cronulla

Cronulla Beach YHA 40 Kingsway ☎ 02 9527 7772, ⓦ www.cronullabeachyha.com. Basic, no-fuss hostel in this unpretentious, surf-oriented suburb, two minutes from the sand and even nearer to the shops

and restaurants of Cronulla Mall. Also well situated for day-trips to Royal National Park; the friendly live-in manager offers surf trips to Garie and drop-offs to Wattamolla. Bunk A$25–30, double/twin ③

The City

Port Jackson carves Sydney in two halves, linked by the Harbour Bridge and Harbour Tunnel. The **South Shore** is the hub of activity, and it's here that you'll find the **city centre** and most of the things to see and do. Many of the classic images of Sydney are within sight of **Circular Quay**, making this busy waterfront area on Sydney Cove a logical – and pleasurable – point to start discovering the city, with the **Sydney Opera House** and the expanse of the Royal Botanic Gardens to the east of Sydney Cove and the historic area of **The Rocks** to the west. By contrast, gleaming, slightly tawdry **Darling Harbour**, at the centre's western edge, is a shiny redeveloped tourist and entertainment area.

Circular Quay

At the southern end of Sydney Cove, **Circular Quay** is the launching pad for harbour and river ferries and sightseeing boats, the terminal for buses from the eastern and southern suburbs, and a major suburban train station to boot (some of the most fantastic views of the harbour can be seen from the above-ground station platforms). Circular Quay itself is always bustling with commuters during the week, and with people simply out to enjoy themselves at the weekend. Restaurants, cafés and fast-food outlets line the Quay, buskers entertain the crowds, and vendors of newspapers and trinkets add to the general hubbub. The sun reflecting on the water and its heave and splash as the ferries come and go make for a dreamy setting – best appreciated over an expensive beer at a waterfront bar. The inscribed bronze pavement-plaques of **Writers' Walk** beneath your feet as you stroll around the Circular Quay waterfront provide an introduction to the Australian literary canon. There are short biographies of writers ranging from Miles Franklin, author of *My Brilliant Career*, through Booker Prize-winner Peter Carey and Nobel Prize-awardee Patrick White, to the feminist Germaine Greer, and quotable quotes on what it means to be Australian. Notable literati who've visited Australia – including Joseph Conrad, Charles Darwin and Mark Twain – also feature.

Having dallied, read, and taken in the views, you could then embark on a sightseeing **cruise** or enjoy a ferry ride on the harbour (see box, p.232). Staying on dry land, you're only a short walk from most of the city-centre sights, along part of a continuous **foreshore walkway** beginning under the Harbour Bridge and passing through the historic area of Sydney's first settlement The Rocks, and extending beyond the Opera House to the Royal Botanic Gardens.

Besides ferries, Circular Quay still acts as a passenger terminal for ocean liners; head north past the Museum of Contemporary Art to Circular Quay West where the **Overseas Passenger Terminal** looks for all the world like the deck of a ship itself. Even if there's no liner to admire, you can take the escalator and the flight of stairs to the upper level – from where many a crowd of well-wishers have waved their hankies – for excellent views of the harbour. The rest of the terminal is given over to swanky restaurants and bars – *Aria*, *Wildfire* and *Cruise* among them.

Leading up to the Opera House is the once-controversial **Opera Quays** development, which runs the length of **East Circular Quay**. Since its opening, locals and tourists alike have flocked to promenade along the pleasant colonnaded lower level with its outdoor cafés, bars and bistros, upmarket shops and Dendy Cinema, all looking out to sublime harbour views. The distasteful building above, dubbed "**The Toaster**" by locals and described by Robert Hughes, the expat Australian art critic and historian, as "that dull, brash, intrusive apartment block which now obscures the Opera House from three directions", caused massive protests, but went up anyway, opening in 1999.

Customs House

The railway and the ugly Cahill Expressway block views to the city from Circular Quay, cutting it off from Alfred Street immediately opposite, with its architectural gem, the sandstone and granite **Customs House**. First constructed in 1845, it was redesigned in 1885 by the colonial architect James Barnet to give it its current Classical Revival-style facade, and its interior revamped in 2005. On the ground floor a **City Exhibition Space** keeps pace with the development of Sydney with an up-to-the-minute detailed 500:1 scale model of the city set into the floor under glass and accompanied by a multimedia presentation. A **public library** (Mon–Fri 10am–7pm, Sat 11am–4pm) is

Harbour cruises

There's a wide choice of **sightseeing cruises**, almost all of them leaving from Circular Quay Wharf 6 and the rest from Darling Harbour. The biggest operators are **Captain Cook Cruises**, with offices at Circular Quay Wharf 6 and King Street Wharf (☎02 9206 111, ⓦwww.captaincook.com.au), and **Matilda**, at Circular Quay Wharf 6 and Darling Harbour Pier 26 (☎02 9264 7377, ⓦwww.matilda.com.au); between them they offer everything from a hop-on-hop-off service between Darling Harbour, Circular Quay, Fort Denison, Taronga Zoo, Shark Island, Watson's Bay and Luna Park (the Matilda *Rocket Explorer*; from A$29 all day, child A$15), to leisurely lunch cruises. In the past, **Harboursights Cruises** run by the State Transit Authority (☎13 15 00, ⓦwww.sydneyferries .info), suspended at the time of writing, were better value: they're worth checking out if the service resumes. For an Aboriginal perspective on the harbour and its history, head out on a cultural cruise from Circular Quay Eastern Pontoon with **Tribal Warrior** (daily 12.45pm; 1hr 45min; A$55, child A$45; ☎02 9699 7377, ⓦwww.tribalwarrior.org). You can book any cruise through **Australian Travel Specialists** (ⓦwww.atstravel.com.au), who have branches at Circular Quay Wharf 6 (☎02 9247 5151) and the Harbourside Shopping Centre, Darling Harbour (☎02 9211 3192).

Ferries and water taxis

If you're happy to do without the (sometimes annoying) running commentary and on-board catering offered by the cruise companies, you can explore the harbour for a lot less by regular **ferry**. The best is the thirty-minute ride to Manly, but there's a ferry going somewhere at almost any time throughout the day. For something more exclusive, take a **water taxi** – Circular Quay to Watsons Bay, for example, costs around A$70 for the first passenger plus A$10 for each extra person. Pick-ups are available from any wharf or jetty if booked in advance; companies to try include Water Taxis Combined (☎02 9555 8888, ⓦwww.watertaxis.com.au), or Watertours, located on Cockle Bay Wharf in Darling Harbour (☎02 9211 7730, ⓦwww.watertours.com.au), who also offer tours on their bright yellow taxis (every 15min; A$15, child A$10 for a speedy ten-minute, one-way spin under the Harbour Bridge to the Opera House).

Tall ships and yachts

For a dash of romance, you can enjoy lunch or twilight drinks and nibbles aboard the **Svanen** (2hr; A$69, child A$29; ☎02 9698 4456, ⓦwww.svanen.com.au), a Danish-built tall ship dating back to 1922, which now sails around the harbour from Campbell's Cove in The Rocks. Sydney's oldest sailing ship is the **James Craig**, an 1874 three-masted iron barque, part of the Sydney Heritage Fleet based at Wharf 7, Pirrama Rd, Pyrmont, near Star City Casino; at weekends, you can become a crew member for the day, with lunch on board (Sat & Sun 9.30am–4pm; A$195, child A$110, over-12s only; ☎02 9298 3888, ⓦwww.shf.org.au). **Sydney by Sail** (☎02 9280 1110, ⓦwww.sydneybysail.com) offers a popular small-group, three-hour Port Jackson Explorer cruise (daily 1pm; A$150, child A$75) onboard a luxury Beneteau yacht, departing from the Australian National Maritime Museum at Darling Harbour (free entry to the museum included).

Jet boats

For maximum thrills (and noise pollution for the locals), head down to Darling Harbour to join **Ocean Extreme** (☎1300 887 373, ⓦwww.oceanextreme.com.au) for a hair-raising, forty-five minute, small-group "Extreme Blast" (daily 11am & 1pm; A$75; max 8 passengers) on a RIB (rigid inflatable boat). At speeds of more than 100kph, the harbour scenery is mostly a blur. **Harbour Jet**, also in Darling Harbour (☎1300 887 373, ⓦwww.harbourjet.com), run the 35-minute "Jet Blast" (Mon & Wed–Sun noon, 2pm & 4pm; A$65, child A$45) on a boat that roars along at 75kph, accompanied by top-volume music.

housed on the first three floors, whilst on the top floor there's a glamorous contemporary brasserie, *Cafe Sydney* (see p.280), with Harbour Bridge views.

Museum of Contemporary Art (MCA)

The **Museum of Contemporary Art** (**MCA**; daily 10am–5pm; free, except for special exhibitions; free tours Mon–Fri 11am & 1pm, Sat & Sun noon & 1.30pm; ⓣ02 9252 2400 for details of special exhibitions and events, ⓦwww.mca .com.au), on the western side of Circular Quay with another entrance on George Street (no. 140), was developed out of a bequest by the art collector John Power in the 1940s to Sydney University to purchase international contemporary art. The growing collection finally found a permanent home in 1991 in the former Maritime Services Building, provided for peppercorn rent by the State Government. The striking Deco-style 1950s building is now dedicated to international twentieth-century art, with an eclectic approach encompassing lithographs, sculpture, film, video, drawings, paintings and Aboriginal art, shown in themed temporary exhibitions. The museum's superbly sited, if expensive, café has outdoor tables overlooking the waterfront and Opera House.

Sydney Opera House

The **Sydney Opera House**, such an icon of Australiana that it almost seems kitsch, is just a short stroll from Circular Quay, by the water's edge on **Bennelong Point**. "Opera House" is actually a misnomer: it's really a performing-arts centre, one of the busiest in the world, with five performance venues inside its shells, plus restaurants, cafés and bars, a stash of upmarket souvenir shops on the lower concourse, and an amphitheatre-like outdoor area. The building, World Heritage listed in 2007, is best seen in profile, when its high white roofs, at the same time evocative of full sails and white shells, give it an almost ethereal quality. Some say the inspiration for the distinctive design came from the simple peeling of an orange into segments, though perhaps Danish architect **Jørn Utzon**'s childhood as the son of a yacht designer had something to do with their sail-like shape – he certainly envisaged a building that would appear to "float" on water. Despite its familiarity, or perhaps precisely because you already feel you know it so well, it's quite breathtaking at first sight. Close up, you can see that the shimmering effect is created by thousands of white tiles.

The feat of structural engineering required to bring to life Utzon's "sculpture", which he compared to a Gothic church as well as to a Mayan temple, made the final price tag A$102 million, more than ten times original estimates. Utzon's design – the winner, in 1957, of the architectural competition that launched the project – incorporated features that were way beyond the technological capabilities of the era. Now almost universally loved and admired, it's hard to believe quite how much controversy surrounded the building in its long haul from conception to completion, a sixteen-year process so plagued by quarrels and scandal that Utzon was forced to resign in 1966 with the building unfinished. Some say he was hounded out of the country by politicians – the newly elected Askin government disagreeing over his plans for the completion of the interior – and xenophobic local architects. Seven years and three Australian architects later the interior was finished, but it never matched Utzon's vision: the focal Concert Hall, for instance, was designed by **Peter Hall** and his team.

In 1999, Utzon was invited to resurrect his active involvement in the building by drawing up a permanent design reference for its conservation and development. Utzon, who has likened the Opera House to "a musical instrument", which "like any fine instrument, needs a little maintenance and fine tuning,

▲ Sydney Opera House

from time to time", went on to act as creative consultant on the refurbishment of one of its rooms, a reception hall, renamed the **Utzon Room** in his honour when it opened to much acclaim in mid-2004. It's hung with a piece of his own artwork, a fourteen-metre tapestry inspired by Bach's *Hamburg Symphonies* and a painting by Raphael, *Procession to Calvary*. He followed this with a colonnade along the western facade, completed in 2006; its design created new windows in the Playhouse and Studio foyer walls, offering panoramic views in keeping with Utzon's guiding desire to have the building embrace its harbour setting. His next project will tackle the western foyers. Opera House CEO Richard Evans is now charged with raising A$700m from government and private funds for further developments and renovations to correct fundamental flaws in the acoustics and arrangement of some of the performance spaces, possibly caused by Utzon's long, enforced absence from the design process.

The building's initial purpose was to provide a home for the Sydney Symphony Orchestra: it was designed with the huge **Concert Hall**, seating 2690, as the focal point. The smaller **Opera Theatre** (1547 seats) is the usual performance base for Opera Australia (seasons Feb–March & June–Nov) and the Australian Ballet (mid-March to May & Nov–Dec); this space may soon close for lengthy renovations. There are three theatrical venues: the **Drama Theatre**, used primarily by the Sydney Theatre Company; The Playhouse, used by travelling performers; and the more intimate **The Studio**. There's plenty of action outside the Opera House, too, with the use of the Mayan temple-inspired **Forecourt** and Monumental Steps as an amphitheatre for free and ticketed concerts – rock, jazz and classical, with a capacity for around five thousand people. Sunday is also a lively day on the forecourt, when the **Tarpeian Markets** (10am–4pm), with an emphasis on Australian crafts, are held.

If you're not content with gazing at the outside, you can join a **guided tour**; a dedicated desk in the foyer handles bookings (℡02 9250 7250, Ⓦwww .sydneyoperahouse.com; discounted rates available online). The Front of House tour gives an overview of the site, looking at the public areas and discussing the unique architecture (daily 9am–5pm; every 30min; 1hr; A$32, child A$23), while early morning backstage tours include access to the scenery docks, rehearsal rooms, technical areas and breakfast in the Green Room (daily 7am; 2hr; A$150). These tours also visit the foyer of The Playhouse where two original Utzon models of the Opera House are displayed, alongside a series of small oil paintings depicting the life of **Bennelong**, the Iora tribesman who was initially kidnapped as little more than an Aboriginal "specimen" but later became a much-loved addition to Governor Arthurs Phillip's household; Phillip later built a hut for him on what is now the site of the Opera House.

The best way to appreciate the Opera House, of course, is to attend an evening **performance**: the building is particularly stunning when floodlit and, once you're inside, the huge windows come into their own as the dark harbour waters reflect a shimmering night-time city – interval drinks certainly aren't like this anywhere else in the world. You could choose to **eat** at what is considered to be one of Sydney's best restaurants, *Guillaume at Bennelong* (see p.281) overlooking the city skyline, or take a **drink** at the *Opera Bar* on the lower concourse with outside tables and an affordable all-day menu (see p.291), plus there's a sidewalk café, a bistro and several theatre bars. The box office offers good-value **packages**, which include tours, meals, drinks and performances.

The Harbour Bridge

The charismatic **Harbour Bridge**, northeast of Circular Quay, has straddled the channel dividing North and South Sydney since 1932; today, it makes the view from Circular Quay complete. The largest arch bridge in the world when it was built, its construction costs weren't paid off until 1988. There's still a toll (A$3) to drive across, payable only when heading south; you can walk or cycle it for free. Pedestrians should head up the steps to the bridge from Cumberland Street, opposite the *Glenmore Hotel* in The Rocks, and walk along the eastern side for fabulous views of the harbour and Opera House (cyclists keep to the western side).

The bridge demands full-time maintenance, protected from rust by continuous painting in trademark steel-grey. Comedian Paul Hogan, of *Crocodile Dundee* fame, worked as a rigger on "the coathanger" before being rescued by a New Faces talent quest in the 1970s. To check out the vista he would have had, you can climb the bridge with **Bridge Climb**, who take specially equipped groups (max 12) to the top of the bridge from sunrise until after dark (min age 10 and 1.2 metres in height; twilight or dawn: A$249–295, child A$189–195; other times: Mon–Fri A$179, child A$109, Sat & Sun A$199, child A$129; ☎02 8274 7777, ⓦwww .bridgeclimb.com). An alternative to the classic route is the Discovery Climb, which takes you up via the suspension arch, through the bridge's inner structure. In each case, the experience takes three and a half hours, of which only two hours are spent on the bridge, gradually ascending and pausing while the guide points out landmarks and offers interesting background snippets. The hour spent checking in and getting kitted up at the "Base" at 5 Cumberland St, The Rocks, and the grey *Star Trek*-style suits designed to blend in with the bridge, make you feel as if you're preparing to go into outer space. It's really not as scary as it looks – harnessed into a cable system, there's no way you can fall off. So that nothing can be dropped onto cars or people below, cameras cannot be taken on the walk (only glasses are allowed, attached by special cords), limiting scope for one of the world's greatest photo opportunities. Though one group photo on top of the bridge is included in the climb price, the jolly strangers, arms akimbo, crowd out the background. To get a good shot showing yourself with the splendours of the harbour behind, taken by the guide, you'll need to fork out another A$16.

If you can't stomach (or afford) the climb, there's a **lookout point** (daily 10am–5pm; A$9.50, child A$4; ⓦwww.pylonlookout.com.au; 5min walk from

Cumberland St then 200 steps) actually inside the bridge's southeastern pylon where, as well as gazing out across the harbour, you can study a photo exhibition on the bridge's history.

The Rocks

The Rocks, immediately beneath the bridge, is the heart of historic Sydney. On this rocky outcrop between Sydney Cove and Walsh Bay, Captain Arthurs Phillip proclaimed the establishment of Sydney Town in 1788, the first permanent European settlement in Australia. Within decades, the area had degenerated into little more than a slum of dingy dwellings, narrow alleys and dubious taverns and brothels. In the 1830s and 1840s, merchants began building fine stone warehouses here, but as the focus for Sydney's shipping industry moved from Circular Quay, the area fell into decline. By the 1870s and 1880s, the notorious Rocks "pushes", gangs of "larrikins" (louts), mugged passers-by and brawled with each other: the narrow street named **Suez Canal** was a favourite place to hide in wait. Some say the name is a version of Sewers' Canal, and indeed the area was so filthy that whole streetfronts had to be torn down in 1900 to contain an outbreak of the bubonic plague. It remained a run-down, depressed and depressing quarter until the 1970s, when there were plans to raze the historic cottages, terraces and warehouses to make way for office towers. However, due to the foresight of a radical building-workers' union which opposed the demolition, the restored and renovated **historic quarter** is now one of Sydney's major tourist attractions and, despite a passing resemblance to a historic theme park, it's worth exploring. It's also the best place for souvenir shopping, especially at weekends when **The Rocks Market** (10am–5pm) takes over the northern end of George and Playfair streets.

There are times, though, when the old atmosphere still seems to prevail: The Rocks has a hefty concentration of pubs, which pack out with after-work revellers on Friday nights; Saturday nights, too, can be thoroughly drunken, while on New Year's Eve it's a place for riotous celebrations to the backdrop of fireworks over the harbour. The best time to come for a drink is Sunday afternoon when many of the pubs here offer live jazz or folk music.

Information, tours and transport

The Rocks Discovery Museum on Kendall Lane (daily 10am–5pm; free; ⓣ1800 067 676, ⓦwww.rocksdiscoverymuseum.com.au) is a good starting point and offers background information and displays of its rich history, from the lives of the original Cadigal inhabitants to the 1970s protests that helped preserve the area from major redevelopment. The small museum is tucked away down Kendall Lane in a restored 1850s sandstone warehouse facing the Rocks Centre, a busy arcade of boutique shops and cafés. Above the arcade is the **Sydney Visitor Centre** (see p.215), where you can pick up *The Rocks Map*, essential material for finding your way around the meandering streets. Another great introduction to the area is the long-running **The Rocks Walking Tours**, starting from 23 Playfair St, Rocks Square (Mon–Fri 10.30am, 12.30pm & 2.30pm, Jan 10.30am & 2.30pm only, Sat & Sun 11.30am & 2pm; 1hr 30min; A$25, child A$11; ⓣ02 9247 6678, ⓦwww.rockswalkingtours.com.au). For online information about other local tours and happenings, visit ⓦwww.therocks.com.

The corner of Argyle and Kent streets, Millers Point, is a terminus for several useful **bus routes**; aim to head here through The Rocks and then catch a bus back: routes 431–434 go along George Street to Railway Square and from there to various locations including Glebe and Balmain, while route 339 goes to the eastern beaches suburb of Clovelly via George Street in the city and Surry Hills.

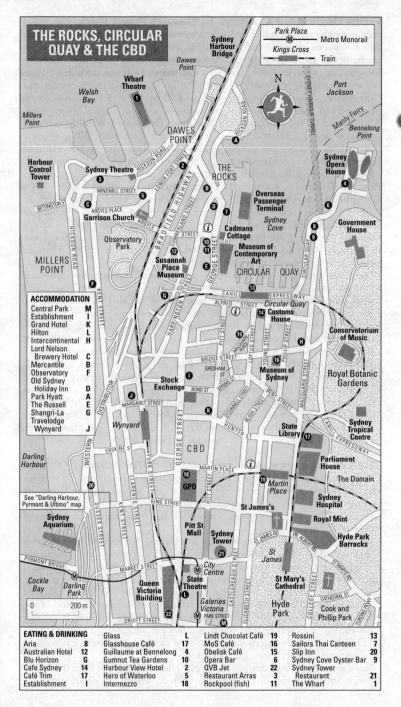

THE ROCKS, CIRCULAR QUAY & THE CBD

Park Plaza **Ⓜ** — Metro Monorail
Kings Cross ▬▬▬▬ — Train

4

SYDNEY

Sydney Harbour Bridge

Dawes Point

Port Jackson

Manly Ferry

Bennelong Point

Walsh Bay

Millers Point

Wharf Theatre ①

DAWES POINT

Sydney Opera House ④

Harbour Control Tower

Sydney Theatre ③

THE ROCKS

Overseas Passenger Terminal

Sydney Opera House

Government House

WINDMILL STREET ⑤

ⒷⒹ ⑦

Cadmans Cottage

Sydney Cove

Garrison Church Ⓒ

Observatory Park

ⓘ

Museum of Contemporary Art

MILLERS POINT

⑫ ⑩ ⑪

Susannah Place Museum Ⓔ

CIRCULAR QUAY ⑬

Ⓕ

Ⓖ CAHILL EXPRESSWAY

ALFRED STREET

Circular Quay

ⓘ

Customs House ⑭

Conservatorium of Music

BRIDGE STREET ⑮

Museum of Sydney ⑯

Royal Botanic Gardens

ACCOMMODATION

Central Park	M
Establishment	I
Grand Hotel	K
Hilton	L
Intercontinental	H
Lord Nelson Brewery Hotel	C
Mercantile	B
Observatory	F
Old Sydney Holiday Inn	D
Park Hyatt	A
The Russell	E
Shangri-La	G
Travelodge	J
Wynyard	

Stock Exchange Ⓘ

Ⓙ

Ⓚ

Wynyard

CBD

State Library ⑰

Sydney Tropical Centre

Parliament House

The Domain

Darling Harbour

Ⓜ

⑳

See "Darling Harbour, Pyrmont & Ultimo" map

MARTIN PLACE

GPO ⑱

ⓘ

⑲ Martin Place

Sydney Hospital

Royal Mint

Sydney Aquarium

St James's

Pitt St Mall

Sydney Tower ㉑

St James

Hyde Park Barracks

Cockle Bay

Darling Park Ⓜ

MARKET STREET

Queen Victoria Building

State Theatre Ⓛ

City Centre Ⓜ

St Mary's Cathedral

Hyde Park

Cook and Phillip Park

Galeries Victoria Ⓜ

㉒ QVB Jet

DRUITT STREET

0 ——— 200 m

N

Port Jackson

EATING & DRINKING

Aria	8	Glass	L	Lindt Chocolat Café	19	Rossini	13
Australian Hotel	12	Glasshouse Café	17	MoS Café	16	Sailors Thai Canteen	7
Blu Horizon	G	Guillaume at Bennelong	4	Obelisk Café	15	Slip Inn	20
Cafe Sydney	14	Gumnut Tea Gardens	10	Opera Bar	6	Sydney Cove Oyster Bar	9
Café Trim	17	Harbour View Hotel	2	QVB Jet	22	Sydney Tower Restaurant	21
Establishment	I	Hero of Waterloo	5	Restaurant Arras	3	The Wharf	1
		Intermezzo	18	Rockpool (fish)	11		

From Cadman's Cottage to Dawes Point Park

Exploring the narrow alleys and streets hewn out of the original rocky spur, which involves climbing and descending several stairs and cuts to different levels, is the area's chief delight. Across George Street from the Discovery Museum, in a small tree-filled reserve, is **Cadman's Cottage**, the oldest private house still standing in Sydney, built in 1816 for John Cadman, ex-convict and Government coxswain (Mon–Fri 9.30am–4.30pm, Sat & Sun 10am–4.30pm; free). You can poke around a few rooms to see how the original settlers lived. Also housed in the cottage is the **National Parks and Wildlife Service** bookshop and information centre (same hours; ☎02 9247 5033, ⓦwww .nationalparks.nsw.gov.au), providing information about the Sydney Harbour National Park and bookings for trips to some of its islands.

From the cottage, head north along the waterfront walkway past the Overseas Passenger Terminal to **Campbell's Cove**, where the beautifully restored 1830s **Campbell's Storehouses**, once part of the private wharf of the merchant Robert Campbell, now house a shopping and eating complex. A replica of Captain Bligh's ship, the *Bounty*, is moored here between cruises, while a luxury hotel, the *Park Hyatt*, overlooks the whole area. The walkway continues adjacent to Hickson Road to **Dawes Point Park**, which sits beneath the Harbour Bridge offering fantastic views, particularly at sunset.

Looking out past the Opera House, you can see **Fort Denison** on a small island in the harbour: "Pinchgut", as the island is still known, was originally used as a special prison for the tough nuts the penal colony couldn't crack. During the Crimean Wars in the mid-nineteenth century, however, old fears of a Russian invasion were rekindled and the fort was built as part of a defence ring around the harbour. The island is one of the stops on the *Rocket Explorer* hop-on-hop-off cruise run by Matilda (see p.232); to disembark, there's a park entry fee of A\$7 (child A\$5). Matilda also run a direct island ferry (A\$17 return, child A\$10 including park fee) from Darling Harbour Pier 26 (9.30am–4pm; every 45min) or Circular Quay Jetty 6 (9.45am–4.15pm; every 45min). Once on the island, you can join a half-hour tour of its Martello tower with a knowledgeable NPWS guide (Mon & Tues 12.15pm & 2.30pm, Wed–Sun 10.45am, 12.15pm & 2.30pm; A\$10); this can be booked in advance with your ferry ticket, or on the spot if there's space. The island's pleasant café is a scenic spot for brunch or lunch.

The old wharves, Millers Point and Observatory Park

On the west side of Dawes Point Park, Hickson Road passes several old wharves and the **Wharf Theatre** (see p.299), home to the Sydney Theatre Company and the Sydney Dance Company. From the restaurant and its bar (see p.281) you can revel in the sublime view across Walsh Bay to Balmain, Goat Island and the North Shore.

Beyond the wharves, looking west towards Darling Harbour, **Millers Point** is a reminder of how The Rocks used to be – with a surprisingly real community feel so close to the tourist hype of The Rocks, as much of the housing is government- or housing association-owned. The area has its upmarket pockets, but for the moment the traditional street-corner pubs and shabby terraced houses on the hill are reminiscent of the raffish atmosphere once typical of the whole area, and the mostly peaceful residential streets are a delight to wander through. This atmosphere is set to change, however, as the old container docks on Darling Harbour's eastern shore have been cleared, ready for redevelopment as waterfront commercial and residential space.

You can reach the area through the Argyle Cut (see p.239) or from the end of George Street, heading onto Lower Fort Street, where you could stop for a drink at the **Hero of Waterloo** at no. 81 (see p.291), built from sandstone excavated from the Argyle Cut in 1844, before peeking in at the **Garrison Church** (daily 9am–5pm) on the corner of Argyle Street, the place of worship for the military stationed at Dawes Point fort (the fort was demolished in the 1920s to make way for the Harbour Bridge) from the 1840s. Beside the church, **Argyle Place** has some of the area's prettiest old terraced houses.

From here, walk up the steps on Argyle Street opposite the church to **Observatory Park** with its shady Moreton Bay figs, park benches and lawns, for a marvellous hilltop view over the whole harbour in all its different aspects – glitzy Darling Harbour and the newer Anzac Bridge in one direction and the older Harbour Bridge, with gritty container terminals, and ferries gliding by, in the other; on a rainy day, you can enjoy it from the bandstand that dominates the park. It's also easy to reach the park from the **Bridge Stairs** off Cumberland Street by the Argyle Cut.

The Italianate-style **Sydney Observatory** from which the park takes its name marked the beginning of an accurate time standard for the city when it opened in 1858, calculating the correct time from the stars and signalling it to Martin Place's GPO and the ships in the harbour by the dropping of a time ball in its tower at 1pm every day – a custom that still continues. Set amongst some very pretty gardens, the building also houses a **museum of astronomy** (daily 10am–5pm; free; ⓣ02 9241 3767, ⓦwww.sydneyobservatory.com.au). A large section is devoted to the Transit of Venus, a rare astronomical event occurring about twice every century; it was the observation of this that prompted Captain Cook's 1769 voyage. The extensive exhibition of astronomical equipment, both obsolete and high-tech, includes the (still-working) telescope installed under the copper dome to observe the 1874 Transit of Venus. Another highlight, in the "Stars of the Southern Sky" section, are three animated videos of Aboriginal creation stories, retellings of how the stars came to be, from the Milky Way to Orion. If you join an evening tour (1hr 45min; daily: Jan & Dec 8.30pm; Feb, March, Oct & Nov 8.15pm; April–Sept 6.15pm & 8.15pm; A$15, child A$10; booking required), you can view the sky through telescopes and learn about the Southern Cross and other southern constellations from an experienced astronomer; there's also a small planetarium, used when the sky is not clear enough for observation.

Argyle Cut and Gloucester Street

From the Observatory, head back to Argyle Street and walk under Bradfield Highway to the **Argyle Cut**, which slices through solid stone connecting Millers Point and Circular Quay. The cut took sixteen years to complete, carved first with chisel and hammer by convict chain-gangs who began the work in 1843; when transportation ended ten years later the tunnel was still unfinished, and it took hired hands to complete it in 1859.

Once you've passed through the cut, look out for the **Argyle Steps**, which lead back up to Cumberland Street. The Harbour Bridge is accessible by foot from here via the pylon staircase or you can sit back and enjoy the splendid views from a couple of fine old boozers, the *Glenmore* and the *Australian*. From the latter, head down **Gloucester Street**; at nos. 58–64 is the **Susannah Place Museum** (Sat & Sun 10am–5pm; school holidays daily 10am–5pm; A$8, child A$4; ⓦwww.hht.net.au), a row of four brick terraces built in 1844 and occupied by householders until 1990. It's now a "house museum" (including a re-created 1915 corner store), which conserves the domestic history of Sydney's working class. There's a fascinating archeological site seen as you exit the museum, which has been in excavation since 1994. The earliest buildings date back to 1795 and the site has revealed over three quarters of a million artefacts – the steps, paths and walls that the early colonizers carved out from the rock are clearly visible.

The Central Business District and Haymarket

From Circular Quay south as far as King Street is Sydney's **CBD** (Central Business District) with **Martin Place** its commercial nerve-centre. A pedestrian mall stretching from George Street to Macquarie Street, lined with imposing banks and investment companies, Martin Place has its less serious moments at summer lunchtimes, when street performances are held at the little amphitheatre, and all-year-round stalls of flower- and fruit-sellers add some colour. The vast **General Post Office (GPO)**, built between 1865 and 1887 with its landmark clock tower added in 1900, broods over the George Street end in all its Victorian-era pomp. The ground and lower ground floors – including the old sorting room and the stables for the mail-delivery horses – have been converted into swish restaurants and bars frequented by city suits, while the upper floors comprise part of a five-star luxury hotel, the *Westin Sydney*, the rest of which resides in the 31-storey tower behind. The old building and the new tower meet in the grand Atrium Courtyard, on the lower ground floor, with its restaurants, bars, classy designer stores, and the **GPO Store**, a gastronome's delight featuring a butchers', fish shop, deli, cheese room, wine merchant and greengrocer. The other end of Martin Place emerges opposite the old civic buildings on lower Macquarie Street. The cramped streets of the CBD itself, overshadowed by office buildings, have little to offer as you stroll through, though a crowd often gathers outside the **Australian Stock Exchange**, opposite Australia Square at 20 Bond St, to gaze at the computerized display of stocks and shares through the glass of the ground floor.

Museum of Sydney

North of Martin Place, on the corner of Bridge and Phillip streets, stands the **Museum of Sydney** (daily 9.30am–5pm; A$10, child A$5; ☎02 9251 5988, ⓦwww.hht.net.au). The site itself is the reason for the museum's existence, for here from 1983 a ten-year archeological dig unearthed the foundations of the first Government House built by Governor Phillip in 1788, which was home to eight subsequent governors of New South Wales before being demolished in 1846. The museum is totally original in its approach, presenting history in an interactive manner, through exhibitions, film, photography and multimedia. A key feature of the museum are the special exhibitions – about four each year – so it's worth finding out what's on before you go.

First Government Place, a public square in front of the museum, preserves the site of the original Government House: its foundations are marked out in different-coloured sandstone on the pavement. The site is best appreciated from the glass lookout on level 3 of the museum, which is also the logical place to start your tour. From up high, you'll notice 29 erect poles near the entrance, **The Edge of the Trees**, an emotive sculptural installation that attempts to convey the complexity of a shared history that began in 1788. Each pole represents one of the original 29 clans that lived in the greater Sydney area, and you can't help but notice the symbolism of the poles, standing quietly to one side, overlooking the comings and goings of Government House. Beside the glass lookout on level 3 is a small but evocative gallery with Aboriginal artefacts, early European writings about their encounters, and a fascinating contemporary video by Aboriginal filmmaker Michael Riley reflecting the clans' own perspective of colonization.

Sydney Sculpture Walk

The specially commissioned artworks of the **Sydney Sculpture Walk** – a City of Sydney Council initiative for the 2000 Olympics and the 2001 Centenary of Federation – form a circuit from the Royal Botanic Gardens, through The Domain, Cook and Phillip Park, the streets of the CBD, Hyde Park and East Circular Quay. One of the most striking of the ten site-specific pieces is Anne Graham's *Passage*, at the eastern end of Martin Place. At timed intervals, a fine mist emerges from grilles marking the outlines of an early colonial home that once stood here, creating a ghostly house on still days. A map showing the sculpture sites is available from Sydney Town Hall (p.242) or the City Exhibition Space (p.231), or there are details at ⓦwww .cityofsydney.nsw.gov.au.

On the same level, a large area is devoted to some rather wonderful **panoramas** highlighting Sydney's evolution into a city. At the dark and creepy **Bond Store** on level 2, holographic "ghosts" relate tales of old Sydney as an ocean port.

There's also an excellent **gift shop** with a wide range of photos, artworks and books on Sydney and the upmarket *MoS Café* (see p.282) on First Government Place.

Sydney Architecture Walks offers various **walking tours**, led by young architects, leaving from here every Wednesday and Saturday at 10.30am (2hr; A\$25, child A\$20, including MoS admission; ⓣ02 8239 2211, ⓦwww .sydneyarchitecture.org).

King Street to Liverpool Street

Further south from Martin Place, the streets get a little more interesting. The rectangle between Elizabeth, King, George and Park streets is Sydney's prime shopping area, with a number of beautifully restored **Victorian arcades** (the Imperial Arcade, Strand Arcade and Queen Victoria Building are all worth a look) and Sydney's two **department stores**, the very upmarket David Jones on the corner of Market and Elizabeth streets, established over 160 years ago, and Myers on Pitt Street Mall.

The landmark **Sydney Tower**, or "Centrepoint" as it is still known to the locals, on Market Street, a giant golden gearstick thrusting up 305m, is the tallest poppy in the Sydney skyline. The 360-degree view from the top is especially fine at sunset, and on clear days you can even see the Blue Mountains, 100km away. Admission to the glass-fronted top-floor Observation Deck (daily 9am–10.30pm, Sat until 11.30pm; A\$24.50, child A\$14.50; ⓣ02 9333 9200, ⓦwww .sydneytoweroztrek.com.au) also allows you to experience OzTrek, a tacky forty-minute virtual-reality show offering a clichéd whirl around Australia. For an extra A\$40 (child A\$30), you can try out the **Skywalk** (daily 9.30am–8.45pm; every 45min; 45min; ⓣ02 9333 9200, ⓦwww.sydneyskywalk.com.au), a tamer but higher version of the Harbour Bridge climb, where you venture out to two glass-floored platforms, 260m up, harnessed to external walkways. Unfortunately, cameras are not permitted for safety reasons. Alternatively, you can see almost the same view, without the crowds and the entry ticket, at the revolving *Sydney Tower Restaurant* (see p.282) below the observation level; it takes about seventy minutes to turn full circle, and all the tables are by the windows.

Nearby, several fine old buildings – the State Theatre, the Queen Victoria Building and the Town Hall – provide a pointed contrast. If heaven has a hallway, it surely must resemble that of the restored **State Theatre**, just across from the Pitt Street Mall at 49 Market St. Step inside and take a look at the ornate and glorious interior of this picture palace opened in 1929 – a lavishly painted, gilded and sculpted corridor leads to the lush, red and wood-panelled foyer. To see more of the interior, you'll need to attend the Sydney Film Festival (see p.301) or other events held here, such as concerts and drama, or you can take a guided tour (monthly 10.30am; 1hr 30 min; A$15; ☎02 9373 6862). Otherwise, pop into the beautiful little *Retro Cafe*, adjacent, for a coffee.

The stately **Queen Victoria Building** (abbreviated by locals to the QVB), taking up the block bounded by Market, Druitt, George and York streets, is another of Sydney's finest. Stern and matronly, a huge statue of Queen Victoria herself sits outside the magnificent building. Built as a market hall in 1898, two years before her death, the long-neglected building was beautifully restored and reborn in 1986 as an upmarket shopping mall with a focus on fashion: from the basement up, the four levels become progressively exclusive (shopping hours Mon–Sat 9am–6pm, Thurs until 9pm, Sun 11am–5pm; building open 24hr). The interior is magnificent, with its beautiful woodwork, gallery levels and antique lifts; Charles I is beheaded on the hour, every hour, by figurines on the ground-floor mechanical clock. From Town Hall station you can walk right through the basement level (mainly bustling food stalls) and continue via Sydney Central Plaza to Myers Department Store, emerging on Pitt Street without having to go outside.

In the realm of architectural excess, however, the **Town Hall** is king – you'll find it across from the QVB on the corner of George and Druitt streets. It was built during the boom years of the 1870s and 1880s as a homage to Victorian England; the huge organ inside its Centennial Hall gives it the air of a secular cathedral. Throughout the interior, different styles of ornamentation compete in a riot of colour and detail; the splendidly dignified toilets are a must-see. Concerts and theatre performances (see p.298) set off the splendiferous interior perfectly.

Haymarket and Chinatown

Between Town Hall and Central Station, **George Street** becomes a more downmarket jumble of clothing shops, discount stores and backpacker travel bureaus. Along the way you'll pass Chinatown, in the area known as **Haymarket**, while a little further west is Darling Harbour (see p.248). The short stretch between the Town Hall and Liverpool Street is for the most part teenage territory, a frenetic zone of **multiscreen cinemas**, pinball halls and fast-food joints, though the **Metro Theatre** is one of Sydney's best live-music venues (see p.295) and *Planet Hollywood* also attracts a keen stream of youngsters and tourists alike. The stretch is trouble-prone on Friday and Saturday nights when there are pleasanter places to catch a film (see cinema listings, p.299). Things change pace at Liverpool Street, where Sydney's **Spanish Corner** consists of a clutch of Spanish restaurants and a cultural centre and venue, the *Spanish Club* (Ⓦwww .spanishclub.com.au).

Sydney's **Chinatown** is a more full-blooded affair than Spanish Corner and probably the most active of the ethnic enclaves in the city. Through the ornate Chinese gates, **Dixon Street** is the main drag, buzzing day and night as people crowd into numerous restaurants, pubs, cafés, cinemas, food stalls and Asian grocery stores. Towards the end of January or in the first weeks of February, Chinese New Year is celebrated here with gusto: traditional dragon and lion dances, food festivals and musical entertainment compete with the noise and smoke from strings of Chinese crackers. Friday nights are also a good time to visit, when a **night market** takes over Dixon and Little Hay streets (6–11pm). A calmer retreat, on the edge of Chinatown, at the southern fringes of Darling Harbour, is the serene **Chinese Garden** (see p.250).

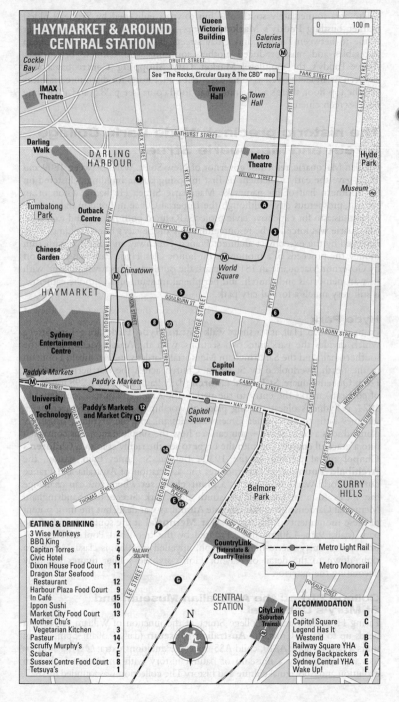

HAYMARKET & AROUND
CENTRAL STATION

Queen Victoria Building

Galeries Victoria

0   100 m

Cockle Bay

DRUITT STREET

PARK STREET

See "The Rocks, Circular Quay & The CBD" map

IMAX Theatre

Town Hall

Town Hall

BATHURST STREET

Darling Walk

DARLING HARBOUR

Metro Theatre

Hyde Park

WILMOT STREET

Museum

SUSSEX STREET

KENT STREET

A

Tumbalong Park

Outback Centre

LIVERPOOL STREET

1

2

3

HARBOUR STREET

4

Chinese Garden

World Square

M

Chinatown

M

HAYMARKET

GOULBURN ST

5

DIXON STREET

GEORGE STREET

PITT STREET

6

Sydney Entertainment Centre

9

8 **10**

7

GOULBURN STREET

SUSSEX STREET

B

11

Capitol Theatre

C

CAMPBELL STREET

CASTLEREAGH STREET

WENTWORTH AVENUE

Paddy's Markets

M HAY STREET

Paddy's Markets

HAY STREET

University of Technology

Paddy's Markets and Market City

12

13

Capitol Square

D

ELIZABETH STREET

FOSTER STREET

SURRY HILLS

DARLING DRIVE

QUAY STREET

ALBION STREET

ULTIMO ROAD

14

GEORGE STREET

PITT STREET

THOMAS STREET

RAWSON PLACE

Belmore Park

E **15**

F

EDDY AVENUE

RAILWAY SQUARE

CountryLink (Interstate & Country Trains)

FOVEAUX STREET

Metro Light Rail

M Metro Monorail

LEE STREET

G

CENTRAL STATION

CityLink (Suburban Trains)

N

The area immediately south of Chinatown is enlivened by Sydney's oldest market, bustling **Paddy's Markets** (Thurs–Sun 9am–5pm), in its undercover home in between Thomas and Quay streets. It's a good place to buy cheap vegetables and mass-produced clothes, souvenirs, and Chinese bric-a-brac. Above Paddy's, the multilevel **Market City Shopping Centre** has a very modern Asian feel as well as some excellent outlet stores for discounted fashion. On the top floor, there's a first-rate Asian food court (see p.282) and a Reading multi-screen cinema.

The historic precinct: Hyde Park, College Street and Macquarie Street

Lachlan Macquarie, reformist governor of New South Wales between 1809 and 1821, gave the early settlement its first imposing public buildings, clustered on the southern half of his namesake Macquarie Street. He had a vision of an elegant, prosperous city – although the Imperial Office in London didn't share his enthusiasm for expensive civic projects. Refused both money and expertise, Macquarie was forced to be resourceful: many of the city's finest buildings were designed by the ex-convict architect Francis Greenway and paid for with rum money, the proceeds of a monopoly on liquor sales. Hyde Park was fenced off by Governor Macquarie in 1810 to mark the outskirts of his township, and with its war memorials and church, and peripheral museum and Catholic cathedral, is still very much a formal city park.

Hyde Park

From the Town Hall, it's a short walk east to **Hyde Park** along Park Street, which divides the park into two sections, with the Anzac Memorial in the southern half, and the Sandringham Memorial Gardens and Archibald Fountain in the north, overlooked by St James' Church across the northern boundary. From Queens Square, **St James' Church** (daily 9am–5pm; see p.298 for details of concerts) marks the entry to the park – the Anglican church, completed in 1824, is Sydney's oldest existing place of worship. It was one of Macquarie's schemes built to ex-convict Greenway's design, and the architect originally planned it as a courthouse – you can see how the simple design was converted into a graceful church. Pop into the crypt to see the richly coloured **Children's Chapel** mural painted in the 1930s. Behind St James train station, the **Archibald Fountain** commemorates the association of Australia and France during World War I; near here is a **giant chess set** where you can challenge the locals to a match. Further south near Park Street, the Sandringham Memorial Gardens also commemorate Australia's war dead, but the most potent of these monuments is the **Anzac War Memorial** at the southern end of the park (daily 9am–4.30pm; free). Fronted by the tree-lined Pool of Remembrance, the thirty-metre-high cenotaph, unveiled in 1934, is classic Art Deco right down to the detail of Raynor Hoff's stylized soldier figures solemnly decorating the exterior.

College Street: the Australian Museum and St Mary's Cathedral

Facing Hyde Park across College Street, at the junction of William Street as it heads up to Kings Cross, the **Australian Museum** (daily 9.30am–5pm; 45min tours 11am & 2pm; A$10, child A$5, special exhibitions extra; Ⓦ www.austmus .gov.au) is primarily a museum of natural history, with an interest in human evolution and Aboriginal culture and history. The collection was founded in 1827, but the actual building, a grand sandstone affair with a facade of Corinthian pillars, wasn't fully finished until the 1860s and was extended in the 1980s. The core of the old museum is the three levels of the **Long Gallery**, Australia's first exhibition gallery, opened in 1855 to a public keen to gawk at the colony's curiosities. Many of the classic displays of the following hundred years remain here, Heritage-listed, contrasting with a very modern approach in the rest of the museum.

On the **ground floor**, the impressive **Indigenous Australian** exhibition looks at the history of Australia's Aboriginal people from the Dreamtime to more contemporary issues of the "stolen generation" and the freedom rides, a series of protests that took place in 1965 by a bus full of protesters travelling around rural NSW towns highlighting the racial discrimination experienced by Aboriginal people. The ground-floor level houses the **Skeletons** exhibit, where you can see a skeletal human going through the motions of riding a bicycle, for example. Level 1 is devoted to **minerals**, but far more exciting are the disparate collections on level 2 – especially the **Birds** and **Insects** exhibit, which includes chilling contextual displays of dangerous spiders such as redbacks and funnel-webs. In the newer section, **Search and Discover** is aimed at both adults and children, a flora and fauna identification centre with Internet access and books to consult, while the **Human Evolution** gallery traces the development of fossil evidence worldwide and ends with an exploration of archeological evidence of Aboriginal occupation of Australia. A separate section, **More Than Dinosaurs**, deals with fossil skeletons of dinosaurs and giant marsupials: best of all is the model of the largest of Australia's megafauna, the wombat-like Diprotodon, which may have roamed the mainland as recently as ten thousand years ago.

On College Street is Catholic **St Mary's Cathedral** (daily 6.30am–7.30pm, Sat 8am–6.30pm; free 1hr tours Sun noon), overlooking the northeast corner of Hyde Park. The huge Gothic-style church opened in 1882, though the foundation stone was laid in 1821. In 1999, the cathedral at last gained the twin stone spires originally planned for the two southern towers by architect William Wardell in 1865. Under the cathedral's impressive forecourt – a pedestrianized terrace with fountains and pools – is the car park for the adjacent **Cook and Phillip Park recreation centre** (Mon–Fri 6am–10pm, Sat & Sun 7am–8pm; A$6, child A$4.40; ☎02 9326 0444), an indoor complex with a fifty-metre swimming pool, gym and an excellent café.

Macquarie Street

Macquarie Street neatly divides business from pleasure, separating the office towers and cramped streets of the CBD from the open spaces of The Domain. The southern end of Governor Macquarie's namesake street is lined with the grand edifices that were the result of his dreams for a stately city: Hyde Park Barracks, Parliament House, the State Library, and the hospital he and his wife designed. The new Sydney – wealthy and international – shows itself on the corner of Bent and Macquarie streets in the curved glass sails of the 41-floor Aurora Place tower, designed by Italian architect Renzo Piano, co-creator of the extraordinary Georges Pompidou Centre in Paris.

At the southern end of the street, bordering Hyde Park, the **Hyde Park Barracks**, designed as convict lodgings by ex-convict Francis Greenway, was built in 1816, again without permission from London, to house six hundred male convicts. Now a museum of the social and architectural history of Sydney (daily 9.30am–5pm; A$10, child A$5; ☎02 8239 2311, ⓦwww.hht.net.au), it's a great place to visit for a taste of convict life during the early years of the colony: start at the top floor, where you can swing in recreations of the prisoners' rough hammocks. Computer terminals allow you to search for information on a selection of convicts' history and background – several of those logged were American sailors nabbed for misdeeds while in Dublin or English ports (look up poor William Pink). After the Barracks closed in 1848, the building was used to house single immigrant women, many of them Irish, escaping the potato famine; an exhibition looks at their lives, and there's a moving monument in the grounds erected by the local Irish community. Look out, too, for the excellent temporary historical exhibitions.

Next door, sandstone **Sydney Hospital**, the so-called "Rum Hospital", funded by liquor-trade profits, was Macquarie's first enterprise, commissioned in 1814 and therefore one of the oldest buildings in Australia. From here it's a short walk through the grounds to The Domain and across to the Art Gallery of New South Wales (see p.247).

One of the original wings of the hospital is now **NSW Parliament House** (Mon–Fri 9am–5pm; ℡02 9230 2111, ⓦ www.parliament.nsw.gov.au), where as early as 1829 local councils called by the governor started to meet, making it by some way the oldest parliament building in Australia. Changing exhibitions in the foyer represent community or public-sector interests and range from painting, craft and sculpture to excellent photographic displays. On Tuesdays, when parliament is sitting, you can join a conducted **tour** (1.30pm; free, booking required) and listen in on Question Time afterwards; on non-sitting days, there are six tours of the house per day.

The other hospital wing was converted into a branch of the **Royal Mint** in response to the first Australian goldrush, and for some time served as a museum of gold mining; most of the building has now been taken over by NSW Historic Houses Trust offices, but a café (Mon–Fri 9am–4pm) extends onto the balcony overlooking Macquarie Street, and some interpretive boards detail the Mint's history.

The **State Library of New South Wales** (Mon–Thurs 9am–8pm, Fri 9am–5pm, Sat & Sun 10am–5pm, Mitchell Library closed Sun; free guided tours Tues 11am & Thurs 2pm, ℡02 9273 1414, ⓦ www.sl.nsw.gov.au) completes the row of public buildings on the eastern side of Macquarie Street. This complex of old and new edifices includes the 1906 sandstone **Mitchell Library**, with an imposing Neoclassical facade gazing across to the verdant Royal Botanic Gardens. Its archive of old maps, illustrations and records relating to the early days of white settlement and exploration in Australia includes the original **Tasman Map**, drawn by the Dutch explorer Abel Tasman in the 1640s. The floor-mosaic in the foyer replicates his curious map of the continent, still without an east coast, and its northern extremity joined to Papua New Guinea. A glass walkway links the library with the modern building housing the General Reference Library. Free exhibitions relating to Australian history, art, photography and literature are a common feature of its vestibules, while lectures, films and video shows take place regularly in the **Metcalfe Auditorium**, which holds free and ticketed events. The library has two excellent **cafés** (see p.281); it's also worth browsing through the impressive collection of Australia-related material in the ground-floor **bookshop**.

The Domain and the Royal Botanic Gardens

Northeast of Hyde Park is **The Domain**, a much larger, plainer open space that stretches from behind the historic precinct on Macquarie Street to the waterfront, divided from the Botanic Gardens by the ugly Cahill Expressway and Mrs Macquarie's Road. In the early days of the settlement, The Domain was the governor's private park; now it's a popular place for a stroll or a picnic, with the Art Gallery of New South Wales, an outdoor swimming pool and Mrs Macquarie's Chair to provide distraction. On Sundays, assorted cranks and revolutionaries assemble here for Speakers' Corner, and every January thousands of people gather on the lawns to enjoy the free open-air concerts of the Sydney Festival (see box, p.212).

Art Gallery of New South Wales

North of St Mary's Cathedral, Art Gallery Road runs through The Domain to the **Art Gallery of New South Wales** (daily 10am–5pm, Wed till 9pm; free except for special exhibitions; free tours Tues–Sun 11am, 1pm & 2pm, Mon 1pm & 2pm; ⊕02 9225 1744, Ⓦwww.artgallery.nsw.gov.au), whose collection was established in 1874. The original part of the building (1897) is an imposing Neoclassical structure with a facade inscribed with the names of important Renaissance artists, and principally contains the large collection of European art dating from the eleventh century to the twentieth; extensions were added in 1988, doubling the gallery space and providing a home for mainly Australian art. On lower level 3 is the **Yiribana Gallery**, devoted to the art and cultural artefacts of Aboriginal and Torres Strait Islanders; one of the most striking exhibits is the **Pukumani Grave Posts**, carved by the Tiwi people of Melville Island. There's also a highly recommended free one-hour tour of the indigenous collection (Tues–Sun 11am). Other highlights include some classic **Australian paintings** on level 4: Tom Roberts' romanticized shearing-shed scene *The Golden Fleece* (1894) and an altogether less idyllic look at rural Australia in Russell Drysdale's *Sofala* (1947), a depressing vision of a drought-stricken town. Works shortlisted for the Archibald Prize, Australia's biggest art competition, are on display from March to May.

In addition to the galleries, there's an auditorium used for art lectures, an excellent bookshop, a good café (Mon, Tues & Thurs–Sun 10am–4.30pm, Wed 10am–8.30pm) and upmarket restaurant (see p.285).

Mrs Macquarie's Chair and "The Boy"

Beyond the Art Gallery is the beginning of one of Sydney's most popular jogging routes – Mrs Macquarie's Road, built in 1816 at the urging of the governor's wife, Elizabeth. The road curves down from Art Gallery Road to Mrs Macquarie's Point, which separates idyllic Farm Cove from the grittier Woolloomooloo Bay. At the end is the celebrated lookout point known as **Mrs Macquarie's Chair**, a seat fashioned out of the rock. From here, Elizabeth could admire her favourite view of the harbour on her daily walk in what was then the governor's private park. On the route down to the point, the **Andrew "Boy" Charlton Pool** is an open-air, chlorinated saltwater swimming pool safely isolated from the harbour waters (daily Sept–May 6am–8pm; A$5.50, child A$3.80; ⊕02 9358 6686) on the Woolloomooloo side of the promontory, with views across to the engrossingly functional Garden Island Naval Depot. "The Boy", as the locals fondly call it, was named after the gold-medal-winning Manly swimmer, who turned 17 during the 1924 Paris Olympics. It's a popular hangout for trendy Darlinghurst types and sun-worshipping gays.

The Royal Botanic Gardens

The **Royal Botanic Gardens** (daily 7am–sunset; free; Ⓦwww.rbgsyd.nsw .gov.au), established in 1816, occupy the area between this strip of The Domain and the Sydney Opera House, around the headland on Farm Cove where the first white settlers struggled to grow vegetables for the hungry colony. While duck ponds, a romantic rose garden and fragrant herb garden strike a very English note, look out for native birds and, at dusk, the fruit bats flying overhead (hundreds of the giant bats hang by day in the Palm Grove area near the restaurant) as the nocturnal possums begin to stir. There are examples of trees and plants from all over the world, although it's the huge, gnarled native Moreton Bay figs that stand out. The gardens provide some of the most stunning **views** of Sydney Harbour, particularly the section between Mrs Macquarie's Point and Main Pond, and are always crowded with workers at lunchtime, picnickers on fine weekends, and lovers entwined beneath the trees.

Many **paths** run through the gardens. A popular and speedy route (roughly 15min) is to start at the northern gates near the Opera House and stroll along the waterfront path. Once you've passed through a second set of gates, walk up the **Fleet Steps** to Mrs Macquarie's Chair (see p.247) with fantastic views of the city skyline through trees.

Within the northern boundaries of the park, the sandstone mansion glimpsed through a garden and enclosure is the **Government House** (built 1837–45), seat of the governor of New South Wales, and still used for official engagements by the governor, who now lives in a private residence. The stately interior is open three days a week for guided tours (Fri–Sun 10.30am–3pm; every 30min; 45min; free; ℡02 9931 5222, Ⓦwww.hht.net.au); you are also free to roam the grounds (daily 10am–4pm).

Further south, just inside the gardens at the end of Bridge Street, the **Conservatorium of Music** is housed in what was intended to be the servants' quarters and stables of Government House. Public opinion in 1821, however, deemed the imposing castellated building far too grand for such a purpose and a complete conversion, including the addition of a concert hall, gave it a loftier aim of training the colony's future musicians.

Below the Conservatorium, the remaining southern area of the gardens has a herb garden, the **Tropical Centre** (daily 10am–4pm; A\$4, child A\$2), where a striking glass pyramid and adjacent glass arc respectively house native tropical plants and exotics, a popular café at Palm Grove Centre and, next door, a small **visitor information outlet** (daily 10am–2.30pm) where free **guided tours** of the gardens commence (daily 10.30am; 1hr 30min; additional tours March–Nov 1pm; 1hr). If you're short of time, the **Trackless Train** runs through the gardens every thirty minutes (Mon–Fri 9.30am–5pm, Sat & Sun 9.30am–6pm; all-day hop-on-hop-off service A\$10, child A\$5) between the visitor centre and the entrance near the Opera House.

Darling Harbour, Ultimo and Pyrmont

Darling Harbour, once a grimy industrial docks area, lay moribund until the 1980s, when the State Government chose to pump millions of dollars into the regeneration of this prime city real estate as part of the 1988 Bicentenary Project. The huge redevelopment scheme around Cockle Bay, which opened that year, included the building of the above-ground monorail – one of only a few in the world – as well as a massive new shopping and entertainment precinct. In many ways it's a thoroughly stylish redevelopment of the old wharves, and Darling Harbour and the surrounding areas of **Ultimo** and **Pyrmont** have plenty of attractions on offer: museums, an aquarium, entertainment areas, a shopping mall, an IMAX cinema, a children's playground, gardens, a casino and a convention and exhibition centre. However, it's only recently that Sydneysiders themselves have embraced it. Sneered at for years by locals as tacky and touristy, it took the Cockle Bay Wharf development – an upmarket café, bar and restaurant precinct on the eastern side of the waterfront – and the most

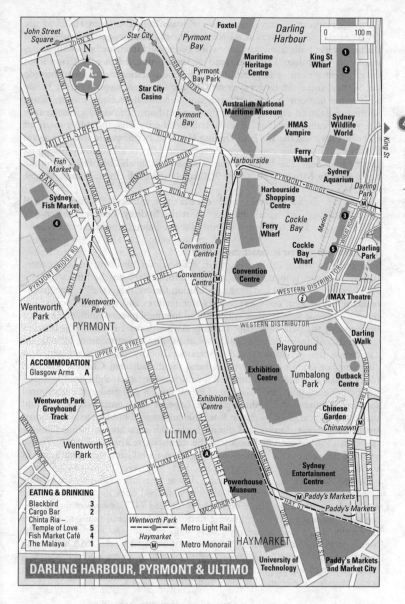

ACCOMMODATION
Glasgow Arms   **A**

EATING & DRINKING
Blackbird	**3**
Cargo Bar	**2**
Chinta Ria –	
Temple of Love	**5**
Fish Market Café	**4**
The Malaya	**1**

Wentworth Park ●━━━●   Metro Light Rail
Haymarket (M)   Metro Monorail

DARLING HARBOUR, PYRMONT & ULTIMO

recent King Street Wharf development to the north of the aquarium to finally lure locals to the much-maligned area.

Behind the development, and accessible from it, is **Darling Park**, with paths laid out in the shape of a waratah flower, the official floral emblem of New South Wales. The western side of Darling Harbour is dominated by rather ugly modern chain hotels, ironically providing some of the view for the stylish Cockle Bay Wharf diners.

Darling Harbour is only a five-minute **walk** from the Town Hall and the QVB: an elevated walkway from Market Street and a pedestrian bridge from Bathurst Street both take you there, while Liverpool Street, further south, brings you in via Tumbalong Park. Alternatively, the **monorail** (see p.219) runs from the city centre to three stops around the harbour. Getting to the wharf outside the Sydney Aquarium by **ferry** from Circular Quay gives you a chance to see a bit of the harbour – Sydney Ferries stop at McMahons Point on the North Shore and Balmain en route, while the hop-on-hop-off *Rocket Explorer* cruiser (see p.232) calls in at Pier 26 and Harbourside. By **bus**, the 443 runs from Circular Quay and the QVB to Darling Harbour, Pyrmont and the casino, and the 449 connects the casino, the Powerhouse Museum, Broadway Shopping Centre and Glebe. The large Darling Harbour site can also be navigated on the dinky **People Mover train** (daily 9.30am–4.30pm; full circuit 20min; A$4.50, child A$3.50).

There are always **festivals and events** here, particularly during school holidays; to find out what's on, drop in at the **Sydney Visitor Centre** (see p.215) near the IMAX Theatre, or visit ⊛ www.darlingharbour.com.au.

Tumbalong Park and around

The southern half of Darling Harbour, just beyond Chinatown and the Entertainment Centre, is focused around **Tumbalong Park**, reached from the city via Liverpool Street. Backed by the Exhibition Centre, this is the "village green" of Darling Harbour, complete with water features and public artworks, and serves as a venue for open-air concerts and free public entertainment. The area surrounding the park is perhaps Darling Harbour's most frenetic – at least on weekends and during school holidays – as most of the attractions, including a carousel, a free playground and a stage for holiday concerts, are aimed at children. For some peace and quiet, head for the adjacent **Chinese Garden** (daily 9.30am–5pm; A$6), completed for the bicentenary as a gift from Sydney's sister city Guangdong; the "Garden of Friendship" is designed in the traditional southern Chinese style. Although not large, it feels remarkably calm and spacious – a great place to retreat from the commercial hubbub to read a book, smell the fragrant flowers that attract birds, and listen to the lilting Chinese music that fills the air. The balcony of the traditional tearoom offers a bird's-eye view of the dragon wall, waterfalls, a pagoda on a hill, and carp swimming in winding lakes.

Darling Walk, the development alongside the harbour's small pleasure-boating lagoon, is packed with tacky, child-pleasing stores and cafés; it's also home to the **Outback Centre** (daily 10am–6pm; free; ☎ 02 9283 7477, ⊛ www.outbackcentre .com.au), featuring a cinema showing films about Aboriginal music and art, live didgeridoo music and a sizeable gallery-shop of paintings and souvenirs. The Southern Promenade of Darling Harbour is dominated by the **IMAX Theatre** (see "Cinemas", p.300). Its giant, eight-storey-high cinema screen shows a constantly changing programme from their 100-film library, with an emphasis on scenic wonders, the animal kingdom and adventure sports.

Sydney Aquarium and Sydney WildlifeWorld

At the bottom of Market Street is **Pyrmont Bridge**, a pedestrian walkway across Cockle Bay, linking the two sides of the harbour. On the eastern side is the fantastic **Sydney Aquarium** (daily 9am–10pm; A$28.50, child A$14.50, discounts available online; ☎ 02 8251 7800, ⊛ www.sydneyaquarium.com.au). If you're not going to get the chance to explore the Great Barrier Reef, the aquarium makes a surprisingly passable substitute. The entry level exhibits freshwater fish from the Murray

Darling basin, Australia's biggest river system, but speed past these to get to the two underwater walkways, where sharks and rays glide overhead. The collection of species from the Great Barrier Reef is truly gigantic, and you'll see plenty of natural behaviour, such as clownfish hovering in anemones and diminutive cleaner wrasses fidgeting around the larger fish. Educational displays highlight the threats to the reef and its conservation. Alongside all the fish, there are also platypus, crocodiles, seals and little penguins in enclosures.

Next door is the equally impressive **Sydney WildlifeWorld** (daily 9am–10pm; A$28.50, child A$14.50, discounts available online; ℡02 9333 9288, ⓦwww.sydneywildlifeworld.com.au), a mesh-domed centre with free-flying birds and a compact collection of over 130 species of animals found throughout Australia. The elegant glass displays are carefully thought out, giving a good impression of the natural environment the animals live in. Koalas, wallabies and kangaroos are the inevitable highlights, but snakes, spiders and other creepy crawlies make interesting viewing and you might even get the chance to handle some nonpoisonous species.

Australian National Maritime Museum and around

On the western side of Pyrmont Bridge is the **Australian National Maritime Museum** (daily 9.30am–5pm, Jan until 6pm; free; tours of the HMAS *Vampire*, the *James Craig*, the HMAS *Onslow* and the replica of the HMB *Endeavour* A$10–30, child A$6–16; ⓦwww.anmm.gov.au). With distinctive modern architecture topped by a wave-shaped roof, it highlights the history of Australia as a seafaring nation, but goes beyond maritime interests to look at how the sea has shaped Australian life, covering everything from immigration to beach culture and Aboriginal fishing methods in seven core-themed exhibitions. Highlights include the "Merana Eora Nora – First People" exhibition, delving into indigenous culture, and "Navigators – Defining Australia", which focuses on the seventeenth-century Dutch explorers. Outside, several vessels are moored: the navy destroyer *Vampire*, and a submarine, HMAS *Onslow*, plus the beautifully restored 1874 square-rigger, the *James Craig*, are permanently on display, while a collection of historic vessels, including a 1970s Vietnamese refugee boat and a replica of Captain Cook's *Endeavour*, are rotated. The pleasant alfresco café here, which you don't have to enter the museum to use, has views of the boats. The bronze **Welcome Wall** outside the museum pays honour to Australia's six million immigrants.

Included in the museum entry is a behind-the-scenes tour of the **Maritime Heritage Centre** at Wharf 7, just beyond the museum off Pirrama Road and beside Pyrmont Bay Park, where conservation and model-making work takes place and some of the collection is stored. Also at the wharf, the Sydney Heritage Fleet's collection of restored boats and ships is moored, the oldest of which was built in 1888.

Slightly south, the two-level **Harbourside Shopping Centre** provides opportunities for souvenir hunting: don't miss the first-floor **Gavala Aboriginal Art Centre** (daily 10am–9pm), which is owned and run by Aboriginal artists selling Aboriginal art, clothing, accessories and music, with proceeds going directly to the makers and musicians.

Ultimo: the Powerhouse Museum and around

From Tumbalong Park, a signposted walkway leads to **Ultimo** and the **Powerhouse Museum** on Harris Street (daily 10am–5pm; A$10, child A$5; special exhibitions extra; free 45min tour daily 11.30am, 12.30pm & 1.30pm; ⓦwww.powerhousemuseum.com). Located, as the name suggests, in a former power station, this is arguably the best museum in Sydney, an exciting place with fresh ideas, combining arts and sciences, design, pop culture and technology under the same roof. There are several big temporary exhibitions each year, with past popular themes as diverse as "The Lord of the Rings" and "The Great Wall of China". The permanent displays are varied, presented with an interactive approach that means you'll need hours to investigate the five-level museum properly. The entrance level is dominated by the huge **Boulton and Watt Steam Engine**, first put to use in 1875 in a British brewery; still operational, the engine is often loudly demonstrated. The **Kings Cinema** on level 3, with its original Art Deco fittings, suitably shows the sorts of newsreels and films a Sydneysider would have watched in the 1930s. Judging by the tears at closing time, the special **children's areas** are a great success. Level 4 houses a transport section brought to life by an impressive sound-and-light show.

Pyrmont: Star City Casino and the Sydney Fish Market

Frantic redevelopment has recently transformed **Pyrmont**, which juts out into the water between Darling Harbour and Blackwattle Bay. The once dilapidated suburb was Sydney's answer to Ellis Island in the 1950s when thousands of immigrants disembarked at the city's main overseas passenger terminal, Pier 13. Today, the former industrial suburb, which had a population of only nine hundred in 1988, has grown into a residential suburb of twenty thousand, housed in groovy renovated warehouses and rather modern units, paid for with A$2 billion worth of investment. With the New South Wales government selling A$97 million worth of property, this has been one of the biggest concentrated sell-offs of land in Australia. Despite complaints from some Sydneysiders about the mediocrity of this new urban landscape, it has certainly become glitzier, with Sydney's casino, Star City, and two TV companies – Channel Ten and Foxtel – based here. Harris Street has filled up with new shops and cafés, and the area's old pubs have been given a new lease of life, attracting the young and mobile. The approach to the spectacularly cabled **Anzac Bridge** (complete with statues of an Australian and New Zealand Army Corps soldier) – Sydney's newest – cuts through Pyrmont and saves between fifteen and twenty minutes' travelling time to Sydney's inner west.

Beyond the Maritime Museum, on Pyrmont Bay, palm-fronted **Star City Casino** is the city's unashamedly tacky 24-hour gambling HQ. As well as the casino, the building houses two theatres, fourteen restaurants, cafés and theme bars, souvenir shops, a convenience store and a nightclub. The casino interior itself is a riot of giant palm sculptures, prize cars spinning on rotating bases, Aboriginal painting motifs on the ceiling, Australian critters scurrying across a red-desert-coloured carpet and an endless array of flashing poker machines. Dress code is smart casual. You can just wander in and have a look around or a drink, without betting.

The best reason to visit this area, though, is the **Sydney Fish Market**, on the corner of Pyrmont Bridge Road and Bank Street (daily 7am–4pm; Ⓦwww .sydneyfishmarket.com.au), only a ten-minute walk via Pyrmont Bridge Road from Darling Harbour. The market is the second-largest seafood market in the world for variety of fish, after the massive Tsukiji market in Tokyo. You need to visit early to see the **auctions** (Mon–Fri only, with the biggest auction floor on Fri; buyers begin viewing the fish at 4.30am, auctions begin 5.30am, public viewing platform opens 7am); buyers log into computer terminals to register their bids.

You can take away oysters, prawns and cooked seafood and eat picnic-style on waterfront tables while watching the boats come in. Everything is set up for throwing together an impromptu meal – there's a bakery, the Blackwattle Deli, with an extensive (and tempting) cheese selection, a bottle shop and a grocer. Alternatively, you can eat in at *Doyles*, the casual and slightly more affordable version of the famous *Doyles* fish restaurant at Watsons Bay; at the excellent sushi bar; or at one of the bustling cafés that have dirt-cheap fish and chips (see p.283). Retail shops open at 7am. The increasingly popular **Sydney Seafood School** (℡02 9004 1111) offers seafood cookery lessons, from Thai-style to French provincial, plus a two-hour, early-morning tour of the selling floor departing from *Doyles* (Mon & Thurs 6.55am; A\$20, child A\$10).

To get to Pyrmont, take the Metro Light Rail from Central to Pyrmont Bay, Star City (for the casino), John Street Square or Fish Market, or take bus 443 from Circular Quay or the QVB.

The inner west

West of the centre, immediately beyond Darling Harbour, the inner-city areas of **Glebe** and **Newtown** surround Sydney University, their vibrant cultural mix enlivened by large student populations. On a peninsula north of Glebe and west of The Rocks, **Balmain** is a gentrified former working-class dock area popular for its village atmosphere, while en route **Leichhardt** is a focus for Sydney's Italian community.

Glebe

Right by Australia's oldest university, **Glebe** has gradually been evolving from a café-oriented student quarter to more upmarket thirty-something territory with a New Age slant. Indeed, it's very much the centre of alternative culture in Sydney, with its yoga schools, healing centres and organic food shops. **Glebe Point Road** is filled with a mix of cafés with trademark leafy courtyards, restaurants, bookshops and secondhand shops as it runs uphill from **Broadway**, becoming quietly residential as it slopes down towards the water of Rozelle Bay. The side streets are fringed with renovated two-storey terraced houses with white-iron lacework verandas. Not surprisingly, Glebe is popular with backpackers and offers several hostels (see "Accommodation", p.227). The **Broadway Shopping Centre** on nearby Broadway, but linked to Glebe by an overhead walkway from Glebe Point Road opposite one of the street's most popular cafés, *Badde Manors* (see p.283), is handy if you're staying in the area, with its supermarkets, speciality food shops, huge food court, record, book and clothes shops and twelve-screen cinema.

Just before the beginning of Glebe Point Road, on Broadway, **Victoria Park** has a pleasant, heated outdoor swimming pool (Mon–Fri 6am–7.15pm, Sat & Sun 7am–5.45pm; A\$4.50, child A\$2.50) with attached gym and a sophisticated café. From the park, a path and steps lead up into **Sydney University**, inaugurated in 1850; your gaze is led from the walkway up to the Main Quadrangle and its very Oxford-reminiscent clock tower and Great Hall. You're welcome to wander round the university grounds, and there are several free museums and galleries to visit. Glebe itself is at its best on Saturday, when **Glebe Market** (10am–4pm), which takes place on the shady primary-school playground on Glebe Point Road (opposite the GNC Live Well healthfood supermarket), is in full swing. On sale are mainly secondhand clothes and accessories, CDs, the inevitable crystals and a bit of bric-a-brac. At 49 Glebe Point Rd, you'll find the excellent **Gleebooks** – one of Sydney's best-loved bookshops. The original, now selling secondhand and children's books, is worth the trek further up to 191 Glebe Point Rd, past St Johns Road and Glebe's pretty park. A few blocks on from here, the action stops and

Glebe Point Road trails off into a more residential area, petering out at **Jubilee Park**. The pleasantly landscaped waterfront park, complete with huge, shady Moreton Bay fig trees, a children's playground and its picturesque Harbour Foreshore Walk around Blackwattle Bay offers an unusual view of far-off Sydney Harbour Bridge framed within the cabled Anzac Bridge.

Buses 431, 433 and 434 run to Glebe from Millers Point, George Street and Central Station; 431 and 434 run right down the length of Glebe Point Road to Jubilee Park, with the 434 continuing on to Balmain, while the 433 runs half-way, turning at Wigram Road and heading on to Balmain. From Coogee beach, the 370 runs to Glebe via the University of NSW and Newtown. The Metro Monorail runs between Central Station and Rozelle stopping at Glebe, just off Pyrmont Bridge Road, and Jubilee Park, Glebe Point. Otherwise, it's a fifteen-minute **walk** from Central Station up Broadway to the beginning of Glebe Point Road.

Newtown and around

Newtown, separated from Glebe by Sydney University and easily reached by train (to Newtown station), is a hip, inner-city neighbourhood. What was once a working-class district – a hotchpotch of derelict factories, junkyards and cheap accommodation – has transformed into a trendy, offbeat area where body piercing, shaved heads and weird fashions rule. Newtown is characterized by a large gay and lesbian population, and a rich cultural mix and healthy dose of students and lecturers from the nearby university. It also has an enviable number of great cafés and diverse restaurants, especially Thai. The Dendy Cinema complex is a central focus, more like a cultural centre than just a film theatre, with its attached bookshop, excellent record store, and streetfront café, all open daily and into the night.

The main drag, gritty, traffic-fumed and invariably pedestrian-laden **King Street**, is filled with unusual secondhand, funky fashion and speciality and homeware shops and a slew of bookshops, old and new. For two weeks in June, various shop windows are filled by irreverent and in-your-face art in the Walking the Street exhibition. The highlight of the year, however, is in November (second Sun) when the huge **Newtown Festival** takes over nearby Camperdown Memorial Park, with over 200 stalls and live music on three stages.

King Street becomes less crowded south of Newtown station as it heads for a kilometre towards St Peters train station, but it's well worth strolling down to look at the more unusual speciality shops (buttons, ribbons, vintage records, Chinese medicine), as well as some small art galleries and yet more retro and funky new clothes shops. It's also stacked with culturally diverse restaurants, including Singaporean, Japanese, Turkish and African, and closer to St Peters station are several colourful businesses aimed at the local Indian community.

Enmore Road stretching west from King Street, opposite Newtown station, is a similar mix of speciality shops with evidence of a migrant population – such as the African International Market at no. 2 and Amera's Palace Bellydancing Boutique at no. 83. It's generally much quieter than King Street, except when a big-name band or comedian is playing at the Art Deco **Enmore Theatre**, at no. 130. Beyond here, the very multicultural, lively but down-at-heel **Marrick-ville** stretches out, known for its Vietnamese and Greek restaurants.

Erskineville Road, extending from the eastern side of King Street, marks the beginning of the adjoining suburb of **Erskineville**, a favourite gay address; the *Imperial Hotel* at 35 Erskineville Rd (see p.294), has long hosted popular drag shows, and is famous as the starting point of the gang in the 1994 hit film *The Adventures of Priscilla, Queen of the Desert*.

Buses 422, 423, 426 and 428 run to Newtown from Circular Quay via Castlereagh Street, Railway Square and City Road. They go down King Street as far as Newtown station, where the 422 continues to St Peters whilst the others turn off to Enmore and Marrickville. From Coogee beach, take the 370 bus to Glebe, which goes via Newtown. Alternatively, catch a **train** to Newtown, St Peters or Erskineville stations.

Leichhardt, Rozelle and Balmain

It takes half an hour on the 440 bus to get from The Rocks to **Leichhardt**, Sydney's "Little Italy", where the famous **Norton Street** strip of cafés and restaurants runs off unattractive, traffic-jammed **Parramatta Road** (buses 436, 437 and 438 from George Street in the city will also take you here). Leichhardt is very much up and coming – shiny, trendy, Italian cafés keep popping up all along the strip. Noron Street's focus is its upmarket cinema complex, The Palace (which hosts a two-week Italian film festival in late Oct), with its attached record store, bookshop and Internet café, and nearby shopping mall. Closer to Parramatta Road is the **Italian Forum**, an upmarket shopping and dining centre and showcase for all things Italian. However, the lively, much-loved and enduring *Bar Italia*, a ten-minute walk further down Norton, is still the best Italian café in Leichhardt (see p.284 for more details on cafés and restaurants in this area).

From Leichhardt, the 445 bus runs along Rozelle High Street and down the hill to Balmain's waterfront. **Rozelle**, once very much the down-at-heel, poorer sister to Balmain, has emerged as a fully-fledged trendy area, with the Sydney College of the Arts and the Sydney Writers' Centre now based here, in the grounds of the 61-hectare waterfront **Callan Park** on Balmain Road. Darling Street has a string of cafés, bookshops, speciality shops, gourmet grocers, restaurants, made-over pubs, and designer home-goods stores, and is at its liveliest on the weekend, when a huge **flea market** (Sat & Sun 9am–4pm) takes over the grounds of Rozelle Primary School, near the Victoria Road end.

Balmain, directly north of Glebe, is less than 2km from the Opera House, by ferry from Circular Quay to Darling Street Wharf, but stuck out on a spur in the harbour and kept apart from the centre by Darling Harbour and Johnston's Bay, it has a degree of separation that has helped it retain its village-like atmosphere and made it the favoured abode of many writers and filmmakers. Like better-known Paddington, Balmain was once a working-class quarter of terraced houses that has gradually been gentrified. Although the docks at White Bay no longer operate, the pubs that used to fuel the dockworkers still abound, and **Darling Street** and the surrounding backstreets are blessed with enough watering holes to warrant a pub crawl – two classics are the *London Hotel* on Darling Street and the *Exchange Hotel* on Beattie Street. Darling Street also rewards a leisurely stroll, with a bit of browsing in its speciality shops (focused on clothes and gifts), and grazing in its restaurants and cafés. The best time to come is on Saturday, when the lively **Balmain Market** occupies the shady grounds of St Andrews Church (7.30am–4pm), on the corner opposite the *London Hotel*. An assortment of books, handmade jewellery, clothing and ceramics, antiques, home-made chocolates, cakes and gourmet foods and organic produce are on sale. The highlight is an eclectic array of food stalls in the church hall where you can snack your way from the Himalayas to Southern India.

For a **self-guided tour** of Balmain and Birchgrove, buy a *Balmain Walks* leaflet (A$2.20) from Balmain Library, 370 Darling St, or the well-stocked Bray's Bookshop, at no. 268. The most pleasurable way **to get to Balmain** is to catch a ferry from Circular Quay to Darling Street Wharf in Balmain East, where the

Just across the water from Balmain East, **Goat Island** is the site of a well-preserved gunpowder-magazine complex. The sandstone buildings, including a barracks, were built by two hundred convicts between 1833 and 1839. Treatment of the convicts was harsh: 18-year-old Charles Anderson, a mentally impaired convict with a wild, seemingly untameable temper who made several escape attempts, received over twelve hundred lashes in 1835 and was sentenced to be chained to a rock for two years, a cruel punishment even by the standards of the day. Tethered to the rock, which you can still see, his unhealed back crawling with maggots, he slept in a cavity hewn into the sandstone "couch". Eventually, Anderson ended up on Norfolk Island (see p.394), where under the humane prisoner-reform experiments of Alexander Maconochie, the feral 24-year-old made a startling transformation.

At the time of writing, the island was closed for a major conservation face-lift by the NPWS to make the buildings more accessible to the public.

442 bus waits to take you up Darling Street to Balmain proper (or it's about a ten-minute walk). Buses 432, 433 and 434 run out to Balmain via George Street, Railway Square and Glebe Point Road and down Darling Street; faster is the 442 from the QVB, which crosses Anzac Bridge and heads to Balmain Wharf.

The inner east

To the **east** of the Royal Botanic Gardens and The Domain, the old **Woolloomooloo** wharf, once a commercial shipping hub, has been rejuvenated as a smart marina complex, while nearby **Potts Point** and **Elizabeth Bay** are pockets of elegant urban style, trading on their harbour views. Inland from here is **Kings Cross**, or "the Cross", a place where cultures collide – streetwalkers, hard-up backpackers and sassy trendsetters rub shoulders in its mixed bag of tawdry shops, seedy bars and cool restaurants. At the heart of the inner east are **Surry Hills**, **Darlinghurst** and **Paddington**; these once-scruffy working-class suburbs have long since been taken over and revamped by the young, arty and upwardly mobile.

Woolloomooloo, Potts Point and Elizabeth Bay

Woolloomooloo occupies the old harbourside quarter between The Domain and the grey-painted fleet of the **Garden Island Naval Depot**. Once a narrow-streeted slum, Woolloomooloo has recently been transformed, though its upmarket apartment developments sit uneasily side by side with problematic community housing, and you should still be careful in the backstreets at night. There are some lively pubs and quieter, more old-fashioned drinking holes, as well as the legendary **Harry's Café de Wheels** on Cowper Wharf Road, a 24-hour pie-cart operating since 1945 and popular nowadays with Sydney cabbies and hungry clubbers (see p.285).

The once picturesquely dilapidated **Woolloomooloo Finger Wharf**, dating from 1917, is now a posh complex comprising a marina, luxury residential apartments, the cool *Blue Sydney* hotel (see p.227) and its funky *Water Bar*, and some slick restaurants offering alfresco dining; inside there's a free exhibition space with changing themes.

Woolloomooloo is best reached **on foot** from the Royal Botanic Gardens by walking south around the foreshore from Mrs Macquarie's Chair, or from Kings Cross by taking the **McElhone Stairs** or the **Butlers Stairs** from Victoria Street; alternatively, take **bus** 311 from Kings Cross, Circular Quay or Railway Square.

Tucked away to the northeast of Woolloomooloo is quieter **Potts Point**, an upmarket area of tree-lined streets, apartment blocks, classy boutique hotels, stylish restaurants, buzzy cafés and occasional harbour glimpses over wealthier **Elizabeth Bay**, its neighbour; this is as close to European living as Sydney gets. The area was Sydney's first suburb, developed land granted to John Wylde in 1822 and Alexander Macleay in 1826. The grand villas of colonial bureaucrats gave way in the 1920s and 30s to Art Deco residential apartments, and in the 1950s big, splendid hotels were added to the scene. The area is heading even further upmarket with the conversion of all the large hotels into luxury apartments.

Kings Cross

The preserve of Sydney's bohemians in the 1950s, **Kings Cross** became an R&R spot for American soldiers during the Vietnam War. Now Sydney's red-light district, it is still frequented by sailors from the Woolloomooloo naval base, and its streets are prowled by prostitutes, drug abusers, drunks and homeless teenagers. Despite this, it is also a bustling centre for backpackers and other travellers, especially around leafy and quieter Victoria Street, and there are lots of fashionable restaurants and cafés, particularly as you head north towards the harbour and the more upmarket Potts Point. The two sides of "the Cross", as locals call it, coexist with little trouble, though some tourists seem somewhat surprised at where they've ended up, and it can be rather intimidating for lone women. However, the constant flow of people (and police officers) makes it relatively safe, and it's always lively, with bars and eating establishments open all hours.

Heading up **William Street** from Hyde Park and past Cook and Phillip Park and the Australian Museum, Kings Cross beckons with its giant neon Coca-Cola sign. By day, William Street looks quite grotty thanks to streams of fast and fumey traffic heading out of the city centre; at night, hardcore transvestite streetwalkers and kerb-crawling patrons go about their business. However, with the Cross City Tunnel easing traffic along here, there are long-term plans for William Street to become a European-style boulevard – tree-lined, traffic-calmed, and with wide pavements for café tables and strolling pedestrians. At the top of the hill, **Darlinghurst Road** is Kings Cross's "action zone". At weekends, an endless stream of suburban voyeurs emerge from Kings Cross station, near the beginning of the Darlinghurst Road "sin" strip, and trawl along the streets as touts try their best to haul them into tacky strip-joints and seedy nightclubs. The strippers and sleaze extend to the end of Darlinghurst Road at the El Alamein fountain in the paved **Fitzroy Gardens**, which, though pleasant-looking, is the usual hangout of some fairly abusive drunks. It's much changed on Sundays, however, when it's taken over by a small arts and crafts market.

Kings Cross is around twenty minutes **on foot** from Central Station or Circular Quay; for a quieter route than William Street, you could head up from The Domain via Cowper Wharf Road in Woolloomooloo, and then up the McElhone Stairs to Victoria Street. By **train**, it's on the line from Central to Bondi Junction; it's also on **bus** routes 311 and 323–326 from Circular Quay, 311 from Railway Square, and 326–327 from Bondi Junction.

Darlinghurst, Paddington and Woollahra

Oxford Street, from Hyde Park to Paddington and beyond, is a major amusement strip. Waiting to be discovered, here and in the side streets, is an array of nightclubs, restaurants, cafés, pubs, cinemas and late-night bookshops. The Oxford Street shopping strip – many would argue Sydney's best for labels and funky style – starts at the corner of Victoria Street in Darlinghurst and doesn't stop until the corner of Jersey Road in Woollahra; around **Darling-hurst**, it is also the focus of Sydney's very active gay and lesbian scene. Hip and bohemian, **Darlinghurst** mingles seediness with a certain hedonistic style. There's another concentration of cafés, restaurants and fashion on Liverpool Street, while Victoria Street is a classic pose strip with the legendary, street-smart *Bar Coluzzi* (see p.285).

Paddington, a slum at the start of the twentieth century, became a popular hangout for hipsters during the late 1960s and 70s. Since then, the young professionals have taken over and turned the area into the smart and fashionable suburb it is today: the Victorian-era terrace houses, with their iron-lace verandas reminiscent of New Orleans, have been beautifully restored. Many of the terraces were originally built in the 1840s to house the artisans who worked on the graceful, sandstone **Victoria Barracks** on the southern side of Oxford Street, its walls stretching seven blocks, from Greens Road to just before the Paddington Town Hall on Oatley Road. **Shadforth Street**, opposite the entrance gates, has many examples of the original artisans' homes. Though the barracks are still used by the army, there are free guided tours (Thurs 10am).

Crossing to the north side of Oxford Street, the small, winding, tree-lined streets running off it are a pleasant place for a stroll. Head via Underwood and Heeley streets to **Five Ways**, where you'll find cafés, speciality shops and a typically gracious old boozer and bistro, the *Royal Hotel* (see p.286). Continuing east there are more shops along Elizabeth Street, while back on Oxford Street the main Paddington action of stylish boutiques and arty homeware stores attracts the "see and be seen" crowd. Always bustling, the area really comes alive on Saturdays, when everyone descends on **Paddington Market** (9am–4pm) in the church grounds at no. 395, opposite Elizabeth Street. The ever-expanding market sells everything from funky handmade jewellery to local artwork, as well as cheap fresh flowers and vintage clothes; you can even get a massage or a tarot reading between a cup of coffee and an organic sandwich.

Woollahra, along Oxford Street from Paddington, is even more moneyed but contrastingly staid, with expensive **antique shops** and **art galleries** along **Queen Street** replacing the fashion and trendy lifestyle focus of Paddington's shops. Leafy Moncur Street hides *Jones the Grocer* (at no. 68), where Woollahra locals gather for coffee at the long central table; it also sells stylishly packaged, outlandishly priced and utterly delicious groceries and gourmet treats.

Transport heading in this direction includes **buses** 333, 380 and 389 from Circular Quay to Bondi via Elizabeth Street, William Street and Oxford Street, and the 378 from Railway Square to Bronte via Oxford Street.

Surry Hills

Surry Hills, directly east of Central Station from Elizabeth Street, was traditionally the centre of the rag trade, which still finds its focus on Devonshire Street. Rows of tiny terraces once housed its original poor, working-class population, many of them of Irish origin. Considered a slum by the rest of Sydney, the dire and overcrowded conditions were given fictional life in Ruth Park's *The Harp in the South* trilogy (see "Books", p.648), set in the Surry Hills of the 1940s. The area became something of a cultural melting pot with European postwar immigration, and doubled as a grungy, studenty, muso heartland in the 1980s, fuelled by cheap bars and cheaper rent. By the mid-1990s, however, the slickly fashionable scene of neighbouring Darlinghurst and Paddington had finally taken over Surry Hills' twin focal points of parallel **Crown Street**, filled with cafés, swanky restaurants, funky clothes shops and designer galleries, and leafy **Bourke Street**, where a couple of Sydney's best

Just beyond Surry Hills, only 2km from the glitter and sparkle of Darling Harbour, is **Redfern**, Sydney's underbelly. Its most notorious district is The Block, a squalid mess of rundown terraced houses and unsolved social problems: in 2004, it made world headlines when, in a short but bitter conflict, local rioters injured over fifty police officers and set Redfern train station ablaze. The Block, just west of the station, is home to Australia's biggest urban **Aboriginal community**, self-managed through a hard-pressed housing co-operative, the Aboriginal Housing Company. It's close enough to the CBD for property developers to be snapping at the co-opera-tive's heels, and the residents, many of whom feel a strong connection to the area, have for some time lived in fear of eviction. The New South Wales government has set up a dedicated department, the **Redfern-Waterloo Authority**, to manage an ambitious programme of urban renewal, but residents are yet to be fully convinced that their needs will be met. A local artists' collective, **SquatSpace** (Ⓦwww.squat space.com), run occasional tours of the area for those keen to look beyond the news reports and discuss the effects of redevelopment and gentrification on inner-city areas – they call it the Redfern-Waterloo Tour of Beauty.

cafés lurk among the trees. As rents have gone up, only **Cleveland Street**, running west to Redfern and east towards Moore Park and the Sydney Cricket Ground (see p.260), traffic-snarled and lined with cheap Lebanese, Turkish and Indian restaurants, retains its ethnically varied population.

Surry Hills is a short **walk** up a steep hill from Central Station (Devonshire St or Elizabeth St exit); take Fouveaux or Devonshire Street and you'll soon hit Crown, or it's an even quicker stroll from Oxford Street, Darlinghurst, heading south along Crown or Bourke streets.

A good time to visit the area is the first Saturday of the month when a lively **flea market**, complete with tempting food stalls, occupies the small Shannon Reserve, on the corner of Crown and Fouveaux streets, overlooked by the **Clock Hotel** (see p.292). The fine balconied pub, which has expanded out of all recognition from its 1840s roots, is emblematic of the new Surry Hills, with its swish restaurant and bar. The area's artistic side can be experienced nearby at the **Brett Whiteley Studio** at 2 Raper St (Sat & Sun 10am–4pm; free; ℡02 9225 1740, Ⓦwww.brettwhiteley.org); walk about three blocks further south down Crown Street, and it's off Davies Street. Whiteley was one of Australia's best-known contemporary painters, with an international reputation by the time he died in 1992 of a heroin overdose at the age of 53; wild self-portraits and expressive female nudes were some of his subjects, but it is his sensual paintings of Sydney Harbour for which he is best known, painted from his home in Lavender Bay. In 1986, Whiteley converted this one-time factory into a studio and living space, and since his death it has become a museum and gallery showing his paintings and memorabilia.

Centennial Parklands

East of Surry Hills and south of Paddington and Woollahra lies the great green expanse of **Centennial Parklands** (daily sunrise to sunset; Ⓦwww .centennialparklands.com.au), comprising Moore Park, Queens Park, and Centennial Park, opened to the citizens of Sydney at the Centennial Festival in 1888. **Centennial Park**, with vast lawns, rose gardens and an extensive network of ponds complete with ducks, resembles an English country park, but is reclaimed at dawn and dusk by distinctly antipodean residents, including possums and flying foxes. It's crisscrossed by walking paths and tracks for cycling, rollerblading, jogging and horse-riding: you can rent a bike or rollerblades nearby (see p.307), or hire a horse from the adjacent equestrian centre, and then recover from your exertions in the café with its popular outside tables or, in the finer months, stay on until dark and catch an outdoor film at the Moonlight Cinema (see p.300). **Moore Park** has facilities for tennis, golf, grass-skiing, bowling, cricket and hockey; it's also home to the Sydney Cricket Ground and the Entertainment Quarter (see below). **Queens Park**, the smallest of the trio, has a variety of sports fields and, in the northeastern corner, three impressively ancient Moreton Bay fig trees. You can pick up a free map of the Centennial Parklands from the Paddington or Woollahra gates on Oxford Street, or the **Parklands Office** inside the park, near the café (Mon–Fri 8.30am–5pm; ☎02 9339 6699). Numerous **buses** stop on the perimeter of the parklands, including the 380, 382 and L82 from Circular Quay, the 372 from Railway Square or Coogee, and the 380 from North Bondi.

The Sydney Cricket Ground (SCG)

The venerated institution of the **Sydney Cricket Ground** or **SCG** (☎02 9360 6601, ⓦwww.sydneycricketground.com.au; match tickets at the gate or from Ticketek ☎13 28 49, ⓦwww.ticketek.com.au) earned its place in cricketing history for Don Bradman's score of 452 not out in 1929, and for the controversy over England's bodyline bowling techniques in 1932. Ideally, proceedings are observed from the lovely 1886 Members Stand, while sipping an icy gin and tonic – but unless you're invited by a member, you'll end up elsewhere, probably drinking beer from a plastic cup. Cricket spectators aren't a sedate lot in Sydney, and the noisiest barrackers will probably come from "the Hill" – or the Doug Walters Stand, as it's officially known. The Bill O'Reilly Stand is comfortable until the afternoon, when you'll be blinded by the sun, whereas the Brewongle Stand provides consistently good viewing. Best of all is the Bradman Stand, with a view directly behind the bowler's arm, and adjacent to the exclusive stand occupied by members, commentators and ex-players. The Test to see here is, of course, **The Ashes**; the Sydney leg of the five tests, each for five days, begins on New Year's Day. Die-hard cricket fans can go on a **tour** of the SCG on non-match days (Mon–Fri 10am, noon & 2pm, Sat 10am; 1hr 30min; A\$25, child A\$17; bookings required on ☎1300 724 737), which also covers the **Aussie Stadium** next door, where the focus is on international and national rugby league and rugby union, and Aussie Rules football matches, when Sydneysiders come out to support their local team, The Swans.

Fox Studios and the Entertainment Quarter

Also within Moore Park, immediately southeast of the SCG, are the Murdoch-owned **Fox Studios** (ⓦwww.foxstudiosaustralia.com), constructed at a cost of A\$300 million within the old Agricultural Showgrounds site. The **Professional Studio**, opened in May 1998, takes up over half the site and has facilities for both film and television production, with six high-tech stages and industry tenants on site providing everything from casting services to stunt professionals. Films made here include *The Matrix* trilogy, *Mission Impossible II*, Baz Luhrmann's *Moulin Rouge*, and episodes I and II of the *Star Wars* saga. The studios themselves are not open to the public, but in the **Entertainment Quarter** immediately south of the site (daily 10am–10pm; ⓦwww.eqmoorepark.com.au), there's a plush **cinema complex** (see "Cinemas", p.299); international film premieres are sometimes held here. The main venue in the quarter is the old Show Ring, once the preserve of wood-chopping competitions and rodeo events, but now hosting everything from open-air cinema and circuses to a Sunday craft and clothing market (10am–4pm) and a fresh-produce Farmers Market (Wed & Sat 10am–3.30pm). Nearby are the gleaming shops, cafés, restaurants and bars of pedestrianized **Bent Street**. There's also a stand-up comedy venue, the *Comedy Store* (see p.299); two music venues, City Live and the Hordern Pavilion (see p.295); and a few family attractions, including a mini-golf course and the indoor **Lollipops Playland** (daily 9.30am–6pm; A$5 includes a coffee, 1–2 years A$9, 3–12 years A$12; ℡02 9331 0811), perfect for a rainy day. Just outside are two free playgrounds and a carousel (A$2.50).

Numerous **buses** stop nearby, including routes 339, 392, 394 or 396 from Central, Wynyard, or Town Hall.

The Harbour

Loftily flanking the mouth of **Sydney Harbour** are the rugged sandstone cliffs of North Head and South Head, providing spectacular viewing points across the calm water to the city 11km away, where the Harbour Bridge spans the sunken valley at its deepest point. The harbour's many coves, bays, points and headlands, and their parks, bushland and swimmable beaches, are rewarding to explore. However, harbour beaches are not as clean as ocean ones, and after storms are often closed to swimmers (see p.269). Finding your way by ferry is the most pleasurable method: services run to much of the **North Shore** and to harbourfront areas of the **eastern suburbs**. The eastern shores are characterized by a certain glitziness and are the haunt of the nouveaux riches, while the leafy North Shore is very much old money. Both sides of the harbour have pockets of bushland that have been incorporated into **Sydney Harbour National Park**, along with five **islands**, one of which – Fort Denison – can be visited on tours (see p.238); Goat Island is currently closed to the public, while the other three – Shark Island, Clark Island and Rodd Island – are bookable for independent visits but you must provide your own transport. The NPWS publishes an excellent free map detailing the areas of the national park and its many walking tracks, available from Cadman's Cottage in The Rocks.

Elizabeth Bay to South Head

The suburbs on the hilly southeast shores of the harbour are rich and exclusive. The area around **Darling Point**, the enviable postcode 2027, is the wealthiest in Australia, supporting the lifestyle of waterfront mansions and yacht-club memberships enjoyed by some-time residents Nicole Kidman and Lachlan Murdoch. A couple of early nineteenth-century mansions, Elizabeth Bay House and Vaucluse House, are open to visitors, providing an insight into the life of the pioneering upper crust, while the ferry to **Rose Bay** gives a good view of the pricey contemporary real estate; the bay is close to beautiful **Nielson Park** and the surrounding chunk of Sydney Harbour National Park. At South Head, **Watsons Bay** was once a fishing village, and there are spectacular views from **The Gap** in another section of the national park. Woollahra Council has brochures (available to download at ⓦ www.woollahra.nsw.gov.au) detailing three **waterside walks**: the 5.5-kilometre (3hr) **Rushcutters Bay** to Rose Bay harbour walk, which can then be continued with the eight-kilometre (4hr 30min) walk to Watsons Bay, and the fascinating five-kilometre cliffside walk from Christison Park in **Vaucluse** (off Old South Head Road) to Watsons Bay and **South Head**, with shipwreck sites, old lighthouses and military fortifications along the way.

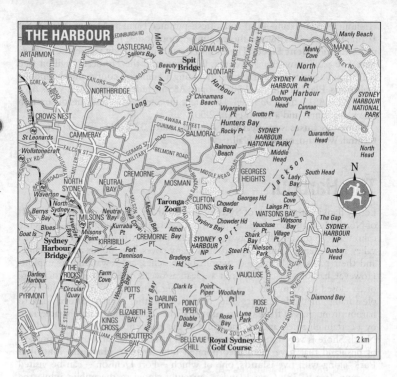

THE HARBOUR

Buses 324 and 325 from Circular Quay via Pitt Street, Kings Cross and Edgecliff cover the places listed below, heading to Watsons Bay via New South Head Road; 325 detours at Vaucluse for Nielson Park. Bus 327 runs between Martin Place and Bondi Junction stations via Edgecliff station and Darling Point.

Elizabeth Bay and Rushcutters Bay

Barely five minutes' walk northeast of Kings Cross, **Elizabeth Bay** is a well-heeled residential area, centred on **Elizabeth Bay House**, at 7 Onslow Ave (Fri–Sun 9.30am–4pm; A\$8, child A\$4; ☏02 9356 3022, ⓦwww.hht.com.au; bus 311 from either Railway Square or Circular Quay, or walk from Kings Cross station), a grand Regency residence with fine harbour views, built in 1835. Heading southeast, you're only a few minutes' walk from **Rushcutters Bay Park**, wonderfully set against a backdrop of the yacht- and cruiser-packed marina in the bay; the marina was revamped for the 2000 Olympics sailing competition. You can take it all in from the tables outside the very popular Rushcutters Bay Kiosk.

Double Bay and Rose Bay

Continuing northeast to **Darling Point**, McKell Park provides a wonderful view across to **Clarke Island** and **Bradleys Head**, both part of Sydney Harbour National Park; follow Darling Point Road (bus 327 from Edgecliff station). Next port of call is the wealthy and snobbish enclave of **Double Bay**, sometimes dubbed "Double Pay". The noise and traffic of New South Head Road are redeemed by several excellent antiquarian and secondhand bookshops, while in the quieter "village", some of the most exclusive shops in Sydney are full of imported designer labels and expensive jewellery. Eastern-suburbs social-ites meet on Cross Street, where the swanky pavement cafés are filled with well-groomed women in impeccable designer outfits. Double Bay's hidden gem is **Redleaf Pool** (Sept–May daily dawn–dusk; free), a peaceful, shady harbour beach enclosed by a wooden pier you can dive off or just laze on; there's also an excellent café here. A ferry stops at both Darling Point and Double Bay; otherwise, catch buses 324, 325 or 327.

A ferry to **Rose Bay** from Circular Quay gives you a chance to check out the waterfront mansions of **Point Piper** as you skim past. Rose Bay itself is a haven of exclusivity, with the verdant expanse of the members-only Royal Sydney Golf Course. Directly across New South Head Road from the course, waterfront **Lyne Park**'s **seaplane** service has been based here since the 1930s. Rose Bay is also a popular **windsurfing** spot; you can rent equipment from Rose Bay Aquatic Hire on Vickery Avenue (☎ 02 9371 7036).

Nielson Park and Vaucluse

Sydney Harbour National Park emerges onto the waterfront at Bay View Hill, where the delightful 1.5-kilometre **Hermitage walking track** to Nielson Park begins; the starting point, Bay View Hill Road, is off South Head Road between the Kambala School and Rose Bay Convent (bus 324 or 325). The walk takes about an hour, with great views of the Opera House and Harbour Bridge, some lovely little coves to swim in, and a picnic ground and sandy beach at yacht-filled **Hermit Point**. Extensive, tree-filled **Nielson Park**, on Shark Bay, is one of Sydney's delights, a great place for a swim, a picnic, or refreshment at the popular café. The decorative Victorian-era mansion, **Greycliffe House**, built for William Wentworth's daughter in 1852 (see below), is now the headquarters of Sydney Harbour National Park (Mon–Fri 10am–noon; ☎ 02 9337 5511, ⓦ www.nationalparks.nsw.gov.au) and provides excellent information and maps on all waterfront walks. With views across the harbour to the city skyline, the park is a prime spot to watch both the New Year's Eve fireworks and the Sydney to Hobart yachts racing out through the heads on Boxing Day.

Beyond Shark Bay, Vaucluse Bay shelters the magnificent Gothic-style 1803 **Vaucluse House** and its large estate on Wentworth Road (Fri–Sun 9.30am–4pm; A\$8, child A\$4; ☎ 02 9388 7922, ⓦ www.hht.net.au), with tearooms in the grounds for refreshment. The house's original owner, explorer and reformer William Wentworth, was a member of the first party to cross the Blue Mountains. In 1831, he invited four thousand guests to Vaucluse House to celebrate the departure of the hated Governor Darling – the climax of the evening was a fireworks display that burned "Down with the Tyrant" into the night sky. To get here, walk from Nielson Park along Coolong Road (or take bus 325). Beyond Vaucluse Bay, narrow **Parsley Bay**'s shady finger of a park is a popular picnic and swimming spot, crossed by a picturesque pedestrian suspension bridge.

Watsons Bay and South Head

On the finger of land culminating in South Head, with an expansive sheltered harbour bay on its west side, and the treacherous cliffs of The Gap on its ocean side, **Watsons Bay** was one of the earliest settlements outside of Sydney Cove. In 1790, Robert Watson was one of the first signalmen to man the clifftop flagstaffs nearby, and by 1792 the bay was the focus of a successful fishing village; the quaint old wooden fishermen's cottages are still found on the tight streets around Camp Cove. It's an appropriate location for one of Sydney's longest-running fish restaurants, *Doyles* (see p.288), by the old Fishermans Wharf, now the ferry terminal (accessible by ferry from Circular Quay, on the *Rocket Explorer* hop-on-hop-off cruise – see box, p.232). In fact, *Doyles* has taken over the waterfront here, with two restaurants, a takeaway, and a seafood bistro in the bayfront beer-garden of *Doyles Palace Hotel*.

Spectacular ocean views are just a two-minute walk away through grassy Robertson Park, across Gap Road to **The Gap** (buses terminate just opposite – the 324, 325, and faster L24 from Circular Quay, and the L82 from Circular Quay via Bondi Beach), whose high cliffs are notorious as a place to commit suicide. You can follow a walking **track** north from here to South Head through another chunk of Sydney Harbour National Park, past the HMAS *Watson* Military Reserve. The track heads back to the bay side, and onto Cliff Street, which leads to **Camp Cove**, a tiny palm-fronted harbour beach popular with families; a small kiosk provides refreshments.

Alternatively, reach Camp Cove by walking along the Watsons Bay beach and then along Pacific Street and through Green Point Reserve. From the northern end of Camp Cove, steps lead up to a boardwalk that will take you to **South Head** (470m circuit), the lower jaw of the harbour mouth; here you'll get fantastic views of Port Jackson and the city, via Sydney's best-known **nudist beach**, Lady Jane (officially "Lady Bay"), a favourite gay haunt. It's not very private, however: a lookout point on the track provides full views, and ogling tour boats cruise past all weekend. From Lady Bay, it's a further fifteen minutes' walk along a boardwalked path to South Head itself, past nineteenth-century fortifications, lighthouse cottages, and the picturesque red-and-white-striped Hornby Lighthouse.

The North Shore

The **North Shore** is generally more affluent than the South. **Mosman** and **Neutral Bay** in particular have some stunning waterfront real estate, priced to match. It's surprising just how much harbourside bushland remains intact here – "leafy" just doesn't do it justice – and superbly sited amongst it all is **Taronga Zoo**. A ride on any ferry lets you gaze at beaches, bush, yachts and swish harbourfront houses, and is one of the chief joys of this area.

North Sydney and around

North Sydney, the district immediately north of the Harbour Bridge, has been associated with "pure fun" since the 1930s – you can't miss the huge laughing clown's face that belongs to **Luna Park**, right beside the bridge's foot at **Milsons Point**. Generations of Sydneysiders have walked through the grinning mouth, and the park's old rides and conserved 1930s fun hall, complete with period wall murals, slot machines, silly mirrors and giant slippery dips, have great nostalgia value for locals (summer holidays Mon–Thurs & Sun 10am–10pm, Fri & Sat 10am–midnight; other holidays Mon–Thurs & Sun 10am–6pm, Fri & Sat 10am–11pm; rest of year Mon & Thurs 11am–6pm, Fri 11am–11pm, Sat 10am–11pm, Sun 10am–6pm; free entry, rides A\$5–8 each or A\$20–48 for an all-day pass; ⓣ02 9033 7676, ⓦwww.lunaparksydney.com). The ferry to Milsons Point Wharf from Circular Quay or Darling Harbour pulls up right outside; otherwise, Milsons Point train station is a short walk away. Beyond the park, a boardwalk goes right around Lavender Bay, offering spectacular views of the Harbour Bridge and Opera House, most notably from McMahons Point Wharf and the adjacent park at Blues Point – which is a photographer's delight.

▲ North Sydney Olympic Pool

Right next door to Luna Park is Sydney's most picturesquely sited public swimming pool, with terrific vistas of the Harbour Bridge – the heated **North Sydney Olympic Pool**, Alfred South Street (Mon–Fri 5.30am–9pm, Sat & Sun 7am–7pm; A$5.50, child A$2.80; ☎02 9955 2309). As well as the fifty-metre outdoor pool, there's a 25-metre indoor pool, plus a gym, sauna, spa and café; an upmarket restaurant with pool and harbour views, *Aqua*, is just outside.

Just east of the Harbour Bridge and immediately opposite the Opera House, **Kirribilli** and adjacent Neutral Bay are mainly residential areas, although Kirribilli hosts a great general **market** on the fourth Saturday of the month in Bradfield Park (see "Markets", p.306). The Prime Minister's official Sydney residence, **Kirribilli House**, is on Kirribilli Point; controversially, former PM John Howard, a native Sydneysider, chose to live in this Gothic-revival mansion full time, costing taxpayers millions of dollars in flights to Canberra. Next door is Admiralty House, home to the Governor General; this is where the British royal family stay when they're in residence.

Following the harbour round you'll come to upmarket **Neutral Bay**. A five-minute walk from Neutral Bay ferry wharf via Hayes Street and Lower Wycombe Road is **Nutcote**, at 5 Wallaringa Ave (Wed–Sun 11am–3pm; A$8, child A$3; ☎02 9953 4453, ⊛www.maygibbs.com.au), the former home for 45 years of May Gibbs, the author and illustrator of the famous Australian children's book, *Snugglepot and Cuddlepie*, about two little gumnuts who come to life; published in 1918, it's an enduring classic. Bush-covered **Cremorne Point**, which juts into the harbour here, is also worth a jaunt. Catching the ferry from Circular Quay brings you in by a quaint open-access sea pool; from here, you can walk right around the point to Mosman Bay (just under 2km), or in the other direction, past the pool, there's a very pretty walk along **Shell Cove** (1km).

Mosman Bay: Taronga Zoo

Mosman Bay's seclusion was first recognized as a virtue during its early days as a whaling station, since it kept the stench of rotting whale flesh from the Sydney Cove settlement. Now the seclusion is a corollary of wealth. The ferry ride into the narrow, yacht-filled bay is a choice one – get off at Mosman Wharf – and fittingly finished off with a beer at the unpretentious *Mosman Rowers' Club* (visitors welcome).

What Mosman is most famous for, though, is **Taronga Zoo** on Bradleys Head Road, with its superb hilltop position overlooking the city (daily 9am–5pm; A$37, child A$18; car park A$10; ☎02 9969 2777, ⊛www.zoo.nsw .gov.au). The wonderful views and the natural bush surrounds are as much an attraction as the chance to get up close to the animals. The zoo houses bounding native Australian marsupials, birds (including kookaburras, galahs and cockatoos) and reptiles, plus sea lions and seals from the sub-Antarctic region. You'll also find exotic beasts from around the world, including giraffes, gorillas and many a playful chimpanzee. The spectacular **Asian Rainforest** exhibit includes a home for Taronga's small herd of Asian elephants.

You can get close to kangaroos and wallabies in the **Australian Walkabout** area, and the **koala house** gives you eye-level views; to get closer, arrange to have your photo taken next to a koala (daily 11am–2.45pm; A$19.95). For a more **hands-on experience**, a VIP Aussie Gold Tour (daily 9.15am & 1.15pm; 1hr 30min–2hr; A$77, child A$41 including zoo entry and koala picture; book 24hr in advance on ☎02 9978 4782) will give you and a small group a session with a zookeeper, guiding you through the Australian animals, some of which can be handled. Keeper talks and feeding sessions – including a free-flight bird show and a seal show – run through the day; details are on the map handed out on arrival.

Two transport-plus-entry options are available: the Sydney Ferries **Zoo Pass**, which includes the return ferry from Circular Quay Wharf 2 (every 30min, 12min each way; A$44, child A$21.50, tickets from the Circular Quay ferry office); and the faster **Zoo Express** run by Matilda (see p.232), cruising from Darling Harbour Pier 26 or Circular Quay Wharf 6 (every 45min; A$44, child A$30). Although there's a lower entrance near the wharf on Athol Road, it's best to start your visit from the upper entrance and spend several leisurely hours winding downhill to exit for the ferry. State Transit buses meet the ferries for the trip uphill, but a better option is to take the **Sky Safari** cable car included in the entry price. **Bus** 247 from Wynyard or the QVB also goes to the zoo.

Bradleys Head

Beyond the zoo, at the termination of **Bradleys Head Road**, Bradleys Head is marked by an enormous mast that once belonged to HMS *Sydney*, a victorious World War II Royal Australian Navy battleship lost (with all 645 hands) in 1941 off Australia's west coast after sinking a German raider. The rocky point is a peaceful spot with a dinky lighthouse and, of course, a fabulous view back over the south shore. A colony of ringtailed possums nests here, and boisterous flocks of rainbow lorikeets visit. The headland comprises another large chunk of Sydney Harbour National Park: you can walk to Bradleys Head via the six-kilometre **Ashton Park walking track**, which starts near Taronga Zoo Wharf, and continues beyond the headland to Taylors Bay and Chowder Head, finishing at **Clifton Gardens**, where there's a jetty and sea baths on **Chowder Bay**. The now defunct military reserve that separates Chowder Bay from another chunk of Sydney Harbour National Park on Middle Head is open to the public (see below), reached by a boardwalk from the northern end of Clifton Gardens.

Middle Harbour

Middle Harbour is the largest inlet of Port Jackson, its two sides joined across the narrowest point at **The Spit**. The Spit Bridge opens regularly to let tall-masted yachts through – much the best way to explore its pretty, quiet coves and bays. Crossing the Spit Bridge, you can walk all the way to Manly Beach along the ten-kilometre Manly Scenic Walkway (see p.275). The area also hides some architectural gems: the mock-Gothic 1889 bridge leading to **Northbridge**, and the idyllic enclave of **Castlecrag**, which was designed in 1924 by **Walter Burley Griffin**, fresh from planning Canberra and intent on building an environmentally friendly suburb – free of the fences and the red-tiled roofs he hated – that would be "for ever part of the bush". Buses 143, 144 and E43 run to Spit Road from Manly, taking in a scenic route uphill overlooking the Spit marina. To get to Castlecrag, take bus 203 from Wynyard.

Between Clifton Gardens and Balmoral Beach, a military reserve and naval depot at **Chowder Bay** blocked coastal access to both **Georges Head** and the more spectacular **Middle Head** by foot for over a century. Since the military's 1997 withdrawal from the site, walkers can now trek all the way between Bradleys Head and Middle Head, with the most popular section being between the six-kilometre stretch between Taronga and Balmoral. The 1890s military settlement is open to visitors as a reserve – the **Headland Park**, managed by the Harbour Trust (℡02 8969 2100, ⓦ www.harbourtrust.gov.au) – which offers tours exploring its underground fortifications (first Sun of the month, morning and afternoon; 2hr; A$8, child A$5). You can reach Headland Park from the northern end of Clifton Gardens (see above) or walk from Balmoral Beach.

The bush of Middle Head provides a gorgeous backdrop to **Balmoral Beach** on Hunters Bay. The shady tree-lined harbour beach is very popular with families. Fronting the beach, there's something very Edwardian and genteel about palm-filled, grassy Hunters Park and its bandstand, which is still used for Sunday jazz concerts or Shakespeare recitals in summer. The antiquated air is added to by the pretty, white-painted **Bathers Pavilion** at the northern end, now converted into a restaurant and café (see p.287). There are two sections of beach at Balmoral, separated by **Rocky Point**, a noted picnicking spot. South of Rocky Point, the "baths" – actually a netted bit of beach with a boardwalk and lanes for swimming laps – have been here in one form or another since

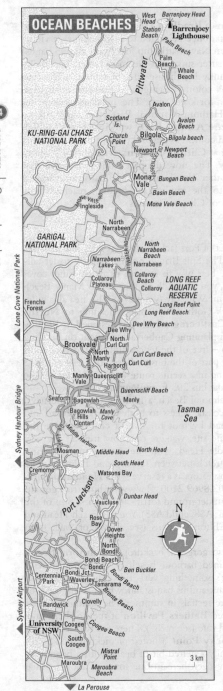

OCEAN BEACHES

West Head Station Beach · Barrenjoey Head · **Barrenjoey Lighthouse**

Palm Beach

Whale Beach

Pittwater

Avalon

Scotland Is. · Avalon Beach

KU-RING-GAI CHASE NATIONAL PARK · Church Point · Bilgola · Bilgola beach

Newport · Newport Beach

Mona Vale · Bungan Beach

MONA VALE Ingleside · Basin Beach

Mona Vale Beach

North Narrabeen

GARIGAL NATIONAL PARK · North Narrabeen Beach

Narrabeen Lakes · Narrabeen

Collaroy Plateau · Collaroy Beach

Frenchs Forest · Collaroy · **LONG REEF AQUATIC RESERVE**

Long Reef Point

Long Reef Beach

Dee Why · Dee Why Beach

Brookvale · North Curl Curl

North Manly · Curl Curl Beach

Manly Vale · Harbord · Curl Curl

Queenscliff

Seaforth · Bagowlah · Queenscliff Beach

Bagowlah Hills · Manly Cove · Manly

Clontarf

Mosman · Middle Head · North Head

Cremorne · South Head

Watsons Bay

Port Jackson

Dunbar Head

Vaucluse

Rose Bay · Dover Heights

North Bondi

Bondi Beach

Centennial Park · Bondi Jct · Ben Buckler

Waverley · Tamarama

Randwick · Clovelly · Bronte Beach

University of NSW · Coogee · Coogee Beach

South Coogee

Mistral Point

Maroubra · Maroubra Beach

Tasman Sea

N

0 ___ 3 km

▼ La Perouse

1899; you can rent sailboards, catamarans, kayaks and canoes and take lessons from Balmoral Sailing Club at the southern end of the beach (see p.305).

On the Hunters Bay side of Middle Head, tiny **Cobblers Beach** is officially **nudist**, and is a much more peaceful, secluded option than the more famous Lady Jane at South Head, and without the sleaze that sometimes troubles the other nudist beach nearby, tiny, south-facing **Obelisk Beach**. The hillside houses overlooking Balmoral have some of the highest price tags in Sydney: for a stroll through some prime real estate, head for **Chinamans Beach**, via Hopetoun Avenue and Rosherville Road. To get to Balmoral, catch a ferry to Taronga Zoo Wharf then bus 238 via Bradleys Head Road, or after 7pm Monday to Saturday the ferry to South Mosman (Musgrave Street) Wharf, then bus 233, or 257 via Military Road (257 originates at Chatswood station).

Ocean beaches

Sydney's **beaches** are among its great natural joys. The water and sand seem remarkably clean – people actually fish in the harbour – and at Long Reef, just north of Manly, you can find rock pools teeming with starfish, anemones, sea-snails and crabs, and even a few shy moray eels. Humpback and southern right whales are regularly sighted from the Sydney headlands on their winter migration from the Antarctic to the tropical waters of Queensland, and southern right whales even occasionally make an unusual appearance in

Sydney Harbour itself – the three southern right whales frolicking under the Harbour Bridge in July 2002 caused a sensation.

Don't be lulled into a false sense of security, however: the beaches do have **perils** as well as pleasures. Some beaches are protected by special shark nets, but they don't keep out stingers (jellyfish) such as bluebottles, which can suddenly swamp an entire beach: listen for loudspeaker announcements that will summon you from the water in the event of any danger. Pacific **currents** can be very strong indeed – inexperienced swimmers and those with small children would do better sticking to the sheltered **harbour beaches** or **sea pools** at the ocean beaches. Ocean beaches are generally patrolled by **surf lifesavers** during the day between October and April (all year at Bondi): red and yellow flags (generally up from 6am until 6 or 7pm) indicate the safe areas to swim, avoiding dangerous rips and undertows. It's hard not to be impressed as **surfers** paddle out on a seething ocean, but don't follow them unless you're confident you know what you're doing. Surf schools can teach the basic skills, surfing etiquette and lingo: see the box on p.305.

The final hazard, despite the apparent cleanliness, is **pollution**. Monitoring shows that it is nearly always safe to swim at all of Sydney's beaches – except after storms, when storm water, currents and onshore breezes wash up sewage and other rubbish onto harbour beaches making them (as signs will indicate) unsuitable for swimming and surfing. To check pollution levels, consult the Beachwatch Bulletin (℡ 1800 036 677, ⓦ www.environment.nsw.gov.au/beach).

Topless bathing for women, while legal, is accepted on many beaches but frowned on at others, so if in doubt, do as the locals do. The **nudist** beaches within reach of central Sydney are not on the open ocean, but just inside the harbour: Lady Bay near Watson's Bay (see p.264) and Cobblers and Obelisk beaches, both near Middle Head (see p.268).

Bondi and the eastern beaches

Sydney's eastern beaches stretch from Bondi down to Maroubra. Heading south from **Bondi**, you can walk right along the coast to its smaller, less brazen but very lively cousin **Coogee**, passing through gay-favourite **Tamarama**, family focused, café-cultured **Bronte**, narrow **Clovelly** and **Gordons Bay**, the latter

---

Bondi's surf lifesavers

Surf lifesavers are what made Bondi famous; there's a bronze sculpture of one outside the Bondi Pavilion. The surf-lifesaving movement began in 1906 with the founding of the Bondi Surf Life Bathers' Lifesaving Club in response to the drownings that accompanied the increasing popularity of swimming. From the beginning of the colony, swimming was harshly discouraged as an unsuitable bare-fleshed activity. However, by the 1890s swimming in the ocean had become the latest fad, and a Pacific Islander introduced the concept of catching waves or **bodysurfing** that was to become an enduring national craze. Although "wowsers" (teetotal puritanical types) attempted to put a stop to it, by 1903 all-day swimming was every Sydneysider's right.

The bronzed and muscled surf lifesavers in their distinctive red-and-yellow caps are a highly photographed, world-famous Australian image. Surf lifesavers (members of what are now called Surf Life Saving Clubs, abbreviated to SLSC) are volunteers working the beach at weekends, so come then to watch their exploits – or look out for a surf carnival; lifeguards, on the other hand, are employed by the council and work all week during swimming season (year-round at Bondi).

with an underwater nature trail. Randwick Council has designed the Eastern Beaches Coast Walk from Clovelly to Coogee and beyond to more downmarket **Maroubra**, with stretches of boardwalk and interpretive boards detailing environmental features. Pick up a free guide-map detailing the walk from the council's Customer Service Office, 30 Francis St, Randwick (℡02 9344 7006; brochures also available to download from Ⓦwww.randwickcitytourism .com.au), or from the beachfront Coogee Bay Kiosk, opposite *McDonald's* on Arden Street. It's also possible to walk north all the way from Bondi to South Head along the cliffs now that missing links in the pathway have been connected with bridges and boardwalk.

Bondi Beach

Bondi Beach is synonymous with Australian beach culture, and indeed the long curve of golden sand must be one of the best-known beaches in the world. It's the closest ocean beach to the city centre; you can take a train to Bondi Junction and then a ten-minute bus ride, or drive there in twenty minutes. Big, brash and action-packed, it's probably not the best place for a quiet sunbathe and swim, but the sprawling sandy crescent really is spectacular.

Red-tiled houses and apartment buildings crowd in to catch the view, many of them erected in the 1920s when Bondi was a working-class suburb. Although still residential, it's long since become a popular gathering place for backpackers from around the world (see box below).

The beachfront **Campbell Parade** is both cosmopolitan and highly commercialized, lined with cafés and shops. For a gentler experience, explore some of the side streets, such as **Hall Street**, where an assortment of kosher bakeries and delis serve the area's Jewish community, and some of Bondi's best cafés are hidden. On Sunday, the **Bondi Beach markets** (10am–5pm), in the grounds of the Bondi Beach Public School on the corner of Campbell Parade and Warners Avenue facing the northern end of the beach, place great emphasis on groovy fashion and jewellery. Between Campbell Parade and the beach, **Bondi Park** slopes down to the promenade, and is always full of sprawling bodies. The focus of the promenade is the arcaded, Spanish-style **Bondi Pavilion** (℡02 8362 3400, Ⓦwww.waverley.nsw.gov.au/info/pavilion), built in 1928 as a deluxe changing-room complex and converted into a community centre hosting an array of workshops, classes and events, from drama and comedy in the theatre and the Seagull Room (the former ballroom) to outdoor film festivals in the courtyard. A community-access **art gallery** on the ground floor (daily 10am–5pm) features changing exhibitions by local artists. In September, the day-long Festival of the Winds, Australia's largest **kite festival**, takes over the beach.

Christmas Day on Bondi

For years, backpackers from colder climes have flocked to Bondi to live out the fantasy of spending Christmas Day on the beach under a scorching sun. It's no longer the drunken free-for-all it once was, though – the council, keen to tame the worst excesses and tempt back local families, have banned alcohol from the beach and its vicinity on 25 December, giving the police the right to make on-the-spot confiscations. However, in the past few years a **dance party** has been organized in the Pavilion, with a bar, DJs, food and entertainment running from 11am to 8pm. Around three thousand revellers cram in, while thousands of others enjoy the alcohol-free beach outside. For tickets, contact Ticketek (℡13 28 49, Ⓦwww.ticketek.com.au).

Surfing is Bondi integral to, the big waves ensuring that there's always a pack of damp young things hanging around, bristling with surfboards. However, the beach is carefully delineated, with surfers using the southern end. There are two sets of flags for swimmers and boogie-boarders, with families congregating at the northern end near the sheltered saltwater pool (free), and everybody else using the middle flags. The beach is netted and there hasn't been a shark attack for over forty years. If the sea is too rough, or if you want to swim laps, there's a seawater swimming pool (plus gym, sauna, massage service and poolside café) at the southern end of the beach under the **Bondi Icebergs Club** on Notts Avenue (Mon–Fri 6am–6.30pm, Sat & Sun 6.30am–6.30pm; A$4.50, child A$2.50; ℡02 9130 4804, ⓦwww.icebergs.com.au). Part of the Bondi legend since 1929, members must swim throughout the winter, and media coverage of their plunge, made truly wintry with the addition of huge chunks of ice, heralds the first day of winter. The clubhouse is a great place for a drink (see p.293).

Topless bathing is condoned at Bondi – a long way from conditions right up to the late 1960s, when stern beach inspectors were on the lookout for indecent exposure. If you fancy a dip but don't have the gear, Beached at Bondi, on the beach in front of the Pavilion, rents out everything from umbrellas, wetsuits, cozzies and towels to surfboards and boogie-boards, and has lockers for valuables.

You can **get to Bondi Beach** on **bus** 333, 380 or 389 from Circular Quay via Oxford Street and Bondi Junction, or take the train to Bondi Junction station, from where several bus routes run to the beach. It's also a stop on the Explorer tour-bus route (see box, p.218).

Tamarama to Gordons Bay

Many people find the smaller, quieter beaches to the south of Bondi more enticing, and the oceanfront and clifftop **walking track** to Clovelly (about 2hr) is popular – the track also includes a fitness circuit, so you'll see plenty of joggers en route. Walk past the Bondi Icebergs Club on Notts Avenue (see above), round Mackenzies Point and through Marks Park to the modest and secluded **Mackenzies Bay**. Next is **Tamarama Bay**, a deep, narrow beach favoured by the smart set and a hedonistic gay crowd ("Glamarama" to the locals), as well as surfers. From Bondi, the beach is a fifteen-minute walk, or a short hop on bus 380 (to Fletcher Street) then a three-hunded-metre stroll. You can also get there by taking bus 361 or 380 from Bondi Junction.

Walking through Tamarama's small park and following the oceanfront road for five minutes will bring you to the next beach along, **Bronte Beach** on Nelson Bay. More of a family affair with a large green park, a popular café strip and sea baths, it's easily reached on bus 378 from Railway Square via Oxford Street and Bondi Junction, where you can also catch bus 360 or 361. The **northern end** has inviting flat-rock platforms, popular as fishing and relaxation spots, and the beach here is cliff-backed, providing some shade. The **park** beyond is extensive with Norfolk Island Pines for shade, electric barbeques, a **mini-train ride** (A$3), here since 1947, and an imaginative children's playground. The secluded and peaceful Bronte Gully lies to the rear where kookaburras are a common sight and brightly coloured lorikeets are often seen bathing in the waterfall. At the **southern end** of the beach, a natural rock enclosure, the "Bogey Hole", makes a calm area for kids to swim in, and there are rock ledges to lie on around the enclosed sea swimming pool known as **Bronte Baths** (open access; free). Nearby, palm trees give a suitably holiday feel as you relax at one of the outside tables of Bronte Road's wonderful café strip (eight to choose from, plus a fish-and-chip shop).

From Bronte, it's a pleasant five-minute walk past the baths to **Waverly Cemetery**, a fantastic spot to spend eternity. Established in 1877, it contains the graves of many famous Australians, with the bush-poet contingent well represented. **Henry Lawson**, described on his headstone as poet, journalist and patriot, languishes in section 3G 516, while **Dorothea Mackeller**, who penned the famous poem *I love a sunburnt country*, is in section 6 832–833.

Beyond here – another five-minute walk – on the other side of Shark Point, is the channel-like **Clovelly Bay**, with concrete platforms on either side and several sets of steps leading into the very deep water. Rocks at the far end keep out the waves, and the sheltered bay is popular with lap-swimmers and snorkellers; you're almost certain to see one of the bay's famous blue groupers (snorkels can be rented up the road at Clovelly). There's also a free swimming pool. A grassy park with several terraces extends back from the beach and is a great place for a picnic. The divinely sited café is packed at weekends, and on Sunday afternoons and evenings the nearby *Clovelly Hotel* is a popular hangout, with free live music and a great bistro, or get rock-bottom-priced drinks and fab views at the *Clovelly Bowling Club*. To get to Clovelly, take **bus** 339 from Millers Point via Central Station and Albion Street, Surry Hills; 360 from Bondi Junction; or the weekday peak-hour X39 from Wynyard.

From Clovelly, it's best to stick to the road route along Cliffbrook Parade rather than rockhop around to equally narrow **Gordons Bay**. Unsupervised, undeveloped Gordons Bay itself is not a pretty beach, but another world exists beneath the sheltered water: the protected **underwater nature trail**, marked out for divers, is home to a range of sea creatures; diving and snorkelling gear can be rented at Clovelly. From here, a walkway leads around the waterfront to Major Street and then onto **Dunningham Reserve** overlooking the northern end of Coogee Beach; the walk to Coogee proper takes about fifteen minutes in all.

Coogee

While **Coogee** has a lively bar, café, restaurant and backpacker scene, and some big hotels, there's just something more laid-back, community-oriented and friendlier about it than Bondi – and it's not totally teeming with trendies. With its hilly streets of Californian-style apartment blocks looking onto a compact, pretty beach enclosed by two cliffy, green-covered headlands, Coogee has a snugness that Bondi just can't match. Everything is close to hand: beachfront Arden Street has a down-to-earth strip of cafés that compete with each other to sell the cheapest cooked breakfast, while the main shopping street, Coogee Bay Road, running uphill from the beach, has a choice selection of coffee spots and eateries, plus a big supermarket.

The ugly high-rise *Holiday Inn* spoilt the southern end of the beach, though its bar does have fabulous views over the water. Other 1990s developments were more aesthetically successful: the imaginatively modernized promenade is a great place to stroll and hang out. Between it and the medium-sized beach is a grassy park with free electric barbecues, picnic tables and shelters. The beach is popular with families (there's an excellent children's playground at the southern end) and travellers, as there's a stack of backpackers' hostels. However, one of Coogee's chief pleasures is its ocean swimming pools, beyond the southern end of the beach. The first, the secluded McIvers Baths, traditionally remains for women and children only and is known by locals as **Coogee Women's Baths** (noon–5pm; entry by donation). Just south of here, at the end of Neptune Street, is the unisex **Wylies Baths** (May–Sept 7am–5pm; Oct–April 7am–7pm; A$3), a saltwater pool on the edge of the sea, with big decks to lie on, and solar-heated showers; it's a fine spot for the excellent coffee made at its kiosk.

You can get to Coogee on **bus** 373 or 374 from Circular Quay via Randwick, or 372 from Railway Square. There are also buses from Bondi Junction via Randwick – 313 and 314 – while the 370 runs from Leichhardt via Glebe and Newtown.

Immediately south of Wylies, **Trenerry Reserve** is a huge green park jutting out into the ocean; its spread of big, flat rocks offers tremendous views and makes a great place to chill out. Probably the most impressive section of Randwick Council's **Eastern Beaches Coast Walk** commences here. The walk, sometimes on boards, is accompanied by interpretive panels detailing the surrounding plant- and bird-life. Steps lead down to a rock platform full of teeming rock pools, and you can swim in a large tear-shaped pool. It's quite thrilling with the waves crashing over – but be careful of both the waves and the dangerous blue-ringed octopus that are found here. At low tide you can continue walking along the rocks around Lurline Bay; otherwise, you must follow the streets inland, rejoining the waterfront from Mermaid Avenue. Jack Vanny Memorial Park is fronted by the cliff-like rocks of Mistral Point, a great spot to sit and admire the ocean, and down by the water the **Mahon Pool**, a small, pleasant open-access sea pool, with waves crashing at its edge and surrounded by great boulders, has an unspoilt, secluded feel.

Manly and the northern beaches

Manly, just above North Head at the northern mouth of the harbour, is doubly blessed with both ocean and harbour beaches. When Captain Arthurs Phillip, the commander of the First Fleet, was exploring Sydney Harbour in 1788, he saw a group of well-built Aboriginal men onshore, proclaimed them to be "manly" and named the cove in the process. During the Edwardian era it became fashionable as a recreational retreat from the city, with the promotional slogan "Manly – seven miles from Sydney, but a thousand miles from care". An excellent time to visit is over the Labour Day long weekend in early October, when the **Jazz Festival** has free outdoor concerts featuring musicians from around the world. Beyond Manly, the **northern beaches** continue for 30km up to the Barrenjoey Peninsula and **Palm Beach**. Pick up the excellent free *Sydney's Northern Beaches Map* from the Manly Visitor Centre (see below). The northern beaches can be reached by regular **bus** from various city bus terminals or from Manly Wharf; routes are detailed throughout the text below.

Manly

A day-trip to Manly, rounded off with fish and chips, offers a classic taste of Sydney life. The ferry trip out here has always been half the fun: the legendary Manly Ferry service commenced in 1854, and the huge old boats come complete with snack bars selling the ubiquitous meat pie. Ferries terminate at **Manly Wharf** in Manly Cove, near a small section of calm harbour beach with a netted-off swimming area popular with families. Like a typical English seaside resort, Manly Wharf had always housed a tacky funfair until a few years ago; now the wharf is all grown up with a slew of cafés and brand shops, including multicultural food stalls and a very swish pub, the *Manly Wharf Hotel*. You'll also find the **Manly Visitor Information Centre** (Mon–Fri 9am–5pm, Sat & Sun 10am–4pm; ☏02 9976 1430, ⓦwww.manlytourism.com.au; lockers A$2) out the front. The wharf is now a hub for adventure activity: three watersports

▲ South Steyne, Manly

companies based here offer parasailing, kayaking and RIB tours through crashing surf to North Head; ask at the tourist office for details.

From the wharf, walk along West Esplanade to **Oceanworld** (daily 10am–5.30pm; A$17.95, child A$9.50; ℡02 8251 7877, Ⓦwww.oceanworld.com.au), where clear acrylic walls hold back the water so you can saunter along the harbour floor, gazing at huge sharks and stingrays. Divers hand-feed sharks three times weekly (Mon, Wed & Fri 11am) and there's always a range of shows and guided tours, including the Dangerous Australians show with local (and deadly) snakes and spiders. You can also dive amongst the **grey nurse sharks** – which can grow up to 160kg – with Shark Dive Xtreme (2hr 30min; qualified diver A$180, unqualified diver A$245; bookings ℡02 8251 7878). Opposite, the screams come from the three giant waterslides of **Manly Waterworks** (Sat & Sun 10am–5pm, daily in school holidays; 1hr A$14.50, all day A$19.50; children must be 120cm or taller; ℡02 9948 1088, Ⓦwww.manlywaterworks.com). Between the slides and Oceanworld, the **Manly Art Gallery and Museum** (Tues–Sun 10am–5pm; A$3.60, child A$1.20; ℡02 9976 1420) has a collection started in the 1920s of Australian paintings, drawings, prints and etchings, and a stash of beach memorabilia including huge, early wooden surfboards and old-fashioned swimming costumes.

Many visitors mistake Manly Cove for the ocean beach, which in fact lies on the other side of the isthmus, 500m down **The Corso**, Manly's busy pedestri-anized main drag filled with surf shops, cafés, restaurants and pubs. The ocean beach, **South Steyne**, is characterized by the stands of Norfolk pine that line the shore. Every summer, a beach-hire concession rents out just about anything to make the beach more fun, from surfboards to snorkel sets, and they also have a bag-minding service. A six-kilometre-long shared pedestrian and **cycle path** begins at South Steyne and runs north to Seaforth, past North Steyne beach and Queenscliff. You can rent mountain bikes from Manly Cycles, a block back from the beach at 36 Pittwater Rd (1hr A$12, all day A$25; ℡02 9977 1189). For a more idyllic beach, follow the footpath from the southern end of South

Steyne around the headland to Cabbage Tree Bay, with two very pretty, protected green-backed beaches at either end: **Fairy Bower** to the west and **Shelley Beach** to the east.

Belgrave Street, running north from Manly Wharf, is Manly's alternative strip, with good cafés, interesting shops, yoga schools and the Manly Environment Centre at no. 41 (Mon–Fri 9am–5pm; ☏02 9976 2842, ⊛www.mec .org.au), whose aim is to educate the community about the local biodiversity and the issues affecting it.

Ferries leave Circular Quay for Manly twice an hour, between about 6am and 11.45pm (30min; A\$6.40). Faster JetCat catamarans (15min; A\$8.20) operate in the morning and evening on weekdays (Mon–Fri 6–9.25am & 4.20–8.30pm) and during the day at weekends (Sat 6.10am–3.35pm, Sun 7.10am–3.35pm).

North Head

You can take in more of the Sydney Harbour National Park at **North Head**, the harbour mouth's upper jaw, where you can follow the short circuitous Fairfax Walking Track to three lookout points, including the **Fairfax Lookout**, for splendid views. A regular 135 **bus** leaves from Manly Wharf for Manly Hospital, from where it's a 25-minute walk through the national park to North Head lookout. Right in the middle of the park is a military reserve with its own **National Artillery Museum** (Wed–Sun 9am–4pm; A\$11, child A\$5) sited in the historic **North Fort**, a curious system of tunnels built into the headland – it takes up to two hours to wander through them with a requisite guided tour.

There's more history at the old **Quarantine Station**, on the harbour side of North Head, used from 1832 until 1984: arriving passengers or crew who had a contagious disease were set down at Spring Cove to serve a spell of isolation at the station, all at the shipping companies' expense. Sydney residents, too, were forced here, most memorably during the plague, which broke out in The Rocks in 1900, when 1828 people were quarantined (104 plague victims are buried in the grounds). The site, its buildings still intact, is now a tourist attraction, with **guided daytime tours** (Wed–Fri 3pm, Sat & Sun 10am & 3pm; 2hr; A\$25, child A\$19; ☏02 9976 6220, ⊛www.q-station.com.au) and spookier **night-time tours** (Mon–Wed 7.30pm; Fri & Sun 6pm; 2hr–2h 30min; A\$25–36 includes light supper), giving an insight not only into Sydney's immigration history but also the evolution of medical science in the last 170 years, often in gory detail. The tours provide the only opportunity to get out to this beautiful isolated harbour spot with its views across to Balmoral Beach. The daytime tours coordinate with the 135 bus from Manly Wharf (bus fare extra); no public transport is available for the night-time visits.

Freshwater, just beyond Manly, sits snugly between two rocky headlands on Queenscliff Bay, and is one of the most picturesque of the northern beaches. There's plenty of surf culture around the headland at Curl Curl, and a walking track at its northern end, commencing from Huston Parade, will take you above the rocky coastline to the curve of **Dee Why Beach** (bus 136, 146, 152, 158 or 169 from Manly Wharf; bus 178 from outside the QVB in the city).

Several other pretty beaches lie up the coast, including the long sweeping **Collaroy Beach**, family-friendly **Mona Vale** and the unusual orange sands of **Bilgola Beach**, from where a trio of Sydney's best beaches, for both surf and scenery, run up the eastern fringe of the mushroom-shaped **Barrenjoey Peninsula**: Avalon and Whale beaches are popular surfie territory, while the more fashionable Palm Beach caters to visiting celebs and Sydney identities getting away from the city.

Backed by bush-covered hills (where koalas can still be found), and reached by 3km of winding road, smallish **Avalon Beach** has a suitably secluded feel and is indeed a slice of paradise on a summer's day. A pleasing set of shops and eateries run at right angles from the beach on Avalon Parade, location of the popular travellers' hangout, *Avalon Beach Hostel* (see p.230).

At the northern point of the peninsula is **Palm Beach**, a hangout for the rich and famous and a popular city escape. It's also the location of "Summer Bay" in the long-running Aussie soap *Home and Away*, with the picturesque Barrenjoey Lighthouse and bush-covered headland – part of **Ku-ring-gai Chase National Park** – regularly in shot. To blend right in, you can stay at the quirky *Palm Beach Bed and Breakfast* at 122 Pacific Rd (see p.230) with lovely views of the ocean. A steep walking path to the summit of Barrenjoey Headland from the car park at the base takes twenty to forty minutes, rewarded by a stunning panorama of Palm Beach, Pittwater and the Hawkesbury River. The NPWS offers weekend tours of the sandstone lighthouse, which dates from 1881 (Sun every 30min, 11am–3pm; 30min; gold coin donation).

Buses 190 and L90 run up the peninsula from Central via Wynyard to Avalon, continuing to Palm Beach via the Pittwater side; change at Avalon for bus 193 to Whale Beach. Buses 188 and L88 go from Central and Wynyard to Avalon, and the 187 and L87 run from The Rocks to Newport.

Botany Bay

The southern suburbs of Sydney, arranged around huge **Botany Bay**, are seen as the heartland of red-tiled-roof suburbia, a terracotta sea spied from above as the planes land at **Mascot**. Clive James, the area's most famous son, hails from Kogarah – described as a 1950s suburban wasteland in his tongue-in-cheek *Unreliable Memoirs*. The popular perception of Botany Bay is coloured by its proximity to an airport, a high-security prison (Long Bay), an oil refinery, a container terminal and a sewerage outlet. Yet the surprisingly clean-looking water is fringed by quiet, sandy beaches and the marshlands shelter a profusion of birdlife. Whole areas of the waterfront, at **La Perouse**, with its associations with eighteenth-century French exploration, and on the **Kurnell Peninsula** where Captain Cook first set anchor, are designated as part of **Botany Bay National Park**, and large stretches on either side of the Georges River form a State Recreation Area. **Brighton-Le-Sands**, the busy suburban strip on the west of the bay, is a hive of bars and restaurants and is something of a focus for

Sydney's Greek community. Its long beach is also a popular spot for windsurfers and kite-surfers.

La Perouse

La Perouse, tucked into the northern shore of Botany Bay where it meets the Pacific Ocean, contains Sydney's oldest Aboriginal settlement, the legacy of a mission. The suburb took its name from the eighteenth-century French explorer, **Laperouse**, who set up camp here for six weeks, briefly and cordially meeting Captain Arthurs Phillip, who was making his historic decision to forgo swampy Botany Bay and move on to Port Jackson. After leaving Botany Bay, the Laperouse expedition was never seen again.

A monument erected in 1825 and the excellent NPWS-run **La Perouse Museum** (Wed–Sun 10am–4pm; A$5.50, child A$3.30; ☏02 9247 5033), which sits on a grassy headland between the pretty beaches of Congwong Bay and Frenchmans Bay, tell the whole fascinating story. There is also an exhibition that looks at the Aboriginal history and culture of the area.

The surrounding headlands and foreshore have been incorporated into the northern half of **Botany Bay National Park** (no entry fee; the other half is across Botany Bay on the Kurnell Peninsula). An **NPWS visitor centre** (☏02 9311 3379) in the museum building provides details of walks including a fine one past Congwong Bay Beach to Henry Head and its lighthouse (5km round trip); ask about the "whale" Aboriginal rock carving. The idyllic veranda of the *Boatshed Cafe*, on the small headland between Congwong and Frenchmans bays, sits right over the water with pelicans floating about below. La Perouse is at its most lively on **Sunday** (and public holidays) when, following a tradition established at the start of the twentieth century, Aboriginal people come down to sell boomerangs and other crafts, and demonstrate snake-handling skills (from 1.30pm) and boomerang-throwing. There are also tours of the nineteenth-century fortifications on **Bare Island** (Sat, Sun & public holidays 1.30pm & 2.30pm; A$7.70; ☏02 9311 3379), joined to La Perouse by a thin walkway; the island, originally built amid fears of a Russian invasion, featured in *Mission Impossible II*.

To **get to La Perouse**, catch bus 394 or 399 from Circular Quay via Darlinghurst and Moore Park, or 393 from Railway Square via Surry Hills and Moore Park, or the L94 express from Circular Quay.

The Kurnell Peninsula and Cronulla

From La Perouse, you can see across Botany Bay to Kurnell and the red buoy marking the spot where Captain James Cook and the crew of the *Endeavour* anchored on April 29, 1770, for an eight-day exploration. Back in England, many refused to believe that the uniquely Australian plants and animals they had recorded actually existed – the kangaroo and platypus in particular were thought to be a hoax. **Captain Cook's Landing Place** is now part of **Botany Bay National Park**, where the informative **NPWS Discovery Centre** (Mon–Fri 11am–3pm, Sat & Sun 10am–4.30pm; car fee A$7; ☏02 9668 9111) looks at the wetlands ecology of the park and tells the story of Cook's visit and its implications for Aboriginal people. Indeed, the political sensitivity of the spot that effectively marks the beginning of the decline of an ancient culture has led to the planned renaming of the park to Kamay-Botany Bay National Park, "Kamay" being the original Dharawal people's name for the bay. Set aside as a public recreation area in 1899, the heath and woodland is unspoilt and there are some secluded beaches for swimming; you may even spot parrots and honeyeaters. To get here, take the train to Cronulla and then Kurnell Bus Services route 987 (☎02 9524 8977).

On the ocean side of the **Kurnell Peninsula** sits Sydney's most southern beach suburb and its longest stretch of beach – just under 5km; the sandy stretch of Bate Bay begins at **Cronulla** and continues as deserted, dune-backed **Wanda Beach**. This is prime **surfing** territory – and the only Sydney beach accessible by train (40min from Central Station on the Sutherland line; surfboards carried free). Steeped in surf culture, everything about Cronulla centres on watersports and a laid-back beach lifestyle, from the multitude of surf shops on Cronulla Street (which becomes a pedestrianized mall between Kingsway and Purley Place), to the outdoor cafés on the beachfront and the surfrider clubs and boating facilities on the bay. Even the *Cronulla Beach YHA* at 40 Kingsway (see p.230) is aimed primarily at surfers with surf excursions to Garie and free use of boogie boards. Unfortunately, the ethnically charged **riots** in December 2005 did much to damage Cronulla's reputation as a chilled beach-resort destination, and tensions between local surfers and Middle Eastern youths from the western suburbs still exist.

Western suburbs

For over sixty years, Sydney has slid ever westwards in a monotonous sprawl of shopping centres, brick-veneer homes and fast-food chains, along the way swallowing up towns and villages, some dating back to colonial times. **Parramatta**, **Liverpool**, **Penrith** and **Campbelltown**, once separate communities scattered between the city and the Blue Mountains, are now satellite towns inside Sydney's commuter belt; here and there amid the latter-day sprawl you'll still find a few eighteenth- and nineteenth-century buildings. For many travellers, however, the main point of interest in this part of the city is the Olympic site at **Homebush Bay**, 8km east of Parramatta.

Parramatta and Penrith

Situated on the Parramatta River, a little over 20km upstream from the harbour mouth, **PARRAMATTA** was the first of Sydney's rural satellites – the first farming community in Australia, in fact. Exploring inland, the European settlers found well-watered, fertile river flats where they quickly established agricultural outposts; their first wheat crop, successfully harvested in 1789, saved the fledgling colony from starvation. Today, dotted among Parramatta's malls and busy roads are a few remnants from that time – eighteenth-century public buildings and original settlers' dwellings that warrant a visit if you're interested in Australian history.

It's a thirty-minute train ride from Central Station to Parramatta, but the most enjoyable way to get here is on the sleek RiverCat ferry from Circular Quay up the Parramatta River (55min; A$7.70 one way). The wharf is on Phillip Street, a couple of blocks away from the helpful **Parramatta Heritage and Visitor Centre** on Church Street, by the convict-built Lennox Bridge (daily 9am–5pm; ☎02 8839 3311, ⓦwww.parracity.nsw.gov.au). The centre hands out free walking-route maps detailing its many historical attractions. Parramatta's most important historic feature is the National Trust-owned **Old Government House** in **Parramatta Park** by the river (Mon–Fri 10am–4pm, Sat & Sun 10.30am–4pm; A$8, child A$5). Entered through the 1885 gatehouse on O'Connell Street, the park – filled with native trees – rises up to the gracious

Sydney Olympic Park at Homebush Bay

The main focus of the much-lauded 2000 Olympic events was the A$470-million **Sydney Olympic Park** at **Homebush Bay**. Virtually the geographical heart of the westward-sprawling city, Homebush Bay already had some heavy-duty sporting facilities – the State Sports Centre and the Aquatic Centre – in place. Since the games, the Park has become a family-oriented sports, recreation and entertainment complex with events such as free outdoor movies, multicultural festivals and children's holiday activities, as well as public sports facilities and professional fixtures.

The **ANZ Stadium**, venue for the Olympic opening and closing ceremonies, track and field events, and marathon and soccer finals, was designed to seat 110,000. Despite an A$68-million overhaul to reduce this number to 83,500 – more realistic for its current use as an Aussie Rules football, cricket, rugby league, rugby union, soccer and concert venue – it's still Sydney's largest stadium. On non-event days, you can take an hour-long tour (4 daily; A$27.50, child A$15; ☏02 8765 2300, ⓦwww.anzstadium.com.au).

Opposite the Olympic site is the huge **Bicentennial Park**, opened in 1988. More than half is conservation wetlands; a boardwalk explores the mangroves, and you can observe the profusion of native birds from a bird hide. There are also around 8km of cycling and walking tracks. Further north, the green-friendly Athletes' Village is now a solar-powered suburb, **Newington**.

To get an overview of the area, there's an **observation centre** on the seventeenth floor of the *Novotel Hotel* on Olympic Boulevard between the Telstra Stadium and the Aquatic Centre (daily 10am–4pm; A$4; ☏02 8762 1111, ⓦwww.novotelsydney olympicpark.com.au). The *Novotel* is Olympic Park's social focus, with several places to eat and drink, including the popular *Homebush Bay Brewery*.

Visiting the venues

The best way to get to Sydney Olympic Park is to take a ferry up the Parramatta River: the **RiverCat** from Circular Quay to the Sydney Olympic Park wharf (Homebush Bay) takes 35 to 50 minutes (A$7.70 one way, child A$3.80). Bus 401 runs from the wharf to the Olympic Centre, the State Sports Centre and the Athletic Centre. Otherwise, direct **trains** from Central to Olympic Park station run four times daily on weekdays; at other times, take a train to Lidcombe, from where connections to Olympic Park depart every ten minutes.

Sydney Olympic Park Visitor Centre, right next to Olympic Park station on the corner of Showground Road and Murray Rose Avenue (daily 9am–5pm; ☏02 9714 7888, ⓦwww.sydneyolympicpark.com.au) can fill you in on events, and hires bikes at weekends (from A$12 for 1hr). A walking tour of the sites, **The Games Trail Tour**, leaves daily from outside the centre at noon, 1.30pm & 3pm (no booking necessary; A$20; 1hr).

Georgian-style building, the oldest remaining public edifice in Australia. It was built between 1799 and 1816 and used as the Viceregal residence until 1855; one wing has been converted into a pleasant teahouse. History aside, Parramatta today is a modern multicultural suburban town with a wealth of international restaurants around Church and Phillip streets, and bargain shops and factory outlets on its outskirts.

Continuing west, the Western Highway and the rail lines head on to **PENRITH**, the most westerly of Sydney's satellite towns, in a curve of the Nepean River at the foot of the Blue Mountains (on the way out here you pass **Featherdale Wildlife Park**; see box, p.333). Penrith has an old-fashioned Aussie feel about it – a tight community that is immensely proud of the

Panthers, its boisterous rugby-league team. The area is also the home of the extensive International Regatta Centre on Penrith Lakes, spreading between Castlereagh and Cranebrook roads north of the town centre, and used in the Olympics; at **Penrith Whitewater Stadium** (T02 4730 4333, Wwww .penrithwhitewater.com.au) you can enjoy a thrilling ninety-minute white-water rafting session (A$80).

Also north of Penrith is an award-winning Aboriginal cultural tourism centre, **Muru Mittigar**, on Castlereagh Road, Castlereagh (Mon–Fri 9am–4pm, Sat 10am–2pm; A$45, child A$34; T02 4729 2377, Wwww.murumittigar.com.au), where Darug guides give talks on their ancestral beliefs and introduce visitors to bush tucker, medicinal plants and the art of boomerang-painting.

Eating and drinking

If the way its chefs are regularly stolen to work overseas is any indication, Sydney has blossomed into one of the great restaurant capitals of the world, offering a fantastic range of cosmopolitan eateries, covering every imaginable cuisine. Quality is uniformly high, with the freshest produce, meat and seafood always on hand, and a culinary culture of discerning, well-informed diners. The restaurant scene is highly fashionable and businesses rise in favour, fall in popularity and close down or change names and style at an astonishing rate. For a comprehensive guide, consider investing in the latest edition of *SydneyEats* or the *Sydney Morning Herald Good Food Guide*.

Sydney's fully fledged **café culture** is at its busiest and best in Potts Point, Darlinghurst, Surry Hills, Glebe, Newtown, Leichhardt and the eastern beaches of Bondi, Bronte and Coogee.

There are many fascinating **ethnic** enclaves, representing the city's diverse communities, where you can eat authentic cuisines Jewish on Hall Street, Bondi Beach; Chinese in Haymarket; Turkish and Indian on Cleveland Street, Surry Hills; Italian in East Sydney, Leichhardt and Haberfield; Greek in Marrickville and Brighton-Le-Sands; Indonesian on Anzac Parade, in Kingsford and Kensington.

All restaurants in the following listings are **open** daily for lunch and dinner, unless otherwise stated. Many cafés open early for breakfast, one of Sydney's most popular meals. Other favourites are weekend brunch, available at some cafés and restaurants, and "high tea" (see p.58), a fad taking over many of the city's look-at-me eateries.

Circular Quay and Sydney Opera House

A tourist magnet, but also stylish enough to be popular with locals, the Circular Quay area has a fine selection of **wharfside eateries** and upmarket restaurants with stunning Harbour Bridge views. For the lisitings below, see map, p.237.

Aria 1 Macquarie St, East Circular Quay T02 9252 2555. One of Sydney's signature, hang-the-expense restaurants, this place can afford to keep its decor restrained and let its unmatched Opera House view provide the glamour. Fans of reality-TV restaurant shows will want to book the Kitchen Table – in the kitchen. Fine cuisine, oodles of style and opera-goer-friendly late opening. Lunch Mon–Fri, dinner daily.

Cafe Sydney Level 5, Customs House, 31 Alfred St, Circular Quay T02 9251 8683. This upmarket brasserie serves wide-ranging food – from tandoori-roasted fish to French- and Italian-inspired dishes – against jaw-dropping views of the Harbour Bridge and Opera House. The atmosphere is fun (the Sun lunchtime jazz is popular). Very much on the tourist agenda. Mains around A$30–38. Closed Sun dinner.

Guillaume at Bennelong Sydney Opera House, Bennelong Point ⊤02 9241 1999. French chef Guillaume Brahimi performs culinary miracles at the Opera House's top-notch restaurant, housed in one of the iconic building's smaller shells. For one splash-out, romantic meal in Sydney, come here. Modern, elegant French fare – and with most mains under A$50, it's not the most expensive place in town. Alternatively, tuck into tapas at the bar. Lunch Thurs & Fri, dinner Mon–Sat.

Rossini Wharf 5, Circular Quay ⊤02 9247 8026. Italian café-restaurant, good for a moderately priced alfresco lunch, or just coffee and a treat: *panzerotti* – big, cinnamon-flavoured and ricotta-filled doughnuts – are a speciality. Daily 7.30am–11pm.

Sydney Cove Oyster Bar 1 East Circular Quay, ⊤02 9247 2937. En route to the Opera House, the outdoor tables right on the water's edge provide a magical location to sample Sydney Rock Pacific oysters (A$20 for half a dozen), or just come for coffee, cake and the view. Daily 8am–11pm.

The Rocks

Though best known for its historic **pubs** (see p.291), many of which serve food, The Rocks has a growing number of expensive restaurants for power-lunchers and cruise-ship passengers on shore leave. For the lisitings below, see map, p.237.

Gumnut Tea Gardens 28 Harrington St ⊤02 9247 9591. Popular lunchtime venue in historic Reynolds Cottage. Munch on delicious gourmet meat pies and ploughman's lunches in the serene leafy courtyard, or sip tea in the antiquated lounge. Live jazz on Fri night and Sun lunch. Mon, Tues, Sat & Sun 8am–5pm, Wed–Fri 8am–9pm.

Restaurant Arras 24 Hickson Rd, Walsh Bay (next to the Sydney Theatre) ⊤02 9252 6285. Distressed decor and witty modern British cuisine. Truly imaginative, the Yorkshire-born chef-owner has found inspiration in all sorts of old-fashioned English favourites, from black pudding to scones and cream, turning them into mouthwatering creations. Mains from A$27. Closed Mon & Sun.

Rockpool (fish) 107 George Str ⊤02 9252 1888. Laid out like a diner – albeit a chic, minimalist

version – but with top-end prices and a superb wine list, this is one of Sydney's best places to splurge on fish and seafood. Lunch Mon–Fri, dinner Mon–Sat.

Sailors Thai Canteen 106 George St ⊤02 9251 2466. Cheaper version of the much-praised, pricey downstairs restaurant, housed in the restored Sailors' Home. The ground-level canteen with a long stainless-steel communal table looks onto an open kitchen, where the chefs chop away to produce simple one-bowl meals. Closed Sun.

The Wharf Pier 4, Hickson Rd, Walsh Bay (next to the Wharf Theatre) ⊤02 9250 1761. Enterprising modern food (lots of seafood), served up in an old dock building with heaps of raw charm and a harbour vista; bag the outside tables for the best views. Good for post-theatre cocktails. Mains from A$26. Closed Sun.

The Central Business District (CBD)

The CBD is good for smart cafés, with plenty of lunchtime spots in its shops, arcades and public buildings: as well as those listed below, check out the **QVB** on George Street, **Myers** on Pitt Street Mall, the **MLC Centre** near Martin Place, and the **Hunter Connection** arcade at 310 George St, opposite Wynyard station. There's a foodie's paradise in the basement of **David Jones** on Market Street, and great Italian espresso bars for quick coffee hits throughout the district. You'll also find superb restaurants here, aimed squarely at top-end tourists and expense-account execs. For the lisitings below, see map, p.237.

Cafés and brasseries

Glasshouse Café & Café Trim State Library of New South Wales, Macquarie St ⊤02 9273 1235. The *Glasshouse Café* on the library's lower ground floor is a relaxing, inexpensive spot for lunch (Mon–Fri noon–3pm) while the smaller *Café Trim* on the ground floor (Mon–Fri 7.30am–5pm, Sat & Sun

10.30am–4.30pm) is equally bright, modern and pleasant, with healthy salads and tempting cakes.

Lindt Chocolat Café 53 Martin Place ⊤02 8257 1600. A chocoholic's dream, this was a world first when it opened; Lindt have since endowed Sydney with two more, on Cockle Bay Wharf and George St. Forget the sensible sandwiches and dive straight into the delectable cakes, macaroons and sundaes for the ultimate chocolate buzz. Mon–Fri 8am–6pm, Sat 10am–5pm.

MoS Café 37 Phillip St, corner of Bridge St ☎02 9241 3636. The stylish, contemporary café-restaurant outside the Museum of Sydney is worth a trip whether you're visiting the museum or not; you can indulge in creative fare such as wild mushroom and spinach lasagne, or scrummy chocolate and Grand Marnier puds. Mon–Fri 7am–9pm, Sat & Sun 8.30am–5pm.

Obelisk Café Shop 1, 7 Macquarie Place ☎02 9241 2141. Fabulous outdoor spot on a historic square with big shady trees, close to Circular Quay. Attracts a working crowd who plunge in for great coffee, *pizzetta*, sandwiches and salads. Mon–Fri 6.30am–5pm, Sat 9am–2pm.

QVB Jet Queen Victoria Building, Druitt St ☎02 9283 5004. Lively, slightly retro Italian café-restaurant, good for people-watching. Popular for breakfast or coffee; the rest of the day, choose from bruschetta, pasta and grills, all reasonably priced. Mon–Wed 7.30am–11pm, Thurs & Fri 7.30am–midnight, Sat 9am–midnight, Sun 10am–7pm.

Restaurants

Glass *Hilton Hotel*, 488 George St ☎02 9265 6068. Luke Mangan, one of Sydney's favourite chefs, uses classic French techniques to conjure up wonderfully theatrical combinations of flavours in this stylish city brasserie. Mains from A$39. Mon–Fri breakfast, lunch & dinner; Sat & Sun breakfast & dinner.

Intermezzo GPO Building, 1 Martin Place ☎02 9229 7788. Packed out with sharply dressed execs, this is one of the sassiest spots in the redeveloped GPO. Far more expensive that the average Italian restaurant, but far more accomplished, too, with a daringly modern Neapolitan menu. Mon–Fri lunch & dinner, Sat dinner.

Sydney Tower Restaurant 100 Market St ☎02 8223 3800. Sydney's revolving restaurant has blockbuster city views, and is permanently packed with Asian tourists. The fixed-price buffet (A$49.95) in the main dining room is reliable; for something more intimate (and expensive), the shimmering *360 Bar and Dining*, one level down (☎02 8223 3883), will also spin you around. Lunch & dinner daily.

Haymarket and around Central Station

The southern end of **George Street** and its backstreets have plenty of cheap restaurants, of variable quality. **Chinatown** around the corner is a better bet: many places here specialize in *yum cha* (dim sum), with several late-night options. The best of the district's many busy, inexpensive **Asian food courts** – with multiple counters serving Thai, Japanese, Vietnamese and, of course, Chinese food – is on the top floor of the Market City Shopping Centre, above Paddy's Markets at the corner of Ultimo Road and Thomas Street (daily 8am–10pm). Others can be found in the Sussex Centre (1st floor, 401 Sussex St; daily 10am–9.30pm); Dixon House (basement level, corner Little Hay and Dixon streets; daily 10.30am–8.30pm) and the Harbour Plaza (basement level, corner Factory and Dixon streets; daily 10am–10pm). A few blocks from Chinatown back toward the city centre, there's a good array of **Spanish eateries** on Liverpool Street, almost all of them boisterous and lively. For the lisitings below, see map, p.243.

BBQ King 18 Goulburn St, Haymarket ☎02 9267 2586. Late-night hangout of chefs, rock stars and students alike, this unprepossessing but always packed Chinese restaurant does a mean meat dish, as suggested by its name and the duck roasting in the window, but there's a big vegetarian menu, too. Communal tables. Daily 11.30am–2am (last orders 1.30am).

Capitan Torres 73 Liverpool St, Haymarket ☎02 9264 5574. Atmospheric and enduring Spanish place specializing in seafood. Freshly displayed catch of the day and an authentic tapas menu, plus great paella. Sit downstairs at the Inexpensive bar or upstairs in the restaurant. Lunch & dinner daily.

Dragon Star Seafood Restaurant Level 3, Market City Shopping Centre, Hay Str, Haymarket ☎02 9211 8988. Sitting proudly aside from the food court, this eight-hundred-seater Cantonese establishment is officially Australia's largest restaurant, but you'll still have to queue at weekends if you haven't booked. Famous for its *yum cha*. Licensed. Daily 10am–3pm.

In Café 11 Rawson Place, Haymarket ☎02 9211 9677. In a district swamped with Asian eateries, this bright little café-restaurant may come as a welcome change, with a cheap menu of international favourites including spaghetti bolognese and well-stuffed burgers. Breakfast, lunch & dinner daily.

Ippon Sushi 404 Sussex St, Haymarket ℡ 02 9212 7669. Fun, cheap Japanese sushi train downstairs, with a revolving choice of delectable dishes (A$2.50–5.50, depending on plate colour), and a proper restaurant menu upstairs. Daily 11am–10.30pm.

Mother Chu's Vegetarian Kitchen 367 Pitt St, Haymarket ℡ 02 9283 2828. Inexpensive Taiwanese Buddhist cuisine in suitably plain surrounds, and – true to its name – family run. Though onion and garlic aren't used, the eats here aren't bland. There's a no-alcohol policy. Closed Sun.

Pasteur 709 George St, Haymarket ℡ 02 9212 5622. Popular Vietnamese cheap-eat specializing in pho, a rice-noodle soup, served with fresh herbs, lemon and bean sprouts. Most noodles (mainly pork, chicken and beef) are A$9, and there's nothing over A$11. Refreshing pot of jasmine tea included. Daily 10am–9pm.

Tetsuya's 529 Kent St, Haymarket ℡ 02 9267 2900. Chef Tetsuya Wakuda takes the voguish concept of degustation dining and flies with it, producing dish after dish of perfection in miniature. Lavished with praise by the critics, it's so popular that despite the sky-high price (A$195 per head), you'll have to book many weeks in advance. Dinner Tues–Fri, lunch & dinner Sat.

Darling Harbour and Pyrmont

Cockle Bay Wharf, the restaurant precinct on the east side of Darling Harbour, has a fine mixture of eateries. Beyond Darling Harbour, you can eat fantastically well at the **Sydney Fish Market**. For the lisitings below, see map, p.249.

Blackbird Cockle Bay Wharf, Darling Harbour ℡ 02 9283 7835. Bar-restaurant with the feel of a modern American diner; sit on stools at the bar or couches out the back, or enjoy the water views from the terrace. Generous, good-value meals to suit all cravings – from dhal to spaghetti, noodles, salads, and pizzas from a hot-stone oven – and breakfast until 4pm. Daily 9am–1am.

Chinta Ria – Temple of Love Roof Terrace, 201 Sussex St, Cockle Bay Wharf, Darling Harbour ℡ 02 9264 3211. People still queue to get in here (bookings lunch only) years after opening, as much for the fun atmosphere – a blues and jazz sound-track, and decor that mixes a giant Buddha, a lotus pond and Fifties-style furniture – as for the yummy, but moderately priced, Malaysian food.

Fish Market Cafe Sydney Fish Market, Pyrmont ℡ 02 9660 4280. Located on the left-hand side after the entrance of the undercover market, this is the pick of the hawkers for its excellent-value seafood platter with Kilpatrick oysters, lobster tails and steamed catch of the day. Mon–Fri 4am–4pm, Sat & Sun 5am–5pm.

The Malaya 39 Lime St, King St Wharf, Darling Harbour ℡ 02 9279 1170. Popular, veteran Chinese-Malaysian place in swish water surrounds, serving some of the best – and spiciest – laksa in town. Mains from A$20.

Glebe

In Glebe, you'll find both cheap and upmarket restaurants, ethnic takeaways, delis and a string of good cafés. **Glebe Point Road** is dominated by cafés – with a cluster of particularly good places at the Broadway end. For the listings below, see map, pp.224 –225.

Badde Manors 1/37 Glebe Point Rd ℡ 02 9660 1835. Staunchly bohemian veteran café with excellent, reasonably priced veggie fare, proper leaf tea, reassuringly tatty furniture and many loyal fans. Mon–Thurs & Sun 7.30am–midnight, Fri & Sat 7.30am–2am.

The Boathouse on Blackwattle Bay End of Ferry Rd ℡ 02 9518 9011. Atmospheric restaurant located above Sydney Women's Rowing Club, with fantastic views across the bay to Anzac Bridge and the fishmarkets, opposite. Fittingly, seafood is the thing here (and this is one of the best places to sample some), from the six different kinds of oysters to the raved-about snapper pie. Expensive at up to A$45 for mains, but worth it. Closed Mon.

Fair Trade Coffee Company 33 Glebe Point Rd ℡ 02 9660 0621. Delightful ambience with funky music and dishes from around the world – Columbia, Morocco, Indonesia and the Middle East are all featured, with nothing over A$12.50. Plenty of vegetarian options, and the all-day cooked breakfast is fantastic. Daily 7am–9pm.

Glebe Point Diner 407 Glebe Point Rd ℡ 02 9660 2646. Locally sourced, organic ingredients, a smart modern design, and amazingly reasonable prices for lovingly hand-made Mod Oz food make this relaxed little place a real find. Lunch Thurs–Sun, dinner Wed–Sat.

No Names 58 Cowper St, corner of Queen St ☎02 9660 2326. Attached to one of Glebe's quirkiest pubs, the *Friend in Hand*, this serves up huge plates of good, cheap pasta (under A$10) and grills (well under A$20) to hungry drinkers. Lunch daily, dinner Mon–Sat.

Osteria dei Poeti 73 Glebe Point Rd ☎02 9571 8955. Lively Italian tavern specializing in classic regional dishes, hand-made cannelloni and a selection of charming Italian wines. Prices are pretty reasonable, too. Closed Sun.

Newtown

On the other side of Sydney University from Glebe, **King Street** in Newtown is lined with cafés, takeaways and restaurants of every ethnic persuasion, particularly Thai.

Green Gourmet 115 King St ☎02 9519 5330. Loud and busy Chinese vegan eatery, which always has plenty of Asian customers, including the odd Buddhist monk. The devout Buddhist owner's creativity is reflected in the divine tofu variations on offer. Order from the menu (mains around A$15) or, to get a taste of everything, choose the a nightly buffet or *yum cha* at weekend lunch. The same owners run the excellent Vegan's Choice Grocery next door. Daily lunch & dinner.

Le Kilimanjaro 280 King St ☎02 9557 4565. Long-running, economical Senegalese-owned place serving authentic and simple dishes that span Africa – from West African marinated chicken to North African couscous. Casual and friendly atmosphere, with African art and craft adorning the walls.

The Old Fish Shop Cafe 239 King St ☎02 9519 4295. This little corner place, decorated with strands of dried garlic and chilli, is pure Newtown: lots of shaven heads, body piercings, tattoos and bizarre fashions. Food is simple – mainly focaccia and mini pizzas – and the excellent raisinloaf goes well with a coffee. Daily 6am–7pm, later in summer.

Sumalee *Bank Hotel*, 324 King St ☎02 8568 1988. Huge portions of gorgeous Thai food, hand-made from fresh ingredients, in a trendy Art Deco pub; the tables are set out in a courtyard decked out with fairy lights. Very busy on Fri & Sat evenings.

Thai Pothong 294 King St ☎02 9550 6277. King Street's best and largest Thai; excellent service and moderate prices (mains on the ever-changing menu are around A$20). Closed Mon lunch.

Balmain and Leichhardt

Leichhardt, Sydney's "Little Italy", has a concentration of cafés and restaurants on **Norton Street**; while the **Darling Street** strip of restaurants runs from Rozelle to upmarket **Balmain**.

Bar Italia 169 Norton St, Leichhardt ☎02 9560 9981. Like a community centre, with the day-long comings and goings of Leichhardt locals, and positively packed at night. The focaccia, served during the day, comes big and tasty, and coffee is spot-on. Some of the best *gelato* in Sydney; pasta from A$11.50; and the extra night-time menu includes more substantial meat dishes. Shady

courtyard out the back. Mon–Thurs 9am–11.30pm, Fri & Sat 9am–midnight.

Circle Café 344 Darling St, Balmain ☎02 9555 9755. Airy building with a shady front courtyard and lots of classic cinema posters plastered on the walls. Hearty breakfasts, home-made pies and delicious savoury crepes are its specialities. Mon–Sat 7am–5pm.

Vegetarian eating

Vegetarians are well catered for on just about every café menu, and most contemporary restaurant menus, too. The following are specifically vegetarian: *Fair Trade Coffee Company* (see p.283), *Bodhi in the Park* (see p.286), *Green Gourmet* (see above) and *Mother Chu's Vegetarian Kitchen* (see p.283).

Woolloomooloo, Potts Point and Kings Cross

There's a cluster of coffee shops and inexpensive eateries, many of which stay open late, in the "**Cross**", and several stylish restaurants nearby, particularly in **Potts Point**.

Cafés and bistros

Cafe Hernandez 60 Kings Cross Rd, Kings Cross ℡ 02 9331 2343. Veteran Spanish-run coffee shop. Relaxed and friendly with an old-time feel; you can dawdle here for ages and no one will make you feel unwelcome. Spanish food is served – *churros*, tortilla, *empanadas* and good pastries – but the coffee is the focus. Open 24hr.

Harry's Café de Wheels Corner of Cowper Wharf Rd & Dowling St, Woolloomooloo. Sometimes, there's nothing like a good old-fashioned pie, and this little cart (open 24hr) has been serving them up for over sixty years. Some gourmet and vegetarian options have made it onto the menu, but the standard meat pie with mashed peas and gravy is still the favourite.

Yellow Bistro 57 Macleay St, Potts Point ℡ 02 9357 3400. Quaint, village-style bistro extremely popular with locals. Delectable fluffy quiches and other mouthwatering savouries served on the ample terrace overlooking Macleay St at lunch, simple but delicious contemporary meals in the cozy dining room at night. Breakfast & lunch daily, dinner Tues–Sat.

Restaurants

Dolcetta 165 Victoria St, Potts Point ℡ 02 9331 5899. Tiny, down-to-earth Italian restaurant with just four tables inside and two more on the street overlooking the fashionable *Dov* restaurant. All dishes under A$15. Mon–Sat 6am–10pm, Sun 7am–4pm.

Fratelli Paradiso 12–16 Challis Ave, Potts Point ℡ 02 9357 1744. This Italian joint has everything, from gorgeous wallpaper and a dark furniture fit-out to flirty waiting staff and a diverse wine list. There's even an adjoining bakery, which runs out of stock before lunchtime most days. And the moderately priced food is amazing, too – calamari, veal, pizzas and pastries – with a blackboard menu that changes daily. Breakfast & lunch daily, dinner Mon–Fri.

Otto The Wharf, 6 Cowper Wharf Rd, Woolloomooloo ℡ 02 9368 7488. *Otto* is the sort of restaurant where agents take actors and models out to lunch, or a well-known politician could be dining at the next table. Trendy and glamorous, with a location not just by the water but *on* the water. The exquisite Italian cuisine – very fresh seafood – coupled with friendly service and a lively atmosphere, is what keeps them coming back. Lunch & dinner daily.

The Restaurant Art Gallery of New South Wales, Art Gallery Rd, The Domain ℡ 02 9225 1819. Well-heeled Sydneysiders flock here for the chic, arty atmosphere; the style is contemporary, the service efficient and the food a well-thought-out version of classic Mod Oz. Good for a weekend brunch. Mon–Fri noon–4pm, Sat & Sun 10am–4pm.

Darlinghurst and East Sydney

Oxford Street is lined with restaurants and cafés from one end to the other. **Taylor Square** and its surroundings is a particularly busy area, with lots of ethnic restaurants and several pubs, whilst **Victoria Street** in Darlinghurst has a thriving café scene. East Sydney, where Crown Street heads downhill from Oxford Street towards William Street, has some excellent Italian restaurants and coffee bars – particularly on **Stanley Street**.

Cafés and bistros

Bar Coluzzi 322 Victoria St, Darlinghurst ℡ 02 9380 5420. Veteran Italian café that's almost a Sydney legend: tiny and always packed with a diverse crew of regulars spilling out onto wooden stools on the pavement, and partaking in the standard menu of focaccias, muffins, bagels and, of course, coffee. Daily 5am–6pm.

Betty's Soup Kitchen 84 Oxford St, Darlinghurst ℡ 02 9380 9698. Soup is obviously the thing here, with continually changing specials that make for a cheap but filling meal, served with damper, but there's also all the simple things your ideal granny might serve: stews, sausages or fish fingers with mash, pasta, salads and desserts. Delicious home-made ginger beer and lemonade.

Nothing over A$15. Daily noon–10.30pm, Fri & Sat to 11.30pm.

Bill and Toni 74 Stanley St, East Sydney ℡ 02 9360 4702. Cheap, atmospheric Italian, where it's worth the queue up the stairs for the huge portions of simple home-made pasta and sauces. The café downstairs serves tasty Italian sandwiches (daily 7am–10pm). Inexpensive. BYO, no corkage. Breakfast, lunch & dinner daily.

Bodhi in the Park Cook and Phillip Park, College St, East Sydney ℡ 02 9360 2523; another branch at Capitol Square, 730–742 George St, Haymarket. Interesting, inexpensive Chinese vegetarian and vegan food, with the focus on delicious *yum cha*, which is served daily until 4pm. Well situated for the local galleries and museums or if you've been for a swim in the park's pool. Organic and biodynamic produce is used. Closed Mon dinner.

Restaurants

A Tavola 348 Victoria St, Darlinghurst ℡ 02 9331 7871. Named after the rallying cry heard at mealtimes in family homes all over Italy, this new restaurant recreates the comforting flavours and aromas of home-made Italian fare – and there's a huge, shared marble table at which to enjoy the convivial atmosphere. Dinner Mon–Sat.

Fishface 132 Darlinghurst Rd, Darlinghurst ℡ 02 9332 4803. This is one place where size doesn't matter – it's tiny – and the excellent

range of seafood and sushi speak for themselves. Everything is fresh: the fish 'n' chips served in a paper cone, the pea soup with yabby tails or the sushi prepared before your eyes. Moderate to expensive. Licensed & BYO. Dinner Mon–Sat.

Oh! Calcutta! 251 Victoria St, Darlinghurst ℡ 02 9360 3650. Certainly not your grungy neighbourhood Indian: the decor was designed by a star interior decorator. *Oh! Calcutta!* keeps getting suitably exclamatory reviews for its authentic – and occasionally inventive – food. Dishes such as quail and goat regularly appear beside more mainstream fare. Try for a balcony table upstairs. Moderate. Dinner Mon–Sat.

Onde 346 Liverpool St, Darlinghurst ℡ 02 9331 8749. People keep returning to this French-owned restaurant, situated in a Darlinghurst sidestreet, which serves outstanding and very authentic bistro-style food: soups and patés to start, mains such as steak and frites or confit of duck, plus a fish dish. Portions are generous, service excellent and desserts decadent. Moderate. Licensed, and all wine is available by the glass. Dinner daily.

Pink Peppercorn 122 Oxford St, Darlinghurst ℡ 02 9360 9922. A moderately priced place that keeps springing up on critics' favourites lists, lured by the unusual Laotian-inspired cooking – including the signature dish: stir-fried king prawns and pink peppercorns. Dinner daily.

Paddington

As **Oxford Street** continues through Paddington, it becomes gradually more upmarket; the majority of restaurants here are attached to gracious old pubs, and most have had a complete culinary overhaul and now offer far more than the steak-and-three-veg option of times past.

Royal Hotel Restaurant *Royal Hotel*, 237 Glenmore Rd, off Five Ways ℡ 02 9331 2604. Grand old triple-storey pub-restaurant serving some of the most mouthwatering steaks in Sydney, non-stop from noon to 11pm (9pm Sun). Eating on the veranda is a real treat, with views over the art gallery and Five Ways action below. There's also the *Elephant Bar* upstairs (see p.292). Moderate.

Sloanes Cafe 312 Oxford St ℡ 02 9331 6717. The emphasis in this veteran café is on good, unusual vegetarian food, moderately priced, but some meatier dishes have slipped onto the menu, including a BLT with guacamole to die for; the fresh juice bar has always been phenomenal. You can check out all the Saturday-market action from the tables in front, or relax in the delightful courtyard. Breakfast & lunch served all day. Daily 6.30am–5pm.

Surry Hills and Redfern

Just east of Central Station, **Cleveland Street** in Surry Hills, running down to Redfern, is lined with inexpensive Turkish, Lebanese and Indian restaurants, which are among the cheapest and most atmospheric in Sydney. **Crown Street** in Surry Hills is home to several funky cafés and some upmarket restaurants.

Cafés and bistros

Erciyes 409 Cleveland St, Redfern ☎ 02 9319 1309. Among the offerings of this busy, cheap family-run Turkish restaurant is delicious *pide* – a bit like pizza – available with 22 different types of toppings, many vegetarian; takeout section, too. Bellydancing Fri & Sat nights, when bookings are essential. Daily 11am–midnight.

Maltese Cafe 310 Crown St, Surry Hills ☎ 02 9361 6942. Established in the early 1940s, this café is known for its delicious and ridiculously cheap Maltese *pastizzi* – flaky pastry pockets of ricotta cheese, plain or with meat, spinach or peas – to eat in or take away. Inexpensive. Mon 10am–4pm, Tues–Sun 8am–6pm.

Mohr Fish 202 Devonshire St, Surry Hills ☎ 02 9318 1326. Tiny but stylish fish 'n' chip bar on the street corner, with stools and tiled walls, which packs in the customers. The modern restaurant next door, owned by the same family, is equally excellent. Moderate. Daily 11am–10pm.

Restaurants

Billy Kwong 355 Crown St, Surry Hills ☎ 02 9332 3300. Traditional Chinese cooking gets a stylish slant at this restaurant owned by celebrity chef Kylie Kwong. The space itself – all dark polished wood and Chinese antiques but brightly lit and with contemporary fittings – complements the often-adventurous combinations of dishes and flavours. Mains A$20–45. Moderate to expensive. Dinner daily. No bookings, so you'll have to queue.

Bird Cow Fish 500 Crown St, Surry Hills ☎ 02 9380 4090. Stylish delicatessen-cum-bistro with a contemporary menu including kangaroo livers and fabulous cheese selections, but wines overly expensive. Usually packed, so book in advance. Mains A$20–35. Daily 8am–10pm.

Longrain 85 Commonwealth St, Surry Hills ☎ 02 9280 2888. Hip – and pricey – restaurant and bar housed in a converted warehouse in the rather subdued north side of Surry Hills off Wentworth Ave. The contemporary Thai flavours are much raved about, with dining on three long community-style wooden tables. Lunch Mon–Fri, dinner daily.

Nepalese Kitchen 481 Crown St, Surry Hills ☎ 02 9319 4264. Peaceful establishment with authentic wooden furniture, religious wall hangings and traditional music. The speciality here is goat curry, served with freshly cooked relishes that traditionally accompany the mild Nepalese dishes, and simple but delicious *momos* (stuffed handmade dumplings). Vegetarian options, too. Lovely courtyard for warmer nights. Inexpensive. Dinner daily.

North Shore

Military Road has an excellent selection of eateries, with quality Asian places towards the Neutral Bay end, gourmet restaurants further east in Cremorne, and Mosman, and a good sprinkling of cafés and well-stocked delis throughout.

Banana Blossom 318 Military Rd, Cremorne ☎ 02 9908 1588. Smart but simple, this contemporary Thai restaurant is committed to making its curries and sauces from scratch, using locally sourced ingredients. For dessert, its sampling plates are the ultimate temptation. Mains around A$30. Lunch Fri, dinner Mon–Sat.

The Bathers Pavilion 4 The Esplanade, Balmoral Beach ☎ 02 9969 5050. Indulgent beach-house-style dining in a 1920s building, originally used as changing rooms. The very pricey restaurant-and-café double-act is presided over by one of Sydney's top chefs, Serge Dansereau. Fixed-price dinner menu in the restaurant is A$115 for three courses (A$90 at lunchtime). The café is a favourite weekend breakfast spot – expect to queue to get in – and there are wood-fired pizzas on offer later in the day. Café daily 7am–midnight, restaurant lunch & dinner daily.

Maisy's Café 164 Military Rd, Neutral Bay ☎ 02 9908 4030. Cool hangout with funky interior and music. The food – all-day breakfasts, nachos and daily specials – is unremarkable, but people keep coming for its buzzy neighbourhood feel. Open 24hr.

Vera Cruz 314 Military Rd, Cremorne ☎ 02 9904 5818. Sleek, modern, edgily minimalist Mexican restaurant – emphatically sombrero-free – serving amazing empanadas, quesadillas and succulent slow-cooked stews. Mains around A$25. Dinner Mon–Sat 6pm–late.

Bondi and Watsons Bay

Bondi is a cosmopolitan centre, with the area's many Eastern European and Jewish residents giving its cafés a continental flair; there are also some fantastic kosher restaurants, delis and cake shops. Bondi Beach is full of cheap takeaways, fish 'n' chip shops and beer gardens, as well as some seriously trendy cafés and restaurants. To the north, **Watsons Bay** is known for its famous seafood restaurant, *Doyles*.

Bondi Social 1st Floor, 38 Campbell Parade, Bondi Beach ☎ 02 9365 1788. You could easily miss the sandwich-board sign pointing you to this hidden gem, but once found, a million-dollar balcony view of the beach awaits those wanting to escape the mêlée of the Campbell Parade pavement. The wood interior is rich and dim-lit at night; the mood promises romance and an interesting dining experience with a worldwide influence. Tapas-style dishes A$10–15. Tues–Fri 6pm–midnight, Sat & Sun 8.30am–9pm.

Bondi Trattoria 34B Campbell Parade, Bondi Beach ☎ 02 9365 4303. Come here to take in the view and the invariably buzzing atmosphere over breakfast, lunch and dinner, or just a coffee. Serves contemporary Australian and Italian food, which, considering the setting – with outdoor seating overlooking the beach – is not at all expensive. Daily 7am–10pm.

Doyles on the Beach 11 Marine Parade, Watsons Bay ☎ 02 9337 1350; also *Doyles Wharf Restaurant* ☎ 02 9337 1572. The former is the original of the long-running Sydney fish-restaurant institution, but both serve great if overpriced seafood (but without the flair and inspiration of

newer places) and have views of the city across the water. The adjacent boozer serves pub-versions in its beer garden. A water taxi can transport you from Circular Quay to Watsons Bay. Daily lunch & dinner.

Gertrude & Alice Cafe Bookstore 46 Hall St, Bondi Beach ☎ 02 9130 5155. Partly a café and partly a secondhand literary bookshop, *Gertrude & Alice* is a homely hangout with generous, affordable light lunches, great cakes, even greater coffee and lots of conversation. Daily 9.30am–late.

Icebergs Dining Room 1 Notts Ave, Bondi Beach ☎ 02 9365 9000. Though much-loved by well-groomed Bondi beach babes, this landmark oceanfront restaurant is not just a place to be seen – its superb Mediterranean-style gourmet cooking has won an embarrassment of accolades. Expensive. Closed Mon.

Three Eggs 100 Brighton Blvd, North Bondi ☎ 02 9365 6262. Groovy, relaxed little café tucked down a quiet residential street around the corner from the North Bondi set of shops. Locals straggle in all day long for eggs cooked any style, or hearty pancakes. Everything under A$15. Daily 7am–3pm.

Bronte, Clovelly and Coogee

South of Bondi, **Bronte**'s beachfront café strip is wonderfully laid back, and **Coogee** has a thriving café scene.

Barzura 62 Carr St, Coogee ☎ 02 9665 5546. Fantastic spot providing up-close ocean views. Both a café and a fully fledged restaurant, with wholesome breakfast until 1pm, snacks until 7pm, and restaurant meals – such as seafood spaghetti or grilled kangaroo rump – served at lunch and dinner. Unpretentious though stylish service encourages a large local crowd. Mains A$14–26. Daily 7am–10pm.

Jack & Jill's Fish Café 98 Beach St, Coogee ☎ 02 9665 8429. This down-to-earth fish restaurant on the north side of the beach is a local legend. Drop in to enjoy delightfully cooked fish, from the basic battered variety to tasty tandoori perch. Mains A$14–20. Tues–Sat from 5pm, Sun from noon.

Melonhead 256 Coogee Bay Rd, Coogee ☎ 02 9664 3319. The smell of fresh fruit wafts down the street from this fantastic juice bar; apart from custom-made smoothies, crushes and

milkshakes, there are enticing salads and Turkish rolls to choose from. Daily 6am–7pm.

Seasalt 1 Donnellan Circuit, Clovelly ☎ 02 9664 5344. Open-fronted café-restaurant, with fabulous views over the beach to cliffs, greenery and houses. *Seasalt* looks really smart, but it's the sort of casual beach joint where you can come in sand-covered and have just a coffee as much as you would a full meal with wine. Cuisine is fresh and modern with a seafood emphasis; takeaway available. Mon–Fri 9am–4.30pm, Sat & Sun 8am–4.30pm, plus, in summer, Fri & Sat 6–10pm.

Swell Restaurant 465 Bronte Rd, Bronte ☎ 02 9386 5001. Sit inside for the latest in sharp interiors, or out on the pavement for a delightful Bronte Beach view, and enjoy tasty Mod Oz fare. There's plenty of competition nearby, so prices are very reasonable for what you're getting. Dinner mains all A$28. Daily 7am–10pm.

Manly

Manly offers something for every taste and budget; there's an upmarket food hall and food stalls on **Manly Wharf**, and loads of good cafés and restaurants on **Belgrave Street**, **Darley Street** and along **South Steyne**.

Café Steyne 14 South Steyne, corner of Victoria Parade ☎02 9977 0116. The laid-back staff and customers epitomize the Manly vibe, and it's easy to spend time over the giant breakfast plates or tucking into the gourmet burgers, including veggie options with tangy chutney. Mon–Fri 8am–10pm, Sat & Sun 7.30am–10pm.

Fishmongers 11 Rialto Square, Wentworth St ☎02 9977 1777. Every bit as popular as its sister establishment in Byron Bay, this inexpensive place redefines fish 'n' chips by delivering gorgeously fresh, immaculate seafood and chunky hand-cut chips, elegantly sprinkled with a garnish of vegetable tempura, in double-quick time.

Pacific Thai Cuisine 2nd floor, 48 Victoria Parade, corner of South Steyne ☎02 9977 7220. With crisp decor and fantastic views of the beach from its upstairs location, this reasonably priced Thai restaurant offers a variety of fresh favourites as well as chef's specials such as Chu Chi Curry (red curry with kaffir lime leaves). Vegetarian options, too.

Entertainment, nightlife and culture

To find out exactly **what's on** in Sydney, you'll get news, features and listings in *Metro*, published with Friday's *Sydney Morning Herald*; *Seven Days*, with Thursday's *Daily Telegraph*; and *Time Out Sydney*. For details of gigs, clubs and alternative goings-on, there's always a plethora of **free listings magazines** in cafés, record shops, boutiques and hostels, particularly in Paddington, Darlinghurst, Glebe and Kings Cross: these include *The Brag*, *Drum Media* and *3D World*. *City Hub*, a politically aware, free, weekly newspaper, also has an excellent events section, as does *TNT Magazine*.

The two main **booking agencies** for ticketed shows and events are Ticketek (☎13 28 49, ⊛www.ticketek.com.au) and Ticketmaster (☎13 61 00, ⊛www .ticketmaster.com.au). There are Ticketek outlets at 50 Park St and at the Theatre Royal on King Street. Ticketmaster outlets include the Capitol Theatre and the Sydney Entertainment Centre, both in Haymarket (see p.295).

Pubs and bars

The differences between a restaurant, bar, pub and nightclub are often blurred in Sydney – some establishments combine of all these under one roof. Sydney's bland pub wilderness has all but disappeared and you'll find a fashionable **bar**

What's on in Sydney: useful websites

General listings
City of Sydney ⊛www.cityofsydney.nsw.gov.au/whatson
Sydney Citysearch ⊛www.sydney.citysearch.com.au
Sydney Morning Herald ⊛www.smh.com.au
Tourism NSW ⊛www.visitnsw.com
What's on in Sydney ⊛www.whatsoninsydney.com.au

Gigs and clubs
3D World ⊛www.threedworld.com.au
Drum Media ⊛www.drummedia.com.au
In the Mix ⊛www.inthemix.com.au

▲ Bar on Oxford Street

on almost every corner, offering everything from poetry readings and art classes to groovy Sunday afternoon jazz or DJ sessions. Not to be outdone, the traditional hotels are getting in renowned chefs and putting on food far beyond the old pub-grub fare. Sydney has many **Art Deco pubs**, their classic 1930s style notably seen in the tilework; we've mentioned some of the best below.

Legendary beer gardens

Many Sydney pubs have an outdoor drinking area, perfect for enjoying the sunny weather – the four listed below, however, are outright legends.

The Coogee Bay Hotel Arden Street, Coogee. Loud, rowdy and packed with backpackers, this enormous beer garden across from the beach is renowned in the eastern suburbs. The hotel has six bars in all, including a big-screen sports bar for all international sporting events; the weekend BBQs always draw a crowd.

Doyles Palace Hotel 10 Marine Parade, Watsons Bay. Still known to locals as the *Watson's Bay Hotel*, the beer garden here gives uninterrupted views across the harbour, which you can enjoy with fresh fish and chips from the renowned *Doyles* kitchen or a steak from the outdoor BBQ.

Newport Arms Hotel 2 Kalinya St, Newport. Famous beer-garden pub established in 1880 with a huge deck looking out over Heron Cove at Pittwater. Good for families, with a children's play area. The bistro's Asian-influenced salads and big seafood servings complement a large wine list.

The Oaks Hotel 118 Military Rd, Neutral Bay. The North Shore's most popular pub takes its name from the huge oak tree that shades the entire beer garden. Cook your own (expensive) steak, or order a gourmet pizza from the restaurant inside.

The Rocks and CBD

Australian Hotel 100 Cumberland St, The Rocks. Convivial corner hotel seemingly always full of Brits. The upstairs veranda has sweeping vistas of Circular Quay and the Opera House; inside, original fittings give a lovely old-pub feel. Known and loved for its Bavarian-style draught beer brewed in Picton, plus gourmet emu, kangaroo and crocodile pizzas.

Blu Horizon 36th floor, *Shangri-La Hotel*, 176 Cumberland St, The Rocks. This hip top-floor hotel bar is mega-expensive but worth it for its stunning 270-degree view – from the Opera House, Darling Harbour and Middle Harbour to Homebush Bay and beyond to the Blue Mountains. Dress smart. Daily 5pm–1am (Sun until midnight).

Establishment 252 George St. Huge, loud and trendy open-fronted bar, in a grand old city building, packed out with well-heeled, off-duty executives in the evenings; to fit in, you'll need to power dress a bit. There are a couple of first-rate restaurants and an achingly cool club (*Tank*, see p.293) in the same venue.

Harbour View Hotel 18 Lower Fort St, The Rocks. This three-storey renovated gem puts you right under the bridge – and close enough from the top balcony cocktail bar to raise a glass to the grey-overall-clad bridge climbers making their way back

from the summit. The crowd is mixed, and better for it, although drinks are a little pricey.

Hero of Waterloo 81 Lower Fort St, Millers Point, The Rocks. One of Sydney's oldest pubs, built in 1843 from sandstone dug out from the Argyle Cut (see p.239), this place has plenty of atmosphere and oozes history. Open fireplaces make it a good choice for a winter drink, and it serves simple meals.

Opera Bar Lower Concourse Level, Sydney Opera House. In summer, you can't move for the people – a mix of concertgoers, tourists and office workers – but that's half the fun of this stunningly located bar with outside tables. Watch the ferries come in, and have a drink next to one of the world's greatest buildings. Jazz on Sun afternoons and a bar-snack menu.

Slip Inn 111 Sussex St. Now famous as the place where Mary Donaldson met her Prince Frederick of Denmark, the *Slip Inn* has several bars, a bistro and a nightclub, *The Chinese Laundry*. Front bars have a pool room, while downstairs a boisterous beer garden fills up on sultry nights, with the quieter, more sophisticated *Sand Bar* beside it. Excellent wine list, with lots available by the glass; bar food includes Thai and pizzas.

Haymarket and Darling Harbour

3 Wise Monkeys 555 George St, corner of Liverpool St. Good mix of Sydneysiders and travellers who come for the relaxed pub

atmosphere, beers on tap, pool tables, live music and late-night DJs (Mon–Thurs to 1am, Fri–Sun to 2am).

Cargo Bar 52–60 The Promenade, King St Wharf, Darling Harbour. Cool, multi-level bar with outdoor seating downstairs, sofas and stools upstairs, and glittering night-time views of Darling Harbour. Drinks are not cheap, but the pizzas are yummy; DJs edge things up a notch at weekends.

Civic Hotel 388 Pitt St, corner of Goulburn St, Haymarket. Beautiful 1940s Art Deco-style pub, its original features in great condition. Upstairs, there's a glamorous dining room and cocktail bar with performance spaces offered to young artistic talent.

Handy meeting point for Chinatown and George St cinema forays.

Scruffy Murphy's 43 Goulburn St, Haymarket. Rowdy, 24hr Irish pub with Guinness on tap, of course; phenomenally popular with travellers and expats, who pop in for some hearty home cooking, too. Just around the corner from Central Station.

Scubar 4 Rawson Place, near Central Station. Aimed squarely at young backpackers. The punters cram in to this basement bar for cheap booze, themed promotions and daft games including weekly crab races.

Glebe, Newtown and Balmain

Bank Hotel 324 King St, next to Newtown station. Smartened-up Art Deco pub, open late and always packed with local arty residents and visiting musos. There's a cocktail bar out back and a great Thai restaurant, *Sumalee* (see p.284), in the leafy beer garden. DJ sessions at weekends.

Exchange Hotel Corner of Beattie & Mullens sts, Balmain. Classic Balmain backstreet corner pub, built in 1885, with a vast wrought-iron balcony. There are four energetic bars, live music in the adjoining nightclub, and the *Bloody Mary Breakfast Club* on Sat and Sun mornings (10am–3pm).

Friend in Hand 58 Cowper St, corner of Queen St, Glebe. Character-filled pub in the leafy backstreets

of Glebe, with all manner of curious objects dangling from the walls and ceilings; a popular haunt for backpackers. Diverse entertainment includes pool, poetry, stand-up comedy and crab racing.

Nag's Head Corner of Lodge St & St Johns Rd, off Glebe Point Rd, Glebe. A good place for a quiet drink, with the decor and atmosphere of a British boozer, and several imported beers on tap – Guinness, Boddingtons, Stella and Becks. Its bistro dishes up excellent steaks and other grills, and there's an extensive bar menu. Pool tables in the loft area upstairs.

Woolloomooloo, Potts Point and Kings Cross

The Bourbon 24 Darlinghurst Rd, Kings Cross. Established in 1968 when it was frequented by US soldiers on R&R, this infamous late-night Kings Cross bistro and drinking hole has been given a swish new upgrade, which hasn't done much to deter some of its more colourful regulars. Retro-disco on Fri, Latin music on Sat.

Soho Bar & Lounge 171 Victoria St, Potts Point. Trendy, Art Deco cocktail bar on leafy Victoria St; the open balcony of the *Leopard Room*, upstairs, is a popular hangout for sharply dressed young locals. At weekends, the whole place becomes a pre-club venue for *Yu* (see p.294), down in the basement.

Darlinghurst, Paddington, Woollahra and Surry Hills

Burdekin 2 Oxford St, Darlinghurst. Well-preserved Art Deco pub with several trendy bars on four levels. The tiny, beautifully tiled, basement bar has table service and generous cocktails, while the spacious ground level sports dramatic columns and a huge round bar. DJ nights Fri & Sat. Closed Mon.

The Clock Hotel 470 Crown St, Surry Hills. This huge hotel has expanded well beyond its 1840s roots (the landmark clock tower was only added in the 1960s). Upstairs, a swish restaurant and bar runs off the huge balcony; downstairs, the booths and tables fill up quickly for after-work drinks, and the four pool tables are ever popular.

Cricketers Arms 106 Fitzroy St, Surry Hills. Just down the road from the live-music scene at the *Hopetoun* (see p.296), this has an equally dedicated clientele. A young, offbeat crowd – plenty of piercings and shaved heads – cram in and fall about the bar, pool room and tiny beer garden, and yell at each other over a funky soundtrack. Hearty bar snacks and a bistro (Tues–Sun 3–10pm).

Elephant Bar *Royal Hotel*, 237 Glenmore Rd, Paddington. The top-floor bar of this beautifully renovated, Victorian-era hotel has knockout views of the city, best appreciated at sunset (cocktail Happy Hour 5.30–6.30pm). The interior is great, too, with its fireplaces, paintings and elephant prints. As it gets crowded later on, people pack onto the stairwell and it feels like a party. **Green Park Hotel** 360 Victoria St, Darlinghurst. A Darlinghurst stalwart, partly because of the stash of pool tables in the back room, but mainly because of the unpretentious vibe. The bar couldn't be more unassuming; there's nothing decorating the walls, and humble bar-tables with stools and a

few lounges out the back accommodate the regular arty crowd.

The Victoria Room Level 1, 235 Victoria St, Darlinghurst. Atmospheric drawing room from the Colonial era with elegant sofas, a grand piano and chandeliers, yet a positively trendy atmosphere popular with the chill-out crowd. Tapas are served from the cocktail bar, and there's High Tea on Sat & Sun afternoons.

Bondi and Coogee

Beach Palace Hotel 169 Dolphin St, Coogee. Home to a young and drunken clientale, made up of locals, beach babes and backpackers. Features seven bars, two restaurants and a great view of the beach from the balcony under the distinctive dome.
Beach Road Hotel 71 Beach Rd, Bondi Beach. Huge, stylishly decorated pub with a bewildering range of bars on two levels, and a beer garden. Popular with both travellers and locals for its good vibe. Entertainment, mostly free, comes from rock bands and DJs.
Bondi Hotel 178 Campbell Parade, Bondi Beach. Huge pub dating from the 1920s, with many of its

original features intact, seating outside and an open bar area where locals hang out with sand still on their feet. Sedate during the day, but at night an over-the-top, late-night backpackers' hangout. Mon–Sat until 4am, Sun until midnight.
Icebergs Bar 1 Notts Ave, Bondi Beach. In the same building as the famous Icebergs winter swimming club (see p.271), this celebrity hangout has a balcony hanging over the pool – a fantastic place to sip a beer and soak up the views and atmosphere of Bondi Beach. To complete the experience, book a table at the restaurant (see p.288).

Clubs

Many of Sydney's best clubs are at **gay** or **lesbian** venues, and although we've listed these separately on p.294, the divisions are not always clear – many places have specific gay, lesbian and straight nights scheduled each week. A long strip of thriving clubs stretches from Kings Cross to Oxford Street and down towards Hyde Park; many stay open until 5am or 6am on Saturday and Sunday mornings. There are also good clubs attached to several of the drinking spots listed on p.289. The scene can be pretty snobby, with door gorillas frequently vetting your style. Below are the bigger venues or places with something unusual to offer.

Candy's Apartment 22 Bayswater Rd, Kings Cross www.candys.com.au. The most happening and unpretentious place in town, this music portal transforms itself every night with cool bands playing early and DJs churning out fresh dance mixes as the night progresses. Thurs–Sun from 9pm, A$10–20.
Club 77 77 William St, East Sydney. The big nights are Thurs–Sat at this intimate and relaxed club. Drinks are cheap, and there's a swag of regulars who come here for the progressive and rare funk, techno and house music. A$10.
Havana Club 169 Oxford St, Darlinghurst www .havanaclub.com.au. Sexy little club with a lounge feel; alternating resident DJs and live musicians/ percussionists ensure that there's always something new happening. The younger crowd comes on Fri for the high-octane beats, while Sat

is predominantly 25- to 30-year-olds. Fri & Sat 10pm–6am. A$15–25.
Home Wheat Rd, Cockle Bay Wharf, Darling Harbour www.homesydney.com. The first really big club venture in Sydney, lavish *Home* can cram two thousand punters into its cool, cavernous interior with outdoor balconies. Decks are often manned by big-name DJs, drinks are expensive, and the staff beautiful. Packed with a younger crowd on Fri for its flagship night Sublime, with four musical styles across four levels. On Sat, Famous plays progressive house and garage. Fri & Sat 11pm till late. A$15–25.
Tank 3 Bridge Lane, off George St, City. This is for the glamorous crowd – if you don't belong, the style police will spot you a mile away. All very funky, from the house music played by regular or guest DJs to the amazing bars. Attire is smart

casual, but attitude and good looks override the dress code. Fri & Sat 10pm–6am. A$15–20.

The World Bar 24 Bayswater Rd, Kings Cross. With cheap drinks on Fri and Sat nights and a relatively relaxed door policy, *The World* is popular with a fun, party-loving crowd of travellers, who jive to a pleasing mix of funk and house grooves in a Victorian-era building with a big front balcony.

Mon–Thurs & Sun noon–4am, Fri & Sat noon–6am. A$15, free before midnight.

Yu 171 Victoria St, Potts Point. One of Sydney's smoothest clubs, pulling in well-groomed party people at weekends. Vast dancefloor, hip decor and stylish colour-block lighting. Mon & Thurs–Sun 10pm–6am. A$20, some nights free.

Gay and lesbian bars and clubs

The last few years have seen a quiet diminishing of specifically gay and lesbian bars: partly thanks to Sydney's highly restrictive liquor-licensing laws, the smaller venues vanish and the large ones just get bigger. Most venues are concentrated in two areas, so it's easy to bar-hop: in the **inner east** around Oxford Street, Darlinghurst, including Surry Hills and Kings Cross; and in the **inner west** in adjoining Newtown and Erskineville. Those wanting a comfortable place to drink with a mixed clientele should also check out pubs already listed, such as the *Green Park Hotel* (see p.293)mor the *Burdekin* (see p.292). Entry is free unless otherwise indicated.

Arq 16 Flinders St, corner of Taylor Square, Darlinghurst ⓦ www.arqsydney.com.au. Huge nine-hundred-person capacity, state-of-the-art club with everything from drag shows and foam parties to pool competitions. Two levels, each with a very different scene: the top floor is mostly gay, while the ground floor is a less crowded mix of gay and straight. Chill-out booths, laser lighting, viewing decks and fishtanks add to the fun, friendly atmosphere. Mon & Thurs–Sun from 9pm, A$10–25.

Columbian Hotel 117 Oxford St, corner of Crown St, Darlinghurst. Mixed-clientele bar where people come to get revved-up in the evenings and renew their energy the day after. The downstairs bar offers an airy, comfortable space to drink, bop and chat, with open windows onto the street. Upstairs (6pm–late) gets very crowded Thurs–Sun nights, attracting a hip and chilled crowd. The music is Hi-NRG upstairs, progressive house downstairs.Daily 10am–late.

Exchange Hotel 34 Oxford St, Darlinghurst. In the downstairs *Phoenix* bar, Sat night's Crash underground "alternative" dance club is mostly gay shirtless men dancing en masse, but on Sun nights there's a happy mix of gays and lesbians. After midnight, it's at its peak with a raunchier, bacchanalian crowd that you won't find anywhere else on the strip. Sat & Sun from 10pm, A$10/A$5.

Imperial Hotel 35 Erskineville Rd, Erskineville. All-week, late-night LGBT venue, with a popular, hot and sweaty dance floor in the basement (progressive, commercial, Hi-NRG), and a riotous drag-show line-up in the *Cabaret Lounge*. The film *The Adventures of Priscilla, Queen of the Desert* both started and ended here; the *Imperial* has basked in the glory ever since.

Midnight Shift 85 Oxford St, Darlinghurst. "The Shift", running for over 25 years, is a veteran of the Oxford St scene. The *Shift Video Bar* is a large drinking and cruising space to a music-video backdrop; pool tables out back. Upstairs, the weekend-only club is a massive space with drag shows, DJs and events. Mainly men. Downstairs bar daily noon–6am, club Fri & Sat 11pm–7am. A$20.

Slide 41 Oxford St, Darlinghurst ⓦ www.slide .com.au. One of the newer clubs on the scene, this fresh and sophisticated dinner, cabaret and dance venue pulls in a loyal crowd with Abba tributes and Sun-night shows featuring exotic acrobatics. Wed–Sun 7pm–3am, A$10–20.

Taxi Club 40 Flinders St, Darlinghurst. A Sydney legend and famous (or notorious) for being the only place you can buy a drink after 10pm on Good Friday or Christmas Day, this bar is the haunt of a strange blend of drag queens, taxi drivers, lesbians and boys (straight and gay). 24hr except for a clean up 6–9am; club Fri & Sat from 1am.

Live music: rock, blues and jazz

For some time, Sydney's **live music** scene was in the doldrums – the cult of the club DJ ruled, inner-city gentrification hounded aspiring musos out of town, and pubs closed their performance spaces to make way for the dreaded pokies (gambling machines). But while it still lags way behind Melbourne and Brisbane, the Sydney scene is getting back on its feet, with a steady stream of acts passing through each month and a well-established summer-festival circuit. Local band nights in pubs and clubs are often free, especially if you arrive early; for touring bands, tickets start at around A$5–15 for small-scale gigs, with most big-name events costing A$50–100. Sunday afternoon and early evening is a mellow time to catch some music, particularly jazz, around town.

There are now several big outdoor rock concerts throughout spring and summer, but Homebake and the Big Day Out are still the best. **Homebake** (around A$80; Ⓦwww.homebake.com.au) is a huge annual open-air festival in The Domain in early December with food and market stalls, rides and a line-up of over fifty famous and underground Australian bands, from Spiderbait to Jet. The **Big Day Out**, on the Australia Day weekend (around A$120; Ⓦwww .bigdayout.com), at the Showground at Sydney Olympic Park, features international names like The Streets, Muse and Scribe as well as big local talent like Something for Kate and The Drones. For jazz fans, the **Manly Jazz Festival** (see box, p.212) is a great way to kick off the season.

Rock, blues and jazz venues

Annandale Hotel 17 Parramatta Rd (corner of Nelson St), Annandale ☏02 9550 1078, Ⓦwww .annandalehotel.com. This pub is a driving force in the revitalization of the city's music scene. The best of Australia's metal, punk and electronica bands play here, and it has hosted sets by big names from the US, including the Dandy Warhols. Daily from 7pm, A$5–30.

The Basement 29 Reiby Place, Circular Quay ☏02 9251 2797, Ⓦwww.thebasement.com.au.

This dark and moody venue is an institution that attracts the great and rising names in jazz, acoustic and world music as well as a roster of the world's most renowned blues performers. To take in a show, book a table and dine in front of the low stage; otherwise, you'll have to stand all night at the bar at the back. A$25–80.

Bridge Hotel 135 Victoria Rd, Rozelle ☏02 9810 1260, Ⓦwww.thebridgehotel.com.au. Legendary inner-west venue specializing in blues and pub rock, with some international but mostly local acts. Also good pub theatre and comedy nights.

Multi-purpose performance venues

Bookings for many major events are handled by Ticketek or Ticketmaster (see p.289).

Capitol Theatre 13 Campbell St, Haymarket ☏02 9320 5000, Ⓦwww.capitoltheatre .com.au

Enmore Theatre 118–132 Enmore Rd, Newtown ☏02 9550 3666, Ⓦwww .enmoretheatre.com.au

The Forum Entertainment Quarter, Errol Flynn Boulevard, Moore Park ☏02 8117 6700, Ⓦwww.forumsydney.com.au

The Hordern Pavilion Entertainment Quarter, Lang Road, Moore Park ☏02 9921 5333, Ⓦwww.playbillvenues.com.au

Sydney Entertainment Centre 35 Harbour St, Darling Harbour ☏02 9320 4200, Ⓦwww.sydentcent.com.au

Sydney Acer Arena Olympic Boulevard, Sydney Olympic Park ☏02 8765 4321, Ⓦwww.acerarena.com.au

Sydney Showground Showground Road, Sydney Olympic Park ☏02 9704 1111, Ⓦwww.sydneyshowground.com.au

Theatre Royal MLC Centre, King Street, City ☏02 9224 8444, Ⓦwww.mlccentre .com.au

Metro Theatre 624 George St, City ☏02 9550 3666, Ⓦwww.metrotheatre.com.au

Sydney is indisputably one of the world's great gay cities – indeed, many people think it capable of snatching San Francisco's crown as the Queen of them all. There's something for everyone – whether you want to lie on a beach during the warmer months or party hard all year round. Gays and lesbians are pretty much accepted, particularly in the inner-city and eastern areas. They have to be – there's too many of them for anyone to argue.

The four-week **Mardi Gras** festival (see below) is world famous: since its beginnings as a gay-rights protest in 1978, it's become the biggest celebration of gay and lesbian culture on the planet, broadcast on national television. In the early 2000s, it hit a rocky patch thanks to financial mismanagement, but it's since cleaned up its act and in 2008, it turned 30. Some stalwarts feel it's become over-commercial and over-inclusive, with too many party-mad straights gatecrashing the main events, but to others, that kind of acceptance is a victory.

Sydney's LGBT community resists ghettoization; even Oxford Street – Sydney's official "pink strip" of restaurants, coffee shops, bookshops, bars and clubs – is not as gay-centric as it used to be, as more and more young gays and lesbians choose to party with their straight friends, or meet people online instead of in bars. Instead, you'll find pockets of activity all over town. There are favourite areas, however: **King Street** in Newtown, and nearby **Erskineville** are centres of gay culture, while lesbian communities have carved out territory of their own in **Leichhardt** (known affectionately as "Dykehardt") and **Marrackville**.

If you've come for the sun, you'll find popular **gay beaches** at Tamarama (see p.271), north Bondi (see p.270), and "clothing-optional" Lady Jane (see p.264), while **pools** of choice are Redleaf at Double Bay (see p.363), the appropriately named Andrew "Boy" Charlton pool in The Domain (see p.247), and the Coogee Women's Baths at the southern end of Coogee Beach (see p.272).

Mardi Gras, Sleaze Ball and Pride

From a queer perspective, the best time of year to visit Sydney is February, when the **Sydney Gay & Lesbian Mardi Gras** (℡02 9568 8600, ⊛www.mardigras.org.au) takes over the city. Four weeks of parties, exhibitions and performances, including the two-week **Mardi Gras Film Festival** in mid-February (see p.301), represent the largest gay and lesbian arts festival in the world, paving the way for the main event, an exuberant three-hour night-time parade down Oxford Street from Hyde Park to Moore Park. Participants devote months to the preparation of outlandish floats and outrageous costumes at Mardi Gras workshops, and even more time is spent on the preparation of beautiful bodies in Sydney's packed gyms.

The Dykes on Bikes, traditional leaders of the parade since 1988, don't set off until 7.30pm, but by mid-morning, up to half-a-million spectators are already jostling for

Hopetoun Hotel 416 Bourke St, corner of Fitzroy St, Surry Hills ℡02 9361 5257. One of Sydney's best venues for the indie band scene, "The Hoey" focuses on new young bands: local, interstate and international acts all play in the small and inevitably packed front bar (Mon–Sat from 7.30pm), and on Sun there are DJs (5–10pm). Popular pool room, drinking pit in the basement, and inexpensive little restaurant upstairs (meals from A$5–10). Closes midnight; A$5–15.

Rose of Australia Hotel 1 Swanson St, Erskineville ℡02 9565 1441. Trendy inner-city types mix with Goths, locals and gays to sample some favourites of the pub circuit. Line-up changes regularly, and bands play Wed–Fri on a rotational basis, so you can catch anything from an original rock act through to a country-and-western cover band. Music is from 9pm (from 6.30pm Sun) and is always free.

Sandringham Hotel 387 King St, Newtown ℡02 9557 1254, ⊛www.sando.com.au. "The Sando" features local and interstate indie bands, who play on the stage upstairs. Thurs–Sat 8.30pm–midnight, Sun 7–10pm; A$5–20.

Sound Lounge Seymour Centre, corner of City Rd & Cleveland St, Chippendale ℡02 9351 7940,

the best viewing positions along the route (brandishing stolen milk crates to stand on for a better view). If you can't get there until late afternoon, your best bet is Flinders Street near Moore Park Road, where the parade ends. Otherwise, reserve yourself one of the three thousand grandstand seats in the **Flinders Street Glamstand**, a fundraiser for AIDS charity The Bobby Goldsmith Foundation (☏02 9283 8666, ⊛www.bgf.org.au; bookings through Ticketmaster, see p.289).

The all-night **dance party** that follows the parade attracts up to 15,000 people and is held in several differently themed dance spaces at The Entertainment Quarter in Moore Park. Tickets, which usually sell out quickly, are released in phases and are sold over the phone by Ticketek (from A$150; see p.289) rather than online, to make it harder for scalpers (touts) to snap them up. Clubs all over town also get in the swing with special celebrations.

Sydney just can't wait all year for Mardi Gras, so the over-the-top **Sleaze Ball,** a fundraiser for the main event, is a very welcome stopgap in early October. Similar to the Mardi Gras party, it's held at The Entertainment Quarter, and goes on through the night (bookings through Ticketek; from A$99). The team at Sydney's **Pride Centre** (☏02 9331 1333, ⊛www.pridecentre.com.au) have been organizing a similarly priced **New Year's Eve party** for the past decade, usually also at The Entertainment Quarter.

For those who miss the parties themselves, the **recovery parties** the next day are nearly as good; virtually all the bars and clubs host all-day sessions, and Darlinghurst is packed with exhausted but deliriously happy party-people.

Information

See also p.228 for gay-friendly **places to stay**, and p.294 for a lowdown on the **club scene**.

ACON (AIDS Council of NSW) 9 Commonwealth St, Surry Hills ☏02 9206 2000, ⊛www.acon.org.au. Counselling, testing and treatment.

Albion Street Centre 150–154 Albion St, Surry Hills ☏02 9332 1090. Counselling, testing clinic, information and library.

Anti-Discrimination Board Level 4, 175–183 Castlereagh St, City ☏02 9268 5544, ⊛www.lawlink.nsw.gov.au.

The Bookshop 207 Oxford St, Darlinghurst ☏02 9331 1103. A good starting point for getting to know gay Sydney, with helpful staff and a complete stock of LGBT-related books, cards and magazines, plus the free gay and lesbian weeklies *Sydney Star Observer* (⊛www.ssonet.com.au) and *SX* (⊛www.eevolution.com.au), and the monthly *LOTL* (*Lesbians on the Loose*; ⊛www.lotl.com).

GLCS (Gay & Lesbian Counselling Service of NSW) ☏02 8594 9596, ⊛www .glcsnsw.org.au. Daily 5.30–10.30pm.

⊛www.seymourcentre.com.au. The University of Sydney's smallest performance venue hosts twice-weekly jazz performances from SIMA (Sydney Improvised Music Association, ⊛www.sima .org.au), plus world music and cabaret. Tapas menu. Tues–Sat.

Vanguard 42 King St, Newtown ☏02 9557 7992, ⊛www.thevanguard.com.au. Intimate venue inspired by New Orleans' dinner-and-jazz clubs; an interesting mixture of jazz, world music and comedy acts take the stage. Tues–Sun from 7pm; A$10–35.

Classical music, theatre and dance

Sydney's **arts scene** is vibrant and extensive, with performances from a good mix of homegrown and visiting talent. The Opera House is the centrepiece venue, but you'll find plenty of intriguing concerts and productions elsewhere; free outdoor performances in The Domain, under the auspices of the Sydney Festival, are a highlight of the year, with crowds gathering to enjoy the music with a picnic.

Orchestras, theatre and dance companies

Australian Ballet ℡03 9669 2700, ⓦwww .australianballet.com.au. When in Sydney, the Melbourne-based national touring company performs at the Sydney Opera House Opera Theatre and the Capitol Theatre.

Bangarra Dance Theatre ℡02 9251 5333, ⓦwww.bangarra.com.au. This touring company's innovative style fuses contemporary movement with the traditional dances and culture of the Yirrkala Community in the Northern Territory's Arnhem Land. Based at the harbour end of Wharf 4/5, Hickson Rd, they also perform in other Sydney venues.

Bell Shakespeare ℡02 8298 9000, ⓦwww .bellshakespeare.com.au. Shakespeare with an Australian accent at the Sydney Opera House.

Company B ℡02 9699 3444, ⓦwww.belvoir .com.au. Creative, edgy and stimulating contemporary theatre company, based at the Belvoir in Surry Hills; its offshoot, B Sharp, is even more radical.

Ensemble Theatre ℡02 9929 0644 ⓦwww .ensemble.com.au. Long-running theatre company, staging contemporary Australian and classic plays in its home venue on the North Shore, and at the York Theatre in the Seymour Centre.

Opera Australia ℡02 9318 8200, ⓦwww .opera-australia.org.au. Divides its attentions between the Sydney Opera House and Melbourne.

Sydney Dance Company ℡02 9221 4811, ⓦwww.sydneydancecompany.com. Australia's leading contemporary dance company performs at the Wharf Theatre, the Theatre Royal and CarriageWorks.

Sydney Symphony Orchestra ℡02 8215 4600, ⓦwww.sydneysymphony.com.au. Directed by Gianluigi Gelmetti, Sydney's world-class orchestra plays at the Sydney Opera House Concert Hall and at the City Recital Hall.

Sydney Theatre Company ℡02 9250 1777, ⓦwww.sydneytheatre.com.au. Based at the Wharf Theatre and specializing in Shakespeare and the classics, this highly regarded company is currently co-directed by Cate Blanchett.

Concert halls

City Recital Hall 2 Angel Place, City ℡02 8256 2222, ⓦwww.cityrecitalhall.com. Opened in 1999, this classical-music venue right next to Martin Place was specifically designed for chamber music. Seats over 1200, but on three levels, giving it an intimate atmosphere.

Conservatorium of Music Royal Botanic Gardens, off Macquarie St, City ℡02 9351 1263, ⓦwww .music.usyd.edu.au. In term time, students of the "Con" give lunchtime recitals every Wed in Verbrugghen Hall (1.10pm; gold coin donation) and there's a varied programme of full-length orchestral, jazz and opera concerts – an opportunity to spot the stars of the future at below-average prices. Tickets on the door or from the City Recital Hall (above). See also p.248.

St James' Church King St, beside Hyde Park, City ℡02 9232 3022, ⓦwww.sjks.org.au. Hosts half-hour lunchtime recitals on Wed (1.15pm; A$5 donation), plus afternoon and evening concerts.

Resident musicians include Australian Baroque Brass, the Alizarin Chamber Ensemble and the highly acclaimed St James' Choir, whose repertoire extends from Gregorian chant to more contemporary pieces.

Sydney Opera House Bennelong Point ℡02 9250 7777, ⓦwww.sydneyoperahouse.com. The Opera House is, of course, *the* place for the most prestigious performances in Sydney, hosting not just opera and classical music but also theatre and ballet in its several auditoriums. Forget quibbles about ticket prices – it's worth going just to say you've been. See also p.233.

Town Hall George St, City ℡02 9265 9189, ⓦwww.cityofsydney.nsw.gov.au. Centrally located concert hall seating two thousand, with a splendid high-Victorian interior complete with grand organ. Hosts everything from chamber orchestras to bush dances and public lectures. Soon to re-open after renovations.

Theatre and dance venues

Belvoir St Theatre 25 Belvoir St, Surry Hills ℡02 9699 3444, ⓦwww.belvoir.com.au. Two-stage venue, showing superb contemporary productions from Company B and B Sharp.

CarriageWorks 245 Wilson St, Eveleigh ℡02 8571 9099 ⓦwww.carriageworks.com.au. Studio theatre in a converted rail yard, with a programme of physical theatre and contemporary dance.

Ensemble Theatre 78 McDougall St, Milsons Point ☎02 9929 0644, ⊛www.ensemble.com.au. Home venue for the long-running Ensemble Theatre Company, staging contemporary Australian and classic plays.

The Footbridge Theatre Parramatta Rd, University of Sydney, Glebe ☎02 9692 9955. Rich and varied repertoire, from cabaret to Shakespeare.

Lyric Theatre Star City Casino, Pirrama Rd, Pyrmont ☎02 9777 9000 or 1300 795 267, ⊛www.starcity.com.au. The place to see those big musical extravaganzas imported from the West End and Broadway. The smaller Star Theatre puts on more off-beat musicals – such as the *Rocky Horror Show* – and comedy.

The Playhouse, Drama Theatre and The Studio Sydney Opera House, Bennelong Point ☎02 9250 7777, ⊛www.sydneyoperahouse .com. The Playhouse and Drama Theatre show modern and traditional Australian and international plays mostly put on by the Sydney Theatre Company, while the Studio, the Opera House's smallest venue (with the most affordable ticket prices), is flexible in design with a theatre-in-the-round format, and offers an innovative and wide-ranging programme of contemporary performance: theatre, cabaret, dance, comedy and hybrid works.

Seymour Centre Corner of City Rd & Cleveland St, Chippendale ☎02 9351 7940, ⊛www .seymourcentre.com.au. The University of Sydney's theatre and music venue contains several modern stages, used by a variety of amateur and professional companies.

Wharf Theatre Pier 4/5, Hickson Rd, Millers Point ☎02 9250 1777, ⊛www.sydneytheatre.com.au. Home to the Sydney Dance Company and the Sydney Theatre Company. Atmospheric waterfront location, two performance spaces and a good restaurant (see p.281), bar and café.

Fringe theatre, comedy and cabaret

Bridge Hotel 135 Victoria Rd, Rozelle ☎02 9810 1260, ⊛www.thebridgehotel.com.au. This famous inner-west blues pub hosts weekly comedy nights (Mon) and cabaret (Tues).

Imperial Hotel 35 Erskineville Rd, Erskineville ☎02 9519 9899, ⊛www.theimperialhotel.com.au. All-week, late-night gay and lesbian venue with brilliant, free drag shows.

New Theatre 542 King St, Newtown ☎02 9519 3403, ⊛www.ramin.com.au/online/newtheatre. Professional and amateur actors (all unpaid) perform contemporary dramas with socially relevant themes.

NIDA Parade Theatres 215 Anzac Parade, Kensington ☎02 9697 7613, ⊛www.nida.edu.au. Australia's premier dramatic training ground – the National Institute of Dramatic Art – where the likes of Mel Gibson, Judy Davis and Colin Friels started out, offers student productions.

Stables Theatre 10 Nimrod St, Darlinghurst ☎02 9361 3817, ⊛www.griffintheatre.com.au. The place to see the Griffin Theatre Company, whose mission is to engage and foster new Australian playwrights.

Sydney Comedy Store Entertainment Quarter, Driver Ave, Moore Park ☎02 9357 1419, ⊛www .comedystore.com.au. International (often American) and Australian stand-up comics. Meals aren't available inside, but nearby restaurants offer discounts for *Comedy Store* ticket-holders. Tues–Sat from 7pm, show 8.30pm; A\$15–29.50.

Cinemas

Sydneysiders are keen movie-goers, and the city hosts several **film festivals** each year (see box, p.301), while summer brings open-air screenings. Many cinemas offer a discount on Mondays or Tuesdays.

Mainstream cinemas

Greater Union 505–525 George St, City ☎02 9273 7431, ⊛www.greaterunion.com. Frenetic seventeen-screen city centre complex packed with teenagers and fast-food outlets.

Hoyts Entertainment Quarter, Bent St, Moore Park ☎02 9332 1300, ⊛www.hoyts.com.au. Spacious, plush complex which sometimes hosts gala events. There's also a humbler Hoyts near Glebe, in the Broadway Shopping Centre, Broadway (☎02 9211 1911).

Reading Cinemas Market City Shopping Centre, Haymarket ☎02 9280 1202, ⊛wwwreadingcinemas.com.au. Busy Chinatown venue with five screens.

Bondi Open Air Bondi Pavilion, Bondi Beach
☎ 02 9130 1235, ⓦ www.bondiopenair.com.au.
Mid-Jan to early March, Tues–Sat, 6.30pm for
8.30pm; A$20, discounted for online booking; bean
bags free. Oldies and new releases in the Pavilion's
amphitheatre-like courtyard, right by the beach.
Moonlight Cinema Belvedere Amphitheatre,
Centennial Park (enter via Woollahra Gate, Oxford
St) ⓦ www.moonlight.com.au. Early Dec to early
March, daily except Mon 7pm for 8.30pm; A$17,

child A$14, discounted for online booking; bean-
bag hire A$6. A different recent classic every night.
St George Open Air Cinema Mrs Macquarie's
Point, Royal Botanic Gardens ☎ 13 61 00
(advance bookings) or 1300 366 649 (on the
day), ⓦ www.stgeorgeopenair.com.au. One-
month season from early Jan to early Feb, daily
except Sat 6.15pm for 8.20pm; from A$23, child
A$22. Recent releases in a picturesque setting
with grandstand seating.

Specialist cinemas

Cinema Paris Entertainment Quarter, Bent St,
Moore Park ☎ 02 9332 1633, ⓦ www.hoyts
.com.au. Four-screen arthouse cinema.
Dendy Newtown 261 King St, Newtown
☎ 02 9550 5699. Trendy four-screen cinema
complex with attached café, bar and bookshop,
showing prestige new-release films.
Dendy Opera Quays 2 East Circular Quay
☎ 02 9247 3800. Classy, superbly sited three-
screen venue with a mixture of quality mainstream
and arthouse offerings.
Govinda's Movie Room 112 Darlinghurst
Rd, Darlinghurst ☎ 02 9380 5155,
ⓦ www.govindas.com.au. Run by the Hare
Krishnas (but definitely no indoctrination), Govinda's
shows classics and recent releases in a pleasantly
unorthodox cushion-room atmosphere. Arrive early
for the popular vegetarian buffet plus movie deal
(A$25.80); film only is A$11.90 but diners are given
preference. Two films Mon–Fri, three Sat & Sun.
Hayden Orpheum 380 Military Rd, Cremorne
☎ 02 9908 4344, ⓦ www.orpheum.com.au.

Charming heritage-listed, six-screen cinema built
in 1935, with a splendid Art Deco interior and old-
fashioned, friendly service. The main cinema has
never dispensed with its Wurlitzer organ recitals
preceding Sat night and Sun afternoon films.
Mainstream, and foreign new releases.
IMAX Theatre Southern Promenade, Darling
Harbour ☎ 02 9281 3300, ⓦ www.imax.com.au.
State-of-the-art giant cinema screen showing a
choice of four films designed to thrill your senses.
Screenings on the hour, 10am–10pm; 45min films
A$18, child A$13; feature-length films A$25/A$18.
Palace Cinemas ⓦ www.palacecinemas.com.au.
Chain of inner-city cinephiles' cinemas showing a
programme of foreign-language, arthouse and new
releases: Academy, 3A Oxford St, corner of South
Dowling St, Paddington ☎ 02 9361 4453; Chauvel,
Paddington Town Hall, corner of Oatley Rd & Oxford
St, Paddington ☎ 02 9361 5398, ⓦ www.chauvel
cinema.net.au; Verona, 17 Oxford St, corner of
Verona St, Paddington ☎ 02 9360 6099; Norton St,
99 Norton St, Leichhardt ☎ 02 9550 0122.

Art galleries and exhibitions

Sydney's artistic epicentres are **Paddington** and **Surry Hills**, with a few
smaller galleries on **King Street**, Newtown. For a directory listing many of
the city's exhibition spaces and dealers, check out the useful *Artfind Guide*
(ⓦ www.artfind.com.au).

Artspace The Gunnery Arts Centre, 43–51 Cowper
Wharf Rd, Woolloomooloo ☎ 02 9356 0555,
ⓦ www.artspace.org.au. In a wonderful location,
showing provocative young artists with a focus on
installations and new media. Tues, Wed, Fri & Sat
11am–5pm, Thurs 11am–8pm.
Australian Centre for Photography 257 Oxford
St, Paddington ☎ 02 9332 1455, ⓦ www.acp
.org.au. Exhibitions of photo-based art from
established and new international and Australian
artists in two galleries. Emerging photographers

are showcased on the Project Wall. There's a
specialist bookshop, photography courses, and a
dark room for hire, plus the very good French-
style *Bistro Lulu*. Tues–Fri noon–7pm, Sat & Sun
10am–6pm.
Australian Galleries: Painting & Sculpture 15
Roylston St, Paddington ☎ 02 9360 5177, ⓦ www
.australiangalleries.com.au. Serene gallery exhibiting and selling contemporary Australian art,
including works by Gary Shead, Jeffrey Smart and
John Coburn. Mon–Sat 10am–6pm.

The once-radical **Sydney Film Festival**, held annually for two weeks in **early June**, has developed into a more mainstream, but nonetheless exciting, programme of features, shorts, documentaries and retrospective screenings from Australia and around the world. The city also hosts several smaller summer festivals, devised with the sort of creative, irreverent approach that first fuelled SFF.

Sydney Film Festival

Founded in 1954 by a group of film enthusiasts at Sydney University, **SFF** (Ⓦwww .sydneyfilmfestival.org) struggled with prudish censors and parochial attitudes until freedom from censorship for festival films was introduced in 1971. From the early, relaxed atmosphere of picnics on the lawns between screenings and hardy film-lovers crouching under blankets in freezing prefabricated sheds, it gradually moved off-campus; since 1974, its main base has been the magnificent State Theatre (see p.241). Over the years, it's provided a springboard for luminaries such as Jane Campion, Baz Luhrmann and Cate Blanchett. These days, alongside the gala screenings and red carpet events at the State Theatre, there's a more provocative programme, aimed at a younger audience, at the Metro Theatre, the Greater Union and the glamorous Dendy Opera Quays (see p.295 & p.300). Single tickets cost A$16.50 (child A$6.50); a choice of passes allow entrance to multiple sessions at a discount, while a reserved seat at every State Theatre screening costs A$220–320. Bookings are handled by Ticketmaster (see p.289).

Flickerfest

The stars above and the sound of waves accompany **Flickerfest** (Ⓣ02 9365 6888, Ⓦwww.flickerfest.com.au), Sydney's nine-day short film festival, held in the amphitheatre of the Bondi Pavilion in early January. Accredited by the US Academy of Motion Pictures, it's a seriously competitive showcase for foreign and Australian productions, including comedy, drama and documentaries. Single session A$15, season pass A$120.

Tropfest

Tropfest (Ⓣ02 9368 0434, Ⓦwww.tropfest.com) is a one-day festival of short films held annually in February. Its name comes from the *Tropicana Cafe* on Victoria Street, Darlinghurst, where the festival began almost by chance in 1993 when a young regular, actor John Polsen, persuaded the owner to show the short film he had made. He encouraged other filmmakers to follow suit, and the following year a huge crowd of punters packed themselves into the café to watch around twenty films. These days, Tropfest is the world's largest short-film competition, with the finalists' offerings relayed to giant screens all over Australia. The centre of the action is The Domain, where a huge crowd gathers for an afternoon and evening of free entertainment. The judges are often famous international actors; Polsen himself, still the festival's director, has made it as a Hollywood director with his films *Swimfan* (2002) and *Hide and Seek* (2005). All entries must be less than seven minutes long and brand new, containing a reference to a signature item announced just months before the closing date; recent items have included "bubble", "sneeze" and "eight".

Other festivals

Mardi Gras Film Festival Ⓦwww.queerscreen.com.au. Two-week showcase for the latest in LGBT cinema, held in mid-February as part of the Gay and Lesbian Mardi Gras (see p.296).

World of Women (WOW) Film Festival Ⓦwww.wift.org/wow. Festival of short films by female directors, held over three days in late October at the Chauvel Cinema, Paddington.

Horse racing in Sydney

There are horse-racing meetings on Wednesday, Saturday and most public holidays throughout the year, but the best times to hit the track are during the **Spring and Autumn Carnivals** (Aug–Sept & March–April), when prize money rockets, and the quality of racing rivals the best in the world. The venues are well maintained, peopled with colourful racing characters and often massive crowds. Principal **racecourses** are: Royal Randwick (Alison Rd, Randwick), which featured in *Mission Impossible II*; Rosehill Gardens (James Ruse Drive, Rosehill); and Canterbury Park (King St, Canterbury), which has midweek racing, plus floodlit Thursday-night racing from September to March. Entry is around A$14, or A$20–25 on carnival days. Contact the Australian Jockey Club (☎02 9663 8400, ⓦwww.ajc.com.au) or the Sydney Turf Club (☎02 9930 4000, ⓦwww.stc.com.au) for details of these and other picturesque country venues. Every Friday, the *Sydney Morning Herald* publishes its racing guide, "The Form". Bets are placed at TAB shops; these are scattered throughout the city, and most pubs also have TAB access.

Australian Galleries: Works on Paper 24 Glenmore Rd, Paddington ☎02 9380 8744, ⓦwww.australiangalleries.com.au. Works for sale here include drawings by William Robinson, Brett Whiteley and Arthurs Boyd, as well as prints and sketches by young Australian artists. Mon–Sat 10am–6pm, Sun noon–5pm.

Hogarth Galleries Aboriginal Art Centre 7 Walker Lane, Paddington ☎02 9360 6839, ⓦwww.aboriginalartcentres.com. Extensive collection of work by contemporary Aboriginal artists, both tribal and urban, and special exhibitions. Tues–Sat 10am–5pm.

Ivan Dougherty Gallery Selwyn St (corner of Albion Ave), Paddington ☎02 9385 0726, ⓦwww.cofa.unsw.edu.au. This is the exhibition space for the College of Fine Arts (COFA), University of NSW.

The ten shows per year focus on international contemporary art with accompanying forums, lectures and performances. Mon–Sat 10am–5pm. Closed Jan.

Josef Lebovic Gallery 34 Paddington St, Paddington ☎02 9332 1840, ⓦwww.joseflebovicgallery.com. Renowned print and graphic gallery specializing in Australian and international prints from the nineteenth, twentieth and twenty-first centuries, as well as vintage photography. Wed–Fri 1–6pm, Sat 11am–5pm.

Ray Hughes Gallery 270 Devonshire St, Surry Hills ☎02 9698 3200, ⓦwww.rayhughesgallery.com. Influential dealer with a stable of high-profile contemporary Australian and New Zealand artists. Openings monthly, with two artists per show. Tues–Sat 10am–6pm.

Shopping

Sydney's main shopping focus is the city centre, in the stretch between Martin Place and the QVB. Apart from its charming old nineteenth-century arcades and two **department stores**, David Jones and Myers, the city centre also has several modern multilevel **shopping complexes** where you can hunt down clothes and accessories without raising a sweat, among them Skygarden (between Pitt and Castlereagh sts) and Centrepoint on Pitt Street Mall, on the corner of Market Street. Much of the area from the QVB to the mall is linked by underground arcades, which will also keep you cool.

Most stores are **open** Monday to Saturday 9am to 6pm, with Thursday late-night shopping until 9pm. Many of the larger shops and department stores in the city are also open on Sunday from 10am to 5pm, as are shopping centres in tourist areas such as Darling Harbour. If you've run out of time to buy presents and souvenirs, don't worry: **Sydney Airport** is attached to one of the biggest shopping malls in Sydney, with outlets for everything from surfwear to R.M. Williams bush outfitters, at the same prices as the downtown stores. **The Rocks** is the best place for souvenir and duty- and GST-free shopping.

Fashion

Oxford Street in Paddington is the place to go for interesting **fashion**, with outlets of most Australian designers along the strip. You'll find more expensive designer gear in the city, at the Strand Arcade, 412 George St, and the David Jones department store on Elizabeth Street. For striking street fashion, check out Crown Street in Surry Hills, with places such as Wheels & Doll Baby at no. 259, and King Street in Newtown running up to St Peters, where you'll also find cheaper styles, retro clothes and other interesting junk. To go with the outfits, funky Australian **jewellery** can be found on Level 1 of the Strand Arcade at Dinosaur Designs (also at 339 Oxford St, Paddington), and at Love and Hatred.

The quality Australian **bush outfitters** R. M. Williams, with branches at no. 71 and no. 389 George St, is great for moleskin trousers, Drizabone coats and Akubra hats. However, for an even wider range of Akubra **hats**, check out Strand Hatters on the ground floor of the Strand Arcade. If it's interesting **surfwear** you're after, head for Mambo at Market City, Hay St, Haymarket (also at 17 Oxford St, Paddington; 80 The Corso, Manly; and 80 Campbell Parade, Bondi Beach), and an array of surf shops at Manly and Bondi Beach.

Arts and crafts

The Rocks is heaving with **Australiana** and **arts and crafts** souvenirs, from opals to sheepskin – weekends are particularly busy when the open-air market takes over George Street. Tourists flock to Ken Done's emporium here at 123 George St and 1–5 Hickson Rd (in the restored Australian Steam and Navigation Building) to buy his colourful designs, which feature Sydney's harbour, boats and flowers; there's a Done Art & Design store at the airport, too, and another at the Market City Shopping Centre. The best place to buy **Aboriginal** art and crafts is the Aboriginal-owned and -run Gavala, in the Harbourside Shopping Centre in Darling Harbour.

Music and books

For a take-home sample of the **Australian music** scene in all its variety, from Aboriginal through to indie and jazz, head for the Australian Music Centre shop, Level 4, The Arts Exchange, 10 Hickson Rd, The Rocks, with very knowledgeable staff and a relaxed listen-before-you-buy policy.

One of the biggest **bookshops** in the city is the long-running, Australian-owned Dymocks, 428 George St, open daily, on several floors with an impressive Australian selection and a café. The small bookshop at the State Library on Macquarie Street has a well-chosen selection of titles on Australia. Book superstores include Kinokuniya in Galleries Victoria, on the corner of George and Park streets; Borders, 77 Castlereagh St, between King and Market streets; and Collins Superstore, Level 2, Broadway Shopping Centre near Glebe. Nearby, Gleebooks, 49 Glebe Point Rd, Glebe, is one of Australia's best bookshops, specializing in academic and alternative books, contemporary Australian and international literature, and is open daily until 9pm; book launches and other literary events are regularly held. Ariel has two large, lively and hip branches, one at 103 George St, The Rocks, and the other at 42 Oxford St, Paddington; both branches open daily until midnight. Macleay Bookshop, 103 Macleay St, Potts Point (daily until 7pm), is a tiny and peaceful choice. The **Travel Bookshop** at 175 Liverpool St, Darlinghurst (closed Sun), is the place to head for maps, guides and travel journals, plus a good selection of Australiana. **Secondhand books** can be found at Glebe and Paddington markets,

Sydney has far more to offer than the standard urban pursuits of sightseeing, shopping, bar-hopping and eating out. Watersports enthusiasts can take to the water (or dive beneath it) right in the city by heading for the **harbour** or the **beach suburbs**, riders can explore the **Centennial Parklands** on horseback, while within easy reach of the centre there are several fine **wilderness areas** where hikers and cyclists can stretch their legs and adventure enthusiasts can test their mettle. **Ku-ring-gai Chase National Park**, the **Hawkesbury River** and the **Royal National Park** are all within easy reach, but **The Blue Mountains** and the **Hunter Valley** wine region are by far the most popular destinations.

Blue Mountains

You'll almost certainly have a better time with one of the small-group adventure outfits than with the commercial bus-tour operators who stick to more sedentary sightseeing. To make the most of your visit, stay at least one night. For more details, see pp.318–331.

Oz Trek ⊕02 9666 4262 or 1300 661 234, ⊛www.oztrek.com.au. Recommended active full-day tours to the Blue Mountains (A$55) including a choice of short bushwalks with a good chance of seeing wildlife. Small groups (max 20). The trip can be extended to overnight packages, staying at the *Blue Mountains YHA* in Katoomba, with either abseiling (A$225) or a Jenolan Caves visit (A$210); meals extra. Pick-ups from Coogee, Bondi, Kings Cross, the CBD and Glebe.

Wildframe Ecotours ⊕02 9440 9915, ⊛www.wildframe.com. Runs hiking trips to less-trodden areas of the Blue Mountains. The Grand Canyon Eco-tour, for fit walkers, includes a small-group bushwalk (max 21) through the Grand Canyon (5km; 3hr). The Blue Mountains Bush Tour is more relaxed, with several short bushwalks. Full day A$85 (child A$55); overnight tours from A$136 including accommodation at the *Blue Mountains YHA* in Katoomba; meals extra. Pick-ups from Coogee, Kings Cross, City and the Blue Mountains.

Diving

Sydney's best dive sites include The Wall, The Apartments and The Cathedral off Long Reef, near Collaroy; The Heads (North Head and South Head) at the mouth of the harbour; Wedding Cake Island near Coogee; and Barrens Hut near Cronulla. The following all offer courses, shore diving and trips.

Pro Dive Coogee 27 Alfreda St, Coogee ⊕02 9665 6333, ⊛www.prodivecoogee .com. Runs boat trips and shore dives anywhere between Camp Cove (Watsons Bay) and La Perouse (4hr double boat dive from A$199; double shore dive A$105).

Aquatic Explorers 40 The Kingsway, under Cronulla Beach YHA, Cronulla ⊕02 9523 1518, ⊛www.aquaticexplorers.com.au. Organizes shore diving on Thursday evenings and Saturday and Sunday mornings (free; gear rental available) plus boat dives, night dives and weekends away up and down the New South Wales coast.

Dive Centre Manly 10 Belgrave St, Manly ⊕02 9977 4355, ⊛www.divesydney .com.au. Offers shore dives at Shelley Beach, Fairlight and Fairy Bower, plus Harbord if conditions are good (daily; single dive A$75, double A$95), and boat dives off Long Reef and The Heads (Fri–Sun; single dive A$90, double A$145). Also night diving (Wed from shore, Fri by boat).

Dive Centre Bondi 192 Bondi Rd ⊕02 9369 3855, ⊛www.divebondi.com.au. Shore dives at North Bondi, Bare Island and Camp Cove (double dive A$95); boat-dive sites include Magic Point, a grey nurse shark habitat (double dive A$145).

Horse-riding

For guided riding around the Centennial Parklands, contact **Moore Park Stables** (A$60/hr; ⊕02 9360 8747, ⊛www.mooreparkstables.com.au) or **Centennial Stables** (A$95/hr; ⊕02 9360 5650, ⊛www.centennialstables.com.au).

4

SYDNEY

Hunter Valley

Prices are for a full day from Sydney, excluding lunch. For more details, see p.335.

Boutique Wine Tours ☎02 9499 5444, ⊛www.boutiquewinetours.com.au. Small-group tours, concentrating on the Lower Hunter Valley's interesting, offbeat wineries, cheesemakers and olive growers, with a flexible itinerary and the option of a light or gourmet lunch stop. A\$99.

Rover Coaches ☎02 4990 1699, ⊛www.rovercoaches.com.au. Operate a once-daily Wine Country Xpress coach service from Central Station and The Rocks to connect with their local Wine Rover hop-on-hop-off winery tour bus, which takes you to many of the major wineries. A\$100.

Wine Country Tours ☎02 9484 0477, ⊛www.winecountrytours.com.au. Master winemaker Richard Everett leads select groups (up to 8) of discerning wine buffs on private cellar visits, sampling special vintages that you won't find in regular tastings. Gourmet lunch stop at *Roberts*. A\$150.

Kayaking

Natural Wanders Kayak Adventures ☎02 9899 1001, ⊛www.kayaksydney.com. Guided kayaking in the harbour: their most popular trips are the short Billy Blue Paddle to Berry's Bay (2hr; A\$65) and, for experienced sea kayakers, the Bridge Paddle (3hr 30min; A\$90), which takes you under the Harbour Bridge from Lavender Bay near Luna Park to explore the North Shore.

Sailing and windsurfing

For general information on sailing courses and yacht rental, contact the NSW Yachting Association (☎02 9660 1266, ⊛www.nsw.yachting.org.au). The main sailing season is October to April.

Balmoral Windsurfing, Sailing and Kayaking School Balmoral Sailing Club, The Esplanade (southern end), Balmoral Beach ☎02 9960 5344, ⊛www.sailboard.net.au. Rents windsurfers and dinghies (A\$40–50/hr) and runs courses (from A\$255 for 2 days) including five-day intensive training for kids (from A\$270).

Sydney by Sail Australian National Maritime Museum, Darling Harbour ☎02 9280 1110, ⊛www.sydneybysail.com. Runs Yachting Australia courses throughout the year, from Level 1 Introductory (18hr including tuition and 2 races; A\$425) to Level 4 Skipper (3-day live-aboard; A\$695). Experienced sailors can charter yachts from A\$495 per half-day.

Scenic flights

Sydney Harbour Seaplanes Rose Bay (☎02 9388 1978 or 1300 732 752, ⊛www.seaplanes.com.au), can take you on a scenic flight over Sydney Harbour and Bondi Beach (15min; A\$160); zoom you up to the Northern Beaches (30min; A\$225); or drop you off for a memorable lunch at Palm Beach or the Hawkesbury River (A\$445–465 including lunch). For helicopter tours, contact **Blue Sky Helicopters** (from A\$190; ☎02 9700 7888, ⊛www.blueskyhelicopters.com).

Surfing

Before you set out, check the current conditions (see p.269).

Let's Go Surfing 128 Ramsgate Ave, North Bondi ☎02 9365 1800, ⊛www.letsgosurfing.com.au. Excellent place to initiate yourself in Bondi surf culture. Group lessons from A\$75 for two hours, private tuition, board sales and rentals.

Manly Surf School North Steyne Surf Club ☎02 9977 6977, ⊛www.manlysurfschool.com. Covers the Northern Beaches, with two-hour lessons from \$A55.

Waves Surf School ☎02 9369 3010 or 1800 851 101, ⊛www.wavessurfschool.com.au. Surfing adventures lasting one to five days, taking you to Royal National Park, Seal Rocks or Byron Bay From A\$79 (1 day) to A\$549 (5 days). City, Bondi and Coogee pick-ups.

at Gleebooks Second Hand Books, 191 Glebe Point Rd (daily until 9pm); upstairs at Lesley McKays Bookshop, 346 New South Head Rd, Double Bay (the ground level, for new books, is open until midnight); and in the secondhand bookshops on King Street, Newtown – in particular, check out the amazingly chaotic piles of books at Gould's Book Arcade, nos. 32–38 (daily 8am–midnight).

Food and drink

There are several handy **supermarkets** in the city centre with extended opening hours, including Woolworths on the corner of Park and George streets, near Town Hall station (Mon–Fri 6am–midnight, Sat & Sun 8am–midnight). Also in the city, there's a large Coles in the World Square shopping centre on George Street and small branches at Wynyard station and at 388 George St; the bigger Coles in the Hyatt Kingsgate shopping centre on Darlinghurst Road in Kings Cross, and in the Broadway Shopping Centre near Glebe, are also handy for travellers (all daily 6am–midnight). In the suburbs, large supermarkets stay open daily until about 10pm or midnight, and there are plenty of (albeit overpriced) 24-hour convenience stores in the inner city and suburbs, often attached to petrol stations. For **delicatessen** items, look no further than the splendid food hall at David Jones on Elizabeth Street. The **Australian Wine Centre** on Alfred Street, Circular Quay (Mon–Sat 9.30am–6.30pm, Sun 11am–5pm), sells more than a thousand **wines** from around Australia and has an in-house wine bar.

Markets

The two best **markets** are the Paddington Market (9am–4pm) and Balmain Market (7.30am–4pm), both on Saturday, while the relaxed Glebe Market (10am–4pm), also on a Saturday, and flea market at Rozelle (Sat & Sun 9am–4pm) are also worth a look. The Rocks Market on George Street (Sat & Sun 10am–5pm) is more touristy but good for a browse, while Paddy's Markets, in Haymarket near Chinatown (Thurs–Sun 9am–5pm), is Sydney's oldest, selling fruit and veg, deli products, meat and fish, plus large quantities of bargain-basement clothes and toys. There's also a series of Saturday markets on the North Shore; Kirribilli Markets (fourth Sat of month 7am–3pm), scenically sited in Bradfield Park, near the foot of the Harbour Bridge, is the best and biggest. Foodies should check out the series of **produce markets**: at Pyrmont Bay Park in front of the Star City Casino (first Sat of month 7–11am); at the Showring at The Entertainment Quarter in Moore Park (Wed & Sat 10am–3.30pm); and at Northside Produce Market at the Civic Centre, Miller Street, North Sydney, between Ridge and McClaren streets (third Sat of month 8am–noon).

Listings

Airlines (domestic) Aeropelican ☎02 4928 9600; Jetstar ☎13 15 38; Norfolkair ☎1800 612 960; Qantas ☎13 13 13; Regional Express ☎13 17 13; Virgin Blue ☎13 67 89.
Airlines (international) Aeroflot, Level 24, 44 Market St ☎02 9262 2233; Air Canada, Level 12, 92 Pitt St ☎02 9232 5222; Air New Zealand, Level 18, 264 George St ☎13 24 76; Air Pacific, Level 10, 403 George St ☎1800 230 150; Alitalia, 64 York St ☎02 9244 2400; British Airways, Level 19, AAP Centre, 259 George St ☎1300 767 177; Cathay Pacific, 8 Spring St ☎13 17 47; Continental, 64 York St ☎02 9244 2242; Delta, Level 9, 189 Kent St ☎02 9251 3211; Finnair, 64 York St ☎02 9244 2299; Garuda, 55 Hunter St ☎1300 365 330; Gulf Air, 12/403 George St ☎02 9244 2199; Japan Airlines, Level 14, 201 Sussex St ☎02 9272 1111; KLM, 13th floor, 115 Pitt St ☎1300 303 747; Korean Air, Level 4, 333 George St ☎02 9262 6000; Luthansa, 143 Macquarie St ☎02 9367 3888;

Malaysia Airlines, 16 Spring St ☎ 02 9364 3500; Olympic, 3rd Floor, 37–49 Pitt St ☎ 02 9251 1048; Qantas, 10 Bridge St ☎ 13 13 13; Scandinavian Airlines, Level 15, 31 Market St ☎ 1300 727 707; Singapore Airlines, 31 Market St ☎ 13 10 11; Thai Airways, 75 Pitt St ☎ 02 9251 1922; Virgin Atlantic, Level 8, 403 George St ☎ 02 9244 2747.

Banks and foreign exchange Head offices of banks are mostly in the CBD, around Martin Place; ATMs are found in all shopping areas. American Express outlets include 105 Pitt St (Mon–Fri 9am–5pm; ☎ 1300 139 060); 296 George St (daily 8.30am–5.30pm); and *Quay Grand Hotel*, Circular Quay East (Mon–Fri 9am–5pm, Sat & Sun 11am–4pm). Lost or stolen travellers' cheques ☎ 1800 251 902. Exchange bureaus include Travelex at the airport and several city locations including 32 Martin Place and 37–49 Pitt St, near Central Station (Mon–Fri 9am–5.15pm, Sat 10am–2.45pm; ☎ 02 9241 5722); UAE Money Exchange, Shop 175 Harbourside Shopping Centre, Darling Harbour (daily 9.30am–9pm; ☎ 02 9212 7124).

Campervan and motorhome hire Some of the following offer one-way hire as an option, and may include a full set of camping gear. All Seasons Campervans, 77 Planthurst Rd, Carlton (☎ 02 9547 0100, ⓦ www.camper.com.au); Britz Campervan Rentals, 653 Gardeners Rd, Mascot (☎ 02 9667 0402 or 1800 331 454, ⓦ www.britz.com.au); Travel Car Centre, 26 Orchard Rd, Brookvale (☎ 02 9905 6928 or 1800 440 300, ⓦ www.travelcar.com.au); Travellers Auto Barn, 177 William St, Kings Cross (☎ 02 9360 1500 or 1800 674 374, ⓦ www .travellers-autobarn.com.au), Wicked Campers, Gate 407, George St, Waterloo (☎ 1800 24 68 69, ⓦ www.wickedcampers.com.au).

Camping equipment Paddy Pallin, 507 Kent St (☎ 02 9264 2685), is the best of the outdoor equipment stores on "Adventure Alley" behind the Town Hall. Cheaper options include army-surplus stores on George St and Pitt St near Central Station, and K-Mart stores at Spring St in Bondi Junction and the Broadway Shopping Centre, Bay St; also check hostel notice boards. Only a few places rent gear: at Alpsport, 1045 Victoria Rd, West Ryde (☎ 02 9858 5844), you can hire tents, sleeping bags and sleeping mats suitable for bushwalking trips.

Car rental Avis, airport (☎ 02 8374 2847) and 200 William St, Kings Cross (☎ 02 9357 2000); Budget, airport (☎ 02 9207 9165) and 93 William St, Kings Cross (☎ 02 8255 9600); Hertz (☎ 13 30 39), airport and corner of William & Riley sts, Kings Cross; Thrifty (☎ 1300 367 227), airport and 75 William St, Kings Cross. Rates at the internationals start at A\$50 per day for a small manual; there are

cheaper deals with the popular Bayswater, 180 William St, Kings Cross (☎ 02 9360 3622, ⓦ www .bayswatercarrental.com.au) and Travellers Auto Barn (see campervan hire).

Car sales Specialists in cars for travellers include Travellers Auto Barn (see campervan hire); Traveller's Mate, 130 Princes Highway, Arncliffe near Mascot airport (☎ 02 9556 2113, ⓦ www .travellersmate.com.au); and the Kings Cross Car Market, Ward Ave, corner of Elizabeth Bay Rd, Kings Cross (daily 9am–6pm; ☎ 02 9358 5000 or 1800 808 188, ⓦ www.carmarket.com.au). All can help with paperwork, contract exchange and insurance, and can advise on buying and selling cars in different states. Paddy's Motor Market at Flemington Market off Parramatta Rd, Homebush West (Sun 8am–4pm; access via Austin Ave near Flemington station; ☎ 1300 361 589, ⓦ www .paddysmotormarket.com.au) is better for buying than selling unless your car is of a type to appeal to local buyers. There are plenty of secondhand dealers on Parramatta Rd from Annandale onwards: check the ads in *Drive*, published with the *Sydney Morning Herald* on Fridays. For private sales, check the ads in *Drive*, on hostel noticeboards, and on the websites listed in Basics on p.43.

Cycle routes Bicycles are carried free on trains outside of peak hours (Mon–Fri 6–9am & 3.30–7.30pm) and on ferries at all times. The Roads and Traffic Authority (RTA; ☎ 1800 060 607, ⓦ www.rta.nsw.gov.au) produces a handy fold-out map, *Sydney Cycleways*, showing both off-road paths and suggested bicycle routes, which they will post out. The best source of information, however, is the organization Bicycle NSW, based at Level 5, 822 George St (Mon–Fri 9am–5.30pm; ☎ 02 9218 5400, ⓦ www.bicyclensw.org.au). The useful book *Bike-It! Sydney* (A\$24.95) details backstreet inner-city bike routes, while *Cycling Around Sydney* (A\$24.95) describes the city's thirty best rides; both come with maps. Popular cycling spots are Centennial Park and the Manly bike path (see p.274). The Sydney branch of international cycling activist group Critical Mass (ⓦ www.bikesarefun.org) meets at 6pm on the last Friday of the month at the Archibald Fountain in Hyde Park for an hour-long mass ride through the city.

Cycle shops For sales: Woolys Wheels, 82 Oxford St, Paddington (☎ 02 9331 2671). For sales and rentals (from A\$33/day): Clarence St Cyclery, 104 Clarence St (☎ 02 9299 4962); Inner City Cycles, 151 Glebe Point Rd, Glebe (☎ 02 9660 6605); Centennial Park Cycles, 50 Clovelly Rd, Randwick (☎ 02 9398 5027). CPC also rents tandems, roller-blades and pedal cars.

Hospitals (with emergency departments)
St Vincent's Hospital, corner of Victoria & Burton sts, Darlinghurst ☎ 02 8382 1111; Royal Prince Alfred, Missenden Rd, Camperdown ☎ 02 9515 6111; Prince of Wales, Barker St, Randwick ☎ 02 9382 2222.

Immigration Department of Immigration, 26 Lee St, near Central Station, City ☎ 13 18 81.

Internet access Access (Wi-Fi and terminals) is free in all City of Sydney libraries. Reasonably priced alternatives (around A$4/hr) include Sydney's YHAs, and Global Gossip, whose branches include 790 George St and 415 Pitt St (both daily 9am–11pm); 14 Wentworth Ave, next to Hyde Park (Mon–Fri 9am–6pm); 61 Darlinghurst Rd, Kings Cross (daily 8am–1am); and 37 Hall St, Bondi (Mon–Thurs 9am–midnight, Fri–Sun 9am–11pm). They also offer cut-rate international calls and parcel post. Phone Net Cafe, 73–75 Hall St, Bondi (Mon–Fri 8am–10pm, Sat & Sun until 9pm; A$3.30/hr), is a lively haunt in its own right.

Left luggage There are lockers at Wanderers' Travel, 810 George St, close to Central Station (daily 7am–8pm; A$4/day) and at Travellers Contact Point, Level 7, Dymocks Building, 428 George St (☎ 02 9221 8744; from A$5). Also locker rooms at the airport and the Sydney Coach Terminal (A$5–15 per 24hr).

Libraries See the State Library, p.246, and Customs House Library, p.231; for details of other Sydney libraries, visit ⊛ www.cityofsydney.nsw .gov.au/library.

Maps Map World, 280 Pitt St (☎ 02 9261 3601, ⊛ www.mapworld.net.au), has Sydney's biggest selection of maps and travel guides; see also "Parks and wildlife information", below.

Medical centres Broadway Medical Centre, 185–211 Broadway, near Glebe (☎ 02 9281 5085) are general practitioners open Mon–Fri 9am–7pm, Sat & Sun 11am–5pm, no appointment necessary; Skin Cancer Centre, 403 George St (☎ 02 9262 4877); Sydney Sexual Health Centre, Sydney Hospital, Macquarie St (☎ 02 9382 7440 or 1800 451 624); The Travel Doctor, 7th Floor, 428 George St (☎ 02 9221 7133, ⊛ www.traveldoctor.com.au).

Motorbike hire Bikescape, 183 Parramatta Rd, Annandale (☎ 1300 736 869, ⊛ www.bikescape .com.au), with scooters from A$70 per day and motorbikes from A$120 (cheaper weekend and longer-term rates available).

Motoring association NRMA 74 King St, City (☎ 13 21 32, ⊛ www.mynrma.com.au; A$55 joining fee plus A$87.30–156.30 annual charge per vehicle; overseas motoring-association members have reciprocal membership); membership entitles you to roadside assistance.

Parks and wildlife information Cadman's Cottage, 110 George St, The Rocks (☎ 02 9247 5033) is the information centre for Sydney Harbour National Park and books tours to its islands; they do not arrange camping permits. For these and information on other national parks around Sydney, go to The National Parks Centre, 102 George St, The Rocks (☎ 02 9253 4600, ⊛ www2 .nationalparks.nsw.gov.au). The Sydney Map Shop, part of the Surveyor-General's Department, 22 Bridge St (☎ 02 9228 6111), sells detailed national park, state forest and bushwalking maps of New South Wales.

Pharmacy (late-night) Crest Hotel Pharmacy, 60A Darlinghurst Rd, Kings Cross (daily 8.30am–midnight; ☎ 02 9358 1822).

Police Headquarters at 14 College St (☎ 02 9339 0277); general assistance ☎ 13 14 44; emergencies ☎ 000.

Post office The General Post Office (GPO) is in Martin Place (Mon–Fri 8.15am–5.30pm, Sat 10am–2pm). Poste restante is located at the post office in the Hunter Connection shopping mall at 310 George St, opposite Wynyard station (Mon–Fri 8.15am–5.30pm). Log your name into the computer to see if you have any post before queueing. Poste Restante, Sydney GPO, Sydney, NSW 2000.

Swimming pools Those detailed in the text are: Cook and Phillip Park Aquatic and Leisure Centre, near Hyde Park (p.245); Andrew "Boy" Charlton in The Domain (p.247); North Sydney Olympic Pool, North Sydney (p.264); Victoria Park, City Rd, next to Sydney University (p.253); and the pool of champions, the Sydney International Aquatic Centre at Homebush Bay (p.279). Sydney's unheated outdoor pools are typically open from the Labour Day weekend in October until Easter.

Taxis Legion ☎ 13 14 51; Premier ☎ 13 10 17; St George ☎ 13 21 66; Taxis Combined ☎ 13 33 00. For water taxis, see box, p.232.

Telephones Outlets for discount-rate phonecards include newsagents and convenience stores, Global Gossip (see "Internet access" above) and most backpacker travel agents.

Travel agents YHA Travel at 422 Kent St (☎ 02 9261 1111) and 11 Rawson Place (☎ 02 9281 9444), both open Mon–Fri 9am–5pm, Sat 10am–2pm (⊛ www.yha.com.au/travel), are excellent for flights and tours. Others include: Backpackers World Travel, 234 Sussex St (☎ 02 8268 6001, ⊛ www .backpackersworld.com.au); Flight Centre, 52 Martin Place (☎ 13 18 66, ⊛ www.flightcentre .com.au); STA Travel, Town Hall Square, 464 Kent St (☎ 02 9262 9763, ⊛ www.statravel.com.au); Student Flights, 140 King St, Newtown (☎ 1300 762 410, ⊛ www.studentflights.com.au); Trailfinders,

8 Spring St (☎1300 780 285; ⓦwww.trailfinders .com.au). All the above have several branches in Sydney.

Women The International Women's Day Development Agency (ⓦwww.iwda.org.au) organizes events to mark International Women's Day in March. Other contacts and resources: Women's Information and Referral Service (Mon–Fri 9am–5pm; ☎1800 817 227); The Women's Library, 8–10 Brown St, Newtown (Tues, Wed & Fri 11am–5pm, Thurs 11am–8pm, Sat & Sun noon–4pm); The Feminist Bookshop, Orange Grove Plaza, Balmain Rd, Lilyfield (☎02 9810 2666).

Work If you have a working holiday visa and appropriate skills, you shouldn't have too much trouble finding some sort of work, particularly in hospitality, retail or office temping. The government employment service, Centrelink (☎13 28 50, ⓦwww.centrelink.gov.au) runs a jobs database (ⓦwww.jobsearch.com.au) and connects jobseekers to employment agencies through the Job Network (ⓦwww.jobnetwork.gov.au). Sydney's many temp agencies include Troys, Level 11, 89 York St (☎02 9290 2955, ⓦwww.troys.com.au), who specialize in hospitality. For a whole range of work, from unskilled to professional, try the multinational Manpower (☎13 25 02, ⓦwww .manpower.com.au). Otherwise, scour the *Sydney Morning Herald*'s employment pages and hostel notice boards; hostel staff may also supply leads.

Moving on from Sydney

Most **bus** services from Sydney depart from **Eddy Avenue**, alongside Central Station, and tickets can be bought from the Sydney Coach Terminal, on the corner of Eddy Avenue and Pitt Street (daily 6am–10pm; ☎02 9281 9366) or direct from bus companies. **Interstate bus services** from Sydney are provided by Greyhound Australia (nationwide); Premier Motor Service (for the East Coast from Cairns to Melbourne); Firefly Express (for Melbourne); and Murray's (for Canberra); see p.35 & p.180 for contact details. Most bus services to **destinations within New South Wales** also depart from Eddy Avenue: in addition to Greyhound and Premier, these include Keans (☎02 6543 1322), daily to the Lower and Upper Hunter Valley; Port Stephens Coaches (☎02 4982 2940 or 1800 045 949, ⓦwww.pscoaches.com.au), daily to Port Stephens via Newcastle outskirts; Rover Coaches (☎02 4990 1699, ⓦwww.rovercoaches.com.au; also

Touring the East Coast from Sydney

Taking a one-way tour from Sydney to another East Coast town or city can be the next best thing to driving yourself: typically, you'll be travelling by minibus with a small group, taking detours to attractions along the way that you'd never be able to reach on public transport.

Ando's Outback Tours ☎02 6842 8286 or 1800 228 828, ⓦwww.outbacktours .com.au. Popular five-day tour from Sydney to Byron Bay but getting well off the beaten track inland via the Blue Mountains, the Warrumbungles, Coonabarabran and Lightning Ridge (A$485 all-inclusive; departs Sydney every Sun); includes a stay on the rural property of the true-blue family who run the tours. Finding farm work is a common bonus.

Autopia Tours ☎03 9419 8878 or 1800 000 507, ⓦwww.autopiatours.com.au. This excellent, long-established Melbourne-based tour company has a three-day Sydney to Melbourne tour via Canberra, Lakes Entrance, Wilson's Promontory and Gippsland (from A$365; includes meals, accommodation). Small-seater buses with the driver acting as guide.

Oz Experience ☎02 9213 1766 or 1300 300 028, ⓦwww.ozexperience.com. A cross between transport and a hard-partying tour, going a little off the beaten track, encompassing beach, surf and bush experiences, with a hop-on-hop-off component lasting six months. Scheduled routes include Sydney to Cairns (A$660); Sydney to Brisbane and Byron Bay (A$310); and Sydney to Melbourne via Canberra and the Snowy Mountains (A$325).

Uluru-Kata Tjuta National Park is the most visited single site in Australia. The park, which encompasses **Uluru** (**Ayers Rock**), Australia's iconic monolith, and **Kata Tjuta** (**The Olgas**), the dome-shaped rock formations nearby, is over 2000km from the East Coast, but only three hours **by air**, making a visit very feasible. If you're wondering whether all the hype is worth it, the answer is an emphatic "yes". The Rock, its textures, colours and not least its elemental presence, is without question one of the world's natural wonders.

Geology and mythology

The reason Uluru rises so dramatically from the landscape is that it is a single piece of coarse-grained **sandstone**, hard enough to resist erosion. Its striking orangey-red hue, enhanced by the rising and setting sun, is the result of superficial **oxidation**; you can get a glimpse of the grey colour of the core in the caves. With its strata pushed up through ninety degrees, it resembles a cut loaf, its layering clearly visible in the pronounced fluting and chasms along the southeast and northwest flanks. Brief, spectacular waterfalls stream down these channels after storms.

To its Aboriginal owners, the **Anangu**, Uluru is also the name of a temporary watering hole near the summit, which lies at a key intersection of many "Dreaming Trails" (or "Songlines", as Bruce Chatwin described them), created by the Anangu's Dreamtime ancestors. There's no truth in the theory that the Rock was once a pre-eminent shrine, to which Aborigines used to flock like prilgrims: instead, its principal significance was as a reliable source of water and food. It was also one of the many landmarks into which the Anangu incorporated ceremonial and burial sites.

Practicalities

The park is in the Northern Territory, southwest of Alice Springs; its **airport**, Ayers Rock (Conellan), served by Qantas, is a little over 10km from the entrance. Obvious starting points are Sydney or Cairns (daily flights), or Melbourne (twice weekly). Alternatively, you can fly from Sydney, Brisbane or Cairns (with Qantas) or Melbourne (with Qantas or Tiger Airways) to **Alice Springs**, departure point for many overland tours of the Red Centre; from here, it's 465km by road to Uluru. Tour operators who can fix you up with a complete trip to the Rock include Qantas Holidays (Ⓦwww.qantas.com.au/holidays) and backpacker-oriented travel agencies such as YHA Travel (Ⓦwww.yha.com.au/travel).

Visitors must stay just outside the park's perimeter in the purpose-built **Ayers Rock Resort** (Yulara), managed by Voyages (bookings Ⓣ1300 134 044, resort Ⓣ08 8957 7888, Ⓦwww.voyages.com.au). Far from the eyesore it could have been, its low-impact, environmentally aware design was way ahead of its time when it was built in the 1980s: eco-friendly features include solar power and efficient water management. Prices are high, but there's plenty of choice, including the surprisingly grassy *Ayers Rock Campground* (camping A$31–36, cabin ❺); the *Outback Pioneer Hotel and Lodge*, which includes small, budget rooms (❻); and the mid-range, boutique-style *Lost Camel Hotel* (❻). For a view of the rock, you'll need to take one of the best rooms at the *Desert Gardens Hotel* (❻), or treat yourself to a stay in the most exclusive option by far, *Longitude 131°* (Ⓦwww.longitude131.com.au; A$2500 per safari tent), a blissfully luxurious ecocamp perched right on the edge of the desert. Within Yulara are a post office, supermarket, laundry, ATM and Information Centre, plus a number of restaurants.

The park, co-managed by its Anangu Aboriginal owners and National Parks, has an **entry fee** of A$25 per person, valid for three consecutive days. Inside the park, 1km before Uluru, is a striking, mudbrick **Cultural Centre** (daily 7am–6pm; Ⓣ08 8956 1128) with displays on Anangu customs and philosophies, details of walking trails, information on the area's natural history, and gallery shops featuring work by local artists.

Tours and activities

All tours can be booked in advance through Voyages, or at Yulara's hotel tour desks or Information Centre; prices quoted exclude the park fee. If you'd prefer to explore the Rock independently, you can jump aboard the **Uluru Express** minibus (from A$40 return, child A$25; ☎02 8956 2152, ⓦ www.uluruexpress.com.au), which shuttles between Yulara, Uluru and Kata Tjuta.

Anangu Tours ☎08 8956 2123 or 08 8950 3030, ⓦ www.ananguwaai.com.au. Unchallenging cultural tours expanding on Dreamtime myths and bushtucker know-how along the Liru, Kuniya and Mala walks, led by a local Aboriginal guide; other options include dot-painting workshops and camel tours. A$75–195, child A$49–129.

Discovery Ecotours ☎08 8956 2563, ⓦ www.ecotours.com.au. Small-group tours around Uluru and Kata Tjuta with local experts. The 9.4-kilometre Uluru Walk (A$115) circling the Rock – perhaps the best tour in the park – is particularly informative, covering both its scientific and cultural significance.

Scenic flights Ayers Rock Helicopters (☎08 8956 2077, ⓦ www.helicoptergroup .com) offer chopper tours of the Rock (from A$105 for 15min), while Ayers Rock Flights (☎08 8956 2345, ⓦ www.ayersrockscenicflights.com.au) will show you the view from a light aircraft (from A$265 for 1hr).

Sounds of Silence Drinks, nibbles and a sophisticated alfresco atmosphere enhance your experience of the Uluru sunset; dinner is served under the stars, and an astronomer gives stargazing tips. Book through Voyages. A$153, child A$77.

To climb or not to climb?

You can appreciate Uluru in any number of ways but to climb or not to climb... that is the question. Some argue that by leaving the climbing route open, the Anangu express implicit approval of its use, since many of the more culturally significant sites along the base of the rock are off-limits to all outsiders. The Anangu counter that they would prefer people to choose for themseleves not to climb, as a gesture of respect.

Far less strenuous, no less satisfying and certainly more in keeping with the spirit of the place are the **walks along the base**, which you can follow independently; park rangers lead free walks. The five-minute stroll from the car park to Mutitjulu, a perennial pool, low-grade rock-art site and scene of epic ancestral clashes, is recommended as long as you hit it between the waves of visiting tour groups. In the other direction from the base of the climb, the two-kilometre Mala Walk to Kantju Gorge is even better, passing unusually eroded caves, more rock art, as well as pools shaded by groves of desert oaks, ending at the huge cliff above Kantju Gorge itself. Best of all is the combination of this and the nine-kilometre walk around the Rock, which takes an easy three hours, offering a look at some Anangu sites (others, indicated by notices, are out of bounds) and the chance to appreciate the Rock's extraordinary textural variations and surface features at close range.

Regardless of Anangu sentiment, many visitors to the Rock do attempt the hour-long **climb to the summit**, but make no mistake, if you do it will be the greatest exertion you will undertake during your trip to Australia. Around a third who try give up, scores need rescuing and, on average, one tourist a year dies, usually from a heart attack. If you slip or collapse you'll roll straight back to the car park. But with a firmly attached hat, plenty of water, secure footwear and frequent rests, you'll safely attain the end of the chain from where the gradient eases off considerably and continues up and down gullies to the summit, often a windy spot, especially in the morning. Most people hang around only long enough for their legs to de-jellify and then climb back down; the daunting view of the car park can cause some freak-outs. The climb is closed during high winds and on days the temperature is expected to exceed 36°C (not as common an occurrence as you might think). The most likely months to find the climb open are January, February, April and August.

from *Four Seasons Hotel*, The Rocks), daily to Cessnock and Hunter Valley resorts. Prior's Scenic Express (℡02 4472 4040 or 1800 816 234) covers the New South Wales south coast including Ulladulla, Batemans Bay and Narooma.

All out-of-town trains depart from the **CountryLink terminal** of Central Station (Travel Centre 6.30am–10pm; ℡13 22 32, ⊛www.countrylink.info). Interstate trains (see p.35) should be booked as early as possible.

If you're **driving**, you'll need an e-toll tag or passes for Sydney's motorway, tunnel and bridge tolls (see p.215). Conveniently, some car-rental companies fit all their vehicles with tags and add the tolls onto your bill.

Travel details

Sydney is very much the centre of the Australian transport network, and you can get to virtually anywhere in the country from here on a variety of competing services. The following list indicates minimum frequencies; as well as the dedicated services listed below, many places will also be served by long-distance services stopping en route.

Trains

Sydney to: Brisbane (twice daily; 14hr 10min); Canberra (twice daily; 4hr 15min); Katoomba (29 daily; 2hr 10min); Maitland (6 daily; 2hr 45min); Melbourne (twice daily; 11hr; plus daily bus/train Speedlink via Albury; 12–13hr); Murwillumbah (3 daily; 13hr 45min); Newcastle (28 daily; 2hr 45min); Windsor (14 daily; 1hr 45min); Wollongong (32 daily; 1hr 30min).

Buses

Sydney to: Batemans Bay (twice daily; 5hr 20min); Bega (twice daily; 8hr); Brisbane (9 daily; 15–17hr); Byron Bay (7 daily; 13hr 15min); Canberra (11–14 daily; 4hr); Cessnock (daily; 2hr 30min); Coffs Harbour (7 daily; 9hr); Eden (twice daily; 8hr 30min– 9hr 30min); Forster (daily; 6hr); Grafton (3 daily; 10hr); Melbourne (6 daily; 12–18hr); Narooma (twice daily; 8hr); Newcastle (8 daily; 3hr); Nowra (twice

daily; 3hr–4hr 20min); Port Macquarie (6 daily; 7hr); Port Stephens (daily; 3hr); Taree (twice daily; 6hr 30min).

Flights

Sydney to: Ballina (4–7 daily; 1hr 40min); Brisbane (42 daily; 1hr 30min); Cairns (8 daily; 3hr 10min); Canberra (20–25 daily; 45min); Coffs Harbour (7 daily; 1hr 15min); Fraser Coast (1–2 daily; 1hr 40min); Gold Coast (17 daily; 1hr 20min); Grafton (daily; 2hr); Hamilton Island (twice daily; 2hr 25min); Lord Howe Island (daily; 1hr 50min); Melbourne (58 daily; 1hr 20min); Merimbula (3 daily; 1hr 35min); Newcastle (daily except Sun; 40min); Norfolk Island (4 weekly; 2hr 20min); Port Macquarie (6 daily; 1hr); Port Stephens (Mon–Fri 1 daily; 1hr); Proserpine (daily; 2hr 30min); Rockhampton (daily; 2hr); Sunshine Coast (4 daily; 1hr 30min); Taree (2–3 daily; 50min); Townsville (daily; 2hr 40min); Uluru (twice daily; 3hr 30min).

North Coast
New South Wales

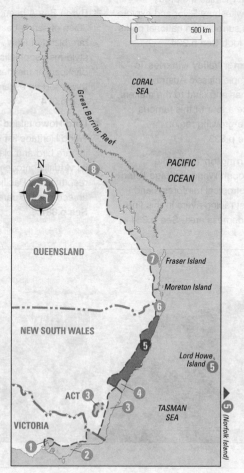

CHAPTER 5 # Highlights

* **The Blue Mountains** Perfect for a short break from Sydney, this craggy wilderness offers inspiring views and superb bushwalking. See p.318

* **Cruising on the Hawkesbury River** Cruise the pretty Hawkesbury River and explore the surrounding national parks on foot. See p.334

* **Hunter Valley wineries** To sample classic Australian wines and chat to the makers, take a tour of this famous vine-growing region. See p.338

* **Barrington Tops** Hike through World Heritage-listed subtropical rainforests and past racing rivers in this fine wilderness area. See p.354

* **Bellingen** Arty, happy little town in the beautiful Bellinger Valley – take a lazy canoe trip, drink great coffee at the enticing cafés and soak up the good vibes. See p.362

* **Byron Bay** A beautiful bay, 30km of sandy beaches and a rare blend of New Age culture, style-mag sophistication and backpacker mayhem make this resort an essential stop. See p.374

* **Lord Howe Island** Making the World Heritage list because of its rare bird and plant life and its virtually untouched coral reef, this tiny Pacific island is an ecotourist's paradise. See p.387

▲ Scenic Skyway, Blue Mountains

North Coast
New South Wales

L
ike its southern counterpart, the **North Coast of New South Wales** is studded with low-rise holiday towns, some perched on wide river mouths, others spread beside coastal lakes or languishing on beautiful bays. While the beaches in this part of the state can't match the magic of those south of Sydney, they're still wild and attractive, with broad, pale sands backed by grassy dunes or paperbark forests. Overlooking the Pacific are breezy headlands topped with Norfolk pines.

For surfers, this is as glittering a destination as Queensland's Gold Coast. The sheer variety of prime breaks between Sydney and the state border is so remarkable that you'll see many a carload of enthusiasts travelling from one great beach to the next, their boards strapped to the roof. Hang-gliders and paragliders use the headlands as launch pads, while sailors, windsurfers and kayakers make good use of the region's many intricate coastal waterways. Inland, there's plenty more space to immerse yourself in nature, with several stunning national parks surrounding Sydney, and lakes and rainforests further north. In essence, the further you go, the better this coast gets: streams tumble down from the Great Dividing Range in mighty waterfalls, creating fertile river valleys and rolling pastures where the predominant agricultural activity is cattle breeding.

Noticeably busier and more populated than the south coast, this section of the state has a strong sense of purpose. Heavy industry, container shipping, mining, wine-making and agriculture all make their mark on the landscape, lending substance to the towns, while the hinterland, particularly in the north, is scattered with appealing country villages populated by artists, musicians and alternative-thinkers.

The magnificent canyons, forests and creeks on Sydney's doorstep bring the city's suburban sprawl to an irrefutable stop. The **Blue Mountains** and **Ku-ring-gai Chase National Park**, both less than two hours' drive from the centre of town, offer bushwalking, scenic viewpoints and a chance to glimpse – or at least hear – native wildlife. The **Hawkesbury River** is perfect for leisurely canoeing or cruising, gliding past historic colonial towns and out to sea through the jagged jaws of Broken Bay, while the **Central Coast** north of Gosford is an ideal spot for a bit of fishing, sailing and lazing around.

Further north, the **Hunter Valley** plays host to cheerfully irreverent parties of wine buffs; this is Australia's oldest, and arguably its best-known, wine-making

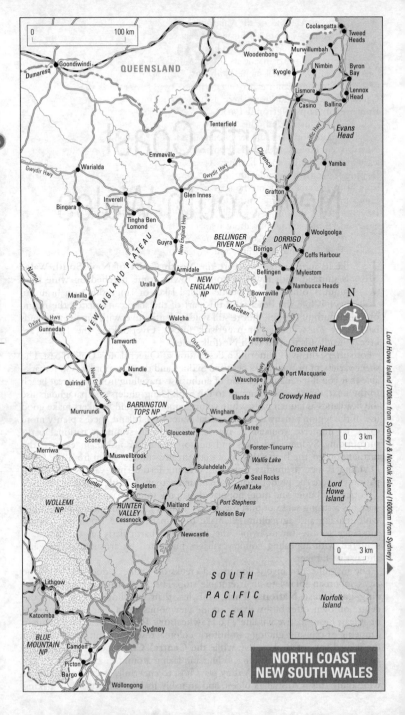

Lord Howe Island (700km from Sydney) & Norfolk Island (1600km from Sydney)

NORTH COAST
NEW SOUTH WALES

region. Downstream from the Valley is **Newcastle**, which, like Wollongong south of Sydney, was once a busy steel-making centre and coal-shipping port; now that the smokestack industries have had their day, it's finding a new identity in commerce and tourism, and its large population of students, surfers and music fans ensure a lively social scene. Within easy reach of the city are the wide bay of **Port Stephens**, home to several pods of dolphins, and the shimmering **Great Lakes**; inland from here is more superb bushwalking country in **Barrington Tops National Park**.

Closer to Queensland, the climate gradually becomes warmer, and the coastline more popular – the series of resorts up here includes **Port Macquarie**, **Nambucca Heads** and **Coffs Harbour** – but in the lush interior there are leafy national parks and charming towns where you can escape it all. The **Bellinger Region** has a delightfully arty and eco-friendly appeal, and **Grafton** has a historic grace. Back on the coast, small towns such as **Yamba** and **Lennox Head** provide a welcome antidote to the busier, blander places, while **Byron Bay** is one of the most enjoyable beach resorts in Australia. This haven of postmodern hippiedom just about manages to retain its slightly offbeat, alternative appeal amid strong competition from affluent stylesetters and raucous backpackers. For a more genuine immersion into New South Wales' committed counterculture, head inland to the lush, hilly **far North-Coast hinterland**, where you'll see plenty of rainbow banners and Tibetan prayer flags fluttering in the wind.

Also included in this chapter are the Pacific islands far off the North Coast of New South Wales: subtropical **Lord Howe Island**, 700km northeast of Sydney, which is part of New South Wales; and **Norfolk Island**, a self-governing external territory of Australia, 900km further northeast. Closer to New Zealand than it is to Australia, it was once a brutally harsh penal colony, and was later settled by descendants of the *Bounty* mutineers.

Regional practicalities

The North Coast is one of Australia's most-travelled regions, but many visitors skip large chunks of it in favour of the hugely popular Blue Mountains and the Hunter Valley – both of which have a good mixture of **accommodation** in hostels, B&Bs and upmarket country hotels – and Byron Bay. Though pleasantly low-rise and compact, Byron has an abundance of places to stay, including an unusually high density of backpackers', plus some interesting luxury retreats. Busy spots for **families**, with good motels and campgrounds, include Nelson Bay on Port Stephens and the Great Lakes resorts. The hinterland villages offer delightful country B&Bs.

Travelling up the North Coast is easy: the Pacific Highway (A1) connects all the coastal towns, supplemented in the south by the faster Sydney–Newcastle Freeway. Off the highway – and even on it – road conditions can be poor, pending repairs. Easy alternatives are the frequent **train** and **bus** services between Sydney and Brisbane. Coastal trains are run by CountryLink (☏13 22 32, ⓦwww.countrylink.info): the Sydney to Brisbane line includes stops at Maitland, Taree, Kempsey, Nambucca Heads, Urunga, Coffs Harbour, Grafton and Casino. There's no service to the coastal region northeast of Grafton, however; these towns are linked to the railway by buses. Greyhound and Premier Motor Service (see p.35) run frequent long-distance bus services along the East Coast from Sydney to Brisbane, stopping at many places en route. Regional operators include Busways (ⓦwww.busways.com.au), Kean's (☏02 6543 1322, ⓦwww.keans.com.au), Blanch's

(☎02 6686 2144, ⒲www.blanchs.com.au), Ryans (☎02 6652 3201, ⒲www
.ryansbusservice.com.au) and Kirklands (⒲www.kirklands.com.au).

There are **regional airports** at Newcastle, Coffs Harbour, Port Macquarie, Grafton, Ballina, Lismore, Norfolk Island and Lord Howe Island; most flights originate in Sydney, Melbourne or Brisbane.

Weather and seasons

The **North Coast** enjoys a consistently mild, subtropical climate. As elsewhere on the coast, however, the **hinterland** is cooler, particularly the highland areas such as Barrington Tops and Dorrigo. Parts of the low-lying Northern Rivers region between the Queensland border and Grafton may **flood** after prolonged heavy rain – the Clarence and Tweed rivers are particularly prone to bursting their banks. The Hunter Valley also sometimes experiences flooding.

Big regional **events** include Newcastle's Surfest in late March, the East Coast Blues and Roots Festival in Byron Bay at Easter, and the Hunter Valley's end-of-harvest celebrations in May. The whale-watching season lasts from May to November; Nelson Bay hosts a whale festival in late September or early October.

The Blue Mountains

From a distance, the section of the Great Dividing Range nearest to Sydney really does look blue – a trick of the light caused by refraction through the fine haze of eucalyptus oil rising from its magnificent forests. The **Blue Mountains**

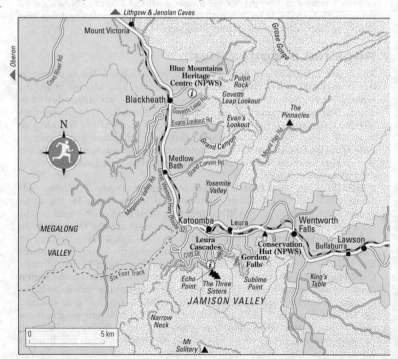

– which are not mountain peaks, but a system of rugged plateaus and escarpments, crisscrossed by canyons and creeks – are close enough to the city to be popular with day-trippers, who come here for the clean air and stunning views, making this by far the most-visited inland region in New South Wales. To really engage with the wilderness, however, you'll almost certainly want to allow longer, perhaps planning a long-distance bushwalking and camping trip, or trying your hand at rock-climbing, abseiling or canyoning.

Some history

At the heart of the Blue Mountains region is a sandstone plateau with an altitude of more than 1000m. Here, over millennia, rivers, waterfalls, winds and driving rain have carved deep ravines, creating a spectacular landscape of sheer precipices and walled valleys. Before white settlement, the **Daruk Aborigines** lived here, dressed in animal-skin cloaks to ward off the cold. In the colony's early days, the mountains were an insurmountable barrier: seeking a route from the coast to the outback, expeditions tried following the streams through the valleys but were defeated by cliff faces rising vertically above them. It was only in 1813 that the Blue Mountains were finally conquered: by following the ridges instead of the valleys, and making use of Aboriginal pathways, the explorers Wentworth, Blaxland and Lawson found a route through to the western plains, opening them up for agricultural settlement – with far-reaching effects on the environment.

An early coal-mining industry, based in Katoomba, was followed by tourism, which snowballed after the arrival of the railway in 1868; by 1900, the first three mountain stations of Wentworth Falls, Katoomba and Mount Victoria had been established as fashionable resorts, extolling the health-giving benefits of

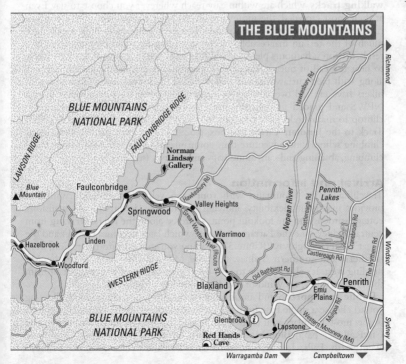

THE BLUE MOUNTAINS

eucalyptus-tinged mountain air. In 2000, the Blue Mountains became a **UNESCO World Heritage Site**, joining the Great Barrier Reef; the listing came after abseiling was finally banned on the mountains' most famous scenic wonder, the **Three Sisters**, after forty years of clambering had caused significant erosion. The Blue Mountains stand out from other Australian forests, in particular for the **Wollemi Pine**, discovered in 1994 (see p.326), a "living fossil" that dates back to the dinosaur era.

"City of the Blue Mountains"

The villages and towns that collectively are rather misleadingly dubbed the "City of the Blue Mountains" lie close to a ridge with spectacular views of the forested canyons of the Blue Mountains National Park, the fourth largest park in New South Wales. The principal settlements are Glenbrook, Springwood, Wentworth Falls, Leura, Katoomba and Blackheath; all are strung out along the Great Western Highway (Route 32), a grinding drive that's not the most auspicious introduction to the region. The townships vary in atmosphere: of the most visited, **Glenbrook**, gateway to the region, is compact, with good access to mountain-biking trails and rock-art sites; **Katoomba**, though rather dour, is closest to the most famous viewpoints and has a good range of accommodation, down-to-earth cafés and an alternative, outdoorsy vibe; **Leura** is chintzy and pretty. **Blackheath** is a quieter spot, with a few characterful guesthouses. The whole region throngs with escapees from the city at weekends and during school holidays, with room rates escalating accordingly.

The main reason to come to the Blue Mountains is not to spend time in the towns, but to use them as a starting point for the tremendous **viewpoints** and **walking tracks**, which are within easy reach wherever you choose to stay. Even at their most crowded, the mountains always offer somewhere where you can find peace and quiet, and even solitude. The deep gorges and high rocks make much of the terrain inaccessible except to bushwalkers and mountaineers; as a result, the forest harbours plenty of **wildlife** and even in a short visit you're likely to hear the call of one of Australia's signature bird species, the superb lyrebird, along with pied currawongs and yellow-tailed black cockatoos. Generations of hikers have created over 140km of wilderness routes, now maintained by the NPWS and graded in difficulty from short, easy one-hour walks along the clifftop to major treks taking two or more days, including the famous Six Foot Track to the **Jenolan Caves** (see box, p.329). For an even grittier experience, climbing schools and adventure tour companies based in the towns offer rock-climbing, abseiling and canyoning trips and courses (see box, p.324).

Arrival and information

Travelling to the mountains with your own vehicle is straightforward and provides maximum flexibility, allowing you to take detours to old mansions, cottage gardens and the lookout points scattered along the ridge. **Driving** from central Sydney, take the Parramatta Road, which later becomes the M4 and the Great Western Highway (Route 32), leading you straight into the region; from northern and southern Sydney, take the M7 and then turn onto the M4 heading west. It's also possible to visit the region as part of a scenic circuit from the Hunter Valley, via Windsor and Richmond, to Lithgow.

Public transport to and around the mountains is also quite good, allowing you to choose a single base from which to explore the entire region; Katoomba is the most popular, as it's particularly well connected and convenient. The CityRail (see p.35) Blue Mountains **train** service to Lithgow via Glenbrook, Wentworth Falls, Leura, Katoomba and Blackheath leaves from Sydney's

Central Station approximately hourly from 4am; the journey to Katoomba takes around two hours (A$12.20 one way, child A$6.10; A$24.20/A$12.20 off-peak day return; last return train from Katoomba Mon–Fri 11.16pm, Sat & Sun 10.55pm). To get around the region, the Blue Mountains Bus Company (ⓣ02 4751 1077 or 13 15 00, ⓦwww.bmbc.com.au) has regular **bus** services from the stops near the *Carrington Hotel* and the *Savoy* in Katoomba to Blackheath, Mount Victoria (Mon–Fri only), Echo Point, Scenic World, Leura and Wentworth Falls. You can also get around the Katoomba and Leura area, and out to Jenolan Caves, by local tour bus (see box, p.325).

The **Blue Mountains Information Centre** on the Great Western Highway at Glenbrook, 44km before Katoomba (daily 9am–4.30pm; ⓣ1300 653 408, ⓦwww.visitbluemountains.com.au) has a huge amount of information on the area, including two free visitor guides: *Blue Mountains Wonderland* (ⓦwww .bluemountainswonderland.com), which has useful colour maps and bushwalking notes, and an events guide, *Imag Monthly*. There's another official visitor information centre at **Echo Point**, near Katoomba (daily 9am–4.30pm; same contact details).

The **Blue Mountains National Park** has its main NPWS ranger station at the **Blue Mountains Heritage Centre** on Govetts Leap Road near Blackheath (daily 9am–4.30pm; ⓣ02 4787 8877); staff can provide comprehensive walking and camping information, and there's a shop selling books, maps and guides. The only point where you must pay vehicle entry into the park is at Glenbrook (A$7).

Accommodation

Aside from the **hostels**, **guesthouses** and **hotels** listed below – of which the options in the popular Katoomba and Leura area are shown on the map on p.322 – the region also has many charming **holiday homes** from around A$400 per weekend or A$600 per week; enquire at Soper Bros, 173 The Mall, Leura (ⓣ02 4784 1633, ⓦwww.soperbros.com.au) or the visitor information centres at Glenbrook and Echo Point (see above). The council runs two **camping and caravan parks**: *Katoomba Falls*, on Katoomba Falls Road, Katoomba (ⓣ02 4782 1835; camping from A$12.45pp; en-suite cabin ❸) and *Blackheath*, on Prince Edward Street, Blackheath (ⓣ02 4787 8101; on-site van ❶); for details of both, see ⓦwww.bmcc.nsw.gov.au. There's also space to camp in the grounds of *Flying Fox Backpackers* (see below). There are car-accessible NPWS campsites near Glenbrook, Woodford, Wentworth Falls, Blackheath and Oberon (A$3, child A$2; for booking information see above). Long-distance hikers can bush-camp in most areas (free; for details, contact the NPWS in Blackheath); since bush fires occur from time to time, it's a good precaution to register your details and itinerary with the local police before setting off, and to carry an emergency locator beacon.

Hostels

Blue Mountains YHA 207 Katoomba St, Katoomba ⓣ02 4782 1416, ⓦwww.yha.com.au. Huge, award-winning hostel in a 1930s building with leaded-light windows, generous communal spaces, an open fireplace and an old-fashioned mountain-retreat ambience. Many rooms are en suite, and there's fast, cheap Internet access. The friendly and helpful reception staff are full of good advice on bushwalking, cycling and other activities. Bunk in four-share or eight-share A$24–29, private twin/double ❸

Flying Fox Backpackers 190 Bathurst Rd, Katoomba ⓣ02 4782 4226, ⓦwww.theflyingfox .com.au. Colourfully painted, homely and laidback bungalow near the station, with spacious dorms and free Wi-Fi. Outside, there's a popular "chill-out" hut with a fire, and a bush-outlook campsite. The knowledgeable managers hire out camping gear, and offer free transport to walking tracks. Camping A$34 (A$17pp), bunk in 7-share $26, private double/twin ❷

No 14 14 Lovel St, Katoomba ⓣ02 4782 7104, ⓦwww.numberfourteen.com. This

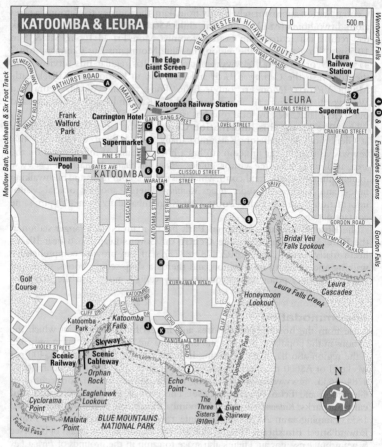

KATOOMBA & LEURA

GREAT WESTERN HIGHWAY (ROUTE 32)

RAILWAY PARADE

Wentworth Falls

0   500 m

Leura Railway Station

The Edge Giant Screen Cinema

LEURA

GT WESTERN HIGHWAY

BATHURST ROAD (MAIN ST)

NARROW NECK ROAD

VALLEY ROAD

Medlow Bath, Blackheath & Six Foot Track

Frank Walford Park

Carrington Hotel

Katoomba Railway Station

GANG GANG STREET

MEGALONG STREET

Supermarket

Supermarket

PARKE STREET

LOVEL STREET

CRAIGEND STREET

Swimming Pool

PINE ST

KATOOMBA

GATES AVE

CLISSOLD STREET

WARATAH STREET

STREET

LEURA MALL

Everglades Gardens

Gordon Falls

MERRIWA STREET

CLIFF DRIVE

GORDON ROAD

CASCADE STREET

KATOOMBA STREET

LURLINE STREET

OLYMPIAN PARADE

Bridal Veil Falls Lookout

Golf Course

KURRAWAN ROAD

Leura Cascades

Leura Falls Creek

Honeymoon Lookout

KATOOMBA FALLS RD

CLIFF DRIVE

Katoomba Park

Katoomba Falls

ECHO POINT ROAD

PANORAMA DRIVE

CLIFF DRIVE

Dardenelles Pass

Skyway

VIOLET STREET

Scenic Railway

Scenic Cableway

Orphan Rock

Federal Pass

Cyclorama Point

Eaglehawk Lookout

Malaita Point

BLUE MOUNTAINS NATIONAL PARK

Echo Point

The Three Sisters (910m)

Giant Stairway

Federal Pass

N

ACCOMMODATION

Blue Mountains YHA	F	Katoomba Falls Caravan Park	I
Carrington Hotel	C	Katoomba Mountain Lodge	E
Cecil Guesthouse	E	La Maison Guesthouse	H
Echoes	J	Lilianfels	K
Flying Fox Backpackers	A	No. 14	B
Jamison House	G	York Fairmont Resort	D

EATING & DRINKING

Arjuna	1	Eucalypt	4
Avalon	3	Fresh	6
Carrington Hotel & Bar	C	Niche Nosh	5
Common Ground Café	8	The Rooster	G
Echoes	J	Siam Cuisine	7
The Elephant Bean	6	Silk's Brasserie	2
		Solitary	9

relaxed hostel, in a charmingly restored house with polished floors, cosy fire, peaceful veranda and original features, is like a home away from home, run by an informative young couple who put in a lot of effort. Some rooms are en suite. Bed in four-share $25, private double/twin ②

Hotels, motels and guesthouses

Carrington Hotel 15–47 Katoomba St, Katoomba ☎02 4782 1111, ⒲www.thecarrington.com.au. When it opened in 1882, the *Carrington Hotel* was the region's finest. Now fully restored, original

features include stained-glass windows, open fireplaces and splendid public rooms. The spacious, well-aired bedrooms and suites vary in size and price; the best ones are beautifully decorated in rich heritage colours. Room ④, suite ⑧

Cecil Guesthouse 108 Katoomba St, Katoomba ☎02 4782 1411, ⒲www.ourguest.com. With great views over the town and Jamison Valley from the common areas and some bedrooms, this place is a little shabby but has charm, with an old-fashioned atmosphere, plus modern touches such as the spa. Most rooms share bathrooms. ④

Echoes 3 Lilianfels Ave, Echo Point, Katoomba ℡02 4782 1966, ⓦwww.echoeshotel.com.au. Much-praised boutique hotel with rather grand decor and stunning views of the Jamison Valley, both from its rooms and from the terrace of its stylish restaurant, also called *Echoes* (see p.330). ❽

Glenella 56 Govetts Leap Rd, Blackheath ℡02 4787 8352. Rather tired but still charming, this guesthouse in a 1905 homestead has antique-furnished rooms, including a few inexpensive share-bathroom options. ❸–❹

Imperial 1 Station St, Mount Victoria ℡02 4787 1878, ⓦwww.hotelimperial.com.au. Nicely restored, sizeable country inn with beautiful leaded-light windows and a range of B&B accommodation, from no-frills pub rooms to spacious en suites, plus good-value bistro meals. ❸–❹

Jamison House 48 Merriwa St, corner of Cliff Drive, Katoomba ℡02 4782 1206, ⓦwww.jamisonhouse .com. Built as a guesthouse in 1903, this seriously charming place has amazing, unimpeded views across the Jamison Valley, and the romantic feel of a small European hotel. Downstairs is a French restaurant, *The Rooster* (see p.330), while upstairs, the breakfast room also has splendid views. ❻

🏃 **Jemby-Rinjah Eco Lodge** 336 Evans Lookout Rd, 4km from Blackheath ℡02 4787 7622, ⓦwww.jembyrinjahlodge.com.au. Accommodation in distinctive one- and two-bedroom timber cabins (with wood fires) in tranquil bushland near the Grose Valley. There's a licensed common area whose focal point is a huge circular fire place. Bushwalks organized for guests. ❺

Katoomba Mountain Lodge 31 Lurline St, Katoomba ℡02 4782 3933, ⓦwww .katoombamountainlodge.com.au. Family-run, central accommodation with budget rooms that share bathrooms and a kitchen. There's also free Wi-Fi, and a veranda with great views. ❷

Lilianfels Lilianfels Ave, Echo Point, Katoomba ℡02 4780 1200, ⓦwww.lilianfels.com.au. Famously glamorous and hugely expensive top-end hotel with a traditional country-house atmosphere, a fine-dining restaurant and a pool. ❽

La Maison 175–177 Lurline St, Katoomba ℡02 4782 4996, ⓦwww.lamaison.com.au. This small, comfortable hotel with spacious, conservatively decorated rooms, obliging management and free Wi-Fi is one of the best-value places in Katoomba. Outside, there's a pretty garden and deck. ❸

York Fairmont Resort 1 Sublime Point Rd, Leura ℡02 4784 4144, ⓦwww.fairmontresort.com.au. Set on an impressive estate next to the Leura golf course and close to good viewpoints, this long-established hotel is gradually being updated; it has a variety of rooms – some exceptionally large – a pool and a good à la carte restaurant, *Eucalypt* (see p.330). ❼–❽

Glenbrook to Wentworth Falls

The first stop off the busy highway from Sydney is **GLENBROOK**, a pleasant village arranged around the train station, with an adventure shop and a strip of cafés on Ross Street. The section of the **Blue Mountains National Park** here is popular for **mountain biking** along the **Oaks Fire Trail** (it's best to start the thirty-kilometre trail higher up the mountain in **WOODFORD** and head downhill, ending up in Glenbrook; bike rental is available at Katoomba, see p.324). Several bushwalks commence from the part-time NPWS office at the end of Bruce Road (Sat & Sun, public and school holidays 8.30am–4.30pm; ℡02 4739 2950). One of the best hikes from here is to see the Aboriginal hand stencils on the walls of **Red Hands Cave** (6km; 3hr return; medium difficulty). With a car or bike you can get there via road and continue to the grassy creekside Eoroka picnic ground and NPWS campsite, where there are lots of Eastern grey kangaroos. In summer, head for the swimmable **Blue Pool** and **Jellybean Pool**, an easy, one-kilometre walk away from Woodford.

The small town of **WENTWORTH FALLS**, 32km further west, was named after William Wentworth, one of the famous trio who conquered the mountains in 1813. A signposted road leads from the Great Western Highway to the **Wentworth Falls Reserve**, with superb views of the waterfall tumbling down into the Jamison Valley. You can reach this picnic area from Wentworth train station by following the easy creekside 2.5-kilometre **Darwin's Walk** – the route followed by the famous naturalist in 1836 to the cliff edge, where he described the view from the great precipice as one of the most stupendous he'd ever seen. Most of the other bushwalks in the area

Adventure activities

Australian School of Mountaineering, at Paddy Pallin, 166 Katoomba St, Katoomba (℡02 4782 2014, Ⓦwww.asmguides.com) is Katoomba's original abseiling outfit, offering day-long intro courses (daily; A$145), plus canyoning in Grand, Empress or Fortress canyons among others (Oct–April daily 9am; A$145); they also run rock-climbing and bush-survival courses.

High 'n' Wild Mountain Adventures, 3–5 Katoomba St, Katoomba (℡02 4782 6224, Ⓦwww.high-n-wild.com.au), another long-established operator, has a good reputation for its beginners' courses in abseiling (half-day A$99) and canyoning (from A$160), plus rock-climbing (from A$159 per half-day), guided bushwalking and bushcraft courses.

Bushwalking tours

Blue Mountains Guides (℡02 4782 6109, Ⓦwww.bluemountainsguides.com.au), though relatively pricey, offer a superb variety of guided walks, including a three-day fully supported trek along the Six Foot Track (see box, p.327).

Blue Mountains Walkabout (℡0408 443 822, Ⓦwww.bluemountainswalkabout .com) is an excellent eight-hour, off-the-beaten-track bush roam led by an Aboriginal guide; expect to look at rock carvings, taste bushtucker and, in summer, swim in waterholes (starts from Faulconbridge station, ends at Springwood station; A$95; BYO lunch and water).

Tread Lightly Eco Tours (℡02 4788 1229, Ⓦwww.treadlightly.com.au) offer highly recommended small-group, expert-guided two-hour, half-day and full-day bushwalk and 4WD tours from Katoomba (A$40–175).

Cycling

Vélo Nova, 182 Katoomba St, Katoomba (℡02 4782 2800), rents mountain bikes from A$28 half day or A$50 full day.

start from the *Conservation Hut* café (see p.330), about 3km from the train station at the end of Fletcher Street.

Leura and around

Just 2km west of Wentworth Falls, wealthy **LEURA**, packed with cafés and antique stores, is a scenic spot with views across the Jamison Valley to the imposing plateau that is **Mount Solitary**. The main shopping strip, **Leura Mall**, has a wide verge lined with cherry trees and makes a popular picnicking spot. Leura is renowned for its beautiful European-style gardens, some of which are open to the public during the **Leura Gardens Festival** (9 days in early Oct; $18 all gardens, or $5 per garden, free for children; Ⓦwww.leuragardensfestival .com.au). There's a fine National Trust-listed garden, open all year, at **Everglades**, 37 Everglades Ave, 2km southeast of the Mall (daily: autumn and winter 10am–4pm; spring and summer 10–5pm; $7, child A$3; ℡02 4784 1938, Ⓦwww.evergladesgardens.info). This country mansion's formal terraces have wonderful Jamison Valley views; there's also an arboretum, a simple tearoom and, in season, a colourful display of azaleas and rhododendrons.

Just over a kilometre south of the Mall is the Gordon Falls picnic area on Lone Pine Avenue, where Leura's mansions and gardens give way to the bush of the **Blue Mountains National Park**; it's an easy ten-minute return walk to the lookout over the falls or there's a canyon walk (2hr circuit; medium difficulty) via Lyrebird Dell and the Pool of Siloam, which takes in some of the Blue

5

Day-trips from Sydney
See p.304.

Horse-riding
Werriberri Trail Rides (①07 4787 9171, ⓦwww.australianbluehorserides.com.au) offer horse-riding and overnight stays for all abilities in the Megalong Valley (pony rides from A$5.50 for 5min, longer rides from A$48 for an hour; full day A$190; pickups from Blackheath train station by prior arrangement).

Local sightseeing tours
An easy way to see all the highlights of the Katoomba and Leura area is to buy a pass for one of the two hop-on-hop-off sightseeing buses whose offices are on Main Street, outside Katoomba train station; both offer commentary en route and discounts to local attractions. **Trolley Tours**, run by Blue Mountains Bus Company (①02 4782 7999 or 1800 801 577, ⓦwww.trolleytours.com.au), are good value: their day pass (A$15) is valid both on ordinary Blue Mountains local buses (see p.321) and on their tour bus, which is decked out like a tram; its stops include Katoomba, Scenic World, the Three Sisters, Leura Cascades and Leura village (full circuit hourly; departing Katoomba Mon–Fri 9.15am–4.15pm, Sat & Sun 9.45am–3.45pm; Katoomba to Echo Point and Scenic World twice hourly 9.20am–4.55pm). The **Blue Mountains Explorer Bus** run by Fantastic Aussie Tours (①02 4782 1866 or 1300 300 915, ⓦwww.explorerbus.com.au), follows a similar route but in a red double-decker London bus (hourly; departing Katoomba 9.45am–4.15pm; day-pass A$33, child A$16.50, including a guide with maps detailing bushwalk and sightseeing options).

Both companies also offer coach transport and day-trips to **Jenolan Caves**: Trolley Tours depart Katoomba at 9.45am daily (one-way transfer A$35; day return A$48; day-trip including cave admission A$65–106); while Fantastic Aussie Tours depart at 11.15am (one-way transfer A$40; day-trip including cave admission A$70–105).

Mountains' distinctive hanging swamps, an Aboriginal rock shelter and cooling rainforest. From Gordon Falls, a 45-minute bushwalk part-way along the Prince Henry Cliff Walk (see p.327) heads to **Leura Cascades** picnic area off **Cliff Drive** (the scenic route around the cliffs that extends from Leura to beyond Katoomba) where there are several bushwalks, including a two- to three-hour circuit walk to the base of the cascading **Bridal Veil Falls** (not to be confused with Bridal Veil Falls on the north side of Leura at Grose Valley – see p.327). To the east of Gordon Falls, Sublime Point Road leads to the aptly named **Sublime Point** lookout, with panoramic views of the Jamison Valley.

Katoomba and around
KATOOMBA, 103km west of Sydney, is the biggest town in the Blue Mountains and the area's commercial heart; it's also the best located for the major sights of Echo Point and The Three Sisters. There's a lively café culture on **Katoomba Street**, which runs downhill from the train station; the street also has a liberal sprinkling of outdoor-clothing shops and secondhand bookstores. When the town was first discovered by fashionable city-dwellers in the late nineteenth century, the grandiose **Carrington Hotel**, prominently located at the top of Katoomba Street, was the height of elegance. It's recently been returned to its former glory, with elegant sloping lawns running down to the street, half of which has been taken over by a new **town square**. A local historian gives tours of the hotel by prior arrangement (1hr–1hr 30min; ①02 4754 5726).

Across the railway line (use the foot-tunnel under the station and follow the signs), a stunning introduction to the ecology of the Blue Mountains can be had at **The Edge Giant Screen Cinema**, 225 Great Western Hwy (℡02 4782 8900, ⓦwww.edgecinema.com.au), whose six-storey-high cinema screen is principally dedicated to daily showings of *The Edge* (10.20am, 11.05am, 12.10pm, 1.30pm, 2.15pm & 5.30pm; $15, child A$10). The highlight of this forty-minute documentary about the region is the segment on "dinosaur trees", a stand of thirty-metre-high **Wollemi Pine** (pronounced "wollem eye"), previously known only from fossil material over sixty million years old. The trees – miraculously still existing – survive deep within a sheltered rainforest gully in the **Wollemi National Park**, north of Katoomba, and they made headlines when they were first discovered in 1994 by a group of canyoners. Since the discovery, the first cultivated Wollemi Pine was planted in 1998 at Sydney's Royal Botanic Gardens.

A thirty-minute walk south from Katoomba train station down Katoomba Street and along Lurline Street and Echo Point Road (or a short hop by local bus or tour bus; see p.321 & p.325) will bring you to **Echo Point**. From the projecting lookout platform between the **information centre** at the Three Sisters Heritage Plaza, breathtaking vistas take in the Kedumba and Jamison valleys, Mount Solitary, the Ruined Castle, Kings Table and the Blue Mountains' most famous landmark, the **Three Sisters** (910m). These three gnarled rocky points take their name from an Aboriginal Dreamtime story that relates how the Kedumba people were losing a battle against the rival Nepean people: the Kedumba leader, fearing that his three beautiful daughters would be carried off by the enemy, turned them to stone, but was tragically killed before he could reverse his spell. The Three Sisters are at the top of the **Giant Stairway** (1hr 45min one way), a very steep eight-hundred-step descent into the three-hundred-metre-deep Jamison Valley below, passing **Katoomba Falls** en route. There's a popular walking route, taking about two hours and graded medium, down the stairway and part-way along the **Federal Pass** to the **Landslide**, and then on to the Scenic Railway or Cableway (see below), either of which will get you up to the ridge.

To experience the Jamison Valley the easy way – with no arduous trekking or climbing – head for the very touristy **Scenic World** the end of Violet Street off Cliff Drive (daily 9am–5pm; ℡02 4780 0200 or 1300, ⓦwww .scenicworld.com.au). The complex houses a small cinema showing a pictorial documentary of the area (free with any ticket), a café with good views, and the base station for the **Scenic Skyway**, a short and pricey glass-bottomed cable-car ride over the valley (A$16 return, child A$8). The main attractions, however, are two modes of transport to and from the valley floor: the extremely steep **Scenic Railway**, adapted from the original haulage mechanism built by the Katoomba miners to carry coal skips up and down the cliff, and the modern and less hair-raising **Scenic Cableway** (A$10 one way by either route, child A$5; return A$19/A$10 or A$28/A$14 including a return trip on the Skyway). The Railway and Cableway both offer fantastic views, and end up close enough to each other for it to be easy to go down by one and up by the other. At the bottom, scenic boardwalks meander through the rainforest with interpretative boards detailing natural features and history along the way (allow 15–50min). For the more energetic, there's a tranquil but moderately difficult twelve-kilometre return bushwalk to the Ruined Castle.

A short walk from the Scenic World complex along Cliff Drive is the **Katoomba Falls picnic area** in Katoomba Park, where there's a kiosk and

The Six Foot Track

Beside the Great Western Highway, about 2.5km west of Katoomba train station, the fenced-in remains of the **Explorers Tree** – initialized by Blaxland, Lawson and Wentworth during their famous 1813 expedition – marks the start of the legendary **Six Foot Track** across the Megalong Valley to Jenolan Caves. Originally a 1.8-metre wide, 42-kilometre-long bridleway, built in the late nineteenth century but impossible to maintain, the track was re-opened as a hiking trail in the 1980s. To join it, leave the highway at Nellies Glen Road, just before the Explorers Tree, and head towards Bonnie Doon Falls.

To walk the entire route, allow two to three days and carry plenty of water. It's also worth taking the precaution of registering your itinerary with the local police, and carrying an emergency locator beacon. To get you on your way, Fantastic Aussie Tours (see p.325) offer a daily transfer service from Katoomba to the start of the track, and pick-ups from Jenolan Caves, while *Blue Mountains YHA* (see p.321) offer a useful deal including a night at the hostel, map, tent hire and transfers for A$110. There are four basic **campsites** along the route, and well-equipped accommodation near Jenolan Caves (see p.329). For detailed bushwalking and camping information, contact the NPWS in Blackheath (see p.321).

Blue Mountains Guides (see p.324) offer a three-day **guided hike** along the track, with a vehicle to carry all the **camping gear** (A$750), while Tread Lightly Eco Tours (see p.324) run a popular morning Wilderness Walk that takes in some of the track (A$30). The truly fit enter Australia's largest annual off-road marathon, the **Six Foot Track Marathon** held in March (more details at ⓦ www.sixfoot.com).

several bushwalking options. The **Prince Henry Cliff Walk** (9km one way; 1hr 30min; easy) is a long, pleasant stroll along the plateau clifftop via Echo Point all the way to **Gordon Falls** with glorious lookouts along the way. A scenic drive following Cliff Drive southwest of Katoomba Falls leads to the approaches to several other spectacular lookouts: Eaglehawk, the Landslide, and Narrow Neck – a great sunset spot, with views into both the Jamison and Megalong valleys.

Blackheath and around

Two train stops beyond Katoomba, and 11km further northwest along the Great Western Highway, there are more lookout points at **BLACKHEATH** – just as impressive as Echo Point and much less busy. One of the best is **Govetts Leap**, at the end of Govetts Leap Road (just over 2km east of the highway through the village centre), near the **Blue Mountains Heritage Centre** (daily 9am–4.30pm; ⓣ02 4787 8877), which doubles as the main regional NPWS office (see p.321). The two-kilometre **Fairfax Heritage Track** from here is wheelchair- and pram-accessible and takes in the Govetts Leap Lookout with its marvellous panorama of the **Grose Valley** and the much-photographed Bridal Veil Falls. Many walks start from the centre, but one of the most popular, **The Grand Canyon** (5km; 3hr 30min; medium difficulty), begins from **Evans Lookout Road** at the south end of town, west of the Great Western Highway.

Govetts Leap Road and its shady cross-street, Wentworth Street, have lots of antique and craft shops, an antiquarian bookshop, and great cafés and restaurants. Ten kilometres southwest of Blackheath, across the railway line, the beautiful unspoilt **Megalong Valley** is reached via winding Megalong Valley Road; it's popular for **horse-riding** (see box, p.325), and there are creeks with swimmable waterholes.

Mount Victoria and around

At the top of the Blue Mountains, secluded and leafy **MOUNT VICTORIA**, 6km northwest of Blackheath along the Great Western Highway and the last mountain-settlement proper, is the only one with an authentic village feel. The great old pub, the *Imperial* (see p.323) has rooms and is good for a drink or meal, while the *Bay Tree Tea Shop* opposite offers traditional scones. Worth a browse are several antique and secondhand bookshops. Some short **walks** start from the Fairy Bower picnic area, a ten-minute walk from the Great Western Highway via Mount Piddington Road.

Beyond Mount Victoria, drivers can circle back towards Sydney via the scenic **Bells Line of Road**, which heads east through the fruit- and vegetable-growing areas of Bilpin and Kurrajong to Richmond, with growers selling their produce at roadside stalls. On the way, **Mount Tomah Botanic Garden** (daily: April–Sept 10am–4pm; Oct–March 10am–5pm; A\$4.40, child A\$2.20; Ⓦ www .rbgsyd.nsw.gov.au) has been the cool-climate outpost of Sydney's Royal Botanic Gardens since 1987; its popular *Garden Restaurant* (see p.330) is a fantastic spot from which to survey the gardens, Wollemi National Park and Bilbin orchards. There's also a kiosk, plus free electric barbecues and picnic tables. By car, you can continue west along the Bells Line of Road to the Zig Zag Railway at Clarence, just over 35km away.

Lithgow and the Zig Zag Railway

En route to Bathurst and the Central West on the Great Western Highway, **Lithgow**, 21km northwest of Mount Victoria, is a coal-mining town nestled under bush-clad hills, with wide leafy streets, quaint mining cottages and some imposing old buildings. About 13km east of the town on the Bells Line of Road, by the small settlement of **Clarence**, is the **Zig Zag Railway** (Ⓣ02 6353 2955, Ⓦwww.zigzagrailway.com.au). In the 1860s, engineers were faced with the problem of how to get the Main Western Line from the top of the Blue Mountains down the steep drop to the Lithgow Valley, so they came up with a series of zigzag ramps. These fell into disuse in the early twentieth century, but tracks were relaid by rail enthusiasts in the 1970s. Served by a variety of old steam trains, the picturesque line passes through two tunnels and over three viaducts on its way from Clarence down to Bottom Points. There are stops along the way where you can get out and rejoin a later train.

To start your journey on the Zig Zag Railway from the upper terminus, Clarence, you'll need to make your way to the station by road. The lower terminus, Bottom Points, can be reached by ordinary CityRail train on the Sydney to Lithgow line by asking the guard to make a special stop at the Zig Zag platform, from where it's a five-minute walk to the departure point for the steam trains. The Zig Zag Railway operates daily (trains depart Clarence at 11am, 1pm & 3pm, returning from Bottom Points 45min later, with extra services during school holidays and some weekends; A\$25 return, child A\$12.50). As a treat for kids, the line holds "Friends of Thomas" and "Wizards Express" days several times a year, decking the trains out as *Thomas the Tank Engine* characters or as the *Hogwarts Express* from *Harry Potter* (A\$35, child A\$25; advance booking required). There are plenty of **motels** in and around Lithgow, especially on the Great Western Highway; the **Lithgow Visitor Information Centre**, 1 Cooerwull Rd, just off the Great Western Highway (daily 9am–5pm; Ⓣ02 6350 3230, Ⓦwww.tourism.lithgow.com) can make bookings and advise on other accommodations.

Jenolan Caves, southwest of Katoomba (30km away across the mountains but over 80km and well over an hour by road; 175km from Sydney) contain New South Wales' most spectacular limestone formations. There are ten "show" caves with walkways leading you among the eerily lit stalactites and stalagmites; entrance is by guided tour, held throughout the day (daily 9.30am–5.30pm; Sat & school holidays 2hr night tours depart 8pm). If you're coming for just a day, plan to see one or two caves: the best general cave is the Lucas Cave (A$23, child A$20.70; 1hr 30min), and a more spectacular one is the Temple of Baal (A$31, child A$27.90; 1hr 30min) while the extensive River Cave, with its tranquil Pool of Reflection, is the longest and priciest (A$37, child A$33.30; 2hr). The system of caves is surrounded by the **Jenolan Karst Conservation Reserve**, a fauna and flora sanctuary with picnic facilities and walking trails to small waterfalls and lookout points. It and the caves are administered by The Jenolan Caves Reserve Trust (☏02 6359 3311 or 1300 763 311, ⓦwww .jenolancaves.org.au), which also holds Saturday **classical music recitals** in the Cathedral Cave, and offers **adventure caving** in various other caves; for this you'll need to be prepared to climb and crawl through narrow gaps (2hr Plughole tour A$60, 7hr Central River tour A$187.50).

The trust also looks after several **places to stay** in the vicinity. The most central is *Jenolan Caves House* (⑤, en-suite ④, suite ⑥), a charming old hotel that found fame as a honeymoon destination in the 1920s. In the old hotel section, there's a good, moderately priced restaurant, a bar and a more casual bistro. About ten minutes by car from the caves in a secluded woodland setting are the *Jenolan Caves Cottages* at Binda Flats, which sleep six (⑥). Other accommodation in the area includes ⚞ *Jenolan Cabins*, 42 Edith Rd, 4km west on Porcupine Hill (☏02 6335 6239, ⓦwww.jenolancabins.com.au; ⑤), whose reasonably priced, well-equipped two-bedroom timber cabins with wood fires accommodate six (BYO linen) – all with magnificent views over the Blue Mountains and Kanangra Boyd national parks and the Jenolan Karst Conservation Reserve; 4WD tours of the area are also offered (from A$80 half-day including lunch).

There's no public transport to the caves; to get there without your own vehicle, you can book coach transfers or a tour with companies based in Katoomba (see p.325) or Sydney (see p.304).

Kanangra Boyd National Park, part of the Greater Blue Mountains World Heritage area, lies immediately southwest of the main section of the Blue Mountains National Park. Much of it is inaccessible, but you can explore the rugged beauty of **Kanangra Walls**, where the Boyd Plateau falls away to reveal a wilderness area of creeks, deep gorges and rivers below. Reached via Jenolan Caves, three **walks** leave from the car park at Kanangra Walls: a short lookout walk, a waterfall stroll and a longer plateau walk – contact the NPWS in **Oberon** for details (38 Ross St; ☏02 6336 1972). Vehicle entry to the park is A$7. *Boyd River* and *Dingo Dell* camping grounds, both off Kanangra Walls Road, have free **bush camping** (pit toilets; limited drinking water at Dingo Dell).

Eating, drinking and nightlife

The region has many well-regarded **restaurants**, and there's a fast-growing **café culture** in Katoomba and Leura (see map, p.322); a few places still pride themselves on their "Devonshire teas" but fashionable fair-trade coffee is more the norm. There are some great bakeries, too: top of the list is *Hominy*, 185 Katoomba St (daily 6am–5.30pm), with public picnic tables just outside.

Nightlife in Katoomba begins to warm up midweek, with a mixture of club nights, karaoke and live music including world, blues and jazz at *TrisElies,* beside the train station at 287 Bathurst Rd (Wed–Sat 9pm–late; from A$10; free jazz from 9pm on Sun; ☎02 4782 4026). The swish *Baroque*, upstairs at the *Carrington Bar* on Main Street, is open from 9pm on Fridays and Saturdays; after 11pm it switches out of cocktail lounge-mode to host live bands and DJs (A$5–10). On the other side of the railway, the huge *Gearin Hotel* (☎02 4782 4395) is a hive of activity, with several bars; it's a hip place to see touring bands or boogie on club nights (Fri & Sat; from A$10).

Cafés

Common Ground Café Katoomba St, corner of Waratah St, Katoomba, ☎02 4782 9744. Blissfully cosy, peaceful and rustic Christian-run place; serene waitresses in floral smocks serve wholesome, comforting fare, from blueberry pancakes to flame-grilled barramundi, at honest prices. Mon–Fri & Sun 9am–late.

The Conservation Hut Fletcher St, Wentworth Falls ☎02 4757 3827. On the site of the Valley of the Waters Conservation Hut, a meeting place for eco-warriors in the 1960s, this is a good place for a light meal before or after a visit to the local lookouts and falls; an NPWS information board gives directions. Mon–Fri 9am–4pm, Sat & Sun 9am–5pm.

The Elephant Bean 159 Katoomba St, Katoomba, ☎02 4782 4620. Small café that serves the best coffee in Katoomba and great all-day breakfasts with eggs every way; there's also a big vegan breakfast. Other good choices include burgers, sourdough sandwiches and salads.

Fresh 181 Katoomba St, Katoomba ☎02 4782 3602. Near the lane heading to the health-food co-op, this airy place is the most popular café with locals, from cops to alternative types. Big on fair-trade coffee, it also serves flatbread wraps and Turkish bread sandwiches for around A$12–14, plus lunchtime specials. Mon–Sat 8am–5pm, Sun 8am–4pm.

Il Postino's 13 Station St, Wentworth Falls ☎02 4757 1615. Great relaxed café in the old post office; the cracked walls have become part of an artfully distressed, light and airy interior. Menu is Mediterranean- and Thai-slanted, with good veggie options. BYO. Daily from 8am, for breakfast & lunch.

Niche Nosh 55–57 Katoomba St, Katoomba ☎02 4782 1622. Funky, arty little café specializing in fabulously light and healthy vegetarian and vegan fare such as tofu burgers, vegetable moussaka and goat's cheese flan. Mon–Sat 9am–9pm, Sun 9am–4pm.

Victory Theatre Café 17 Govetts Leap Rd, Black-heath ☎02 4787 6777. A very pleasant space in the front of an old Art Deco theatre now converted into an antiques centre, offering gourmet sandwiches and café favourites with an interesting spin, including plenty for vegetarians. Daily 8.30am–5pm.

Restaurants

Arjuna 16 Valley Rd, Katoomba ☎02 4782 4662. Excellent, authentic Indian restaurant. A bit out of the way but well positioned for spectacular sunset views, so get there early. Good veggie choices, too. Evenings from 6pm; closed Tues & Wed.

Avalon 18 Katoomba St, Katoomba ☎02 4782 5532. Stylish place with the ambience of a quirky café, in the dress circle of the old Savoy Theatre, with many Art Deco features, and beautiful valley views. Moderately expensive menu, but generous servings and to-die-for desserts – or come here just for a drink. Lunch & dinner Wed–Sun.

Carrington Hotel 15–47 Katoomba St, Katoomba ☎02 4782 1111. The hotel's splendid *Grand Dining Room* has columns and decorative inlaid ceilings; its Sunday "high tea" is a treat and dinner is elegant, with prices to match, plus there are several bars and classic Kentia-palm-filled lounges in which to enjoy a pre- or post-dinner drink. At the front of the hotel, the *Old City Bank Brasserie* is more moderate, with a reasonable wine list.

Echoes 3 Lilianfels Ave, Echo Point, Katoomba ☎02 4782 1966. A chic setting and first-rate Mod Oz cuisine make this a firm favourite of well-heeled city escapees. Breakfast, lunch & dinner, daily.

Eucalypt *York Fairmont Resort*, 1 Sublime Point Rd, Leura ☎02 4784 4144. Specializing in beautiful renditions of straightforward dishes such as crispy-skin barramundi or rack of lamb with spinach and sweet potato, this is a safe place to splurge. Mains A$30–35. Daily 6–9.30pm.

Garden Restaurant Mount Tomah Botanic Garden, Mount Victoria ☎02 4567 2060. Popular spot with a pricey contemporary Australian menu and fantastic north-facing views over the gardens and beyond. Cheaper light lunches are also available. Lunch daily.

The Rooster *Jamison House*, 48 Merriwa St, corner of Cliff Drive, Katoomba ☎02 4782 1206. French restaurant in a gorgeous dining room full of original fixtures, with big picture windows and above-average prices. Lunch Sat & Sun, dinner daily.

Siam Cuisine 172 Katoomba St, Katoomba ☎02 4782 5671. One of three much-of-a-muchness Thai restaurants interspersed along Katoomba St. This one is popular, inexpensive, and offers cheap lunchtime specials. Closed Mon.

Silk's Brasserie 128 The Mall, Leura ⊤02 4784 2534. Parisian-style bar with excellent service and a moderately priced menu including sophisticated European-style dishes, from confit of duck to Tasmanian salmon. Lunch & dinner daily.

Solitary 90 Cliff Drive, Leura Falls ⊤02 4782 1164. Perched on a hairpin bend on the mountains' scenic cliff-hugging road, the views of the Jamison Valley and Mount Solitary from this unassuming Mod Oz restaurant are sublime. Expect beautifully laid tables, eager service, a well-chosen and reasonably priced wine list, jazz soundtrack, and gourmet food. Lunch Sat & Sun, dinner Tues–Sat.

Listings

Camping equipment Paddy Pallin, 166 Katoomba St, Katoomba (⊤02 4782 4466), sells camping gear and a good range of topographic maps and bushwalking guides and supplies. For cheap gear, go to K-Mart (next to Coles supermarket, Katoomba St). Flying Fox Backpackers and Blue Mountains YHA in Katoomba (see p.321) rent gear to guests.

Car rental Explore the Blue Mountains c/o Fantastic Aussie Tours, 283 Main St, Katoomba ⊤02 4780 0000 or 4782 1911.

Festivals Katoomba's Blue Mountains Music Festival (mid-March; ⊛www.bmff.org.au) is a three-day folk, roots and blues event, with performances from Australian and international musicians on several indoor and outdoor stages (A$65–95 for one evening's concerts; A$165 for the whole festival). The Winter Magic Festival (⊛www.wintermagic.com.au), held in Katooomba on or close to the winter solstice in late June, features music, markets and a costume parade.

Fire bans Serious bush fires in the Blue Mountains region have made headline news in the past; for current information regarding camp-fire restrictions, see ⊛www.bushfire.nsw.gov.au.

Hospital Blue Mountains District Anzac Memorial, Katoomba ⊤02 4784 6500.

Internet access Blue Mountains YHA terminals and Wi-Fi are fast, cheap and available to non-guests; other options include Katoomba Book Exchange, 34 Katoomba St, Katoomba.

Laundry The Washing Well, K-Mart car park, Katoomba. Daily 7am–7pm.

Pharmacies Blooms Springwood Pharmacy, 161 Macquarie Rd, Springwood (Mon–Fri 8.30am–9pm, Sat & Sun 9am–7pm); Greenwell & Thomas, 145 Katoomba St, Katoomba (Mon–Fri 8.30am–7pm, Sat & Sun 9am–6pm).

Post office Katoomba Post Office, Pioneer Place, off Katoomba St, Katoomba, NSW 2780.

Supermarket Coles, Pioneer Place, off Katoomba St, Katoomba (daily 6am–midnight).

Swimming pool Katoomba Aquatic Centre, Gates Ave, Katoomba (Mon–Fri 6am–8pm, Sat & Sun 8am–8pm, winter weekends closes 6.30pm; ⊤02 4782 1748; swim A$4.90, child A$3.50), has an outdoor and indoor complex with toddlers pool, sauna, spa and gym.

Taxis Taxis wait outside the main Blue Mountains train stations to meet arrivals; otherwise, for the upper mountains call Katoomba Radio Cabs (⊤02 4782 1311), or for the middle mountains call Blue Mountains Taxi Cab (⊤02 4759 3000).

Trains General enquiries ⊤13 15 00, ⊛www.131500.info.

The Hawkesbury River and Central Coast regions

The **Hawkesbury River** widens and slows as it approaches the South Pacific, joining Berowra Creek, Cowan Creek, Pittwater and Brisbane Water in the system of flooded valleys that form **Broken Bay**. The bay and its inlets are a haven for anglers, sailors and windsurfers, while the adjoining bushland is virtually untouched. **National parks** surround the river's lower reaches, among them **Ku-ring-gai Chase** to the south and **Dharug**, inland to the west.

The **Pacific Highway** here, partly supplanted by the **Sydney–Newcastle Freeway**, is fast and efficient, with picturesquestretches as it passes Ku-ring-gai Chase. The **railway** follows the road almost as far as Broken Bay, before taking a scenic diversion through the **Central Coast**, passing Brooklyn, Woy Woy and Gosford en route to **Newcastle**.

Ku-ring-gai Chase National Park

Only 24km from the centre of Sydney, **Ku-ring-gai Chase** is one of the best-known of New South Wales' national parks and, with the Pacific Highway running all the way up one side, also the easiest to get to. The bushland scenery is crisscrossed by walking tracks, which you can explore to seek out Aboriginal rock carvings, or just to get away from it all and see the forest and its wildlife.

At the northeastern corner of the park, West Head juts into Broken Bay at the entrance to **Pittwater**, a deep, sheltered, ten-kilometre-long inlet. From the West Head lookout, reached via West Head Road, there are superb views across to Barrenjoey Head and Barrenjoey Lighthouse near Palm Beach, the northernmost of Sydney's Northern Beaches, on the eastern shore of Pittwater. The **Garigal Aboriginal Heritage Walk** (3.5km circuit) leads from West Head to an Aboriginal rock-engraving site.

Practicalities

There are four **road entrances** to the park, two in the southwest and two in the southeast, with an A$11 fee for cars. Without your own transport, you can take the **train** to Turramurra and then Shorelink Bus 577 (℡02 9457 8888, ⓦwww .shorelink.com.au) to the Bobbin Head Road entrance in the southwest, a good area for picnic sites and walking tracks. To reach the Pittwater side of the park, you can take a **ferry** or **water taxi**, both operated by Palm Beach Ferry (ferries run hourly and take 20min; A$12.60 return, child A$6.30; ℡02 9974 2411, ⓦwww .palmbeachferry.com.au) from Palm Beach to the *The Basin* (see below). **Buses** 190 and L90 run up to Palm Beach from central Sydney. Alternatively, you can make the short crossing from Church Point Wharf, 10km northwest of Colloroy, to Halls Wharf with Church Point Ferry (Regular daily departures; A$11 return, child A$6.70; ℡02 9999 3492) or by water taxi (A$21; hail by calling from the freephone at Church Point Wharf). Bus E86 from Sydney's Central Station (weekdays only) and bus 156 from Manly Wharf both run to Church Point.

The **Kalkari Visitor Centre** on Ku-ring-gai Chase Road in the southwest corner of the park, 2.5km from the Pacific Highway (daily 9am–5pm; ℡02 9472 9300), and the **Sydney North Region Information Centre**, also on Ku-ring-gai Chase Road but closer to the Bobbin Head Road entrance (daily 10am–4pm; ℡02 9472 8949), have details of walking trails.

Accommodation in the park is available at the very popular *Pittwater YHA*, a fifteen-minute walk uphill from Halls Wharf (℡02 9999 5748, ⓦwww.yha .com.au; bunk in shared room A$25–28, private double/twin ❷; advance bookings required). It's one of New South Wales' most scenically sited hostels – a rambling old house overlooking the Pittwater (kayaks available) and surrounded by spectacular bush walks. Bring supplies with you – the last food (and bottle) shop is at Church Point. Alternatively, you can **camp** at *The Basin* on the Pittwater foreshore, further north (A$10, child A$5; ℡02 9974 1011 for bookings; ⓦwww.basincampground.com.au); facilities at the site are minimal.

The Hawkesbury River

One of New South Wales' prettiest rivers, lined with sandstone cliffs and bush-covered banks for much of its course, and with some interesting old settlements alongside, the **Hawkesbury River** has its source in the Great Dividing Range and flows out to sea at Broken Bay. For information about the many **national parks** along the river, contact the NPWS in Sydney (℡02 9247 5033, ⓦwww .nationalparks.nsw.gov.au/sydney) or at 370 Windsor St in Richmond (℡02 4588 2400). Short of chartering your own boat, the best way to explore the

It is no longer legal for visitors to New South Wales' wildlife parks to hold koalas – for that, you'll need to travel up to Queensland – but photo-opportunity "patting" sessions are still on offer. Below are several hands-on wildlife experiences in the region immediately north of Sydney.

The **Koala Park Sanctuary**, around 25km north of Sydney (daily 9am–5pm; A\$19, child A\$9; ℡02 9484 3141, ⓦwww.koalaparksanctuary.com.au) was established as a safe haven for koalas in 1935 and has since opened its gates to wombats, possums, kangaroos and native birds of all kinds. Koala-feeding, patting and photo sessions take place daily at 10.20am, 11.45am, 2pm and 3pm. It's not far from the Pacific Highway on Castle Hill Road, West Pennant Hills; take the train to Pennant Hills then Hillsbus route 631–637.

One of Sydney's oldest wildlife reserves, **Waratah Park Earth Sanctuary**, about 36km north of Sydney (℡02 9986 1788, ⓦwww.waratahpark.com.au), sits in stunning bush scenery on the edge of Ku-ring-gai Chase National Park. Closed for major renovations at the time of writing, Waratah is most famous as the one-time home of 1960s television star Skippy the bush kangaroo. The park is reached via Mona Vale Road – it's signposted from Terrey Hills.

Featherdale Wildlife Park, 30km west of Sydney (daily 9am–5pm; A\$19, child A\$9.75; ℡02 9622 1644, ⓦwww.featherdale.com.au) is home to an assortment of Australian species; patting koalas and hand-feeding all manner of marsupials are the main attractions. It's located at 217 Kildare Rd, Doonside, off the M4 between Parramatta and Penrith; take the train to Blacktown, then bus 725.

The **Australian Reptile Park**, 65km north of Sydney (daily 9am–5pm; A\$22.50, child A\$11.50; ℡02 4340 1022, ⓦwww.reptilepark.com.au), just off the Pacific Highway before the Gosford turn-off, offers yet more koala photo-ops, and has kangaroos roaming the park that you can tickle and hand-feed, though its real stars are the reptiles, with native Australian species well represented and visible all year round thanks to heat lamps in the enclosures. The highlights are Eric, New South Wales' largest saltwater crocodile, and perenties, a species of monitor lizard found in central Australia; they can grow to over 2.5m in length. You can also watch snakes and funnel web spiders being milked for their venom for the Commonwealth Serum Laboratories. There's no public transport; eight companies offer day-tours, including Oz Trek (see p.304).

river system is to take a **cruise** (see box, p.334); the *Riverboat Postman* service from Brooklyn, just above the western mass of Ku-ring-gai Chase National Park, is the most interesting.

Upstream: Wiseman's Ferry

WISEMAN'S FERRY is a popular recreational spot for day-trippers from Sydney – just a little over an hour from the city centre by car, and with access to the **Dharug National Park** over the river via a free 24-hour car ferry. Dharug's rugged sandstone cliffs and gullies shelter Aboriginal rock engravings, which can be visited only on ranger-led trips (to book, contact Gosford NPWS ℡02 4320 4203). There are NPWS camping areas at Mill Creek and at Ten Mile Hollow (A\$5, child A\$3; see p.54 for booking information); the latter lies on the **Old Great North Road**, carved out of the rock by hundreds of convicts from 1829 and now open to walkers, cyclists and horse riders but not vehicles.

The settlement of Wiseman's Ferry was based around ex-convict Solomon Wiseman's home, **Cobham Hall**, built in 1826. Much of the original building still exists in the *Wiseman's Ferry Inn* on the Old Great North Road (℡02 4566 4301; ❸), with character **rooms** upstairs sharing bathrooms, and en-suite,

Exploring the Hawkesbury River system

The **Riverboat Postman** service run by Hawkesbury River Ferries in Brooklyn (☏02 9985 7566) still carries letters up and down the river; it also takes tourists. It departs from Brooklyn Wharf on Dangar Road (Mon–Fri 9.30am; 4hr; A$45, child A$25 including morning tea; book in advance). Brooklyn is around 52km north of Sydney via the Pacific Highway or Sydney–Newcastle Freeway (Mooney Mooney exit); it's also easily reached by train from Sydney's Central Station or from Gosford.

The sizeable **MV Lady Kendall** (☏02 4323 1655, ⊛www.starshipcruises.com.au) cruises both Brisbane Waters and Broken Bay (daily during school holidays, otherwise Sat–Wed; A$27, child A$23; book in advance). You can join the boat at Gosford's Public Wharf at 10.15am or 1pm, or at Woy Woy at 10.40am or 12.10pm.

The **Hawkesbury Paddlewheeler**, based in Windsor (☏02 4575 1171, ⊛www .paddlewheeler.com.au), offers a touch of Mississippi-style romance; the Sunday Jazz Cruise with a live band on board is good value at A$30 including lunch (12.30– 3pm; book in advance).

Houseboat rentals

Houseboats can be good value if you can get a group together, with prices for four people starting from around A$500 for two days (one night) or A$1100 for a week. The Sydney Visitor Centres (see p.215) have details; well-known operators include Able Hawkesbury River Houseboats, on River Road, Wiseman's Ferry (☏1800 024 979, ⊛www.hawkesburyhouseboats.com.au) and Ripples Houseboats, 87 Brooklyn Rd, Brooklyn (☏02 9985 5534, ⊛www.ripples.com.au).

motel-style rooms outside at the back. Other accommodation in the surrounding area includes *Del Rio Riverside Resort* (☏02 4566 4330, ⊛www .delrioresort.com.au; camping from A$25, self-catering villa or cabin ❸–❺), a campsite in Webbs Creek reached via the Webbs Creek car ferry, 3km south of Wiseman's Ferry; facilities include a bistro, swimming pool, tennis court and golf course. *Rosevale Farm Resort*, 3km along Wiseman's Ferry Road en route to Gosford (☏02 4566 4207; camping A$20–30, self-catering unit ❷), is set in extensive bushland close to Dharug National Park.

Taking the ferry across the river from Wiseman's Ferry, it's then a scenic nineteen-kilometre river drive north along Settlers Road, another convict-built route, to **St Albans**. Here you can partake of a cooling brew (or stay a while) at a pub built in 1836, the attractive, hewn sandstone *Settlers Arms Inn* (☏02 4568 2111, ⊛www.settlersarms.com.au; ❹). It's set on two and a half acres, and many of the vegetables and herbs for the delicious home-cooked food are organically grown on site (in-house guests can order breakfast and dinner; the daily lunch and Fri–Sun dinner menu are available to all).

The Upper Hawkesbury: Windsor and beyond

About 50km inland from Sydney and easily reached by train from Central Station via Blacktown, **WINDSOR** is probably the best preserved of all the historic Hawkesbury towns, with a lively centre of narrow streets, spacious old pubs and numerous historic colonial buildings. It's terrifically popular on Sundays, when a **market** takes over the shady, tree-lined mall end of the main drag, George Street, and the *Macquarie Arms Hotel*, which claims to be the oldest pub in Australia, sponsors live rock'n'roll on the adjacent grassy village green. Near the pub, the **Hawkesbury Museum** at 7 Thompson Square (daily 11am–3pm; A$2.50, child A$0.50; ☏02 4577 2310, ⊛www.hawkesburyhistory .org.au) has a small local history collection; it also houses the town's

Visitor Information Centre (Ⓦwww.hawkesburyvalley.com). Art exhibitions and cultural events are held at the striking new **Hawkesbury Regional Gallery** on George Street (Mon & Wed–Fri 10am–4pm, Sat & Sun 10am–3pm; free; Ⓣ07 4560 4441). From Windsor, Putty Road (Route 69) heads north through beautiful forest country, along the eastern edge of the Wollemi National Park, to Singleton in the Hunter Valley.

From Richmond, just 7km northwest of Windsor, the **Bells Line of Road** (Route 40) goes to Lithgow via Kurrajong and is a great scenic drive; all along the way are fruit stalls stacked with produce from the valley. There's a wonderful view of the Upper Hawkesbury Valley from the lookout point at **Kurrajong Heights**, on the edge of the Blue Mountains. Another scenic drive from Richmond to the Blue Mountains, emerging near Springwood is south along the Hawkesbury Road, with the **Hawkesbury Heights Lookout** halfway along providing panoramic views. Not far from the lookout, the small, modern, solar-powered *Hawkesbury Heights YHA* (Ⓣ02 4754 5621; bed in twin-share A$23–28, private double/twin ❷) also has lovely views from its secluded bush setting.

The Central Coast

The shoreline between Broken Bay and Newcastle, known as the **Central Coast**, is characterized by large **coastal lakes** – saltwater lagoons almost entirely enclosed, but connected to the ocean by small waterways. The northernmost, **Lake Macquarie**, is the biggest saltwater lake in New South Wales. Most travellers bypass the Central Coast altogether on the Sydney–Newcastle Freeway, which runs some way inland; to see a bit more of the coastal scenery and the lakes, take the older Pacific Highway.

North of the Australian Reptile Park (see p.333) and **Gosford**, Tuggerah and Munmorah lakes meet the sea at **THE ENTRANCE**, a favourite fishing spot with anglers – and with swarms of pelicans, which descend upon Memorial Park for the afternoon fish-feeds (3.30pm; free). The beaches and lakes along the coast from here to Newcastle are crowded with caravan parks, motels and outfits offering the opportunity to fish, windsurf, sail or water-ski: although less attractive than places further north, they make a great day-trip or weekend escape from Sydney. **The Entrance Visitors Centre**, Marine Parade (daily 9am–5pm; Ⓣ02 4385 4430 or 1800 806 258; Ⓦwww.cctourism.com.au) has regional information and a free accommodation-booking service. Within the Central Coast area there's a well-developed **bus service**: Red Bus Services (Ⓣ02 4332 8655, Ⓦwww.redbus.com.au) run between The Entrance, Gosford and Wyong, while the Busways network (Ⓣ02 4368 2277, Ⓦwww.busways .com.au), which covers several sections of the coast between Campbelltown to Grafton, serves Gosford and the western shore of Lake Tuggerah.

The Hunter Valley

New South Wales' best-known wine-making region and Australia's oldest, the **Hunter Valley** is an area synonymous with fine **wine** – in particular, its golden, citrusy **Sémillon** and soft and earthy **Shiraz**. The drive from Sydney takes just over two hours, making the Hunter an easy and popular getaway for urban wine-buffs, who come here to stock up at the region's cheerfully informal cellar doors (winery tasting and sales rooms), indulge at elegant country hotels and restaurants, or just chill out at a concert. The first vines were planted in 1828, and some local wine-maker families, such as the Draytons, have been here since

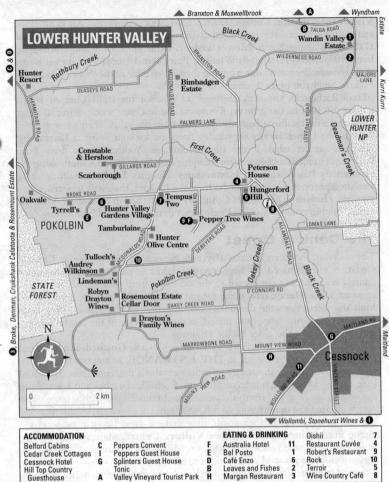

LOWER HUNTER VALLEY

ACCOMMODATION				EATING & DRINKING			
Belford Cabins	**C**	Peppers Convent	**F**	Australia Hotel	**11**	Oishii	**7**
Cedar Creek Cottages	**I**	Peppers Guest House	**E**	Bel Posto	**1**	Restaurant Cuvée	**4**
Cessnock Hotel	**G**	Splinters Guest House	**D**	Café Enzo	**6**	Robert's Restaurant	**9**
Hill Top Country		Tonic	**B**	Leaves and Fishes	**2**	Rock	**10**
Guesthouse	**A**	Valley Vineyard Tourist Park	**H**	Margan Restaurant	**3**	Terroir	**5**
						Wine Country Café	**8**

the 1850s. In what might seem a bizarre juxtaposition, this is also a long-established **coal-mining region**, though the blue-collar character of its towns is steadily changing as wine-making and tourism grab the spotlight.

Arrival, regional transport and information

Travelling **by car** from Sydney, the Lower Hunter Valley is 150km north via the Sydney–Newcastle Freeway; for a more scenic route, turn off the freeway at the Peats Ridge exit near Calga, 60km north of Sydney, and drive northwest through the Wollombi Valley. A meandering route from the Blue Mountains via Putty Road is popular with **motorcyclists**. From Newcastle, the gateway town of Cessnock is 51km inland via the Pacific Highway and route 132; from Port Macquarie, it's 264km south. Rover Coaches in Cessnock (℡02 4990 1699, Ⓦwww.rovercoaches.com.au) run a once-daily **bus** service from Central Station and The Rocks, dropping off at Cessnock and Pokolbin in the late morning (A$70 return, child A$35). Kean's run a service from Sydney to Scone in the Upper Hunter Valley (departs Central Station Mon–Fri 3pm), stopping at Cessnock and Pokolbin (A$64 return, child A$32). The slow and infrequent CityRail (see p.35) Hunter Line **trains** from Newcastle to Scone run through the northern Lower Hunter, stopping at Maitland and Branxton.

Considering the perils of drink-driving, a good alternative are the numerous **tours** on offer (for trips from Sydney, see box, p.305; for local tours, see box, pp.340–341) or hiring a **taxi** (Cessnock Radio Cabs; ☎02 4990 1111) or booking a **shuttle bus** (Vineyard Shuttle Service; ☎02 4991 3655).

Try to tour the wineries during the week; crowds and room rates peak at weekends, particularly if there's a concert on. The end-of-harvest celebrations during May are also busy. There are well over a hundred wineries to choose between, plus makers of cheese, chocolate and other gourmet goodies; to plan a route, pick up the excellent free *Hunter Valley Wine Country* guide and map from the **Hunter Valley Wine Country Visitor Information Centre**, Main Road, Pokolbin (Mon–Sat 9am–5pm, Sun 9am–4pm; ☎02 4990 0900, ⓦ www .winecountry.com.au), scenically sited amongst vineyards, with an affordable café (see p.343).

Accommodation

The rates indicated below are for a one-night stay on Friday or Saturday, though in practice some places require you to book at least two nights at weekends; most also offer substantial **discounts** midweek.

Belford Cabins 659 Hermitage Rd, Pokolbin ☎02 6574 7100, ⓦ www.belfordcabins.com.au. These fully equipped, self-catering two- and four-bedroom bushland cabins, each with its own BBQ, are good value if there's more than two of you. Comfy, spacious and clean, they share a games room, pool and playground. ⑥

Cedar Creek Cottages Stonehurst Vineyard, Wollombi Rd, Cedar Creek, 12km northwest of Wollombi ☎02 4998 1576, ⓦ www .cedarcreekcottages.com.au. An idyllic choice away from the busy Pokolbin area on a 550-acre farm, these country cottages have stunning vineyard views; all were artfully designed using reclaimed doors, windows and fireplaces to lend a charming, lived-in feel. Breakfast hamper, port and chocolate included; civilized noon check-out. ⑤

Cessnock Hotel 234 Wollombi Rd, Cessnock ☎02 4990 1002, ⓦ www.cessnockhotel.com.au. Renovated pub with a great bistro-cum-bar, the *Kurrajong Restaurant*. Rooms all share bathrooms but have high ceilings, fans and really comfy beds. Big veranda to hang out on; cooked breakfast included in the rate. ❸

Hill Top Country Guesthouse 288 Talga Rd, Rothbury ☎02 4930 7111, ⓦ www .hilltopguesthouse.com.au. Rural retreat on 300 acres of the Molly Morgan range, with fantastic views. Explore the property by foot, horse, mountain bike or 4WD tour and then retreat for a massage. The family home, with six guest

bedrooms on top of the ridge in wooded gardens, has the feel of an old-fashioned homestead, with a piano, billiard table and wood fire in the communal rooms. The "*Lovenest*" villas on the valley floor have private balconies with unobstructed views of Lower Hunter farmland. Light breakfast included (lunch & dinner available). Room ❹, villa ⑥

Peppers Convent Halls Rd, Pokolbin ☎02 4998 7764, ⓦ www.peppers.com.au/convent. The swankiest place to stay in the Hunter Valley, with a price to match. Converted from an old nunnery, it has cosy fireplaces, low beams and masses of cachet. Located on the Pepper Tree estate (see box, p.338), a short stroll from *Robert's Restaurant* (see p.334). ❽

Peppers Guest House Ekerts Rd, Pokolbin ☎02 4993 8999, ⓦ www.peppers.com .au/guest-house. This gracious hotel, on a large area of parkland where kangaroos graze, has the air of an overgrown country house, with welcoming lounges and excellent dining in the posh restaurant or on the greenery-draped veranda. There's also an indoor pool. ❼

Splinters Guest House 617 Hermitage Rd, Pokolbin ☎02 6574 7118, ⓦ www .splinters.com.au. Built and run by an affable former woodwork-teacher, the mezzanine-bedroomed cottages on this 25-acre property feature heaps of timber, slate floors, leadlight windows and New Guinea artefacts, and come with wood-combustion stove, leather armchairs and kitchen with espresso machine (cook-your-own breakfast supplied). Also en-suite rooms with a mini-espresso machine and an egg-cooker (light breakfast included); everyone gets port and chocolate in their room. There's a covered BBQ area with fountain, a telescope, guest-lounge massage chairs, a practice golf green, gazebo, walking tracks, dogs and horses. Wineries and restaurant within wandering distance. Best value around, especially mid-week. Room ❹, cottage ❽

Tonic 251 Talga Rd, Lovedale ℡02 4930 9999, Ⓦwww.tonichotel.com.au. Fresh and fun, this is easily the Hunter's coolest offering. Its seven bright, funky shed-style rooms, set beside a pond and

furnished with a whimsical twist, are scattered with little luxuries (all for sale); each also has a fridge stuffed with breakfast treats (included in the room rate). Over-15s only. ❼

Valley Vineyard Tourist Park 137 Mount View Rd, 2km west of Cessnock ℡02 4990 2573, Ⓦwww.valleyvineyard.com.au. This reasonably priced family-friendly option – a rarity in the Hunter – is tidily kept, with two pools, a BBQ area and an on-site Thai restaurant. There's a choice of tent or van space, simple cabins (linen hire available) and roomier, fully equipped cottages. Camping A$30–40, cabin ❸, cottage ❺

Lower Hunter Valley wineries

Almost all of the Lower Hunter's 120 or so wineries offer **free cellar-door wine-tastings** – unstuffy and unintimidating affairs, which are all about enjoyment and appreciation, with minimal hard-sell. Virtually all wineries are open daily between 10am and 4pm at least, and many offer **guided tours** at set times for no more than A$5 per person. Below are a few of our favourites, but by meandering you'll discover your own gems.

Constable & Hershon Gillards Road, Pokolbin ℡02 4998 7887, Ⓦwww .constablehershon.com.au. Founded in 1981 by two best friends from England, this small establishment at the foot of the Brokenback Range produces limited-edition wines and offers unhurried wine-tastings, plus garden tours (Mon & Wed–Fri, 10.30am). Daily except Tues, 10am–5pm.

Drayton's Family Wines Oakey Creek Road, Pokolbin ℡02 4998 7513, Ⓦwww .draytonswines.com.au. Friendly, down-to-earth winery, established in 1853. Everything from vine-pruning to bottling is still done here; excellent tours (Mon–Fri 11am; 45min; free) show the whole process. A pretty picnic area with wood-fired barbecue overlooks a small dam and vineyards. Mon–Fri 8am–5pm, Sat & Sun 10am–5pm.

Hungerford Hill Broke Road, Pokolbin ℡02 4990 0711, Ⓦwww.hungerfordhill .com.au. This space-station-like, state-of-the art establishment with a chic restaurant, *Terroir* (see p.343), turns winery style on its head, but the wines themselves are still hand-made. Mon–Wed 9am–5pm, Thurs & Fri 9am–7pm, Sat & Sun 9am–7pm.

Hunter Resort Hermitage Road, Pokolbin ℡02 4998 7777. Home both to a winery and to the Bluetongue brewery, producer of respected speciality beers. Winery tours held daily (9am, 11am & 2pm; 45min).

Pepper Tree Wines Halls Road, Pokolbin ℡02 4998 7359, Ⓦwww.peppertreewines .com.au. This multiple-award-winning boutique winery has a French-rustic feel and beautiful gardens. Mon–Fri 9am–5pm, Sat & Sun 9.30am–5pm.

Peterson House Corner of Broke and Branxton roads, Pokolbin ℡02 4998 7881, Ⓦwww.petersonhouse.com.au. The only Hunter Valley winery to specialize in sparkling wines, they also use their *méthode champenoise* expertise to produce for other wineries. The pretty pond-side building is a pleasant tasting spot with a fantastic eatery, the *Restaurant Cuvée* (see p.342). For more indulgence, the Hunter Valley Chocolate Company is right next door. Daily 9am–5pm.

Rosemount Estate Cellar Door McDonalds Road, Pokolbin ℡02 4998 6670, Ⓦwww.rosemountestate.com. This converted church, built in 1909, is the Lower Hunter tasting room for Rosemount, one of Australia's best-known, award-winning wineries; their vineyards are in the Upper Hunter. Daily 10am–5pm.

Scarborough Gillards Road, Pokolbin ℡02 4998 7563 or 1300 888 545, Ⓦwww .scarboroughwine.com.au. Small, friendly winery with a reputation for outstanding

The Lower Hunter Valley

By far the best-known wine area in the Hunter is the **Lower Hunter Valley**, nestled under the picturesque **Brokenback Range** and reached via the main town of **CESSNOCK**, where even the jail and high school have their own vineyards. The town itself is uninteresting, and surprisingly unsophisticated given the wine culture surrounding it, though the main drag, Vincent Street, has been landscaped in an attempt to improve things. It's a good choice of base if you're on a budget, however, as it features some big old country pubs that offer a taste of Australian rural life.

The main wine-tasting district of **Pokolbin**, twelve to fifteen kilometres northwest, has some very desirable accommodation and a fine-dining scene. It's also home to the **Hunter Valley Gardens Village** on Broke Road, an unashamedly commercial complex of wine merchants and gift shops, with a

wines, specializing in Chardonnay. Pleasantly relaxed sit-down tastings are held in a small cottage with wonderful valley views. Daily 9am–5pm.

Stonehurst Wines Wollombi Rd, Cedar Creek, 12km northwest of Wollombi ☎02 4998 1576, ⓦwww.stonehurst.com.au. Delightfully right-on organic winery – one of the few in the valley whose grapes are entirely handpicked and insecticide-free – producing well-regarded Chambourcin and Golden Dessert Semillon. In keeping with their philosophy, their tiny chapel-like tasting room was constructed using reclaimed materials.

Tamburlaine McDonalds Road, Pokolbin ☎02 4998 7570, ⓦwww.mywinery.com. The jasmine-scented garden outside this organic, eco-conscious outfit provides a hint of the flowery, elegant wines within. Tastings are well orchestrated and delivered with a heap of experience. Daily 9.30am–5pm.

Tempus Two Broke Road, Pokolbin ☎02 4993 3999, ⓦwww.tempustwowinery .com.au. This huge, contemporary winery and performance venue – all steel, glass and stone – has a high-tech urban-chic design. It's owned by Lisa McGuigan, of the well-known wine-making family, whose unique-tasting wines are the result of using lesser-known varieties such as Pinot Gris, Viognier and Marsanne. Daily 10am–5pm.

Tyrrell's Broke Road, Pokolbin ☎02 4993 7000, ⓦwww.tyrrells.com.au. The oldest independent family vineyards – and one of the best – producing consistently fine Sémillon wines. The tiny ironbark slab hut, where Edward Tyrrell lived when he began the winery in 1858, is still in the grounds, and the old winery with its cool earth floor is much as it was. Beautiful setting against the Brokenback Range. Mon–Sat 8.30am–5pm, winery tours 1.30pm.

Wandin Valley Estate Corner of Wilderness and Lovedale roads ☎02 4930 7317. Picturesquely sited on a hundred acres of vineyards with magnificent views, this produces a variety of wines but is best known for its hot-selling rosé. There's a European-style restaurant, *Bel Posto* (see p.342), next door. Free tours on demand. Mon–Fri 9am–5pm, Sat & Sun 10am–5pm.

Wyndham Estate Dalwood Road, Dalwood ☎02 4938 3444, ⓦwww .wyndhamestate.com. A scenic drive through the Dalwood Hills leads to the Lower Hunter's northern extent, where Englishman George Wyndham first planted Shiraz in 1828. Now owned by multinational Pernod Ricard, there's an excellent guided tour (daily 11am; free), which covers the vines and wine-making techniques and equipment, including the original basket press. The idyllic riverside setting – grassy lawns, free barbecues – makes a great spot for picnics and the annual opera concert. There's also a restaurant and outdoor café. Daily 10am–4.30pm.

formal garden to visit (daily 9am–5pm; A$19.90, child A$11; ☎02 4990 4000, ⊛www.hvg.com.au).

The Pokolbin area can seem like an exhausting winery theme park, however, with its hot-air balloons, horse-and-carriage rides and wall-to-wall cellar doors, B&Bs and resorts, all screaming out their attractions. To experience the real appeal of the Hunter Valley wine country – its charming bush and farming feel and its vast vineyards seemingly lost among forested ridges, red-soiled dirt tracks, and paddocks with grazing cattle – take Lovedale Road into the **Lovedale/North Rothbury area** north of Cessnock, or visit towns such as

Hunter Valley activities, events and tours

Carriage rides
Hunter Valley Classic Carriages (☎02 4991 3655, ⊛www.huntervalleyclassic carriages.com.au) have an assortment of vintage-style wagons and landaus to trot you round the wineries in style (from A$54 per half day). Horribly tacky or huge fun – you decide.

Concerts and events
Every year over a mid-May weekend, seven or eight wineries in the scenic Lovedale district team up with local restaurants to host the **Lovedale Long Lunch** (☎02 4930 7611, ⊛www.lovedalelonglunch.com.au), a gourmet event in which you skip from venue to venue, tucking into a course at each.

In summer, Bimbadgen Estate hosts broad-appeal rock nights in their amphitheatre, as part of the **A Day on the Green** touring concert series (⊛www.adayonthegreen .com.au; tickets through Ticketmaster, ⊛www.ticketmaster.com.au). Uber-chic winery **Tempus Two** (see p.339) hosts outdoor rock concerts in its grassy grounds throughout the summer.

In October, Wyndham Estate (see p.339) hosts **Opera in the Vineyards**, an evening recital on the banks of the Hunter River (tickets A$70–160 through Ticketek ☎02 4921 2121 or 13 28 49). Also in October, **Jazz in the Vines** (tickets A$45; ☎02 4930 9190, ⊛www.jazzinthevines.com.au) is a day of fine food, wine and music based at Tyrrell's (see p.339).

Cycling
Hunter Valley Cycling offer **mountain bikes** and **tandems** with free delivery and collection within the Hunter Valley (from A$30 per day; ☎0418 281 480, ⊛www .huntervalleycycling.com.au).

Gourmet tastings
The Hunter olive-growing industry has taken off: check out the **Hunter Olive Centre** (Pokolbin Estate Vineyard, McDonalds Rd, Pokolbin; daily 10am–5pm; ☎02 4998 7524), where you can sample different olives and oils from around the valley. Among several places where you can try artisan-made cheese, chocolates and other tasty fare are, on Broke Road, **The Hunter Valley Cheese Company** and the **Smelly Cheese Shop**, both passionate about cheese, and the **Pokolbin Chocolate and Jam Company**, which makes chocolates flavoured with Hunter Valley liqueurs.

Horse-riding
Hunter Valley Horse Riding Adventures (☎02 4930 7111, ⊛www.huntervalley horseriding.com.au) at *Hill Top Country Guesthouse* (see p.337) offer cross-country riding over the Molly Morgan Range (from A$50).

Hot-air ballooning
Balloon Aloft (☎02 4938 1955 or 1800 028 568, ⊛www.balloonaloft.com), a Hunter Valley institution, will float you over the vines any morning you like,

Wollombi (pronounced "wollom-bye"), 28km southwest; **Broke**, 35km northwest; **Branxton**, 22km north; and the still unspoilt **Upper Hunter**, west of Muswellbrook, with its marvellous ridges and rocky outcrops.

Eating and drinking

Many of the Hunter's excellent **restaurants** are attached to wineries; in the towns, the Hunter's large old **pubs** dish out less fancy but more affordable grub. Just about every winery and accommodation place in the valley has a barbecue;

conditions permitting – with champagne to finish, of course (A$320, A$295 midweek; child A$200).

Scenic flights
From Cessnock's tiny airport, **Hunter Valley Aviation** (℡02 4991 6500, ⓦwww.huntervalleyaviation.com) will whirl you over the valley in a light aircraft (from A$60 for 20min); alternatively, Hunter Wine Helicopters (℡02 4991 7352, ⓦwww.hunterwinehelicopters.com.au) will buzz you about in a chopper (from A$70 for 10min).

Tours
Rover Coaches (ⓦwww.rovercoaches.com.au) offers a daily hop-on-hop-off Wine Rover service around the Lower Hunter; stops include the tourist office, some eighteen wineries, eating places (Mon–Fri A$30, Sat & Sun A$40). The excellent **Hunter Valley Day Tours** (℡02 4951 4574, ⓦwww.huntervalleydaytours.com.au) offer a wine- and cheese-tasting tour with informative commentary (A$89 including lunch). The long-established, family-run **Hunter Vineyard Tours** (℡02 4991 1659, ⓦwww.huntervineyardtours.com.au) drops in at five wineries (A$80–85 including lunch). Also recommended are **Trekabout 4WD Tours** (℡02 4990 8277; from A$45) and **Aussie Wine Tours** (℡02 4991 1074, ⓦwww.aussiewinetours.com.au; from A$50), both flexible and supportive of small local wineries.

Wine appreciation
The **Hunter Resort** on Hermitage Road, Pokolbin runs an excellent two-hour **wine course** (daily 9am; A$25; booking required; ℡02 4998 7777, ⓦwww.hunterresort.com.au), that includes a winery tour and a tasting tutorial. Brian Metcalfe of **Hunter Valley Boutique Wine Tours** (℡02 4990 8989, ⓦwww.huntervalleytours.com.au) and ex-Londoner James Myles of **James' Vineyard Tours** (℡0437 151 500, ⓦwww.vineyardtours.com.au) will guide you around a selection of small wineries for private tastings.

Winery museums
The **Hunter Valley Wine Interpretive Centre**, attached to the tourist office, has a wealth of background information on local viticulture. There are collections of historical photos and artefacts at the following Pokolbin wineries, all of which are open daily, from 10am to 5pm (free): **Lindeman's** (McDonalds Rd), where Dr Lindeman first planted his vines in 1842; the swish **Tulloch's** (Debeyers Rd), whose display includes early twentieth-century photos by famous Australian photographer Max Dupain, a family friend; **Robyn Drayton** (Pokolbin Mountains Rd), whose archive dates back to 1853; and **Audrey Wilkinson** (DeBeyers Rd), which also has panoramic views of the Hunter landscape. At **Oakvale** (Broke Rd), you can look at a reconstruction of a nineteenth-century general store, stuffed with paraphernalia.

▲ Vineyards, Hunter Valley

you can pick up self-catering supplies at the Coles **supermarket** at 1 North Ave, Cessnock (Mon–Sat 6am–midnight, Sun 8am–8pm), the convenience store in the Hunter Valley Gardens Village (daily 8.30am–5pm) or the Australian Regional Food Store at the Small Winemakers Centre on McDonalds Road (daily 10am–5pm).

Australia Hotel 136 Wollombi Rd, Cessnock. The bistro at this down-to-earth town-centre pub with coal-mining connections has above-average fare, with most mains, including stir-fries and grills, under A\$25.

Bel Posto Wilderness Rd ☏ 02 4930 9199. This restaurant specializes in recipes from Italy, Spain and Portugal (mains A\$29) and serves wine from the nearby Wandin Valley Estate at cellar-door prices. With magnificent views across the Wategos and the Brokenback Range, the balcony is a great spot for lunch. Tues–Thurs 10am–4pm; Fri–Sun 10am–4pm & 6.30–9.30pm.

Café Enzo Peppers Creek Antiques, Broke Rd, Pokolbin ☏ 02 4998 7233. Relaxing courtyard café that feels like it's been lifted from the south of France; start the day here with a delicious cooked breakfast or excellent coffee; for lunch there's a light Mediterranean menu at restaurant, rather than café, prices. Daily 9am–5pm.

Leaves and Fishes 737 Lovedale Rd ☏ 02 4930 7400. Fabulously fresh seafood

– from simple buckets of prawns with hand-cut chips to stacks of oysters – is the star of the ever-changing gourmet menu at this delightfully casual and airy timber-cabin restaurant with tranquil water views. Breakfast Sat & Sun, lunch Wed–Sun, dinner Fri–Sat.

Margan Restaurant 1238 Milbrodale Rd, Broke ☏ 02 6579 1372. Experienced wine-maker Andrew Margan turns out some tasty wines, and his latest Mediterranean-influenced gourmet eatery has won plenty of plaudits, too. Dishes use seasonal, local produce, and the flavours are kept deliciously simple. Fri & Sat lunch & dinner, Sun breakfast & lunch.

Oishii Broke Rd, Pokolbin ☏ 02 4998 7051. This Japanese-Thai restaurant serves succulent sushi and sashimi, sauteed prawns and aromatic curries at refreshingly moderate prices (many dishes under A\$20). Mon–Wed 11.30am–3pm & 5–9pm, Thurs–Sun 11.30am–9pm.

Restaurant Cuvée Peterson House, corner of Broke & Branxton rds, Pokolbin ☏ 02 4998 7881.

The Champagne House veranda is the perfect place to indulge in a glass of fizz for breakfast, perhaps with eggs Benedict or syrup pancakes. Breakfast (from 10am) & lunch daily, dinner Thurs–Sun.

Robert's Restaurant Pepper Tree Wines, Halls Rd, Pokolbin ☎ 02 4998 7330. *Robert's* is a long-established Hunter Valley fine-dining institution, as much for the setting in a charming 1876 wooden farmhouse filled with flowers and antiques, and shaded by a huge peppertree, as for the French rustic-style food, cooked in a wood-fired oven.

Rock 576 DeBeyers Rd, Pokolbin ☎ 02 4998 6968. A recent arrival that's wowed critics and punters alike, this place does magical things with fresh, regional produce in a very cool, post-industrial-style space; well worth the splurge (Thurs–Sat from 6.30pm). By day, you can eat at the *Firestick Café* – more casual, but still supreme, with a nice line in pizzas (daily 9.30am–5pm).

Terroir Hungerford Hill winery, Broke Rd, Pokolbin ☎ 02 4998 7666. *Terroir* set the trend for gourmet dining in strikingly modern surroundings and, little by little, others in the Hunter are following. For a real treat, push the boat out and order the degustation menu. Mon & Tues lunch, Wed–Sat lunch & dinner.

Wine Country Café 455 Wine Country Drive, Pokolbin. Attached to the Wine Country tourist office, this bright, airy place offers good-value gourmet sandwiches and light lunches. Mon–Sat 9am–5pm, Sun 9am–4pm.

Newcastle

New South Wales' second oldest city, with a population of over a quarter of a million, **NEWCASTLE** can never hope to rival the glamour, exuberance and sheer diversity of Sydney, which lies only 159km away. It has a strong sense of its own identity, however – there's a rough-edged brashness to the place, a legacy of its proud blue-collar past, mixed with a vibrant student/surfer culture – and for a former centre of heavy industry, it's surprisingly attractive, a fact now being more widely recognized.

The city was founded in 1804 as a penal colony for convicts too hard even for Sydney to cope with. Its site, at the mouth of the Hunter River, was carefully chosen: **coal**, crucial to Australia's economic development, had already been discovered in abundance beneath the Hunter Valley, around 50km upstream. Even today, Newcastle remains the world's largest coal-exporting port – there may be a couple of dozen bulk carriers queued off the beaches at any one time – though if Queensland's mining industry continues to grow it will soon be overtaken by Gladstone. Ironically, Newcastle also has a reputation as being one of the most environmentally progressive places on earth.

The heyday of Newcastle's other heavy industries has passed – its massive steelworks ceased operation in 2000 – forcing the city to reinvent itself. The last few years have seen a **real-estate boom** in the city centre: hundreds of apartments and hotels have gone up, and architectural icons are being redeveloped, from characterful late-nineteenth-century terraces to the grand old *Great Northern Hotel* on Scott Street, first built in 1938, which has recently undergone a A$3 million facelift. Many of the city's stately buildings have been spruced up, fine riverside parklands have been created right in the city centre, and a former goods yard has been converted into a waterside cultural, eating and bar-hopping venue. The city is taking to tourism in a big way, trading on its location, poised beside both river and ocean – there are wonderfully breezy **surf beaches** within strolling distance of the centre and milder beaches around the rocky promontory at the mouth of the Hunter River, while the extraordinary **dunes** of Stockton Beach are just a ferry ride away. You might not choose to spend your entire holiday here, but it can be a good base for excursions, particularly for the wineries of the nearby Hunter Valley.

Arrival, city transport and information

Newcastle lies on the Pacific Highway, but the fastest route from Sydney **by road** is to take the Sydney–Newcastle Freeway. If you're travelling by **train**, you'll arrive at Newcastle's main train station, right in the heart of the city on Scott Street; **long-distance buses** arrive at nearby Watt Street. There are flights to Newcastle Airport (NTL; ⓦ www.newcastleairport.com.au) from Melbourne

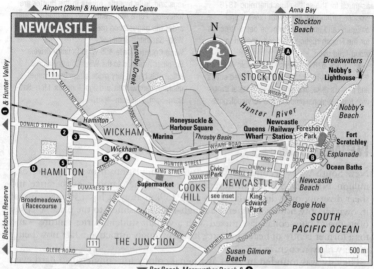

ACCOMMODATION		EATING & DRINKING					
Crowne Plaza	E	Bali Corner	13	Grind	17	Produce Café	10
Great Northern Hotel	F	Bar on the Hill	1	Harry's Café de		Silo	7
Hamilton Heritage B&B	D	The Beach Hotel	6	Wheels	11	Supply	16
Newcastle Backpackers	C	The Brewery	9	Hotel Delany	18	Sydney Junction	
Newcastle Beach YHA	G	Cambridge Hotel	4	The Kent	3	Hotel	2
Quality Hotel Noah's		Crown & Anchor	12	The Last Drop		Terminal One	8
on the Beach	B	EuroBar	5	Espresso Bar	15		
Stockton Beach Tourist Park	A	Goldbergs Coffee House	19	MJ Finnegan's	14		

(Jetstar, Qantas, Tiger Airways and Virgin Blue), Sydney (Aeropelican and Qantas), Canberra (Brindabella Airlines), Brisbane (Brindabella Airlines, Jetstar, Qantas and Virgin Blue), the Gold Coast (Jetstar), Coffs Harbour (Brindabella Airlines), Port Macquarie (Brindabella Airlines) and Norfolk Island (Norfolkair); the **airport** is at Williamtown, 28km north of the centre, between Newcastle and Port Stephens. Port Stephens Coaches (T 02 4982 2940, W www.pscoaches .com.au) run buses to Newcastle station, but it's a skeleton service; **taxis** (Newcastle Taxis; T 02 4904 5900 or 13 10 08) or shuttles (Network All Travel; T 02 4956 9299, W www.alltravel.com.au) are more convenient.

Heading west from the station, Scott Street joins Hunter Street, the city's main thoroughfare. Newcastle's hub is the pedestrianized, tree-lined **Hunter Street Mall**, with its department store, shops, fruit stalls, buskers and elevated walkway to the harbour foreshore. From the mall, as you continue west along Hunter Street, Civic train station marks the city's cultural and administrative district, centred around City Hall, the Civic Theatre and Civic Park. A short walk south of here are the cafés, restaurants and offbeat boutiques of **Darby Street**, Cooks Hill. East of the station lies Newcastle East, with Fort Scratchley, Nobby's Lighthouse and the city beaches.

It's easy to get around using Newcastle's **public transport** system, Newcastle Buses and Ferries (T 13 15 00, W www.newcastlebuses.info); by day (7.30am–6pm), buses are free within the long, narrow central zone east of Wickham station. Elsewhere in the city, bus fares are time-based, allowing transfers (1hr A$3; 4hr A$5.90; all-day A$9; children half-fare). All-day tickets are also valid on the Stockton ferry, which otherwise costs A$2.10 each way (departs Queens Wharf Mon–Sat 5.15am–midnight, Sun 8.30am–10pm). All bus and ferry tickets can be bought on board. Passenger trains serve the suburbs; the Sydney line has handy stops at Civic for Darby Street and Hamilton for Beaumont Street (fares from A$2.60 single).

The very helpful **Newcastle Visitor Information Centre** at 361 Hunter St, roughly opposite Civic station (Mon–Fri 9am–5pm, Sat & Sun 10am–3pm; T 02 4974 2999 or 1800 654 558, W www.visitnewcastle.com.au), can provide other local information and maps.

You can familiarize yourself with the city sights on a one-hour tour aboard **Newcastle's Famous Tram** (Mon–Fri; departs Newcastle station and the *Crowne Plaza* at 11am & 1pm, or Queens Wharf at 10.55am & 12.55pm; A$12, child A$6; T 02 4977 2270, W www.famous-tram.co.au), a twee but fun bus-done-out-as-a-tram deal; the same company also offers Hunter Valley tours at weekends (see box, p.349).

Accommodation

Crowne Plaza Wharf Rd T 02 4907 5000, W www .crowneplaza.com.au. The city's top-end option, with great river views from the best rooms, this hotel also has a lap pool alongside the waterfront promenade, and a restaurant specializing in dishes to pair with Hunter Valley wines. Variable rates. ⑤–⑥

Great Northern Hotel 83–89 Scott St T 07 4927 5728, W www.leisureinnhotels.com. This Newcastle landmark – a favourite drinking hole for local workers since the 1930s – has been given a total makeover to provide comfortable, contemporary rooms. ⑤

Hamilton Heritage B&B 178 Denison St, Hamilton T 02 4961 1242. Characterful option in a house

dating back to the 1900s, set in a leafy part of town. There's a choice of three old-fashioned but cosy rooms. ④

Newcastle Backpackers 42 & 44 Denison St, Hamilton T 02 4969 or 1800 333 436 3436, W www.newcastlebackpackers.com. An outstanding home-style hostel and guesthouse with a heated swimming pool, run by a friendly family. The owners offer free pick-ups and beach transfers, and set up surfing lessons (boogie-boarding free, surfing A$25 including gear). Camping A$24 (A$12pp), bunk in six-share or four-share A$27, private double/twin ②

Newcastle Beach YHA 30 Pacific St ☏ 02 4925 3544, ⓦ www.yha.com.au. Fantastic hostel in a spacious old building, once a gentlemen's club, with huge common areas including a lounge with fireplace and leather armchairs, and all the usual facilities. On the quiet side of the town centre, it's just a stroll from the surf, with boogie-boards to borrow, surf boards to hire (A$5/hr) and plenty of other offers. Bunk in room sleeping three to ten A$27–30, private double/twin ❷

Quality Hotel Noah's on the Beach Shortland Esplanade, corner of Zaara St ☏ 02 4929 5181, ⓦ www.noahsonthebeach.com.au. Middle-market multi-storey hotel right opposite Newcastle Beach. The rooms are rather small but most have great ocean views. ❺

Stockton Beach Tourist Park Pitt St, Stockton Beach ☏ 02 4928 1393. Picturesquely sited campground right on the extensive beach with a camp kitchen. Two-minute ferry ride from the city. Camping A$22–27, basic cabin ❷, en-suite cabin ❸

The City

Newcastle has whole streetscapes of beautiful **Victorian terraces** that put Sydney's to shame – pick up a free guide from the tourist office to steer you around some of the old buildings. Newcastle East, the site of the original settlement, has its own signposted heritage walk. A couple of buildings overlooking the **Foreshore Park**, the district's waterfront gardens, typify Newcastle's trend for recycling its wealth of public architecture: on one corner of the gardens stands the beautiful Italianate brick **Customs House** and the **Paymaster's Office**, with wide, colonial-style timber verandas; both are now popular restaurants.

From the Foreshore Park, you can walk or cycle right along the south bank of the Hunter River, past the city centre; on the way you pass the restored **Queens Wharf**, with its distinctive iron observation tower (8am–dusk; free) and popular waterfront drinking spot *The Brewery* (see p.350). Further along is the **Honeysuckle** development, an assortment of renovated rail sheds, wharves, pristine walkways and smart new apartments centring on Harbour Square. You'll find a string of cafés and restaurants here, and on Sunday there's a produce and craft market boasting some interesting food alternatives such as gourmet *pizzettas*. One of the old rail sheds houses an excellent organic produce café and shop (see p.348); another is earmarked as a site for the **Newcastle Regional Museum**, due to open in 2009, with exhibits on the area's industrial heritage and on the 1989 earthquake, which shattered the city, claiming thirteen lives.

Beaches and wildlife reserves

Newcastle Beach, only a few hundred metres from the city centre on Shortland Esplanade, has patrolled swimming between flags, a sandy saltwater pool perfect for children, shaded picnic tables, and good surfing at its southern end. At the northern end, the beautifully painted Art Deco-style, free **Ocean Baths** houses the changing pavilions for the huge saltwater pool, which has its own diving board.

North of Newcastle Beach, beyond Fort Scratchley, is the long, uncrowded stretch of **Nobby's Beach**, with a lovely old beach pavilion. A walkway leads to Nobby's Head and its nineteenth-century lighthouse, with a good chance of spotting dolphins and (in season) whales en route.

Turning south once more, it's possible to follow **The Bathers Way** all the way down to the Merewether Ocean Baths, a five-kilometre coastal path with a few steep stretches; it takes a couple of hours in all. On the way, south of Newcastle Beach, you'll come to the huge expanse of King Edward Park, which has good walking paths and cliff views over a rocky stretch of waterfront. One section of the rock ledge holds Australia's first man-made ocean pool, the **Bogie Hole**, chiselled out of the rock by convicts in the early nineteenth century for the Military Commandant's personal bathing pleasure. The cliffs are momentarily intercepted by **Susan Gilmore Beach** – secluded enough to indulge in some nude bathing – then further around the rocks is **Bar Beach**, a popular surfing spot that's floodlit at night. The longer **Merewether Beach** is the location for Surfest (Ⓦ www.surfest.com.au), one of Australia's biggest annual pro-surfing events, held in late March. Overlooking the water is *The Beach Hotel*, a fine place for a drink and a spot of surf-watching, while at the southern end is the fabulous Merewether Ocean Baths and a separate children's pool.

Just two minutes by ferry from Queens Wharf across the Hunter River, the beachside suburb of **Stockton** is the starting point for the vast, extraordinary **Stockton Beach**, which extends 32km north to **Anna Bay**. Two kilometres wide at some points and covered in moving sand dunes, some of which are up to 30m high, Stockton Bight, as it's officially known, looks strikingly like a mini-desert and has been the location for a Bollywood film. In recent years it's become something of an adventure playground for quad-bikers, sandboarders and horse riders (see box, p.348).

Inland, **Blackbutt Reserve** is a large slab of bushland in the middle of Newcastle suburbia in New Lambton Heights about 10km southwest of the city (daily 9am–5pm; free; koala talks Sat & Sun 2.30pm, koala feeding daily 2–3pm; Ⓣ 02 4904 3344); consisting of four valleys, it includes a remnant of rainforest, creeks, lakes and ponds and 20km of walking tracks to explore them. En route you'll see kangaroos, koalas, wombats, emus and other native animals in the reserve's wildlife enclosures. To get here from the city, take bus 222 or 363 to the Lookout Road entrance, or bus 224 to the Carnley Avenue entrance (which is also a short walk from Kotara train station).

Northwest of the city, the **Hunter Wetlands Centre**, Sandgate Road, Shortland (daily 9am–5pm; A$6, child A$3; Ⓣ 02 4951 6466, Ⓦ www.wetlands .org.au), situated on Hexham Swamp, by Ironbark Creek, is a community-owned conservation area that features on the Ramsar list of internationally significant wetland areas. Modelled on Slimbridge in the UK, it's home to a mass of waterfowl and reptiles. There are walking and cycling trails here, a visitor information centre from which you can rent canoes (from A$7.50 for 2hr), and a busy programme of activities and events. You can reach the centre by train from Newcastle to Sandgate, from where it's a ten-minute walk.

Eating

The two streets to head for are **Darby Street** in Cooks Hill, close to the city centre, an arty, bohemian quarter with a multicultural mix of restaurants and some very hip cafés; and **Beaumont Street** in Hamilton, 3km northwest of the city centre (train to Hamilton station or bus 260), with a concentration of Italian places, as well as Turkish, Lebanese, Japanese and Indian – it's jam-packed on Friday and Saturday nights. Other good spots are **Market Square Foodcourt**, upstairs in the Hunter Street Mall, with a range of food bars, or the **Honeysuckle** foreshore, for showy modern dining and drinking.

Bali Corner 65 Hunter St Ⓣ 02 4929 5961. Simple restaurant with a Balinese chef, offering a rare chance to try authentic Balinese recipes such as *rendang* curry or *nasi campur* (a tasting plate of delicately flavoured dishes). It's good value, with plenty for veggies. Mon–Wed 8am–3pm, Thurs & Fri 8am–10pm, Sat 5–10pm.

EuroBar 79 Beaumont St, Hamilton Ⓣ 02 4962 3053. Spacious (and very trendy) interior with outdoor tables to check out the busy street action,

but it still gets packed; Italian risottos, Greek pastas and Kilpatrick oysters ensure a European flavour, with nothing over A$20. Licensed & BYO. Daily 7.30am–11pm.

Goldbergs Coffee House 137 Darby St, Cooks Hill Ⓣ 02 4929 3122. This perennially popular Darby St institution is big, buzzy and airy, with polished wooden floors. The emphasis is on the excellent coffee, plus very reasonably priced eclectically modern

Newcastle and **Nelson Bay**, the most popular destination on the bay of Port Stephens, are around 60km apart, making each within easy day-trip distance of the other. Both have a vibrant watersports culture, while between the two are the magnificent dunes of Stockton Bight, a favourite destination for a variety of adventure activities.

Hang-gliding and paragliding

Air Sports (ⓣ0412 607 815, ⓦwww.air-sports.com.au) offer tandem flights around the Newcastle area (20–30min; A$165).

Horse-riding

You can set off on horseback with **Sahara Trails Horse Riding**, based in Anna Bay (ⓣ02 4981 9077, ⓦwww.saharatrails.com), for an amble through the bush or a canter along Stockton Beach, with options for everyone.

Kitesurfing and windsurfing

Kiteworks, 548 Glebe Rd, Adamstown (ⓣ0413 387 991, ⓦwww.kiteworks.com.au), can provide all the kitesurfing gear you need; trainer kite hire is A$30/hr, while one-to-one lessons are A$65/hr. A short trip south of Newcastle, **Board Crazy** at Belmont (ⓣ02 4947 7131, ⓦwww.boardcrazy.com.au) offer kitesurfing and windsurfing on Lake Macquarie.

Rugby matches

Newcastle's NRL rugby team, the **Knights**, play at the Energy Australia Stadium, five minutes from Broadmeadow station.

Sandboarding, quad-biking and 4WD tours of Stockton Bight

Adventure tours may take in the dunes, the wreck of the *Sygna Bergen* (which has been rusting offshore since 1974) and the region's World War II anti-tank defences – black, metallic pyramids rising out of the sand to give the scene a sci-fi twist.

   Dawsons Scenic Tours, Soldiers Point (ⓣ02 4982 0602, ⓦwww.portstephens adventure.com.au), offer short 4WD beach tours, with sandboarding as a highlight (1hr; A$20, child A$15) and longer tours (3hr 30min–4hr; A$75, child A$40); they start from Stockton Wharf or from Birubi Point, at the northeast end of Stockton Beach. **Quad Bike King**, Taylors Beach (ⓣ02 4919 0088, ⓦwww.quadbikeking.com.au), offer thrilling quad-bike tours (from A$85 for 1hr). **Port Stephens 4WD Tours**, 35 Stockton St, Nelson Bay (ⓣ02 4984 4760, ⓦwww.portstephens4wd.com.au), run a variety of trips to the giant slopes (from A$45 for 2hr, child A$25).

Scuba diving

Dive sites around Nelson Bay include Broughton Island, haunt of grey nurse sharks, and the sponge and coral gardens of the marine reserve between Fly Point and Halifax Park. There are also a couple of wrecks within two hours travelling time by boat. **Pro Dive** at the D'Albora Marina, Nelson Bay (ⓣ02 4981 4331,

---

meals. Also outside courtyard. Licensed. Daily 7am–midnight.

🏃 **Grind** 127 Darby St, Cooks Hill ⓣ07 4929 4710. Packed-out coffee shop and bistro with a bohemian feel, serving delicious, mid-priced daily specials such as *nori* and herb-crumbed Atlantic salmon, plus gorgeous puddings. Daily 7.30am–late.
Harry's Café de Wheels 199 Wharf Rd ⓣ02 4926 2165. Popular franchise of the Sydney legend, this

retro-styled fast-food van serves hot pies to hungry mouths at all hours. Mon, Tues & Sun until 11pm, Wed & Thurs until 1am, Sat & Sun until 4am.
The Last Drop Espresso Bar 37 Hunter St ⓣ02 4926 3470. Great little café, which serves excellent coffee, fresh juices, frappés and smoothies and tasty gourmet sandwiches. Daily 7am–4pm.
Produce Café Honeysuckle Railway Buildings, Merewether ⓣ02 4927 5366. Champion of the

@www.prodivenelsonbay.com), run trips and courses (shore dives from A$70; single boat dive A$120 including gear).

Sea kayaking
Blue Water Sea Kayaking (⏂0405 033 518, @www.kayakingportstephens.com.au) specialize in guided trips, from short paddles, launching from the sheltered Nelson Bay Marina (1hr; A$25, child A$15) to longer tours timed to catch the sunset. They also run overnight kayaking and camping excursions in the Myall Lake region (A$125 per day).

Surfing
Key to Newie's alternative feel is its hefty dose of **surf culture** – many surfwear companies, surfboard-makers and world champions, including Mark Richards, Matt Hoy and Luke Egan, hail from here. On a good day, the waves can exceed 2.5m, attracting hardcore enthusiasts. Favourite breaks that are jealously guarded by the locals (some of whom tend to give tourists a cool reception) include Nobby's Reef, a consistent left-hand break; Bar Beach, one of Australia's most celebrated spots; and Merewether, a classic right-hand reef break. Redhead Beach and Blacksmiths Breakwall are quieter options, further south. For **lessons**, try Redhead Mobile Surf School in Newcastle (⏂02 4944 9585, @www.redheadsurfscholl.com.au) or Anna Bay Surf School at One Mile Beach, Port Stephens (⏂02 4981 9919, @www .annabaysurfschool.com.au); recommended **surf shops** include PD Surfboards at 7 Darby St. *Newcastle Beach YHA* and *Newcastle Backpackers* (see p.345) can also fix up gear hire and tuition.

Whale- and dolphin-watching
Between May and November you might see whales as they migrate first north then south along the Pacific Coast, while dolphin cruises are available all year round; try **Moonshadow Cruises**, 35 Stockton St, Nelson Bay (⏂02 4984 9388, @www .moonshadow.com.au; 2hr dolphin-spotting A$21, child A$11; 3hr whale-watching A$60, child A$25), or **Simba II Cruises** at Tea Gardens, on the north side of the bay (3hr dolphin-spotting: A$25, child A$10; ⏂02 4997 1084).

Much more satisfying than a motor cruise, though, are the eco-friendly trips aboard a fifteen-metre catamaran run by **Imagine Cruises** out of Nelson Bay (⏂02 4984 9000, @www.imaginecruises.com.au; 1hr 30min dolphin cruise A$30, child A$15; 3hr whale-and-dolphin cruise A$60, child A$30).

To search for dolphins by kayak, contact **Blue Water Sea Kayaking** (see above); for the excitement of spotting whales from a helicopter, contact **Heliservices** (⏂02 4962 5188, @www.heliservices.com.au).

Wine tours
Newcastle's Famous Tram (Sat & Sun 10am–4pm; A$45; ⏂02 4977 2270, @www .famous-tram.co.au), a bus in the livery of a 1920s tram, will whisk you around the Hunter Valley vineyards, stopping for tastings and a BBQ lunch.

area's produce, this café uses local poultry, sourdough bread, organic milk and vegetables to rustle up gourmet breakfasts, sandwiches and delicious meals. Daily 7am–3pm.

Silo The Boardwalk, Honeysuckle Drive ⏂02 4926 2828. As close as Newcastle's regenerated wharfside gets to cool, this bistro with lounge touches (modish flock wallpaper and chandeliers) serves mid-priced fare such as duck risotto or king prawn spaghetti, and hosts DJ sessions and wine-tasting events.

Supply 25 King St ⏂02 4929 2222. With a light, modern and airy interior and groovy music playing, this is a good place to clear a hangover. Breakfasts, pastas, salads and dinner served at very reasonable prices. Mon–Fri 7.30am–5pm, Sat & Sun 8.30am–4pm.

Entertainment and nightlife

The cultural precinct, near Civic Park on King, Hunter and Auckland streets, is the location for two refurbished Art Deco venues: at the **University Conservatorium of Music** on Auckland Street (☎02 4921 8900), there are often free lunchtime concerts as well as evening performances; while the grand **City Hall**, 290 King St (☎02 4974 2948), has occasional classical-music events such as the Australian Chamber Orchestra. The Newcastle Visitor Information Centre (see p.345) publishes monthly details of what's on. Mainstream **cinema** is on offer at the three-screen Greater Union, nearby at 183 King St (A$14.50, child A$10.50; all seats A$9 on Tues; ☎02 4926 2233). Both art-house and mainstream releases are shown around the corner at the three-screen Showcase City Cinemas, 31–33 Wolfe St, off Hunter Street Mall (A$12–12.50, child A$9–10; ☎02 4929 5019).

For **nightlife listings**, check out *TE* (the Wednesday supplement to the *Post*), free monthlies *Reverb* and *Drum Media*, or ⍟www.newcastlemusic.com. During term time, the students of Newcastle University add a lot of life to the city but there is always a thriving live-music scene; local heroes include Silverchair and the Screaming Jets.

Pubs, bars and clubs

Bar on the Hill University Drive, Callaghan (12km west of the city via bus 226 to University Drive or train to Warabrook station) ☎02 4921 5000. Uni bar, a hub of the student social scene: in term time, it hosts regular gigs.

The Beach Hotel Opposite Merewether Beach ☎02 4963 1574. With a huge beachfront beer garden, this is popular all weekend and is the place to go on Sunday nights when there are live bands (free).

The Brewery Queens Wharf, 150 Wharf Rd. Popular waterfront drinking hole with good beer and three bars – grab tables right on the wharf or on the upstairs balcony. Food from the busy bistro can be eaten outside (weekend breakfasts, too). Live music or DJs Wed–Sun (free).

Cambridge Hotel 789 Hunter St, West Newcastle ☎02 4962 2459. One of Newcastle's big venues for touring bands.

Crown & Anchor 189 Hunter St. Well-known city boozer, with outdoor tables alongside the classic, beautifully tiled exterior. Popular balcony upstairs, overlooking the street. The nightclub, *Frost Bites* (Wed–Sun; free), specializes in lethal sno-cone alcoholic drinks.

Fanny's 311 Wharf Rd ⍟www.fannys.com.au. Up-for-it club with a wild reputation, hosting everything from CD launches to bikini-modelling contests. Wed 8pm–3am, Fri 8pm–4am, Sat 8pm–5am.

Hotel Delany 134 Darby St, Cooks Hill ☎02 4929 1627, ⍟www.thedelany.com. Cool spot to catch a small-scale live gig (Wed–Sat) or jamming session (Sun).

The Kent 59 Beaumont St, corner of Cleary St, Hamilton ☎02 4961 3303. Beautifully renovated old pub and music venue, which is busy most nights – pool comps, quizzes, karaoke, a rock duo (Fri–Sun nights), and Sunday afternoon jazz (4.30–8.30pm) – but with several refuges, including a plant-filled beer garden and a great bistro.

MJ Finnegan's 21–23 Darby St, Cooks Hill. Newcastle's obligatory Irish theme pub. Always lively and popular, especially with travellers, as they often put on free-food nights to pack them in.

Sydney Junction Hotel 8 Beaumont St, Hamilton ☎02 4961 2537. *SJ's* is a young and lively pub in an equally animated strip. Usually free but entry up to A$15 for major gigs. Open to 1am most nights, Fri & Sat to 4am.

Terminal One Harbour Square, Honeysuckle Drive ☎02 4927 1722. Swanky bar, haunt of Newcastle's would-be glitterati, with a contemporary cocktail-lounge feel and low upholstered cubes to chat on.

Listings

Banks and exchange There are ATMs in Hunter St Mall. American Express is at 49 Hunter St, ☎1300 139 060. Commonwealth Bank, 136 Hunter St Mall (☎02 4927 2777) has foreign exchange.

Car rental ARA ☎1800 243 122 or 02 4962 2488, ⍟www.ararental.com.au; Thrifty, Newcastle Airport ☎02 4965 1535.

Internet access Battle Ground, 169 King St (daily 10am–10pm); *Newcastle Beach YHA*, 30 Pacific St;

Backpackers By The Beach, 34 Hunter St; free public Wi-Fi on Beaumont St, Hamilton. **Left luggage** At the train station (daily 8am–5pm). **Post office** 1 Market St, Newcastle East; Shop 30, Marketown Shopping Centre, Parry St, Newcastle West.

Supermarket Coles, corner of King & National Park sts; IGA, Hunter St; both open daily until late. **Taxi** Newcastle Taxis (℡02 4904 5900 or 13 10 08, 🌐www.newcastletaxis.com.au).

Port Stephens

Just north of Newcastle, the wide bay of **Port Stephens**, which extends inland for some 25km, offers calm waters and numerous coves ideal for swimming, watersports and fishing, while the ocean side has good surf and wide, sandy beaches. In January, thousands of families arrive to take their annual holiday in the area dubbed "Blue Water Paradise". The main township of **NELSON BAY** is perched near the tip of the bay's southern arm, the Tomaree Peninsula, together with the quieter settlements of Shoal Bay and Fingal Bay; further inland are the low-key resorts of Corlette and Soldiers Point, while Tea Gardens lies on the opposite side of the bay. To the south is Anna Bay and the giant dunes of Stockton Beach (see p.347), the largest on the eastern Australian mainland and a target for adventure enthusiasts. For waterborne action, you can choose between surfing, parasailing, sea-kayaking and jet-skiing, all available at various locations around the bay, along with dolphin-spotting and, in season, whale-watching in the open ocean. For details of these and other activities, see the box on p.348; the visitor information centre (see below) can also give pointers. During peak whale-watching time, from late September to early October, Nelson Bay hosts a festival of whale-related talks and family events (🌐www.whalefest.com.au).

Practicalities

Getting around the bay is easiest if you have your own vehicle, though Busways (🌐www.busways.com.au) call at Tea Gardens en route between Sydney and Taree, and Greyhound and Premier Motor Service (see p.35) stop at Karuah, midway around the bay. Port Stephens Coaches (℡02 4982 2940, 🌐www.pscoaches.com.au) links all the smaller beach settlements with Nelson Bay, and runs an express service from Sydney and Newcastle. The Port Stephens Ferry Service (A\$20, child A\$10 return; pay on board; ℡0412 682 117) crosses from Nelson Bay's public jetty to Tea Gardens and back three times a day, with extra crossings during holidays. The **visitor information centre** (daily 9am–5pm; ℡02 4980 6900 or 1800 808 900, 🌐www.portstephens.org.au) on Victoria Parade in Nelson Bay offers an accommodation-, tour- and cruise-booking service.

Good **accommodation** options include the bright, attractively designed *Nelson Bay B&B* at 81 Stockton St, Nelson Bay (℡02 4984 3655, 🌐www.nelsonbaybandb.com.au; ❹), which has three comfortable en-suite rooms, set among leafy bushland, ten minutes' walk from town; and the top-end *Peppers Anchorage,* Corlette Point Road, Corlette (℡02 4984 2555, 🌐www.peppers.com.au/anchorage; ❻, suite ❼), overlooking yacht moorings and boasting wonderfully bright and comfortable rooms and unusually attractive split-level "loft" suites. The best budget options are *Melaleuca Surfside Backpackers*, 2 Koala Place, One Mile Beach (℡02 4982 1248, 🌐www.melaleucabackpackers.com.au), which has appealing one-room timber bungalows (❸), camping (A\$30) and six-share bunkhouses (A\$28pp) set in tranquil bushland roamed by koalas and possums; and the excellent rainforest-garden *Samurai Beach Bungalows YHA*, Frost Road, Anna Bay (☎02 4982 1921, ⓦwww.yha.com.au), with shared cabins (A$25–34) en-suite "deluxe" bungalows (❷–❹), a roofed-over "bush" kitchen, free boards and bikes, Wi-Fi and a nice pool.

All the resort areas have a good sprinkling of **restaurants** catering for holidaymakers; the best regarded is *Zest* at 16 Stockton St, Nelson Bay (Tues–Sat from 6.30pm; ☎02 4984 2211), famous for its delicate, imaginative cooking.

⑤

The Great Lakes

The **Great Lakes**, north of Port Stephens, is a region of stunning coastal waterways, backed by forested mountains and separated from the ocean by pristine, beach-fringed bush. Its highlight, the beautiful **Myall Lakes National Park**, well rewards a day or so of exploration. From the Pacific Highway, which skirts the region on the inland side, a heavenly two-hour drive loops east to take you through the southern part of the park – if approaching from the south, turn right onto Tea Gardens Road and continue through Tea Gardens and Hawks Nest for the very scenic drive to **Mungo Brush**, between the shores of **Myall Lake** and the ocean. There are plenty of gentle walking tracks around here, while a more challenging 21-kilometre hike leads back to Hawks Nest. Just after Mungo Brush, the charming Bombah Point Ferry (daily 8am–6pm; every 30min; A$4) takes you and your car over Myall Lake; from here the partly unsealed Bombah Point Road leads you back to the highway at **Bulahdelah**, 30km from your starting point.

Further north is another scenic route: the 120-kilometre **Lakes Way** (Tourist Drive 6) via Forster–Tuncurry. This road, which is completely sealed, heads east off the highway 5km north of Bulahdelah, and rejoins it around 80km south of Port Macquarie. From Bungwahl, in the southern section of the route, a turn-off leads down mostly unsealed roads to **SEAL ROCKS**, a remote, unspoilt fishing village and the only settlement in the **national park**. The first beach you come to, **Number One Beach**, is truly beautiful, with crystal-clear waters marooned between two headlands. Two minutes to the south, there are great waves for surfing. **Sugar Loaf Point Lighthouse** is around ten minutes' walk up a steep path; the grounds offer fantastic 360-degree views, and the lookout below leads down to a deserted, rocky beach. Seal Rocks' seasonal agglomerations of nurse sharks make it one of the best **dive sites** in New South Wales (see below).

Activities in Forster-Tuncurry

Amaroo Cruises at the end of Memorial Drive, Forster (☎0419 333 445, ⓦwww .amaroocruise.com.au), run daily dolphin-watching trips (2hr; A$40, child A$25), while **Forster Dive Centre** on the waterfront at 11 Little St, Forster (☎02 6555 4477, ⓦwww.forsterdivecentre.com.au), take the dolphin experience a stage further by taking you out to snorkel with them (2hr; A$60): they run several trips a week and almost always find a sizeable, inquisitive pod. They also offer a full programme of scuba courses and diving trips to Seal Rocks. **Forster Luxury Boat Hire** at the nearby Boatshed Number One, 1 Little St (☎02 6554 7733) rents out boats, canoes and wave skis (racing kayaks with a surfboard shape).

North of Seal Rocks, the exhilarating drive past the pleasant, unpretentious beach resort of **Pacific Palms** and on through the tiny **Booti Booti National Park** takes you through dramatic forests; as you cross the narrow spit of land between Wallis Lake and Elizabeth Bay it's hard to keep your eyes on the road, especially at sunset. Ten kilometres further north, a bridge connects the twin holiday towns of **FORSTER–TUNCURRY**, the former set on the strip of land separating **Wallis Lake** from the ocean. While the lake is very pretty, Forster itself decidedly isn't, being somewhat blighted by unimaginative development. It's a good base for all manner of cruises and watersports, though, and famous for its **oysters** and playful resident **oceanic bottlenose dolphins**. You can meet local Aboriginal artists at **Tobwabba Gallery** at 10 Breckenridge St (Mon–Fri 9am–5pm; free; ℡02 6554 5755, ⓦwww.tobwabba.com.au), which has some great contemporary work.

Practicalities

To explore Myall Lakes National Park in your own time you really need a **car**: the vehicle entry fee is A\$7. **Public transport** into the region includes Busways route 150 between Sydney and Tuncurry and route 151 between Newcastle and Taree, which both travel along the Lakes Way. Greyhound and Premier Motor Service (see p.35) buses both serve Forster, with Greyhound also stopping at Bulahdelah. The well-organized **Great Lakes Visitor Information Centre** on Little Street in Forster (daily 9am–5pm; ℡02 6554 8799 or 1800 802 692, ⓦwww.greatlakes.org.au), offers an accommodation-booking service.

If you want to **stay** in the area overnight, bushcamping in Myall Lakes National Park is an attractive option, particularly if you have a boat to get you to the remotest spots (A\$10, child A\$5; ⓦwww.nationalparks.nsw .gov.au). Otherwise, there's centrally located *Forster Beach Caravan Park* on Reserve Road, Forster (℡02 6554 6269 or 1800 240 632, ⓦwww .forsterbeachcaravan.com.au; camping A\$22–29, cabin ❸–❺), which has spotless amenities, a playground and beach frontage; or the beautifully located *EcoPoint Myall Shores Resort*, by the Bombah Point Ferry on the northern side of Myall lake, 16km southeast of Bulahdelah (℡02 4997 4495 or 1300 769 566, ⓦwww.myallshores.com.au; camping A\$20–26, cabin or villa ❷–❼). This tranquil resort – the best in the national park – boasts stylish waterfront villas and a good café-restaurant, plus canoe and boat rental. For a spot right on the beach, head 16km south of Forster to *Sundowner Tiona Tourist Park*, The Lakes Way, Tiona (℡02 6554 0291 or 1800 636 452, ⓦwww.sundownerholidays.com; camping A\$22–35, bunk in shared lodge A\$22.50, cabin ❷–❺), right on Seven Mile Beach, in the Booti Booti National Park; or to *Seal Rocks Camping Reserve* on Kinka Road, Seal Rocks (℡02 4997 6164 or 1800 112 234, ⓦwww.sealrockscampingreserve.com.au; camping A\$24–28, cabin ❷–❹), a glorious, unspoilt site on the beautiful Number One Beach, with basic facilities. Although there's a small general store in the settlement, you should bring supplies in with you.

Wharf Street, the main strip in Forster, has numerous cafés, **restaurants** and takeaways; nearby lakefront options include *Bella Bellissimo* on Memorial Drive (closed Mon; ℡02 6555 6411), offering gourmet Italian fare and a buzzy atmosphere, and *Casa del Mundo*, 8 Little St (Tues–Sat 6pm–late; ℡02 6554 5906), which is run by a Menorcan chef and specializes in Balearic-style seafood dishes.

Barrington Tops National Park and Ellenborough Falls

The World Heritage-listed **Barrington Tops National Park**, 60km inland from Forster–Tuncurry, is one of the state's most spectacular hiking regions. The Tops themselves are two high, cliff-ringed plateaus, **Barrington** and **Gloucester**, which rise steeply from the surrounding valleys. The changes in altitude within the park are so great – the highest point is 1586m – that within a few minutes you can pass from areas of subtropical rainforest to high, windswept plateaus covered with snow gums, meadows and subalpine bog.

From the coast, there are two **road routes** into the park. If you're heading north from Sydney, Newcastle or Port Stephens, the most direct route is via Dungog; alternatively, you can leave the Pacific Highway at Nabiac, 22km from Forster–Tuncurry and 103km southwest of Port Macquarie, and approach via the country town of Gloucester, a route that takes you through gentle, hilly farmland. All the park's roads are unsealed; in good weather conditions you can tackle most of them in a 2WD vehicle, but if you're heading for one of the more remote campsites, or if there's heavy rain or snow (common up on the plateau from end April to early Oct), you'll need 4WD – contact the NPWS in Gloucester (☏02 6538 5300; ⊛www.nationalparks.nsw.gov.au) for advice. The closest you'll get to the park with public transport is to take the **train** to Gloucester or Dungog.

The **Visitor Information Centres** on Dowling Street in Dungog (Mon–Fri 9am–5pm, Sat & Sun 10am–3pm; ☏02 4992 2212, ⊛www.barringtons .com.au), at 27 Denison St in Gloucester (Mon–Fri 9am–5pm, Sat & Sun 9am–3.30pm; ☏02 6558 1408, ⊛www.gloucester.org.au), and in Forster (see p.353) can help with specific routes or organized 4WD tours into the national park. There are plenty of picnic grounds, walking trails and scenic **lookouts** to explore. It's possible to bushcamp in some areas for free; there are also several NPWS **campsites** (A$5–10, child A$3–5 per night; see p.54 for booking information). The other **accommodation** in the area is relatively pricey, but there are lots of options. One of the closest places to the park itself is *Salisbury Lodges*, at 2930 Salisbury Rd in Salisbury, 40km northwest of Dungog (☏02 4995 3285, ⊛www.salisburylodges.com.au; ⑤). This wilderness retreat is perfect for a quiet country weekend and has lovely timber lodges, a great restaurant and a gorgeous rainforest setting. A slightly cheaper alternative is *The Barringtons Country Retreat* on Chichester Dam Road, 23km north of Dungog (☏02 4995 9269, ⊛www.thebarringtons.com.au; ⑤), a collection of cabins and lodges with log fires and spa baths.

Between Barrington Tops and Port Macquarie, north of Wingham, is the two-hundred-metre-high **Ellenborough Falls**, one of the most spectacular waterfalls on the whole coast; you can get there by cutting across from Gloucester via unsealed roads, or by taking Tourist Drive 8 from Taree to Elands and then continuing along Bulga Forest Drive.

Port Macquarie

The fast-growing town of **PORT MACQUARIE**, at the mouth of the Hastings River, has a beautiful natural setting. Long, sandy **beaches** extend far along the coast, pelicans and dolphins bob about in the harbour, and the surrounding hinterland is dotted with forests, mountains and pretty towns.

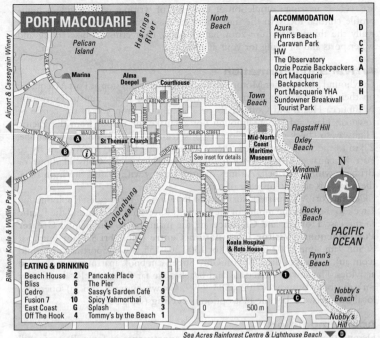

PORT MACQUARIE

Hastings River

North Beach

Pelican Island

Airport & Cassegrain Winery

Marina

Alma Doepel

Courthouse

PARK STREET

BAY ST

HASTINGS RIVER DRIVE

WAUGH ST

BULLER ST

St Thomas' Church

OXLEY HWY

SHORT ST

HOLLINGWORTH STREET

GORE STREET

LAKE ROAD

Kooloonbung Creek

CLARENCE STREET

HORTON STREET

MUNSTER STREET

HAY ST

CHURCH STREET

HILL STREET

GRANT STREET

LORD STREET

OWEN STREET

Town Beach

Flagstaff Hill

PACIFIC DRIVE

Oxley Beach

Windmill Hill

Rocky Beach

PACIFIC OCEAN

Mid-North Coast Maritime Museum

See inset for details

Koala Hospital & Roto House

FLYNN ST

OCEAN ST

Flynn's Beach

Nobby's Beach

Nobby's Hill

Billabong Koala & Wildlife Park

Town Beach

ACCOMMODATION

Azura	D
Flynn's Beach Caravan Park	C
HW	F
The Observatory	G
Ozzie Pozzie Backpackers	A
Port Macquarie Backpackers	B
Port Macquarie YHA	H
Sundowner Breakwall Tourist Park	E

EATING & DRINKING

Beach House	2	Pancake Place	5
Bliss	6	The Pier	7
Cedro	8	Sassy's Garden Café	9
Fusion 7	10	Spicy Yahmorthai	5
East Coast	G	Splash	3
Off The Hook	4	Tommy's by the Beach	1

N

0   500 m

Sea Acres Rainforest Centre & Lighthouse Beach ▼ D

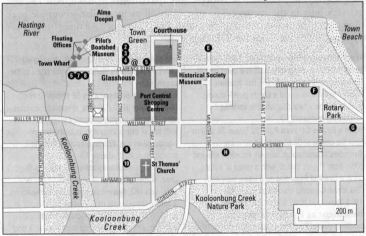

Hastings River

Floating Offices

Town Wharf

Alma Doepel

Pilot's Boatshed Museum

Town Green

Courthouse

Town Beach

6 7 8

Glasshouse

2 3 4

5

@

CLARENCE STREET

SUGAR STREET

HORTON STREET

MURRAY ST

Historical Society Museum

Port Central Shopping Centre

E

STEWART STREET

F

Rotary Park

G

BULLER STREET

HOLLINGWORTH STREET

Kooloonbung Creek

@

WILLIAM   STREET

HAY STREET

MUNSTER STREET

GRANT STREET

LORD STREET

CHURCH STREET

H

9

10

St Thomas' Church

HAYWARD STREET

GORDON   STREET

Kooloonbung Creek Nature Park

Kooloonbung Creek

0   200 m

The town was established in 1821 as a place of secondary punishment for convicts who continued their criminal ways after arrival in New South Wales; by the late 1820s, the penal settlement was closed and the area opened up to free settlers. For some time, Port has been saddled with a rather plodding image: it's best known as a pleasant but doggedly uncool resort for young families and retirees. It's keen to change gear, however, and edge its way upmarket: the town centre already has a few good restaurants and the ambitious new **Glasshouse** arts centre, nearing completion at the time of writing, will provide a high-profile cultural focus. In the meantime, the easy-going **activities** on offer are really the thing, with mini-zoos, nature parks, river cruises, horse-riding and watersports and all vying for your attention.

Arrival and information

Greyhound and Premier Motor Service **buses** (see p.35) stop at Port Macquarie on their runs between Sydney and Brisbane, while Kean's run to Tamworth, Nambucca Heads and Coffs Harbour. They should drop you in the centre of town on Hayward Street, although not all make the detour from the Pacific Highway, so check carefully. CountryLink **trains** (see p.35) stop in Wauchope, 22km to the west, from where there's a connecting bus service. You can **fly** to Port Macquarie Airport (PQQ) direct from Newcastle, Coffs Harbour or Brisbane with Brindabella Airlines, or from Sydney with Qantas or Virgin Blue; the airport is about 6km west of town.

Central Port Macquarie is surrounded by water on three sides: Kooloonbung Creek to the west, the mouth of the Hastings River to the north, and the Pacific to the east. **Horton** and **Clarence** are the main streets. The helpful **Greater Port Macquarie Visitor Information Centre** (Mon–Fri 8.30am–5pm, Sat & Sun 9am–4pm; ℡02 6581 8000 or 1300 303 155, ⓦwww.portmacquarieinfo.com.au), just out of the CBD on Gore Street, can book apartments, rooms and activities. The town's attractions and beaches are far flung, and local transport isn't the best; Busways (℡02 6583 2499, ⓦwww.busways.com.au) operate a local **bus** network but the best option is **cycling** (see p.358).

Accommodation

Despite the huge number of **motels** and **apartments** in town, Port can still get very busy in the summer. The motels are all pretty similar, so outside peak time just cruise around town to see which takes your fancy. All three backpacker options do free pick-ups from the bus stop.

Azura 109 Pacific Drive ℡02 6582 2700, ⓦwww.azura.com.au. A lovely little B&B in a quiet part of town close to Shelly Beach. The four modern, stylish rooms have use of a comfy guest-lounge; breakfast is on a beautiful wooden veranda, overlooking rainforest. ❹

Flynn's Beach Caravan Park 22 Ocean St, 2.5km from the centre ℡02 6583 5754, ⓦwww.flynnsbeachcaravanpark.com.au. Excellent site just 200m from Flynn's Beach, with a range of cabins set in a forest of ferns and gum trees, pool and BBQ areas. Camping from A$25, cabin ❸

HW 1 Stewart St ℡02 6583 1200, ⓦwww.hwmotel.com.au. In a fine location on the low headland overlooking Town Beach, this comfortable place with executive-friendly amenities, such as Wi-Fi and a great room-service breakfast menu, at reasonable prices. ❺

The Observatory 40 William St ℡02 6586 8000 or 1300 888 305, ⓦwww.observatory.net.au. This smart modern block represents a new trend in Port; its quality open-plan apartments have well-equipped kitchens, flat-screen televisions, Wi-Fi

and contemporary decor. Many also have great views through Port's signature Norfolk pines to the ocean. ❺

Ozzie Pozzie Backpackers 36 Waugh St ℡02 6583 8133 or 1800 620 020, ⓦwww.ozziepozzie.com. Friendly, brightly decorated place, small but with lots of extras thrown in including boogie-boards, bikes and a basic breakfast. Bunk in shared room A$30, double ❸

Port Macquarie Backpackers 2 Hastings River Drive, corner of Gordon St ℡02 6583 1791 or 1800 688 882, ⓦwww.portmacquariebackpackers.com.au. Great hostel run by an ex-backpacker in an 1888 Victorian Gothic weatherboarded building with colourful dorms, fine communal areas, a pool and BBQ area, plus a fun atmosphere. There's free use of bikes and boogie-boards. Bunk in shared room A$27, double ❷

Port Macquarie YHA 40 Church St ℡02 6583 5512, ⓦwww.yha.com.au. Very compact and very yellow YHA in a quiet part of town, with an atmosphere to match. Decent rooms and shared areas are supplemented by free boogie-boards, cheap bike hire and a programme of trips. Bunk in four- or six-share A$23–37, private double/twin ② **Sundowner Breakwall Tourist Park** 1 Munster St ☎ 02 6583 2755 or 1800 636 452, ⓦ www .sundownerholidays.com. Right next to the town, river and beach, this family-oriented site is

superbly located and feels roomy despite the number of cottages and cabins packed into it. Lots of activities – including surf trips – are offered in case the pool and kids club lose their appeal. Bunk in shared cabin A$25, camping A$35.50–$42, cabin ③, cottage ⑤

The town and around

Port Macquarie has a tendency to destroy reminders of its past, though a few early buildings survive (you can get a historic-walk leaflet at the tourist office). The **Historical Society Museum** on Clarence Street, opposite the courthouse (Mon–Sat 9.30am–4.30pm; A$5), illuminates early life in the penal settlement, and houses a rather gruesome convict whipping stool complete with fake blood that should frighten the kids into good behaviour. The main **Mid-North Coast Maritime Museum** at 6 William St (Mon–Sat 11am–3pm; A$5) contains the usual mix of nautical artefacts and model boats; there's more at its outpost, the **Pilot Boatshed** at the far western end of Clarence Street (Mon–Fri 10am–2pm; free).

The river foreshore, with its anglers and pelican colony, is a pleasant place for a peaceful sunset stroll or to grab some fish 'n' chips. Floating offices where you can book anything from dolphin tours to seaplane flights (see box, p.358) are found at the western end of Clarence Street, while at Lady Nelson Wharf on Town Square, at the northern end of Horton Street, you can step aboard the **Alma Doepel** (daily 9am–dusk; A$3, child A$1; ⓦ www .almadoepel.com.au), a wonderfully restored timber schooner built in 1903. Inland, on Clarence Street, is the **Glasshouse** (☎ 02 6581 8888, ⓦ www .glasshouse.org.au), a promising new regional arts, entertainment and conference venue whose construction ran way over budget and schedule, amid much local controversy; it's set to host an impressive programme of opera, theatre, concerts and exhibitions.

Another fine attraction in the town centre is the **Kooloonbung Creek Nature Park**, a large bushland reserve remarkably close to the CBD. From the entrance at the corner of Horton and Gordon streets, you can step onto trails among casuarinas, eucalypts and swampy mangroves, visit a cemetery containing the graves of eminent early settlers, or sweat through a small patch of rainforest – were it not for the boardwalks and faint hum of traffic, it would be amazingly easy to believe that you were lost in the bush.

A string of fine **beaches** backed by grassy or wooded slopes run down the ocean-facing side of town (Town, Flynn's and Lighthouse are patrolled); perhaps the best way to spend a day in Port Macquarie is to rent a bike and explore the cliff-top paths and roads that link them all. On the way you can call in at the **Sea Acres Rainforest Centre** on Pacific Drive, between Shelly Beach and Miners Beach (daily 9am–4.30pm; free guided walks at regular intervals; A$8, child A$4; ☎ 02 6582 3355) – this impressive park includes three different types of rainforest, which can be inspected at close quarters from a boardwalk; there's also a café.

Back towards the town centre on Lord Street, in the grounds of **Roto House**, is Australia's oldest **koala hospital** (daily 8am–4.30pm; free; guided tour 3pm; ☎ 02 6584 1522, ⓦ www.koalahospital.org.au). It's a great place to learn about koalas, and you can even adopt one of the "patients" if you get particularly attached; most are recovering from road accidents, dog attacks or disease, and all but a handful of long-termers end up back in the wild. For yet more cuddly creatures, the **Billabong Koala & Wildlife Park** at 61 Billabong Drive, off the

Oxley Highway west of town (daily 9am–5pm; koala encounters at 10.30am, 1.30pm & 3.30pm; A\$15, child A\$10; ☏02 6585 1060), has emu chicks, kangaroos, spider monkeys, koalas and an assortment of reptiles including venomous snakes.

You'll find the **wines** produced at Cassegrain Winery on Fernbank Creek Road, off the Pacific Highway west of town (daily 9am–5pm; ⓦwww .cassegrainwines.com.au), on many a wine list in the area; the award-winning restaurant here, *Ça Marche* (daily noon–3pm & Fri 6–9pm; ☏02 6582 8320, ⓦwww.camarche.com.au), is a great spot for a long lunch overlooking the vineyards.

Eating and drinking

Beach House 1 Horton St ☏02 6584 5692. This large riverfront bar has unquestionably the best location in town, perfect for breakfast, a long lunch, or best of all, early evening drinks soaked up with a gourmet pizza or pasta. It's not classy, but it's always packed in summer.

Bliss 74 Clarence St ☏02 6584 1422, ⓦwww .blissrestaurant.com. The sunset views across the river at this stylish, imaginative Mod Oz eatery are blissful indeed. Daily from 6.30pm & Mon–Fri 11.30am–2pm.

Activities in Port Macquarie

Boating and canoeing

The **Settlement Point Boatshed** (☏02 6583 6300), 2km north of the CBD next to the Settlement Point Ferry (follow Park St north over the road bridges), rents out canoes and boats at reasonable rates.

Cycling

Graham Seers Cyclery, Shop 2, Port Marina, Bay St (☏02 6583 2333) offers bike hire for A\$25/half-day or A\$40/full day; **Gordon Street Cycles**, 163 Gordon St (☏02 6593 3633) are slightly cheaper (both Mon–Fri 9am–5pm, Sat 9am–1pm).

Camel safaris

Port Macquarie Camel Safaris (☏0437 672 080, ⓦwww.portmacquariecamels .com.au) offer short ambles along the sand, starting from Lighthouse Beach (mornings, daily except Sat; from A\$23 for 30min, child A\$17).

Cruises

Port Macquarie Cruise Adventures, Clarence St foreshore (☏02 6583 8483 or 1300 555 890, ⓦwww.cruiseadventures.com.au), will take you along the coast or upriver in search of dolphins, pelicans, waterlilies and rainforest; prices range from A\$15 (child A\$10) for a short sunset cruise (1hr 30min) to A\$75 (child A\$50) for a trip to the Maria River Everglades (5hr 30min). For a Hastings River cruise with a historical theme, book a tour on the **MV Wentworth** based at the Pilot Boatshed on the Clarence Street foreshore (Tues & Thurs; ☏02 6584 2987); there's a two-hour tour at 10.30am (A\$15, child A\$10) and a one-hour tour at 1pm (A\$10, child A\$6).

Day-trips and tours

Waves n Wilderness (☏0427 880 485, ⓦwww.wavesnwilderness.com.au) offer small-group coastal and hinterland tours, with the option of designing your own itinerary (half day from A\$200 per group, full day A\$300); **Gondwana Tours** (☏02 6583 2341, ⓦwww.gondwanatours.com.au) run larger-group trips (half day A\$66, full day A\$88), including winery tours and a full-day run out to Ellenborough Falls and the Kindee Suspension Bridge over the Hastings River nearby. With **Coast**

Cedro 70 Clarence St ☎02 6583 5529. The enticing breakfast menu at this elegantly minimalist café includes ricotta hotcakes with banana, walnuts and maple syrup, while for lunch there may be spicy lamb burgers or crab linguini – good value at A$15–17. Daily 7.30am–2.30pm.

East Coast 40 William St ☎02 6583 9300. Run by a British, Michelin-starred restauranteur on a mission to bring quality food to regional Australia, this smart but unpretentious place has a simple menu of affordable, brilliantly prepared classics. Daily for breakfast, lunch & dinner.

Fusion 7 6/124 Horton St ☎02 6584 1171. In the hands of one of Port's top chefs, this laidback spot serves enticing Mod Oz combinations such as spicy Thai prawns with green papaya, or barramundi with apple and pomegranate. Thurs & Fri lunch, Tues–Sat dinner.

Off The Hook Horton St ☎02 6584 1146. Handily located thirty seconds from Town Green, this takeaway serves the best fish 'n' chips in town. Daily from 11am.

Pancake Place Clarence St, corner of Hay St ☎02 6583 4544. Heaven for hungry young families, this cheerful place will load your plate with maple syrup and bacon pancakes at breakfast time, while lunch and dinner pancake specials include satay chicken or tasty meatballs, all under A$20. Daily 8am–2pm & 6–9pm.

The Pier 72 Clarence St ☎02 6584 2800. About as trendy as Port Macquarie gets, this large, airy bar has an impressive range of Belgian and European designer beers on tap.

Sassy's Garden Café 1/124 Horton St. Funky café with good coffee and cookies to enjoy in a lovely little tropical garden, opening onto the street. Mon–Fri 8am–4pm, Sat 8am–2pm.

and **Country Trike Tours** (from A$40; ☎0409 829 474) you can blast along the coast in a Harley trike.

Diving
Rick's Dive School, 19 Granite St (☎02 6584 7759, ⓦwww.ricksdiveschool.com.au) run a full programme of PADI courses.

Horse-riding
Bellrowan Valley Horse Riding (☎02 6587 5227, ⓦwww.bellrowanvalley.com.au), 28km inland from Port Macquarie, offer trail rides through beautiful bushland. Rides range from a one-hour trip (A$55) to a two-day tour, spending the night at a country pub or a rustic homestead (A$299). Beginners welcome.

Scenic flights
Akuna Seaplanes (☎1300 369 216 or 0412 507698, ⓦwww.akunaseaplanes.com .au) take off from the Town Green boat ramp (from A$50 for 12min, min 2 people); between June and October, they'll take you whale-watching. If you'd rather feel the breeze, you can go microlighting with **Midcoast Microlights** (☎0428 850 062).

Surfing
Port Macquarie Surf School (☎02 6585 5453, ⓦwww.portmacquariesurfschool .com.au) and **NSW Institute of Surfing** (☎02 6584 1477, ⓦwww.nswios.com.au) are the busiest local training outfits, with two-hour beginner lessons on Town Beach for A$30–45. For something a little different, check out **Soul Surfing** (☎02 6582 0114, ⓦwww.soulsurfing.com.au) who offer half-day surfing safaris, driving you off in search of that perfect off-beat spot (from A$48), and three- to five-day retreats, an inspired combination of surfing, yoga and restaurant-hopping (from A$615) with accommodation at *The Observatory* (see p.356).

Waterskiing and wakeboarding
Inland at **Stoney Park** (☎02 6585 0080, ⓦwww.stoneypark.com.au) on Hacks Ferry Road, Telegraph Point, 20km northwest of town, you can take to the water on purpose-built lakes.

Spicy Yahmorthai Clarence St, corner of Hay St
☏02 6583 9043. Busy local Thai serving good-
value favourites including red, green and yellow
curries, stir-fries and Thai salads. Daily 5.30–10pm.
Splash 3/2 Horton St ☏02 6584 4027, ⓦwww
.restaurantsplash.com. Newish but already one of
Port's best restaurants, this upmarket place has a
fresh interior and a large outdoor dining area

overlooking the river. The delicious, Mod Oz menu
is notable for its oysters and a well-thought-out
wine list. Mon–Fri lunch & dinner, Sat dinner only.
Tommy's by the Beach 4 Flynn St ☏02 6583
5477. Hugely popular for its cabaret and music
nights, this party restaurant serves up hearty
steaks and good seafood. Dinner from 6pm
Mon–Sat.

Listings

Car rental Hertz, 102 Gordon St ☏02 6583 6599;
Thrifty, 101 Hastings River Drive ☏02 6584 2122.
Festivals A two-week regional Heritage Festival
(☏02 6581 8623) takes place in March or April,
featuring concerts, walking tours and local-history
talks. In Dec, the Sundowner Breakwall Tourist Park
hosts a two-day music event, the Festival of the
Sun (ⓦwww.fotsun.com).
Hospital Port Macquarie Hospital, Wright's Rd
☏02 6581 2000.
Internet access Port PC & Electronic Service,

2/15 Short St (daily 9am–7pm); Port Surf Hub, 57
Clarence St (daily 9am–6pm).
NPWS 152 Horton St ☏02 6586 8300.
Police ☏02 6583 0199.
Post office Shop 2, Palm Court Centre, 14–16
Short St.
Supermarkets and provisions Coles, corner of
Short & Hayward sts (daily 6am–midnight). The
Fishermen's Co-op, near the town wharf, sells fresh
fish and seafood.
Taxis Port Macquarie Taxicabs ☏02 6581 0081.

The Macleay Valley and Nambucca Heads

The coastline between Port Macquarie and Nambucca (pronounced "nam bucker") Heads, 115km to the north, has some magical spots. **KEMPSEY**, though not one of them, is a large service-town on the Macleay River, 49km from Port Macquarie, and home to a prominent Aboriginal population, the **Dunghutti** people. The Dunghutti's ability to demonstrate continuous links with their territory led in 1996 to a successful native title claim for a portion of land at **CRESCENT HEAD**, 21km southeast of Kempsey. The agreement was both the first recognition of native title by an Australian government on the mainland, and the first time that an Australian government negotiated an agreement with indigenous people to acquire their land. There are some wonderful waterfront **campsites** around Crescent Head, including *Delicate Nobby Camping Ground* on Point Plomer Road (☏02 6566 0144; A$20–22), set in secluded bushland ten minutes' drive from the township.

Slightly further up the coast is **Hat Head National Park** and the small town of **SOUTH WEST ROCKS**, perched on a picturesque headland. The excellent *Hat Head Holiday Park* (☏02 6567 7555 or 1800 006 600, ⓦwww.4shoreholidayparks.com.au; camping A$25–28, cabin ❸) is the best place to stay. Further north, back on the Pacific Highway, you'll pick up signs for **TAYLORS ARM** and *The Pub with No Beer*, one of the two hostelries that market themselves as the inspiration for the popular Australian folk song of the same name, recorded in the 1950s by Kempsey's most famous son, the late Slim Dusty. While the song is indeed about the *Taylors Arm Hotel*, the poem on which it was based is about the *Day Dawn Hotel* in Ingham, Queensland, destroyed by fire some time ago (see p.555).

Further north again is the laid-back family-holiday town of **NAMBUCCA HEADS**, which overlooks the sandy, island-strewn mouth of the Nambucca

River and is backed by the Nambucca State Forest. Though many travellers pass it by, it has a very pretty setting, with great **swimming** in the crystal-clear lagoon at the rivermouth and good **surf** on Main Beach, patrolled and easy to reach from town, and even better waves at Beilby's and Shelly beaches, nearer the rivermouth. South of town, an easy 28-kilometre drive away by road, is the popular surfing spot of **Scotts Head**, which is also a good place for whale-watching (June–Sept).

Nambucca Heads is on the main Sydney–Brisbane **bus** and **train** routes, with Greyhound, Premier Motor Service and CountryLink (see p.35) calling in: long-distance buses stop just off the Pacific Highway, a couple of kilometres from the town centre, near the **Nambucca Valley Visitor Information Centre** (daily 9am–5pm; ☎02 6568 6954, ⓦwww.nambuccatourism.com). Busways operate a skeleton bus service between Nambucca Heads and Urunga, Coffs Harbour and Bellingen.

To explore the river at a gentle pace, you can hire a **houseboat** from Nambucca River Houseboats (☎02 6568 9313, ⓦwww.nambuccariverhouse boats.com); a boat sleeping six costs A$495 for a weekend (Fri–Mon) or A$825 per week in high season. A good **place to stay** in town is *Oceanview*, 2 Fraser St (☎02 6568 6138, ⓦwww.oceanviewnambucca.com), which has simple but modern rooms (❸) and fresh, stylish apartments (❺). For families, the exceptionally well-located *White Albatross Holiday Resort* (☎02 6568 6468 or 1800 152 505, ⓦwww.whitealbatross.com.au; camping A$42–52, van ❷, cabin ❹, villa ❺) at the end of Wellington Drive is a great choice, right on the lagoon and ocean beach. Alternatively, *Marcel Towers Beach House* at 12 Wellington Drive (☎02 6568 7041, ⓦwww.marceltowers.com.au; ❹), a three-storey building on the waterfront, has reasonably priced, though somewhat frumpy, apartments. *Bluewater Brasserie* (lunch & dinner daily; ☎02 6568 6344) on Wellington Drive serves good pub **food** on a veranda overlooking the lagoon and river. Slightly upriver but also on Wellington Drive, 🍴 *Matilda's* (Mon–Sat lunch & dinner; ☎02 6588 6024) is a long-standing favourite with locals, serving up delicious Mod Oz food in a cute yet classy building.

The Bellinger Region

The **Bellinger Region**, just south of Coffs Harbour, is a beautiful area that truly has something for everyone. It comprises the pristine seaboard around **Urunga** and **Mylestom**, the charming, arty country town of **Bellingen**, the lush **Bellinger Valley** and the village of **Dorrigo** near the spectacular, rainfor-ested **Dorrigo National Park**. Leading you into the heart of the region is the **Waterfall Way** (Route 78), a picturesque drive that climbs through pastoral landscapes up to the Dorrigo Plateau.

Urunga and Mylestom

URUNGA, 20km north of Nambucca Heads and 30km south of Coffs Harbour, is a small town on the wide Kalang River, close to the ocean. For travellers using public transport, it's the closest stop on the Pacific Highway or CountryLink North Coast railway to Bellingen: long-distance buses (see p.35) stop beside the highway at the **Bellingen Shire visitor information centre** (Mon–Sat 9am–5pm, Sun 10am–2pm). Nearby **MYLESTOM**, 12km north via the highway, is an undeveloped backwater that occupies a beautiful spot, sandwiched between the final reaches of the Bellinger River and the beach. You can take advantage of its riverside setting at the **Alma Doepel Reserve**'s sheltered, sandy river beach. Two minutes' walk to the east is a gorgeous sweep of surf beach – often gloriously deserted. There's a **campsite** in Mylestom, the *North Beach Caravan Park* on Beach Parade (☎02 6655 4250, ⓦwww.nbcp.net; camping A\$30–36, cabin ❸), along with a couple of restaurants, but you're really better off just stopping for a quick swim, then heading inland up into the valley.

Bellingen

Around 4km north of Urunga and 25km south of Coffs Harbour on the Pacific Highway, the Waterfall Way turn-off takes you 12km west to the bewitching little town of **BELLINGEN**, one of the most characterful spots in New South Wales – many people who come to "Bello" for a day-trip end up staying a week. It has a strong community feel and is full of thriving small businesses with a palpable alternative bent; you'll discover plenty of fair-trade clothing companies, organic food shops, therapy studios and creative cooperatives as you explore. It's also scattered with a superb selection of independently run, eco-minded cafés, restaurants and country B&Bs.

Arrival and information

If you're travelling to Bellingen by public transport it's best to ask your accommodation to arrange a transfer from Urunga's long-distance bus stop or train station, as local **bus** connections aren't great. Busways operate a skeleton daily service from Coffs Harbour, Urunga, Mylestom and Nambucca Heads, while Kean's run from Coffs and Dorrigo twice a week – the bus stop is at the corner of Hyde and Church streets, by the mural. The **tourist office**, at the Old Butter Factory (daily 9am–5pm; ☎02 6655 1522, ⓦwww.bellingermagic.com), can book accommodation, activities and festival tickets.

Each August, Bellingen hosts a lively three-day **Jazz and Blues Festival** (ⓦwww.bellingenjazzfestival.com.au), followed by the **Global Carnival** (ⓦwww.globalcarnival.com) of world music in late September or early

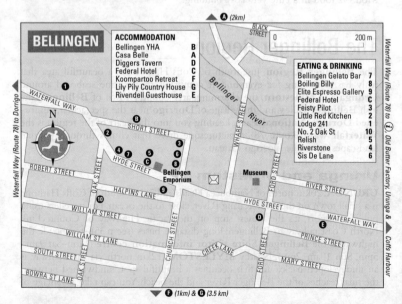

October. In January, **Camp Creative** (Ⓦwww.campcreative.com.au) takes over for five days, featuring an inspiring mixture of creative workshops, from Bollywood dancing, scriptwriting or mosaic-making to crash courses in clarinet.

Accommodation

For Bellingens events, you'll need to book **accommodation** well in advance.

Bellingen YHA 2 Short St Ⓣ02 6655 1116, Ⓦwww.bellingenyha.com.au. With views towards the Bellinger River, this beautiful two-storey timber house is one of Australia's most relaxed and atmospheric hostels. It appeals to creative, back-to-nature types: the sleeping options include bunks on a balcony. By day, you can join an affably guided excursion to Dorrigo National Park or the alternative, mostly nudist, community at Bundagen, or go tubing on the river. Bunk in shared room A$25–30, private double ➋

Casa Belle 90 Gleniffer Rd Ⓣ02 6655 9311, Ⓦwww.casabelle.com. Gorgeous B&B in an Italian-style villa, like a nugget of Tuscany transported to North Bellingen. Everything – from the tranquil atmosphere to the generously late check-out – is geared towards total relaxation. ➎

Diggers Tavern 30 Hyde St Ⓣ02 6655 0007, Ⓦwww.diggerstavern.com.au. This large town-centre pub has a block of en-suite motel rooms at the back – they're very plain for Bellingen, but comfortable, orderly and cheap. ➌

Federal Hotel 77 Hyde St Ⓣ02 6655 1003 Ⓦwww.federalhotel.com.au. The town's favourite hostelry has above-average pub rooms with shared bathrooms, including some with dorm-style bunks. Bunk in shared room A$25–40, private double ➋

Koompartoo Retreat Dudley St Ⓣ02 6655 2326, Ⓦwww.koompartoo.com.au. Tucked away on the south side of town amongst five acres of fragrant forest, rich in birdlife, are these four hardwood chalets. Furnished in country-cottage style, they have mini-kitchens, BBQs and fabulous elevated balconies. ➎

Lily Pily Country House 54 Sunny Corner Rd Ⓣ02 6655 0522, Ⓦwww.lilypily.com.au. This tranquil farmland retreat has a strikingly modern, eco-sensitive shell, while the interior feels like a traditional, but luxurious, country B&B. The lovely rooms and verandas have views of forest and rolling countryside. Art lessons by arrangement. ➏

Rivendell Guesthouse 10–12 Hyde St Ⓣ02 6655 0060, Ⓦwww.rivendellguesthouse.com.au. Welcoming Federation-style house, with a small pool and pretty rooms with shady verandas; a full cooked breakfast plus after-dinner port and choccies are included. ➍

The Town

Just off Waterfall Way on the eastern approach to town is the **Old Butter Factory** (daily 9am–4.30pm; Ⓣ02 6655 1522, Ⓦwww.bellingen.com /butterfactory): well worth a browse, this renovated dairy houses galleries and craft shops representing Bellingen's many painters, ceramicists and leather-workers; there's also a pleasant café. Bellingen Park, just south of the centre, is the site of an interesting monthly **market** (third Sat of the month 7am–2pm) with buskers, crafts and organic food, while a predominantly foodie Growers' Market is held on the second and fourth Saturday.

Hyde Street in the town centre has a quirky, villagey, Federation feel. There's eclectic shopping for right-on designer clothing and ethnic housewares at the **Bellingen Emporium**, in the former Hammond and Wheatley department store, its grand interior gloriously restored. At **Heartland Didgeridoos**, opposite the Shell garage (Ⓦwww.heartlanddidgeridoos.com.au), you can make your own didj, try one out in front of the presumably long-suffering owner, or book a masterclass. Also on Hyde Street is the town's local history **museum** (A$2), run by volunteers and stuffed with old photos.

For a cooling break from crafts and culture, head down to the tranquil Bellinger River; the **rope swings** on the riverbank are great fun, and you can **swim** back into town (or float if you're staying at the *YHA* and borrow one of their tubes). **Bellingen Canoe Adventures**, based just east of town in Fernmount (☎02 6655 9955, ⊚www.canoeadventures.com.au), are much-recommended; their daily river meanders bring sightings of koalas, eagles and the odd dolphin. Half-day tours cost A$44 (child A$22), and sunset and full-moon trips with champagne are also available (A$22).

At dusk, as the flying foxes flap their way across the rooftops, you may see a fairy-lit **horse-drawn carriage** roaming the streets – thirty-minute rides cost A$15, while short ghost tours are A$10 (☎02 6655 0270, ⊚www.fairytaletours.com.au).

Eating, drinking and entertainment

For a night out, the place to head is the *Federal Hotel* on Hyde Street, where there's nearly always a local band or singer performing. The Bellinger population includes an unusually high proportion of **musicians** – David Helfgott (whose life was dramatized in the 1996 film, *Shine*) lives nearby, and if you're very lucky, you might catch one of his rare piano performances somewhere in town.

Bellingen Gelato Bar 101 Hyde St ☎02 6655 1870. Stylish *gelateria* with Fifties-style decor, a cool old jukebox, funky lighting, delicious cakes and mouthwatering Italian-style ice cream, hand-made on the premises using all-natural ingredients. Mon & Tues 11am–6pm, Wed 10am–6pm, Thurs–Sat 10am–8pm, Sun 10am–6pm.

Boiling Billy 7F Church St ☎02 6655 1947. Cosy place serving good coffee, warming porridge, Turkish breakfasts and wholesome veggie lunches. Mon–Fri 8am–4pm, Sat & Sun 8am–2pm.

Elite Espresso Gallery 62 Hyde St ☎0402 364 705. Spacious and buzzing, with local art on the walls and jazz on the stereo. You'll find masses of healthy breakfast and lunch options here; there's also web access (terminals and Wi-Fi). Mon–Fri 9am–5pm, Sat 9am–noon.

Federal Hotel 77 Hyde St ☎02 6655 1003. This animated, heritage-listed pub is Bello's social hub, with excellent live music in the bar and good, hearty brasserie food in the stylish and hugely popular restaurant, *Relish* (lunch & dinner daily).

Feisty Pilot 5 Church St ☎02 6655 0840. With characteristic Bello wackiness, this sushi bar has a New Age-meets-manga feel, selling an assortment of Japanese oddments and offbeat clothing as well as good sushi. Mon–Sat 9am–4pm.

Little Red Kitchen 111 Hyde St ☎02 6655 1551. Good for an evening meal on a budget, this bohemian spot offers tasty pizza (A$15–25) and

pasta (A$15–17) to eat in or take away. Mon & Wed–Sun 5–9pm.

🏃 **Lodge 241** 117 Hyde St ☎02 6655 2470. This striking, balconied, Federation-style building houses a fabulous gallery-café with bucolic views over hills and creeks – a perfect place to relax with a coffee and newspaper. Lunchtime specials (around A$15) may include baked polenta with ratatouille, or wild game pâté. A chess club holds open meetings here on Sundays. Wed–Sun 8.30am–4pm.

🏃 **No. 2 Oak St** ☎02 6695 5000. Locals get a glazed look in their eyes when you mention this one; the multiple-award-winning restaurant is everyone's favourite, and rustles up some truly stunning contemporary Australian food in a cute heritage cottage. At A$30–35 for a main course, it's well worth the treat. Tues–Sat from 6.30pm; booking advisable.

Riverstone 105–109 Hyde St ☎02 6655 9099, ⊚www.riverstonecafe.com.au. Funky open-fronted café run by an organic coffee expert who dedicated months to creating the perfect blend; it also offers wholesome light meals, interesting beers and a short-but-sweet wine list. Daily 8am–2.30pm, also Fri 6–9pm.

Sis De Lane 7C Church St ☎02 6655 2973. Appealing café offering ricotta pancakes with grilled banana and honey for breakfast, quality antipasto at lunchtime and amazing carrot cake for afternoon tea.

Dorrigo National Park

From Bellingen, the Waterfall Way continues northwest, winding steeply past spectacular lookouts to the Dorrigo Plateau and **DORRIGO NATIONAL PARK**. This World Heritage-listed area contains startlingly beautiful remnants of rainforest that have been protected since 1901; prior to that, much of the surrounding region had been decimated by loggers, lured by its valuable stocks of red cedar and hoop pine.

The **Rainforest Centre**, 4km southeast of town via Waterfall Way and Dome Road (daily 9am–4.30pm; free; ☎02 6657 2309), is a great facility, which makes the national park unusually accessible; it has displays on flora and fauna, a café and maps of **walking trails**. Several trails start right behind the centre: the **Skywalk**, an elevated boardwalk extending high over the rainforest canopy for 200m, is the most spectacular and also the least strenuous. Others range from the Satinbird Stroll (a 600-metre circuit) up to the Wonga Walk (6.6km return), which winds through the rainforest and underneath the Crystal Shower and Tristania falls. It's cool, misty and slightly eerie down on the forest floor, and easy to believe you're miles from anywhere as huge trees and vines soar overhead. All the walks starting behind the centre are open from 5am to 10pm daily, so visitors can observe the forest's nocturnal creatures; by day, you're likely to hear the calls of regent bowerbirds, eastern whipbirds and superb lyrebirds. Wilder trails, with more majestic waterfalls and great escarpment views, begin from the Never Never Picnic Area, a further 10km down Dome Road. There are no campsites in the park, but **bushcamping** is allowed.

Dorrigo

DORRIGO is a sleepy rural village with cool highland air and wide streets. Compared to Bellingen it's little visited, but its main strip, Hickory Street, has some appealing gallery shops, cafés and delis, and there are excellent bushwalking trails nearby. **Dorrigo National Park** should be first on your list of places to visit; with more time, you could set out to explore some of the other natural attractions within day-trip distance, including Cathedral Rock, Mount Hyland, Guy Fawkes River and the New England National Park. Nearer to the village, there's a magnificent waterfall, **Dangar Falls**, just 2km north of the centre. The three-day **Dorrigo Folk and Bluegrass Festival** (Ⓦwww.dorrigo.com /festival) is held at the town's Showgrounds in late October each year.

Practicalities

The only way to get to Dorrigo on **public transport** is with Kean's (see p.317), whose buses run here from Coffs Harbour via Bellingen twice a week, stopping at the corner of Hickory and Cudgery streets. The **tourist office** at 36 Hickory St (daily 10am–4pm; ☎02 6657 2486, Ⓦwww.dorrigo.com) can advise you on **accommodation** in the area. Options include farmstays, holiday houses and pleasant country B&Bs such as *Gracemere Grange*, 325 Dome Rd, near the national park (☎02 6657 2630, Ⓦwww.gracemeregrange.com.au; bed in shared room A$30, private double ❸), a comfortable place owned by an inveterate traveller with a collection of keepsakes from around the world; or *Tallawalla Retreat*, 113 Old Coramba Rd (☎02 6657 2315, Ⓦwww.tallawalla.com; ❸), which has a seven-acre garden and a solar-heated pool. In town, you can rent a simple cottage with bedroom, bathroom and kitchenette at *Misty's*, 33 Hickory St (☎02 6657 2855; ❹), which is Dorrigo's favourite **restaurant**, serving gorgeous contemporary regional cuisine in a charming 1920s weatherboarded house (lunch Tues–Fri, dinner Fri & Sat). The *Lick the Spoon Café* at *Waterfall Way Winery*, 51–53 Hickory St (☎02 6657 1373, Ⓦwww.waterfallwaywinery.com), offers gourmet deli lunches and home-made gluten-free cakes, while aperitif-style fortified wines ferment in vast steel drums out the back – persimmon and other fruity flavours are the house specialities (available for tasting Mon–Fri 10am–4pm & Sat 10am–noon).

Coffs Harbour

Back on the Pacific Highway, **COFFS HARBOUR** is beautifully set at a point where the mountains of the Great Dividing Range fall almost directly into the South Pacific Ocean, and boasts glorious expanses of white sand to the north. Stunning eucalyptus forests signal the approach to Coffs on the Pacific Highway; the town itself, though far less pretty, is a lot of fun, with more activities than you can shake a stick at. Offshore, the **Solitary Islands** are notable for diving, with fringing coral reefs and a plethora of fish, while migrating whales pass by between June and October or November.

Arrival, orientation and information

All long-distance buses stop at the **bus station** on the corner of McLean Street and the Pacific Highway: Greyhound and Premier Motor Service (see p.35) stop here on their East Coast runs. Kean's link the town with Bellingen and Dorrigo; Busways run to Bellingen, Urunga and Nambucca Heads; and Ryans to Grafton (see p.317). The **train station**, down at the harbour, is on the CountryLink North Coast line (see p.35). You can fly direct to Coffs from Sydney (Qantas or Virgin Blue), Brisbane or Port Macquarie (both Brindabella); the Coffs Coast regional **airport** (CFS; ☎02 6648 4837) is a very short taxi journey south of town.

Coffs is rather spread out; **to get around**, the options include renting a car or bike (see p.39 & p.44), hiring taxis (☎13 10 08), or travelling by local bus. The town is split into three distinct sections: the CBD and mall; the jetty area, around 2km to the east; and the northern suburbs of Sapphire Beach, Moonee Beach Reserve and Emerald Beach. Busways route 365 covers the CBD and jetty areas (once or twice hourly Mon–Sat, skeleton service Sun; ☎02 6652 2744), while Ryans run up to the beaches (4 daily Mon–Fri, 2 daily Sat).

The helpful **tourist office**, just off the Pacific Highway, next to the bus station (daily 9am–5pm; ☎02 6648 4990 or 1300 369 070, ⊛www.coffscoast .com.au), can book accommodation for you.

Accommodation

As well as the options below, Coffs has an abundance of **self-catering** places, particularly along Ocean Parade. Many of these require you to make a booking of at least a week during the busy Christmas and Easter holidays.

Hostels

Aussitel Backpackers 312 Harbour Drive ☎02 6651 1871 or 1800 330 335, ⊛www .aussitel.com. Very friendly backpackers', bursting with "all down the pub together" spirit. Good facilities, plus helpful management, heated pool, free use of canoes, boogie-boards and surfboards, cheap bike hire and lots of activities. Bunk A$28, private double/twin ❷

Barracuda Backpackers 19 Arthur St ☎02 6651 3514, ⊛www.backpackers.coffs.tv. Small, chilled-out place close to the best surfing spots in town, with free use of boogie-boards and surfboards, and low rates. Bunk A$22, private double/twin ❷

Coffs Harbour YHA 51 Collingwood St ☎02 6652 6462, ⊛www.yha.com.au. This huge, modern hostel has faultless facilities and very helpful staff who can sign you up for an avalanche of activities. Bikes are available to rent (A$10) and there's a pleasant pool area. Bunk A$25–33, en-suite double/twin ❷

Holiday parks

Moonee Beach Holiday Park Moonee Beach Rd (east of the Pacific Hwy) ☎02 6653 6552 or 1800 184 120, ⊛www.moonee.com.au. Magical tent or van sites and well-equipped cabins in bush surroundings, with beach, estuary and headlands to explore. Camping A$25–37, cabin ❸

Park Beach Holiday Park Ocean Parade ☎02 6648 4888 or 1800 200 111, ⊛www .parkbeachholidaypark.com.au. Huge, well-ordered and highly family-oriented campsite, close to the beach, with BBQ, pool and playground, plus kids'

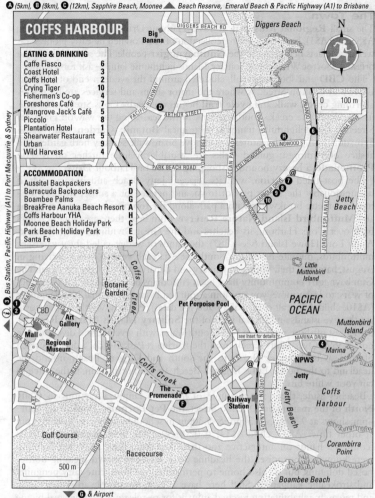

COFFS HARBOUR

Big Banana

Diggers Beach

Diggers Beach Rd

N

0   100 m

EATING & DRINKING

Caffe Fiasco	6
Coast Hotel	3
Coffs Hotel	2
Crying Tiger	10
Fishermen's Co-op	4
Foreshores Café	7
Mangrove Jack's Café	5
Piccolo	8
Plantation Hotel	1
Shearwater Restaurant	5
Urban	9
Wild Harvest	4

ACCOMMODATION

Aussitel Backpackers	F
Barracuda Backpackers	G
Boambee Palms	A
BreakFree Aanuka Beach Resort	H
Coffs Harbour YHA	C
Moonee Beach Holiday Park	E
Park Beach Holiday Park	B
Santa Fe	B

Jetty Beach

Little Muttonbird Island

PACIFIC OCEAN

Muttonbird Island

Botanic Garden

Coffs Creek

CBD

Art Gallery

Mall

Regional Museum

Pet Porpoise Pool

see Inset for details

Marina

NPWS

Jetty

Coffs Harbour

The Promenade

Railway Station

Corambirra Point

Golf Course

Racecourse

Boambee Beach

0   500 m

G & Airport

A (5km), B (9km), C (12km), Sapphire Beach, Moonee Beach Reserve, Emerald Beach & Pacific Highway (A1) to Brisbane

Bus Station, Pacific Highway (A1) to Port Macquarie & Sydney

activities during the holidays. Camping A$27–$46, cabin ❷, villa ❹

B&Bs and resort hotels

Boambee Palms 5 Kasch Rd, Boambee (west of the Pacific Hwy, 7km south of Coffs) ☏02 6658 4545, ⓦwww.boambeepalms.com.au. Luxury B&B aimed at couples, just inland from the delightful village of Sawtell. The four suites are very stylishly done out, and there's tennis, a pool and BBQ, plus yummy breakfasts. ❺

BreakFree Aanuka Beach Resort 11 Firman Drive ☏02 6652 7555, ⓦwww.aanuka.com.au.

A comfortable, family-friendly option in a leafy spot right on the beachfront, this resort has attractively decorated rooms with ethnic touches, plus tennis courts and a prettily landscaped swimming pool. ❺

Santa Fe 235 The Mountain Way, Sapphire Beach (off Gaudrons Rd, west of the Pacific Hwy) ☏02 6653 7700, ⓦwww.santefe.net.au. This designer B&B with a Mexican feel boasts three beautifully decorated guest-suites with private decks, lush gardens, a pool, hammocks and gourmet breakfasts – a great place to spoil yourself. ❺

The Town

The small **Regional Museum**, at 191A Harbour Drive (Tues–Sat 10am–4pm; A\$3, child A\$1), has an interesting collection of relics owned by early pioneers, as well as artefacts belonging to the **Gumbaynggirr** people. The star exhibit is the original, Doctor Who-esque Solitary Islands lighthouse lamp – ask for a demo.

The **CBD** and shopping mall, clustered around the western end of Harbour Drive and Grafton Street, is where the major shops and services are located. A charming **creek walk** and **cycle trail** begins on nearby Coffs Street and winds its way down the creek's southern bank to the sea. Along the way, off Hardacre Street, is the delightfully tranquil, subtropical **Botanic Garden** (daily 9am–5pm; donation), which features a mangrove boardwalk, sensory herb garden and a slice of rainforest; guided walks are available. A little further on is **The Promenade**, a breezy boutique shopping centre on Harbour Drive.

The boat-filled **marina**, with its adjacent Jetty Beach and historic pier, is unquestionably the nicest part of town, and perfect for a sunset stroll. A five-hundred-metre breakwater with a path along the top runs between the marina and **Muttonbird Island Nature Reserve**; from here, there are fantastic views back over Coffs Harbour, its beaches and the Great Dividing Ranges beyond. As on Lord Howe Island (see p.387), thousands of wedge-tailed shearwaters, or muttonbirds, migrate here from Southeast Asia each year to breed, arriving in August, hatching their young in January and departing once again in April. The Gumbaynggirr commmunity have been custodians of the colony for thousands of years; to learn more, you can join a tour led by an Aboriginal NPWS ranger (A\$10, child A\$5; call ☎02 6652 0900 for dates). Partially visible to the north are the five islands and several islets of the **Solitary Islands Marine Reserve**, the largest offshore reserve in New South Wales, with several good dive sites (see box, p.369). Over Coffs Creek from the marina is Park Beach, a decent stretch of sand, as is Boambee Beach to the south and Digger's Beach around the headland to the north. Little Digger's Beach, to the north again, is the place to tan your white bits.

Beaches aside, there are a couple of must-see family attractions in Coffs. North of the marina on Orlando Street, the **Pet Porpoise Pool** (daily 9am–4pm; shows at 9.30am, 12.30pm & 3.30pm in school holidays, or 10am & 1pm at other times; A\$27, child A\$14; ☎02 6659 1900, ⓦwww.petporpoisepool.com) is a hands-on, interactive zoo that dates from the days when dolphins were known as porpoises; the headline act is a cast of crowd-pleasing bottle-nosed dolphins, but it's also home to performing sea lions, cute fairy penguins, and strokeable kangaroos. Staff here have a background role in conservation and research, rehabilitating rescued animals for re-release. The other real biggie in town is the **Big Banana** amusement park, 3km north of Coffs on the Pacific Highway (daily 9am–4.30pm; free entry, rides and shows from A\$5 each; ☎02 6652 4355, ⓦwww.bigbanana.com), announced by a hideous, inexplicably iconic concrete banana. Most visitors skip the multimedia show about the banana industry and get straight down to the serious business of ice-skating, tobogganing down the giant slide, buying banana-related merchandise and eating chocolate-covered bananas.

Eating, drinking and nightlife

The Harbour Drive mall has a wealth of daytime-only **cafés**, which are good for a sandwich, albeit in less-than-scenic surrounds; in the evening, head for the **restaurants** on the creekside or at the jetty end of the drive. **Nightlife** is covered by the *Plantation*, *Coffs* and *Coast* hotels on Grafton Street (the Pacific Highway), catering for locals, backpackers and classier punters, respectively

The Coffs Coast is a great place for active people, with plenty of watersports on offer; for land-based adventure, the beautiful rivers and hiking trails of the Bellinger Region (see p.361) are within easy reach.

Canoeing, kayaking and rafting

For a wild experience, you'll want to hit the ocean, or head inland to raft the spectacular Nymboida River, north of Dorrigo: by camping in the wilderness overnight, you can reach some truly bracing spots. **Liquid Assets Adventure Tours**, 38 Marina Drive (℗02 6658 0850, ⓦwww.surfrafting.com) will take you sea-kayaking or surf-rafting in the Pacific (half day A$50); they'll also run you up to the Nymboida for river-kayaking (half day A$50) or white-water rafting (1 day A$160, 2 days A$360). **Wildwater Adventures** on Hubbard St, Woolgoolga (℗02 6654 1114, ⓦwww.wildwateradventures.com.au), run river-rafting trips lasting two or four days (A$360–600). If you'd rather just potter about on Coffs Creek in town, you can hire a canoe or pedal-boat from **Promenade Canoes**, The Promenade, 321 Harbour Drive (A$12–25/hr; ℗02 6651 1032, ⓦwww.promenadecanoes.com.au).

Circus skills

Zip Circus (℗02 6656 0768, ⓦwww.zipcircus.com.au) run fun flying-trapeze classes for all ages (3yr+) in the grounds of the *Novotel Pacific Bay Resort*, on the north side of town (A$50).

Diving

The mingling of tropical and temperate waters draws a huge variety of sealife – including grey nurse sharks and, in summer, manta rays – to the **Solitary Islands Marine Reserve**. Certified divers can get there with Jetty Dive Centre, 398 Harbour Drive (℗02 6651 1611, ⓦwww.jettydive.com.au) for A$95 plus A$35 for gear (two dives); snorkellers can come along for A$55. This 5-star PADI centre offers a full training programme (4-day Open Water course A$395).

Horse-riding

Valery Trails, Valery Rd, 20km southwest of Coffs off the Pacific Highway at Bonville (℗02 6653 4301, ⓦwww.valerytrails.com.au) will take you out for a two-hour ride through the Bongil Bongil rainforest (daily; A$50); they also run weekend trips through the Bellinger Region, staying overnight at the *Federal Hotel* in Bellingen (A$300).

Scenic flights

You can zoom around in a chopper with **Strath Air Helicopters**, based at the airport (from A$49 for 8min; ℗02 6652 7508, ⓦwww.coffsharbourhelicopters.com.au).

Sky diving

Coffs City Skydivers (℗02 6651 1167, ⓦwww.coffsskydivers.com.au) do tandem dives from 3050m (A$325), plus solo-jump training courses. Great views of the Coffs Coast and the Great Dividing Range on the way down – if you can bear to look.

Surfing

There are over twenty surfable beaches on the Coffs Coast. For lessons, contact **East Coast Surf School** at Diggers Beach (℗02 6651 5515, ⓦwww.eastcoastsurfschool.com.au), or **Lee Winkler** at Coffs Harbour Surf Life Saving Club on Park Beach (℗02 6650 0050, ⓦwww.leewinklersurfschool.com.au): both offer intro sessions for A$45–55, and coaching to advanced levels.

Whale- and dolphin-watching

Cruise companies base themselves at the marina. **Pacific Explorer**, a sailing catamaran with a highly responsible and experienced crew, will take you whale-watching in season (June–Oct; A$30; ℗02 6652 8988). **Spirit Of Coffs Harbour Cruises** (℗02 6650 0155) also run whale-watching trips (A$39), plus daily dolphin-spotting cruises (A$35).

– all are pretty lively in summer, and between them you'll find live music most nights.

Caffe Fiasco 22 Orlando St ☏02 6651 2006. Hip, noisy, family-run Italian restaurant delivering delicious traditional fare – including wonderful focaccia and pizza from the wood-fired oven – in a contemporary setting. Pizza under A$20; other mains A$24–34. Dinner Tues–Sun, plus Sun breakfast & lunch (7.30am–3pm).

Crying Tiger Harbour Drive ☏02 6650 0195. Contemporary Thai with a very Zen interior. A little pricier than average, but the beautiful curries and stir-fries more than justify it. Daily from 5.30pm.

Fishermen's Co-op 69 Marina Drive ☏02 6652 2811. Famously good fish 'n' chips, using nothing but fresh, wild-caught seafood; you can eat on the deck or take away. Daily until early evening.

Foreshores Café 394 Harbour Drive ☏02 6652 3127. Large, airy place where they stack their burgers with extras; other brunch or lunch options include pasta dishes and Greek salad. Daily 7.30am–3pm.

Mangrove Jack's Café The Promenade, 321 Harbour Drive ☏02 6652 5517. The decor isn't quite as polished as at the *Shearwater* (see opposite), but there are the same fine creek views and slightly flashier, more expensive food. Daily from 7am for breakfast & lunch, Tues–Sat dinner.

Piccolo 390 Harbour Drive ☏02 6651 9599. Stylish Italian eatery that wouldn't look out of place in Sydney or Melbourne. The low-level lighting, scarlet floor and cushion-stuffed window seats create an intimate atmosphere, complemented by delicious food. Mains under A$30. Tues–Sat from 6pm.

Shearwater Restaurant The Promenade, 321 Harbour Drive ☏02 6651 6053. Grab a veranda table overlooking Coffs Creek and feast on fabulous Mod Oz-style dishes, including seafood specials such as smoked tuna or beautifully dressed scallops. Mains A$22–28. Daily 8am–late.

Urban 384A Harbour Drive ☏02 6651 1989. Upbeat and extremely red coffee lounge serving top-notch lattes, "mugachinos" and espressos; favourites for lunch include pumpkin or Thai beef salad, fresh calamari and tasty wraps. Daily 7am–4pm.

Wild Harvest 69 Marina Drive ☏02 6651 6888. In this stylish, breezy spot with the ocean on one side and the marina on the other, you can tuck into bacon and eggs or pancakes for breakfast, or super-fresh seafood (sourced from the *Fishermen's Co-op* next door) for lunch. Daily 7am–4.30pm.

Listings

Bike rental Bob Wallis Cycles, 13 Orlando St (corner of Collingwood St) ☏02 6652 5102. A$18/half day, A$25/full day, A$40/two days.

Car rental Coffs Harbour Rent-a-Car ☏02 6651 5022; Europcar ☏02 6651 8558; Hertz ☏02 6651 1899; Thrifty ☏02 6652 8622.

Hospital 345 Pacific Hwy ☏02 6656 7000.

Internet access Public Library, corner of Coffs & Duke sts (Mon–Fri 9.30am–6pm, Sat 9.30am–2pm; free); there's cheap access at *Café Bonne Santé*,

38 Moonee St (Mon–Fri 7.30am–4pm; Wi-Fi and terminals) and Jetty Dive Centre, Harbour Drive (daily 8am–5pm; terminals).

NPWS 32 Marina Drive ☏02 6652 0900.

Police 22 Moonee St ☏02 6652 0299.

Post office In the CBD: U1, The Palms Centre, 35 Harbour Drive; in the jetty area: 354 Habour Drive, corner of Camperdown St.

Taxi ☏13 10 08.

Grafton and the Clarence River

GRAFTON, 83km north of Coffs Harbour and 169km south of Byron Bay via the Pacific Highway, is a pleasant district capital on a bend of the wide **Clarence River**, which almost encircles the city. Grafton is a genteel, old-fashioned town with wide, tree-lined avenues – head down Victoria and Fitzroy streets, lined with pretty, Federation-style houses, rather than the workaday main strip, Prince Street. The week-long **Jacaranda Festival** (late Oct to early Nov; Ⓦwww.jacarandafestival.org.au) celebrates the town's stunning jacaranda and flame trees, which come ablaze with purple, mauve and red blossoms in the spring. Out of festival time this is a quiet place, where the historic atmosphere is the main attraction. **Schaeffer House** at 190 Fitzroy St (Tues–Thurs & Sun 1–4pm; A$3; ☎02 6642 5212) is listed by the National Trust and lovingly preserved by the local historical society; it has a collection of beautiful china, glassware and period furniture. On the same street at no. 158 is the **Grafton Regional Gallery** (Tues–Sun 10am–4pm; free; ☎02 6642 3177), which has some fine temporary exhibitions and local artwork.

Practicalities

The staff at the **Clarence River Tourism Visitor Centre** on the Pacific Highway at the corner of Spring Street in South Grafton (daily 9am–5pm; ☎02 6642 4677, ⓦwww.clarencetourism.com), can give you information on scenic drives, out-of-town cruises and nearby national parks. CountryLink **train** services along the North Coast stop at Grafton station, close to the river crossing in South Grafton, while **long-distance buses** stop near the tourist office. Either way, it's a half-hour walk into the town proper, across a fine, split-level road-and-rail bridge. Grafton is on the main Sydney–Brisbane Greyhound and Premier Motor Service routes (see p.35); Ryans (see p.318) run buses to Coffs Harbour, while Busways (see p.317) run a regular service connecting South Grafton with the town centre. The Clarence Valley regional **airport** is 17km south of Grafton; you can fly there from Sydney with Regional Express, and take a taxi into town for around A$15 (☎13 10 08).

There's some decent **accommodation** in Grafton, notably in the two grand old pubs: the *Roches Family Hotel* at 85 Victoria St (☎02 6642 2866, ⓦwww.roches.com.au; ❶) and the *Crown Hotel Motel* at 1 Prince St (☎02 6642 4000, ⓦwww.crownhotelmotel.com; ❷–❸); both offer great-value rooms and pub food. The food is better at the former, and the location, right next to the river, more pleasant at the latter. More in keeping with the town's Victorian style is the delightful, though thoroughly chintzy, *Arcola B&B* at 150 Victoria St (☎02 6643 1760, ⓦwww.arcola.com.au; ❻), a heritage house on the banks of the river; included in the rate is a delicious, home-made afternoon tea and breakfast.

The best place to **eat** is *Georgie's* (Wed–Sat 10am–late, Sun 10am–4pm; ☎02 6642 3177) at the Regional Art Gallery; this much-praised place serves excellent sandwiches, light meals and treats in a leafy courtyard or inside amongst the art. Smart, contemporary Australian cuisine (mains A$20–25) is on the menu in the evenings. There are cafés, bistros and take-aways on Prince and Fitzroy streets.

Maclean, Yamba, Iluka and around

North of Grafton, the Pacific Highway runs close to the lower reaches of the Clarence River before looping away through open fields and then crossing the Clarence via the Harwood Bridge, around 50km downstream, 120km south of Byron Bay. Just west of the bridge is the small delta town of **Maclean**, which proclaims its Scottish heritage with tartan lampposts and street signs in Gaelic. For a scenic, riverside route between Grafton and Maclean, take Tourist Drive 22 via Lawrence.

East of Maclean, the drive continues to the coast, passing under the foot of the Harwood Bridge then following the Clarence to the pretty holiday village of **YAMBA**, an up-and-coming place with a fresh, surfie vibe. Facing it across the mouth of the river is its twin settlement, **ILUKA**; Busways run daily services to both from Grafton. Clarence River Ferries shuttle foot passengers between the two communities four times a day (A$6, child A$3; ☎02 6646 6423) and also run river cruises: on Sundays, they offer a four-hour lunchtime jazz cruise with a live band (A$25, child A$20), which you can join at either Yamba or Iluka. To go cruising in a sailing catamaran, hook up with Rockfish at the Yamba marina, who are on the water daily; they'll take you whale-watching in season (standard cruises from A$20; whale cruises A$100, child A$70; ☎02 6645 8153 or 0447 458 153, ⓦwww.rockfish.com.au).

In sun-drenched Yamba, far nicer than the many **motels** (❹) is the idyllic *Calypso Holiday Park* on Harbour Street (☎02 6646 8847, ⓦwww .calypsoyamba.com.au; camping A$27–31, cabins ❸). The *Pacific Hotel* commands a terrific location overlooking the picturesque Main Beach at 18 Pilot St (☎02 6646 2125, ⓦwww.pacifichotelyamba.com.au; basic double ❷, en-suite motel room ❺), and has decent pub rooms, great live music (Thurs–Sat), and an excellent, inexpensive **restaurant**. Other outstanding places to eat include the funky *Caper Berry Café* at 25 Yamba St for lunch (daily 6.30am–5pm; ☎02 6646 2322), *Gormans* on Yamba Bay for good, simple seafood and a pleasantly old-fashioned atmosphere (daily for lunch & dinner; ☎02 6646 2025) and *Sea Spray* on Clarence Street (daily for dinner; ☎02 6646 8336) for more stylish Mod Oz fare.

A few kilometres south of Yamba is **Yuraygir National Park**, with places to **bushcamp** (free) and numerous basic but attractive campsites (A$10, child A$5; vehicle fee A$7 per day; book via Grafton NPWS ☎02 6441 1500) and a spectacular strip of sand at Angourie Point, which became New South Wales' first **surfing reserve** in 2007. Eighty kilometres west of Grafton, the **Gwydir Highway** runs through the rugged and densely forested **Gibraltar Range** and **Washpool** national parks, both with walking tracks, bushcamping, lookout points and waterfalls galore.

Ballina and Lennox Head

Aroud 133km north of Grafton and 91km south of the state border, the Pacific Highway passes the old port of **Ballina**. It's largely ignored by the young holidaymakers who fly into its airport – Byron Bay, further north, is a far bigger draw – but it's a pleasant enough place, with waterways to explore. The fastest way between Ballina and Byron is via the highway, but a far more scenic alternative is to take the coast road, Tourist Drive 38, which offers stunning ocean views en route to **Lennox Head**, as laidback a beach town as Byron Bay is hectic.

Ballina

The old port of **BALLINA**, at the mouth of the Richmond River, is a quiet town with plenty of holiday accommodation, but very little glitz; it hasn't escaped the clutches of the "big things" though, with the **Big Prawn** marking the entrance to town on the highway from Grafton.

Arrival and information

Greyhound and Premier Motor Service (see p.35) connect Ballina by **long-distance bus** to all stops between Sydney and Brisbane; Kirklands run from Byron Bay, Brisbane, Lismore and Lennox Head. You can **fly** to Ballina Byron Gateway airport (BNK), 5km north of central Ballina, from Sydney with Virgin Blue, Regional Express or Jetstar (see p.35), who also have flights from Melbourne. Rental cars, taxis (☎02 6686 9999) and Byron Bay shuttle services (see p.376) can be picked up at the airport, while Blanch's (see p.317) run

local buses into town (A$3.40, child A$1.70 one way), as well as to Lennox Head, Byron Bay and Mullumbimby. To get around Ballina, you can rent **bikes** from Jack Ransom Cycles at 16 Cherry St (T02 6685 3485). The **Ballina Visitor Information Centre** (Mon–Fri 9am–5pm; T02 6686 3484, Wwww .discoverballina.com) in Las Balsas Plaza can book accommodation, river cruises and other tours.

Accommodation

Ballina Lakeside Holiday Park North of the river on Fenwick Drive T02 6686 3953 or 1800 888 268, Wwww.ballinalakeside.com.au. Good holiday park, right next to the lagoon with plenty of decent facilities. Camping A$27–39, cabins and villas ②–⑤

Ballina Manor 25 Norton St T02 6681 5888, Wwww.ballinamanor.com.au. This very grand, colonial-style place is the most upmarket hotel in town. ⑥

Ballina YHA Travellers Lodge 36 Tamar St T02 6686 6737, Wwww.yha.com.au. Clean hostel with a swimming pool, cheap bike hire and free use of boogie-boards, snorkel gear and skateboards. Bunk in four-share A$25–28, double/twin ②

Brundah B&B 37 Norton St T02 6686 8166, Wwww.brundah.com.au. Extremely pretty B&B set in a stunning heritage-listed Federation house with a beautiful garden. ⑤

Flat Rock Tent Park 38 Flat Rock Rd (just off the coast road, 5km north of Ballina) T02 6686 4848, Wwww.bscp.com.au. This unspoilt, unpowered site for tents only is set right on Angels Beach, perfect for a back-to-nature stay. Camping A$26.

The town and around

Four kilometres north on Gallans Road, east of the Pacific Highway, the tea trees of the **Thursday Plantation** (daily 9am–5pm; free; Wwww.thursday plantation.com) produce the all-healing oil; the plantation – with a sculpture park and tea-tree maze in the grounds, and a shop full of soothing goodies – makes for an interesting visit. On Regatta Avenue by Las Balsas Plaza is the **Maritime Museum** (daily 9am–4pm; donation; Wwww.ballinamaritime museum.org.au). Its star exhibit is a raft – with a sail painted with talismans designed by Salvador Dalí – from the 1973 Las Balsas expedition, in which three vessels set sail from Ecuador in an aim to prove that ancient South American civilizations could have traversed the Pacific. A mere 179 days and nine thousand miles later the twelve-strong crew arrived in Ballina, sporting some choice facial hair. A few doors down is **Richmond River Cruises** (from A$25, child A$12.50; T02 6687 5688), who run trips downriver. For the more actively inclined, **Ballina Kayak Tours** on River Street offer eco-tours, paddling through mangrove creeks (from A$45; T02 6685 3722, Wwww .ballinakayaks.com). To go it alone, call **Ballina Boat Hire**, also on River Street (T02 6681 6115 or 0403 810 277), who rent out tinnies and barbecue boats (from A$40/2hr).

Eating

For tasty alfresco **food**, *Shelly's on the Beach* at 6 Shelly Beach Rd (daily 7.30am–5pm; T02 6686 9844) has a variety of breakfasts and lunches, enticing cakes, and great views over Shelly's Beach – follow the bridge and sea wall 2km north of town. The *River Thai*, at 5 River St (Tues–Sat from 6pm; T02 6686 9774), serves excellent curries, stir-fries and the like, while for very civilized fine-dining try the restaurant at *Ballina Manor* (breakfast & dinner daily; see above). *Sandbar* (Wed–Sat dinner & drinks, Sat & Sun breakfast & lunch; T02 6696 6602), on Compton Drive just over the river, is the first designer-style place to hit Ballina and an excellent spot for early-evening drinks.

Lennox Head

LENNOX HEAD, 11km north of Ballina, is a relaxed place with a surfie feel and oodles of innocent, small-town charm. At the southern end of the fabulous Seven Mile Beach, The Point rates among the best **surfing** spots in the world, and professionals congregate here for the big waves in May, June and July. Catapult Boardsports on the beachfront (℡02 6687 5301) have gear for hire, and offer lessons in surfing, windsurfing and kiteboarding (from A$65). There are also great places to **hang-glide** along the coast between here and Byron Bay (see box, p.382). Adding to Lennox Head's appeal is the calm, fresh water of **Lake Ainsworth**; stained dark by the tea trees around its banks, it's a popular swimming spot for families seeking refuge from the crashing surf in the soft, practically medicinal water (it's effectively diluted tea-tree oil).

Practicalities

Since Lennox Head is off the Pacific Highway, no **long-distance buses** call here: the nearest stop is at Ballina. Two local bus services pass through: Blanch's (see p.317), running between Ballina Byron Gateway airport, Ballina and Byron Bay (8 daily Mon–Fri, 6 Sat, 3 Sun), and Kirklands (see p.318), from Lismore and Ballina (skeleton service).

There are a couple of inexpensive places to **stay** in town. *Lennox Head Beach House YHA* at 3 Ross St (℡02 6687 7636, ⓦwww.yha.com.au; bunk in four-share A$26–29, double ❷), is a great little hostel ideally situated between the lake and the beach, close to the bus stop; Reiki massage, reflexology and Bowen therapy are available in-house, and there's watersports gear to borrow or hire, plus a herb garden for creative cooks. *Lake Ainsworth Caravan* on Pacific Parade Park (℡02 6687 7249, ⓦwww.bscp.com.au; camping A$26–33, cabin ❸) is a fairly standard holiday park but superbly located right by the water. *Randall's on Ross* is a great B&B option at 9 Ross St (℡02 6687 7922; ❻), with excellent breakfasts and very comfy queen-sized beds, while the two fabulously hip luxury apartments at *Sanbah*, 16 Rayner Lane (℡02 6685 3844, ⓦwww.swellproperty .com.au; ❼) couldn't be better located: they're right on the beachfront in town.

The busiest part of Lennox Head is Ballina Street, set back from the beach at the south end of town; this is where you'll find the town's most stylish **restaurant**, *Quattro* (Mon 6–10pm, Tues–Sun 8am–10pm; ℡02 6687 6950), good for oysters, or pasta with rustic bread; a reliable Asian eatery, *Mi Thai* (Wed–Sun from 6pm); and *Café Bella* (breakfast & lunch daily; ℡02 6687 6893), a cute little place set back from the road, rustling up huge, succulent Turkish bread sandwiches, burritos and pancakes, with nothing over A$15. The *Lennox Point Hotel* on Pacific Parade, at the junction of the beachfront and the road from Byron Bay, serves good food in its bistro, *Ruby's by the Sea* (Wed–Sat lunch & dinner, Sun lunch; ℡02 6687 5769), while the pub itself is a convivial sort of place, with live music from Thursday to Sunday. Further north along the beachfront, *Seven Mile* on Pacific Parade (Tues–Sat dinner, Sun lunch; ℡02 6687 6210) has great sea views, a very bright colour scheme and bold Mod Oz food to match.

Byron Bay

Situated at the end of a long sweeping bay, within easy reach of over 30km of almost unbroken sandy beaches, the township of **BYRON BAY** is a crossroads for young backpackers, a hotspot for gay travellers and a "must do" on the

BYRON BAY

N

PACIFIC OCEAN

Cape Byron

Little Watego's Beach

Watego's Beach

MARINE PARADE

CAPE BYRON HEADLAND RESERVE

Lighthouse ●

Cosy Corner

Tallow Beach

Byron Bay

The Pass

PALM VALLEY DRIVE

LIGHTHOUSE ROAD

BAY STREET

BAY LANE

FLETCHER STREET

MIDDLETON STREET

P

R

S

MARVELL STREET

CARLYLE STREET

U

T

17

18

The Plaza

JONSON STREET

BUTLER STREET

16

Disused Railway Station

Swimming Pool

N

M

3

●

LAWSON STREET

15

BYRON STREET

LAWSON STREET

12 14 13

8 6 5 7 9 10 11

4

Clarke's Beach

F ●

Main Beach

The Wreck

Belongil Beach

Belongil Creek

The Epicentre ●

BORDER ST

CHLOE STREET

EWINGSDALE ROAD

KENDALL STREET

SHIRLEY STREET

BYRON STREET

SKINNERS RD

SCHOOL RD

Arts Factory ● G

E ●

D ●

see inset for detail

LAWSON STREET

MASSINGER STREET

CARLYLE STREET

COWPER ST

COWPER ST

BANGALOW RD

BROWNING ST

RUSKIN STREET

KINGSLEY STREET

TENNYSON ST

MARVELL ST

MIDDLETON ST

BYRON ST

FLETCHER ST

BAY STREET

L ●

J ●

@

2

JONSON ST

i

Disused Railway Station

Byron Cinemas

H ●

Arts and Industry Estate, Pacific Highway, A (3km), B (3km) & C (5km)
K (4km), L (6km), Lennox Head & Ballina

0   500 m
0   200 m

— Disused Railway

ACCOMMODATION

Amber Gardens Guesthouse	C
Amigos	I
Aquarius Guesthouse	P
Arcadia Guesthouse	J
Arts Factory Lodge	G
Backpackers Inn	D
Beach Hotel	M
Breakfree Eco Beach	E
Broken Head Holiday Park	L
The Byron at Byron	K
Byron Bathers	S
Byron Bay Beach Resort	A
Byron Bay Bunkhouse	T
Byron Bay YHA	U
Cape Byron YHA	R
Clarke's Beach Holiday Park	F
First Sun Holiday Park	N
Hotel Great Northern	Q
Holiday Village Backpackers	H
Main Beach Backpackers	O
Planula	B

EATING & DRINKING

Asia Joe's	7
The Balcony	8
Bay Leaf Café	17
Beach Hotel	M
Buddha Bar	G
Byron Street Bistro	15
Byronian Café	14
Cheeky Monkey	2
Cocomangas	13
Earth 'n' Sea	9
Fish Heads	3
Fishmongers	6
Fresh	5
Hotel Great Northern	Q
La La Land	11
Olivo	13
Orient Express	4
O-Sushi	18
Rae's on Watego's	1
The Rails	16
Twisted Sista Café	10
Why Not!	12

5

regular tourist circuit. Such is its cachet that an American magazine recently voted its main beach one of the sexiest in the world. Like many towns on the East Coast, it's in a state of change: once famously progressive, its small-community feel, free-for-all atmosphere and New Age ideals have faded under ever-encroaching commercialism, leaving it about as radical as MTV. But while the barefoot hippies have been priced out of town, the alternative therapists and organic provedores are thriving: little by little, Byron is morphing into a playground for dressed-down, yoga-loving, style-mag-reading city escapees, drawn here because it's beautiful – and a lot of fun.

Arrival and information

Trains no longer call into Byron; the closest station is Casino on the Sydney–Brisbane CountryLink line, from where you can catch a bus into town. There are also bus connections to Byron from Grafton station. **Long-distance bus** companies Greyhound and Premier Motor Service include Byron Bay on their East Coast runs; the stop is on Jonson Street, near the old train station. The J&B Coaches Byron Bay Surfers Express (℡07 5592 2655, ⓦwww.byronbayexpress.com.au), a speedy (1hr 10min) transfer service between Surfers Paradise and Byron via Coolangatta, operates four times a day. Oz Road Trip (℡07 3395 8891, ⓦwww.ozroadtrip.com.au) run a backpacker bus to Byron Bay from Brisbane via Surfers Paradise and Nimbin or Coolangatta three times a week. Regional bus services include Kirklands, who run from Brisbane, Surfers, Tweed Heads, Murwillumbah, Brunswick Heads, Lennox Head and Ballina; and Blanch's, from Ballina, Lennox Head and Mullumbimby.

The closest **airport** is Ballina Byron Gateway (BNK), 39km south, served by flights from Sydney with Jetstar, Regional Express and Virgin Blue, and from Melbourne with Jetstar. Blanch's run a bus service from the airport to town (8 daily Mon–Fri, 6 Sat, 3 Sun). Alternatively, a shuttle bus costs around A$15 one way with Byron Easybus (℡02 6685 7447, ⓦwww.byronbayshuttle.com.au) or Airport Transfers (℡02 6685 5008 or 1800 135 660, ⓦwww.airporttransfersbyronbay.com.au). Relatively few flights land at Ballina; for a greater choice, you can fly to the Gold Coast or Brisbane and travel overland from there. The 67-kilometre journey to Byron from Gold Coast airport, Coolangatta, costs around A$25 with Kirklands (2–3 daily) or Brisbane 2 Byron (1–2 daily; ℡07 5429 8759 or 1800 626 222, ⓦwww.brisbane2byron.com) or A$30–36 with Byron Easybus or Airport Transfers. Brisbane Airport is 177km away; fast connections for around A$45 include Byron Easybus or Brisbane 2 Byron, who also pick up in central Brisbane (A$34).

The helpful **Byron Visitor Centre**, at 80 Jonson St near the bus stop (daily 9am–5pm; ℡02 6680 8558, ⓦwww.visitbyronbay.com), has a huge range of printed information and a free accommodation-booking service (℡02 6680 8666, ⓦwww.byronbayaccom.net) for everything except campsites and hostels. Byron's many travel shops and hostel tour desks can fix up car hire, tickets, trips and activities.

Accommodation

Demand for rooms in Byron Bay often exceeds supply, and it's essential to book well in advance for all holidays and festivals – think weeks rather than days for hostels, and months for hotels and apartments, some of which impose minimum-stay rules. Byron's very mixed bag of **backpackers'** includes some of Australia's liveliest dives; all are packed in summer, despite steep prices. For groups, a **holiday apartment** (booked through the tourist office or real-estate

Take the plunge!

Counting every bay, inlet and island, Australia's eastern seaboard extends well over 18,000km. To locals and visitors alike, this adds up to one giant playground, perfect for watersports of every description. East Coast Australians of all ages are utterly united in their love of the water, and many are keen to share their expertise: if you'd like to try surfing, scuba diving or island-hopping by yacht, this is a superb place to learn the ropes. Just make sure you're fully clued-up about tides, currents, waves and wildlife, and you'll have the

Surfing

Surfing is the quintessential East Coast activity: Australians have been riding the waves with gusto since the early twentieth century, when Hawaiians showed them how. Some of those brought up on the coast have made surfing their livelihood; for many more, it's simply their life.

Practically every coastal town from Agnes Water to Melbourne has good breaks nearby; when conditions are right, a surf beach without surfers is a rare sight. Luckily for beginners, the waves tend to be far more manageable than the giant rollers that pound the other side of the Pacific. Particularly **prized locations** are those where the shoreline faces in different directions, so there's always something going on, whichever way the wind is blowing – Byron Bay is a perfect example.

Australian **surfing culture** has working-class, macho roots, and it's common for East Coast surfies to be fiercely territorial. To get in with the locals, try signing up for some lessons – the coast has dozens of instructors, some of them former champions - or head for a surf club. You'll find these in every surfing town; their club houses, open to all, usually have spectacular ocean views and are great places to get the low-down on the scene.

Surfing at Manly Beach ▲

Surfers in winter, East Coast Australia ▼

Best surf spots

▶▶ Bell's Beach, VIC
▶▶ Coolangatta, QLD
▶▶ Currumbin, QLD
▶▶ Newcastle, NSW
▶▶ Byron Bay, NSW
▶▶ South Stradbroke Island, QLD
▶▶ Manly, NSW
▶▶ Bondi Beach, NSW
▶▶ Wollongong, NSW
▶▶ Noosa, QLD

Swimming

You'll find glorious **outdoor public pools** throughout the region. On **Bondi Beach**, the Icebergs pool is famous for its year-round swimming tradition (see p.271), and there's another stunning saltwater pool, the Merewether Ocean Baths, perched on the shore in **Newcastle**. **Cairns** and **Townsville** both have appealing waterfront lagoons, **Brisbane** has a man-made beach and pool in its riverside parklands, and the **North Sydney Olympic Pool** – right beside the harbour, near the foot of the Harbour Bridge – must be one of the most stunningly located city-centre swimming spots in the world.

▲ North Sydney Olympic Pool

▼ Sailing around the Whitsundays

Boating

Of all the many beautiful **sailing** harbours and marinas along Australia's East Coast, there are three that reign supreme on the visitor itinerary: **Abel Point Marina** and **Shute Harbour** near Airlie Beach, starting points for yachting trips around the **Whitsundays**; and Port Jackson, otherwise known as **Sydney Harbour**, surely one of the world's most glamorous places to spend a day on the water.

Windsurfing and **kitesurfing** are popular throughout the region, as are the more environmentally dubious sports of powerboating, wakeboarding, waterskiing and buzzing about on jet-skis. For a waterborne experience that's peaceful, eco-friendly and fantastic exercise, try **kayaking** or **canoeing**, an excellent way to explore lakes, inlets and bays; with luck, you may see dolphins, dugongs, pelicans or penguins, depending on the region. On **Lake Tinaroo** in the Atherton Tablelands, you can join an after-dark trip, spotting nocturnal animals along the way – a truly magical experience.

Close-up encounter with a potato cod ▲

Snorkelling through coral ▼

Diving and snorkelling

The **Great Barrier Reef**, which extends a mind-boggling 2300km from Lady Elliott Island to New Guinea, is the largest marine park in the world. Every site is different: while some teem with pelagics and others throng with tiny nudibranchs, the majority are remarkable for their sheer variety. For more information, see p.500.

If you've never dived before, this is an excellent place to learn, though there's plenty of diversity and drama for **snorkellers**, too: in some areas, you'll see as much from the surface as you would from below. It's common for diving trips to cater for both divers and snorkellers, with separate staff members looking after each group; the best outfits also have **marine ecologists** on hand to give talks illustrated with photos of the most engaging species.

Starfish, Great Barrier Reef ▼

Top 5 sites

▶▶ **Bougainville Reef, Coral Sea, QLD**
Beyond the outer edge of the Reef but well worth the long trip, with grey reef sharks, white-tip reef sharks and turtles.

▶▶ **Wreck of the SS Yongala, QLD**
You'll see a tremendous variety of schooling fish around the hull of this century-old passenger liner.

▶▶ **Lord Howe Island, NSW**
The merging of temperate and tropical currents over the world's southernmost reef ensures a fascinating variety of species, including lobsters and kingfish.

▶▶ **Mornington Peninsula, VIC**
Snorkel among wild dolphins and seals in the cool waters of Port Phillip Bay.

▶▶ **Heron Island, QLD**
The Reef has very few cays where you can step straight off the beach to explore the coral gardens: this is one of them.

agents in town) might be a more practical option. If all the places in town are full, try Brunswick Heads, a quiet coastal resort about 18km north, or Lennox Head (see p.374), about 19km south. Except for the weekend of **Splendour in the Grass** (see p.381), you can expect a substantial discount on the rates below from May to September.

Campsites

Broken Head Holiday Park Beach Rd, Broken Head ☎1800 450 036 or 02 6685 3245, ⓦwww.brokenhd.com.au. The best of the bay's holiday parks, this site has good facilities and gentle, wooded inclines that afford great sea views over the southern end of Tallow Beach and the aptly named Broken Head Rocks. Camping A$42–48, cabin ❸–❺

Clarke's Beach Holiday Park Off Lighthouse Rd ☎02 6685 6496, ⓦwww.byroncoast.com.au/clarkes. Pleasant wooded site with standard amenities but a fantastic setting right on fabulous Clarke's Beach. Camping A$42–45, cabin ❹–❺

First Sun Holiday Park Lawson St ☎02 6685 6544, ⓦwww.bshp.com.au/first. Excellent central location on Main Beach. Cabins range from basic to fully self-contained. Camping A$42–58, cabin ❹–❺

Hostels

Aquarius Backpackers 16 Lawson St ☎02 6685 7663 or 1800 029 909, ⓦwww.aquarius-backpackers.com.au. Excellent motel-style hostel boasting characterful, split-level en-suite dorms with fridge, and some cute apartments. Good communal areas, attractive pool, and a bar with a daily happy hour. Bunk A$33, basic double ❸, apartment ❻

Arts Factory Lodge Skinners Shoot Rd ☎02 6685 7709, ⓦwww.artsfactory.com.au. In a bushland setting, this unusual place is a sprawling riot of sculpture, crafts and old buses. If you value a hippie atmosphere, you'll love it, but it's so popular it can be a bit of a scrum. You can camp, or sleep in a dorm, tepee or wagon; facilities include a pool, sports kit, poi-twirling classes and plenty of hammocks. Camping A$36, bunk A$30, double ❸, chalet ❻

Backpackers Inn 29 Shirley St ☎02 6685 8231, ⓦwww.backpackersinnbyronbay.com.au. Sociable hostel with direct access to Belongil Beach, a cosy cushion-strewn lounge, large clean dorms, pool and – almost uniquely in backpacker territory – a bath. Bunk A$34, double ❸

Byron Bay Bunkhouse 1 Carlyle St ☎02 6685 8311 or 1800 241 600, ⓦwww.byronbay-bunkhouse.com.au. Basic, colourfully decorated hostel linked to a language school. Big veranda and decent kitchen; *Oska's Cafe* is just underneath for quick breakfast fixes. Bunk A$30.

Byron Bay YHA 7 Carlyle St ☎02 6685 8853, ⓦwww.yha.com.au. Large, bright, relatively peaceful option with a BBQ area and pool, comfy dorms, plus free boogie-boards and bikes. Pricier than most, but a good choice if you're not that into Byron's party-hostel scene. Bunk A$39, double ❹

Cape Byron YHA Middleton St, corner of Byron St ☎02 6685 8788, ⓦwww.yha.com.au. Relaxed hostel with a pleasant pool, games room and fairly standard dorms. BBQ once a week, plus free bikes and boogie-boards. Highish prices but a solid option. Bunk A$38, double ❹

Holiday Village Backpackers 116 Jonson St ☎02 6685 8888. Well-equipped, motel-style hostel with standard dorms, a pool, BBQ and free boards and bikes. Bunk A$30–33.

Main Beach Backpackers 19 Lawson St ☎02 6685 8695, ⓦwww.mainbeachbackpackers.com. Safe hostel in a handy location, with standard dorms, a great sundeck and pool, BBQ nights twice a week, and low rates. Bunk A$29, double ❷

Pubs, guesthouses and B&Bs

Amber Gardens Guesthouse 66 Plantation Drive, Ewingsdale ☎02 6684 8215, ⓦwww.ambergardens.net. This discreetly run, out-of-town B&B has four impeccably styled rooms, a pretty garden and a small, chic pool area; breakfast is a masterpiece. ❺

Amigos 32 Kingsley St ☎02 6680 8662, ⓦwww.amigosbb.com. Charming, peacefully located guesthouse just five minutes' walk from the town centre. Colourful, Latin-influenced decor, polished wood floors, a sunny kitchen/lounge, hammocks, newspapers and a tranquil garden make this the perfect haven. ❹

Arcadia Guesthouse 48 Cowper St ☎02 6680 8699, ⓦwww.arcadiaguesthouse.com.au. Fresh, contemporary guesthouse in a Federation-era homestead; most of the brightly decorated rooms are en-suite and have spa- or clawfoot baths. Guests can use the funky pink bikes for free. ❺

Byron Bathers 2 Fletcher Lane ☎02 6680 7775, ⓦwww.byronbathers.com.au. The most central of Byron's B&Bs, this is extremely stylish, with a modern, sun-drenched feel and an enticing pool, just big enough to cool off in. ❻

Hotel Great Northern Jonson St, corner of Byron St ☎02 6685 6454. The clean, no-frills pub rooms

here are amongst the cheapest in town, and worth considering if you can cope with the noise from the street and the bands playing below. ②
Planula 1 Melaleuca Drive ☏ 02 6680 9134, ⓦ www.planula.com.au. Attractive, unfussy guesthouse set in a large, lush tropical garden, with highly eco-conscious owners who have a wealth of knowledge on the local scuba scene, and can fix up diving trips and training. ④

Hotels, motels and resorts

Beach Hotel Bay Lane ☏ 02 6685 8758, ⓦ www.beachhotel.com.au. This beachfront landmark has a pleasant pool, comfortable rooms and generous suites, all within stumbling distance of Byron's favourite pub. A good choice if you want to be right in the thick of things. ⑦
Breakfree Eco Beach 35–37 Shirley St ☏ 02 6639 5700, ⓦ www.ecobeachbyron.com.au. Clean,

stylish motel free of the dreadful interior-design tendencies that always used to bedevil this type of place. Pristine pool and BBQ area. All motels should be like this. ⑤
🏃 **The Byron at Byron** 77–97 Broken Head Rd, Suffolk Park ☏ 02 6639 2000 or 1300 554 362, ⓦ www.thebyronatbyron.com.au. Utterly fabulous, top-end apartment-resort; you'll feel you're wandering through the pages of a luxury magazine. A curtain of coastal forest provides a spectacular, close-to-nature backdrop to the swish pool, deck and open-sided restaurant; the rooms are in strikingly modern buildings tucked among the trees. ⑦
Byron Bay Beach Resort Bayshore Drive ☏ 02 6685 8000, ⓦ www.byronbaybeachresort.com.au. Lovely complex set in subtropical gardens and rainforest; accommodation is in wooden chalets, and there's also a great pool, bar, restaurant, tennis courts and golf course. ⑤

The town and around

There's plenty of opportunity to soak up the local atmosphere – and the often bizarre mix of countercultures as surfie meets soap-starlet meets hippy – simply by wandering the streets. If you want to explore, one of the first places to visit is the rocky, tussocky promontory of **Cape Byron**, the easternmost point of the Australian mainland and a popular spot for the spiritually inclined to greet the dawn; a walking track leads there from Lighthouse Road, on the northeastern edge of town. With a bit of luck you'll see **dolphins**, who like to sport in the surf off the headland, or **humpback whales**, which pass this way heading north in June or July and again on their return south in September or October. On the crest of the cape is Byron's famous **lighthouse**; to look inside and admire its impressive eight-ton lens, you can join a warden-led tour (3–5 daily; 30min; A$8, child A$6).

Main Beach in town is as good as any to swim from, and usually has relatively gentle surf. One reason why Byron Bay is so popular with surfers is because its beaches face in all directions, so there's almost always one with a good swell; conversely, you can usually find somewhere for a calmer swim. West of Main Beach, you can easily find a spot to yourself on **Belongil Beach**, from where there's sand virtually all the way to **Brunswick Heads**.

To the east, Main Beach curves round towards Cape Byron to become **Clarke's Beach**; **The Pass**, a famous surfing spot, is at its eastern end. This and neighbouring **Watego's Beach** – beautifully framed between two rocky spurs – face north, and usually have the best surf. On the far side of the cape, **Tallow Beach** extends towards the **Broken Head Nature Reserve**, 6km south of the town centre at Suffolk Park; there's good surf at Tallow just around the cape at Cosy Corner, and also at Broken Head. From the car park here, a short stroll through rainforest leads down to the secluded, nudist **Kings Beach**.

Lying at a crossroads between tropical and temperate currents, the diversity of marine life in the waters of Byron Bay makes this a prime place to **dive** (for operators, see box, p.382). The reefs here are rock, rather than coral: there are several sites to explore within the aquatic reserve surrounding

▲ Byron Bay lighthouse

Julian Rocks, a clump of granite outcrops 3km offshore; the **Cod Hole**, an extensive underwater cave inhabited by large moray eels and other fish, is particularly impressive.

Eating

Byron Bay is a great place to eat, with cafés, delis and restaurants galore sprinkled down Jonson Street and the roads leading off it.

Cafés and takeaways

Asia Joe's Bay Lane ☎02 6680 8787. Come early to snag one of the few tables at this popular, funky café/takeaway, famous for its *laksa* and other bargain stir-fries and noodles. Daily 5–9.30pm.

Bay Leaf Café Marvell St ☎02 6685 8900. Busy little spot with a variety of casual perches at which to enjoy a fabulous breakfast of ricotta and marscapone pancakes with berry compote, or a juicy lunchtime sandwich. Daily 7.30am–3pm.

Byronian Café 58 Jonson St ☎02 6685 6754. There's a taste of the old Byron in this iconically hippyish streetside spot, serving herbal tea and mango *lassi*; lunch specials may include scrummy roast veggies and *tahini* in pitta. Daily 6am–3pm.

Fishmongers Bay Lane (behind the *Beach Hotel*) ☎02 6680 8080. Locals rave about this gourmet fish 'n' chip shop, and justifiably so: its delectably battered fish, posh chips and tasty

tempura would put many a restaurant to shame. Daily noon–9.30pm.

Twisted Sista Café Lawson St ☎02 6685 6810. Unctuous banana smoothies and really quite gigantic cakes, plus the usual sandwiches, wraps and burgers. Daily 7am–5.30pm.

Restaurants

The Balcony 3 Lawson St ☎02 6680 9666. An early-evening cocktail on the balcony of this beautiful, eclectically decorated bar-restaurant is the most relaxing way to kick off a night in Byron. Succulent food is served all day; in the evening, the style is Mod Oz with a Spanish twist. Booking essential, sometimes even for drinks. Daily 8am–12.30am.

Buddha Bar Arts Factory, Skinners Shoot Rd ☎02 6685 5833. Excellent gourmet pub-food in arty environs: eat in 1950s-style booths, cushion-stuffed

379

You'll find a huge variety of alternative therapists, yoga teachers, healers, palmists and tarot readers in Byron Bay – particularly during the lucrative summer months. The alternative culture also attracts artists and artisans in droves, and supports a thriving gay scene. The tourist office can provide information on special classes and events.

Alternative therapies, spa treatments, meditation and yoga

Noticeboards around town advertise no end of treatments and classes for mind, body and soul, from the conventional to the frankly wacky. For a very luxurious few hours in sublime surroundings, you could book into **The Spa** at *The Byron at Byron* (see p.378), which offers an excellent range of facials, full-body treatments, meditation, yoga and astrology sessions, or head out to **Amala** (Mon–Fri 9am–5.30pm, Sat & Sun 9am–2pm; ☎02 6687 1216, ⓦwww.gaiaretreat.com.au) at *Gaia*, the exclusive wellbeing retreat founded by Olivia Newton John, deep in the countryside at Brooklet, 19km southwest of town. **Quintessence**, 8/11 Fletcher St (daily; ☎02 6685 5533, ⓦwww .quintessencebyron.com.au), and **Buddha Gardens**, near the Arts Factory at 15 Gordon St (daily; ☎02 6680 7844, ⓦwww.buddhagardensdayspa.com.au), each offer slightly more affordable menus of aromatherapy, massage and beauty treatments.

Heading off the deep end of the purple spectrum, the **Ambaji Wellness Centre** at 6 Marvell St (☎02 6685 6620, ⓦwww.ambaji.com.au) is very New Age, with a wide range of treatments from massage and reflexology to tarot readings, crystal healing and chakra clearing.

The longest-established yoga school in town is **Byron Yoga Centre** at The Epicentre, 51 Border St, Belongil Beach (☎02 6687 2230, ⓦwww.byronyoga.com); there are dozens of other options. Specialist holiday company **Samudra** (☎02 6685 5600 or 1800 828 888, ⓦwww.samudra.com.au) offers week-long Byron retreats with yoga in the morning, surfing in the afternoon, and vegetarian meals in between – a great, healthy way to relax (A$2450 full board).

Creative arts

There are arts and crafts stalls galore at the **Byron Bay market**, held on the first Sunday of each month on Butler Street, behind the train station, and at the hinterland markets: The Channon and Alstonville on the second Sunday, Mullumbimby on the third Saturday, Uki (north of Nimbin) and Ballina on the third Sunday, and Bangalow on the fourth Sunday. Around 3km west of town on Bayshore Drive, off Ewingsdale Road (the road to the Pacific Highway), the **Arts and Industry Estate** is a browser's dream, with over three hundred studios run by local artisans selling furniture, jewellery, art and glassware. Back in town, Jonson Street and its side streets have plenty of shops dealing in funky, fair-trade clothes, beads, hand-made shoes and locally made crafts, particularly jewellery.

The **Byron Bay Writers' Festival** (☎02 6685 5115, ⓦwww.byronbaywriters festival.com.au), held annually in July or August, features readings, workshops and film screenings.

Gay and lesbian Byron Bay

Byron Bay and its hinterland towns, which together have the second-largest gay and lesbian community in New South Wales after Sydney, have long been favourite destinations for LGBT travellers. There's not much gay/straight segregation in Byron, but **Kings Beach** (see p.378) is unofficially a gay nudist beach, while **Cocomangas** (see p.381) hosts wild club nights including drag shows and special post-Mardi Gras parties. Recommended **accommodation** for a getaway à deux includes *The Byron at Byron Bay*, *Byron Bathers* and the gay-owned *Amber Gardens Guesthouse* (see p.377). For upcoming events in Byron and the hinterland, check the listings at ⓦwww.tropicalfruits.org.au.

conservatories or on leather sofas, surrounded by hippy types. BYO. Also a great drinking den, with live music and fire-twirling galore. Mon–Sat 4pm–midnight, Sun 4–10pm.

Byron Street Bistro 8 Byron St ⊤02 6685 5324. Aiming to recreate a little corner of France in the heart of Byron, this quiet, intimate spot serves elegant breakfasts and light lunches, while the evening menu features classic cuisine. Mon & Sat breakfast & lunch, Tues–Fri breakfast, lunch & dinner.

Earth 'n' Sea 11 Lawson St ⊤02 6685 6029 or 6685 5011. The huge menu at this perennially popular pizza restaurant includes all the classics and some more off-the-wall hand-made combos such as the Beethoven, an alarming medley of prawn, banana and pineapple. Daily from 5.30pm.

Fish Heads 1 Jonson St ⊤02 6680 7632. Smart-casual seafood restaurant that would be entirely perfect were it not for its views of the beachfront car park. Still, you can hear the sea from the deck, and the food's very good. Daily 7.30am–11pm.

Fresh 7 Jonson St ⊤02 6685 7810. Practically a Byron institution, this funky, mid-priced place caters for all your daily eating needs, from organic sweetcorn-fritter stacks and salsa at breakfast, to pork belly and kingfish curry in the evening. Daily 7.30am–10pm.

Olivo 34 Jonson St ⊤02 6685 7950. A good wine list and adventurous Mediterranean-inspired dishes, with plenty of veggie options, attract an upmarket clientele to this stripped-down, modern space. Daily from 6.30pm.

Orient Express 1/2 Fletcher St ⊤02 6680 8808. Hugely popular Asian-fusion restaurant, serving wonderfully textured delicacies inspired by traditional Thai, Vietnamese and Sichuan recipes. Low tables and oriental oddments lend bags of atmosphere. Mains A$20–30. Daily noon–10pm.

O-Sushi 15 The Plaza, Jonson St ⊤02 6685 7103. The best of Byron's sushi-train restaurants, with young, keen staff, high standards and low prices. Takeaway available. Daily 11am–9.30pm.

Rae's on Watego's 8 Marine Parade, Watego's Beach ⊤02 6685 5366. Open to all for lunch and dinner, the restaurant at this uber-exclusive hotel has an idyllic, special-occasion atmosphere and a short, simple menu – entirely luxurious, with prices to match (around A$45 for a main course).

Why Not! 18 Jonson St ⊤02 6680 7994. This acclaimed café-restaurant offers Aussie-style tapas, cocktails (Happy Hour 5–7pm Mon–Sat & all day Sun) and a great-value Mod Oz evening menu (mains A$24–28) in a welcoming, contemporary area. Daily 6am–midnight.

Entertainment and nightlife

The weekly free community newspaper, *The Byron Shire Echo*, has a comprehensive gig guide; many of the best are in tiny venues out in the hinterland. **New Year's Eve** is such a big event that the council has taken to closing the town off, so come early. Huge crowds also roll up for Byron's two annual music festivals: the wide-ranging **East Coast Blues and Roots Festival** (Easter; ⊛www.bluesfest.com.au) and the more indie-oriented **Splendour in the Grass** (late July or early Aug; ⊛www.splendourinthegrass.com). In the Arts Factory complex, **The Lounge Cinema** (⊤02 6685 5828) must be up there in the world's coolest cinema competition. Pigskin-covered seats are sprinkled with light by a large disco ball, and three or four art-house or mainstream films are screened daily, at very reasonable prices; get there early to slouch on one of the cushions at the front. Byron Cinemas at 108 Jonson St (⊤02 6680 8555) is the local multi-screen venue.

Beach Hotel Bay St ⊤02 6685 6402. This huge bar, superbly sited right opposite Main Beach, has a large terrace and bistro, and attracts a cross-section of locals and visitors. There's live music every night in high season, including big-name bands, plus jazz sessions on Sun afternoon.

Cheeky Monkeys 115 Jonson St ⊤02 6685 5886. Renowned backpacker party zone, with loud music, lots of frolicking, and A$5 meals from 7pm to see you through to closing time eight hours later. Closed Sun.

Cocomangas 32 Jonson St ⊤02 6685 8493, ⊛www.cocomangas.com.au. Lively, long-running nightclub serving up a rich mix of hip-hop, rap and funk, with occasional drag nights. Mon–Sat 5pm–3am.

Hotel Great Northern Jonson St, corner of Byron St ⊤02 6685 6454. Huge and occasionally raucous Aussie pub with nightly live music in high season, plus comedy and cabaret. The bistro does A$10 pizza-and-pasta deals Mon–Thurs. Closes anywhere between 1am and 3am, depending on the crowd.

La La Land The Bay Centre, 6 Lawson St ℡ 02 6680 7070. The little sister of the Melbourne institution, this is the hippest nightspot in town, and a major stop on the international DJ circuit. The cavernous, chandelier-bedecked interior is fairly chilled until 10.30pm, after which it gets reliably rammed with locals and well-heeled backpackers. A$10–25 cover, depending on the DJ. Mon–Sat 9pm–3am, Sun 8pm–midnight.

The Rails The old train station, Jonson St ℡ 02 6685 7662. Good local bands rock the mike at this busy place a few times a week, and with its covered outdoor area, it's a better bet than the pub.

Tours and activities around Byron Bay

Surfing is huge in Byron Bay – you'll see locals of all ages riding the waves whenever and wherever conditions are right, and they're far less territorial than the hard-cases around Sydney, Newcastle and Queensland's Gold Coast. The steady influx of up-for-it backpackers also helps sustain a wealth of **other activities**, including trips out to the lush hinterland.

Cycling

Most hostels have bikes that can either be used free or rented by guests; otherwise, try **Byron Bay Bicycles** in The Plaza, Jonson St (Mon–Fri 8.30am–5.30pm, Sat 9am–4pm; A$15/4hr or A$22/8hr; ℡ 02 6685 6067, ⓦ www.byronbaybicycles.com .au). **Mountain Bike Tours** (℡ 1800 122 504 or 0429 122 504, ⓦ www .mountainbiketours.com.au) will send you along the coast or into the hinterland rainforest, with routes to satisfy both the casual cyclist and the rabid downhiller. Options range from one-day rides through Mount Jerusalem or Nightcap national parks (A$99) to six-day coastal tours (A$1650).

Circus skills

Circus Arts at the Byron Entertainment Centre on Centennial Circuit (℡ 02 6685 6566, ⓦ www.circusarts.com.au) will have you swinging from the chandeliers and generally clowning about in no time. Ninety-minute trapeze workshops (A$45), and circus-skills taster courses (from A$20), including plenty of kids' sessions.

Diving and snorkelling

Julian Rocks, the local diving destination, is within sight of shore, just five minutes by boat; dive or snorkel there and you're likely to encounter dolphins, turtles, moray eels and a good variety of fish, from perky clownfish to blushing cuttlefish. In summer, you may see leopard sharks; in autumn, manta rays; while in winter, grey nurse sharks cruise in. The water is clearest and warmest from March to June; July to August is calmer, while the September to November plankton bloom reduces visibility but brings in masses of wildlife. There are two PADI outfits in town, running similar programmes of courses and trips, including whale-watching in season: **Byron Bay Dive Centre**, 9 Marvell St (℡ 02 6685 8333 or 1800 243 483, ⓦ www .byronbaydivecentre.com.au) and **Sundive** on Middleton Street (℡ 02 6685 7755 or 1800 008 755, ⓦ www.sundive.com.au). A four-day Open Water course costs A$395–475, plus A$60 for the compulsory medical check; snorkel trips are around A$50. The owners of *Planula* (see p.378) are the main organizers of the annual **Byron Underwater Festival** (ⓦ www.underwaterfestival.com.au), held in late April/early May, with workshops, presentations and photo competitions.

Hang-gliding, gliding and skydiving

Byron Airwaves Hang Gliding School (℡ 02 6629 0354) and **Flight Zone** (℡ 02 6685 8768) both offer thirty-minute tandem hang-gliding flights over the Cape Byron Headland Reserve or Lennox Head, south of Byron, for A$145. **Byron Bay Gliding** (℡ 02 6684 7572, ⓦ www.byronbaygliding.com) provide glider trips (from A$95) and pilot training, while **Skydive Byron Bay** (℡ 02 6684 1323,

Listings

Car rental Earth Car Rentals, 18 Fletcher St ☏02 6685 7472; Hertz, 5 Marvell St ☏02 6621 8855; several international firms have desks at Ballina Byron Gateway airport.

Farmer's market Butler St (Mon 8am–11am).

Hospital Wordsworth St, off Shirley St ☏02 6685 6200.

Internet access There are plenty of options including cheap terminals at Peter Pan's, 87 Jonson St; new Wi-Fi hotspots are appearing all the time.

ⓦwww.skydivebyronbay.com) offer Australia's highest jump – 4267m, with spectacular views over Cape Byron – for A\$299.

Hot-air ballooning

For inspiring views of the hinterland inland from Byron Bay, set off at sunrise with **Byron Bay Ballooning**, based in Tyagarah, 11km outside town (A\$295, child A\$145 including Byron pick-up; ☏02 6684 7880, ⓦwww.byronbayballooning.com).

Horse-riding

With **Pegasus Park** (☏02 6687 1446, ⓦwww.pegasuspark.com.au) you can trot through the hinterland (A\$50/hr or A\$70/1hr 30min) or fulfil that galloping-down-a-deserted-beach fantasy (A\$70/hr or A\$110/2hr).

Kayaking

You can set out to sea with the expert guides from **Cape Byron Kayaks** (☏02 6680 9555, ⓦwww.capebyronkayaks.com) to paddle among dolphins and turtles, and get some free Tim Tams into the bargain (A\$60/3hr).

Surfing

Black Dog Surfing in The Plaza, Jonson St (☏02 6680 9828, ⓦwww.blackdogsurfing.com), is the best of many outlets offering gear hire and tuition; they guarantee you'll stand up on your first lesson, a bold claim worth testing out. With a maximum of five students per instructor, everyone receives individual attention. Options include a three-hour intro lesson (A\$60), or two-hour private lesson (A\$120). Other busy schools include **Surfing Byron Bay** (☏02 6685 7099, ⓦwww.gosurfingbyronbay.com) and **Mojosurf** (☏02 6639 5100, ⓦwww.mojosurf.com).

Tours

Byron Bay Wildlife Tours (☏0429 770 686, ⓦwww.byronbaywildlifetours.com) will take you to see 'roos, koalas, wallabies, flying foxes and parrots in the wild near Byron (from A\$50, child A\$25).

Jim's Alternative Tours (☏02 6685 7720, ⓦwww.jimsalternativetours.com) are one-day bus trips giving a genuinely interesting insight into the hinterland's alternative way of life, visiting Nimbin, Minyon Falls and The Channon, with cool tunes en route (A\$35). Options for a quick jaunt into Nimbin include the **Nimbin Shuttle Bus** (☏02 6680 9189, ⓦwww.nimbintours.com), **Green Triangle** (☏1800 503 475, ⓦwww.greentriangle.com.au) and the **Happy Coach** (☏02 6685 3996, ⓦwww.happycoach.com.au), all A\$22–28 return. Bear in mind, however, that your fellow-tourers may be more interested in buying dope than anything else.

Surfaris (☏02 6684 8111, ⓦwww.surfaris.com) offer full-on surfing trips between Byron Bay and Sydney. If you really want to learn to surf, this is a great way of doing it: you'll be living with gnarly wave-riders who'll chuck you in the water every day until you get it (4–8 days; from A\$449 all inclusive).

Yoga and meditation

See box, p.380.

Left luggage The Byron Visitor Centre will store luggage during the day for A$3; Byron Bus & Backpacker Travel, 84 Jonson St, have lockers (A$4/5hr or A$8/24hr).
Police 2 Shirley St ⌾02 6685 9499.

Post office 61 Jonson St.
Supermarket Woolworths, The Plaza, Jonson St (Mon–Fri 8am–9pm, Sat & Sun 8am–8pm).
Taxi ⌾02 6685 5008; there's a rank on Jonson St, opposite *Hotel Great Northern*.

Far North Coast hinterland

The beautiful **far North Coast hinterland** lies between the major service town of **Lismore**, in the fertile Richmond River valley to the south, and **Murwillumbah**, in the even lusher valley of the Tweed River near the Queensland border. Much of the area dances to a different tune, with hippies, craft markets, communes and Kombi vans very much the norm in this "Rainbow Region". The hinterland's three rainforest national parks and several reserves are World Heritage listed: **Mount Warning National Park** rises in the middle of a massive caldera, on whose northwest and southern rims lie the **Border Ranges and Nightcap national parks**, the latter near countercultural **Nimbin** and **The Channon**, home to the largest and most colourful market in the area.

You need **your own vehicle** to get the best out of the area, particularly to complete one of the most **scenic drives** in New South Wales – the short round-trip over the mountainous, winding country roads north and northeast of Lismore to Nimbin, The Channon and Clunes, and then via Eltham and Bexhill, with superb views from the ridges and hilltops. The way into the region by **train** is via Casino, which is on the Sydney–Brisbane CountryLink line, with bus connections to Lismore and Murwillumbah; **long-distance buses** also stop at Murwillumbah, but most bus travellers head into Byron Bay and pick up a hire car or a bus tour from there. Lismore has a regional **airport**.

Nimbin and around

Fifty kilometres inland from Byron via Lismore is **NIMBIN**, site of the famed Aquarius Festival that launched Australian hippy culture in 1973; it's a friendly little place and synonymous with the country's alternative life. The surrounding rainforest is dotted with as many as fifty communes, while the town itself is famous for live music, crafts and New Age therapies, but mainly **marijuana**. Visitors are invariably offered dope as soon as they set foot in town and you'll see it smoked openly on the streets; however, that doesn't mean to say you can wave joints around and expect not to get arrested should the police make one of their infrequent visits. Try to time your visit to coincide with the annual **Mardi Grass and Cannabis Law Reform Rally** (Ⓦwww.nimbinmardigrass .com), held on the first weekend in May, when the town becomes a tent city and a high proportion of the temporary population have dreadlocks – bong throwing, joint rolling and campaigning rallies are amongst the activities on offer. Alternatively, aim to make it here on a **market** day (third and fifth Sun of the month), where you'll catch some music, crafts and great organic food.

Arrival and information

There's no regular **public transport** to Nimbin, but plenty of tour buses head up from Byron Bay (see p.383). The town has its own remarkably efficient **visitor centre** at 80 Cullen St (Mon–Sat 10am–4pm; ⌾02 6689 1764), with Internet terminals.

Accommodation

There are a number of **places to stay** in and around Nimbin, though during Mardi Grass the place is booked up well in advance, so be prepared to **camp**; all the hostels have pitches available.

Granny's Farm Backpackers & Camping ☏ 02 6689 1333. In a peaceful farm setting a short walk from town, this extremely pretty little hostel has a converted old train carriage you can sleep in down by the creek, two pools, and a general emphasis on having a good time. Bunk A$20, double ❶

Grey Gum Lodge 2 High St ☏ 02 6689 1713. Right in town, the very comfortable and beautifully decorated *Grey Gum Lodge* is about as smart as it gets hereabouts, with a saltwater swimming pool and a very toned-down Nimbin vibe – a plus for some people. ❷

Nimbin Rox YHA 74 Thorburn St ☏ 02 6689 0022, ⊛ www.yha.com.au. Slightly shambling but still the pick of the hostels, this small and friendly place is set in a superb rural location just outside town and has basic dorms, a charming double and an enchanting garden. Camping A$24, bunk A$24–27, room, yurt, or tepee ❷

Rainbow Retreat 75 Thorburn St ☏ 02 6689 1262, ⊛ www.rainbowretreat.net. Just outside Nimbin and the hippiest place of all, with accommodation either in a dorm, an old VW Kombi, a gypsy wagon or a cheap double, plus camping space. It shares a stretch of Goolmanger Creek with the resident platypus, while horses munch between the tent spaces. Camping A$26 (A$13pp), bunk A$20, double ❷

The Town

Like a parody of itself, Nimbin's tiny main strip, Cullen Street, is aglow with small stores painted in bright, psychedelic designs, selling health food, incense sticks and ethnic clothing. The **Nimbin Museum** (daily 9am–5pm; gold coin donation) is a decidedly weird, visually chaotic folk-art installation run by hippies, with a Kombi van left where it was driven through the front wall, lots of way-out graffiti and a ceiling mobile made from hand whisks – it nevertheless manages to impart a message of sorts about the value of Bundjalung Aboriginal culture and the benefits of cannabis use. If you have Green leanings, the **Nimbin Environmental Centre** might be of interest – they campaign on environmental issues, and can arrange visits to the **Djanbung Gardens Permaculture Centre** (⊛ www.permaculture.com.au), a showcase for a system of sustainable agriculture that is gaining ground worldwide. The **Hemp Embassy** (daily 10am–5pm; ⊛ www.hempembassy.net) too is worth a look; learn why the Hemp Party believe the herb should be legalized (you can even join if you want) and browse through some of their previous campaigns and press releases. The **Nimbin School of Arts Gallery** (daily 10am–4pm) is worth a browse for the sake of the odd piece of genuinely original work you'll find amongst its motley array of more derivative paintings and sculptures.

Eating, drinking and nightlife

Cullen Street is full of good **places to eat**, including the legendary, grungey *Rainbow Café* (daily 9am–5pm), which serves all-day breakfasts, burgers and salads, and *The Coffee House* (Mon–Sat 8am–4pm, Sun 9am–4pm), which has lots of tasty munchies – Turkish bread with dips, healthy treats and good local coffee. *Nimbin Pizza & Pasta* (daily from 5pm; ☏ 02 6689 1427), a long-established favourite, offers gargantuan pizzas topped with local organic produce, while *The Spangled Drongo* (Wed–Fri, Sun & Mon lunch & dinner, Sat lunch only; ☏ 02 6698 0033) has a good menu of curries, *laksas* and stir-fries from a chef who's passionate about Thai cooking. For **nightlife and entertainment** there's the *Nimbin Hotel*, which sees plenty of live music and some interesting local characters; the *Rainbow Retreat* (see above), with more live bands; and the *Hemp Bar*, next to the Hemp Embassy, a cozy, Amsterdam-esque drinking hole. *The Nimbin Bush Theatre* (☏ 02 6689 1111), located in an old butter factory over the bridge opposite *Granny's Farm Backpackers*, serves fabulous food and is home to a charming little cinema – call or check the notice boards in town for screenings.

The Channon and the Nightcap National Park

THE CHANNON, a 26-kilometre drive south of Nimbin, is a pretty village on the banks of **Terania Creek**. It's home to the **Channon Craft Market** (second Sun of the month), the best – and the first – of its type in the Rainbow Region. Begun in 1976 to provide the rapidly starving hippies with some cash, the rule that you have to "make it or bake it" still holds fast – it's a colourful spectacle and well worth a trip. The funky, heritage-listed *Channon Tavern* is set within an old butter factory, and serves up hearty dinners and local gossip.

A fourteen-kilometre drive into the **Nightcap National Park**, along the unsealed Terania Creek Road, brings you to **Protestors Falls** and a rainforest valley filled with ancient brush box trees, saved by the 1979 protest, which was the first successful anti-logging campaign in Australia. You can walk down to the bottom of the falls, named after the dispute, to the Terania Creek Picnic Area. Also within the park are the one-hundred-metre cascades of **Minyon Falls**, often more of a trickle in summer; a steep walk (2hr return) leads down to the base. You're allowed to **camp** at the *Rummery Park Camping Ground* (A$3pp) in nearby **Whian Whian State Conservation Area**, 2km from Minyon Falls along Peates Mountain Road; for something more comfortable, try the arty *Havan's Ecotourist Retreat* (T02 6688 6108, W www.rainbowregion .com/havan; ❹), just off Terania Creek Road on Lawler Road, overlooking the creek and rainforest.

Murwillumbah and around

MURWILLUMBAH is a quiet, inland town on a bend of the Tweed River, a little over 30km northwest of Byron Bay. It has some well-preserved Art Deco facades, and is a good starting point for exploring the beautiful Tweed Valley and the mountains that extend to the Queensland border. It's well worth dropping by the **Tweed River Regional Art Gallery**, at the corner of Tweed Valley Way and Minstral Road (Wed–Sun 10am–5pm; free), which displays the work of local artists and travelling exhibitions.

At the Murwillumbah exit on the Pacific Highway, the **Big Avocado** lures the visitor towards **Tropical Fruit World** (daily 10am–4.30pm; A$32, child A$15; W www.tropicalfruitworld.com.au), slightly to the south on Duranbah Road. A plantation that has been turned into a miniature theme park, it grows avocados, macadamia nuts and many kinds of tropical fruit; you can ride around in open-air buses and miniature trains, or cruise around on man-made "tropical canals". There are canoes and aqua-bikes for rent, as well as a fruit market selling plantation produce.

The **Tweed Valley** and the surrounding land close to the Queensland border are among the most beautiful areas of New South Wales, ringed by mountain ranges that are actually the remains of an extinct volcano. Some twenty million years ago a huge shield **volcano** spewed lava through a central vent onto the surrounding plain. Erosion carved out a vast bowl around the centre of the resultant mass of lava, while the more resistant rocks around the edges stood firm. Right at the bowl's heart is **Mount Warning** (1157m)–Wollumbin ("Cloud Catcher") to the local **Bundjalung Aborigines** – the original vent of the volcano, whose unmistakable, twisted profile rises like a sentinel from the Tweed Valley. The mountain is a place of great cultural significance to the

Bundjalung, who believe that only expressly chosen people may attempt the steep three-hour path to the summit; however, as at Uluru, many visitors can't resist the dazzling views on offer.

North of Murwillumbah is Tourist Drive 40, a 57-kilometre **scenic drive** through the **Tweed Valley**, which takes in some of its best features en route from Murwillumbah up to Tweed Heads and the state border.

Practicalities

Greyhound and Premier Motor Service **long-distances buses** stop in town. The excellent **visitor information centre**, located in the Rainforest Heritage Centre on Alma Street (Mon–Sat 9am–4.30pm, Sun 9.30am–4pm; ℡02 6672 1340 or 1800 674 414, ⓦwww.tweedtourism.com.au), has detailed displays and an accommodation-booking service.

Places to stay in Murwillumbah include the Art Deco *Imperial Hotel* at 115 Main St (℡02 6672 1036; ❶), a grand old building right in the centre of town, with good-value singles and doubles, an excellent bistro and local bands at weekends. *Mount Warning Riverside YHA*, at 1 Tumbulgum Rd (℡02 6672 3763, ⓦwww.yha.com.au; bunk A\$26–29, double ❷), is a truly wonderful find; a cosy hostel in a house leaning over the river, it has bikes for rent, free canoes and rowing boat, plus free ice cream every evening at 9pm – stay for two nights and you'll get a free trip to Mount Warning. Alternatively, make the most of the countryside by staying in rural accommodation: *Mount Warning Forest Hideaway* on Byrill Creek Road near the village of Uki, southwest of town (℡02 6679 7277, ⓦwww.foresthideaway.com.au; ❸), occupies a hundred acres of lush forest and offers motel-style units with cooking facilities, plus a swimming pool.

Places to eat include the excellent *New Leaf Café* at 47 Main St (breakfast & lunch; ℡02 6672 4073), with delicious and original South Asian- and Mediterranean-inspired organic veggie nibbles at very reasonable prices; *Blue Frog* at 4 Wharf St (Mon 9am–5pm, Tues–Fri 8am–5pm, Sat 8am–12.30pm; ℡02 6672 7474), a French-run patisserie with tables outside, scrummy sandwiches and tempting little pots of mousse; and the *Imperial Hotel*, for good bistro food.

Lord Howe Island

I would strongly urge preserving this beautiful island from further intrusions of any kind...

Government Expedition, 1882

World Heritage-listed **LORD HOWE ISLAND** is a kind of Australian Galapagos – a perfect eco-destination, attracting dedicated natural-history enthusiasts and outdoor types with its rugged beauty. Situated 700km northeast of Sydney, and roughly in line with Port Macquarie, it's technically a part of New South Wales, despite its distance from the mainland.

Just 11km long and 2.8km across at its widest point, the crescent-shaped island's only industry other than tourism is its plantations of **kentia palms** (see p.389); two-thirds of the island is designated as Permanent Park Reserve. As you fly in, you'll get a stunning view of the whole of the volcanic island: the towering summits of rainforest-clad **Mount Gower** and **Mount Lidgbird** at the southern end; the narrow centre with its idyllic lagoon and a **coral reef** extending about 6km along the west coast; and a group of tiny islets off the lower northern end of the island providing sanctuary for the abundant **birdlife**.

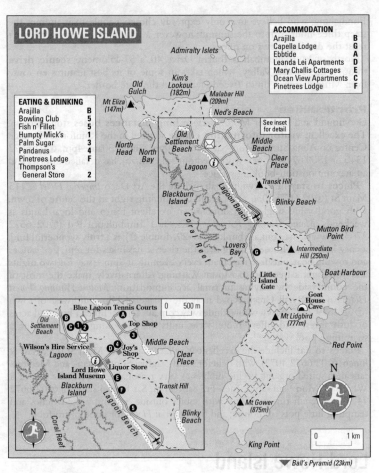

LORD HOWE ISLAND

ACCOMMODATION

Arajilla	B
Capella Lodge	G
Ebbtide	A
Leanda Lei Apartments	D
Mary Challis Cottages	E
Ocean View Apartments	C
Pinetrees Lodge	F

EATING & DRINKING

Arajilla	B
Bowling Club	5
Fish n' Fillet	5
Humpty Mick's	1
Palm Sugar	3
Pandanus	4
Pinetrees Lodge	F
Thompson's General Store	2

Admiralty Islets

Kim's Lookout (182m)

Old Gulch

Malabar Hill (209m)

Mt Eliza (147m)

Ned's Beach

See inset for detail

Old Settlement Beach

Middle Beach

North Head *North Bay*

Clear Place

Lagoon

Transit Hill

Blackburn Island

Blinky Beach

Coral Reef

Lagoon Beach

Mutton Bird Point

Lovers Bay

Intermediate Hill (250m)

Little Island Gate

Boat Harbour

Goat House Cave

Mt Lidgbird (777m)

Red Point

Ball's Pyramid (23km)

Blue Lagoon Tennis Courts

Top Shop

0   500 m

Old Settlement Beach

Wilson's Hire Service

Joy's Shop

Middle Beach

Lagoon

Liquor Store

Clear Place

Lord Howe Island Museum

Blackburn Island

Transit Hill

Lagoon Beach

Coral Reef

Blinky Beach

Mt Gower (875m)

0   1 km

King Point

N

The emphasis here is on tranquillity: there are only 350 islanders; no rowdy nightclubs spoiling the peace; no mobile-phone coverage; and most of the four hundred visitors allowed at any one time are couples and families. Even disregarding the island's ecological attractions, it's a fascinating place to stay: most visitors are intrigued by the small details of island life, such as how children are schooled and food is brought from the mainland, and are generally eager to sample life in this egalitarian paradise where no one locks their car (or even takes the key out of the ignition), bike or house. Though it's expensive to get to the island – and accommodation and eating out are far pricier than on the mainland – cruises, activities and bike rental are all relatively affordable. The island's **climate** is subtropical, with temperatures rising from a mild 19°C in winter to 26°C in the summer, and an annual rainfall of 1650mm. It's cheaper to visit in the winter, though some places are closed.

Some history

Lord Howe Island was discovered in 1788 by Lieutenant Henry Lidgbird Ball (who named the island after the British admiral Richard Howe), commander of

Lord Howe ecology

Seven million years ago, a volcanic eruption on the sea floor created Lord Howe Island and its 27 surrounding islets and outcrops – the island's boomerang shape is a mere remnant (around two percent) of its original form, mostly eroded by the sea. While much of the **flora** on the island is similar to that of Australia, New Zealand, New Caledonia and Norfolk Island, the island's relative isolation has led to the evolution of many **new species** – of the 241 native plants found here, 105 are endemic, including the important indigenous **kentia palm** (see below).

Similarly, until the arrival of settlers, fifteen species of flightless **land birds** (nine of which are now extinct) lived on the island, undisturbed by predators and coexisting with migrating sea birds, skinks, geckos, spiders, snails and the now-extinct giant horned turtle. However, in the nineteenth century Lord Howe became a port of call for ships en route to Norfolk Island, whose hungry crews eradicated the island's stocks of **white gallinule** and **white-throated pigeon**. The small, plump and flightless **woodhen** managed to survive, protected on Mount Gower, and an intensive captive breeding programme in the early 1980s saved the species (there are now about 350). About one million **sea birds** – fourteen species – nest on Lord Howe annually: it is one of the few known breeding-grounds of the providence petrel; has the world's largest colony of red-tailed tropic birds; and is the most southerly breeding location of the sooty tern, the noddy tern and the masked booby. Cats have now been eradicated from the island, as a result of which bird numbers have soared, and a plan to exterminate rats and mice is under way. Nervous travellers can rest in peace on Lord Howe, safe in the knowledge that there are none of the poisonous spiders and snakes that blight the mainland.

The cold waters of the **Tasman Sea**, which surround Lord Howe, host the world's southernmost **coral reef**, a tropical oddity which is sustained by the warm summer current sweeping in from the Great Barrier Reef. There are about sixty varieties of brilliantly coloured and fantastically shaped coral, and the meeting of warm and cold currents means that a huge variety of both **tropical and temperate fish** can be spotted in the crystal-clear waters. Some of the most colourful species include the yellow moon wrasse, parrotfish and the yellow-and-black banner fish. Unique to Lord Howe is the doubleheader, with its bizarre, bulbous forehead and fat lips. Beyond the lagoon, the water becomes very deep, with particularly good diving in the seas around the **Admiralty Islets**, which have sheer underwater precipices and chasms. The diving season lasts from May to November (for information on dive companies, see p.393).

the First Fleet ship *Supply*, during a journey from Sydney to found a penal colony on Norfolk Island. The island wasn't inhabited for another 55 years, however; the first **settlers came** in 1833, and others followed in the 1840s. In 1853 two white men arrived with three women from the Gilbert Islands in the central Pacific, and it is from this small group that many of Lord Howe's present population are descended. In the 1840s and 1850s the island served as a stopover for **whaling ships** from the US and Britain, with as many as fifty ships a year passing through. In 1882, a government expedition from the mainland recommended that in order to preserve the island, no one other than the present "happy, industrious" leaseholders and their families be allowed to make permanent settlement.

With the decline of whaling, economic salvation came in the form of the "thatch" palm, one of the four endemic species of the **kentia palm**. Previously used as roofing for the islanders' homes, it began to be exported as a decorative interior plant, boosting the island's economy. The profits from the kentia trade were shared out equally amongst the Lord Howe residents, each of whom was in turn expected to take on an equal share of the (not overly hard) work on the kentia plantations. In 1918, however, the kentia industry was damaged by the appearance of **rats**, which escaped onto the island from a ship. **Tourism** was eventually to become the mainstay of the island – Lord Howe became a popular stopover on the cruise-ship circuit before World War II, and after the war it began to be visited by holiday-makers from Sydney, who came by seaplane.

Today, rats still pose a hazard to the palms, but the **kentia industry** is nonetheless in resurgence, with profits going towards the preservation of the island's unique ecosystem. Seeds are no longer exported but instead cultivated in the Lord Howe Island Board's own **nursery**, which sells two and a half million plants annually; they also grow seedlings here for regeneration around the island. You can visit the nursery, as well as other parts of the island on guided walks with Ron's Rambles (see p.392). Ron will have you sniffing herbs, feeling rocks and believing some tall stories about the early islanders' bushcraft.

Getting there

You can **fly** to Lord Howe Island with Qantas (see p.35) from Sydney (at least daily for most of the year), Brisbane (twice weekly) and Port Macquarie (weekly in summer) from about A$900 return in peak season, or A$650 return in the winter months. Overseas visitors can fly to Lord Howe as an add-on fare on an air pass. Your accommodation must be arranged before you book your air travel, as there's a limit on the number of tourists staying each night. It's often much easier – and better value – to go on a **package tour**. Prices for seven nights start at around A$830 in winter and A$1060 in summer: try Oxley Travel (ⓣ02 6583 1955 or 1800 671 546, ⓦwww.oxleytravel.com.au) or Talpacific Holidays (ⓣ1300 665 737, ⓦwww.talpacific.com).

Arrival, information and transport

There's no official transport from the **airport**, located in the narrow central part of the island, but wherever you're staying, you'll be met on arrival by your lodge-owner. The island's **tourist office** is located inside the Lord Howe Island Museum at the junction of Lagoon and Middle Beach roads (Mon–Fri 9.30am–3pm, Sun 9am–2pm; ⓣ02 6563 2114 or 1800 240 937, ⓦwww.lordhoweisland .info): all tours and activities can be booked here, and the useful *Ramblers Guide to Lord Howe Island* (A$9), which covers all the island's walks in great detail, is also available.

Lord Howe has few **roads** and only a small number of cars. There are sporadic streetlights down Lagoon Road, but you'll need to bring a torch with you, or buy one from one of the stores, if you want to venture far at night – in wet conditions, you might see some glow-in-the-dark fungi. The most common ways to get around are by **bicycle**, boat or on foot. Most lodges offer **bikes** to guests, but they don't have lights either, so if you want to ride at night attach a torch; if your lodge has exhausted its supply, then you can also rent cycles from Wilson's Hire Service at 3 Lagoon Rd, opposite Lagoon Beach (closed Sat; A$8/day; ⓣ02 6563 2045). **Cars** can be rented from around A$50 per day at Wilson's and *Leanda Lei Apartments* (ⓣ02 6563 2195); pre-booking is essential.

Crossing the centre of the island to the north, Ned's Beach Road has a cluster of **shops** and **services**, including Thompson's General Store (daily 8am–6pm; ⓣ02 6563 2155), where you can book most activities, order roast chooks, and rent fishing or snorkelling gear. You'll also find a community hall-cum-summer cinema and a **post office** (Mon–Fri 10am–3pm) on this road. It's a good idea to bring all the **cash** you'll need with you – there are no ATMs on the island, although Larrup's beachwear shop on Ned's Beach Road and Joy's Shop, opposite *Leanda Lei Apartments* on Middle Beach Road (daily 9am–6.30pm), give A$50 to A$100 cash out on credit cards to customers.

There are three places to buy **groceries** and sundries on the island: Thompson's General Store; Joy's Shop; and Top Shop, tucked away on Skyline Street off Mutton Bird Drive (Mon–Fri 9am–12.30pm & 4.30–6pm, Sun 9am–12.30pm), where you can buy fresh meat and vegetables. Inevitably, transport costs make things more expensive than on the mainland.

Accommodation

Most of the accommodation on Lord Howe Island is **self-catering** and of a good standard. All the lodges are centrally located, with the exception of *Capella Lodge*, where the privacy, views and air of luxury more than compensate.

Arajilla Lagoon Rd ☎02 6563 2002 or 1800 063 928, ⊛www.arajilla.com.au. This intimate, chic, chocolates-on-your-pillow kind of place nestles amongst kentia palms and banyan forest; the stylish suites and two-bed apartments have private decks with leafy views. Spa treatments are administered in a timber yurt, and delicious meals are taken in the beautiful Balinese-style bar-restaurant. Full board only. ❽

Capella Lodge Lagoon Rd ☎02 9544 2273, ⊛www.lordhowe.com. Nestling under Mount Gower and Mount Lidgbird, this is the most luxurious and exclusive place to stay on the island. The stunning bar and infinity pool overlook the mountains, and the suites and loft apartments are all interior-designed to within an inch of their lives. There's also an indulgent spa and a residents-only restaurant with jaw-dropping views. Breakfast, sunset drinks and canapés, and contemporary fusion-style evening meals are included in the price. ❽

Ebbtide Muttonbird Drive ☎02 6563 2023, ⊛www.ebbtide-lhi.com.au. Nestling up on the cliff by Searles Point, this very friendly place has simple, stylish apartments and cottages set in a tropical garden of pawpaw and banana (guests can help themselves). A private bush-track leads down to Ned's Beach. ❻–❼

Leanda Lei Apartments Middle Beach Rd ☎02 6563 2095, ⊛www.leandalei.com.au. Smart, clean and run with friendly efficiency by the Riddle family. The studios and one- or two-bedroom apartments are set in lush manicured grounds with BBQs, close to Lagoon Beach. ❻–❼

Mary Challis Cottages Lagoon Rd ☎02 6563 2076. Situated right by Lagoon Beach, these two cute cottages have everything you'll need, plus some home-baked goodies on arrival – and a couple of docile cows. ❺

Pinetrees Lodge Lagoon Rd ☎02 9262 6585, ⊛www.pinetrees.com.au. The island's first guesthouse is a family-friendly place, set in rigorously maintained, forested grounds. Accommodation is in motel-style units or newer "garden cottages" grouped around the original lodge. Delicious meals are included in the price. There's also a tennis court, and a boatshed on Lagoon Beach, a delightful place for a sundowner from the honesty bar. ❽

The island

A good way to kick off your island idyll is with a trip to the **Lord Howe Island Museum** on the corner of Middle Beach and Lagoon roads (Mon–Fri 9am–3pm, Sat & Sun 9.30am–2pm), which goes a long way to answering all those "so who's related to who?" questions you inevitably bore your lodge-owner with. The museum hosts very good slide-shows on island history and ecology a few evenings a week, narrated by the island naturalist, Ian Hutton (days and times vary, check at the tourist office; A$6), as well as irregular cultural nights.

Walking trails and activities

At the island's **northern end**, you can walk all the way from North Bay or Old Settlement Beach on the western side to Ned's Beach on the east, stopping at various lookout points – allow a good five hours. Relaxed, educational half-day **guided walks** are available from personable local resident Ron (for a bit of folklore and local colour; ☎02 6563 2010) or Ian Hutton (for an informed look at the island's ecology; ⓦwww.lordhowe-tours.com.au); book at Thompson's Store for either. If you simply want to take in the beautiful views, it's very easy to do it yourself. From the path behind **Old Settlement Beach**, it's a steep two-kilometre climb over a hill to **North Bay**, where there's a picnic area and BBQ; you start the twenty-minute trek to the summit of **Mount Eliza** (147m) from behind the huts here. It's worth taking a boat to **North Bay** with Islander Cruises (☎02 6563 2021; A\$15) and beginning the walk from there, as the initial hike from Old Settlement Beach takes a lot out of you without giving much back. The summit of Mount Eliza is the most accessible place to see **sooty terns** in their southernmost breeding grounds. When the colony visits the island (Sept–March) each female lays a single speckled egg on the bare ground, which means that the actual summit has to be closed for the birds' protection.

Back at the base at **North Bay**, a five-minute walk through forest leads to **Old Gulch**, a beach of boulders, where at low tide you can rock-hop to the **Herring Pools** at the base of the cliff front and examine the colourful marine life before returning to the picnic area. Walking back up the hill towards Old Settlement Beach you can take the path east to **Kim's Lookout** (182m), which provides a good view of the settlement and the lagoon beaches and islets. Heading along the cliff edge from here, you come to **Malabar Hill** (209m), which gives access to one of the world's largest nesting concentrations of **red-tailed tropic birds**, who between September and May make their homes in the crannies of the cliff face below, laying only one egg and looking after the chick for twelve weeks until it can fly. From the summit, you can just see Ball's Pyramid way down to the south around the corner of Mount Lidgbird. To complete the walk, you drop down to **Ned's Beach**, where you'll probably need a long drink. There are more walks in the centre of the island – maps are available from the tourist office and at your accommodation.

Slightly less energetic activities are available at the *Blue Lagoon Lodge*'s **tennis courts** on Ned's Beach Road (book at Thompson's General Store; balls and rackets available to rent), and the nine-hole **golf course** near *Capella Lodge* (A\$20 with your own clubs, A\$35 with theirs; balls A\$1). For something even less strenuous, Whitfield's Island Tours (☎02 6563 2115) run a half-day tour of the island in their air-conditioned bus, with a tea break included (A\$28, child A\$15).

Mount Gower

The ultimate view on the island is at its **southern end**, where the lofty summit of **Mount Gower** (875m) gives vistas over the whole island and out to sea towards the world's tallest sea stack, **Balls Pyramid** (548m), a spike of volcanic rock that breaks dramatically up out of the ocean 23km from Lord Howe. Mount Gower is high enough to have a true **mist forest** on its summit, with a profusion of ferns, tree trunks and rocks covered in mosses. This extremely strenuous walk can be undertaken only with a licensed **guide** (Jack Shick is the most experienced; 8hr; A\$50, BYO lunch; booking required; ☎02 6563 2218) and is definitely not for the faint-hearted – one section of the walk runs precariously along a narrow cliff-face above the sea, and in parts the track is so steep that you have to pull yourself up the guide ropes. The path to the top was blazed by botanists in 1869, who took two days to get there, but they were rewarded with the discovery of a plant seen nowhere else on earth – the **pumpkin tree**, bearing fleshy orange flowers. You can see other rare endemic plants here, including the island apple and the blue plum, as well as birds such as the providence petrel and the woodhen.

To join the walk, you have to be at the Little Island Gate on the south of the island by 7.30am: you can get a lift there with Whitfield's Island Tours (see p.392; A\$6 return), or it's about a half-hour cycle ride from the north of the island.

Water-based activities

The island has some sensational swimming, snorkelling and diving sites, as well as a large number of boat trips. The beaches here are lovely, though the white sand isn't the soft, powdered stuff you find on the mainland, but rather rough little bits of broken-up coral. There's stunning snorkelling at **Sylphs Hole**, off Old Settlement Beach, and on the east side of the island at Ned's Beach, where corals lie only 10m from the shore. The combination of temperate and tropical waters make double-headed wrasse, lobsters and angelfish a common sight. **Snorkelling gear** and wetsuits can be borrowed cheaply from the hut at the back of Ned's Beach (put your money in the honesty box); sets are also available from most lodges and at Wilson's Hire Service (A\$4/day). Every day around an hour after low tide, Ned's Beach is the scene of a **fish-feeding** frenzy, when people gather to throw fish scraps into the water, attracting a throng of big trevally, kingfish and reef sharks.

If you want to **surf** on the island, it's best to bring your own board (Qantas can accommodate them if you call in advance), although Larrup's have a few available for rent (A\$20/half-day, A\$30/full day). Blinky Beach is the best for surfing, although you can also paddle out 1.5km into the lagoon to the break beyond the reef to catch a few waves with the locals.

Glass-bottom boat cruises over the beautiful reef are available from Lagoon Beach with Lord Howe Environmental Tours (2hr; A\$30, child A\$15; ☏02 6563 2214), based on Lagoon Road. If you're interested in **diving**, **fishing**, **snorkelling tours**, **kayaking**, or any kind of **boat trip**, one of the two adjacent boatsheds on Lagoon Road will sort you out. **Busty's Boatshed** is a one-stop shop for Islander Cruises (☏02 6563 2021), the locally owned Howea Divers (☏02 6563 2290, ⓦwww.howeadivers.com .au), Lord Howe Nature Tours (☏02 6563 2447) and Sea to Summit Expeditions (☏02 6563 2218). The **Pro Dive Boatshed** next door is home to Pro Dive (☏02 6563 2253, ⓦwww.prodivelordhowe.com.au), Marine Adventures (☏02 6563 2253, ⓦwww.marineadventures.com.au) and Lulawai Cruises (☏02 6563 2195). Both sheds offer a bewildering array of magical experiences, from North Bay barbecue trips and sunset tours in the lagoon, to snorkelling excursions, dive courses, leisurely fishing jaunts, and cruises around the awe-inspiring Ball's Pyramid.

Eating and drinking

Bookings are necessary at all **eating** places for evening meals (not much vegetarian food is available, so ask beforehand). The **Co-op** (closed Wed & Sat) on Ned's Beach Road, opened in an attempt to reduce the amount of packaging brought onto the island, is a great place to stock up on bulk items like muesli and pasta. There's no **pub** on Lord Howe; the closest thing is the *Bowling Club* (daily from 4.30pm), which serves pub-style grub (Mon–Thurs) and hosts a popular disco on Friday nights (8pm–midnight).

Arajilla Lagoon Rd ☏02 6563 2002. This luxury resort has an excellent restaurant serving delicious Australian cuisine, although due to full board being offered to guests it only rarely has space for non-residents. Dinner daily.

Fish 'n' Fillet ☏02 6563 2208. These guys hold fish-fry nights at the bowling club on Tues & Thurs from 5.30pm. They also run a great scheme where you leave your order in the boxes outside *Humpty Mick's* or Joy's Shop by 3pm, and the fish is delivered straight to your door between 5pm & 6.30pm – just leave the money on your table if you're out.

Humpty Mick's Ned's Beach Rd ☏02 6563 2287. An essential lunch or snack stop offering affordable salads, speciality burgers, focaccias and daily fish specials. Daily 9am–7.30pm.

Palm Sugar Skyline Drive ☏02 6563 2120. Afternoon tea, amazing cakes, and some excellent evening meals are served on the colourful, tranquil veranda. Private lunches, beach picnics and BBQs available on request. Mon–Sat from 2pm.

Pandanus Anderson Rd ☏02 6563 2240. This pleasant, minimalist restaurant has wooden floors, starchy white table linen and beachy artwork, and serves pizza, pasta and mains with an Italian flavour. Daily from 6pm. lunch Thurs–Sat.

Pinetrees Lodge Lagoon Rd ☏02 6563 2177. The Mon-night fish-fry here is the best of several on the island; it's well worth booking for this quintessential Lord Howe experience, including as it does vast plates of sushi, fried kingfish, chips, salads and groaning tables of desserts. Go early and have a glass of wine over at the lodge's boatshed on the lagoon, where you can watch the often-spectacular sunset.

Thompson's General Store Ned's Beach Rd. Inexpensive takeaway sandwiches, fish and beef burgers at lunchtime only.

Norfolk Island

Just 8km long and 5km wide, tiny, isolated **NORFOLK ISLAND** is an External Territory of Australia located around 1600km from Sydney and 1450km from Brisbane – closer to New Zealand than to mainland Australia – on a similar latitude to Yamba. The island has had an eventful history, being linked with early convict settlements and later with the descendants of Fletcher Christian and other "mutiny-on-the-*Bounty*" rebels. It's a unique place, forested with grand indigenous pine trees, and with a mild subtropical **climate** ranging between 12°C and 19°C in the winter and from 19°C to 28°C in the summer; Norfolk is also said to have the world's **cleanest air** after Antarctica. The island's **tax-haven** status makes it a refuge for millionaires, and most visitors spend a fortune in its numerous **duty-free stores**.

Norfolk mainly attracts honeymooners or retired Australians and New Zealanders ("newly weds and nearly deads"). All visitors require a **passport** to visit the island, which has its own Legislative Assembly. A thirty-day **visitor permit**, extendable to 120 days, is granted automatically on arrival. The island has no income tax, finances being raised from sources such as departure tax (A$30) and a road levy included in the price of petrol. Most of the 1900 local people remain unaffected by tourism, maintaining their friendly attitude, amusing nicknames (confusingly used in the island's telephone directory) and the remnants of their dialect, **Norfolk**, a mixture of old West Country English and Tahitian (see p.545). While the crime rate on Norfolk is for the most part very low, two **murders** in 2002 and 2004 (the second that of the Deputy Chief Minister) subjected the island to unprecedented and unwelcome media attention.

Much of the land is cleared for cultivation, as islanders have to grow all their own fresh food; cattle roam freely and are given right of way, creating a positively bucolic atmosphere. At the centre of the island is its only significant settlement, **Burnt Pine**; on the south coast, picturesque **Kingston** is the sightseeing focus. Scenic winding roads provide access to the **Norfolk Island**

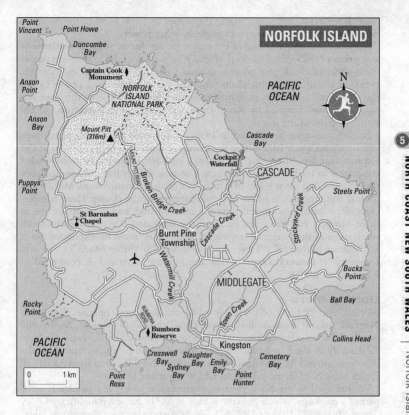

NORFOLK ISLAND

Point Vincent
Point Howe
Duncombe Bay
Captain Cook Monument
NORFOLK ISLAND NATIONAL PARK
Anson Point
Anson Bay
Mount Pitt (316m)
PACIFIC OCEAN
N
Cascade Bay
Cockpit Waterfall
CASCADE
Steels Point
MOUNT PITT ROAD
Broken Bridge Creek
Puppys Point
St Barnabas Chapel
Burnt Pine Township
Cascade Creek
Stockyard Creek
Bucks Point
Watermill Creek
MIDDLEGATE
Ball Bay
BUMBORA ROAD
Rocky Point
Town Creek
Collins Head
PACIFIC OCEAN
Bumbora Reserve
Kingston
Cemetery Bay
Cresswell Bay
Slaughter Bay
Emily Bay
Sydney Bay
Point Hunter
Point Ross

0   1 km

National Park and the **Botanic Garden** in the northern half of the island, which together cover twenty percent of Norfolk's area with subtropical rainforest. Norfolk Island is also an ornithologist's paradise, with nine endemic **bird** species, including the endangered **Norfolk Island green parrot**, with its distinctive chuckling call. The two small, uninhabited islands immediately south of Norfolk, **Nepean** and **Phillip** islands, are important **seabird** nesting sites.

Some history

A violent **volcanic eruption** three million years ago produced the Norfolk Ridge, extending from New Zealand to New Caledonia (Norfolk Island's closest neighbour, 700km north), with only Norfolk, **Phillip** and **Nepean islands** remaining above sea level. **Captain Cook** "discovered" the islands in 1774, but it's now believed that migrating Polynesian people lived here in the fourteenth or fifteenth centuries – their main settlement at Emily Bay has been excavated and stone tools found. Cook thought the tall **Norfolk pines** would make fine ships' masts, with accompanying sails woven from the native flax. Norfolk Island was settled in 1788, only six weeks after Sydney. However, plans to use the fertile island as a base to grow food for the starving young colony of Australia floundered when, in 1790, a First Fleet ship, the *Sirius*, was wrecked on a reef off the island, highlighting its lack of a navigable harbour. This **first settlement** was proved unviable when the pines were found not to be strong enough for masts, and it was finally abandoned in 1814. Most of the buildings were destroyed to discourage settlement by other powers.

Norfolk's isolation was one of the major reasons for its **second settlement** as a **prison** (1825–55), described officially as "a place of the extremest punishment short of death"; up to two thousand convicts were held on Norfolk, overseen by sadistic commandants who had virtually unlimited power to run the settlement and inflict punishments as they saw fit. Some of the imposing stone buildings designed by Royal Engineers still stand in **Kingston**, on the southern coast of the island.

Norfolk was again abandoned in 1855, but this time the buildings remained and were used a year later during the **third settlement**, which consisted of 194 Pitcairn Islanders (the entire population), who left behind their overcrowded conditions to establish a new life here. The new settlers had only eight family surnames among them – five of which (Christian, Quintal, Adams, McCoy and Young) were the names of the original mutineers of the *Bounty*. These names – especially Christian – are still common on the island, and today about one in three islanders can claim descent from the mutineers. These descendants still speak some of their original language to each other: listen for expressions such as "Watawieh Yorlye?" ("How are you?") and "Si Yorlye Morla" ("See you tomorrow"). **Bounty Day**, the day the Pitcairners arrived, is celebrated in Kingston on June 8.

Getting there

Norfolk Air (☎1300 663 913, ⓦwww.norfolkair.com) operate **flights to Norfolk Island** from Sydney (4 weekly), Brisbane (3 weekly), Melbourne (weekly), Newcastle (weekly) and Hamilton in New Zealand, while Air New Zealand fly to the island twice weekly from Auckland – flights from Australia cost from around A$700 return, and those from New Zealand from A$550; all flights from Norfolk are subject to a A$30 departure tax.

Visitors need to pre-book their accommodation, either independently or as part of a **package**, which can cost as little as A$819 for seven nights: try Oxley Travel (☎02 6583 1955 or 1800 671 546, ⓦwww.oxleytravel.com.au) or Talpacific Holidays (☎1300 665 737, ⓦwww.talpacific.com).

Information, transport and tours

The **airport** is on the western side of the island, just outside **Burnt Pine**, the main service centre; here you'll find the **tourist office** (Mon, Tues, Thurs & Fri 8.30am–5pm, Wed 8.30am–4pm, Sat 8.30am–3pm; ☎+6723 22147, ⓦwww .norfolkisland.com), which books tours and activities; the liquor bond store, which sells discounted alcohol on production of your airline ticket; the **post office**; the Communications Centre, where you go to make international **phone calls**; and two banks, Westpac and Commonwealth (the latter has the island's only ATM).

There's no public transport on Norfolk Island and it's rather hilly, so getting around **by car** is much the best option. Many accommodation places offer a car as part of the package or give you a big discount on **car rental**. It's very cheap anyway, with rates between A$20 and A$25 per day – Aloha Rent A Car (☎+6723 22510) is based at the airport. No one bothers with seat belts or even driving mirrors, and the maximum speed limit is only 50kph (40kph in town). There are also a limited number of **bikes** for rent, which can be arranged through the tourist office or your accommodation.

Tours

Pinetree Tours has an office on the main street next to the Commonwealth Bank (℡+6723 22424, ⓦwww.pinetreetours.com); they offer a slew of **tours**, including an introductory half-day bus trip around the island (A$28), a convict tour (A$28) and meals in islanders' homes (A$56). Bounty Excursions (℡+6723 23693, ⓔbounty@norfolk.nf) also runs a range of cultural and historic trips, while Culla & Co, on Rooty Hill Road (℡+6723 22312), offers shire–horse-drawn carriage rides of the island.

Norfolk is surrounded by a coral reef and pristine waters, so at least one waterborne tour is a must; the volcanic sea floor is full of caves and swim-throughs and the whole area is a marine reserve – commercial fishing is banned. There are several glass–bottomed **boat cruises** (A$20) on Emily Bay, including on the *Bounty Glass Bottomed Boat* (℡+6723 22515) and *Christian's Glaas Bohtam Boet* (℡+6723 23258). For fishing trips, call Advance Fishing (℡+6723 23363, ⓦwww.nf/advancefishing). Bounty Divers (℡+6723 24375, ⓦwww.bountydivers.com) run PADI **diving** courses (Open Water A$550) and trips (A$120 per dive, including gear), have **snorkelling** and **diving** gear for rent, and lead guided reef-walks. Tropical Sea Kayaks (℡+6723 80508, ⓦwww.seakayaking.nf) runs an easy **kayak** tour (1hr 30min; A$25) and a beautiful, longer paddle taking in tall cliffs, tiny islands, sea stacks and arches before culminating in a swim in the tranquil lagoon (A$45).

Accommodation

Anson Bay Lodge Bullock's Hut Rd ℡+6723 22897, ⓦwww.ansonbaylodge.com. Small, blue weatherboard cottage for two to four people. One of the cheapest places on the island but not for anyone offended by pine furniture. ❸

Christians of Bucks Point Ball Bay ℡+6723 23833, ⓦwww.christians.nf. Frilly, historic property on the southeast coast, where much of the timber used is from original convict buildings. You're welcomed with champagne; the rate also includes use of a car. ❼

Forrester Court Clifftop Cottages Mill Rd, Cascade ℡+6723 22838, ⓦwww.forrestercourt.com. Lovely boutique cottages with great views over Cascade Bay and a tennis court. Car rental

and a breakfast basket is included in the price. ❼

Shearwater Scenic Villas Point Ross ℡+6723 22539, ⓦwww.shearwater.nf. Self-contained accommodation in extensive grounds, with terrific water views over Bumbora Reserve. ❻

Tintoela of Norfolk Cascade ℡+6723 22946, ⓦwww.tintoela.nf. Large, luxury wooden house, and adjacent cottages sleeping up to ten, with panoramic views of Cockpit Valley and Cascade Bay. Car included. ❻

Whispering Pines Mount Pitt Rd ℡+6723 22114, ⓦwww.norfolk-pines-group.nf/whisper.html. Another place that won't break the bank, with charming, hexagonal timber cottages hidden in thickly wooded gardens. ❹

The island

Norfolk's main settlement, **BURNT PINE**, is a fairly modern affair crammed with shops selling everything from cosmetics to stereos, all at duty-free prices; most shops are closed on Wednesday and Saturday afternoons and all day Sunday. The island's ecotourism attraction, **A Walk in the Wild** (daily 2–5pm; free), is based here at Taylor's Road, educating visitors about the fragile, disappearing rainforest and its bird life.

KINGSTON is Norfolk's administrative centre, with the Legislative Assembly meeting in the military barracks, and the old colonial Government House now home to the island's Administrator. There's an excellent view from the **Queen Elizabeth Lookout** over the **Kingston and Arthur's Vale Historic Area** and the poignant seafront **cemetery**, containing a number of graves from the brutal second settlement and detailed interpretative boards. You can tour the remaining buildings and their museums separately (A$8) or with a combined ticket (A$21.80), which allows multiple access to all the town's museum sites over several days (daily 11am–3pm; Ⓦwww .museums.gov.nf). **Quality Row** bears some of the world's most impressive examples of Georgian **military architecture**, and looking at the buildings now it's difficult to imagine the suffering that took place behind their walls. This is the place to come for a taste of Norfolk Island history: there are four museums housed under the umbrella of the **Norfolk Island Museum**. The **Archeological Museum** is located in the basement of the former Commissariat, which was built in 1835; the upstairs was converted to the All Saints Church by the Pitcairners. Close by, in the **No. 10 House Museum**, there are examples of Norfolk pine furniture made by convicts. The worthwhile **Social History Museum**, in the Pier Store, outlines the story of the island through its three settlements. Perhaps most interesting, though, is the **Maritime Museum**, in what was once the Protestant chapel; various artefacts recovered from the 1790 wreck of the *Sirius* are on display, including its huge anchor, but more compelling is the *Bounty*-related paraphernalia brought here by Pitcairners, including the ship's cannon and even the kettle that was used on Pitcairn Island for everything from fermenting liquor to boiling sea water for salt.

The Kingston area is also the site of the island's main swimming **beaches**, protected by a small reef. Immediately in front of the walls of the ruined barracks is **Slaughter Bay**, which has a sandy beach dotted with interestingly gnarled and eroded basalt rock formations; the small hard-coral reef is excellent for **snorkelling**. At low tide you can take a cruise in a glass-bottomed boat (see "Tours", p.397) from nearby Emily Bay, which is also a beautiful, safe swimming area backed by a large pine forest.

In **Bumbora Reserve**, just west of Kingston, reached by car via Bumbora Road, you can see the natural re-growth of Norfolk pines; from the reserve you can walk down to Bumbora Beach, a shady little strip of sand where you'll find some safe pools for children to swim in at low tide. There's another track down to **Crystal Pool**, which has more swimming and snorkelling.

The west coast

West of Burnt Pine, along Douglas Drive, you'll find the exquisite **St Barnabas Chapel**, once the property of the Melanesian Mission (Anglican), which relocated gradually here from New Zealand between 1866 and 1921. The chapel's rose window was designed by William Morris and some of the others by Sir Edward Burne-Jones; the altar was carved by Solomon Islanders – ancestral masters of the craft.

Further along the **west coast** there's a scenic picnic area with tables and barbecues high over **Anson Bay**, from where it's a satisfying walk down to the beach. Immediately north of here, **Norfolk Island National Park** has 8km of walking trails, many of them old logging tracks. Many walks start from **Mount Pitt** (320m), a pleasing drive up a fairly narrow and winding sealed road surrounded by palms and trees – worth it for the panoramic views. The most enjoyable walk from here is the three-kilometre route to the **Captain Cook Monument** (1hr 45min), which starts as a beautiful grassy path but soon becomes a downward-sloping dirt track with some steps. Just south of the national park, on Mount Pitt Road, the tranquil rainforest of the **Botanic Gardens** is worth a stroll. Here you can observe the forty endemic plant species, including the pretty native hibiscus, the native palm, and the island's best-known symbol, the **Norfolk pine**, which can grow as high as 57m with a circumference of up to 11m. Camping isn't allowed in the national park or the gardens, although they're both open around the clock.

Eating, drinking and entertainment

Island **food** is plain and fresh, with an emphasis on locally caught fish and home-grown seasonal produce. Tahitian influence remains in the tradition of big fish-fries, and in some novel ways of preparing bananas. As most accommodation is self-catering, you'll need to head to the Foodland Supermarket in Burnt Pine (daily to 6pm). On Sunday afternoon, **fresh fish** is sold at the Kingston pier.

The best, and most expensive, **restaurant** is *Mariah's*, at *Hillcrest Gardens Hotel* on Taylor's Road (℡ +6723 22255), for à la carte dining with spectacular views of Phillip Island. *Dino's* on Bumboras Road (℡ +6723 24225) is a quality licensed Italian place with a pleasant ambience, while the *South Pacific Resort* on Taylor's Road (℡ +6723 23154) puts on big fish-fries, smorgasbord nights, carveries and musical shows at various times during the week; on other nights, an ordinary brasserie menu is available from 5.30pm. A superb spot for **lunch** is the extremely popular *Café Pacifica* on Cutters Corn Road (℡ +6723 23210), set in a leafy nursery and serving exquisite brunches and afternoon teas.

The **clubs** on the island provide good places to eat, drink and mingle with the locals. Facing each other across Burnt Pine's main street are the *Sports and Workers Club* and the *Norfolk Island Bowling Club*. The *Golf Club* in Kingston has a popular bar that also serves meals. The only **pub** is the *Brewery* on Douglas Drive, opposite the airport, with local ales such as "Bee Sting" and "Bligh's Revenge", pool tables and a rough, late-night crowd that can be a bit intimidating for single women.

Travel details

Trains

Blue Mountains (Blackheath, Katoomba and Leura) to: Sydney (hourly; 2hr–2hr 20min).
Casino (for Byron Bay and Hinterland) to: Brisbane (daily; 2hr 40min); Sydney (daily; 11hr 15min).
Coffs Harbour to: Brisbane (daily; 5hr 20min); Sydney (daily; 8hr 40min).
Grafton to: Brisbane (daily; 3hr); Sydney (daily; 10hr).
Nambucca Heads to: Brisbane (daily; 6hr); Sydney (daily; 8hr).
Newcastle to: Sydney (hourly; 2hr 40min).
Wauchope (near Port Macquarie) to: Brisbane (daily; 8hr); Sydney (daily; 6hr 30min).

Buses

Byron Bay to: Ballina (13–22 daily; 40min); Brisbane (9 daily; 2hr 30min); Brunswick Heads (10–13 daily; 15min); Buladelah (6 daily; 9hr 20min); Coffs Harbour (8 daily; 4hr); Forster (daily; 8hr 45min); Grafton (8 daily; 3hr); Karuah (7 daily;

9hr 45min); Lennox Head (8–12 daily; 25min); Lismore (6–10 daily; 2hr 5min); Maclean (5 daily; 2hr 15min); Murwillumbah (5 daily; 55min); Nambucca Heads (6 daily; 3hr 30min); Port Macquarie (5 daily; 8hr); Surfers Paradise (9 daily; 1hr 20min); Sydney (4 daily; 14hr 15min); Tweed Heads (4–5 daily; 1hr 20min); Urunga (6 daily; 3hr 20min).
Coffs Harbour to: Bellingen (Mon–Fri 4–5 daily, Sun daily; 1hr); Byron Bay (8 daily; 3hr 50min); Dorrigo (Tues, Thurs & Sun daily; 1hr 10min); Grafton (8–12 daily; 1hr 10min); Nambucca Heads (6–11 daily; 1hr); Port Macquarie (6–7 daily; 2hr 40min); Urunga (6–11 daily; 40min).
Murwillumbah to: Ballina (1–2 daily; 1hr 40min); Byron Bay (5 daily; 55 min); Casino (1–2 daily; 2hr 50min); Lennox Head (1–2 daily; 1hr 30min); Lismore (1–2 daily; 2hr 20min).
Port Macquarie to: Ballina (5 daily; 6hr); Bellingen (Tues, Thurs & Sun; 3hr 15min); Byron Bay (6 daily; 7hr); Coffs Harbour (6 daily; 2hr 40min); Dorrigo (Tues, Thurs & Sun; 3hr 50min); Grafton (5 daily; 4hr 10min); Wauchope (2–6 daily; 1hr).

Flights

Ballina to: Melbourne (2–6 per week; 2hr 5min); Sydney (5 daily; 1hr 50min).
Coffs Harbour to: Brisbane (1–2 daily; 1hr); Lord Howe Island (1 per week, summer only; 2hr) Port Macquarie (1–2 daily; 1hr 30min); Sydney (6–7 daily; 1hr 25min).
Lismore to: Sydney (3–4 daily; 1hr 50min).
Lord Howe Island to: Brisbane (1–2 per week; 1hr 35min); Port Macquarie (summer only; 1 per week; 1hr 20min); Sydney (1–3 daily; 1hr 30min).

Newcastle to: Brisbane (5–7 daily; 1hr 5min); Canberra (1–4 daily; 1hr 10min); Melbourne (5 daily; 1hr 35min); Sydney (3–8 daily; 45min).
Norfolk Island to: Brisbane (3–4 per week; 2hr 25min); Newcastle (1 per week); Sydney (4 per week; 2hr 30min).
Port Macquarie to: Coffs Harbour (1–2 daily; 30min); Lord Howe Island (summer only; 1 per week; 1hr 20min); Sydney (3–8 daily; 1hr).

6

Brisbane and southeast Queensland

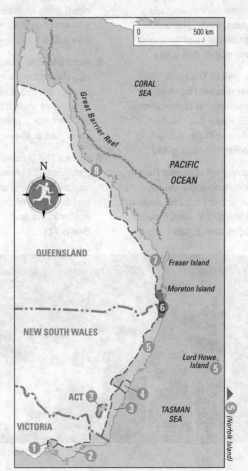

CORAL
SEA

Great Barrier Reef

PACIFIC
OCEAN

N

QUEENSLAND

Fraser Island

Moreton Island

NEW SOUTH WALES

Lord Howe
Island

ACT

TASMAN
SEA

VICTORIA

(Norfolk Island)

0   500 km

Highlights

✳ **Surfing the Gold Coast** This perennially popular holiday region is a boardrider's dream, with superb waves and a buzzing social scene. See p.407

✳ **Q1 Deck, Surfers Paradise** Zoom up to the seventy-seventh floor of Australia's highest building for unforgettable views of southeast Queensland. See p.419

✳ **Australian Outback Spectacular** Excellent showmanship and equestrian skills make this celebration of Aussie ideals a cracking evening out. See p.422

✳ **Lamington National Park** A compelling region to explore, with ancient forests, abundant wildlife and inviting mountain lodges. See p.426

✳ **Tangalooma, Moreton Island** Spot dugongs and turtles in Moreton Bay, then join the wildlife rangers in feeding wild dolphins. See p.436

✳ **Brisbane's South Bank** The River City's sleek modern-arts complex has real cultural clout, while its urban beach is a touch of genius. See p.449

✳ **Australia Zoo** Exactly how a zoo should be – with happy, healthy animals and upbeat, informative staff, it's a credit to its creator, the late Steve Irwin. See p.464

✳ **Noosa** The Sunshine Coast's most desirable resort offers elegant shopping and dining, and a chance of seeing koalas in the wild. See p.471

▲ Q1 tower, Surfers Paradise

6

Brisbane and southeast Queensland

T he southeastern corner of Queensland is holiday central, with a superb climate and a legendary coastline. Long, broad, sandy and fringing an emerald ocean, the region's **beaches** are as popular with picnic-toting families, strolling couples and partying backpackers as with the legions of hard-bodied, live-to-surf locals who contrive to spend as much time as possible outdoors.

This is by far the most developed section of the state, with a population that's rocketed over recent years; if you've already seen some of central and northern Queensland, where the coast is much wilder, or are travelling north from the relatively low-rise New South Wales coast, you'll be struck by the accommodation blocks punctuating the skyline close to shore. Few of southeast Queensland's coastal towns are completely free of high-rise blocks, but it's in the **Gold Coast**, the strip adjoining the state border, that large-scale development reaches a resounding crescendo – notably in Surfers Paradise, home to the tallest building in Australia, Q1, whose spire can be seen 200km away. If you choose to stay here, by far the best plan is to embrace the thoroughly three-dimensional environment – stay in a tower, admire the staggering ocean views, and enjoy the way the urban vibe follows through at street level in a buzz of energetic shopping, bar-hopping and out-of-town theme park rides.

An hour inland, the green heights of the **Gold Coast Hinterland**, which includes part of the World Heritage-listed Central Eastern Rainforest Reserves of Australia, offer a complete contrast – here there's a chain of national parks to explore on foot with stunning views of forested slopes and valleys. The parks are home to rare and threatened flora, including ancient Antarctic beech trees, some with root systems over 5000 years old, and more species of frog, snake, bird and marsupial than any other similarly sized area of Australia. **Lamington National Park**'s pioneering mountain lodges, founded in the late 1920s and early 1930s, are an ideal base for hikers and wildlife-watchers, while **Tamborine**

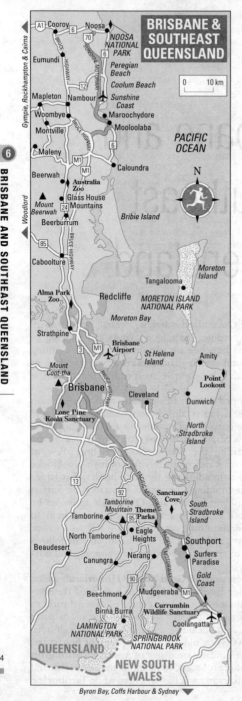

BRISBANE & SOUTHEAST QUEENSLAND

Gympie, Rockhampton & Cairns

Woodford

0   10 km

PACIFIC
OCEAN

N

Cooroy
Noosa
NOOSA NATIONAL PARK
Eumundi
Peregian Beach
Coolum Beach
Mapleton
Nambour
Sunshine Coast
Woombye
Maroochydore
Montville
Mooloolaba
Maleny
Caloundra
Beerwah
Australia Zoo
Glass House Mountains
Mount Beerwah
Beerburrum
Bribie Island
Caboolture
Tangalooma
Moreton Island
Alma Park Zoo
Redcliffe
MORETON ISLAND NATIONAL PARK
Moreton Bay
Strathpine
Brisbane Airport
St Helena Island
Amity
Mount Coot-tha
Brisbane
Point Lookout
Cleveland
Dunwich
Lone Pine Koala Sanctuary
North Stradbroke Island
Tamborine Mountain
Sanctuary Cove
Tamborine
Theme Parks
South Stradbroke Island
Eagle Heights
North Tamborine
Beaudesert
Nerang
Southport
Canungra
Surfers Paradise
Gold Coast
Beechmont
Mudgeeraba
Binna Burra
Currumbin Wildlife Sanctuary
LAMINGTON NATIONAL PARK
Coolangatta
SPRINGBROOK NATIONAL PARK
QUEENSLAND
NEW SOUTH WALES

Byron Bay, Coffs Harbour & Sydney

Mountain has several attractive luxury retreats, perfect for touring the region's food and wine trails.

Brisbane, the state capital, is a relaxed riverside city with a manageably compact centre and a thriving social scene, focussed around a glut of good restaurants and a feast of live music venues. For those planning an extended stay, it's a good place to hunt down casual work. Offshore, **South Stradbroke**, **North Stradbroke** and **Moreton Island** are southeast Queensland's answer to Fraser Island – giant sand dunes surrounded by waters patrolled by dolphins, dugongs and whales. North of Brisbane, fruit and vegetable plantations behind the gentle **Sunshine Coast** benefit from rich volcanic soils and a subtropical climate, overlooked by the spiky, isolated peaks of the **Glass House Mountains**. Nearby is **Australia Zoo**, one of the country's most enjoyable animal attractions, while **Noosa** in the far north of the region is a highly appealing resort town with an upmarket atmosphere, a pristine coastal park, and more famous surf.

Regional practicalities

Accommodation in southeast Queensland includes an abundance of reasonably priced self-catering apartments and pricier resort hotels in the coastal and island resorts, a good mix of executive-friendly hotels and more modest city B&Bs in Brisbane, and a scattering of delightful hiking lodges and rural retreats in the hinterland. The centres with the greatest choice of backpacker accommodation are Surfers Paradise and Brisbane.

The region's international **airport** is in Brisbane; there are smaller airports near Coolangatta on the Gold Coast and just north of Maroochydore on the Sunshine Coast, both served by internal flights. The Brisbane-to-Cairns **Bruce Highway (A1/M1)** is the main transport artery for the north of the region; in Brisbane it becomes the **Pacific Motorway**, linking the city with the Gold Coast and New South Wales. Brisbane is the hub of a **rail**, **bus** and **long-distance bus** network which extends north to Noosa and south to Coolangatta; the railway runs 12–15km inland, with bus connections to the coastal towns. Oddly, perhaps, there's no direct line between Brisbane and the northern New South Wales coast – bus is the only public transport option for this route. **Car hire** is a good investment if you'd like to explore the quietest stretches of the coast and hinterland; a wide choice of **day-trips** can show you the blockbuster attractions such as Lamington National Park, Australia Zoo and the Gold Coast theme park. The offshore islands are served by **ferries** operated by their resorts.

Weather and seasons

Southeast Queensland enjoys a pleasant subtropical **climate**; with around three hundred days of sunshine each year there's little "off-season" as such. In summer (November to March), temperatures can be high, but humidity and rainfall are moderate compared to the north of the state – the heavy rains of late 2007 and early 2008 were a much-needed break in a long drought that necessitated severe restrictions on domestic, industrial and agricultural water usage. If you're staying in the hinterland mountains in winter (April to November), you'll be glad of some warm clothing.

The most popular resorts, including Noosa and Surfers Paradise, are always packed over Christmas and New Year and at Easter, but seasonal festivals and events bulk up the crowds throughout the year. The Gold Coast is a notorious **Schoolies Week** destination, with thousands of high-school leavers from across the country ditching their exam rooms in mid-November for a few days of hard partying in Surfers Paradise. Other busy events include the **Quiksilver Roxy Pro Surf Championships** hosted by Kirra Beach in February; the week-long **Noosa Festival of Surfing** in March and month-long **Noosa Mayfiesta** in May; the **Blues on Broadbeach** festival in late May; the **Coolangatta Wintersun Festival** – ten days of rock & roll nostalgia – in June; the **Brisbane Festival** in July (even years) and **Riverfestival** in late August; the **Gold Coast Indy** car race in October; and the **Woodford Folk Festival** in late December. **Whale-watching** season is roughly June to November.

The Gold Coast

Beneath a jagged skyline shaped by scores of high-rise beachfront apartments, the **Gold Coast** is Australia's Miami Beach or Costa del Sol, a striking contrast to dignified, business-like Brisbane, only an hour away to the north. Aggressively superficial, it's not the place to go if you're seeking peace and quiet, but its sheer brashness can be fun for a couple of days – perhaps as a weekend break from Brisbane. There's little variety in the beach and nightclub scene, however, and if you're concerned this will leave you jaded, bored or broke, you'd be better off avoiding this corner of Queensland altogether.

The coast is blessed with a virtually unbroken beach, 40km long, from **Coolangatta** at Queensland's southern border, past **Burleigh Heads**, **Broadbeach** and **Surfers Paradise** to **Main Beach** and **The Spit** just clear of South Stradbroke Island. The wide, golden **sands**, nominally why everyone comes to the Gold Coast, swarm with bathers and **surfers** all year round: board-riding first blossomed here in the 1930s and the key breaks at Coolangatta, Currumbin and Burleigh Heads still pull daily crowds. In the meantime, other attractions have sprung up, notably the **pub-and-club scene** centred on Surfers Paradise, a slew of **adrenaline activities** from bungee jumping to V8 Supercar racing, and the action-packed, out-of-town **theme parks**, perennially popular with the young Australians and Asians who visit the region in their hordes.

Getting there and around

The nearest major international **airport** to the Gold Coast is in Brisbane; the regional Gold Coast Airport (OOL; ⓦwww.goldcoastairport.com), 3km west of Coolangatta, is served by Air Asia, Freedom Air, Jetstar, Qantas, Tiger Airways and Virgin Blue (see p.35), with domestic flights from Newcastle, Sydney, Melbourne and Adelaide and international flights from New Zealand and Malaysia. Surfside Buslines and Gold Coast Tourist Shuttle (see below) run **buses** between the airport and the resorts. All the main coastal suburbs are served by long-distance **buses** run by Greyhound and Premier (see p.35).

From Brisbane, the Pacific Motorway (M1) leads straight down to the Gold Coast. Local buses from Brisbane Transit Centre on Roma Street include Kirklands (ⓣ02 6626 1499, ⓦwww.kirklands.com.au), which run about eight times daily to Southport, Surfers, Burleigh Heads and Coolangatta. Coachtrans (ⓣ07 3358 9700 or 1300 664 700, ⓦwww.coachtrans.com.au) and Gold Coast Con-x-ion (ⓣ07 5556 9888, ⓦwww.con-x-ion.com) both organize door-to-door transfers from Brisbane to Gold Coast lodgings or theme parks; the fare from Brisbane airport to Surfers Paradise is around A$38 (child A$19). You can also get to the Gold Coast from central Brisbane by taking the TransLink Citytrain **rail service**, which stops at Coomera, Helensvale, Nerang and Robina, all of which have local bus connections to the coast; a one-way trip to Surfers Paradise costs around A$11. From Brisbane airport, the Airtrain (ⓦwww.airtrain.com.au) runs direct to the same stops; the fare including an onward bus trip is around A$28, or A$37 including a transfer to the door of your final destination.

From New South Wales, the coastal highway enters Queensland at Coolangatta; Kirklands buses (see above) cover this route, while J&B Coaches (ⓣ02 5592 2655, ⓦwww.byronbayexpress.com.au) run a daily service between Byron Bay and Surfers Paradise. In summer, New South Wales **time** is an hour ahead of Queensland, so you'll have to adjust your watch on crossing the border. There's no **railway line** from the New South Wales coast to the Gold Coast; the nearest line is the Sydney–Brisbane CountryLink, which runs some distance inland, with no stops between Kyogle in New South Wales and Brisbane.

Getting around, Surfside Buslines run a 24-hour bus service (up to six times hourly; timetables available from bus drivers, on ⓣ1300 655 655 or at ⓦwww .surfside.com.au) along the Gold Coast Highway from Tweed Heads and Coolangatta to Surfers Paradise and Southport and out to all the theme parks. Their various **passes** give unlimited bus travel for between three and fourteen days (A$26–63, child A$13–31.50). Their transfer division, Gold Coast Tourist Shuttle, offers passes for unlimited door-to-door trips in the Gold Coast area, including to and from the theme parks and Gold Coast Airport (A$58–132, child A$29–66). The alternative is to take **taxis** (℡13 10 08) or **hire a car** (see p.421).

Orientation and information

The term "Gold Coast" is variously used to describe the unbroken urban development that stretches all the way from Coolangatta to Sanctuary Cove, or the broader region that also includes the inland theme parks (see box, p.422), the hinterland national parks (see p.423) and the offshore islands (see p.432). The urban area is referred to as a city but with little industry apart from tourism it's fairer to think of it as an overgrown string of resorts – the principal is Southport, but the best known by far is the skyscraper-heavy Surfers Paradise.

Surfing the Gold Coast

The locals will assure you that the Gold Coast has the best **surfing beaches** in the world. In terms of consistency, this might be true – on any given day there will be good surf somewhere along the coast, with two-hundred-metre-long sand-bottom point breaks, and rideable waves peaking at about four metres in prime conditions.

The coast is known for its **barrels**, particularly during the summer storm season when the winds shift around to the north; in winter, the swell is smaller but more reliable, making it easier to learn to surf. A rule of thumb for finding the best surf is to **follow the wind**: head to the north end of the coast when the wind blows from the north, and the south when it comes from the south. Generally, you'll find the **best swell** along the southern beaches – favourite spots include **Snapper Rocks** in Coolangatta, **Burleigh Heads** and **Currumbin Alley**. Other famous breaks are found off **South Stradbroke Island**, just beyond the Gold Coast to the north (see p.432).

Sea temperatures range between 26°C in December and 17°C in June, so a 2–3mm wetsuit is adequate. Hard-core surfers come for Christmas and the cyclone season, though spring is usually the busiest time. Major international and state **championships** are held in the Burleigh Heads and Coolangatta areas between December and March, with local **competitions** and events taking place all along the coast on most weekends, advertised through local surf shops.

All beaches between Coolangatta and Main Beach are **patrolled** – look for the signs – and while sharks might worry you, more commonplace hostility is likely to come from the locals, who form tight-knit cliques with very protective attitudes towards their patches.

For expert **tuition**, **tours**, or **advice** on the Gold Coast surfing scene, contact Go Ride a Wave on Cavill Mall, Surfer's Paradise (℡1300 132 441, ⓦwww .gorideawave.com.au); a two-hour beginners' session costs around A$70, or less if you book in advance. They also offer **board hire**, as do numerous surf shops in Surfers Paradise, Coolangatta and elsewhere on the coast; typical prices are A$25–45 a day or from A$75 a week for board rental, plus credit-card deposit. Other local tutors include former world champion Cheyne Horan at Surfers Paradise Surf Lifesaving Club (℡1800 227873, ⓦwww.cheynehoran.com.au; 2hr group lesson A$45) and international pro Nancy Emerson (℡07 5559 5902 or 0413 380 933, ⓦwww.surfclinics.com; 2hr group lesson A$85), whose team works in various areas. Walkin' on Water (℡07 5534 1886, ⓦwww.walkinonwater.com) teach beginners in Cooolangatta.

To try your hand at **kitesurfing**, another popular Gold Coast pastime, get in touch with Pureaqua (℡0416 267 654 or 0414 944 354, ⓦwww.pureaqua.com.au) on the Broadwater at Southport, who offer beginners a three-hour intro package for A$185; other outfits include Kitesurf (℡0405 197 870, ⓦwww.kitesurfgoldcoast.com) and Kamikaze Kites on Mermaid Beach, south of Broadbeach (℡07 5592 5171, ⓦwww.kamikazekites.com).

The Gold Coast is no place to sit still and do nothing – key to its huge popularity with young, energetic holidaymakers is the plethora of activities on offer, with the emphasis on high-octane thrills, and new options popping up all the time. Most of the theme parks, racing tracks and airfields lie twenty to thirty minutes northwest of Surfers Paradise, clustered around the Pacific Motorway (M1). Hikers, wildlife enthusiasts and birdwatchers will find plenty of stretches of beautiful wilderness within day-trip distance, from the offshore islands north of town to the mountains and vineyards of the hinterland to the west and south.

Brisbane day-trips
Gray Line Tours (Brisbane; ☎07 3489 6401 or 1300 360 776, ⊛www.graylinetours .com.au) will pick you up from the Gold Coast and whisk you around the city sights including Mount Coot-tha and Lone Pine (full day A$98, child A$62).

Bungee jumping
Bungy Australia (19 Palm Ave, Surfers Paradise; ☎07 5570 4833, ⊛www .bungyaustralia.com; A$99) has a thirty-metre rig, equivalent to fourteen storeys.

Go-karting
Karting in Paradise (Peachy Rd, Ormeau; ☎07 3382 6000, ⊛www .kartinginparadise.com.au; from A$27 for 10min) lets you loose to race your mates around a 1.3-kilometre track, the longest in Queensland. The site is a 25-minute drive northwest of Surfers, off the Pacific Motorway. There's another track in Pimpama (**Le Mans Kart Racing**; 232 Old Pacific Highway ☎07 5546 6566, ⊛www.lemanskarting .com) with a seven-hundred-metre circuit.

Great Barrier Reef
Seair will fly you straight to **Lady Elliot Island** from Coolangatta in 1hr 45 minutes, by special arrangement with *Lady Elliot Island Resort* (see p.498). You can drop in for the day or stay overnight. For a good choice of other reef destinations, head to Brisbane and fly to Proserpine, Hamilton Island or Cairns.

Hinterland and Sunshine Coast day-trips and tours
The following tour companies, based on the Gold Coast, offer day-trips for A$55–135 (child A$25–75); some also organize longer tours:
Coast to Bush Tours (13 Kurrawa Ave, Mermaid Beach; ☎0410 611 589 or 07 5572 3171) will take you to Tamborine Mountain and Lamington National Park or Springbook National Park; they charge more than most, but you'll be with a small group.
The Mountain Coach (Coolangatta; ☎07 5524 4249 or 1300 762 665, ⊛www .mountaincoach.com.au) run daily day-trips from numerous points on the Gold Coast to Tamborine Mountain and *O'Reilly's* in Lamington National Park.
Mountain Trek Adventures (Nerang; ☎07 5578 3157 ⊛www.bigvolcano.com .au/custom/mtntrek) organize small-group 4WD day-tours of the hinterland parks with a barbecue lunch instead of the standard picnic; they also offer late-afternoon wildlife-spotting trips in Springbrook National Park.
Scenic Hinterland Tours (Beach Rd, Surfers Paradise; ☎07 5531 5536, ⊛www .hinterlandtours.com.au) offer comfortable, reasonably priced coach trips to most hinterland national parks; they'll also take you up to the Sunshine Coast or down to Byron Bay.
Southern Cross (Labrador; ☎07 5574 5041 or 1800 067 367, ⊛www.sc4wd.com .au) will drive you around Tamborine Mountain or Lamington National Park, visiting waterfalls and tackling offbeat tracks by rugged 4WD bus.

The following, based elsewhere in southeast Queensland, will pick you up from the Gold Coast or Brisbane on request:

Araucaria Eco Tours (℡07 5544 1283, ⊛www.learnaboutwildlife.com) specialize in wildlife-watching tours of a day or longer throughout southeast Queensland.

Australian Day Tours (℡07 3489 6444, ⊛www.australiandaytours.com.au) have a dozen or so day-trips to the Sunshine Coast, Lamington National Park, Tamborine Mountain and south to Byron Bay in NSW.

Boots A'Walkin' (℡07 3398 2404, ⊛www.bootsawalkin.com.au) offer the chance to hike around the Gold Coast Hinterland national parks in the company of a highly experienced bushwalking guide.

Bushwacker Ecotours (℡1300 559 355, ⊛www.bushwacker-ecotours.com.au) are highly recommended for hiking day-trips to various parts of the Gold Coast Hinterland and north to the Glass House Mountains, featuring plenty of wildlife, rainforests, bushtucker and swimming holes.

Green Triangle Experiences (℡0402 623 736 or 1800 503 475, ⊛www .greentriangle.com.au) offer small-group guided tours to Springbrook National Park, catering for a young crowd.

Hot-air ballooning

Balloon Down Under (Burleigh West; ℡07 5593 8400, ⊛www.balloondownunder .com.au; A$295, child A$200 including transfers from Gold Coast hotels) will float you over the Gold Coast Hinterland at sunrise for stunning views.

Island tours

Island destinations within easy reach of the city include **Moreton Island** (see p.436), **North Stradbroke** (see p.433) and **South Stradbroke** (see p.432).

Paragliding

The **Paragliding Centre** in the Gold Coast Hinterland (3/40 Christie St, Canungra; ℡07 5543 4000, ⊛www.paraglidingcentre.com.au) offers tandem flights and courses in the Tamborine Mountain area.

Parasailing (parascending) and jetboating

You can take off over the ocean with **Seabreeze Sports** (Seaworld Drive, Main Beach; ℡07 5527 1099, ⊛www.seabreezesports.com.au; A$65), who also offer jet-skis and speed-boat rides, while **Extreme Jetboating** (℡07 5531 6176) specialize in no-holds-barred boat trips.

River cruises

For a fun way to explore the Nerang River and the Broadwater, **Aquaduck** (℡07 5539 0222, ⊛www.aquaduck.com.au; A$32, child A$26), an amphibious bus, departs five times daily from Orchid Avenue, Surfers Paradise for an hour-long trip; alternatively, **BlueFire Cruises** (℡07 5557 8888, ⊛bluefirecruisesqld.com.au; from A$75) offer dinner cruises with entertainment from Rio-style samba dancers; and **Wyndham Cruises** (℡07 5539 9299 or 1300 733 274, ⊛www.wyndhamcruises.com.au; A$42, child A$22), based at the Tiki Village Wharf at the river end of Cavill Avenue, spend a relaxed couple of hours on the water each morning and afternoon.

Scenic flights

Gold Coast Helitours (Marina Mirage Heliport, Main Beach; ℡07 5591 8457, ⊛www.goldcoasthelitours.com.au; from A$44 for 5min) offer sightseeing trips by helicopter. For a scenic flight with a touch of vintage glamour, **Tigermoth Joy Rides**

(Pimpama; ☏0418 787 475 or 1300 650 355, ⓦwww.tigermothjoyrides.com.au; from A$150 for 15min) will kit you out in Biggles-style helmet and goggles and take you for a spin over Surfers Paradise, South Stradbroke Island or the Gold Coast Hinterland in a 1930s biplane.

Skydiving

Jump out of a perfectly good helicopter with **Sky Dive Queensland** (Mariners Cove Marina, Main Beach; ☏07 5546 2877 or 1300 767 790, ⓦwww.skydiveqld.com.au), who offer tandem jumps onto the Surfers beach, and all the tuition you need to go solo.

Surfing

See box, p.407.

Theme parks

See box, p.422.

V8 Supercars and rally driving

At the **Holden Performance Driving Centre** in Norwell (☏07 5546 1366, ⓦwww.performancedriving.com.au) you can strap yourself into the passenger seat of a V8 SS Commodore for an adrenaline-pumping set of laps; book a driver-training session if you'd like to learn how it's done (from A$449). **WRX Experience** in Pimpama offer the full-on thrill of high-speed rally driving (☏1300 550 979, ⓦwww.wrxdrift.com.au; from A$195).

Vintage motorbike, classic car and performance car hire

For a novel way to tour Brisbane and southeast Queensland, **Adrenalin Harley Tours** (☏0414 239 668, ⓦwww.adrenalinharleytours.com.au) and **Adrenalin Motorcycle and Trike Tours** (☏0423 757 272 or 07 5579 8507, ⓦwww.triketours.net, from A$40 for 30min) will let you blast around on a Harley or Harley-Davidson Harley trike; **Retro Rides** (☏07 3256 6490, ⓦwww.retro-rides.com.au) will set you up with a chauffeur-driven vintage Chevvy; **Ferrari Experience** will hand you the keys of a stunningly engineered convertible for a brief ride around Surfers (☏0408 720 038; from A$220 for 40min); while with **Marque 1** (☏07 3391 0831, ⓦwww.marque1.com.au) you can indulge your millionaire fantasies in a shiny Porsche or Maserati.

Whale-watching

Spirit of Gold Coast (Mariners Cove Marina, Main Beach; ☏07 5572 7755, ⓦwww.goldcoastwhalewatching.com; half day A$89, child A$50, full day A$119/A$80) run daily cruises during the humpback migration season (June–Nov), boasting a 99.3 percent sighting success rate.

Winery tours

Coast to Bush Tours (13 Kurrawa Ave, Mermaid Beach; ☏0410 611 589 or 07 3372 3171; half day A$125, day A$85) operate chauffeur-driven wine-tasting trips around the Tamborine Mountain region, with detours to gardens and craft shops. **Australian Day Tours** (see p.409) and Brisbane-based winery-tour specialists **Cork'n'Fork** and **Winery Escape Tours** (see p.461) will pick you up from the Gold Coast for their tasting trips.

The Gold Coast Tourism Corporation (☏1300 309 440, ⓦwww.verygc .com) has **information centres** at 2 Cavill Ave, Surfers Paradise (Mon–Fri 8.30am–5.30pm, Sat 8.30am–5pm, Sun 9am–4pm; ☏07 5538 4419) and at

South of Surfers Paradise

The southern section of the Gold Coast is a haphazardly developed string of beach resorts – the busiest of which are Coolangatta, Currumbin, Burleigh Heads and Broadbeach – facing some of the best **surf** in the country. If you're not into surfing, you may well be underwhelmed: a mess of crowded, multi-lane traffic systems and uninspiring buildings make the urban landscape as forgettable as the **beaches** are remarkable. Explore a little further, though, and you'll find two **wildlife sanctuaries** and – unbelievably amidst all the commotion – a tiny **national park**, which preserves a remnant of the coast's original environment.

Coolangatta

On the Queensland–New South Wales border 66km north of Byron Bay and 102km south of Brisbane, **COOLANGATTA** merges seamlessly with its twin town, Tweed Heads (in New South Wales), along Boundary Street. With only a giant concrete plinth just off the main road marking the border, you'll probably make the crossing without realizing it. Unless it's New Year, when everyone takes advantage of the one-hour time difference between the states to celebrate twice, most travellers bypass Coolangatta completely; in doing so, they miss some of the best surf, least crowded beaches and the only place along the Gold Coast that can boast a real "local" community. New holiday apartment developments are beginning to have an impact on the skyline, but for now the general ambience remains that of a small seaside town.

Arrival and information

Gold Coast Airport is 3km west of Coolangatta – see p.406 for local transport connections. There are two **long-distance bus stops**: Premier set down in Bay Street, just over the border in Tweed Heads (and inside the NSW time zone), while Greyhound use a bus shelter at the corner of Warner and Chalk streets, in Coolangatta (and QLD). Coolangatta's helpful **tourist office** is about halfway down Griffith Street (Mon–Fri 8.30am–5.30pm, Sat 9am–3pm; ☏07 5569 3380, ⊛www.verygc.com). **Taxis** can be booked on ☏13 10 08. **Car rental** is available through Coolangatta Car Rentals, inside the Coolangatta Place complex halfway down Griffith Street (☏07 5536 9960); prices start at around A$40 a day.

Accommodation

Accommodation is concentrated near the state border, where apartment buildings overlook the sea on Marine Parade and Point Danger.

Coolangatta YHA 230 Coolangatta Rd, Bilinga ☏07 5536 7644, ⊛www.coolangattayha.com. Clean facilities and helpful management, who include breakfast in the rate. The position, 3km north of central Coolangatta, is a bit far from town, but handy for the airport and the quieter beaches. Bunk in shared room A$25–28, private double/twin ❷

Kirra Beach Hotel 128 Marine Parade, Kirra Point ☏07 5536 3411, ⊛www.kirrabeachhotel .com.au. Ideal location for board-riders, with low prices for reasonably spacious rooms with TV and fridge. ❷

Kirra Beach Tourist Park Charlotte St, Kirra ☏07 5581 7744, ⊛www.gctp.com.au/kirra. Around 1km inland on the north side of town, this

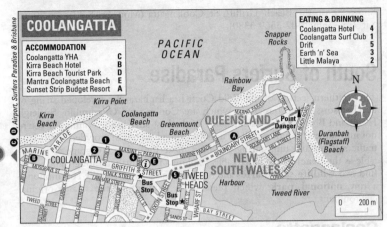

is probably the cheapest place in the area, with four- and two-person cabins, and tent sites. Reduced rates for longer stays. Camping A$27–30, cabins ②–④

Mantra Coolangatta Beach 88 Marine Parade ☏ 07 5506 8787, ⓦ www.mantracoolangattabeach .com.au. Smart, modern holiday apartments, many of them with stunning views over Greenmount

Beach, in a complex with a tennis court, fitness centre and pool. ⑤–⑥

Sunset Strip Budget Resort 199 Boundary St ☏ 07 5599 5517, ⓦ www.sunsetstrip.com.au. Offers singles, doubles and family rooms with a huge shared kitchen and lounge area, plus simple apartments. There's also a shared twenty-metre pool and sundeck. ②–③

The Town

Central Coolangatta's main thoroughfare, **Griffith Street**, lies one block back from the ocean, parallel to the shore, and is lined with banks, shops and eateries. It's connected by a handful of short streets to the oceanfront road, **Marine Parade**, which overlooks a string of glorious north-facing beaches – **Kirra**, **Coolangatta**, **Greenmount** and **Rainbow Bay**. The most popular with sun worshippers is Coolangatta, which is right in town; continue west beyond Kirra Point to Kirra Beach, and you'll find yourself at the start of a six-kilometre stretch of sand that is less crowded. Far in the distance to the northwest, the view over sand and sea ends with the jagged teeth of the Surfers Paradise skyscrapers.

Point Danger, the small headland on the eastern edge of town, lies half in Queensland and half in New South Wales: the state border cuts through it along Boundary Street, then continues along Griffith Street and Dixon Street. Marking the headland is a strikingly modernist **lighthouse**, built in 1971 and named after Captain Cook.

Twenty-five metres below the lighthouse, crowds of **surfers** make the most of the swell at **Duranbah Beach** (also known as Flagstaff Beach). Pros regularly visit Coolangatta to test out the "D-bah" beach break, a Gold Coast classic that's otherwise monopolized by hard-core locals. Other good, challenging spots to surf include **Snapper Rocks** at Point Danger's northern tip, ideal for longboarding, and **Kirra Point**, location of one of Australia's most famous point breaks, a favourite of world surfing champion Kelly Slater. For beginners, the reliable conditions at Greenmount Beach and Rainbow Bay are generally a good bet. **Surfboards and information** are available from Pipedream, 24 Griffith St (☏ 07 5599 1164), and Mount Woodgee, 122 Griffith St (☏ 07 5536 5937). You'll

▲ Surfing at Snapper Rocks, Coolangatta

find plenty of decent secondhand gear for sale, though local boards tend to be too thin and lightweight to use elsewhere. For **tuition**, see the box on p.407.

Eating, drinking and nightlife

There are plenty of **snack bars** and **restaurants** on Griffith Street and Marine Parade. The bistro at the *Coolangatta Surf Club* on Marine Parade (☏07 5536 4648; daily noon–8pm, plus Sun breakfast from 8am), which has a long shaded balcony overlooking the beach, is fantastic value. Also on Marine Parade is *Earth 'n' Sea* (☏07 5536 3477; lunch & dinner daily); like its namesake in Byron Bay, this is a great place for pizza. *Little Malaya*, at the western end of Marine Parade, serves up large noodle soups with chicken or seafood for next to nothing; while for more of a splurge, the casually stylish *Drift*, Griffith Plaza, 152 Griffith St (☏07 5536 6601; lunch & dinner daily) is good for seafood and Mod Oz meat dishes. The place to catch bands is the *Coolangatta Hotel*'s **nightclub**, on the corner of Marine Parade and Warner Street. If you're doing your own cooking, there's a 24-hour NightOwl convenience store at the Showcase Shopping Centre beside the *Coolangatta Hotel*, and bigger **supermarkets** across the border at the main shopping centre on Wharf Street, in Tweed Heads.

Currumbin

CURRUMBIN, 8km north of Coolangatta and 18km south of Surfers Paradise, is a low-key leftover from the days before high-density development. The focus is **Currumbin Wildlife Sanctuary**, off the Gold Coast Highway at Tomewin Street (daily 8am–5pm; A\$32, child A\$21; Wildnight Adventure 7pm daily; A\$49, child A\$27; ℡07 5534 1266 or 1300 886 511, Ⓦwww.cws.org.au), which was started in 1947 by local beekeeper and flower-grower Alex Griffiths, who began by feeding **rainbow lorikeets** to keep them away from his precious blooms, and went on to develop a seventy-acre reserve of woodlands and waterways into a native bird refuge. Today, the tradition of lorikeet feeding is still alive and well, the centre cares for sick and injured wildlife, and the sanctuary is a permanent home to marsupials including kangaroos, wallabies, possums and sugar gliders, reptiles including death adders and frilled dragons, and birds including emus and cassowaries. The park's strongest point is its beautiful natural setting, best experienced from the **elevated walkways** through the forest, where you'll see koalas, tree kangaroos and birds at eye-level. Visit in the evening, and you'll see some of the species that haven't adjusted their nocturnal habits; there's also music and dancing from an Aboriginal troupe. A Saturday morning **farmers' market** sets up opposite the sanctuary once or twice a month.

On the north side of town between Currumbin Point and Elephant Rock, **Currumbin Beach** is a good, relatively undeveloped stretch of coast; given a breeze there are usually some decent rollers to ride. **Currumbin Alley** near the mouth of Currumbin Creek is a favourite right-hand break that's within the grasp of rookie surfers. Just to the north, **Palm Beach** is more sheltered. Both the Currumbin and Palm Beach Surf Life Saving Clubs on the seafront are good places to stoke up on hearty **food**, while *The Boatshed*, 2 Thrower Drive, a little inland from the Gold Coast Highway (℡07 5534 3888; closed Mon) is a great spot for breakfast and Mod Oz fare.

Burleigh Heads

Around 19km north of Coolangatta and 7km south of Surfers Paradise, **Burleigh Heads** consists of a traffic bottleneck where the highway dodges between the beach and a rounded headland; there can be very good surf here, making it a favourite spot for local pros to try out their moves, but the rocks make it rough for novices. Sixty years ago, before the bitumen and paving took over, this was all dense eucalypt and vine forest, the last fragment of which survives as **Burleigh Head National Park**. Entrance is from the car park on Goodwin Terrace, on the north side of the park, or from the Gold Coast Highway, on the south side, where there's a QPWS information centre (daily 10am–3pm).

Geologically, the headland stems from the prehistoric eruptions of the Mount Warning volcano (p.386), 30km to the southwest. Lava surfaced through vents, cooling to tall hexagonal basalt columns, now mostly tumbled and covered in vines. Rainforest colonized the richer volcanic soils, while stands of red gum grew in weaker sandy loam; along the eastern seafront there's a patch of exposed heathland bordered by groups of pandanus, and a beach along the mouth of Tallebudgera Creek. This diversity is amazing considering the minimal space. While urban encroachment has seriously affected the **wildlife**, you can still see butterflies, brush turkeys and sunbathing dragons. Apart from the park, Burleigh Heads has little to detain you, but for a treat there's good **seafood** on offer at *Oskars on Burleigh* on the beachfront at 43 Goodwin Terrace (℡07 5576 3722).

Less than 2km inland, on West Burleigh Road and accessible by Surfside bus, the state-managed **David Fleay Wildlife Park** (daily 9am–5pm; A\$15.40, child A\$7.20; ☎07 5576 2411, ⓦwww.epa.qld.gov.au) is an informal environmental education park and wildlife breeding centre with boardwalks through forest pens and plenty of rangers on hand to answer your questions. The late David Fleay was the first person to persuade platypus to breed in captivity, and the park has a special section devoted to this curious animal. Also in residence are crocodiles, koalas, gliders, Lumholtz's tree kangaroos (endangered in the wild and rarely seen in captivity) and plenty of birds including cassowaries, eagles and gouldian finches. There are various guided tours through the day; a highlight is the **nocturnal house** – a chance to see normally somnambulant Australian wildlife such as acrobatic yellow-bellied gliders and comical-looking bilbies in action.

Broadbeach

BROADBEACH lies just south of Surfers Paradise, and is rather overshadowed by its brash, tower-cluttered neighbour. Nonetheless, it has its own, distinct character: there's a sedate, suburban feel to its spacious streets, pedestrian precinct and generous green spaces, and its beach is rarely overcrowded. It also has a large shopping centre, **Pacific Fair** on Hooker Boulevard, home to the Gold Coast's Myer department store and a good selection of fashion boutiques.

While central Surfers Paradise has so many tower blocks that only the oceanfront properties and the highest storeys of the mega-towers have unobstructed Pacific vistas, the views from Broadbeach's handful of high-rise **accommodation** options are superb. You can bag yourself amazing panoramas, and enjoy them in luxury, at *Air*, 159 Old Burleigh Rd (☎07 5555 3000, ⓦwww.airbroadbeach.com.au; ❺; seven-day minimum stay in peak season), a sleek modern apartment block with up-to-the minute decor; an alternative is *Beach Haven*, 1 Albert Avenue (☎07 5570 3888 or 1800 074 041, ⓦwww.bhaven.com.au; ❺), a classic tower-block complex of conservatively furnished ocean-view apartments, close to the Broadbeach Mall (Victoria Ave). Broadbeach's relatively sophisticated selection of places to eat and drink include cosmopolitan, European-style cafés and restaurants, all of which are positively humming during **Blues on Broadbeach**, the resort's five-day live blues festival, held in late May (ⓦwww.bluesonbroadbeach.com).

For **food**, the local Italian deli, ⚹ *MBD*, 19 Albert Ave (daily 6am–6pm; ☎07 5538 8233) is worth a special trip – stuffed with amazing goodies, it has a few sought-after café tables where you can tuck into fabulous toasted sandwiches and eclectic lunches for under A\$20. Self-confident café-bar *Alto Cucina*, The Oasis, Victoria Ave (Mon–Thurs & Sun 7am–11pm, Fri & Sat 7am–2pm; ☎07 5539 0377) specializes in antipasti to share, and stretches its modern-Italian theme to the limit – there's even egg and bacon pizza for breakfast. Broadbeach's warmly hospitable French eatery, *Champagne Brasserie*, 2 Queensland Ave (Tues–Fri lunch & dinner, Sat 6–9.30pm; ☎07 5538 3877) has a passionate local following; it serves excellent food prepared in traditional French style, with main courses around A\$31. *Yellowfin* at 20 Queensland Ave (daily lunch & dinner; ☎07 5504 5335) is a fresh, modern and relaxed restaurant offering beautifully presented fish and seafood at reasonable prices, while busy streetside café *Crema Espresso*, The Wave Building, Surf Parade, corner of Victoria Mall (daily 7am–10pm; ☎07 5526 9488) is excellent for coffee and wraps.

Surfers Paradise

While other Gold Coast resorts may have better shops, cafés and restaurants – and even better surf breaks – **SURFERS PARADISE** grabs all the glory. Stunningly located on a narrow strip of land between the Nerang River and the ocean, Surfers is a tourism hotspot, bristling with skyscrapers, buzzing with energy, and, in places, seething with commercialism at its most jaded and trashy.

Spiritually (though not geographically) the true heart of the coastal strip, Surfers is the place where the aims and aspirations of the region are most evident. A large proportion of its residents make their living by providing services and entertainment for tourists; visitors reciprocate by parting with their cash. All around and irrespective of what you're doing – sitting on the beach, partying in one of the frenetic nightclubs along Orchid or Cavill avenues, shopping in the malls for clothes or even finding a bed – the pace is brash and glib. Don't come here expecting to be allowed to relax; subtlety is nonexistent and you'll find that your enjoyment (or loathing) of Surfers will depend largely on how much it bothers you to have its hedonistic mood rammed down your throat.

The town's enduring popularity – particularly with Japanese, Chinese and Indian tourists, and with backpackers from all over the world – is a tribute to the successful marketing of the ideal Aussie lifestyle as one long beach party. Some would argue, however, that most visitors don't come here for the ultimate in sun and sand – but simply because everyone else does.

Some history

Surfers' beaches have been attracting tourists for over a century. Originally called Elston, the embryonic resort town was renamed Surfers Paradise in 1925 thanks to a successful campaign led by canny local hotelier and entrepreneur **Jim Cavill**; it's a moniker that still raises wry smiles among the Gold Coast surfing community, who know that there are far better waves to ride elsewhere. It was during the 1950s that the town started developing along overtly commercial lines, with the first high-rise beachfront apartment building appearing in 1959; within a decade, Australians were taking more annual leave than ever before, a growing number of families owned cars and were using them to take holidays away from home, and Surfers was booming.

The demand for views over the ocean led to ever-higher towers, which began to encroach on the dunes; together with the sheer volume of people attracted here, this has caused **erosion** problems along the entire Gold Coast. Nonetheless, **development** continues unabated. Today, complexes dating back to the late 1980s are considered sufficiently outmoded to be ripe for demolition, making way for something shinier and, inevitably, taller. At 322.5m high, the eighty-storey Q1 tower in central Surfers, completed in 2005, is Australia's tallest building; by 2010, it will be joined by three more gigantic skyscrapers.

Arrival and information

Surfers' **bus station** (daily 6am–10pm) is on Beach Road, which runs between the Gold Coast Highway and Surfers Paradise Boulevard, one street south of Cavill Avenue. Coachtrans (℡07 3358 9700 or 1300 664 700, ⓦwww .coachtrans.com.au) run here from Brisbane; J&B (℡07 5592 2655; ⓦwww .byronbayexpress.com.au) from Byron Bay; Kirklands (℡02 6626 1499, ⓦwww.kirklands.com.au) from Brisbane, Byron Bay and Lismore; and Greyhound and Premier (see p.35) from numerous points on the East Coast. Oz Road Trip (℡07 3395 8891, ⓦwww.ozroadtrip.com.au) run a backpacker bus from Byron Bay three times a week. At the bus station you'll find luggage lockers, bus-company desks and an accommodation-information counter. The **tourist information centre** is in a booth at 2 Cavill Ave (Mon–Fri 8.30am–5.30pm, Sat 8.30am–5pm, Sun 9am–4pm; ☎07 5538 4419, ⊛www.verygc.com), but the accommodation desk is usually just as well informed.

Security is worth bearing in mind; petty thieves are active all year round but particularly at the busiest times: Christmas, New Year, Easter, and Schoolies Week in November. Don't leave vehicles unlocked, don't take valuables onto the beach, and don't wander alone at night; instead, book taxis or take advantage of the courtesy buses run by hostels and resorts.

Accommodation

Surfers' **accommodation** is split between high-end, high-rise **hotels**; lower-rise **apartment blocks** that can be an excellent deal for a group, though you usually have to stay for a minimum of three nights; and **backpacker hostels**, which tend to be very hard-sell – don't expect any peace until you've signed up for trips to nightclubs, parties and beach events. Whatever you choose, **book in advance**. There are simply too many possibilities to give a comprehensive list; those below are central and good value. If you want to **camp**, you'll have to head to the quieter sections of the Gold Coast such as Southport to the north and Miami to the south; all campsites get booked solid at peak times.

Hostels

Aquarius 44 Queen St, Southport ☎07 5527 1300 or 1800 229 955, ⊛www.aquariusbackpackers.com.au. Homely place with a decent pool; it's some distance from the action, but there's a free bus to Surfers. Bunk in six-share or quad-share A$26–31, private double or twin ❸

Backpackers in Paradise 40 Peninsula Drive ☎1800 268 621, ⊛www.backpackersinparadise.com. More relaxed than the places nearer the beach, this has a bright, funky courtyard with hammocks to lounge in, en-suite dorms of various sizes and a pool. Bunk in shared room A$22–30, private double/twin or apartment ❸

Surfers Paradise Backpackers Resort 2837 Gold Coast Hwy ☎1800 282 800, ⊛www.surfersparadisebackpackers.com.au. Purpose-built, sparklingly clean and efficient, with lots of space and handy freebies including laundry facilities and boxes to lock away valuables. Bunk in shared room A$26–31, private room or apartment ❸

Surf n Sun Beachside Backpackers 3323 Surfers Paradise Blvd, corner of Ocean Ave ☎1800 678 194, ⊛www.surfnsun-goldcoast.com. Though cramped and barrack-like, this low-rise hostel is very close to the ocean. Bunk in shared room A$26–31, private double or twin ❸

Trekkers Hostel 22 White St, Southport ☎1800 100 004, ⊛www.trekkersbackpackers.com.au. Restored old house 3km from the centre, with heaps of deals and trips. Price includes a basic breakfast and a shuttle bus to the beach. Bunk in shared room A$26–31.

Hotels, motels and apartments

Chateau Beachside Elkhorn Ave ☎07 5538 1022, ⊛www.chateaubeachside.com.au. Right in the heart of Surfers and overlooking the beach, this ageing tower-block motel is a decent mid-range deal, with good-sized rooms and studios with mini-kitchens. ❹

Courtyard Marriott Hanlan St ☎07 5579 3499 or 1800 251 259, ⊛www.marriott.com.au/oolcy. Flash, very central international chain hotel offering a variety of rooms, all good value for a high degree of comfort. ❹–❻

Enderley Gardens 38 Enderley Ave ☎07 5570 1511, ⊛www.stellaresorts.com.au. Quite an oasis, this relatively low-rise, modest apartment complex is arranged around a pretty, curvy pool fringed with palms and tropical greenery. ❺

Holiday Inn 22 View Ave ☎07 5579 1000 or 1800 007 697, ⊛www.holidayinnsurfersparadise.com.au. Smart hotel from a reliable brand: far more stylish than you might expect thanks to an ambitious contemporary makeover. Rates vary by date. ❻–❼

Iluka Corner of Hanlan St & Esplanade ☎1800 073 333 or 07 5539 9155 ⊛www.ilukabeachresort.com.au. Medium-sized tower with rooms and mini-apartments; the decor is nothing special, but most of the apartments look straight out to the ocean. ❹

Q1 Resort and Spa Hamilton Ave
☎ 07 5630 4500 or 1300 792 008, ⓦ www
.q1.com.au. Surfers' record-breakingly colossal
tower has lagoon-style swimming pools and plush
apartments with one, two or three bedrooms. All
are decorated in a cold, clean, contemporary style
and have specially designed balconies from which

to enjoy the spectacular views. Guests can access
the *Q1 Deck* (see p.419) at a small discount. ❼

Vibe 42 Ferny Ave ☎ 07 5539 0444,
ⓦ www.vibehotels.com.au. Unbeatable for
designer styling on a budget, this urban hotel has a
small pool on a great little riverside deck, and bags
of funky attitude. ❺

The City

Central Surfers Paradise is a thin ribbon of partially reclaimed land between the ocean and the **Nerang River**, which – as the Broadwater – flows north, parallel with the beach, past The Spit and South Stradbroke Island into the choked channels at the bottom end of Moreton Bay. Reclaimed land in the river forms islands whose names reflect the fantasies of their founders – Isle of Capri, Sorrento, Miami Keys – and that have become much-sought-after real estate.

From its dingiest club to its best restaurant, Surfers exudes entertainment, and at times – most notoriously at Christmas and New Year – you can spend 24 hours a day out on the town. Another thing you'll spend is money: the only free venue is the beach and with such a variety of distractions it can be financial suicide venturing out too early in the day – the city is full of tourists staggering around at noon with terrible hangovers and empty wallets, complaining how expensive their holiday has become. The area around **Orchid Avenue** and partially pedestrianized **Cavill Avenue** is a bustle of activity from early morning – when the first surfers head down to the beach and the shops open – to after midnight, when there's a constant movement of bodies between the bars and nightclubs. If you spend any length of time larging-it in town, you'll get to know the district intimately.

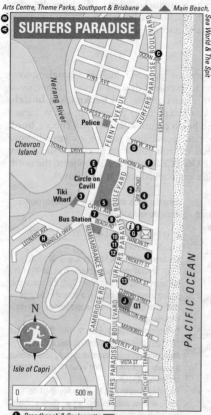

Arts Centre, Theme Parks, Southport & Brisbane ▲ ▲ Main Beach, Sea World & The Spit

SURFERS PARADISE

ACCOMMODATION
Aquarius	A	Q1 Resort and Spa	J
Backpackers in Paradise	H	Surf n Sun Beachside	
Chateau Beachside	F	Backpackers	C
Courtyard Marriott	G	Surfers Paradise	
Enderley Gardens	K	Backpackers Resort	L
Holiday Inn	D	Trekkers Hostel	B
Iluka	I	Vibe	E

EATING & DRINKING
Absynthe	J	La Paella	11
Bavarian Haus	5	Melbas	7
The Bedroom	2	Mybar	6
Captain's Table	2	Q1 Skybar	J
Cocktails and Dreams	6	The Rice Paddy	12
Crema Deli Bar	J	Shooters	6
Elsewhere	4	Surfers Beergarden	9
Grumpy's Wharf	J	The Tandoori Place	13
Howl at the Moon	9	Titanium Bar	1
Kookoo Tapas and Lounge Bar	10	Zarraffa's Coffee	8

6

BRISBANE AND SOUTHEAST QUEENSLAND | Surfers Paradise

418

Surfers' tower-block cityscape makes an immediate impression, but the stakes in who can build highest and so block their neighbours' view of the beach seem to be rising all the time. Occupying an entire block on Surfers Paradise Boulevard between Clifford Street and Hamilton Avenue, **Q1**, 78 storeys high and 322.5m to the top of its spire, was briefly the world's tallest residential building until it was overtaken by the 23 Marina and Princess towers in Dubai. The entire seventy-seventh and seventy-eighth floors are given over to an **observation deck** (Mon–Thurs & Sun 9am–9pm, Fri & Sat 9am–midnight; A\$17.50, child A\$10; Fri & Sat after 8pm A\$10; ☏07 5630 4700, ⓦwww .Q1observationdeck.com), reached by a non-stop lift that whisks you up in a breathtakingly brief 42.7 seconds. Huge plate-glass windows allow you to drink in stupendous views of the Gold Coast's urban landscape – the ostentatious riverfront villas and puny-looking high rises below you, the golden beach stretching as far as you can see, and, inland, the cloud-topped mountains of the hinterland, with Mount Warning in New South Wales in the far distance. To top the experience, there's a café-bar (see below), which oozes sleek urban cool.

Across the Esplanade, the **beach** is all you could want as a place to recover from your night out; it runs north from here to **Main Beach** (see p.421) and beyond, so finding empty sand is rarely difficult. If you're feeling energetic, seek out a game of volleyball or head for the surf: the swell here is good in a northerly wind, but most of the time it's better for boogie-boards.

Shopping

Cavill Avenue area is the shopping hub; as you'd expect, it's good for boards, boardies and bikinis, with a sprinkling of international luxury names among the places peddling cheap clothing and trashy souvenirs. For discount shopping, the place to head for is **Harbour Town**, an out-of-town mall just off the Gold Coast Highway in Biggera Waters northwest of the city, which is stuffed with outlets stocking major brands at knockdown prices. For **food and drink**, there are supermarkets and delis in the Circle on Cavill mall between Ferny Avenue and Surfers Paradise Boulevard and in the Centro Centre on Cavill Avenue, plus a scattering of convenience stores in the same central area.

Eating and drinking

Surfers has somewhere to **snack** wherever you look but the selection, with a few notable exceptions, lags way behind its neighbours Broadbeach (see p.415) and Main Beach (see p.421) in the quality stakes.

Cafés and bars

Crema Deli Bar Q1, Hamilton Ave ☏07 5538 0866. In a prime spot at the foot of the Q1 tower, but not overpriced, this café serves tasty wraps and bagels, plus milkshakes and hot drinks, and opens for breakfast at 7am.

Kookoo Tapas and Lounge Bar 3120 Surfers Paradise Blvd ☏07 5538 0217. The first of its kind in Surfers, this smooth, retro-modern hangout offers seductive cocktails, vintage wines and champagne, along with tasty tapas for under A\$10 a plate. Daily 11am–late.

Q1 Skybar Q1 observation deck, Hamilton Ave ☏07 5630 4700. Highly stylish in a subtle way, to avoid upstaging the tremendous

views, this is fabulous for coffee and cakes by day, and a stunning venue for sunset cocktails. Breakfast on Sun mornings is quite an event. Admission fees apply (see above).

Titanium Bar 30–34 Ferny Ave ☏07 5538 9677. Sharp urban bar with river views – a place to knock back cocktails and shooters while watching sport on the big screen. Occasional live music.

Zarraffa's Coffee Cavill Ave, corner of Surfers Paradise Blvd ☏07 5538 1519. This popular little coffee and cake shop is open all night on Fri & Sat.

Restaurants

Absynthe Q1, Hamilton Ave ☏07 5504 6466. Raising Gold Coast culinary standards at a stroke, this is the region's most celebrated restaurant, with a feted chef, a mouthwatering *degustation* menu, expertly prepared à la carte dishes for A$22–40 featuring seafood, venison and prime beef, and a clean modern style to fit its location at the foot of Q1. Mon–Fri lunch & dinner, Sat dinner only.

Bavarian Haus 41 Cavill Ave ⊤07 5531 7150. Wood-panelled theme restaurant, where you can wolf down steins of beer and plates of beef while staff dressed in leather and lace pump away on Bavarian brass instruments. Fair value and good fun if you're in the mood. Lunch & dinner daily.

Captain's Table Upstairs at 26 Orchid Ave ⊤07 5531 5766. Award-winning restaurant with excellent seafood variations – the delicious barbecued Moreton Bay bugs shouldn't be missed. Get in early for a table with a view.

Grumpy's Wharf Tiki Village, at the river end of Cavill Ave ⊤07 5531 6177. Casual Pacific

Island-style decor and views over the Nerang River make a great setting for this relatively pricey seafood restaurant.

La Paella 3114 Gold Coast Hwy ⊤07 5527 5940. Tiny yet lively Spanish restaurant with excellent tapas, sangría by the bucket, and sumptuous veal casserole at moderate prices. Daily, dinner only.

The Rice Paddy 3100 Gold Coast Hwy ⊤07 5592 1390. Far better than the other Asian restaurants in Surfers, this Vietnamese place has great house specialities including sizzling scallops and pork with sesame seeds and plum sauce, and a surprisingly good wine list. Lunch Mon–Fri, dinner daily.

The Tandoori Place 30 Laycock St ⊤07 5592 1004. Unexceptional, but just the job when nothing but a curry will do, with a decent selection of classic meat and vegetarian choices. Daily for lunch, dinner and takeaway.

Nightlife and entertainment

Along with the beach, Surfers' **pubs and clubs** – mostly located in Orchid Avenue – are its *raison d'être*. Initially, particularly if you're staying at a hostel or have picked up a free pass somewhere, your choice will most likely be influenced by the various **deals** on entry and drinks. In addition, there are booze-cruise nightclub **tours** offered by various places for around A$60, including transport and often a club pass valid for the rest of your stay. Opening times are from around 6pm to 3am or later, with the usual 3am lockout after which you can't enter; bars are open daily and clubs from Thursday to Sunday.

As well as the nightspots below, the Gold Coast often hosts **dance parties** and live **music festivals** (Good Vibrations, in February, is one of the biggest), usually held at outdoor venues such as Doug Jennings Park at The Spit. You can find out the latest in the free Brisbane **listings magazines** *Scene*, *Rave* and *Time Off* and the more regionally oriented *Tsunami*.

The Bedroom 26 Orchid Ave Ⓦwww.thebedroom .net.au. One of the best places for house and dance on the coast, with an ever-changing array of local and international DJs.

Cocktails and Dreams The Mark Complex, Orchid Ave. Nightly dance crowd in the late-teen bracket, who party against a background of neon and disco lighting.

Elsewhere 23 Cavill Ave Ⓦwww.elsewherebar .com. Intimate bar with a very funky retro-chic vibe, hosting live bands and DJ nights. Fri–Sun.

Howl at the Moon Upstairs at Centro Centre on Cavill Ave. Hugely popular restaurant, bar and nightclub with two live pianists performing their own sing-along renditions of popular hits. Daily 8pm–2am, bookings advisable.

Melbas 46 Cavill Ave. Big and relatively upmarket nightclub with a monstrous, atmospherically lit bar and powerful sound system – plus a noticeably older crowd than the rest of Surfers' clubs.

Mybar The Mark Complex, Orchid Ave Ⓦwww .mybar.com.au. Dance bar playing massive club hits, with occasional international DJ sets.

Shooters The Mark Complex, Orchid Ave. Crowds heading for more serious dance spots start out here for a game of pool and a few drinks; it's a favourite stop on the backpacker bar-crawl trail. Daily 8pm–5am.

Surfers Beergarden Upstairs on Cavill Ave, opposite Orchid Ave. Good for live music, with local and visiting bands on Thurs & Sat nights.

Listings

Car, scooter and bike rental CY Rent a Car, 9 Trickett St ☎07 5570 3777, ⓦwww.cyrentacar .com.au; East Coast Car Rentals, 25 Elkhorn Ave ☎07 5592 0444 or 1800 028 881, ⓦwww .eastcoastcarrentals.com.au; Surfers Paradise Car Hire, Transit Centre ☎07 5570 1200 or 1800 671 361, ⓦwww.surfersparadisecarhire.com; Red Back Car Rentals, Transit Centre ☎07 5592 1655 or 1800 811 268, ⓦwww.redbackrentals.com.au; Red Rocket, Centre Arcade, Orchid Ave ☎07 5538 9074, ⓦwww.redrocketrentals.com.au.

Hospitals and medical centres Gold Coast Hospital, Nerang St, Southport ☎07 5571 8211;

Gold Coast Medical Centre and Travel Clinic, 3211 Gold Coast Hwy, near Cavill Ave ☎07 5538 8099.

Pharmacy Day/Night Pharmacy, Piazza Shopping Plaza, corner of Elkhorn Ave & Gold Coast Hwy (daily 7am–midnight).

Post office The main branch is in the Centro Shopping Centre on Cavill Ave (Mon–Fri 9am– 5.30pm, Sat 9am–12.30pm).

Surfing tuition and board rental See box, p.407.

Taxis ☎13 10 08.

Tours See box, pp.408–409.

North of Surfers Paradise

The Gold Coast ribbon development continues to hog the seaboard for a little over 20km north of Surfer's Paradise, with the skyscrapers petering out in favour of modest apartment buildings and estates. The northernmost stretch of Gold Coast beach – **Main Beach** and **The Spit** – has excellent surf but is far quieter than the urban areas around Surfers, and arguably much more attractive, too. North of here, the coast is sheltered by South Stradbroke Island (see p.432), which can be reached by ferry services from the low-key marinas at Runaway Bay and Hope Harbour. There's another marina at upmarket riverside development **Sanctuary Cove**, a pleasant, peaceful place to stay. Inland, clustered around the motorway to the northwest, are the bulk of the Gold Coast's famous **theme parks**, which can't really compare to the blockbuster attractions of Florida and California but are, nonetheless, enormous fun.

Main Beach and The Spit

Backed by casuarinas and low-rise buildings, the peaceful, powder-soft sand of **MAIN BEACH** has surf that's good enough to please the pros; there's more of the same on the ocean side of **THE SPIT**, a five-kilometre sliver of land that's home to the Gold Coast's original theme park, Sea World (see box, p.423) but is otherwise largely undeveloped. Two of the Gold Coast's plushest **places to stay** are found towards the southern end of The Spit. *Palazzo Versace* (Sea World Drive; ☎07 5509 8000 or 1800 098 000, ⓦwww.palazzoversace .com; ❾) is a huge, extravagant concoction of glittering pools, lofty colonnades and brocaded soft furnishings designed by Donatella Versace to emulate a Renaissance palace. Breathtakingly expensive, it fits well with the Gold Coast's ambition of becoming a playground for top-flight jetsetters. The *Sheraton Mirage Gold Coast* (Sea World Drive; ☎07 5591 1488, ⓦwww.starwoodhotels .com; ❻–❽) can't really compete with all this opulence, but nor does it have the same sky-high rates; its rooms, some of which have stunning ocean views, are extremely comfortable, and its swimming pools are magnificent. There's also a hostel in this area: *Surfers Paradise YHA* (70 Sea World Drive; ☎07 5571 1776, ⓦwww.yha.com.au; bunk in quad-share A$26–29, private double /twin ❷) has good facilities, plus a lively bar and grill serving up beer and pub fare till late. For a break from the resort scene, there's an appealing clutch of trendy **cafés and restaurants**, popular with Porsche-driving locals, on Main

Gold Coast theme parks

All the **theme parks** are a bundle of fun, especially for children. Several of them offer enough diversions to swallow up a whole day, particularly during the school summer holidays, when you can expect long queues for the most popular rides; at the busiest times, opening hours may be extended by an hour or so. Each of the parks has a distinct character, so it's worth splurging on a **multi-park pass** and trying a few, but if the weather's hot, a day getting soaked at Wet 'n' Wild or WhiteWater World takes some beating. For the latest **special offers**, check out the park websites at ⓦwww .myfun.com.au and ⓦwww.themeparksgoldcoast.com.au.

The closest park to Surfers Paradise is SeaWorld, 5km immediately north of town on The Spit. Dreamworld and WhiteWater World are beside the Pacific Motorway (M1) in Coomera, 23km northwest of Surfers and 56km south of Brisbane. All the other parks are just west of the Pacific Motorway in Helensvale, 16km northwest of Surfers and 63km south of Brisbane. **Local buses** from the Gold Coast hotels run by Surfside Buslines and Gold Coast Shuttle will take you to any of the parks, or you can sign up for a **theme-park tour** from Surfers or Coolangatta with Gold Coast Con-x-ion (ⓣ07 5556 9888, ⓦwww.con-x-ion.com) or from Brisbane with Coachtrans (ⓣ07 3238 4700, ⓦwww.coachtrans.com.au). Both Coomera and Helensvale are on the TransLink Citytrain Brisbane–Gold Coast **railway** line.

The parks

Australian Outback Spectacular (Tues–Sun, doors open 3.30pm for the 4.30pm show and at 6.15pm for the 7.30pm show; A$95, child A$65, advance booking required; ⓣ13 33 86 or 07 5519 6200, ⓦwww.outbackspectacular.com.au) is a thoroughly enjoyable arena show with dinner thrown in. Set in a giant recreation of an Outback cattle station, it features stunning demonstrations of horsemanship, livestock herding and even camel racing, with some great comedy moments.

Dreamworld (daily 10am–5pm; A$66, child A$43; ⓣ07 5588 1111, ⓦwww .dreamworld.com.au) has a fairground atmosphere that has been pulling in the crowds since the early eighties; top of the bill are the Cyclone, the southern hemisphere's tallest high-speed gravity rollercoaster, and Wipeout, the world's fastest vertical thrill ride. There's also a large enclosure of hand-reared tigers and a collection of friendly native animals including wombats and kangaroos.

Beach's Tedder Avenue; among the most tempting are Mod Oz eatery *Café Roxx* (ⓣ07 5591 3033) and small but perfectly formed wine bar *Chill on Tedder* (ⓣ07 5528 0388), while *Coffee on Tedder* (ⓣ07 5528 1966) is a first-rate café.

Sanctuary Cove

For property investors, **SANCTUARY COVE**, 23km north of Surfers Paradise and 65km south of Brisbane, is the Gold Coast's answer to Noosa on the Sunshine Coast: a network of freshwater inlets lined with yacht moorings and swish waterfront houses, few of which would leave you change from a couple of million dollars. Tucked away near the mouth of the Coomera River, this quiet enclave is a popular holiday spot for well-off families who want to steer clear of the brash bustle of Surfers Paradise but be close to the child-pleasing Gold Coast theme parks, most of which are only fifteen minutes' drive away. The **place to stay** is the large, elegant ⛤ *Hyatt Regency Sanctuary Cove* (Manor Circle; ⓣ13 12 34 or 07 5530 1234, ⓦwww.sanctuarycove.regency.hyatt .com; room ❻, suite ❼). With a grand main building styled like a Queensland manor house, sweeping waterfront lawns, good sports facilities, a swimming

Paradise Country Aussie Farm Tour (tours daily at 9.30am, 10.30am, 11.15am & 1pm; A$57.50, child A$41 including lunch; ⓣ 13 33 86 or 07 5573 8270, ⓦ www .paradisecountry.com.au) gives you an up-close introduction to life in rural Australia, with a chance to get friendly with piglets, lambs, calves, horses, koalas and kangaroos and to try your hand at sheep-shearing, whip-cracking and boomerang-throwing.

Sea World (daily 10am–5pm; A$66, child A$43; ⓣ 13 33 86 or 07 5588 2205, ⓦ www .seaworld.com.au), the longest running of the parks, features immaculately trained performing dolphins and sea lions, and aquaria for sharks, turtles, rays and other species. This is one of the few places where you can see dugongs at close quarters. The centre's rehabilitation units help prepare injured seabirds and stranded wild dolphins for release. Alongside the animal attractions are various stomach-churning rides.

Warner Bros Movie World (daily 10am–5pm; A$66, child A$43; ⓣ 13 33 86 or 07 5573 8485, ⓦ www.movieworld.com.au) has rollercoasters and thrill-rides themed around Hollywood blockbusters, plus stunt demonstrations and parading cartoon characters.

Wet 'n' Wild Water World (daily 10am–4pm or later; A$45, child A$29; ⓣ 13 33 86 or 07 5573 2255, ⓦ www.wetnwild.com.au) has a series of pools linked by water slides – some are so gentle your granny would love them, while others are high-speed and, to the fainthearted, thoroughly vicious. The star attraction is the "mad 'n' massive" forty-metre tunnel of the Tornado; another real thriller is the Black Hole, which sends you spiralling down a tube in total darkness. During school holidays, there's a daily Hollywood movie screening at dusk; you can watch the show while floating around in the wave pool.

WhiteWater World (daily 10.30am–4.30pm or later; A$43, child A$29; ⓣ07 5588 1111, ⓦ www.whitewaterworld.com.au) is the most recent addition; it's all about getting wet in the most adrenalin-inducing way possible. The Super Tubes HydroCoaster uses "hydro-magnetism" to propel you uphill before shooting you down a flume, while The Rip sends you hurtling around a massive whirlpool at breathtaking speed. Technologically advanced, this is one of the world's most water-efficient water parks, so you can expect all the rides to be running at full blast even during drought periods.

lagoon and excellent service, it's a very pleasant choice. There's excellent in-house dining at *The Fireplace*, where chefs roasting juicy steaks and vegetables in the open kitchen's wood-fired oven add a touch of theatre. Just beyond the resort is a small riverside complex of boutiques, gift shops and restaurants, with a cinema; the social focus is the *Waterfront Tavern*, a down-to-earth marina pub with a huge deck overlooking the moorings, and good-value counter meals.

The Gold Coast Hinterland

Beginning around 30km inland from the Gold Coast's jangling excesses, the **Gold Coast Hinterland** is a mountainous, rainforested plateau encompassing a series of beautifully wild **national parks**, with enough walking tracks to keep you occupied for days. In **Springbrook National Park**, there are magnificent waterfalls to visit and panoramic views from mountain lookouts, while **Lamington National Park** is prime hiking and bird-watching country, with atmospheric trails leading through pristine forests of Antarctic beech, a Gondwanan relic also found in South America. The two parks are linked by a spectacular new 54-kilometre hiking trail, the **Gold Coast Hinterland Great Walk**, with simple campsites along the way. Further north, **Tamborine Mountain**'s easy hill-walking tracks and pleasant country lodges are close enough to both Brisbane and Surfers Paradise to be perfect for a short, relaxing escape from the city.

Practicalities

You can dip into the region for a day by booking a short **tour** from the Gold Coast or Brisbane – see the boxes on p.408 and p.460 – but to explore to any degree you'll need your own vehicle, which will also work out the cheapest option for a group. Access to the region is via routes leading west and south off the Pacific Motorway (M1) between Brisbane and the Gold Coast. If you're **driving**, carry a good road map, and allow plenty of time to tackle the narrow, steep and winding mountain roads.

Weather ranges from very wet in summer (when there are small, mildly irritating leeches in abundance, and some hiking trails are closed) to fairly cool

---

Queensland's Great Walks

The QPWS has committed A$10m since 2004 to the creation of six new **long-distance wilderness hiking routes**, five in the coastal hinterland and one on Fraser Island, by upgrading and connecting existing tracks and bush campgrounds. Serious hikers can tackle entire trails – an unbeatable way of experiencing some of the state's most beautiful bush savanna, forests and mountains – while those with less time to spare can choose from a number of recommended short sections of each trail. Either way, unless you decide to double back on yourself, you'll need to arrange to be picked up at your end point, as the routes are linear, not circular.

The **best time of year** for walking is April to September; some sections may be closed at the peak of the rainy season between late January and late March. Facilities are basic, so be ready to rough it: most walkers' campgrounds have running water and barbecues or firewood, but not all have showers. Most require that you limit the size of your group to eight and stay for no more than two nights, to minimize the impact of your visit. For **route maps** and further details, visit ⓦwww.epa.qld .gov.au/greatwalks; to arrange camping permits, call ⓣ13 13 04 or visit ⓦwww.qld .gov.au/camping.

Once you're underway, it's important that you stick to the marked trails, for the sake of the environment and for your own safety: you'll be walking through remote regions where mobile-phone reception may be patchy or non existent.

Gold Coast Hinterland Great Walk

Green Mountains to Springbrook National Park (54km; 4 campgrounds; 4–5 days). This new mountain trail, not quite complete at the time of writing, connects the well-established hiking areas of Lamington National Park with the Numinbah Valley and the Springbrook plateau, taking you through spectacular forest scenery.

Sunshine Coast Hinterland Great Walk

Lake Baroon to Delicia Road Conservation Park (58km; 3 campgrounds; 4–6 days). Taking you through the Blackall Range just west of Montville and Mapleton and east

and dry in winter, though **rain** is a year-round possibility. If you're planning to **hike**, you'll need good footwear for the slippery paths, although trails are well marked. **Accommodation** is in country lodges, mountain retreats and campsites, all of which usually require booking in advance. You'll find some of southeast Queensland's loveliest places to stay tucked among the trees; prices are generally high, though, so if you're on a tight budget bring a **tent** or travel by **campervan**. Not all campsites provide barbecues or firewood, so it's best to have a **gas stove**, as collecting your own firewood in national parks is forbidden.

Springbrook National Park

At the edge of a plateau along the New South Wales border, but only accessible from the Queensland side, **Springbrook National Park** comprises several separate fragments – the best of which are **Purling Brook** and **Natural Bridge** – featuring abundant forest, waterfalls and swimming holes.

To get there with your own wheels, turn off the Pacific Motorway (M1) at **Mudgeeraba** (from the north, take exit 79, 79km southeast of Brisbane; from the south, take exit 80, 24km northwest of Coolangatta) and then follow the steep, narrow and winding Route 99 as it twists its way to a junction 20km southwest; here you turn right to take Route 97 to Natural Bridge, a looping 24km to the south (see below), or left to continue due south along Route 99 to the Purling Brook section of the park, about 8km from the junction.

of Kenilworth, this route leads past waterfalls and across rocky creeks through warm subtropical rainforest and open eucalyptus woods, with seven- to eight-hour stretches between camps.

Fraser Island Great Walk
Dilli Village to Happy Valley (90km; 8 campgrounds; 6–8 days).
Looping inland from Seventy-Five Mile Beach to the perched lakes of the interior and back to the coast, this takes you over coastal dunes, through scribbly gum woodland and subtropical rainforest; there's a chance of spotting dingoes en route.

Mackay Highlands Great Walk
Pine Grove to Mount Britton (56km; 4 campgrounds; 5 days).
This trail starts at Eungella and takes in Broken River (excellent for platypus-spotting), the Crediton State Forest and the Denham Range. Some sections are remote and extremely challenging; the whole trail is best walked from north to south to avoid hot and steep uphill climbs.

Whitsunday Great Walk
Brandy Creek to Airlie Beach (30km; 2 campgrounds; 3 days).
Relatively easy-going, with no more than six hours between camps, this route heads through the tulip oaks, bloodwoods and gum trees of Conway State Forest, with views of the Whitsunday Islands along the way.

Wet Tropics Great Walk
Wallaman Falls to Henrietta Gate or Blencoe Falls (110km; 5 campgrounds; 3–6 days).
Most walkers just tackle a part of this hefty hike, which leads you through the rainforested Girringun National Park, west of Cardwell and Ingham. The central section, along the Herbert River Gorge, has no tracks or facilities and is strictly for hardcore hikers. Permanent residents of the region include cassowaries and estuarine crocodiles.

The 109-metre **Purling Brook Falls** are very impressive after rain has swollen the flow; a four-kilometre track zigzags down the escarpment and into the rainforest at the base of the falls before curving underneath them (expect a soaking from the spray) and going back up the other side. In the plunge pool at the foot of the falls, the force of the water is enough to push you under; swimming is more relaxed in a couple of pools downstream, picturesquely encircled by lianas and red cedar. A couple of kilometres south of the falls there's a basic QPWS **campground**, *The Settlement* (for booking information, see p.54), a new site with space for tents and vans. Another 10km south, the road drive brings you to **Best of All Lookout** right on the New South Wales border, offering a broad vista south to Mount Warning.

Natural Bridge is a dark, damp and hauntingly eerie place, where a collapsed cave ceiling beneath the riverbed has created a subterranean waterfall. You can walk in through the original cave-mouth some 50m downstream; from the back of the cave outside the forest frames the waterfall and blue plunge pool, surreally lit from above – **glow worms** illuminate the ceiling at night.

Lamington National Park

Lamington National Park occupies the northeastern rim of a vast 1156-metre-high caldera centred on Mount Warning, 15km away in New South Wales. An enthralling world of rainforest-flanked rivers, open heathland and ancient eucalypt woods, Lamington's position on a crossover zone between subtropical and temperate climes has made it home to a staggering variety of plants, animals and birds, with isolated populations of species found nowhere else in the world. Rarities to look out for include Albert's lyrebirds, spotted-tailed quolls, red-necked pademelons and the Lamington spiny crayfish, a startlingly blue, creek-dwelling crustacean.

There are two possible bases for exploring the park: **Binna Burra** on the drier northern edge, and **Green Mountains** (location of the well-publicized *O'Reilly's Rainforest Retreat* and a QPWS campground) in the thick of the forest. While both bases are surrounded by stunning wilderness, each has a distinctive atmosphere: Binna Burra's lodge and campsite have a low-key, down-to-earth rusticity that suits committed hikers, while Green Mountains is busier, more upmarket and more commercial, catering for hordes of day-trippers and non-walkers as well as hikers. A twenty-kilometre-long path links the two, and continues a further 33km southeast to Springbrook National Park; this 53-kilometre route is the newest of the Queensland Great Walks (see box, p.424).

Practicalities

The journey **by road** from the Gold Coast to Binna Burra takes just over an hour (1hr 45min from Brisbane); getting to Green Mountains takes about half an hour longer. It's simplest to first aim for **Nerang**, inland from Surfers Paradise at junctions 69 and 71 on the Pacific Motorway. From here, Binna Burra is 36km southwest (start by following Route 90, turn left along Route 97 and right along Route 84, continue through tiny **Beechmont**, and keep going to the end of the road), while *O'Reilly's* is about 65km away (take Route 90 all the way to the village of **Canungra** then turn left for the tortuous but scenic mountain road; again, continue right to the end).

Beechmont and Canungra are the last proper sources of **fuel**, cash and camping provisions before the national park; Canungra also has a **visitor information centre** (daily 9.30am–4pm; ☎07 5543 5156 or 1300 88 11 64, ⓦwww.queenslandshiddenoasis.com) offering advice, accommodation bookings and Internet access.

▲ Lamington National Park

If you don't have a car, you can book a **pick-up** with *Binna Burra Mountain Lodge* (from A\$77 for 4 people in a taxi from Nerang station, served by direct trains from Brisbane and buses from the Gold Coast) or *O'Reilly's* (daily shuttle from Surfers Paradise, Brisbane or Gold Coast Airport from A\$38 per person one way; taxis on request). Some of the tour operators running day-trips to Lamington (see p.408 & p.460) will allow you to travel up one day and down another if requested in advance.

Once in the park, Lamington has to be explored on foot: most of the tracks described below are clearly signposted and **free maps** are available from the information centres near Binna Burra (1.5km downhill from the lodge and campsite) and at *O'Reilly's*.

Binna Burra

Binna Burra is a massive tract of highland forest where, overlooking the Numinbah Valley from woodland on the crown of Mount Roberts, you'll find **accommodation** at *Binna Burra Mountain Lodge* (T07 5533 3622 or 1800 074 260, W www.binnaburralodge.com.au; ○). Founded in 1933, the emphasis here is, naturally enough, on outdoor activities, with superb guided walks and light-hearted evening entertainment such as family quizzes and bush dancing included in the price. While it's all rather dated – the timber rooms need a revamp and the restaurant only offers stodgy set menus – it's a homely, unpretentious and relaxing place to rest up between hikes, with superb views of the forested Coomera Valley. A stroll away is the lodge's **campsite**, which has hot showers (camping A$24, safari tent ○; campers can join the lodge's guided walks for A$15–50), and its **café**, the *Binna Burra Tea House* (Mon–Fri 9am–4pm, Sat & Sun 7.30am–5pm; takeaway pizza available Fri 5–7.30pm), which has a much more contemporary style than the restaurant, serving frittata, tasty sandwiches and mod-Oz light meals. There's no other accommodation in the immediate area, but hikers can **bushcamp** inside the national park between February and November by applying in advance to the Binna Burra QPWS rangers' office (Mon–Fri 1–3.30pm; T07 5533 3584, E binna.burra@epa.qld.gov.au).

Of the **walks**, try the easy five-kilometre **Caves Circuit**, which follows the edge of the Coomera Valley past the white, wind-sculpted Talangai Caves to remains of Aboriginal camps, strands of *psilotum nudum* (a rootless ancestor of the ferns), and a hillside of strangler figs and red cedar. The 11-kilometre circuit to the foot of the **Ballunjui Falls** is a little more demanding, with some vertical drops off the path; key features along the way include views from **Bellbird Lookout** of Egg Rock, at its most mysterious when shrouded in dawn mists, and a stand of majestic forty-metre-tall box brush trees. For a full day's exercise, the trail can be extended out to **Ships Stern**, adding a tiring and dry 10km to the loop, but rewarding you with wonderful views of the Numinbah Valley. **Dave's Creek Circuit** is similar but about half as long, crossing bands of rainforest and sclerophyll before emerging onto heathland. Look for tiny clumps of red **sundew** plants along the track, which supplement their nitrogen intake by trapping insects in sticky globules of nectar.

By far the best of the longer tracks is the **Border Track**, a relatively easy 21-kilometre, nine-hour route through the rainforest and groves of Antarctic beech trees between Green Mountains and Binna Burra. A couple of times a week, *Binna Burra Mountain Lodge* runs a bus to the head of the track near *O'Reilly's* for anyone who wants to walk back, charging A$35 per person one way.

Green Mountains

The **Green Mountains** region is Lamington at its best, a huge spread of cloud forest filled with ancient, moss-covered trees and a mass of wildlife including so many birds that you hardly know where to look first. The winding road up from Canungra leads you past the **Rosemount Alpaca Farm**, worth a stop for its café, with glorious valley views, and its gallery shop, which sells alpaca fleeces and clothing. After a long ascent through mature mountain forests – as impressive as any in Queensland – you reach *O'Reilly's Rainforest Retreat* (T07 5502 4911 or 1800 688 722, W www.oreillys.com.au; room ○, suite ○), Lamington's most comfortable place to stay, with a packed programme of guided hikes and natural history walks (A\$10–45, child A\$5–23 per activity; no charge for self-guided walks). Run by the O'Reilly family since 1926, its rooms, suites and villas have been modernized over the years and are fairly nondescript, but there's a potent whiff of history in the cosy lounge with its fireside chairs, grand piano and displays of memorabilia. Elsewhere, the day-trip trade saddles *O'Reilly's* with a theme-park atmosphere – coachloads of visitors come here at lunchtime to eat in the **café** and hand-feed the crimson rosellas, king parrots and brush turkeys that hang around in flocks.

If you're just here for the hiking and would like a more back-to-basics experience, you can pitch a tent or park a campervan at the QPWS-run Green Mountains **campground**, a two-minute walk from *O'Reilly's* (see p.54 for booking information), which has hot showers and coin-operated barbecues; alternatively, you could plan a long-distance walk and camp in the bush (permits to bushcamp must be obtained in advance from the Green Mountains QPWS rangers' office at *O'Reilly's*; Mon, Wed & Thurs 9–11am & 1–3.30pm, Tues & Fri 1–3.30pm; ☎07 5544 0634, ✉green.mountains@epa.qld.gov.au). Another option, through rather isolated, is *Cainbable Mountain Lodge*, 21km from Canungra on the road to *O'Reilly's* (☎07 5544 9207, ⓦwww.cainbable .com; ④–⑦), whose attractive, self-contained chalets sleep from four to eight people and have splendid views.

The **birdlife** around *O'Reilly's* is a major attraction: determined twitchers can clock up over fifty species, including the spectacular black-and-gold regent bowerbird, without even reaching the forest. But it's worth pushing on to the **treetop walk** just beyond the clearing, where a suspended rope-bridge hangs 15m above ground level. At the halfway anchor point, you scale a narrow ladder to vertigo-inducing mesh platforms 30m up the trunk of a strangler fig to see the canopy at eye level. Soaking up the increased sunlight at this height above the forest floor, tree branches become miniature gardens of mosses, ferns and orchids. By night, the walkway is the preserve of possums, leaf-tailed geckoes and weird stalking insects.

If you manage only one day-walk at Lamington, make it the exceptional fifteen-kilometre **Blue Pool–Canungra Creek** track (5hr return), which features fantastic trees, river crossings and countless opportunities to fall off slippery rocks and get soaked. The first hour is dry enough as you tramp downhill past some huge red cedars to Blue Pool, a deep, placid waterhole where platypuses are sometimes seen on winter mornings; this makes a good walk in itself. After a dip, head upstream along Canungra Creek; the path traverses the river a few times (there are no bridges, but occasionally a fallen tree conveniently spans the water) – look for yellow or red arrows painted on rocks that indicate where to cross. Seasonally, the creek can be almost dried up; if the water is more than knee-deep, you shouldn't attempt a crossing and will need to retrace your steps. Follow the creek as far as Elabana Falls and another swimming hole, or bypass the falls; either way, the path climbs back to the guesthouse.

Another excellent trail (17.5km return) takes six hours via **Box Creek Falls** to the eastern escarpment at **Toolona Lookout**, on the Border Track to Binna Burra; rewards are a half-dozen waterfalls, dramatic views into New South Wales, and encounters with clumps of moss-covered Antarctic beech trees.

Tamborine Mountain

Tamborine Mountain, a volcanic plateau about 40km west of the Gold Coast and 80km south of Brisbane, is a patchwork of rainforest, farmland, wineries and lookouts with commanding views, interspersed with the country villages of **Eagle Heights**, **North Tamborine** and **Tamborine**. Once the haunt of the Wangeriburra Aborigines, Tamborine Mountain's forests were targeted by the timber industry in the late nineteenth century until locals succeeded in getting the area around **Witches Falls** declared Queensland's first national park in 1908; other scattered pockets of forest have since been protected, together comprising **Tamborine National Park**. A trip to the plateau provides a pleasant escape from the city, with a surplus of tearooms, country accommodation and easy walking tracks through accessibly small, jungley stands of timber.

Practicalities

Tamborine Mountain's main access road is Route 95, which loops up the north side of the plateau to Eagle Heights and North Tamborine and then winds its way down again. **Driving** from the coast, turn off the Pacific Motorway (M1) at exit 57 (Oxenford, north of the theme parks) and follow Route 95 up to Eagle Heights; from Brisbane, turn off the motorway at exit 35 (South Beenleigh) and take Route 92 to Tamborine, followed by the section of Route 95 called Tamborine Mountain Road; this leads up to North Tamborine. You can also access the mountain from Nerang or Canungra by taking the signposted turnings off Route 90. All routes to the mountain have steep, winding stretches.

The region's **visitor information centre** is in Doughty Park, North Tamborine, on the way into the village from the Tamborine Mountain Road or Eagle Heights (Mon–Fri 10am–2.30pm, Sat & Sun 9.30am–2.30pm; ☏07 5545 3200).

Some companies running **day-trips** from Brisbane and the Gold Coast (see p.408 & p.460) will take you up the mountain on the way to Lamington National Park, with just enough time for a stop at the Gallery Walk craft shops; others offer **winery tours**, visiting the district's boutique vineyards and often including a stop at the respected Tamborine Mountain Distillery (see p.431). If you'd prefer to plan your own winery circuit, you can pick up information and maps from the tourist office or at Ⓦwww.goldcoastwinecountry.com.au.

Accommodation

Clustered in and around the village of North Tamborine, the mountain's abundant **country lodges**, **inns** and **retreats** are mostly of a romantic-getaway nature: comfortable little places hidden away in forest gardens.

The Bearded Dragon Tamborine Village ☏07 5543 6888, Ⓦwww.beardeddragon.com.au. At the foot of the mountain, this is one of the best-value options in the region, with above-average pub rooms. The tavern holds beer tastings and doubles as a cane-toad-racing venue. ④
The Cottages 23 Kootenai Drive ☏07 5545 2574, Ⓦwww.thecottages.com.au. Cute little villas, conservatively furnished, in a lush garden. ⑤
Hillside Bed and Breakfast 25 Leona Court ☏07 5545 3887, Ⓦwww.hillsidebedandbreakfast.com. This homely place offers a choice of rooms in the main house, or a self-contained cottage with a wood stove in the lounge and wonderful views from the deck; all are modestly priced for North Tamborine. ⑤
Maz's Ambience Retreat 25 Eagle Heights Rd ☏07 5545 1766, Ⓦwww.mazsretreat.com. Run by

a music-lover, this is possibly the only lodge in Queensland with an array of instruments – tambourines, of course, but also pianos and guitars – in its guest cottages, which are elaborately decorated with four-posters, feather boas, swags and chintz. There's also a pool. ⑦
Pethers Rainforest Retreat 28B Geissman St ☏07 5545 4577, Ⓦwww.pethers.com.au. Wonderfully stylish, this forest hideaway has an upmarket restaurant and ten very comfortable wooden pole-frame guest lodges; very good value mid-week. ⑥
The Polish Place 333 Main Western Rd ☏07 5545 1603, Ⓦwww.polishplace.com.au. Unsurprisingly Polish-run, this has cosy self-contained chalets and a well-regarded restaurant serving traditional Polish cuisine (see p.431). ⑥

Songbirds in the Forest Tamborine Mountain Rd ☎07 5545 2563, ⓦwww.songbirds.com.au. One of the best places to stay in the hinterland, this is a gorgeous, relaxing retreat set amongst lush greenery, alive with the calls of kookaburras and tree frogs. It has just six luxury timber villas with Balinese touches – each with a gas fire for cool evenings – and a superb restaurant (see below). ❼

Tamborine Mountain Caravan and Campsite Thunderbird Park, Tamborine Mountain Rd ☎07 5545 0034, ⓦwww.tamborine.info. This leafy site is an affordable, family-friendly option with room for tents, caravans and campervans, plus ready-pitched safari tents to rent. Camping A$18–22, safari tent ❷

The villages

EAGLE HEIGHTS is the largest settlement on Tamborine Mountain, though it's not much more than a five-hundred-metre-long strip, **Gallery Walk**, lined with touristy cafés and craft showrooms. The **botanic gardens** (free), off Long Road, are very pretty, with small picnic lawns surrounding a pond overlooked by tall trees; for something a little more energetic, head to **Palm Grove Circuit** at the end of Palm Grove Avenue, a 2.5km-long mix of dry forest, a few small creeks, and a limpid, eerie gloom created by an extensive stand of elegant piccabean palms. Hidden 20m up in the canopy are elusive wompoo pigeons, often heard but seldom seen, despite their vivid purple-and-green plumage and onomatopoeic call.

A few kilometres west, the village of **NORTH TAMBORINE** has more of a community feel; Main Street is a pleasant, spacious stretch with a few cafés plus a post office, ATMs and fuel. Next door to each other on Beacon Road, a short walk from the tourist office or Main Street, are the Tamborine Mountain Distillery (Wed–Sat 10am–3pm; ☎07 5545 3452, ⓦwww.tamborinemountaindistillery .com), where you can sample award-winning schnapps and liqueurs, and the Witches Chase Cheese Company (daily 10am–4pm; ☎07 5545 1696, ⓦwww .witcheschasecheese.com.au), which specializes in artisan-made camembert, blue cheese and ice cream, and also offers tastings.

The best walk from North Tamborine is an easy three-kilometre track, which starts from Main Western Road, about a kilometre south of the tourist office, and slaloms downhill through open scrub and rainforest to **Witches Falls**, with impressive views off the plateau on the way. The falls themselves are usually only a trickle; far more dramatic are **Cedar Creek Falls**, a good swimming spot a couple of kilometres north of North Tamborine, reached via Tamborine Mountain Road and Cedar Creek Falls Road. Finally, down near **Mount Tamborine** – which is otherwise purely residential – there's a stand of primitive, slow-growing cycads (see box, p.554) and a relatively dry climate at **Lepidozamia National Park** on Main Western Road.

Eating and drinking

Eagle Heights has no shortage of places churning out scones and cream, mostly clustered along Gallery Walk. For something more substantial, you could try *Eagle Thai* on Southport Avenue (☎07 5545 4445; from 6pm daily except Wed), which also does take-aways, but the **best places to eat** on the mountain are in and around North Tamborine. Around 2km north of the village, ⚘ *Songbirds in the Forest* on Tamborine Mountain Road (lunch daily, dinner Thurs–Sat; ☎07 5545 2563, ⓦwww.songbirds.com.au) is one of Queensland's finest restaurants, specializing in delicately flavoured meat and fish accompanied by homegrown organic produce; it's masterminded by a chef who has worked at some of Australia's top dining venues. On the south side of the village, *The Polish Place*, 333 Main Western Rd (☎07 5545 1603, ⓦwww.polishplace.com.au) serves traditional Polish cuisine such as dumplings and chocolate torte; in the centre, *Forest*, 13

Main St (℗07 5545 4916), a characterful bistro with private nooks and shelves of books to browse, is good for steaks and burgers. For something quick and inexpensive, *Spice of Life*, 28 Main St (daily from 7am; ℗07 5545 3553) is a cosy little deli that's great for breakfast or imaginative, healthy salads.

South Stradbroke and the Moreton Bay Islands

Bordering the northern Gold Coast and Brisbane's eastern fringes are the shallow, island-scattered waters of the Broadwater and Moreton Bay. A string of sand islands lie parallel to the mainland, the largest of which, **South Stradbroke Island**, **North Stradbroke Island** and **Moreton Island**, are wild, peaceful holiday destinations with an interesting mixture of native flora and fauna and challenging surf. Like Fraser Island further north, they were formed when sand swept up from the southeastern continental shelf anchored against rocky pivot points: Point Lookout on North Stradbroke and Cape Moreton on Moreton are the equivalent of Indian Head on Fraser. All three islands are generously endowed with dunes and beautiful sandy beaches, and are just the right distance from the mainland to be accessible but seldom crowded. They're favourite destinations for Brisbane residents looking for a quick, back-to-basics getaway.

Closer to Brisbane, the prison ruins on the island of **St Helena**, which recall the convict era, make for an interesting day-trip.

Moreton Bay itself is famous throughout Australia as the home of the unfairly named Moreton Bay bug, a small, delicious variety of lobster. The bay's sheltered conditions and abundant seagrass also provide a perfect environment for dugongs, turtles and dolphins. Humpback whales pass the islands in late winter en route to and from their calving grounds around the Whitsundays, and can often be spotted from dry land, even without binoculars; if you take a wildlife-watching boat trip at this time, you'll be practically guaranteed close-up sightings.

South Stradbroke Island

SOUTH STRADBROKE ISLAND is a twenty-kilometre-long, narrow strip of sand, separated from North Stradbroke Island by the 1896 cyclone. It's the third-largest sand island in the world after Fraser Island and North Stradbroke, with broadly similar woodland vegetation to its larger cousins, but a slightly flatter profile. Its cabbage-palm wetlands harbour some rare flora, including the endangered swamp orchid.

Getting to South Stradbroke

Each of South Stradbroke's three main resorts run **passenger ferries** from the mainland. Anyone can use these, whether booked to stay overnight or not; in each case, you can choose between a basic ticket or a day-trip that includes lunch at the resort. The crossing to *South Stradbroke Island Resort* from Runaway Bay Marina, 10km north of Surfers on Bayview Street, takes 25 minutes (Mon–Thurs 10.30am & 4pm, Fri & Sat 10.30am, 4pm & 6pm, returning Sun 9.30am, 3.30pm & 5pm, Mon–Fri 8am, 2.30pm & 5.30pm, Sat 8am, 3.30pm & 5pm; day return A$30, child A$15; overnight or longer return A$25/A$15; day-trip A$45/A$22). It's advisable to book through the resort in advance, but tickets are also sold at *Café on C* near the jetty. Return minibus transfers from the Surfers Paradise Transit Centre to Runaway Bay Marina cost A$6.

Couran Cove Resort runs ferry transfers from Hope Harbour near Sanctuary Cove, 23km north of Surfers and 65km south of Brisbane, (4–6 departures daily; 40min; A$45 return, child A$25; day-trip A$70/A$40). The daily boat to *Couran Point Island Beach Resort* leaves from Marina Mirage, 3km north of Surfers at Main Beach (A$25 return, child A$10; day-trip A$65/A$30).

The island

Until recently, some believed that South Straddie, which is not a national park, was doomed to become an extension of the Gold Coast, complete with skyscrapers and rollercoasters, but the Gold Coast City Council have declared a large parcel of land a **conservation area** in order to stem the tide of development. For now, the island is relatively isolated with just the thinnest scattering of houses, its quiet beaches of blond sand offering something of an escape from the mainland. **Golden wallabies**, unique to the Stradbroke islands, are used to being hand-fed by visitors (you can buy suitable food by the bag), and are easy to spot. There's also some of the coast's finest **surf** to ride along the southeast shore, though note that the locals are notoriously protective of the best spots.

Despite all these natural attractions, many visitors come over for the day purely to get gently plastered in the bar and restaurant at *South Stradbroke Island Resort* (☏07 5577 3311, ⓦwww.ssir.com.au; ❹), which has simple but pretty palm bungalow-style rooms for overnight stays. For the more active, there's paragliding, canoeing, speedboat riding and bushwalking to choose from. *Couran Cove Resort* (☏07 5509 3000 or 1800 268 726, ⓦwww.couran.com; room ❻, villa ❽), towards the north of the island, offers a more exclusive atmosphere, a marina, a spa and a host of activities, along with luxurious waterfront accommodation; *Couran Point Island Beach Resort* (☏07 5501 3555, ⓦwww.couranpoint .com.au; ❺) is a fairly modest alternative in the same area. For self-sufficient campers, there are a few basic campgrounds: *Currigee* and *North Currigee* (☏07 5577 3932) in the south, and *Tipplers* and *Bedrooms* (☏07 5577 2849) in the north; all charge A$17 per night for an unpowered tent site.

North Stradbroke Island

At 40km long, **North Stradbroke Island** is the largest of the Moreton Bay islands; it's also the most developed, with sealed roads and three fully serviced townships: Dunwich, Amity and Point Lookout. The main concentration of the island's tourist accommodation – and the best land-based whale-watching opportunities – is at Point Lookout.

Ninety percent of Straddie is given over to **mining** the island's titanium-rich sands: the majority of the two thousand or so permanent residents are employees of Consolidated Rutile Ltd. The mine sites south of Amity, and in the central west and south, are far from exhausted but their future is precarious, thanks to an oversupply on the world market. Other industries focus on timber, a by-product of preparing land for mining, and, increasingly, tourism.

Stradbroke's **diving** is renowned for congregations of the increasingly rare grey nurse shark, along with moray eels, dopey leopard sharks, and manta rays; the latter cruise by in the summer months, November to March. Courses and dives can be arranged through *Manta Lodge* (see p.435). Between June and October, you'll get good views of migrating humpback whales while you're out on the water.

Getting there and around

Three **ferry** companies operate services from the mainland to the port at Dunwich; if you're taking a vehicle, you need to book in advance. All the boats leave from Toondah Harbour at **Cleveland**, 29km southeast of central Brisbane; to get there from Brisbane by public transport, take the TransLink Citytrain Doomben–Cleveland train, then catch the red-and-yellow National Bus from Cleveland station to the harbour (A$2). Stradbroke Ferries (℡07 3286 2666, ⓦwww.stradbrokeferries.com.au) run water taxis (12 crossings daily, 30min; A$17 return, child A$10) and vehicle ferries (11 crossings daily; 45min; A$122 return per car). Sea Stradbroke (℡07 3488 9777, ⓦwww.seastradbroke.com) run a car and passenger ferry (8 crossings daily; 45 min; A$122 return per car, pedestrian A$10 return, child A$5). Gold Cats Stradbroke Flyer (℡07 3286 1964, ⓦwww.flyer.com.au) run a fast passenger catamaran service (14 crossings daily, 25min; A$17 return, child A$10).

To **get around** the island, the Stradbroke Island Buses' Dunwich–Point Lookout **bus** connects with all water taxis (A$9.50 return, child A$5), and various operators offer **4WD safaris**: Sunrover Expeditions (℡07 3880 0719 or 1800 353 717, ⓦwww.sunrover.com.au) and Straddie Kingfisher Tours (℡07 3409 9502, ⓦwww.straddiekingfishertours.com.au) are both recommended. Some roads on Stradbroke are open to mining vehicles only, so drivers should look out for the signs. **Off-roading** through the centre on non-designated roads is not advised: quite apart from the damage caused to the dune systems, the sand is very soft and having your vehicle pulled out will be very expensive. Driving on the beach requires a 4WD and a **permit**, which can be obtained from the ferry offices or from Stradbroke Island Tourism on Junner Street in Dunwich (℡07 3409 9555, ⓦwww.stradbroketourism.com); the cost is A$15 for 48 hours or A$30 for a year.

Those with limited time can visit Straddie on a **day-trip** from Brisbane or the Gold Coast: tour companies running trips to the island include Sunrover Expeditions (see above) and Moreton Bay Escapes (℡07 3236 1126 or 1300 559 355, ⓦwww.moretonbayescapes.com.au).

The island

Unless you need to fuel up or visit the bank, there's little to keep you at **DUNWICH**, Straddie's ferry port on the west coast. Two sealed roads head out of town, east through the island's centre towards Main Beach, or north to Amity and Point Lookout. The road through the centre passes two lakes – the second and smaller of these, **Blue Lake**, is a national park and source of fresh water for the island's wildlife, which is most visible early in the morning. Beyond Blue Lake you have to cross **Eighteen Mile Swamp** to reach **Main Beach** and, though there's a causeway, the rest of the route is for 4WDs only. You can **camp** behind the beach anywhere south of the causeway (north of it is mining-company land), but be prepared for the mosquitoes that swarm around the mangroves; the southernmost point is an angling and wildlife Mecca, with birdlife and kangaroos lounging around on the beaches.

Heading north from Dunwich, it's 11km to where the road forks left for a further 6km to **AMITY**, a sleepy place built around a jetty at the northwestern point of the island; there's a store, **campsite** and a small, low-key **resort**, *Sea Shanties*, at 9A Cook St, Amity Point (☎07 3409 7161, ⓦwww.seashanties .com.au; ❷), which offers beachfront cabins sleeping four; they're self-contained but fairly basic, and you'll need to bring your own bedding.

Stay on the road from Dunwich past the Amity turn-off, and it's another 10km to **POINT LOOKOUT**, at Straddie's northeastern tip. The township spreads out around the island's single-rock headland, overlooking a string of beaches, a sports pub, a takeaway-pizza place, a store, some cafés and various **places to stay**. Top of the range are *Samarinda*, Samarinda Drive (☎07 3409 8785, ⓦwww.samarinda.com.au; ❺) with pleasant apartments very close to the sea, available for stays of two or more nights, and *Straddie Views B&B* at 26 Cumming Parade (☎07 3409 8875; ❹), with a nice veranda offering ocean views. A cool choice for a family or small group is *C-Shack* on 16 Galeen St (☎07 3409 8455, ⓦwww.cshackholidays.com; ❺), a beautifully designed and quirkily decorated holiday house with a retro surf-culture feel, available for two nights or more, with discounts for longer stays. The YHA-affiliated *Manta Lodge* at 1 Eastcoast Rd (☎07 3409 8888, ⓦwww.stradbrokeislandscuba.com.au; bunk in shared room A$25–28) is the local budget option, with surfboards, bikes and fishing gear for rent; they also have a PADI dive centre and organize 4WD, walking and trail-riding trips. There are several camping and caravan parks in the area, all managed by *Stradbroke Holiday Parks* (☎1300 551 253; camping A$18–25). The best **place to eat** is *Amis at Pandanus Palms Resort*, 21 Cumming Parade (☎07 3409 8600), a gem of a restaurant with superb sea views and good seafood prepared by highly experienced chefs.

Point Lookout's **beaches** are picturesque, with shallow, protected swimming along the shore. Home and Cylinder beaches are both patrolled and, therefore, crowded during holiday weekends; to find some empty sand, head for the more easterly Deadman's Beach or Frenchman's Bay, bearing in mind that these are unwatched waters. On the headland above the township, there are fine views and the chance to see loggerhead turtles and dolphins; from the walking track around North Gorge down to Main Beach you might see whales during the migration season.

St Helena Island

Small, low and triangular, **St Helena Island** sits 8km from the mouth of the Brisbane River, and from the 1850s until the early twentieth century served as a **prison**. The government found it particularly useful for political trouble-makers, such as the leaders of the 1891 shearers' strike and, with more justice, a couple of slave-trading "Blackbirder" captains.

A tour of the penal settlement, tagged the "Hell Hole of the South Pacific" during its working life, leaves you thankful you missed out on the "good old days". Escape attempts (there were only ever three) were deterred by sharks, whose presence was actively encouraged around the island. Evidence of the prisoners' industry and self-sufficiency is still to be seen in the stone houses, as well as in the remains of a sugar mill, paddocks, wells, and an ingenious lime kiln built into the shoreline. The Deputy Superintendent's house has been turned into a bare **museum** (reached from the jetty on a mini-tramway), displaying a ball and chain lying in a corner and photographs from the prison era. Outside, the two cemeteries have been desecrated: many headstones were carried off as souvenir coffee tables, and the corpses dug up and sold as medical specimens. The remaining stones comprise simple concrete crosses stamped with a number for the prisoners, or inscribed marble tablets for the warders and their children.

AB Sea Cruises offer **day-trips** aboard the *Cat-o'-Nine-Tails* catamaran (Wed 9.15am, returning at 2.15pm, Sun 10am, returning at 3pm; A$69, child A$39 including lunch; ☎07 3893 1240, ⓦwww.sthelenaisland.com.au) and **night tours** (Sat 7pm, returning at 11.15pm; A$79 including dinner and *son et lumière* show). Advance bookings are required. The trips leave from **Manly**, on the coast due east of central Brisbane; to get there from the city by public transport, take the TransLink Citytrain Doomben–Cleveland train to Manly station, from where it's a ten-minute walk to the jetty.

Moreton Island

A 38-kilometre-long narrow band of stabilized, partly wooded sand dunes, **Moreton Island** is blessed with faultless beaches that are distinctly underpopulated for much of the year, and perfect for lounging, surfing or fishing. For most visitors, the big draws are the wild but habituated dolphins that show up at the island's jetty each evening to be fed fish by the wildlife rangers of *Tangalooma Wild Dolphin Resort*: anyone can watch, or even join in. Other marine creatures that cruise around the area include dugongs, turtles and, as elsewhere in the bay, migrating whales. Many people living or staying in Brisbane, the Gold Coast or the Sunshine Coast just come over for the day, with or without a vehicle, to explore beyond Tangalooma (the island tracks and beaches are suitable for 4WDs only) – most notably at Christmas and Easter, when up to a thousand vehicles crowd onto the island all at once – but it's also possible to stay at the resort or camp.

If you're planning to stay a while, note that there are **no banks** on the island, and supplies are expensive – it's best to be self-sufficient and have enough water if you're camping. Before you go in the sea, remember that the beaches aren't patrolled and there are no shark nets.

Getting there

Tangalooma Wild Dolphin Resort (enquiries ☎07 3637 2000 or 1300 652 250, resort 07 3410 6000, ⓦwww.tangalooma.com) operate **passenger ferries** direct to the resort from Holt Street Wharf off Kingsford Smith Drive, Pinkenba, 12km east of central Brisbane and just south of the airport (3 or 4 departures daily; 75min; overnight guest A$70 return, child A$36; day-trip from A$40/A$25). For an extra fee, you can book door-to-door transfers from any point on the Gold Coast (A$40, child A$20) or Brisbane (A$10, child A$5).

The island's **vehicle ferry** service is run by Micat (☎07 3909 3333, ⓦwww.micat.com.au), whose huge modern catamaran carries cars and foot passengers to the Tangalooma Wrecks ramp just north of the resort. It leaves daily at 8.30am, with extra departures at 6.30pm on Friday and 2.30pm on Sunday, from the wharf near their office at 14 Howard Smith Drive, Lytton – you can get here from central Brisbane in an hour by catching the TransLink Citytrain Doomben–Cleveland train to Wynnum Central station, from where there's a bus connection. The open return fares are A$180 per vehicle with two passengers and A$45 or A$30 (child) per pedestrian.

Micat also offer a **day-trip** from the mainland including a 4WD bus tour and a spot of sandboarding for A$114 (child A$103), and can organize QPWS **camping permits** for the standard A$4.50 per person per night, plus vehicle-access permits (required if you're bringing a 4WD to the island) for A$34.40 per visit.

Other recommended **tour companies** include Sunrover Expeditions (see p.434), while Dolphin Wild (☎07 3380 444, ⓦwww.dolphinwild .com.au; A$110, child A$100 including lunch) offer daily **cruises** from Redcliffe, on the coast north of Brisbane, visiting a few of Moreton's beaches and snorkelling spots; for an extra charge, you can book transfers to Redcliffe from central Brisbane (A$25) or the Sunshine or Gold coasts (A$35).

The island

The main arrival point on the island is **TANGALOOMA** on the west coast, where the beachfront is entirely given over to *Tangalooma Wild Dolphin Resort* (see p.436; ⓪) a casual, cheerfully middle-market place with pleasant gardens and a good range of rooms and apartments plus decent, unfussy places to eat and drink. The resort is built on the site of a former **whaling station** that last saw active service in the early 1960s, and grim reminders of the past linger on: a harpoon is preserved as a commemorative sculpture, and the remains of the carcass-processing platform, unsightly by any standards, is used as a shelter for ping-pong tables and volleyball. But despite these macabre features, the resort is an upbeat place with a strong conservation ethic; the excellent wildlife rangers run an eco-information station with a library, and take guests out on wildlife-watching cruises for an extremely good chance of spotting dugongs, turtles and (in season) whales.

Offshore, a set of wrecks, deliberately sunk to create an artificial reef and windbreak, provide fine **snorkelling** at high tide. Other activities organized by the resort include **4WD bus tours**, **quad-biking** and **sandboarding** trips to the dunes to the south of the resort, but the undisputed highlight of the day is the **dolphin-feeding session** held each evening, which is both charming and informative. The resort rangers have been monitoring the progress of a pod of inshore bottlenose dolphins for some years by tempting them close to the beach with handouts of fish – enough to keep them interested, but not so much that they become dependent. Visitors can take part by hand-feeding dolphins under careful supervision.

North of the resort are a couple of national-park **campsites** with basic facilities (water, showers and toilets); they get as crowded as anywhere on the island – permits are available from the QPWS booking service (see p.54) or the Moreton Island National Park office on the island (☎07 3408 2710).

With your own vehicle, or on foot if you don't mind hiking, you can take the ten-kilometre track from Tangalooma across to Moreton's wild and attractive eastern side, where the beach has good **surf** and it's less crowded. At **Eagers Creek**, at the end of the track, there's another campsite and a five-kilometre return trip up sandy **Mount Tempest**'s 280-metre peak – an exhausting climb. Head 10km north up the beach from Eagers Creek, and you'll find Blue Lagoon, the largest of the island's freshwater lakes, only 500m from the beach and adjacent to the smaller, picturesque **Honeyeater Lake**. Blessed with shady trees, the dunes behind the beach here make an ideal place to camp, and the site is supplied with water, showers and toilets. Dolphins come in close to shore, a habit that Moreton's Ngugi Aborigines learned to exploit by using them to chase fish into the shallows – pioneer settler Tom Petrie was so impressed by the efficiency of dolphin-assisted spear-fishing that he recorded the practice when writing about his life in Brisbane in the 1870s.

The north and south ends of the islands are only accessible from the Tanga-looma area by 4WD, though there are tiny settlements at both: **BULWER**, on the island's northeast corner, comprises a cluster of weatherboard "weekenders" and a store stocking fuel and beer and providing basic **accommodation** in cabins, for which you need to bring bedding (bookings through Combie Trader; ☎07 3203 6399, ⓦwww.moreton-island.com; ➌); while right at Moreton's southern tip, tiny **KOORINGAL** has a store offering fuel, supplies and drinks from their bar (daily 8am–midnight).

Brisbane

As the fast-growing capital of a state whose fortunes are booming, **BRISBANE** (pronounced "briz-b'n") is simmering nicely. Gone are the days when urbanites from Sydney and Melbourne dismissed Queensland's first city as a chronically languid country town. Well on the way out, too, is the gauche self-deprecation with which Brisbanites used to play down their city's rapid development with jokey names such as "Bris Vegas" or "Brisneyland". Their relaxed outlook survives – for the present – but it's mixed with a new pride in a city that now boasts world-class galleries, museums, heritage buildings, a buzzing restaurant and music scene, and a quality of life attractive enough to pull in settlers from all over the nation. Its climate is enviable, and its riverside boardwalks and green spaces – seasonally adorned with jacaranda, jasmine and frangipani flowers – lend themselves to outdoor living. Prime Minister Kevin Rudd, a Queenslander who grew up 100km north of Brisbane in Nambour, seems set to make his home capital a political powerhouse, too.

By far the largest city in Queensland, with well over a million and a half residents, Brisbane's urban sprawl covers over 60km of the Moreton Bay coastline, but central Brisbane, 20km inland, remains compact and walkable. The city's main trading, business and cultural centre is squeezed onto the peninsulas formed by a series of lazy loops of the **Brisbane River**, with most of the high-rise buildings confined to just one pocket, the **City district**. Brisbane is a city with relatively few great landmarks, and the river is in many ways its defining feature: its meanderings require that journeys between districts often include a bridge or ferry crossing. In recent years, the riverbanks have become a social focus, dotted with waterfront restaurants and bars, cultural venues, gardens and even a man-made beach.

As a base for wider explorations, Brisbane is a good choice, with the Sunshine Coast, the Gold Coast, the Moreton Bay Islands, Tamborine Mountain and Lamington and Springbrook national parks all an easy journey away by road, rail or ferry. Meanwhile, for those looking to enjoy an urban experience, the city is unlikely to disappoint: its healthy sociability and abundance of casual, short-term employment opportunities tempt many travellers to stay longer than planned.

Some history

In 1823, responding to political pressure to shift the "worst type of felons" away from Sydney, the New South Wales government sent Surveyor General **John**

John Oxley recorded that the **Brisbane Aborigines** were friendly; in the early days, they even rounded up and returned runaways from the settlement. In his orders to Oxley on how to deal with the indigenous peoples, Governor Brisbane admitted, though in a roundabout way, that the land belonged to them: "All uncivilized people have wants ... when treated justly they acquire many comforts by their union with the more civilized. This justifies our occupation of their lands."

But future governors were not so liberal, and things had soured long before the first squatters moved into the Brisbane area and began leaving out "gifts" of poisoned flour and calling in the Native Mounted Police to disperse local Aborigines – a euphemism for exterminating them. In the later part of the nineteenth century, survivors from these early days were dispossessed by the **Protection Act** (in force until the 1970s), which saw them rounded up and relocated onto special reserves away from traditional lands.

A trace of Brisbane's Aboriginal past is found at the **Nudgee Bora Ring** about 12km north of the centre at Nudgee Waterhole Reserve, at the junction of Nudgee and Childs roads. Last used in 1860, two low mounds where boys were initiated form little more than an icon today, and you'll probably feel that it's not worth the trip. More rewarding are the several **Aboriginal walking trails** at Mount Coot-tha; the City Hall information desk has leaflets on these that explain traditional uses of the area.

Oxley north to find a suitable site for a new prison colony. Sailing into **Moreton Bay**, he was shown a previously unknown river by three shipwrecked convicts who had been living with Aborigines. He explored it briefly, named it "Brisbane" after the governor, and the next year established a convict settlement at **Redcliffe** on the coast. This was immediately abandoned in favour of better anchorage further upstream, and by the end of 1824 today's city centre had become the site of Brisbane Town.

Twenty years on, a land shortage down south persuaded the government to move out the convicts and free up the Moreton Bay area to settlers. Immigrants on government-assisted passages poured in and Brisbane began to shape up as a busy **port** – an unattractive, awkward town of rutted streets and wooden shacks. As the largest regional settlement of the times, Brisbane was the obvious choice as capital of the new state of Queensland on its formation in 1859, though the city's first substantial buildings were constructed only in the late 1860s, after fire had destroyed the original centre and state bankruptcy was averted by Queensland's first gold strikes at Gympie. Even so, development was slow and uneven: new townships were founded around the centre at Fortitude Valley, Kangaroo Point and Breakfast Creek, gradually merging into a city.

After World War II, when General Douglas MacArthur used Brisbane as his headquarters to coordinate attacks on Japanese forces based throughout the Pacific, Brisbane stagnated, earning a reputation as a dull, underdeveloped backwater – not least thanks to the Bjelke-Petersen regime. More recently, escalating development has transformed the city's skyline. Since 2001, Brisbane has boasted the country's highest internal migration figures and a quarter of the national **population growth**, resulting in a booming property market, with house-price inflation topping twenty percent in 2007. To help satisfy the demand for upmarket apartments, dilapidated inner-city and riverfront areas have been razed and redeveloped, and there are ever-more ambitious urban-renewal plans in the pipeline – the latest, the North Quarter scheme near Roma Street, will involve extensive land reclamation and the building of a new footbridge across the river from the north bank to the South Bank Cultural Centre.

▲ Teneriffe

▲ ❶, ⑲, ⑳ & ㉑

▲ The Emporium & Airport

NEW FARM

FORTITUDE VALLEY

Brunswick Street Station

BRUNSWICK ST MALL

Story Bridge

BRADFIELD HIGHWAY

St John's Cathedral

Customs House

Riverside Centre

Riverside

Holman Street

Eagle Street Pier

Polo Club

SPRING HILL

Boundary Street

Wharf Street

Central Station

ANZAC SQUARE

Museum of Brisbane

City Hall

Wickham Park

Observatory

Victoria Park

Albert Park

PETRIE TERRACE

Brisbane Transit Centre & Roma Street Station

William Jolly Bridge

CORONATION DRIVE

250 m

0

ACCOMMODATION

Acacia	K
Annie's Shandon Inn	L
Astor	M
Banana Bender	J
Brisbane Manor Hotel	A
Bunk	D
Central Brunswick	F
Chifley at Lennons	W
City Backpackers	O
Cloud 9	N
Emporium Hotel	B
Explorers Inn	U
Hilton	V
Homestead	I
Kookaburra Inn	G
The Marque	Y
Palace Backpackers	Q
Rendezvous	P
Sebel	T
Snooze Inn	C
Sportsman Hotel	H
Stamford Plaza	X
Thornbury House	E
Tinbilly	S
Yellow Submarine	R

▲ & Sunshine Coast

❸ ❶ ❷ ❸ ❹

❶ ❶ ❷ ❸ ❹

▲ Sanctuary

▲ Milton, Toowong, Castlemaine Perkins Brewery & Mount Coot-tha

▲ Paddington & Rosalie

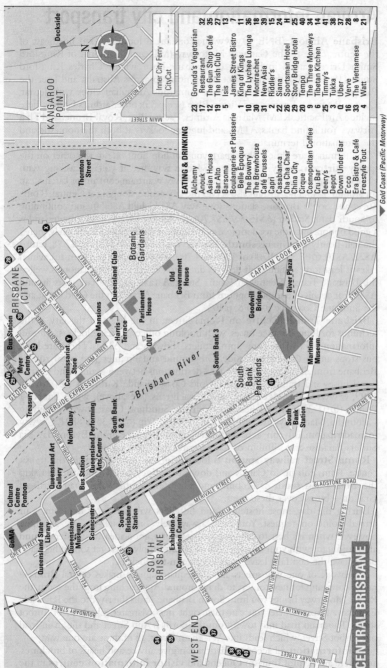

EATING & DRINKING

Alchemy	23
Anouk	17
Asian House	12
Bar Alto	19
Barsoma	5
Boulangerie et Patisserie Belle Epoque	1
The Bowery	10
The Brewhouse	30
Café Brussels	31
Capri	2
Casablanca	22
Cha Cha Char	26
China City	29
Cirque	20
Cosmopolitan Coffee	9
Cru Bar	25
Deery's	3
Depot	0
Down Under Bar	16
Ecco	33
Era Bistro & Café	4
Freestyle Tout	21
Govinda's Vegetarian Restaurant	32
The Gun Shop Café	35
The Irish Club	27
Isis	13
James Street Bistro	7
King of Kings	11
The Lychee Lounge	36
Montrachet	18
New Asia	39
Riddler's	15
Siana	24
Sportsman Hotel	H
Story Bridge Hotel	25
Tempo	40
The Three Monkeys	34
Tibetan Kitchen	14
Timmy's	41
Tukka	38
Uber	37
Verve	28
The Vietnamese	8
Watt	21

CENTRAL BRISBANE

Ipswich, St Lucia & Lone Pine

Gold Coast (Pacific Motorway)

Arrival, information and city transport

Brisbane Airport (BNE; ⓦ www.bne.com.au) is located 14km northeast of the centre, close to the Gateway Motorway (M1) and just north of Kingsford Smith Drive, named in honour of Brisbane-born aviator Charles Kingsford Smith (1897–1935), the first pilot to fly nonstop across Australia and later the Pacific. You can fly to Brisbane from numerous Australian cities with Jetstar, Qantas, Regional Express and Virgin Blue (see p.35); other airlines landing here include Air Pacific, KLM, Malaysia Airlines, Pacific Blue, Royal Brunei and Thai Airways. You'll find banks, ATMs and luggage lockers at both the domestic and the international terminals.

The terminals are almost 3km apart; you can hop from one to the other on the speedy **Airtrain** (every 15–30min; A$4 one way; free if you're travelling with Qantas or Virgin and just changing planes; ⓦ www.airtrain.com.au) or catch a cab for around A$13. The Airtrain also serves the city centre, stopping at Central, Roma Street and South Brisbane stations (one way A$13, child A$6.50) and continuing to South Bank Station (A$15.30/A$7.70); it takes twenty to thirty minutes and is a good option, since the road route is notorious for traffic jams. Alternatively, there's the half-hourly Coachtrans **shuttle bus** service (one way A$12, child A$8; return A$22/A$10; ⓣ07 3358 9700 or 1300 664 700, ⓦ www.coachtrans.com.au), which takes at least forty minutes but delivers direct to central accommodation as well as the Brisbane Transit Centre on Roma Street. A **taxi** into the city costs around A$35. For details of transport options from Brisbane Airport to the Gold Coast and the Sunshine Coast, see p.406 & p.463.

Brisbane Transit Centre on Roma Street, in the heart of the city, is the terminus for long-distance buses, with booking offices, luggage lockers, a hostel information desk (daily 8am–5pm), toilets, showers and ATMs. There are local bus stops and a taxi rank outside. Greyhound and Premier (see p.35) run to Brisbane from all the major East Coast destinations between Sydney and Cairns. Local buses and transfers from the Gold Coast include Kirklands (ⓣ02 6626 1499, ⓦ www.kirklands.com.au) and Coachtrans (see above); while Suncoast Pacific (ⓣ07 3236 1901) head in from the Sunshine Coast towns including Caloundra, Maroochydore and Noosa. Oz Road Trip (ⓣ07 3395 8891, ⓦ www.ozroadtrip.com.au) run a backpacker bus to Brisbane from Byron Bay via Surfers Paradise and Nimbin or Coolangatta three times a week.

Roma Street railway station is located on the ground floor of the transit centre. Trains run up to Cairns and down to Sydney and Melbourne, but skip the Gold Coast south of Robina, and the New South Wales coast north of Grafton – buses cover these areas.

During the day, most hosteliers and hoteliers will pick you up from your arrival point on request. You can't always rely on a pick-up late at night, however, when it's best to take a taxi – it's not a good idea to wander around after midnight with your luggage in tow. If you simply must get somewhere and don't have the taxi fare, leave your luggage in the lockers.

A network of one-way streets and inadequate signage makes central Brisbane rather confusing for newcomers to **drive** around. Approaching from the south, the Pacific Motorway brings you from South Brisbane across the river to the Riverside Expressway, from where you can turn right into Margaret, Elizabeth or Turbot streets. The main road into town from the north is Ann Street and the main road out Turbot Street, which leads into Wickham Street; all of these are one way.

For **information**, all accommodation can give advice and heaps of brochures, and there are helpful Tourism Queensland **visitor information centres** in the domestic terminal at Brisbane Airport (daily 8.30am–2.30pm; ⓣ07 3406 3193,

Ⓦwww.southernqueensland.com) and near the Wintergarden on Queen Street Mall (Mon–Thurs 9am–5.30pm, Fri 9am–7pm, Sat 9am–5pm, Sun 9.30am–4.30pm; ℡07 3006 6290, Ⓦwww.ourbrisbane.com).

City transport

Although Brisbanites complain about traffic congestion and inadequate public transport services, they're far better served than many cities of comparable size. All public local bus, train and ferry services within Greater Brisbane are efficiently operated by **TransLink** (℡13 12 30, Ⓦwww.translink.com.au), whose network extends all the way north to Noosa and south to Coolangatta. There's a TransLink information desk at the Queen Street Mall visitor information centre. **Fares** are the same for all services – boat, bus and train – and are calculated by zone: the more zones you cross, the more you pay. For example, an adult single fare in the central zone is A$2.30, while a ride out to the inner suburbs costs a little over A$4. **Daily tickets**, which offer unlimited bus, ferry and train travel for a day, are cheaper if you're taking more than one trip. The options are a Daily (A$4.60 one zone, A$5.40 two zones; valid for one calendar day until midnight) or an Off-Peak Daily (A$3.50 one zone, A$4.10 two zones; valid for one calendar day Mon–Fri 9am–3.30pm & 7pm–midnight, Sat & Sun all day). Singles and dailies can be bought on any bus or ferry, at Citytrain stations or newsagents. For multiple trips over several days, you can buy a weekly or monthly **pass**, valid on all services, from newsagents and stations. A convenient alternative if you're planning to make several journeys over the course of several days is the new Translink **go card**, a smart card that you can use across the entire city and suburban transport network; you're charged the standard single fare for the first six journeys you make in any seven-day period and half price for the rest of the week. You can buy one and charge it up with credit at Citytrain stations, over the phone (℡13 12 30) or online (Ⓦwww.translink.com.au/go).

Buses run from about 5am to 11.30pm, with NightLink buses connecting the Central Business District and Fortitude Valley with the suburbs all night on Fridays and Saturdays. The hubs for most services are the Queen Street Bus Station below the Myer Centre and the Cultural Centre Busway Station on the South Bank. Drivers give change.

The City, including Central Station, Riverside, Eagle Street Pier and Queen Street Mall, is covered by a free service, the ten-stop **City Loop** (red stops and buses, running every 10min both clockwise and anticlockwise; Mon–Fri 7am–5.50pm).

The electric **Citytrain** network, which extends right out to the distant suburbs and the Gold Coast, provides a faster service than the buses, but is not as frequent or comprehensive. Trains through central Brisbane run every few minutes, but for the more distant suburbs you may have to wait an hour. The last trains leave Central Station at about 11.45pm.

Brisbane's **ferries** zigzag across the river at high speed and are an enjoyable and efficient way of getting around the city. Running every ten to thirty minutes between 5.50am and 10.30pm, the **Inner City** and **CityCat** services are the most useful, the latter sailing at a bracing 27 knots between the University of Queensland campus in the southwest to Bretts Wharf, with stops including North Quay (for Queen Street Mall), South Bank (for the Cultural Centre and Parklands), Riverside (for the riverside restaurants) and New Farm Park (for the park and Brisbane Powerhouse).

After dark, **taxis** (℡13 10 08 or 13 19 24) tend to cruise round the clubs and hotels; during the day, Roma Street is a good place to find one. A short hop in town is likely to cost A$5–8. **Cyclists** have a good number of bike routes from which to choose, with maps available from the tourist information booths and libraries. A few hostels **loan** bikes, or they can be easily rented elsewhere (see p.460).

Accommodation

Brisbane's inner-city **accommodation** is varied and excellent value, with hostels, motels, apartments and international-style hotels spread right across the centre, catering for a broad mix of business travellers and tourists. The following is just a small selection of the options; beds are only scarce during major sports events such as the annual Brisbane Cup horse race in June, and the Royal Queensland Show (the "Ekka"; www.ekka.com.au) in August. Hostellers have masses of choice, with many backpackers' places running jobfinder and travel and tour desks. Most hostels are very security-conscious, and some will only offer their dorm beds to "genuine backpackers", defined as those travelling with a rucksack. Prices at executive-orientated hotels vary day by day and typically drop at weekends.

City district and Petrie Terrace

All the following are within walking distance of Central Station, Roma Street Station and Brisbane Transit Centre.

Hostels

Banana Bender 118 Petrie Terrace ☎ 07 3367 1157, www.bananabenders.com.au. A small, friendly hostel with a homely, easy-going feel. There's a little kitchen and BBQ area, a casual TV lounge and a deck for dining. Bunk in triple, quad or dorm A$26–28, private double/twin ❷

City Backpackers 380 Upper Roma St ☎ 07/3211 3221, www.citybackpackers.com.au. Big, busy, well-run hostel with bargain rates, clean facilities, fair-sized rooms, a bar with budget meal deals and BBQ nights, swimming pool and free undercover parking. Bunk in shared room A$19–28, private double/twin ❷

Cloud 9 350 Upper Roma St ☎ 07 3236 2333 or 1800 256 839, www.cloud9backpackers.com.au. Small, eco-friendly and fresh as paint, with very cheap beds in the largest dorm and good views from the roof terrace, this is one of the best of the clutch of hostels west of the Transit Centre. Bunk in shared room A$17–27, en-suite twin ❸

Palace Backpackers Corner of Ann & Edward sts ☎ 07 3211 2433 or 1800 676 340, www .palacebackpackers.com.au. Huge City landmark, purpose-built in 1911 (its ancient lift still survives). A few rooms are spacious but the noise from the *Down Under Bar* prompts some travellers to move elsewhere for some sleep. Bunk in dorm, quad or triple A$25–28, private double/twin ❷

Tinbilly 446 George St (corner of Herschel St) ☎ 07 3258 5888 or 1800 446 646, www.tinbilly .com. Modern party-hostel and bar almost directly opposite the Transit Centre; facilities are good, though doubles are expensive and the noise can build in the evening. Bunk in dorm or quad-share A$25, private double/twin ❸

Yellow Submarine 66 Quay St ☎ 07 3211 3424, www.yellowsubmarinebackpackers.com. Small, comfortable hostel in an 1860s building with landscaped courtyard and all the usual facilities, plus trips and BBQs organized by the owners, ensuring a sociable atmosphere. Bunk in shared room A$25–27, private double/twin ❷

Pubs, inns and B&Bs

Acacia 413 Upper Edward St ☎ 07 3832 1663 or 1800 773 63. An austere brick exterior disguises this plain but clean and orderly B&B, offering simple rooms, some en suite, at low prices. ❸

Annie's Shandon Inn 405 Upper Edward St ☎ 07 3831 8684, www.babs.com.au/annies. An old-fashioned budget option, chintzy but cosy, with a choice of en-suite or non en-suite rooms. ❷

Explorers Inn 63 Turbot St (corner of George St) ☎ 07 3211 3488, www.explorers.com.au. Friendly low-cost lodgings with small double rooms and large twins and triples, all en suite. ❹

Kookaburra Inn 41 Phillips St, Spring Hill
⊕07 3832 1303, ⊛www.kookaburra-inn.com.au.
Essentially a cross between a B&B without the
breakfast and a hostel without the dorms, this
characterful Queenslander is a cheap and peaceful
place to stay, with simple twins, doubles and
singles, and a shared kitchen. ❷
Sportsman Hotel 130 Leichhardt St, Spring Hill
⊕07 3831 2892, ⊛www.sportsmanhotel.com.au.
Gay-friendly pub with cheap rooms. Predominantly
male clientele, but both sexes welcome. ❷
Thornbury House 1 Thornbury St, Spring Hill
⊕07 3839 5334, ⊛www.babs.com.au/thornbury.
Charming little B&B in a lovingly maintained
Queenslander with a pretty veranda and leafy
courtyard. ❹

Hotels and apartments

Astor 193 Wickham Terrace ⊕07 3144 4000,
⊛www.astorhotel.com.au. Mid-price hotel in a
characterful nineteenth-century building attached to
a newer block with a small rooftop pool. Some rooms
are tired but rates are low. Room ❸, studio ❹
Chifley at Lennons 66 Queen St Mall ⊕07 3222
3222, ⊛www.chifleyhotels.com. Bang in the City's
main shopping centre, this modern place offers tidy

hotel rooms with a great range of discounts and
deals. ❹
Hilton 190 Elizabeth St ⊕07 3234 2000, ⊛www
.brisbane.hilton.com. While the interior is a little
austere, the five-star rooms are perfect for
business travellers, the pool is bigger than most,
breakfast is brilliant, and you can't fault the Queen
St Mall location. ❻
The Marque 103 George St ⊕07 3221 6044,
⊛www.marquehotels.com. Very central, with a funky
reception area, plain but decent rooms, a small pool
and very reasonable rates at weekends. ❺
🏃 **Rendezvous** 255 Ann St ⊕07 3001 9888,
⊛www.rendezvoushotels.com/brisbane.
Spacious, classically furnished hotel rooms and
apartments and regular special offers make this
one of the best options in the centre of town. ❺
Sebel King George Square ⊕07 3229 9111,
⊛www.mirvachotels.com.au. Huge hotel with
comfortable, affordable rooms and a heated rooftop
pool. ❺
Stamford Plaza Edward St ⊕07 3221 1999,
⊛www.stamford.com.au/spb. Top-notch hotel with
a grand mix of colonial and modern buildings
overlooking the river and Botanic Gardens. Rates
drop at weekends. ❼

Fortitude Valley and New Farm

If you stay in the Valley, you'll be within stumbling distance of all the best clubs
and live-music venues. Some streets can be noisy and seedy late at night, but the
northern end of the district is quieter, as is New Farm to the east. To get here
from the centre, take the Citytrain to Brunswick Street Station or catch a bus
from Adelaide Street.

Hostels

Bunk 11 Gipps St (corner of Ann St) ⊕07 3257
3644 1800 682 865, ⊛www.bunkbrisbane.com.au.
Warehouse-sized backpackers' whose noisy road-
junction location and late-night bar are compensated
buy good facilities. The studios are far smarter than
you'd expect from a hostel. Bunk in shared room
A$26–29, private double/twin ❸, studio ❹
Homestead 57 Annie St ⊕1800 658 344. A large
house converted into a hostel, with a quiet atmosphere, a pool and plenty of outdoor space, plus
bikes to borrow. The hostel also arranges local trips.
Bunk in shared room A$22–26, private double ❷

Hotels and apartments

Brisbane Manor Hotel 555 Gregory Terrace
⊕07 3252 4171 or 1800 800 589, ⊛www
.brisbanemanor.com. Good-value guesthouse in a
quirky heritage building some distance from the
centre, with a good range of en-suite rooms and
use of laundry and kitchen facilities. ❷

Central Brunswick 455 Brunswick St ⊕07 3852
1411, ⊛www.centralbrunswickhotel.com.au.
Sparkling modern building with comfortable en-
suite rooms and studios with mini-kitchens. Shared
amenities include a small spa, sauna and gym. ❹
🏃 **Emporium Hotel** 1000 Ann St ⊕07 3253
6888, ⊛www.emporiumhotel.com.au.
Surrounded by great restaurants and shops, this
aparthotel is the showpiece of the stunning new
Emporium urban village. It oozes contemporary
boutique style, and is faultlessly comfortable –
there's even a pillow menu. Upstairs, the gym and
rooftop lap pool will have you stepping up your
exercise routine in a flash. ❻
Snooze Inn 383 St Pauls Terrace ⊕1800 655 805,
⊛www.snoozeinn.com.au. Fresh, modern place
offering smart, little en-suite rooms and a "grab-
and-go" breakfast, with useful extras such as free
broadband Internet access. Handy for the station,
and great value. ❹

The City

Central Brisbane is focused around the broad bends of the **Brisbane River**, with the triangular wedge of the business centre on the north bank surrounded by community-oriented suburbs. The heart of **City district** is the busy, upmarket commercial and administrative area around Queen Street and George Street, whose glass towers, cafés and century-old sandstone facades extend southeast to the Botanic Gardens on the river. Radiating **north**, the polish gives way to less conservative shops, accommodation and eateries around Spring Hill, Fortitude Valley and New Farm, and the aspiring suburbs of Petrie Terrace, Paddington and Rosalie. To the west is a blaze of riverside homes at Milton and Toowong and the fringes of Mount Coot-tha. **South of the river**, the major landmarks are the South Bank Cultural Centre and Parklands, with a pleasant riverside walkway stretching right around Kangaroo Point, linked to the north bank by the Story Bridge. South of South Bank are the open, bustling streets of the West End and South Brisbane, more relaxed than their northern counterparts.

City district

The **City district** may be Brisbane's most business-like quarter, with hordes of commuters flooding off the buses and trains in the morning and afternoon rush hours, but there's a laidback slant to commercial life here – think open-necked shirts rather than jackets and ties. While the office blocks are individually uninspiring, collectively they're impressive, especially when reflected in the river. At ground level, the hard edges are softened by splashes of public sculpture and art, including a wacky series of one-offs by local painters, commissioned by the City council to brighten up all the street-corner traffic-signal boxes.

Queen Street Mall

Queen Street is Brisbane's oldest thoroughfare, and is still its shopping hub: the stretch between Brisbane Square and Edward Street is a **pedestrian mall** flanked by multistorey shopping centres including the heritage-listed **Brisbane Arcade**, built in the 1920s and home to celebrated local fashion houses. The mall is always busy with people running errands, eating at the many cafés, window shopping or just socializing, and there's usually some kind of entertainment, too: either informal efforts – acrobats, buskers and the occasional soap-box orator – or more organized events such as dancing or jazz sessions on the small stage about halfway towards the southwest end of the street.

The Museum of Brisbane, the Observatory and the Central Business District

North from the mall along Albert Street, you arrive at **King George Square**, with its fountains and bronze sculptures of swaggies, native wildlife and what look like large pieces of futuristic circuitry. Facing the square to the west is **City Hall**, a stately 1920s building ruined by an ugly clock tower. Inside, the **Museum of Brisbane** (daily 10am–5pm; free) has a smattering of paintings with regular shows by prominent Australian artists and a varied programme of exhibitions and installations related to the city's social history and aspirations. The **clock tower** is open, too, for a view of the city centre (Mon–Fri 10am–3pm, Sat 10am–2pm; free); access is through the City Hall foyer and then up by lift.

Flanked by roads further up Albert Street, tiny **Wickham Park** is overlooked by the grey cone of Brisbane's oldest building, a windmill known as the

Observatory, built by convicts in 1829 to grind corn for the early settlement. The original wooden sails were too heavy to turn but found use as a gallows until being pulled off in 1850, and all grinding was done by a treadmill – severe punishment for the convicts who had to work it. After the convict era the building became a signal station and now stands locked up and empty, held together with a cement glaze.

East between here and the river lies Brisbane's **Central Business District**, which was heavily developed in the 1990s and left with a legacy of glassy high-rises sprouting alongside the restaurants and shops of the Riverside Centre; the few surviving old buildings are hidden among the modern ones. The copper-domed **Customs House** (daily 10am–4pm; free) at the upper end of Queen Street, built in 1889, harbours a small collection of Chinese antiques and hosts free concerts given by the Queensland University Orchestra every month, while the neo-Gothic **St John's Cathedral** (daily 9.30am–4.30pm; donation) on Ann Street has some elegant stained-glass windows and the only fully stone-vaulted ceiling in Australia.

Wedged between the City, Petrie Terrace and Spring Hill on the edge of the new North Quarter is **Roma Street Parkland**, the world's largest subtropical urban garden, home to a lush assortment of ferns, succulents and pandanus trees, with free guided walks led by volunteers every day at 10am and 2pm.

The historic precinct

The southern section of the City between Queen Street and the Botanic Gardens contains some of Brisbane's finest architecture, dating from the earliest days of settlement until the late nineteenth century. Between Elizabeth Street and Queen Street, occupying an entire block, is the former **Treasury** with its classical facade. Built in the 1890s, its grandeur reflects the wealth of Queensland's gold mines (though by this point most were on the decline) and was a slap in the face to New South Wales, which had spitefully withdrawn all financial support from the fledgling state on separation some forty years previously, leaving it bankrupt. With irony typical of a state torn between conservatism and tourism, the building is now Brisbane's 24-hour **casino**.

South along William Street, the **Commissariat Store** is contemporary with the Observatory, though in considerably better shape. Originally a granary, it's now a **museum** (Tues–Sun 10am–4pm; A$4) and headquarters of the Royal Historical Society of Queensland; the knowledgeable staff pep up an otherwise dusty collection of relics dating back to convict times. Further south along George Street you pass **Harris Terrace** and **The Mansions**, two of the city centre's last surviving rows of Victorian-era terraced houses, the latter guarded by stone cats on the parapet corners. Nearby, on the corner of George and Alice streets, the **Queensland Club** was founded in 1859, just four days before the separation of Queensland from New South Wales. Heavy walls, columns and spacious balconies evoke a tropical version of a traditional London club; entrance and membership – women are still not allowed to join – are by invitation only. Diagonally opposite, **Parliament House** (Mon–Fri 9.30am–4pm, Sat & Sun 10am–2pm; free guided tours when parliament not in session) was built to a design by Charles Tiffin in 1868, in an appealingly compromised French Renaissance style that incorporates shuttered north windows, shaded colonnades and a high, arched roof to allow for the tropical climate. You can see the grand interior on an hour-long guided tour, and there's access to the chambers when there's no debate in progress.

South of Parliament House, George Street becomes a pedestrian lane along the western side of the Botanic Gardens and home to the Queensland

University of Technology. Here you'll find **Old Government House** (Mon–Fri 10am–4pm; free), the official residence of Queensland's governors and premiers between 1862 and 1910. Another of Tiffin's designs, the building has been comprehensively restored to its stately, early twentieth-century condition, and is well worth a look for its furnishings.

The Botanic Gardens

Bordered by Alice Street, George Street and the river, Brisbane's **Botanic Gardens** overlook the cliffs of Kangaroo Point and, while more of a park than a botanic garden, provide a generous arrangement of flowers, shrubs, bamboo thickets and green grass for sprawling on, all offering an easy escape from city claustrophobia. Free **guided tours** (Mon–Sat 11am & 1pm except mid-Dec to Jan) leave from the rotunda, 100m inside the gardens' main entrance, halfway along Alice Street.

Once a vegetable patch cultivated by convicts, formal gardens were laid out in 1855 by Walter Hill, who experimented with local and imported plants to see which would grow well in Queensland's then untried climate. Some of his more successful efforts are the oversized **bunya pines** around the Edward Street entrance at the east end of Alice Street, planted in 1860, and a residual patch of the **rainforest** that once blanketed the area, at the southern end of the park. **Mangroves** along the river, accessible by a **boardwalk**, are another native species more recently protected. During the day, cyclists, joggers and rollerbladers flock to the park, as it's at one end of a popular track that follows the north bank of the river south to St Lucia and the University of Queensland. At the southern end of the gardens, classical music recitals and other events are held on an open-air stage in the summer, beyond which the pedestrian **Goodwill Bridge** crosses over the river to South Bank Parklands.

The northern neighbourhoods

North of the river, just beyond Brisbane's Central Business District, are several former suburbs that have been absorbed by the city sprawl: **Paddington** and **Petrie Terrace** to the west, **Spring Hill** and **Fortitude Valley** to the north, **New Farm** and **Teneriffe** to the east. Houses in these areas are popular with Brisbane's aspiring professional class, and while office buildings, woolshed-conversions and one-way streets are beginning to encroach, there's also an older character reflected in the many high-set, wooden-balconied Queenslanders lining the quieter streets.

Queenslanders

Single-storey, colonial-style timber houses with shady verandas and corrugated-iron roofs are an iconic element of the urban landscape in older Queensland towns such as Brisbane, Rockhampton and Cairns – so much so that Brisbane's Queensland Museum (see p.449) recently created an exhibit about the uses found for one of their most treasured features, the "under-the-house" space. Designed long before air-conditioning was invented, **Queenslanders** were built on sturdy "stumps", leaving an open space at ground level to help air circulate. In some houses, this space serves as a park for cars, kayaks or surfboards; in others, it's a studio, a kids' den or a place to sling hammocks. Some of the finest hundred-year-old Queenslanders in Brisbane's leafy inner suburbs have filigree ironwork or timber lattices and fretwork on the balconies and parapets; in recent years, many have been painstakingly restored, while others have been snapped up by investors, uprooted, and transported out of town for a new life in the country.

Fortitude Valley

While the other northern neighbourhoods are mainly residential, **Fortitude Valley** – better known as just **The Valley** – is Brisbane's unofficial centre of artistic, gastronomic and alcoholic pursuits. A tangled, eclectic mix of the gay, the groovy and the grubby, The Valley spans out from partially pedestrianized **Brunswick Street** into **Ann Street** and **Wickham Street**. At its heart is a mélange of offbeat shops, boutiques and galleries; pubs, nightclubs and live-music venues; a compact Chinatown complete with the usual busy restaurants and stores; and a burgeoning European-style street-café scene. Some of Australia's most interesting fashion designers and contemporary art dealers base themselves here, and The Valley's vibrant music culture has nurtured many leading lights of the country's rock, folk and jazz scene.

The area is in a state of inner-city gentrification, with the urban poor making way for a mixture of hip students, cool creatives and, in the case of the spruced-up northeastern quarters such as **James Street** and **The Emporium**, the upwardly mobile, drawn partly by some of the best restaurants in the city. Brunswick Street itself, however, has yet to embrace the wine-bar and deli culture that's moved in elsewhere, and remains a good spot to enjoy an evening out among Brisbane's young, fun and adventurous. It's best at weekends when cafés buzz and musicians compete for your attention. On Saturdays, there's a market in the Brunswick Street mall selling vintage and locally designed clothing, vinyl and oddments.

South Brisbane

Across the river from the city centre, the main points of interest are the **South Bank Cultural Centre** and the nearby **South Bank Parklands**, which lie either side of Victoria Bridge, connecting Queen Street and Melbourne Street. The district can be reached by ferry to the South Bank wharves or Citytrain to South Brisbane Station, while plenty of buses from all parts of the city stop on Melbourne Street. It's also possible to cross Victoria Bridge or Goodwill Bridge, at the southeast end of the Parklands, on foot.

Southwest of here is the **West End**, South Brisbane's answer to Fortitude Valley or New Farm; it has no sights as such but does have a relaxed, low-rise, multi-ethnic vibe and is popular for its escalating number of **restaurants** and **cafés** strung out along Boundary Street.

The South Bank Cultural Centre

The superb **South Bank Cultural Centre**, a row of modern riverfront buildings linked by Grey Street and a waterside boardwalk, comprises the Queensland Performing Arts Centre, Queensland Museum and Sciencentre, Queensland Art Gallery, State Library and Brisbane's proudest recent addition, the Gallery of Modern Art (GoMA). The buildings themselves are substantial blocks of clean-edged concrete and glass, designed not to upstage the collections within; all have suitably stylish gallery shops and cafés.

The **Queensland Museum** (daily 9.30am–5pm; main collection free, Sciencentre A\$10, child A\$8; ☎07 3840 7555, ⓦwww.southbank.qm.qld .gov.au) is essentially a natural history museum with a little social history thrown in. It kicks off with life-size models of humpback whales and excellent displays of distinctive regional artefacts – from Mister Fourex and the Bundy polar bear to cane toads, sand from Fraser Island and photos of Queenslander houses – then takes you past displays of finds from the state's fossil sites, including a reconstruction of Queensland's own *Muttaburrasaurus*, and various historic planes, boats and automobiles. There's also a little bit on the marine environment, particularly turtles, and the **Museum Zoo**, where hundreds of

▲ Brisbane's South Bank

models, skeletons and remains of wildlife are arranged in a long conga line in order of size. The topmost floor has an exhibition on **Aboriginal Queensland**, with the usual cases of stone tools and boomerangs enlivened by photos, accounts by early settlers and Aboriginal elders, interactive videos and Dreamtime stories. The ground floor **Sciencentre** is good for those who prefer to prod and dismantle exhibits rather than peer at them through a protective glass case. It's great for children, with favourites including the "perception tunnel", which gives the impression of rotating although you remain stock still, and the "Thongophone", a set of giant pan pipes played by whacking the top with a flip-flop – all good rainy-day material.

The adjoining **Queensland Art Gallery** (Mon–Fri 10am–5pm, Sat & Sun 9am–5pm; free, except for special exhibitions; ℡07 3840 7303, ⓦwww.qag .qld.gov.au) houses a collection of Australian painting from the early days of local settlement up to the present, with most important artists represented. Top of the bill are astounding works by Sidney Nolan from his series on **Mrs Fraser** (of Fraser Island fame), watercolours by Aboriginal artists Albert Namatjira and Joe Rootsey, Bribie Islander Ian Fairweather's abstract canvases, and a nineteenth-century **stained-glass window** of a kangaroo hunt. The selection is broad enough to trace how Australian art began by aping European tastes and then, during the twentieth century, found its own style in the works of Nolan, Boyd and Whiteley, who were all inspired by Australian landscape and legends.

The redeveloped **Queensland State Library** (Mon–Thurs 10am–8pm, Fri–Sun 10am–5pm; ℡07 3840 7666, ⓦwww.slq.qld.gov.au) is thoroughly forward-looking, with a large Internet-access area downstairs (free), a busy programme of talks and events, a Heritage Collections section including significant letters, maps, photographs and artefacts, a ground-breaking Indigenous Knowledge Centre and an excellent general-reference library.

At the northwest end of the complex is Australia's largest modern art gallery, **GoMA** (Mon–Fri 10am–5pm, Sat & Sun 9am–5pm; free, except for special exhibitions; ℡07 3840 7303, ⓦwww.qag.qld.gov.au), a huge, flexible, airy space with a permanent collection covering the last thirty years. Since its inauguration in late 2006, it has hosted several blockbuster multimedia shows by twentieth- and twenty-first-century artists, including the 2008 season's headline-grabbing Andy Warhol retrospective.

The South Bank Parklands

The **South Bank Parklands** date back to 1988, when the site hosted the Brisbane World Expo; they have since been altered and redeveloped and are

The Brisbane River

The **Brisbane River** is, at four hundred million years old, one of the world's most ancient waterways. It flows from above Lake Wivenhoe – 55km inland – past farmland, into quiet suburbs and through the city before emptying 150km downstream into Moreton Bay. Once an essential trade and transport link with the rest of Australia and the world, it now does little but separate the main part of the city from South Brisbane, with the maritime industries long-since transferred to Port of Brisbane out on the coast.

Today, the river is superficially active around the city centre, with ferries and dredgers keeping it navigable, but most of the old wharves and shipyards lie derelict or buried under parkland. Nonetheless, Brisbanites, who call their home town the **River City**, are immensely proud of their waterfront, and large urban regeneration funds have been directed at enhancing it with new bridges, bankside boardwalks and places to walk, cycle, eat, drink or just hang out. For ten days each year from late August, the city celebrates its relationship with its river at the **Riverfestival** (Ⓦ www.riverfestival.com.au), a highly enjoyable series of performances, fireworks and events at waterfront venues.

In Brisbane's early days, the river was a liability. In February 1893, cyclonic rains swelled the flow through the city, carrying off Victoria Bridge and scores of buildings: eyewitness accounts stated that "debris of all descriptions – whole houses, trees, cattle and homes – went floating past". This has since been repeated many times, notably in January 1974 when rains from **Cyclone Wanda** completely swamped the centre, swelling the river to a width of 3km at one stage. Brass plaques at **Naldham House Polo Club** on Eagle Street mark the depths of the worst floods. Today, however, some of Brisbane's poshest real estate flanks the river, with waterfront mansions at Yeerongpilly, Graceville and Chelmer, southwest of the centre. They're all banking on protection from the Lake Wivenhoe dam, completed in 1984.

The **riverbanks** are great to explore on foot, with stunning, ever-changing views: the circuit from Brisbane Square, across Victoria Bridge to South Bank, under the Kangaroo Point cliffs, across the Story Bridge (access to which is from the south end of Main Street at Kangaroo Point, and from the riverside path on the north bank), along Riverside, through the Botanic Gardens and back to Brisbane Square makes a very pleasant walk of two or three hours. You can shorten the loop by using Goodwill Bridge, and in due course there will be another new pedestrian bridge from Tank Street to GoMA.

Another enjoyable way to explore the city-centre reaches of the river is simply to ride up and down on the **CityCat** (see p.443); this is so popular that the boats can get very crowded during holidays. You can also take ninety-minute **sightseeing cruises** from the South Bank Cruise Terminal, South Bank Parklands with River City Cruises (A\$25, child A\$15; bookings required; ☏0428 278 473, Ⓦ www.rivercitycruises.com.au); lunch, tea or dinner cruises aboard the *Kookaburra River Queens* (from A\$30; ☏07 3221 1300, Ⓦ www.kookaburrariverqueens.com); or book a **gondola tour** followed by dinner for an evening with a dash of Venetian-style romance (Golden Gondolas; ☏0419 400 944, Ⓦ www.gondola.com.au; A\$330 for two). The more actively inclined can **canoe** the river with Riverlife, based under the Kangaroo Point Cliffs (☏07 3891 5766, Ⓦ www.riverlife.com.au; A\$29 for 1hr 30min).

among the most pleasant parts of the city. Intended as a giant play zone for residents and visitors alike, they parklands are wonderfully varied: you can promenade under shady fig trees along the riverfront; meditate at an intricately carved **Nepalese pagoda**, built for the Expo; picnic under rainforest plants and bamboo on lawns lining the banks of shallow, stone-lined man-made streams (which are convincing enough to attract large, sunbathing water dragons and birds); relax at the **artificial beach** and accompanying saltwater pool; or browse the stalls of the weekend **craft market** (see p.454). Among the other attractions are the exhibits at the **Maritime Museum** (daily 9.30am–4.30pm; A$7, child A$3.50; ☏07 3844 5361, ⓦwww.maritimemuseum.com.au), including a ninety-year-old Torres Strait pearling lugger and a World War II frigate, *Diamantina*, on show in the dry dock.

The parklands are a favourite venue for **public celebrations**, such as New Year and Australia Day firework displays. Open-air film screenings are held on the Rainforest Green during November and December (ⓦwww .brisbaneopenair.com.au). **Bands** play most Saturday nights, either on the outdoor stage or at the *Plough Inn*, a restored, century-old pub on the cobbled high street. There are also several **cafés and restaurants** open all day, every day.

You can reach South Bank Parklands on Citytrain to **South Bank Station**; by ferry or CityCat; or by taking the pedestrian Goodwill Bridge from the Botanic Gardens to the Maritime Museum.

Southwest of the centre

A few worthwhile sights lie southwest of the city centre, some of which – such as Lone Pine Sanctuary – you can reach **by boat** along the Brisbane River, though all are also accessible by other forms of public transport.

The Castlemaine-Perkins Brewery and XXXX Ale House

Just west from Petrie Terrace on Milton Road (take the Citytrain to Milton and it's just across the street), the **Castlemaine Perkins Brewery** (☏07 3361 7597, ⓦwww.xxxx.com.au) has been making Queensland's own beer since 1878. Their famous yellow-and-red **XXXX** emblem is part of the Queensland landscape – it's splashed across T-shirts, the roofs of Outback hotels, and the labels of countless discarded bottles and cans. For enthusiasts, the brewery's **XXXX Ale House** visitor centre on Paten Street runs tours (Mon–Fri 10am–4pm on the hour, Sat 10.30am, 11am & noon; A$20, child or non-beer-drinker A$12; visitors must wear shoes, not sandals) providing a one-hour overview of the brewery's history and processes followed by a tasting of four different beers.

Drinks for women: the Regatta Hotel

Though Australian **pubs** still tend towards being all-male enclaves, women were once legally barred to "protect" them from the corrupting influence of foul language. On April 1, 1965, Merle Thornton (mother of the actress Sigrid Thornton) and her friend Rosalie Bogner chained themselves to the footrail of Brisbane's **Regatta Hotel** bar in protest; the movement they inspired led to the granting of "the right to drink alongside men" in the mid-1970s. The grand, ornate-balconied colonial hotel, now a trendy place for a riverside drink after work on Fridays, is about 2km west of the city centre on Coronation Drive in Toowong, right by the Regatta CityCat ferry stop.

Queensland is the only Australian state in which you're **allowed to hold a koala**, albeit briefly: it's the classic animal-encounter photo opportunity, heavily promoted at just about every wildlife park on the Queensland coast. The practice is strictly regulated, with koala keepers required to run a rota to ensure that no animal suffers stress through over-handling (or being kept up past its bed-time). Among the best places to find out how it feels to hug a koala are Lone Pine Koala Sanctuary near Brisbane (see below), Australia Zoo on the Sunshine Coast (see p.464), Billabong Sanctuary near Townsville (see p.544), Bungalow Bay Koala Sanctuary on Magnetic Island (see p.553) and The Rainforest Habitat in Port Douglas (see p.601). In other Australian states, the closest you can get to one of these furry fellows is to pat one under the supervision of a handler, and feel its coat – surprisingly coarse, but unmistakably eucalyptus-scented.

Mount Coot-tha

The lower slopes of **Mount Coot-tha**, about 7km west of the city centre (bus 471 from Adelaide Street runs hourly 9.15am–3.15pm), are the setting for Brisbane's second **botanic gardens** (daily: April–Aug 8am–5pm; Sept–March 8am–5.30pm; free). Sunday picnickers are a common sight in this leafy haven, where careful landscaping and the use of enclosures have created a variety of climates – dry pine and eucalypt groves, a cool subtropical rainforest complete with waterfalls and streams, and the elegant Japanese Gardens with bonsai and fern houses. The steamy **tropical plant dome** contains a pond stocked with lotus lilies and fish, overhung by lush greenery dripping with moisture. Informative **free guided walks** depart from the information kiosk at 11am and 1pm daily.

The other dome in the gardens does duty as a **planetarium** (Tues–Fri 10.30am–4.30pm, Sat 11am–8.15pm, Sun 11am–4.15pm; A$12.10, child A$7.10). While the foyer display is dated, the audio-visual show, which you view lying back under the dome's ceiling, gives a unique perspective of the key features of Brisbane's night sky. There's also an observatory, for which you need to book (☎07 3403 2578; A$13, child A$8).

After visiting the botanic gardens most people head up the road to Mount Coot-tha's **summit** for panoramas of the city and, on a good day, the Moreton Bay Islands. Walking tracks from here make for moderate hikes of an hour or two through dry gum woodland, and include several **Aboriginal trails** – the best of these branches off the Slaughter Falls track with informative signs pointing out plants and their uses.

Lone Pine Koala Sanctuary

Lone Pine Koala Sanctuary, on Jesmond Road in Fig Tree Pocket, 11km from the city centre (daily 8.30am–5pm; A$22, child A$17; ☎07 3378 1366, Ⓦwww.koala.net), has been a popular upstream destination since it first opened its gates in 1927. Here you can see native Australian fauna in their natural state – which, in the case of the sanctuary's 130 or so koalas, involves being asleep all day but for a few hours in the late afternoon, unless they're on koala-hug photo duty. In nearby enclosures you'll find other slumbering animals, including wombats, Tasmanian devils, fruit bats, blue-tongued lizards and dingoes; there's also a paddock where tolerant wallabies and kangaroos are fed by visitors.

You can get to Lone Pine by **bus** 445 from Ann Street or bus 430 from George Street, but the most enjoyable way is to take an eighty-minute **river trip** from the Cultural Centre pontoon in front of the Queensland State Library, past Brisbane's waterfront suburbs, with Mirimar Cruises (daily 10am, returning at 1.30pm; A$48, child A$27, including entry to Lone Pine; boat only A$46 return, child A$20; ☎0412 749 426 or 1300 729 742, ⊛www.mirimar.com). The CityCat and other public ferries do not go as far upstream as Lone Pine.

Shopping

Brisbane's primary shopping street, **Queen Street Mall**, is the place to go for department stores and branches of mainstream chains including electrical and clothing shops.

For something original, head for the buzzing districts of **Fortitude Valley** and **New Farm**. TCB on Duncan Street, near Brunswick Street Mall, is the retail headquarters for many local fashion designers including Chelsea de Luca, George Wu and Gail Sorronda, while nearby you'll find small, urban boutiques selling clubwear and a couple of eminently practical shops specializing in camping and hiking gear. On James and Ann streets, former transport depots have been reborn as "style zones", stuffed with chic clothing outlets, food and wine shops: Emporium on Ann Street has a row of great boutiques and other tempting shops, while James Street has one-offs such as Artes de Mexico.

On the other side of town, the suburbs of **Paddington** and **Rosalie** are good for characterful, bohemian fashion and homeware shops selling bric-a-brac, vintage jewellery and designer originals. The city's main **discount outlet** centre is DFO, out of town, on Airport Drive, just off the Gateway Motorway.

The city centre has several weekend **markets** for contemporary crafts, jewellery, leatherwork and oddments – too trendy for bargains, but good for gifts – at the South Bank Parklands (Fri 5–10pm, Sat 11am–5pm, Sun 9am–5pm), Brunswick Street Mall (Sat & Sun 8am–4pm), Riverside and Eagle Street (Sun 8am–4pm) and King George Square (Sun 10am–4pm).

For **provisions**, there's a supermarket in Queen's Plaza at the northeast end of Queen Street Mall, and fabulously fresh produce, including sushi and artisan-style cheese, at Fresh on Melbourne Street in South Brisbane and the James Street Market in The Valley.

Most city-centre shops are open seven days a week, with extended hours on Fridays. For details of bookshops and pharmacies, see p.462.

Eating, drinking and nightlife

Brisbane has no gastronomic tradition to exploit, but in recent years its foodie credentials have improved at a prodigious rate, in step with its growing affluence. As in Melbourne and Sydney, the driving trend has been towards clean-lined, contemporary design and modern Australian or "**Mod Oz**" cuisine involving creative use of local produce with an Asian or Mediterranean twist. However, the city also retains plenty of down-to-earth haunts – the slightly tatty but much-loved neighbourhood cafés and Chinese, Vietnamese, Turkish and Italian restaurants that have been around for ages – ensuring genuine variety.

Restaurants, **cafés** and **bars** are scattered all over the city, with a fine selection of true gastro-havens along the riverbanks, a dense grouping of Asian restaurants in Fortitude Valley's Chinatown, pockets of urban cool in The Valley's club zone, fashionable café and cocktail society in the Emporium and James

Street areas and a more bohemian, multi-ethnic flavour along South Brisbane's Boundary Street. All the main shopping centres have **food courts**, busy with shoppers and workers, while traditional Aussie **hotels** in the inner-city suburbs offer cheap and filling counter meals – washed down with the local brew, Castlemaine XXXX, of course.

Restaurants

City district, Petrie Terrace and Paddington

Alchemy 175 Eagle St ☎07 3229 3175. Run by a chef who has worked with Jamie Oliver and Marco Pierre White, this riverside theatre of gastronomy has a menu so experimental that the results are hit and miss, but this doesn't deter Brisbane's affluent set, who crowd the place out. The best dishes are the simpler ones, such as sashimi with sorbet. Lunch and dinner Mon–Fri, dinner only Sat.

Cha Cha Char Eagle St Pier ☎07 3211 9944. With an owner who is well connected to the beef industry, this blokey riverside place is heaven for carnivores: A$40 will buy you one of the best steaks you'll ever eat, and you'll find excellent wines to match. Mon–Fri 11.30am–late, Sat & Sun 5.30am–late.

China City 76 Queen St Mall ☎07 3211 1999. Relatively expensive but probably the most authentic Cantonese food in Brisbane; especially good for its seafood and *yum cha* (dim sum).

🏃 **E'cco** 100 Boundary St ☎07 3831 8344. With an impressive awards list and their own cookbooks, this established temple to Mod Oz excellence is not cheap (all main courses cost A$37.50), but you're guaranteed gorgeous ingredients, simply but expertly prepared. Lunch and dinner Mon–Fri, dinner only Sat.

Govinda's Vegetarian Restaurant First floor, 99 Elizabeth St. This Hare Krishna-run canteen is one of the city's best bargains – you can fill up on delicately spicy fare for A$10. Mon–Thurs 11am–3pm & 4.30–7pm, Fri 11am–8.30pm, Sat 11am–2.30pm.

🏃 **Montrachet** 224 Given Terrace, Paddington ☎07 3367 0030. Run by a chef from Lyon, this painstaking recreation of a classic French city restaurant delivers sumptuous cuisine and is madly popular. Lunch and dinner Mon–Fri.

Riddler's 124 Leichhardt St ☎07 3831 8399. Cavernous, budget Italian restaurant with huge pizzas and small but filling pasta favourites. Daily, dinner only.

Siana Riparian Plaza, 71 Eagle St ☎07 3221 3887. This Asian-fusion restaurant is owned by an interior designer, and it shows. Elegant dining and a superbly stocked bar that takes the art of cocktail creation to new heights. Lunch and dinner Mon–Fri, Sat 4pm–late.

Verve 109 Edward St ☎07 3221 5691. In the basement of the Metro Arts building, this modern Italian with funky music and art serves enticing pasta and risottos for under A$20. Closed Sun.

Fortitude Valley and New Farm

Asian House 165 Wickham St ☎07 3852 1291. Good, filling, reasonably priced Chinese, such as roast pork or greens in oyster sauce. Lunch and dinner daily.

Bar Alto Brisbane Powerhouse, Lamington St ☎07 3358 1063. Riverside bar-restaurant at Brisbane's funkiest arts centre, serving top-class Italian food at surprisingly moderate prices. Tues–Sun 11am–late.

Capri The Emporium, 1000 Ann St ☎07 3257 0401. Great little restaurant in a precinct bursting with excellent options. This one has a simple formula: it concentrates on top-quality pizza and pasta at down-to-earth prices.

Freestyle Tout The Emporium, 1000 Ann St ☎07 3876 2288. With pasta and salads on the menu, there's nothing to stop you having a full meal here, but many people drop in simply to gorge on the scene-stealing signature desserts – an affordable treat at under A$15.

Isis 466 Brunswick St ☎07 3852 1155. Smart, popular, long-running brasserie with a calm atmosphere, a French-influenced menu and above-average prices. Lunch and dinner Tues–Sat, dinner only Sun.

James Street Bistro 39 James St ☎07 3852 5155. One of a fine collection of places in the James St area, serving stylish food such as grilled halloumi salad, braised lamb-shank pie or roast pumpkin pizza to a discerning local crowd. Daily from 7am for breakfast and lunch, and for dinner Thurs–Sun.

King of Kings 169 Wickham St ☎07 3012 8898. Huge, tacky Chinese, popular thanks to its fine *yum cha* (dim sum) selections. Lunch and dinner daily.

🏃 **Tibetan Kitchen** 454 Brunswick St ☎07 3358 5906. This attractive place offers a cheap, tasty menu of "traditional Tibetan, Sherpa,

Nepalese foods" including The Valley's best samosas and curries. Daily 5.30–9.30pm.

The Vietnamese 194 Wickham St ☏07 3252 4112. Genuine Vietnamese food in a plain and unassuming setting. The steamboat is excellent, as are the spring rolls; two can eat well for A\$30. Lunch, dinner and take-aways daily.

Watt Brisbane Powerhouse, Lamington St ☏07 3358 5464. Delicious juxtapositions abound at this excellent theatre eatery – white tablecloths against a gritty urban setting; zippy wasabi, pistachio and lemon alongside delicately flavoured meat and seafood flavours. Well worth a visit whether you're seeing a show or not. Tues–Fri 10am–late, Sat & Sun 8am–late.

West End, South Bank and Kangaroo Point

Deery's 200 Main St, Kangaroo Point 07 3391 2266. Just the way a pub restaurant should be, with good, honest food such as steak or fish and chips, fine wine and excellent service. Lunch and dinner daily.

Era Bistro & Café 102 Melbourne St, South Bank ☏07 3255 2033. Two fine venues in one sleek, contemporary package: a café for quick, fresh breakfasts (from 7am) and lunches including super-fresh salads, and a bistro for stylish, leisurely daytime or evening meals. Both are open daily.

New Asia 153 Boundary St, West End ☏07 3846 3569. The best Vietnamese restaurant in the West End, this offers prawns grilled on sugar cane, deep-fried quail, rice-noodle dishes – most for less than A\$10 a dish. Daily for lunch, dinner and takeaways.

Tempo 181 Boundary St, West End ☏07 3846 3161. An old favourite for great Italian-style home cooking, with fresh salads and fine seafood pasta at low prices. Even humble sandwiches come with a salad big enough to be a meal in itself. Tues–Sun 9am–late.

Timmy's Galleria, 240 Grey St, South Bank ☏07 3846 0322. With wonderful views over the Parklands lily pools, this is a fresh, cheerful spot serving modern, moderately priced Thai fare, including excellent duck. Tues–Fri 11am–late, Sat 8am–late, Sun 8am–3pm.

Tukka 145 Boundary St, West End ☏07 3846 6333. Run by a creative chef who applies French-style cooking techniques to native Australian fruits, seeds, herbs and meats with genuinely original results. Most main courses are under A\$30. Daily from 6pm.

Cafés and bars

City district, Paddington and Spring Hill

Anouk 212 Given Terrace, Paddington ☏07 3367 8663. Neighbourhood café with a trendy, dressed-down style and many loyal fans; great for delicious breakfasts and light lunches. Daily 7am–5pm.

The Brewhouse 142 Albert St ☏07 3003 0098. Microbrewery producing British-style ale, bitter and stout, plus a sports bar and grill with live bands or DJs at weekends. Daily 11.30am–1am.

Café Brussels Corner of Mary & Edward sts ☏07 3221 0199. European-style bar with century-old wooden panelling and a lengthy menu of chilled beers imported from Belgium. Daily 11am–late.

Casablanca 52 Petrie Terrace ☏07 3369 6969. Inexpensive brasserie and café with a multi-ethnic tapas menu and beer list; an equally eclectic music selection, from hip-hop to reggae to salsa, gets the youthful crowd moving. Closed Mon.

Down Under Bar *Palace Backpackers*, corner of Ann & Edward sts. Hugely popular drinking hole for travellers behaving badly. Mon–Fri noon–late, Sat & Sun 5pm–late.

The Irish Club 171 Elizabeth St ☏07 3221 5699. Not a theme-bar clone but the genuine deal, with regular Irish band nights, and cheap pub lunches and dinners. Mon–Sat 10am–midnight.

Sportsman Hotel 130 Leichhardt St ☏07 3831 2892, ⊛www.sportsmanhotel.com.au. Gay, lesbian and straight crowds fill the two floors of this gay-owned (and operated) pub, which has pool tables, bands and a bistro, and features karaoke, drag nights and dance shows. Daily 10am–late.

Fortitude Valley and New Farm

BarSoma 22 Constance St ☏07 3252 9550. Supercool but unintimidating, with gritty vintage decor, good tapas, and a nice line in Latin and soul, this is a bar for grown-ups. Thurs–Sat 6pm–late.

Boulangerie et Patisserie Belle Epoque The Emporium, 1000 Ann St ☏07 3852 1500. A rarity in Brisbane, this serves French-style sandwiches stuffed with goats' cheese or salami, plus tarts and coffee.

The Bowery 676 Ann St ☏07 3252 0202. Superb cocktails mixed by masters in a cool city bar with a deliberately inconspicuous entrance, designed to make you feel as if you're sneaking into a Prohibition-era speakeasy. Tues–Sun 5pm–3am.

Cirque 618 Brunswick St ☏07 3254 0479. Packed all morning with breakfasters enjoying good coffee and imaginative offerings such as French toast with mascarpone and pears. Daily 7am–3pm.

Cosmopolitan Coffee 322 Brunswick St Mall. This no-frills favourite opens early for breakfast and serves good coffee and basic Italian-style fare all day.

Cru Bar 22 James St ☎07 3252 2400. Chic open-sided wine, champagne and oyster bar, much loved by the darlings of the James St neighbourhood's new sophisticated set. Mon–Fri 11.30am–1am, Sat & Sun 8.30am–1am.

Depot The Emporium, 1000 Ann St ☎07 3666 0188. This roofed-over outdoor café oozes casual style and is popular with local power-breakfasters, bar-lunchers, wine-lovers and anyone in search of an afternoon coffee fix. Mon–Sat 7am–late, Sun 7am–5pm.

West End and Kangaroo Point

The Gun Shop Café 53 Mollison St, West End ☎07 3844 2241. West Enders happily queue to have breakfast at this shabby-chic little place, which also does excellent lunches such as warm duck salad, smoked trout with asparagus or seafood-stuffed zucchini flowers. Daily 7am–10pm.

The Lychee Lounge 92 Boundary St, West End ☎07 3846 0544. Brilliant cocktail bar, famous for its chilli-infused cocktails and edgy, arty decor; it gets clubby late in the evening, with occasional DJ sets. Daily 3pm–2am.

Story Bridge Hotel Main St, Kangaroo Point ☎07 3391 2266. Historic Brisbane hotel so loved by local drinkers that when building the Story Bridge they bent the highway around it, rather than send in the demolition men; it's still popular today. Closes midnight Mon–Thurs & Sun, 1.30am Fri & Sat.

The Three Monkeys 58 Mollison St, West End ☎07 3845 6044. Bohemian coffee shop decorated with a funky assortment of African oddments; the food here is forgettable but the drinks are delicious. Daily 9.30am–late.

Uber 100 Boundary St, West End ☎07 3846 6680, ⓦwww.uber.net.au. Stylish late-night cocktail lounge with local DJs spinning the tunes. Wed–Sun 4pm–late.

Fortitude Valley music venues and clubs

Brisbane's **Fortitude Valley** is one of the best places in Australia to catch live music, with an explosion of home-grown talent including bands and artists such as Savage Garden, Powderfinger, Regurgitator, George, Custard, Keith Urban, Pete Murray and The Veronicas, and an impressive variety of **venues**. Some of The Valley music bars double as nightclubs with DJs swapping places with the bands; there's also a crowd of dedicated dance venues.

The scene is very fluid, with places tending to open and close in the blink of an eye. Those listed below should be here to stay, but check with **music stores** such as Rocking Horse, just off Queen Street Mall in Albert Street, or weekly **free magazines** for up-to-the-minute reviews and listings – *Rave* for general music news, *Time Off* for live bands and *Scene* for dance. Entrance fees generally hover around the A\$5–15 mark: some nights are free, but big names command hefty cover charges. Many venues stay open until 5am or even later but, as elsewhere in the state, there's a 3am lockout, after which nobody is allowed to enter, even if they've been inside previously.

Some of The Valley's streets can be somewhat sleazy after dark, with an element of drug-related petty crime – if you've any distance to go on your own, take a taxi.

Alhambra Lounge 12 McLachlan St ☎07 3126 0226, ⓦwww.alhambralounge.com. Richly decorated in the style of a Moorish palace, this is Brisbane's most sophisticated club and function venue, featuring R&B, soul, hip-hop and Latin nights. Thurs–Sun 9pm–5am.

The Arena 210 Brunswick St ☎07 3252 5690. Large, long-established venue hosting popular DJs and dance parties as well as local and international touring bands.

The Beat 677 Ann St ☎07 3852 2661, ⓦwww .thebeatmegaclub.com.au. Studiously relaxed gay/ straight techno and dance venue. Upstairs is the *Cockatoo Club*, a screamingly gay venue with loud commercial dance music and drag shows. Daily 9pm–5am.

Family 8 McLachlan St ☎07 3852 5000, ⓦwww .thefamily.com.au. Big-name resident and visiting DJs spin groovy soul, house and disco on the thumpingly good sound systems at this heavyweight venue with two giant dance floors. Fri–Sun 9pm–5am.

Fringe Bar Ann St, corner of Constance St ☎07 3252 9833, ⓦwww.fringebar.net. With a refreshingly unintimidating open frontage, this after-work drinking spot turns into a funky dance club and live-music venue later on. Wed–Sat.

Globe Theatre 220 Brunswick St ☎07 3844 4751, ⓦwww.globetheatre.com.au. Unique venue mixing live-music sessions and club nights with cult-film screenings.

GPO 740 Ann St ☎07 3252 1322, ⓦwww .gpohotel.com.au. Trend-setting dance-bar and function venue on two floors inside a beautiful old post-office building – shaping up to rival *The Press Club* for fashion-conscious clientele. Thurs–Sun.

The Met 256 Wickham St ☎07 3527 2557, ⓦwww.themet.com.au. Full-on dance venue with stunning lighting, featuring star DJs from Brisbane and beyond; Boy George is among the luminaries who have appeared here.

Monastery 621 Ann St ☎07 3527 7081, ⓦwww .monastery.com.au. Local DJ venue attracting a relaxed, young party crowd, with occasional live-music slots.

The Press Club 339 Brunswick St ☎07 3852 4000, ⓦwww.pressclub.net.au. Dressed-up cocktail bar playing relaxed and funky Latin/swing dance beats. Rather a "fabulous" crowd, out to see

and be seen, with drinks prices to match. Daily from 7pm.

Ric's Bar 321 Brunswick St ☎07 3854 1772, ⓦwww.ricsbar.com.au. Narrow, crowded place that draws a hard-edged crowd – getting to the bar takes some effort. Nightly mix of live Aussie bands and DJ-driven techno; hefty fry-ups and pizzas at *Fatboys'* pavement tables outside.

The Tivoli 52 Costin St ☎07 3852 1711, ⓦwww.thetivoli.net.au. Originally an Art Deco theatre, now one of Brisbane's best and most popular live venues for big-name bands and acoustic artists.

The Troubadour 322 Brunswick St ☎07 3552 2626. A place to make musical discoveries, with nightly live sessions, usually acoustic or offbeat rock, and a relatively quiet, low-key atmosphere.

The Wickham 308 Wickham St, corner of Alden St ☎07 3852 1301, ⓦwww.thewickham.com.au. Classic Queenslander-style hotel, home to the state's most popular gay and lesbian pub. Drag show on Thursdays, Sunday afternoon sessions from 2pm, and DJs every night.

The Zoo 711 Ann St ☎07 3854 1382, ⓦwww .thezoo.com.au. One of the best and longest-established clubs in The Valley, offering a hectic night out featuring local indie rock, folk, electronic and jazz bands. Wed–Sat 8pm–late, plus some Sundays.

Gay and lesbian Brisbane

Brisbane's gays and lesbians revel in a loud and energetic scene, which gets better every year. In June, the annual Brisbane **Pride Festival** (ⓦwww.pridebrisbane.org.au) is held, a diverse three-week event with a rally, fair, art exhibitions, a film festival, sports events, and general exhibitionism at a huge dance party – the Queen's Birthday Ball. The **Sleaze Ball** (ⓦwww.sleazeball.com.au) in November, an all-day party at the RNA Showgrounds, is another opportunity to indulge in hedonism of all kinds.

The **LGBT scene** is largely clustered around the suburbs of Spring Hill, Fortitude Valley, New Valley, New Farm and Paddington. For up-to-the-moment information, listen to the weekly Queer Radio show on Station 4ZZZ 102.1FM (Wed 8.30–10pm) or pick up a copy of the fortnightly *Qnews* (ⓦwww.qnews.com.au) or *Queensland Pride* (ⓦwww.qlp.e-p.net.au) from gay nightclubs, street distributors and some coffee shops.

For **gay-friendly accommodation**, there are apartments at the *Central Brunswick* and rooms at the *Sportsman Hotel* (see p.445); nightlife focuses on *The Wickham*, the *Sportsman Hotel* and the *Cockatoo Club* above *The Beat* (see p.457). Bent Books, 205A Boundary St, on the corner of Vulture St in the West End, is the longest-established **gay bookshop** in Brisbane (Mon–Fri 9am–6pm, Sat & Sun 9am–5pm); gay and lesbian **healthcare advice** is available at the Brunswick Street Medical Centre, 665 Brunswick St, New Farm (Mon–Sat 8am–4pm; ☎07 3358 1977).

Theatres, cinemas and performance venues

The city's vibrant **cultural scene** received a real boost with the recent refurbishment of the Brisbane Powerhouse and the opening of a new art-house cinema, the Dendy. All of the city's cultural venues have restaurants or café-bars, with exceptionally good ones at the Powerhouse. From time to time, stadium-style events are held outdoors at RiverStage in the Botanic Gardens, or indoors at the massive Brisbane Exhibition and Convention Centre, South Bank (℡07 3308 3000).

Billie Brown Studio 78 Montague Rd, South Brisbane ℡07 3010 7600, ⓦwww.qldtheatreco .com.au. Home to the Queensland Theatre Company, which stages work by established and emerging Australian playwrights, plus international classics.

Birch Carroll & Coyle Myer Centre, 167 Queen St Mall ℡07 3027 9999, ⓦwww.greaterunion. au. Mainstream multiscreen cinema, slap bang in the city centre.

Brisbane Jazz Club 1 Annie St (near Holman St ferry), Kangaroo Point ℡07 3391 2006, ⓦwww .brisbanejazzclub.com.au. Long-established riverside music venue with just the kind of laidback, respectful vibe you'd expect. Live sessions are open to non-members for an entry fee of A$15. Evenings, Thurs–Sun.

Brisbane Powerhouse 119 Lamington St, New Farm ℡07 3358 8622 (enquiries) or 07 3358 8600 (box office), ⓦwww.brisbanepowerhouse.org. Cutting-edge alternative performing-arts space hosting theatre productions from all over the world, with free foyer performances of music (from 3.30pm) and comedy (from 6.30pm) on Sundays. Outdoor screenings of current and classic films are held in the park outside the venue throughout the summer (ⓦwww.moonlight.com.au).

Conservatorium 16 Russell St, South Bank ℡13 62 46 (bookings), ⓦwww.griffith.edu.au. Part of the Griffith University campus, this is one of the city's best venues for opera and classical music, with an acoustically excellent theatre and a smaller recital hall.

Dendy 346 George St ℡07 3211 3244 and Portside Wharf, Remora Rd, Hamilton (5min from the Brett's Wharf ferry) ℡07 3137 6000, ⓦwww .dendy.com.au. Upmarket cinemas showing international art-house releases, with discounted entrance on Mondays. The George St cinema dates back to the 1940s; the Portside venue is brand new.

Judith Wright Centre of Contemporary Arts 420 Brunswick St ℡07 3872 9018, ⓦwww .jwcoca.qld.gov.au. Interesting performance venue featuring an edgy selection of contemporary dance, physical theatre and world music.

Queensland Performing Arts Centre (QPAC) Melbourne St, South Bank ℡07 3840 7444 or 13 62 46 (bookings), ⓦwww.qpac.com.au. Dignified complex in modern premises including the Lyric, Playhouse and Cremorne theatres, the large Concert Hall, and exhibition spaces. Performances by Queensland Opera, the Ballet Theatre of Queensland and the Queensland Orchestra and Youth Orchestra are held here; it also hosts visiting companies and orchestras from Australia and overseas, plus mainstream musicals.

Sit Down Comedy Club Paddo Tavern, 186 Given Terrace, Paddington ℡07 3369 4466. Stand-up comedy shows at 8pm most days of the week.

Southbank Cinemas 167 Grey St, South Bank ℡07 3846 5188, ⓦwww.cineplex.com.au. Mainstream cinema complex, including Brisbane's largest screen.

Listings

Airlines Air New Zealand ℡13 24 76, airport ℡07 3860 4405; Air Niugini ℡07 3229 5844, airport ℡07 3860 4161; Air Pacific ℡1800 230 150, airport ℡07 3860 4203; Air Vanuatu ℡1300 780 737, airport ℡07 3114 1240; British Airways ℡1300 767 177; Cathay Pacific ℡13 17 47, airport ℡07 3860 4455; Emirates ℡1300 303 777, airport 07 3860 6777; Etihad ℡07 3229 +8000; Freedom Air ℡1800 122 000; Japan

Airlines ℡1300 525 287; Jetstar ℡13 15 38; Korean Air ℡07 3226 6000, airport ℡07 3860 5222; MacAir ℡1800 622 247; Malaysia Airlines ℡13 26 27, airport ℡07 3860 4615; Pacific Blue, ℡13 65 45; Qantas ℡13 13 13; Rex ℡07 13 17 13; Royal Brunei ℡07 3017 5000, airport ℡07 3860 5177; Singapore Airlines ℡13 10 11, airport ℡07 3860 4196; Thai Airways ℡1300 651 960, airport ℡07 3860 4163; Virgin Blue ℡13 67 89.

Aboriginal culture

The **Riverlife Adventure Centre** on the riverbank under the Kangaroo Point cliffs (☎07 3891 5766, ⓦwww.riverlife.com.au), hosts weekly Dreamtime story-telling, music and dance sessions with descendants of the Yuggera tribe (Thurs noon–1pm; A$39, child A$25), while the **Australian Indigenous Tribal Gallery** (376 George St ☎07 3236 1700, ⓦwww.indigenousgallery.com.au) stages art shows and workshops.

Abseiling and rock climbing

Few cities in the world have a natural rock wall within a few minutes' walk of the centre; Brisbane is one of them. You can sort out all the equipment and instruction you may need to tackle the Kangaroo Point cliffs, which are floodlit after dark, with **Torre Outdoor Adventure** (☎07 3870 0643, ⓦwww.torremountaincraft.com.au) or **Riverlife** (see above).

City tours

TransLink's hop-on-hop-off **City Sights** tourist bus is a great way to get around (every 45min; 9am–5pm daily; all-day ticket A$25, child A$20; route maps available from the Queen Street Mall Visitor Information Centre or at ⓦwww.citysights.com.au). With running commentary from the driver, it covers a nineteen-stop route including the Central Business District, Roma Street Parkland, Suncorp Stadium, Mount Coot-tha Lookout, *Regatta Hotel*, Southbank, Story Bridge and Chinatown, taking around ninety minutes for a complete loop. You can hail the blue buses at any of their specially marked stops and buy tickets on board; same-day travel on the CityCat is thrown in as a bonus. Alternatively, **Gray Line Tours** (Transit Centre, Roma St; ☎07 3489 6401 or 1300 360 776, ⓦwww.graylinetours.com.au) offer day-trips that whisk you around the sights including Mount Coot-tha and Lone Pine (A$98, child A$62).

Cycling

Brisbane has masses of cycleways, following the riverbanks and crisscrossing the city. **Valet Cycle Hire**, operating from a van inside the Botanic Gardens off Alice Street (A$15/hr, A$35/day, discounts for longer; ☎0408 003 198, ⓦwww.cyclebrisbane.com), can deliver bikes direct to your accommodation. You can also hire bikes (and rollerblades) from Riverlife (see above).

Hinterland and coast day-trips and tours

Australian Day Tours (Transit Centre, Roma St; ☎07 3489 6444, ⓦwww.australiandaytours.com.au) have a dozen or so day-trips to the Sunshine Coast, Gold Coast theme parks, Lamington National Park, Tamborine Mountain and south to Byron Bay in NSW, mostly costing around A$80–90 (child A$45–55). **Green Triangle Experiences** (35 Fern St, Woolloongabba; ☎0402 623 736 or 1800 503 475, ⓦwww.greentriangle.com.au) offer small-group guided tours from Brisbane to Tamborine Mountain and Lamington National Park, the Gold Coast Hinterland or the Gold Coast beaches, or down to Byron Bay and Nimbin in NSW, catering for a young crowd. For details of out-of-town companies that will pick you up from Brisbane on request, see box, p.408.

Great Barrier Reef

Lady Elliot Island is a seventy-minute flight away from the Redcliffe airstrip in north Brisbane with Seair, by special arrangement with *Lady Elliot Island Resort* (see p.498); you can drop in for the day or stay overnight. Proserpine and Hamilton Island airports, for the Whitsundays, and Cairns, for the northern stretches of the Reef, can also be reached by direct flight from Brisbane.

Hot-air ballooning

Balloons Over Brisbane (West End; ☎07 3844 6671, ⓦwww.balloonsoverbrisbane.com.au) and **Fly Me To The Moon** (☎07 3423 0400, ⓦwww.flymetothemoon.com.au) offer the rare treat of ballooning over the city at dawn, while **Floating Images**, based 40km out of town near Ipswich (☎07 3294 8770, ⌨www.floatingimages .com.au), will take you drifting over the Greater Brisbane countryside. Prices start at A$255, with pick-ups from central Brisbane on request.

River activities and cruises
See box, p.451.

Scenic flights
To charter a bespoke aerial sightseeing trip by helicopter, talk to **Solitair Helicopters** in Archerfield, south of Brisbane (☎07 3275 3798, ⌨www.solitairhelicopters.com.au); they can suggest itineraries and arrange pick-ups from the airport or the city.

Sporting fixtures
Queensland's sport is **rugby league**, and the stomping ground of the local side – the Brisbane Broncos (⌨www.broncos.com.au) – is the **Suncorp Stadium** on Castle-maine St, Milton, five minutes' walk west of the City (⌨www.suncorpstadium.com .au); the event of the year is the State of Origin series in May or June. Soccer and international test cricket feature here as well. Local **cricket** team the QLD Bulls (⌨www.bulls.com.au) play at **The Gabba** on Vulture Street, Woolloongabba, south of Kangaroo Point (⌨www.thegabba.org.au), which in winter hosts **Aussie rules football** matches featuring the Brisbane Lions (⌨www.lions.com.au). The Queens-land Reds **rugby union** team (⌨www.qru.com.au/reds) play at the Suncorp or at their home ground, **Ballymore Stadium**, Clyde Road, Herston. Match tickets cost A$25–85 from Ticketek (☎13 28 49, ⌨www.ticketek.com.au) or Ticketmaster (☎1300 136 122, ⌨www.ticketmaster.com.au).

Story Bridge Adventure Climb
Though billed as an adventure, anybody of average fitness can tackle the walk to the top of **Story Bridge**, Brisbane's landmark cantilevered road bridge (from A$110, child A$82.50; ☎1300 254 627, ⌨www.sbac.net.au). If you have a slight fear of heights, all worries should be dispelled by the lengthy and rigorous pre-climb briefing at "base camp", 170 Main Street, Kangaroo Point, and the fact that you're firmly clipped to a safety line throughout. At 74m above the river, the summit is similar to the height of a 22-storey building, with splendid views, but the climb is a fairly gentle ascent up shallow steps of iron mesh. It's small fry compared to the Sydney Harbour BridgeClimb (see p.235), and rather overpriced, but worth it for rarity value: the only other comparable experience in the world is the tour of the Auckland Harbour Bridge, New Zealand.

Wildlife parks
Brisbane's best-loved animal attraction is **Lone Pine Koala Sanctuary** (see p.453); also worth a trip is **Alma Park Zoo** at Dakabin (daily 9am–5pm; A$28, child A$19; ☎07 3204 6566, ⌨www.almaparkzoo.com.au), which is home to kangaroos, koalas and cassowaries, plus a few non-native inmates including monkeys and baboons. The park is signposted off the Bruce Highway (A1), 28km north of town; the nearest railway station is Caboolture.

Winery tours
There are a couple of dozen relatively undiscovered wineries within an hour so of Brisbane, some of which – such as **Canungra Valley Vineyards** near Lamington National Park, and **Sirromet Wines**, Mount Cotton – have produced international award-winners. Canungra Valley (☎07 5543 4011, ⌨www.oreillys.com.au/cvv) is open to day-visitors, while Australian Day Tours (see p.460) run twice-weekly trips to Sirromet (A$55). Winery-tour specialists **Cork 'n' Fork** (☎07 5543 6584, ⌨www .corknfork.com.au) and **Winery Escape Tours** (☎0416 838 694, ⌨www .wineryescapetours.com.au) run tasting trips to Sirromet and **Tamborine Mountain**'s boutique wineries and distillery.

Banks Queensland banking hours are Mon–Fri 9.30am–4pm; major branches in the centre are around Queen & Edward sts.

Books Borders, 162 Albert St, for a broad selection; Coaldrakes, The Emporium, 1000 Ann St, for chunky photographic volumes; Avid Reader Book Store, 193 Boundary St, West End, for a neighbourhood shop run by booklovers; Bent Books, 205A Boundary St, West End, for gay and lesbian-interest titles; Queensland State Library, (see p.450), for reference.

Brisbane Festival Seventeen days of arts events, held biennially (even years) in July. ⓦwww .brisbanefestival.com.au.

Car rental You'll pay from around A$40 for a single-day's compact-car rental; longer terms cost from A$30 a day. All the major internationals are represented in Brisbane; alternatives include Abel (ⓣ13 14 29, ⓦwww.abel.com.au); East Coast (ⓣ1800 028 881, ⓦwww.eastcoastcarrentals .com.au); and Ezy (ⓣ1300 661 938, ⓦwww .ezycarhire.com.au). For campervans, try Travellers Auto Barn (ⓣ1800/674 374, ⓦwww.travellers -autobarn.com.au) and Wicked (ⓣ1800 246 869, ⓦwww.wickedcampers.com.au); special offers may bring the price down to A$30 per day.

Consulates Britain, 1 Eagle St ⓣ07 3223 3200; China, 79 Adeleide St ⓣ07 3219 6509; Japan, 12 Creek St ⓣ07 3221 5188; Malaysia, 239 George St ⓣ07 3210 2833; Papua New Guinea, 320 Adelaide St ⓣ07 3221 7915; The Philippines, 126 Wickham St, Fortitude Valley ⓣ07 3252 8215; South Africa, Level 38, Central Paza 1, 345 Queen St, ⓣ07 3258 6666; Thailand, 87 Annerley Rd ⓣ07 3846 7771.

Emergencies Fire, police and ambulance ⓣ000.

Hospitals and medical centres The main public hospital is the Royal Brisbane, Herston (ⓣ07 3636 8111; buses 126, 144 or 172 from outside City Hall); Travellers' Medical Service, Level 1, 245 Albert St (ⓣ07 3211 3611, ⓦwww.travellers medicalservice.com), for general services, vaccinations and women's health.

Internet Most hostels have terminals where you can log on from around A$4 an hour; other lodgings may charge over A$10 per hour. For free access via terminals or Wi-Fi, go to the Queensland State Library, South Bank Cultural Centre (see p.450).

Left luggage None at the airport, but available at the Transit Centre on Roma St for A$6 per day per locker.

Pharmacies Transit Centre Pharmacy (daily 7am–6pm); Day & Night Pharmacy, 141 Queen St Mall (Mon–Sat 8am–9pm, Sun 10am–5pm).

Police Queensland Police Headquarters is opposite the Transit Centre on Roma St (ⓣ07 3364 6464).

Post office 261 Queen St (Mon–Fri 7am–6pm; ⓣ13 13 18 for poste restante.

Swimming pools The open-air Olympic-size Valley Pool on Wickham St is heated in winter (Mon–Fri 5.30am–7pm, Sat 6am–6pm, Sun 7.30am–5pm; hours may be extended in summer; A$3.90, child A$2.70). The South Bank Parklands swimming lagoon and beach are open daily (free). Brisbane's hotel pools tend to be small.

Taxis Black and White ⓣ13 10 08; Yellow Cabs ⓣ13 19 24.

Travel agents Backpackers World Travel, 131 Elizabeth St ⓣ07 3211 8900; Flight Centre, 327 George St ⓣ07 3005 1444; STA, 59 Adelaide St ⓣ07 3229 2499; Student Flights, 126 Adelaide St ⓣ07 3229 8449; Trailfinders, 101 Adelaide St ⓣ07 3229 0887.

Work Many hostels run effective ad-hoc agencies for their guests; for out-of-town farm work, try Brisbane's WWOOF office at Banana Benders (see p.444).

The Sunshine Coast

The **Sunshine Coast**, stretching north of Brisbane to Noosa, is a mild-mannered counterpart to the Gold Coast to the south. While the region's larger towns are clogged with dull developments and noisy highways and are as bland as Surfers Paradise is racy, the smaller resorts and country towns are pleasantly quiet, with a few genuinely interesting and elegant spots. For the Australian families who flock to the region for beach holidays, and the retirees who settle here to enjoy its mild climate, the relaxed, low-key atmosphere is a major attraction.

The coastal towns of **Caloundra**, **Mooloolaba** and **Maroochydore** are unlikely to rock your world, but they have good beaches and surf, and easy access to some very worthwhile inland attractions – **Australia Zoo**, the striking scenery of the **Glasshouse Mountains**, and the pretty hill country of the **Sunshine Coast Hinterland**, scattered with hamlets peddling cream teas and crafts. There's also an unbeatable diving destination offshore, the **HMAS Brisbane**, deliberately wrecked off the coast near Mooloolaba. Further north, **Coolum** has one of the region's most beautiful stretches of sand, while **Noosa** is easily southeast Queensland's most refined beach resort, a gem of a place nestled among creeks and lakes at the mouth of the River Noosa.

Getting there and around

The nearest arrival point for international flights is Brisbane; the regional airport, **Sunshine Coast Airport** (MCY; ⊛www.maroochy.qld.gov.au /sunshinecoastairport) at Mudjimba, 3.5km north of Maroochydore, handles domestic flights from Sydney, Melbourne and Adelaide with Jetstar and Virgin Blue. A public **bus** (Sunbus route 622, operated by TransLink) runs from the airport to Maroochydore and Mooloolaba (A$2.70, child A$1.40 one way), or Coolum (A$3.60/A$1.80), with connections to Noosa (A$4.60/A$2.30). Alternatively, local **airport-shuttle** company Henry's will get you to Coolum or Noosa ($10–20, child A$5–10 one way; ☎07 5474 0199, ⊛www.henrys.com .au), while Sun-Air cover Maroochydore, Mooloolaba and Caloundra (A$9–33, child A$8 one way; ☎07 5477 0888, ⊛www.sunair.com.au); taxis cost considerably more. Sun-Air can also drive you to the Sunshine Coast from Brisbane Airport (from A$29 to transit centres, or from A$45 to your accommodation). You're required to book shuttles in advance.

Brisbane's **Citytrain** network (☎13 12 30, ⊛www.translink.com.au) can take you into the region; the line is convenient for the hinterland, with stops at Caboolture, the Glass House Mountains, Woombye, Nambour and Eumundi. The national **long-distance bus** companies run to all the major towns in the region, though not to the hinterland villages. For details of rail, bus and self-drive routes to Australia Zoo, see p.465.

As elsewhere in Queensland, hiring a vehicle allows you maximum freedom to explore. The Sunbus network covers much of the region, but some buses only run a couple of times a day; useful routes in addition to the bus from the airport include Noosa and Noosaville to Eumundi, and Maroochydore and Mooloolaba to Australia Zoo. If you'd prefer to take **guided bus tours**, companies to try include Noosa Hinterland Tours in Coolum (☎07 5446 3111, ⊛www.noosahinterlandtours.com); Storeyline Tours in Tewantin (☎07 5474 1500, ⊛www.storeylinetours.com.au) and Sun-Air at Kunda Park (see above); the destinations on offer include Australia Zoo, the Glass House Mountains, the hinterland villages and Eumundi markets. See also p.408 and p.460.

Woodford and the Glass House Mountains

The southernmost town in the Sunshine Coast region is the otherwise unremarkable **Caboolture**, 48km north of Brisbane and 84km south of Noosa. Around 20km northwest of here, around an hour's drive from Brisbane, is the two-street town of **WOODFORD**, which draws thousands of revellers each year for its six-day late-December folk festival (☎07 5496 1066, ⊛www .woodfordfolkfestival.com) culminating in spectacular New Year's Eve and New

Year's Day celebrations. The festival, Queensland's low-profile answer to Glastonbury (complete, more often than not, with mud) always has a great line-up of music, cabaret and comedy.

North of Caboolture, a relatively new road, route 24 (Steve Irwin Way/Glass House Mountains Tourist Drive), turns off the Bruce Highway towards **Glass House Mountains National Park**: nine dramatic, isolated pinnacles jutting out of a flat plain, visible from as far away as Brisbane. To the Kabi Aborigines, the mountains are the petrified forms of a family fleeing the incoming tide, though their current name was bestowed by Captain Cook because of their "shape and elevation" – a resemblance that's obscure today. The peaks themselves vary enormously: some are rounded and fairly easy to scale, while a couple have vertical faces and sharp spires requiring competent climbing skills. It's worth conquering at least one of the easier peaks, as the views are superb: **Beerburrum**, overlooking the township of the same name, and **Ngungun**, near the Glass House Mountains township, are two of the easiest to tackle, with well-used tracks that shouldn't take more than two hours return; the latter's views and scenery outclass some of the tougher peaks, though the lower parts of the track are steep and slippery. **Tibberoowuccum**, a small peak at 220m just outside the national-park boundary, must be climbed from the northwest, with access from the car park off Marsh's Road. The taller mountains – **Tibrogargan** and **Beerwah** (the highest at 556m) – are at best tricky, requiring specialist skills, while **Coonowrin** is completely off-limits due to the possibility of rock falls.

For maps of the region and local climbing conditions, ask the experienced volunteers at the **visitor information van** in Matthew Flinders Park, 2km north of Beerburrum town and about 20km north of Caboolture (a new information centre is planned). The most convenient **accommodation** in the area is at *Glasshouse Mountains Holiday Village* on route 24, south of Glass House Mountains township and 25km north of Caboolture, at the foot of Mount Tibrogargan (T07 5496 9338, Wwww.glasshousemountainsholidayvillage.com.au; camping A$22–24, cabins ③). There's also a QPWS campsite at Coochin Creek off Roys Road, east of the Bruce Highway (see p.54 for booking information).

Australia Zoo

Australia Zoo (daily 9am–4.30pm; A$49, child A$29 for admission and shows; optional extras include guided tours from A$15, animal encounters and photo sessions A$20–55; T07 5436 2000 or 1300 274 539, Wwww.australiazoo.com .au), just north of Beerwah, became famous through the efforts of its late director, "Crocodile Hunter" **Steve Irwin** (see box, p.466). The staff continue Irwin's tradition of exuberant exhibitionism, and it remains one of the largest and most enjoyable commercial zoos in Australia.

Irwin's guiding principles were that close-up, interactive encounters with animals and birds engender respect for the planet's wildlife – and that by allowing healthy animals to demonstrate what they're naturally good at, you can put on a highly entertaining and educational show. The zoo's gung-ho **Crocoseum** spectaculars are a highlight of any visit – you can expect parrots flying across the arena at speed, star appearances from fearsome-looking reptiles, and a strident but chirpily presented conservation message.

The **animal collection**, which includes cheetahs, tigers and elephants as well as native species, is extremely well kept, in visitor-friendly surroundings. Just as Irwin's exuberance rubbed off on his staff, you won't find many shy, retiring individuals

▲ Crocodile at Australia Zoo

among the Australia Zoo inmates. More or less all are treated as pets, so instead of glimpsing wombats snoozing in shady hideaways as they would in the wild, you'll see them promenading through the park on leads; and instead of bored crocodiles lurking immobile in pens, you'll see outrageously fit-looking specimens leaping for chunks of meat dangled by their handlers as bait. There are hands-on photo opportunities aplenty: apart from the usual camera-confident koalas, you can get friendly with echidnas, dingoes, possums and giant pythons. It's a credit to the genuinely caring zoo staff that all survive with their dignity intact.

Adjacent to the zoo is the **Australian Wildlife Hospital**, founded by Irwin and his wife Terri in 2004; it cares for around 5000 injured reptiles, birds and marsupials a year and has already grown to cope with demand. A daily tour takes you behind the scenes; the cost (A\$30, child A\$20) helps fund its programme of rescue and rehabilitation work.

A free **Australia Zoo bus** picks visitors up from Noosa, Coolum, Maroochydore, Mooloolaba and Caloundra each morning; contact the zoo to book. You can also get there by **public transport**. From Maroochydore and Mooloolaba, Sunbus route 615 departs for the zoo twice each morning (45–55min; A\$4.60, child A\$2.30 one way). From Brisbane or the Gold Coast, take the Citytrain to Caboolture, then the Citytrain Caboolture–Nambour Railbus to the zoo; this takes around ninety minutes from central Brisbane (A\$8.40, child A\$4.20 one way) or up to three hours from Nerang,

Steve Irwin

The sudden death in 2006 of khaki-clad naturalist **Steve Irwin** – stabbed in the heart by the barb of a two-metre bull ray while swimming near Batt Reef on a filming trip in Far North Queensland – shocked Australia. It seemed deeply ironic that somebody so vital, whose trademark was a respectful but fearless rapport with dangerous animals, should have been the victim of a freak attack from a non-aggressive species. Stingray wounds are rare enough; death by stingray is almost unknown.

The accident plunged the nation into mourning; even those who considered Irwin something of a buffoon for his over-the-top action-man antics stopped to reassess. Tributes to his outstanding contribution to education and conservation flooded the media, and the space under Australia Zoo's Crocoseum became a memorial site, hung with row upon row of khaki shirts signed by distraught fans.

Irwin grew up among animals: in 1970, when he was eight years old, his parents – a herpetologist and a wildlife vet – founded the reptile park that later became Australia Zoo. Young Stevo quickly developed a knack for managing reptiles – every crocodile in the zoo was either captured by him and his father in northern Queensland, or bred on site. In 1991, Irwin took over directorship of the zoo, and his parallel career as a television presenter took flight a year later with the making of the first *Crocodile Hunter* documentary. He later became a vocal spokesman for Australia's anti-poaching movement, and was instrumental in setting up a conservation organization, **Wildlife Warriors Worldwide** (Ⓦ www.wildlifewarriors.org.au), whose projects include the Australian Wildlife Hospital and an international crocodile rescue and research programme.

In his lifetime, Irwin's image and personality were integral to the Australia Zoo brand. Since his departure, his American wife Terri and precocious daughter Bindi have begun to up their profile as figureheads for the operation, but in the meantime you'll still see Stevo everywhere on site – in photographs, signage, namechecks and videos played on a continuous loop. One such clip preserves a perfect example of the man at his irrepressible best: immediately after dodging a terrifying lunge from a pair of komodo dragons, Irwin, breathless, turns to camera. "Crikey, that was too close!" he says, and then, without missing a beat, "Let's follow them!"

depending on connections (A\$9.40/A\$4.70). A slightly faster but less frequent alternative is to take the Citytrain to Beerwah (same fares as above), from where it's a five-minute drive to the zoo; free Australia Zoo buses meet most incoming trains, or can be ordered by calling Ⓣ07 5436 2000.

Australia Zoo Travel (Ⓣ07 5436 2000, Ⓦ www.australiazootravel.com) run **bus tours** from Brisbane, the Gold Coast or the Sunshine Coast, with commentary about the Irwins and the zoo en route; for other tour companies offering zoo itineraries, see p.408, p.460 and p.463. If you're **driving**, access is on route 24 (Steve Irwin Way/Glass House Mountains Tourist Drive); this runs roughly parallel to the Bruce Highway. Approaching from the south, leave the highway at the Beerburrum/Glass House Mountains exit; the zoo is 18km north of here, about 3km beyond Beerwah. From Brisbane, the drive takes around an hour. From points north, take the Landsborough/Glass House Mountains exit, from where it's approximately 11km.

Caloundra

On the coast 20km east of Landsborough – there's a local bus from Landsborough railway station – **CALOUNDRA** (pronounced "cal-ow-ndra") has managed to resist the worst of the over-development that blight its neighbours to the north, Mooloolaba and Maroochydore. While the town has its share of towering apartment blocks, central, tree-lined **Bulcock Street** has only low-rise buildings and a small seaside-town atmosphere. A craft and gift market is held here on Sunday mornings. The **bus terminal** on Cooma Terrace, one street south of Bulcock, has a tourist information desk; Caloundra also has two **visitor information centres**, at 7 Caloundra Rd, on the edge of town as you drive in from the Sunshine Motorway, and at 77 Bulcock St, in the centre (Mon–Fri 8.30am–5pm; ☎07 5420 8718 or 1800 644 969 ⓦwww.caloundratourism.com.au).

The most central of Caloundra's very pleasant **beaches** is Bulcock Beach, immediately south of Bulcock Street. Perpetually breezy, it's popular with windsurfers and kitesurfers; you can hire or buy gear and book lessons with local specialists Caloundra Wind and Surf (☎0419 670 913, ⓦwww.caloundrawindandsurf.com.au) or Kitethrills (☎07 5492 6108, ⓦwww.kitethrills.com). Kings Beach, to the east of the centre and separated from Bulcock Beach by Deep Water Point, is considered the first true surfing beach north of Brisbane; it's crammed on windy weekends. Shelley Beach and Moffat Beach, further north, are much quieter.

Caloundra is situated at the head of a network of saltwater channels and inlets including **Pelican Waters**, a creekmouth real-estate hotspot 4km south of town, and **Pumicestone Passage Marine Park**, the stretch of water between **Bribie Island** and the mainland. Caloundra Cruises (☎07 5492 8260, ⓦwww.caloundracruise.com) offer a weekly cruise that takes you close enough to Bribie Island to spot shorebirds, Brahminy kites and, with luck, dugongs (departs Thurs 9.45am from Pelican Waters jetty; A$35, child A$20 for 2hr 30min).

For **accommodation**, *Caloundra City Backpackers*, 84 Omrah Ave (☎07 5499 7655, ⓦwww.caloundracitybackpackers.com.au; bed in shared room A$25, private double/twin ❷), is a real find – clean, well run, and just two minutes from Bulcock Beach. Equally handy for the town centre and beach are the reasonably priced self-catering apartments at *Belaire Place*, 38 Minchinton St (☎07 5491 8688, ⓦwww.belaireplace.com; ❹–❺); they're simple but bright, and there's the option of paying extra for a top-floor sea view. Central Caloundra has a decent scattering of resort-style **restaurants** and a great handmade ice cream shop, *Gelateria Milano* at 82 Bulcock St.

Mooloolaba

North of Caloundra, the Sunshine Coast's holiday mood gets into full swing in **MOOLOOLABA**, 98km from Brisbane; this is the first town served by the Sunshine Motorway, which branches off the Bruce Highway near Buderim and heads up towards Noosa, 43km further north. Mooloolaba is a mess of high-rise accommodation blocks, boutiques and flashy, forgettable dining experiences; for holidaying Australian families, the beaches – long, sandy and excellent for surfing – are the main draw. The town's sole inland attraction is **UnderWater World** on Parkyn Parade (daily 9am–5pm; A$26.50, child A$15; extras include behind-the-scenes tours for A$10/A$8; ☎07 5444 8488, ⓦwww.underwaterworld.com.au), a large aquarium complex with a fascinating, beautifully lit collection of cold-water species such as seadragons and cow fish, a bizarre crew of primordial looking billabong-dwellers and, as an amusing gimmick, a fish tank made out of a car. In pride of place is a 2.5-million-litre

Diving the wreck of the HMAS Brisbane

Deliberately sunk in 2005 to create a new marine conservation park and diving destination, the former **HMAS Brisbane**, a 133-metre-long Royal Australian Navy destroyer that served in both the Vietnam and Gulf wars, lies in 28m of open water 7.5km northeast of Mooloolaba. It's already well on the way to becoming a good place to spot reef-dwelling flora and fauna; the first coral colonies, starfish, molluscs and fish were quick to move in. For now, however, what makes it remarkable is the fact that you, too, can get right inside the hull; by contrast, you can only admire the famous *SS Yongala*, wrecked near Ayr (see p.531), from the outside: the interior is a grave site and out of bounds.

The *Brisbane* was carefully scuttled with divers in mind: entrances and light wells were cut in the hull and decks and internal passageways were cleared, preserving as much as possible of the original layout. A well-versed dive guide should be able to identify each section, from the engine and boiler rooms to the sleeping quarters and laundry, as you swim through. Since some of the passageways are tight and gloomy, and the currents and surges can be strong, this is a challenging site and not recommended for novice wreck divers. Visibility tends to be best in the winter months.

Dive operators

Scubaworld, a highly efficient diving and training outfit located on the Parkyn Parade wharf close to UnderWater World in Mooloolaba (☏07 5444 8595, ⓦwww .scubaworld.com.au) will, after a thorough briefing, take certified divers out in their RIB to dive the *Brisbane* (A$184 for two dives including gear). Other operators running trips to the wreck include **Sunreef**, 110 Brisbane Rd, Mooloolaba (☏07 5444 5656, ⓦwww.sunreef.com.au).

basement oceanarium with a viewing tunnel running through it, offering superb views of nonchalant nurse sharks, reef sharks, turtles and rays. If you'd like to jump in with them, you can book a Shark Dive through nearby Scubaworld (daily except Tues; certified divers A$165, non-divers A$195 for 30min, including admission and gear; ☏07 5444 8595, ⓦwww.scubaworld .com.au), who also run **wreck-diving trips** to the remains of the *HMAS Brisbane*, which lies offshore, twenty minutes away by inflatable launch (see box above).

Buses set down on Smith Street, a short way back from the shops and restaurants lining the hundred-metre-long seafront Esplanade; the **visitor information centre** is on the corner of First Avenue and Brisbane Road (daily 9am–5pm; ☏07 5478 2233, ⓦwww.maroochytourism.com). The Esplanade has plenty of modern high-rise **holiday apartment buildings**, all charging A$250–300 for a two-bedroom, self-contained unit, with rising discounts the longer you stay. One of the smartest is *Sirocco* (☏07 5444 1400, ⓦwww .mantrasirocco.com.au; ⑥), with rooms decked out in white marble and Italian leather, and great ocean views. Alternatively, *Sandcastles*, on the corner of Esplanade and Parkyn Parade, next to the Surf Club (☏07 5478 0666, ⓦwww .sandcastlesonthebeach.com.au; ⑤) offers a choice of older one-bed apartments, some with ocean views and a few with private roof terraces. For **budget accommodation**, *Mooloolaba Beach Backpackers* at 75 Brisbane Rd (☏07 5444 3399, ⓦwww.mooloolababackpackers.com; bunk in quad-share A$26–29, en-suite double ②) is a bright, clean and upbeat option with a pool; the price includes breakfast, barbecue nights and loan of bikes, kayaks and boogie-boards. **Eating** places are everywhere, though the best deals and sea views are at *Mooloolaba Surf Club's* smart café, bar and restaurant on The Esplanade (daily

Maroochydore

Mooloolaba's immediate neighbour is **MAROOCHYDORE**; their centres are only 3km apart – you can walk from one to the other along an ocean path – and their fringes merge seamlessly. If you approach Maroochydore from the Sunshine Coast Motorway, which skirts the town, or via the multi-lane highway, which tears right through it, first impressions will suggest it's not an immediately attractive place. However, regeneration programmes have lent a gentle buzz to the spacious and pleasant waterside districts at the mouth of the Maroochy River, where you'll find a good scattering of cafés, delis, wine bars and restaurants. Away from the centre, pelicans perch on the lamp posts, the beaches and suburban streets are quiet, and the surf – as usual – is great.

Buses set down outside a shopping mall on First Avenue, close to The Esplanade; there's a **visitor information centre** on Sixth Avenue, at the corner of Melrose Parade (daily 9am–5pm; ⊕07 5479 1566, ⓌWww.maroochytourism.com) and fast **Internet** at Email Central, 19 The Esplanade (daily 9am–8pm). The best **accommodation** and **eating** options are concentrated along and around the waterfront on Duporth Avenue, The Esplanade and Cotton Tree Parade.

Accommodation

Cotton Tree Backpackers 15 The Esplanade ⊕07 5443 1755, ⓌWww.cottontreebackpackers.com. The best budget option: a bright, airy old beach house offering free use of bikes, surfboards and kayaks. Bunk in shared room A$23, private double ❷

Cotton Tree Caravan Park Cotton Tree Parade ⊕07 5443 1253 or 1800 461 253, ⓌWww.maroochypark.qld.gov.au. Tent and van site in a great beachfront location, close to the public swimming pool. Camping A$25–32, cabin ❹

Heritage Motor Inn 69 Sixth Ave ⊕07 5443 7355. A classic motel set-up, with plain rooms arranged around courtyard parking, this is a decent, inexpensive option. ❹

Space 45 The Esplanade ⊕07 5430 0000, ⓌWww.spaceholidayapartments.com. Excellent-value, attractively furnished luxury apartments sleeping two or up to four, in a modern block facing the waterfront park. ❺–❻

Waves 36–38 Duporth Ave ⊕07 5479 4600, ⓌWww.thewaves.net. Smart, comfortable apartment block with good sea views; not as stylish as *Space*, but with a better pool. ❺

Eating and drinking

The Deli Co 14 Duporth Ave ⊕07 5479 2558. Maroochydore's best deli, serving tasty gourmet treats. Mon–Fri 8am–4pm, Sat 8am–3pm.

Envy 31 Cotton Tree Parade ⊕07 5443 8494. Down-to-earth café, good for healthy and creative salads, veggie lunches and hand-blended juices. Daily 6.30am–6pm, plus a set menu on Friday evenings from 6pm.

Govinda's 7 First Ave ⊕07 5451 0299. Simple café that's a thorough bargain for its aromatic South Asian cooking, served canteen-style. Mon–Thurs 11.30am–2.30pm, Fri 11.30am–2.30pm & 5–8pm, Sun 5–8pm.

Habits 45 The Esplanade ⊕07 5452 7722. Contemporary tapas bar with a multi-ethnic menu that includes Coffin bay oysters, sushi and pizza. Tues–Sun 11.30am–late.

Hunt 6 Duporth Ave ⊕07 5479 5188. The most appealing of a new crop of sleek contemporary eateries, popular with well-heeled lunchers for its daily specials; regular main courses hover around A$30. Lunch and dinner Tues–Sat.

Mio Spazio 45 The Esplanade ⊕07 5451 1243. Excellent European-style café, serving gourmet sandwiches and good coffee, at the foot of the *Space* building. Mon–Fri 8.30am–5pm, Sat 9am–2pm.

The Sunshine Coast Hinterland

Inland from Maroochydore, a turning off the Bruce Highway takes you past Woombye's renowned **Big Pineapple** – as ridiculous as any of the East Coast's Big Things, and only notable for being the second oldest after the Big Banana at Coffs Harbour – to the functional sugar-farming town of Nambour, 102km north of Brisbane and 69km south of Gympie. From here, a ninety-kilometre (2hr) circuit drive takes you through the **Sunshine Coast Hinterland**, a rural idyll of rolling hillsides and fields of dairy cattle, with occasional far-reaching views over green valleys out to the coast. This is attractive walking country, ringing with kookaburra calls; a pleasant way to explore is to follow the **Sunshine Coast Hinterland Great Walk** along the Blackall Range (see box, p.424). The **visitor information centres** for the area (ⓦwww .maroochytourism.com) are at 198 Main St, Montville (daily 10am–4pm; ⓣ07 5478 5544) and 787 Landsborough–Maleny Rd, Maleny (daily 9am–5pm; ⓣ07 5499 9788 or 1800 644 169), and there's a **QPWS office** at 61 Bunya St, Maleny (ⓣ07 5494 3983).

The painstakingly prettified village of **Montville** suffers from an overdose of craft shops and twee tearooms, but there are some genuinely lovely places to stay in the surrounding countryside; one of the best is the charming 🔱 *Spotted Chook*, 176 Western Ave, Montville (ⓣ07 5442 9242, ⓦwww.spottedchook .com; ⑥), a rural B&B designed and run by Francophiles, with rooms decorated in beautiful shabby-chic style. Not quite as romantic, but wonderfully located 4km north of Montville on the edge of Kondalilla National Park, is *Tree Houses of Montville* (ⓣ07 5445 7650 or 1800 444 350, ⓦwww.treehouses.com.au; ⑤), which has pole cabins built among rainforest. To stretch your legs, it's worth taking the rainforest track from the car park near the lodge to **Kondalilla Falls**, where Skene Creek plunges 90m; the 4.6-kilometre circuit takes under two hours. You can see another respectably sized waterfall, **Mapleton Falls**, from the lookout a quick stroll away from the entrance to Mapleton Falls National Park, just west of the sleepy village of **Mapleton**, north of Montville.

As a break from scones and cream, there are a few good **restaurants**, **pubs** and contemporary **cafés** in and around Montville. *The Edge* in the Mayfield Centre (ⓣ07 5442 9344; breakfast & lunch daily) has fabulous valley views, quality Asian-Australian cooking and a good wine list; *The Penefathings Inn*, 96 Main St, makes a cheerful attempt at recreating an English country pub, with live jazz and blues on Sunday evenings; there's authentic French cuisine, a moderate set menu and a warm welcome at *Relais Bressan* on Flaxton Drive in the hamlet of Flaxton, between Montville and Mapleton (ⓣ07 5445 7157; lunch & dinner Mon & Thurs–Sun); while *Sister* at 18–20 Margaret St in Palmwoods, 8km east of Montville (ⓣ07 5445 0655; Mon–Sat 7.30am–4pm plus a set dinner from 6pm Fri) is a cool café run by a chef who has worked with Jamie Oliver and is passionate about flavoursome organic food.

Maleny, the largest village in the region, has a more workaday atmosphere, tempered by its community of ageing hippies; the *Upfront Club* at 31 Maple St (Mon 7.30am–10pm, Tues,Wed & Sun 7.30am–3pm, Thurs–Sat 7.30am–late) has good food with a healthy inclination and live folk, roots and soul on Friday and Saturday evenings. About 5km south out of town, **Mary Cairncross Park** (summer 9am–5pm; winter 10am–4pm; donation) is a small patch of rainforest inhabited by snakes, wallabies and plenty of birds; there's a fantastic view south over the Glass House Mountains from the entrance. There are several **accommodation** options outside Maleny on the road to Montville, including the simple but friendly *Maleny Hills Motel*

(☎07 5494 2551, ⓦwww.malenyhills.com.au; ❹) and *Lyndon Lodge B&B*
(☎07 5494 3307, ⓦwww.lyndonlodge.com.au; ❹), with superb views and
very helpful owners.

Just off the Bruce Highway around 20km north of Nambour, on the way to
Noosa, is **EUMUNDI**, a tiny country town known for its enormous **markets**
selling handmade clothing, jewellery, crafts and produce (Wed 8am–1pm, Sat
6.30am–2pm). An appealing place to **stay overnight** here is *Hidden Valley B&B
and Cookery School*, 39 Caplick Way (☎07 5442 8685, ⓦwww.eumundibed
.com; ❼), an old Queenslander home with great decor and gourmet food; in
the huge garden, there's a pool and a 1940s railway carriage, beautifully
converted into a guest room sleeping up to four. For a light lunch, there are
food stalls in the market and a few cafés and delis in town, typically with a
wholefood/veggie leaning; *Modern Primitive* in the Old Bakery on the main
street (☎07 5442 7946; Wed–Sun) is good for eclectic tapas and pizza.

Coolum

The stretch of coast between the Maroochy and Noosa Rivers is dotted with
small, low-key holiday resorts; all are within easy reach of the Bruce Highway
and Sunshine Coast Airport, making them popular with Australian families.
COOLUM, 90km north of Brisbane and 15km south of Noosa, is the largest
of these, a growing destination that nonetheless remains peaceful and
uncrowded. The gorgeous swimming and surfing beach is Coolum's main
attraction; it's ablaze with colour during the two-day Coolum **kite festival**
in October (ⓦwww.coolumkitefestival.com), which features kitesurfing as
well as kite flying. The *Hyatt Regency Coolum*, Warran Road (☎07 5446 1234,
ⓦwww.coolum.regency.hyatt.com; ❽), Coolum's large luxury resort, is on
the south side of town; there are also plenty of family-friendly holiday apartments to rent, which you can book through the **visitor information
centre** at Tickle Park just off the seafront road (David Low Way) near the
southern end of the beach (daily 9am–5pm; ☎07 5459 9050, ⓦwww
.maroochytourism.com).

Noosa

Spread elegantly along the creeks and inlets at the mouth of the placid **Noosa
River**, **NOOSA** – the low-rise, exclusive end of the Sunshine Coast – is an
established celebrity hangout, and a haven for gourmets, surfers, boating types
and conservationists; the latter recently succeeded in their bid to have Noosa
Shire and its coastal waters listed as a UNESCO **biosphere reserve**.

Sheltered by an enviably beautiful forested headland and wafted with the
scent of frangipani and expensive sunscreen, the town has the feel of an
affluent Mediterranean resort. It's fringed by beaches on two sides, the best
of which are long, lovely **Sunshine Beach** to the east, and, just off the main
shopping strip, **Main Beach** on **Laguna Bay** which, though compact, is one
of the most appealing north-facing urban beaches in Queensland. Much of
the headland is national park, with well-kept walking tracks from which
you'll almost certainly see wild **koalas**, while out of town to the north there
are a couple of shallow **lakes** – **Cooroibah** and **Cootharaba** – with good
paddling potential.

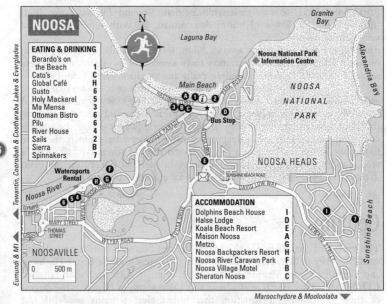

Maroochydore & Mooloolaba ▼

Information and accommodation

The **long-distance bus stop** is at the junction of Noosa Parade and Noosa Drive. More useful than the commercially driven information desks scattered all over Noosa is the official **visitor information centre** by the roundabout on Hastings Street (daily 9am–5pm; ☎07 5447 4988 or 1300 066 672, ⓦwww.visitnoosa.com.au).

Noosa has an abundance of quality mid-range and top-end **accommodation**, plus a handful of good hostels and van parks, but the town is so popular that there can be a shortage of rooms during school holidays, despite steep price hikes, so it's wise to pre-book.

Dolphins Beach House 14 Duke St, Sunshine Beach ☎1800 454 456, ⓦwww.dolphinsbeach house.com. Colourful self-contained units with a distinctly mellow, New Age feel and surfboards to rent, about 5min walk from the sea. ❸

Halse Lodge 17 Noosa Drive, Noosa Heads ☎1800 242 567 or 07 5447 3377, ⓦwww .halselodge.com.au. Giant, sprawling, immaculate 1888 Queensland building in large grounds close to Noosa Beach; a place for relaxing rather than partying. Often full, so book in advance. Bunk in shared room A$29–35, double/twin ❷

Koala Beach Resort 44 Noosa Drive, Noosa Heads ☎07 5447 3355 or 1800 357 457, ⓦwww .koalaresort.com.au. Central budget accommodation in dorms and motel units. Nowhere near the beach, but the party atmosphere and live music might compensate. Bunk in shared room A$27, double ❷

Maison Noosa 5 Hastings St, Noosa Heads ☎07 5447 4400, ⓦwww.maisonnoosa.com.au. Superbly sleek and luxurious new apartments in an unbeatable location right on the beach. ❻

Metzo 152–158 Noosa Parade, Noosaville ☎07 5440 7500, ⓦwww.metzonoosa.com.au. Modern apartments with two or three bedrooms, on the main road into Noosa Heads, a short hop from Gympie Terrace; all are spacious and very well decorated, and there's a small pool. ❼

Noosa Backpackers Resort 9–13 William St, Noosaville ☎07 5449 8151 or 1800 626 673, ⓦwww.noosabackpackers.com. With basic rooms and dorms – which, though small, are bright – this is an upbeat spot, right behind the fab *Global Café* (see p.475). Close to the river, with free use of kayaks, boogie-boards and surfboards. Bunk in shared room A$28, double ❷

Noosa River Caravan Park Russell St, Noosaville
☎07 5449 7050. Large site for tents, caravans and
camper vans, with splendid river views. Camping
A$24–31.

Noosa Village Motel 10 Hastings St, Noosa Heads
☎07 5447 5800, ⓦwww.noosavillage.com.au.
Unpretentious, tidy motel that's an extraordinarily
good deal given its location on Noosa's most glitzy,

upmarket street. Rooms are not huge, though some
have balconies. ❺

Sheraton Noosa 14–16 Hastings St, Noosa
Heads ☎07 5449 4888, ⓦwww.sheraton
.com/noosa. Classy hotel with a large pool, a
basement spa and top-notch catering (see below).
The best rooms have wonderful views over the river;
all have beds you'll want to sleep in forever. ❼

The Town

The name Noosa is applied to a seven-kilometre-long stretch of merging settlements on the south side of the Noosa River – **Tewantin**, **Noosaville** and
Noosa Heads – plus the Pacific coast suburbs of **Sunshine Beach** and neighbouring **Sunrise Beach**. All are connected by the regular and efficient Sunbus
bus network; there are several departures an hour between 5am and 8pm,
followed by a more limited evening service. Noosa Heads is the hub, with a chic
and brash European-style shopping-and-dining enclave along beachside
Hastings Street, while there's a far more down-to-earth area of shops, banks
and cafés with a cinema, 1km inland along **Sunshine Beach Road**.

From Hastings Street, it's an easy walk east along the coastal boardwalks that skirt
around the headland – or a short drive – into **Noosa National Park**. The
pathways, which start from the information and picnic area at the end of Park
Road, a continuation of Hastings Street, take you through an attractive mix of
mature rainforest, eucalypt woodlands (home to a healthy population of koalas),
coastal heath and fine **beaches**. On the far side of the headland, east-facing,
"swimwear optional" Alexandria Bay has good sand pounded by unpatrolled surf.

Noosaville, west of Noosa Heads, is a mainly residential district, though more
and more restaurants are popping up along **Gympie Terrace** on the riverfront.
In the late afternoon, half of Noosa promenades along this pleasant strip as the
sinking sun colours a gentle tableau: mangroves on the opposite shore, pelicans
eyeing anglers for scraps and landing clumsily midstream, and everything from
cruise boats to windsurfers, kayaks and jet-skis out on the water.

Shopping

After eating out, surfing and cruising, **shopping** is a favourite pastime in Noosa.
Pedestrian-friendly Hastings Street is lined with a glut of tempting swimwear
boutiques, jewellery shops and homeware stores: top names include *Witchery*,
Signature and *Pearls for Girls*. Also in Noosa Heads, *Honey Ant Gallery* on 11
Stevens St (Thurs–Sat 10am–4pm; ☎07 5455 4334, ⓦwww.honeyantgallery
.com) is a good place to browse Outback Aboriginal art. For organic produce,
head to *Organika* at 205 Weyba Rd; for fresh bread, you can't do better than *La
Miche Patisserie*, 11 Sunshine Beach Rd.

Eating

Noosa's **nightlife** is pretty restrained: **eating out** is the main pastime. Hastings
Street has long been the place to wine and dine, but soaring rents have seen
some excellent eateries relocate to Gympie Terrace in Noosaville.

Berardo's on the Beach Hastings St ☎07 5448
0888. The casual, relatively inexpensive offshoot of
Berardo's, one of Noosa's most celebrated (and
priciest) restaurants, this is the best spot in town

for breakfast or lunch on the beach. Daily from
7.30am.

Cato's *Sheraton Noosa*, 14–16 Hastings St ☎07
5449 4888. The *Sheraton*'s amazing breakfast

Most of Noosa's diversions involve messing around on the water; the staff at your accommodation can help with bookings and itineraries. For details of tour companies running day-trips to **Australia Zoo** and the **Sunshine Coast Hinterland**, see p.463 and 466; for **Fraser island**, see p.490.

Cruising the Noosa River, the Lakes and the Everglades

Cruising is a pleasantly sedate way to explore the area's lakes and waterways. The best bet for a short trip, with the chance to ogle Noosa's fabulous waterside properties, is the **Noosa Ferry** (regular daily departures; one way from A\$6, child A\$3; all-day pass A\$17.50/A\$5; ☎07 5449 8442, ⓦwww.noosaferry.com), which runs from the Sheraton jetty off Hastings Street to Tewantin. To get as far as Lake Cooloola, via lakes Cooroibah and Cootharaba, **Noosa River Cruises** in Noosaville (☎07 5449 7362, ⓦwww.noosaevergladescruises.com) have day-tours for A\$80. **Beyond** in Tewantin (☎07 5449 9177 or 1800 657 666, ⓦwww.beyondnoosa.com.au) has six-hour cruises upriver for A\$84 (child A\$50) and full-day tours for A\$149 (child A\$100), which combines a cruise through the Everglades with a 4WD run along the sandy shore between Noosa and Rainbow Beach.

Cycling

Noosa Bike Hire (☎07 5474 3322, ⓦwww.bikeon.com.au), who have mountain and road-bike hire stations at points all over town, also run guided tours.

Kayaking

Noosa Kayak Tours (A\$66 for 2hr; ☎0418 787 577, ⓦwww.noosakayaktours.com) will guide you along the Noosa River or take you sea-kayaking around Noosa National Park and Laguna Bay, where you might spot dolphins; their meeting place is the Visitor Information Centre.

Kitesurfing

Adventure Sports Kitesurf Australia (203 Gympie Terrace; ☎07 5455 6677, ⓦwww .adventuresports.net.au) offers starter lessons (2hr; A\$150), and intensive coaching in a helmet rigged up with a two-way radio system (2hr 30min; A\$220).

Surfing

Surfing was Noosa's original reason to be – surfers have been flocking here since the 1960s – and the best waves are found around Noosa Heads; you'll find all the necessary gear at **Surf World** (34 Sunshine Beach Rd; ☎07 5447 3538). If you're a novice try a lesson with **Merricks Learn to Surf** (19 Waterside Court, Noosaville; ☎0418 787 577, ⓦwww.learntosurf.com.au), **Go Ride A Wave** (77 Noosa Drive, Noosa Heads; ☎1300 132 441, ⓦwww.gorideawave.com.au); or **Wavesense** (corner of Duke & Douglas sts, Sunshine Beach; ☎07 5474 9076, ⓦwww.wavesense.com.au); costs are around A\$55 for a two-hour introduction, or A\$220–550 for a five-day course.

Trips to Fraser Island

See p.487. Overland tours leaving from Noosa often start by four-wheel-driving to Rainbow Beach via Cooloola Beach, a forty-kilometre run of uninterrupted sand.

Waterskiing, jet-skis and boat hire

Pro Ski, on the river bank at Gympie Terrace in Noosaville (☎07 5449 7740), has water-skiing (A\$90 for 30min or A\$140 for 1hr including instruction) and jet-skis (A\$65 for 30min); next door, **Pelican Boat Hire** (☎07 5449 7239, ⓦwww.pelicanboathire .com.au) has small outboard boats for hire (A\$34 for the first hour and A\$14 for each additional hour) as well as canoes and surf skis.

buffet, which includes gravad lax, fresh banana bread and delicious pastries, is open to all for a princely A\$35 – well worth the splurge. The bar is stuffed with well-heeled locals by night. From 6.30am daily.

🏃 **Global Café** 13 William St ☎07 5474 1844. Superb little all-day café serving up full breakfasts and lovely lunches such as smoked pork cutlets with sweet potato, or baked salmon and asparagus, at basic prices. Wi-Fi hotspot. Mon & Tues 8am–2pm, Wed–Sun 8am–2pm & 6–9pm.

🏃 **Gusto** 257 Gympie Terrace ☎07 5449 7144. Understated but utterly fabulous, this relaxed spot offers thoughtfully prepared contemporary dishes full of delicate textures and zingy colours; main courses are under A\$30. Lunch and dinner daily, plus breakfast on Sun.

Holy Mackerel 187 Gympie Terrace ☎07 5449 9519. Unquestionably the place for fish and chips – try the sensational coconut prawns and handmade ice cream. Daily 10am–late.

Ma Mensa Hastings St ☎07 5449 2328. This large, well-worn, family-oriented Italian bistro is inexpensive for the location, with lots of pasta dishes for around A\$20. Lunch and dinner daily.

Ottoman Bistro 249 Gympie Terrace ☎07 5447 1818. Tagines, couscous and seafood mezze receive a contemporary twist at this comfortable,

mid-range restaurant, and there's belly dancing on Sat. Lunch & dinner Tues–Sun.

Pilu 257 Gympie Terrace ☎07 5449 0961. Upmarket but relaxed waterfront restaurant, which gives Italian cooking a light, modern reinterpretation. Lunch & dinner daily.

River House 301 Weyba Rd ☎07 5449 7441. One of Noosa's gastronomic wonders. The ever-changing menu includes mad new ideas such as pork and pistachio terrine, or pot-roasted quince and apple pie – which invariably work. Most main courses are under A\$30. Dinner daily, plus lunch on Sun.

Sails 75 Hastings St ☎07 5447 4235. This quiet beachfront seafood restaurant, romantic but far from schmaltzy, is a great place to catch the sunset. The wine list is outstanding. Main courses around A\$28–35.

Sierra 8 Hastings St ☎07 5447 2414. Cool streetside people-watching hangout with newspapers and excellent coffee; also good for chunky, gourmetstyle burgers and steak sandwiches, or a leisurely daiquiri, the house speciality. Daily 8am–midnight.

Spinnakers Surf Life Saving Club, corner of Duke St & Belmore Terrace, Sunshine Beach ☎07 5447 5491. Spacious bar and restaurant with unbeatable views and big servings of seafood, steaks, pasta and salad, all reasonably priced. Call for the free bus on Tues, Wed & Fri evenings and Sun afternoons.

Lake Cooroibah and Lake Cootharaba

As it winds its way south into Noosa, a six-kilometre stretch of the Noosa River pools into a pair of tidal saltwater lakes – **Cooroibah** and **Cootharaba**. Placid, shallow and fringed with paperbarks and reedbeds, the lakes look their best at dawn before there's any boat traffic.

You can **cruise** the lakes from Noosa (see box, p.474), or drive up from Tewantin; turn off the main road onto Werin Street at the school, then turn left again and follow the signposts. About 6km along is **Cooroibah township** on Cooroibah's western shore, where there's a boat ramp from where it's 10km by water to Lake Cootharaba, the larger of the two. Tucked away on Cooroibah's northern shore is a rustic backpackers' bush-camp, *Gagaju* (☎07 5474 3522; bunk in timber bunkhouse A\$15, camping A\$10 per person; call in advance to book a pick-up from Noosa); canoe trips and evenings spent around the fire are among the attractions. Tiny **BOREEN POINT** on the shore of Lake Cootharaba, 18km from Tewantin, offers another basic place to stay, the colonial-era wooden *Apollonian Hotel* (☎07 5485 3100; bunk in shared room A\$30; double ❷), which oozes character and serves cold drinks and pub lunches. Boreen Point also has fuel, a general store and a council-run **campsite**.

After another 4km the road runs out at **Elanda Point** (where there's another small store), from where there's a footpath to Cootharaba's northernmost edge at **Kinaba**, basically a tourist office set where Kin Kin Creek and the Noosa River spill lazily into the lake through thickets of mangroves, hibiscus and tea trees – the so-called **Everglades**. A boardwalk from Kinaba leads to a hide where you can spy on birdlife. The picnic area here is a former **corroboree ground**. **Canoes** and kayaks can be rented at all the townships from around A\$40 a day.

Travel details

Trains

Brisbane to: Ayr (6 weekly; 22hr); Bowen (6 weekly; 20hr); Bundaberg (6 weekly; 6hr); Caboolture (6 weekly; 1hr); Cairns (5 weekly; 31hr); Cardwell (5 weekly; 26hr 30min); Gladstone (6 weekly; 9hr); Ingham (5 weekly; 25hr 30min); Innisfail (5 weekly; 29hr); Mackay (6 weekly; 17hr); Proserpine (6 weekly; 19hr); Rockhampton (6 weekly; 11hr 30min); Townsville (6 weekly; 23hr); Tully (5 weekly; 27hr 30min).

Buses

Brisbane to: Agnes Water (daily; 11hr); Airlie Beach (5 daily; 18hr 30min); Ayr (5 daily; 22hr 30min); Bowen (5 daily; 20hr 30min); Bundaberg (5 daily; 9hr); Burleigh Heads (6 daily; 1hr 30min); Byron Bay (10 daily; 4hr); Cairns (5 daily; 28hr 30min); Cardwell (6 daily; 26hr); Childers (5 daily; 8hr); Coolangatta (8 daily; 2hr 30min); Gladstone (4 daily; 11hr); Hervey Bay (7 daily; 5hr); Ingham (5 daily; 24hr); Innisfail (7 daily; 27hr); Mackay (8 daily; 15hr 30min); Mission Beach (5 daily; 26hr 25min); Mooloolaba (6 daily; 2hr 30min); Noosa (9 daily; 2hr 50min); Rockhampton (5 daily; 11hr 30min); Surfers Paradise (every 30min; 1hr 30min); Sydney (7 daily; 17hr 30min); Townsville (5 daily; 24hr); Tully (5 daily; 27hr).

Noosa to: Agnes Water (daily; 9hr); Airlie Beach (daily; 16hr 45min); Ayr (daily; 20hr); Brisbane (9 daily; 2hr 50min); Bundaberg (twice daily; 7hr); Cairns (twice daily; 27hr 30min); Cardwell (twice daily; 24hr); Childers (twice daily; 5hr 30min); Hervey Bay (4 daily; 4hr); Ingham (twice daily; 23hr); Innisfail (twice daily; 26hr); Mackay (twice daily; 14hr); Mission Beach (twice daily; 25hr); Rainbow Beach (twice daily; 3hr); Rockhampton (twice daily; 10hr); Tin Can Bay (daily; 2hr 30min); Townsville (twice daily; 21hr); Tully (twice daily; 25hr).

Surfers Paradise to: Brisbane (every 30min; 1hr 30min); Burleigh Heads (every 10min; 30min); Byron Bay (10 daily; 3hr); Coolangatta (every 10min; 1hr); Sydney (7 daily; 15hr 30min).

Ferries

Brisbane to: Moreton Island (twice daily; 2hr); North Stradbroke Island (11 daily; 30min); St Helena (3 or more weekly; 2hr).

Surfers Paradise to: South Stradbroke Island (3 or more daily; 30min).

Flights

Brisbane to: Adelaide (many daily; 3hr 30min); Alice Springs (twice daily; 4hr 30min); Bundaberg (twice daily; 50min); Cairns (many daily; 2hr 10min); Canberra (many daily; 2hr); Charleville (daily; 2hr); Darwin (twice daily; 3hr 40min); Emerald (twice daily; 1hr 40min); Gladstone (4 daily; 1hr 15min); Hervey Bay (twice daily; 1hr 15min); Hobart (many daily; 3hr 50min); Longreach (daily; 3hr); Mackay (9 daily; 3hr); Maroochydore–Sunshine Coast (many daily; 30min); Melbourne (many daily; 2hr 25min); Mount Isa (twice daily; 4hr); Norfolk Island (4 weekly; 3hr 45min); Perth (many daily; 5hr); Proserpine (twice daily; 1hr 50min); Rockhampton (4 daily; 1hr 5min); Roma (daily; 1hr 10min); Sydney (many daily; 1hr 35min); Townsville (6 daily; 1hr 50min).

Gold Coast–Coolangatta to: Adelaide (many daily; 3hr 35min); Canberra (12 daily; 2hr 40min); Melbourne (many daily; 3hr 35min); Sydney (many daily; 1hr 15min).

Sunshine Coast–Maroochydore to: Brisbane (many daily; 30min); Melbourne (daily; 3hr); Sydney (daily; 1hr 45min).

7

The Fraser Coast to the Whitsundays

CHAPTER 7 # Highlights

* **Fraser Island** Explore the giant dunes, pristine lakes and stunning beach of this sand island on an action-packed 4WD safari. **See p.487**

* **Mon Repos Conservation Park** Watch loggerhead turtles struggle up the beach to nest, or witness hatchlings making their maiden dash into the ocean. **See p.497**

* **Southern Great Barrier Reef** One of the world's most beautiful coral complexes – an absolute must for snorkellers and scuba divers. **See p.500**

* **Eungella National Park** Australia's best platypus-watching spot, its luxuriant forests also teem with birds, possums and sugar gliders. **See p.511**

* **The Whitsundays** Stay in style at an island resort, or enjoy some of Australia's most picturesque sailing in the archipelago's turquoise seas. **See p.519**

* **Whitehaven Beach** With powder-soft sand so pure it squeaks, this is an essential stop for tours out of Airlie Beach. **See p.525**

* **Heart Reef** Rediscover your inner romantic by soaring over this iconic reef in a seaplane, looking out for turtles, rays and sharks. **See p.529**

* **SS Yongala** Queensland's classic wreck-dive is patrolled by huge groupers and giant schools of barracuda and trevally. **See p.531**

▲ Lake McKenzie, Fraser Island

The Fraser Coast to the Whitsundays

There's an unmistakable shift between subtropical and tropical landscapes along the central Queensland coast, with the northern stretches noticeably stickier than the south. The **Tropic of Capricorn** runs right across the region, heralding a transition in vegetation, climate and atmosphere. Hugging the coast and its river mouths is a loosely scattered string of towns and cities, all relaxed and friendly but staunchly provincial; by far the biggest attractions lie offshore: wildlife-rich reefs and pristine cays with strand after strand of unspoilt beach; the challenging terrain of Fraser Island, excellent for four-wheel driving and bush camping; and the lure of the Whitsundays, a glittering archipelago caressed by fresh breezes.

The **Fraser Coast** covers over 190km of the seaboard between Noosa and Bundaberg, a world of giant dunes, forests, coloured sands and freshwater lakes where fishing and off-roading are the activities of preference. But your visit doesn't have to be a macho tangle with the elements: it's relatively easy and inexpensive to rent tents and an air-conditioned vehicle and set off to explore in some comfort. The main destination for all of this is **Fraser Island**, an enormous, elongated and largely forested sand island of wooded dunes and freshwater lakes, which has just about enough room for the crowds of tourists who visit each year. On the mainland off the island's southernmost tip, the small towns of **Rainbow Beach** and **Tin Can Bay** offer a laidback alternative, with a long strip of beach and the chance to come into contact with wild **dolphins**, while the well-preserved Victorian town of **Maryborough nearby** gives you a glimpse into the region's past. You can catch a ferry to Fraser Island from the Rainbow Beach area or from the main access point and tourist hub, **Hervey Bay**. Between August and November, the waters between here and Fraser Island become a giant swimming pool for migrating **humpback whales**, with several operators running whale-watching cruises.

Further north, sand carried up the coast by ocean currents is swept out to sea by Fraser Island's massive outwards-leaning edge, eventually being deposited 80km offshore as a cluster of tiny, coral-fringed sand islands – **cays** – which mark the southernmost tip of Queensland's mighty **Great Barrier Reef**. The coastal settlements of **Bundaberg**, the **Discovery Coast** (**Agnes Water** and **Town of 1770**) and **Gladstone** between them offer access to a few of these cays – **Lady Elliot Island**, **Lady Musgrave Island**, **Heron**

FRASER COAST TO THE WHITSUNDAYS

Sunshine Coast & Brisbane

Island and **Wilson Island** – on day-trips or overnight stays in a resort; either way, there's the chance to do some excellent **scuba diving**. In its southernmost reaches, the reef is only a partial barrier to the Pacific swell, and the coast is correspondingly windblown; Agnes Water has the northernmost of Australia's long string of East Coast **surfing** beaches. Bundaberg – along with the nearby hamlet of **Childers** – lies at the heart of a rich sugar cane-, fruit- and vegetable-farming area, and both are popular places to find short-term **crop-picking work**.

Rockhampton, capital of the **Capricorn Coast**, sits right on the Tropic of Capricorn. It started out as a prosperous town, built with gold-mining money in the nineteenth century, and has ridden a rollercoaster of good and bad fortunes ever since; it's currently on an upswing. Like most of the other towns set back from the central Queensland coast, Rockhampton is not particularly geared up for tourism, but is a good place to soak up the atmosphere of a provincial city: here the speciality is bucking bull-riding at the weekly **cattle rodeo** in the centre of town.

Views from the volcanic outcrops overlooking the Capricorn Coast, some 40km east of Rockhampton, stretch across graziers' estates and pineapple plantations to exposed headlands, estuarine mudflats and the Keppel Islands. The small coastal towns of **Yeppoon** and **Emu Park**, 20km apart and settled by cattle barons in the 1860s, were soon adopted by Rockhampton's elite as places to beat the summer temperatures, and retain a pleasantly dated holiday atmosphere – besides being much nicer places to stay than Rockhampton itself. **Great Keppel Island** is the coast's main draw, however, accessed from **Rosslyn Bay**, just south of Yeppoon, and ringed by pretty beaches.

Inland from the mineworkers' town of **Mackay**, the cool, luxuriant slopes of **Eungella National Park** offer a dramatic first glimpse of tropical rainforest, a rich natural environment that's far more commonplace further into northern Queensland, while in **Cape Hillsborough National Park**, forest tumbles down to a beach where wallabies forage at dawn. Between this stretch of coast and the reef is a wealth of beautiful granite islands covered in thick pine forests, the pick of which are the **Whitsundays**, near the tourist and sailing hub of **Airlie Beach**. Many of the islands are accessible on day-trips or longer sailing excursions, though some offer everything from campsites to luxury resorts if you fancy a change of pace. The more northern islands have beautiful fringing reefs, and good Great Barrier Reef **dive sites** are a boat trip away to the east, but the undisputed highlight for experienced scuba divers is the wreck of the **SS Yongala** further north. Back on the mainland, you'll find yourself deep in market-gardening territory; around the towns of **Bowen** and **Ayr** those running low on funds can recharge their bank balances with a spot of **fruit- and vegetable-picking**.

Regional practicalities

This section of the Queensland coast offers plenty of **accommodation** options; you'll find the most choice, with a corresponding selection of **restaurants**, **bars** and **shops**, in the tourist hubs of Hervey Bay and Airlie Beach, both of which are highlights of the independent travellers' circuit. The islands, also highly popular, each have a different character: while some are the exclusive preserve of gorgeous luxury establishments, others offer a choice of middle-market resorts – still pricey compared to the mainland – and bush camping in national-park sites. **Eco-retreats** are thin on the ground compared to Far North Queensland, but you'll find a few on the islands and in the wilderness areas of Eungella and Cape Hillsborough.

The closest international **airports** to the region are at Brisbane and Cairns; internal flights serve Hervey Bay, Gladstone, Rockhampton, Mackay, Proserpine and Hamilton Island. The single-lane Brisbane–Cairns **Bruce Highway** is the region's transport artery, generally covering the considerable distances between most towns through forests or fields ten or twenty kilometres from the ocean; it tends to be quiet (only slightly busier than in Far North Queensland) but the locals have a habit of tailgating each other for many kilometres. Long-distance **buses** stop at all the major towns and many of the smaller ones. The Brisbane–Cairns **railway** line also traverses the entire region, with stops at Maryborough, Bundaberg, Gladstone, Rockhampton, Mackay, Proserpine, Bowen and Ayr. A few out-of-the-way spots are covered by **local bus** networks, and **guided tours** will take you to Fraser Island, Eungella and the Whitsundays, but if you don't have your own wheels it's worth **hiring a car** from time to time to reach some of the less accessible parks and beaches such as Cape Hillsborough or the Discovery Coast. From the Bundaberg area north, you need to watch out for **cane trains** that cross roads during the sugar-crushing season (roughly June– Dec); crossings are usually marked by flashing red lights.

Weather and seasons
Winters on the central Queensland coast (April–Nov) are dry and pleasant; you'll rarely need a second layer by day, though nights can be fresh and chilly, especially in the mountainous areas: Eungella National Park, where it can drop

From Agnes Water north, **dangerous jellyfish** (see p.47) may be present in the coastal waters from November to May. To minimize the risk of being stung, you should wear a protective Lycra suit when swimming in the ocean at this time, even inside jellyfish-resistant "stinger nets". It's not advisable to swim in isolated areas.

to below zero on winter nights, is a favourite destination for "Christmas in July" parties. The transitions from winter to summer and back again are gradual and barely discernible to those used to the showy seasonal changes of spring and autumn in temperate climes. In **summer** (Dec–March), temperatures in the tropical towns of Rockhampton and Mackay can shoot up to over 40°C, with humidity increasing the further north you travel. During the **cyclone season** (Nov–April), there's always a possibility of torrential rain and devastating storms, though the harshest cyclones, strong enough to rip apart forests and buildings, are relatively rare.

Whale-watching season in the Hervey Bay and Fraser Coast area is August to November; in the Whitsundays, it's June to September. **Turtles nest** on the islands of the southern Great Barrier Reef and the Bundaberg coast from mid-November to early February, with the hatchlings making an appearance between late January and March. **Scuba diving** and snorkelling on the Great Barrier Reef is good all year round, but visibility is best during the calm weather from April to October. The best time of year to find **farm work** picking mangoes, tomatoes and vegetables is March to November in the Bundaberg and Childers area, and May to December in the Bowen and Ayr area.

Rainbow Beach, Tin Can Bay and Maryborough

The small, slowly developing coastal townships of **Rainbow Beach** and **Tin Can Bay**, just north of Noosa and south of Hervey Bay, can be reached by back roads from either town, or from the Bruce Highway (A1) by turning off at Gympie. **RAINBOW BEACH**, 80km from Gympie and 48km from Tin Can Bay, is a very casual knot of streets set back from a fantastic **beach** facing into **Wide Bay**. The township lies either side of **Rainbow Beach Road**, which ends above the surf at a small **shopping complex** housing a post office, service station and store – Greyhound and Premier **buses** (seep.35) pull in nearby on Spectrum Street. **Accommodation** includes *Rainbow Beach Holiday Village*, 13 Rainbow Beach Rd (☎07 5486 3222, ⓦwww.beach-village.com.au; camping A$22–30, villas ❸), and *Fraser's on Rainbow Beach*, 18 Spectrum St (☎07 5486 8885, ⓦwww.frasersonrainbow.com; bunk in shared room A$24–30, private double ❷), an upbeat hostel with a 24-hour Internet café; the tour staff can fix you up with a trip to Fraser Island. There's a lively **pub** on the main road serving huge steaks at around A$20, while *Coloured Sands Café* in the shopping complex does good coffee, cooked breakfasts, pancakes and fish and chips.

The main recreations here are **fishing**, **paragliding**, **surfing** and **kite-boarding** – there's almost always a moderate southeasterly blowing – but you can also take a 4WD (when the tide is right) or walk 10km south along the beach to the coloured sand cliffs at **Double Island Point**, whose streaks of red, orange and white are caused by minerals leaching down from the cliff-top; beyond the point, you can drive all the way down the beach to Tewantin, just outside Noosa, by 4WD – an exhilarating thirty-kilometre run. On the far side of the point lies the rusty frame of the *Cherry Venture* **shipwreck**, beached during a storm in 1973. Offshore, Wolf Rock, a group of four volcanic pinnacles named by Captain Cook's crew, offer some exciting **scuba diving**, with swim-throughs and ledges patrolled by grey nurse sharks and a giant grouper: Wolf Rock Dive Centre on Karoonda Road (℡07 5486 8004, ⓦwww.wolfrockdive .com.au) will take you there.

Rainbow Beach is one of the transit points for trips to **Fraser Island** (see p.487). Well-prepared hikers can visit as pedestrians, while confident drivers can take a 4WD across – the island is inaccessible to 2WD vehicles – by catching a barge (vehicle ferry; see box, p.488) from **Inskip Point**, 10km north of town. Safari, 5 Karoonda Rd (℡07 4124 4244 or 1800 689 819, ⓦwww .safari4wdhire.com.au), offer basic off-roaders from about A\$125 per day and LandCruisers from A\$175 per day for a three-day rental, and can sort out **packages** including complete camping kits and the required permits (see p.489). If you'd prefer to have somebody else show you the sights, you can join an organized tour – see box, p.490.

Some 55km from Gympie and 48km from Rainbow Beach, **TIN CAN BAY** occupies a long, wooded spit jutting north into a convoluted inlet; the main drag, **Tin Can Bay Road**, runs for a couple of kilometres past a small shopping centre, post office and a few places to stay and eat before petering out at the Yacht Club. There's no beach here, and not much going on: the main reason to stop is to see the wild **indo-pacific humpback dolphins** who pull in early each morning at **Barnacle Point** jetty, just short of the Yacht Club. Two habituated dolphins are hand-fed fish at 8am so that visitors can get a closer look, as an educational exercise; you can participate if you follow strict guidelines, which include making sure your hands are clean and you don't touch these rare animals.

Greyhound **buses** (see p.35) set down just off the main road, in Bream Street. The town's **accommodation** won't entice you to stay long: the options include the *Sleepy Lagoon Motel* near the bus stop (℡07 5486 4124, ⓦwww.tincanbay.gday.com.au; bed in shared room A\$25, private double ❷, motel room ❸), a fairly basic place attached to the pub; *Dolphin Waters* at 40–41 The Esplanade (℡07 5486 2600; ❹), a small complex of modern holiday apartments with a pool that's just big enough to swim in; and *Kingfisher Caravan Park*, also on The Esplanade (℡07 5486 4198; camping A\$19–20, cabin ❶), one of a couple of cramped camping and caravan sites with a few cabins. For **eating**, *Barnacles*, at the dolphin-feeding station at Barnacle Point, does good, inexpensive lunches.

Maryborough, a handsome little town on the banks of the Mary River, just off the Bruce Highway (A1) 264km north of Brisbane and 113km south of Bundaberg, is one of Queensland's oldest settlements. In the mid-nineteenth century, its port was the engine of the Fraser Coast economy, second only to Sydney in importance. Today, there's a quiet, old-fashioned feel to the place, and a good number of impeccably preserved Victorian buildings to admire. For a civilized **lunch** stop, *Muddy Waters Café* (℡07 4121 5011) at the old wharf offers creative cooking and a relaxed waterfront terrace, while *The Port Residence* on Wharf Street (℡07 4123 5001; closed Mon), in the former riverside customs house, rustles up good salads and pasta; it's also open for dinner and weekend breakfasts. Maryborough has a regional **airport**.

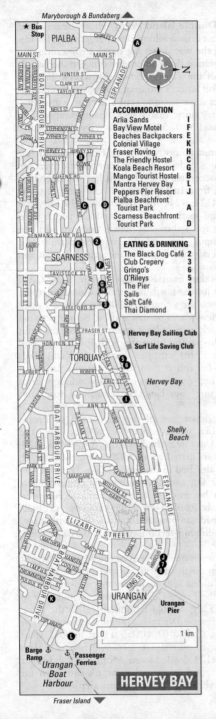

Maryborough & Bundaberg ▲

★ Bus Stop

PIALBA

CHARLES ST

A

MAIN ST

MAIN ST

N

HUNTER ST

CLARK ST

TAYLOR ST

NEILS ST

ACCOMMODATION

STEPHENSON ST

ZYPHER ST   ZYPHER ST

Arlia Sands   I
Bay View Motel   F
Beaches Backpackers   E
Colonial Village   K
Fraser Roving   H
The Friendly Hostel   C
Koala Beach Resort   G
Mango Tourist Hostel   B
Mantra Hervey Bay   L
Peppers Pier Resort   J
Pialba Beachfront
  Tourist Park   A
Scarness Beachfront
  Tourist Park   D

HERVEY ST   HERVEY ST

B

MCNALLY ST

DOWN

QUEENS RD

I

TORQUAY RD

C   D

DENMANS CAMP ROAD

GARRY ST

SCARNESS

2

EATING & DRINKING

The Black Dog Café   2
Club Crepery   3
Gringo's   6
O'Rileys   5
The Pier   8
Sails   4
Salt Café   7
Thai Diamond   1

TAVISTOCK ST

EXETER ST

F

ESPLANADE

G   H

RIDEFORD ST

3

FRASER ST

4

Hervey Bay Sailing Club

Surf Life Saving Club

TORQUAY

HONITON ST

ROBERT ST

ROBERT ST

5   6

Hervey Bay

ERIC ST

ANN ST

I

HERBOT ST

Shelly Beach

ALEXANDER ST

CUNNINGHAM ST

MARGARET ST

MARGARET ST

WILLIAM ST

RICHARD ST

ELIZABETH STREET

SHELL ST

CORAL ST

ESPLANADE

SMITHS ST

HANSEN ST

BOOL COOROY

HIBISCUS ST

KING ST

EDWARD ST

URANGAN

K

Urangan Pier

0   1 km

BOAT HARBOUR DRIVE

L

Barge ⚓ Ramp

⚓ Passenger Ferries

Urangan Boat Harbour

484

HERVEY BAY

Fraser Island ▼

Hervey Bay

On a breezy stretch of coast between Noosa and Bundaberg, around 35km northeast of Maryborough, **HERVEY BAY** is a rapidly expanding sprawl of suburbs that used to be known locally as "God's Waiting Room" due to the large number of retirees living here. These days, its population is expanding and diversifying, as young professionals priced out of larger cities are choosing to move here for in search of a relaxed lifestyle. Though very spread out, with acres of commercial and light industrial estates on the outskirts, it's a straightforward enough place, somewhere to pull up for only as long as it takes to join the throng crossing to **Fraser Island**, or to venture into the bay to spot **whales** in the spring.

Pialba is Hervey Bay's commercial centre, an ugly blob of car parks, shopping malls and industrial estates where the road from Maryborough enters the west side of town. It's about 1km from here to **The Esplanade**, a pleasant seven-kilometre string of motels and shops facing a wooded foreshore, running east through the conjoined coastal suburbs of **Scarness**, **Torquay** and **Urangan**, the departure point for whale-watching trips and ferries to Fraser Island.

Practicalities

Driving from the south, you turn off the Bruce Highway (A1) at Maryborough to take route 57 into town; from the north, you can leave the Bruce Highway by way of route 12 from Howard past cane and pineapple fields to the Burrum Coast, entering Hervey Bay from the west, or take the faster but less scenic route from Torbanlea to the Maryborough–Hervey Bay road.

Long-distance buses (see p.35) wind up in Pialba, at the Centro shopping centre, just off Boat Harbour Drive. The helpful visitor information centre (℡07 4124 4000 or 1800 811 728, ⓦwww.visitherveybay.info; Mon–Fri 6am–5.30pm, Sat & Sun 6.30am–1pm) is on the Maryborough Road (Route 57), near the junction with Urraween Road. Hervey Bay airport (HVE) is about 5km south of Urangan off Booral Road, with direct flights from Brisbane and Sydney with Qantas, Jetstar and Virgin Blue (see p.35). The nearest train station is Maryborough West, on the main line between Brisbane and Cairns; a Trainlink bus service into town meets every train. Hervey Bay also has a decent local bus service, circuiting around town between about 6am and 6pm, though you'll need a taxi for the airport (℡13 10 08; around A$15). Most lodgings offer Internet

Whale-watching from Hervey Bay

Humpback whales are among the most exciting marine creatures you can encounter: growing to 16m long and weighing up to 36 tonnes, they make their presence known from a distance by their habit of "breaching" – making spectacular, crashing leaps out of the water – and expelling jets of spray as they exhale.

Prior to 1952, an estimated ten thousand whales made the annual journey between Antarctica and the tropics to breed and give birth in shallow coastal waters; a decade later, whaling had reduced the population to just two hundred. Now protected, their numbers have increased to over five thousand, many of which migrate along the eastern coast of Australia. An estimated two thirds enter the channel between Hervey Bay and Fraser Island, with each family spending anything up to three weeks relaxing in its sheltered waters, making this the best whale-watching spot in the country. The season lasts from August to November, a little later than in northern waters because Fraser Island leans outwards, deflecting the creatures away from the bay as they migrate north, but funnelling them into the constricted waters on their return from their breeding grounds in the Whitsundays.

In the early months you're more likely to see mature bulls who, being inquisitive, swim directly under the boat and raise their heads out of the water, close enough to touch. You may even see them fighting over mating rights and hear their enchanting mating songs; of course, you may also see and hear nothing at all. The later part of the season sees mothers and playful calves coming into the bay to rest before their great migration south, a good time to watch the humpbacks breaching. Whether all this voyeurism disturbs the animals is unclear, but they seem at least tolerant of the attention paid to them.

The town makes the most of their visit with an August Whale Festival, and operators are always searching for new gimmicks to promote whale-watching cruises and flights. For an aerial view, try Air Fraser Island (℡1800 247 992, ⓦwww.airfraserisland.com.au), costing from A$85 per person (depending on the number of passengers) for a thirty-minute buzz. Cruises from Urangan Boat Harbour or Fraser Island last a morning or full day and cost from A$100 per person. Some boats can take up to 150 passengers; this doesn't necessarily mean they feel overcrowded but check the boat size, viewing space, speed of vessel and how many will be going before committing yourself. Quick Cat (℡07 4128 9611 or 1800 671 977, ⓦwww.herveybaywhalewatch.com.au) and Blue Horizon (℡07 4125 3600 or 1800 247 992, ⓦwww.bluehorizoncruises.com.au) work with a spotter plane to almost guarantee sightings; Spirit of Hervey Bay (℡07 4125 5131 or 1800 642 544, ⓦwww.spiritofherveybay.com) has underwater portals to view the whales if they come close; while Whalesong Cruises (℡1800 689 610, ⓦwww.whalesong.com.au), Tasman Venture (℡07 4124 3222 or 1800 620 322, ⓦwww.tasmanventure.com.au) and the sailing catamaran Blue Dolphin (℡07 4124 9600, ⓦwww.bluedolphintours.com.au) also come recommended.

access at varying rates; *Koala Beach Resort* on The Esplanade (see below) has a cheap and convenient Internet café, open to all, in its reception.

Hervey Bay is the principal departure point for passenger and vehicle ferries to World Heritage-listed **Fraser Island** (see p.487). The island's roads are 4WD only; Hervey Bay has no shortage of companies renting suitable vehicles (see p.487) or offering guided tours (see p.490).

Accommodation

Hervey Bay has a good range of **accommodation**, from decent budget options to characterful B&Bs and smart apartments; the selection below is just a fraction of what's on offer on the beachfront Esplanade and its immediate vicinity. The town is packed during the whale-watching season and at Christmas and Easter, when many motels hike up their prices. Most places will pick you up from the bus station, and all can help organize tours to Fraser Island, with the hostels specializing in putting together budget self-drive packages: Hervey Bay is a backpacker hub and a good place to meet potential co-travellers. If you're **camping**, the best sites are right on the beach at *Pialba Beachfront Tourist Park* (℡ 07 4128 1399) and *Scarness Beachfront Tourist Park* (℡ 07 4128 1274), both on the ocean side of The Esplanade (A$21–29.90 per pitch).

Arlia Sands 13 Ann St, Torquay ℡ 07 4125 4360, ⓦ www.arliasands.com.au. Extremely comfortable, well-equipped apartments sleeping from two to four people in a quiet street off The Esplanade – an ideal family option. ❹

Bay View Motel 399 The Esplanade, Torquay ℡ 07 4128 1134, ⓦ www.thebayviewmotel .com.au. This historic guesthouse with wooden floors and colourful interior boasts spotless rooms and friendly owners who can't do enough to please. ❸

Beaches Backpackers 195 Torquay Terrace, Torquay ℡ 07 4124 1322 or 1800 655 501, ⓦ www.beaches.com.au. Excellent, busy party hostel with lively bar/bistro and cheerful staff, one street back from The Esplanade. Bunk in shared room A$22, private double ❷

Colonial Village 820 Boat Harbour Drive, Urangan ℡ 07 4125 1844 or 1800 818 280, ⓦ www.yha .com.au. Leafy and peaceful YHA-affiliated hostel, within easy reach of Urangan Boat Harbour. Bunk or bed in shared room A$28–32, private double ❷

Fraser Roving 412 The Esplanade, Torquay ℡ 07 4125 6386 or 1800 989 811, ⓦ www .fraserroving.com. Barracks-like but clean and efficient backpackers' specializing in Fraser trips, with more beds than bunks, a large, sociable bar area and a pool. Bunk or bed in shared room A$20–30, private double ❷

The Friendly Hostel 182 Torquay Rd, Scarness ℡ 1800 244 107, ⓦ www.thefriendly.com.au.

Relaxed, intimate guesthouse, with comfy three-bed self-contained dorms and a nice, family atmosphere. Bunk in shared room A$24–27, private double ❷

Koala Beach Resort 408 The Esplanade, Torquay ℡ 07 4125 3601 or 1800 354 535, ⓦ www .koalaadventures.com. Large hostel with party vibe in a great location close to shops, with an Internet café and its own fleet of 4WDs for Fraser trips. Bunk in shared room A$24–27, private double ❷

🏃 **Mango Tourist Hostel** 110 Torquay Rd, Torquay ℡ 07 4124 2832, ⓦ www .mangohostel.com. Delightful old Queenslander house with polished floors and just three rooms. The hosts are extremely knowledgeable about Fraser Island and can organize alternative nature-based walking tours, ecotours or sailing trips. Bunk in shared room A$22, private double ❶

Mantra Hervey Bay Buccaneer Drive, Urangan ℡ 07 4197 8200, ⓦ www.mantraherveybay .com.au. Plain rooms and apartments with marina views down at the boat harbour, useful if you've just stepped off the ferry from Fraser or are planning an early crossing. Room ❹, apartment ❺–❽

🏃 **Peppers Pier Resort** The Esplanade, Urangan ℡ 07 4194 9700, ⓦ www.peppers .com.au/pier-resort. Stylish, cosy and comfortable modern mini-apartments of various sizes, in a large seafront complex with secure underground parking and a great pool. ❻–❽

Eating and drinking

Apart from snack bars and fast-food joints in Pialba, most of the **places to eat** and spend the evening are along The Esplanade in Torquay.

The Black Dog Café 389 The Esplanade, Torquay ⊤07 4124 3177. Small, smart restaurant with heavy Asian leanings – mostly Japanese. Udon soup, sushi, and beef teriyaki sit strangely alongside Cajun fish and Caesar salad. Good value, with mains at A$18–25.

Club Crepery 417 The Esplanade, Torquay ⊤07 4194 6488. Fresh, tasty juices, rolled-to-order sushi and filling crepes make this cool, contemporary café a good choice. Daily from 9am.

Gringo's 449 The Esplanade, Torquay ⊤07 4125 1644. Good Mexican menu with enchiladas, chilli con carne and nachos with either beans or meat, spiced to order. Main courses cost around A$20. Tues–Sun from 5.30pm.

O'Rileys 446 The Esplanade, Torquay ⊤07 4125 3100. Savoury pizza, pasta and crepes, but best for fruit pancakes and cream. Tues–Sun from 5.30pm, Sun breakfast 8–11am.

The Pier 573 The Esplanade, Urangan ⊤07 4128 9699. Upmarket seafood restaurant with old-fashioned, high standards. Daily from 6pm.

Sails 433 The Esplanade, Torquay ⊤07 4125 5170. This Mediterranean/Asian brasserie is a good place to splash out a little. Good choices are the Shanghai noodles and seafood risotto, and there are some decent vegetarian options, too. Closed Sun.

Salt Café 569 The Esplanade, Urangan ⊤07 4124 9722. Stylish breakfast and lunch joint attached to *Peppers Pier Resort*, but open to all. Daily 7am–5pm.

Thai Diamond 353 The Esplanade, Scarness ⊤07 4124 4855. Inexpensive yet filling dishes, with cheerful service in an unassuming cafeteria-style setting. Licensed and BYO. Daily 10am–midnight.

Listings

Airlines Air Fraser Island (⊤1800 247 992, ⓦwww.airfraserisland.com.au) for whale-spotting and flights to Fraser; Jetstar, Qantas and Virgin Blue for intercity flights. For Lady Elliot Island, contact the resort direct (see p.498).

Banks Most banks are in Pialba, with a few scattered along The Esplanade at Torquay.

Camping equipment Some 4WD operators rent camping equipment.

Car rental Nifty (463 The Esplanade ⊤1800 627 583) has decent runarounds from A$35 a day. For 4WD, Fraser Magic (Kruger Court, Urangan ⊤07 4125 6612, ⓦwww.fraser-magic-4wdhire .com.au) has the lowest rates and has been going forever; Bay 4WD Hire Centre (54 Boat Harbour Drive, Pialba ⊤07 4128 2891, ⓦwww.bay4wd .com.au) offers much the same deal. Aussie Trax

(56 Boat Harbour Drive, Urangan ⊤07 4124 4433 or 1800 062 275, ⓦwww.fraserisland4wd.com.au) has a good range of vehicles and packages. For more information about 4WD rental for Fraser Island, see box, p.491.

Internet access Several hostels can oblige, as can the tourist office near the bus station at Pialba's Centro shopping complex (A$4/hr).

Pharmacy Day and Night Pharmacy, 418 The Esplanade, Torquay (daily 8am–8pm).

Post office On The Esplanade, Torquay.

Taxi ⊤13 10 08.

Watersports Torquay Beach Hire, 415 The Esplanade, Torquay (⊤07 4125 5528), offers surf skis, windsurf boards and outboard-driven tinnies for a day's fishing.

Fraser Island

With a length of 123km, **Fraser Island** is the world's largest sand island, but this dry fact does little to prepare you for the experience. Accumulated from sediments swept north from New South Wales and beyond over the last two million years, the scenery ranges from silent forests and beaches sculpted by wind and surf to crystal-clear streams and dark, tannin-stained lakes. The east coast forms a ninety-kilometre razor-edge from which Fraser's tremendous scale can be absorbed as you travel its length; with the sea as a constant, the dunes along the beach seem to evolve before your eyes – in places low and soft, elsewhere hard and worn into intriguing canyons. By contrast, slower progress through the forests of the island's interior creates more subtle impressions of its age and permanence – a primal world predating European settlement – brought into question only when the view opens suddenly onto a lake or a bald sandblow. In 1992, the entire island was recognized as a UNESCO **World Heritage Site**, with almost all but a few pockets of freehold land and the tiny townships of Eurong and Happy Valley being national park.

Fraser Island has become a highly popular destination for adventure travellers drawn by the idea of tackling challenging 4WD-only sand tracks; barrelling along a long, remote beach; fishing; swimming in freshwater lakes; and camping in remote coastal and forest sites. It's also a magnet for ecotourists and wildlife enthusiasts: the island is well protected and has a thriving number of birds, insects, frogs, reptiles and small marsupials, and, most famously, a two-hundred-strong population of pure-bred dingoes. Regular visitors include dolphins, dugongs and humpback whales and their calves, which breach in the waters of Platypus Bay, in the northwest, between August and October.

All this interest means that the island, large though it is, is always busy with tour groups covering a standard circuit. While these offer an excellent introduction to the island's highlights, your best chance of snatching a few days in peaceful solitude is to travel independently; this requires some careful planning.

Some history

To the Butchulla (or Kabi) Aborigines, Fraser Island is **K'gari**, a beautiful woman so taken with the earth that she stayed behind after creation, her eyes becoming lakes that mirrored the sky and teemed with wildlife so that she wouldn't be lonely. European settlers named the island after Eliza Fraser, wife of the captain of the doomed *Stirling Castle*; having survived the shipwreck, she made it to dry land at Waddy Point, only to be enslaved by the Aboriginal inhabitants. The exact details of Eliza's captivity remain obscure as she produced several conflicting accounts, but her role as an "anti-Crusoe" inspired the work of novelist Patrick White and artist Sidney Nolan.

Ferries to Fraser Island

Several ferry companies connect Fraser Island with the mainland. There's a daily **passenger ferry** from Urangan Boat Harbour in Hervey Bay to *Kingfisher Bay Resort* on Fraser's west coast (℡07 4120 3333 or 1800 072 555; 6 crossings daily; 45min; A\$55 return, child A\$28). The most useful **barges** (vehicle ferries) run from River Heads, 10km south of Hervey Bay, to Wanggoolba Creek, south of Kingfisher Bay (℡07 4194 9222; 3 crossings daily at 8.30am, 10.15am and 3.30pm, returning at 9.30am, 2.30pm and 4.30pm; 30min; A\$75 one way per vehicle), which is the **easiest place to land**, recommended for inexperienced 4WD drivers. Separate barge services also run from River Heads to Kingfisher Bay (℡07 4120 3333 or 1800 072 555; three crossings daily; 45min; A\$75 one way per vehicle) and from Inskip Point, 10km north of Rainbow Beach, to Hook Point on Fraser's southern tip (℡07 5486 3227; throughout the day, 6am–5.30pm; 15min; A\$80 one way per vehicle), though this is a difficult landing and not for novice drivers. There's also a twice-daily barge service from Urangan to Moon Point at the north end of Kingfisher Bay (℡07 4194 9222; 8.30am and 3.30pm, returning at 9.30am and 4.30pm), but a tricky onward route means this can only be used by private, rather than rented, vehicles.

All the vehicle ferries also take foot passengers. They all operate independently, and the Urangan and River Heads services should be pre-booked. If you plan to enter the island at one point and exit from another, you'll need separate one-way tickets.

7

THE FRASER COAST TO THE WHITSUNDAYS | Fraser Island

Practicalities

The easiest way to get a taste of Fraser – albeit a very small fragment – is to take the daily **passenger ferry** from Urangan Boat Harbour in Hervey Bay to *Kingfisher Bay Resort* (see box, p.488). There's a beach here where dingoes are sometimes spotted, and the resort has a pool and restaurant for the use of day visitors; resort staff also operate **one-day guided tours** of the island (A$155, child A$85) and shorter wildlife walks. Agents based in Hervey Bay or Rainbow Beach run one-day tours that start with a ferry crossing and then whip around the main sights – usually some of the forest, a couple of lakes, and the beach as far as Indian Head – but the wildlife and overall feel of the area are elusive unless you get away from the more popular places, camp for the night and explore early on in the day.

For a more in-depth visit, you can join a **two- or three-day tour** or, if you're a confident driver, take the cheaper option of assembling a group and **renting a 4WD**, either independently or through accommodation, buying a Queensland Parks and Wildlife Service **vehicle permit** (available for A$33.45 on ☎13 13 04 or at ⓦ www.epa.qld.gov.au) and then catching a **barge** (vehicle ferry) to the island. For details of tours and ferries, see the boxes on p.488 and p.490.

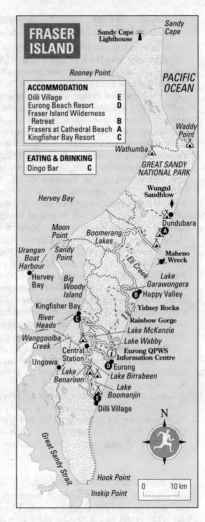

FRASER ISLAND

Sandy Cape Lighthouse
Sandy Cape
Rooney Point
PACIFIC OCEAN

Waddy Point
Wathumba
GREAT SANDY NATIONAL PARK
Wungul Sandblow
Hervey Bay
Dundubara
Moon Point
Boomerang Lakes
Maheno Wreck
Urangan Boat Harbour
Sandy Point
Eli Creek
Hervey Bay
Big Woody Island
Lake Garawongera
Happy Valley
Kingfisher Bay
Yidney Rocks
River Heads
Rainbow Gorge
Lake McKenzie
Wanggoolba Creek
Lake Wabby
Central Station
Eurong QPWS Information Centre
Ungowa
Eurong
Lake Benaroon
Lake Birrabeen
Lake Boomanjin
Dilli Village
N
Great Sandy Strait
Hook Point
Inskip Point
0   10 km

Once on the island, there are a few **safety points** to bear in mind. Fraser's wild **dingoes** (see box, p.493) are intelligent opportunists; though rarely harmful to humans, they can behave very aggressively and should be treated with caution. Don't approach them, and don't feed them or leave anything edible lying around. You should also be aware that **sharks** and severe currents make Fraser a dangerous place to get in the sea; if you want to swim, stick to the freshwater lakes. If you're driving, make sure your vehicle is adequately equipped for the road conditions and you have a good supply of **water** at all times; it's very easy to get stuck in the soft sand. Lastly, pack some powerful **insect repellent**.

For **supplies**, the west-coast resort at Kingfisher Bay and the east-coast settlements of Happy Valley and Eurong have basic stores, telephones, bars and fuel; there's another store at *Frasers at Cathedral Beach* but no shops or restaurants at

There's a tremendous choice of guided trips to Fraser Island, most of which start with a boat transfer from Hervey Bay's Urangan Boat Harbour to Kingfisher Bay. Others use the ferry from Inskip Point, near Rainbow Beach, to Hook Point, and will pick you up from Rainbow Beach, or Noosa on the Sunshine Coast.

For day-trips, **The Fraser Island Company** in Torquay, Hervey Bay (ⓣ07 4125 3933 or 1800 446 655, ⓦwww.fraserislandco.com.au; standard tour A$145, child A$85; small-group tour A$179, child A$125), offer an excellent barbecue lunch and use new vehicles and first-rate guides. They also seem to work out of sync with rival tours' schedules, so you don't keep bumping into busloads of other visitors. **Fraser Explorer Tours** in Urangan, Hervey Bay (ⓣ07 4194 9222 or 1800 249 122, ⓦwww .fraserexplorertours.com.au; A$145, child A$85) are also recommended for tours from Hervey Bay or the Sunshine Coast. **Fraser Island Excursions** in Noosa (ⓣ07 5449 0393, ⓦwww.fraserislandexcursions.com.au; A$189) run upmarket small-group tours by LandCruiser, with superior catering.

For those who would like to **spend a night on the island**, The Fraser Island Company run two-day trips with accommodation in safari tents at *Frasers at Cathedral Beach* (A$269); Fraser Explorer Tours offer trips with a choice of rooms at *Eurong Beach Resort* (A$253–305); whilst Cool Dingo (ⓣ07 4120 3333 or 1800 072 555, ⓦwww.cooldingotour.com; A$289–339), who cater for a young crowd, include a stay in a double or four-share room at the *Wilderness Lodges*, which are part of *Kingfisher Bay Resort*. For three-day all-inclusive packages covering just about the whole island, the best is again offered by The Fraser Island Company (A$435), along with Cool Dingo (A$359–409). In Rainbow Beach, *Fraser's on Rainbow Beach*, 18 Spectrum St (ⓣ07 5486 8885, ⓦwww.frasersonrainbow.com) offer a three-day guided tour for A$409.

Optional extras on all tours include a quick **scenic flight** with Air Fraser Island (ⓣ07 4125 3600 or 1800 247 992, ⓦwww.airfraserisland.com.au; A$70) – a rare opportunity to take off from and land on a beach in a light aircraft, and very reasonably priced.

Outside the whale-watching season, Hervey Bay's boat operators (see box, p.485) offer more generalized **cruises** in the vicinity of Fraser Island, spending about four hours searching for dolphins, turtles and – with real luck – dugongs (sea cows) at around A$100–125 per person. In addition, Krystal Clear (ⓣ07 4124 0066; A$70, child A$35) run glass-bottomed-boat day trips.

Dilli Village. You'll save money by bringing whatever you need with you; and make sure you **take all rubbish home** or place it in the large, wildlife-proof metal skips you'll find along the way. The island **taxi** service, based at Eurong (ⓣ07 4127 9188 or 0429 379 188), charges around A$70 for a trip from the east to the west coast.

Getting around

Driving on the island requires a **4WD vehicle**. The east beach serves as the main highway, with roads running inland to popular spots; make sure you pick up a **tide timetable** from barge operators, as parts of the beach are only reliably negotiable at low tide. Other tracks, always slower than the beach, crisscross the interior; the main tracks are often rough from heavy use, and minor roads tend to be in better shape.

General 4WD advice is to lower your **tyre pressure** to around 12psi to increase traction on the sand, but this isn't normally necessary (if you get bogged down, however, try it first). Rain and high tides harden sand surfaces, making driving easier.

Fraser Island is simply too large and varied to appreciate fully on a day-trip, and with competition in Hervey Bay keeping prices to a minimum it's a great opportunity to learn how to handle a **4WD**. See p.487 for some recommended outfits; a stipulation of the Fraser Coast 4x4 Hire Association is that the company should take time to protect both itself and you with a full briefing on the island and driving practicalities. Renting a 4WD over three days, expect to pay around A\$135 per day for a two-seater such as a Suzuki, up to A\$200 per day for an eight-seater Land Rover Defender or Toyota LandCruiser, including insurance.

Conditions include a minimum driver age of 21 and a A\$500 deposit, payable in plastic or cash – note that advertised prices are normally for renting the vehicle only, so tents, food, fuel, the ferry and vehicle and camping permits for the island are extra, available separately or as part of a self-drive tour package. To help cut costs, you'll want to form a **group** of five or six. All hostels naturally want to sell you their tour but will normally fill the car to capacity (usually eight) to maximize their profit, which can be very uncomfortable on the bumpy tracks around Fraser. A three-day, two-night camping trip works out at about A\$150–190 per person plus provisions.

Road rules are the same as those on the mainland, with a speed limit of 80kph on the eastern beach, strictly enforced by the island police. Most **accidents** involve collisions on blind corners, rolling in soft sand (avoid hard braking or making sudden turns, as you don't have to be going very fast for your front wheels to dig in, turning you over), and trying to cross apparently insignificant creeks on the beach at 60kph – 4WDs are not invincible. Don't drive your vehicle into the surf; you'll probably get stuck and even if you don't, this much saltwater exposure will rust out the bodywork within days (something the rental company will notice and charge you for). Noise from the surf means that pedestrians can't hear vehicles on the beach and won't be aware of your presence until you barrel through from behind, so give them a wide berth.

Walking is an excellent way to see the island. A well-marked but under-used trail, the Fraser Island Great Walk (see p.425), covers a little under 90km of the island's best bits between Happy Valley and Dilli Village in six- to eight-kilometre chunks; highlights include circumnavigating the lakes, wandering through scribbly-gum forests, and chance encounters with goannas and dingoes. A good week-long hike, which by each sundown will render you virtually unconscious after all that walking across soft sand, it requires no special skills beyond endurance and the ability to set up camp before you pass out. There's also an established circuit from Central Station south past lakes Birrabeen and Boomanjin with an energetic burst up Wongi Sandblow for sweeping views out to sea, then up the coast and back to Central Station via lakes Wabby and McKenzie. Again, don't underestimate the effort required to cover so much sand: you should allow at least three days. The Queensland Parks and Wildlife Service (Ⓦ www.epa.qld.gov.au) issues practical advice for hikers and campers.

Accommodation

All **accommodation** needs to be booked in advance. Top of the range are the spacious hotel rooms and self-contained villas at ⚘ *Kingfisher Bay Resort* (Ⓣ 07 4120 3333, Ⓦ www.kingfisherbay.com; ❺, villa ❼) on the west coast. This award-winning ecolodge is set in stunning coastal wetlands that are excellent for wildlife-watching: resident rangers run early morning bird walks and after-dark spotlighting tours of the vicinity, as well as day-trips around the island. There's a very good restaurant specializing in gourmet cooking with a bush-tucker twist, and a more informal nightly buffet. Uphill are the resort's excellent budget *Wilderness Lodges* (single bed or bunk in shared twin or quad room A\$33), which have a roomy, outback-cabin feel and are within strolling distance of a backpacker-friendly bar-restaurant, the *Dingo Bar*; it can get pretty rowdy, but is out of earshot of the main complex.

It's a tough 15km across the island from *Kingfisher Bay* to **Seventy-Five Mile Beach** on the east coast, where most of the other options are found. The southernmost (and first if you're coming up from Hook Point) is friendly and low-key *Dilli Village* (℡07 4127 9130, ⓦwww.dillivillage.com; camping A\$20–25, bunkhouse room ❶, cabin ❸), not far from Lake Boomanjin. Further north up the beach towards the road to Central Station, *Eurong Beach Resort* (℡07 4127 9122 or 1800 111 808, ⓦwww.eurong.com; ❹, apartment ❺) has motel-style accommodation sleeping up to six per unit, and a pool. From here, it's a good way to *Fraser Island Wilderness Retreat* at Happy Valley (℡07 4127 9144, ⓦwww.fraserislandco.com.au; ❺, five-bed cabin ❻), which provides comfortable accommodation with a pool and good food.

With a Queensland Parks and Wildlife Service **camping permit** (see p.54), you can **camp** in any of the marked camping zones along the eastern foreshore, or if you need tank water, showers, toilets and barbecue areas, use the main **national park campsites** at Central Station, Dundubara and Waddy Point or the smaller sites at Lake Boomanjin, Wathumba and Ungowa. There are also **privately run campsites** at *Frasers at Cathedral Beach* (℡07 4127 9177; camping A\$20–30, cabin ❸) and the nicer *Dilli Village* (see above).

Around Central Station

Most people get their bearings by making their first stop at **Central Station**, an old logging depot with campsite, telephone and information hut under some monstrous bunya pines in the middle of the island, halfway between the landing at Wanggoolba Creek and Eurong on the east coast. From the station, take a stroll along **Wanggoolba Creek**'s upper reaches, a magical, sandy-bottomed stream so clear that it's hard at first to see the water as it runs across the forest floor. It's a largely botanic walk from here to **Pile Valley**, where satinay trees humble you to insignificance as they reach 60m up to the sky. The trees produce a very dense timber, durable enough to be used as sidings on the Suez Canal, and are consequently in such demand that the trees on Fraser were already almost logged out before conservationists intervened; felling continued right up to the early 1990s.

There are several freshwater **lakes** around Central Station, all close enough to walk to and all along main roads. A nine-kilometre track leads north to **Lake McKenzie**, the most popular on the island and often very crowded: ringed by white sand, with clear water reflecting a blue sky, it's perfect for swimming and a wonderful place to spend the day. Eight kilometres to the south, **Birrabeen** is quieter and mostly hemmed in by trees, while **Boomanjin**, 8km further, is open and perched in a basin above the island's water-table – there's a national park campsite here (see p.54 for booking details), or it's not too far to the coast at *Dilli Village* if you want to spend the night in the area.

Seventy-Five Mile Beach

East-coast **Seventy-Five Mile Beach** is Fraser's main road and camping ground, and one of the busiest places on the island. Vehicles hurtle along, pedestrians and anglers hug the surf, and tents dot the foredunes; this is what beckons the crowds over from the mainland. Coming from Central Station, you exit

Fraser's **dingoes** are thought to have lived on the island for over two thousand years; as they have never had the opportunity to inter-breed with domestic dogs, they are considered Australia's purest strain. They used to be a common sight but are becoming more and more elusive; after one killed a child in 2001, any dingoes that frequented public areas were culled, and the Queensland Parks and Wildlife Service stepped up its efforts to educate visitors in dingo-aware behaviour. Even now, it's a battle to dissuade unthinking visitors from feeding the animals or leaving food, such as fish scraps, as litter. Rangers have been doing all they can to re-instill a healthy fear of humans in the dingoes, including shouting at pups who seem to be getting "too friendly", and even pelting them with slingshots. This seemingly harsh behaviour is based on sound conservation principles: the dingoes' greatest chance of survival lies in self-sufficiency, and human-dingo conflict situations are unlikely to arise if both parties keep a respectful distance.

As things stand, you'll see plenty of "Be dingo-safe" notices around the island, but few dingoes. If you do encounter some, keep your distance; if approached, behave assertively by standing tall and shouting or clapping your hands above your head, then back off calmly; don't wave your arms about or run. Dingoes are closely related to wolves and have a similar pack-mentality; they tend to respect signals of dominance, but may attack humans who display submissive behaviour such as offering food. Despite the misleadingly scrawny appearance of some individuals, the island has ample natural food supplies for the colony, so don't feed them, ever.

onto the beach at **Eurong**, a small complex of lodges and shops; 6km north, **Hammerstone Blow** is slowly engulfing **Lake Wabby**, a small but deep patch of tannin-stained blue below the dunes with excellent swimming potential – another century and it will be gone. Another 10km along at **Rainbow Gorge**, a short trail runs between two sandblows, through a hot, silent desert landscape where sandblasted trees emerge denuded by their ordeal. Incredibly, a dismal spring seeps water into the valley where the sand swallows it up; "upstream" are the gorge's stubby, eroded red fingers.

Another five kilometres brings you to **Happy Valley**, another source of supplies and beds, and then after the same distance again you cross picturesque **Eli Creek**, where water splashes briskly between briefly verdant banks before spilling into the sea. Sand-filtered, it's the nicest swimming spot on the island, though icy-cold. Back on the beach, another 4km brings you to the *Maheno* **shipwreck**, beached in 1935 and now a skeleton almost consumed by the elements, and the start of a line of multicoloured sand cliffs known as the **Cathedrals**. About 5km up the beach from here is the **Dundubara campsite**, behind which is the tiring, hot four-kilometre walk up Wungul Sandblow through what may as well be the Sahara; turn around at the top, though, and the glaring grey dune-scape is set off by distant views of a rich blue sea.

Approximately 20km north from Dundubara, **Indian Head** is a rare – and pretty tall – rocky outcrop, the anchor around which the island probably formed originally. It's not a hard walk to the top, and on a sunny day the rewards are likely to include views down into the surf full of dolphins, sharks and other large fish chasing each other; in season, you'll certainly see pods of whales, too, breaching, blowing jets of spray, or just lying on their backs, slapping the water with outstretched fins. From here there's a tricky bit of soft sand to negotiate for a final nine-kilometre run around to **Champagne Pools**, an attractive cluster of shallow rock pools right above the surf line, which mark as far north as vehicles are allowed to travel.

The interior, west coast and far north

Fraser's wooded **interior**, a real contrast to the busy coast and popular southern lakes, gets relatively few visitors. It encloses **Yidney Scrub**, the only major stand of rainforest left on the island. While the name may not conjure up a very appealing image, the trees are majestic and include towering kauri pines. There's a circuit through Yidney from Happy Valley, taking in the Boomerang Lakes and Lake Allom on the long way back to the beach near the *Maheno*. Allom, a small lake surrounded by pines and cycads, is completely different in character from its flashy southern cousins.

The island's **northwest coast** is a mix of mangrove swamp and treacherously soft beaches, both largely inaccessible to vehicles. Rough tracks to this part of the island lead off the road that crosses from Happy Valley to the minor ferry terminus at Moon Point.

Bundaberg and the Coral Coast

Around 50km off the Bruce Highway from the pretty, heritage town of **Childers** or from Gin Gin, **Bundaberg**, close to the coast and surrounded by canefields and fruit farms, is famous for its **rum**. Such is the scale of the surrounding area's agricultural operations that those wanting farm **work** are virtually guaranteed seasonal employment, particularly between February and November, picking avocados, tomatoes, snow peas and zucchini. You can fly from Bundaberg to the southernmost Barrier Reef cay, **Lady Elliot Island**, which offers a resort and good scuba diving, or head east to the **CORAL COAST**, an important place for **marine turtles**, who mass in huge numbers every summer to lay their eggs on the beaches: the best place to witness their nocturnal activities is **Mon Repos**, northeast of town.

Childers

On the Bruce Highway about 60km north of Maryborough on the way to Bundaberg, **CHILDERS** is a very attractive, one-horse highway town, with a high street lined with well-preserved Queenslanders with ornate verandas, and shops seemingly transported from another era. Sadly, it's also known for the terrible **fire** that burned down the old *Palace Backpackers* in 2000, killing fifteen people. The town has moved on, however, and the site of the tragedy has been rebuilt as a tasteful, low-key memorial and **visitor information centre** (72 Churchill St; ☏07 4126 3886; Mon–Fri 9am–4pm, Sat & Sun 9am–3pm).

Childers' core of heritage-listed buildings offers an excuse to pull up and stretch your legs; these include the photogenic *Federal Hotel*, a wooden pub built in 1907, and the musty, bottle-filled **Childers Pharmaceutical Museum** (Mon–Fri 8.30am–4pm, Sat 8.30am–noon; A\$4). Just west of Childers at Apple Tree Creek, **Flying High Bird Habitat** (daily 10am–3pm; A\$18, child A\$8; ☏07 4126 3777) is a huge aviary with just about every type of Australian parrot and finch zipping around, squawking or chewing the furnishings.

If you're after **farm work**, it's available from March to November, sometimes continuing to January; *Sugar Bowl Caravan Park* (☏07 4126 1521, ⓦwww .sugarbowlchilders.com; cabin ❷; weekly rates for workers: camping A\$90, bunk in bunkhouse A\$120), on the Bruce Highway just west of town, a spacious site with a pool but not much shade, can help with contacts and transport. Other **places to stay** include *Palace Motel* at 72 Churchill St (☏07 4126 2244,

7

@www.palacemotel.com.au; ❷), a new-build on the restored site of the old *Palace Backpackers*, which has tidy rooms and a small pool; and *Hotel Childers* at 59 Churchill St (☏07 4126 1719; ❷), a great option, with very cute "country-style" rooms and a spacious beer garden. It also serves the best **meals** in Childers; the *Laurel Tree Cottage*, 89 Churchill St, at the Bundaberg end of town, comes a close second, with traditional fare including delightful pies. Childers is also the home of Mammino, producers of fabulous macadamia nut fudge and handmade ice cream (115 Lucketts Rd; daily 9am–5pm).

Bundaberg

BUNDABERG, or "**Bundy**" as it's more affectionately known, is synonymous with rum cocktails throughout Australia and if you believe their advertising pitch, the town's **Bundaberg Rum distillery** on Whittred Street, about 2km east of the centre on the way to Bargara (visitor centre Mon–Fri 9am–4pm, Sat & Sun 9am–3pm; tours Mon–Fri 10am–3pm, Sat & Sun 10am–2pm; A$10; ☏07 4131 2999), accounts for half the country's annual rum consumption. A distillery tour allows fans to wallow in the overpowering pungency of raw molasses, and ends, of course, with a free sample – though you probably won't need to drink much after inhaling the fumes in the vat sheds, where electronic devices are prohibited in case a spark ignites the vapour. Another famous local company, also called **Bundaberg**, brews and mixes soft drinks; they, too, have a visitor centre, in a building shaped like a giant ginger beer barrel (147 Bargara Rd; ☏07 4154 5480 or 1800 629 923; Mon–Sat 9am–4.30pm, Sun 10am–3pm;).

Bundaberg town centre is a quiet, humdrum place; its handful of highlights include an interesting **Arts Centre** on Barolin St (Mon–Fri 10am–3pm, Sat & Sun 11am–3pm), showcasing local painters and ceramicists; a few heritage-listed buildings; and a museum to **Bert Hinkler**. Flying 1270km from Sydney to Bundaberg in 1921, Hinkler set a world record for continuous flight in his flimsy wire-and-canvas Baby Avro, demonstrating its potential as transport for remote areas and so encouraging the formation of Qantas the following year. In 1983, the house where Hinkler lived at the time of his death was transported to Bundaberg and rebuilt in the Botanic Gardens as the **Hinkler House Museum**, 4km from the centre over the Burnett Bridge towards Gin Gin, sharing its desirable surroundings with a Sugar Museum, Historical Museum and a steam train (all daily 10am–4pm; A$5, child A$2 for the house; ☏07 4152 0222). Outside the house, landscaped gardens flank ponds where Hinkler was supposedly inspired to design aircraft by watching ibises in flight.

Bundaberg is not known for its diving, but, unusually for Queensland, it has an artificial reef to explore – **Cochrane Reef**, near Elliott Heads, southeast of town. Created by a local fishing and scuba diving association, by planting a motley assembly of scrap including planes, barges, prisms and pipes on the ocean floor, it is an impressive structure, which has gradually acquired a covering of coral and sponges, attracting a good variety of fish. Dive companies running trips there include Aqua Scuba (☏07 4153 5761, @www.aquascuba.com.au).

Practicalities

Bundaberg lies along the south bank of the **Burnett River**, about 15km from the coast. **Bourbong Street**, the main thoroughfare, runs parallel to the river and is where you'll find banks and the post office, as well as the **tourist office**, at no. 271 (daily 9am–5pm; ☏07 4153 8888, @www.bundabergregion.info). There's a good Internet café on Barolin Street, just north of Bourbong. The **bus**

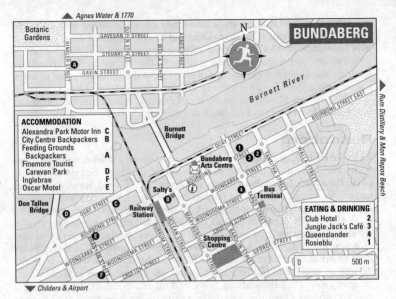

▲ Agnes Water & 1770

BUNDABERG

Botanic Gardens

GAVEGAN STREET

QUEEN STREET

STEUART STREET

AGNES STREET

WILLA STREET

HINKLER AVENUE

GAVIN STREET

N

Burnett River

BOURBONG STREET EAST

Rum Distillery & Mon Repos Beach

ACCOMMODATION
Alexandra Park Motor Inn **C**
City Centre Backpackers **B**
Feeding Grounds
  Backpackers **A**
Finemore Tourist
  Caravan Park **D**
Inglebrae **F**
Oscar Motel **E**

Burnett
Bridge

QUAY STREET

Bundaberg
Arts Centre

TANTITHA STREET

WALLA STREET

Salty's

BOURBONG

WOONGARRA STREET

Bus
Terminal

Don Tallon
Bridge

QUAY STREET

Railway
Station

BOURBONG STREET

WOONGARRA STREET

WOONDOOMA STREET

BURRUM STREET

McLEAN STREET

MARYBOROUGH STREET

TARGO STREET

CROFTON STREET

BARLIN STREET

Shopping
Centre

GEORGE STREET

EATING & DRINKING
Club Hotel **2**
Jungle Jack's Café **3**
Queenslander **4**
Rosieblu **1**

0   500 m

▼ Childers & Airport

7

terminal is on Targo Street, with the **railway station** 500m west on McLean Street. The **airport** (BDB), for departures to Lady Elliot Island amongst other places, is 4km from the centre on the Childers Road. **Moving on**, trains and long-distance buses – Greyhound (T 13 20 30) and Premier (T 13 34 10) – head up the coast to Gladstone and south to Childers and beyond; Greyhound also runs to Agnes Water daily.

Accommodation

Most of Bundaberg's **motels** are strung out along Bourbong Street and Takalvang Street, which becomes the Childers Road, west of the centre. The city's **hostels** cater for itinerant workers, and can put you in touch with local farms. There are **campsites** on the Burnett River and on Mon Repos Beach (see p.498).

Alexandra Park Motor Inn 66 Quay St
T 07 4152 7255. A mock-Queenslander-style place with huge rooms: dated but comfortable. **④**

City Centre Backpackers 216 Bourbong St, near the train station T 07 4151 3501. Workers' hostel, fairly central but on a busy, noisy main road. Bunk in shared room A$25, private double **②**

Feeding Grounds Backpackers 4 Hinkler Ave
T 07 4152 3659, W www.footprintsadventures .com.au. A much more relaxed place to stay than the other backpackers' in town; runs turtle tours in Jan. Bunk in quad room A$25.

Finemore Tourist Caravan Park Quay St
T 07 4151 3663. Tidy site for tents, caravans and campervans, in a pleasant location overlooking the Burnett River. Camping A$16–18, cabin **②**

Inglebrae 17 Branyan St T 07 4154 4003,
W www.inglebrae.com. Elegant B&B in a homely, 100-year-old Queenslander, decorated in classic country-house style. **③**

Oscar Motel 252 Bourbong St T 07 4152 3666,
W www.oscarmotel.com.au. Motel just west of the centre, with very reasonable prices for good-sized rooms with Internet access, plus a pool and barbecue area. **③**

Eating and drinking

For **eating**, *Jungle Jack's Café* on Bourbong Street opens at 6.30am for big breakfasts and all-day fry-ups, while *Rosieblu*, also on Bourbong Street, opens at 8.30am and rustles up healthier options including deli-style sandwiches at lunchtime. *Club Hotel*, on the corner of Bourbong and Tantitha streets, is a traditional pub that's had a contemporary makeover on the inside, serving filling counter meals for lunch and dinner. *Queenslander*, a brash **bar** on Targo Street, pulls in young backpackers and local workers.

Mon Repos Conservation Park and the turtle rookery

Mon Repos Conservation Park is on the Coral Coast 15km east of Bundaberg, reached by initially following Bourbong Street out of town towards the port and looking out for small brown signposts for the beach (or larger ones for the *Turtle Sands Tourist Park*). Once the site of a French telegraph link to New Caledonia, today Mon Repos' reputation rests on being Australia's most accessible **loggerhead turtle rookery**. From November to February, female loggerheads clamber laboriously up the beaches after dark, excavate a pit with their hind flippers in the sand above the high-tide mark, and lay about a hundred parchment-shelled eggs. During the eight-week incubation period, the ambient temperature of the surrounding sand will determine the sex of the entire clutch; 28.5°C is the change-over point between male and female. On hatching, the endearing, rubbery-brown youngsters stay buried in the nest until after dark, when they dig themselves out en masse and head for the sea. In season, about a dozen turtles lay each night, and watching the young leave the nest and race towards the water like clockwork toys is both comical and touching. Your chances of seeing both laying and hatching in one evening are best during January, but hatching may continue into early April. The loggerhead's future doesn't look too bright at present: since 1980, Mon Repos' rookery population has halved, most likely due to net-trawling offshore.

The Queensland Parks and Wildlife Service at Mon Repos runs **guided tours** (bookings ℡07 4153 8888; A$8.70, child A$4.60) at 7pm each evening

▲ Turtle hatchling, Mon Repos Conservation Park

from November to late March, when the beach is otherwise off limits between 6pm and 6am; most lodgings can book you on a tour-and-transport package. For **accommodation** at Mon Repos Beach, the first-rate 🔱 *Turtle Sands Tourist Park* (℡ 07 4159 2340, 🌐 www.turtlesands.com.au; camping A$20–22, cabin ➊, villa ➋) is right next to the turtle rookery and a kilometre of beach.

Lady Elliot Island

The Great Barrier Reef's southernmost outpost, **Lady Elliot Island** is a two-kilometre-square patch of casuarina and pandanus trees stabilizing a bed of coral rubble, sand and – as with all the southern cays – a thick layer of **guano**, courtesy of the generations of birds that have roosted here. The elegant **lighthouse** on Lady Elliot's west side was built in 1866 after an extraordinary number of wrecks on the reef; on average, one vessel a year still manages to come to grief here. Wailing shearwaters and the occasional suicide of lighthouse staff didn't endear Lady Elliot to early visitors, but a low-key **resort** and excellent reef have now turned the island into a popular escape.

Shearwaters aside, there's a good deal of **birdlife** on the island; residents include thousands of black noddies and bridled terns, along with much larger frigate birds and a few rare **red-tailed tropicbirds** – a white, gull-like bird with a red beak and wire-like tail – which nest under bushes on the foreshore. Both loggerhead and green **turtles** frequent the beaches, too, and in a good summer there are scores laying their eggs here each night. The main reason to come to Lady Elliot, however, is to go **scuba diving**: the best spots are out from the lighthouse, but check daily currents with the dive staff at the resort first. The Blowhole is a favourite with divers, with a descent into a cavern (keep an eye out for the "gnomefish" here), and there's also the 1999 wreck of the yacht *Severence* to explore. You've a good chance of encountering harmless leopard sharks, sea snakes, barracuda, turtles and gigantic manta rays wherever you go. Shore dives cost A$35 per person, boat dives A$50 and night dives A$70, plus gear rental at up to A$40 per day.

Lady Elliot can only be reached **by air**, on daily flights with Seair from Bundaberg or Hervey Bay (overnight return A$219; morning tour plus lunch and transfers: A$275/child A$146 from Bundaberg or Hervey Bay; A$599/A$330 from Maroochydore; A$699/A$349 from Brisbane and the Gold Coast; book through your resort). **Accommodation** is at the comfortable, eco-friendly 🔱 *Lady Elliot Island Resort* (℡ 1800 072 200, 🌐 www.ladyelliot.com.au; safari tent ➌, room ➐, suite ➒; all rates half board), which has basic four-person safari-tent-style cabins as well as motel-like rooms, and suites with ocean views. The focus here is firmly on the natural environment, with gadget-free rooms (none have TVs, radios or phones and most are not air-conditioned). As well as underwater activities, there's a regular programme of bird walks and glass-bottom-boat tours, plus turtle spotting in season.

For advice on **swimming** in northern Queensland's coastal waters during the "stinger season", see p.47.

The Discovery Coast

On the coast 122km north of Bundaberg and 125km south of Gladstone, the tiny **DISCOVERY COAST** settlements of **Agnes Water** and nearby **Town of 1770** mark the place where Captain Cook first set foot in Queensland on 24 May, 1770; today, the locals re-enact the event in an annual community festival of parties and parades. For the most part, this stretch of coast is a pretty, chronically quiet resort area with a cul-de-sac atmosphere, but a spate of holiday-home development means things might be set to change. Natural attractions include pockets of mangrove, fan palm and paperbark wetlands, and Queensland's northernmost **surf beach** at Agnes Water. Town of 1770 is the closest mainland point to **Lady Musgrave Island** and the reefs nearby, and there are regular boat trips for divers and snorkellers. Greyhound Australia (see p.35) operates a **daily bus** between Bundaberg and Agnes Water, stopping on Spring Road.

AGNES WATER consists of a service station, a surf shop, post office and supermarket, a few cafés, several clusters of holiday accommodation and, on the way into town, the *Agnes Water Tavern* (T07 4974 9468), an upbeat country pub that does excellent counter meals. The town is fronted by a stunning, sweeping **beach** backed by sand dunes, and there are some delightful coastal walks in the area, including the three-kilometre trail from Agnes Headland along the wooded ridge to Springs Beach, which is best reached from the museum on Spring Road. **Accommodation** includes *Mantra Pavillions Mirage on 1770* on Beaches Village Circuit, halfway to Town of 1770 (T07 4902 1000, Wwww.pavillionsresort.com.au; ⑤–⑦), with fabulously spacious new one-, two- or three-bed apartments right behind the windy beach; *Sandcastles 1770* (T07 4974 9428, Wwww.sandcastles1770.com.au; ④) on Spring Road, featuring nicely designed suites and apartments in landscaped gardens; and *Mango Tree Motel* on Agnes Street (T07 4974 9132, Wwww .mangotreemotel.com; ❸), with simple motel rooms close to the beach. Popular with young travellers are *1770 Backpackers* (T07 4974 9849 or 1800 121 770, Wwww.the1770backpackers.com; bunk in shared room A$25, private double ❷), a funky but cramped hostel on Captain Cook Drive, and the cool-by-nature *Cool Bananas* on Springs Road (T07 4974 7660 or 1800 227 660, Wwww.coolbananas.net.au; bunk in shared room A$25). Scooter Roo on Bicentennial Drive (T07 4974 7697, Wwww.scooterroo tours.com) has **cars and scooters for rent**, and hosts fun scooter tours.

Town of 1770 is even smaller, occupying the foreshore of a narrow promontory some 6km to the north. At the end of the road is windswept Round Hill, with exposed walking trails and coastal views, though the main reason to come here is to take a **day-trip to the reef**. Boats leave from the marina: *Spirit of 1770* (T1800 631 770, Wwww.spiritof1770.com.au; A$145, plus A$50 per dive, child A$70) takes 75 minutes to reach **Lady Musgrave Island**, allowing up to five hours to explore the island, reef and deep-water lagoon. At 1770, **places to stay** include *The Beach Shacks* (T07 4974 9463, Wwww.1770beachshacks.com; ⑤), which has four beautiful and comfortable pole homes with a tropical island feel, facing the ocean; a budget alternative are the simple cabins and tent sites in spacious, wooded grounds at *Captain Cook Holiday Village* (T07 4974 9219, Wwww.1770holidayvillage.com; camping A$24–27, cabin ❷), which has a bistro, store and pool. For **eating**, *Saltwater Café* on Captain Cook Drive, overlooking the beach, does excellent fish and chips and pizzas for around A$20, and lights a campfire on chilly winter nights. There's a lively **bar** next door.

Whether you're a novice snorkeller or a highly experienced scuba diver, little can prepare you for the thrill of your first underwater glimpse of the **Great Barrier Reef** – drifting over colourful coral and perhaps coming face to face with starfish, Christmas tree worms, lugubrious-looking turtles or fidgety clownfish – in the knowledge that the section you're exploring is just one scrap of a system that extends for a colossal 2300km. The Barrier Reef, which is the largest living structure on earth and the largest World Heritage area, is to Australia what rolling savannas and game parks are to Africa: a fragile wilderness of outstanding ecological drama and diversity. There's so little relation to life above the surface that distinctions normally taken for granted – such as that between animal, plant and plain rock – seem blurred, while the respective roles of observer and observed are constantly challenged by curious fish peering at you or even following you about.

Beginning with **Lady Elliot Island**, northeast of Bundaberg, and extending north to New Guinea, the Reef follows the outer edge of Australia's continental plate, running closer to land as it moves north: in the Gladstone area, the main structures are over 300km offshore, but near Cairns, the reef is just 50km away. Far from being a continuous, unified barrier, the Reef consists of around three thousand discrete sections of varying type. The greater part is made up of an intricate maze of individual, disconnected patch reefs, which – especially in the southern sections – sometimes act as anchors for the formation of low sand islands known as **cays**. In the north, sections form long ribbons. Adding to the overall picture are the fringing reefs surrounding continental islands (which were once part of the mainland).

All of it, however, was built by one animal: the tiny **coral polyp**. Simple organisms, related to sea anemones, polyps grow together like building blocks to create modular colonies – **corals** – which form the framework of the reef's ecology by providing food, shelter and hunting grounds for larger, more mobile species. Around their walls and canyons flow a bewildering assortment of creatures: large rays and turtles glide effortlessly by, fish dodge into nooks and between coral branches, snails sift the sand for edibles, and brightly coloured nudibranchs dance above rocks.

The Reef is a national park (the largest tropical marine park in the world), administered by the **Marine Parks Authority**, which has designated separate zones in each area for uses such as fishing, tourism and research. It also battles against – or at least attempts to gauge – the effects of overfishing, pollution, agricultural runoff, environmental fluctuations and tourism. All these things are beginning to have a serious effect on the Reef, with many formerly colourful coral gardens reduced to weed-strewn rubble. Don't let this put you off going, though – the Reef is still unquestionably worth seeing, and if the government realizes how much tourism will be lost if the Reef dies, they may do more to protect it.

Visiting the Reef

Since the Reef lies some distance off shore, access is usually by **boat**, though some sections can be reached by **light aircraft** or **helicopter**: Lady Elliot Island has an airstrip, and there are floating helipads in a few spots. By far the most-used access points are Cairns (see p.590) and Port Douglas (see p.602) in northern Queensland, followed by Airlie Beach and the Whitsundays in central Queensland (see p.514). While there are plenty of day-trips to choose from, giving you anything between two and four hours to explore one or more sites, by far the most satisfying way to experience the underwater environment, if you're serious about diving and snorkelling, is to book a **live-aboard** trip lasting several days. Staying out at sea overnight, you get the chance to travel to the less-frequented sites of the Outer Reef and be in the water at arguably the most interesting times of day: dawn, when the fish are most active, and after dark, when the "night shift" of nocturnal species emerge from their daytime hiding places.

Diving and other ways of seeing the Reef

Scuba diving is the best way to get to grips with the Reef, and **dive courses** are on offer right along the coast. Four or five days is the minimum needed to safely cover the course work – two or three days pool and theory, two days at sea – and secure you the all-important C-card that must be shown each time you dive. The quality of training and the price you pay vary; before signing up, ask others who have taken courses about specific businesses' general attitudes and whether they just seem concerned about processing as many students in as short a time as possible – you need to know that any problems you may encounter while training will be taken seriously. Another consideration is whether you ever plan to dive again: if this seems unlikely, **resort dives** (a single dive with an instructor) will set you back only A\$85 or so, and are usually available on day-trips to the Reef and island resorts. **Qualified divers** can save on rental costs by bringing some gear along; tanks and weightbelts are always covered in dive packages but anything else may be extra.

Snorkelling is a good alternative to diving, particularly since it gives you access to the very shallow waters where the sunlight is brightest and the colours most vivid: you can pick up the basics in five minutes. If you think you'll do a fair amount, buy your own mask, snorkel and fins – they're not dramatically expensive – as rental gear usually comes from the most basic range. Look for a silicone rubber and toughened glass mask and ask the shop staff to show you how to find a good fit. If getting wet just isn't for you, try **glass-bottomed boats** or semi-submersibles.

Reef hazards

Stories of shark attacks, savage octopuses and giant clams all make good press, but are mostly the stuff of fiction. However, there are a few things at the Reef capable of putting a dampener on your holiday, and it makes sense to be careful. The best protection is simply to **look and not touch**, as nothing is actively out to harm you.

Seasickness and **sunburn** are the two most common problems to afflict visitors to the Reef, so take precautions. Coral and shell **cuts** become badly infected if not treated immediately by removing any fragments and dousing with antiseptic. Some corals can also give you a nasty **sting**, but this is more a warning to keep away in future than something to worry about seriously. Animals to avoid tend to be small. Conical **cone shells** are home to a fish-eating snail armed with a poisonous barb, which has caused fatalities. Don't pick them up – there is no "safe" end to hold them. Similarly, the shy, small, **blue-ringed octopus** has a fatal bite and should never be handled. **Stonefish** are camouflaged so that they're almost impossible to distinguish from a rock or lump of coral. They spend their days immobile, protected from attack by a series of poisonous spines along their back. If you tread on one, you'll end up in hospital – an excellent argument against reef-walking. Of the larger animals, **rays** are flattened fish with a sharp tail-spine capable of causing deep wounds – don't swim close over sandy floors where they hide. At the Reef, the most commonly encountered **sharks** are the black-tip and white-tip varieties, and the bottom-dwelling, aptly named carpet shark, or wobbegong – all of these are inoffensive unless hassled.

In general, snorkellers and divers are more of a hazard to the reef than vice versa. In order to **minimize damage**, you should exercise buoyancy control, be very careful not to kick the coral with your fins, and never stand on or hold onto reefs; even if you don't break off branches, you'll certainly crush the delicate polyps.

Reef tax

The Marine Parks Authority levies an Environmental Management Charge (EMC; currently A\$5 per person per day) commonly referred to as **reef tax**, to help fund monitoring and management of human impact on the Reef. On most tours and boat trips, the reef tax is not included in the cost of the tour and you'll be asked to pay once you're on board.

Eurimbula National Park, on the west side of 1770 across Round Hill Creek, abounds with birdlife. You can **tour** the region aboard *The Larc* **amphibious bus** (☎07/4974 9422, ⓦwww.1770larctours.com.au; full day A$115, child A$70, sunset cruise A$30/A$15), which spends the day exploring the remote coastline. For 4WD road access to the park, head 10.5km back towards Miriam Vale from Agnes Water, where you'll see the track and national-park sign to the north of the road. You can **bushcamp** about 15km inside the park in the dunes behind Bustard Beach, but beware of sand flies.

Lady Musgrave Island

Lady Musgrave Island is another tiny, low sand cay covered in soft-leaved **pisonia trees**, which hosts the usual throng of roosting birdlife and (in season) breeding green and loggerhead turtles. Unusually, the cay is ringed by a coral wall that forms a large turquoise **lagoon**. Diving inside the lagoon here is safe but pretty tame (though snorkelling is good); outside the wall is more exciting. Relatively easy, inexpensive access means that Lady Musgrave is the best of the southern cays on which to **camp**; the QPWS site is pleasantly shaded by casuarina trees but there are **no facilities**, so make sure you bring absolutely everything you need with you, including all camping and cooking gear, a fuel stove, food and more water than you need (at least five litres a day). Up to forty people are allowed to camp here at any one time (see p.54 for booking information), but the whole island is off-limits during the peak of the turtle- and seabird- nesting season (from Australia Day, 26 Jan, to Easter), when you're not allowed to land.

The only way over to Lady Musgrave is aboard 1770 Barrier Reef Cruises' *Spirit of 1770*, which runs out from Town of 1770 daily for snorkelling and scuba diving in the lagoon (see p.499). The crew take out campers, too (A$290, child A$140 return), and offer scuba-gear hire; they'll arrange for fresh provisions to be brought over if you're planning a long stay. There's free parking at the marina; alternatively, 1770 Barrier Reef Cruises can organize secure parking for a moderate charge.

Gladstone and around

Around 90km up Highway 1 from the Miriam Vale turn-off, **GLADSTONE** is a busy port and industrial hub, home to cement works and the Boyne Island processing plant, which refines aluminium from ore mined at Weipa on the Cape York Peninsula. Glaringly hot, there's no reason to visit unless you're trying to reach **Heron Island** or **Wilson Island**. If you've time to spare en route, the **Tondoon Botanic Gardens**, about 7km south of town (April–Sept Mon–Fri 8.30am–5.30pm, Sat & Sun 7am–5.30pm; Oct–March Mon–Fri 9am–6pm, Sat & Sun 7am–6pm; free), comprise a partly wild spread of wetlands, woodlands, forests and native shrubs, all expertly laid out – you'll probably clock up wallabies and birdlife here, too.

The main strip is **Goondoon Street**, where there's a semi-pedestrian mall – just the usual high-street shops, post office and banks – plus a couple of hotels and motels. You'll find a helpful **tourist office** (Mon–Fri 8.30am–5pm, Sat & Sun 9am–5pm) inside the ferry terminal at the marina, about 2km north of the centre on Bryan Jordan Drive. The long-distance bus stop and the train station are both close to the centre; Gladstone Airport (GLT) is a ten-minute drive out of town. *Gladstone Reef Hotel*, 38 Goondoon St (☎07 4972 1000; ❸), has ordinary **motel rooms** and good views from a rooftop pool, while *Gladstone Backpackers* on 12 Rollo St (☎07 4972 5744, bunk in shared room A$25, private double ❷) has typical hostel facilities and is close to the river. Places to **eat** on Goondoon Street Mall include *Scotties*, 46 Goondoon St (☎07 4972 4711), which offers contemporary cooking at gourmet prices.

Heron Island and Wilson Island

Famous for its diving, **Heron Island** is small enough to walk around in an hour, with half the cay occupied by a comfortable, eco-friendly **resort** and **research station**, and the rest covered in groves of pandanus, coconuts and shady pisonias. You can literally step off the beach and into the reef's maze of coral, or swim along the shallow walls looking for action. The eastern edges of the lagoon are accessible for snorkelling at any time, but **scuba diving** must be arranged through the resort, which charges A$55 for a standard dive and A$80 to venture out at night; you can also spend a day touring some more isolated reefs for A$320 a person – equipment is extra. A drift along the wall facing Wistari reef to Heron Bommie covers about everything you're likely to encounter. The coral isn't that good but the amount of life is astonishing: tiny boxfish hide under ledges; turtles, cowries, wobbegong, reef sharks, moray eels, butterfly cod and octopuses secrete themselves among the coral; manta rays soar majestically; and larger reef fish gape vacantly as you drift past. The bommie itself makes for first-rate **snorkelling**, with an interesting swim-through if your lungs are up to it, while the Tenements along the reef's northern edge are good for bigger game – including sharks.

There's a price to pay for all this natural wonder – namely, no day-trips and no camping. 🍴 *Voyages Heron Island* (☎07 4972 9055, ⓦ www.heronisland .com; ❼, suite ❾) is excellent, though; its rates, coupled with the ferry charge (A$200 return) are pretty steep, but not out of line with Queensland's other island resorts. **Ferries** leave from Gladstone Marina up to three times a day – there's free parking here, or a car lockup (A$12 a day) operated by the tackle shop (8am–5pm) – and there's also the option of flying in by **helicopter** with Australian Helicopters (☎07 4978 1177, ⓦ www.austheli.com).

Heron's sister cay, **Wilson Island**, is even tinier and more exclusive: 🍴 *Voyages Wilson Island* (reservations ☎1300 134 044, ⓦ www.wilsonisland.com.au; ❽) is a delightful little desert-island eco-retreat hosting no more than twelve guests at a time in supreme, but elegantly rustic and casual, comfort. Again, you can snorkel straight off the beach. A full-board stay in a safari tent costs A$990 per night for two, including the return boat transfers from Heron Island (40min each way), with a minimum two-night booking, and no children allowed. You can watch the nocturnal activities of marine turtles on the beach during the nesting and hatching season, but the island is closed in February while the resident seabirds are rearing their chicks.

Rockhampton and the Capricorn Coast

Right on the Tropic of Capricorn, 108km north of Gladstone and 336km south of Mackay, **ROCKHAMPTON** is a substantial, spread-out town; impressive Victorian quayside buildings line the south bank of the **Fitzroy River**, and grand, century-old Queenslanders hog the best views – and the best chance of a breeze in the stifling summer months – in the hills on the south side of town.

Outside the centre, the highway is flanked by a faceless sprawl of motels, tyre dealers, workshops and industrial units.

The city was founded after a false gold rush in 1858 left hundreds of miners stranded at a depot 40km inland on the banks of the sluggish, humid river, and their rough camp was adopted by local stockmen as a convenient port. The iron trelliswork and sandstone buildings fronting the river recall the balmy 1890s, when money was pouring into the city from a prosperous cattle industry and nearby gold and copper mines, which went on to fund the fledgling BP company. Both the meat and the mining industries have suffered serious dips in past decades but today are in good financial health, which means Rockhampton is enjoying an upswing. All this money hasn't bought much class, however: you'll see plenty of wide boys roaring through town in custom-trimmed cars, and, with the exception of a small riverside art gallery, the city's social and cultural scene is sparse. Bearing this in mind, it is best seen as a springboard for the adjacent **Capricorn Coast**, which includes **Emu Park**, **Yeppoon** and **Great Keppel Island**.

Arrival and information

Rockhampton is divided by the Fitzroy River, with all services clustered directly south of its two bridges along Quay and East streets; the Bruce Highway runs right through town. Greyhound and Premier **buses** (see p.35) stop at the service station on the highway just north of Fitzroy Bridge; **local buses** to or from Yeppoon and the Capricorn Coast set down, amongst other places, along Bolsover Street. The **railway station** is 1km south of the centre on Murray Street, and **Rockhampton airport** (ROK) is 4km to the southwest at the end of Hunter Street – Jetstar, Qantas and Virgin Blue fly in from Brisbane, and Tiger Airways flies four times a week from Melbourne (see p.35). **Banks**, the post office and other services,

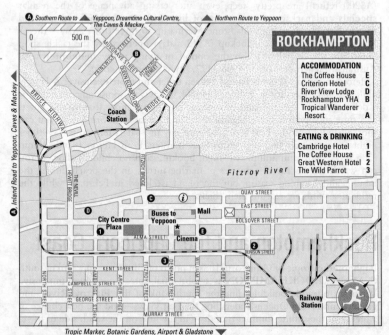

including Internet cafés, are mostly along East Street. The **tourist office** is in the old riverside customs house on Quay Street (℡07 4922 5339; Mon–Fri 8.30am–4.30pm, Sat & Sun 9am–4pm). Recent reports of nasty incidents involving gangs of teenagers are unfortunately too numerous to ignore; there's no need for paranoia, but do follow local advice and don't walk alone at night.

Accommodation

If your only reason for being in Rockhampton is to get to **Great Keppel**, there's little reason to stay over: it's easy enough to catch a local bus to the ferry dock at Rosslyn Bay (see p.507), and nearby Yeppoon and Emu Park are breezier places to spend a night. For a rural alternative within driving distance, there's **farmstay accommodation** at Myella (℡07 4998 1290, ⓦwww .myella.com; full board ❸), 124km southwest of town, a working farm that you can explore by motorbike or on horseback.

The Coffee House 51 William St ℡07 4927 5722, ⓦwww.coffeehouse .com.au. With smart new rooms and apartments, and a good café-bistro downstairs, this is the pick of the city's accommodation choices. ❺–❻
Criterion Hotel Quay St (corner of Fitzroy St) ℡07 4922 1225, ⓦwww.thecriterion.com.au. Historic pub with reasonably priced though often noisy rooms and suites overlooking the river. ❶, suite ❷–❹
River View Lodge 48 Victoria Parade ℡07 4922 2077. Simple rooms with shared facilities in a pleasant and central location. Bunk in shared room A$20, private double ❶

Rockhampton YHA 60 MacFarlane St ℡07 4927 5288, ⓦwww.yha.com.au. In a slightly shabby but spacious compound north of the river, handy for the long-distance bus stop, this is a good hostel with down-to-earth staff, and the option of paying extra for an en-suite cabin. Bunk in quad room A$22–24.50, private double ❶
Tropical Wanderer Resort 394 Yaamba Rd ℡07 4926 3822 or 1800 815 563, ⓦwww .bestonparks.com.au. On the highway 3km north of the river, this van park and motel has a restaurant and pool set in attractive gardens. Camping A$26, cabin ❷, motel room/villa ❹

The city and around

It doesn't take long to look around the city itself. The **Tropic Marker**, 3km from the river at Rockhampton's southern entrance, is just a spire informing you of your position at 23° 26' 30" S. Apart from a riverside stroll to take in the early twentieth-century architecture or the brown-stained boulders midstream that gave the city its name, there's little else to detain you. Rockhampton's cattle business lends a Wild-West feel: dotted around town are jokey fibreglass bulls, and the highlight of the week is the Friday-night **cattle rodeo** at the *Great Western Hotel* on the corner of Stanley and Denison streets (℡07 4922 3888), with high-adrenaline professional bucking-bull-riding and nerve-soothing country music. For gentler animal encounters, the Botanic Gardens on the southern edge of town has a small zoo run by volunteers; while some of the inmates, particularly the chimps, are a little forlorn, you're guaranteed close-up sightings of emus and koalas. The zoo is also home to an important research centre devoted to the rare northern hairy-nosed wombat; the centre hopes to open a visitor facility in due course.

About 5km north of town on the Bruce Highway, the **Dreamtime Cultural Centre** (℡07 4936 1655, ⓦwww.dreamtimecentre.com.au; Mon–Fri 10am–3.30pm; tours with an Aboriginal guide at 10.30am and 1pm; A$12.75, child A$6) offers a good introduction to central Queensland's Aboriginal heritage. Inside, chronological and Dreamtime histories are intermingled, with a broad dissection of the archeology and mythology of Carnarvon Gorge, the dramatic sandstone rock site southwest of Rockhampton in Queensland's Central

Highlands. Outside, surrounded by woodland, gunyahs (shelters of bark and branches) and stencil art, you'll find an unlikely walk-through dugong (sea cow), and the original stone rings of a **bora ground** that marked the main camp of the Darumbal, whose territory reached from the Keppel Bay coastline inland to Mount Morgan. The tour also discusses plant usage and introduces boomerang, dance and didgeridoo skills – audience participation is definitely encouraged.

The limestone hills north of Rockhampton are riddled with a **cave system**, thick with tree roots encased in stone after forcing their way down through rocks, "cave corals" and "frozen waterfalls" – minerals deposited by evaporation after annual floods. The **ghost bat** (Australia's only carnivorous species) and the **little bent-winged bat** – both now endangered – seasonally use the caves for roosts, and you might catch the odd group huddled together on the ceilings, eyes peering down at you over leaf-shaped noses. Two sets of caverns are open to the public, both reached by turning off the Bruce Highway 25km north of Rockhampton at **The Caves** township and following the signs. The **Etna Caves**, which are undeveloped but none too extensive, are open seasonally: from December to February you can go on a **bat tour** with a Queensland Parks and Wildlife Service ranger (four evenings a week; A\$8, child A\$4; book through QPWS Rockhampton on ☎07 4936 0511), and between March and October you can explore on your own (6am–8pm; take a torch and durable shoes). The **Capricorn Caves** (☎07 4934 2883, ⓦwww.capricorncaves.com.au; daily 9am–4pm; free, one-hour guided tour A\$20, child A\$10, "wild caving" adventure tour A\$65, day-trips including transfers available on request) are impressive, with plenty of spotlights illuminating their interiors.

Eating and drinking

A **steak** of some kind is the obvious choice in Australia's beef capital, and any of the hotels can oblige. There's a smattering of cafés around the mall, while the *Great Western Hotel* over on Stanley Street (☎07 4922 3888) serves quality steak, as does the *Cambridge Hotel* on Cambridge Street. A perch at the *Criterion*'s bar on Quay Street, overlooking the Fitzroy River, is recommended for less flamboyant steak and beer, along with elbow-to-elbow closeness with a few locals. For a more refined experience, 🍴 *The Coffee House* on William Street (☎07 4927 5722) is open all day for amazing gourmet breakfasts, great coffee and wine-bar-style lunches and evening meals, while *The Wild Parrot* on Denham Street (Tues–Fri 9am–5pm, Sat & Sun 9am–10pm; ☎07 4921 4099) is a pleasant café with a leafy courtyard and relaxed atmosphere.

Emu Park and Yeppoon

There are **two roads** to the **Capricorn Coast** from Rockhampton; together they make a circuit that regional marketeers like to call the "Scenic Loop". The southern route starts at Bridge Street on the north bank of the river, from where it's 50km to Emu Park; the northern route starts 5km further up the Bruce Highway, heading coastwards for the forty-kilometre run to Yeppoon. Young's **buses** run from Rockhampton to Yeppoon, Emu Park and Rosslyn Bay (☎07 4922 3813; ⓦwww.youngsbusservice.com.au; 6–12 services daily from the stop beside the car park in Bolsover Street, near the junction with William Street).

EMU PARK comprises a pleasant sandy beach and breezy hillside covered by scattered Queenslander houses. Up on a promontory, complex chords ring out from the **Singing Ship**, an inspired abstract monument to Captain Cook unveiled at the 1970 bicentenary of the great navigator's arrival in Queensland. The statue is a ship-like installation painted white and strung with wind-catching wires and organ pipes: visit on a blustery day to hear it at its most resonant. A decent, motel-like **place to stay** is *Endeavour Inn* on Hill Street (☏07 4939 6777 or 1800 252 112, ⓦwww.endeavourinn.com.au; ③); or there's spruce resort-style accommodation at *Emus Beach House*, 92 Pattison St (☏07 4939 6111, ⓦwww.emusbeachhouse.com), closed for refurbishment at the time of writing.

Heading north up the coast from here, it's 18km via **Rosslyn Bay** to **YEPPOON**'s quiet handful of streets, which face the Keppel Islands over a blustery expanse of sand and sea. All services are on **Normanby Street**, at right angles to the seafront Anzac Parade. **Buses** pull into the depot on Hill Street, which also runs off Anzac Parade parallel with Normanby. For **accommodation**, *Driftwood*, about 2km north of town at 7 Todd Ave (☏07 4939 2446, ⓦwww.driftwoodunits.com.au; ③), has straightforward but smartly equipped self-contained rooms overlooking the beach, whilst *Bayview Tower*, in the centre of town at 4 Adelaide St (☏07 4939 4500, ⓦwww .bayviewtower.com.au; ④), has good though plain rooms and excellent sea views from the upper floors. There are also basic beds at *Yeppoon Backpackers*, in town at 30 Queen St (☏07 4939 8080; bunk in shared room A$22), and inexpensive, self-contained cabins and shady tent sites at *Poinciana Tourist Park* (☏07 4939 1601, ⓦwww.poincianatouristpark.com; camping A$20–23, cabin ①), just south of town off the Emu Park road.

Yeppoon prides itself on its fresh **fish**, and there are plenty of **restaurants** where you can sample it. The pick of the lot is the no-frills *Seagulls Seafood* on Anzac Parade, which specializes in local Spanish mackerel dishes; its bucket of seafood is excellent value at A$15. The nearby *Keppel Bay Sailing Club* has a cheaper bar with long views of the islands, while their restaurant offers budget all-you-can-eat lunches and dinners. The mall-like Normanby Street has a couple of cafés serving up good breakfasts and coffee. For weekend **entertainment**, try *Bonkers Nightclub*, one road back from Anzac Parade on Hill Street.

Great Keppel Island

Great Keppel, the largest of the eighteen Keppel islands, is a windswept hillock covered in casuarinas and ringed by white sand so fine that it squeaks when you walk through it, all surrounded by an invitingly clear blue sea – just the place for a few days of indolence.

A daily catamaran **ferry service** to Great Keppel run by Freedom Fast Cats leaves from Keppel Bay Marina at **Rosslyn Bay**, 5km south of Yeppoon, three times daily, taking less than half an hour (☏07 4933 6244 or 1800 336 244; A$41, child A$22.50 return). Youngs (☏07 4922 3813; ⓦwww .youngsbusservice.com.au) runs a regular **bus** service between the marina and Rockhampton; the alternative is Rothery's Coaches (☏07 4922 4320). There's exposed **free parking** at the harbour; for protection from salt spray, leave your car undercover at Great Keppel Island Security Car Park (A$10/day; ☏07 4933 6670), opposite the Rosslyn Bay junction on the main road. It's also possible

For advice on **swimming** in northern Queensland's coastal waters during "stinger season", see p.47.

to fly from Rockhampton to the *Great Keppel Island Resort* airstrip in twenty minutes (booking through the resort).

Arriving at Great Keppel, the ferry leaves you near several **accommodation** choices; most can offer last-minute discounted packages. *Great Keppel Island Holiday Village* (☏1800 180 235, ⓦwww.gkiholidayvillage.com.au; single in four-share A$33, safari tent ❸, cabin ❹) is a spruce, friendly place with a first-rate kitchen; nearby is the *Keppel Haven YHA*, which, at the time of writing, was closed for refurbishment. A short walk away on Fisherman's Beach, *Keppel Lodge* (☏07 4939 4251, ⓦwww.keppellodge.com.au; ❹) is a pleasant, motel-like affair; on a prime spot on the same bay are the large grounds of the *Great Keppel Island Resort* (☏07 4925 1600 or 1800 245 658, ⓦwww.greatkeppelresort.com.au; ❺), which, at the time of writing, was being remodelled and upgraded from three-star to five-star. For **food** outside the holiday village and resort, there's a late-opening pizza shack, *Island Pizza*, much frequented after the bars close. The scuba centre on Putney Beach hires **snorkelling gear** to allow exploration of Great Keppel's fringing reef and sea-grass fields, home to turtles and dugongs, and runs trips further afield.

Great Keppel's main **beaches**, Putney and Fisherman's, are remarkably pleasant considering the number of people lounging on them at any one time, but a half-hour walk will take you to more secluded spots. Reached by a woodland path past the resort, Long Beach attracts sun-worshippers, while snorkellers make the short haul over sand dunes at the western end to shallow coral on Monkey Beach. **Middens** (shell mounds) on Monkey Beach were left by Woppaburra Aborigines, who were enslaved and forcibly removed to Fraser Island by early settlers.

Mackay

Coastal Queensland's fifth-largest city, **MACKAY** (pronounced "mc-eye") lies on the banks of the broad, brown Pioneer River, some 336km north of Rockhampton and 146km south of Airlie Beach. If you've just travelled north along the famously long and unremarkable Rockhampton–Mackay stretch of the Bruce Highway (Highway 1), where the only roadside distraction is the hope of seeing a wild koala in the dry eucalyptus woodland, the fertile Pioneer Valley comes as an appealing break. Despite encounters with aggressive Juipera Aborigines, John Mackay was impressed enough to settle the valley in 1861, and within four years the city was founded and the first **sugar cane** plantations were established; sugar remains one of the region's main industries today.

After years in the doldrums, Mackay is currently enjoying an economic boom driven by the **coal mines** out west in the Bowen Basin, for which the city has become a dormitory town and service centre. Most of Mackay's visitors are here on business; the city is barely geared up for tourism, with few specific sights apart from the odd **Art Deco** building, a **botanical garden** on the south-western edge of town, and **Artspace**, a small contemporary art centre in a strikingly modern building on Gordon Street (☏07 4957 1755, ⓦwww.artspacemackay.com.au; Tues–Sun 10am–5pm; free). However, the city's proximity to two alluring national parks – coastal **Cape Hillsborough** and rainforested **Eungella** in the Mackay Highlands – makes it a good starting point from which to explore.

Sugar cane on the Tropical Coast

Sugar cane, grown in an almost continuous belt between Bundaberg and Mossman, north of Cairns, has long been the Tropical Coast's economic pillar of strength, but a global price crash has now left the Queenslanders struggling to compete with growers in South America and elsewhere.

First introduced in the 1860s, the crop subtly undermined the racial ideals of British colonialists when farmers, planning a system along the lines of the southern United States, employed Kanakas – Solomon Islanders – to work the plantations. Though only indentured for a few years, and theoretically given wages and passage home when their term expired, Kanakas on plantations suffered greatly from unfamiliar diseases, while the recruiting methods used by "Blackbirder" traders were at best dubious and often slipped into wholesale kidnapping. Growing white unemployment and nationalism through the 1880s eventually forced the government to ban black-birding and repatriate the islanders. Those allowed to stay were joined over the next fifty years by immigrants from Italy and Malta, who mostly settled in the far north and today form large communities scattered between Mackay and Cairns.

After cane has been planted in November, the land is quickly covered by a blanket of dusky green; even before the cane is full height, roadside canefields block the view of the surrounding landscape. Before cutting, seven to ten months later, the fields were traditionally set on fire at dusk to burn off leaves and maximize sugar content in a brief, photogenic blaze. This practice is now rare – the best way to be at the right place at the right time is to ask at a mill.

Cut cane is then transported to the mills along a rambling rail network. The mills themselves are incredible buildings, with machinery looming out of makeshift walls and giant pipes that belch out steam around the clock when the mill is in operation. Cane is juiced for raw sugar or molasses, as the market dictates; crushed fibre becomes fuel for the boilers that sustain the process; and ash is returned to the fields as fertilizer. **Farleigh Mill** (T07 4963 2700), north of Mackay, is open for **tours** (Mon–Fri 1pm; A$17) during the crushing season (June–Nov); sturdy shoes, a long-sleeve-shirt and long trousers are essential. **Polstone Sugar Farm** (T07 4959 7298) near Homebush in the Pioneer Valley also opens for visits (Mon, Wed & Fri afternoons) at harvest time (June–Oct).

Practicalities

Central Mackay lies immediately south of the Forgan Bridge, spanning the Pioneer River, around **Victoria Street**, **Sydney Street** and **Gordon Street**, with the **bus station** – just a set-down point outside Mackay Travelworld – near the corner of Victoria and Macalister streets. Con-x-ion (T07 5556 9888, W www.con-x-ion.com) run a twice-daily shuttle between Airlie Beach, Cannonvale, Proserpine and Mackay. Both **trains** (the station is on Connors Rd, 3km south off Milton St along Boundary Rd or Paradise St) and **planes** arrive south of town; a taxi into town from either will set you back around A$15. Jetstar, Qantas, Tiger Airways and Virgin Blue (see p.35) have, between them, direct flights from Mackay Airport (MKY; T07 4955 8155, W www .mackayports.com) to Sydney, Melbourne, Brisbane, Cairns, Townsville, Rockhampton and Gladstone. Mackay Travelworld (Mon–Fri 7am–6pm, Sat 7am–2pm; T07 4944 2144) is the **ticket agent** for bus, train and air travel. **Taxis** can be booked on T13 10 08.

The **tourist office** (T07 4952 2677, W www.mackayregion.com) is poorly located 3km southwest of the centre at 320 Nebo Rd (A1 Highway); you're better off consulting the staff wherever you're staying. For details of operators running day-trips to Eungella National Park and the Pioneer Valley, see p.512.

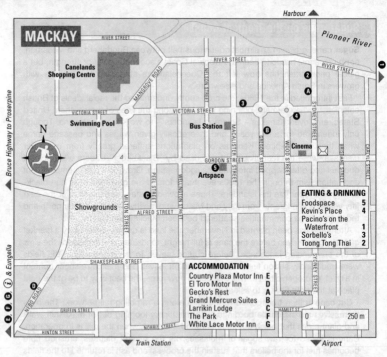

Aviation Mackay (☎07 4951 4300; A\$130 for 1hr) offers **scenic flights** over the city and surrounding area, including the highlands and coast.

On Sunday, market day in Sydney and Victoria streets (8.30am–1pm), a free **Mackay Explorer** bus service shuttles passengers around the city centre.

Accommodation

Although Mackay has plenty of **motels**, **hotels** and **holiday apartments** scattered around the city fringes and the northern suburbs (particularly at the marina and Bucasia Beach), it's sometimes hard to find a bed in the city centre, as demand from visiting workers can be high.

Country Plaza Motor Inn 40 Nebo Rd ☎07 4957 6526, ⓦwww.countryplaza.com.au. Family-friendly motel with good facilities for the price, not too far from the centre. ❸

El Toro Motor Inn 14 Nebo Rd ☎07 4951 2722. Welcoming motel with a pool, playground, and babysitting on request. ❸

Gecko's Rest 34 Sydney St ☎07 4944 1230, ⓦwww.geckosrest.com.au. This central, modern budget option has spacious rooms with air-con and a large, well-equipped kitchen, but little natural light. Single bed in quad room A\$22, private double ❶

Grand Mercure Suites 19 Gregory St ☎07 4969 1000, ⓦwww.mackaygrandmercure.com.au. Well-appointed chain-hotel-style suite hotel in the city centre, with a gym and pool. Studio ❺, suite ❻

Larrikin Lodge 32 Peel St ☎07 4951 3728, ⓦwww.larrikinlodge.com.au. Comfortable Queenslander house with a laid-back feel. The staff are very knowledgeable about the region, and run trips to Eungella. Bunk or single in shared room A\$21, private double ❶

The Park Nebo Rd ☎07 4952 1211. Two kilometres south of the centre on the highway to Rockhampton, this is a tidy, well-maintained caravan park with self-contained units. Camping A\$18–25, cabin ❷

White Lace Motor Inn 73 Nebo Rd ☎07 4951 4466 or 1800 075 107, ⓦwww.whitelace.com.au. In a pretty building with a "white lace" balcony, this has more character than most of the city-fringe places, and useful extras such as broadband Internet. ❹

Eating

Aside from the following, several downtown **pubs** and **restaurants** offer filling week-time lunch specials for under A$10.

Foodspace Artspace Mackay, Gordon St ☏ 07 4957 1719. Suitably creative and modern light cooking plus sandwiches, cakes and cocktails at the city's cultural focal point. Tues–Fri 10am–4pm, Sat & Sun 9am–4pm.

Kevin's Place 79 Victoria St ☏ 07 4953 5835. Singaporean-Chinese restaurant with fixed-price lunches (try the *laksa* – a colossal bowl of noodles, seafood and spicy coconut soup) and à la carte dinners with mains around A$22, featuring five-spice squid and whole fried fish. Closed Sun evenings.

Pacino's on the Waterfront 8 River St ☏ 07 4957 8131. With moderately priced seafood, pasta and pizzas from the wood-fired oven, this is a popular spot in a great riverside location.

Sorbello's 166 Victoria St ☏ 07 4957 8300. Good choice for pastas and other Italian dishes for around A$20 per person.

Toong Tong Thai 10 Sydney St ☏ 07 4957 8051. Long-established, cheerful Thai restaurant and takeaway with authentically hot and spicy food. There's a selection of appealing lunchtime specials, or it's around A$25 a head for a full meal.

Around Mackay

An easy drive from Mackay are two beautiful national parks: to the west, rainforested **Eungella** (pronounced "young g'lla") in the Mackay Highlands, an excellent area to see platypuses, amphibians, insects and birds, and to the north, coastal **Cape Hillsborough**, where wallabies bounce along the beach in the early hours.

Eungella National Park

Some 80km west of Mackay and reached by way of a scenic drive through the lush green **Pioneer Valley**, the magical rainforest and rivers of **EUNGELLA NATIONAL PARK** are worth the journey even if you weren't almost guaranteed to see **platypuses**. There are two sections to visit: lowland swimming holes

▲ Kangaroo at Eungella National Park

and tropical rainforest at **Finch Hatton Gorge**, and highland rainforest at **Broken River**. The park's isolation has produced several unique species, including the Mackay tulip oak, the Eungella honeyeater and the much-discussed but probably now extinct **gastric brooding frog**, known for incubating its young in its stomach.

Day-trips from Mackay taking in both sections of the park can be arranged with Reeforest Adventure Tours (A\$99; ⓣ07 4959 8360 or 1800 500 353, ⓦwww.reeforest.com) or Jungle Johno at the *Larrikin Lodge* (ⓣ07 4951 3728 or 07 4957 5477; A\$65). Both run only if they have sufficient numbers; otherwise, you'll need your own vehicle. Driving yourself **from Mackay**, head south down Nebo Road (Bruce Highway/A1) in the direction of Sarina to the city limits then turn west along the Peak Downs Highway and west again onto the Eungella Road. If you're coming **from Proserpine**, follow the signs directing you south off the highway just beyond tiny Kuttabul, around 30km before Mackay; if you're travelling north **from Rockhampton**, you can turn off the highway just north of Sarina and take the Sarina–Homebush and Marian–Eton roads to the Eungella Road.

Much of the national park is inaccessible by road; to get an aerial overview, including stunning views of the rainforest-clad peaks, you can take a **scenic flight** by light aircraft with Mackay Aviation (ⓣ07 4951 4300).

Finch Hatton Gorge

The Eungella Road cuts through prime cane country and past several **sugar mills** as it runs the length of the Pioneer Valley, past the townships of **Marian** (one-time home of legendary opera singer Dame Nellie Melba) and **Mirani**. Some 60km from Mackay, signposts just before Finch Hatton township mark the turn-off to **Finch Hatton Gorge**, 12km from the main road across several fords; access depends on the season, though generally it's negotiable by all vehicles. Immediately across the first creek, *Platypus Bush Camp* (ⓣ07 4958 3204, ⓦwww.bushcamp.net; camping A\$15 or A\$7.50 per person, bed in shared cabin A\$25, private cabin ❷) provides woodland tent space and basic accommodation in a handful of open-sided, tree-house-style wooden cabins: bed, amenities and kitchen are supplied; camping gear is available to hire and the rest (including food) is up to you. This is probably the most authentic rainforest experience you can have anywhere in Queensland: you'll see an astonishing array of bird- and animal life (including the elusive platypus), sit by a fire under the stars, shower in the rainforest amidst fairy-like fireflies, and be lulled to sleep by a gurgling creek.

For a highly original perspective on the forest, it's well worth booking a zipline session with **Forest Flying** (ⓣ07 4958 3359, ⓦwww.forestflying.com; daily 10.30am & 1pm; A\$45). Their custom-built wire, pulley and harness system, starting 25m up in the trees, has a rope-operated brake that allows you to go as slow as you like, and even stop mid-slide – perfect for the environment they have chosen, an attractive stretch of forest inhabited by hundreds of fruit bats. Depending on where they're roosting on the day of your visit, you may have outstandingly close views of the bats as they hang from the branches and squabble amongst themselves, with babies wrapped under their mothers' wings.

Back on the main track, about a kilometre – and three creeks – further on you'll find camping space and three plain but comfortable self-catering units at *Finch Hatton Gorge Cabins* (Gorge Rd; ⓣ07 4958 3281, ⓦwww .finchhattongorgecabins.com.au; cabin ❸). Nearby is the *Gorge Kiosk*, which serves home-made juice and ice cream. Another kilometre beyond, the road ends at a picnic area, from where graded **walking tracks** ascend through a hot jungle of palms, vines and creepers to where the gorge winds down the side of Mount Dalrymple as a rocky creek pocked with swimming holes. **Araluen Falls** (1.5km from the picnic area), a beautiful – if icy – pool and cascade, is the perfect place to spend a summer's day; further up (3km from the picnic area) is an even more attractive cascade at the **Wheel of Fire Falls**, where you can sit up to your neck in the water.

Finch Hatton, Eungella and Broken River

FINCH HATTON is the most attractive village in the Pioneer Valley, with a characterful old country railway station and pretty houses strung out along the road. For a restful stop, *Bowerbird Café* (Wed–Fri from 9am, Sat & Sun from 8am) offers coffee, juice and healthy snacks. About 15km beyond the township, the valley comes to a dramatic close as the main road makes an unforgettably steep and twisting ascent up the range to **EUNGELLA**. This spread-out hamlet comprises a general store, a couple of cafés and the *Eungella Chalet* (℡07 4958 4509), whose back-lawn beer garden and swimming pool sit just metres from a seven-hundred-metre drop into the forest, with a fantastic panorama down the valley. The best **place to stay** here is the friendly *Eungella Holiday Park* (℡07 4958 4590; camping A$16–20, cabin ❷, large guesthouse ❹) – take the first right at the top of the climb – which has log cabins, units and campsites, more great views, plus its own store and an ATM.

South of the hamlet, the landscape takes on an alpine look, with patches of forest and rolling dairy pasture. Around 5km beyond Eungella is the excellent ⚓ *Broken River Mountain Resort* (℡07 4958 4000, ⓦwww.brokenrivermr.com.au; room or cabin ❹, two-bedroom lodge ❺). Perfect for natural-history enthusiasts, with plain but immaculately kept rooms and cabins sleeping two or four, the lodge has a restaurant for hearty evening meals, a lounge with a fireplace for chilly winter nights (the temperature can drop well below zero in the mountains), and resident naturalists who conduct fascinating morning or after-dark nature rambles four times a week. It's close to a small bridge over **Broken River**, the best river in Australia (and, it's claimed, the world) to see platypus. Nearby is the **Queensland Parks and Wildlife Service office**, which is usually unattended but has maps of the area, and a QPWS **campsite** for tents only (see p.54 for booking information) with cold showers and a picnic area. Be prepared for **rain**: Eungella translates as "Land of Cloud".

The best vantage point for **platypus-watching** is the purpose-built **platform** by the picnic area; normally fairly timid creatures, here they've become quite tolerant of people, and you can often see them right through the day; you're almost guaranteed to see at least one if you visit at dawn or dusk. The real star of Broken River, though, is the **forest** itself, whose ancient trees with buttressed roots and immensely high canopies conceal a floor of rich rotting timber, ferns, palms and vines. Local cabbage palms, with their straight trunks and crown of large, fringed leaves; huge, scaly-barked Mackay cedar; and tulip oaks are all endemic – many other shrubs and trees here are otherwise only found further south, indicating that Eungella may have once been part of far more extensive forests. It can be difficult to see **animals** in the undergrowth, but the sun-splashed paths along riverbanks attract goannas and snakes, and you'll certainly hear plenty of birds. The best two **walking tracks** either follow the river upstream to Crediton and then return along the road (16km return), or head through the forest and down to *Eungella Chalet* (13km return). There's also an easy **forty-minute circuit** from the picnic grounds upstream to Crystal Cascades. For dedicated hikers, a challenging long-distance track leads from

Eungella south to Mount Britton (56km); best spread over five days, this is one of the QPWS Great Walks (see p.424).

Cape Hillsborough National Park

Cape Hillsborough, about an hour's drive north of Mackay, is the site of a pretty beachfront national park; you'll probably need your own vehicle to reach it, but Reeforest Adventure Tours in Mackay (☎07 4959 8360 or 1800 500 353, ⓦwww.reeforest.com) sometimes include the area in their itineraries. From the Bruce Highway (A1) north of Mackay, the turning to the cape, 20km out of town, is signposted to Cape Hillsborough National Park and **Seaforth**; this road runs past cane fields and the imposing bulk of Mount Jukes for a further 30km to the park.

The main area of the national park is set around a broad two-kilometre **beach**, backed by a good picnic area and framed by the beautifully wooded cliffs of Cape Hillsborough to the north and Andrews Point to the south; the shallow bay is good for swimming (outside the stinger season). Hidden in bushland at the end of the road, the 🏊 *Cape Hillsborough Resort* (☎07 4959 0152, ⓦwww .capehillsboroughresort.com.au; camping A$20–25, cabin ❷, motel room ❷) has a pool, basic store (closes 6pm) and restaurant. It's an excellent choice for self-sufficient wildlife enthusiasts, with plenty of information about the local fauna, including birds, butterflies and the agile and whip-tail wallabies that are often seen on the beach just after sunrise, feeding on washed-up vegetation. A good **walk** heads out 2km past here to **Hidden Valley**, a patch of cool, shady forest on a rocky beach where you'll find the outline of an Aboriginal fish trap; keep your eyes peeled for dolphins, turtles and pelicans out in the bay.

Five hundred metres back up the road towards Mackay, an excellent two-kilometre trail follows a **boardwalk** through coastal mangroves (bring insect repellent) and then snakes up to a ridge for views over the area from open gum woodland peppered with grevillias, cycads (see box, p.554) and grasstrees – the latter identified by their tall, spear-like flower spike. There's also a huge **midden** up here, the remains of Aboriginal shellfish feasts, and plenty of reptiles sunning themselves around the edges of the path.

The Whitsunday Coast

Such is the romantic allure of the Whitsundays, the attractive clutch of continental islands close to the coast between Mackay and Townsville, that the **Whitsunday Coast**, the stretch of mainland closest to the archipelago, has gradually grown from a launch-point for island-hoppers to a busy resort area in its own right.

The inland gateway to the region is **PROSERPINE** (pronounced "prosser-pyne"), 123km north of Mackay and 264km south of Townsville, a small workaday sugar town on the turn-off from the Bruce Highway (A1) to Whitsunday, and site of the regional **railway station** and mainland **airport** – Whitsunday Coast Airport (PPP), 10km south of town, served by intercity flights from Brisbane and Sydney with Jetstar, Qantas and Virgin Blue (see p.35). Arriving by **long-distance bus** (see p.35)there's no need to get out at

For advice on **swimming** in northern Queensland's coastal waters during the "stinger season", see p.47.

Proserpine as all services turn off the A1 to continue the extra 23km to Airlie Beach on the coast. If you do wind up in town, Whitsunday Transit (T 07 4946 1800, W www.whitsundaytransit.com.au) run a regular **local bus** service between Proserpine and Shute Harbour, stopping at Cannonvale and Airlie Beach; contact them in advance to arrange railway-station or airport **pick-ups**. Late arrivals can stay at the functional *Proserpine Motor Lodge*, 184 Main St (T 07 4945 1788; ❷), which is right on the highway, or at the van park on Jupp Street.

WHITSUNDAY is the cover-all name for the string of coastal communities northeast of Proserpine including Cannonvale, Airlie Beach and Shutehaven, jumping-off points for the **Whitsunday Islands** (see p.519). **Cannonvale** and **Airlie Beach** are the service centres, while island ferries and some boat trips leave from Shute Harbour, signposted as Shutehaven, 10km on from Airlie Beach past Conway National Park. Other boat trips leave from **Abel Point Marina** on the Cannonvale side of Airlie Beach.

Airlie Beach and around

Coming from Proserpine, you enter Whitsunday at **CANNONVALE**, a scattering of modern buildings fringing the highway for about a kilometre or so, overlooked by luxury homes set higher up on the wooded slopes of the Conway Range. Just around the headland past Abel Point Marina, **AIRLIE BEACH** is nestled between the sea and a steep, forested hillside, its lower slopes covered in a growing number of apartment buildings. Airlie Beach's mixed bag of resort shops, bars and restaurants are crammed into one short stretch of **Shute Harbour Road** and the hundred-metre-long **Esplanade**. Despite the name, Airlie Beach has only a couple of gritty stretches of sand, which get covered at high tide – though the deep turquoise bay, dotted with yachts and cruisers, is gorgeous. To make up the shortfall, there's a free, open-air **swimming lagoon** between Shute Harbour Road and the sea, complete with landscaped lawns, showers, changing rooms, communal hotplate barbecues, benches and a little sand.

There's a strong backpacker presence in Airlie Beach – this is one of the standard coastal stops for young travellers journeying between the Gold Coast and Cairns – and the little strip gets pretty lively after dark. This is also a meeting point for yachties, who gather at Abel Point Marina, the Whitsunday Sailing Club on Airlie Bay and Shute Harbour before setting off around the Whitsunday Islands; a new marina for Airlie Beach was under construction at the time of writing, with another at Shute Harbour in the pipeline.

Airlie Beach's biggest daytime preoccupation is with **organizing cruises** (see box, p.522), but you can also rent **watersports gear** from the kiosk on the beach; organize half-day to six-day **sea-kayaking** expeditions with Salty Dog (T 07 4946 1388, W www.saltydog.com.au); or visit **Bredl's Wildlife Park** (daily 9am–4.30pm; A$25), a ten-acre bush-zoo 4km from Airlie Beach towards Shutehaven, which has an excellent reptile collection. A **flea market** is held on the waterfront near the long-distance bus stop on Saturday mornings, for local produce and souvenirs (7am–1pm). Hikers can spend a few days out of town exploring the Whitsunday Great Walk, one of the QPWS Great Walks (see p.425), which takes you along marked trails through the pristine **Conway State Forest**, immediately south of Airlie Beach. **Conway National Park**, a stretch of forested mountains and mangroves facing the islands, is mostly inaccessible but there's a small roadside parking area about 7km from Airlie Beach on Shute Harbour Road, from where an easy walking track climbs Mount Rooper to an observation platform giving views of the islands' white peaks jutting out of the unbelievably blue sea.

A final 3km on, **SHUTEHAVEN** comprises a cluster of houses with stunning views overlooking the islands from wooded hills above **Coral Point**; its harbour, **Shute Harbour**, is one of Australia's busiest for small craft, with most of the island ferries and bareboat charters departing from here.

Practicalities

Airlie Beach's **long-distance bus stop**, served by Greyhound and Premier (see p.35), is at the eastern end of town, off The Esplanade on the road to the Whitsunday Sailing Club. Mackay-based Con-x-ion (see p.509) run a twice-daily shuttle to Cannonvale and Airlie Beach from Mackay. The **railway station** is at Proserpine, with services up and down the coast between Brisbane and Cairns.

The nearest mainland **airport** is Whitsunday Coast Airport (PPP) at Proserpine, served by intercity flights from Jetstar, Qantas and Virgin Blue; the other commercial airport in the area is Great Barrier Reef Airport (HTI) on Hamilton Island (see p.520). Private transfers between the mainland and the islands run from Whitsunday Airport on Shute Harbour Road, about half way between Airlie Beach and Shute Harbour.

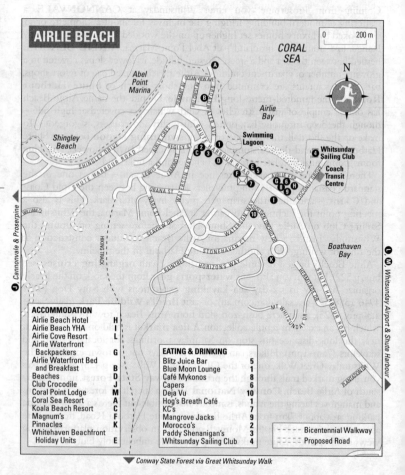

AIRLIE BEACH

0   200 m

CORAL SEA

N

Abel Point Marina

Shingley Beach

Airlie Bay

Swimming Lagoon

Whitsunday Sailing Club

Coach Transit Centre

OCEAN VIEW AVE

SHUTE HARBOUR ROAD

SHINGLEY DRIVE

AIRLIE CRES

BEGLEY ST

LEWIS ST

WATERSON WAY

QRANA ST

MARS ST

SEAVIEW DR

WILLIAM CT

HIKING TRACK

STONEHAVEN CT

RAINTREE

HORIZONS WAY

WATERSON WAY

VON ORCHARD ST

COCONUT GROVE

AIRLIE ESP

Boathaven Bay

MT WHITSUNDAY DR

SHUTE HARBOUR ROAD

PLANTATION

◀ **○** Cannonvale & Proserpine

○ ○ Whitsunday Airport & Shute Harbour ▶

ACCOMMODATION
Airlie Beach Hotel	H
Airlie Beach YHA	I
Airlie Cove Resort	L
Airlie Waterfront Backpackers	G
Airlie Waterfront Bed and Breakfast	B
Beaches	D
Club Crocodile	J
Coral Point Lodge	M
Coral Sea Resort	A
Koala Beach Resort	C
Magnum's	F
Pinnacles	K
Whitehaven Beachfront Holiday Units	E

EATING & DRINKING
Blitz Juice Bar	5
Blue Moon Lounge	
Café Mykonos	8
Capers	6
Deja Vu	10
Hog's Breath Café	1
KC's	
Mangrove Jacks	9
Morocco's	2
Paddy Shenanigan's	3
Whitsunday Sailing Club	4

- - - - Bicentennial Walkway
═════ Proposed Road

▼ Conway State Forest via Great Whitsunday Walk

For advice on **swimming** in northern Queensland's coastal waters during the "stinger season", see p.47.

The Whitsunday Transit **bus** (℡07 4946 1800, Ⓦwww.whitsundaytransit .com.au) runs between Cannonvale, Airlie Beach, Abel Point, Whitsunday Airport and Shute Harbour roughly twice an hour from about 6am to 6pm, and around once an hour between Cannonvale and Airlie Beach from 6pm until 10.30pm.

Staff at the town's hotels, hostels and other places offer limitless **information**, though don't expect it to be unbiased; the Whitsundays Central Reservations Centre at the Cannonvale end of Airlie Beach (259 Shute Harbour Rd; ℡07 4946 5299 or 1800 677 119, Ⓦwww.airliebeach.com) is probably the most objective source, but it's a good idea to ask other visitors about which cruises they recommend before making a decision.

Accommodation

Unless you're in town during the September Whitsunday Fun Race, Schoolies Week in November, or Christmas and New Year, you'll have little trouble finding **accommodation**, which is concentrated in Airlie Beach itself. **Hostels** are all cramped, but a pool and kitchen are standard amenities; **motels** and **resorts** often insist on minimum stays of three nights during Christmas and Easter, though might offer discounted rates at other times. All places act as booking agents for tours and transport.

Airlie Beach Hotel Corner of The Espanade & Coconut Grove ℡07 4964 1999 or 1800 466 233, Ⓦwww.airliebeachhotel.com.au. Since being refurbished, this is one of the smarter places to stay in Airlie Beach, with a choice of motel-style suites or higher-priced four-star beachfront rooms. ❹–❺

Airlie Beach YHA 394 Shute Harbour Rd ℡07 4946 6312, Ⓦwww.yha.com.au. Generally busy and somewhat crowded, with tidy dorms and doubles. Bunk in shared room A$24–27, private double ❷

Airlie Cove Resort Shute Harbour Rd ℡07 4946 6727, Ⓦwww.airliecove.com.au. Camping, van sites, simple cabins and luxury timber villas in a plot with an attractive, wilderness feel, 3km outside Airlie Beach. Camping A$32–48, cabin ❸, villa ❹

Airlie Waterfront Backpackers The Esplanade ℡07 4948 1300 or 1800 247 543, Ⓦwww .airliewaterfront.com. With a brilliant beachfront location, this has a variety of rooms, including dorms with more space than most hostels provide. Bunk in shared room A$25–27, single bed in quad room A$30, private double ❷

Airlie Waterfront Bed and Breakfast Corner of Broadwater & Mazlin sts ℡07 4946 7631, Ⓦwww.airliewaterfrontbnb.com.au. Four characterful serviced apartments in a modern timber house with fantastic bay views; all the rooms have luxury touches and two have private spa baths. ❺

Beaches 356 Shute Harbour Rd ℡07 4946 6244 or 1800 636 630. Lively backpackers' hostel with plenty of youth appeal; dorms and rooms are all en suite. Bunk in shared room A$25, private double ❸

Club Crocodile Shute Harbour Rd ℡07 4946 7155, Ⓦwww.oceanhotels.com.au. Large family-orientated resort with plenty of facilities including a baby-sitting service, and good discounts. ❸

Coral Point Lodge 54 Harbour Ave, Shute Harbour ℡07 4946 9500, Ⓦwww .coralpointlodge.com.au. Delightful, excellent-value apartments sleeping four to six, with great views. The attached café-restaurant is well worth a stop even if you're not staying here. ❺

Coral Sea Resort 25 Oceanview Ave ℡07 4946 6458, Ⓦwww.coralsearesort .com. Airlie Beach's only real full-blown resort has smart rooms in a great location right on the water-front; some have ocean views. ❼

Koala Beach Resort Shute Harbour Rd ℡07 4946 6001 or 1800 800 421, Ⓦwww .koalaadventures.com. Basic six-bunk dorms, each with shower and TV, in a lively hostel with a pool in pleasant landscaped grounds; you can also camp here. Camping A$20 (A$10pp), bunk in shared room A$27, private double ❷

Magnum's Shute Harbour Rd ℡1800 624 634, Ⓦwww.magnums.com.au. This party hostel has tidy cabins with en-suite bathrooms, pleasantly sheltered tropical lawns, and a loud bar. Camping A$18–20, bunk in shared room A$17–20, private double ❷

Pinnacles 16 Golden Orchid Drive ☎07 4948 4800, ⓦwww.pinnaclesresort.com. Up in the hills above town, these fresh, modern five-star apartments – sleeping two to six – have private spa

baths and share an ozone pool and a gym with sea views. ❺–❼

Whitehaven Beachfront Holiday Units 285 Shute Harbour Rd ☎07 4946 5710. Plain but quiet mini-apartments, very centrally located, right on the beach. ❸

Eating and entertainment

As with accommodation, the majority of the Whitsunday Coast **restaurants**, as well as the liveliest **nightclubs**, are in Airlie Beach. In addition to the places below, *Beaches* and *Magnum's* backpacker hostels both have late night bars that host club sessions and live-music nights.

Blitz Juice Bar Shute Harbour Rd. Tiny place with healthy options including a long list of fresh juices and sandwiches.

Blue Moon Lounge Mango Terrace, 263 Shute Harbour Rd. Open all day every day, but best after dark, this cocktail bar has a chilled, hippyish vibe, with regular acoustic music sessions.

Café Mykonos 287 Shute Harbour Rd. No-frills Greek café/takeaway offering cheap and cheerful kebabs, souvlaki, dolmades and salads, with nothing over A$12. Daily 11am–8pm.

Capers The Esplanade ☎07 4964 1777. This Mod Oz restaurant takes its wines and cocktails very seriously. The outdoor tables are good for lunch, while inside there's a large lounge-style bar that wakes up in the evenings. Breakfast, lunch and dinner daily.

Deja Vu *Water's Edge Resort*, 4 Golden Orchid Drive ☎07 4948 4309. With Mediterranean and Asian influences, this poolside place offers a set-menu "long lunch" on Sundays – excellent value at under A$40 if you're very hungry and have four hours to spare. Wed–Sat noon–2.30pm & 6–9pm, Sun noon–4pm.

Hog's Breath Café 261 Shute Harbour Rd. The original of this chain of Tex-Mex grill restaurants, still serving good grub. Main courses cost around A$24.

KC's 50 Shute Harbour Rd. Unpretentious, noisy grill where you can blow out on chargrilled steak, kangaroo, croc and seafood. Live bands at weekends. Breakfast, lunch and dinner till 3am.

Mangrove Jacks 297 Shute Harbour Rd ☎07 4964 1888. Easy-going wood-fired pizza joint. Daily 11.30am–2.30pm & 5.30–9.30pm.

Morocco's Shute Harbour Rd. Lively bar with a huge video screen, party atmosphere, and cheap Mexican and Cajun dishes. Daily 3pm–2am.

Paddy Shenanigan's 352 Shute Harbour Rd. Irish pub that makes a popular place to down a few pints and set the mood before heading onto one of Airlie's clubs.

Whitsunday Sailing Club Off The Esplanade. The club bar, open to non-members for drinks and pub food, has an old-school feel and good views out over the bay. Daily 10am–late.

Listings

Banks NAB and Commonwealth in Airlie Beach, plus ANZ and Westpac in Cannonvale.

Boat charters See box, p.522.

Car and scooter rental Airlie Beach Budget Autos, 285 Shute Harbour Rd ☎07 4948 0300; Avis, 366 Shute Harbour Rd ☎07 4946 6318; Europcar, 398 Shute Harbour Rd ☎07 4946 4133; Fun Rentals, Shute Harbour Rd ☎07 4948 0489; Tropic Car Hire, 15 Commercial Close ☎07 4946 5216; We Do Scooters ☎07 4946 5425. Cars cost around A$50 a day, scooters from A$35.

Car lockup Available at Shute Harbour Secured Parking (☎07 4946 9666) or Whitsunday Airport Secured Parking (☎0419 790 995).

Diving See box, p.528.

Doctor Opposite *McDonald's*, Shute Harbour Rd, Airlie Beach (daily 8am–7pm; 24hr phoneline ☎07 4948 0900).

Internet If your accommodation or tour booking office can't help out, airliebeach.com, up near the *Hog's Breath Café* at the Cannonvale end of Airlie Beach, has a stack of terminals.

Left luggage Lockers available 24 hours a day at The Locker Room on the corner of Shute Harbour Rd & The Esplanade (A$4–6 per day).

Pharmacy Airlie Day and Night Pharmacy (daily 8am–8pm).

Police Shute Harbour Rd, Cannonvale ☏ 07 4948
8888.
Post office In the centre of town, near
McDonald's.
Queensland Parks and Wildlife Service Corner
of Shute Harbour & Mandalay rds, 3km from Airlie
Beach towards Shutehaven (☏ 07 4946 7022,
ⓦ www.epa.qld.gov.au; Mon–Fri 9am–5pm). Island
camping permits and a small environmental
display.

Scenic flights See box, p.529.
Skydiving Skydive Airlie Beach, Whitsunday Airport
☏ 07 4946 9115, ⓦ www.skydiveoz.com.
Supermarket The biggest are in Cannonvale and
Jubilee Pocket, though Airlie Beach has a well-
stocked local food store about halfway through
town on Shute Harbour Rd.
Taxi ☏ 13 10 08; there are ranks in the main
shopping areas.

The Whitsundays

The Cumberland Islands, popularly known as the **Whitsundays**, look just like
the granite mountain peaks they once were before rising sea levels cut them off
from the mainland between six and ten thousand years ago. They were seasonally inhabited by the Ngaro Aborigines when Captain Cook sailed through in
1770; he proceeded to name the area after the day he arrived, and various
locations after his expedition's sponsors.

Today, dense green hoop pine forests, tropical jungle, vivid blue water and
roughly contoured coastlines give the islands instant appeal, and the surrounding
seas bustle with yachts and cruisers. The islands' steep topography leaves little
room for **beaches** but there are a few fine ones, notably **Catseye Bay** on
Hamilton Island and **Whitehaven Beach** on Whitsunday Island; the latter
regularly features on "Best Beach in the World" lists.

The archipelago comprises 74 islands in four groups: the Sir James Smith
Group (including Brampton Island) in the south, the Anchor Islands in the
southwest, the Lindeman Group further north and, east of Airlie Beach, the
Whitsunday Group, where most of the resorts are found. The first of these
opened in the 1930s; today, there are resorts on eight of the islands (Daydream,
South Molle, Long, Hayman, Hook, Hamilton, Lindeman and Brampton),
accessible by regular connections from the mainland, but most of the islands lie
within the Whitsunday Islands National Park and remain undeveloped. While
some of the islands were once used for livestock grazing, others are thickly
forested. Resorts aside, the few islands left in private hands are mainly uninhabited and largely the domain of local yachties.

There are three ways to explore the Whitsundays: dropping in for the day from
the mainland, staying on the islands or, best of all, cruising around them. **Day-
trips**, whether by small ferry, motor cruiser or yacht, give a taste of one or more
islands, with time to snorkel and swim. **Staying** allows you to choose between
camping (there are over thirty nationalpark campsites on the islands) and resort
facilities, with bushwalks and beach sports to pass the time. The resorts vary a
great deal in size and atmosphere, but most cater for middle- to high-budget
travellers; Hamilton even has a six-star resort. While prices may seem high
compared to mainland Queensland, stand-by deals can be good value, and polite
bargaining is always worth a try. **Cruises** ply the clear waters around the islands
for a few days of relaxing, snorkelling and diving, perhaps putting ashore at
times (check this, if it's the islands themselves you want to see). While it's

For advice on **swimming** in northern Queensland's coastal waters during the
"stinges season", see p.47.

possible to join a powerboat cruise, the classic way to experience the archipelago is by **yacht**, with or without a professional skipper, depending on your experience and inclinations.

Wildlife on the most visited islands tends to be bold and easy to spot – you're likely to see plenty of sulphur-crested cockatoos, bush stone curlews, rainbow lorikeets, goannas and flying foxes plus, on some islands, wallabies and brush turkeys. For **snorkelling**, the best fringing reefs are around Hayman Island and the north side of Hook Island. Don't miss the chance to do some **whale-watching** (see p.529) if you're in the archipelago between June or July and September, when humpbacks arrive from the Antarctic to give birth and raise their calves before heading south again.

Island practicalities

The islands' main commercial **airport**, Great Barrier Reef Airport (HTI) on Hamilton Island, is served by Jetstar, Qantas and Virgin Blue with direct flights from Melbourne, Sydney, Brisbane and Cairns. The other resort islands have helipads and landing facilities for light aircraft and seaplanes. The mainland base

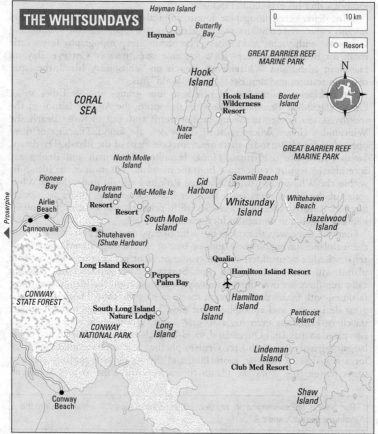

THE WHITSUNDAYS

Hayman Island

Butterfly Bay

Hayman

0   10 km

○ Resort

GREAT BARRIER REEF MARINE PARK

N

Hook Island

CORAL SEA

Hook Island Wilderness Resort

Border Island

Nara Inlet

GREAT BARRIER REEF MARINE PARK

North Molle Island

Cid Harbour

Sawmill Beach

Pioneer Bay

Daydream Island   Mid-Molle Is

Whitsunday Island

Whitehaven Beach

Airlie Beach

Resort   Resort
South Molle Island

Proserpine

Cannonvale

Shutehaven (Shute Harbour)

Hazelwood Island

Long Island Resort

Qualia

Peppers Palm Bay

Hamilton Island Resort

CONWAY STATE FOREST

Hamilton Island

Dent Island

Penticost Island

South Long Island Nature Lodge

CONWAY NATIONAL PARK

Long Island

Lindeman Island

Club Med Resort

Conway Beach

Shaw Island

520

Brampton Island (20 nautical miles southeast) ▼

for private transfers to the islands is Whitsunday Airport on Shute Harbour Road, about half way between Airlie Beach and Shute Harbour; it's used by Aviation Tourism Australia (℡07 4946 9102, ⓦwww.avta.com.au), Air Whitsunday (℡07 4946 9111, ⓦwww.airwhitsunday.com.au) and Aviation Adventures (℡07 4946 9988, ⓦwww.av8.com.au) for flights to Daydream, Hayman, South Molle, *Club Med* on Lindeman, and *Peppers Palm Bay* and *South Long Island Wilderness Lodge* on Long. The nearest mainland commercial airports are Proserpine's Whitsunday Coast Airport (PPP) and Mackay Airport (MKY). Australasian Jet (ⓦwww.ausjet.com.au) fly from Mackay to Brampton Island.

The transport hubs for **ferries and cruisers** are Shute Harbour on the mainland (with some boats using Abel Point Marina) and Hamilton Island. Local ferry and cruise company Fantasea (Shute Harbour; ℡07 4946 5111, ⓦwww.fantasea.com.au) offers ferry transfers between Shute Harbour and Daydream (A$27 one way), Long (A$27) and Hamilton (A$40–50). Voyager (℡07 4946 5255) ferry passengers from Shute Harbour to Hook Island. Cruise Whitsundays (℡07 4946 4662, ⓦwww.cruisewhitsundays.com) run transfers between Abel Point Marina and Daydream, South Molle and Hamilton. If you'd like to see more than one island, however, it's cheaper to choose a **cruise** from either Shute Harbour or Abel Point Marina (see box, p.522) than to shuttle between islands by ferry.

The resorts on Hayman and Brampton run **private ferry transfer services** for their guests: to Hayman, luxury launches run from Hamilton Island Airport or Shute Harbour (1hr; A$410 return); to Brampton, there's a daily boat from Mackay Marina (1hr 15min; A$110 return). *Peppers Palm Bay* on Long Island has its own ferry from Shute Harbour.

The nearest **long-distance bus stop** to the islands is Airlie Beach. The nearest **railway station** is Proserpine, with services up and down the coast between Brisbane and Cairns. Whitsunday Transit (℡07 4946 1800, ⓦwww .whitsundaytransit.com.au) runs a regular local bus service connecting Proserpine, Cannonvale, Airlie Beach, Abel Point, Whitsunday Airport and Shute Harbour roughly every half hour from 6am to 6pm. Parking at Shute Harbour costs A$10 per day or $40 for a week; there's also secure parking at Whitsunday Airport.

If you're planning to make use of the **national park campsites**, you'll need to arrange **camping transfers** as the ferries won't get you close enough to the sites; to arrange to be dropped on the quieter corners of the resort islands, or on isolated islands such as Planton, Tancred and Denman islands, contact Island Camping Connections (℡07 4946 1388) or Camping Whitsundays (℡07 4948 0933 or 1800 550 751, ⓦwww.campingwhitsundays.com), who can get you to the Molle group, northern Hook Island, and Cid Harbour or Whitehaven Beach on Whitsunday Island and lend you camping gear and water containers. You'll also need to book **QPWS camping permits**; see p.54 for information. The campsites have very basic facilities – pit toilets, picnic tables and rainwater tanks – so take everything you'll need with you, especially insect repellent, a gas stove (wood fires are prohibited) and drinking water. If you're planning a long stay, you can arrange for cruise boats to ferry in extra supplies.

The **Whitsundays Information Centre** is on the mainland in Cannonvale (1/5 Carlo Drive; ℡07 4948 5900 or 1800 801 252, ⓦwww .tourismwhitsundays.com.au).

Brampton Island and Lindeman Island

The southernmost of the Whitsundays, closer to Mackay than Airlie Beach, **Brampton Island** has more national park than most, home to fruit bats and

Exploring the Whitsunday archipelago by **yacht** is a quintessential East Coast experience. Sheltered by the Great Barrier Reef and by the islands' own mountains, the seas here tend to be smooth and safe, with plenty of protected anchorages, but there's no shortage of interesting challenges: skippers need to be confident navigators to steer safely round the reefs, while the average wind speed of 15–25 knots makes for some serious sailing.

Day-trips usually take in two or more islands, and offer a mixture of skippered sailing and motoring, with the chance to experience the thrills of boom-netting – sitting in a large rope hammock stretched above the water at the front of the boat so that you can catch the full soaking force of the waves – and do some snorkelling. Some may concentrate on a single theme, such as whale-watching, fishing or lazing on Whitehaven Beach. **Multi-day cruises** cover much the same territory but at a slower pace, typically spending a couple of nights at sea. A three-day, two-night sailing trip from Abel Point Marina is likely to take you to Hook Island via Nara Inlet, then on to Whitehaven Beach on Whitsunday Island; there may be an opportunity for sailing lessons along the way. **Scuba diving** is available to certified divers on some cruises (see box, p.501); on others, you can make arrangements for a dive boat to pick you up en route and take you out to the best sites.

The list of operators below is far from exhaustive; word of mouth is the best method of finding out about current deals and whether operators live up to their publicity. The **Whitsunday Charter Boat Industry Association** (℡07 4948 0601, ⊛www.wcbia .com) may be able to advise.

When **choosing a trip**, check the length – "three days" might mean one full day and two half-days – along with how much time is spent sailing and how much at anchor, how many people will be on board, and the size of the vessel. There are scores of beautiful boats, so you'll be swayed by your preference, be it for a performance racing yacht or a fun trip with lots of deck space on which to lounge. Bear in mind that a cheerful crew who are prepared to take your interests into account can make all the difference. As you'd expect, you get what you pay for: some of the "backpacker boats" are cramped, with very basic catering, and attract a hard-drinking crowd. Some yachts also have poor environmental practices and pump waste directly into the sea, so it's wise to ask probing questions. Finally, if you want to save money, shop around as close to departure times as possible, when advertised prices may drop. Keep an eye on the **weather forecast**, too, as itineraries may change in extreme conditions.

Groups with yachting experience might consider a **bareboat charter**. Making a booking is much like hiring a car. You're briefly shown how everything works; provisioning, itinerary-planning and navigation are all up to you, though radio back-up is available should you need advice along the way. Bareboat charter companies won't necessarily ask for a boat licence but will usually require the skipper and first mate in your group to provide proof of sailing proficiency; if you're inexperienced, they'll suggest you book some tuition or hire a skipper. Small yachts sleeping a family of four start at around A$400 a day; add about 25 percent during holiday seasons. A five-day minimum booking is standard.

Day-trips

Cruise Indigo ℡07 4946 8613, ⊛www.cruiseindigo.com.au (A$112, child A$80). Sailing trip from Hamilton Island to Whitehaven Beach and Chalkies Beach in an eighteen-metre Sydney-to-Hobart yacht, with lunch on the beach. Also sunset cruises.

Cruise Whitsundays ℡07 4946 4662, ⊛www.cruisewhitsundays.com.au (A$140, child A$80). Sailing trip from Abel Point Marina, South Mille, Daydream and Long to Whitehaven Bay aboard a fast, modern 26-metre catamaran.

Longer sailing trips

Two major sailing companies manage the majority of vessels: **Oz Adventure Sailing** (2/293 Shute Harbour Road; ☎07 4940 2000 or 1300 653 100, ⓦwww.ozsailing.com .au) and **Cruise Whitsunday**, comprising **Australian Tall Ship Cruises** and **Southern Cross** (☎07 4946 4999 or 1800 675 790, ⓦwww.australiantallships.com and ⓦwww .soxsail.com.au). Both have classic tall ships, vintage-style schooners and racing maxi yachts in their fleets and cater for a wide range of interests, from sedate cruising to livelier trips for a young crowd. **Sunsail** on Hamilton Island (Marina Village; ☎07 4948 9509 or 1800 803 988, ⓦwww.sunsail.com.au) offer small-group catamaran cruises with a skipper and cook.

Anaconda III (☎1800 677 199, ⓦwww.airliebeach.com; A$539 for three nights). The largest party yacht in the Whitsundays, taking up to 32 passengers in comfort. Relatively expensive, but you do get three full days aboard.

Bahia Melissa (Sunsail; A$1400 sharing a double cabin, A$2200 single occupancy, for three nights' full board). Flexible-itinerary sailing aboard a 14-metre-long catamaran, with first-class catering and service. A very comfortable option for a small group (maximum eight passengers plus two professional crew), and good value, compared to bareboating, if there are only two of you (as you book a cabin, rather than the whole boat).

Derwent Hunter (Oz Adventure Sailing; from A$499 for two nights). Ninety-foot schooner built in 1945 and totally refurbished with timber decking and fittings after years spent as a research vessel and a film set, and yet more time engaged in dubious activities in the South China Sea.

Siska (Southern Cross; A$409 for two nights). A race-winning 25-metre maxi yacht with room for twenty passengers.

Solway Lass (Australian Tall Ship Cruises; from A$449 for three nights). Classic three- or six-night adventures aboard a famous tall ship, over a century old.

Southern Cross (Southern Cross; A$409 for two nights). The company's flagship: a high-speed, 21-metre-long America's Cup challenger accommodating fourteen passengers. Aimed at couples.

Waltzing Matilda (Oz Adventure Sailing; from A$439 for two nights). A more modern design than most of Oz's fleet, this eighteen-metre ketch is not that roomy, but has a great atmosphere.

Whitsunday Magic (Australian Tall Ship Cruises; from A$629 for three nights). Large, characterful luxury schooner with diving facilities, sailing to the islands and Outer Reef.

Sailing tuition

Sunsail (see above). Weekly five-day/six-night RYA Competent Crew courses for beginners, with a maximum of five students per yacht (A$1200 per person) They also offer more advanced courses: RYA Day Skipper and Coastal Skipper Practical each take five days (A$1200).

Oz Adventure Sailing (see above). Liveaboard "Learn to Sail" courses lasting three (A$549) or six days (A$1100).

Bareboat charters

Whitsunday Rent-a-Yacht (Shute Harbour; ☎07 4946 9232 or 1800 075 000, ⓦwww .rentayacht.com.au) and **Queensland Yacht Charters** (Abel Point Marina; ☎07 4946 7400 or 1800 075 013, ⓦwww.yachtcharters.com.au) have been going for years and are thoroughly reliable, as are **Sunsail** (see above), who offer an excellent fleet of comfortable and well-maintained 10- to 15-metre mono-hull yachts sleeping four to ten, and catamarans sleeping up to eight, including two top-end air-conditioned models.

kangaroos, and an overnighters-only resort, *Voyages Brampton Island* (☎07 4951 4499, ⓦwww.brampton-island.com; ❻) aimed primarily at couples: there are no dedicated family facilities. It's a little tired so doesn't quite count as luxurious, but it's comfortable and peaceful, with a beautiful seawater pool seemingly hanging over the ocean. On offer are the usual selection of watersports (including jet-skis, dinghies and snorkelling, but not diving), plus a guided trip across to neighbouring Carlisle Island to visit its highly atmospheric "1000-year-old" melaleuca forest.

Lindeman Island suffered as a victim of feral goats, though their eradication has seen native plants making a comeback in a small melaleuca swamp and on the wooded northeast side. **Mount Oldfield** offers panoramic views, while other walking tracks lead to swimming beaches on the north shore. The family-friendly *Club Med* **resort** (☎1800 258 263, ⓦwww.clubmed.com.au; all-inclusive ❸), Australia's first and only, has all the services you'd expect and no day-trippers.

Hamilton Island

Hamilton Island claims to be Australia's most popular island holiday destination, and it's certainly always busy; at times, its tiny road network is positively clogged with visitors pottering about in the standard mode of transport, electric buggies. There are echoes of the Gold Coast in the small row of slab-like hotel and apartment buildings dominating the best beach, **Catseye Bay**, and while not everyone you'll meet here will be a holiday-maker – Hamilton has around two thousand permanent residents – no attempt is made to disguise the fact that the island is wholly devoted to tourism.

Hamilton is privately owned by a multimillionaire wine magnate, and most of its businesses belong to the same umbrella company. Near the marina, a cluster of village amenities including a small supermarket, a bakery and a few restaurants line the quaint **colonial-style waterfront**; uphill from here are holiday villas with fine views of the sea (to let through Accom Hamilton Island; ☎1800 466 600, ⓦwww.accomhamiltonisland.net.au). Beyond these, tucked away on the island's northern point, is the recent luxury **accommodation** addition of ⚶ *Qualia* (reservations ☎02 9433 3349, ⓦwww.qualia.com.au; ❾), a medium-sized six-star resort and spa, which offers the ultimate in secluded relaxation in a setting designed to blend in with the island landscape, with imaginative use of local stone and timber. As you'd expect, the cost of staying here is high, even for the Whitsundays.

Most visitors opt to stay at the *Hamilton Island Resort* on Catseye Bay (☎07 4946 9999 or 13 73 33, ⓦwww.hamiltonisland.com.au), which has a kids' club, several large, good-looking pools and a good mix of accommodation including the attractive *Palm Bungalows* (❼) for self-caterers, impressively spacious rooms with commanding views in the towering *Reef View Hotel* (❼) and luxury beach suites in the *Beach Club* (❽). Even if you're not staying there, it's worth dropping in to the *Reef View* just to zoom up to the top floor in one of the glass-walled lifts and admire the view, assuming you can stomach the fact that the towers exist at all: completed in 1990, these nineteen-storey shockers can be explained, though not excused, as a product of less-enlightened times.

The **places to eat** scattered around the Marina Village and the hotel area all offer resort-style fare, most of which is either disappointing, overpriced or both; the best of the bunch is the upmarket Mod Oz *Beach House* on Catseye Bay (☎07 4946 8580; Tues & Wed 5.30pm–late, Fri–Sun noon–2pm & 5.30pm–late).

To circuit the island's roads, **buggy rental** costs A$45 for one hour or A$70 per day; there's also a free – and frequent – **bus service** that runs from 7am to 11am. Hamilton's sole visitor attraction is a small and rather cramped zoo, the **Koala Gallery** (daily 7.30am–5pm; A$17.50, child A$8.50; ℡07 4946 8266), which, in addition to koalas, houses wombats, crocs and other native species. Activities on offer on the island include the **Wire Flyer** (A$50; ℡07 4946 8780, child A$40), a hang-glider attached to a zip-line; **high-speed catamaran sailing** with Adrenalin Rush (A$60, child A$50; ℡07 4946 8286, ⓦwww .adrenalinrush.com.au), **kayaking** around the island with Sea Kayaking Whitsundays (from A$39; ℡07 4946 8305, ⓦwww.kayakwhitsunday.com); guided snorkelling with H2O Sportz (A$85, child A$65; ℡07 4946 9888, ⓦwww.h2osportz.com.au); plus windsurfing and dinghy sailing. Yachting is also, naturally, a popular pastime; the liveliest time is during **Hamilton Island Race Week** in August, a relatively new event.

Hamilton is not the most rewarding of the islands for wildlife-watchers – along with gulls and crows, the island's voluble colonies of sulphur-crested cockatoos and fruit bats are the most conspicuous species you'll encounter – but there are a few pleasant bushwalks through the forested hills beyond the resort.

Long Island

Long Island is exactly that, being not much more than a narrow, ten-kilometre ribbon almost within reach of the mainland forests. You feel closer to the wilderness here than on most of the other resort islands, and there are worthwhile hikes through the rainforest to **Sandy Bay** (where there's a nationalpark campsite) up **Humpy Point**, or around the northern end of the island, home to agile wallabies and flying foxes.

The island has three **resorts**, all quite separate from each other and each with a distinct character. *Long Island Resort* at Happy Bay (℡07 4946 9400, ⓦwww .oceanhotels.com.au; full board ❸–❼) is an ageing, family-orientated place with a low-budget feel that makes it seem poor value, even though it's one of the least expensive of the island resorts; there's plenty of entertainment on offer but the atmosphere is regularly shattered by helicopters flying people to the upmarket alternatives. ⚑ *Peppers Palm Bay* (℡07 4946 9233, ⓦwww.peppers .com.au; full board ❾), half a kilometre south at the island's waist, is a more exclusive upmarket retreat with a handful of very pretty cabins right on the beach, but for a real escape, head to ⚑ *South Long Island Nature Lodge* at Paradise Bay (℡07 4946 9777, ⓦwww.southlongisland.com; full board ❽; 5-night minimum stay), an intimate option whose six comfortable, eco-friendly beach houses, superb food and attentive service are only accessible by helicopter.

Whitsunday Island

The largest island in the group, uninhabited and managed by Queensland Parks and Wildlife Service, **Whitsunday Island** is also one of the most enjoyable. On its east coast is **Whitehaven Beach**, easily the finest in all the islands, and on the itinerary of just about every cruise boat in the region. Long, blindingly white, icing-sugar-soft and still clean despite the numbers of day-trippers and campers, it's a beautiful spot so long as you can handle the lack of distractions – there's no resort on Whitsunday, and the beach is entirely undeveloped. The **campsite** is at the south end of the beach, just above the tide line, with minimal shelter provided by whispering casuarinas. Snorkellers should also head down to this end of the beach, facing Haslewood Island, while at the north end there's

▲ Sailing in the Whitsundays

a short bushwalk up to a lookout with spectacular views over **Hill Inlet**, its emerald and sapphire waters marbled with white sand.

Over on Whitsunday's west side, **Cid Harbour** is a quieter hideaway that lacks a great beach but instead enjoys a backdrop of giant granite boulders and tropical forests, with several more campsites above coral and pebble shingle. **Dugong Beach** is the nicest, sheltered under the protective arms and buttressed roots of giant trees; it's a twenty-minute walk along narrow hill paths from **Sawmill Beach**, where you're likely to be dropped off.

The Molles and nearby islands

South Molle Island was a source of fine-grained stone for Ngaro Aborigines, a unique material for the tools that have been found on other islands and may help in mapping trade routes. The rather shabby and overpriced **resort**

(T07 4946 9433 OR 1800 075 080, Wwww.southmolleisland.com.au; full board ●) in the north of the island offers heaps of extras such as sports and guided walks. **Walking tracks** from behind the golf course lead to gum trees and rainforest, encompassing vistas of the islands from the top of Spion Kop and Mount Jeffreys, and some quiet beaches at the south end.

South Molle's resort can sometimes organize a lift to the **campsite** on uninhabited **North Molle Island**, only 2km away (otherwise, contact Camping Whitsundays; see p.521); the beach here is made up of rough coral fragments, but the snorkelling is fairly good. There are another couple of campsites on **Mid-Molle Island**, joined to South Molle by a low-tide causeway about half a kilometre from the resort.

Daydream Island is little more than a tiny wooded rise between South Molle and the mainland, with a narrow beach running the length of the east side, and coral to snorkel over at the north end. The large **resort** (T07 4948 8488 or 1800 075 040, Wwww.daydreamisland.com; ●) offers fine food and hospitality plus a good range of facilities including a man-made outdoor aquarium and an outdoor cinema. It's hardly in harmony with its surroundings, though: regimented lines of 1960s-style blocks dominate views of the island from the sea and detract from an otherwise very pretty scene.

Tiny **Planton**, **Tancred** and **Denman** islands are just offshore from South Molle – with no facilities and limited camping at national park campsites, they're about as isolated as you'll get in the Whitsundays. All three are surrounded by reef, but be careful of strong currents.

Hook Island

Directly north of Whitsunday Island, **Hook Island** is the second largest in the group. The low-key and fairly basic *Hook Island Wilderness Resort* (T07 4946 9380, Wwww.hookislandresort.com; camping A$35, bunk in shared room A$45, private cabin ●), at the island's southeastern end, is the only place on the Whitsundays offering budget beds. It has fine views over the channel to Whitsunday, as well as a bar, a small store, and a cafeteria serving meals and snacks. There are also several national park **campsites** around the island, the pick of which is at southern **Curlew Beach** – sheltered, pretty and accessible only with your own vessel or by prior arrangement with a tour operator.

Cruises often pull into southern **Nara Inlet** for a look at the **Aboriginal paintings** on the walls of a small cave above a tiny shingle beach. Though not dramatic in scale or design, the art is significant for its net patterns, which are otherwise found only in the Queensland Outback at central highland sites such as Carnarvon Gorge.

Snorkelling on the reef directly in front of the resort is a must; snorkelling gear and surf skis are free (with deposit) to guests. The water is cloudy on large tides, but the coral outcrops are all in fairly good condition and there's plenty of life around, from flatworms to morays and parrotfish. Day-cruises run from Airlie to the top-rate fringing coral at **Butterfly Bay**, **Maureen's Cove**, **Luncheon Bay** and **Manta Ray Bay** on the northern and northeastern tips of the island – visibility can be poor here, but on a good day these sites offer some of the best diving and snorkelling in the Whitsundays.

Hayman Island

Small and with a jealously guarded luxury-private-island atmosphere, there's not much to **Hayman Island** beyond its large resort, ⚐ *Hayman*

(☎07 4940 1244, ⊛www.hayman.com.au; ⑧). The extremely high price of staying at this multi-award-winning hotel pales into insignificance when compared to the cost of building it, which topped A$300 million. Having shelled out between A$700 and A$4500 just to be here for the night, guests can relax in spacious rooms or browse the in-house art collection, while porters move about through underground tunnels to preserve the peace. The centrepiece of the resort is an immense swimming-pool complex fronted by

Tours and activities in the Whitsundays

Diving and snorkelling trips

There's stunning coral in fairly shallow water around the more northerly Whitsundays, and a cluster of sites, with better visibility – including Bait Reef, Knuckle Reef and Hardy Reef – within day-trip distance on the Whitsunday section of the Great Barrier Reef.

H2O Sportz Marina Village, Hamilton Island ☎07 4946 9888, ⊛www.h2osportz .com.au (full day A$169 plus A$100–120 for two dives; half day A$85 plus A$70–90 for one dive). Diving and snorkelling trips to rewarding sites on the north coast of Hook Island, at Border Island east of Whitsunday, and at Bait Reef in the Coral Sea. They also offer PADI scuba training.

Fantasea Shute Harbour ☎07 4946 5111, ⊛www.fantasea.com.au (A$195, child A$90; two dives A$100). Owns a permanent pontoon, Reefworld, at Hardy Reef, east of Hayman Island, for snorkelling, diving, semi-submersible rides and helicopter flips. Their cruiser sails there from Shute Harbour at 8am daily, picking up passengers from Daydream and Hamilton on the way and getting back at 5.35pm; if you're staying on Long Island, you can join the trip by crossing to Shute Harbour first. It's possible to stay at sea for a night by booking a Reefsleep package (from A$400) – a good alternative if you don't have time to take a live-aboard trip.

Cruise Whitsundays 263 Shute Harbour Rd, Airlie Beach ☎07 4946 4662, ⊛www .cruisewhitsundays.com.au (A$189, child A$90; two dives A$154). Luxury day-trips by cruiser from Abel Point Marina to their pontoon at the excellent Knuckle Reef Lagoon snorkel and dive site, northeast of Hayman Island.

Oz Adventure Sailing 2/293 Shute Harbour Rd ☎07 4940 2000 or 1300 653 100, ⊛www.ozsailing.com.au. This sailing-trip company offers on-board scuba diving facilities on a number of their live-aboards, including racing yacht *Spank Me* (two nights A$479); ketch *Kiana* (three nights A$549); sail/dive catamarans *Pacific Star* (three nights from A$479) and *Wings* (two nights from A$375); classic yacht *Summertime* (three nights from A$495); power cruiser *Powerplay* (two nights from A$395) and maxi yachts *Matador* and *Freight Train* (two nights from A$495). These trips include one dive, with additional dives costing A$60–65.

Power-launch day-trips

Cruise Whitsundays (see above). Day visits to Daydream or South Molle, or twin-island cruises to both islands, with full use of the resort facilities (A$80, child A$45; both islands for A$105/A$60).

Fantasea (see above). Offers trips from Shute Harbour to *Long Island Resort* (A$67, child A$47), *Daydream Island Resort* (A$71–77, child A$41–47), Hamilton Island (A$101, child A$59), including lunch in each case, or to all three for A$80 (child A$44) plus lunch. Their daily Whitehaven Beach Cruise takes you from Shute Harbour (A$125, child A$30) or from Hamilton, Daydream or Long (A$79, child A$30) to Whitehaven Beach by air-conditioned catamaran, for a leisurely day out. They also offer a three-night live-aboard cruise around the islands and reef aboard the luxury *MV Ammari* (⊛www.fantaseaammari.com).

a blond beach fringed with palms. The restaurants are all superb, and the spa, *Spa Chakra*, is world class.

Access to the island is by helicopter, seaplane or luxury high-speed cruiser (with complimentary fizz and nibbles) from Hamilton Island or Shute Harbour. Families with kids are welcome as guests, but day-trippers aren't allowed anywhere near the place. Some cruises and diving trips do sail quite close, though, stopping for a look at the coral in **Blue Pearl Bay** on the island's west coast.

Mantaray ℡07 4946 4321 or 1800 816 365, ⊛www.mantaraycharters.com (A$130, child A$65). Fast and relatively roomy boat out to Whitehaven Beach, where you spend around three hours at leisure before heading north for Mantaray Bay and some good snorkelling.

Ocean Rafting ℡07 4946 6848, ⊛www.oceanrafting.com (A$103, child A$66). Great-value, action-packed cruise on a zippy inflatable to Whitehaven Beach, with a walk to the Hill Inlet lookout or the Aboriginal caves at Nara Inlet. Maximum 25 passengers.

Reefjet ℡07 4946 5366, ⊛www.reefjet.com.au (A$130, child A$65). Long-established operator making a fast run out to Whitehaven Beach and Hook Island for sand and snorkelling.

Whitehaven Xpress ℡07 4946 1585, ⊛www.whitehavenxpress.com.au (A$133, child A$67). Small-group trips to Whitsunday Island, stopping for scenery at Hill Inlet before a spot of snorkelling and a beach barbecue at Whitehaven Beach.

Sailing trips
See box, p.522.

Scenic flights
The islands look stunning from the air. **Aviation Tourism Australia** (Whitsunday Airport; ℡07 4946 9102, ⊛www.avta.com.au) and their Hamilton division, **Hamilton Island Aviation** (℡07 4946 8249) offer a variety of scenic flights by helicopter, light aircraft or seaplane, the latter touching down on the shores of Whitehaven Beach for an hour or so on the sand. You'll zoom over scudding yachts, their sails dazzling white against the luminous indigo, turquoise and aquamarine Coral Sea and the deep green of the forests. To add to the romance, your pilot will head out to the Great Barrier Reef east of Hayman Island to buzz over the appropriately named Heart Reef, icon of many a Whitsunday wedding brochure. **Air Whitsunday** (Whitsunday Airport; ℡07 4946 9111, ⊛www.airwhitsunday.com.au) offers scenic flights and day trips by sea plane, **Aviation Adventures** (Whitsunday Airport; ℡07 4946 9988, ⊛www.av8 .com.au) will zip you around by helicopter, and **Tigermoth Adventures** (Whitsunday Airport; ℡07 4946 9111, ⊛www.tigermothadventures.com.au) will take you up in a vintage biplane. All can arrange pick-ups from mainland or island accommodation.

Watersports
All the island resorts offer at least some of the following: sea kayaking, jet skiing, powerboating, inflatable rides, dinghy sailing, windsurfing and snorkelling; some include non-powered activities in their room rates.

Whale-watching
The sheltered waters of the Whitsundays become a calving and nursery ground for humpback whales between July and September. Operators that offer whale-watching trips at this time include **Fantasea** (see opposite; A$99, child A$49, family A$247) and **Sea Kayaking Whitsundays** (℡07 4946 8305, ⊛www.kayakwhitsunday.com; A$119). Alternatively, book a scenic flight for a good chance of watching the whales from

Bowen and Ayr

BOWEN, a quiet seafront settlement 60km northwest of Proserpine, 204km from Townsville and around 45 minutes' drive from Airlie Beach, is one of Queensland's oldest towns; it was once under consideration as the site of the state capital, but it floundered after Townsville's foundation. Today, stark first impressions created by the sterile bulk of the saltworks on the highway are offset by some pretty beaches to the north and a certain small-town charm. Murals in the town centre act as a local-history primer, depicting scenes from the town's earliest days to its time as a World War II seaplane base. Celebrated Australian movie director Baz Luhrmann chose to film his historical drama *Australia* (2008) in and around Bowen, largely because the jetty looks as if it has barely changed since the 1930s.

The main attraction for many travellers is the prospect of seasonal **farm work**: Bowen's mangoes and tomatoes are famous throughout Queensland, and there's a large floating population of itinerant pickers in town between April and January. In peak harvest season (May–Nov), the backpacker hostels (see below) can sometimes help with finding work.

Bowen's attractive **beaches** lie a couple of kilometres north of the town centre. **Queens Beach**, which faces north, is sheltered, long and has a stinger net for the jellyfish season, but the best is **Horseshoe Bay**, small, and hemmed in by some sizeable boulders, with good waters for a swim or snorkel – though the construction of an oversized resort nearby threatens to ruin the atmosphere.

With **your own transport**, it might be worth **skipping Bowen** in favour of the ranch-style *Bogie River Bush House* (T07 4785 3407, W www .bogiebushhouse.com.au; ❹), about 60km inland from town towards Collinsville. This splendid farmstay retreat has good cooking, a pool and offers the chance to go horse-riding, fishing, or to meet tame wildlife, rescued as orphans; you can also organize farm work here. Alternatively, for coastal seclusion on the opposite side of Edgecumbe Bay from Bowen, there's the ✈ *Cape Gloucester Eco-Resort* at Hydeaway Bay (T07 4945 7242, W www.whitsundayecoresort.com; ❹, cabin ❻), with a saltwater pool and just ten self-contained rooms and cabins on a large plot overlooking clear blue water fringed by an empty beach.

Bowen practicalities

Bowen's centre overlooks **Edgecumbe Bay**, with all the shops and services spaced out along broad, quiet **Herbert Street**. The **railway station** is a few kilometres west of town near the highway, while **long-distance buses** run by Greyhound and Premier (see p.35) stop outside Bowen Travel (T07 4786 2835), just off Herbert on Williams Street, which can organize tickets. There's a **visitor centre** 4km south of town on the Bruce Highway (T07 4786 4222, W www.tourismbowen.com.au).

Budget **accommodation** – which should be booked in advance and is usually offered at weekly rates only – is offered by *Bowen Backpackers*, at the beach end of Herbert Street (T07 4786 3433; bunk in shared room A$18– 26.50, private double ❷; sometimes closes after the end of the picking season in December), which has a huge pool at the back of the building; and *Reefers* at

For advice on **swimming** in northern Queensland's coastal waters during the "stinger season", see p.47.

the corner of Soldiers and Horseshoe Bay roads (℗07 4786 4199, ⓦwww
.reefers.com.au; bunk in shared room A$22, private double ❶), a spacious place
with a pool, 3km from town near the beaches. **Mid-range** choices include
Castle Motor Lodge, 6 Don St (℗07 4786 1322, ⓦwww.castlemotorlodge
.com.au; ❸), about the closest option to the centre of town. You can **eat** at the
century-old *Grandview Hotel* at 5 Herbert St, down near the Harbour Office, or
at *McDee's Coffee Shop* on the corner of Herbert and George streets, or climb
up to *Three Sixty on the Hill* (1 Margaret Reynolds Drive, Flagstaff Hill ℗07
4786 6360; Mon & Sun 8.30am–4.30pm, Wed–Sat 9.30am–9pm) for fresh, light
meals and wraparound views; alternatively, stock up at the **supermarket** on
Williams Street and at the town's numerous fruit and vegetable stalls.

Ayr

On the Bruce Highway between Bowen and Townsville are the towns of
Home Hill and **Ayr**, separated by a mill, a few kilometres of cane fields and
the iron framework of the **Burdekin River Bridge** – the Burdekin River, one
of the north's most famous landmarks, is still liable to flood during severe wet
seasons, despite having to fight its way across three weirs and a dam. On the

Diving the SS Yongala

The **SS Yongala** was a 109-metre-long passenger ship, which, for reasons that
remain a mystery, sank with all hands during a cyclone in 1911, just eleven nautical
miles offshore, near Cape Bowling Green. The water in this area is rich in nutrients
but exposed to the powerful ocean currents, so marine species quickly adopted the
structure as a safe haven. It lay undiscovered for over fifty years, becoming thickly
encrusted in coral, and remains remarkably intact. Home to a diverse population of
turtles, rays, moray eels, giant groupers and huge schools of barracuda, mackerel
and trevally, the wreck now makes a staggeringly good **dive site**, considered Australia's best by experienced divers, many of whom count it amongst the world's top
five.

Depths are manageable – the wreck lies in 14 to 29 metres of water – but because
of its exposed location, it's not much fun diving here if the weather is rough. Even in
calm conditions, this can be a demanding site, with strong currents and startlingly
big fish, so it's best not to go unless you've logged twenty dives or more and your
skills are up to date. Unlike the wreck of the HMAS *Brisbane* near Mooloolaba (see
p.468), it's not possible to enter the *Yongala* – you can only swim over and around
the ship.

Operators who take certified divers out to the wreck include **Yongala Dive** (56
Narrah St, Alva Beach, Ayr; ℗07 4783 1519, ⓦwww.yongaladive.com.au; daily two-
dive trips from A$204 or A$234 including gear; nitrox fills A$20), who are just thirty
minutes by RIB from the site. They can arrange transfers to Alva Beach from Airlie
Beach for A$45; for those planning to stay overnight, they also have very comfortable
accommodation with breakfast included (*Yongala Divers Lodge*; bed in shared room
A$27, private double ❸). Townsville-based **Adrenalin Dive** (9 Wickham St, Towns-
ville; ℗07 4724 0600 or 1300 664 600, ⓦwww.adrenalindive.com.au) run trips to the
wreck three times a week from Townsville and Magnetic Island (A$205–240 for two
dives, depending on whether you need gear), while **Prodive Townsville** (252 Walker
St Townsville; ℗07 4721 1760 or 1300 131 760, ⓦwww.prodivetownsville.com.au)
offer two-dive *Yongala* day-trips (A$235), plus three-night live-aboard trips including
a total of ten dives on the *Yongala* and other sites (A$775).

Prodive also run PADI courses including a five-day eco-course (A$885), which gives
beginners the chance to dive the *Yongala*.

northern side, **AYR**, 85km south of Townsville, is a compact farming town fast becoming another popular stop on the **farm work** trail. The highway, which runs through town as Queen Street, is where you'll find the **bus stop** and all essential services, as well as workers' hostels, which can find you employment picking and packing capsicums, amongst other things – *Ayr Backpackers* at Wilmington House on Wilmington Street (℡07 4783 5837; phone in advance for pick-up; bunks from A$110 per week; single nights only available outside of the fruit-picking season and on special request), is the best option.

Ayr's other attraction is quick and easy access to the wreck of the **Yongala**, offshore near Alva Beach (see box, p.531).

❼ Travel details

Trains

Ayr to: Bundaberg (6 weekly; 9hr 30min); Mackay (6 weekly; 5hr); Proserpine (6 weekly; 2hr 30min); Rockhampton (5 weekly; 11hr).

Bowen to: Bundaberg (6 weekly; 14hr); Mackay (6 weekly; 3hr 30min); Proserpine (6 weekly; 45min); Rockhampton (6 weekly; 9hr 30min).

Bundaberg to: Ayr (6 weekly; 9hr 30min); Bowen (6 weekly; 14hr); Brisbane (6 weekly; 6hr); Caboolture (6 weekly; 5hr 45min); Cairns (5 weekly; 24hr); Cardwell (5 weekly; 19hr 30min); Gladstone (6 weekly; 2hr 15min); Ingham (5 weekly; 17hr 45min); Innisfail (5 weekly; 23hr); Mackay (6 weekly; 10hr 15min); Proserpine (6 weekly; 12hr 15min); Rockhampton (6 weekly; 4hr 15min); Townsville (6 weekly; 17hr); Tully (5 weekly; 21hr).

Gladstone to: Bundaberg (6 weekly; 2hr 15min); Mackay (6 weekly; 8hr); Proserpine (6 weekly; 10hr); Rockhampton (6 weekly; 2hr 30min).

Mackay to: Ayr (6 weekly; 5hr); Bowen (6 weekly; 3hr 30min); Brisbane (6 weekly; 17hr); Bundaberg (6 weekly; 10hr 15min); Caboolture (6 weekly; 16hr); Cairns (5 weekly; 14hr); Cardwell (5 weekly; 10hr); Gladstone (6 weekly; 8hr); Ingham (5 weekly; 8hr 45min); Innisfail (5 weekly; 12hr 30min); Proserpine (6 weekly; 2hr); Rockhampton (6 weekly; 6hr); Townsville (6 weekly; 6hr 30min); Tully (5 weekly; 10hr 30min).

Proserpine to: Ayr (6 weekly; 2hr 30min); Bowen (6 weekly; 45min); Brisbane (6 weekly; 19hr); Bundaberg (6 weekly; 12hr 15min); Caboolture (6 weekly; 18hr); Cairns (5 weekly; 12hr); Cardwell (5 weekly; 8hr); Gladstone (6 weekly; 10hr); Ingham (5 weekly; 6hr 30min); Innisfail (5 weekly; 9hr 30min); Mackay (6 weekly; 2hr); Rockhampton (6 weekly; 8hr 30min); Townsville (6 weekly; 4hr 30min); Tully (5 weekly; 8hr 30min).

Rockhampton to: Ayr (5 weekly; 11hr); Bowen (6 weekly; 9hr 30min); Brisbane (6 weekly; 11hr

30min); Bundaberg (6 weekly; 4hr 15min); Caboolture (6 weekly; 10hr 30min); Cairns (5 weekly; 8hr); Cardwell (5 weekly; 16hr 15min); Gladstone (6 weekly; 2hr 30min); Ingham (5 weekly; 15hr); Innisfail (5 weekly; 18hr 15min); Mackay (6 weekly; 6hr); Proserpine (6 weekly; 8hr 30min); Townsville (6 weekly; 12hr); Tully (5 weekly; 16hr).

Buses

Agnes Water to: Bundaberg (daily; 1hr 30min); Hervey Bay (daily; 4hr).

Airlie Beach to: Ayr (6 daily; 3hr 30min); Brisbane (5 daily; 18hr); Bundaberg (3 daily; 12hr 30min); Cairns (6 daily; 10hr); Cardwell (6 daily; 6hr 45min); Childers (5 daily; 13hr 15min); Hervey Bay (5 daily; 14hr); Ingham (6 daily; 6hr); Innisfail (6 daily; 9hr); Mackay (6 daily; 2hr 15min); Mission Beach (6 daily; 8hr); Mooloolaba (daily; 17hr 30min); Noosa (daily; 16hr 45min); Rockhampton (5 daily; 7hr 30min); Townsville (6 daily; 4hr); Tully (6 daily; 7hr 35min).

Ayr to: Airlie Beach (6 daily; 3hr 30min); Bundaberg (5 daily; 14hr); Hervey Bay (5 daily; 15hr 30min); Mackay (6 daily; 5hr); Rockhampton (5 daily; 10hr).

Bundaberg to: Agnes Water (daily; 1hr 30min); Airlie Beach (5 daily; 10hr 30min); Ayr (5 daily; 14hr); Brisbane (5 daily; 6hr 30min); Cairns (6 daily; 20hr 30min); Cardwell (6 daily; 17hr); Childers (5 daily; 50min); Hervey Bay (5 daily; 1hr 45min); Ingham (5 daily; 19hr); Innisfail (5 daily; 3hr); Mackay (5 daily; 9hr); Mission Beach (5 daily; 20hr); Noosa (twice daily; 7hr); Rainbow Beach (daily; 4hr 30min); Rockhampton (5 daily; 3hr 30min); Townsville (5 daily; 15hr 30min); Tully (5 daily; 19hr 30min).

Childers to: Airlie Beach (5 daily; 13hr 15min); Bundaberg (5 daily; 50min); Hervey Bay (5 daily; 50min); Mackay (5 daily; 11hr); Rockhampton (5 daily; 5hr).

Hervey Bay to: Agnes Water (daily; 4hr); Airlie Beach (5 daily; 14hr); Ayr (5 daily; 15hr 30min); Brisbane (7 daily; 5hr); Bundaberg (5 daily; 1hr 45min); Cairns (6 daily; 20hr 30min); Cardwell (5 daily; 20hr); Childers (5 daily; 50min); Ingham (5 daily; 19hr); Innisfail (5 daily; 22hr); Mackay (5 daily; 10hr 30min); Mission Beach (5 daily; 21hr); Noosa (4 daily; 4hr); Rainbow Beach (daily; 2hr); Rockhampton (5 daily; 6hr); Townsville (5 daily; 19hr); Tully (5 daily; 20hr 30min).

Mackay to: Airlie Beach (6 daily; 2hr 15min); Ayr (6 daily; 5hr); Brisbane (8 daily; 15hr 30min); Bundaberg (5 daily; 9hr); Cairns (5 daily; 13hr); Cardwell (6 daily; 9hr); Childers (5 daily; 11hr); Hervey Bay (5 daily; 10hr 30min); Ingham (6 daily; 9hr); Innisfail (6 daily; 12hr); Mission Beach (6 daily; 10hr 30min); Noosa (twice daily; 14hr); Rockhampton (5 daily; 5hr); Townsville (6 daily; 6hr 30min); Tully (6 daily; 10hr).

Rockhampton to: Airlie Beach (5 daily; 7hr 30min); Ayr (5 daily; 10hr); Brisbane (5 daily; 11hr 30min); Bundaberg (5 daily; 3hr 30min); Cairns (5 daily; 17hr 30min); Cardwell (5 daily; 14hr); Childers (5 daily; 5hr); Hervey Bay (5 daily; 6hr); Ingham (5 daily; 11hr 30min); Innisfail (5 daily; 16hr); Mackay (5 daily; 5hr); Mission Beach (4 daily; 16hr); Noosa (twice daily; 10hr); Townsville (twice daily; 11hr); Tully (5 daily; 14hr).

Ferries

Airlie Beach/Shute Harbour to: Daydream Island (1–2 daily; 45min); Hamilton Island (1–3 daily; 1hr); Hook Island (1–2 daily; 1hr 30min); Lindeman Island (twice daily; 1hr 30min); South Molle Island (twice daily; 45min); Whitsunday Island (daily; 2hr).

Hervey Bay to: Fraser Island (8 daily; 30min–1hr).

Mission Beach to: Dunk Island (10 or more daily; 15min).

Rosslyn Bay to: Great Keppel Island (3 daily; 45min–1hr).

Flights

Bundaberg to: Brisbane (3 daily; 1hr); Cairns (twice daily; 4hr 50min); Gladstone (weekly; 35min); Lady Elliot Island (daily; 45min); Mackay (daily; 2hr); Rockhampton (daily; 50min).

Gladstone to: Bundaberg (weekly; 35min); Rockhampton (5 weekly; 25min).

Mackay to: Bundaberg (daily; 2hr); Cairns (twice daily; 2hr 45min); Rockhampton (twice daily; 45min); Townsville (4 daily; 1hr).

Rockhampton to: Bundaberg (daily; 50min); Cairns (twice daily; 3hr); Gladstone (5 weekly; 25min); Great Keppel Island (3 daily; 25min); Mackay (twice daily; 45min); Townsville (twice daily; 1hr 50min).

Far North Queensland

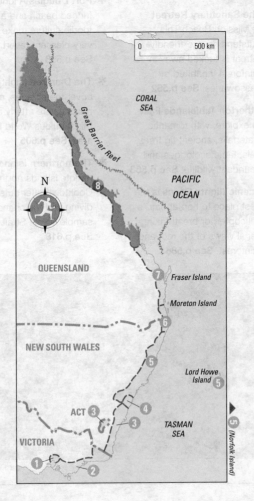

CHAPTER 8 # Highlights

* **Magnetic Island** Nip around this laid-back island in a moke, swim from picturesque coves, and go koala-watching in beautiful eucalyptus forests. See p.547

* **The Sanctuary Retreat** at Mission Beach This outstanding eco-friendly retreat is tucked away in rainforest inhabited by cassowaries. See p.562

* **Atherton Tablelands** Easy to explore, with romantic waterfalls, ancient fig trees, delectable ecolodges and abundant wildlife. See p.568

* **Scenic flights** Cairns is the best place to hop aboard a helicopter for breathtaking aerial views of the reef and rainforest. See p.586

* **Northern Great Barrier Reef** In the far north, the mighty reef runs close to the coast and is easily accessible by day-trip. See p.590

* **Port Douglas** A long, palm-fringed beach and a thriving foodie culture make this a very pleasant resort. See p.598

* **The Daintree** Mighty trees cover the hillsides, and the beaches are utterly unspoilt in this fabulous World Heritage area. See p.605

* **The northern islands** The remote islands north of Cooktown offer outstanding diving and the chance to sample Torres Strait culture. See p.618

▲ Great Barrier Reef

8

Far North Queensland

The tropical coast from Townsville to Cooktown offers easy access to some of Australia's most outstanding natural attractions: lush rainforest, rolling highlands, empty beaches, idyllic cays and, of course, the mighty Great Barrier Reef, a magnet for divers and snorkellers. It's prime territory for anyone who enjoys the great outdoors, with outstanding hiking, cycling, canoeing, birding and wildlife-watching opportunities, along with a healthy sprinkling of extreme sports, from zip-lining and bungee-jumping to off-road four-wheel driving.

This stretch of northern Queensland has a wealth of **national parks**, with rainforest holding its own against agricultural land; the further north you travel, the fewer sugar and fruit farms you encounter, and the more wilderness. The Great Dividing Range edges coastwards as it progresses north, dry at first, but gradually acquiring a green sward that culminates in the steamy, rainforest-draped scenery around **Cairns**.

Life moves at a languid pace in the region's small towns, where people consider their location both a privilege and a selling point – "tropical" is easily the most frequently used adjective in local slogans and company names. Even **Townsville**, in the dry, southern belt, talks up its tropical attractiveness and has recently spent a fortune on transforming its seafront esplanade into a beautiful tourist-friendly park of palm-shaded swimming pools, lawns and beaches.

Just off shore, an easy ferry ride from Townsville, lies **Magnetic Island**, a laid-back holiday spot that used to be the sole preserve of families and budget travellers. These days, developers are giving it a makeover to upgrade its appeal, but it still has plenty of quiet corners, from clothing-optional coves to eucalyptus forests where you have an excellent chance of spotting wild koalas. There's more peace and quiet in the area around **Paluma**, where the tropical greenery really kicks in and you can get back to nature in simple forest lodges or visit impressive waterfalls including the **Wallaman Falls**, Australia's tallest.

Hinchinbrook Island, one of the region's largest offshore national parks, has superb hiking trails, while nearby **Orpheus**, **Dunk** and **Bedarra** islands have perfect beaches and luxury resorts to lure lotus-eating tourists. The mainland beaches can be lovely, too, and far less rarified; at **Mission Beach**, after a morning flaked out on the sand, you can lose yourself in coastal rainforest and perhaps glimpse one of the region's population of endangered cassowaries.

There's a swathe of farmland around **Innisfail** – a good place to look for work picking fruit and vegetables – and, inland from here, in the **Atherton Tablelands**, a rolling highland region of pastures and waterfalls, with spectacular rainforest-clad mountains to the north around **Kuranda**.

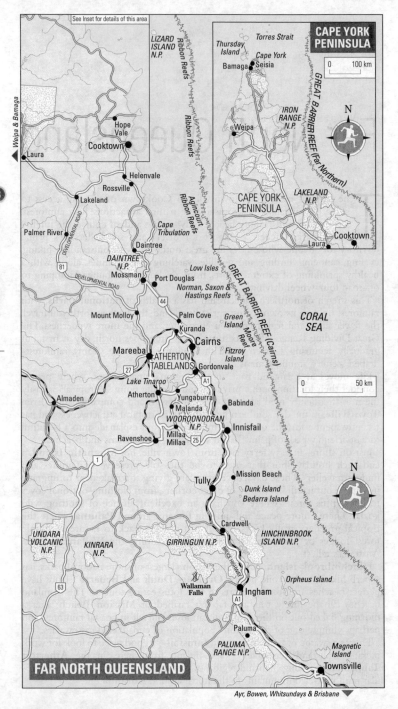

See Inset for details of this area

LIZARD ISLAND N.P.

Ribbon Reefs

Ribbon Reefs

Weipa & Bamaga

Hope Vale

Cooktown

Laura

Helenvale

Rossville

Lakeland

Palmer River

81

DEVELOPMENTAL ROAD

DEVELOPMENTAL ROAD

Agincourt Ribbon Reefs

Cape Tribulation

Daintree

DAINTREE N.P.

Mossman

Port Douglas

Low Isles

Norman, Saxon & Hastings Reefs

Mount Molloy

44

Palm Cove

Kuranda

Cairns

Green Island

Mareeba

ATHERTON TABLELANDS

Gordonvale

Moore Reef

CORAL SEA

27

Lake Tinaroo

A1

Fitzroy Island

Almaden

Atherton

Yungaburra

Malanda

WOOROONOORAN N.P.

Babinda

Innisfail

Ravenshoe

Millaa Millaa

25

Tully

Mission Beach

Dunk Island

Bedarra Island

UNDARA VOLCANIC N.P.

KINRARA N.P.

Cardwell

GIRRINGUN N.P.

HINCHINBROOK ISLAND N.P.

1

63

Wallaman Falls

Orpheus Island

Ingham

A1

BRUCE HIGHWAY

Paluma

PALUMA RANGE N.P.

Magnetic Island

Townsville

GREAT BARRIER REEF (Cairns)

CAPE YORK PENINSULA

0   100 km

N

Torres Strait

Thursday Island

Cape York

Bamaga

Seisia

Weipa

IRON RANGE N.P.

GREAT BARRIER REEF (Far Northern)

CAPE YORK PENINSULA

LAKELAND N.P.

Laura

Cooktown

N

0   50 km

FAR NORTH QUEENSLAND

Ayr, Bowen, Whitsundays & Brisbane ▼

From here, it's a short hop to **Cairns**, the cheerful regional hub, hemmed in by forested mountains and the sea. What the city lacks in conventional sights, it more than makes up for in opportunities for wider exploration: it's the perfect springboard for trips to the highlands, the rainforest and the Great Barrier Reef. North of the city is a string of attractive coastal resorts, some of them, such as **Palm Cove** and **Port Douglas**, dripping in A-list appeal.

The **Daintree** and **Cape Tribulation**, north of Cairns, comprise an outstanding wilderness region of cloud-cloaked coastal forest ringing with the calls of insects and birds. North of here, the rainforested ranges ultimately give way to the savanna of the huge, triangular **Cape York Peninsula**, a sparsely populated setting for what is widely regarded as the most rugged 4WD adventure in the country. The cape's offshore islands and reefs are little visited but excellent for diving, while the **Torres Strait Islands** have an independent spirit that makes them culturally distinct from the rest of Australia.

Regional practicalities

The Far North Queensland coast has an excellent variety of **accommodation** options. Independent travellers tend to zone in on Mission Beach, Cairns, the Daintree and Cape Tribulation, which have a good mix of budget lodgings and stripped-down wilderness retreats, but if you're thinking of treating yourself, options to consider include the more exclusive island resorts, some of which are highly eco-friendly; the Atherton Tablelands' delightful ecolodges; Cairns' swanky waterfront properties; and the glitzy spas and mega-resorts of Palm Cove and Port Douglas. Cairns and Port Douglas have by far the best selection of **restaurants**, **bars** and **shops**.

The region's international **airport** is in Cairns; there's a smaller airport in Townsville with connections to many Australian cities. The quiet, single-lane **Bruce Highway** concludes its run up from Brisbane at Cairns, hugging the coast and connecting all major towns in the region. North of the city, the traffic is even lighter, and the tarmac runs out altogether halfway to Cooktown if you're travelling up from Mossman via the coastal road, or just beyond Cooktown if you've taken the alternative, inland road. For the rest of the Cape York Peninsula, you'll need a **4WD**. During the sugar-crushing season (roughly June–Dec), you may occasionally be held up at cane-train level crossings; look out for the flashing red lights.

Long-distance **buses** stop at all the major towns and many of the smaller ones. The Brisbane–Cairns **railway** line also traverses the entire region, with stops at Townsville, Ingham, Cardwell, Tully, Innisfail, Babinda, Gordonvale and Cairns. Townsville, Cairns and their suburbs are covered by **local bus** networks. **Guided tours** will take you to the Atherton Tablelands, the Daintree, Cape Tribulation and Cape York, but it's worth **hiring a car** from time to time to reach some of the less accessible parks or beaches. To get out to the Great Barrier Reef, you need to join a **boat trip**: the best places to pick one up are Cairns, Port Douglas and Mission Beach.

Weather and seasons

Winters on the northern Queensland coast (April–Nov) are generally dry and pleasant, with bright, sunny weather, but in the rainforest it can pour at any time of year. These showers are often followed by sunshine, but the sky can be grey for days at a time. The transitions from winter to summer and back again are gradual and barely discernible to those used to the showy seasonal changes of spring and autumn in temperate climes. In **summer** (Dec–March), rain falls more frequently and the humidity increases, particularly north of Cairns, though

Dangerous jellyfish (see p.47) may be present in the coastal waters from November to May. To minimize the risk of being stung, you should wear a protective Lycra suit when swimming in the ocean at this time, even inside jellyfish-resistant "stinger nets". It's not advisable to swim in isolated areas.

the ocean breezes rarely fail. The peak of the wet season is from January to March. Both Townsville and Cairns have average summer temperatures of 31°C. During the cyclone season (Nov–April), there's a strong possibility of torrential rain and devastating storms, but destructive cyclones are relatively rare.

Scuba diving and snorkelling on the Great Barrier Reef is good all year round but visibility is best during the calm weather from April to October. The best time of year to find **farm work** picking vegetables in the Ingham, Tully and Innisfail area is May to December, while tobacco season in Mareeba is September to November. Banana picking work is often available all year.

Townsville

Regional capital **TOWNSVILLE** sprawls around a broad spit of land between the isolated hump of Castle Hill and swampy Ross Creek. The hot, muggy, salty air, the old pile houses on the hills, and the esplanade lined with palms and fig trees mark it out as a decidedly tropical city. While its biggest draw is **Magnetic Island**, just off shore, Townsville does have its moments: there's a visible maritime history, some good visitor attractions and an interesting architectural mix from Victoriana to Art Deco to 1970s modernism, with a decent sprinkling of twenty-first-century development thrown in. To see the city in its best light, head down to **The Strand**, Townsville's family-friendly beach promenade; long and leafy with well-kept lawns, it has been spruced up in recent years and is now arguably the most attractive urban seafront in Queensland.

Townsville was founded in 1864 by John Melton Black and Robert Towns, entrepreneurs who felt that a settlement was needed for northern stockmen who couldn't reach Bowen when the Burdekin River was in flood. Despite an inferior harbour, the town soon outstripped Bowen in terms of both size and prosperity, its growth accelerated by **gold** finds inland at Ravenswood and Charters Towers. Today, Townsville is the gateway to Far North Queensland and a transit point for routes west; it's also an important military centre, seat of a university (which ensures a lively bar and club scene) and home to substantial Torres Strait Islander and Aboriginal communities, as well as tourists looking for a lower-key, less commercialized alternative to Cairns. But despite this diverse cultural mix, there's a certain drabness to the city centre, accentuated by the mass of car showrooms, retail sheds and industrial units that surround it. Desperate to shake off its old "Brownsville" image and reinvent itself as a modern, dynamic metropolis, Townsville has regeneration plans aplenty, but for now there's a pervasive sense of nothing much going on, particularly after 2pm on Saturday, when the shops all close for the weekend.

Orientation, arrival and information

Townsville's roughly triangular city centre is hemmed in by Cleveland Bay to the north, Ross Creek to the southeast and Castle Hill to the southwest. The

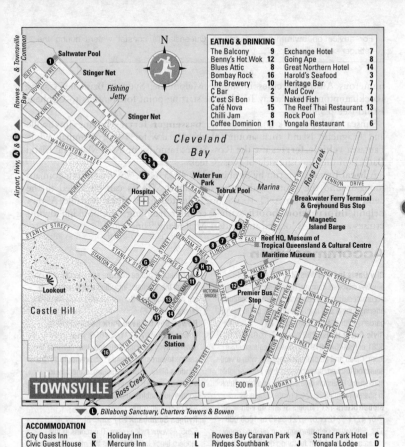

EATING & DRINKING

The Balcony	9	Exchange Hotel	7
Benny's Hot Wok	12	Going Ape	8
Blues Attic	8	Great Northern Hotel	14
Bombay Rock	16	Harold's Seafood	3
The Brewery	10	Heritage Bar	7
C Bar	2	Mad Cow	7
C'est Si Bon	5	Naked Fish	4
Café Nova	15	The Reef Thai Restaurant	13
Chilli Jam	8	Rock Pool	1
Coffee Dominion	11	Yongala Restaurant	6

TOWNSVILLE

L, Billabong Sanctuary, Charters Towers & Bowen

ACCOMMODATION

City Oasis Inn	G	Holiday Inn	H	Rowes Bay Caravan Park	A	Strand Park Hotel	C
Civic Guest House	K	Mercure Inn	L	Rydges Southbank	J	Yongala Lodge	D
Globetrotters	F & I	Reef Lodge Backpackers	E	Seagulls	B		

main shopping street is **Flinders Street**, which follows the north bank of Ross Creek. Its central section, **Flinders Mall**, is a pedestrian precinct that's rather run-down (though set for a revamp), while its last five-hundred-metre stretch, **Flinders Street East**, leads to the Reef HQ Aquarium. The main waterfront boulevard, **The Strand**, leads northwest from the centre. On the south side of Ross Creek, **Palmer Street** has a growing number of restaurants.

Long-distance buses run by Greyhound stop north of the centre at the (see p.35) Breakwater Ferry Terminal on Sir Leslie Thiess Drive (℡07 4772 5100 or 1300 473 946; ticket office Mon–Fri & Sun 6am–7.30pm, Sat 6am–4pm), while Premier buses (see p.35) pull in on Plume Street in South Townsville, from where it's a short walk across the bridge to the city centre. The **railway station**, serving points between Cairns and Brisbane, is just southwest of the centre along Flinders Street. **Townsville Airport** (TSV; ⓦwww.townsvilleairport .com.au) is 5km northwest of town; it's a short hop into the centre by taxi or by the Abacus shuttle bus (A$8 single, A$14 return; book in advance on ℡07 4775 5544 or 1300 554 378) and there are also car-rental desks in the terminal building. No international flights land here at present but Virgin Blue and Jetstar fly in from Melbourne, Sydney and Brisbane, and Qantas run services from

For advice on **swimming** in northern Queensland's coastal waters during the "stinger season", see p.47.

numerous Australian cities including Melbourne, Sydney, Brisbane, Cairns, Rockhampton and Mackay. It's also the starting point for transfers to Orpheus Island (see p.556).

Sunsea **cruise boats** and Sunferries **passenger ferries** linking Townsville and Magnetic Island turn around at the Breakwater Ferry Terminal, while Fantasea **vehicle ferries** use the Ross Street ramp (signposted Magnetic Island Barge) on the opposite side of Ross Creek.

A **local bus** service run by Sunbus (ⓣ07 4725 8482, ⓦwww.sunbus.com.au) loops around the centre and serves the suburbs. **Taxis** can be hailed in the centre or booked on ⓣ13 10 08. Some hostels have **bikes** available. A very helpful **information booth** with a counter handling and booking diving, cruises and tours is located in Flinders Mall (daily 9am–5pm).

Accommodation

City Oasis Inn 143 Wills St ⓣ07 4771 6048, ⓦwww.cityoasis.com.au. Resort-style accommodation in a reasonably central location, offering rooms and mini-apartments set in jungly gardens with a landscaped pool. ❺

Civic Guest House 262 Walker St ⓣ07 4771 5381 or1800 646 619, ⓦwww.civicguesthouse .com. Clean and helpful backpackers' with a well-equipped kitchen, spa pool and free Friday-night barbecues. Deals on dive courses and trips. Bunk in shared room A\$22–24, private double ❷

Globetrotters 121 Flinders St and 45 Palmer St ⓣ07 4771 3242 or 07 4721 5945 or 1800 008 533, ⓦwww.globetrottersinn.com.au. Amazingly cheap accommodation featuring decent motel-style rooms on Flinders St and hostel-style dorms on Palmer St; rates include breakfast and dinner. Bunk in shared room A\$18–25, private double ❷

Holiday Inn 334 Flinders Mall ⓣ07 4729 2000, ⓦwww.townsville.holiday-inn.com. There's nothing special about most of the rooms in this tired 1970s tower, catering mainly for business travellers, but the views from the upper-floor balconies and the rooftop pool are unbeatable. Rates vary daily. ❹–❻

Mercure Inn Woolcock St ⓣ07 4725 2222, ⓦwww.accorhotels.com.au. Situated 4km outside the city centre, this is a comfortable option for the price if you're just passing through; the better rooms have been given a contemporary makeover, and there's a good resort-style pool. ❸–❺

Reef Lodge Backpackers 4–6 Wickham St ⓣ07 4721 1112, ⓦwww.reeflodge.com.au. One of

the cheapest places in town, and friendly enough with all the facilities, including a girls-only dorm, but a bit cramped. Bunk in shared room A\$19–23, private double ❷

Rowes Bay Caravan Park Heatley Parade, Rowes Bay ⓣ07 4771 3576, ⓦwww .rowesbaycp.com.au. Situated 3km north of the centre towards Pallarenda (on bus route #7 from Flinders Mall), with views across the bay to Magnetic Island, this popular place offers good-value cabins and camping sites. Camping A\$21–27, cabin ❷

Rydges Southbank 23 Palmer St ⓣ07 4726 5265, ⓦwww.rydges.com. The rooms in this modern block look dated but the mini-apartments are fresh, contemporary and good value; there's also a great saltwater pool. ❹

Seagulls 74 The Esplanade ⓣ1800 079 929, ⓦwww.seagulls.com.au. Seafront resort-hotel on the edge of town, with lush, spacious tropical gardens. ❹

Strand Park Hotel 59–60 The Strand ⓣ07 4750 7888, ⓦwww.strandparkhotel .com.au. Beachfront apartments in Townsville's prettiest area, offering self-contained suites with either garden or sea views. One-bedroom suite ❹; two-bedroom suite ❻

Yongala Lodge 11 Fryer St ⓣ07 4772 4633, ⓦwww.historicyongala.com.au. A welcoming place, named after the city's most famous shipwreck, with slightly past-their-best motel rooms joined to a historic old Queenslander with original furnishings. ❸

The city and around

Funded by inland gold mines during the late nineteenth century, some of Townsville's solid stone colonial **architecture** is quite imposing, especially along Flinders Street East. More recent additions to the urban landscape include its Art Deco clock towers and former hospital, and the 1970s *Holiday Inn*, an impressive cylindrical building that dominates Flinders Mall. The city council has published a series of *Heritage Trails* leaflets to guide visitors around the notable spots.

On the corner of Flinders Mall and Denham Street, the **Perc Tucker Art Gallery** (Mon–Fri 10am–5pm, Sat & Sun 10am–2pm; free; ☏ 07 4727 9000) is another grand old building, featuring travelling exhibitions of antique and indigenous art. On Sunday mornings (8.30am–1pm), the Mall itself hosts **Cotters Market**, a busy event with a friendly local feel and plenty of arts, crafts and seasonal produce from North Queensland to browse.

Castle Hill looms over the city centre, an obvious target if you're after clear views of the region. There's a road to the top from Stanley Street; on foot, head along Gregory Street to Stanton Terrace and join a walking path of sorts that climbs to the lookout, for grand vistas to the distant Hervey Range and Magnetic Island.

The Strand runs northwest from the marina (the departure point for dive trips) along Cleveland Bay. An evening **craft market** is held here on the first Friday of each month from May to December (5–9.30pm). The southern end of the esplanade is lined with mighty fig trees, a Victorian-style park with an impressive Anzac war memorial, and elegant old buildings. Beyond the marina, the waterfront strip, which looks out to Magnetic Island, is a beautiful stretch of palms, sandy beach and shady lawns with an excellent children's waterpark, communal hotplate barbecues, a fishing jetty, a swimming pool, and two stinger nets (Nov–May), plus a good variety of cafés and restaurants.

Reef HQ Aquarium, The Cultural Centre and Museum of Tropical Queensland

The excellent **Reef HQ Aquarium**, on Flinders Street East (daily 9.30am–5pm; A\$21.50, child \$10.50, or A\$32.50/17.50 including IMAX admission; ☏ 07 4750 0800, ⊛ www.reefhq.com.au), houses huge tanks containing the world's largest living recreation of a coral reef. Walking through the viewing tunnel, you can watch schools of fish drifting over the coral, clownfish hiding among anemones' tentacles and myopic-looking turtles or slinky reef sharks cruising past. Between the main tanks are smaller ones for oddities – sea snakes, deep-sea nautiluses, baby turtles and lobsters. Upstairs, videos about the reef are shown, and you can handle some inoffensive invertebrates including tiny clams, sea cucumbers and starfish. Reef HQ's **IMAX cinema** projects films with a popular science theme onto a domed ceiling to create an overwhelming, wrap-around image.

In the same complex, **The Cultural Centre** (Mon–Fri 9.30am–4.30pm; A\$16.50, child A\$9; ☏ 07 4772 7679, ⊛ www.cctownsville.com.au) showcases Aboriginal and Torres Strait Island culture through art, artefacts, music and dance. Attached is a gallery shop with a great range of original paintings, textiles and handmade toy animals that make superior souvenirs.

Next door, an innovative building houses the Queensland Government-run **Museum of Tropical Queensland** (daily 9.30am–5pm; A\$12, child A\$7; ☏ 07 4726 0600, ⊛ www.mtq.qld.gov.au), which showcases the Queensland Museum's maritime archeology collection. The centrepiece is a full-sized, cut-away replica – figurehead and all – of the front third of the **Pandora**, a British frigate tied up in the tale of the **Bounty mutiny**, which sank on the Outer Reef in 1791 (see box on p.545 for the full tale). Accompanying artefacts salvaged off the wreck since its discovery in 1977 include water jars and bottles, tankards owned by the crew, and the surgeon's pocket watch, with glass face and finely chased gold and silver mountings. Dioramas recreate life on board, with views into the cramped captain's cabin and a dramatic reconstruction of the sinking, while a life-sized blueprint of the *Pandora*'s upper deck is mapped out on the carpet. You can also join in the twice-daily "Running Out the Gun", the loading and mock firing of a replica cannon from the ship. Other sections of the museum cover **coral–reef ecology** and Outback Queensland's extensive **fossil finds** (including several life-sized dinosaur models).

Townsville Town Common Conservation Park and Billabong Sanctuary

The **Townsville Town Common Conservation Park** (daily 6.30am–6.30pm; free) is 6.5km north of the centre, on the coast at **Pallarenda**. The Bohle River pools into wetlands below the Many Peaks Range, a habitat perfect for wildfowl, including brolga, the stately symbol of the northern marshes. Less popular – with rice farmers anyway – are the huge flocks of magpie geese that visit after rains and are a familiar sight over the city. You need a vehicle to reach the park, but once there you can get about on foot, although a car or bike makes short work of the less interesting tracks between lagoons. Camouflaged **hides** at Long Swamp and Pink Lily Lagoon let you clock up a few of the hundred or more bird species in the park: egrets stalk frogs around waterlilies, ibises and spoonbills strain the water for edibles and geese honk at each other, undisturbed by the low-flying airport traffic – bring binoculars.

Seventeen kilometres south of Townsville towards Ayr on the Bruce Highway, **Billabong Sanctuary** (daily 8am–5pm; A\$27, child A\$16; ℡07 4778 8344, Ⓦwww.billabongsanctuary.com.au) is a well-kept collection of Australian fauna in a mixture of rainforest and eucalyptus woodland laid out around a large waterhole. The owners' mission is to raise awareness of conservation issues by inviting visitors to interact with the animals, so there's a non-stop daily programme of talks about various species, with opportunities to stroke, pat and cuddle the inmates. This is one of the few remaining places in Australia where you're allowed to hold koalas and wombats; proceeds from photo sales help fund species survival programmes. Opportunistic wallabies and whistling ducks range freely and are always on the make for handouts; the more dangerous animals, such as saltwater crocs, cassowaries (bred for release into the wild), dingoes, wedge-tailed eagles and snakes are securely penned. A swimming pool and accompanying snack bar make the sanctuary a fine place to spend a few hours.

Eating, drinking and entertainment

There are plenty of good **eating** options in Townsville, with restaurants grouped in three main areas: in the centre on Flinders Street; south on Palmer Street; and out along The Strand. For evening **entertainment**, many of the town's hotels and bars cater to the sizeable military and student presence and have regular live music, for which you might have to pay a cover charge.

The Balcony 287 Flinders Mall (upstairs) ℡07 4771 2255. Overlooking the Mall, this upstairs café-restaurant specializes in unfussy Mediterranean-style salads, grills and open sandwiches, plus homemade cakes. Mon–Fri 7am–3pm, Sat & Sun 8am–3pm.

Benny's Hot Wok 17 Palmer St ℡07 4721 1474. Stylish, popular and reasonably priced Singaporean

In 1788, the British Admiralty vessel **Bounty** sailed from England to Tahiti, with a mission to collect **breadfruit** seedlings, intended to provide a cheap source of food for Britain's plantation slaves in the West Indies. But the stay in Tahiti's mellow climate proved so much better than life on board that on the return journey in April 1789 the crew **mutinied**, led by the officer **Fletcher Christian**. Along with eighteen crew who refused to join in the mutiny, **Captain William Bligh** was set adrift in a longboat far out in the Pacific, while the mutineers returned to Tahiti, intending to settle there.

Things didn't go as planned, however. After an incredible feat of navigation over 3600 nautical miles of open sea, Bligh and all but one of his companions reached the Portuguese colony of Timor in June, emaciated but still alive, from where Bligh lost no time in catching a vessel back to England, arriving there in March 1790. His report on the mutiny immediately saw the Admiralty dispatch the frigate **Pandora** off to Tahiti under the cold-hearted **Captain Edwards**, with instructions to bring back the mutineers to stand trial in London.

Meanwhile in Tahiti, Christian and seven of the mutiny's ringleaders – knowing that sooner or later the Admiralty would try to find them – had, along with a group of Tahitians, taken the *Bounty* and sailed off into the Pacific. Fourteen of the *Bounty*'s crew stayed behind on Tahiti, however, and when the *Pandora* arrived there in March 1791, they were rounded up, clapped in chains and incarcerated in the ship's brig, a three-metre-long wooden cell known as **"Pandora's Box"**.

Having spent a fruitless few months island-hopping in search of the *Bounty*, Captain Edwards headed up the east coast of Australia where, on the night of August 29, the *Pandora* hit a northern section of the Great Barrier Reef. As waves began to break up the vessel on the following day, Edwards ordered the longboats to be loaded with supplies and abandoned the ship, leaving his prisoners still locked up on board; it was only thanks to one of the crew that ten of them managed to scramble out as the *Pandora* slid beneath the waves.

In a minor replay of Bligh's voyage, the *Pandora*'s survivors took three weeks to make it to Timor in their longboats, and arrived back in England the following year. Edwards was castigated for the heartless treatment of his prisoners, but otherwise held blameless for the wreck. The ten surviving mutineers were court-martialled: four were acquitted, three hanged, and three had their death sentences commuted. Captain Bligh was later made Governor of New South Wales, where he suffered another mutiny known as the **"Rum Rebellion"** (see "History", p.628). To add insult to injury, the *Bounty*'s whole project proved a failure; when breadfruit were eventually introduced to the West Indies, the slaves refused to eat them.

Seventeen years later, the American vessel *Topaz* stopped mid-Pacific at the isolated rocky fastness of **Pitcairn Island** and, to the amazement of its crew, found it settled by a small colony of English-speaking people. These turned out to be the descendants of the *Bounty* mutineers, along with the last survivor, the elderly **John Adams** (also known as Alexander Smith). Adams told the *Topaz*'s crew that having settled Pitcairn and burned the *Bounty*, the mutineers had fought with the Tahitian men over the women, and that Christian and all the men – except Adams and three other mutineers – had been killed. The other three had since died, leaving only Adams, the women, and their children on the island. After Adams' death, Pitcairn's population was briefly moved to Norfolk Island (see p.394) in the 1850s, where some settled, though many of their descendants returned and still live on Pitcairn.

and Asian café-restaurant, with tasty bowls of noodle soup and Indonesian or Thai curries. Daily 5pm–late. **The Brewery** 252 Flinders St ⊕07 4724 2999, Ⓦwww.townsvillebrewery.com.au. Café-bar,

boutique brewery and club, housed in the old post office building. The beer and ambience are good by night, but the self-consciously cool club atmosphere grates a bit by day. Daily 11am–late.

C Bar Gregory St Headland, The Strand ☏ 07 4724 0333. One of Townsville's coolest café-restaurants, right on the seafront with outside tables looking out towards Magnetic Island. Good for anything from a coffee or beer to succulent char-grilled steak or lamb kebabs and salad.

Café Nova 2 Blackwood St. Long-running student venue, with generous helpings and meals, including tasty salads, for under A$15. Tues–Fri 10.30am–midnight, Sat & Sun 6pm–midnight.

C'est Si Bon 48 Gregory St ☏ 07 4772 5828. Much loved by locals, this stylish café serves what is arguably the best coffee in town, plus juices and snacks. Daily 7am–5pm.

Chilli Jam 205 Flinders St East. Pan-Asian café with speedy service, serving reasonably priced noodles, stir-fries and satays. Closed Mon & Sun.

Coffee Dominion 1 Stokes St ☏ 07 4724 0767. Brews quality roasted coffee for early birds from 5.30am on weekdays.

Going Ape 215 Flinders St East. Funky and fun café-bar that gives *yum cha* (dim sum) an Aussie twist, with plates of emu spring rolls and kangaroo satay to share. Closed Mon.

Great Northern Hotel 500 Flinders St ☏ 07 4771 6191. The downstairs bar in this landmark Queenslander pub has lots of character, and serves huge, cheap meals.

Harold's Seafood 58 The Strand ☏ 07 4724 1322. If you can't catch your own from the nearby fishing jetty, console yourself with a takeaway of local barramundi from this excellent establishment.

Heritage Bar 137 Flinders St East. Drop in on Frid for local oysters at A$9.50 a dozen, or on Thurs for prawns at A$9.50 per half kilo. Tues–Sat 5pm–late.

Naked Fish 59–60 The Strand ☏ 07 4724 4623. Upmarket modern seafood with mains from A$20 to A$30, excellent calamari and a broad wine list. Daily 5pm–late.

The Reef Thai Restaurant 455 Flinders St ☏ 07 4721 6701. Char-grilled seafood, green curry, satays, vegetarian fare and a chilli-packed beef dish known as "crying tiger". Mains A$15–22. Daily 5.30–10pm; licensed and BYO; takeaway available.

Rock Pool Kissing Point, The Strand. Cheerful café overlooking the swimming lagoon at the north end of the city beach.

Yongala Restaurant 11 Fryer St, at the *Yongala Lodge* ☏ 07 4772 4633. Historic, authentically furnished surroundings where you can enjoy live music and good, Greek-influenced food. The building's architect was on board the *Yongala* when it sank. Daily from 6.30pm.

Pubs, bars and clubs

Townsville's after-dark scene is concentrated on **Flinders Street East**, where clubs and bars come and go, or just revamp themselves, on a regular basis; there are also a few nightspots on **Palmer Street** in South Townsville.

Blues Attic 221 Flinders St East. Live blues most nights, from 9pm.

Bombay Rock 719 Flinders St. In an imposing building vaguely reminiscent of a Maharajah's palace, this place pulls in a young crowd with live bands and regular DJ nights.

Exchange Hotel 151 Flinders St East. This pub is a real locals' watering-hole, with occasional live bands.

Mad Cow 129 Flinders St East. Pool tables and dancing to cheesy pop – packed at weekends.

Listings

Banks All located on Flinders Mall. There are ATMs in most pubs.

Car rental Avis has offices at the airport (☏ 07 4725 6522) and the centre (☏ 07 4721 2688); other agencies at the airport include Budget, Europcar, Hertz and Thrifty. Independent Rentals (☏ 07 4772 6850 or 1800 678 843, ⊛www .independentrentals.com.au) has basic models from A$35 a day.

Hospital Townsville General Hospital, Eyre St ☏ 07 4781 9211 (emergencies ☏ 000).

Internet There's enough competition in town to ensure prices are reasonable. Best value at $2 per hour is Globetrotters, 121 Flinders St East (daily 9am–7pm); other cheap options include Internet-on-the-Mall, 313 Flinders Mall (daily 7am–late) and The Internet Den, 265 Flinders Mall (daily 9am–5pm).

The main diving attraction out from Townsville is the **Yongala shipwreck** (see p.531), just under 90km southeast of the city near Cape Bowling Green. Experienced divers can book a day-trip with Adrenalin Dive from Townsville and Magnetic Island (9 Wickham St; ℡1300 664 600 or 07 4724 0600, ⊛www.adrenalindive.com.au; A$205–240 for two dives, depending on whether you need gear), while **Prodive Townsville** (252 Walker Street; ℡1300 131 760 or 07 4721 1760, ⊛www .prodivetownsville.com.au) offer two-dive *Yongala* day-trips for A$235 and three-day/three-night liveaboard trips including a total of ten dives on Wheeler Reef and the *Yongala* for A$775. Prodive also run **PADI courses**.

There's also access from Townsville to the local stretch of the Great Barrier Reef – the best option for **Reef day-trips** is **Sunsea** (℡1800 447 333 or 07 4726 0888, ⊛www.sunferries.com.au), a friendly outfit that runs from the Breakwater Ferry Terminal on Sir Leslie Thiess Drive to Kelso Reef, picking people up from Magnetic Island on the way and allowing around three and a half hours on the reef for diving, snorkelling and lunch; the trip costs A$145 (child A$90), plus A$105–135 for two dives including gear. Kelso has an interesting collection of coral bommies in 12–15m of water, with plenty of marine species in residence. Alternatively, snorkellers and novice divers can head out to Wheeler Reef with **Adrenalin Dive** (A$165 plus A$40–120 for two dives, depending on whether you need gear and tuition).

8

Police 30 Stanley St ℡07 4760 7777 (emergencies ℡000).
Post office Behind Flinders Mall on Sturt St, near the junction with Stanley St.
Sailing Freedom (℡0438 225820) offer cruises to Magnetic Island or around Cleveland Bay aboard a twelve-metre sailing catamaran.
Scenic flights Fly Scenic (℡07 4725 5884, ⊛www.flyscenic.com.au) will spin you over Magnetic Island, the Palm Islands and the Great Barrier Reef in a light aircraft (from A$199 for 30min), or fly you along The Strand in a Tiger Moth (from A$150 for 30min).

Taxi The main rank is just off Flinders Mall on Stokes St (℡13 10 08).
Tours Detours (℡07 4728 5311, ⊛www .detourcoaches.com) run coach trips to the old gold-mining town of Charters Towers (A$115, child A$45) and the rainforest at Paluma (A$98, child A$45); Kookaburra Tours (℡0448 794798, ⊛www .kookaburratours.com.au) offer regular heritage tours of the city plus trips to the old gold-mining railway tunnels outside Townsville, or to Charters Towers, the Wallaman Falls or Paluma; Tropicana (℡07 4728 1800, ⊛www.tropicanatours.com.au) will show you around the city in a stretch jeep (A$75, child A$40).

Magnetic Island

Another island named by Captain Cook in 1770 – after his compass played up as he sailed past – **MAGNETIC ISLAND** is a beautiful triangular granite core around 10km from Townsville. There's much to be said for a trip here: lounging on a beach, swimming over coral, bouncing around in a moke from one roadside lookout to another, and enjoying the sea breeze and the island's vivid colours. Compact enough to drive around in half a day, but large enough to harbour a few small settlements, Magnetic Island's accommodation and transfer costs are considerably lower than on many of Queensland's other islands, and if you've ever wanted to spot a **koala** in the wild, this could be your chance – they're often seen wedged into gum trees up in the northeast corner of the island.

Originally part of the mainland, but separated from it by rising sea levels between 6000 and 7500 years ago, Magnetic's dry tropical landscapes are far more varied than those of the coral cays and the smaller Whitsundays. Seen from the sea, the island's apex, **Mount Cook**, hovers above eucalyptus woods variegated with patches of darker green vine forest. The north and east coasts are pinched into shallow **sandy bays** punctuated by **granite headlands** and **coral reefs**, while the western part of the island is flatter and edged with mangroves. Impressive granite tors, some as large as a house and seemingly precariously perched, bear testament to Magnetic's volcanic prehistory; in the rainy season, waterfalls tumble down the rocky hillsides.

Just over half the island – the centre, northwest and far northeast – is a **national park** and a well-marked series of **bush trails**, particularly in the northeast, allow you to explore. The winning combination of unspoilt, varied coastline, satisfying hiking country and rewarding wildlife-watching and birding opportunities makes "Maggie", as the locals call it, an appealing destination for nature lovers. Backpackers have been coming here for years, and they're now being joined by tourists with a little more money to spend, lured by the island's sparkling new marina and luxury accommodation complexes.

Four sleepy villages, **Picnic Bay**, **Nelly Bay**, **Arcadia** and **Horseshoe Bay**, are dotted along the east coast. These have a sprinkling of shops, bars and restaurants, so there's no need to bring anything with you.

Arrival and island transport

Two **ferry services** shuttle passengers and vehicles between Townsville on the mainland and Nelly Bay on Magnetic's southeast coast; some islanders use them to commute to work in Townsville each day. **Sunferries passenger ferries** leave from the Breakwater Ferry Terminal on Sir Leslie Thiess Drive around sixteen times daily (℗07 4726 0800, ⓦ www.sunferries.com.au; A\$26.70 return, child A\$13.30); you can pick up a **timetable** from any information booth. There's no need to book, just turn up fifteen minutes before departure to buy a ticket at the terminal and hop on board; the ten-kilometre crossing takes around 25 minutes. Parking at the terminal costs A\$5 per day. The **Fantasea Cruising Magnetic car and passenger ferry** (℗07 4772 5422, ⓦ www .magneticislandferry.com.au; A\$144 return per car carrying up to four people, pedestrian A\$22 return, child A\$13) leaves from Ross Street in South Townsville seven or eight times a day; this option takes forty minutes.

Magnetic Island has around 35km of road and is straightforward to navigate. The main road, which winds its way from Picnic Bay in the south to Horseshoe Bay in the northeast, is tarmac; there are also a number of unsealed roads, including a track from Picnic Bay to West Point, which are out of bounds to rental vehicles. **Magnetic Island Bus Service** (℗07 4778 5130) meets all ferries on its run along the main road, more or less hourly between 6.45am and 9.30pm, with services to 11.55pm at weekends. Tickets can be purchased from the bus driver or outside the Nelly Bay Ferry Terminal: a single to Picnic Bay or Arcadia costs A\$2 (child A\$1), Horseshoe Bay A\$3 (child A\$1.50), a day-pass A\$11 (child A\$5.50), and if you're checking into a hostel, you're allowed to buy a return for the price of a single. For **rental transport**, Moke Magnetic near Nelly Bay Ferry Terminal (℗07 4778 5377, ⓦ www.mokemagnetic.com) rents out fun mini-mokes for a flat A\$68 a day including fuel, while Tropical Topless, also in Nelly Bay (℗07 4758 1111) charge A\$60 a day plus fuel. Some lodgings rent out **bicycles** for around A\$15 a day, as do Magnetic Island Bike Hire (℗0425 244 193), who have push bikes and electric bikes and will deliver anywhere on the island.

For advice on **swimming** in northern Queensland's coastal waters during the "stinger season", see p.47.

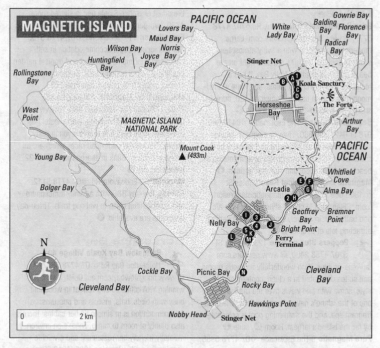

MAGNETIC ISLAND

PACIFIC OCEAN

Gowrie Bay
Balding Bay
White Lady Bay
Florence Bay
Radical Bay
Lovers Bay
Maud Bay
Norris Bay
Joyce Bay
Wilson Bay
Huntingfield Bay
Rollingstone Bay

Stinger Net

Koala Sanctury

Horseshoe Bay

The Forts

West Point

MAGNETIC ISLAND NATIONAL PARK

Arthur Bay

PACIFIC OCEAN

Mount Cook ▲ (493m)

Young Bay

Whitfield Cove

Bolger Bay

Arcadia

Alma Bay

Nelly Bay

Geoffrey Bay
Bremner Point
Bright Point

Ferry Terminal

N

Cockle Bay
Picnic Bay

Cleveland Bay

Cleveland Bay

Rocky Bay

Hawkings Point

Nobby Head   Stinger Net

0   2 km

ACCOMMODATION			
Arcadia Beach Guest House	**H**	Marshall's	**E**
Base Backpackers	**N**	New Friends	
Beachside Palms	**M**	Bed & Breakfast	**D**
Bungalow Bay Koala Village	**C**	Peppers Blue on Blue	**J**
Foresthaven	**F**	Pure Magnetic	**K**
Magnetic Island		Sails	**B**
Tropical Resort	**L**	Segara Villas	**I**
Magnum's on Magnetic	**G**	Shaws on the Shore	**A**

EATING & DRINKING	
Banister's Seafood Restaurant	**2**
Barefoot	**1**
Boardwalk	**J**
Fat Possum Café	**5**
Le Paradis	**3**
Man Friday	**4**
Marlin Bar	**1**
Noodies	**1**

Practicalities

The island's four main villages – Picnic Bay, Nelly Bay, Arcadia and Horseshoe Bay – are rather scattered, but Horseshoe Bay has a small but tight cluster of **shops** and **restaurants** on its beachfront road, Pacific Drive. Many lodgings will rent out **snorkelling gear**, bikes and watersports equipment, make tour bookings and provide Internet access; there is also a wireless **Internet** hotspot at the post office shop on Sooning Street in Nelly Bay (Mon–Fri 9am–5pm, Sat 9–11am), and an Internet café in Arcadia (The Lounge on Bright Ave).

Island accommodation

Magnetic Island has a good range of **hotels**, **lodges** and **apartments**, with options for all budgets. Once best known as a low-cost holiday resort for families and backpackers, the addition of a budget ecolodge and new five-star developments have broadened the island's appeal. Most lodgings are easily accessible by bus, but may also be able to pick you up if you call in advance.

Nelly Bay

Base Backpackers 1 Nelly Bay Rd ☏07 4778 5777, ⓦwww.basebackpackers.com. Large, modern backpackers' with a lively atmosphere, sizeable pool, bar and DJ, situated right on the beach at the far south of Nelly Bay. It has a restaurant serving cheap meals, and there's a full-moon rave once a month. Camping A$20, bunk in shared room A$26–30, private double ❸

Beachside Palms 7 The Esplanade ☏0419 660 078 or 0427 750 680, ⓦwww.magnetic-island -qld.com. Four straightforward and low-key but spacious one- and two-bedroom apartments on the beach road, with pool and laundry facilities. ❹

Magnetic Island Tropical Resort Yates St ☏1800 069 122, ⓦwww.magneticislandresort .com. Clean, simple chalet-style cabins with a/c and bathroom, in a lovely eight-acre bush setting attracting lots of birdlife. ❹

🏃 **Peppers Blue on Blue** 123 Sooning St ☏07 4758 2400, ⓦwww.peppers.com .au/blue-on-blue. With wonderfully spacious rooms and suites decorated in a clean, contemporary style, some with fine views over the marina, this is one of the island's newer luxury options. There's a fragrant spa, and the swimming pool is colossal – by far the island's largest. Room ❻, suite ❼

Pure Magnetic 9 The Esplanade ☏07 4778 5955, ⓦwww.puremagnetic.com. Swish, contemporary two-bedroom, two-bathroom Balinese-style villas crammed into a beachfront plot with a small pool. Stylish but very pricey unless four share. ❽

Segara Villas 20 Mango Parkway ☏07 4778 5151, ⓦwww.segara.com.au. Beautiful, peaceful Balinese-style villas decorated in bold colours, with polished wooden floors, set around a pool amidst tropical gardens. ❺

Arcadia

Arcadia Beach Guest House 27 Marine Parade ☏07 4778 5668, ⓦwww.arcadiabeach guesthouse.com.au. Bright rooms with a slightly quirky touch, and studios aimed at couples on romantic getaways. Guests can use a kitchen, wood-fired pizza oven and barbecue, or order breakfast or dinner. Single bed in shared room A$30, two-person tent ❶, private double ❸

Foresthaven 11–13 Cook Rd ☏07 4778 5153. Old-fashioned budget accommodation in self-contained apartments with pool and tropical garden backing onto the national park. Single bed in shared room A$15, private apartment ❸

Magnum's on Magnetic 7 Marine Parade ☏07 4778 5177 Or 1800 663 666, ⓦwww .magnums.com.au. This large beach hostel has three late-night bars and draws a young party crowd. The weekly cane-toad races (Wed) are an island institution. Bunk in shared room A$18–22, private double ❷

Marshall's 3 Endeavour Rd ☏07 4778 5112. Friendly, low-key B&B with a family atmosphere and quiet garden close to walking trails. Three-day discounts are available. ❸

Horseshoe Bay

🏃 **Bungalow Bay Koala Village** 40 Horseshoe Bay Rd ☏07 4778 5577, ⓦwww.bungalowbay.com.au. Quiet, award-winning YHA-affiliated eco-retreat in woodland busy with birds, bats, insects and possums. Accommodation is in simple timber cabins; there's also plenty of room to camp. There's an environ-mentally friendly bar/restaurant and a wildlife sanctuary on site. Camping A$25 (A$12.50pp), bunk in shared cabin A$27, private double ❷

New Friends Bed & Breakfast Horseshoe Bay Rd ☏07 4758 1220. Spacious, well-furnished apartments in large grounds, 5min walk from the beach. ❹

Sails 13 Pacific Drive ☏07 4778 5117, ⓦwww .sailsonhorseshoe.com.au. Comfortable self-contained apartments and villas with a pool and outdoor barbecue area, at the quiet end of Horseshoe Bay. ❻

Shaws on the Shore 7 Pacific Drive ☏07 4758 1900, ⓦwww.shawsontheshore.com.au. Though rather chintzy, these holiday apartments (with one, two or three bedrooms) have good views out over Horseshoe Bay; the larger ones are good value for sharers. ❺–❻

The southeast coast

Set on the southernmost tip of the island, **PICNIC BAY** is a languid spot, well shaded by surrounding gum woodland and beachfront fig trees, with a nice beach facing Townsville. Once the main ferry terminal (which has since relocated to Nelly Bay), this tiny settlement at the end of the sealed road is now facing an identity crisis, and there's not really much to do here except lounge on the sand: the village has a main beach with a stinger net in season (Nov–May), and a smaller, quieter clothing-optional beach, **Rocky Bay**, reached by a walking track off the road to Nelly Bay.

▲ Exploring Magnetic Island by mini moke

Further up the coast, **NELLY BAY** is thriving thanks to the new marina complex and ferry terminal; local resistance to island development has kept building work in check for a couple of decades, but it's now become a property hotspot, with luxury residential and holiday complexes springing up along the waterfront. In September 2007, the marina hosted the inaugural **Magnetic Island Race Week**, set to become an annual maritime event; also in September is the three-day **Great Tropical Jazz Party**. To the east and south of the harbour is a sprawl of houses fronted by a good beach, with a little reef some way out. Nelly Bay's amenities are growing rapidly: there's a supermarket near the ferry terminal, a bakery and post office on Sooning Street, and more shops planned. The smartest **places to eat** here are the *Boardwalk* restaurant and cocktail bar at *Blue on Blue*, 123 Sooning St (☎07 4758 2400; breakfast, lunch and dinner, daily) and *Le Paradis* on Sooning Street (☎07 4778 5044; daily 11.30am–2.30pm and 6pm–late), an acclaimed French restaurant where, if you're willing to push the boat out, you can share a huge platter of *fruits de mer* or *chateaubriand*. For a more casual evening out, you can tuck into burritos and enchiladas at *Man Friday* off Kelly Street (☎07 4778 5658; Mon & Wed–Sun 6pm–late), or pies, burgers, cakes and smoothies at the delightfully named *Fat Possum Café* at 55 Sooning St (☎07 4778 5409; daily 8am–5pm).

A little further along the coast, **ARCADIA** surrounds Geoffrey Bay and counts the good-value *Banister's Seafood Restaurant* at 22 McCabe Crescent (☎07 4778 5700) among its attractions. At Arcadia's northern end is the perfect swimming beach of **Alma Bay**, sheltered by cliffs and boulders, and with good snorkelling over the coral just offshore. The lifeguard post here is manned all year, making it a safe option for families. A **walking track** from the end of Cook Road leads towards Mount Cook and the track to Nelly Bay, or up to Sphinx Lookout for sea views. At dawn or dusk, you might see diminutive island **rock wallabies** on an outcrop or boulder near Arcadia's jetty.

North of Arcadia the road forks at a small car park, with the right branch (prohibited to rental vehicles) leading via **Arthur Bay** and tiny, pretty **Florence Bay** to Radical Bay, while the main road carries on to Horseshoe Bay. Leave your car at the car park and continue uphill on foot to **the Forts**, built during World War II to protect Townsville from attack by the Japanese. The walking track climbs gently for about 1.5km through gum-tree scenery to gun emplacements (now just deserted blockhouses) set one above the other among granite boulders and pine trees. The best views are from the slit windows at the command centre, right at the pinnacle of the hill. The woods around the Forts are the best place on the island and, some argue, in Australia, to see **wild koalas**, introduced to the island in 1930. Since they sleep during the day, tracking them down is usually a matter of wandering around, looking carefully at crooks in trees – although if you visit in the early morning or late afternoon, you may see them scrambling surprisingly speedily along branches in search of the freshest and greenest eucalyptus leaves.

Horseshoe Bay and around

The road ends in the north at **HORSESHOE BAY** on the island's longest and busiest beach, half of which is developed and half of which remains blissfully secluded, with views north beyond the bobbing yachts to distant Palm Island. The sand is narrow but pretty, shaded by palms and casuarinas, while off shore there's enough seagrass to guarantee regular sightings of turtles and the occasional appearance of dugongs.

Horseshoe Bay's cluster of beachfront shops along Pacific Drive features a general store and a few **places to eat,** including one of the best on the island: the chic, arty *Barefoot* (11.30am–late, closed Tues & Wed). Nearby is *Noodies* (Mon–Wed & Fri 11.30am–late, Sat 8am–late, Sun 8am–3pm) a Latin-style joint serving up burritos, nachos, margaritas and shooters, and a regular pub, the *Marlin Bar* (daily from 11am), with cheap steaks, several beers on tap and

Tours and activities on Magnetic Island

For a **tour of the island by boat**, you could spend a day **sailing** to hard-to-reach beaches and bays on *Jazza*, a 13 metre yacht (Horseshoe Bay; ℗07 4778 5530, ⓦwww.jazza.com.au; day-trip A$100); or cast off aboard the gaff-rigged schooner *Providence V* (Nelly Bay; ℗07 4778 5580, ⓦwww.providencesailing.com.au; day-trip A$129). Alternatively, try your hand at **sea-kayaking** with **Magnetic Island Sea Kayaks** (Horseshoe Bay; ℗07 4778 5424, ⓦwww.seakayak.com.au; A$69 including breakfast).

Relatively murky waters don't make Magnetic Island the most dramatic place to learn to **scuba dive**, but with easy shore access it's very cheap – certification courses start at A$299 – and on a good day there's some fair coral, a couple of small shipwrecks and decent fish-life. **Pleasure Divers** (10 Marine Parade, Arcadia; ℗07 4778 5788 or 1800 797 797, ⓦwww.divemagneticisland.com) run courses, dive around the island, and can also arrange dives to the *Yongala* (see p.531) for experienced divers. **Reef EcoTours** (Nelly Bay; ℗0419 712579, ⓦwww.reefecotours.com) organizes specialist snorkelling trips to the island's most interesting coastal spots, run by a coral-reef ecology expert. It's also possible to head out to the **Great Barrier Reef** on one of the diving and snorkelling trips run by the operators in Townsville (see p.547): they will pick you up from Nelly Bay on their way out to the Reef.

Other diversions include **horse rides** with the experienced **Bluey's Horseshoe Ranch** (58 Gifford St, Horseshoe Bay; ℗07 4778 5109, ⓦwww.blueyshorseranch.com; A$85 for 2hr).

cocktails by the jug. The beach, which is good for swimming most of the year, with a stinger net from November to May, is also a great place for activities – several beachfront operators **rent** out jet-skis, kayaks, surf-skis and boats, and provide joyrides on inflated tubes and water skis.

Steep and rocky **hiking tracks** lead over the headland to secluded, clothing-optional **Balding Bay**, one of the smallest and prettiest on the island; you can spend a perfect day here snorkelling around the coral gardens just off shore. Further on, **Radical Bay** – half a kilometre of sandy beach sandwiched between two huge, pine-covered granite fists – is another attractive spot, but since it's accessible by private vehicles, it doesn't have quite the same magic as Balding; though presently uninhabited, its character is likely to change completely if a proposed new luxury resort development gets underway.

On the way into Horseshoe Bay, the bus stops at *Bungalow Bay Koala Village* and the island's excellent **Koala Sanctuary** (℡07 4778 5577, ⓦwww .bungalowbay.com.au; A\$19, child A\$10). To visit the sanctuary, you need to join one of their leisurely guided tours (daily 10am, noon & 2.30pm) which teach you about the island's ecology and introduce you to the resident crocs, lizards, cockatoos and pythons, as well as the stars of the show – captive-bred koalas. Proceeds from the sales of koala-cuddling photos help support island-wide wildlife-welfare projects. Three days a week before the morning tour there's a gourmet breakfast of guava champagne, reef fish with bush tomatoes, honey-comb and other local produce (Wed, Fri & Sun 8.30am, possibly more frequently in future; A\$25, child A\$12.50). The woodlands near the sanctuary are rich in wildlife including birds, insects and large colonies of fruit bats.

North of Townsville

The coastal region just an hour to the **north of Townsville** is the southern-most outpost of Queensland's wet tropics, with dramatic, dark green plateaus shrouded in cloud. The forests here once formed a continuous belt; while logging has thinned them to a disjointed necklace of national parks, it still seems as if almost every side-track off the highway leads to a waterhole or falls surrounded by jungle. This is where it really pays to have your own vehicle. There's deep forest around **Paluma** and superlative scenery at **Wallaman Falls**, the tallest single-drop waterfall in Australia, inland from **Ingham**. There are also a handful of **islands** to explore, including the wilds of **Hinchinbrook** and the small, exclusive resort-islands of **Orpheus**, **Bedarra** and **Dunk**.

Paluma and Jourama Falls

Some 60km north of Townsville and 290km south of Cairns, the Mount Spec road turns west off the Bruce Highway (A1) and climbs a crooked 21km into the hills to **Paluma** township, where the tropical highland climate really kicks in; if you've travelled here from the south, you'll notice a drop in temperature and a jump in humidity. Halfway there, a solid stone bridge, built by relief labour during the Great Depression of the 1930s, spans **Little Crystal Creek**, with some picnic tables and barbecue hotplates by the road, and deep swimming holes overshadowed by rainforest just up from the bridge – beware of slippery rocks and potentially strong currents. Look out, too, for large, metallic-blue **Ulysses butterflies** bobbing around the canopy.

PALUMA itself consists of a handful of weatherboard cottages in the rainforest at the top of the range. A couple of **walking tracks** (from 500m to

Cycads are extremely slow-growing, fire-resistant plants found throughout the tropics, with tough, palm-like fronds – relics of the age of dinosaurs. Female plants produce large cones that break up into bright orange segments, each containing a seed; these are eaten (and so distributed) by emus, amongst other creatures. Despite being highly toxic to humans – almost every early Australian explorer made himself violently ill trying them – these seeds were a staple of Aborigines, who detoxified flour made from the nuts by prolonged washing. They also applied "fire-stick farming" techniques, encouraging groves to grow and seed by annual burning.

2km in length) take you into the gloom, including a ridgetop track to Witt's Lookout. Keep your eyes open for **chowchillas**, plump little birds with a dark body and white front that forage by kicking the leaf litter sideways; you'll also hear whipbirds and the snarls of the black-and-blue **Victoria riflebird**, a bird of paradise – they're fairly common in highland rainforest between here and the Atherton Tablelands, but elusive. For a good glimpse of these, head for *Ivy Cottage Tearooms* (℡07 4770 8533; Tues–Fri 10.30am–4pm, Sat & Sun 10am–5pm), whose garden and birdtable is the local riflebird population's favourite afternoon haunt – their Devonshire cream teas aren't bad either. They offer self-catering **accommodation** (❹); alternatives include self-contained cabins at *Misthaven Units* (℡07 4770 8607; ❷) and *Paluma Rainforest Cottages* (℡07 4770 8520, ⓦwww.palumarainforest.com.au; ❸), or bed and breakfast at *Forestmist Cottages* (℡07 4770 8578; ❸).

Beyond Paluma the range descends west, leaving the dark, wet coastal forest for open gum woodland. *Hidden Valley Cabins* (℡07 4770 8088 or 1800 466 509, ⓦwww.hiddenvalleycabins.com.au; room ❸, cabin ❺), an ecolodge 24km beyond Paluma on a dirt road near Running River, provides simple timber cottages, a spa, pool, beer, meals and packed lunches. Nearby is **The Gorge**, a lively section of river with falls, rapids and pools – drive down in a 4WD or walk the last kilometre.

The *Frosty Mango* roadhouse (daily 8am–6pm), on the Bruce Highway (A1) north of Paluma and 65km north of Townsville, is well worth a stop for curry, cakes, and ice cream made from locally grown fruit. Further north, a six-kilometre part-asphalt road leads west off the highway towards **Jourama Falls**. The road ends at the low-key Paluma Range National Park (Jourama Falls) **campsite** (see p.54 for booking information) set amongst gum and wattle bushland peppered with huge **cycads**. From here an hour-long walking track follows chains across the rocky riverbed to swimming holes surrounded by gigantic granite boulders and cliffs, finally winding up at the falls themselves – which are fairly insignificant by the end of the dry season but impressive in full flood.

Ingham and around

Home to Australia's largest Italian community, the small town of **INGHAM**, 110km north of Townsville and 240km south of Cairns, is well placed for trips inland to **Girringun National Park** – home to Australia's highest waterfall – and also gives access to the tiny port of **Lucinda**, the southern terminus for ferries to Hinchinbrook Island (see p.557). The other offshore attraction near Ingham is the tiny **Orpheus Island National Park**.

Pasta and wine are to be had in abundance during the May **Italian Festival**, but the town is better known for events surrounding the former *Day Dawn*

Hotel (since replaced by *Lee's Hotel*) on Lannercost Street, one of the pubs that claims to be the legendary "**Pub without Beer**". Local lore has it that during World War II, Ingham was the first stop for servicemen heading north from Townsville, and in 1941 they drank the bar dry, a momentous occasion recorded by local poet Dan Sheahan and later turned into the popular ballad, *The Pub With No Beer*. If you've an hour to kill in town, there's a nice easy **walk** around the well-signposted **Tyto Wetlands** on the southern outskirts. Named after the eastern grass owls (*Tyto capensis*) that live here, this network of waterways, ponds and grasslands has bird hides, walkways and an interpretive centre with interactive displays and local wildlife photography. Birdwatchers have recorded over two hundred species in the area, and there's also a colony of agile wallabies.

The Bruce Highway (A1) curves through Ingham as Herbert Street, though most services are located slightly to the west along **Lannercost Street**. Information is available at the well-informed **Hinchinbrook Visitor Centre** (Mon–Fri 8.45am–5pm, Sat & Sun 9am–2pm; ℡07 4776 5211, ⓦwww .hinchinbrooknq.com.au), on the corner where the highway from Townsville and the south meets Lannercost Street; they also stock brochures on local national parks. Long-distance **buses** (see p.35) stop nearby ten times daily; the **railway station** is 1km east on Lynch Street – you can buy **tickets** from Ingham Travel at 28 Lannercost St (℡07 4776 5666).

Accommodation options include *Palm Tree Caravan Park*, off the Bruce Highway, south of the town centre (℡07 4776 2403; camping A\$17–22, cabin ❷), straightforward pub rooms at *Lee's Hotel* (58 Lannercost St; ℡07 4776 1503, ⓦwww.leeshotel.com.au; ❷ including continental breakfast), or basic dorm beds at the *Royal Hotel* (46 Lannercost St; ℡07 4776 2024; A\$14) on Lannercost Street. *Lee's* does filling budget **meals**, and the bar hasn't run out of beer since the 1940s. Ingham's sizeable Italian community ensures it's a good place for delis and Italian restaurants; the *Olive Tree Coffee Lounge*, just a few doors along from the Visitor Centre, has great home-made pizza and pasta.

Leaving, the Bruce Highway (A1) is well marked, but for the various sections of **Girringun National Park**, turn west down Lannercost Street and follow the **Trebonne** road (lucidly signposted, "This road is not Route 1"); for **Lucinda**, follow the signs for Forest Beach and Halifax from the town centre.

Girringun National Park and Wallaman Falls

Several disconnected areas of wilds west of Ingham together form **Girringun National Park**, named after a mythical storyteller from the local Aboriginal tribe. The road from Ingham divides 20km along at Trebonne, with separate routes from here to either Mount Fox or Wallaman Falls. For **Mount Fox**, stay on the road for 55km as it crosses cattle country to the base of this extinct volcanic cone; the last 2km are dirt and can be unstable. A rocky, unmarked path climbs to the crater rim through scanty forest; it's hot work, so start early. The crater itself is only about 10m deep, tangled in vine forest and open woodland. With prior permission, you might be able to camp at the nearby township's cricket grounds – either ask at the school, or call ℡07 4777 5104.

The signposted, forty-kilometre route to **Wallaman Falls** runs along a mostly sealed road up the tight and twisting range. Tunnelling through thick rainforest along the ridge (where cassowaries are commonly sighted), the road emerges at the Girringun National Park (Wallaman Falls) QPWS **campsite** (see p.54 for booking information) home to a great many bettongs, before reaching a picnic area at the falls **lookout**. The falls – at 268m, Australia's tallest single drop – are spectacular, leaping in a thin ribbon over the sheer cliffs of the plateau opposite and appearing to vaporize by the time they reach the gorge floor. A walk down a narrow and slippery path from the lookout to the base dispels this impression, as the mist turns out to be from the force of water hitting the plunge pool. Birdwatchers may find tooth-billed bowerbirds in this area between September and January, and Victoria's riflebirds between August and December. If you're staying the night, walk from the campsite along the adjacent quiet stretch of **Stoney Creek** at dawn or late afternoon to see platypuses. Wallaman Falls is the start of one of Queensland's most challenging wilderness hikes, the 110km Wet Tropics Walk (see p.424); if you don't have the time or the stamina for the longest section, a very rugged long-distance track north to Blencoe Falls, you could try one of the shorter routes to Yamanie (37.5km, manageable in 2 days) or Henrietta Gate (57km, 3 days).

Orpheus Island

Orpheus is a scrap of an island, 24km offshore, 45km east of Ingham. Thickly vegetated, its only development, *Orpheus Island Resort* (☎07 4777 7377, ⓦwww .orpheus.com.au; ⓞ), is one of the most understated of Queensland's exclusive island hideaways, and suits those looking for a back-to-nature luxury escape, with empty beaches and good snorkelling. As it's not owned by a chain, it has a one-off atmosphere, but rates are terrifically high (full board from A\$1450 per night for two people, plus flights from Townsville). There's also a QPWS **campsite** (see p.54 for booking information) accessible only by private boat or charter.

Cardwell

Some 50km north of Ingham and 190km south of Cairns lies the modest little truckstop town of **CARDWELL** – just a quiet string of shops on one side of the Bruce Highway (A1), with a windblown beach on the other. It's made attractive by the outline of **Hinchinbrook Island**, which hovers just off shore, so close that it almost seems to be part of the mainland. The main reason to stop here is to plan a trip to the island, though you can also buy very cheap **lychees** from roadside stalls in December.

Cardwell spreads for about 2km along the highway, with banks, the post office, supermarket and hotel all near or south of the **old jetty**, itself about halfway along the road. Just north of the jetty, the QPWS-run **Rainforest and Reef Information Centre** (daily 8am–4.30pm; free; ☎07 4066 8601) has a walk-through rainforest and mangrove display, plus a QPWS ranger on hand to answer questions on the area, in particular on mountain-access approval for hikers wishing to tackle Mount Bowen or Mount Diamantina on Hinchinbrook Island (see p.557).

Ferries to Hinchinbrook leave not from Cardwell itself but from the shiny new Port Hinchinbrook Marina, south of town, or from Lucinda northeast of Ingham; for details see p.557. If you'd like to spend a few days **cruising** around Hinchinbrook's coastline, perhaps looking for crocodiles and dugongs, instead of hiking its trails, you can hire a bareboat **yacht** or **houseboat** sleeping from six to twelve people from Hinchinbrook Rent a Yacht, based at Port Hinchinbrook Marina (☎07 4066 8007, ⓦwww.hinchinbrookrentayacht.com .au; from A\$500 per day for a minimum four-day charter). Port Hinchinbrook also has a **scuba** centre, HDive (☎07 4066 0091, ⓦwww.hdive.com.au).

For advice on **swimming** in northern Queensland's coastal waters during the "stinger season", see p.47.

Buses pull up just off the highway on Brasenose Street, beside the BP service station and *Seaview Café*; the **railway station** is about 200m further back. You can buy bus **tickets** at *Seaview Café* (daily 8am–late).

Accommodation options include nice gardens and cute rooms at *Cardwell Bed & Breakfast*, two streets behind the bus stop at 18 Gregory St (℡07 4066 8330, ⓦwww.cardwellhomestay.com.au; ❸); self-contained, simple units at *Cardwell Beachfront Motel*, 1 Scott St (℡07 4066 8776; ❸); modern hostel accommodation close to the bus stop and tips on local work opportunities at *Cardwell Central Backpackers*, 6 Brasenose St (℡07 4066 8404, ⓦwww .cardwellbackpackers.com.au; bunk in shared room A$20, private double ❶); or camping and cabins at *Kookaburra Holiday Park and YHA*, 175 Bruce Hwy (℡07 4066 8648, ⓦwww.kookaburraholidaypark.com.au; camping A$20–24, bunk in shared room A$18, room or cabin ❷). There are also attractive modern apartments and cabins with a pool at *Port Hinchinbrook Resort* (℡1800 22 00 77, ⓦwww.porthinchinbrook.com.au; ❺) in the rather sterile surroundings of the marina. For **food**, *Annie's Kitchen* (daily 7am–7.45pm), just up the highway from the bus stop, is the best of the town's roadside cafés; fish and chips can be had from *Seafood Fish & Chips* opposite the Rainforest and Reef Information Centre. If you're **self-catering**, head for the small supermarket on the north side of town.

Hinchinbrook Island

Across the channel from Cardwell, **HINCHINBROOK ISLAND** looms huge and green, with mangroves rising to forest along the mountain range that forms the island's spine, peaking at **Mount Bowen**. The island's drier east side, hidden behind the mountains, has long beaches separated by headlands and the occasional sluggish creek. This is Bandjin Aboriginal land, and though early Europeans reported the people as friendly, attitudes later changed and nineteenth-century "dispersals" had the same effect here as elsewhere. The island was never subsequently occupied, and apart from a single resort, Hinchinbrook remains much as it was two hundred years ago. At nearly 40,000 hectares, it's one of Australia's largest national parks; its main attraction is the superb **Thorsborne Trail**, a moderately demanding 32-kilometre hiking track along the east coast, which takes in forests, mangroves, waterfalls and beaches.

Practicalities

Ferries from Port Hinchinbrook Marina, just south of Cardwell, to Ramsay Bay at Hinchinbrook's **north end** are run by Hinchinbrook Island Ferries (℡07 4066 8585 or 1800 777 021, ⓦwww.hinchinbrookferries.com.au; A$66 one way, A$90 return); while Hinchinbrook Wilderness Safaris in Lucinda, northeast of Ingham (℡07 4777 8307, ⓦwww.hinchinbrookwildernesssafaris .com.au), run to George Point at the **south end** (A$46 one way, A$57 return); they can also take you to other points in the south such as Mulligan Bay (A$66 one way, A$77 return) or Bluff Creek (A$57 return). You can book a **bus** between Lucinda and Ingham or Cardwell for A$25 per person with Ingham Travel (℡07 4776 5666).

The Thorsborne Trail needs some **advance planning**. You should arrange Queensland Parks and Wildlife Service hiking and camping permits (see p.54) as far ahead as possible – since visitor numbers on the island are restricted, the trail is often booked solid. QPWS allows a maximum group size of six with no more than forty people in total on the trail at one time. Trail maps can be downloaded from their website (ⓦwww.epa.qld.gov.au) where, nearer the time of your trip, you can read current warnings – permits can be suspended if a "prescribed burn" of the eucalyptus forest is due to take place. The trail is managed under a minimal-impact bushwalking, no-trace camping ethic, and you're required to watch a QPWS video on this subject before setting out. If you're planning to climb one of the mountains, particularly Mount Bowen (1121m) or Mount Diamantina (995m), you need to get mountain-access approval from the Rainforest and Reef Information Centre in Cardwell (see p.556). Finally, you need to decide whether to start at the north or south end of the island and book **ferry transfers** accordingly, though note there may be **no ferries** in February and March.

The drier winter months (June–Oct) provide optimum **hiking conditions**, though it can rain throughout the year. **Hiking essentials** include water-resistant footgear, pack and tent, a lightweight raincoat and insect repellent. Wood fires are prohibited, so bring a **fuel stove**. *Kookaburra Holiday Park* in Cardwell (see p.557) rents out camping gear. Although streams with **drinking water** are fairly evenly distributed, they might be dry by the end of winter, or only flowing upstream from the beach – collect from flowing sources only. As for **wildlife**, you need to beware of crocodiles in lowland creek systems. Less worrying are the white-tailed rats and marsupial mice that will gnaw through tents to reach food; there are metal food-stores at campsites, though hanging anything edible from a branch may foil their attempts.

If you're not interested in a serious hike, then Hinchinbrook Island Ferries offers an excellent **day-trip** (A\$90, child A\$45), departing daily at 9am from Port Hinchinbrook Marina, cruising after **dugong** and stopping for a three-kilometre beach-and-rainforest walk before winding up with a dip in the pool at the island's sole proper **accommodation**, ⚘ *Hinchinbrook Island Wilderness Lodge* (☎07 4066 8270 or 1800 777 021, ⓦwww.hinchinbrookresort.com.au; cabins sleeping up to four ❺, luxury pole-cabin doubles ❼). The lodge is set on Cape Richards at Hinchinbrook's northernmost tip and makes a comfortable retreat. If you just want ferry transfers to the lodge, the fare with Hinchinbrook Island Ferries is A\$96 return for the scheduled service (departs daily 9am, returns 4pm) or A\$180 one way for a special charter at other times. **Diving trips** can be arranged through Port Hinchinbrook's scuba centre, HDive (see p.556).

The Thorsborne Trail

The 32-kilometre **Thorsborne Trail** is manageable in three days, though at that pace you won't see much: some parts of the route are hard-going, and it's far better to allow between four and seven. **Trailheads** are at Ramsay Bay in the north and George Point in the south, and the route is marked with orange triangles (north–south), or yellow triangles (south–north). The north to south route, described below, is considered slightly more forgiving as it eases into ascents, although the advantage of ending up in the north is that the pick-up with Hinchinbrook Island Ferries includes a welcome few hours unwinding at the *Wilderness Lodge's* bar and pool.

Boats from Port Hinchinbrook Marina, south of Cardwell, take you through the mangroves of Missionary Bay in the north to a boardwalk that crosses to the eastern side of the island at **Ramsay Bay**. The walk from here to **Nina Bay**, which takes a couple of hours, is along a fantastic stretch of coast with rainforest sweeping right down to the sand and Mount Bowen and Nina Peak as a backdrop. If long bushwalks don't appeal, you could spend a few days camped at the forest edge at Nina instead; a creek at the southern end provides drinking water and Nina Peak can be climbed in an hour or so. Otherwise, continue beyond a small cliff at the southern end of Nina, and walk for another two hours or so through a pine forest to **Little Ramsay Bay** (drinking water from Warrawilla Creek), which is about as far as you're likely to get on the first day.

Moving on, you scramble over boulders at the far end of the beach before crossing another creek (at low tide, as it gets fairly deep) and entering the forest beyond. From here to the next camp at **Zoe Bay** takes about five hours, following creek beds through lowland casuarina woods and rainforest, before exiting onto the beach near Cypress Pine waterhole. A clearing and pit toilets at the southern end of Zoe Bay marks the **campsite** – though you'll need to check with the QPWS rangers in Cardwell (see p.556) about the safest areas to camp, as **crocodiles** have been seen here. This is one of those places where you'll be very glad you brought insect repellent.

Next day, take the path to the base of **Zoe Falls** – the waterhole here is fabulous but not safe for swimming – then struggle straight up beside them to the cliff top, from where there are great vistas. Across the river, forest and heathland alternate: the hardest part is crossing **Diamantina Creek**, a fast-flowing river with huge, slippery granite boulders. **Mulligan Falls**, not much further on, is the last source of fresh water, with several rock ledges for sunbathing around a pool full of curious fish – stay off the dangerously slippery rocks above the falls. Zoe to Mulligan takes around four hours, and from here to George Point is only a couple more if you push it, but the falls are a better place to camp and give you the chance to backtrack a little to take a look at the beachside lagoon at **Sunken Reef Bay**.

The last leg to **George Point** is the least interesting: rainforest replaces the highland trees around the falls as the path crosses a final creek before arriving at unattractive Mulligan Bay. The campsite at George Point has a table and toilet in the shelter of a coconut grove but there's no fresh water, nothing to see bar Lucinda's sugar terminal, and little to do except wait for your ferry.

Murray Falls and Tully

Twenty kilometres north of Cardwell and 170km south of Cairns, a side road leads off the Bruce Highway (A1) and heads another 20km inland past banana plantations to attractive **Murray Falls**, right at the edge of the Cardwell Range. It's really just worth a look to break your journey, but there's a large QPWS **camping area** here (see p.54 for booking information) and tracks through the forest to permanent swimming holes and lookouts across the bowl of the valley. There's a basic store on the approach road, some distance from the falls, but it's best to stock up in Cardwell beforehand.

Some 45km north of Cardwell, **TULLY** lies to the left of the highway on the slopes of **Mount Tyson**, whose 450-centimetre annual rainfall is the highest in Australia. Chinese settlers pioneered banana plantations here at the beginning of the twentieth century, and it's now a stopover for **white-water rafting** day-trips out of Cairns and Mission Beach on the fierce and reliable Tully River, 45km inland. Otherwise, the town is nothing special, a triangle of narrow streets with cultivated lawns and flowerbeds backing onto roaring jungle at the end of Brannigan Street, a constant reminder of the colonists' struggle to keep chaos at bay. Though most people drive the extra thirty minutes to Mission Beach, there's **accommodation** here at *Green Way Caravan Park* (☏07 4068 2055; camping A\$20, cabin ❷) or the well-managed *Banana Barracks* hostel at 50 Butler St (☏07 4068 0455, ⓦwww.bananabarracks.com; bunk in shared room A\$24, private double ❷), which has excellent **farm-work** connections, plus free trips and deals for guests staying a week or more.

Mission Beach

Branching coastward off the Bruce Highway (A1) a couple of kilometres north of Tully – and again from the truckstop town of El Arish, around 20km further north – is a loop road that leads through canefields and patches of rainforest to **MISSION BEACH**, the collective name for four peaceful hamlets strung out along a fourteen-kilometre stretch of sand. Though very tourism-orientated, it's a pleasantly unspoilt area, appealing to those whose idea of a perfect break is cooking over a barbie in the backyard of a holiday house, a stone's throw from the ocean. The quiet, palm-fringed coast offers plenty of opportunities for laidback lounging, while not far off shore lies **Dunk Island**, whose idyllic beaches and rainforest track can be explored on a pleasant day-trip, and its exclusive little neighbour, **Bedarra Island**. Mission Beach is also a good spot for nature enthusiasts and ecotourists: the coastal forest is home to the largest surviving **cassowary** population in Australia, and you'll have a reasonable chance of seeing one if you stay in one of the area's forest retreats.

The area owes its name to the former Hull River Mission, destroyed by a savage **cyclone** in 1918. In 2006, **Cyclone Larry** stripped the rainforest canopy and flattened farms between here and Cairns, wiping out the entire year's banana crop; to the tutored eye, the effects will be visible for years, but the community is back on its feet and the forest is already well on the way to recovery.

Arrival and information

From south to north, Mission Beach comprises the communities of **South Mission Beach**, **Wongaling Beach**, **Mission Beach** and **Bingil Bay**, each around four or five kilometres from its neighbours. **Long-distance buses** set down near the Big Cassowary at Wongaling Beach shopping centre; your accommodation might collect you from the stop if forewarned. A **local bus**, the Beach Bus, plies the route between South Mission and Bingil Bay (roughly hourly Mon–Sat 8.30am–6pm; ☎07 4068 7400, ⓦ www.transnorthbus.com); for a **taxi**, call ☎07 4068 8155 or 0429 689 366. Le Tour Bikes on Cassowary Drive just north of the Big Cassowary (☎07 4068 9553, ⓦ www.letourbikes .com.au) rents mountain bikes for A\$25 per day and also offers scooter hire.

The **Mission Beach Visitor Centre** (Mon–Fri 9am–5pm; ☎07 4068 7099, ⓦ www.missionbeachtourism.com) is on the main road, Porter Promenade, between the Mission Beach village shops and Clump Point; right behind it, the **C4 Environmental Information Centre** (Mon–Fri 10am–5pm; free) has a display on local habitats and environmental issues, along with a nursery growing seeds collected from cassowary droppings, with the aim of safeguarding the giant bird's food supply for the future. A local produce and craft **market** is held in the nearby parkland on the first and third Sundays of each month (6.30am–noon). There are **Internet** cafés at Wongaling Beach and Mission Beach.

Accommodation

Accommodation is fairly evenly distributed along the coast and covers everything from camping to resorts, with an emphasis on small-scale places. One of the most popular choices is to rent a house from an agency such as *Mission Beach Holidays* (☎07 4088 6699, ⓦ www.missionbeachholidays.com. au); they have a huge number of properties to choose from, most of them very close to the beach.

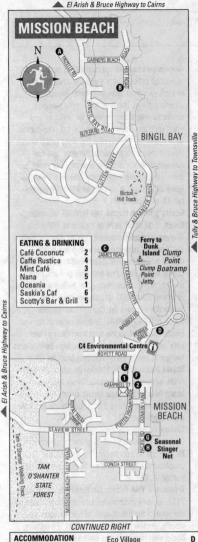

MISSION BEACH

BINGIL BAY

TAM O'SHANTER STATE FOREST

Bicton Hill Track

Ferry to Dunk Island

Clump Point

Clump Point Boatramp

Clump Point Jetty

EATING & DRINKING

Café Coconutz	2
Caffe Rustica	4
Mint Café	3
Nana	5
Oceania	1
Saskia's Caf	6
Scotty's Bar & Grill	5

C4 Environmental Centre

MISSION BEACH

Seasonal Stinger Net

TAM O'SHANTER STATE FOREST

MISSION CIRCLE

Tam O'Shanter Walking Track

Tully & Bruce Highway to Townsville

Big Cassowary

Bus Stop

Dunk Island Water Taxis

Ferry to Dunk Island

WONGALING BEACH

TAM O'SHANTER STATE FOREST

WEBB STREET

Seasonal Stinger Net

Hull River Mission (site of)

SOUTH MISSION BEACH

Hull River

Kennedy Walking Track

Not to scale

8

ACCOMMODATION

Beachcomber Coconut Caravan Village	**O**	Eco Village	**D**	Licuala Lodge	**I**	Sejala	**H**
Cassawong Cottages	**N**	Hibiscus Lodge	**J**	Mission Beach Retreat	**F**	Taihoa	**P**
Castaways	**G**	Hideaway Holiday Village	**E**	Sanctuary Retreat	**B**	Treehouse YHA	**A**
		Honeyeater B&B	**M**	Scotty's Beach House	**K**	The Wongalinga	**L**
		The Horizon	**Q**	Sealord's	**C**		

Beachcomber Coconut Caravan Village
Kennedy Esplanade, South Mission Beach
☏07 4068 8129, ⊛www.beachcombercoconut
.com. Tidy though rather crowded beachfront site
close to the South Mission stinger net, with a
variety of self-catering units and space for tents,
vans and caravans, plus a café-restaurant.
Camping A$29–35, cabin ②, villa ④

Cassawong Cottages Reid Rd, Wongaling Beach
☏07 4098 8500, ⊛www.cassawongcottages
.com.au. Pricey for the area, but pretty, these self-
catering bungalows are comfortable and set among
a leafy little garden. ⑤

Castaways Pacific Parade, Mission Beach
☏07 4068 7444, ⊛www.rydges.com. Overlooking
the beach, right by the stinger net, this place has a

For advice on **swimming** in northern Queensland's coastal waters during the "stinger season", see p.47.

good location. The rooms are ordinary and the pool is rather uninviting, but the beachside gardens are lovely. Room ❹, apartment ❻

Eco Village Clump Point ☏07 4068 7534, ⓦwww.ecovillage.com.au. Though not particularly eco-friendly, this offers smart rooms just back from the beach amongst pandanus, native nutmeg trees and tropical gardens with a natural rock pool. The luxury rooms have Jacuzzis. ❺

Hibiscus Lodge 6 Kurrajong Close, Wongaling Beach ☏07 4068 9096. Welcoming B&B with three guest rooms in a large house with a sweeping front lawn and a small pool. Breakfast is served on the veranda. ❹

Hideaway Holiday Village Porter Promenade, Mission Beach ☏07 4068 7104, ⓦwww.missionbeachhideaway.com.au. Large roadside site with self-catering cabins to rent and plenty of room to camp. Camping A$29–37, cabin ❷, villa ❸

Honeyeater B&B 53 Reid Rd, Wongaling Beach ☏07 4068 8741, ⓦwww.honeyeater.com.au. Attractive, Bali-inspired house with a lovely open-plan lounge, a pool set in lush tropical gardens, and quiet guest rooms. ❹

The Horizon Explorer St, South Mission Beach ☏1800 079 090, ⓦwww.thehorizon.com.au. The service at this upmarket hotel can be indifferent, but you can't fault the location – on a steep hillside with gorgeous views of tropical vegetation and sparkling sea – and the pool is by far the most attractive in Mission Beach. ❺

Licuala Lodge 11 Mission Circle, Mission Beach ☏07 4068 8194, ⓦwww.licualalodge.com.au. Delightful tropical-style B&B with airy wooden verandas and traditional, high-ceilinged interior; the landscaped garden and pool are worth a stay in themselves, and the huge breakfast will keep you going all day. ❸

Mission Beach Retreat Porter Promenade, Mission Beach ☏07 4088 6229, ⓦwww.missionbeachretreat.com.au. Small, basic hostel conveniently located next to the Mission Beach shops and restaurants, with low prices. Bunk in shared room A$19, private double ❶

Sanctuary Retreat Holt Rd, Bingil Bay ☏07 4088 6064 or 1800 777 012,

ⓦwww.sanctuaryretreat.com.au. An outstanding eco-lodge set on a very steep hill amid fifty acres of thick rainforest, alive with birds, insects and other creatures. The huts are simple sleeping platforms with insect screens for walls, so you wake up surrounded by greenery; the pole-cabins have balconies looking over the trees to the ocean. Healthy meals are served in the very cool bar-restaurant, which also has breathtaking views, and there's a pool and yoga studio. You won't want to leave. Single bed in shared hut A$32.50, private hut ❷, pole-cabin ❹

Scotty's Beach House 167 Reid Rd, Wongaling Beach ☏07 4068 8676 or 1800 665 567, ⓦwww.scottysbeachhouse.com.au. Popular party backpackers' near the coach stop and beach, behind a lively bar-restaurant with regular DJs and games nights. Colourful and arranged around a pool, its bunkhouses sleep up to twelve each. Bunk in shared room A$21–26, private double ❶

Sealord's 4 James Rd, Clump Point, Mission Beach ☏07 4088 6444, ⓦwww.sealords.com.au. Elegant B&B just up the road from Clump Point jetty, with polished wooden floors, high ceilings and two guest rooms full of luxurious touches. ❹

Sejala Pacific Parade, Mission Beach ☏07 4088 6699, ⓦwww.sejala.com.au. These "boutique beach huts" – Bali-style timber cabins hidden in a tropical garden – have a great beachside location and a small pool. ❺

Taihoa 24 Kennedy Esplanade, South Mission Beach ☏07 4068 9446, ⓦwww.taihoa.com.au. Modern studio apartments for singles and couples (no kids), with a small pool and shared barbecue. ❹

Treehouse YHA Frizelle Rd, Bingil Bay ☏07 4068 7137, ⓦwww.yha.com.au. Like an alpine chalet on the edge of the forest, open to wildlife such as insects, geckos and cane toads, this is a relaxing hostel with hammocks to lounge in and a small but pleasant pool. Camping A$24 (A$12pp), bunk in shared room A$22, private double ❷

The Wongalinga 64 Reid Rd, Wongalinga Beach ☏07 4068 8221. Set in a beautiful beachfront garden with lawns running right down to the sand, these spacious, breezy apartments are perfect for a relaxing and comfortable stay. ❻

South Mission Beach, Wongaling Beach, Mission Beach and Bingil Bay

Tucked between Hull River National Park and the ocean, **SOUTH MISSION BEACH** is a quiet, mostly residential spot, with a long, clean beach. Signposted off the main road on Mission Drive is a monument to the original site of the **Hull River Mission**; after the 1918 cyclone, the mission was relocated to safer surroundings on Palm Island. At the southern end of beachfront Kennedy Esplanade, the **Kennedy Walking Track** weaves through coastal swamp and forest for a couple of hours to Edmund Kennedy's original landing place near the mouth of the Hull River – a good place to spot coastal birdlife and, quite likely, crocodiles.

The next hamlet north is **WONGALING BEACH**, a slowly expanding settlement based around a small shopping centre whose roadside mascot is a giant statue of a cassowary. A further 5km lands you at **MISSION BEACH** itself, the focus of which is the cluster of shops, boutiques, restaurants, banks and a post office one block back from the beach on Porter Promenade. Inland between the two, a six-kilometre walking track weaves through **Tam O'Shanter State Forest**, a dense maze of muddy creeks, vine thickets and stands of licuala palms (identified by their frilly, saucer-shaped leaves). If you don't see **cassowaries** here – sometimes leading their knee-high, striped chicks through the undergrowth – you'd be very unlucky. Continuing 6km north of Mission township past the **Clump Point** boat ramp and lookout – a black basalt outcrop with views south down the beach – and **Clump Point Jetty**, the road winds along the coast to sleepy **BINGIL BAY**. Just before, there's a parking bay on the roadside for the excellent **Bicton Hill track**, a four-kilometre hilly walk through wet tropics forest where encounters with cassowaries are again likely. From here, the road continues inland alongside the **Clump Mountain National Park** and back to the main highway.

There are stores and **places to eat and drink** in all four hamlets, though Mission Beach has the most choice, including *Oceania* (closed Wed), which specializes in fish and grills, and backpacker favourite *Café Coconutz* (daily from 4pm), a fun place for globally-inspired light meals, juices and beer. Other good choices include ⚑ *Saskia's Café* on South Mission Beach Rd, South Mission Beach (Tues–Thurs 9am–4pm, Fri & Sat 8am–4pm), an excellent little spot for

Cassowaries

The forests around Mission Beach are a reliable place to spot **cassowaries**, a blue-headed and bone-crested rainforest version of the emu, whose survival is being threatened as their habitat is carved up – estimates suggest that there are barely 1200 birds left in tropical Queensland (though they are also found in New Guinea and parts of Indonesia). Cyclones have had a disastrous effect on cassowary populations – researchers believe that the 2006 cyclone wiped out all that year's chicks in Mission Beach, and forced older birds to broaden their foraging range, leading to an increase in road accidents and attacks from dogs. Many larger trees rely on the cassowary to eat their fruit and distribute their seeds, meaning that the very make-up of the forest hinges on the bird's presence. Unfortunately, cassowary conservation is chronically underfunded, perhaps partly because these stern-looking birds don't have the charisma of, say, the koala.

Unlike emus, cassowaries are not timid and may attack if they feel threatened, particularly males, who are in charge of guarding the chicks. If you see a cassowary, remain quiet and keep a safe distance.

Among local tours worth seeking out, **Raging Thunder's Xtreme Team** (☎1800 337 116, ⓦwww.rtextreme.com; A$165), exclusive to Mission Beach, offers the best-value **river rafting** down the Tully River in small groups, getting to the river (70km away) before the bus-loads arrive from Cairns. **Jump The Beach** (☎1800 444 568, ⓦwww.jumpthebeach.com.au) can take you to more then 4000m for **freefall** fun with a beach landing (A$295), and also offers accelerated solo freefall training (A$595). If you'd like to take to the water, you can go **paddling around Dunk Island** for the day with **Coral Sea Kayaking** (☎07 4068 9154, ⓦwww.coralseakayaking.com; A$118) or **The Kayak Company** (☎0429 469 330; A$50), who also offer shorter trips (from A$15). For **reef trips**, **Quick Cat** (☎07 4068 7289, ⓦwww.quickcatcruises.com.au; A$144, child A$72; two certified dives A$95) run a motor catamaran to Beaver Cay on the Barrier Reef for coral-viewing and snorkelling, while **Calypso Dive Centre** (20 Wongaling Beach Rd; ☎07 4068 8432, ⓦwww.calypsodive.com; A$120; two certified dives A$75) run diving and snorkelling trips to Eddy Reef, plus PADI courses. Both operate daily and stop at Dunk Island on the way to and from the reef.

classy deli-style breakfasts and lunches; *Nana* on Reid Rd, Wongalinga Beach (Mon–Sat from 6pm), which serves Thai standards to eat in or take away; *Caffe Rustica* on Wonglalinga Beach Rd (Wed–Sat from 5pm, Sun 11am–9pm), an intimate trattoria with an interesting wine list; and *Mint Café* on Cassowary Drive, Wongalinga Beach, a fresh, chic and friendly little place serving healthy, home-made breakfasts, quiches and salads, including good veggie options, at reasonable prices. There are also a few permanent and temporary **galleries** dotted around, run by Mission Beach's small community of laid-back, arty locals.

Dunk Island

In 1898, Edmund Banfield, a Townsville journalist who had been given only weeks to live, waded ashore on **Dunk Island**. He spent his remaining years – all twenty-five of them – as Dunk's first European resident, crediting his unantici-pated longevity to the relaxed island life. A tiny version of Hinchinbrook, Dunk attracts far more visitors to its resort and camping grounds. While there's a satis-fying track over and around the island, it's more the kind of place where you make the most of the beach – as Banfield discovered.

Vessels from the Mission Beach area put ashore on or near the jetty, next to the *Jetty Café*, which sells sandwiches, hot meals and fresh seafood; there's no store on the island. On the far side is the shady QPWS **campsite** (see p.54 for booking information) with toilets, showers and drinking water. Five minutes along the track is the **resort**, *Voyages Dunk Island* (☎07 4068 8199, ⓦwww.dunk-island.com; ❼), with a stunning beach setting; day-guests can pay to use the resort facilities and have lunch either at the resort restaurant or the *Jetty Café*. The best places to relax are on **Brammo Bay**, in front of the resort, or **Pallon Beach**, behind the campsite. Note that the beaches are narrow at high tide and the island is close enough to the coast to attract box jellyfish in season, but you can always retreat to the resort pool.

Before falling victim to incipient lethargy, head into the interior past the resort and **Banfield's grave** for a circuit of the island's west. The full nine-kilometre **trail** up Mount Cootaloo, down to Palm Valley and back along the coast is a three-hour rainforest trek, best tackled clockwise from the resort. You'll see green pigeons and yellow-footed scrubfowl foraging in leaf litter, vines, trunkless palms and, from the peak, a vivid blue sea dotted with hunchbacked islands.

Two **ferry** operators make the five-kilometre crossing from Mission Beach to Dunk daily; you can book direct or through your accommodation. Quick Cat (℡07 4068 7289, ⓦwww.quickcatcruises.com.au; 20min, A\$21 one way or A\$42 return) depart from Clump Point Jetty at 8.30am, 10am, 2pm and 4pm; the last ferry leaves Dunk at 4.30pm. Water Taxis (℡07 4068 8310; 10min; A\$30 day return) leave from Wongaling Beach at 8.30am, 9.30am, 11am, 12.30pm, 2.30pm and 4.15pm, with the last boat leaving Dunk at 4.30pm; these are small and not really suitable if you have much luggage. It's also possible to fly direct to Dunk from Cairns with Hinterland Aviation (ⓦwww.hinterlandaviation .com.au); this takes around 45 minutes.

Camping gear can be rented from the complex next to the post office in Mission Beach; you can also leave surplus equipment with them. Dunk Jet Sports at the Calypso Dive office on Wongaling Beach Road, Mission Beach (℡07 4068 8432, ⓦwww.dunkjetsports.com.au) offers jet-ski tours of Dunk for A\$230 per jet-ski (for up to two people).

Bedarra Island

Tiny Bedarra Island, south of Dunk, offers the ultimate in desert-island luxury. Its resort, ⚓ *Voyages Bedarra Island* (℡07 4068 8233, ⓦwww.bedarraisland .com; ❽), is one of Australia's most exclusive and expensive: rates start at around A\$1500 a night and rise to around A\$3000 for a large pavilion complete with private plunge pool and fully equipped rainforest office. All sixteen villas are secluded, with views of a groomed beach. Access is via Dunk Island, by helicopter or light aircraft (with Hinterland Aviation from Cairns; see above) or ferry (with Quickcat or Water Taxi from Mission Beach; see above), followed by a twenty-minute crossing from Dunk to Bedarra in the resort launch.

South of Cairns

Between Tully and Cairns, the Bruce Highway (A1) runs right through the heart of the Coastal Queensland Wet Tropics. Much of the coastline along this stretch is inaccessible – the highway keeps a steady course eight to twelve kilometres inland – but you're thrillingly close to rainforest-clad mountainsides threaded with waterfalls. Along the way, the eccentric remains of **Paronella Park**, near the fruit-farming town of **Innisfail**, make an interesting detour, and the **Bellenden Ker Range** offers some challenging trails for hikers.

The Wet Tropics and World Heritage

Queensland's **Wet Tropics** – the coastal belt from the Paluma Range, near Townsville, to the Daintree north of Cairns – are **UNESCO World Heritage**-listed, as they contain one of the oldest surviving tracts of rainforest anywhere on earth. Whether this listing has benefited the region is questionable, however; logging has slowed, but the tourist industry has vigorously exploited the area's status as an untouched wilderness, constantly pushing for more development so that a greater number of visitors can be accommodated. The clearing of mangroves for the Port Hinchinbrook marina and resort at Cardwell is a worst-case example; Kuranda's **Skyrail** was one of the few projects designed to lessen the ultimate impact (another highway – with more buses – was the alternative).

Paronella Park

On the Bruce Highway (A1) around 25km north of Tully and 31km south of Innisfail, tiny **Silkwood** marks the turn inland for the 23-kilometre run through canefields to **Paronella Park** at Mena Creek, 120km from Cairns (daily 9am–7.30pm; A$28, child A$14; ☏07 4065 3225, ⓦwww.paronellapark.com.au). This extraordinary estate was laid out by José Paronella, a Spanish immigrant who settled here in 1929 and, to fulfill a childhood, dream, constructed a **castle** complete with florid staircases, water features and avenues of exotic kauri pines amongst the tropical forests. In its day, the castle hosted parties, weddings and movie nights, its ballroom adorned with velvet drapes, paintings of toreadors and a giant mirrorball.

Wrecked by floods, cyclones and a fire and left to moulder for twenty years, the castle and park were reclaimed from the jungle during the 1990s and given a new lease of life as a splendidly romantic theme park, with half-ruined buildings artfully part-covered in undergrowth, lush gardens and arrays of tinkling fountains – all gravity-fed from the adjacent Mena Creek. A former walk-through aquarium has become the roost of endangered little bent-winged bats, and native vegetation includes a bamboo forest and dozens of *angiopteris* ferns, rare elsewhere. Fifteen-minute indigenous cultural performances held four times a day and educational bushtucker walking tours add to the park's appeal, so you'll need a good couple of hours to do the place justice; the after-dark tour, daily at 6.20pm, is particularly atmospheric and evocative. There's a **restaurant** on site, or you can eat at the old pub on the other side of Mena Creek.

Innisfail

INNISFAIL, a small but busy town on the Johnstone River, 90km south of Cairns and 52km north of Tully, was hard hit by Cyclone Larry in 2006; as a result, government-funded restoration work has now revitalized its old Art Deco facades. There's a thriving fruit-farming industry here, and it's a good spot to find work **picking bananas** between September and April: the specialists are *Innisfail Budget Backpackers*, on the highway on the northern side of town (125 Edith St; ☏07 4061 7833, ⓦwww.jobsforbackpackers.com.au; bunk in shared room A$140 per week); and the much smarter *Codge Lodge*, in a large Queenslander near the pale pink Catholic church on Rankin Street (☏07 4061 8055; bunk in shared room A$25 or A$140 per week, private room ❷). Innisfail is worth a quick stop anyway as a reminder that modern Australia was in no way built by the British alone: there's a sizeable **Italian community** here, represented by the handful of delicatessens displaying herb sausages and fresh pasta along central Edith Street. The tiny red **Lit Sin Gong temple** on Owen Street (and the huge longan tree next to it) was first established in the 1880s by migrant workers from southern China, who cleared scrub and created market gardens here; many of Innisfail's banana plantations have been bought up recently by **Hmong** immigrants from Vietnam.

The Bellenden Ker Range, Babinda and Gordonvale

Just north of Innisfail, where the Palmerston Highway starts its ascent from the Bruce Highway (A1) to the southern Atherton Tablelands (see p.568), is the southern limit of the **Bellenden Ker Range**, which dominates the region immediately south of Cairns and includes Queensland's highest mountain, **Bartle Frere**. While the fifteen-kilometre, two-day return climb through **Wooroonooran National Park** to the 1600-metre summit is within the reach of fit, well-prepared bushwalkers, you should check the QPWS website first (Ⓦwww.epa.qld.gov.au) or contact the Wooroonooran park ranger in Bartle Frere township (☎07 4067 6304) for accurate information about the route.

Whether or not you decide to climb to the peak, it's worth visiting **Josephine Falls**, at the start of the summit track, which forms wonderfully enclosed jungle waterslides; it's signposted off the highway 19km north of Ingham or 72km south of Cairns at one-horse **Pawngilly**, from where you continue for 8km via Bartle Frere township. The **summit track** itself – which runs through an area hard-hit by Cyclone Larry in 2006 – is marked from here with orange triangles and passes through rainforest, over large granite boulders and out onto moorland with wind-stunted vegetation. Much of the summit is blinded by scrub and usually cloaked in rain, but there are great views of the Atherton Tablelands and coast during the ascent.

North of here, there's a detour off the highway at **Babinda** township – dwarfed by a huge sugar mill – to another waterhole 7km inland at **The Boulders**, where an arm of Babinda Creek forms a wide pool before spilling down a collection of house-sized granite slabs. Cool and relatively shallow, the pale blue waterhole is an excellent place to swim in the dry season, though dangerous when the water is high: several deaths have been caused by subtle undertows dragging people over the falls. You can also **camp** here for free.

Nearing the northern limit of the range is **Gordonvale**, the place where the notorious **cane toad** was first introduced to Australia (see box below). Just outside town is **Walsh's Pyramid**, a natural formation that really does look like an overgrown version of its Egyptian counterpart; the locals organize a hill-running race to the top once a year. Inland from here, the tortuous Gillies Highway climbs to Lake Barrine and Lake Eacham on the Atherton Tablelands. North of the pyramid is the northernmost section of the Bruce Highway (A1): a thirty-minute drive through the suburbs of Edmonton and White Rock to Cairns.

Cane toads

Native to South America, the huge, charismatically ugly **cane toad** was recruited in 1932 to combat a plague of greyback beetles, whose larvae were wreaking havoc on Queensland's sugar cane. The industry was desperate – beetles had cut production by ninety percent in plague years – and resorted to seeding tadpoles in waterholes around Gordonvale. They thrived, but it soon became clear that toads couldn't reach the insects (who never landed on the ground), and they didn't burrow after the grubs. Instead, they bred whenever possible, ate anything they could swallow, and killed potential predators with poisonous secretions from their neck glands. Native wildlife suffered: birds learned to eat nontoxic parts, but snake populations have been seriously affected. Judging from the quantity of flattened carcasses on summer roads (running them over is an unofficial sport), there must be millions lurking in the canefields, and they're gradually spreading into New South Wales and the Northern Territory – they arrived in Darwin, via Kakadu, in 2006. Given enough time, they seem certain to infiltrate most of the country.

The toad's outlaw status has generated a cult following, with its warty features and nature the subject of songs, toad races, T-shirt designs, a brand of beer and the award-winning **film** *Cane Toads: An Unnatural History* – worth seeing if you come across it on video. The record for the largest specimen goes to a 1.8-kilogram monster found in Mackay in 1988.

The Atherton Tablelands

The **ATHERTON TABLELANDS** behind Cairns, also known as the Cairns Highlands, are named after **John Atherton**, who opened a route between the coast and the highlands in 1877 to transport tin out of the Herberton mines. Dense forest once covered these highlands, but over the course of the twentieth century most of the trees were felled for timber – a lucrative source of income for the growing settlement of Cairns – and the land given over to dairy cattle, tobacco and grain. Most of the landscape is now rolling and pastoral, but the remaining pockets of forest are magnificent, with some particularly fine swathes in the north around **Kuranda**, the region's ever-popular day-trip destination.

It's the Tablelands' understated beauty that draws most visitors today. A legacy of the region's volcanic prehistory are some interesting cone-shaped forested hills between the quiet country towns of **Atherton** and **Yungaburra**, and picturesque crater lakes, notably **Lake Eacham** and **Lake Barrine**. The several quiet national parks harbour rare species such as **gouldian finches** and **tree kangaroos**, while to the south a driveable circuit takes you to a series of romantic **waterfalls**. You could spend days here, driving or hiking, staying in one of the region's several outstanding **ecolodges**, or simply camping out for a night and searching for wildlife with a torch.

Arrival and getting around

You really need **your own vehicle** to explore widely. Drivers can make the steep climb up to the Tablelands via the Palmerston Highway (Route 25) from Innisfail to Ravenshoe; the twisty Gillies Highway from Gordonvale to Atherton; the Kennedy Highway (Route 1) from Smithfield to Kuranda; or the Mossman–Mount Molloy and Peninsula Developmental roads from Mossman to Mareeba.

Alternatively, numerous **tours** visit the Tablelands from Cairns (see box, p.586), and there's a limited **bus service** with Whitecar Coaches (☏07 4091 1855) from their Cairns stop at 46 Spence St to Kuranda, Mareeba, Atherton, Herberton and Ravenshoe (four times a day Mon–Fri, two on Sat, one on Sun).

If you're just visiting Kuranda or are exploring by public transport, two unforgettable ways to ride up from Cairns are to take the **Kuranda Scenic Railway** or the **Skyrail Rainforest Cableway** (see p.577), both of which are worthwhile attractions in themselves. Both offer several standard packages combining these and other sights, with transfers from hotels in Cairns or Port Douglas if required.

The Central and Southern Tablelands

The heart of the Atherton Tablelands is a **pastoral region** of rolling green landscapes, which, after the rainy season, are as lush as the hills and farms of Ireland or Wales. The climate is refreshingly cool compared to the coast, and there's an abundance of fresh water: the central highlands are dotted with lakes, and the southern region is laced with waterfalls, hidden in leafy gorges. The pockets of **native rainforest** that still remain are home to mighty, other-worldly strangler figs, along with layer upon layer of epiphytic growth including creepers, vines and ferns. Patient observers will find platypus in the creeks and Lumholtz's tree kangaroos in the forests, while the more common marsupials such as brushtail possums, bandicoots and red-legged pademelons are widespread. Birds are abundant, among them interesting species such as the buff-breasted paradise kingfisher and an assortment of frogmouths and owls. Best of all, the region has

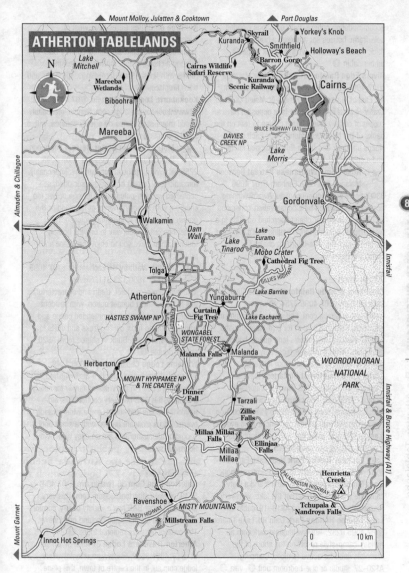

some of Queensland's best **rural retreats**, many of them secluded, highly eco-friendly and set in outstanding areas for birding and wildlife-watching.

Accommodation

Ravenshoe

The Old Convent 23 Moore St ☏ 07 4097 6454, ⓦ www.theoldconvent.com.au. Elegantly old-fashioned B&B with masses of character. ③

Malanda and around

Fur 'n' Feathers Hogan Rd, Tarzali ☏ 07 4096 5364, ⓦ www.rainforesttreehouses .com.au. One of the Tablelands' superlative accommodation options, with gorgeous wooden pole-frame houses set amongst a hundred acres of thick rainforest, rich in wildlife. Brick lodge ⑤, timber cabin ❼

Rivers Edge Rainforest Retreat Near Malanda ☏ 07 4095 2369, ⓦ www.riversedgeretreat.com.au. East of Malanda, the owners of *Mount Quincan Crater Retreat* in Yungaburra (see opposite) have a couple of equally lovely forest cabins to rent on the banks of the North Johnstone River. Each one sleeps up to six and has a fully-equipped kitchen and a cosy wood-burning stove. ⑥

Rose Gums Wilderness Retreat Between Malanda and Lake Eacham ☏ 07 4096 8360, ⓦ www.rosegums.com.au. Award-winning eco-retreat designed by a conservation-conscious architect, with timber chalets perched on stilts in a wonderfully secluded forest setting that's excellent for bird-watching. One-bedroom chalet ⑥, two-bedroom chalet ❼

The lakes

Chambers Wildlife Rainforest Lodges Near Lake Eacham ☏ 07 4095 3754, ⓦ www.rainforest-australia.com. Self-contained cabins in a forested area that's good for bird-watching and wildlife-viewing; the owners lend guests books and binoculars. Minimum three-night stay. One-bedroom lodge ④, five-bedroom lodge ⑤

Crater Lake Rainforest Cottages Near Lake Eacham ☏ 07 4095 2322, ⓦ www.craterlakes.com.au. Four cosy and charmingly decorated forest cottages, each different: the *Pioneer* cottage has corrugated iron panels and bric-a-brac evoking a settler's shack, while the *Tuscan* cottage has romantic drapes and chandeliers. ⑤

Lake Eacham Tourist Park Near Lake Eacham ☏ 07 4095 3730, ⓦ www.lakeeachamtouristpark.com. Simple but welcoming cabins and a leafy campsite within easy reach of the lake, with very reasonable prices. Camping A$13–19, cabin ②

Lake Tinaroo Holiday Park Dam Rd, Lake Tinaroo ☏ 07 4095 8232, ⓦ www.ltholidaypark.com.au. Holiday-camp-style resort on the shore of the reservoir, good for active families. Camping A$20–27, studio or one-bedroom unit ③, villa ④

Yungaburra and around

Eden House 20 Gillies Hwy ☏ 07 4095 3355, ⓦ www.edenhouse.com.au. In the centre of the village, this upmarket country hotel is a favourite for wedding parties. The best rooms, with pretty courtyards, are decorated in a sleek, modern style, and there's a spa. ⑤

Gumtree on Gillies Gillies Hwy, west of Yungaburra ☏ 07 4095 3105, ⓦ www.gumtreeongillies.com.au. Quality country B&B offering a choice of four individually designed rooms with lavish ethnic furnishings, spa baths and open fireplaces. ⑤

Kookaburra Lodge Eacham Rd ☏ 07 4095 3222, ⓦ www.kookaburra-lodge.com. Simple, reasonably priced motel-style rooms off a leafy veranda, with a small swimming pool. ⑤

Mount Quincan Crater Retreat Peeramon Rd, southeast of Yungaburra ☏ 07 4095 2255, ⓦ www.mtquincan.com.au. This impeccably romantic rural retreat has just six secluded, self-contained wooden-pole houses for one or two (no children) with sweeping views of farmland or the grassy caldera of a long-extinct volcano. The owners go out of their way to provide homely touches, then leave you to enjoy the peace and privacy. ⑥

On the Wallaby 34 Eacham Rd ☏ 07 4095 2031 or 1800 123 311, ⓦ www.onthewallaby.com. Quiet, clean and characterful, this is an excellent budget option, with resident guides who run highly recommended canoe and wildlife-spotting trips, cycling treks and visits to lakes and waterfalls. Bunk in shared room A$20, private double ❶

Williams Lodge Cedar St ☏ 07 4095 3449, ⓦ www.williamslodge.com. In a distinguished house that's been in the Williams family for nearly a century, this B&B has very comfortable, old-fashioned rooms and suites, and a wide veranda overlooking a pleasant garden with a small pool. Yungaburra's restaurants are an easy walk away. Room ④, suite ⑤

Atherton

Atherton Blue Gum 36 Twelfth Ave ☏ 07 4091 5149, ⓦ www.athertonbluegum.com. This very pleasant, timber B&B has a variety of airy, comfortable rooms, a small heated pool and good views. The owners organize regional tours. ④

Atherton Travellers Lodge 37 Alice St, off Vernon St ☏ 07 4091 3552, ⓦ www.athertontravellerslodge.com.au. In the centre of town, this place specializes in finding farm work for travellers; you don't get much space to yourself, but it's hospitable. Bunk in shared room A$20, private double ②

Atherton Woodlands Tourist Park 141 Herberton Rd ☏ 07 4091 1407, ⓦ www.woodlandscp.com.au. Green and spacious campsite on the edge of town with useful facilities including free Wi-Fi. Camping A$20–29, cabin ②

Mareeba and around

Jabiru Safari Camp Mareeba Tropical Savanna and Wetland Reserve ⊤07 4093 2514, ⓦwww.mareebawetlands.com. The reserve offers wilderness enthusiasts bed and breakfast in en-suite safari tents, with the option of canoeing, guided wildlife walks and a twilight dinner. ❻

Jackaroo Motel 340 Byrnes St ⊤07 4092 2677, ⓦwww.jackaroomotel.com. Comfortable motel with tidy rooms and a good swimming pool. ❸
Mareeba Riverside Caravan Park 13 Egan St ⊤07 4092 2309. Situated on the Barron River within walking distance of Mareeba town centre, this is a quiet, shady site. Camping A$16–20.

Millaa Millaa and the waterfall circuit

Climbing up to the Tablelands by way of the Palmerston Highway, scenic and slung with rope bridges to allow tree-kangaroos to cross at canopy height, the first village you come to, 59km from Innisfail, is **MILLAA MILLAA**, its centre a quiet, five-hundred-metre street with the usual hotel and general store. A thirteen-kilometre waterfall circuit loops off the highway just east of the village, passing three small but atmospheric cascades. **Ellinjaa Falls** are hidden away in a forested gorge, reached by way of a steep flight of steps, at the bottom of which is a pool you can wade in; **Zillie Falls**, a few kilometres north of here, can be admired obliquely from a roadside lookout at the top. The loveliest of the three are the emblematic **Millaa Millaa Falls**, a romantic curtain of water tumbling into a broad, dark pool: you can swim right up to the cascade to feel the energy of the falling water. There's a QPWS **campsite** at Henrietta Creek in the southern section of the Wooroonooran National Park, about 27km southeast of Millaa Millaa (standard camping fees apply, payable on-site), from where walking tracks lead to mossy **Tchupala Falls** and the impressive **Nandroya Falls**.

Ravenshoe, the Misty Mountains and Herberton

West of Millaa Millaa, the Kennedy Highway takes you to **RAVENSHOE**, the highlands' southernmost town, notable for the *Tully Falls Hotel*, Queensland's highest pub, and **Millstream Falls**, Australia's broadest waterfall, 5km southwest. There's also a restored full-size **steam railway** here, the Millstream Express (A$15, child A$7.50; ⊤07 4097 6005, ⓦwww.steamloco.nq.nu), with a train to the tiny siding of Tumoulin, Queensland's highest railway station, departing on Saturdays, Sundays and public holidays at 1.30pm and returning at 3pm. Ravenshoe's **visitor centre** is on Moore Street (daily 9am–4pm; ⊤07 4097 7700).

Southeast of town, a series of marked **hiking trails** through the **Misty Mountains**' forests and streams offer walks of between a day and a week in length, some of which follow traditional walking routes of the Jirrbal and Ma: Mu Aboriginal people, with campsites laid out at regular intervals – for practical information, check out ⓦwww.mistymountains.com.au, or call the QPWS in Cairns on ⊤07 4046 6600.

Southwest, the road drops off the Tablelands past **Innot Hot Springs** – with its huge anthills and steamy upwellings behind the *Hot Springs Hotel* – and the township of **Mount Garnet**, to the start of the Gulf Developmental Road.

North of Ravenshoe, the main road passes **Mount Hypipamee National Park** and **The Crater**, a 56-metre vertical rift formed by volcanic gases blowing through fractured granite that's now filled with deep, weed-covered water. Walking tracks take you to a crater lookout, or to **Dinner Falls** in the headwaters of the Barron River. There are picnic tables in the park, but no campsite. **Wongabel State Forest**, further north, also has easy walking tracks.

On the way north to Atherton, the road circles west via **HERBERTON**, a quaint, one-time timber and mining town without a modern building in sight. During the 1880s, there were thirty thousand people here (a century before Cairns' population numbered so many), and the railway from Atherton was built to service the town. If you happen to be in Herberton at lunchtime on a Sunday, it's worth checking out the huge outdoor **barbecues** at the *Royal Hotel*'s beer garden. Herberton's **visitor centre** is on Grace Street (℡07 4096 2244).

Malanda

About 23km north of Millaa Millaa and 25km southeast of Atherton, the **dairy** at **MALANDA** provides milk and cheese for the whole of Queensland's far north, plus most of the Northern Territory and even New Guinea. **Malanda Dairy Centre** on James Street in the middle of town offers factory tours (Mon–Fri 10.30am & 11.30am; A$10.50, child A$6; ℡07 4095 1234) and has a café and deli selling local dairy specialities such as cheesecake, smoothies, Mungalli Creek cheese (made near Millaa Millaa) and, of course, fresh milk. The town's other central landmark is the venerable *Malanda Hotel*, built in 1911 to sleep three hundred people. It claims to be the **largest wooden building** in the southern hemisphere and its old furnishings and excellent restaurant are worth a look, though the bar is so cavernous it always feels empty.

On the edge of town towards Atherton, there's a concrete-rimmed roadside swimming hole and a short rainforest walk at **Malanda Falls Conservation Park**; the display at the **visitor centre** here (daily 9.30am–4.30pm; ℡07 4096 6957) gives a rundown of the Tablelands' volcanic origins, rainforest ecology, and the region's Aboriginal and settler history. Further towards Atherton on the same road is **Gallo Dairyland** (daily from 9.30am; free; ℡07 4095 2388, ⓦwww.gallodairyland.com.au), a working dairy farm where visitors can watch cattle being milked, cheese and chocolates being made, or settle down to enjoy fresh scones in the café. Lactose-free cheese and Swiss-style chocolates are for sale in the deli.

Lake Eacham and Lake Barrine

A few kilometres east of Yungaburra at the start of the Gillies Highway down to Gordonvale are the **crater lakes**, or "maars", of Barrine and Eacham – blue, still discs surrounded by thick rainforest that seems to be recovering well following its battering by **Cyclone Larry** in 2006. Each of the craters was formed when a body of superheated water trapped underground exploded like a prehistoric water bomb. **Lake Eacham** has a picnic area, pontoons you can swim from and an easy four-kilometre forest trail around its shores, where inoffensive **amethystine pythons** – Australia's largest snake – sun themselves down by the water.

For its part, **Lake Barrine** has a waterside tearoom serving good cream teas and canteen-style meals, and a **cruise boat** (daily 10.15am, 11.30am, 1.30pm, 2.30pm & 3.30pm; A$14, child A$7; ℡07 4095 3847), which spends an hour circuiting the lake, sharing the water with freshwater eels, grebes and pelicans. To get away from the crowds, follow the signs for the two enormous coarse-barked kauri pines; though midgets compared to North America's great sequoias, they're among Australia's largest trees, and thought to be over a thousand years old. These mark the start of a quiet five-kilometre **walking track** around the lake; keep your eyes peeled for spiky-headed water dragons, more pythons and hordes of musky rat-kangaroos, which look exactly as you'd expect them to.

Yungaburra

Around 13km east of Atherton and 40km west of Gordonvale on the Gillies Highway, the self-consciously pretty village of **YUNGABURRA** makes an excellent base to explore the Tablelands. Though its claims to be a historic town are a little far-fetched, it is over a century old and has a good number of quaint buildings, including the *Yungaburra Pub* in the old *Lake Eacham Hotel*, several picturesque chapels, and well-kept timber homes whose gardens flow onto the grassy verges that line the streets. The village is also the venue for a huge morning **market** of Tablelands produce, plants, art and crafts on the last Saturday of each month (7.30am–12.30pm), and a famous folk-music festival, held annually in late October. The local **visitor information centre** is on Cedar St (daily 10am–6pm; ☎07 4095 2416).

This region is unusually rich in native fauna; good places for wildlife-watching include Mount Quincan and the shores of Lake Tinaroo on the edges of town, and, more centrally, the **platypus-viewing hide** by the bridge where the road to Atherton crosses Peterson Creek. As a platypus hotspot, it doesn't really compare to Broken River in Eungella National Park (see p.513), but nonetheless you have a fair chance of seeing some activity here around dawn and dusk. Also worth a visit is the remarkable **Curtain Fig Tree**, signposted off the road to Atherton, an extraordinarily large specimen whose base is entirely overhung by a stringy mass of aerial roots drooping off the higher branches.

Informative **wildlife guides** can help you spot some of the rare endemic birds and nocturnal marsupials found in this region, if you're lucky, such as scrub wrens, Lumholtz's tree kangaroos and green ringtail possums. You can also expect to see red-legged pademelons, brushtail possums and bandicoots. Highly recommended are the after-dark lake canoeing trips run by the guides at *On the Wallaby* (see p.570): paddling across the dark water of Lake Tinaroo under a dome of stars, scanning the banks for wildlife, you will almost certainly pick out several species with your torch. Tablelands local Alan Gillanders runs regular nocturnal walks and daytime birding (Alan's Wildlife Tours; ☎07 4095 3784, ⓦwww.alanswildlifetours.com.au; from A\$60 for two).

Yungaburra has several good **places to stay** (see p.570); while few of these have swimming pools, the lakes are within easy reach. It also has the widest selection of **eating places** of all the Central Tablelands villages; the best are ⅍*Flynn's* on Eacham Road (☎07 4095 2235; Mon, Tues & Fri–Sun 6pm–late), a slow-food bistro with imaginative dishes such as chicken poached in Australian champagne, and *Eden House*, Gillies Highway (☎07 4095 3355; Mon & Thurs–Sun 6.30pm–late), which serves handmade sausages and other upmarket renditions of local fare, with main courses around A\$33. For something quick and filling, *Whistlestop Café* on Gillies Highway opens at 7am for breakfast and offers sandwiches, salads and cakes all day, while *Quincan Cottage and Café* (8am–4pm) has good, classic Aussie pies. Also on Gillies Highway, *Nick's Swiss-Italian Restaurant and Yodellers' Bar* (lunch Wed & Fri–Sun, dinner Tues–Sun) is themed to the rafters with everything from cow bells and skis to oompah music, and carries a menu of bratwurst, rösti, sauerkraut and pasta. The adjacent *Chalet Rainforest Gallery* is a twee little gift shop with, upstairs, an unspeakably kitsch display of mannequins dressed as rainforest goblins.

Lake Tinaroo

From the Gillies Highway east of Yungaburra, and from **Tolga**, north of Atherton, turn-offs lead to **Lake Tinaroo**, a convoluted reservoir formed by damming the Barron River's headwaters. Like many reservoirs, it has a rather sterile atmosphere, but it offers plenty of opportunities for watersports, including sailing, water skiing and year-round fishing for barramundi and redclaw (an abundant freshwater crayfish). On the northwest shore is the lake holiday park (see p.570), which rents out canoes. Past here, a road runs 25km around the lake to the Gillies Highway, 15km east of Yungaburra, passing five very cheap **campsites** on the north shore before cutting deep into native forests. It's worth stopping along the way for the short walks to bright green **Mobo Crater**, spooky **Lake Euramo**, and the highly impressive **Cathedral Fig Tree**, a giant parasitic strangler fig some 50m tall and 43m around the base; the thick mass of tendrils supporting the crown have fused together like molten wax.

Atherton

Thirty kilometres south of Mareeba, **ATHERTON** is the largest town in the Tablelands. Though centrally placed for forays to most of the area's attractions, it's a humdrum spot; if you're thinking of staying in a town, Yungaburra is a far prettier choice. It was founded in part by Chinese miners who settled here in the 1880s after being chased off the goldfields: 2km south of the centre on Herberton Road, the corrugated-iron **Hou Wang Temple and Chinatown Museum** (daily 10am–4pm; A\$7, child A\$2; ☏07 4091 6945) is the last surviving building of Atherton's old **Chinatown**, a once-busy enclave of market gardens and homes that was abandoned after the government gave the land to returning World War I servicemen. The temple was restored in 2000, with an accompanying museum containing photographs and artefacts found on site – the excellent **birds of prey show** is also held here (Mon, Thurs, Sat & Sun 11am & 2.30pm; A\$12).

The other reason to come to Atherton is to catch the authentically grubby 1920s **steam train** to Herberton, which leaves on Wednesday and Sunday from Platypus Park, just south of town (departs 10.30am, returns 3pm; A\$27.50); along the way you travel through tunnels and forest, and past the pretty Carrington Falls, then have an hour or so to look around Herberton (see p.572) before the return trip. Otherwise, you can clock up more local **birdlife** at **Hasties Swamp**, a big waterhole and two-storey observation hide about 5km south of town. While nothing astounding, it's a peaceful place populated by magpie geese, pink-eared ducks, swamp hens and assorted marsh tiggets.

Atherton's banks and shops can be found along and around Main Street, with a supermarket at the south end past the post office and a few **cafés**, the best of which is *Gallery 5* near the junction with Robert Street. Nearby is a friendly **visitor information centre** (daily 9am–5pm; ☏07 4091 4222).

Just north of Atherton is *The Humpy*, a long-established roadside store selling wonderfully fresh regional produce. It's also worth stopping at the village of **Tolga**, on the Kennedy Highway 5km north of Atherton, to visit the **Tolga Woodworks Gallery and Café** (daily 9am–5pm; ☏07 4095 4488), where you can watch woodturners at work. The gallery sells beautiful burlwood bowls and intricately carved boxes, and stocks chunks of raw red cedar, canary ash, rosewood and mahogany, ready to carve should inspiration strike; the excellent café offers healthy soups and salads, wood-fired-oven-baked bread, and tempting cakes.

Mareeba and around

MAREEBA, 34km north of Atherton and 39km southwest of Kuranda, is a quiet place and the Tablelands' oldest town, founded in the 1900s after the area was opened up for **tobacco**-farming; there's a small collection of historic artefacts to browse at the **Mareeba Heritage Centre** on Byrnes

Street (℡07 4092 5674), which doubles as a **tourist information centre**. **Coffee** has largely replaced tobacco now – *The Coffee Works*, on Mason Street at the southern end of town (daily 9am–4pm; ℡1800 355 526, Ⓦwww.coffeeworks.com.au), is one of several places where you can take a "tasting experience" tour (hourly; A\$12), buy fresh beans, or just try a brew at the café. The *Jaques Coffee Plantation* east of Mareeba offers tours with a twist, swooping over the coffee fields and the surrounding area, including Lake Mitchell, by microlight (A\$80 for a 20min flight, A\$160 for 40min; ℡07 4093 3284, Ⓦwww.jaquescoffee.com).

In Mareeba itself, all the shops and banks can be found on Byrnes Street, with the **tourist office** (daily 8am–4.30pm; ℡07 4091 4222) about a kilometre south of town along the Atherton road, marked by a memorial to James Venture Mulligan, the veteran prospector who discovered the Palmer River Goldfields. The town is pretty seedy **after dark**, with plenty of drunks staggering around even early on.

Fruit plantations have become a profitable business in the Mareeba area, with several farms recently branching out into **tropical fruit wine** production and opening cellar doors to promote their mango wines, coffee liqueurs and banana brandy – try *Golden Drop Winery* (daily 8am–6.30pm; ℡07 4093 2750), found by turning off the highway at Biboohra, 9km north of Mareeba.

Just beyond Biboohra, the **Mareeba Tropical Savanna and Wetland Reserve** (Wed–Sun 10am–4pm, closed Jan–March; A\$10; ℡07 4093 2514, Ⓦwww.mareebawetlands.com) is a stunning five-thousand-acre reserve of tropical savanna woodlands with grass-fringed lagoons that attract seasonal flocks of brolgas, jabiru storks and black cockatoos, along with resident walla-bies, kangaroos and goannas. The wetlands are part of a breeding programme for rainbow-coloured **gouldian finches**, a formerly common bird now virtually extinct in the wild, but which you can see in the aviary here. You can also follow self-guided walking tracks, rent timber canoes, join a boat tour or book a twilight ranger-led wildlife-watching ramble.

Kuranda and the Northern Highlands

A constant stream of visitors arriving from the coast has turned the formerly atavistic community of **KURANDA** into a stereotypical tourist village. Even so, it's a pretty spot, tucked away in the forest beside the **Barron River**, and good for a half-day excursion, particularly if you take the opportunity to travel by the **Kuranda Scenic Railway** or the **Skyrail Rainforest Cableway**.

Practicalities

The road from Cairns comes in at the top of town, while trains and the Skyrail cable car arrive 500m downhill; **essential services** – post office, store, bank, cafés – are laid out between them along Coondoo Street. **Kuranda Information Centre** is on Therwine Street (℡07 4093 9311, Ⓦwww.kuranda.org). Kuranda has plenty of **cafés** serving lunch or tea and cream scones, though most are pricey: *Annabel's Pie Shop*, across from the main markets, has excellent pasties and pies; while *Nevermind Café* halfway down Coondoo Street does tasty organic sandwiches, pancakes and salads.

Accommodation

Given its accessibility from Cairns, Kuranda doesn't tempt many people to stay overnight; it's virtually a ghost town after the markets close, and its **lodgings** tend to be very peaceful.

Kuranda Backpackers' Hostel 6 Arara St ☎07 4093 7355, ⓦwww .kurandabackpackershostel.com. Just up from the Skyrail terminus and railway station, this is a quiet, laid-back hostel with large grounds, a kitchen and laundry. Bunk in shared room A$19, private double ❶

Kuranda Hotel Motel ☎07 4093 7206, ⓦwww .kurandahotel.com.au. Reasonably priced, with rooms behind an incongruous-seeming Irish pub. ❸

Kuranda Rainforest Accommodation Park ☎07 4093 7316, ⓦwww.kurandarainforestpark.com.au.

The nearest place to camp, just out of town across the Mareeba road, with pleasant shade. Camping A$22–26, room with shared bathroom ❶, bungalow ❸

Kuranda Resort and Spa ☎07 4093 7556, ⓦwww.kurandaresortandspa.com. The upmarket option, with spacious log cabins with spa baths and rainforest views, swimming pools linked by waterfalls, a poolside restaurant with a cosy fireplace, and a day spa offering Hawaiian-inspired massage. Room ❹, apartment ❺

Kuranda Scenic Railway and Skyrail Rainforest Cableway

You can drive up to Kuranda by way of the steep and winding Kennedy Highway, but a more popular option is to take the Kuranda Scenic Railway from Cairns or the Skyrail Rainforest Cableway from Smithfield just north of Cairns; it's possible, and recommended, to arrive by one of these, and depart by the other.

The **Kuranda Scenic Railway** (daily from Cairns Station at 8.30am & 9.30am, stopping at Freshwater, north of Cairns, 20min later, returning from Kuranda at 2pm & 3.30pm; standard fares A$39 single or A$56 return; Gold Class A$82/A$99 including drinks and nibbles; ☎07 4036 9333, ⓦwww.ksr .com.au) is a lovingly maintained vintage railway, built in the late nineteenth century as a crucial supply route for the miners of Herberton up on the Tablelands. Winding its way through steep gorges and dense rainforest, the train slows down at the most scenic spots, and stops for ten minutes at a lookout with fine views of the Barron Falls (see p.578) before pulling into Kuranda's pretty, orchid-shrouded station.

▲ Kuranda Scenic Railway

While the railway gives you good views of the World Heritage-listed rainforest southeast of Kuranda, a ride in one of the green gondolas of the **Skyrail Rainforest Cableway** (daily from Smithfield or Kuranda 8.15am–5.15pm; A$39 single, A$56 return; ⊕07 4038 1555, ⓦwww.skyrail.com.au) gives you a sense of total immersion; you glide over the canopy to the sound of frogs, insects and birds and are treated to aerial views of orchids, basket ferns and the tops of trees. The construction of the cableway was an astonishing feat of eco-friendly engineering, with towers lowered in by helicopter to minimize damage to the delicate forest floor. There are two midway stations: at Red Peak friendly and knowledgeable guides will escort you around a boardwalk trail, pointing out interesting botanical details, while at Barron Falls there's a visitor centre to fill you in on rainforest ecology. Allowing time for these, a one-way journey takes around ninety minutes.

Kuranda and around

For many visitors, the journey to and from **Kuranda** is a bigger attraction than the village itself, but some come specifically for the much-hyped **markets**, a spread of permanent stalls whose numbers are boosted by the arrival of travelling traders on Wednesday, Thursday, Friday and Sunday mornings (from 9am). Many of these do the rounds of the North Queensland markets, including those at Port Douglas, Yungaburra and Mission Beach. Among the usual array of souvenirs are stalls selling local fruit wine and natural cosmetics; there's also an interesting didgeridoo stall offering some good examples of the genuine article and the opportunity to sign up for masterclasses (from A$15 for 30min).

Kuranda also has a number of good nature parks and wildlife enclosures. **RainForeStation** (daily 9am–4pm; A$39, child A$19.50; ⊕07 4085 5008, ⓦwww.rainforest.com.au) combines a taste of Pamagirri Aboriginal culture – boomerang-and spear-throwing, and a *corroboree* (music and dance performance) – with a riverboat trip, an exotic orchard and a small zoo, home to a cassowary and some wombats, kangaroos, dingoes and koalas (available for koala-cuddling photos). The **Australian Butterfly Sanctuary** (daily 9.45am–4pm; A$14, child A$7.50; ⊕07 4093 7575, ⓦwww.australianbutterflies.com), the country's largest, specializes in breeding giant Ulysses and Cairns birdwing butterflies, which flutter around in large aviaries; and **Birdworld** (daily 9am–4pm; A$14, child A$7.50; ⊕07 4093 9188, ⓦwww.birdworldkuranda.com), is a superb aviary with realistically arranged vegetation and nothing between you and a host of native and exotic rarities. At the **Koala Gardens** next door (daily 9am–4pm; A$15, child A$7.50; ⊕07 4093 9953, ⓦwww.koalagardens.com), you can hold koalas and see wallabies, wombats, snakes and crocodiles in a rather bland environment; at **Batreach** (Tues–Fri 10.30am–2.30pm; entry by donation), you can get close to rehabilitated flying foxes; while the **Australian Venom Zoo** (daily 9am–4pm; A$16, child A$10; ⊕07 4093 8905, ⓦwww.tarantulas.com.au) has the rather ghoulish mission of showcasing poisonous spiders, scorpions, snakes and centipedes, on the pretext that a greater understanding of these animals and their venom could lead us to some medical breakthroughs.

Around 9km southwest of Kuranda down the Mareeba road, **Cairns Wildlife Safari Reserve** (daily 9am–4.30pm; A$28, child A$14; ⊕07 4093 7777, ⓦwww.cairnswildlifesafarireserve.com.au) has a few native species but draws the crowds with tigers, cheetahs, white rhinos and ring-tailed lemurs in pretty authentic, savanna surroundings – there are guided tours and feeding sessions throughout the day. In the same area, Blazing Saddles (⊕07 4093 9100, ⓦwww.blazingsaddles.com.au) offer **horseback tours** of a working farm, suitable for anyone from beginner up.

Barron River

Kuranda sits on a bend in the **Barron River** near the top of the **Barron Gorge**, a wildlife corridor used by cassowaries, spotted quolls and Lumholtz's tree kangaroos. The **Barron Falls**, a two-kilometre walk away, are tamed by a hydroelectric dam upstream but are still spectacular in the wet season, when the river rages down. Cross the railway bridge next to the station and take a path leading down to the river, where Smiley's Adventure Hire offers 45-minute **cruises** (5 daily Wed–Sun; A$14; ☏0412 775 184) that take you close to the riverbank to look for wildlife, or canoe rentals to explore the river at your leisure. **Walking tracks** lead through the pretty riverside forest and back into the village, or down to cold swimming spots. Other trails follow the road beyond the falls through the **Barron Gorge National Park** and down to Kamerunga, near Cairns – see p.596 for details.

Cairns

Low-rise, upbeat and unpretentious, **CAIRNS** is the hub of the Far North Queensland tourist circuit. It has few significant landmarks – it doesn't even have a beach worthy of the name – but it does have unrivalled access to mountains, rainforest and the **Great Barrier Reef**, and a profusion of tour companies ready to take you there.

It also has a thoroughly tropical flavour: mynah birds chatter in the fig trees in the city centre, the palm-lined seafront Esplanade buzzes round the clock and the mountains of the Great Dividing Range make for a dramatic backdrop. The place to be seen is **Marlin Wharf**; settle yourself on the deck of a harbourside bar for sundowners and watch boats pull into the city marina after a day on the Reef.

The city was pegged out over the site of a sea-cucumber fishing camp when gold was found to the north in 1876, but it was the Atherton Tablelands' tin and timber resources that established the town and kept it ahead of its nearby rival, Port Douglas (see p.598). The harbour remained the focus of the north's fish and prawn concerns, and tourism began modestly when marlin fishing became popular after World War II. With the "discovery" of the reef in the 1970s and the appeal of the local climate, the tourist industry snowballed, and development has continued fairly steadily ever since.

For visitors primed by hype, Cairns may fall short of expectations, crowded as it is with tacky souvenir shops and booking agencies, all stacked high with brochures advertising tours of the Atherton Tablelands, the Daintree, Cape Tribulation and the many islands and dive sites within day-trip distance. However, if you can accept the tourist industry's intrusiveness and the fact that you're unlikely to escape the crowds, you'll find the city a convenient base with a great deal on offer.

Arrival, orientation and city transport

Cairns International Airport (CNS; Ⓦwww.cairnsairport.com) is about 7km north of the centre off the Captain Cook Highway. Air New Zealand fly here from Auckland, Cathay Pacific from Hong Kong, Air Niugini from Papua New Guinea and Qantas from Japan and Singapore. Domestic services to Cairns are provided by Qantas, Jetstar and Virgin Blue (see p.35) from, between them, numerous cities including Adelaide, Brisbane, Melbourne and Sydney. The small, easy-going arrivals terminal has an ATM and foreign exchange desk, car-rental desks, an Internet café and a mobile-phone rental desk. A taxi into Cairns city centre costs around A$15 by day and A$20–25 by night. A cheaper alternative, if you don't mind being taken by a circuitous route, is to take a Sun Palm **shuttle bus** (Ⓣ07 4087 2900, Ⓦwww.sunpalmtransport.com). These operate like shared taxis, taking you to your door in Cairns for A$10 (A$15 return); they also run to Port Douglas for A$30 (A$55 return) or to Cape Tribulation for A$65 (A$110 return).

Long-distance buses to and from Cairns turn around at the stops next to Fogarty Park; the Greyhound office (see p.35) is nearby, outside the Reef Fleet Terminal (Mon–Fri 8.30am–5.30pm, Sat 8.30am–3pm; Ⓣ07 4051 5899). Premier (see p.35) set down at the south end of Lake Street. Whitecar Coaches (Ⓣ07 4091 1855) run daily to Sheridan St and 46 Spence St in Cairns from Kuranda, Mareeba, Atherton, Herberton and Ravenshoe in the Atherton Tablelands. Country Road Coachlines (Ⓣ07 4045 2794, Ⓦwww .countryroadcoachlines.com.au) run three times a week between Cairns and Cooktown along each of the two alternative routes: the coast road via Port Douglas, Cape Tribulation and the Bloomfield Track, and the inland road via Mount Molloy, Mareeba and Lakeland Downs. Coral Reef Coaches (Ⓣ07 4098 2800, Ⓦwww.coralreefcoaches.com.au) operate a daily service between Cairns, the Northern Beaches, Port Douglas and Mossman; while Sun Palm (see above) run daily to Port Douglas, Mossman, the Daintree and Cape Tribulation.

The **railway station** is 750m from the Esplanade, under the Cairns Central shopping mall between Bunda and McLeod streets. This is the northernmost terminus for the Sunlander and Tilt Trains, which cover the 1681-kilometre route along the Queensland coast between Cairns and Brisbane via Townsville, Proserpine, Mackay, Gladstone, Rockhampton, Bundaberg and Hervey Bay, a journey that takes thirty hours and fifteen minutes in total. The Kuranda Scenic Railway, a vintage train service from Cairns to Kuranda on the Atherton Tablelands (see p.576), runs from here twice daily.

Some hotels and hostels offer their guests **free transfers** from their arrival point; many of these can be contacted via the freephone service in the airport arrivals terminal.

Downtown Cairns, the grid of streets behind the Esplanade overlooking Trinity Bay and Trinity Inlet, is easy enough to navigate on foot. The main roads into town are, from the south, the Bruce Highway, which becomes Mulgrave Road, and, from the north, the Captain Cook Highway, which becomes

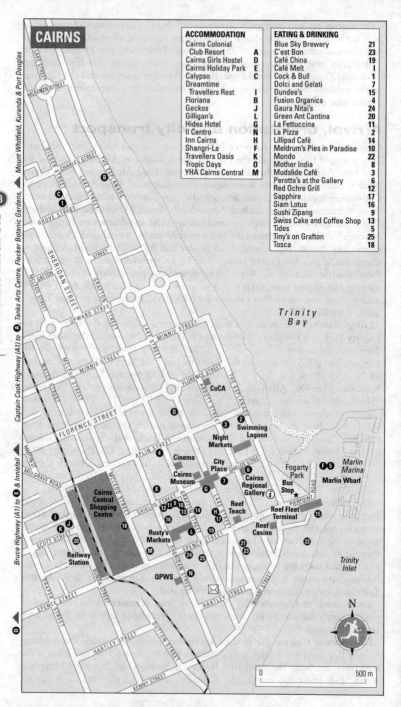

CAIRNS

ACCOMMODATION

Cairns Colonial Club Resort	A
Cairns Girls Hostel	D
Cairns Holiday Park	E
Calypso	C
Dreamtime Travellers Rest	I
Floriana	B
Geckos	J
Gilligan's	L
Hides Hotel	G
Il Centro	N
Inn Cairns	H
Shangri-La	F
Travellers Oasis	K
Tropic Days	O
YHA Cairns Central	M

EATING & DRINKING

Blue Sky Brewery	21
C'est Bon	23
Café China	19
Café Melt	I
Cock & Bull	1
Dolci and Gelati	7
Dundee's	15
Fusion Organics	4
Gaura Nitai's	24
Green Ant Cantina	20
La Fettuccina	11
La Pizza	2
Lillipad Café	14
Meldrum's Pies in Paradise	10
Mondo	22
Mother India	8
Mudslide Café	3
Perotta's at the Gallery	6
Red Ochre Grill	12
Sapphire	17
Siam Lotus	16
Sushi Zipang	9
Swiss Cake and Coffee Shop	13
Tides	5
Tiny's on Grafton	25
Tosca	18

Sheridan Street. For **getting around** the city and its suburbs, the **local bus** service, run by Sunbus from the Transit Mall on Lake St, City Place (℡07 4057 7411, ⓦwww.sunbus.com.au), serves the city and suburbs as far south as Gordonvale and as far north as Palm Cove; you can buy all-day, weekly and monthly passes, and **timetables** are available online or from the drivers. You may be able to **rent bikes** at your accommodation; otherwise, check out the rental outfits on p.44. If you want to buy a **secondhand car**, try Travellers' Auto Barn at 123–125 Bunda St (℡07 4041 3732, ⓦwww.travellers-autobarn .com) or one of the many dealers on Mulgrave Road, or check the classified ads in the Wednesday and Saturday editions of the local paper, the *Cairns Post*.

Information

Cairns' official **visitor information centre** is the Gateway Discovery Centre, housed in the old Shire Offices at 51 Esplanade (℡07 4051 3588, ⓦwww.tropicalaustralia.com.au); they have a wealth of brochures and flyers. Other places around town with prominent blue "i" signs, along with the backpacker agents on Shields Street, tend to focus on selling the tours that they'll make the most commission on – don't expect them to provide unbiased, informed opinions.

Accommodation

Cairns has a huge number of **places to stay** in every price bracket: the following is just a selection. Most are pretty central, though there's also a knot of recommended backpacker hostels west of the railway station, an easy fifteen minutes' walk from the Esplanade. If you'd prefer to base yourself in a beach resort with access to the city's amenities, you could consider staying out of town at the Northern Beaches beyond the airport (see p.597).

The nearest large **campsite** is the excellent-value *Cairns Holiday Park* on Little St (℡07 4051 1467 or 1800 259 977, ⓦwww.cairnscamping .com.au; camping A\$20–28, cabin ❶), with good amenities including free Wi-Fi and a pool.

Hotels, motels and guesthouses

Cairns Colonial Club Resort 18–26 Cannon St ℡07 4053 5111, ⓦwww.cairnscolonialclub .com.au. Large suburban resort hotel, popular with families and retirees, with attractively landscaped swimming pools in well-established tropical gardens and a holiday-camp feel. Room ❺, suite ❼

Floriana 183 Esplanade ℡07 4051 7886, ⓦwww .florianaguesthouse.com. Creaky old guesthouse on the quiet northern Esplanade, with old-fashioned furnishings; rooms vary in quality, but the best ones have pleasant sea views. ❸

Hides Hotel 87 Lake St ℡07 4051 1266, ⓦwww .clubcroc.com.au. Venerable, old city-centre hotel,

slightly tatty but with low rates. Some rooms have had a recent makeover, but the cheaper ones are unadorned, with ancient fittings. ❷–❹

Il Centro 26–30 Sheridan St ℡07 4031 6699 or 1800 066 399, ⓦwww.ilcentro.com.au. Modern and fairly spacious self-contained apartments bang in the centre, with broadband Internet and a pool. ❹

Inn Cairns 71 Lake St ℡07 4041 2350, ⓦwww .inncairns.com.au. Smart city apartments each with kitchen and laundry facilities. There's also a pool and barbecue area, plus rooftop views out to sea. ❺

Shangri-La The Marina ℡07 4031 1411, ⓦwww.shangri-la.com. The most luxurious address on the waterfront, with a cathedral-like

---

For advice on **swimming** in northern Queensland's coastal waters during the "stinger season", see p.47.

lobby, sleek, contemporary styling, immaculate service and beds as soft as a cloud – well worth the expense. Room ⑥, suite ⑦–⑧

Hostels

Cairns Girls Hostel 147 Lake St ⓣ 07 4051 2016, ⓦ www.cairnsgirlshostel.com.au. Renovated 1930s Queenslander for females only, with tidy rooms and shared facilities, and a secure feel. Bunk in shared room A$20, private twin ①

Calypso 5–9 Digger St ⓣ 07 4051 7518, ⓦ www.calypsobackpackers.com. Large, cheerful hostel with small but jauntily decorated rooms and a canteen (the *Zanzibar Bar*) serving breakfast, dinner and Sun lunch at rock-bottom prices. Bunk in shared room A$24, private double/twin ②

Dreamtime Travellers Rest 4 Terminus St ⓣ 07 4031 6753 or 1800 058 440, ⓦ www.dreamtime travel.com.au. Small, quiet hostel with pleasant rooms and a relaxed tropical atmosphere, behind the recommended *Café Melt* (see p.584). Bunk in shared room A$22–25, private double/twin ②

Geckos 187 Bunda St ⓣ 1800 011 344 or 07 4031 1344, ⓦ www.geckosbackpackers.com.au. Friendly hostel in a characterful 1930s Queenslander with wooden floors and a small pool. The rooms, though rather gloomy and airless, are more spacious than most. Single bed in quad-share A$21, private double/twin ①

Gilligan's 57–89 Grafton St ⓣ 07 4041 6566, ⓦ www.gilligansbackpackers.com.au. Massive backpackers' resort with every conceivable facility – there's even a two-thousand-capacity bar hosting DJs and live bands. Very central, but impersonal. Bunk or single bed in shared room A$22–27, private double/twin ④

Travellers Oasis 8 Scott St ⓣ 07 4052 1377, ⓦ www.travoasis.com.au. Lovingly restored old Queenslander, among the best budget options in Cairns, with a small, pleasant pool, jaunty decor and a relaxed, sociable atmosphere. The owners also run *Tropic Days*. Single bed in shared room A$24, private double/twin ②

Tropic Days 28 Bunting St ⓣ 07 4041 1521, ⓦ www.tropicdays.com.au. Excellent, colourful hostel; the staff, who go out of their way to be helpful, run a courtesy bus service (ample compensation for being outside the centre) and throw a weekly barbecue of local game – great value and loads of fun. Single bed in shared room A$24, private double/twin ②

YHA Cairns Central 20–26 McLeod St ⓣ 07 4051 3158, ⓦ www.yha.com.au. Popular not just with young backpackers but also families and older travellers, this is large and busy – the shared kitchen has banks of fridges and hobs, and there's always a sense of something going on. Though not particularly characterful, it's very central. Bunk in shared room A$23–26, private double/twin ②

The City

Cairns' strength is in doing, not seeing: there are few monuments, natural or otherwise. This is partly because the Cape York goldfields were too far away and profits were channelled through Cooktown, and partly because Cairns was remote, lacking a rail link with Townsville until 1924; people came here to exploit resources, not to settle. Your best introduction to the region's heritage is at the **Cairns Historical Museum** on Shields Street, City Place (Mon–Sat 10am–4pm; A$5, child A$2; ⓣ 07 4051 5582, ⓦ www .cairnsmuseum.org.au), which uses photos and small artefacts to explore maritime history, the Bama Aborigines of the Tablelands, and Chinese involvement in the city and Palmer goldfields.

City Place, the pedestrian convergence of Lake and Shields streets, is Cairns' central square, a magnet for young travellers, with a rash of bars, cafés, Internet outlets and tacky souvenir shops selling boardies, bikinis and boomerangs. Local performers do their best at the small **sound shell** here from time to time.

Futher to the east, the seafront **Esplanade** is packed through the day and into the night with people cruising between their accommodation and the shops and restaurants. Grabbing an early morning coffee here, you'll witness a quintes-sentially Cairns scene: fig trees framing the waterfront, with a couple of trawlers, cruise boats and seaplanes bobbing at anchor in the harbour. Joggers jog, and others promenade along the edge at low tide to watch birds feeding in the shallows – there's an identification chart in Fogarty Park – while an excellent **skateboard park** is thoughtfully located up towards the hospital.

Cairns' well-planned **swimming lagoon**, which sits above the tide-line where Shields Street meets the Esplanade, is fringed by an artificial beach, grassy parkland and communal hotplate barbecues; it's always busy, particularly at weekends. At the southern end of the Esplanade is the Reef Casino building, topped by **Cairns Wildlife Dome** (daily 8am–6pm; A$22; combined ticket for this and other attractions available; ☎07 4031 7250, ⓦwww.cairnsdome.com .au). There's no hiding the artificiality of this mini rainforest park but it's the only place to get close-up views of pademelons, bettongs, koalas, crocodiles and a good variety of exotic birds in the city centre. Nearby, the **Reef Fleet Terminal** houses the booking and check-in desks for the day-cruises to the reef departing from Marlin Marina. **Marlin Wharf**, the boardwalk alongside Cairns' three plushest waterside hotels, the *Hilton*, the *Sebel Harbour Lights* and the *Shangri-La*, is always buzzing at lunchtime and in the early evening – recently redeveloped, it's a fine place to eat and drink. The buzz, however, has yet to rub off on its shopping plaza, **The Pier**, which is somewhat lifeless with a subterranean feel.

A short stroll from the Esplanade, on the corner of Shields and Abbott streets, **Cairns Regional Art Gallery** (Mon–Sat 10am–5pm, Sun 1–5pm; A$5; ☎07 4046 4800, ⓦwww.cairnsregionalgallery.com.au) is worth a look if Cairns' crasser commercial side is beginning to grate; exhibitions include both local contemporary artists' work and travelling shows. The city's other main cultural venue is the Centre for Contemporary Arts, **CoCa**, at 96 Abbott St (Tues–Thurs & Sat 10am–5pm, Fri 10am–6pm; free; ☎07 4050 9400), which shows modern art and sculpture from Far North Queensland and incorporates an arthouse cinema and theatre space; while out in the suburbs, the **Tanks Arts Centre** at 46 Collins Ave (Mon–Fri 10am–4pm; ☎07 4032 2349, ⓦwww .tanksartscentre.com) hosts visual arts exhibitions and also specializes in alternative performance.

Even if you're not thinking of going to the reef, it's worth spending the early evening at the superb **Reef Teach** multimedia show at the Bolands Centre, 14 Spence St (Mon–Sat 6.30–8.30pm; A$13, child A$7; ☎07 4031 7794, ⓦwww .reefteach.com.au), in which eccentric marine biologist Paddy Colwell gives more essential background than the dive schools and tour operators have time to impart.

Beyond the centre, the city's natural attractions include the wonderful **Flecker Botanic Gardens** (Mon–Fri 8.30am–5.30pm; free guided walks Mon–Fri 1pm) and adjacent **Mount Whitfield Environmental Park**, whose cool, tranquil rainforest is dense enough for wallabies. Both are accessed via Collins Avenue on the north edge of town; several buses run up here from City Place Transit Mall, or it's a fifty-minute walk. Also worth a look are the **mangrove walks** on the airport approach road nearby, whose boardwalks and hides give you a chance to see different varieties of mangrove trees, mudskippers and red-clawed, asymmetric fiddler crabs. Take some insect repellent or you'll end up giving the flies a free lunch. South of the city, there's aquatic fun to be had at **Sugarworld Waterslides** (weekends and school holidays 10am–4.30pm; A$10.50, child A$8.50; ☎07 4055 5477, ⓦwww.sugarworld.com.au), which has four giant waterslides set among one-hundred-year-old trees, plus a wading pool for toddlers.

Shopping

Cairns has a busy, though fairly downmarket, shopping scene. The stalls at the **night markets** between the Esplanade and Abbott Street (daily 4.30–11pm) are typical of the type of tourist-trap outlets found all over the city, peddling sarongs, beads, animal skins, and mass-produced boomerangs. But just when you think Cairns has nothing but cheap clothing and tacky souvenirs on offer, you'll happen across something interesting, such as Sacred Sounds on Aplin Street, near the Esplanade, which has an excellent selection of quality **didgeridoos** painted by Aboriginal artists, plus local-music CDs. You'll also find several good **jewellers** in town focusing on opals and freshwater pearls, the regional speciality. The main indoor shopping mall, **Cairns Central**, covers the basics such as mobile phones, electrical goods, clothes and luggage, with a Myers department store at one end. There's also an Australian Geographic store here selling telescopes, binoculars and expedition gadgets, and an Aussie Bush Hats and Oilskins shop with a sideline in cane-toad purses, shark-tooth pendants and croc-tooth hatbands.

The stallholders at **Rusty's Markets** between Grafton and Sheridan streets (Fri 6am–6pm, Sat 6am–3pm, Sun 6am–2pm) sell a fantastic range of local produce including tropical fruit and veg, herbs, coffee yoghurt and fish. For maximum choice, Friday is the best day, but you'll find amazing discounts just before the traders start packing up on Sunday. Dotted around the edge of the large market hall are some good healthy fast-food and juice stands.

Eating and nightlife

Cairns has no shortage of **places to eat**. Least expensive are the Esplanade takeaways serving anything from coffee and croissants to Chinese food, falafel, kebabs and pasta, some of which open early and close very late. The **night markets** and **Cairns Central** both house fast-food plazas, with a choice ranging from fish and chips to pizza or sushi; there are healthier options at **Rusty's Markets**. Alternatively, you can stock up at the **supermarkets** on Abbott Street or in Cairns Central.

The **pub and club** culture is struggling to adjust to Queensland's relatively new smoking restrictions; an unexpected casualty was landmark blues bar *Johnos*, now closed. Clubs typically start warming up around 9pm with a 3am "lockout" (last entry; if you're already inside, you can usually stay until 5am). Many pubs also feature regular live-music sessions – reviews and details are given in Cairns' free weekly **listings magazine**, *Time Out*. **Petty thieves** work some bars and nightclubs: try not to make yourself an obvious target.

Cafés

Café Melt 189 Bunda St ☏ 07 4031 6754. Aimed at backpackers from the nearby hostels but attracting others too, this informal café-restaurant and Internet lounge has an eclectic menu including juices, stir-fries, and interesting pizzas such as smoked chicken and almond.

Dolci and Gelati Shields St. Generous scoops of yummy, artisan-style ice cream made from tropical fruit and berries, plus excellent coffee. Daily 11am–10pm, Thurs–Sun till 11pm.

Fusion Organics Corner of Aplin St & Grafton St ☏ 07 4051 1388. Inspirational wholefood café with multicultural staff and a global-village atmosphere. The healthy breakfast options include home-made muesli and organic raisin toast, and there are fresh salads for lunch

and juices with New Age names such as "Make me glow". Mon–Fri 7am–4.30pm, Sat 7am–2pm.

Lillipad Café 72 Grafton St ☏ 07 4051 9565. Another of Cairns' excellent organic cafés, with plenty of healthy goodies on offer, including fabulous breakfasts and vegetarian lunches, and a strong alternative vibe.

Meldrum's Pies in Paradise 97 Grafton St. Award-winning pies and artisan bread with tasty ingredients such as beetroot and poppy seeds.

Mudslide Café Aplin St. Tiny place whose coffee was recently voted best in Cairns by local radio listeners; they also offer juices, wraps and toasted focaccia.

Swiss Cake and Coffee Shop 93 Grafton St ☏ 07 4051 6393. Always busy, this top-notch patisserie serves crisp strudels, rich cakes and fine coffee. Tues–Fri 7am–5pm, Sat 7am–2pm.

Tiny's on Grafton 45 Grafton St ☎ 07 4031 4331. This no-frills health-food joint mixes fabulous juices and smoothies and offers good vegetarian food including juicy tofu and satay wraps. Mon–Fri 7.30am–4pm.

Restaurants, pubs and bars

Blue Sky Brewery Palm Court Building, Lake St. Sleek and stylish new microbrewery restaurant catering for discerning drinkers.

Café China 32 Spence St ☎ 07 4041 2028. With an inexpensive noodle house and a more sophisticated Cantonese restaurant with great main dishes from A$15, plus daily *yum cha* sessions, this gets the seal of approval from visiting Chinese.

C'est Bon 20 Lake St ☎ 07 4051 4488, ⓦ www.cestbon.com.au. Delicious French cuisine in the elegant, airy surroundings of a hexagonal Queenslander with a mini Eiffel Tower perched on top. Tues–Fri noon–2.30pm & 6pm–late, Sat 6pm–late.

Cock & Bull 6 Grove St ☎ 07 4031 1160. Large pub aiming for an Anglo-Irish atmosphere, serving up draught Guinness plus cheap, hearty counter meals, including A$5 lunchtime specials. Daily 8am–3am.

Dundee's Marlin Parade ☎ 07 4051 0399. It may have migrated to the waterfront, but this established upmarket grill still leans towards native fauna with dishes such as kangaroo satay, garlic Tablelands yabbies (small crayfish) or bugtails (large crayfish) in champagne sauce. Mains start at around A$28. Daily 6.30–10.30am, 11.30am–2pm & 5.30–10.30pm.

La Fettuccina 41 Shields St ☎ 07 4031 5959. Superb home-made pasta and classic *secondi* make this the most popular Italian restaurant in town. Daily 5pm–late.

Gaura Nitai's 55 Spence St ☎ 07 4031 2255. Hare Krishna restaurant offering vegetarian fare – satays, dumplings, dahls and rice – at rock-bottom prices. Daily 11am–2.30pm & 6–8pm.

Green Ant Cantina 183 Bunda St ☎ 07 4041 5061. This quirky, informal hangout serves cheap and tasty evening meals with a Mexican theme – fajitas, tortillas and enchiladas – and deliciously classic-tasting burgers. Arrive early for their unbeatable pre-7pm specials. Live bands and DJs at weekends. Daily 4pm–late.

Mondo *Hilton*, 34 Esplanade ☎ 07 4052 6780. With tables shaded by palm trees on the quiet Trinity Inlet waterfront, this is a perfect spot for a

relaxed, moderately priced lunch of tacos or seafood, or a civilized sundowner.

Mother India 2/80 Sheridan St ☎ 07 4041 1000. Reliable restaurant offering decent Indian fare in a no-frills setting.

Perotta's at the Gallery 38 Abbott St ☎ 07 4031 5899. Stylish for brunch or lunch and romantic by night, this streetside terrace attracts an arty crowd with specialities such as Tasmanian oysters with vodka mascarpone and chocolate and chilli pannacotta. Main courses around A$30. Daily 10am–midnight.

La Pizza 93 Esplanade ☎ 07 4031 2646. Versatile all-day eatery serving everything from light breakfasts to blow-out pizza feasts.

Red Ochre Grill 43 Shields St ☎ 07 4051 0100. Long-running Mod Oz restaurant with a menu revolving around unmistakably Australian ingredients such as kangaroo and crocodile. Above-average prices, particularly for the enticing "tasting plates". Mon–Fri noon–3pm & 6–10pm, Sat & Sun 6–10pm.

Sapphire 39 Lake St ☎ 07 4052 1494. Gay-owned and operated meeting and eating place, offering coffee and tapas in a stylish lounge setting. Daily 8am–late.

Siam Lotus 76 Sheridan St ☎ 07 4041 1800. Serves unfussy, authentic and reasonably priced Thai classics. Tues–Sun 5.30pm–late; licensed and BYO; takeaway available.

Sushi Zipang 39 Shields St ☎ 07 4051 3328. The best place in town for sushi, which parades across a conveyor belt and is remarkably good value at A$2.80 a portion. Tues–Sat 11.30am–2pm & 5.30–9pm.

Tides Pier Boardwalk, The Marina ☎ 07 4052 7670. Smart Mod-Oz-meets-Asian eatery attached to the *Shangri-La* on Cairns' stylish waterfront strip.

Tosca Cairns Central, 50 McLeod St ☎ 07 4041 0822. One of the better places in the mall, this trattoria-bar with a bistro feel has an outside terrace and is good for breakfast, risottos and pizzas.

Nightlife

12 Bar Blue 62 Shields St ☎ 07 4041 7388, ⓦ www.12barblue.com. Live blues and jazz, with an over-30s night on Saturdays. Tues–Sun 5pm–midnight.

Brothers 99 Anderson St ☎ 07 4053 1053. Large suburban entertainment venue, the most likely place in Cairns to host well-known bands.

Casa De Meze Corner of Aplin St & Esplanade. This weekday karaoke venue perks up at weekends with live band sessions on Fridays and salsa dance classes on Saturdays.

FAR NORTH QUEENSLAND ⑧

The following all operate in, or within easy reach of, Cairns. Most can arrange to pick you up from your accommodation in Cairns or the Northern Beaches, often at no extra charge. If you book several activities at once, you may qualify for discounted rates. You can also join the activities run by the Port Douglas-based operators (see p.602) by paying extra for transfers.

Aboriginal culture
Book a day with **M & J Aboriginality** (from A$165; ☎07 4067 1660) and you'll be invited into Mat and Judy's family home in Babinda, south of Cairns, to paint or burn a design onto a didgeridoo, then learn to play it. For an insight into Aboriginal bushlore, tour the rainforest between Cairns and Port Douglas with botanist, bush-tucker and natural-medicines expert Warren Whitfield of **Fire Stick Tours** (A$149, child A$120; ☎07 4055 8971, ⓦwww.firesticktours.com.au). Several tour companies can arrange day-trip packages including a visit to the excellent **Tjapukai Aboriginal Culture Park** (see p.597).

Bicycle tours
Traffic is thin in Far North Queensland, making this rewarding cycling country. On weekdays, **Bandicoot** run easy-going guided cycle tours around the Atherton Table-lands (A$99; ☎07 4055 0155, ⓦwww.bandicootbicycles.com), or you can get stuck into some moderate to extreme off-road biking around Cairns and Cape Tribulation with Dan's Mountain Biking (A$85–120; ☎07 4032 0066, ⓦwww.cairns.aust .com/mtb); both are highly recommended.

Bungee jumping
AJ Hackett's Bungy (A$104 per jump; ☎07 4057 7188 or 1800 622 888, ⓦwww .ajhackett.com) is a fifty-metre purpose-built platform, a world first when it was built in 1990. Surrounded by rainforest, it's in the hills off the Captain Cook Highway near Smithfield, 8km north of Cairns. Spectators are welcome.

Bushwalking
Wooroonooran Safaris (☎07 4051 5512, ⓦwww.wooroonooran-safaris.com.au) spends a moderately strenuous day hiking through thick rainforest just north of Bartle Frere, where you're guaranteed to see wildlife and get wet crossing creeks (A$159, child A$89.50 all-inclusive).

Diving, snorkelling and cruising
See the boxes on p.592 and p.594.

Fishing
To fish for barramundi and other estuary species, **Fishing Cairns** (☎07 4041 1169, ⓦwww.fishingcairns.com.au) charges A$155 for a full day on a charter boat, while sport fishing for marlin, wahoo and tuna costs A$375 per day.

Hot-air ballooning
You can float over the Atherton Tablelands with **Hot Air** (from A$180, child A$99; ☎07 4039 9900, ⓦwww.hotair.com.au).

Overland tours and safaris
See box, p.588.

Scenic flights
A twenty-minute low-altitude helicopter or light-aircraft flight out of Cairns gives you just enough time to see the nearby rainforest and coast from above. On a longer trip, you could head out over the Great Barrier Reef and its islands as well, but if it's the reef that interests you most, it's more economical to book a cruise to one of the Outer Reef pontoons with a helipad – such as Great Adventures, Reef Magic Marine World

or Sunlover (see p.592) – and then take to the air to check out the surrounding area. Swooping over the reef is a fascinating and thrilling way to size up the coral formations: on calm days, you may see turtles, manta rays, dugongs and sharks, tiny but unmistakable, in the water below, and from July to September you can search for whales. For an exclusive day out, you can arrange to land on a sand cay: your own desert island for the duration of your visit.

Barrier Aviation (℡07 4035 9359, ⓦwww.barrieraviation.com.au) have very keen prices for their flights to Green Island and the Outer Reef by light aircraft (from A$69 for 30min).

Cairns Seaplanes (℡07 4031 4307, ⓦwww.cairnsseaplanes.com) cover Green Island and the reef and charge from A$235 (child A$250) for 25 minutes, or A$361 (child A$270) for a brief sand-cay trip.

Daintree Air Services (℡07 4034 9300, ⓦwww.daintreeair.com.au) charge A$199 for a sixty-minute flight over the Reef by twin-prop plane; they also buzz up to Lizard Island (A$590) or Cape York (A$990) for the day, and run a four-day flying safari of Cape York (A$3100).

Down Under Helicopters (℡07 4034 9000, ⓦwww.downunderheli.com) is a dynamic aviation company with a fleet of helicopters ranging from tiny two- to seven-seaters. They will fly you over Cairns, the Barron Gorge, the Atherton Tablelands or the Great Barrier Reef (from A$90 for a 10min flip to $1190 for a three-day luxury excursion including two nights at *Rose Gums Wilderness Retreat*; see p.570). They can also transfer you to or from Hastings Reef (from A$245 including return cruise), land you on a remote sand cay for a private lunch and snorkelling, or give you a taste of flying a dual-control helicopter.

GBR Helicopters (℡07 4035 9669, ⓦwww.gbrhelicopters.com.au) provide scenic flights over the Outer Reef for cruise companies including Quicksilver and Sunlover (A$125 for 10min; A$295 for 30min); they also operate air transfers between Cairns and Green Island, the Outer Reef pontoons, Cape Tribulation and various luxury destinations including Lizard Island and Orpheus Island.

Skydiving

Skydive Cairns (℡07 4031 5466, ⓦwww.skydivecairns.com.au) dare you to chuck yourself out of a plane with an instructor for A$210–295, depending on how high you go; a two-day solo training course will set you back A$595.

White-water rafting

Hurtling over the rapids on the reliable Tully River near Tully or the slightly less turbulent Barron River behind Cairns is wild fun despite being a conveyor-belt business: as you pick yourself out of the river, the raft is dragged back for the next busload. A "day" means around five hours rafting; a "half-day" about two. Agents include **RnR** (℡07 4041 9444, ⓦwww.raft.com.au), **Raging Thunder** (℡07 4030 7990, ⓦwww.ragingthunder.com.au) and **Foaming Fury** (℡07 4031 3460, ⓦwww.foamingfury.com.au); day-trips cost around A$155 and multi-day expeditions up to A$1300, plus a compulsory rafting levy of A$25 per day. For better value, consider the Raging Thunder Xtreme Team tour from Mission Beach (see p.564), which gets you on the river before the Cairns day-trippers arrive and with smaller groups.

Wildlife-watching and birding

Natural-history tours focusing on the Atherton Tablelands' platypus, tree kangaroos and rare possums are run by **Wait-a-While Tours** (℡07 4098 2422, ⓦwww.waitawhile.com.au) and **NatureTour** (℡07 4093 7287, ⓦwww.australiawildlifetours.com); expect to pay A$95 for a four-hour trip and A$200–300 for an afternoon and evening excursion. Wait-a-While also offer specialized birding trips, as does **Cassowary Tours** (℡07 4034 1202, ⓦwww.cassowarytours.com.au), who can put together week-long packages.

The following tour operators will generally pick you up from your accommodation in Cairns or the Northern Beaches, often at no extra charge, and may offer a discount if you book more than one trip. For excursions starting from Port Douglas, see p.602; you can join these by paying extra for transfers.

Atherton Tablelands, the Daintree and Cape Tribulation

The following tour companies are highly recommended. **Uncle Brian** (day-trip A$109; ☎07 4050 0615, ⓦwww.unclebrian.com.au) cover the coastal forest and Tableland waterfalls by bus and cater for a young, up-for-it crowd. **On the Wallaby** (A$95–185; ☎07 4050 0650, ⓦwww.onthewallaby.com) run active adventures lasting one to three days, taking in waterfalls, lakes, canoeing and cycling. **Cape Trib Connections** (from A$109 for a one-day trip; ☎07 4041 7447 or 1800 838 757, ⓦwww .capetribconnections.com) run whistle-stop tours of Port Douglas, Mossman Gorge, the Daintree and Cape Trib. **Trek North Safaris** (☎07 4033 2600, ⓦwww.treknorth .com.au) use smaller vehicles and visit Kuranda or the Daintree and Cape Trib region. **Billy Tea Bush Safaris** (A$150, child A$100; ☎07 4032 0077, ⓦwww.billytea.com .au) run day-trips to the Daintree, Cape Tribulation and the Bloomfield Track by 4WD. With **Fire Stick Tours** (☎07 4055 8971, ⓦwww.firessticktours.com.au), you can walk through the rainforest of the Northern Highlands with an Aboriginal botanist.

It's also possible to map out **your own tour** by hiring a car, which can cost as little as A$50 per day for up to four people, plus fuel and provisions – though, of course, you'll miss out on the local knowledge of a guide.

Cooktown and Cape York

The following organize trips to the tip by 4WD, boat and plane, and have reliable reputations. **Heritage Tours** (☎07 4054 7750 or 1800 775 533, ⓦwww.heritage tours.com.au) run a variety of trips, from a seven-day camping tour by bus (A$990),

---

Gilligans 57–89 Grafton St. House music and rave in a large, popular venue.

Nu Trix 55 Spence St ☎07 4051 8225. Cairns' only dedicated gay club, with drag/diva shows on Saturdays. Fri–Sun 9pm–3am.

PJ O'Brien's City Place. Loud, brash Irish bar attracting a mix of locals and young, up-for-it tourists, especially on Fri, Sat & Sun nights.

Shenannigans Shields St. Rowdy Irish bar with live bands at weekends.

Soho Shields St ☎07 4051 2666. Hip-hop and

house DJs pack out this small venue from Wednesday to Saturday nights.

Velvet Underground Reef Casino, 35 Wharf St ☎07 4030 8888. Dance music for a young crowd.

Woolshed 22 Shields St ☎07 4031 6304. Budget backpackers' pub, with huge, cheap meals (hostels issue vouchers for these), beer and cocktails by the jug and party fever. Conscientious objectors to wet T-shirt competitions should steer well clear. Daily till 5am.

Listings

Airlines All of the following fly to and from Cairns: Airlines PNG ☎1300 764 696; Air New Zealand ☎13 24 76; Air Niugini ☎07 4080 1600; Cathay Pacific ☎13 17 47; Jetstar ☎13 15 38; MacAir Airlines ☎07 4035 9505; Qantas ☎13 13 13; Virgin Blue ☎13 67 89.

Banks and exchange Banks and ATMs are scattered throughout the city centre. Some booths around the Esplanade also offer bureau de change facilities, though rates are lower than at the banks.

Bike rentals Bandicoot Bicycle Hire & Tours, 59 Sheridan St ☎07 4055 0155 (from A$18 per day); Cairns Scooter World, 47 Shields St ☎07 4031 3444 (from A$12 per day).

Books Exchange Book Shop, 78 Grafton St, has an excellent range of secondhand books to buy or exchange.

Camping equipment Adventure Equipment, 133 Grafton St, and It's Extreme, Cairns Central and 32 Spence St, stock and rent out all types of outdoor

to sixteen days travelling by luxury cruise ship (A$4650). **Exploring Oz** (☎1300 888 112, ⓦwww.exploring-oz.com.au) run a six-day Cairns to Cape York bushcamping tour by bus (A$875). **Billy Tea Bush Safaris** (see above) run overland tours from A$710 for three days to A$2750 for two weeks. **Wilderness Challenge** (☎07 4035 4488, ⓦwww.wilderness-challenge.com.au) have Cape York ecotours of one to fourteen days, taking in Cooktown and Jowalbinna, the Aboriginal rock-art sites around Laura. **The Bama Way** (☎07 4053 7001, ⓦwww.bamaway.com.au) run short overland tours introducing you to local Aboriginal history and legend, from A$399 for two days. You can also **fly** with the mail to remote stations across Cape York from Monday to Friday with **Aero-Tropics Air Services** (☎07 4040 1222, ⓦwww.aero-tropics.com.au) for A$375–550 return depending on destination. If you're self-sufficient, you can plan a **self-drive trip** by hiring a 4WD from around A$120 per day (see p.000).

Green Island and Fitzroy Island
See p.594.

Kuranda by Kuranda Scenic Railway and Skyrail Rainforest Cableway
See p.576.

Trinity Inlet
Cairns Habitat Cruises (A$59, child A$29.50; ☎07 4031 4007, ⓦwww .cairnshabitatcuises.com.au) run informative and relaxing daily half-day tours of the calm waters just south of the city centre, exploring the mangroves and visiting the Cairns Crocodile Farm. They also offer ninety-minute Twilight Cruises three times a week (Tues, Fri & Sat 5.30–7pm).

gear and even kayaks; City Place Disposals, on the corner of Shields & Grafton sts, has more down-to-earth, non-brand-name equipment.

Car rental Typical one-day rates start at A$50 for a four-person runaround, though longer rentals might come in at only A$45 a day. 4WDs cost from A$120 per day. Several international agencies have desks at the airport and offices in town; local companies include: A1 Car Rental, 141 Lake St ☎07 4031 1326 or 1300 301 175; Cairns Older Car Hire, 422 Sheridan St ☎07 4053 1066, ⓦwww.cairnsoldercarhire.com; All Day, 151 Lake St ☎07 4031 3348, ⓦwww.cairns-car -rentals.com; East Coast Car Rentals, 146 Sheridan St ☎1800 028 881, ⓦwww .eastcoastcarrentals.com.au.

Cinemas There are BCC multi-screen venues at 108 Grafton St and in Cairns Central, and arthouse screenings at CoCa, 96 Abbott St.

Hospital and medical centres Cairns Medical Centre, on the corner of Florence & Grafton sts (☎07 4052 1119) is open 24hr for vaccinations and GP consultations (free if you have reciprocal national-health cover). Hospitals include Base Hospital, at the northern end of the Esplanade

(☎07 4050 6333), or Cairns Private Hospital (☎07 4052 5200) on the corner of Upward & Lake sts, if you have insurance.

Internet access Most lodgings have facilities, but some hotels overcharge; cheap options in town include the various Global Gossip outlets around City Place, Cairns Fast Internet on Abbott St, and the public library, also on Abbott St.

Laundromats 147B Lake St, 113 Sheridan St and 227 Sheridan St. Many hostels, hotels and holiday apartments provide coin-operated laundries or an in-house laundry service for their guests.

Pharmacy Cairns Day and Night Pharmacy and Medical Centre, 29B Shields St (daily 8am–9pm).

Police 5 Sheridan St ☎07 4030 7000.

Post office 13 Grafton St (Mon–Fri 9am–5pm); upstairs in Orchid Plaza, Abbott St (Mon–Fri 9am–5.30pm, Sat 9am–12.30pm); and in Cairns Central shopping mall, McLeod St (Mon–Fri 9am–5.30pm, Sat 9am–12.30pm).

QPWS At the southern end of Sheridan St, just past the police station (Mon–Fri 8.30am–5pm; ☎07 4046 6600). Staff are very helpful, and have plenty of free brochures on regional parks, plus books for sale on wildlife and hiking.

RACQ breakdown service ☎ 13 11 11.

Shopping hours Most city-centre shops are open Mon–Fri 9am–5pm & Sat 9am–noon; Cairns Central shopping mall is open until 9pm on Thurs and 10.30am–4pm on Sun.

Taxis The main rank is on Lake St, west of City Place, or call ☎ 13 10 08. A 3km hop costs around A$8, with higher rates at night (midnight–5am) and on public holidays.

Travel agents Flight Centre, 24 Spence St ☎ 07 4052 1077; STA, 125 Abbott St ☎ 07 4041 3798;

Trailfinders, Hides Corner, Lake St ☎ 07 4050 9600.

Work The backpacker contact points along Shields St or your accommodation may be able to help out with WWOOF placements in the Atherton Tablelands.

Yacht Club 4 Esplanade ☎ 07 4031 2750, ⓦ www .cairnsyachtclub.com.au. Worth contacting for hitching/crewing north to Cape York and the Torres Strait, south to the Whitsundays and beyond, and even to New Guinea and the Pacific.

The Great Barrier Reef near Cairns

The **Great Barrier Reef** attracts thousands of visitors to Cairns each year. Since there's no shore-diving from Cairns, and the closest part of the 34-kilometre-wide reef system lies around 30km offshore, your first step towards experiencing the remarkable underwater landscape is to find a suitable boat to take you there (see box, p.592). Cairns is much closer to the reef and its islands than most other Queensland cities, making day-trips a breeze.

Reef tourism is big business in Cairns, and new visitors may feel overwhelmed by the sheer number of cruise or dive options that seem to be on offer. In fact, most of the outlets touting trips in town are just agents, all selling the same products: to get a clearer idea of what's actually available, head down to the **Reef Fleet Terminal** on Spence Street, near Marlin Wharf, where all the major boat companies have desks.

A lot of fuss is made about the differences between the **Inner Reef** (closer to the coast, and visited by slower boats), the **Outer Reef** (closest to the open sea and the target of most speedy operators) and the **fringing reefs** (surrounding Fitzroy Island and Green Islands). As a rule, the inner and island sites, though easy to get to (45–60min is typical) offer the least satisfying diving – they're vulnerable to silting from the nearby rivers, and the most-visited sites have been degraded by human traffic. The mid-reef sites such as Hastings, Saxon and Norman are generally in better condition, but serious divers prefer the outer sites such Thetford, Flynn, Milln and Pellowe reefs almost due east of Cairns, and the Agincourt Ribbon Reefs to the northeast. The faster boats can make it out to any of these in under three hours; most visitors return to Cairns the same day, but it's also possible to stay out at sea on a **live-aboard** in order to experience the interesting changes in marine activity that take place at dawn, dusk and after dark.

If you look beyond the generalizations, however, the coral and fishlife at any point in the reef system can be either excellent or tragic. The state of Cairns' coral is the subject of much debate: years of agricultural run-off and recent **coral-bleaching** events and cyclones – not to mention the sheer number of visitors – have had a visibly detrimental effect, even in a few of the remoter sections. Some of the damaged areas are recovering faster than others. That said, almost everywhere is still packed with stunning hard and soft coral formations and vibrant marine life, ranging from tiny gobies to squid, turtles, and beautiful giant clams. Pelagics are relatively rare, but only seasoned divers who want to only see sharks, or who limit themselves to just one or two sites, might come away disappointed.

Reef cruises and **diving trips** lasting from a day to over a week, aboard anything from an old trawler to a racing yacht or a high-speed, state-of-the-art twin-hull cruiser with sun decks and air-conditioned lounges, depart regularly from Marlin Wharf or the Marlin Marina in Cairns (for details of boats based further up the coast in Port Douglas, from which the journey to the Agincourt Ribbon Reefs is shorter, see box, p.602). If you're serious about diving, it's best to opt for an outfit with a well-respected scuba team. The best companies have enthusiastic, tightly drilled, multilingual staff, including experienced British and Japanese instructors as well as Australians. Many divemasters and instructors are highly safety-conscious and ecologically aware, taking an interest in your preferences and pointing out relevant species once you're underwater. A few, however, treat their customers like objects on a conveyor belt, leaving all but the most basic safety procedures up to you and doing nothing to enhance the submarine experience; these tend to work at the sites where the diving is unremarkable by any standards.

If you're just planning to cruise, one way to choose the right boat is simply to check out the **price** and whether this includes any **extras**: small, cramped, slow tubs are the cheapest, while roomy, faster catamarans are more expensive; to narrow things down further, find out which serves the best **food**.

On some trips, your boat is your base for the day; it may visit several sites. On others, you will dock at a private **pontoon**; these include fixed platforms from which even the most nervous snorkellers and divers can enter the water with ease.

Before going to the reef, take in the excellent two-hour **Reef Teach** multimedia and interactive show (see p.583) – this is one of the most worthwhile things anyone interested in marine ecology can do in Cairns.

Inner and Outer Reef dive sites

The dozen or more **Inner Reef** sites within easy reach of the city are all good for snorkelling, though scuba divers will find them much of a muchness. Concentrated day-tripping means that you'll probably be sharing the experience with several other boatloads of people, with scores of divers in the water at once. You'll see plenty of damaged coral; marine life abounds, but it's patchily distributed, particularly in areas where unscrupulous operators feed the fish.

Michaelmas Cay, a small, vegetated crescent of sand, is worth a visit: over thirty thousand sooty, common and crested terns roost on the island, while giant clams, sweetlips and reef sharks can be found in the surrounding waters. Nearby **Hastings Reef**, another novice-level dive, has better coral, a resident moray eel and bulky maori wrasse, and plenty of sea stars in the sand beneath. The two are often included in dive-trip packages, providing shallow, easy and fun diving. Another favourite, **Norman Reef**, tends to have very clear water, and some decent coral gardens with abundant marine life.

One of the best-value options for diving the **Outer Reef** is to take an overnight live-aboard trip to a nearby section such as **Moore Reef**, which, at 40km from Cairns, takes between ninety minutes and two hours to reach. It's rather generalized terrain, but the advantages over a simple day-excursion are that you get longer in the water plus the opportunity for night dives. Moore is a great choice for beginners, with a good chance of seeing a variety of wildlife species, including a giant maori wrasse, in straightforward conditions.

Cairns-based diving schools often take their intermediate and advanced students out to **Thetford**, **Flynn**, **Milln** and **Pellowe** reefs, east of the city, where there are coral bommies to examine and interesting swim-throughs to explore.

Most of the **cruise companies** running day-trips from Marlin Wharf in Cairns offer their passengers a variety of activities including snorkelling, glass-bottomed boat or semi-submersible tours, scenic flights by helicopter and plain old cruising, either under motor or sail. The basic tour price covers snorkelling equipment and lunch, with guided snorkelling and other activities available at extra cost. If you're keen to get underwater, you can book a try-dive (around A$120) or, if you're already qualified, guided diving (around A$60–75 for one dive or A$80–120 for two). Many of the cruise-company divemasters and instructors are excellent guides. On request, experienced Paddy Colwell, a marine biologist at Reef Teach (see p.583), can accompany you on your dives for around A$200 per day all inclusive; this comes highly recommended.

Live-aboard trips cater for more serious divers, last from three days upwards and cover the best of the reefs. All costs below include berth, meals, dives and gear rental.

In all cases, it's best to book at least a day in advance, and be aware that trips may be cancelled in unfavourable weather. Be wary, too, of "expenses only" boat trips offered by word of mouth; if in doubt, find out from any booking office in town if you're dealing with a registered operator.

Sailing-boat day-trips

Ocean Free Edge Hill ✆07 4050 0550, ⊛www.oceanfree.com.au. Small-group day-trips to Green Island aboard a 16.5-metre schooner. A$109, child A$70.

Ocean Spirit Cruises ✆07 4031 2920, ⊛www.oceanspirit.com.au. Large vessel that holds up to a hundred passengers – it sails out to Upolu Cay and Oyster Reef near Michaelmas Cay daily, anchors for diving and snorkelling, and then returns. A$110, child A$75.50.

Passions of Paradise ✆07 4050 0676 or 1800 111 346, ⊛www.passions.com.au. This highly respected operator runs a roomy, stable and eco-friendly sailing catamaran that motors out to Michaelmas Cay and Breaking Patches on the Outer Reef for bird-watching, snorkelling, diving and glass-bottom boating, then sails back. Committed staff offer a personal service, and diving is reasonably priced. A$119, child A$70.

Powerboat day-trips

Compass ✆1800 815 811, ⊛www.reeftrip.com. Slow boat, not very stable in windy conditions but one of the cheapest, cruising to Hastings Reef and Breaking Patches. A$75.

Down Under Osprey V 287 Draper St ✆1800 079 099, ⊛www.downunderdive.com.au. Speedy vessel that runs out to the outer Norman, Saxon and Hastings reefs for five hours of snorkelling and diving; comfortable ride, chirpy crew and good meals. A$119, child A$60.

Down Under Super Cat ✆1800 079 099, ⊛www.downunderdive.com.au. Well-organized budget option, visiting two Outer Reef locations per trip. A$85, child A$85.

Great Adventures Reef Fleet Terminal, Spence St ✆07 4044 9944 or 1800 079 080, ⊛www.greatadventures.com.au. Large, fast catamarans depart three times a day for day-trips to Green Island (from A$67, child A$33.50; activities and lunch available at extra cost), with the option of continuing to a private pontoon at Moore Reef or Norman Reef.

Ocean Freedom Edge Hill ✆07 4050 0550, ⊛www.oceanfree.com.au. Small-group day-trips to Upulo Cay aboard a luxury cruiser, with five hours to enjoy two separate diving and snorkelling sites. A$165, child A$80.

Ocean Quest, **Reef Quest** and **Sea Quest** 319 Draper St ✆07 4046 7333, ⊛www.diversden.com.au. Stable, well-equipped catamarans that take snorkellers and divers (including PADI students) to any number of Outer Reef sites depending on weather conditions. A$115, child A$80.

Quicksilver Silverswift ☏07 4087 2100, ⓦwww.silverseries.com.au. Large, comfortable 24-metre catamaran (sister vessel to *Silversonic*, based in Port Douglas), which speeds to the Outer Reef in just an hour, giving you more time there than any other day-trip boat – up to five hours on three different sites chosen from Flynn, Pellowe, Milln and Thetford reefs, allowing you to do plenty of snorkelling or up to three dives. A$148, child A$107.

Reef Magic Marine World Reef Fleet Terminal, Spence St ☏07 4031 1588 or 1300 666 700, ⓦwww.reefmagiccruises.com. High-speed luxury catamaran that spends five hours at the Marine World pontoon at Moore Reef, for diving, snorkelling, glass-bottom boating and quick helicopter flights. A$165, child A$85.

Seastar 75 The Esplanade ☏07 4041 6218, ⓦwww.seastarcruises.com.au. Long-established family-run business with permits for some of the best sections of Hastings Reef (Outer Reef) and Michaelmas Cay. The boat takes a maximum of forty passengers and spends five hours on the reef each trip – 2hr 30min at both Hastings and Michaelmas – to allow time for up to three dives plus snorkelling. A$165, child A$110.

Sunlover Reef Cruises Reef Fleet Terminal, Spence St ☏07 4050 1333 1800 810 512, ⓦwww.sunlover.com.au. Fast catamaran to a pontoon at Moore Reef for scuba diving, snorkelling, seawalker helmet diving and scenic flights by helicopter. Well-trained, caring staff manage to look after all comers, whatever their interests, with great efficiency and humour. A$175, child A$90.

Tusa Corner of The Esplanade & Spence St ☏07 4047 9100, ⓦwww.tusadive.com. Custom-built diving vessel taking a maximum of sixty passengers; a roving permit means each trip could go to any of ten separate reefs. A$145 or A$205 for certified divers including two dives and gear rental, child A$90.

Live-aboard trips

Mike Ball Dive Expeditions 143 Lake St ☏07 4031 5484 or 07 4053 0500, ⓦwww.mikeball.com. Luxury diving with one of Queensland's best-equipped and longest-running operations; fly/dive destinations include the Cod Hole (from A$1160 for three nights) and the Coral Sea (from A$1251 for four nights or A$2252 for seven nights).

Nimrod Explorer ☏07 4031 5566, ⓦwww.explorerventures.com. Motorized catamaran with basic or plush cabins carrying up to eighteen guests; four- to eight-day Cod Hole, Osprey Reef, Ribbon Reefs and Far Northern Reef trips cost A$1745–2645 including flights to or from Cooktown.

ProDive Corner of Shields & Abbott streets ☏07 4031 5255 or 1800 353 213, ⓦwww.prodivecairns.com. This highly respected outfit runs three-day/two-night trips to Thetford, Flynn, Milln and Pellowe reefs (Outer Reef); you travel aboard a dedicated dive boat carrying up to 32 passengers and have time to dive up to 11 times, including two night dives. They also sell equipment. A$560.

Santa Maria ☏07 4055 6130, ⓦwww.reefcharter.com. Twenty-metre, replica nineteenth-century gaff-rigged schooner with a maximum of ten passengers for three-day trips to Thetford and Moore reefs. A$560.

Spirit of Freedom ☏07 4047 9150, ⓦwww.spiritoffreedom.com.au. Huge 33-metre vessel with superlative facilities, sailing to Cod Hole, the Ribbons and Coral Sea. Three days from A$1950, four days from A$2250, seven days from A$3950.

Taka ☏07 4051 8722, ⓦwww.takadive.com.au. Fast, thirty-metre vessel with four decks and advanced facilities including photography tuition and nitrox. Four days to Cod Hole and Ribbon reefs from A$1000; five days to Cod Hole and the Coral Sea from A$1280.

Vagabond ☏07 4059 0477, ⓦwww.vagabond-dive.com. Twenty-metre sailing yacht with a maximum of eleven passengers and a roving permit to suit weather conditions. Two days from A$290, certified dives A$35 each.

Cairns' various **dive schools** run PADI courses, from Open Water (A$370–700 for four or five days) to Divemaster level (up to A$2000 for eighteen days), with Instructor courses available by arrangement. Standards are universally sound but costs may vary, largely depending on whether your tutors stick to Inner Reef sites or take you out to the Outer Reef by live-aboard. Before starting your course, you need a dive medical; this costs around A$50. The schools may take non-students to the reef, but experienced divers may want to avoid these trips unless they have checked that it will be possible to dive separately from the heavily shepherded groups of beginners.

Diving schools

CDC 121 Abbott St ☎07 4051 0294, ⓦwww.cairnsdive.com.au. This school sees record-breaking numbers of students through their Open Water training every year.

Deep Sea Divers Den 319 Draper St ☎07 4046 7333, ⓦwww.diversden.com.au. Reliable outfit that's been operating for over 25 years and sometimes offers interesting specials, such as night dives during coral-spawning season.

Down Under Cruise & Dive 287 Draper St ☎07 4052 8300 or 1800 079 099, ⓦwww .downunderdive.com.au. This outfit makes a point of trying to keep prices low.

Pro-Dive Corner of Shields & Abbott streets ☎07 4031 5255 or 1800 353 213, ⓦwww.prodivecairns.com. Not the cheapest, but highly respected; their five-day Open Water course, including three nights on a live-aboard, costs A$725.

Longer trips of three days or more venture further from Cairns into two areas: a circuit north to the **Cod Hole** and the **Ribbon Reefs**, or straight out into the **Coral Sea**. The Cod Hole, near Lizard Island (see p.619), has no coral but is justifiably famous for the mobs of hulking potato cod that rise from the depths to receive hand-outs; currents here are strong, but having these monsters come close enough to cuddle is awesome. The Ribbons are a two-hundred-kilometre string boasting relatively pristine locations and good visibility, the southernmost of which, the Agincourt Reefs, are within a couple of hours of Port Douglas (see box, p.602). Further out, the Coral Sea sites are isolated, vertically walled reefs some distance from the main structure and surrounded by open water teeming with seasonal bundles of pelagic species including mantas, turtles and minke whales. The most-visited Coral Sea sites are **Osprey** and **Holmes** reefs, but try to get out to **Bougainville Reef**, home to everything from garden eels and brightly coloured fan coral to whitetip reef sharks.

Green Island and Fitzroy Island National Park

The two offshore islands nearest Cairns, **Green Island** and **Fitzroy Island**, are popular day-trip destinations: they're easily accessible by boat and have enough sand and snorkelling to compensate for the lack of both along Cairns' urban coastline. Though not technically part of the Great Barrier Reef, they're fringed by coral; much of this is in poor condition, but you'll still see plenty of fish.

Green Island

Heart-shaped and tiny, **Green Island** is easy to reach, making it an ideal day-trip from Cairns – a standard excursion that's a hit with Japanese tourists, who visit in large numbers. If your main aim is to find a pleasant beach within easy reach of the city, you'll find better options in Cairns' northern suburbs (see p.597), which are far cheaper to get to; if you're looking for a quiet island escape, you'll probably prefer Fitzroy; and if you're an experienced diver, you'll find the sites near the island disappointing. Although Green Island lies within a protected area, its popularity has, inevitably, taken its toll on the underwater landscape and on the behaviour of its wildlife (which are fed), while its smallness means that it can be difficult to escape other visitors.

For an easy-going day out, though, it's an appealing-enough destination. Unusually for the coral cays, the island is thickly vegetated, with its own mini-rainforest. Part of this can be explored by following a short boardwalk; well-written information panels guide you along. There's also a swimming pool and a small nautical museum with a few crocodiles (A$12.50), but the island's main attractions are its ring of sandy beach, and the tropical fish and turtles that feed among the coral and weedbeds just offshore. Even if you're not a snorkeller, you need only take a trip in a **semi-submersible** or a **glass-bottomed boat** (a device that was first invented in Far North Queensland in the 1930s) to see plentiful marine life. Alternatively, you could visit the **underwater observatory** at the end of the pier (A$10); the world's first, it has graced the pier since 1954.

If you'd like to experience the island's quieter side, the answer is to stay over at the *Green Island Resort* (☎07 4031 3300, ⓦwww.greenislandresort .com.au; ❽), which is off-limits to day-trippers and has five-star suites arranged around the attractive pool or looking out onto oceanside forest. The rates, though high, include transfers and activities, and compare reasonably well with those of Queensland's remoter island resorts.

Daily cruise services to the island from Marlin Wharf in Cairns include Great Adventures (Reef Fleet Terminal, Spence St; ☎07 4044 9944 or 1800 079 080, ⓦwww.greatadventures.com.au), departing at 8.30am, 10.30am and 1pm; the fifty-minute outward cruise includes an informative talk from a marine ecologist (from A$67, child from A$33.50). Big Cat Green Island Reef Cruises (from A$66, child from A$37; ☎07 4051 0444, ⓦwww.bigcat-cruises.com.au) depart daily at 9am, 11am and 1pm. Both companies run courtesy buses that will collect you from your accommodation; for an extra charge, you can book lunch, escorted snorkelling, touring by "Yellow Submarine" semi-submersible, seawalker helmet diving and scuba diving. Alternatively, **Ocean Free** (A$109, child A$70; ☎07 4050 0550, ⓦwww.oceanfree.com.au) offers small-group **sailing tours** to Green Island with offshore snorkelling. Booking and check-in desks for all boat services are found in the Reef Fleet Terminal on Spence Street, opposite Marlin Wharf.

Day-trippers on a **budget** might want to bring their own provisions, as the only options on the island are a mediocre buffet bar and the pricey resort restaurant.

Green Island looks particularly attractive from the air, but scenic flights to and from the island are limited to just a few a day for conservation reasons. **Cairns Seaplanes** (☎07 4031 4307, ⓦwww.cairnsseaplanes.com) will fly you there and back from Cairns by twin-prop plane for A$250 (child A$187); between the brief flights, you have two hours to explore. **Cairns Heli-Scenic** (from A$125 for 10min; ☎07 4031 5999, ⓦwww.cairns-heliscenic.com.au) run helicopter

For advice on **swimming** in northern Queensland's coastal waters during the "stinger season", see p.47.

transfers and tours, bookable in advance from their rep on the boat to the island or their desk the island itself.

Fitzroy Island National Park

Fitzroy Island is a continental island, not a cay like Green Island; the locals tend to prefer it, as it's far quieter, larger and wilder. Fitzroy Island Ferries (Reef Fleet Terminal; ☏07 4030 7907, ⓦwww.fitzroyisland.com.au) operate a **ferry service** from Marlin Wharf to the island twice a day, crossing in 45 minutes for A$42 return (child A$21). Day-trips including lunch and snorkelling or glass-bottomed boating cost around A$67. The island resort is, at the time of writing, being redeveloped into a luxury retreat; the ferry staff can fill you in on its progress.

To escape the sunbathers, you can set off on one of several worthwhile walks through highland greenery. If you make the two-hour trek to the disused lighthouse, you'll be rewarded with excellent, far-reaching views of the reef, its cays and islands. Fitzroy rises to 269m, offering good vantages for whale-watching during the humpback migration season in winter.

Separated from the main island by a narrow channel is tiny **Little Fitzroy Island**. You can explore both islands by sea kayak with Raging Thunder (☏07 4030 7907, ⓦwww.ragingthunder.com.au).

North of Cairns

Cairns is the perfect springboard from which to explore what is arguably Australia's most scenically diverse region: rainforests, mangrove creeks, waterfalls, mountains, beaches, sand cays and coral reefs are all within easy reach, making this excellent territory for hiking, cycling, diving, snorkelling, kayaking, wildlife-watching, extreme sports and much more besides. The **Barron Gorge National Park**, northwest of the city, is good hiking country, with well-marked trails and natural swimming holes. For those whose idea of bliss is to splash out on a few days of utter relaxation beside the ocean, the **Northern Beaches** offer laid-back luxury just beyond the city limits.

Most of the areas below can be reached by **local bus** from City Place in Cairns with Sunbus (☏07 4057 7411, ⓦwww.sunbus.com.au). Coral Reef Coaches (☏07 4098 2800, ⓦwww.coralreefcoaches.com.au) run daily bus transfers between Cairns and Palm Cove (A$20 one way).

Crystal Cascades and Barron Gorge National Park

About 12km northwest of Cairns near Redlynch, **Crystal Cascades** (Wongalee Falls) is a narrow forest gorge gushing with rapids, small waterfalls and swimming opportunities – somewhere to picnic rather than explore. It's important to heed warnings about the large, serrated, heart-shaped leaves of the stinging tree (also known locally as "dead man's itch") found beside the paths here; the stories about this plant's sting may seem exaggerated, but if stung you'll believe them all.

Near **Kamerunga** township, 15km from Cairns, there's a marked, fairly steep one-kilometre track through the **Barron Gorge National Park** along Stoney Creek, with swimming holes on the way. Tall rainforest trees arch over the creek, and you'll spot plenty of epiphytic basket ferns clinging to branches and to the creekside boulders. The trail is popular with bird-watchers, as in summer, from early November, buff-breasted paradise kingfishers are regularly seen here.

Cairns' Northern Beaches

Cairns' variously developed **Northern Beaches** all lie off the southern stretch of the Captain Cook Highway that connects Cairns and Mossman. These well-to-do suburbs offer a slower pace than the city, while still being close enough for easy access: all but distant Ellis Beach are on bus routes. Fringing this twenty-kilometre stretch of coast is an almost continuous swathe of attractive, northeast-facing, palm-shaded natural sandy beach – one asset that central Cairns has to manage without.

HOLLOWAYS BEACH, around 10km north of Cairns, is a handful of suburban streets fronting a long strip of sand, quiet except for the airport 3km to the south. *Strait on the Beach* **café** has fairly ordinary food but great views from its shaded beachfront terrace, while *Billabong B&B* on Caribbean Street (☎07 4037 0162, ⓦwww.cairns-bed-breakfast.com; ❹) is a delightful and secluded spot set on a man-made inland island, surrounded by water and full of birdlife – the tariff includes a gourmet breakfast.

On the Captain Cook Highway about 12km north of Cairns and 53km south of Port Douglas, the township of **SMITHFIELD** marks the point at which the Kennedy Highway branches off and begins its ascent to Kuranda in the Atherton Tablelands. Just under 1km south of the junction, a large roadside complex houses the lower terminal of the **Skyrail Rainforest Cableway** (see p.577). Close enough to the Skyrail terminal for it to be easy to hop from one to the other is **Tjapukai Aboriginal Cultural Park**, (daily 9am–5pm plus evening shows at 7–10pm; day visit A$31, child A$15.50; evening show and buffet, A$87, child A$43.50; various packages including transfers and other attractions such as the Skyrail, Bare Hill sacred site and Green Island available; ☎07 4042 9999, ⓦwww.tjapukai.com.au). The park offers a dignified, humorous and highly creative survey of local Aboriginal history, bushlore, music and contemporary culture; highlights are an audiovisual presentation on the fate of the indigenous Australians at the hands of the European settlers, a theatrical rendition of Tjapukai folklore using holograms to conjure images from Dreamtime tales, hands-on boomerang- and spear-throwing demonstrations and some stunning artwork. You should allow a couple of hours to see everything.

YORKEYS KNOB, 14km from Cairns, has one of the best **kite-surfing** beaches in Australia; Kiterite at 471 Varley St (☎07 4055 7918, ⓦwww.kiterite.com.au) offer lessons for A$79 per hour. The beach also has an stinger net from November to May. *Villa Marine*, 8 Rutherford St (☎07 4055 7158, ⓦwww.villamarine.com.au; ❸–❹), has self-contained, spacious units set 50m back from the beach beside a cool patch of rainforest; the manager here is a mine of useful information about the Cairns region. You can **eat** at the sailing club in the picturesque **Half Moon Bay Marina**, a favourite locals' spot for Sunday breakfast or brunch.

North of Yorkeys Knob are the upmarket tourist areas of **Trinity Beach**, **Kewarra Beach**, **Clifton Beach** and **Palm Cove**, all with spotlessly clean, palm-fringed beaches and lots of luxury holiday apartments, beach resorts, cafés, boutique shops, restaurants and watersports operators. Palm Cove, 24km from Cairns and 41km from Port Douglas, is one of Far Northern Queensland's honeypot resorts, its accommodation and restaurants attracting wealthy holidaymakers and minor celebrities. You can expect to pay well over A$400 per room per night at many of the resorts here, with minimum stays enforced during the high seasons, but, like Port Douglas further north, the Northern Beaches wear their affluence lightly – you can stroll around barefoot without feeling out of place. A planned new precinct of shops, restaurants, cafés, cultural centre and arthouse cinema, The Village, will make the resort even more pedestrian-friendly. There's a stinger net here from November to May, so you can swim in the sea all year round.

The 𝔐 *Sebel Reef House & Spa* (99 Williams Esplanade, Palm Cove; ☎07 4055 3633, ⓦwww.reefhouse.com.au; ❸), in lush oceanfront gardens, and *Kewarra Beach Resort* (Kewarra Beach; ☎07 4057 6666, ⓦwww.kewarrabeachresort .com.au; ❻–❽), tucked away in a patch of rainforest on the quietest stretch of beach, are for now the grandest and most secluded, respectively, of all the resorts along the coast, but are soon to be outshone by *The Royal Palm Cove* (ⓦwww .theroyalpalmcove.com), described by its developers as Australia's first seven-star resort. Palm Cove has more spas than any other resort in Queensland; among the best is *Angsana Great Barrier Reef* (1 Veivers Rd; ☎07 4055 3000, ⓦwww .angsana.com; ❽). The top-end hotels all have suitably elegant eateries, but there are a few good, moderate places, too: in Trinity Beach, *Atlantis* (47 Vasey Esplanade; ☎07 4057 8550) serves wonderful fish, and in Palm Cove, *Cairns Surf Club* (135 Williams Esplanade; ☎07 4059 1244) is good for pasta and steaks, *Reef House* (99 Williams Esplanade; ☎07 4055 3633) serves unfussy gourmet food, while 𝔐 *Nu Nu* (123 Williams Esplanade; ☎07 4059 1880) does amazing breakfasts, gorgeous sandwiches and the best coffee around.

Cairns Tropical Zoo (daily 8.30am–5pm; A$29, child A$14.50; ☎07 4055 3669, ⓦwww.cairnstropicalzoo.com), on the Captain Cook Highway between Clifton Beach and Palm Cove, showcases native species, allowing visitors the chance to stroke a wombat, feed a kangaroo, pat a python or have their photo taken cuddling a koala. It also houses a few exotics from abroad, such as Himalayan red pandas. The "Night Zoo" after-dark tour (Mon–Thurs & Sat 7–10pm; A$89, child A$44.50) is particularly recommended; it offers close-up views of Australia's often-elusive nocturnal fauna, and includes a barbecue with live music.

If you want to escape for a few days, you couldn't ask for a finer place to unwind than the long and lovely strip of sand at **ELLIS BEACH**, 28km north of Cairns and 37km south of Port Douglas (and unfortunately beyond the reach of bus services) with a pleasant place to stay, 𝔐 *Ellis Beach Bungalows* (☎07 4055 3538, ⓦwww.ellisbeach.com; camping A$26–32, cabin ❷, bungalow ❹). On a private beach a few kilometres north of here is *Turtle Cove Resort* (☎07 4059 1800, ⓦwww.turtlecove.com; ❺–❼), a relaxed little place that has a reputation as one of Australia's best gay and lesbian beach retreats.

Port Douglas and around

North of Cairns and south of Cape Tribulation, the Captain Cook Highway runs close to the coast, winding its way around rocky cliffs, over forested bluffs and past isolated beaches. This beautiful route takes you deep into the region where, as the tourist literature loves to put it, "the rainforest meets the reef". By turning east off the highway 64km north of Cairns you drive into **Port Douglas**, one of Queensland's most pleasant coastal towns, while strung out along the highway further north is **Mossman**, a fairly humdrum town that's the last sizeable centre before the Far North's most celebrated pocket of rainforest, the Daintree.

Port Douglas

Perched on the Coral Sea coast, 67km north of Cairns, **Port Douglas** is a growing resort town with a relaxed outlook and an upmarket appeal: the type of celebrities who like to keep things fairly low-key drop into the more exclusive hotels here from time to time.

Once a bustling gold-rush settlement and sugar transit centre, the town had been half-asleep for the best part of a century when, in recent years, luxury-hotel developers began to take an interest. Now, the road into town is lined with resort complexes, and every other building in the leafy backstreets near the beach has holiday apartments to let, but the centre still has a reassuringly villagey feel. Port is unmistakably a tourist hub, with a main street full of boutiques and souvenir shops, but its laidback community of eccentrics and ex-urbanites continue to make their presence felt; in particular, they're ardent supporters of the town's vibrant restaurant and café scene.

For most visitors, Port Douglas' appeal lies in its safe, quiet atmosphere and tourist-friendly facilities. There's a modern **marina** on Dickson Inlet, and a huge beach, **Four Mile Beach**, just east of the centre, with a stinger net from November to May. Well-placed for excursions to the Daintree and the Great Barrier Reef, Port is also getting to be as good a place as Cairns to pick up a regional tour or dive trip.

Arrival, orientation and information

Coral Reef Coaches (℡07 4098 2800, ⓦwww.coralreefcoaches.com.au) run a daily **shuttle bus service** between Cairns, the Northern Beaches, Port Douglas and Mossman, as well as charter services and local tours. Sun Palm (℡07 4084 2626, ⓦwww.sunpalmtransport.com) link Port Douglas with Cairns, the Northern Beaches, Mossman, the Daintree and Cape Tribulation. Most of the town's shops and services are found on or just off the main street, **Macrossan Street**, including a supermarket and a post office (on Owen St; Mon–Fri 8.30am–5.30pm, Sat 9am–2pm). As in Cairns, a proliferation of businesses offer tourist information; the Port Douglas **tourist office** at 23 Macrossan St (daily 8.30am–5.30pm; ℡07 4099 5599, ⓦwww.tourismportdouglas.com.au) can sort out everything from Aboriginal-guided tours of Mossman Gorge to sailing trips and buses to the Daintree. There are several **car rental** options in town, including Thrifty, 50 Macrossan St (℡07 4099 5555); while you can pick up bikes for A$19 per day at Bike Shop, also on Macrossan Street. The best places to get **online** are Wicked on Macrossan Street (daily 8.30am–10pm), which has plenty of terminals for A$5 per hour, or Re:hab, also on Macrossan (see p.604).

Accommodation

Port has a great range of convenient, modern **self-catering options**, from tidy studios to large serviced apartments with a shared pool. If you find a place close to the restaurants and shops in the centre of town, you're unlikely to miss the facilities of a hotel, but there are also several large out-of-town **hotel complexes** to choose from.

For advice on **swimming** in northern Queensland's coastal waters during the "stinger season", see p.47.

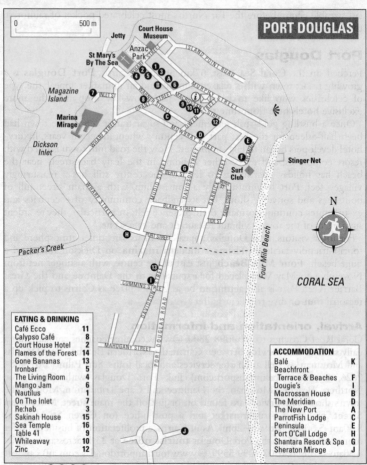

0   500 m

Jetty   **Court House Museum**

St Mary's By The Sea   **Anzac Park**

Magazine Island

Marina Mirage

Dickson Inlet

Packer's Creek

Stinger Net

Surf Club

CORAL SEA

Four Mile Beach

N

EATING & DRINKING

Café Ecco	11
Calypso Café	8
Court House Hotel	2
Flames of the Forest	14
Gone Bananas	13
Ironbar	5
The Living Room	4
Mango Jam	6
Nautilus	1
On The Inlet	7
Re:hab	3
Sakinah House	15
Sea Temple	16
Table 41	9
Whileaway	10
Zinc	12

ACCOMMODATION

Balé	K
Beachfront Terrace & Beaches	F
Dougie's	B
Macrossan House	D
The Meridian	A
The New Port	C
ParrotFish Lodge	E
Peninsula	H
Port O'Call Lodge	G
Shantara Resort & Spa	I
Sheraton Mirage	J

14, **15**, **16**, **K**, *Rainforest Habitat*, ▼ *Captain Cook Highway to Mossman & Cairns*

Balé 1 Balé Drive ☎07 4084 3000, ⓦwww.peppers.com.au/bale-resort. Spread over a vast estate on the edge of town, this is Port's most exclusive option, with celebrity-friendly private houses, complete with their own plunge pools, starting at A$900 for two. **⑧**

Beachfront Terrace & Beaches The Esplanade ☎07 4099 6070 or 1800 463 325, ⓦwww .latitude16.com.au. Large complex of self-catering apartments overlooking Four Mile Beach, a very short walk from the centre. **④–⑥**

Dougie's Davidson St ☎07 4099 6200 or 1800 996 200, ⓦwww.dougies.com.au. Simple but decent rooms, two-person tents to rent by the day, and space for your own tent or campervan among tropical trees. Camping A$24, bunk in shared room A$26, private double **③**

Macrossan House 19 Macrossan St ☎07 4099 4366, ⓦwww.macrossanhouse-port-douglas.com .au. Reasonably priced, conservatively furnished mini-apartments with a shared pool, bang in the centre of town. **⑤**

The Meridian 15–17 Davidson St ☎07 4084 2400, ⓦwww .portdouglasmeridian.com. These pristine, well-designed apartments with secure parking are an excellent choice for self-caterers; Macrossan Street is an easy walk away. Reduced rates in low season. No children. Studio **⑤**, one-bedroom **⑥**

The New Port 16 Macrossan St ☎07 4099 5700, ⓦwww.thenewport.com.au. Comfortable apartments in various sizes, from studios to two bedrooms, at good rates for the convenient location. **④–⑤**

ParrotFish Lodge 37 Warner St ☏ 07 4099 5011 or 1800 995 011, ⓦ www.parrotfishlodge.com.au. Aimed firmly at young backpackers – and a bit slapdash – this is the closest hostel to the centre of town. Bunk in shared room A$25–33, private double ❸

Peninsula 9–13 The Esplanade ☏ 07 4099 9100 or 1800 676 674, ⓦ www.peninsulahotel.com.au. Pricey mini-apartments with hotel service on a cramped but beautifully located plot overlooking Four Mile Beach. ❼

Port O'Call Lodge Port Street ☏ 07 4099 5422 or 1800 892 800, ⓦ www.portocall.com.au. Pleasant, colourful YHA-affiliated budget option about 1km from the centre, with solar panels to lend eco-friendliness. Free bus from other YHA hostels and Cairns Airport. Bunk in a shared room A$26.50–31.50, private double ❸

Shantara Resort & Spa 27–31 Davidson St ☏ 07 4084 1400, ⓦ www.shantara.com.au. This attractive complex of fresh studios and apartments with modern styling offers you the option of maid service, and there's a spa on the premises. Reduced rates in low season. No children. ❻–❽

Sheraton Mirage Port Douglas Rd ☏ 07 4099 5888, ⓦ www.starwoodhotels.com. This, the first of Port's upmarket resort complexes, set a high standard for others to follow. Complete with golf course, tidy palm trees and an impressive beach-front location, it has all the comforts you'd expect. Room ❼, villa ❽

The Town

The town centre lies on a peninsula between Dickson Inlet and Four Mile Beach, and comprises a small grid of streets centred around **Macrossan Street**, which runs from the north end of Four Mile Beach to Anzac Park, with the **marina** a couple of blocks west. Macrossan is a pleasant shopping street, shaded with mango trees and palms; here you'll find plenty of good "resort wear" boutiques and a few excellent **gallery shops**, such as Candlenut Gallery, which sells beautifully carved and polished objects made from local gum trees and L'Dream, with a gorgeous range of original silver, opal and pearl jewellery. The best place in town for **art**, with a good selection of canvases from talented locals, is Australian and Oceanic Art on the corner of Grant and Warner streets.

Anzac Park is the scene of an increasingly busy Sunday **market** (8am–2pm), with traders from the region selling fresh tropical fruit, vegetables and herbs, local gagarra honey, sugar-cane juice, orchids, paintings, strings of pearls and organic insect repellent. Near the park's **jetty** you'll find the whitewashed timber church of **St Mary's by the Sea**, built after the 1911 cyclone carried off the previous structure, while on Wharf Street is the restored **Court House**, now a small museum housing memorabilia from the gold-rush days of the late nineteenth century.

On the way into town, **The Rainforest Habitat**, just off the highway on Port Douglas Road (daily 8am–5.30pm; A$29, child A$14.50; ☏ 07 4099 3235, ⓦ www.rainforesthabitat.com.au) is an excellent little wildlife park with rainforest, wetland and grassland zones, home to kangaroos, wallabies, koalas, lorikeets, cassowaries and a great many wading birds. It's also one of only two zoos in Australia to keep tree kangaroos; these have been breeding successfully, so you may get a glimpse of a youngster. "Breakfast with the birds", served buffet-style in the wetland aviary café for an extra A$10 (child A$5) on top of the standard entrance fee, is fantastic value.

Eating and drinking

Port Douglas is becoming quite a gourmet destination, with masses of good **restaurants** to choose from. It's not a late-night town, though: the streets are quiet well before midnight. Self-caterers will find it easy to stock up with a large **supermarket** on Macrossan Street, a great pie shop on Grant Street, an organic grocer on Warner Street and excellent produce stalls at the Sunday morning **market**.

The following operators run enjoyable trips to destinations and attractions within easy reach of Port Douglas. Most can arrange to pick you up from your accommodation in town, often at no extra charge. Alternatively, it's possible to join the trips and activities run by the Cairns-based operators (see box, p.592) by paying extra for transfers.

Boat hire

Port Douglas Boat Hire Marina Mirage ☎07 4099 6277. Rent out small, stable fishing boats, equipped with fishing kits, barbecues, eskies (coolers) and ice, allowing you to explore Dickson Inlet, and try a little fishing, at your own pace.

Day-trips to the Daintree and Cape Tribulation

A day is just enough time to get a taste of the coastal rainforest, stopping at lookouts, boardwalk trails, creeks, empty beaches and pretty picnic spots.

Back Country Bliss ☎07 4099 3677, ⓦwww.backcountrybliss.com. Offer a 4WD trip to Cape Tribulation and the Bloomfield Falls (A$189), or a whistle-stop day-trip all the way to Cooktown and back (A$899 for up to 5 people).

De Luxe Safaris ☎07 4099 6406, ⓦwww.deluxesafaris.com.au. Run comfortable small-group tours, travelling by bio-diesel LandCruiser or minibus with a genial guide. A$155–165, child A$125.

Tony's Tropical Tours ☎07 4099 3230, ⓦwww.tropicaltours.com.au. Highly environmentally aware outfit with enthusiastic guides, running small-group tours of Mossman Gorge, the Daintree and Cape Tribulation (A$155, child A$126) or through the region and on to Bloomfield Falls (A$172, child A$130).

Day-trips to the Low Isles and Outer Reef

Out to sea, the vegetated sand cays known as the **Low Isles**, around 18km offshore in the Great Barrier Reef Marine Park, make a good day-trip by cruise vessel, with a lighthouse dating back to 1878 and fine snorkelling and turtle-spotting opportunities in a blue lagoon, while the spectacular dive and snorkel sites of the **Agincourt Ribbon Reefs** on the **Outer Reef**, 70km northeast of Port Douglas, are within manageable cruising distance by high-speed catamaran.

Calypso Marina Mirage ☎07 4099 6999, ⓦwww.calypsocharters.com.au. Reef trips taking in three sites per day, for diving and snorkelling.

Poseidon Reef Adventure Centre, Corner of Macrossan & Grant streets ☎07 4099 4772 or 1800 085 674, ⓦwww.poseidon-cruises.com.au. Highly professional company with a large, comfortable catamaran that cruises to a variety of sites at the Agincourt Ribbon Reefs, for diving and snorkelling straight off the boat. The scuba team are attentive, informative and very safety-conscious, and the sites they visit are first rate; you'll have time for up to three dives. A$165, child A$125, three dives (certified diver) A$220.

Café Ecco 1/43 Macrossan St ☎07 4099 4056. With streetside tables, a quiet terrace at the back, and world music on the stereo, this is a good place to stop for freshly squeezed juice or a sandwich. Tues–Sun 8am–5pm.

Calypso Café Corner of Warner & Grant sts. Brilliant for breakfast, this little place serves beautifully presented bacon, tomato and spinach melts and vanilla French toast. Mon–Sat 8.30am–3pm, Sun 8.30am–noon.

Court House Hotel Corner of Macrossan & Wharf sts ☎07 4099 5181. A local landmark, this Queenslander-style corner house pub is busy all day, with sports on TV and live music most nights.

🏃 **Flames of the Forest** Mowbray River Rd ☎07 4099 3144, ⓦwww.flamesoftheforest .com.au. Utterly romantic, this is as much an outing as an eating experience; guests gather in a candlelit forest clearing for sparkling wine, then sit

Quicksilver Silversonic Marina Mirage ⓣ07 4087 2100, ⓦwww.silverseries.com.au. Large 24-metre catamaran (sister vessel to *Silverswift*, based in Cairns) whose speed means that you get longer at the Agincourt Ribbon Reefs – up to five hours on three different sites, allowing you to do plenty of snorkelling or up to three dives. Departs 8.30am daily. Operates whale-watching trips in season (roughly May–Sept), with the opportunity to swim with dwarf minke and humpback whales. A$158, child A$117.

Quicksilver Wavedancer Marina Mirage ⓣ07 4087 2100, ⓦwww.quicksilver-cruises.com. Luxurious catamaran with sails, cruising to the Low Isles daily at 10am; the crossing takes under an hour, and the rest of your day can be spent snorkelling, sunbathing on the beach, or taking a glass-bottom boat tour. Try-dives are also available. A$127, child A$66, intro dive A$112.

Quicksilver Wavepiercer Marina Mirage ⓣ07 4087 2100, ⓦwww.quicksilver-cruises.com. Fast, state-of-the-art catamaran, which departs 10am daily, cruising to a private pontoon on the Agincourt Ribbon Reefs, for snorkelling, "Ocean Walker" helmet diving, scuba diving (intro A$134, one certified dive A$92, two dives A$134) and "dry" wildlife-watching in the underwater observatory and semi-submersible boat. A$191, child A$98.

Sailaway Reef Adventure Centre, corner of Macrossan & Grant streets ⓣ07 4099 4772 or 1800 085 674, ⓦwww.sailawayportdouglas.com. Luxury-style catamaran sailing trip to the Low Isles, with over five hours to snorkel and explore, and room for no more than 33 guests. A$150, child A$90.

Shaolin Reef Adventure Centre, corner of Macrossan & Grant streets ⓣ07 4099 4772 or 1800 085 674, ⓦwww.shaolinportdouglas.com. Romantic Chinese junk that cruises to the Low Isles for lunch and a lazy afternoon, carrying up to 23 guests. A$150, child A$90.

Undersea Explorer 4 Princes Wharf ⓣ07 4099 5911, ⓦwww.undersea.com.au. Scientific research vessel on which guests can participate in exciting projects such as monitoring sharks and dwarf minke whales; destinations include Osprey Reef, Cod Hole and the Ribbons, with occasional trips to the historic *Pandora* wreck (see p.545). Weekly departures. From A$2600 for a six-day live-aboard expedition.

Kite-surfing

Windswell Barrier St ⓣ07 4098 2167, ⓦwww.windswell.com.au. This outfit based at the southern end of Four Mile Beach will teach you to kite-surf (A$99–150 for 2hr) and lend out gear. There's wakeboarding on calm days.

Scenic flights

Quicksilver Helicopters Sunbird Centre, Sheraton Mirage ⓣ07 4099 6034. Aerial tours of the Great Barrier Reef.

around creekside tables for a tasty banquet followed by Dreamtime tales from Aboriginal story-tellers. A$195, child A$120 including wine and transfers. Mid-March to mid-Jan Thurs, Fri & Sun 7.30–10.30pm.

Gone Bananas 87 Davidson St ⓣ07 4099 5400. Men and women are handed separate cocktail lists at this tropical-oriental bar/restaurant – pink fruity concoctions for her, "Marlon Brando" with Kahlua and Drambuie for him. On the menu are Aussie-Asian dishes such as emu carpaccio and crocodile curry. Mon–Sat 6pm–late.

Ironbar 5 Macrossan St ⓣ07 4099 4776. This large drinking shack knocked together from a hotchpotch of found timber and corrugated iron is a Port Douglas institution, with cane-toad racing upstairs at 7.30pm every evening (A$5).

The Living Room 22 Wharf St ⓣ07 4099 4011. With an outdoor deck tacked onto a renovated Queenslander house, this place has an Asian-fusion menu thick with seafood specialities such as blue swimmer crab and tiger prawns. Tues–Sun 6.30pm–late.

Mango Jam 24 Macrossan St ☎07 4099 4611. Informal and family-friendly – so often busy, with slow service – *Mango Jam* serves good pancakes and pizzas. Daily 7.30am–late.

Nautilus 14 Macrossan St ☎07 4099 5330. To find this long-established, upmarket place, turn off Macrossan along a path through rainforest foliage. The ultimate treat is the six-course food- and wine-tasting menu (A$149).

On The Inlet 3 Inlet St ☎07 4099 5255. This fish restaurant is better at lunchtime, when you can enjoy its waterside views, than in the evening. A giant grouper lurks near the wharf and is fed by the staff every afternoon. Daily noon–late.

Re:hab 18 Macrossan St ☎07 4099 4677. No lunch, just the best coffee in town, and a mellow, funky vibe. Mon–Sat 8am–10pm, Sun 9am–10pm.

Sakinah House *Rydges Sabayah*, 87–109 Port Douglas Rd ☎07 4099 8900. Swanky but not over-expensive, this hangout for well-heeled tourists and minor celebrities serves Aussie-Asian dishes such

as lemongrass chicken with banana blossom and crispy snapper with chilli, tamarind and coriander sauce. Daily breakfast & dinner.

Sea Temple Mitre St ☎07 4099 1572. Top-end presentation and creative combinations of fine ingredients make this Mod-Oz-meets-Asia hotel restaurant a memorable choice. Daily breakfast, lunch & dinner.

Table 41 41 Macrossan St ☎07 4099 4244. One of Macrossan Street's swankier eateries, this place is famous for its seafood medley featuring Moreton Bay bugs, Tableland red claw crayfish, seared scallops and more, for two to share. Daily 6pm–late.

Whileaway 43 Macrossan St ☎07 4099 4066. Cool and contemporary bookshop café serving excellent coffee. Mon–Fri 8am–5pm, Sat & Sun 9am–3pm.

Zinc Corner of Macrossan & Davidson sts ☎07 4099 6260, ⓦwww.zincportdouglas .com. Brisk, friendly and stylish, this is currently the cool place to be seen in Port. There's a fantastic cocktail list and an imaginative, contemporary menu, with mains around A$30. The tropical aquarium is a witty touch.

Mossman and Mossman Gorge

MOSSMAN, 14km north of Port Douglas, is a quiet town that looks as if it has hardly changed since the 1950s; rail lines between the canefields and mill still run along the main street, Front Street. With banks, fuel, shops, organic lunches at *Goodies* and Internet access at *Temptations*, it's a useful stop if you're on the way to or from the Daintree and Cape Tribulation.

Ten minutes inland by way of the turning just south of town, **Mossman Gorge** looks like all rainforest river valleys should; steep-sided and overhung with mossy branches, the boulder-strewn flow with deep natural pools is good for messing around in on a quiet day, but attracts streams of tour buses in peak season. There are plenty of **walking trails** taking in the gorge and rainforest, lasting from a few minutes to a couple of hours. **Kuku Yalanji**, the local Aboriginal community, have a cooperative of guides (Kuku Yalanji Dreamtime) who conduct **tours** of the gorge explaining its history and local plant usage (Mon–Sat, 4 tours daily; A$27.50, child A$16; ☎07 4098 2595, ⓦwww.yalanji.com.au). If you want to stay somewhere plush but peaceful in this area, book in at the exclusive *Silky Oaks Lodge* (☎07 4098 1666 or 1300 134 044, ⓦwww.silkyoakslodge.com.au; ⓞ), 7km northwest of Mossman through the canefields; there's not much rainforest here, but the rooms have good views of tropical gardens and the Mossman River, there's an in-house spa, and you get very well looked after.

North of Mossman, the highway continues to Daintree village; if you're heading for the Daintree ferry to Cape Tribulation, you need to turn right 9km after the hamlet of Wonga, which is the last place to buy petrol before the Daintree. South of Mossman, the inland road takes you up to **Mount Molloy** for the route either south to Mareeba or north to Cooktown by the Peninsula Developmental Road – longer than the coastal Bloomfield Track (see p.613) but a much easier drive.

▲ Mossman Gorge

The Daintree and Cape Tribulation

Just a couple of hours' drive from Cairns, 35km north of Mossman, lie the **Daintree** – a loose term encompassing **Daintree Village**, the **Daintree River** and the **Daintree National Park** – and **Cape Tribulation**. The tamed south-eastern fringe of the Cape York Peninsula, it's a dramatic, quintessentially tropical region: thick, dark vine-draped rainforest tumbles down hillsides to meet palm-fringed beaches; cassowaries and brush turkeys patrol the shady forest floor; and six-metre crocodiles lurk in the creeks.

While Far North Queensland has numerous pockets of beautiful rainforest rich in flora and fauna, the Daintree, at 1200 square kilometres, is the largest and longest-surviving expanse. It catches the imagination of **ecotourists** and wilderness-seekers to such a degree that it's by far the busiest forest destination in the state, but it's extensive enough to allow plenty of space for peaceful wanderings. The range of accommodation is excellent, with a high proportion of properties designed in complete sympathy with the environment, and there are plenty of outdoor activities on offer, from sea kayaking and zip-lining to birding and rambling.

There has been rainforest vegetation in this area for at least 200 million years, making it the **oldest rainforest in the world** – more than twenty times older than the Amazon. To date, over three thousand plant species have been identified in the Daintree, seven hundred of them endemic to the region, and the forest also supports two thirds of Australia's bat and butterfly species, plus nearly a third of the country's frog, reptile and marsupial species including rarities such as tree kangaroos and the Daintree River possum.

Exploited for many years by loggers ripping out silky oak, satin ash, red cedar and mahogany, the forest received its **World Heritage** listing surprisingly recently, in 1988. Until the early 1980s, the only road through the region was a track, while north of Cape Tribulation there was no road at all; when regional and federal governors commissioned the construction of a new road through the forest to link Cooktown with Cairns, environmentalists responded by chaining themselves to trees and burying themselves in the path of bulldozers. Though unsuccessful in their primary purpose, their protest drew attention to the fragility of the forest and the vulnerability of the adjacent Great Barrier Reef: during the construction works, floodwaters washed tonnes of excavated soil into the ocean. Even now, there's a struggle to rein in **development**: roads have been surfaced, land has been subdivided and the main route through the forest is dotted with lodges and other amenities. In a recent move, Aboriginal communities have campaigned successfully to reclaim territories they consider to be their birthright; this may result in new construction projects in some areas.

Some day-trip visitors are disappointed that the closest they get to immersion in the rainforest is driving along the tarmac of the Cape Tribulation Road or walking rather tame boardwalk-trails; you have to **stay overnight** to tune into the region's natural majesty. The deep forest has few hiking trails and offers little opportunity to explore independently, but **after-dark walks** around the forest fringes reveal an intriguing variety of birds, insects, reptiles and shy, nocturnal marsupials. Early morning is a good time to explore the boardwalks – as well as admiring strangler figs, fan palms, wait-a-while palm vines and rare orchids, you'll see the forest birds at their busiest.

The region receives an impressive three metres of **rain** a year – sometimes as much as five. While you can expect occasional showers whenever you visit, the wet season gives the forest a battering – between January and March, creeks can burst their banks for hours at a time and the Bloomfield Track north of Cape Tribulation may be impassable for days or even weeks. Despite the inconvenience, there's nothing quite like witnessing the rainforest come alive after rain – and it's never as humid as you might imagine, thanks to cooling sea breezes.

Getting there and around

There's an unsealed airstrip for light aircraft and helicopters at Cow Bay but the nearest **airport** to the region is at Cairns. For maximum flexibility, the best way to visit is to book a **tour** from Cairns or Port Douglas, including a few nights' accommodation, or to plan a **self-drive** trip, designing your itinerary independently. As long as you're happy to tackle fairly narrow, steep and winding roads, you can drive as far as Cape Tribulation in a 2WD car; it's only north of Emmagen Creek on the Bloomfield Track that you really need a 4WD. The main road is still relatively new and the wildlife has yet to adjust to its dangers, so it's important to drive carefully and heed the variable speed limits. There's only one **fuel station** in the region: the roadhouse south of Cooper Creek.

Day-trips from Cairns and Port Douglas will show you some of the sights, but you really need longer to take in the rich scenery and atmosphere – and you obviously have to stay overnight if you want to see nocturnal animals. If you only have a day to spare, however, Port Douglas' De Luxe Safaris (℡07 4099 6406, ⓦwww.deluxesafaris.com.au; A$165, child A$125) or Tony's Tropical Tours (℡07 4099 3230, ⓦwww.tropicaltours.com.au; A$155–172, child A$126–130) are good choices, running comfortable small-group guided tours of Mossman Gorge, the Daintree and Cape Tribulation, with plenty of interesting stops at creeks, beaches and boardwalks. Mason's Tours at Myall Creek, Cape Tribulation (℡07 4098 0070, ⓦwww.masonstours.com.au) run local tours, including wildlife walks (see p.606). For operators based in Cairns, see the box on p.588.

For those who don't have their own transport but want more independence than a tour can offer, Sun Palm (℡07 4084 2626, ⓦwww.sunpalmtransport .com) and Coral Reef Coaches (℡07 4098 2800, ⓦwww.coralreefcoaches .com.au) both run daily **shuttle buses** from Cairns to the Daintree and Cape Tribulation (A$45–50 one way), via Port Douglas and Mossman. Sun Palm also run a **local bus** serving Cow Bay, Cooper Creek, Coconut Beach and Cape Tribulation. Several lodgings hire out **mountain bikes**.

Practicalities

There are small **grocery shops** at Cooper Creek, Myall Creek and Cape Tribulation, but no post office between Mossman and Cooktown – you can hand post in at your accommodation but there may be a delay of up to a week before it reaches the postal system. The region has no banks but there are **ATMs** at Myall Creek and Cape Tribulation. Mobile phone coverage in the region is almost nil. The Cape Trib Shop at Myall Creek and a couple of the hostels offer **Internet access** but it's slow and expensive.

Wildlife attracts many visitors to the area, but should be treated with respect. Cassowaries can be dangerous if they, or their young, feel threatened: remain calm and back off. Crocodiles inhabit the creeks and river mouths in the region (see box below). Dangerous snakes such as death adders are present, though it's extremely rare to see one.

Accommodation

The Daintree has an abundance of **accommodation** and all, even the more sophisticated places, immerse you in the wilderness – you'll fall asleep to a chorus of insects and wake to the sound of birdsong.

Be croc-wise!

Crocodile sightings in the Daintree are a regular occurrence. Most creeks are marked by warning signs whether crocs live there or not, but the locals know all their haunts, so always seek their advice before wading or swimming. Stand back from the edge when fishing, and when camping, choose a site at least 2m above the high-water mark. Never prepare food or wash dishes at the water's edge, or leave food scraps lying around.

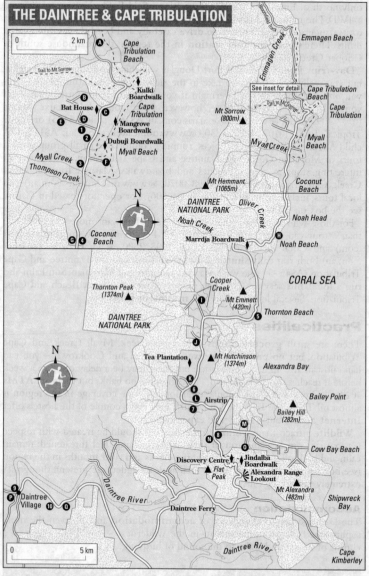

THE DAINTREE & CAPE TRIBULATION

0 — 2 km

0 — 5 km

FAR NORTH QUEENSLAND

ACCOMMODATION				EATING & DRINKING			
Cape Trib Beach House	**A**	Epiphyte Bed and Breakfast	**O**	Café on Sea	**5**	Fanpalm Café	**6**
Cape Trib Exotic Fruit Farm	**B**	Ferntree Rainforest Lodge	**D**	The Cape	**4**	Floravilla	**8**
Cape Tribulation Camping	**F**	Heritage Lodge	**I**	Cassowary Café	**D**	Julaymba	**Q**
Coconut Beach Resort	**G**	Julaymba	**Q**	Cycad	**L**	Myall Creek	
Crocodylus Village	**M**	Lync-Haven Retreat	**K**	Daintree Ice		Takeaway	**3**
Daintree Eco Lodge & Spa	**Q**	Noah Beach Camping	**H**	Cream Company	**7**	Papaya Café	**9**
Daintree Rainforest Retreat	**N**	PK's Jungle Village	**C**	Daintree Tea House	**10**	Whet	**2**
Daintree Wilderness Lodge	**L**	Rainforest Hideaway	**E**	Dragonfly			
Deep Forest Lodge	**J**	Red Mill House	**P**	Gallery Café	**1**		

Daintree Village

Daintree Eco Lodge & Spa Daintree Rd, near Daintree Village ☏07 4098 6100, ⓦwww .daintree-ecolodge.com.au. Imaginatively run in partnership with the local community, and hyped as one of the finest eco-retreats in Queensland, but the reality may disappoint – it's close to the road, and the cabins and spa, though comfortable, have a neglected look. Only the restaurant, *Julaymba* (see p.612), with lovely views over a lily pool, is truly atmospheric. ❽

Red Mill House Stewart St ☏07 4098 6233, ⓦwww.redmillhouse.com.au. Set in a leafy garden, this has comfortable en-suite rooms, decorated with style, a separate self-contained house, and a good pool. Room ❺, house ❻

Cow Bay and Hutchinson Creek

🏃 **Crocodylus Village** Buchanan Creek Rd, Cow Bay ☏07 4098 9166, ⓦwww .crocodyluscapetrib.com. Tucked under the forest canopy with sunlight only penetrating in patches, this friendly wilderness hostel has very large en-suite safari tents, good home-made food, and walking trails that feel much more natural than the boardwalks found elsewhere. Bunk in shared tent A$23, private en-suite double ❷

Daintree Rainforest Retreat Cape Tribulation Rd, near Cow Bay ☏07 4098 9101, ⓦwww .daintreeretreat.com.au. This unpretentious, homely, eco-friendly place has a good variety of doubles and self-contained family rooms, and a small pool. ❸

Daintree Wilderness Lodge Near Hutchinson Creek ☏07 4098 9105, ⓦwww.daintree wildernesslodge.com.au. With pretty cabins deep in a lovely fan palm forest, connected by boardwalks, this is an atmospheric choice, with a good restaurant (see p.613). ❻

🏃 **Epiphyte Bed and Breakfast** 22 Silkwood Rd, Cow Bay ☏07 4098 9039, ⓦwww .rainforestbb.com. Laid-back, open-plan house, outside the forest fringes, with tidy rooms and a glorious shared veranda from were there are sweeping views across a colourful garden to Thornton's Peak. Eco-friendly and very good value. Room ❸, cabin ❹

Lync-Haven Retreat Cape Tribulation Rd, near Bailey's Creek ☏07 4098 9155, ⓦwww .lynchaven.com.au. The cabins here are fairly basic, but there's also room to camp. The owners

run a small wildlife orphanage. Camping A$19–24, cabin ❹

Cooper Creek and Noah Creek

Deep Forest Lodge Cape Tribulation Rd ☏07 4098 9162, ⓦwww.daintreedeepforestlodge .com.au. Well-furnished, self-contained cabins sleeping up to three or five set in a pleasant garden, fringed by forest. ❹

Heritage Lodge Cape Tribulation Rd ☏07 4098 9138, ⓦwww.heritagelodge.net.au. Fairly upmarket lodge with simple but attractive cabins, plus a spa and a good restaurant, close to the Cooper Creek swimming holes and walking trails. ❺

Noah Beach Campground Noah Beach ☏13 13 04, ⓦwww.epa.qld.gov.au. QPWS site with space for tents only, in the woodland behind Noah Beach; prone to flooding after heavy rain, it may be closed in the wet season. Camping A$9 (A$4.50 per person).

Coconut Beach to Cape Tribulation

Cape Trib Beach House Cape Tribulation Rd ☏07 4098 0030 or 1800 111 124, ⓦwww .capetribbeach.com.au. Not strictly a beach house, this is a collection of cabins in a forested coastal plot, their price ascending as you descend towards the sea. The top-end cabins, though simple, have atmosphere. Bunk in shared room A$25, room ❷, cabin ❹–❻

Cape Trib Exotic Fruit Farm Nicole Drive ☏07 4098 0057, ⓦwww.capetrib.com.au. Two pretty creekside cottages close to the orchard. Pricier than the other Daintree B&Bs, but it offers a pleasantly secluded location and an elaborate fruit breakfast. ❺

Cape Tribulation Camping Off Cape Tribulation Rd, Myall Beach ☏07 4098 0077, ⓦwww. capetribcamping.com.au. Within metres of the pristine beach, this is the best spot to camp on the Daintree coast. Two-person camping A$24–30, two-person safari tent ❷

🏃 **Coconut Beach Resort** Cape Tribulation Rd ☏07 4098 0033, ⓦwww .coconutbeachresort.com.au. This large, upmarket resort straddles the road, with a gorgeous, lofty, cedarwood poolside restaurant (*The Cape*) and spa on the beach side and rooms on the forest side; best are the gorgeous cabins

There are no stinger nets on the Daintree coast; for advice on **swimming** in northern Queensland's coastal waters during the "stinger season", see p.47.

with large screens you can open to enjoy the forest noises. ⑥

Ferntree Rainforest Lodge Camelot Close, Cape Tribulation ☎07 4098 0033, ⓦwww .ferntreerainforestlodge.com.au. In a large, sunny garden plot, unusual for the Daintree, this has a broad choice of rooms, from small multi-shares to large private villas. Bunk in shared room A$30, private double ⑤, suite ⑥

PK's Jungle Village Cape Tribulation Rd ☎1800 232 333, ⓦwww.pksjunglevillage.com.

Backpacker central, lively and often noisy and crowded. Camping A$30, bunk in shared room A$25, cabin ❸, private en-suite double ❹

Rainforest Hideaway Camelot Close ☎07 4098 0108, ⓦwww.rainforesthideaway.com. Designed and built by the owner, this eco-friendly lodge is a one-off, with rustic but characterful and comfy timber cabins hidden among trees up on a hillside. ❹

Daintree Village and the Daintree River

Set on the south bank of the Daintree River, inland from the Mossman–Cape Tribulation road, **DAINTREE VILLAGE** – a former timber camp – is now little more than a clutch of pubs and stores with poignant views of deforested countryside. Separated from the Daintree coast by the river, there's a forgotten feeling about the place. Most visitors travelling up from Mossman bypass the village completely and instead, before reaching it, turn right to cross to the north bank of the Daintree River and follow the road up to Cape Tribulation.

The main reason to spend time on the south bank is to take a **riverboat cruise**. Birders will want to contact Chris Dahlberg at Daintree River Tours and Cruises (☎07 4098 7997, ⓦwww.daintreerivertours.com.au) for his exceptional two-hour dawn **birding and wildlife-watching tours** (A$55). In the village, you'll find several other operators offering more mainstream trips; one of the better options is Daintree River Electric Boat Cruises (A$20, child A$10; ☎1800 686 103), who take small groups out for a one-hour trip in a quiet boat.

With no bridge across the Daintree River, taking the **Daintree River ferry** (6am–midnight; vehicle A$10 single, A$18 return, pedestrian A$1 each way) is a key part of the ritual of approaching the national park. The 25-vehicle-capacity cable-ferry runs on demand but can be busy in peak season (July & Aug), with queues on either side.

The Alexandra Range to Hutchinson Creek

Across the river is the start of the **Daintree National Park** and the 35-kilometre scenic drive along Cape Tribulation Road to the tiny settlement of the same name, north of which the sealed road ends and becomes the 4WD-only Bloomfield Track to Cooktown.

Soon after the Daintree River ferry crossing, you can start to appreciate the sounds and colour of the rainforest as the road cuts a winding and steeply undulating swathe over the convoluted **Alexandra Range**. There's a break in the trees at the Walu Wugirriga Alexandra Range Lookout, where you can stop to admire the view of the coast for an immediate sense of the forest tumbling right down to the shore.

Around 8km from the ferry is the turn-off to the **Jindalba Boardwalk**, a well-planned and maintained forest walk that's excellent for bird-watching, and is one of the locations where cassowaries are sometimes seen. On the way is the **Discovery Centre** (daily 8.30am–5pm; A$25, child A$10; ☎07 4098 9171, ⓦwww.daintree-rec.com.au), a superb eco-education centre and forest park with an elevated walkway and a five-level, 23-metre-high observation tower with fabulous views. Climbing to the top, you'll see different species of flora and fauna at different heights, from ground-dwelling brush turkeys and scrub fowl, to the trunk-clinging birdsnest ferns and dun-coloured insectivorous birds of the mid-section, right up to the colourful canopy feeders – wompoo pigeons, metallic starlings, double-eyed fig parrots and flamboyant Ulysses butterflies. You may also be lucky enough to see a cassowary, as there's a high concentration of the birds in this area.

North of here and just before the airstrip, a six-kilometre side road leads through tamed forest, most of which is privately owned and not part of the national park, to **Cow Bay**'s excellent **beach**. Offshore is croc-shaped Snapper Island, an uninhabited chunk of the Great Barrier Reef Marine Park, significant to its traditional owners, the Kuku Yalanji people. You can explore this quiet stretch of coast by sea kayak with *Crocodylus* (see p.609), whose guides have permission to paddle out to the island and bush camp overnight.

The main road continues to **Hutchinson Creek**, which has a couple of good swimming holes within reach of the road bridge, one just downstream and the other reached by wading upstream.

Cooper Creek to Myall Creek

Moving north along the main Cape Tribulation Road, the landscape opens out as you pass a tea plantation at the foot of Mount Hutchinson. Further on, near the mouth of Cooper Creek, you can go **croc-spotting** by boat with Cape Tribulation Wilderness Cruises (A\$23, child A\$16 for a 1hr trip; ☏07 4033 2052, Ⓦwww.capetribcruises.com): the guide knows the creek extremely well, so you have a good chance of seeing several large estuarine crocodiles.

The Cape Tribulation Road meets the coast for the first time at **Thornton Beach**, a beautifully broad expanse of sand scattered with dot-patterns left by crabs and backed by stunningly dramatic forested mountains.

From here it's another few kilometres to the **Marrdja Botanical Walk**, where concrete paths and boardwalks follow Oliver Creek, a tributary of the Noah River, through a mixture of coastal forest to mangroves at the river mouth on **Noah Beach**. Look for spiky wait-a-while (lawyer cane), lianas twisted into corkscrew shapes where they once surrounded a tree, and the spherical pods of the cannonball mangrove – dried and dismembered, they were used as puzzles by Aboriginal peoples, the object being to fit the irregular segments back together.

North of Coconut Beach is the **Cape Trib Shop**, also the base for **Mason's Tours** (☏07 4098 0070, Ⓦwww.masonstours.com.au), who organize 4WD safaris – they publish a very detailed map of the Bloomfield Track to Cooktown, useful if you're heading that way – and local walks with knowledgeable guides. Particularly recommended are their after-dark wildlife walks, looking for snakes, crocodiles, bandicoots and possums. Near the store is a path leading to a natural swimming hole in Myall Creek. Opposite the store, a short track heads through thick forest to **Myall Beach** (see p.612).

Cape Tribulation

Cape Tribulation – a fifty-minute drive from the ferry crossing, and two and a half hours or so in total from Cairns – was named when Captain Cook's vessel hit a reef off shore in June 1770. His black mood saddled the region with a catalogue of gloomy names, including Mount Sorrow and Weary Bay. The cleared area below the steep, forested slopes of **Mount Sorrow** has a café, store, ATM, pharmacy and a **Bat House** (Tues–Sun 10.30am–3.30pm; A\$2), worth a visit to handle tame, orphaned flying foxes.

The coastal area is best explored on foot, for the simple pleasure of walking through the forest with the sea breaking on a beach not five minutes distant. Taking the **path** to the Cape Lookout, you may see brilliantly coloured pittas (small, tailless birds with a buff chest, green back and black-and-rust heads) bouncing around in the leaf litter, or even a crocodile sunning itself on the beach. The nearest beach to the township, **Myall Beach**, is attractive, with communal barbecues; you can walk there via the **Dubuji Boardwalk** which leads off the main road for a 1.2-kilometre-long replay of Marrdja, though with greater botanical variety and some particularly impressive trees. Alternatively, take the Mangrove Boardwalk over the coastal swamp. You can reach Cape Tribulation Beach, north of the headland, from the Kulki Boardwalk. Serious hikers can take the **Mount Sorrow Trail**, which turns off the road at roughly the point where the tarmac ends and leads through the forest to a lookout high up on the mountain; it's a steep ascent, so you should start early in the morning when it's cool, and take enough water to last you for the return trip of up to seven hours.

The area has a good reputation for **adventure activities**; lodge and hostel staff can organize reef trips, horse-riding, mountain biking, river snorkelling, sea kayaking and guided forest walks. Also on offer is the exhilarating experience of zip-lining through the forest, 22m up, with **Jungle Surfing Canopy Tours** (A$80; ℡07 4098 0043, ⓦwww.junglesurfing.com.au). Conducted by highly professional guides well-versed in forest ecology, this is part joy ride, part nature tour, with wonderful elevated views of the trees.

For a more sedate experience, the appealingly eccentric owner of the **Cape Trib Exotic Fruit Farm** (℡07 4098 0057, ⓦwww.capetrib.com.au; A$20) hosts educational fruit-tasting sessions each afternoon at 2pm, followed by an amble through the orchard to see what's fruiting or flowering. Thanks to the rainy equatorial-style microclimate created by Mount Sorrow, it's possible to grow an astounding variety of fruit here, including black sapote, custard apple, mangosteen, sourop and miracle fruit (little berries that temporarily suppress sensitivity to acid – making lime taste sweet and the roughest wine taste like a vintage Shiraz).

Cape Tribulation marks the start of the Bloomfield Track to Cooktown (see p.613). The tarmac gives way to gravel about a kilometre before the *Cape Trib Beach House*, and if you carry on driving, the first waterway you'll have to ford is **Emmagen Creek**, about 6km north of the Cape. This small creek runs halfway up Mount Sorrow and is recommended for its safe swimming holes; following it, you can penetrate the forest in a way that the boardwalks don't allow. However, since crocodiles' movements can be unpredictable, get local advice before setting out.

Eating and drinking

As well as the places listed below, all the hostels and most of the larger hotels have **restaurants** and **bars**, which are open to non-residents. Although plenty of backpackers come here, they tend to be in nature-loving mode; everything shuts down early in the evening, with the bar at *PK's* the only place that sometimes gets rowdy at night.

Daintree Village

Daintree Tea House Daintree Rd, near Daintree Village ℡07 4098 6161. More of a restaurant than a teahouse, this place has an old-fashioned chintzy feel and dedicated staff; the speciality is barramundi, steamed in banana leaves or sauteed in white wine with chives.

Julaymba *Daintree Eco Lodge & Spa*, Daintree Rd, near Daintree Village ℡07 4098 6100. This upmarket restaurant has a short, well-chosen menu of dishes flavoured with rainforest ingredients such as wild lime, torch ginger flower and lemon myrtle. Lunch and dinner.

Papaya Café Stewart St ☎07 4098 6173. One of a clutch of basic, reasonably priced village eateries, this serves wild-caught fish, homemade pies and Asian-style dishes. Lunch daily 11am–3pm, dinner Wed–Sun from 6pm.

Cow Bay and Hutchinson Creek

Cycad *Daintree Wilderness Lodge*, near Hutchinson Creek ☎07 4098 9105, ⓦwww.daintreewilderness lodge.com.au. Intimate restaurant serving dishes such as kangaroo in red wine or rib-eye with portobello mushrooms; main courses are around A$30.

Daintree Ice Cream Company Cape Tribulation Rd, Hutchinson Creek. Roll up here and you'll be handed four scoops of the flavours of the day for A$5. Popular varieties include black sapote and wattleseed; all are made with fruit from the orchard. Daily noon–5pm.

Fanpalm Café Cape Tribulation Rd, Bailey's Creek ☎07 4098 9243. Friendly café-bar with tasty smoothies and wraps, and good, moderately priced evening specials such as curry or cajun chicken salad. Afterwards, allow at least 20min to walk around their fan-palm forest boardwalk. Daily 9am–5pm, dinner Thurs–Sat from 6pm.

Floravilla Corner of Buchanan Creek Rd, Cow Bay ☎07 4098 9100. Licensed garden café offering sandwiches, drinks and ice cream, with a small gallery shop.

Cooper Creek and Noah Creek

Café on Sea Thornton Beach. This licensed café is the only place in the Daintree that is, as the name suggests, right on the beach; it serves light meals, organic coffee, wine and cold beer. Breakfast, lunch and dinner.

Coconut Beach to Cape Tribulation

The Cape *Coconut Beach Resort*, Coconut Beach ☎1300 134 044. Elegant restaurant in an airy timber longhouse, serving gourmet Aussie-Asian specialities. Daily 6–8.30pm.

Cassowary Café *Ferntree Rainforest Lodge*, Camelot Close, Cape Tribulation ☎07 4098 0033, ⓦwww.ferntreerainforestlodge.com.au. Breakfast, pizza and pasta (A$12–24) in an attractive timber pavilion. Daily 7–9.30am and 6–9pm.

Dragonfly Gallery Café Camelot Close, Cape Tribulation ☎07 4098 0121. A wooden stilt-house in a pretty glade, with waterfalls tumbling through the garden, this restaurant uses local produce and has a round table big enough for a party. Breakfast, lunch and dinner.

Myall Creek Takeaway Cape Tribulation Rd, Myall Creek ☎07 4098 0086. Offers simple stop-gaps such as sandwiches, chips and cake, a short walk from the Myall Creek swimming hole.

Whet Cape Tribulation Rd, Cape Tribulation ☎07 4098 0007. Smart and contemporary but a tad pretentious, this place offers gourmet tapas in the afternoons and late evenings, and mains such as barramundi with roast peppers and smoked scallop dumplings for around A$30 at other times.

The Bloomfield Track and Peninsula Developmental Road

There are two overland routes to Cooktown from Mossman: the **coastal route** via the Daintree ferry, Cape Tribulation Road and Bloomfield Track, which takes around three hours in the dry season, but has a rough patch that's impassable after storms; and the longer and less pretty, but easier, **inland route** along the Peninsula Developmental Road via Lakeland, which is tarmac all the way and takes around four hours. With a 4WD, you can circuit the entire region by taking one route north and the other south.

Spanning 80km from Cape Tribulation to where it joins the Cooktown Road at Black Mountain, the **Bloomfield Track** is completely impassable after heavy rain and otherwise requires a **4WD**. The trickiest section is the middle, between **Emmagen Creek** and the **Bloomfield River**: the northern and southern stretches are firm gravel, with no creeks to ford, and can be tackled in an ordinary 2WD car. If you want to cover the whole distance and don't have your own 4WD, you can catch the Country Road Coachlines **bus** (T07 4045 2794, W www.countryroadcoachlines.com.au), which travels up and down the track three times per week on its Cairns–Cooktown run, weather permitting – contact them in advance for a pick-up anywhere along the Cape Tribulation Road.

As you head north, **Emmagen Creek** is the first of several fords, followed by drastic gradients as the road climbs and plunges through virgin rainforest towards the tidal **Bloomfield River**, which has to be crossed at low water. Beyond the **Wujal Wujal Aboriginal community** on the north side, the road flattens out to run past *Haley's Cabins and Camping* (T07 4060 8207, W www.bloomfieldcabins.com; camping A$20, cabin ❷), where there's plentiful camping space and basic cabins. *Home Rule Rainforest Lodge*, at **ROSSVILLE** (T07 4060 3925, W www.home-rule.com.au; camping A$16, room ❶), offers rooms with shared washing and kitchen facilities and inexpensive meals; alternatively, you could splash out on the exclusive *Bloomfield* (T07 4035 9166, W www.bloomfieldlodge.com.au; full board ❼–❽, minimum stay 4 nights), a luxury lodge with a variety of gorgeous timber cottages surrounded by forest. Moving on, it's not far now to the more down-to-earth *Lions Den* **pub** at Helenvale near Black Mountain (see below), about thirty minutes from Cooktown.

The 260-kilometre **Peninsula Developmental Road**, the inland road from the Captain Cook Highway to Cooktown and points north, was only completed in 2006; previously, parts were slow-going gravel. It leaves the highway just before Mossman and climbs to the drier scrub at **MOUNT CARBINE**, a former tungsten mine whose roadhouse and *Mt Carbine Motel* (T07 4094 3108; ❷), with simple but clean roadside rooms, fulfil all basic functions. Next up is the *Palmer River Goldfields Roadhouse* (T07 4060 2020; camping A$16.50), a fuel stop, campground and pub with a tiny museum of gold-mining implements. Further north is the junction stop of **LAKELAND**, with a motel (T07 4060 2142; ❷), an excellent coffee shop (open from 6am) and a fuel station. From here, the Peninsula Developmental Road heads north-west via Laura, while the road to Cooktown continues northeast, past cataracts at the **Annan River Gorge**, and the mysterious **Black Mountain (Kalkajaka)**, two huge dark piles of lichen-covered granite boulders near the road. Aborigines reckon the formation to be the result of a building competition between two rivals fighting over a girl, and tell stories of people wandering into the eerie, whistling caverns, never to return. A more commonplace hazard on the Cooktown road are the cattle, kangaroos and wallabies that venture onto the carriageway; it's best not to drive after dark.

Just south of Black Mountain, it's worth making the four-kilometre detour south along an easy stretch of the Bloomfield Track to the *Lions Den* at **HELENVALE** (T07 4060 3911, W www.lionsdenhotel.com.au; camping A$16–24, safari tent ❷). The *Den* is an old-style pub complete with iron sheeting and beam decor, and nasty exhibits in glass bottles on the piano; it plays up for tourists during the day, but the atmosphere's one-hundred-percent authentic at night. Those with 4WD vehicles can follow the track south to Cape Tribulation (see p.605), while back on the main road it's another twenty minutes to Cooktown, past the birdlife-packed waterholes of **Keatings Lagoon Conservation Park**, just 5km short of town.

Cooktown

COOKTOWN is the East Coast's northernmost town of any size; until very recently, it was beyond the reach of the highway, and it still has an intriguingly idiosyncratic frontier-town feel. The locals take pride in the history of the settlement, and there are echoes of its early prosperity in the broad, though deathly quiet, streets. Much of the workforce has recently been lured northwest to the mines at Weipa, but for those who remain, fishing is a favourite occupation – locals complain that it's impossible to find anyone at work when the barramundi are biting.

Some history

After the *Endeavour* nearly sank at Cape Tribulation in 1770, Captain Cook landed at a natural harbour to the north, where he spent two months repairing the vessel, observing the "Genius, Temper, Disposition and Number of the Natives". There's no truth in the old rumour that he named the kangaroo after an Aboriginal word for "I don't know", but misunderstandings certainly common enough. Tempers wore thin on occasion, as when the crew refused to share a catch of turtles with local Aborigines and Cook commented: "They seem'd to set no value upon any thing we gave them."

The region lay dormant until **gold** was discovered southwest on the **Palmer River** in 1872; within months a harbour was being surveyed at the mouth of the **Endeavour River**, and the tented camp of **Cooktown** was finding its feet. Within two years, it was a boom town. A wild success while gold lasted, the settlement once boasted a main street alive with hotels and a busy port doing brisk trade with Asia through thousands of Chinese prospectors and merchants. But the reserves were soon exhausted and by 1910 Cooktown was on the decline.

Arrival and information

Country Road Coachlines **buses** (℡07 4045 2794, 🌐www.countryroad coachlines.com.au) run three times a week between Cairns and Cooktown along each of the two alternative routes: the coast road via Port Douglas, Cape Tribulation and the Bloomfield Track, and the Peninsula Developmental Road via Mount Molloy and Lakeland.

Cooktown has a **supermarket**, laundromat, fuel stations and a bank with an ATM. The **tourist office**, with helpful, informed staff, is at Nature's PowerHouse in the Botanic Gardens (℡07 4069 6004, 🌐www.cook.qld.gov.au). The only time you might have trouble finding **accommodation** is during the **Discovery Festival** on the Queen's Birthday weekend in early June, which re-enacts Cook's landing – wooden boat, redcoats, muskets and all.

Those moving on up the **Cape York Peninsula** have two options: vehicles other than 4WDs have to head southwest to Lakeland for Laura and points north; stronger sets of wheels can reach Lakefield National Park more directly by heading towards the Hope Vale community and then taking the Battle Camp road. The **last fuel** this way until Musgrave is about 32km from Cooktown at the *Endeavour Falls Tourist Park*, but Cooktown is the last source of fresh provisions before Weipa.

Accommodation

Cooktown Caravan Park 14–16 Hope St ℡07 4069 5536, 🌐www.cooktowncaravan park.com. Leafy, pleasant site for vans, caravans and tents, with Wi-Fi. Camping A$20–25. **Endeavour Falls Tourist Park** ℡07 4069 5431, 🌐www.endeavourfallstouristpark.com.au.

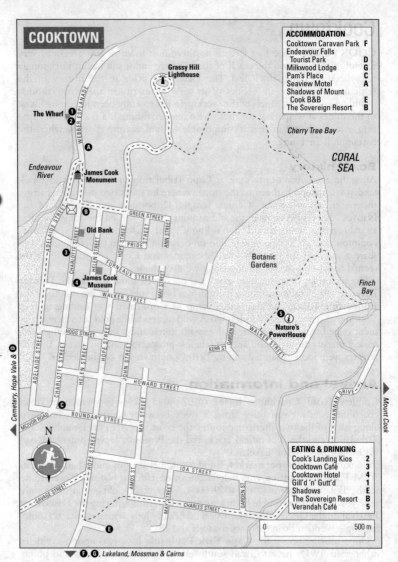

COOKTOWN

ACCOMMODATION
Cooktown Caravan Park   F
Endeavour Falls
   Tourist Park   D
Milkwood Lodge   G
Pam's Place   C
Seaview Motel   A
Shadows of Mount
   Cook B&B   E
The Sovereign Resort   B

Grassy Hill Lighthouse

The Wharf   ❶ ❷

Ⓐ

Endeavour River

James Cook Monument

Cherry Tree Bay

CORAL SEA

Ⓑ

Old Bank

GREEN STREET
HOPE STREET
PRIDE STREET
ANN STREET

❸

WEBBER ESPLANADE

ADELAIDE STREET
CHARLOTTE STREET
HELEN STREET

FURNEAUX STREET

James Cook Museum   ❹

Botanic Gardens

WALKER STREET

MAY STREET

Finch Bay

HOGG STREET

Nature's PowerHouse   ❺ ⓘ

WALKER STREET

KERR ST
GARDEN ST

JOHN STREET
HOPE STREET
HELEN STREET
CHARLOTTE STREET
ADELAIDE STREET

HOWARD STREET

MAY STREET

Ⓒ

BOUNDARY STREET

MCIVOR ROAD

N

Cemetery, Hope Vale & Ⓓ

HANNAN DRIVE

Mount Cook

EATING & DRINKING
Cook's Landing Kios   2
Cooktown Café   3
Cooktown Hotel   4
Gill'd 'n' Gutt'd   1
Shadows   E
The Sovereign Resort   B
Verandah Café   5

IDA STREET
AMOS ST
MAY STREET
GARDEN ST

CHARLES STREET

SAVAGE STREET

Ⓔ

0   500 m

▼ Ⓕ, Ⓖ, Lakeland, Mossman & Cairns

Around 32km northwest of Cooktown via the gravel road to Hope Vale, this family-friendly oasis on the Endeavour River has pine-shaded gardens and a freshwater pool. Camping A\$20–24, cabin ❷
Milkwood Lodge Annan Rd ☏ 07 4069 5007, ⓦ www.milkwoodlodge.com. Two kilometres out of town off the main road, this lodge is hidden on a secluded, forested hillside. Its cabins are a little dated but you feel close to the

wilderness, with good forest and valley views from the verandas. ❹
Pam's Place Corner of Charlotte St & Boundary St ☏ 07 4069 5166, ⓦ www .cooktownhostel.com. With a friendly, community feel, this place has motel units, simple budget rooms, a kitchen and shady grounds that you'll share with noisy birds and orphaned wallabies. Bed in triple room A\$25, private double ❷

Seaview Motel 178 Charlotte St ☎07 4069 5377. Popular with anglers, this two-storey hotel has a pool, and tidy rooms with views of the water. ❸

🏃 Shadows of Mount Cook B&B Off Hope St ☎07 4069 5584, ⓦwww.shadowsof mtcook.com.au. Two delightfully decorated rooms adorned with original art, in a peaceful oasis just

south of town, with a pretty pool and fine, intimate restaurant (see below). ❹

The Sovereign Resort Corner of Charlotte & Green sts ☎07 4043 0500, ⓦwww.sovereign -resort.com.au. Cooktown's upmarket option, *The Sovereign Resort* has spacious rooms, a very attractive pool and a breezy café-bar-restaurant. ❺

The Town

Cooktown's neat, quiet high street, Charlotte Street, is fronted by **Endeavour Park**, the site of Cook's landing, now graced by a statue of the great navigator. Among monuments on the lawn are the remains of defences sent from Brisbane in the nineteenth century to ward off a threatened Russian invasion: one cannon, three cannonballs and two rifles.

The best **views** of the town and river are from the top floor of the old brick-built Sisters of Mercy Convent on Helen Street, now the **James Cook Museum** (daily 9.30am–4pm; A$7.50, child A$2; ☎07 4069 5386), containing a bit of everything, elegantly displayed: artefacts jettisoned from the *Endeavour*; a reconstructed joss house; a display on pearling around Thursday Island; and an account of the "hopelessly insolvent" Cooktown–Laura railway. For further historical photos and artefacts, it's worth dropping in at the **Cooktown Archives** in the Old Bank on Charlotte Street.

There are more views of the district from the red-and-white, corrugated-iron cone of **Grassy Hill Lighthouse**, reached on a concrete track from the end of Hope Street. **Mount Cook** is a rather tougher proposition, a two-hour return hike through thick forest on meagre paths – follow the orange triangles from the nondescript starting point beyond Ida Street. At the end of Walker Street, the **Botanic Gardens** date back to 1880 and are a good place to look for Cooktown orchids, emblem of Queensland, a delicate rose-pink and cream variety. Its education centre, **Nature's PowerHouse**, includes the Charles Tanner Gallery of Cape York Wildlife, the legacy of a passionate local zoologist, and a collection of botanical illustrations (daily 9am–5pm; A$3). The road past the gardens runs down to sandy **Finch Beach** on Cherry Tree Bay; although it's reputedly a safe swimming beach, you should heed the home-made warning signs with a picture of a croc underneath.

Anglers gather at the wharfside at the mouth of the Endeavour River; boat owners in this area charge around A$200 per day for a **sport-fishing** trip.

Just outside town, 500m along Endeavour Valley Road, Cooktown's half-wild **cemetery**, divided into Jewish, Chinese, Protestant and Catholic sections, suggests how cosmopolitan the town once was. The cemetery's most famous resident is **Mary Watson** of Lizard Island, whose grave near the entrance is decorated with seashells and a painting of a pietà.

To learn about the area's Aboriginal history and culture, you can book a walking tour with local enthusiast Willie Gordon at Guurrbi Tours (☎07 4069 6259, ⓦwww.guurrbitours.com), who guides visitors around nearby rock-art sites and chats engagingly about bush tucker and native wildlife (from A$60, child A$30).

Eating and drinking

The best place to **eat and drink** in Cooktown is 🏃 *Shadows* (Tues–Sat from 6.30pm; ☎07 4069 5584) at the *Shadows of Mount Cook B&B*, off Hope Street,

For advice on **swimming** in northern Queensland's coastal waters during the "stinger season", see p.47.

The **Cape York Peninsula** points north towards the Torres Strait and New Guinea, and tackling the rugged tracks and hectic river crossings on the "Trip to the Tip" is an adventure – besides being a means to reach **Australia's northernmost point** and the communities at **Bamaga** and **Thursday Island**, so different from anywhere else in Australia that they could easily be in another country. But it's not all four-wheel driving across the savanna: during the dry season, the wetlands at **Lakefield National Park** and **Laura's** Aboriginal heritage are only a day's journey from Cairns in any decent vehicle. Given longer you might visit the magnificent **Iron Range National Park** and get as far as the mining company town of **Weipa**, but don't go further than this without off-road transport; while some have managed to reach the Tip in family sedans, most who try fail miserably.

Traffic on the peninsula, though sparse, is on the increase with the expansion of Weipa's aluminium and bauxite mining operations. The Queensland government has set aside a large development fund for the Cape York region, so you can expect to see improvements in the region's infrastructure over the coming years.

Practicalities

With thousands making the overland journey between May and October, a breakdown won't necessarily leave you stranded, but the cost of repairs will make you regret it. **Bikers** should travel in groups and have off-roading experience. Those without their own vehicle can take an **overland tour** all the way to Cape York (see box, p.588), or get as far as Cooktown by **bus** (see p.615). It's also possible to travel up to Thursday Island by **cargo ship** (see p.621). **Airlines** serving the Cape from Cairns include Aero-Tropics (℡07 4040 1222, ⊛www.aero-tropics.com.au), Skytrans (℡1800 818 405, ⊛www.skytrans.com.au) and Regional Pacific Airlines (℡07 4040 1400, ⊛www.regionalpacific.com.au). **Daintree Air Services** (℡07 4034 9300, ⊛www.daintreeair.com.au) will fly you up from Cairns for the day by twin-prop plane (A$990); they also offer a four-day flying safari taking in Cooktown, Thursday Island, the Cape, Weipa, Karumba, Lawn Hill and the Undara Lava Tubes (A$3100).

It's not allowed to take a regular rental car beyond Cooktown, where the tarmac ends, but specialist agents can offer fully equipped **4WD vehicles**, suitable for the journey. **Essential items** for any vehicles heading to the Tip include a first-aid kit, a comprehensive tool kit and spares, extra fuel cans, and a tarpaulin for creek crossings. A winch, and equipment for removing, patching and inflating tyres may also come in handy.

which offers fresh, tropical dishes such as mango and avocado salad or local barramundi in herb sauce, in arty surroundings. The *Sovereign* (℡07 4069 5400) has a smart, airy upstairs bar-restaurant with good fish and views of the Endeavour River, and the *Cooktown Hotel* does decent counter meals. The *Verandah Café* at the Botanic Gardens (daily 10am–4pm) is excellent for light lunches, while for something speedy, there are all-day fry-ups at *Cooktown Café* on Charlotte Street, sandwiches and gossip at *Cook's Landing Kiosk* on Webber Espanade, or fish and chips at *Gill'd 'n' Gutt'd* further along (daily till 7.30pm).

Islands north of Cooktown

The northernmost outpost of the Cairns section of the Great Barrier Reef Marine Park is **Lizard Island**, a tiny national park graced by an exclusive resort. Beyond here lies the Far Northern Section, tricky to get to except on

While Cape York's crocodiles make the standard 4WD procedure of walking **creek crossings** before driving them potentially dangerous, wherever possible you should make some effort to gauge the water's depth and find the best route. *Never* blindly follow others across. Make sure all rescue equipment – shovel, winch, rope, and so on – is easy to reach, outside the vehicle. Electrics on petrol engines need to be waterproofed. On deep crossings, block off air inlets to prevent water entering the engine, slacken off the fan belt and cover the radiator grille with a tarpaulin; this diverts water around the engine as long as the vehicle is moving. Select an appropriate gear (changing it in midstream will let water into the clutch) and drive through at walking speed; clear the opposite embankment before stopping again. In deep water, there's a chance the vehicle might float slightly, and so get pushed off-track by the current – though there's not much you can do about this. If you stall, switch off the ignition immediately, exit through windows, disconnect the battery (a short might restart the engine) and winch out. Don't restart the vehicle until you've made sure that water hasn't been sucked in through the air filter – which will destroy the engine.

You'll find a few **roadhouses** and **motels** along the way, with lodges at Musgrave (*Lotus Bird Lodge*; ☏07 4060 3400, ⓦwww.lotusbird.com.au; ⑥), Archer River (*Archer River Roadhouse*; ☏07 4060 3266; ④) and near the Iron Range National Park at Portland Roads (*Portland House*; ☏07 4060 7193, ⓦwww.portlandhouse .com.au; ⑤). Close to the Tip, you'll find en-suite rooms and a pool at *Resort Bamaga* in Bamaga (☏07 4069 3050, ⓦwww.resortbamaga.com.au; ⑤) while in Seisia, the departure point for ferries to Thursday Island in the Torres Strait (see p.621), there's the well-equipped, palm-shaded *Seisia Holiday Park* (☏07 4069 3243 or 1800 653 243, ⓦwww.seisiaholidaypark.com; camping A$20, cabin ④). Between Weipa and Bamaga, accommodation on the Cape is mostly limited to **camping**, and it's inevitable if you head right to the Tip that one night at least will be spent in the bush. Settlements also supply meals and provisions, but there won't be much on offer, so take all you can carry. Don't turn bush campsites into rubbish dumps: take a pack of bin liners and remove all your garbage. **Estuarine crocodiles** are present throughout the Cape: read the warning under "Wildlife dangers" in Basics (p.000). There are few **banks**, so take enough cash to carry you between points – some roadhouses accept plastic. In Cairns, the QPWS office stocks **maps** and brochures on the Cape's national parks, whilst the RACQ (ⓦwww.racq.com) has up-to-date information regarding current road conditions.

an extended voyage by live-aboard: fewer than 9000 visitors a year make it up here, compared to the 900,000 who visit the area around Cairns. Partly thanks to its isolation, the region is rich in pristine coral and rare wildlife, including dugongs and six species of turtle. Like crumbs broken off Australia's northeastern tip, **Thursday Island** and the other **Torres Strait Islands** dot the gap between the Coral Sea and the Arafura Sea.

Lizard Island

There are six continental islands in Lizard Island National Park, the principal of which, **Lizard Island**, is one of the remotest resort islands in Australia, a granite rise covered in stunted trees and grassy heath, 90km north of Cooktown and 30km off shore, within sight of the Outer Reef. **Divers** and **snorkellers** rave about the fringing reef here, the coral in the Blue Lagoon and the clam gardens in Watson's Bay.

Shell middens show that Lizard was regularly visited by Aboriginal peoples, but the island was uninhabited when **Robert Watson** built a cottage and started a beche-de-mer (sea cucumber) processing operation here in the 1870s, accompanied by his wife **Mary** and two Chinese servants, Ah Sam and Ah Leong. Aborigines, affronted at this intrusion on hallowed ground, attacked the house while Robert was at sea in October 1881, killing Ah Leong and forcing Mary, her baby and Ah Sam to flee in a beche-de-mer boiling tank; they survived for nine days before dying of thirst.

The only regular access to Lizard Island is on **flights from Cairns** with Hinterland Aviation (A$398 return; ☎ 07 4035 9323) or with Daintree Air Services (☎ 07 4034 9300, ⊛ www.daintreeair.com.au), who offer day-trips for A$590. It's also possible to charter a helicopter from one of the Cairns-based operators. **Accommodation** is available in a swish but heartbreakingly expensive barefoot-luxury lodge, ⚡ *Voyages Lizard Island* (☎ 1300 134 044, ⊛ www.lizardisland.com.au; full board ⑨), which has private beach houses decorated in a sleek, unfussy, contemporary style, excellent catering, and a dive station.

Alternatively, there's a basic **QPWS campsite** (see p.54 for booking information) on Watson Beach. Campers should be self-sufficient in food and bring charcoal beads for cooking (gas cylinders are not allowed on the plane); there are also communal gas burners at the site. There's a bar (the *Marlin Bar*), but the lodge is off-limits apart from in serious emergencies.

The Torres Strait Islands

The **Torres Strait Islands** are a collection of dozens of populated and uninhabited specks of land that lie scattered across the two-hundred-kilometre-wide **Torres Strait**, which separates Australia from New Guinea. Little **Thursday Island**, the region's administrative centre, is easily reached from Cape York by ferry or from Cairns by air, and offers a fascinating glimpse into an all-but-forgotten corner of Australia whose inhabitants, the **Torres Strait Islanders**, have a very different world view from the country's white population. Thursday Island and its neighbour, **Horn Island**, are the best known of the group, but there's also a resort on remote **Poruma Island** (⊛ www.poruma.com; ⑨).

The strait is named after **Luís Vaez de Torres**, who navigated its waters in 1606; at this time, the different Torres Strait Islands existed in a complicated state of trade and warfare, which was brought to an end when the islanders enthusiastically embraced the arrival of Christianity – known here as the "**Coming of the Light**" – in 1871. **Pearling** (for mother of pearl) was the main source of employment here from this point until after World War II, when the advent of plastics saw the industry collapse and a mass migration of islanders to the Australian mainland. Those who chose to stay formed a movement to establish an Islander Nation, which bore its first fruit on June 3, 1992, when the **Mabo Decision** acknowledged the Merriam as traditional owners of easterly Murray Island, thereby setting a precedent for mainland Aboriginal claims and sending shock waves through the establishment.

Coming over by ferry from the mainland, you pass **Possession Island** and come within sight of a plaque commemorating James Cook's landing here on 22 August 1770, when he planted the flag for George III and Great Britain. Then it's into the shallow channel between Horn Island and **Prince of Wales Island**, the strait's largest, stocked with deer and settled by an overflow population unable to afford Thursday's exorbitant land premiums.

Thursday Island and Horn Island

A three-square-kilometre dot within sight of the mainland, **Thursday Island** wears a few aliases: known simply as TI in day-to-day use, it was coined "Sink of the Pacific" for the variety of peoples who passed through in pearling days, and the local tag is Waiben or (very loosely) "Thirsty Island" – once a reference to the availability of drinking water and now a laconic aside on the quantity of beer consumed. The hotel clock with no hands hints at the pace of life, and it's only for events like Christmas, when wall-to-wall aluminium punts from neighbouring islands make the harbour look like a maritime supermarket car park, that things liven up. Other chances to catch Thursday in carnival spirit are during the annual **Coming of the Light festivities** on July 1, and the full-bore **Island of Origin** rugby-league matches later in the same month – in one year, 25 players were hospitalized, and another killed.

In Thursday Island's town centre, there are traces of the **old Chinatown** district around Milman Street, and a reminder of Queensland's worst shipping disaster in the **Quetta Memorial Church**, way down Douglas Street, built after the ship hit an uncharted rock in the straits in 1890 and went down with virtually all hands onboard. The Aplin Road **cemetery**, where two of the victims are buried, has tiled Islander tombs and depressing numbers of **Japanese graves**, all victims of pearl diving during the early twentieth century. As a by-product of the industry, Japanese crews had accurately mapped the strait before World War II, and it's no coincidence that the airstrip was **bombed** when hostilities were declared in 1942; fortifications are still in place on Thursday's east coast. Bunkers and naval cannon at the **Old Fort** on the opposite side date from the 1890s.

The **Gab Titui Cultural Centre** across from the ferry terminal provides an interesting insight into island affairs and has a daily dance performance (Mon–Sat 9am–5pm, Sun 2–5pm, reduced opening times Jan–Feb; A\$6; ☎07 4090 2130); the town's only **café** is inside.

Horn Island, another small chunk of land surrounded by mangroves and coral, is just a few minutes from Thursday Island's wharf by water taxi (A\$15). It's also the site of an open-cut gold mine and the **regional airport** (with regular flights to and from Cairns). The main reason to take a trip across is to visit the **pearling museum**, run by an ex-diver and stocked with his memorabilia – including an old-fashioned bronze dive helmet.

Practicalities

Ferries to Thursday Island run from Seisia, just south of Cape York, with Peddell's (June–Sept Mon–Sat; Oct–May Mon, Wed & Fri; A\$47, child A\$27.50 one way; ☎07 4069 1551, ⓦwww.peddellsferry.com.au). Peddell's also offer **bus tours** of TI and neighbouring Horn Island. It's also possible to travel up from Cairns aboard the Trinity Bay **cargo ship** (☎07 4035 1234, ⓦwww .seaswift.com.au). The ship departs Cairns at 2pm every Friday, arriving at Horn Island on Sunday morning and Thursday Island in the afternoon. Accommodation is in air-conditioned four-bed cabins, which cost from A\$500 per person; taking along a 4WD vehicle costs an additional A\$690.

Flying, Aero-Tropics (☎07 4040 1222, ⓦwww.aero-tropics.com.au) and Regional Pacific Airlines (☎07 4040 1400, ⓦwww.regionalpacific.com.au) both serve Thursday Island Airport (TIS) on Horn Island daily from Cairns via Bamaga, with water-taxi connections over to nearby Thursday Island. To get to Poruma Island, you'll need to book a charter flight from Cairns or Horn Island through the resort (see p.620).

Thursday's **wharf** sits below the colonial-style Customs House, a minute from the **town centre** on Douglas Street. Here you'll find a post office with payphones, a **bank** and two of the island's **bars**: the *Torres* just beats the neighbouring *Royal* as Australia's northernmost. Facing the water on Victoria Parade, there are clean **lodgings** at the *Federal Hotel* (℡07 4069 1569, Ⓦwww.federalhotelti.com.au; ❺), while on Douglas Street, *Mura Mudh* (℡07 4069 2050; ❶) is a cheap and cheerful **hostel** run by Thursday Islanders. **Horn Island**'s sole place to stay and eat is the *Gateway Torres Strait Resort* (℡07 4069 2222, Ⓦwww.torresstrait.com.au; ❹).

Travel details

Trains

Cairns to: Ayr (5 weekly; 9hr); Bowen (5 weekly; 11hr); Brisbane (5 weekly; 31hr); Bundaberg (5 weekly; 24hr); Caboolture (5 weekly; 30hr); Cardwell (5 weekly; 4hr); Gladstone (5 weekly; 22hr); Ingham (5 weekly; 4hr); Innisfail (5 weekly; 2hr); Kuranda (twice daily; 1hr 45min); Mackay (5 weekly; 14hr); Proserpine (5 weekly; 12hr); Rockhampton (5 weekly; 8hr); Townsville (5 weekly; 7hr); Tully (5 weekly; 3hr).

Ingham to: Ayr (5 weekly; 3hr 30min); Bowen (5 weekly; 5hr 30min); Brisbane (5 weekly; 25hr 30min); Bundaberg (5 weekly; 17hr 45min); Caboolture (5 weekly; 24hr 30min); Cairns (5 weekly; 4hr); Cardwell (5 weekly; 1hr); Gladstone (5 weekly; 16hr 30min); Innisfail (5 weekly; 3hr 15min); Mackay (5 weekly; 8hr 45min); Proserpine (5 weekly; 6hr 30min); Rockhampton (5 weekly; 15hr); Townsville (5 weekly; 2hr); Tully (5 weekly; 1hr 45min).

Townsville to: Ayr (6 weekly; 1hr 30min); Bowen (6 weekly; 3hr); Brisbane (6 weekly; 23hr); Bundaberg (6 weekly; 17hr); Caboolture (6 weekly; 22hr); Cairns (5 weekly; 7hr); Cardwell (5 weekly; 3hr); Gladstone (6 weekly; 14hr 30min); Ingham (5 weekly; 2hr); Innisfail (5 weekly; 5hr); Mackay (6 weekly; 6hr 30min); Proserpine (6 weekly; 4hr 30min); Rockhampton (6 weekly; 12hr); Tully (5 weekly; 4hr).

Buses

Cairns to: Airlie Beach (5 daily; 11hr); Atherton Tablelands (twice daily Mon–Fri); Ayr (5 daily; 7hr 30min); Brisbane (5 daily; 28hr 30min); Bundaberg (6 daily; 20hr 30min); Cape Tribulation (twice daily; 5hr); Cardwell (6 daily; 3hr); Childers (5 daily; 23hr); Cooktown (up to 6 weekly; 12hr); Hervey Bay (5 daily; 24hr); Ingham (6 daily; 3hr 30min); Innisfail (6 daily; 1hr 15min); Mackay (5 daily; 13hr); Mission Beach (4 daily; 2hr 30min); Noosa (twice daily; 27hr 30min); Port Douglas (twice daily;

2hr); Rockhampton (5 daily; 17hr 30min); Townsville (6 daily; 6hr); Tully (6 daily; 2hr 45min).

Mission Beach to: Airlie Beach (6 daily; 8hr); Ayr (5 daily; 5hr 30min); Brisbane (5 daily; 26hr 25min); Bundaberg (5 daily; 20hr); Cairns (4 daily; 2hr 30min); Cardwell (5 daily; 1hr); Childers (4 daily; 21hr); Hervey Bay (5 daily; 21hr); Ingham (5 daily; 2hr); Innisfail (5 daily; 1hr); Mackay (6 daily; 10hr 30min); Noosa (twice daily; 25hr); Rockhampton (4 daily; 16hr); Townsville (5 daily; 3hr 30min); Tully (5 daily; 30min).

Townsville to: Airlie Beach (6 daily; 4hr); Ayr (5 daily; 1hr); Brisbane (5 daily; 24hr); Bundaberg (5 daily; 15hr 30min); Cairns (5 daily; 6hr); Cardwell (5 daily; 2hr); Childers (5 daily; 18hr); Hervey Bay (5 daily; 19hr); Ingham (5 daily; 1hr 30min); Innisfail (5 daily; 4hr 30min); Mackay (6 daily; 6hr 30min); Mission Beach (5 daily; 3hr 30min); Noosa (twice daily; 17hr); Rockhampton (twice daily; 11hr); Tully (5 daily; 3hr).

Ferries

Cairns to: Thursday Island (weekly; 36hr).
Cape York to: Thursday Island (Mon–Fri 2 daily; 1hr 15min–2hr).
Cardwell to: Hinchinbrook Island (twice daily; 1–2hr).
Mission Beach to: Dunk Island (10 or more daily; 15min).
Townsville to: Magnetic Island (10 or more daily; 45min).

Flights

Cairns to: Bamaga (daily; 1hr 45min); Bundaberg (twice daily; 4hr 50min); Cooktown (daily; 45min); Dunk Island (daily; 45min); Lizard Island (twice daily; 1hr); Mackay (twice daily; 2hr 45min); Proserpine (6 weekly; 2hr); Rockhampton (twice daily; 3hr); Thursday Island/Horn Island (1–2 daily; 2hr); Townsville (twice daily; 1hr); Weipa (daily; 1hr 15min).
Townsville to: Cairns (twice daily; 1hr); Mackay (4 daily; 1hr); Rockhampton (twice daily; 1hr 50min).

Contexts

Contexts

Early history

I t's difficult for visitors to Australia's **East Coast** to form an idea of the pre-colonial era, as two centuries of European rule shattered traditional Aboriginal life, and evidence of those earlier times mostly consists of cryptic art sites and legends. As soon as the Europeans arrived in the late eighteenth century, they made the East Coast their power centre, and the region remains the seat of government and the principal focus of national development.

The following account covers the early years of the **Aboriginal and European presence** in the region, up to Federation in 1901. Histories of the cities of **Melbourne**, **Sydney** and **Brisbane** are given on pp.88, 210 and 438, and further information on **Aboriginal history** appears on p.630.

Origins

After the break-up of the supercontinent **Gondwana** into India, Africa, South America, Australasia and Antarctica, Australia moved away from the South Pole, reaching its current geographical location about fifteen million years ago. Though the mainland was periodically joined to New Guinea and Tasmania, there was never a land link with the rest of Asia. Successive Ice Ages dried out the climate; by six thousand years ago, the oceans had stabilized at their present levels and Australia's environment was much as it appears today: an arid centre with a relatively fertile eastern seaboard.

Decades of archeological work, the reports of early settlers, and oral tradition have established that **Aboriginal people** have lived in Australia for at least forty thousand years. The early arrivals most likely took advantage of low sea levels to cross the Timor Trough into northern Australia, or island-hop from Indonesia onto what is now the Cape York Peninsula via New Guinea. Exactly when this happened, how many times it happened and what they did next are debatable. The oldest known remains from central Australia are only 22,000 years old, so it's possible that initial colonization occurred around the coast, followed by later exploration of the interior.

The earliest inhabitants used crude **stone implements**, gradually replaced by a more refined technology based around lighter tools, **boomerangs**, and the use of core stones to flake blanks, which were then fashioned into spearheads, knives and scrapers. As only certain types of stone were suitable for the process, tribes living further away from quarries had to trade with those living near them. **Trade networks** for rock, **ochre** (a red clay used for ceremonial purposes) and other products – shells and even wood for canoes – eventually stretched from New Guinea to the heart of the continent, following river systems away from the coast. **Rock art**, preserved in an ancient engraved tradition, and other more recent painted styles, seem to indicate that cultural links also travelled along these trade routes – similar symbols and styles are found in widely separated regions.

It's probable that the disappearance of Australia's prehistoric megafauna was accelerated by Aboriginal hunting, but the most dramatic change wrought by the original Australians was the controlled use of **fire** to clear areas of forest. Burning promoted new growth and encouraged game, indirectly expanding grassland and favouring certain plants – cycads, grasstrees, banksias and eucalypts – which evolved fire-reliant seeds and growth patterns. But while the Aboriginal people modified the environment for their own ends, their belief that land, wildlife and people were an interdependent whole engendered a sympathy for natural processes, and maintained a balance between the population and natural resources.

Tribes were organized and related according to complex kinship systems, reflected in the three hundred different **languages** known to exist at that time. Legends about the mythical **Dreamtime**, when creative forces shaped the landscape, provided verbal maps of tribal territory and linked natural features to the actions of these Dreamtime ancestors, who often had both human and animal forms. This spiritual and practical attachment to tribal areas was expedient in the use of resources, but was the weak point in maintaining a culture after white dispossession – separated from the lands they related to, legends lost their meaning, and the people their sense of identity.

Cook and the Endeavour

In 1768, **Lieutenant James Cook** (later Captain Cook) set sail from Plymouth aboard the *Endeavour* with a commission from the Royal Society to observe the 1769 Transit of Venus in the South Pacific, and additional instructions to locate **Terra Australis Incognita**, the "Unknown Southern Land"

▲ James Cook Statue, Cooktown

charted on maps acquired in the captured Spanish port of Manila in the Philippines, six years earlier. With him on the *Endeavour* were botanists Joseph Banks and Daniel Solander. Voyaging via Brazil and Tierra del Fuego to Tahiti, where the transit was duly recorded, the expedition proceeded to map New Zealand's coastline before continuing west.

The crew first sighted the East Coast in April 1770 and sailed north from Cape Everard, with Cook naming their first landing place **Botany Bay** after the interesting specimens Banks and Solander collected there: flowering plants were so profuse they assumed the bay would make good, fertile ground for later settlement. On their arrival, they had been confronted by two Eora Aborigines armed with spears but drove them off with musket fire. The party continued north up the Queensland coast, passing Moreton Bay and Fraser Island before entering the treacherous passages of the Great Barrier Reef where, on June 11, the *Endeavour* ran aground north of a point that Cook named **Cape Tribulation**, "because here begun all our troubles". Cook managed to beach the ship safely at the mouth of the Endeavour River (present-day **Cooktown**), where the expedition set up camp while the ship was repaired.

Contact between Aborigines and whites during the following six weeks was tinged with a mistrust that never quite erupted into antagonism, and Cook took the opportunity to make notes in which he tempered romanticism for the "noble savage" with the sharp observation that European and Aboriginal values were mutually incomprehensible. The expedition was intrigued by some of Australia's wildlife, but otherwise unimpressed with the country, and were glad to sail onwards on August 5. With imposing skill, Cook successfully managed to navigate the rest of the reef, finally claiming possession of the country – which he named **New South Wales** – for King George III on August 21, 1770, at Possession Island in the Torres Strait, before sailing off to Timor.

The convict colonies

The expedition's reports didn't arouse much enthusiasm in London. However, after the loss of its American colonies following the **American War of Independence** in 1783, Britain was deprived of a handy location to offload convicted criminals. They were temporarily housed in prison ships or "hulks", moored around the country, while the government tried to solve the problem. **Sir Joseph Banks**, botanist on the *Endeavour*, advocated Botany Bay as an ideal location for a **penal colony** that could soon become self-sufficient. The government agreed (perhaps also inspired by the political advantages of gaining a foothold in the Pacific), and in 1787 the **First Fleet**, packed with over seven hundred convicts, set sail for Australia on eleven ships under the command of **Captain Arthur Phillip**. Reaching Botany Bay in January 1788, Phillip deemed it unsuitable and instead proceeded to **Camp Cove**, on Port Jackson's fine natural harbour, landing on January 26, 1788; it was here that they founded the settlement of **Sydney**.

Sydney's early years were unpromising: the colonists suffered erratic weather and starvation, Aboriginal hostility, soil that was too hard to plough, and timber so tough it dented their axes. In 1790, supplies ran so low that a third of the population had to be transferred to a new colony on **Norfolk Island**, 1600km northeast. Even so, in the same year, Britain dispatched a second fleet with a thousand more convicts – 267 of whom died en route. To ease the situation, Phillip granted packages of farmland to marines and former convicts before he returned to Britain in 1792. The first **free settlers** arrived the following year, and Britain's preoccupation with the French Revolutionary Wars meant a reduction in the number of convicts being transported to the colony, thus allowing a period of consolidation, and further exploration – **Matthew Flinders** explored the coastline south of Sydney in 1796, travelled north to Moreton Bay and Hervey Bay in 1798, and circumnavigated the entire continent between 1800 and 1803, charting it scrupulously and proposing a name for it: "**Australia**".

In the early 1800s, the foundations of the New South Wales wool industry were laid with the import of livestock from South Africa, but corruption set in, coming to a head in 1808 when **John Macarthur**, controller of the colony's illicit rum trade, ousted **Governor William Bligh** (former captain of the *Bounty*) in an uprising dubbed the **Rum Rebellion**. Britain responded by appointing the firm-handed **Colonel Lachlan Macquarie**, backed by the 73rd Regiment, as Bligh's replacement in 1810. Macquarie settled the various disputes – Macarthur had fled to Britain a year earlier – and brought eleven years of disciplined progress to the colony.

Labelled the "Father of Australia", for his vision of a country that could rise above its convict origins, Macquarie implemented enlightened policies towards former convicts or **emancipists**, enrolling them in public offices. He also attempted to educate, rather than exterminate, Aboriginal people and was the driving force behind New South Wales becoming a productive, self-sufficient colony. But he offended the landowner **squatters**, who were concerned that emancipists were being granted too many favours, and also those who regarded the colony solely as a place of punishment. In fact, conditions had improved so much that by 1819 New South Wales had become the major destination for voluntary emigrants from Britain.

In 1821, Macquarie was replaced as governor, and his successor, **Sir Thomas Brisbane**, was instructed to segregate, not integrate, convicts. To this end, when New South Wales officially graduated from being a penal settlement to a new British colony in 1823, the convicts were packed off to newly explored regions, as far away from Sydney's free settlers as possible. In 1824, the year the British Admiralty officially adopted the name "Australia" for the continent, John Oxley, the Surveyor General, chose the **Brisbane River** as the site of a new penal settlement; within fourteen years, free settlers also began to move there. Meanwhile, townships had been founded elsewhere around the coast including, in 1835, a settlement on the **Yarra River** that went on to become Melbourne. In the 1850s, the regions to the north and south of present-day New South Wales broke away to become independent states: **Victoria** in 1851, and **Queensland** in 1859.

While the relationship between the British and the Aboriginal people started reasonably amicably, it soured as the tribes began to realize the newcomers were depriving them of natural resources: Governor Phillip reported that "the natives now attack any straggler they meet unarmed". Forced off their traditional hunting grounds, which were taken by the settlers for agriculture or grazing, Aboriginal groups began stealing crops and spearing cattle. Response from the British was brutal: **"dispersals"** – a euphemism for violent assaults and even massacres – became commonplace wherever indigenous people resisted white intrusion. Insidious methods such as poisoning waterholes or lacing gifts of flour with arsenic were also employed by pastoralists angered over stock losses. The Aboriginal people were not a single, unified society, and in 1837 the British exploited existing divisions by creating the notorious **Native Mounted Police**, an Aboriginal force that aided and abetted the extermination of rival groups.

Gold, nationalism and Federation

The discovery of **gold** in 1851 by Edward Hargraves, fresh from the California fields, had a dramatic bearing on Australia's future. The first major strikes in New South Wales and Victoria brought an immediate rush of hopeful miners from Sydney and Melbourne and, once the news spread overseas, from the

USA and Britain. The British government, realizing the absurdity of spending taxes on shipping criminals to a land of gold when there were plenty of people willing to pay for their passage, finally **ended transportation** in 1853.

A new "level society", based on a work-and-mateship ethic, evolved on the goldfields, where education had little bearing on an ability to endure hard work and spartan living conditions. Yet the **diggers** were all too aware of their poor social and political rights. At the end of 1854, frustrations over mining licences erupted at **Eureka**, on the outskirts of Ballarat in Victoria, where miners built a stockade and ended up being charged by mounted police. Twenty-two of the miners were killed in the event, which is commonly regarded as a turning point in Australian history. The surviving rebels – put on trial for high treason – were vindicated, and rights, including the vote, were granted to miners.

The Victorian goldfields also saw **racial tensions** directed against a new minority, the **Chinese**, who first arrived there during the 1850s. Disheartened by diminishing returns and infuriated by the Chinese ability to find gold in abandoned claims, diggers stormed a Chinese camp at **Lambing Flat** in 1861. Troops had to be sent in to stop the riots, but the ringleaders were later acquitted by an all-white jury. The general resentment towards the Chinese went unchallenged, despite the fact that they improved life by running stores and market gardens in mining towns.

Throughout the country, **nationalism** and its bitter side, racial discrimination, were on the increase. Citing a perversion of Darwinian theory that held that Aboriginal people were less evolved than whites and so doomed to extinction, most states began to follow Tasmania's example of "**protection**" (see p.631), relocating Aborigines into reserves that were frequently a long way from their traditional lands – in Queensland, for instance, Rockhampton Aborigines were moved to Fraser Island, 500km away. Ostensibly to prevent slavery, but driven by recession and growing white unemployment, the Queensland government forced the repatriation of the **Solomon Islanders** who had been shipped in to work on the sugar plantations, and taxed the Chinese out of the country.

By the 1890s, the state governors were beginning to see the advantages to **Federation**, not least as a way to control indentured labour and present a united front against French, German and Russian expansion in the Pacific. A decade of wrangling to ensure equal representation irrespective of population saw the formation of a **High Court** and a two-tier **parliamentary system** consisting of a House of Representatives and Senate, presided over by a Prime Minister. Each state would have its own premier, and Britain would be represented by a Governor-General. Approved by Queen Victoria shortly before her death, the **Commonwealth of Australia** came into being on January 1, 1901.

Society

Modern Australian **society**, though dominated by white, English-speaking communities with Western attitudes and ideologies, is composed of individuals from many different ethnic backgrounds. Unlike most other nations, in Australia, citizens who consider themselves indigenous are a tiny minority – around 2.5 percent – and attempts to correct their marginalization are a major political and social preoccupation. Of the remainder of the population, around 24 percent were born overseas; the rest can trace their heritage to a vast array of different nations. East Coast Australia is highly **urbanized**: the majority of the region's residents live in the state capitals Melbourne, Canberra, Sydney and Brisbane, or their suburbs, with most of the rest concentrated in the provincial coastal towns.

Indigenous Australians

Despite evident diversity in appearance, language and custom, the first white Australians didn't distinguish between the country's indigenous peoples, lumping them together under the generic name Aborigines. They also largely ignored the tribes' intimate relationship with the land, an accord that had enabled them to survive Australia's challenging conditions for many thousands of years. These days, some individuals consider Aborigine to be a derogatory label and prefer the terms **indigenous Australians** or **Aboriginal people** and **Torres Strait Islanders**, while clearer channels of communication mean that each community, be they urbanized Koories from Melbourne or Sydney or the rural Guugu Yimithirr of Far North Queensland, can find an individual voice. Very loosely woven cultural and linguistic threads link these groups, but their main point of commonality lies in the long-running struggle to improve their communities' health, education and economic prospects, factors that overshadow the undisputed richness of their cultural heritage.

Colonial attitudes

Estimates suggest that Australia had 750,000 indigenous inhabitants prior to colonization. Captain James Cook, exploring the East Coast in 1770, noted the Aboriginal presence, but saw no evidence of them using the land in a manner that implied ownership; he therefore declared the continent **terra nullius**, or unclaimed wasteland, available for appropriation. From the arrival of the First Fleet in 1788, indigenous Australians were gradually dispossessed of their lands and livelihoods – and, in many cases, their lives – at the hands of the British colonists.

A shortage of documentation makes it hard to measure the full pattern of events, but historians estimate that twenty thousand Aborigines may have died in unrecorded **battles**, sparked by attempts to defend their traditional sources of food and water. Many more perished from European **diseases**, such as smallpox, to which they had no immunity: the diaries of the First Fleet record the rapid decimation of the Aboriginal camps in the Sydney hinterland. Those who survived, fled, unwittingly infecting neighbouring groups as they went; when Governor Hunter made an exploratory expedition to western New

South Wales in the 1820s, he recorded evidence of smallpox epidemics among Aboriginal groups who had not previously come into contact with Europeans.

As **farming and settlement** expanded during the nineteenth and twentieth centuries, so did the pressure on food and water supplies: livestock such as cattle, goats, sheep and rabbits between them reduced fragile pastures to dustbowls, while other introduced animals such as foxes and cats hunted native animal species that had traditionally sustained the Aboriginal people.

In the late nineteenth century, indigenous Australians began to be subjected to systematic imprisonment under the guise of **protection** from the devastating impact of colonization. However, parliamentary records of the time suggest the Europeans felt that they needed to be shielded from the Aborigines, rather than vice versa, and this was the motivation behind the appointment of official Protectors, who removed indigenous Australians to apartheid-style rural reserves. In some cases, these were on traditional lands, allowing people to continue to live relatively undisturbed. Elsewhere, notably Queensland, people were forcibly removed from their home areas and relocated, breaking up families and shattering spiritual and physical ties with the land. The indigenous Australians were the wards of their so-called protectors, and, despite not being recorded as part of the population, they required permits to marry or to move from one reserve to another. Aboriginal children fathered by Europeans but born to black mothers were removed and put into state institutions or with white foster parents as part of a policy of assimilation that produced a sub-group known as the **Stolen Generations**: some received exemplary care, but many, inevitably, suffered extreme cultural disorientation. This treatment persisted in some areas until the late 1960s, and its aftermath still haunts the Aboriginal community today.

Voting and land rights

The revitalization of Aboriginal people and their culture effectively began in 1967, when a constitutional referendum overwhelmingly endorsed the rights of indigenous Australians as **voting citizens**, and gave the federal government the power to legislate for Aboriginal people. The referendum ushered in a new era of **self-determination**, evidenced by the establishment of the first Ministry for Aboriginal Affairs in the Whitlam Labor Government of 1972–75. After more than a hundred years of agitation, **land rights** were accorded to Aboriginal groups in the Northern Territory in 1976 under federal legislation. Since then, other states have legislated to vest title over various pieces of state-owned land to their traditional Aboriginal owners. All the mainland states and territories now have provisions for Aboriginal land rights.

Along with ownership of land – and some control over funding – came opportunities for economic self-sufficiency, enterprise and expansion previously unavailable to Aboriginal groups. Some turned their attention specifically to **land management**: cooperative agreements with the Australian Nature Conservation Agency led in 1985 to Aboriginal ownership and joint management of two of Australia's most important conservation reserves – Uluru–Kata Tjuta and Kakadu national parks in the Northern Territory. These arrangements recognize that Aboriginal owners retain an enormous understanding about the ecology of their traditional lands.

However, the spectre of *terra nullius* persisted until the High Court judged in the 1992 **Mabo** case that native title to land existed in Australia unless it had been extinguished by statute or by some use of the land that was inconsistent with the continuation of native use and ownership. The **Wik Decision** of 1996 went a step further, acknowledging that native title also exists on pastoral leases, though with the proviso that "pastoral interest will prevail over native title rights, wherever the two conflict".

Citizenship and social problems

Despite these successes, indigenous Australians have continued to face considerable disadvantages. Along with citizenship in 1967 came **unemployment** (black workers were now entitled to a wage, but few station owners were willing to pay them the same as white people), together with the legal right to purchase **alcohol**, a disastrous combination. Institutionalized welfarism compounded feelings of futility and ethnic shame, and substance abuse was – and still is – heavily implicated in the destructive spiral often observed by visitors to Aboriginal communities. The negative repercussions were evident in sickness and death, violence and despair, exclusion from education, and families in disarray.

Successive federal governments set up various representative bodies, including the notorious **Aboriginal and Torres Strait Islanders Commission** (ATSIC; 1990–2004). This statutory authority gave elected Aboriginal representatives effective control over many of the federal funding programmes directed at Aboriginal organizations and communities, including employment schemes and improved health education. Running at around A$2 billion per annum, this should have seen Aboriginal people thriving right across Australia. The reality was entirely different: corruption, nepotism and flawed or hare-brained projects all helped bring about ATSIC's abolition and a return to greater federal government control.

The vast over-representation of Aboriginal people in the criminal justice system, largely as a result of alcohol-related crime, compounded community fragmentation. In 1991, the **Royal Commission into Aboriginal Deaths in Custody** called for wide-ranging changes in police and judicial practice, and for social programmes aimed at improving Aboriginal health, education, economic prospects and empowerment. But despite considerable government lip-service to these recommendations, they didn't result in any substantial change to incarceration rates.

Poor health continues to substantially reduce the life expectancy of Aboriginal people: on average, non-indigenous Australians live seventeen years longer than Aboriginal Australians. A survey released by the Australian Bureau of Statistics in 2006 revealed that 22 percent of Aboriginal people considered themselves in fair health at best. Seven percent felt seriously depressed, and 65 percent had at least one long-term health problem such as trouble with vision or hearing, asthma or diabetes; the figures for other Australians are considerably lower on all counts.

On the **positive** side, many families and communities are confronting the problems that alcohol is causing. Between them they are putting pressure on problem drinkers to limit their drinking, and are now able to implement new laws to reduce the damage alcohol is doing to the people around them.

Reconciliation

The process of reconciliation with an emphasis on **rights**, as initiated in the early 1990s by the Labor government under Paul Keating, was always anathema to John Howard, prime minister from 1996 to 2007. As he saw it, "symbolic measures" such as an official national apology or treaty were an insult to the present generation of non-Aboriginal people who were not responsible for past mistakes, and did nothing to address problems in Aboriginal communities such as alcoholism, appalling health, and lack of access to education. Instead, in 1998 he launched a programme of "**practical reconciliation**" based around the delivery of improved welfare services through mainstream channels: to this end, he pledged A$63 million over four years for counselling and "link-up" services for those who had been removed from their families, though, thanks to the dubious practices of the ATSIC, not all of this filtered through.

In 2004, "**mutual obligation**" and "**shared responsibility**" became the new buzzwords: Aboriginal communities were invited to sign voluntary **Shared Responsibility Agreements** (SRAs) with the government, committing to positive behaviour or actions – such as better attention to general hygiene or school attendance – in exchange for funding for specified community-infrastructure needs such as the installation of petrol bowsers or a new swimming pool. Though considered patronizing by some, SRAs produced positive results and at first glance, seemed an efficient, common-sense system – no more wasteful one-size-fits-all solutions. However, their success was hampered by a confusing and costly bureaucratic structure with inadequate mechanisms to check whether community responsibilities are fulfilled and funds fairly distributed.

In the run-up to the **2007 federal election**, both Liberal-National Coalition leader John Howard and his Australian Labor Party opponent Kevin Rudd built carefully worded pledges into their election campaigns – Howard said he would hold a referendum on whether the rights of indigenous Australians should be enshrined in the constitution, while Rudd made a commitment to narrowing the gap between indigenous and non-indigenous Australians in health, education and economic development. Both skirted the unpopular issue of **financial compensation** for past injustices. Within months of taking office, Prime Minister Kevin Rudd made history when, on February 13, 2008, speaking on behalf of the Australian parliament, he issued a **formal apology** to all indigenous Australians over the Stolen Generations. It was a cathartic moment for many, but for indigenous leaders bent on reparations, it did not go nearly far enough.

National identity

In just a few generations, Australia has morphed from a country that used to pride itself on its **Britishness** – or, more accurately, its quirky, independent-minded brand of Britishness – into a multicultural, highly urbanized society defined at least in part by its ethnic and ideological **diversity**. Many of the trappings of colonial heritage still exist: a language that, though peppered with idiosyncratic words and expressions, hails from the "mother country"; national institutions, from parliament to the ABC, which follow a British model; and Queen Elizabeth II, who – inexplicably to some – remains the country's sovereign. The first **migrants** to make Australia their home – some willingly, some unwillingly, transported here for at least five years each as punishment for crimes as petty as stealing handkerchiefs, or for life in the case of serious assault – were almost all English, and as recently as the 1930s, around 98 percent of new settlers still came from the UK. But since World War II, Australia has welcomed successive waves of labour migrants and refugees from other territories, in particular from Italy, Ireland, Greece, Lebanon, Turkey, Vietnam, Poland and China.

Today, only six percent of the population were born in the UK, and fifteen percent speak a language other than English at home. The people that make up modern Australia are the offspring of individuals from well over one hundred different nations, and the country records a net gain of more than 180,000 new immigrants a year – which averages more than one every three minutes. On the East Coast, many settle in cultural pockets – there are strong, localized **Greek** and **Jewish** communities in Melbourne, numerous ethnic quarters in Sydney, and vibrant **Chinese** communities in Melbourne, Sydney and Brisbane – but integration is on the increase. **Italians**, the first group of continental Europeans to arrive in large numbers, have a particularly strong presence, with Italian the most taught and studied modern language in Australian schools. The Asian and Pacific nations – Australia's natural trading partners – are also strongly represented. With cultural integration has come a general shift in lifestyles and tastes; one example that's immediately obvious to visitors is the Australian passion for good coffee and fusion cooking, inspired by Mediterranean and Asian influences.

The more complex the cultural mosaic, the more elusive, inevitably, the definition of **national identity** becomes. Nonetheless, there are a number of qualities and values that Australians themselves consider particularly Australian. Core to these are the concepts of egalitarianism and a "**fair go**", whereby every individual has the right to make the best of any opportunity that comes their way, and "**mateship**", a fierce loyalty to one's peers. Active participation in society is considered essential: this is a country where voting has been compulsory in all states since 1942. Australians also have a strong anti-establishment streak and a healthy mistrust of misplaced authority; even in business, attitudes are as informal and relaxed as practicality allows. Inevitably, some of these qualities have a downside – the Australian belief in egalitarianism and anti-elitism can foster mediocrity and anti-intellectualism, as few wish to be seen as overachievers. Social commentators scratch their heads in despair at the tendency for ordinary Australians to hold their sportsmen in far higher regard than their noteworthy painters and Nobel-prize-winning scientists. Meanwhile, relaxed, "no worries – she'll be right" attitudes can sometimes translate as fatalism, heartlessness or insensitivity.

Perhaps because of a deep-seated discomfort about certain elements of their early history, or perhaps because the harshness of the natural environment has honed the collective survival instinct, Australians have a relish for competition; and as a young nation in a remote corner of the globe, they have a heightened need to prove themselves. One manifestation of this is an ever-increasing use of the stiflingly judgmental term "**un-Australian**": forcefully applied to an individual, organization or policy exhibiting socially unacceptable qualities, this has become the ultimate insult, more wounding than any profanity.

Sport

A ustralians are **sports** mad. The overwhelming majority love the outdoors and enjoy a challenge, making training, playing and spectating popular ways to spend time. A collective desire for recognition and respect in the outside world means that Australians take **international sporting events** extremely seriously, and are highly successful: it's been claimed that their gold-and-green-garbed representatives achieve more victories per capita than any other nation. At home, any fixture – be it from Aussie Rules football to cane-toad racing – always draws an enthusiastic crowd, ready for a good bout of barracking, followed by some hard partying once the final whistle blows. Thousands more gather round to watch the action on TV.

Two of the apparent paradoxes of the national psyche – a fiercely competitive nature, set against an ardent belief in egalitarianism, mateship and the right to a fair go – make Australians **natural team players**. There are few people an Australian admires more than the supremely gifted sportsman or woman who excels without unseemly effort, yet downplays their talent and lives a modest life – cricketing hero Don Bradman, swimmer Dawn Fraser, runner Cathy Freeman, speed skater Steven Bradbury and cyclist Ryan Bayley are all perfect examples.

The chance to see excellence in action draws people to stadiums and screens up and down the East Coast, with **Aussie Rules** the biggest crowd-puller in Victoria, and **rugby league** the sport of heroes in New South Wales and Queensland; these are followed, in order of general preference, by cricket, tennis, horse racing, motor sports, rugby union, basketball, football (soccer) and netball. Even unpromising-sounding activities such as **surf lifesaving** events and **yacht racing** are tremendously popular – lifesavers hold entertaining annual regional carnivals at which teams compete in a series of gruelling races through the water, while in Sydney Harbour, the start of the Sydney-to-Hobart yacht race just after Christmas is cause for a massive social event.

Football

Australian Rules football, better known as **Aussie Rules** or just footy, is an extraordinary, anarchic, no-holds-barred, eighteen-a-side brawl related to Gaelic football. The game is huge in Melbourne, home of the **Australian Football League** (AFL; ⊛www.afl.com.au), but less popular north of the Victorian border, where it's sometimes dismissed as "aerial ping pong". The season runs through the winter from March, culminating in two teams battling it out for the AFL Flag at the **Grand Final** in September. Victorian sides are always the favourites to win.

Aussie Rules is played with a ball similar to that used in rugby or American football, on a large oval ground that often doubles as a cricket ground. At each end are four uprights, the inside two (the goal posts) taller than the outside two (the behind posts). The ball can be propelled by any means necessary except throwing; the aim is to get it through the goal (six points). Other ways to score points include hitting a goal post or getting the ball between a goal and a behind post (one point in each case). There are four twenty-minute quarters, plus lots of time added on for injury or the ball being out of play.

The image of the game is overwhelmingly macho. Its players, chunkily built and kitted out in butt-hugging shorts and bicep-revealing guernseys (sleeveless

C

CONTEXTS | Sport

jumpers), aren't sent off for misconduct, ensuring a lively, skilful and, above all, gladiatorial confrontation. However, despite the apparent violence on the pitch (or perhaps because of it), Aussie Rules fans tend to be loyal and well behaved, trading colourful insults but not blows.

Australians also play **football** (soccer), but until recently it's been thoroughly overshadowed both by Aussie Rules, a game for "real Australians", and rugby. Football was first brought to the continent by the British; successive groups of postwar immigrants including the Greeks, Yugoslavs and Italians joined the fray by each forming their own National Soccer League club, typically incorporating their old home country's flag into their logo and stirring up fervent nationalistic support. As such, the game was marginalized as "ethnic" and politically charged. In 2004, in an attempt to promote national interest in the sport, the NSL was disbanded and replaced by the **A-League** competition (⊛www.a-league.com.au), now run by Football Federation Australia. Eight teams take part: seven from Australia's major cities and regions, and one from New Zealand.

Given the shortage of home-turf opportunities, the best players invariably head off to play overseas but return to play in Australia's national team, the **Socceroos**, interest in which has increased significantly since their appearance at the 2006 World Cup – their first for thirty years – where they (controversially) lost to eventual champions Italy in the second round.

Rugby

In New South Wales and Queensland, **rugby league** attracts the fanatics, especially for the hard-fought State of Origin matches. The thirteen-a-side game is one at which the Australians – known as the **Kangaroos** – seem permanent world champions, despite having a relatively small professional league, the **National Rugby League** (NRL; ⊛www.nrl.com). Partly controlled by Rupert Murdoch's News Limited, it's exclusively an East Coast game, and the sport of choice of Greater Sydney, home to ten of the league's seventeen clubs. The biggest scorers in the league are the Brisbane Broncos and Melbourne Storm; Canberra, Wollongong, Newcastle, Gold Coast and Townsville also have clubs. Firmly rooted in urban working-class culture, rugby league draws huge crowds and television audiences throughout the winter season (from March), peaking for the **Grand Final** in late September. Its star players command multimillion dollar contracts and sponsorship deals, and the NRL manages to sell more merchandise than any other Australian sports league.

Rugby union, by comparison, has an elitist image and a minority following. It's still more popular in Australia than football, though, and well-publicized competitions between teams from Australia, New Zealand and South Africa have sparked a growth in interest. The hugely popular national team, the **Wallabies**, have their training base at Coffs Harbour on North Coast New South Wales. The main competition is the **Super 14**, a battle between four teams from Australia, five from South Africa and five from New Zealand. The Australian Rugby Union (⊛www.rugby.com.au) also participates in the **Bledisloe Cup**, an annual three-match series between the Wallabies and New Zealand's All Blacks, and the Rugby World Cup, held every four years.

Cricket

Cricket, played from October to March, is a great spectator sport – for the crowd, the summer sunshine and the beer as much as the play. Every state is involved, and the four-day matches of the **interstate series** (traditionally known as the Sheffield Shield, but renamed the Pura Cup by its sponsors in 1999 and likely to have another name change soon) are interspersed with one-day games and internationals, as well as full five-day international test matches.

The international competition that still arouses greatest interest is that between Australia and England – **The Ashes** – a series of five test matches held biennially, alternating between the Australian and the English summer (making the gap between series either eighteen or thirty months). In January 2007, Australia took the Ashes back Down Under after demolishing England in the first series whitewash since 1920.

Having been around since the 1880s, The Ashes is perhaps the oldest rivalry between nations in international sport. The name of the series is purely figurative (the current trophy is made of crystal) but has an interesting provenance: in 1882, an Australian touring side defeated England at the Oval in South London by seven runs, and the *Sporting Times* was moved to report, in a mock obituary, that English cricket had "died at the Oval… deeply lamented by a large circle of sorrowing friends" and "the body will be cremated and the ashes taken to Australia". The England captain, Ivo Bligh, picked up on the theme and vowed that in the next series, he would recover the ashes. When his team outclassed the Aussies in Melbourne in 1883, he was presented with a funerary urn containing the ashes of a set of bails; he later bequeathed this to the MCC.

Tennis

All of Australia is glued to the small screen for the fortnight of the **Australian Open** (@www.australianopen.com), held at Melbourne Park each year from mid-January. Like the other three Grand Slam tennis tournaments, it includes singles, doubles, junior and masters' competitions; the male and female singles title winners each bag well over A$1.3m. The matches are played on hard courts surfaced with cushioned acrylic, and the main venues (the Rod Laver Arena and Vodafone Arena) have retractable roofs – essential during the heatwaves that would otherwise wither players and spectators alike.

Australia has bred a few **tennis legends**, including Rod Laver, who won all the Grand Slam mens' singles titles in both 1962 and 1969; Margaret Court, who won a total of 62 Grand Slam titles and was one of only three players ever to have won every possible title (singles, doubles and mixed doubles) at all four Grand Slam events; Evonne Cawley, who took multiple titles in the 1970s; Pat Cash, who shone during the 1980s; and Pat Rafter, the dual Grand Slam winner who famously donated half his winnings from the 1997 and 1998 US Open championships to an Australian children's charity.

Environment, flora and fauna

Australia's East Coast contains vast tracts of accessible, picturesque **natural scenery** – not just the beautiful beaches and dunelands you might expect, but also stately, fragrant forests, glittering lakes, rugged escarpments, and plateaus dotted with the cones of long-dead volcanoes.

Isolated from the other continents and from human interference, Australia's primeval flora and fauna adapted by taking an evolutionary route that was unique. In response to the irregular rhythms of fire, drought and flood, some mammals, birds and reptiles survived by developing opportunistic, as opposed to seasonal, breeding patterns; others became nomadic grazers, specialist leaf-feeders or brutally efficient predators.

Humans have made the East Coast their home for over forty thousand years but it's only in the last two hundred or so that the **relationship between man and nature** has shifted from largely cooperative to highly manipulative. The European settlers, ignorant of the fragility and profound "otherness" of Australian ecosystems, hacked down ancient trees for timber and farmland, planted unsuitable crops, trees and shrubs and allowed cattle and sheep to drink pastures dry, tearing up the resulting desert with their hooves. The challenging terrain and shortage of fresh water in a great many areas limited the settlers' movements, but even so, more native animals became extinct in nineteenth- and twentieth-century Australia than on any other continent.

Despite this tragedy, the East Coast's many pristine landscapes and ecosystems remain fascinatingly distinctive. These days, **conservationists** advocate zero tolerance for invasive animals and plants, particularly notorious non-natives such as fast-breeding rabbits, rampant, choking lantana and the infamous cane toad.

It takes time to appreciate the subtleties of the East Coast environment – and the sheer scale of the rainforests and reefs and the relentlessness of the eucalyptus groves can be overwhelming – but the excellent network of well-staffed national parks and committed tour guides mean that enriching explorations are possible, even within a short visit to the region.

Native habitats, trees and plants

Six wilderness regions on Australia's East Coast – all of them substantial and three of them vast – appear on the **UNESCO World Heritage list** of places of exceptional natural beauty, aesthetic importance and ecological or geological significance. One designated region, the Gondwana Rainforests of Australia, comprises large pockets of forested highlands in northeast New South Wales and southeast Queensland, including Barrington Tops, Dorrigo, Lamington and Springbrook national parks. The entire Great Barrier Reef and the Wet Tropics of Queensland, which includes all the rainforest between Townsville and Cooktown, are also listed, as are the Greater Blue Mountains Area, Fraser Island and the Lord Howe Island Group. The region also has four **UNESCO**

Biosphere Reserves, protected areas in which conservation and sustainable use of natural resources work hand in hand: Croajingolong National Park, Mornington Peninsula and Western Port, Wilsons Promontory Marine Park and Reserve, and Noosa Biosphere Reserve.

Australia's most distinctive and widespread **trees** are those that developed a dependence on fire. Some, like the seemingly limitless varieties of **eucalypts** or gum trees, need extreme heat to burst open button-shaped pods and release their seeds, and encourage fires by annually shedding bark and leaves, depositing a thick layer of tinder on the forest floor. Other shrubs with similar habits are **banksias**, **grevillias** and **bottlebrushes**, with their distinctive bushy flowers and spiky seed-pods, while those prehistoric survivors, palm-like **cycads** (see p.554) and **grasstrees**, similarly depend on regular conflagrations to promote new growth. For thousands of years, Aborigines used controlled burn-offs to make the land more suitable for hunting, thereby possibly enhancing these fire-reliant traits.

Mangrove swamps, found along the tropical and subtropical coasts, are tidal zones of thick grey mud and mangrove trees, whose interlocked, aerial roots make an effective barrier to exploration. They've suffered extensive clearing for development, and it wasn't until recently that their importance to the estuarine life-cycle won them limited government protection; Aboriginal people have always found them a rich source of animal and plant products.

Rainforest once covered much of the continent, but today only a small portion of its former abundance survives. There are three types found in the coastal region: the temperate rainforests of New South Wales and the high-altitude areas of southeast Queensland; the subtropical rainforest of coastal southeast and central Queensland; and the tropical rainforest of northern Queensland, which conforms more to the classic image of a lush, dark, humid rainforest complete with **strangler figs**, **mosses** and **orchids**. Where it's well-preserved, it's astoundingly impressive; trees, competing for light, grow to gigantic heights, supporting themselves with buttress roots, and hosting a huge number of plant species: tangled, trailing **vines**, **elkhorns**, **basket ferns** with their giant, delicately curled fronds, and other epiphytes. **Fan palms** are found in more open forest, where there's regular water.

Some forest types illustrate the extent of Australia's prehistoric flora. **Antarctic beech** or *Nothafagus*, found south of Brisbane and also in South America, along with **kauri pines** from Queensland, which also occur in New Zealand, are all relict evidence of the prehistoric supercontinent, Gondwana. Another famous "living fossil" is the **wollemi pine**, found in Wollemi National Park in the Blue Mountains region.

As long as you don't eat them or fall onto the pricklier versions, most Australian plants are harmless – though in rainforests you'd want to avoid entanglement with spiky **lawyer cane** or **wait-awhile vine** (though it doesn't look like it, this is a climbing palm) and steer well clear of the large, pale-green, heart-shaped leaves of the **stinging tree** (see p.46).

Wildlife

In the years after the demise of the dinosaurs, Australia split away from the rest of the world, and the animals here evolved along different lines to anywhere else. As placental mammals gained the ascendancy in South America, Africa, Europe and Asia, it was the **marsupials** and **monotremes** that took over in Australia: among the megafauna that flourished on the continent until around thirty thousand years ago – well into Aboriginal times – were a rhino-sized wombat, carnivorous kangaroos and thylacaleo, a marsupial lion. While marsupials and monotremes also found a niche in New Guinea and South America, it's in Australia that they reached their greatest diversity and numbers. Less distinctive, but impressive by virtue of sheer amount of species, are the other mammals – principally **bats** and **rodents** – while tropical Queensland, in particular, harbours a rainbow of **reptiles**, **amphibians** and **insects**. Ornithology enthusiasts with time to travel can tick off a fascinating variety of habitats, home to wading, woodland, field and rainforest **birds**. The underwater landscape is rich in interest, too, with a scintillating assortment of **marine species**.

Australians love to regale visitors about the **dangers** of the bush and the deep. However, while the possibility of encountering a life-threatening spider, snake, jellyfish or shark is certainly not to be taken lightly (see "Health", p.46, for general advice), lurid tales of fearsome "drop bears" lurking in gums, tree trunks revealing themselves to be giant snakes, bloodthirsty wild pigs rampaging through the bush and other terrors are mostly the product of suburban paranoia laced with a surprising naivety about the great outdoors. For the well prepared, there's little to fear from Australia's wildlife, and if you spend any time in the wilderness, you'll undoubtedly end up far better informed than the yarn-spinners.

For a visual identity guide to some of the East Coast's most common species, see the *East Coast wildlife* colour section.

Marsupials

Marsupials are mammals that give birth to a partially formed embryo, which then develops in a **pouch** on the mother; this allows a higher breeding rate in good years. Australia's East Coast is home to a surprising variety of species – nearly fifty in all, ranging from small creatures easily mistaken for mice or rats, to kangaroos, wallaroos and wallabies, the country's answer to deer and antelope. Since Australia has very few large carnivores, the marsupials have hardly any predators, and the main threat to their survival is the shrinkage of food supplies through habitat reduction and climate change. Many of the smaller species belie their rodent-like appearance by hunting insects, reptiles and birds, but the larger species are mainly **herbivorous**, feeding on grass and, in some cases, leaves, tubers and fungi. All are highly adapted to cope with Australia's arid conditions – some can survive without drinking at all, obtaining all the water they need from their food.

Kangaroos, which have an unofficial claim to the title of Australia's national animal, are plentiful and surprisingly diverse – on the coastal strip between Melbourne and Cape York, there are around twenty different species of kangaroo, wallaroo, wallaby and tree kangaroo, all of which belong to the same family, *Macropodidae* (meaning big-footed). While some are nocturnal, a number of species are semi-diurnal, constantly switching between bouts of grazing and snoozing, and are therefore not as difficult to spot by daylight as you might expect. Female kangaroos have four teats; the pouch may hold young at different stages of their development, with the mother producing a different type of milk for each. It's believed that the kangaroo's distinctive bipedal hopping evolved in direct response to food shortages: it's an energy-efficient method of covering long distances in search of fresh grazing. But because they're unable to move their hind legs in a walking motion, they're far less nimble over short distances – putting their fore feet down and steadying themselves with their tail as they jump their hind feet forward – and they have trouble moving backwards. Interestingly, however, when swimming (rare but occasionally seen), they kick their hind legs separately.

The **common wallaroo**, the East Coast's largest species, is a widespread, solitary animal with dark grey fur and a black nose, typically found in rocky areas. **Eastern grey kangaroos**, which have lighter grey fur and are more gregarious, appear to have a great fondness for the easy grazing of golf courses, quiet coastal foreshores, and grassy verges in small country towns. Wallabies are smaller; the commonest East Coast species is the **agile wallaby**, which is sandy brown with a pale stripe on each cheek and flank. Other common species include **whiptail wallabies** (large for a wallaby, with a long slim tail) and **swamp wallabies** (with dark grey fur and a lighter, gingery chest). On rainforest fringes in Queensland and New South Wales, you may see **black-striped wallabies**, **red-legged pademelons** and **red-necked pademelons**, small, solitary wallabies that eat leaves and grasses. **Tree kangaroos** (Bennett's and Lumholtz's) are distinctive and rare, found only in small pockets of coastal forest in Queensland, notably the Atherton Tablelands and the Daintree, and occupying a niche similar to that of the monkeys found on other continents. Uniquely among kangaroos, these shy, nocturnal species spend most of their time off the ground, and can move forwards or backwards in trees by using their limbs independently; they can also leap between branches and either hop, walk or run along the ground.

Easiest to find of all the marsupials because they're well adapted to life in suburban and urban areas, **common ringtail possums** (which have a long prehensile tail, often held in a loop, and are roughly rabbit-sized) and **common brushtail possums** (slightly larger, with a stubbier tail) are often seen foraging boldly in gardens and campsites. Their timid relatives the **greater glider** and the diminutive **sugar glider** may, with a little persistence, be spotted in trees on the edges of forests at dusk or after dark; the stretchy membranes of skin and fur between their fore and hind feet allow them to plane for around 100m between branches.

The arboreal, eucalyptus-chewing **koala** (found in forests throughout the region) is sensitive to disturbance; this has made them relatively elusive, and has placed them on the endangered list as their habitat is cleared. The koala is also, famously, at risk due to its highly selective diet of leaves, with a preference for fibrous, toxin-packed eucalyptus, which are energy draining to digest. Koalas have thick fur to protect them from heat, cold and rain, particularly in the south – the koalas in Victoria are noticeably larger and thicker-coated than those in Queensland – and their brains are markedly smaller than their skull capacity, possibly as an energy-saving adaptation. They live in social groups, and the bellowing of territorial males sounds not unlike water emptying down a drain. Exceptionally among non-primates, every koala's fingerprints are unique. Since koalas seem relatively unfazed by captivity, practically every wildlife park on the coast has a few in residence; they're also fairly easy to spot in the wild on Raymond Island, in Noosa National Park and on Magnetic Island.

The koala's closest relative is the tubby, ground-dwelling, burrow-digging **wombat**, two species of which are found on the East Coast: the **common wombat** (limited to coastal New South Wales and Victoria) and the **northern hairy-nosed wombat** (critically endangered and the subject of an intensive research and conservation programme in Rockhampton).

Other marsupials found on many parts of the coastal strip include rat-like **bandicoots** and tiny, mouse-like **dunnarts** and **antichinuses**, which are insectivorous. The fiercest of the marsupials, though harmless to humans, are the vaguely ferret-like **quolls** (the spotted-tail quoll in the south and the northern quoll in Queensland), which are carnivorous.

Monotremes

Platypuses and echidnas are the only **monotremes**, egg-laying mammals that suckle their young through specialized pores. Once considered a stage in the evolution of placental mammals, they're now recognized as a specialized branch of the family. Neither is particularly rare, but being nocturnal, shy and, in the case of the platypus, aquatic, they can be difficult to find. **Ant-eating echidnas** resemble a long-nosed, thick-spined hedgehog or small porcupine, and are found countrywide; **platypuses** are confined to the eastern ranges, notably Eungella National Park and the Atherton Tablelands, and look like a blend of duck and otter, having a grey, rubbery bill, webbed feet, short fur, and a poison spur on males. This combination seemed too implausible to nineteenth-century biologists, who initially denounced stuffed specimens as a hoax, assembled from pieces of other animals.

Other mammals

Animals that have been introduced to Australia, deliberately or unwittingly, are generally considered the rogues of the wildlife world, but it seems a little unfair to apply the same opprobrium to **dingoes** (see p.493), who have made the continent their home for nigh on twelve thousand years. They're considered a pest, however, as they attack native wildlife, livestock and, on rare occasions, people. A 5400-kilometre fence from South Australia into northwest Queensland and down again to New South Wales blocks their movements, but you can see them on Fraser Island, which has a long-isolated and therefore unusually pure-bred population. Elsewhere, dingoes interbreed with domestic dogs. They are believed to be the descendants of a type of a dog-like wolf, brought to Australia from Southeast Asia, where very similar animals are still found.

Huge colonies of **bats**, whose many common varieties include blossom, horseshoe, freetail, bentwing, long-eared and tube-nosed bats, congregate in caves and fill entire trees all over the region. **Fruit bats**, or **flying foxes**, are especially common in the tropics, where evenings can be spent watching colonies of the one-metre-winged monsters heading out from their daytime roosts on feeding expeditions.

The East Coast has relatively few **rodent** species – small marsupials are, presumably, better adapted to the region's cycle of droughts and floods – but one that sometimes shows up at forest lodges and camps is the **melomys**, which looks like a large mouse. The cane fields, woodlands and grasslands also support several species of **rat** and Australia's smallest native rodent, the **delicate mouse**.

Reptiles, frogs, insects and spiders

Australian **reptiles** come in all shapes and sizes. In the tropical parts of the country, the pale **lizards** you see wriggling across the ceiling on Velcro-like pads are **geckos**, and you'll find fatter, sluggish **skinks** – such as the stumpy blue-tongued lizard – everywhere. Other widespread species are **frill-necked**

lizards, known for fanning out their necks and running on their hind legs when frightened, and the ubiquitous **goannas** (the Australian name for monitor lizards).

Crocodiles are confined to the tropics and come in two types: the shy, inoffensive **freshwater crocodile** grows to around 3m in length and feeds on fish and frogs, while the larger, bulkier, and misleadingly named saltwater or **estuarine crocodile** can grow to 7m, ranges far inland (often in freshwater) and is the only Australian animal that constitutes an active threat to humans. Highly evolved predators, they should be given a very wide berth (see p.47).

Despite their bad press, **snakes** are generally timid and pose far less of a problem, even though the East Coast has everything from **constricting pythons** to seriously venomous species including **death adders**, **taipans**, **copperheads**, **common browns**, **king browns** and **tiger snakes**.

Australia has no native toads but plenty of **frogs**: their after-sunset croaking, trilling and chiming lend a delightful soundscape to streams, waterholes and wetlands on the East Coast – particularly after rain, which is a frog's cue to mate. Numerous species of tree frog are found here, including the very beautiful **Blue Mountains tree frog**, which is light brown with chocolate and crimson markings. Others include the **striped rocket frog**, named for its supercharged leaping ability, and the **northern banjo frog**, which has a high-pitched call like the "plunk" of a banjo string.

The sound of male **cicadas** chirping to attract a mate is, to many Australians, the sound of summer. Australia has over two hundred species altogether, some of which emit a sound that is ear-splitting enough to repel birds, their principal predator – the cicadas concerned have a way of blocking their own hearing organs so that they're not deafened by their own call. High season is also the best time to see **butterflies**, one of the loveliest of which is the **Ulysses butterfly**, a large, electric blue swallowtail found in the rainforests of northern Queensland. Another Queensland stunner is the **Cairns Birdwing**, Australia's largest butterfly, with a wingspan of over 16cm.

Australians are rightly cautious of **spiders**, as some – such as the redback and the funnel web – can deliver a dangerous bite (see p.47), but the majority of the 10,000 species that researchers have identified to date are harmless, and some, such as the bizarre-looking, brooch-like **shiny spider**, are very striking.

Birds

With a climate that extends from temperate zones well into the tropics, Australia's **birdlife** is abundant and varied. **Little penguins** and **albatrosses** live along the southeast coast, while **riflebirds**, related to New Guinea's birds of paradise, and the **cassowary**, a colourful version of the ostrich, live in the tropical rainforests. Among the birds of prey, the countrywide **wedge-tail eagle** and the coastal **white-bellied sea eagle** are most impressive in their size. Both share their environment with the stately grey **brolga**, an Australian crane, and the even larger **jabiru stork**, with its chisel beak and pied plumage. **Parrots**, arguably the country's most spectacular birds, come in over forty varieties, and no matter if they're flocks of green budgerigars, outrageously coloured rainbow lorikeets or white sulphur-crested cockatoos, they'll deafen you with their noisy calls. Equally raucous are **kookaburras**, giant kingfishers found near permanent water. The quieter **tawny frogmouth**, an incredibly camouflaged cousin of the nightjar, has one of the most disgruntled expressions ever seen on a bird.

Non-native fauna

Feral **rabbits**, **goats** and **pigs** are considered a pest on the East Coast, as they degrade the environment and compete with indigenous fauna for food and shelter. Feral **foxes** and **cats** are even more unpopular – they present a major threat to small marsupials and birds. An introduced amphibian, however, has turned out to be the most insidious and rapacious invader of all: the highly poisonous **cane toad**, introduced in the 1930s in an unsuccessful attempt to combat a plague of greyback beetles, has no natural enemies and is on a relentless march from the north Queensland sugar-cane fields, southwards along the coast and across northern Australia. For more on the cane toad, see the box on p.567.

Marine life

As diverse a cradle of life as the rainforests, the off shore marvel that is the **Great Barrier Reef** harbours hundreds of species of coral, invertebrates and fish. Species well worth looking out for range from tiny, colourful flatworms and spindly shrimps to mighty napoleon wrasses, potato cod and manta rays. Simple lifeforms such as giant clams, sea squirts and starfish add vivid colour to the Reef, as do Christmas tree worms, which retract their feathery tentacles if you get too close. Among the most decorative of the **fish** are butterflyfish, angelfish and feather-fin bullfish, which flit around the reef in pairs, while you'll often see colourful parrotfish lumbering from one patch of coral to another, munching at outcrops. Skittish triggerfish dart about, and the equally highly strung clownfish – still the most popular fish on the Reef, thanks to *Finding Nemo* – hover nervously among the tentacles of their host anemones. You may also see schooling fish such as goatfish or barracuda, crevice-dwellers such as moray eels, and bottom-dwellers such as stingrays and sea cucumbers. Non-aggressive **sharks** such as whitetip reef sharks, leopard sharks and grey nurse sharks may be encountered in deep water.

Marine mammals and **reptiles** – in particular migratory **humpback whales**, **turtles**, **bottlenose dolphins**, **Australian fur seals** and **dugongs** – are also part of the East Coast's abundant marine life; there are numerous places to see these animals between Melbourne and central Queensland.

Books

Australian writing first came into its own in the 1890s when, in the run-up to Federation, a strong **nationalistic movement** produced writers such as Henry Lawson and Banjo Paterson, who romanticized the bush and glorified the mateship ethos. In the following decade, outstanding **women writers** such as Miles Franklin and Barbara Baynton gave a feminine slant to the bush tale and set the trend for strong female authorship.

In the 1970s, Australian novelists came to be recognized in the **international arena**: Patrick White was awarded a Nobel Prize in 1973, Peter Carey won the Booker in both 1988 and 2001, and Kate Grenville won the 2001 Orange Prize for Fiction. Other notable Australian writers who have aroused interest further afield include David Malouf, Julia Leigh, Tim Winton (twice nominated for the Booker), Thomas Keneally, Richard Flanagan, Chloe Hooper and Robyn Davidson.

Literary journals such as *Meanjin*, *Southerly*, *Westerly* and *Heat* provide exposure for new and established writers by publishing short fiction, essays and reviews. The big **prizes** in Australian fiction include the Vogel Literary Award for the best unpublished novel written by an author under the age of 35, and the much-coveted Miles Franklin Award. Some Australian books are not available overseas, but Gleebooks, one of Australia's best literary booksellers, delivers worldwide (ⓦwww.gleebooks.com.au).

Contemporary fiction

Murray Bail *Eucalyptus* (1998). Beautifully written novel with a fairytale-like plot: New South Wales farmer, Holland, has planted nearly every type of eucalyptus tree on his land. When his extraordinarily beautiful daughter Ellen is old enough to marry, he sets up a challenge for her legion of potential suitors, to name each tree.

John Birmingham *He Died with a Felafel in His Hand* (1994). A collection of squalid and very funny tales emerging from the once-dissolute author's experience of flat-sharing hell in Brisbane.

Anson Cameron *Tin Toys* (2000). The Aboriginal Stolen Generations issue explored through the tale of Hunter Carolyn, an unintentional artist who can change skin colour at will.

Peter Carey *Bliss* (1981). Carey's first and perhaps best novel is the story of a Sydney ad executive who drops out to New Age New South Wales. Other novels by Carey to look out for include his two Booker Prize-winners *Oscar and Lucinda* (1988) and *True History of the Kelly Gang* (2000), about the bushranger Ned Kelly; his bizarre short stories, *The Fat Man in History* (1974), with which he launched his career; and his quirky recent novels *Theft: A Love Story* (2007) and *His Illegal Self* (2008).

Tom Gilling *Miles McGinty* (2001). Nineteenth-century Sydney comes alive in this riotous, entertaining love story of Miles, who becomes a levitator's assistant and begins to float on air, and Isabel, who wants to fly.

Kate Grenville *The Idea of Perfection* (1999), set in the tiny, fictional New South Wales town of Karakarook, and about two unlikely characters who fall in love, won the 2001 Orange Prize for Fiction. *The Secret River* (2005) was shortlisted for the Man Booker Prize in 2006 and won the Commonwealth Writers' Prize. This historical novel explores the uneasy terrain of early white contact with Aborigines, telling the story of freed convict William Thornhill taking up land in the Hawkesbury with his family.

Linda Jaivin *Eat Me* (1995). Billed as an "erotic feast", this novel opens with a memorable fruit-squeezing scene (and this is only the shopping) as three trendy Sydney women (fashion editor, academic and writer) swap stories of sexual exploits.

David Malouf *The Conversations at Curlow Creek* (1996). One of Australia's most important contemporary writers charts the developing relationship between two Irishmen the night before a hanging; one is the officer appointed to supervise the execution and the other the outlaw facing his death. Malouf's earlier novel *Remembering Babylon* (1993) is the moving story of a British cabin boy in the 1840s who, cast ashore, lives for sixteen years amongst the Aboriginal people of Far North Queensland before finally re-entering the British colonial world.

Andrew McGahan *The White Earth* (2004). Set in Queensland's Darling Downs wheatfields; it's 1992, and the Mabo land-rights case fills the news. After the death of his father,

8-year-old William is drawn into his discontented uncle's White League. Questions of Aboriginal dispossession and white belonging reverberate. More recently, McGahan raised the ire of neo-conservative reviewers with the polemical tone of his dystopian novel *Underground* (2006), set in a not too distant future in totalitarian Australia.

Alex Miller *Journey to the Stone Country* (2002). A betrayed wife leaves her middle-class Melbourne existence and returns to tropical north Queensland, setting out on a journey with a childhood Aboriginal acquaintance into the stone country that is his tribe's remote heartland. However, dark secrets from the lives of their grandparents threaten what future they may have together.

Elliot Perlman *Seven Types of Ambiguity* (2003). The chain of events, secrets and lies stretching back a decade that lead to Simon Heywood kidnapping his ex-girlfriend's son are related by seven different narrators. Probing middle-class anxiety in a consumeristic, market-driven society, Perlman's conscience-driven writing can be moralistic at times, but at its best is clever and insightful, providing an intense social portrait of contemporary Melbourne from Toorak to St Kilda.

Australian classics

Barbara Baynton *Bush Studies*. A collection of nineteenth-century bush stories written from the female perspective.

Rolf Boldrewood *Robbery Under Arms*. The story of Captain Starlight, a notorious bushranger and rustler around the Queensland borders.

Miles Franklin *My Brilliant Career*. A novel about a spirited young girl in early twentieth-century Victoria who refuses to conform.

May Gibbs *Snugglepot and Cuddlepie*. A timeless children's favourite: the illustrated adventures of two little creatures that live inside gumnuts.

George Johnston *My Brother Jack*. The first in a disturbing trilogy set in Melbourne suburbia between the wars, which develops into a semi-fictional attempt to dissipate the guilt Johnston felt at being disillusioned with, and finally leaving, his native land.

Thomas Keneally *The Chant of Jimmie Blacksmith*. A prize-winning novel that delves deep into the psyche of an Aboriginal outlaw, tracing his inexorable descent into murder and crime. Sickening, brutal and compelling.

Henry Lawson Ballads, poems and stories from Australia's best-loved chronicler come in a wide array of collections. A few to seek out are: *Henry Lawson Bush Ballads*, *Henry Lawson Favourites* and *While the Billy Boils – Poetry*.

Norman Lindsay *The Magic Pudding*. A whimsical tale of some very strange men and their grumpy, flavour-changing and endless pudding; a children's classic with very adult humour.

Ruth Park *The Harp in the South*. First published in 1948, this first book in a trilogy is a well-loved tale of inner-Sydney slum life in 1940s Surry Hills. The spirited Darcy family's battle against poverty provides memorable characters.

A.B. ("Banjo") Paterson Australia's most famous bush balladeer, author of *Waltzing Matilda* and *The Man from Snowy River*, who helped romanticize the bush's mystique. Some of the many titles published include *Banjo Paterson's Favourites* and *Man from Snowy River and Other Verses*.

Henry Handel Richardson *The Getting of Wisdom*. A gangly country girl's experience of a snobby boarding school in early twentieth-century Melbourne. Like Miles Franklin (see p.647), Richardson was actually a female writer.

Christina Stead *For Love Alone*. Set largely around Sydney Harbour, where the late author grew up, this novel follows the obsessive Teresa Hawkins, a poor but artistic girl from a large, unconventional family, who scrounges and saves to head for London and love.

Kylie Tennant *Ride on Stranger*. First published in 1943, this is a humorous portrait of Sydney between the two world wars, seen through the eyes of newcomer Shannon Hicks.

Aboriginal writing

Faith Bandler *Welou, My Brother* (1984). A novel by a well-known black activist describing a boy's early life in Queensland, and the tensions of a racially mixed community.

John Muk Muk Burke *Bridge of Triangles* (1994). Powerful, landscape-driven images in this tale of a mixed-race child growing up unable to associate with either side of his heritage, but refusing to accept the downward spiral into despair and alcoholism adopted by those around him.

Ruby Langford *Don't Take Your Love to Town* (1988). An autobiography demonstrating a black woman's courage and humour in the face of

tragedy and poverty lived out in northern New South Wales and inner-city Sydney.

Mudrooroo *Wildcat Falling* (1965). The story of a black teenage delinquent coming of age in the 1950s.

Leah Purcell *Black Chicks Talking* (2002). In an effort to overcome Aboriginal stereotypes, indigenous actor and writer Purcell gives insight into the lives of contemporary black women with this collection of lively, lengthy interviews, conducted with nine young females including the first Aboriginal Miss Australia (and now politician) Kathryn Hay, dancer Frances Rings and actor Deborah Mailman.

Archie Weller *The Day of the Dog* (1992). Weller's violent first novel came out in an angry burst after he was released, aged 23, from jail. The protagonist, in a similar situation, is pressured back into a criminal world by his Aboriginal peers and by police harassment. Searing pace and forceful writing. His second novel, *Land of the Golden Clouds* (1998), is an epic science-fiction fantasy, set three thousand years in the future, which portrays an Australia devastated by a nuclear holocaust and populated by warring tribes.

Travel writing

Bill Bryson *Down Under* (2000). Vintage Bryson, a sketchy but affectionate and readable account of a quick hop around a country that "from time to time sends us useful things... but nothing we can't actually do without". Much puzzled amusement over venomous wildlife and cultural peculiarities.

Peter Carey *30 Days in Sydney: a wildly distorted account* (2001). Part of Bloomsbury Publishing's "The Writer and the City" project, where "some of the finest writers of our time reveal the secrets of a city they know best". Carey hangs out with old friends, and it is their lives, their tales and their often nostalgic trips around Sydney that form the basis of this vivid city portrait.

Bruce Chatwin *The Songlines* (1987). A semi-fictional account of an exploration into Aboriginal nomadism and mythology that turns out to be one of the more readable expositions of this complex subject.

Larry Habegger (ed) *Travelers' Tales Australia* (2000). Excerpts and essays from some of the world's best travel writers – Bruce Chatwin, Tim Cahill, Jan Morris, Tony Horwitz, Pico Iyer and Paul Theroux – as well as new talents.

Mark McCrum *No Worries* (1997). Knowing nothing of the country except the usual clichés, McCrum arrives in 1990s Australia and makes his way around by plane, train, thumb and Greyhound, meeting a surprising cast of characters along the way. As he travels, the stereotypes give way to an insightful picture of modern Australia.

Ruth Park *Ruth Park's Sydney* (1999). Revised and expanded edition of prolific novelist Park's classic guide to the city. A perfect walking companion, full of personal insights, anecdotes and literary quotations.

History and politics

Robyn Annear *Nothing But Gold: the Diggers of 1852* (1999). With an eye for interestingly obscure details, this is a wonderfully readable account of the gold rushes of the nineteenth century, a period that perhaps did more than any other to shape the Australian character.

John Birmingham *Leviathan: the unauthorised biography of Sydney* (1999). Birmingham's tome casts a contemporary eye over the dark side of Sydney's history, from nauseating accounts of Rocks' slum life and the 1900 plague outbreak, through the 1970s traumas of Vietnamese boat people (now Sydney residents) to scandals of police corruption.

Manning Clark *A Short History of Australia* (2006). A condensed and revised edition of this leading historian's multi-volume tome, focusing on dreary successions of political administrations over two centuries, and cynically concluding with "An Age of Ruins, 1969–1986".

Inga Clendinnen *Dancing With Strangers* (2003). Empathetic, almost poetically written account of the interaction of the British and the Aborigines (whom Clendinnen calls "Australians") in the five years after the arrival of the First Fleet.

Ann Curthoys *Freedom Ride: A Freedom Rider Remembers* (2002). History professor Curthoys was one of the busload of young, idealistic white university students who accompanied Aboriginal activist Charles Perkins (only 29 himself) on his revolutionary trip through northern New South Wales in 1965, to look at Aboriginal living conditions and root out and protest against racial discrimination.

David Day *Claiming a Continent: a New History of Australia* (2001). Award-winning, general and easily readable history, concluding in 2000. The possession, dispossession and ownership of the land – and thus issues of race – are central to Day's narrative. Excellent recommended reading of recent texts at the end of each chapter will take you further.

Bruce Elder *Blood on the Wattle: Massacres and Maltreatment of Aboriginal Australians Since 1788* (3rd ed, 2003). A heart-rending account of the horrors inflicted on the continent's indigenous peoples, covering infamous nineteenth-century massacres as well as more recent mid-twentieth-century scandals of the Stolen Generations children.

Robert Hughes *The Fatal Shore* (1986). A minutely detailed epic of the origins of transportation and the brutal beginnings of white Australia.

Dianne Johnson *Lighting the Way: Reconciliation Stories* (2002).

Twenty-four very personal stories, written in a simple, engaging style, show Aboriginal and non-Aboriginal Australians working with each other, from community artworks to political activism. Positive and inspiring.

Mark McKenna *Looking for Blackfellas Point: an Australian History of Place* (2002). This prize-winning book uncovers the uneasy history of Aboriginals and European settlers on the far south coast of New South Wales and widens its scope to the enduring meaning of land to both Aboriginal and white Australians.

Rosemary Neill *White Out: How Politics is Killing Black Australia* (2002). Outspoken book that asserts that the rhetoric of self-determination and empowerment excuses the wider society from doing anything to reduce the disparity between black and white Australian populations. Busting taboos about indigenous affairs, Neill criticizes ideologies of both Left and Right.

Henry Reynolds *Why Weren't We Told?* (1999). An autobiographical journey by a revisionist historian showing how he, like many generations of Australians, imbibed a distorted, idealized Australian history, and describing his path to becoming an Aboriginal-history specialist.

Portia Robinson *The Women of Botany Bay* (1988). The result of painstaking research into the records of every female transported from Britain and Ireland between 1787 and 1828, Robinson tells with conviction and passion who these women really were.

Eric Rolls *Sojourners* (1993) and *Citizens* (1996). The first and second volumes of *Flowers and the Wide Sea*, farmer-turned-historian Rolls' fascinatingly detailed history of the Chinese in Australia.

Anne Summers *Damned Whores and God's Police* (2nd ed, 2002). Stereotypical images of women in Australian society are explored in this ground-breaking reappraisal of Australian history from a feminist point of view.

Watkin Tench and Tim Flannery (ed) *1788* (1996). One of the most vivid accounts of early Sydney was written by a twenty-something captain of the marines, Watkin Tench, who arrived with the First Fleet. Tench's humanity and youthful curiosity shine through as he brings alive the characters who peopled the early settlement, such as the Aboriginal Bennelong.

Linda Weiss, Elizabeth Thurbon and John Mathews *How to Kill a Country* (2004). Australia's leading policy analysts examine the Free Trade Agreement with the United States, predicting that Australia's interests and identity would be damaged by the quest for a "special relationship".

Autobiography and biography

A.B. Facey *A Fortunate Life* (1981). A hugely popular autobiography of a battler, tracing his progress from a bush orphanage to Gallipoli, through the Depression, another war and beyond.

David Malouf *12 Edmondstone Street* (1985). An evocative autobiography-in-snatches of one of Australia's finest literary novelists, describing, in loving detail, the eponymous house in Brisbane where Malouf was born, life in the Tuscan village where he lives for part of each year, and his first visit to India.

Hazel Rowley *Christina Stead: a Biography* (revised ed, 2007). Stead (1902–83) has been acclaimed as Australia's greatest novelist. After spending years in Paris, London and New York with her American husband, she returned to Australia in her old age.

Society and culture

Geoffrey Blainey *Triumph of the Nomads* (1976). A fascinating account portraying Aboriginal people as masters and not victims of their environment. One of the best books on the subject.

David Dale *Who We Are* (2006). A compelling snapshot of ordinary peoples' lives in Australia, presented through a compilation of contemporary quotes, lists and miscellany.

Peter Dunbar-Hall and Chris Gibson *Deadly Sounds, Deadly Places* (2004). Comprehensive guide to contemporary Aboriginal music in Australia, from Archie Roach to Yothu Yindi; includes a handy discography.

Peter Goldsworthy (ed) *True Blue? On Being Australian* (2008). An easy-going but thought-provoking collection of short essays, literary sketches and photographs pinpointing the contradictions and insecurities inherent in Australia's sense of identity.

Donald Horne *The Lucky Country: Australia in the Sixties* (1964). This seminal collection of essays challenged Australian ideals and political practices, suggesting that it was through luck, not skill, that the country was holding its own on the world stage – a message forgotten by those who now use the label Horne coined, "the lucky country", in a wholly positive sense.

Peter Singer and Tom Gregg
How Ethical is Australia? An Examination of Australia's Record as a Global Citizen (2004). Eminent philosopher and professor of bioethics Peter

Singer teams up with researcher Tom Gregg to examine Australia's policies on foreign aid, the United Nations, overseas trade, the environment and refugees.

Ecology, wildlife and environment

Leonard Cronin *Australian Mammals* (2008). Beautifully illustrated and laid out field guide with clear, useful notes on each species.

David Doubilet *Great Barrier Reef* (2002). Stunning portrait of the marine park from one of the world's leading underwater photographers, who has dived it from north to south.

Tim Flannery *The Future Eaters* (1994). Paleontologist and environmental commentator Flannery poses the theory that as the first human beings migrated down to Australasia, the Aborigines, Maoris and other Polynesian peoples changed the region's flora and fauna in startling ways, and began consuming the resources needed for their own future; the Europeans made an even greater impact on the environment, continuing this "future eating" of natural resources.

Drew Hutton and Libby Connors *A History of the Australian Environmental Movement* (1999). Written by a husband-and-wife team, Queensland academics and

prominent in Green politics, this well-balanced book charts the progress of conservation attempts since 1860.

Ann Moyal *Platypus* (2001). When British and French naturalists were first introduced to the platypus, they were flummoxed. Was it bird, reptile or mammal? And did it really lay eggs? Moyal, a science historian, provides a captivating look at Australian nature through European eyes.

Peter and Pat Slater *The Slater Field Guide to Australian Birds* (2003). Pocket sized, and the easiest to use of the many available guides to Australian birds.

Mary White *The Greening of Gondwana* (1986). Classic work on the evolution of Australia's flora and geography.

James Woodford *The Wollemi Pine* (2000). An award-winning environment writer tells the story of the Wollemi pine, assumed to have been extinct since the age of the dinosaurs, until specimens were discovered in the Blue Mountains in 1994.

Language

Language

Australian English

Based on British English but unmistakably Antipodean, the **Australian language** is colourful, dynamic and idiomatic; the spoken version, in particular, is full of cultural clues. Its assorted ingredients include the archaic English and Irish dialects of the colony's early convicts, the mid-twentieth century Queen's English of the ABC and BBC, and numerous Aboriginal languages. Words derived from a host of folk tales and legends have worked their way into the vocabulary, as have resonant brand names and, more recently, terms and expressions borrowed from global culture, including American and European music, films and TV. True Australian slang, "strine", is more common in the outback than on the relatively moderately spoken East Coast, but you'll hear snippets of it in the urban vernacular.

One of the most distinctive Australian **linguistic habits**, and one that's extremely infectious, is the tendency to add an interrogative-sounding rising inflection to the end of statements, as if asking whether the listener agrees. Another is to opt for jovial informality at every opportunity – calling objects "him" or "her" rather than "it", abbreviating names of people, places and things into something ending in "-o" or "-ie" (as in "arvo" or "Brissie") and peppering sentences with mild swear words. Many Australians use words like "bloody", "bugger" and "bastard" innocently and even affectionately; there was much bemusement when the slogan chosen by Tourism Australia in 2006 for a two-year international ad campaign abroad – "So where the bloody hell are you?" – caused quite a stir.

Australian TV soap operas, films such as *Crocodile Dundee*, and personalities such as the late Steve Irwin are credited with spreading strine throughout the English-speaking world, not least the versatile and agreeable "No worries". Other classic **Australianisms** such as Aussie, barbie, joey, boomerang, didgeridoo, Down Under, walkabout and "G'day!" are, of course, thoroughly familiar. British and Australian English are particularly closely entwined: both nations use understatement and irony with great relish, and share a host of **slang words and expressions** such as "ta", "do a U-ey", "have a crack", "throw a wobbly", "hang on a tick", "dodgy", "knackered", "piece of piss", "ear-bashing", "whinger", "wuss", "mozzie", "sickie", "brekkie" and "bloke". Americans may feel more at sea when faced with a barrage of Australian idioms, though some of the above are shared, as are others such as "ankle-biter" and "rugrat".

Surprisingly, perhaps, Australia doesn't really have **regional accents**, though Queenslanders are noted for their laid-back tone and for adding "eh?" to the end of assertions. Aboriginal accents, too, have a distinctive edge. Among other speakers, noticeable class and gender differences belie Australia's claim to be an egalitarian society: interestingly, the cultivated Australian accent is much more common among women than Aussie blokes, many of whom pride themselves on their broad ocker delivery.

Glossary

Akubra Wide-brimmed felt hat; a brand name.

ANZAC Australia and New Zealand Army Corps.

Are you right? Are you OK?

Arvo Afternoon.

Back o' Bourke Outback.

Banana bender Resident of Queensland.

Barrack Cheer on, support (a sports team).

Bathers Swimsuit or swimming trunks/shorts, also called a cossie, swimmers or togs.

Battler Someone who struggles to make a living, as in "little Aussie battler".

Beaut! or **You beauty!** Exclamation of delight.

Beg yours? Excuse me, pardon?

Beyond the Black Stump Outback; back of beyond.

Bikkies Biscuits; "It costs big bikkies" means it's expensive.

Billabong Oxbow lake, or any waterhole in a dry riverbed.

Billy Can used to boil water over a campfire.

Blowies Blow flies.

Bludger Someone who does not pull their weight, or a scrounger, from an archaic slang word for a pimp.

Blue Fight; blue or bluey is also a nickname for a red-haired person.

Blundstones or **Blundies** Leather, elastic-sided workmen's boots.

Boardies Boardshorts – essential surfwear.

Bonzer Good, great.

Boom netting Riding in the net or trampoline at the bow of a yacht.

Bottle shop Off-licence or liquor store.

Brass razoo Something of minuscule value, as in "not worth a brass razoo".

Brumby Feral horse.

Buckley's chance Extremely slim odds. "Hasn't got a Buckley's" means hasn't a hope.

Budgie smugglers Speedos.

Bug Moreton Bay bug or Balmain bug – a very tasty crayfish.

Bunyip Monster of Aboriginal legend; bogey-man that inhabits billabongs.

Burl Trial; as in "Give it a burl".

Bush Unsettled country area, or untamed vegetation.

Bush lawyer Person keen to give advice, whether they're qualified to comment or not.

Bushranger Runaway convict; nineteenth-century outlaw.

Bushwhacker Someone lacking in social graces, a hick.

Chook Chicken.

Clayton's Used adjectivally to mean in name only.

Cobber Old-fashioned word for a friend.

Cocky Small farmer; a cow cocky is a dairy farmer.

Coo-eee! Aboriginal long-distance greeting or call, now widely adopted.

Corroboree Aboriginal ceremony.

Crim Criminal.

Crook Sick or broken.

Cut lunch Sandwiches.

Dag Scrap of excrement caught in the wool on a sheep's backside; uncool, slobbish or nerdy person (adj. daggy).

Daks or **strides** Trousers/pants.

Dam A man-made body of water or reservoir; not just the dam itself.

Damper Bread cooked in a pot on embers.

Darl Friendly term of address, short for darling.

Dekko Look; as in "Take a dekko at this".

Derro Derelict or destitute person.

Digger Old-timer, especially an old soldier.

Dill Idiot.

Dilly bag Aboriginal carry-all made of bark, or woven or rigged twine.

Dinky-di Straight up, authentic.

Disposal store Store that sells used army and navy equipment, plus camping gear.

Donga Basic country cabin.

Doona Quilt.

The Dreaming The process of passing Aboriginal cultural information from one generation to the next.

Dreamtime Cycle of Aboriginal myths and stories explaining the origins of the world.

Drizabone Waxed cotton raincoat, originally designed for horse riding; a brand name.

Drongo Fool.

Drover Cowboy or station hand.

Dunny Outside pit toilet.

Esky Portable, insulated box to keep food or beer cold, originally a brand name.

Fair go Equal opportunity.

Feral A hippy or an uncivilized person.

Fisho Fisherman or fishmonger.

Fossick To search for gold or gems in abandoned diggings.

Furphy A rumour, lie or false story.

Galah Noisy or garrulous person; after the bird.

Galvo Corrugated iron.

Garbo Garbage or refuse collector.

Gibber Rock or boulder.

Give away To give up or resign; as in "I used to be a garbo but I gave it away".

Grey nomad Retiree on a long trip around Australia by motorhome or caravan.

Grog Alcohol, beer.

Grommet Child surfer.

Gub or **gubbah** Aboriginal terms for a white person.

Guernsey Aussie Rules footballer's team shirt. "To get a guernsey" means to be applauded, honoured or selected.

Gutless wonder Coward.

Heaps Favourite Aussieexpression for "a lot".

Holy dooley! Expression of surprise.

Hoon A yob, delinquent.

Humpy Temporary shelter used by Aborigines and early pioneers.

Jackeroo Male station-hand.

Jilleroo Female station-hand.

Koori or **Koorie** Generic term for Aboriginal people from southeastern Australia.

Lair it up Dress, behave or decorate something in a flash, vulgar way.

Larrikin Mischievous youth.

Lay by Practice of putting a deposit on goods until they can be fully paid for.

Lollies Sweets or candy.

Manchester Household linen.

Mate A sworn friend; also used as a general-purpose term of address to both friends and strangers, male or female.

Mateship Camaraderie, warmth and loyalty.

Mexicans Queensland term for residents of New South Wales, and New South Wales term for Victorians (that is, those south of the border).

Middy A standard (285ml) glass of beer (NSW).

Milk bar Corner shop, and often a small café.

Minimum chips Fish 'n' chip-shop term for a (relatively) small portion of fries.

Mob Collective term for kangaroos, adopted by some Aborigines to mean an Aboriginal kinship group or community.

Mod Oz Modern Australian, Mediterranean-Asian fusion cooking.

Moleskins Strong cotton trousers worn by bushmen.

Mug Layabout or naïve idiot, as in "'Ave a go, ya mug".

Murri Generic term for Aboriginal people from Queensland.

Nature strip Grass verge.

Nipper Young, trainee lifesaver.

Never Never Outback, wilderness.

Ocker Uncultivated Australian – can be considered either cute or crass.

Op shop Short for Opportunity Shop; a charity shop or thrift store.

Outback Remote, unsettled, inland Australia.

Paddock Field for livestock or a sports pitch.

Panel van Van with no rear windows and front seating only.

Pashing Kissing or snogging, often in the back of a panel van.

Perve To leer or act as a voyeur; as in "What are you perving at?"

Piss Beer.

Piss head Drunkard.

Pissed Drunk.

Pokies One-armed bandits; gambling machines.

Pommie or **Pom** Person of English descent – not necessarily abusive.

Pot A standard (285ml) glass of beer (VIC & QLD).

Queenslander Traditional-style, wooden house with a veranda, built on stilts or piles (QLD).

Rack off! Get lost!

Raincheck Voucher issued by a shop for a running special offer, allowing you to buy the item later at the offer price.

Rapt Very pleased, delighted.

Rash vest or **rashie** Surfing top, worn with boardies or under a wetsuit.

Ratbag An eccentric person; also a term of mild abuse.

Ratshit or **shithouse** How you feel after a night on the piss.

Raw prawn Something hard to swallow; to "come the raw prawn" is to try and deceive or make a fool of someone.

Reckon! Absolutely!

Rego Vehicle registration document.

You little ripper! Rather old-fashioned exclamation of enthusiasm.

Rock up Arrive.

Rollies Roll-up cigarettes.

Root Vulgar term for sexual congress.

Rooted To be very tired or to be beyond repair; interchangeable with "buggered".

Ropable Furious to the point of requiring restraint.

Rouseabout An unskilled rural labourer, such as a woolshed hand.

RSL Returned and Services League of Australia, a support group for ex-servicemen, with a network of social clubs.

Schooner A large glass of beer (VIC 485ml, NSW & QLD 425ml).

Send her down, Hughie An exclamation before or during heavy rain.

Shark biscuit Novice surfer.

Sheila Woman, now considered a pejorative term.

She'll be right or **she'll be apples** Everything will work out fine.

Shoot through To pass through or leave hurriedly.

Shout To pay for someone, on the assumption that they'll reciprocate later, as in "I'll shout you a beer" or "It's my shout, mate".

Singlet Sleeveless cotton vest. The archetypal Australian working man's singlet, in navy, is produced by Bonds.

Skivvy Polo (roll) neck.

Slab 24-can carton of beer.

Slouch hat Soldier's hat with the brim turned up on one side.

SLSC Surf Life Saving Club. Surf Lifesavers wear red and yellow and are volunteers; lifeguards wear blue and are city council or resort employees.

Smoko Tea break.

Snag Sausage.

Speedo Famous Australian brand of athletic swimming costume; speedos refers to men's swimming briefs (nicknamed budgie smugglers or sluggos), as opposed to trunks (shorts) or boardies (boardshorts).

Squiz Glance; as in "Have a squiz at this".

Station Very large pastoral property or ranch.

Sticky beak Nosy person, or to be nosy; as in "Let's have a sticky beak".

Stockman Cowboy or station hand.

Stubby Small bottle of beer.

Sunbake Sunbathe.

Swag Large bedroll, or one's belongings.

Tall poppy Someone who excels or is eminent but self-important. "Cutting down tall poppies" means bringing overachievers back to earth – a national pastime.

Thongs Flip-flops, beach sandals.

Tinnie Can of beer, or a small aluminium boat.

Gone troppo Deranged, originally used for people driven mad by tropical heat and humidity.

Tucker Food.

Two-up Old gambling game based on the tossing of coins.

Un-Australian Much-used critical jargon for any Australian who doesn't embrace values such as mateship and the right to a fair go.

Unit Flat or apartment.

Ute Short for utility vehicle: a pick-up truck or open-backed van.

Walkabout Temporary migration undertaken by Aborigines; also has the wider meaning of a journey for its own sake. "Gone walkabout" can mean gone missing.

On the wallaby Living a nomadic life in the bush.

Warm fuzzies Feeling of contentment.

Waxhead Surfer.

Weatherboard Traditional-style, wooden house (NSW).

Woop-woop The outback.

Wowser Killjoy or prude.

Yabbie Freshwater crayfish.

Yakka Work, as in "hard yakka".

Yobbo Uncouth person.

Youse You (plural).

Travel
store

Put yourself in the Picture

Discover Australia with YHA AUSTRALIA

Friendly, clean, secure, affordable accommodation!

More than **100** hostels and **700** discounts

Jump on board, jump online at yha.com.au

Small print and

Index

A Rough Guide to Rough Guides

Published in 1982, the first Rough Guide – to Greece – was a student scheme that became a publishing phenomenon. Mark Ellingham, a recent graduate in English from Bristol University, had been travelling in Greece the previous summer and couldn't find the right guidebook. With a small group of friends he wrote his own guide, combining a highly contemporary, journalistic style with a thoroughly practical approach to travellers' needs.

The immediate success of the book spawned a series that rapidly covered dozens of destinations. And, in addition to impecunious backpackers, Rough Guides soon acquired a much broader and older readership that relished the guides' wit and inquisitiveness as much as their enthusiastic, critical approach and value-for-money ethos.

These days, Rough Guides include recommendations from shoestring to luxury and cover more than 200 destinations around the globe, including almost every country in the Americas and Europe, more than half of Africa and most of Asia and Australasia. Our ever-growing team of authors and photographers is spread all over the world, particularly in Europe, the USA and Australia.

In the early 1990s, Rough Guides branched out of travel, with the publication of Rough Guides to World Music, Classical Music and the Internet. All three have become benchmark titles in their fields, spearheading the publication of a wide range of books under the Rough Guide name.

Including the travel series, Rough Guides now number more than 350 titles, covering: phrasebooks, waterproof maps, music guides from Opera to Heavy Metal, reference works as diverse as Conspiracy Theories and Shakespeare, and popular culture books from iPods to Poker. Rough Guides also produce a series of more than 120 World Music CDs in partnership with World Music Network.

Visit www.roughguides.com to see our latest publications.

Rough Guide travel images are available for commercial licensing at www.roughguidespictures.com

Rough Guide credits

Text editor: Keith Drew
Layout: Anita Singh
Cartography: Ashutosh Bharti
Picture editor: Mark Thomas
Production: Vicky Baldwin
Proofreader: Samantha Cook
Cover design: Chloë Roberts
Editorial: **London** Ruth Blackmore, Alison
Murchie, Andy Turner, Edward Aves, Alice Park,
Lucy White, Jo Kirby, James Smart, Natasha
Foges, Róisín Cameron, Emma Traynor, Emma
Gibbs, James Rice, Kathryn Lane, Christina
Valhouli, Monica Woods, Mani Ramaswamy,
Joe Staines, Peter Buckley, Matthew Milton,
Tracy Hopkins, Ruth Tidball; **New York** Andrew
Rosenberg, Steven Horak, AnneLise Sorensen,
April Isaacs, Ella Steim, Anna Owens, Sean
Mahoney, Paula Neudorf, Courtney Miller;
Delhi Madhavi Singh, Karen D'Souza
Design & Pictures: **London** Scott Stickland,
Dan May, Diana Jarvis, Nicole Newman,
Chloë Roberts, Sarah Cummins, Emily Taylor;
Delhi Umesh Aggarwal, Ajay Verma, Jessica
Subramanian, Ankur Guha, Pradeep Thapliyal,
Sachin Tanwar, Nikhil Agarwal

Production: Rebecca Short
Cartography: **London** Maxine Repath, Ed
Wright, Katie Lloyd-Jones; **Delhi** Jai Prakash
Mishra, Rajesh Chhibber, Rajesh Mishra,
Animesh Pathak, Jasbir Sandhu, Karobi Gogoi,
Alakananda Roy, Swati Handoo, Deshpal Singh
Online: Narender Kumar, Rakesh Kumar,
Amit Verma, Rahul Kumar, Ganesh Sharma,
Debojit Borah, Ravi Yadav
Marketing & Publicity: **London** Liz Statham,
Niki Hanmer, Louise Maher, Jess Carter,
Vanessa Godden, Vivienne Watton, Anna
Paynton, Rachel Sprackett, Libby Jellie, Jayne
McPherson, Holly Dudley; **New York** Geoff
Colquitt, Katy Ball;
Delhi Ragini Govind
Manager India: Punita Singh
Reference Director: Andrew Lockett
Operations Manager: Helen Phillips
PA to Publishing Director: Nicola Henderson
Publishing Director: Martin Dunford
Commercial Manager: Gino Magnotta
Managing Director: John Duhigg

Publishing information

This first edition published October 2008 by
Rough Guides Ltd,
80 Strand, London WC2R 0RL
345 Hudson St, 4th Floor,
New York, NY 10014, USA
14 Local Shopping Centre, Panchsheel Park,
New Delhi 110017, India
Distributed by the Penguin Group
Penguin Books Ltd,
80 Strand, London WC2R 0RL
Penguin Group (USA)
375 Hudson Street, NY 10014, USA
Penguin Group (Australia)
250 Camberwell Road, Camberwell,
Victoria 3124, Australia
Penguin Group (Canada)
195 Harry Walker Parkway N, Newmarket, ON,
L3Y 7B3 Canada
Penguin Group (NZ)
67 Apollo Drive, Mairangi Bay, Auckland 1310,
New Zealand
Cover concept by Peter Dyer.

Typeset in Bembo and Helvetica to an original
design by Henry Iles.

Printed in China

© Emma Gregg 2008

680pp includes index

A catalogue record for this book is available from
the British Library

ISBN: 978-1-85828-885-7

1   3   5   7   9   8   6   4   2

Help us update

We've gone to a lot of effort to ensure that the
first edition of **The Rough Guide to East Coast
Australia** is accurate and up to date. However,
things change – places get "discovered", opening
hours are notoriously fickle, restaurants and
rooms raise prices or lower standards. If you
feel we've got it wrong or left something out,
we'd like to know, and if you can remember the
address, the price, the hours, the phone number,
so much the better.

Please send your comments with the subject
line "**Rough Guide East Coast Australia
Update**" to ✉ mail@roughguides.com. We'll credit
all contributions and send a copy of the next
edition (or any other Rough Guide if you prefer)
for the very best emails.
   Have your questions answered and tell others
about your trip at
ⓦ community.roughguides.com

SMALL PRINT

Acknowledgements

The author, Emma Gregg, would like to thank everyone who made researching this book in Australia such a pleasure. Particularly warm thanks go to Anna Catchpole at Hills Balfour Synergy; Gabe and Cathy Thallon at Tropic Days and Travellers Oasis in Cairns; Dan and Heidi Degen in Brisbane; Felicity Gallimore, Martin Poole, Charlotte, Ross and Juliet in Sydney; Janet McGarry at YHA Australia; and Helen Marsden in Melbourne. Thanks also go to Danny Adam at Jemby-Rinjah Eco Lodge; Charlie Allcorn at Sunlover Reef Cruises; Jocelyn Amey and Rebecca Ham at Tjapukai; Tania Anderson at Norfolk Island Tourism Marketing; Jeff Aquilina at Coral Sea Resort, Airlie Beach; Angelo Barra at Zinc, Port Douglas; Evie Bear at Management and Publicity; Michelle Behsman, Tolita Dukes, Eva Grabner, Nick Moon and Justin Philip at Ocean Hotels; Megan Bell and Andrea Campbell at Quicksilver, Cairns; Paula Bennet, Fraser Coast South Burnett Tourism; Vera Bloxam at Milkwood Lodge, Cooktown; Danielle Boniface at Rainforestation; Marianna and Luigi Bonomi at Shantana Resort, Port Douglas; Brian Bowers at Coffs Coast Visitor Information Centre; Susan Boyd, Deborah Friend, Katie Cahill and Karen Smith at Infront Communications; Julie Brown at Q1, Surfers Paradise; Matt Bruton at Great Barrier Reef Helicopters; Gabe Burgess and Angela Sweeney at Tangalooma, Moreton Island; Sally Burleigh at Qualia; Sherrilyn Charles at Daintree Eco Lodge; Jodi Clark at Kingfisher Bay Resort; Cleo, Damien, Gaelle and Paul at On The Wallaby, Yungaburra; Alison Cole at Great Keppel Island; Damien Condon and Belinda Edwards at Brisbane Marketing; Bree Corbett, Louise Longman and Judith Watson at Voyages; Matt Cross at Dolphin Watch Cruises, Huskisson; Megan Czisz and Katy Woods at YHA; Greg Daven at the Kuranda Scenic Railway; Susan Davis, Stephen Ferrino and Deborah McDiarmid at Sheraton Noosa; Karen Doane and Dion Eades at Tourism Tropical North Queensland; Fern Duffie and Therese Toy at Townsville Enterprise; Luke Edwards at Capricorn Tourism; Philip Edwards and Bonnie Rodwell at Songbirds Rainforest Retreat; Brett and Janelle Flemming at Bungalow Bay, Magnetic Island; Greg Floyd at Binna Burra Mountain Lodge; Rebecca Freestun at Accor; Paolo Gambino at the Cairns Colonial Club Resort; Andrea Gibson at Poseidon, Port Douglas; Willie Gordon at Gurrbi Tours; Bill Gray at MG Media Communications; Scott and Margaret Greer at Riviera Backpackers YHA, Lakes Entrance; Shelley Griffiths at the Discovery Centre, Daintree; Paul Grossman at Noosa Ferry; Peter Harman at Peppers Guest House and Convent, Pokolbin; Ben Harnwell at Shoalhaven Visitors Centre, Nowra; John and Sue Haymes at The Meridian, Port Douglas; Phillipa Heslop at Cedar Creek Cottages; Chris and Wendy Hillier at Narooma YHA; Jon Hutchinson at Sydney Central YHA; Leeroy and Jane Hutton at The Spotted Chook, Montville; Julie Johnston at Skyrail; Daniel Jones at Brampton Island; Kate Jones, Sharon Kennedy and Sandy Tepli at Shangri-La Hotels and Resorts; Owen Jones and Sally Morgan at Hayman; Barb and Kerry Kehoe at Mount Quincan Crater Retreat; Shelley-Ann Kelly at Gladstone Area PDL; Paula Kennett at Hamilton Island; Nicola Kleijn, Kris McIntyre and Bernadette Wazir at Peppers; Jade Leece and Michael Mallin at York Fairmont Resort, Leura; Kim Lehmann at Sunsail, Hamilton Island; Adam Letson at Skyrail Rainforest Cableway; Deni Linforth at Whitsunday Rent a Yacht; Annmarie Mansour at Tourism New South Wales; Sarah McAtamney at Australia Zoo; Ken McBryde at Caloundra Cruise; Kelly McCarthy at YHA Victoria; Graham and Jo McIntyre at Bellingen YHA; Ian McKinnon at Scubaworld, Maroochydore; Erin Millar at Hyatt Regency, Sanctuary Cove; Chris Morris at SunFerries, Townsville; Liz Mulacaster at Austravel; Jon and Peta Nott at Rose Gums Wilderness Retreat; Gemma O'Brien and Laurren McAtamney at Tourism Sunshine Coast; Nikki Otton at Mackay Tourism; Chris Owen at Peppers Blue on Blue, Magnetic Island; Lyn Parché and Melinda Dunn at The Byron at Byron, Byron Bay; Ollie Philpot at Tourism Queensland; Maree Reason-Cain at C4 Marketing; Wayne and Linda Retchford at Metzo Noosa; Jovanka Ristich at Independent PR; Adrian and Jenny Robertson at Jervis Bay Getaways; Peter Savoff and Kath Rose at Emporium Hotel; Natalie Schofield at Gold Coast Tourism; Steve Spinaze at HeliCharter, Cairns; Andy Spittall at The Horizon at Mission Beach; Brian Stokes at Bellingen Shire Tourism; Kirsten Taylor at The Rainforest Habitat; Amanda Tidmarsh at O'Reilly's; Kim Tolhurst at The Horizon; Wayne Tuckfield at Wandarrah Lodge YHA, Merimbula; Paul Verity and Susan Kelly at Sancturay Retreat, Mission Beach; Helen Vine at Railway Square YHA, Sydney; Sheena Walshaw at Jungle Surfing, Cape Tribulation; Konstanze Werhahn-Mees at Eight Hotels; Ann Westgate at Blue Mountains YHA, Katoomba; Warren Whitfield and Leonie Young at Fire Stick Tours; Peter Williams at Williams Lodge, Yungaburra; Shelley Winkel at Dreamworld and WhiteWater World. Thanks too to the many others who kindly offered me advice and assistance during my research. In London, I would like to thank Keith Drew, Mani Ramaswamy, Mark Thomas and all the team at Rough Guides. Finally, I am indebted to Nathan Pope without whose unswerving understanding, good sense and good humour I would have been up a gum tree.

SMALL PRINT

Photo credits

All photos © Rough Guides except the following:

Cover
Front cover image: Fraser Island © John Warburton-Lee Photography/Alamy
Back cover image: Koala road sign © Nicole Newman
Inside back picture: Surf-lifesaver flag © Rough Guides

Introduction
Great Barrier Reef © Ted Mead/Getty Images
View of Melbourne © Cadaphoto/Getty Images
Detail of beach huts © Annie Griffiths Belt/Getty Images
Restaurant on Sydney Harbour © Ian Cumming/Axiom
Rock climbing in the Blue Mountains © Chris Bradley/Axiom
Manly Beach © Sally Mayman/Getty Images
Aerial view of the Great Barrier Reef © Emma Greg
Road sign © Emma Gregg
Lifeguards on beach © Peter Adams/Getty Images

Things not to miss
02 Melbourne Cup © Michael Coyne/Axiom
03 Wilson's Promontory National Park © Ern Mainka/Alamy
04 Green turtle © Darryl Torckler/Getty Images
05 Bondi Beach © Jacobs Stock Photography/Getty Images
07 Café in Melbourne © Jenny Acheson/Axiom
08 The Daintree and Cape Tribulation © Emma Gregg
09 Humpback breaching © Jason Edwards/Getty Images
10 Platypus © Dave Watts/Alamy
11 Whitsundays's © Emma Gregg
12 Gold Coast surfing © David Wall/Alamy
14 The Blue Montains © DK Images
15 Fraser Island © Emma Gregg
16 Australia Zoo © Emma Gregg
17 South Bank Brisbane © Emma Gregg
18 Koala © Emma Gregg
19 Feeding Dolphins © Emma Gregg
20 Highland waterfalls © Emma Gregg
21 New Year celebrations Sydney © Robin Smith/Getty
22 Whitehaven Beach © Peter Hendrie/Getty Images
23 Possum at night © Getty Images
24 Phillip Island penguins © JTB Photo Communications/Alamy
26 Scuba diving, Great Barrier Reef © Jeff Hunter/Getty Images

27 Lord Howe Island © Paul Miles/Axiom
28 Mardi Gras © Kristian Dowling © Getty Images

Take the plunge! colour section
Fish swimming in spiral pattern © Pete Atkinson/Getty Images
Surfer on Manly © Christophe Launay/Getty Images
Surfers on beach © Anthony Webb/Axiom
Sydney Olympic Pool © DK Images
Sailing in the Whitsundays © Emma Gregg
Diver and potato grouper © Pete Atkinson/Getty Images
Woman snorkelling © Pete Atkinson/Getty Images
Sea star © Norbert Wu/Getty Images

East Coast Ecotourism colour section
Ancient melaleuca forest, the Whitsundays © Emma Gregg
Daintree National Park © Emma Gregg
Mission Beach © Emma Gregg
Egret, Fraser Island © Emma Gregg
Water lily © Emma Gregg
Humpback whale © Dave Watts/Alamy
Moreton Island © Emma Gregg]

Wildlife section colour section
Dolphins, Great Barrier Reef © Thomas Schmitt/Getty Images
Racoon butterfly fish © Maximilian Weinzierl/Alamy
Anemone fish © Fred Bavendam/Getty Images
Feather fin © Carol Buchanan/Alamy
Surf parrot fish © Suzanne Long/Alamy
Humpheaded maori wrasse © Richard Smith
Bluespotted stingray © NHPA
Whitetip reef shark © NHPA
Green turtles © NHPA
Dugong © NHPA
Humpback whale © NHPA
Esturine crocodile © NHPA
Eastern grey kangaroo © NHPA
Red-necked pademelon © NHPA
Agile wallaby © NHPA
Brushtail possum © NHPA
Koala © NHPA
Common wombat © NHPA
Sugar glider © NHPA
Flying fox © NHPA
Platypus © Dave Watts/Alamy
Rainbow Lorikeet © NHPA
Laughing Kookaburra © NHPA
Southern Cassowary © NHPA
Superb Lyrebird © NHPA

Index

Map entries are in colour.

C

D

T

Map symbols

maps are listed in the full index using coloured text

-----	International boundary	Ⓜ	Metro station
—·—·—	State/territorial boundary	Ⓣ	Tram stop
— — —	Chapter division boundary	★	Bus/taxi stop
═════	Motorway	⚓	Ferry/boat stop
═══	Main road	♦	Point of interest
══	Minor road	@	Internet access
▬▬▬	Pedestrianized street	ⓘ	Information office
- - - - -	Path/track	⊠	Post office
—■—	Railway	⊞	Hospital
— — —	Ferry route	Ⓟ	Parking
——	River/coast	♦	Museum
⌒	Bridge	🏛	Monument
▲	Mountain peak	⛳	Golf course
⌂⌂	Mountain range	⚠	Campsite
〰	Gorge	🚢	Shipwreck
〰	Rock	☩	Church (regional maps)
〰	Reef	⬭	Stadium
⩡	Viewpoint	▬	Building
⚘	Waterfall	✝	Church/cathedral
◠	Cave	⬚	Beach
⬧	Conservation hut	⊞	Cemetery
⚲	Lighthouse	⬚	Park
✈	Airport	⬚	Forest
╲	Airfield